Okyay Kaynak   Ethem Alpaydin
Erkki Oja   Lei Xu (Eds.)

Artificial Neural Networks and Neural Information Processing – ICANN/ICONIP 2003

Joint International Conference ICANN/ICONIP 2003
Istanbul, Turkey, June 26-29, 2003
Proceedings

Springer

Series Editors

Gerhard Goos, Karlsruhe University, Germany
Juris Hartmanis, Cornell University, NY, USA
Jan van Leeuwen, Utrecht University, The Netherlands

Volume Editors

Okyay Kaynak
Ethem Alpaydin
Bogazici University
Bebek, 34342 Istanbul, Turkey
E-mail: {kaynak,alpaydin}@boun.edu.tr

Erkki Oja
Helsinki University of Technology
Laboratory of Computer and Information Science
P.O.B. 5400, 02015 HUT, Finland
E-mail: erkki.oja@hut.fi

Lei Xu
The Chinese University of Hong Kong
Department of Computer Science and Engineering
Shatin, Hong Kong
E-mail:lxu@cse.cuhk.edu.hk

Cataloging-in-Publication Data applied for

Bibliographic information published by Die Deutsche Bibliothek
Die Deutsche Bibliothek lists this publication in the Deutsche Nationalbibliografie;
detailed bibliographic data is available in the Internet at <http://dnb.ddb.de>.

CR Subject Classification (1998): F.1, I.2, I.5, I.4, G.3, J.3, C.2.1, C.1.3, C.3

ISSN 0302-9743
ISBN 3-540-40408-2 Springer-Verlag Berlin Heidelberg New York

This work is subject to copyright. All rights are reserved, whether the whole or part of the material is concerned, specifically the rights of translation, reprinting, re-use of illustrations, recitation, broadcasting, reproduction on microfilms or in any other way, and storage in data banks. Duplication of this publication or parts thereof is permitted only under the provisions of the German Copyright Law of September 9, 1965, in its current version, and permission for use must always be obtained from Springer-Verlag. Violations are liable for prosecution under the German Copyright Law.

Springer-Verlag Berlin Heidelberg New York
a member of BertelsmannSpringer Science+Business Media GmbH

http://www.springer.de

© Springer-Verlag Berlin Heidelberg 2003
Printed in Germany

Typesetting: Camera-ready by author, data conversion by PTP-Berlin GmbH
Printed on acid-free paper   SPIN: 10928790   06/3142   5 4 3 2 1 0

Preface

This book constitutes a collection of papers presented at the joint *International Conference on Artificial Neural Networks* and *International Conference on Neural Information Processing*, ICANN/ICONIP 2003, from June 26–29, 2003 in Istanbul, Turkey. The conference was organized by Boğaziçi University, Istanbul in cooperation with the Soft Computational Intelligence Society, Turkey. The ICANN conferences were initiated in 1991 and have become the major European meeting in the field of neural networks. Similarly, the ICONIP conferences were initiated in 1994 and have become the major Asian meeting in the field. This conference was the first one combining the two. Being held in Istanbul, Turkey, it bridged the two continents and brought together the researchers from them in a joint meeting.

From 346 submitted papers, the program committee selected 102 for publication as long papers. There were also 36 papers presented in the special sessions. We would like to thank all the members of the program committee, special session organizers, and reviewers for their great effort in the reviewing process and for helping us to organize a scientific program of high quality.

We would like to thank the Asia Pacific Neural Network Assembly (APPNA) and the European Neural Network Society (ENNS) for their support. We acknowledge the financial support of the Boğaziçi University Foundation, the European Office of Aerospace Research and Development of the USAF, and the Turkish Scientific and Technical Research Council (TÜBİTAK). We would like to thank Levent Akın, Gökhan Aydın, Cem Say, and Uğur Yıldıran for their help with the local organization and Aleksander Malinowski for the web submission support. The conference and the proceedings would not have been possible without their contributions.

April 2003

Okyay Kaynak

Organization

ICANN/ICONIP 2003 was organized by Boğaziçi University, Istanbul in cooperation with the Soft Computational Intelligence Society, Turkey.

Executive Committee

Conference Chair: Okyay Kaynak, Turkey

Program Co-chairs: Ethem Alpaydın, Turkey
                        Erkki Oja, Finland
                        Lei Xu, Hong Kong

Organizing Committee: Levent Akın, Turkey
                        Gökhan Aydın, Turkey
                        Cem Say, Turkey
                        Uğur Yıldıran, Turkey

Tutorials: Nikola Kasabov, New Zealand

Honorary Co-chairs: Shunichi Amari, Japan
                        Erol Gelenbe, USA
                        Teuvo Kohonen, Finland

Advisory Board: Jose Dorronsoro, Spain
                        Kunihiko Fukushima, Japan
                        Michael Jordan, USA
                        Lalit Mohan Patnaik, India
                        Terrence Sejnowski, USA
                        David Willshaw, UK
                        Yi-Xin Zhong, China
                        Jacek Zurada, USA

Program Committee

Learning Algorithms:	M.O. Efe (USA), M. Ishikawa (Japan), A. Sperduti (Italy)
SVM and Kernel Methods:	R. Herbrich (UK), K.-R. Müller (Germany), N. R. Pal (India)
Statistical Data Analysis:	W. Duch (Poland), A. Galushkin (Russia), F. Yarman-Vural (Turkey)
Pattern Recognition:	S.Y. Bang (Korea), R. Duin (The Netherlands), U. Halıcı (Turkey)
Vision:	L. Akarun (Turkey), K. Fukushima (Japan), H. Mallot (Germany)
Speech Recognition:	L. Arslan (Turkey), P. Gallinari (France), N. Kasabov (New Zealand)
Robotics and Control:	L. Akın (Turkey), T. Gedeon (Australia), S. Gielen (The Netherlands)
Signal Processing:	O. Ersoy (USA), C. Y. Liou (Taiwan), O. Simula (Finland)
Time-Series Prediction:	L.W. Chan (Hong Kong), K. Cılız (Turkey), G. Dorffner (Austria)
Intelligent and Hybrid Systems:	F. Gürgen (Turkey), P. Sincak (Slovakia), L. P. Wang (Singapore)
Neural Network Hardware:	B.B. Chaudhuri (India), G. Dündar (Turkey), U. Ruckert (Germany)
Cognitive Science:	P. Erdi (Hungary), H.G. Tekman (Turkey), S. Usui (Japan)
Computational Neuroscience:	W. Gerstner (Switzerland), A.K. Guo (China), M. Özkan (Turkey)

Referees

Rafal Adamczak	Sina Balkir	Narendra Chaudhari
Fabio Aiolli	Igor Belikh	Sanjay Chawla
L. Akarun	Anton Belousov	Dingguo Chen
H.L. Akin	Yoshua Bengio	Genshe Chen
Esa Alhoniemi	Tasos Bezerianos	P. Y. Chen
Ethem Alpaydin	Monica Bianchini	S.H. Chen
Bruno Apolloni	Jacek Biesiada	Philip E. Cheng
Oya Aran	Gilles Blanchard	S.B. Cho
L. Arslan	Roelof Brouwer	Chong-Ho Choi
Hideki Asoh	Nicolas Brunel	Ugur Cilingiroglu
Volkan Atalay	Paola Campadelli	K. Ciliz
Bulent Ayhan	Barbara Caputo	Jens Christian Claussen
Mahmood R. Azimi	Andre Carvalho	Bruno Cremilleux
Rauf Baig	L. W. Chan	D.N. Davis

Hakan Delic
Zumray Dokur
G. Dorffner
Guido Dornhege
Jose Dorronsoro
W. Duch
Robert P.W. Duin
G. Dundar
M.O. Efe
Issam El Naqa
P. Erdi
O. Ersoy
Armando Fernandes
Arthur Flexer
K. Fukushima
Ryoko Futami
P. Gallinari
Junbin Gao
T. Gedeon
W. Gerstner
S. Gielen
Mark Girolami
Berk Gokberk
Huseyin Goksu
Thore Graepel
C. Gruber
Nilgun Guler
Suat Gumussoy
A.K. Guo
F. Gurgen
Masafumi Hagiwara
Ugur Halici
Ari Hamalainen
Barbara Hammer
James Henderson
R. Herbrich
Carlos Hernandez-
    Espinosa
Kazuyuki Hiraoka
Wolfgang Hoermann
Wolfgang Huebner
Heikki Hyotyniemi
Jukka Iivarinen
Shiro Ikeda
Hirotaka Inoue

S. Iplikci
Shin Ishii
Masumi Ishikawa
Thorsten Joachims
Ulf Johansson
Piotr Juszczak
Ata Kaban
Ryotaro Kamimura
Samuel Kaski
Cosku Kasnakoglu
Motoaki Kawanabe
Richard Kempter
Mustafa E. Keskin
Daijin Kim
Heinrich Klar
Konrad Koerding
Tamara G. Kolda
Irena Koprinska
Jozef Korbicz
Raghu Krishnapuram
Koji Kurata
Franz J. Kurfess
Takio Kurita
James Kwok
Timo Laakso
Jorma Laaksonen
Sampsa Laine
Heba Lakany
Pavel Laskov
Yusuf Leblebici
M. Kemal Leblebicioglu
Stephane Lecoeuche
Lutz Leistritz
Achim Lewandowski
Shuhui Li
Zhaoping Li
C.T. Lin
Daw-Tung Lin
C.Y. Liou
Michelle Liou
Fu-Sheng Lu
Teresa Bernarda
    Ludermir
Wolfgang Maass
Christopher MacLeod

Marco Maggini
H. Mallot
Simone Marinai
Francesco Masulli
Yasuo Matsuyama
Grant Maxwell
Alessio Micheli
Sebastian Mika
Jose del Millan
Mehmet Kerem
    Muezzinoglu
K.R. Muller
Joseph Murray
Selcuk Ogrenci
Gulay Oke
Oleg Okun
Manfred Opper
Pavel Paclik
A. Pal
N. R. Pal
Elzbieta Pekalska
Matti Pietikainen
Faruk Polat
Mario Porrmann
Gunnar Raetsch
Kimmo Raivio
Kiruthika Ramanathan
Marina Resta
Constantino Carlos
    Reyes
Dick de Ridder
Stefano Rovetta
Joseph Rudman
Albert Ali Salah
Brian Sallans
Bulent Sankur
Bilge Say
Franco Scarselli
Christin Schafer
R. Schuffny
Gursel Serpen
Rudy Setiono
Bernhard Sick
Ivan Nunes da Silva
Marina Skurichina

Diego Sona
Lambert Spaanenburg
A. Sperduti
Inna Stainvas
Ivilin Stoianov
Wolfgang Stuerzl
Mu-Chun Su
P.N. Suganthan
Martin Szummer
Roberto Tagliaferri

David M.J. Tax
H.G. Tekman
Peter Tino
Aruna Tiwari
Arnaud Tonnelier
Edmondo Trentin
Ah Chung Tsoi
Harri Valpola
Ricardo Vigario
Carl van Vreeswijk

Jung-Hua Wang
L.P. Wang
Sumio Watanabe
Jiann-Ming Wu
Olcay Taner Yildiz
Junichiro Yoshimoto
Pao-Ta Yu
Hugo Zaragoza
Michael Zibulevsky

Sponsoring Institutions

Boğaziçi University Foundation
European Office of Aerospace Research and Development of the USAF
Turkish Scientific and Technical Research Council (TÜBİTAK)

Table of Contents

Learning Algorithms

Adaptive Hopfield Network 3
    Gürsel Serpen

Effective Pruning Method for a Multiple Classifier System Based
on Self-Generating Neural Networks 11
    Hirotaka Inoue, Hiroyuki Narihisa

Structural Bias in Inducing Representations for Probabilistic
Natural Language Parsing 19
    James Henderson

Independent Component Analysis Minimizing Convex Divergence 27
    Yasuo Matsuyama, Naoto Katsumata, Ryo Kawamura

Selecting Salient Features for Classification Committees 35
    Antanas Verikas, Marija Bacauskiene, Kerstin Malmqvist

Fast and Efficient Training of RBF Networks 43
    Oliver Buchtala, Alexander Hofmann, Bernhard Sick

Loading Temporal Associative Memory Using the Neuronic Equation 52
    Cheng-Yuan Liou, Un-Cheong Sou

Learning Compatibility Functions for Feature Binding and
Perceptual Grouping 60
    Sebastian Weng, Jochen J. Steil

Differential ICA 68
    Seungjin Choi

A Comparison of Model Aggregation Methods for Regression 76
    Zafer Barutçuoğlu, Ethem Alpaydın

Linear Least-Squares Based Methods for Neural Networks Learning 84
    *Oscar Fontenla-Romero, Deniz Erdogmus, J.C. Principe,
    Amparo Alonso-Betanzos, Enrique Castillo*

Optimal Hebbian Learning: A Probabilistic Point of View 92
    Jean-Pascal Pfister, David Barber, Wulfram Gerstner

Competitive Learning by Information Maximization: Eliminating
Dead Neurons in Competitive Learning 99
    Ryotaro Kamimura

Approximate Learning in Temporal Hidden Hopfield Models............. 107
  Felix V. Agakov, David Barber

Finite Mixture Model of Bounded Semi-naive Bayesian Networks
Classifier.. 115
  Kaizhu Huang, Irwin King, Michael R. Lyu

System Identification Based on Online Variational Bayes
Method and Its Application to Reinforcement Learning 123
  Junichiro Yoshimoto, Shin Ishii, Masa-aki Sato

Dimension Reduction Based on Orthogonality – A Decorrelation
Method in ICA 132
  Kun Zhang, Lai-Wan Chan

Selective Sampling Methods in One-Class Classification Problems 140
  Piotr Juszczak, Robert P.W. Duin

Learning Distributed Representations of High-Arity Relational
Data with Non-linear Relational Embedding........................... 149
  Alberto Paccanaro

Meta-learning for Fast Incremental Learning........................... 157
  Takayuki Oohira, Koichiro Yamauchi, Takashi Omori

Expectation-MiniMax Approach to Clustering Analysis 165
  Yiu-ming Cheung

Formal Determination of Context in Contextual Recursive Cascade
Correlation Networks 173
  Alessio Micheli, Diego Sona, Alessandro Sperduti

Confidence Estimation Using the Incremental Learning Algorithm,
Learn++ 181
  Jeffrey Byorick, Robi Polikar

Stability and Convergence Analysis of a Neural Model Applied in
Nonlinear Systems Optimization 189
  Ivan Nunes da Silva

SVM and Kernel Methods

Generalization Error Analysis for Polynomial Kernel Methods –
Algebraic Geometrical Approach 201
  Kazushi Ikeda

Regularized Kriging: The Support Vectors Method Applied to Kriging ... 209
  José M. Matías, Wenceslao González-Manteiga

Support Vector Machine Classifiers for Asymmetric Proximities 217
  Alberto Muñoz, Isaac Martín de Diego, Javier M. Moguerza

Fuzzy Model Identification Using Support Vector Clustering Method 225
  Ayşegül Uçar, Yakup Demir, Cüneyt Güzeliş

Human Splice Site Identification with Multiclass Support Vector
Machines and Bagging... 234
  Ana Carolina Lorena, André C.P.L.F. de Carvalho

Statistical Data Analysis

Optimizing Property Codes in Protein Data Reveals Structural
Characteristics 245
  Olaf Weiss, Andreas Ziehe, Hanspeter Herzel

Multicategory Bayesian Decision Using a Three-Layer Neural Network ... 253
  Yoshifusa Ito, Cidambi Srinivasan

Integrating Supervised and Unsupervised Learning in Self
Organizing Maps for Gene Expression Data Analysis 262
  *Seferina Mavroudi, Andrei Dragomir, Stergios Papadimitriou,
  Anastasios Bezerianos*

Prior Hyperparameters in Bayesian PCA............................... 271
  Shigeyuki Oba, Masa-aki Sato, Shin Ishii

Relevance and Kernel Self-Organising Maps 280
  Emilio Corchado, Colin Fyfe

Pattern Recognition

Hierarchical Bayesian Network for Handwritten Digit Recognition 291
  JaeMo Sung, Sung-Yang Bang

A Novel Neural Network Approach to Solve Exact and Inexact Graph
Isomorphism Problems 299
  Brijnesh J. Jain, Fritz Wysotzki

Evolutionary Optimisation of RBF Network Architectures in a
Direct Marketing Application....................................... 307
  Peter Neumann, Bernhard Sick, Dirk Arndt, Wendy Gersten

Intrusion Detection in Computer Networks with Neural and Fuzzy
Classifiers 316
  Alexander Hofmann, Carsten Schmitz, Bernhard Sick

Optimal Matrix Compression Yields Storage Capacity 1 for Binary
Willshaw Associative Memory 325
  Andreas Knoblauch

Supervised Locally Linear Embedding 333
  Dick de Ridder, Olga Kouropteva, Oleg Okun, Matti Pietikäinen,
  Robert P.W. Duin

Feature Extraction for One-Class Classification 342
  David M.J. Tax, Klaus-R. Müller

Auto-adaptive and Dynamical Clustering Neural Network 350
  Stéphane Lecoeuche, Christophe Lurette

Transformations of Symbolic Data for Continuous
Data Oriented Models 359
  Krzysztof Grąbczewski, Norbert Jankowski

Comparing Fuzzy Data Sets by Means of Graph Matching Technique 367
  Giuseppe Acciani, Girolamo Fornarelli, Luciano Liturri

How to Do Multi-way Classification with Two-Way Classifiers 375
  Florin Cutzu

Vision

Sparse Coding with Invariance Constraints 385
  Heiko Wersing, Julian Eggert, Edgar Körner

Restoring Partly Occluded Patterns: A Neural Network Model with
Backward Paths 393
  Kunihiko Fukushima

The InfoMin Criterion: An Information Theoretic Unifying
Objective Function for Topographic Mappings 401
  Yoshitatsu Matsuda, Kazunori Yamaguchi

Short-Term Memory Optical Flow Image............................. 409
  Satoru Morita

A Hybrid MLP-PNN Architecture for Fast Image Superresolution 417
  Carlos Miravet, Francisco B. Rodríguez

Recognition of Gestural Object Reference with Auditory Feedback 425
  Ingo Bax, Holger Bekel, Gunther Heidemann

Multi-chip Implementation of a Biomimetic VLSI Vision Sensor
Based on the Adelson-Bergen Algorithm 433
  Erhan Ozalevli, Charles M. Higgins

Speech Recognition

Client Dependent GMM-SVM Models for Speaker Verification 443
  Quan Le, Samy Bengio

Frequency and Wavelet Filtering for Robust Speech Recognition 452
  Murat Deviren, Khalid Daoudi

Robotics and Control

Unsupervised Learning of a Kinematic Arm Model 463
  Heiko Hoffmann, Ralf Möller

A Design of CMAC Based Intelligent PID Controllers 471
  Toru Yamamoto, Ryota Kurozumi, Shoichiro Fujisawa

Learning to Control at Multiple Time Scales 479
  Ralf Schoknecht, Martin Riedmiller

The Evolution of Modular Artificial Neural Networks for Legged
Robot Control... 488
  Sethuraman Muthuraman, Grant Maxwell, Christopher MacLeod

Dimensionality Reduction through Sensory-Motor Coordination......... 496
  Rene te Boekhorst, Max Lungarella, Rolf Pfeifer

Learning Localisation Based on Landmarks Using Self-Organisation 504
  Kaustubh Chokshi, Stefan Wermter, Cornelius Weber

Signal Processing

Spatial Independent Component Analysis of Multitask-Related
Activation in fMRI Data... 515
  *Zhi-ying Long, Li Yao, Xiao-jie Zhao, Liu-qing Pei, Gui Xue,
  Qi Dong, Dan-ling Peng*

Closed Loop Stability of FIR-Recurrent Neural Networks 523
  Alex Aussem

Selective Noise Cancellation Using Independent Component Analysis 530
  Jun-Il Sohn, Minho Lee

Expert Mixture Methods for Adaptive Channel Equalization 538
  Edward Harrington

A Relaxation Algorithm Influenced by Self-Organizing Maps 546
  Michiharu Maeda

A Gradient Network for Vector Quantization and Its Image
Compression Applications.. 554
  Hatice Doğan and Cüneyt Güzeliş

Multi-scale Switching Linear Dynamical Systems..................... 562
  Onno Zoeter, Tom Heskes

Time-Series Prediction

Model Selection with Cross-Validations and Bootstraps –
Application to Time Series Prediction with RBFN Models 573
  Amaury Lendasse, Vincent Wertz, Michel Verleysen

A Hybrid Neural Architecture and Its Application to Temperature
Prediction 581
  Srimanta Pal, Jyotirmay Das, Kausik Majumdar

Risk Management Application of the Recurrent Mixture Density
Network Models 589
  Tatiana Miazhynskaia, Georg Dorffner, Engelbert J. Dockner

Hierarchical Mixtures of Autoregressive Models for Time-Series
Modeling 597
  Carmen Vidal, Alberto Suárez

Intelligent and Hybrid Systems

A Simple Constructing Approach to Build P2P Global Computing
Overlay Network 607
  Dou Wen, Jia Yan, Liu Zhong, Zou Peng

Option Pricing with the Product Constrained Hybrid Neural Network ... 615
  Paul Lajbcygier

Self-Organizing Operator Maps in Complex System Analysis 622
  Pasi Lehtimäki, Kimmo Raivio, Olli Simula

Optimization of a Microwave Amplifier Using Neural Performance
Data Sheets with Genetic Algorithms................................ 630
  Filiz Güneş, Yavuz Cengiz

Adaptive Stochastic Classifier for Noisy pH-ISFET Measurements 638
  Tong Boon Tang, Hsin Chen, Alan F. Murray

Comparing Support Vector Machines, Recurrent Networks, and Finite
State Transducers for Classifying Spoken Utterances.................. 646
  Sheila Garfield, Stefan Wermter

Selecting and Ranking Time Series Models Using the
NOEMON Approach 654
  Ricardo B.C. Prudêncio, Teresa B. Ludermir

Optimization of the Deflection Basin by Genetic Algorithm and
Neural Network Approach... 662
  Serdal Terzi, Mehmet Saltan, Tulay Yildirim

Inversion of a Neural Network via Interval Arithmetic for Rule
Extraction 670
    Carlos Hernández-Espinosa, Mercedes Fernández-Redondo,
    Mamen Ortiz-Gómez

Implementation of Visual Attention System Using Bottom-up
Saliency Map Model... 678
    Sang-Jae Park, Sang-Woo Ban, Jang-Kyoo Shin, Minho Lee

A Self-Growing Probabilistic Decision-Based Neural Network for
Anchor/Speaker Identification 686
    Y.H. Chen, C.L. Tseng, Hsin-Chia Fu, H.T. Pao

Unsupervised Clustering Methods for Medical Data: An Application
to Thyroid Gland Data 695
    Songül Albayrak

Protein Sequence Classification Using Probabilistic Motifs and
Neural Networks 702
    Konstantinos Blekas, Dimitrios I. Fotiadis, Aristidis Likas

On a Dynamic Wavelet Network and Its Modeling Application 710
    Yasar Becerikli, Yusuf Oysal, Ahmet Ferit Konar

Neural Network Hardware

Low Power Digital Neuron for SOM Implementations 721
    Roberta Cambio, David C. Hendry

Direction Selective Two-Dimensional Analog Circuits Using
Biomedical Vision Model..................................... 729
    Masashi Kawaguchi, Kazuyuki Kondo, Takashi Jimbo,
    Masayoshi Umeno

Review of Capacitive Threshold Gate Implementations 737
    Valeriu Beiu, Maria J. Avedillo, Jose M. Quintana

Constructive Threshold Logic Addition (A Synopsis of the Last Decade) . 745
    Valeriu Beiu

CrossNets: Neuromorphic Networks for Nanoelectronic Implementation .. 753
    Özgür Türel, Konstantin Likharev

Cognitive Science

The Acquisition of New Categories through Grounded Symbols:
An Extended Connectionist Model 763
    Alberto Greco, Thomas Riga, Angelo Cangelosi

A Neural Model of Binding and Capacity in Visual Working Memory 771
  Gwendid T. van der Voort van der Kleij, Marc de Kamps, Frank van der Velde

Neural Network: Input Anticipation May Lead to Advanced
Adaptation Properties 779
  Andrei Kursin

Acceleration of Game Learning with Prediction-Based Reinforcement
Learning – Toward the Emergence of Planning Behavior –.............. 786
  Yu Ohigashi, Takashi Omori, Koji Morikawa, Natsuki Oka

Computational Neuroscience

The Interaction of Recurrent Axon Collateral Networks in the
Basal Ganglia 797
  Mark D. Humphries, Tony J. Prescott, Kevin N. Gurney

Optimal Coding for Naturally Occurring Whisker Deflections 805
  Verena Vanessa Hafner, Miriam Fend, Max Lungarella, Rolf Pfeifer, Peter König, Konrad Paul Körding

Object Localisation Using Laterally Connected "What" and
"Where" Associator Networks 813
  Cornelius Weber, Stefan Wermter

Influence of Membrane Warp on Pulse Propagation Time 821
  Akira Hirose, Toshihiko Hamano

Detailed Learning in Narrow Fields – Towards a Neural Network
Model of Autism 830
  Andrew P. Papliński, Lennart Gustafsson

Online Processing of Multiple Inputs in a Sparsely-Connected
Recurrent Neural Network 839
  Julien Mayor, Wulfram Gerstner

The Spike Response Model: A Framework to Predict Neuronal Spike
Trains 846
  Renaud Jolivet, Timothy J. Lewis, Wulfram Gerstner

Roles of Motion and Form in Biological Motion Recognition 854
  Antonino Casile, Martin Giese

Special Sessions

Semantic and Context Aware Intelligent Systems

Improving the Performance of Resource Allocation Networks through
Hierarchical Clustering of High-Dimensional Data 867
  Nicolas Tsapatsoulis, Manolis Wallace, Stathis Kasderidis

Learning Rule Representations from Boolean Data 875
  B. Apolloni, A. Brega, D. Malchiodi, G. Palmas, A.M. Zanaboni

Weighted Self-Organizing Maps: Incorporating User Feedback 883
  Andreas Nürnberger, Marcin Detyniecki

Classification and Tracking of Hypermedia Navigation Patterns 891
  Patrick Gallinari, Sylvain Bidel, Laurent Lemoine, Frédéric Piat, Thierry Artières

Self-Aware Networks and Quality of Service 901
  Erol Gelenbe, Arturo Núñez

Drawing Attention to the Dangerous 909
  Stathis Kasderidis, John G. Taylor, Nicolas Tsapatsoulis, Dario Malchiodi

ASK – Acquisition of Semantic Knowledge 917
  Trevor P. Martin

An Adaptable Gaussian Neuro-Fuzzy Classifier 925
  Minas Pertselakis, Dimitrios Frossyniotis, Andreas Stafylopatis

Knowledge Refinement Using Fuzzy Compositional Neural Networks 933
  Vassilis Tzouvaras, Giorgos Stamou, Stefanos Kollias

Complex-Valued Neural Networks: Theories and Applications

Phase Singular Points Reduction by a Layered Complex-Valued
Neural Network in Combination with Constructive Fourier Synthesis 943
  Motoi Minami, Akira Hirose

Quantum Adiabatic Evolution Algorithm for a Quantum Neural
Network 951
  Mitsunaga Kinjo, Shigeo Sato, Koji Nakajima

Adaptive Beamforming by Using Complex-Valued Multi Layer
Perceptron 959
  Andriyan Bayu Suksmono, Akira Hirose

A Complex-Valued Spiking Machine 967
  Gilles Vaucher

The Behavior of the Network Consisting of Two Complex-Valued
Nagumo-Sato Neurons 977
  Iku Nemoto

On Activation Functions for Complex-Valued Neural Networks –
Existence of Energy Functions – 985
  Yasuaki Kuroe, Mitsuo Yoshida, Takehiro Mori

The Computational Power of Complex-Valued Neuron 993
  Tohru Nitta

Computational Intelligence and Applications

Recommendation Models for User Accesses to Web Pages 1003
  Şule Gündüz, M. Tamer Özsu

A Spectral-Spatial Classification Algorithm for Multispectral
Remote Sensing Data.. 1011
  Hakan Karakahya, Bingül Yazgan, Okan K. Ersoy

Neural Network Based Material Identification and Part Thickness
Estimation from Two Radiographic Images........................... 1018
  Ibrahim N. Tansel, Reen Nripjeet Singh, Peng Chen,
  Claudia V. Kropas-Hughes

Selection of Optimal Cutting Conditions by Using the Genetically
Optimized Neural Network System (GONNS) 1026
  W.Y. Bao, Peng Chen, Ibrahim N. Tansel, N.S. Reen, S.Y. Yang,
  D. Rincon

Building RBF Neural Network Topology through Potential Functions.... 1033
  Natacha Gueorguieva, Iren Valova

Use of Magnetomyographic (MMG) Signals to Calculate the
Dependency Properties of the Active Sensors in Myometrial Activity
Monitoring 1041
  C. Bayrak, Z. Chen, J. Norton, H. Preissl, C. Lowery, H. Eswaran,
  J. D. Wilson

Speed Enhancement with Soft Computing Hardware.................... 1049
  Taher Daud, Ricardo Zebulum, Tuan Duong, Ian Ferguson,
  Curtis Padgett, Adrian Stoica, Anil Thakoor

Neural Networks Applied to Electromagnetic Compatibility (EMC)
Simulations 1057
  Hüseyin Göksu, Donald C. Wunsch II

Sliding Mode Algorithm for Online Learning in Analog Multilayer
Feedforward Neural Networks 1064
    Nikola G. Shakev, Andon V. Topalov, Okyay Kaynak

Exploring Protein Functional Relationships Using Genomic
Information and Data Mining Techniques 1073
    Jack Y. Yang, Mary Qu Yang, Okan K. Ersoy

Predicting Bad Credit Risk: An Evolutionary Approach............ 1081
    Susan E. Bedingfield, Kate A. Smith

Indirect Differentiation of Function for a Network of Biologically
Plausible Neurons.. 1089
    Amber D. Fischer, Cihan H. Dagli

Application of Vision Models to Traffic Sign Recognition 1100
    X.W. Gao, L. Podladchikova, D. Shaposhnikov

Emotion Recognition

An Intelligent Scheme for Facial Expression Recognition 1109
    Amaryllis Raouzaiou, Spiros Ioannou, Kostas Karpouzis,
    Nicolas Tsapatsoulis, Stefanos Kollias, Roddy Cowie

Signal Enhancement for Continuous Speech Recognition 1117
    Theologos Athanaselis, Stavroula-Evita Fotinea, Stelios Bakamidis,
    Ioannis Dologlou, Georgios Giannopoulos

Emotion in Speech: Towards an Integration of Linguistic,
Paralinguistic, and Psychological Analysis..................... 1125
    Stavroula-Evita Fotinea, Stelios Bakamidis, Theologos Athanaselis,
    Ioannis Dologlou, George Carayannis, Roddy Cowie, E. Douglas-Cowie,
    N. Fragopanagos, John G. Taylor

An Emotional Recognition Architecture Based on Human
Brain Structure.. 1133
    John G. Taylor, N. Fragopanagos, Roddy Cowie, E. Douglas-Cowie,
    Stavroula-Evita Fotinea, Stefanos Kollias

Neural Networks for Bio-informatics Applications

Neural Network Ensemble with Negatively Correlated Features for
Cancer Classification 1143
    Hong-Hee Won, Sung-Bae Cho

Feature Analysis and Classification of Protein Secondary
Structure Data 1151
    S.Y.M. Shi, P.N. Suganthan

Recognition of Structure Classification of Protein Folding by NN
and SVM Hierarchical Learning Architecture 1159
   I-Fang Chung, Chuen-Der Huang, Ya-Hsin Shen, Chin-Teng Lin

Machine Learning for Multi-class Protein Fold Classification
Based on Neural Networks with Feature Gating 1168
   Chuen-Der Huang, I-Fang Chung, Nikhil Ranjan Pal, Chin-Teng Lin

Some New Features for Protein Fold Prediction 1176
   Nikhil Ranjan Pal, Debrup Chakraborty

Author Index 1185

Learning Algorithms

Adaptive Hopfield Network

Gürsel Serpen, PhD

Electrical Engineering and Computer Science Department
The University of Toledo, Toledo, OH 43606 USA
gserpen@eng.utoledo.edu
http://www.eecs.utoledo.edu/~serpen

Abstract. This paper proposes an innovative enhancement of the classical Hopfield network algorithm (and potentially its stochastic derivatives) with an "adaptation mechanism" to guide the neural search process towards high-quality solutions for large-scale static optimization problems. Specifically, a novel methodology that employs gradient-descent in the error space to adapt weights and constraint weight parameters in order to guide the network dynamics towards solutions is formulated. In doing so, a creative algebraic approach to define error values for each neuron without knowing the desired output values for the same is adapted.

1 Introduction

Classical Hopfield networks (CHN) have been applied to a surprisingly large spectrum of problems in optimization literature in numerous disciplines citing their ability to compute locally optimal solutions in constant time for any size problem for a hardware realization of the search algorithm [1]. The type and class of problems subjected to solution with CHNs is unaccountably large and rich given the all-encompassing nature of the field of optimization. This promise, which can be improved vastly, has been fulfilled to some degree for a significant set of problems considered. Often, difficulties in converging to feasible solutions were overcome with problem specific ad hoc or heuristic remedies while theoretical insight gained into the convergence properties provided reasonable avenues as well. As to the quality of feasible solutions computed by CHNs, simulated annealing or mean-field annealing mechanisms offered dramatic improvements at the expense of introducing serialization into an otherwise highly parallel algorithm thereby compromising one of fundamental computational features of CHNs, which is constant computation time for any size of a given problem.

This paper proposes an innovative and novel adaptation mechanism to dramatically improve ability of the CHN to locate high-quality solutions for large-scale static optimization problems. Adaptive Hopfield network (AHN), which embodies the proposed adaptation mechanism, is poised to deliver the true computational promise of the Hopfield network by guiding it towards feasible and high-quality solutions of a given optimization problem while preserving the inherent parallelism embedded in the algorithm itself. Implications of developing a massively-parallel search algorithm for optimization problems, which consistently produces feasible and high-quality solutions in constant time for any problem size instance when realized in hardware, are clear: promise is revolutionary for its potential improvements to the solutions of a vast array of real-life problems. Next sections will present the basic mathematical models for the classical Hopfield network, the proposed adaptive Hopfield network with all its adaptive and innovative features, and a preliminary simulation study.

2   Classical Hopfield Network

A Hopfield network is a nonlinear dynamical system [2], whereby the definition of the continuous Hopfield network is as follows. Let z_i represent a node output and $z_i \in [0,1]$ with $i = 1,2,....,K$, where K is the number of network nodes. Then,

$$E = -\frac{1}{2}\sum_{i=1}^{K}\sum_{j=1}^{K}w_{ij}z_i z_j + \frac{1}{\lambda}\sum_{i=1}^{K}\int_{0}^{z_i} f^{-1}(z)dz - \sum_{i=1}^{K}b_i z_i \qquad (1)$$

is a Liapunov function for the system of equations defined by

$$\frac{du_i(t)}{dt} = -u_i(t) + \sum_{j=1}^{K}w_{ij}z_j(t) + b_i \text{ and } z_i = f(u_i), \qquad (2)$$

where w_{ij} is the weight between nodes z_i and z_j subject to $w_{ij} = w_{ji}$, b_i is the external input for the i-th node whose state is represented by u_i, and $f(\cdot)$ is a nonlinearity, typically the sigmoid function with steepness defined by a parameter λ. Note that the second term in the Liapunov function vanishes for very large positive values of the parameter λ for cases where the activation function is sigmoid.

The set of formulas given in Equation 2 seek out through gradient descent a local minimum of the Equation 1 as dictated by the initial values of the neurons, neuron update order, and the basins of attractions of stable equilibrium points in the state space of the network dynamics. It has been shown that many local minima in the Liapunov space are not feasible solutions while those local minima associated with feasible solutions are far from the optimal solution, which is much more clearly noticeable particularly when the problem size instance grows [3], [4].

An adaptation mechanism that extracts the required information from previous unsuccessful search attempts in order to incorporate it into the neural network dynamics so that it is less likely for the CHN to repeat the same failed search process is of much utility. The proposed adaptation algorithm as detailed in the next sections follows this overall line of reasoning to guide the CHN towards feasible and high-quality solutions of large-scale static optimization problems.

3 Adaptive Hopfield Network

The CHN has two sets of parameters that can be adapted: weights and constraint weighting coefficients. Gradient descent based adaptation offers a computationally and mathematically feasible option for the both. Specifically, recurrent backpropagation algorithm for the weights and direct gradient descent for the constraint weighting coefficients are two reasonable choices and will be employed to demonstrate the adaptation concepts being proposed.

3.1 Adaptation Algorithm for Weights: Recurrent Backpropagation

The full derivation of the recurrent backpropagation (RBP) algorithm can be found in [5], [6], [7]. The RBP training algorithm requires an adjoint network, which is topologically identical to the CHN with the exception that all signal directions are reversed, to be set up and relaxed to compute updates for the weights of the CHN. The adjoint network accepts the error, which is computed using the stable values of neurons of the CHN upon convergence to a fixed point.

The RBP training algorithm for the CHN is implemented as follows. Upon convergence of the CHN dynamics given by Equations 1 and 2 to a fixed point, error values for output nodes need to be computed. The error for an output node is computed by the following formula:

$$e_i = \tau_i - z_i(\infty), \qquad (3)$$

where $z_i(\infty)$ is the stable output value of i-th neuron upon convergence to a fixed point with $i = 1, 2, \ldots, K$, K is the number of neurons in the CHN, and τ_i is the desirable value of the i-th neuron output. It should be noted that the value of τ_i is not normally known but can be derived indirectly through a novel procedure as will be demonstrated in a later section of this paper.

Next, an adjoint network, the topology of which is identical to that of the CHN with all signal directions reversed, is set up with the following linear dynamics:

$$\frac{dz_i^*(t)}{dt} = -z_i^*(t) + \sum_{j=1}^{K} f'(u_j(\infty)) w_{ji} z_j^*(t) + e_i \qquad (4)$$

for $i = 1, 2, \ldots, K$, where $z_j^*(t)$ represents the output of j-th node in the adjoint network, while noting that nodes in the adjoint network do not possess an output nonlinearity for the activation function and the weight w_{ij} in Hopfield network is replaced by $f'(u_j(\infty)) w_{ji}$ in its adjoint network.

Noting that local stability of the recurrent network dynamics is a sufficient condition for the convergence of the adjoint network dynamics, once the adjoint network converges, weight updates can be computed as

$$\Delta w_{ij} = -\eta \frac{\partial E}{\partial w_{ij}} = \eta f'[u_i(\infty)] z_i^*(\infty) z_j(\infty) \text{ and } \Delta w_{ij} = \Delta w_{ji} \text{ for } i, j = 1, 2, \ldots, K, \quad (5)$$

where η is the learning rate, which is a positive real, and f' is the derivative of the neuron activation function f.

It is critical to note that weight matrix symmetry needs to be preserved for global stability of Hopfield network dynamics. Therefore, the weight matrix can simply be maintained as an either upper triangular or lower triangular, which also happens to reduce memory storage requirement by half.

3.2 Adaptation Algorithm for Constraint Weighting Coefficients

A typical static optimization problem can be mapped to a single layer neuron topology of the CHN through empirical development of an error function [2]. This error function might be in the form of sum of linear and quadratic error terms, where each error term is associated with a particular constraint of the problem. In a generalized sense, the following format for the problem specific error function, which is defined to resemble the generic template given by the Liapunov function in Equation 1, is pursued:

$$E(\mathbf{z}) = -\frac{1}{2} \sum_{\alpha=1}^{|S_\alpha|} g_\alpha \sum_{i=1}^{K} \sum_{j=1}^{K} d_{ij}^\alpha \delta_{ij}^\alpha z_i z_j - \sum_{\beta=1}^{|S_\beta|} g_\beta \sum_{i=1}^{K} \delta_i^\beta z_i \quad (6)$$

where $i \neq j$; the set of constraints is given by $S_\varphi = \{C_1, C_2, \ldots, C_\varphi\}$ with S_α and S_β representing sets of quadratic and linearly formulated constraints, respectively, $S_\varphi = S_\alpha \cup S_\beta$, $S_\alpha \cap S_\beta = \phi$ and $|S_\varphi| = |S_\alpha| + |S_\beta|$; $g_\alpha \in R^+$ if the hypothesis nodes z_i and z_j each represent for a constraint α in S_α are mutually supporting and $g_\alpha \in R^-$ if the same hypotheses are mutually conflicting; the term δ_{ij}^α is equal to 1 if the two hypotheses represented by nodes z_i and z_j are related under the constraint α and is equal to 0 otherwise; similarly, the term δ_i^β is equal to 1 or 0 to facilitate mapping of the constraint β in S_β to the network topology; and the d_{ij}^α term is equal to 1 for all i and j under a hard constraint (which cannot be violated by definition) and is a predefined cost for a soft constraint (which can be violated in degrees), which is typically associated with a cost term in optimization problems.

Upon comparison of this generic error function given by Equation 6 with the Liapunov function in Equation 1, weight and bias terms are defined in terms of constraint weighting coefficients as follows:

$$w_{ij} = \sum_{\alpha=1}^{|S_\alpha|} g_\alpha \delta_{ij}^\alpha d_{ij}^\alpha \text{ and } b_i = \sum_{\beta=1}^{|S_\beta|} g_\beta \delta_i^\beta \text{ for } i, j = 1, 2, \ldots, K. \quad (7)$$

An earlier study derived bounds on initial values of the constraint weighting coefficients in Equation 7 to induce solutions of a given static optimization problem as stable equilibrium points in the state space of the classical Hopfield network dynamics [4]. It was further noted in the same study that in many cases the set of solutions tend to become a much smaller and proper subset of the set of all stable equilibrium points. Furthermore, it is well-known that values of constraint weighting coefficients often require adaptation throughout the overall search process: this issue has been addressed through predetermined heuristic update schedules to date [8]. It is possible to modify values of these coefficients in a more mathematically rigorous and "adaptive" manner utilizing the procedure of gradient descent in the error space. Following discussion presents details of such an approach.

Gradient descent based update rule when applied to adapt the constraint weighting coefficients is given by

$$g_\varphi(t_{k+1}) = g_\varphi(t_k) - \mu \frac{\partial E(\mathbf{z}, t_k)}{\partial g_\varphi(t_k)}, \tag{8}$$

where μ is the learning rate parameter that is a positive real, $g_\varphi(t_k)$ is the constraint weighting coefficient associated with constraint φ for $\varphi = 1, 2, ..., |S_\varphi|$ at discrete update time t_k, and $E(\mathbf{z}, t_k)$ is the value of error function at discrete time t_k, and t_k is the discrete time instant representing the conclusion of k-th relaxation of the network dynamics throughout an adaptation cycle.

Partial derivatives of the problem specific error function can easily be computed in most cases since the form of this function obeys a generic template, which lends itself to relatively easy manipulation, and is given by

$$E(\mathbf{z}, t_k) = E_1(\mathbf{z}, t_k) + E_2(\mathbf{z}, t_k) + \cdots + E_{|S_\varphi|}(\mathbf{z}, t_k)$$
$$= g_1(t_k) E_1'(\mathbf{z}, t_k) + \cdots + g_{|S_\varphi|}(t_k) E_{|S_\varphi|}'(\mathbf{z}, t_k), \tag{9}$$

where E_φ' is the unweighted error term, a scalar quantity readily computable throughout the search process, associated with the constraint φ for $\varphi = 1, 2, ..., |S_\varphi|$ at discrete time t_k. Then, partial derivatives of the error function with respect to constraint weighting coefficients assume the form of

$$\frac{\partial E(\mathbf{z}, t_k)}{\partial g_\varphi(t_k)} = E_\varphi'(\mathbf{z}, t_k) \text{ for } \varphi = 1, 2, ..., |S_\varphi|. \tag{10}$$

Consequently, the update equation for constraint weight parameters becomes

$$g_\varphi(t_{k+1}) = g_\varphi(t_k) - \mu E_\varphi'(\mathbf{z}, t_k) \text{ for } \varphi = 1, 2, ..., |S_\varphi|. \tag{11}$$

3.3 Derivation of Terms Required by Weight Update Formulas

Derivation of required quantities needed for weight and constraint parameter updates in Equations 5 and 11 will be demonstrated using a simplified example, which can easily be extended to more comprehensive cases with relative ease [9]. Consider a two dimensional $N{\times}N$ neuron array for the Hopfield network topology and assume the error term for the row constraint, which enforces each row to have exactly one active neuron, is defined by

$$E_{row} = g_{row} \sum_{i=1}^{N}\sum_{j=1}^{N}\left[1-\sum_{n=1}^{N}z_{nj}(\infty)\right]^2, \qquad (12)$$

where i and j are the indices for rows and columns, respectively, n is the index for rows of the network, $z_{nj}(\infty)$ is the stable value of nj-th neuron output upon convergence to a fixed point, and g_{row} is a positive real weight parameter. When each column of the output array has exactly one active neuron, this error term will be zero. The first summation over the indexing variable i is included because the error function needs to be defined for each neuron in the output layer.

We developed a novel procedure to define "desired" error values for each neuron in the output layer of the network to facilitate application of a supervised training algorithm for the classical Hopfield network. Note that desirable values of individual neurons of the classical Hopfield network for a solution are not known. What is known instead is the error function value for complete output array instance. Using the error function, it is feasible to compute desired or target values for each individual neuron. The error function E is defined in terms of the error value for each individual neuron, e_i, in the output layer by

$$E = \frac{1}{2}\sum_{i=1}^{N\times N} e_i^2, \qquad (13)$$

where the dimensions of the output neuron array is $N{\times}N$ and error is computed as in Equation 3.

The derivative of error function E with respect to some weight w_{kl}, where w_{kl} is the weight between k-th and l-th nodes for $k,l=1,2,\ldots,N{\times}N$, can be conveniently defined in terms of the error value for each individual output neuron, e_i, by

$$\frac{\partial E}{\partial w_{kl}} = -\sum_{i=1}^{N\times N} e_i \frac{\partial z_i(\infty)}{\partial w_{kl}}. \qquad (14)$$

This equation can be rewritten in terms of an output node array with N rows and N columns, where i, the index of the output layer neurons, is related to row and column indices q and r by $i = (q-1)N + r$,

$$\frac{\partial E}{\partial w_{kl}} = -\sum_{q=1}^{N}\sum_{r=1}^{N} e_{qr} \frac{\partial z_{qr}(\infty)}{\partial w_{kl}} \qquad (15)$$

Note that, from Equation 9, we have

$$\frac{\partial E}{\partial w_{kl}} = \frac{\partial}{\partial w_{kl}}\left(E_1 + E_2 + \cdots + E_{|S_\varphi|}\right) = \frac{\partial}{\partial w_{kl}}E_1 + \frac{\partial}{\partial w_{kl}}E_2 + \cdots + \frac{\partial}{\partial w_{kl}}E_{|S_\varphi|}. \quad (16)$$

Thus, the derivative of total error function can be computed by adding the derivatives of individual error terms. Using the error term due to the row constraint in Equation 12 and taking the derivative with respect to the w_{kl} yields

$$\frac{\partial E_{row}}{\partial w_{kl}} = -2g_{row}\sum_{q=1}^{N}\sum_{r=1}^{N}\left(1 - \sum_{n=1}^{N}z_{qn}(\infty)\right)\frac{\partial z_{qr}(\infty)}{\partial w_{kl}},$$

while noting that

$$\frac{\partial z_{qn}(\infty)}{\partial w_{kl}} \neq 0 \quad \text{when } n = r \text{ or } l=(q\text{-}1)N+r.$$

The desirable form for this error term is then given by

$$\frac{\partial E_{row}}{\partial w_{kl}} = 2g_{row}\sum_{q=1}^{N}\sum_{r=1}^{N}\left(\sum_{n=1}^{N}z_{qn}(\infty) - 1\right)\frac{\partial z_{qr}(\infty)}{\partial w_{kl}}. \quad (17)$$

Comparing Equations 15 and 17 results in

$$e_{qr} = 2g_{row}\left(\sum_{n=1}^{N}z_{nr}(\infty) - 1\right), \quad (18)$$

which is the quantity needed to adapt the weights through Equations 4 and 5.
The partial needed in Equation 10 to adapt constraint weighting coefficients through the Equation 11 is easily obtained from Equation 12 as follows:

$$\frac{\partial E(\mathbf{z},t_k)}{\partial g_{row}} = \sum_{i=1}^{N}\sum_{j=1}^{N}\left[1 - \sum_{n=1}^{N}z_{nj}(\infty)\right]^2. \quad (19)$$

4 Simulation Study

We have done a preliminary simulation study on the Traveling Salesman problem with city counts up to 400 and results indicate that the proposed adaptation procedure is feasible and promising in guiding the Hopfield network towards solutions. Solutions tend to be significantly higher quality on the average compared to those computed by the classical Hopfield network.

The algorithm at the moment presents a few evidently challenging obstacles for simulation purposes: the weight matrix size makes it practically impossible to test very large problem instances even on Supercomputing platforms [10] and the computational cost of the recurrent backpropagation algorithm is high. We are currently attempting to minimize the computational complexity of the overall adaptive Hopfield network. We anticipate results of a comprehensive simulation study to appear in an upcoming journal paper.

5 Conclusions

An adaptation mechanism, which modifies constraint weighting coefficient parameter values and weights of the classical Hopfield network, was proposed. A mathematical characterization of the adaptive Hopfield network was presented. Preliminary simulation results suggest the proposed adaptation mechanism to be effective in guiding the Hopfield network towards high-quality feasible solutions of large-scale static optimization problems. We are also exploring incorporating a computationally viable stochastic search mechanism to further improve quality of solutions computed by the adaptive Hopfield network while preserving parallel computation capability.

Acknowledgements. Simulation study for this project has been funded in part through a computing grant (No. PJS0254-1) by the State of Ohio Supercomputer Center in Columbus, OH, USA.

References

1. Smith, K.: Neural Networks for Combinatorial Optimization: A Review of More Than A Decade of Research. INFORMS J. on Computing. **11** (1999) 15–34
2. Hopfield, J. J., Tank, D. W.: Neural Computation of Decision in Optimization Problems. Biological Cybernetics. 52 (1985) 141–152
3. Serpen, G., Parvin, A.: On the Performance of Hopfield Network for Graph Search Problem. Int. J. Neurocomputing. 14 (1997) 365–381
4. Serpen, G., Livingston, D. L.: Determination of Weights for Relaxation Recurrent Neural Networks. Int. J. Neurocomputing. **34** (2000) 145–168
5. Pineda, F. J.: Generalization of Back-Propagation to Recurrent Neural Networks. Physical Review Letters. **59** (1987) 2229–2232
6. Almeida, L. B.: A Learning Rule for Asynchronous Perceptrons with Feedback in a Combinatorial Environment. Proc. of IEEE 1st Int. Conf. on Neural Networks. San Diego, CA. (1987) 609–618
7. Werbos, P. J.: Generalization of Backpropagation with Application to A Recurrent Gas Market Model. Neural Networks. **1** (1988) 234–242
8. Serpen, G., Livingston, D. L.: An Adaptive Constraint Satisfaction Network. Proc. ASILOMAR Conf. Signals, Systems and Circuits. Monterey, California. (1990) 163–167
9. Serpen, G., Patwardhan, A., Geib, J.: Simultaneous Recurrent Neural Network Addressing the Scaling Problem in Static Optimization. Neural Systems. **11** (2001) 477–487
10. OSC – Ohio Supercomputer Center, Columbus, Ohio, USA, 2002.

Effective Pruning Method for a Multiple Classifier System Based on Self-Generating Neural Networks

Hirotaka Inoue[1] and Hiroyuki Narihisa[2]

[1] Department of Electrical Engineering and Information Science,
Kure National College of Technology,
2-2-11 Agaminami, Kure-shi, Hiroshima, 737-8506 Japan
hiro@kure-nct.ac.jp

[2] Department of Information and Computer Engineering,
Okayama University of Science,
1-1 Ridai-cho, Okayama-shi, Okayama, 700-0005 Japan
narihisa@ice.ous.ac.jp

Abstract. Recently, multiple classifier systems (MCS) have been used for practical applications to improve classification accuracy. Self-generating neural networks (SGNN) are one of the suitable base-classifiers for MCS because of their simple setting and fast learning. However, the computational cost of the MCS increases in proportion to the number of SGNN. In this paper, we propose a novel pruning method for the structure of the SGNN in the MCS. Experiments have been conducted to compare the pruned MCS with an unpruned MCS, the MCS based on C4.5, and k-nearest neighbor method. The results show that the pruned MCS can improve its classification accuracy as well as reducing the computational cost.

1 Introduction

Classifiers need to find hidden information in the given large data effectively and classify unknown data as accurately as possible [1]. Recently, to improve the classification accuracy, multiple classifier systems (MCS) such as neural network ensembles, bagging, and boosting have been used for practical data mining applications [2,3]. In general, the base classifiers of the MCS use traditional models such as neural networks (backpropagation network and radial basis function network) [4] and decision trees (CART and C4.5) [5].

Neural networks have great advantages of adaptability, flexibility, and universal nonlinear input-output mapping capability. However, to apply these neural networks, it is necessary to determine the network structure and some parameters by human experts, and it is quite difficult to choose the right network structure suitable for a particular application at hand. Moreover, they require a long training time to learn the input-output relation of the given data. These drawbacks prevent neural networks being the base classifier of the MCS for practical applications.

Self-generating neural networks (SGNN) [6] have simple network design and high speed learning. SGNN are an extension of the self-organizing maps (SOM) of Kohonen [7] and utilize the competitive learning which is implemented as a self-generating neural tree (SGNT). The abilities of SGNN make it suitable for the base classifier of the MCS. In order to improve in the accuracy of SGNN, we proposed ensemble self-generating neural networks (ESGNN) for classification [8] as one of the MCS. Although the accuracy of ESGNN improves by using various SGNN, the computational cost, that is, the computation time and the memory capacity increases in proportion to the increase in number of SGNN in the MCS.

In this paper, we propose a novel MCS pruning method to reduce the computational cost for classification. This method is constructed from two stages. First, we introduce an on-line pruning algorithm to reduce the computational cost by using class labels in learning. Second, we optimize the structure of the SGNT in the MCS to improve the generalization capability by pruning the tedious leaves after learning. In the optimization stage, we introduce a threshold value as a pruning parameter to decide which subtree's leaves to prune and estimate with 10-fold cross-validation [9]. After the optimization, the MCS can improve its classification accuracy as well as reducing the computational cost. We use bagging [10] as a resampling technique for the MCS.

We investigate the improvement performance of the pruned MCS by comparing it with the MCS based on C4.5 [11] using ten problems in the UCI repository [12]. Moreover, we compare the pruned MCS with k-nearest neighbor (k-NN) [13] to investigate the computational cost and the classification accuracy. The optimized MCS demonstrates higher classification accuracy and faster processing speed than k-NN on average.

2 Pruning a Multiple Classifier System Based on SGNN

In this section, we describe how to prune tedious leaves in the MCS. We implement the pruning method as two stages. First, we mention the on-line pruning method in learning of SGNN. Second, we show the optimization method in constructing the MCS.

2.1 Self-Generating Neural Networks

SGNN are based on SOM and implemented as a SGNT architecture. The SGNT can be constructed directly from the given training data without any intervening human effort. The SGNT algorithm is defined as a tree construction problem of how to construct a tree structure from the given data which consist of multiple attributes under the condition that the final leaves correspond to the given data.

Before we describe the SGNT algorithm, we denote some notations.

- input data vector: $\boldsymbol{e}_i \in \mathbb{R}^m$.
- root, leaf, and node in the SGNT: n_j.
- weight vector of n_j: $\boldsymbol{w}_j \in \mathbb{R}^m$.

```
Input:
  A set of training examples E = {e_i}, i = 1, ... , N.
  A distance measure d(e_i,w_j).
Program Code:
  copy(n_1,e_1);
  for (i = 2, j = 2; i <= N; i++) {
    n_win = choose(e_i, n_1);
    if (leaf(n_win)) {
      copy(n_j, w_win);
      connect(n_j, n_win);
      j++;
    }
    copy(n_j, e_i);
    connect(n_j, n_win);
    j++;
    prune(n_win);
  }
Output:
  Constructed SGNT by E.
```

Fig. 1. SGNT algorithm

- the number of the leaves in n_j: c_j.
- distance measure: $d(e_i, w_j)$.
- winner leaf for e_i in the SGNT: n_{win}.

The SGNT algorithm is a hierarchical clustering algorithm. The pseudo C code of the SGNT algorithm is given in Figure 1. In Figure 1, several sub procedures are used. Table 1 shows the sub procedures of the SGNT algorithm and their specifications.

In order to decide the winner leaf n_{win} in the sub procedure choose(e_i,n_1), the competitive learning is used. This sub procedure is recursively used from the root to the leaves of the SGNT. If an n_j includes the n_{win} as its descendant in the SGNT, the weight w_{jk} ($k = 1, 2, \ldots, m$) of the n_j is updated as follows:

$$w_{jk} \leftarrow w_{jk} + \frac{1}{c_j} \cdot (e_{ik} - w_{jk}), \quad 1 \leq k \leq m. \tag{1}$$

Table 1. Sub procedures of the SGNT algorithm

Sub procedure	Specification
$copy(n_j, e_i/w_{win})$	Create n_j, copy attributes of e_i/w_{win} as weights w_j in n_j.
$choose(e_i, n_1)$	Decide n_{win} for e_i.
$leaf(n_{win})$	Check n_{win} whether n_{win} is a leaf or not.
$connect(n_j, n_{win})$	Connect n_j as a child leaf of n_{win}.
$prune(n_{win})$	Prune leaves if the leaves have the same class.

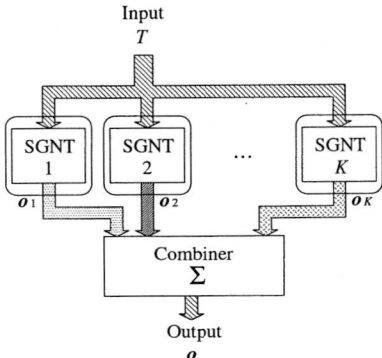

Fig. 2. An MCS which is constructed from K SGNTs. The test dataset T is entered each SGNT, the output o_i is computed as the output of the winner leaf for the input data, and the MCS's output is decided by voting outputs of K SGNTs

After all training data are inserted into the SGNT as the leaves, the leaves have each class label as the outputs and the weights of each node are the averages of the corresponding weights of all its leaves. The whole network of the SGNT reflects the given feature space by its topology. For more details concerning how to construct and perform the SGNT, see [6]. Note, to optimize the structure of the SGNT effectively, we remove the threshold value of the original SGNT algorithm in [6] to control the number of leaves based on the distance because of the trade-off between the memory capacity and the classification accuracy. In order to avoid the above problem, we introduce a new pruning method in the sub procedure prune(n_win). We use the class label to prune leaves. For leaves connected to the n_{win}, if those leaves have the same class label, then the parent node of those leaves is given the class label and those leaves are pruned.

2.2 Optimization of the Multiple Classifier System

The SGNT has the capability of high speed processing. However, the accuracy of the SGNT is inferior to the conventional approaches, such as nearest neighbor, because the SGNT has no guarantee to reach the nearest leaf for unknown data. Hence, we construct an MCS by taking the majority of plural SGNT's outputs to improve the accuracy (Figure 2).

Although the accuracy of the MCS is superior or comparable to the accuracy of conventional approaches, the computational cost increases in proportion to the increase in the number of SGNTs in the MCS. In particular, the huge memory requirement prevents the use of MCS for large datasets even with latest computers.

In order to improve the classification accuracy, we propose an optimization method of the MCS for classification. This method has two parts, the merge

```
1 begin    initialize j = the height of the SGNT
2   do for each subtree's leaves in the height j
3     if the ratio of the most class ≥ the threshold value α,
4     then merge all leaves to parent node
5     if all subtrees are traversed in the height j,
6     then j ← j − 1
7   until j = 0
8 end.
```

Fig. 3. The merge phase

```
1 begin initialize α = 0.5
2   do for each α
3     evaluate the merge phase with 10-fold cross validation
4     if the best classification accuracy is obtained,
5     then record the α as the optimal threshold value
6     α ← α + 0.05
7   until α = 1
8 end.
```

Fig. 4. The evaluation phase

phase and the evaluation phase. The merge phase is performed as a pruning algorithm to reduce dense leaves (Figure 3). This phase uses the class information and a threshold value α to decide which subtree's leaves to prune or not. For leaves that have the same parent node, if the proportion of the most common class is greater than or equal to the threshold value α, then these leaves are pruned and the parent node is given the most common class.

The optimum threshold values α of the given problems are different from each other. The evaluation phase is performed to choose the best threshold value by introducing 10-fold cross validation (Figure 4).

3 Experimental Results

We investigate the computational cost (the memory capacity and the computation time) and the classification accuracy of MCS based on SGNN with bagging for ten benchmark problems in the UCI repository [12]. We evaluate how the MCS is pruned using 10-fold cross-validation for the ten benchmark problems. In this experiment, we use a modified Euclidean distance measure for the MCS. To select the optimum threshold value α, we set the different threshold values α which are moved from 0.5 to 1; $\alpha = [0.5, 0.55, 0.6, \ldots, 1]$. We set the number of SGNT K in the MCS as 25 and execute 100 trials by changing the sampling order of each training set. All computations of the MCS are performed on an IBM PC-AT machine (CPU: Intel Pentium II 450MHz, Memory: 323MB).

Table 2. The average memory requirement and classification accuracy of 100 trials for the bagged SGNT in the MCS. The standard deviation is given inside the bracket on classification accuracy ($\times 10^{-3}$)

	memory requirement			classification accuracy		
Dataset	pruned	unpruned	ratio	pruned	unpruned	ratio
balance-scale	113.62	860.61	13.2	0.869(5.68)	0.848(7.93)	+2.1
breast-cancer-w	28.9	897.81	3.2	0.972(2.45)	0.968(2.66)	+0.4
glass	104.77	297.95	35.1	0.721(11.77)	0.716(13.73)	+0.5
ionosphere	54.52	472.18	11.5	0.893(8.24)	0.868(7.79)	+2.5
iris	14.65	208.7	7	0.965(4.83)	0.961(4.74)	+0.4
letter	6213.52	27052.43	22.9	0.956(0.76)	0.956(0.75)	0
liver-disorders	155.17	471.71	32.8	0.624(14.88)	0.608(17.01)	+1.6
new-thyroid	49.5	298.4	16.5	0.952(6.32)	0.949(6.76)	+0.3
pima-diabetes	212.81	1045.4	20.3	0.749(7.34)	0.730(8.71)	+1.9
wine	14.69	239.21	6.1	0.965(4.73)	0.96(4.2)	+0.5
Average	696.22	3184.44	16.9	0.866	0.856	+1

Table 2 shows the average memory requirement and classification accuracy of 100 trials for the MCS based on SGNN. As the memory requirement, we count the number of units which is the sum of the root, nodes, and leaves of the SGNT. The memory requirement is reduced from 64.9% to 96.8% and the classification accuracy is improved from 0% to 2.5% by pruning the MCS. This supports that the pruned MCS can be effectively used for all datasets with regard to both the computational cost and the classification accuracy.

To evaluate the pruned MCS's performance, we compare the pruned MCS with the MCS based on C4.5. We set the number of classifiers K in the MCS as 25 and we construct both MCS by bagging. Table 3 shows the improved performance of the pruned MCS and the MCS based on C4.5. The results of the SGNT and the pruned MCS are the average of 100 trials. The pruned MCS has a better performance than the MCS based on C4.5 for 6 of the 10 datasets. Although the MCS based on C4.5 degrades the classification accuracy for iris, the pruned MCS can improve the classification accuracy for all problems. Therefore, the pruned SGNT is a good base classifier for the MCS on the basis of both the scalability for large scale datasets and the robust improving generalization capability for the noisy datasets comparable to the MCS with C4.5.

To show the advantages of the pruned MCS, we compare it with k-NN on the same problems. In the pruned MCS, we choose the best classification accuracy of 100 trials with bagging. In k-NN, we choose the best accuracy where k is 1,3,5,7,9,11,13,15,25 with 10-fold cross-validation. All methods are compiled by using gcc with the optimization level -O2 on the same computer.

Table 4 shows the classification accuracy, the memory requirement, and the computation time achieved by the pruned MCS and k-NN. Next, we show the results for each category.

Table 3. The improved performance of the pruned MCS and the MCS based on C4.5 with bagging

	MCS based on SGNT			MCS based on C4.5		
Dataset	SGNT	MCS	ratio	C4.5	MCS	ratio
balance-scale	0.781	**0.869**	+8.8	0.795	0.827	+3.2
breast-cancer-w	0.957	**0.972**	+1.5	0.946	0.963	+1.7
glass	0.641	0.721	+8	0.664	**0.757**	+9.3
ionosphere	0.853	0.894	+4.1	0.897	**0.92**	+2.3
iris	0.949	**0.965**	+1.6	0.953	0.947	−0.6
letter	0.879	**0.956**	+7.7	0.880	0.938	+5.8
liver-disorders	0.58	0.624	+4.4	0.635	**0.736**	+10.1
new-thyroid	0.935	**0.952**	+1.7	0.93	0.94	+1
pima-diabetes	0.699	0.749	+5	0.749	**0.767**	+1.8
wine	0.95	**0.965**	+1.5	0.927	0.949	+2.2
Average	0.822	0.866	+4.4	0.837	**0.874**	+3

Table 4. The classification accuracy, the memory requirement, and the computation time of ten trials for the best pruned MCS and k-NN

	classification acc.		memory requirement		computation time (s)	
Dataset	MCS	k-NN	MCS	k-NN	MCS	k-NN
balance-scale	0.882	**0.899**	**100.41**	562.5	**1.27**	2.52
breast-cancer-w	**0.977**	0.973	**26.7**	629.1	1.69	**1.31**
glass	**0.756**	0.706	**115.97**	192.6	0.48	**0.04**
ionosphere	**0.915**	0.875	**25.62**	315.9	1.7	**0.25**
iris	**0.973**	0.960	**10.9**	135	0.18	**0.05**
letter	0.958	**0.961**	**6273.15**	18000	**220.52**	845.44
liver-disorders	**0.666**	0.647	**150.28**	310.5	0.77	**0.6**
new-thyroid	**0.968**	0.968	**53.57**	193.5	0.34	**0.05**
pima-diabetes	**0.768**	0.753	**204.11**	691.2	**2.47**	3.41
wine	**0.978**	0.977	**12.2**	160.2	0.36	**0.13**
Average	**0.884**	0.872	**697.29**	2119.1	**22.98**	85.38

First, with regard to the classification accuracy, the pruned MCS is superior to k-NN for 7 of the 10 datasets and gives 1.2% improvement on average. Second, in terms of the memory requirement, even though the pruned MCS includes the root and the nodes which are generated by the SGNT generation algorithm, this is less than k-NN for all problems. Although the memory requirement of the pruned MCS is totally used K times in Table 4, we release the memory of SGNT for each trial and reuse the memory for effective computation. Therefore, the memory requirement is suppressed by the size of the single SGNT. Finally, in view of the computation time, although the pruned MCS consumes the cost of K times of the SGNT, the average computation time is faster than k-NN. In the case of letter, in particular, the computation time of the pruned MCS is faster than k-NN by about 3.8 times. We need to repeat 10-fold cross validation many times to select the optimum parameters for α and k. This evaluation consumes much computation time for large datasets such as letter. Therefore, the pruned MCS based on the fast and compact SGNT is useful and practical for large datasets. Moreover, the pruned MCS has the ability of parallel computation because each classifier behaves independently. In conclusion, the pruned MCS is practical for large-scale data mining compared with k-NN.

4 Conclusions

In this paper, we proposed a new pruning method for the MCS based on SGNN and evaluated the computational cost and the accuracy. We introduced an on-line and off-line pruning method and evaluated the pruned MCS by 10-fold cross-validation. Experimental results showed that the memory requirement reduces remarkably, and the accuracy increases by using the pruned SGNT as the base classifier of the MCS. The pruned MCS is a useful and practical tool to classify large datasets. In future work, we will study an incremental learning and a parallel and distributed processing of the MCS for large scale data mining.

References

1. J. Han and M. Kamber. *Data Mining: Concepts and Techniques*. Morgan Kaufmann Publishers, San Francisco, CA, 2000.
2. J. R. Quinlan. Bagging, Boosting, and C4.5. In *Proceedings of the Thirteenth National Conference on Artificial Intelligence*, pages 725–730, Portland, OR, 1996.
3. G. Rätsch, T. Onoda, and K.-R. Müller. Soft margins for AdaBoost. *Machine Learning*, 42(3):287–320, 2001.
4. C. M. Bishop. *Neural Networks for Pattern Recognition*. Oxford University Press, New York, 1995.
5. R. O. Duda, P. E. Hart, and D. G. Stork. *Pattern Classification*. John Wiley & Sons Inc., New York, 2nd ed., 2000.
6. W. X. Wen, A. Jennings, and H. Liu. Learning a neural tree. In *the International Joint Conference on Neural Networks*, Beijing, China, 1992. This paper is available at ftp://ftp.cis.ohio-state.edu/pub/neuroprose/wen.sgnt-learn.ps.Z.
7. T. Kohonen. *Self-Organizing Maps*. Springer-Verlag, Berlin, 1995.
8. H. Inoue and H. Narihisa. Improving generalization ability of self-generating neural networks through ensemble averaging. In T. Terano, H. Liu, and A. L P. Chen, eds, *The Fourth Pacific-Asia Conference on Knowledge Discovery and Data Mining*, vol. 1805 of *LNAI*, pages 177–180, Springer-Verlag, 2000.
9. M. Stone. Cross-validation: A review. *Math. Operationsforsch. Statist., Ser. Statistics*, 9(1):127–139, 1978.
10. L. Breiman. Bagging predictors. *Machine Learning*, 24:123–140, 1996.
11. J. R. Quinlan. *C4.5: Programs for Machine Learning*. Morgan Kaufmann, San Mateo, CA, USA, 1993.
12. C.L. Blake and C.J. Merz. UCI repository of machine learning databases, University of California, Irvine, Dept of Information and Computer Science, 1998. Datasets is available at http://www.ics.uci.edu/~mlearn/MLRepository.html.
13. E. A. Patrick and F. P. Fischer. A generalized k-nearest neighbor rule. *Information and Control*, 16(2):128–152, 1970.

Structural Bias in Inducing Representations for Probabilistic Natural Language Parsing

James Henderson

Dept. of Computer Science, University of Geneva, Genève, Switzerland
James.Henderson@cui.unige.ch,
http://cui.unige.ch/~henderson/

Abstract. We present a neural network based natural language parser. Training the neural network induces hidden representations of unbounded partial parse histories, which are used to estimate probabilities for parser decisions. This induction process is given domain-specific biases by matching the flow of information in the network to structural locality in the parse tree, without imposing any independence assumptions. The parser achieves performance on the benchmark datasets which is roughly equivalent to the best current parsers.

1 Introduction

Processing structured data, and particularly natural language parsing, has been a challenge for artificial neural networks. Recurrent neural network architectures are potentially useful in this domain, due to their ability to recursively compress unbounded structures into a finite hidden representation. But this potential has been muted by their strong bias towards only including recent information in a hidden representation and ignoring information earlier in the recursion. This bias has prevented many attempts at parsing with neural networks from scaling up to long sentences with large parse trees [1], and is probably responsible for the poor performance when neural networks have been applied to broad coverage parsing [2]. Rather than trying to avoid this bias, in this work we exploit this bias to help the network's training induce hidden representations which are appropriate to the domain. We propose a method for neural network structure processing which matches recency in the network's recursive computation to a domain-dependent notion of locality in the structure.

We apply this locality principle to the design of Simple Synchrony Networks (SSNs) [3,4] for estimating the probabilities of parser decisions. The resulting statistical parsers achieve performance roughly equivalent to the state-of-the-art. Performance with part-of-speech tags as input is better than any other such parser. With words as input, performance (89.1% F-measure) is only 0.6% below the best current parser, despite using a relatively small vocabulary.

2 Inducing History Representations with SSNs

Natural language parsing takes a string of words of unbounded length (the sentence) and produces a tree structure of unbounded size (the parse). In statistical parsing, the objective is to estimate the probability of each possible tree structure for the input sentence, and choose the most probable one. To handle the unbounded size of the trees, the probability of a parse tree is broken down into a sequence of probabilities for individual decisions about the tree, such as choosing the label of a node in the tree or deciding which node is the parent of another node. This sequence of decisions is called the tree's derivation. Assuming that there is a one-to-one mapping between trees and derivations, we can use the chain rule for conditional probabilities to derive the probability of a tree as the multiplication of the probabilities of each derivation decision d_i conditional on that decision's prior derivation history $d_1,..., d_{i-1}$.

$$P(tree(d_1,...,d_m)) = P(d_1,...,d_m) = \Pi_i P(d_i|d_1,...,d_{i-1})$$

Given such a probability model, we want to design a neural network for estimating the model's parameters $P(d_i|d_1,...,d_{i-1})$.

The most challenging problem in estimating $P(d_i|d_1,...,d_{i-1})$ is how to represent the unbounded amount of information in the derivation history $d_1,..., d_{i-1}$. We would like to have a finite representation $h(d_1,..., d_{i-1})$ of this history. The standard practise in statistical parsing is to make a priori independence assumptions which allow us to ignore all the information about $d_1,..., d_{i-1}$ except a finite set of history features [5,6]. Holistic approaches to neural network parsing avoid such independence assumptions by applying a neural network architecture for sequence processing directly to the history sequence $d_1,..., d_{i-1}$ [1]. Training automatically induces a hidden representation which is used for $h(d_1,..., d_{i-1})$. We take a similar approach, but use a neural network architecture, Simple Synchrony Networks [3,4], which is capable of exploiting both the sequential ordering of the derivation history and the underlying structural nature of the tree which the derivation specifies.

SSNs allow us to exploit the underlying tree structure because they do not treat a derivation as a single holistic sequence, but as a set of sub-derivations. Each one of these sub-derivations is associated with a node in the tree, and structural relationships between nodes are used to determine how information is passed from one of these sub-derivations to another. The unbounded number of nodes in a parse tree is not a problem for this approach, because SSNs can process an unbounded set of sub-derivations, as well as handling the unbounded length of each sub-derivation.

A SSN processes each of the sub-derivations in its set in the same way as a Simple Recurrent Network (SRN) [7]. At each step $s_{j,k}$ in the sub-derivation s_j for node j, a context layer is used to record the hidden layer activations from the previous step $s_{j,k-1}$ in s_j, and these activations plus the new inputs at step $s_{j,k}$ are used to compute new hidden layer activations and the outputs for step $s_{j,k}$. The vector of new hidden layer activations at step $s_{j,k}$ is the history representation $h(d_1,..., d_{s_{j,k}-1})$ for the derivation decision $d_{s_{j,k}}$. The outputs for step $s_{j,k}$ are the estimates for the probability distribution $P(d_{s_{j,k}}|d_1,..., d_{s_{j,k}-1})$. The new inputs at position $i = s_{j,k}$ are a set of pre-defined features of the derivation history $f(d_1,..., d_{i-1})$ and a set of history representations $\{rep_{i-1}(l) | l \in D(j)\}$ for nodes $D(j)$ which are in pre-defined structural relationships to node j, where $rep_{i-1}(l) = h(d_1,..., d_{\max(k|k \leq i \wedge N(k)=l)})$ is the most recent previous history representation assigned to node l, and $N(k)$ is the node for the sequence to which step k is assigned.

To avoid making independence assumptions we need $f(d_i|d_1,...,d_{i-1})$ to always include d_{i-1} and $D(N(i))$ to always include N(i-1). In this case, any information about the derivation history $d_1,...,d_{i-1}$ could in principle be included in the history representation $h(d_1,...,d_{i-1})$ (by induction). However, in practice some information is much more likely to be included than other information. During training, the error which is back-propagated through the network's recursive computation quickly vanishes as it passes from hidden layer computation to hidden layer computation. This means that training will tend to ignore correlations between inputs and outputs which are separated by many hidden layer computations, and focus on correlations between inputs and outputs which are close together. However, this inductive bias can actually be very useful. Inducing a finite hidden representation of an unboundedly large history is a very difficult optimization problem, so it is important to bias the learning towards representations which we know a priori to be good ones.

We achieve this bias by placing inputs which we know to be relevant to a given output close to that output in the flow of information between history representations. Features of the derivation history $d_1,...,d_{i-1}$ which are expected to be directly relevant to the derivation decision d_i are included in the pre-defined inputs $f(d_1,...,d_{i-1})$. And if two derivation decisions d_i and d_{i+k} are expected to be dependent on the same features of the derivation history, then the node $N(i)$ for the earlier decision is included in the set of nodes $D(N(i_k))$ whose history representations are input to the computation for the later decision. This approach differs from the approach of making independence assumptions primarily in that these biases are soft while independence assumptions are hard. Sufficiently strong correlations which contradict our expectations will still be discovered by the training.

3 The SSN Statistical Parser

The complete parsing system uses the probability estimates computed by the SSN to search for the derivation $d_1,...,d_m$ with the highest probability $P(d_1,...,d_m)$. The search incrementally constructs partial derivations $d_1,...,d_i$ by taking a derivation it has already constructed $d_1,...,d_{i-1}$, using the SSN to estimate a probability distribution $P(d_i|d_1,...,d_{i-1})$ over possible next decisions d_i, and computing $P(d_1,...,d_i) = P(d_1,...,d_{i-1})P(d_i|d_1,...,d_{i-1})$. In general, the partial derivation with the highest probability is chosen as the next one to be extended, but to perform the search efficiently it is necessary to prune the search space (see [8] for details). We find that the search is still tractable with sufficiently little pruning that it has virtually no effect on parser accuracy.

The parameters $P(d_i|d_1,...,d_{i-1})$ which the SSN estimates are determined by the order in which derivation decisions are made. The derivation ordering which we use here is that of a form of left-corner parser [9], illustrated by the numbering in the left half of figure 1. The parsing of a subtree proceeds bottom-up from its leftmost terminal, and introduces the node for the root of the subtree after the root's first child has been parsed. This root node is then placed on a stack, where it provides top-down information for the parsing of the root's remaining children, as illustrated in the right half of figure 1. More detail about the derivations used can be found in [8].

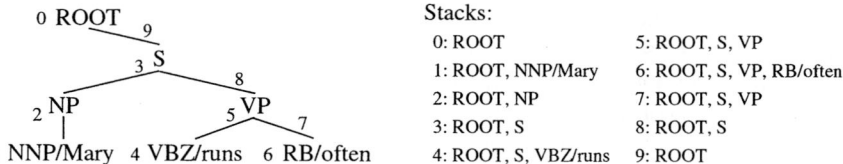

Fig. 1. The order in which aspects of the parse tree are specified in a derivation (left) and the derivation's stack after each decision (right).

The SSN uses standard methods [10] to estimate a probability distribution over the set of possible next decisions d_i given the SSN's history representation $h(d_1,..., d_{i-1})$. Due to the need to choose node labels and predict input words, there are a very large number of possible next decisions. For this reason we separate the computation of $P(d_i|d_1,..., d_{i-1})$ into several sub-computations, and use mixture models to combine them. Each sub-computation uses the normalized exponential output function. The first computation has one output for each of the three basic types of decisions: predict the next tag-word pair $P(predict|\alpha)$, introduce a new node $P(introduce|\alpha)$, or pop the stack $P(pop|\alpha)$, where $\alpha = h(d_1,..., d_{i-1})$. The second computation has one output for each node label.

$$P(introduce(l)|\alpha) = P(introduce(l)|introduce, \alpha)P(introduce|\alpha)$$

When computing the probability of predicting the next word, we avoid the need to normalize over the entire set of words by first computing a probability distribution over tags, and then computing a probability distribution over tag-word pairs conditioned on the tag.

$$P(predict(t/w)|\alpha) = P(predict(t/w)|predict(t/), \alpha)P(predict(t/)|predict, \alpha)P(predict|\alpha)$$

This means that only the tag-word computation for the correct tag needs to be performed. We also reduced the computational cost of word prediction by replacing the very large number of lower frequency tag-word pairs with a tag-"unknown-word" pair. This method also has the advantages of training an output to be used for words which were not in the training set, and smoothing across tag-word pairs whose low frequency would prevent accurate learning by themselves. A variety of frequency thresholds were tried, as reported in section 5. The inputs for tag-word pairs also include separate inputs for tags and the same tag-"unknown-word" pairs.

4 The Linguistically Appropriate Inductive Bias

As discussed in section 2, we can impose domain-dependent biases on the induction of history representations through the choice of $N(i)$, $D(N(i))$, and $f(d_1,..., d_{i-1})$. In particular, we want information from the history representations for the nodes $D(N(i))$ to be relevant to the history representation for the node $N(i)$. We match recency in this flow of information between history representations to a linguistically appropriate notion of structural locality.

We assign a derivation step i to the node $N(i) = top_i$ which is on the top of the stack prior to that step. This means that $h(d_1,..., d_{i-1})$ will always receive as input the history representation of the most recent previous step which also had top_i on the top of the stack. This imposes an appropriate bias because the induced history features which are relevant to previous derivation decisions involving top_i are likely to be relevant to future decisions involving top_i as well. As a simple example, in figure 1, the prediction of the leftmost terminal of the VP node (step 4) and the decision that the S node is the root of the whole sentence (step 9) are both dependent on the fact that the node on the top of the stack in each case has the label S (chosen in step 3).

Given that $N(i) = top_i$, we want to define $D(N(i))$ to be a set of nodes which are structurally local to top_i. We define $D(N(i))$ to be the left-corner ancestor of top_i (which is below top_i on the stack), top_i's leftmost child, and top_i's most recent child (which is top_{i-1}, or none). The history representations for these nodes always include that for the previous derivation step $i - 1$, so we are not imposing any independence assumptions by this choice of $D(N(i))$.

The pre-defined features $f(d_1,...,d_{i-1})$ which are input directly to $h(d_1,...,d_{i-1})$ are those which we think are directly relevant to the decision to be made at step i. In the parser presented here, these inputs are the last decision d_{i-1} in the derivation, the label or tag of the sub-derivation's node top_i, the most recently predicted tag-word pair, and the tag-word pair for top_i's leftmost terminal.

5 The Experimental Results

We tested this SSN parsing model on the standard corpus (the Penn Treebank [11]), thereby allowing us to compare its performance directly to other broad coverage parsing models in the literature. To test the effects of varying the vocabulary size on performance and tractability, we trained three different models. The simplest model (SSN-Tags) includes no words in the vocabulary, using only part-of-speech tags as input. The second model (SSN-200) uses all tag-word pairs which occur at least 200 times in the training set, plus the tag-"unknown-word" pairs. This resulted in a vocabulary size of 512 tag-word pairs. The third model (SSN-20) thresholds the vocabulary at 20 instances in the training set, resulting in 4242 tag-word pairs.[1]

We determined appropriate training parameters and network size based on intermediate validation results and our previous experience with networks similar to the models SSN-Tags and SSN-200. We trained two or three networks for each of the three models and chose the best one based on their validation performance. We then tested the best models for each vocabulary size on the testing set.[2] Standard measures of performance are shown in table 1.[3]

The left panel of table 1 lists the results for the SSN-Tags model and for two other models which only use part-of-speech tags as inputs: another neural network parser (Cost01) [2], and a probabilistic context free grammar (Char97) [13]. The SSN-Tags

---

[1] We used a publicly available tagger [12] to provide the tags used in these experiments.
[2] All the best networks had 80 hidden units. Weight decay regularization was applied at the beginning of training but reduced to 0 by the end of training.
[3] All our results are computed following the standard criteria in [6], and using the standard training, validation, and testing sets [6]. F-measure is a combination of recall and precision. The F-measures values for previous models may have rounding errors.

Table 1. Standard performance measures on labeled constituents in the testing set.

	Cost01	Char97	SSN-Tags	Ratn99	Coll99	Coll00	SSN-200	SSN-20
recall	57.8	70.1	83.3	86.3	88.1	89.6	88.3	88.8
precision	64.9	74.3	84.3	87.5	88.3	89.9	89.2	89.5
F-measure	61.0	72.1	83.8	86.9	88.2	89.7	88.8	89.1

model achieves performance which is much better than the only other broad coverage neural network parser, Cost01. The SSN-Tags model also does better than any other published results on parsing with just part-of-speech tags, as exemplified by the results for Char97.

The right panel of table 1 lists the results for the two SSN models which use words, SSN-200 and SSN-20, and three recent statistical parsers: Ratn99 [5], Coll99 [6], and Coll00 [14]. The performance of the SSN models fall near the top of this range, only being beaten by the best current parsers, which all achieve performance roughly equivalent to Coll00. The best current parser, Coll00, has only 4% less precision error, only 7% less recall error, and only 6% less F-measure error than the best SSN model. The SSN parser achieves this performance using a much smaller vocabulary than other approaches, which all use a frequency threshold of at most 5 plus morphological analysis, and without any explicit notion of a phrase's head word, which has proved to be important in other models [6].

6 Related Work

Much previous work on parsing with neural networks has taken the approach of modeling the derivation sequence directly [1]. The problem with this approach is that when a parse tree is flattened into a single derivation sequence, some decisions which are structurally local in the tree will inevitably end up being far apart in the derivation. This implies an inductive bias in the neural network which is not appropriate for the domain, as discussed in section 2. As the parse tree grows larger the distance in the derivation between adjacent decisions in the tree also grows larger, which we believe is the main reason this approach has not been successfully scaled up beyond small parse trees [1].

Two neural network architectures have been developed specifically for application to structured representations, SSNs and Recursive Neural Networks (RNNs) [15]. The RNN architecture models structures by mapping the nodes and edges of the structure's graph directly to hidden layers and links in the neural network. When applied to natural language parsing [2], this mapping is applied to the partial parse trees produced during an incremental parse of a sentence. The RNN learns to estimate the probability that a partial parse tree is correct. For the purposes of broad coverage parsing the results are not very good, as shown in table 1 under Cost01. Based on the arguments made in section 2, we believe this is because the distance between an input and the output in the RNN's recursive computation is a function of the structural distance from the input's node to the tree's root, rather than the structural distance between the input's node and the node where a decision needs to be made.

The Simple Synchrony Network architecture was originally motivated by a neuroscientific hypothesis about how the timing of neuron activation spikes is used to represent objects [16]. The units of an SSN pulse, which provides them with two temporal dimensions for encoding information, period and phase. Phases are used to represent objects, and periods are used to represent the time course of computation. The key property of this architecture from the point of view of learning is that timing is used to represent objects, so the same link weights can be used for each object, resulting in the ability to generalize to unbounded sets of objects [3]. In this paper the objects are the nodes of the tree, so each phase includes the hidden and output unit activations for one node's sub-derivation. There is one period for each word in the sentence, but unlike in previous work, there may be periods in which a phase has no output and simply copies its previous hidden activations. We use the simplest version of the SSN architecture, which has no holistic representation of state (non-pulsing units) [3], only the hidden activations for individual sub-derivations. In this form the SSN architecture is a special case of the RNN architecture, but the RNN would be applied to the graph of the information flow between SSN sub-derivations, rather than to the tree structures as is done in [2]. Previous work on applying SSNs to parsing [4] has not been general enough to be applied to the standard corpus, so it is not possible to compare results directly to this work.

7 Conclusions

This paper has presented the design of a Simple Synchrony Network for statistical parsing. The SSN is trained to estimate the probabilities of derivation decisions conditioned on the previous derivation history, and these estimates are used to search for the most probable parse. When trained and tested on the standard datasets, the parser's performance (89.1% F-measure) is only 0.6% less than the best current parser [14], despite using a smaller vocabulary size (4242 inputs) and less prior linguistic knowledge.

This level of performance is achieved due to the Simple Synchrony Networks' success in inducing a good hidden representation of the unbounded derivation history. Crucial to this success is the use of domain-dependent biases which focus the induction process on structurally local aspects of the derivation history. In addition to demonstrating the usefulness of this approach to neural network structure processing, this work demonstrates the ability of neural network structure processing to successfully scale up to unrestricted structures, large datasets, and fairly large vocabularies.

References

1. E.K.S. Ho and L.W. Chan. How to design a connectionist holistic parser. *Neural Computation*, 11(8):1995–2016, 1999.
2. F. Costa, V. Lombardo, P. Frasconi, and G. Soda. Wide coverage incremental parsing by learning attachment preferences. In *Proc. of the Conf. of the Italian Association for Artificial Intelligence*, 2001.
3. Peter Lane and James Henderson. Incremental syntactic parsing of natural language corpora with simple synchrony networks. *IEEE Transactions on Knowledge and Data Engineering*, 13(2):219–231, 2001.

4. James Henderson. A neural network parser that handles sparse data. In *Proc. 6th Int. Workshop on Parsing Technologies*, pages 123–134, Trento, Italy, 2000.
5. Adwait Ratnaparkhi. Learning to parse natural language with maximum entropy models. *Machine Learning*, 34:151–175, 1999.
6. Michael Collins. *Head-Driven Statistical Models for Natural Language Parsing*. PhD thesis, University of Pennsylvania, Philadelphia, PA, 1999.
7. Jeffrey L. Elman. Distributed representations, simple recurrent networks, and grammatical structure. *Machine Learning*, 7:195–225, 1991.
8. James Henderson. Inducing history representations for broad coverage statistical parsing. In *Proc. joint meeting of North American Chapter of the Association for Computational Linguistics and the Human Language Technology Conf.*, Edmonton, Canada, 2003.
9. D.J. Rosenkrantz and P.M. Lewis. Deterministic left corner parsing. In *Proc. 11th Symposium on Switching and Automata Theory*, pages 139–152, 1970.
10. Christopher M. Bishop. *Neural Networks for Pattern Recognition*. Oxford University Press, Oxford, UK, 1995.
11. Mitchell P. Marcus, Beatrice Santorini, and Mary Ann Marcinkiewicz. Building a large annotated corpus of English: The Penn Treebank. *Computational Linguistics*, 19(2):313–330, 1993.
12. Adwait Ratnaparkhi. A maximum entropy model for part-of-speech tagging. In *Proc. Conf. on Empirical Methods in Natural Language Processing*, pages 133–142, Univ. of Pennsylvania, PA, 1996.
13. Eugene Charniak. Statistical parsing with a context-free grammar and word statistics. In *Proc. 14th National Conference on Artificial Intelligence*, Providence, RI, 1997. AAAI Press/MIT Press.
14. Michael Collins. Discriminative reranking for natural language parsing. In *Proc. 17th Int. Conf. on Machine Learning*, pages 175–182, Stanford, CA, 2000.
15. P. Frasconi, M. Gori, and A. Sperduti. A general framework for adaptive processing of data structures. *IEEE Transactions on Neural Networks*, 9:768–786, 1998.
16. Lokendra Shastri and Venkat Ajjanagadde. From simple associations to systematic reasoning: A connectionist representation of rules, variables, and dynamic bindings using temporal synchrony. *Behavioral and Brain Sciences*, 16:417–451, 1993.

Independent Component Analysis Minimizing Convex Divergence

Yasuo Matsuyama, Naoto Katsumata, and Ryo Kawamura

Department of Computer Science, Waseda University,
Tokyo 169-8555, Japan
yasuo2@waseda.jp, {katsu,ryo}@wizard.elec.waseda.ac.jp

Abstract. A new class of learning algorithms for independent component analysis (ICA) is presented. Starting from theoretical discussions on convex divergence, this information measure is minimized to derive new ICA algorithms. Since the convex divergence includes logarithmic information measures as special cases, the presented method comprises faster algorithms than existing logarithmic ones. Another important feature of this paper's ICA algorithm is to accept supervisory information. This ability is utilized to reduce the permutation indeterminacy which is inherent in usual ICA. By this method, the most important activation pattern can be found as the top one. The total algorithm is tested through applications to brain map distillation from functional MRI data. The derived algorithm is faster than logarithmic ones with little additional memory requirement, and can find task related brain maps successfully via conventional personal computer.

1 Introduction

Optimization of information measures is a rich resource of learning algorithms. This is mainly because observed data are often probabilistic in nature. Independent component analysis (ICA) [1] is a typical case obtained from such optimization. Usually, the performance measure for the optimization is based upon logarithmic information measures [1], [2], [3]. But, there is a wider class of information measure called the convex divergence or the f-divergence [4][1].

Starting from discussions on the basic properties of the f-divergence, we derive a new class of ICA algorithms called the f-ICA by minimizing this information measure. Contribution of this paper can be previewed as follows.
(i) New properties of the f-divergence and related information measures are presented.
(ii) The f-ICA contains usual logarithmic ICA as a special case. Convergence speed is faster than the logarithmic one.
(iii) Obtained algorithms are modifiable to be partially supervised learning.
(iv) Corresponding software is executable on a personal computer. Applications to human brain map distillation from functional Magnetic Resonance Imaging (fMRI) are successfully made.

---
[1] Equation (4.20) of [5] is a forerunner of the f-divergence.

2 Convex Divergence and New Properties

2.1 Definition and Properties

Convex divergence is a measure of information which gives a directed distance between two probability densities p_ψ and p_φ by using an adjustable convexity. Here, ψ and φ are generic parameters. Let $f(r)$ be convex on $r \in (0, \infty)$, and let $g(r) \stackrel{\text{def}}{=} rf(1/r)$ be its dual convex function. Then, the convex divergence, or f-divergence, is defined as follows [4].

$$D_f(\psi\|\varphi) \stackrel{\text{def}}{=} \int_y p_\varphi(y) f(p_\psi(y)/p_\varphi(y)) dy$$
$$= \int_y p_\psi(y) g(p_\varphi(y)/p_\psi(y)) dy \stackrel{\text{def}}{=} D_g(\varphi\|\psi) \geq g(1) = f(1) \stackrel{\text{def}}{=} 0 \quad (1)$$

We are interested in the case that $f(r)$ is twice continuously differentiable. This assumption makes it possible to discuss information matrices and gradient style learning. Differential properties are as follows.

$$D_f(\varphi\|\varphi) = D_g(\varphi\|\varphi) = 0 \quad (2)$$
$$\partial^{10} D_f(\varphi\|\varphi) = \partial^{10} D_g(\varphi\|\varphi) = 0 \quad (3)$$
$$\partial^{20} D_f(\varphi\|\varphi) = f''(1) F_Y(\varphi) = g''(1) F_Y(\varphi) = \partial^{20} D_g(\varphi\|\varphi) \quad (4)$$

Here, ∂^{ij} stands for i and j times partial differentiation with respect to ψ and φ, respectively. $F_Y(\varphi)$ is the Fisher information matrix.

Next, we define the following constant[2].

$$c \stackrel{\text{def}}{=} \frac{f''(1)}{f'(1)} = -\frac{g''(1)}{g'(1)} \in (-\infty, \infty). \quad (5)$$

Then, the following expansion holds around $r = 1$.

$$\frac{f(r)}{f''(1)} = \left(\frac{1}{c} r^c\right) \left\{\frac{1}{1-c}(r^{1-c} - 1)\right\} + o(1) \quad (6)$$

$$\frac{g(r)}{g''(1)} = \left(\frac{-1}{c}\right) \left\{\frac{1}{1-c}(r^{1-c} - 1)\right\} + o(1) \quad (7)$$

Here, $o(1)$ is the higher order term. From Equations (6) and (7), we find that

$$L^{(c)}(r) = \frac{1}{1-c}(r^{1-c} - 1) \quad (8)$$

is regarded as an extended class of logarithm. In fact, $L^{(1)}(r) = \log r$ in the limit. This "c-logarithm" has relationships to the Fisher information matrix and the Cramér-Rao bound. Let L_c be an abbreviated notation of $L^{(c)}(p_\varphi)$. Then, we have

$$M_Y^{(c)}(\varphi) \stackrel{\text{def}}{=} E_{p_\varphi}\left[c p_\varphi^{-2(1-c)} \left(\frac{\partial L_c}{\partial \varphi}\right)\left(\frac{\partial L_c}{\partial \varphi^T}\right)\right] = -E_{p_\varphi}\left[p_\varphi^{-(1-c)} \left(\frac{\partial^2 L_c}{\partial \varphi \partial \varphi^T}\right)\right]. \quad (9)$$

---
[2] If we add a set of assumptions that $f(xy) = kf(x)f(y)$ and $f''(1) = g''(1) = 1$, then the α-divergence [6], [7] is obtained. In this case, $c = \frac{1-\alpha}{2}$ holds. The symbol $o(1)$ in (6) and (7) becomes unnecessary.

The case of $c = 1$ is reduced to the Fisher information matrix $F_Y(\varphi)$:

$$M_Y^{(c)}(\varphi) = cM_Y^{(1)}(\varphi) = cF_Y(\varphi). \tag{10}$$

Because of Equations (10), the use of the information matrix $M_Y^{(c)}(\varphi)$ does not deteriorate the Cramér-Rao bound [8], [9], [10]. We assume that underlying problems are regular, so that $M^{(c)}(\varphi) > 0$, $F(\varphi) > 0$, and $c > 0$.

2.2 Optimization Transfer

Equations (4), (8), (9) and (10) mean that the f-divergence and the c-logarithm can be used as targets of optimizations instead of logarithmic information measures. That is, optimizations can be transferred to the f-divergence and/or to the c-logarithm [10], [11]. From the next section, independent component analysis is discussed through the minimization of the f-divergence between the observed joint probability density p and the independent probability density q.

3 The f-ICA Algorithm

3.1 Derivation of the Algorithm

In the problem of ICA, we are given a set of vector random variables.

$$\boldsymbol{x}(n) = [x_1(n), \cdots, x_K(n)]^T = A\boldsymbol{s}(n), \quad (n = 1, \cdots, N). \tag{11}$$

Here, the matrix A and the vector

$$\boldsymbol{s}(n) = [s_1(n), \cdots, s_K(n)]^T \tag{12}$$

are all unknown but the following: (i) The components $s_i(n)$, $(i = 1, \cdots, K)$, are non-Gaussian except for at most one i. (ii) The components $s_i(n)$ and $s_j(n)$ are independent each other for $i \neq j$.

Under the above conditions, we want to estimate a demixing matrix

$$W = \Lambda \Pi A^{-1} \tag{13}$$

so that the components of

$$W\boldsymbol{x}(n) \stackrel{\text{def}}{=} \boldsymbol{y}(n) = [y_1(n), \cdots, y_K(n)]^T \tag{14}$$

are independent each other for every n. Here, Λ is a nonsingular diagonal matrix and Π is a permutation matrix, both of which are unknown too.

For the independent component analysis of this paper, we minimize the following f-divergence.

$$I_f(\bigwedge_{i=1}^K Y_i) \stackrel{\text{def}}{=} D_f\left(p(y_1, \cdots, y_K) \| \prod_{i=1}^K q_i(y_i)\right)$$
$$= D_g\left(\prod_{i=1}^K q_i(y_i) \| p(y_1, \cdots, y_K)\right) \stackrel{\text{def}}{=} I_g(\bigwedge_{i=1}^K Y_i) \tag{15}$$

This quantity counts how the joint probability density $p(y_1,\cdots,y_K)$ is close to $\prod_{i=1}^{K} q_i(y_i)$. Traditional methods [1], [2], [3] minimize the mutual information or maximize the differential entropy, which corresponds to $c = 1$.

For the estimation of the demixing matrix W, we use a gradient descent. In this case, we obtain

$$-\nabla I_g(\wedge_{i=1}^{K} Y_i) \stackrel{\text{def}}{=} -\frac{\partial I_g(\wedge_{i=1}^{K} Y_i)}{\partial W} = \int_{\mathcal{X}} |W| q(\boldsymbol{y}) g'\left(\frac{|W|q(\boldsymbol{y})}{p(\boldsymbol{x})}\right) \left\{W^{-T} - \boldsymbol{\varphi}(\boldsymbol{y})\boldsymbol{x}^T\right\} d\boldsymbol{x}. \tag{16}$$

Here,

$$\boldsymbol{\varphi}(\boldsymbol{y}) = [\varphi_1(y_1),\ldots,\varphi_K(y_K)]^T = -\left[\frac{q_1'(y_1)}{q_1(y_1)},\ldots,\frac{q_K'(y_K)}{q_K(y_K)}\right]^T \tag{17}$$

is a nonlinear function assumed to be such as $\varphi_i(y) = y^3$ or $\tanh(y)$. For the natural gradient [12], [13], [14], we multiply $cW^T W$. Then, we have

$$-\tilde{\nabla} I_g(\wedge_{i=1}^{K} Y_i) \stackrel{\text{def}}{=} -\frac{\partial I_g(\wedge_{i=1}^{K} Y_i)}{\partial W}(cW^T W)$$
$$= -c \int_{\mathcal{Y}} q(\boldsymbol{y}) g'\left(\frac{q(\boldsymbol{y})}{p(\boldsymbol{y})}\right) \left\{I - \boldsymbol{\varphi}(\boldsymbol{y})\boldsymbol{y}^T\right\} d\boldsymbol{y}\, W$$
$$= f''(1)\left[c\left\{I - E_{p(\boldsymbol{y})}[\boldsymbol{\varphi}(\boldsymbol{y})\boldsymbol{y}^T]\right\} W + (1-c)\left\{I - E_{q(\boldsymbol{y})}[\boldsymbol{\varphi}(\boldsymbol{y})\boldsymbol{y}^T]\right\} W\right] + o(1) \tag{18}$$

Here, the last equality is obtained by the expansion of $qg'(q/p)$ around $p \approx q$. Then, the update equation is

$$W(t+1) = W(t) + \tilde{\Delta}_g W(t), \tag{19}$$

with

$$\tilde{\Delta}_g W(t) = \rho(t)\left\{-\tilde{\nabla} I_g(\wedge_{i=1}^{K} Y_i)\right\}_{W=W(t)}. \tag{20}$$

Here, $\rho(t)$ is a small positive number called the learning rate. We call the learning algorithm (19) and (20) the f-ICA. Note that $c = 1$ is the case of the minimum mutual information ICA [2], [3]. The region $0 < c < 1$ gives faster convergence with the ratio of $1 + \frac{1-c}{c}\frac{q}{p}$.

3.2 Realization Using Past and Future Information

Equation (18) is a resource of f-ICA algorithms. The next important step is to find effective interpretations of this expression. Since we are given sample observations, the expectation $E_{p(\boldsymbol{y})}$ can be approximated by repeated applications of given data in either a batch or a successive style. But, the expectation $E_{q(\boldsymbol{y})}$ contains an unknown probability density function $q(\boldsymbol{y})$ because of the semi-parametric formulation of ICA. Since "$p(\boldsymbol{y}) \to q(\boldsymbol{y})$" holds as the update is repeated, $p(\boldsymbol{y})$ and $q(\boldsymbol{y})$ can be considered as two time-ordered states extracted from learning iterations [15]. Therefore, we can use a time-shifted version of p for the sake of unknown q. This interpretation leads to the following versions which are readily programmable for computer software.

[Momentum f-ICA]

If we use $p(\boldsymbol{y})$ as $p^{(t-\tau)}(\boldsymbol{y})$ and $q(\boldsymbol{y})$ as $p^{(t)}(\boldsymbol{y})$ at the t-th iteration, then the sample-based learning is realized as follows.

$$\tilde{\Delta}_g W(t) \stackrel{\text{def}}{=} \tilde{\Delta} W(t) + \mu_c \tilde{\Delta} W(t-\tau)$$
$$= \rho(t)\left[\{I - \varphi(\boldsymbol{y}(t))\boldsymbol{y}(t)^T\}W(t) + \mu_c\{I - \varphi(\boldsymbol{y}(t-\tau))\boldsymbol{y}(t-\tau)^T\}W(t-\tau)\right] \quad (21)$$

Here, $\mu_f = \frac{c}{1-c}$. Thus, we add a momentum term $\tilde{\Delta} W(t-\tau)$ weighted by μ_c.

[Turbo (Look-ahead) f-ICA]

If we use $p(\boldsymbol{y})$ as $p^{(t)}(\boldsymbol{y})$ and $q(\boldsymbol{y})$ as $p^{(t+\tau)}(\boldsymbol{y})$ at the t-th iteration, then the sample-based learning is realized as follows.

$$\tilde{\Delta}_g W(t) \stackrel{\text{def}}{=} \tilde{\Delta} W(t) + \nu_c \tilde{\Delta} \hat{W}(t+\tau)$$
$$= \rho(t)\left[\{I - \varphi(\boldsymbol{y}(t))\boldsymbol{y}(t)^T\}W(t) + \nu_c\{I - \varphi(\boldsymbol{y}(t+\tau))\boldsymbol{y}(t+\tau)^T\}\hat{W}(t+\tau)\right] \quad (22)$$

Here, $\nu_c = \frac{1}{\mu_c} = \frac{1-c}{c}$, and $\hat{W}(t+\tau)$ is a predicted future value.

3.3 Batch and Semi-batch

Since we are given $\{\boldsymbol{x}(n)\}_{n=1}^N$ as a set of source vectors, the expectation $E_p[\cdot]$ is approximated by $\frac{1}{T}\sum_{i=1}^T[\cdot]$, where T is the number of samples in a selected window. The case of $T = N$ is the full batch mode. If we use $T < N$ as a window, it becomes a semi-batch mode. If $T = 1$, the case is an incremental learning. It is possible to choose a window size smaller than N for the look-ahead part so that the computation is alleviated. This style of semi-batch mode is recommended for the turbo f-ICA.

3.4 Partial Supervision

Because of the unknown permutation matrix Π, the resulting matrix W still requires users to identify which source is which. This aggravates undesirable off-line nature of the algorithm. Therefore, we consider to inject partially supervising data so that the target information is recovered as the top source.

From Equation (14), the observed signal $\boldsymbol{x}(n)$ is expressed as a transformation of $\boldsymbol{y}(n)$ by

$$\boldsymbol{x}(n) = W^{-1}\boldsymbol{y}(n) \stackrel{\text{def}}{=} U\boldsymbol{y}(n). \quad (23)$$

Let

$$U \stackrel{\text{def}}{=} [\boldsymbol{u}_1, \cdots, \boldsymbol{u}_K] \quad (24)$$

and

$$\boldsymbol{u}_j = [u_{1j}, \cdots, u_{Kj}]^T. \quad (25)$$

Then,

$$\boldsymbol{x}(n) = \boldsymbol{u}_1 y_1(n) + \cdots + \boldsymbol{u}_K y_K(n). \quad (26)$$

Thus, the vector $\{u_j\}_{j=1}^K$ possesses the information on the mixture. Therefore, we consider to control the ordering of u_j. Suppose we have a set of teacher signals or a target pattern, say $\bar{R}$. Then, this teacher signal can be incorporated into the iterative minimization [16]. The method is to add a descent cost term

$$F(U, \bar{R}) = tr\{(\bar{R} - U)^T(\bar{R} - U)\}. \tag{27}$$

For this cost function, the gradient descent term is

$$\Delta U = \gamma(\bar{R} - U), \tag{28}$$

where γ is a small positive constant. If $\bar{R}$ is nonsingular, the following approximation can be used

$$\Delta U = \gamma \bar{R}\{I - (W\bar{R}^{-1})\} \approx \gamma \bar{R}(W\bar{R} - I). \tag{29}$$

Since we have to use the effect of ΔU with the main increment $\tilde{\Delta}_g W$ of (20), the following transformed version is used.

$$\Delta V = -W\{\Delta U\}W. \tag{30}$$

This equation comes from an expansion of an the update matrix U^{-1} [11], [16], [17]. Since we applied the natural gradient to obtain the main update term (20), we need to use the same method to ΔV. But, the natural gradient in this case is the same as ΔV becase of the following equality:

$$\tilde{\Delta} V = -W\{\Delta U\}(U^T U)W(W^T W) = \Delta V. \tag{31}$$

4 Real-World Applications of the f-ICA: Brain Map Distillation

The purpose of this experiment is to find independent spatial patterns in the brain functional magnetic resonance imaging (fMRI) using a conventional personal computer. Since Equation (26) holds, we can regard each column vector of $U = W^{-1}$ as an activation pattern of separated brain maps [18]. The fMRI data are measured by assigning a series of "on-off" stimuli to a tested person.

Figure 1 illustrates convergence speed. The dotted line shows the speed of the usual logarithmic method (minimum mutual information with natural gradient). The solid line is the presented method using the momentum strategy with constant learning rates. Thus, the presented method in this paper is successful. Note that, placed between these two lines is the curve using Hestenes-Stiefel type learning rate adjustment. Because the true cost function is semi-parametric in ICA, time-dependent adjustment of the learning rate may not always be effective. Figure 2 is the extracted activation pattern (a time course) which corresponds to an assigned on-off task to a subject (a young male)[3]. This pattern is the top one, i.e., u_1. The prior knowledge injection of Section 2.4 was so successful. Figure 3

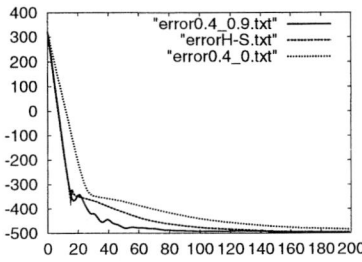 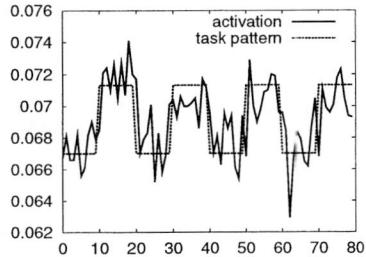

Fig. 1. Learning speed.   **Fig. 2.** Corresponding activation.

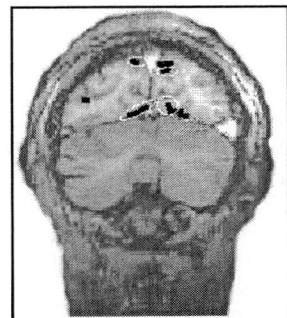

Fig. 3. Separation of V1 and V2.

is the resulting brain map. This map clearly separates the edges of visual regions V1 and V2.

Experiments were executable by a conventional personal computer. This is due to the increased speed of the presented algorithm which exploits the second term of Equation (18). A usual memory size is sufficient since the presented algorithm requires very little memory increase.

5 Concluding Remarks

In this paper, the concept of the optimization transfer to an information measure which is more general than the logarithmic one was explained. This paper showed (i) basic properties of the f-divergence and related information measures, (ii) derivation of a general class of ICA algorithms based upon the convex divergence, (iii) reduction of indeterminacy in ICA by using a partially supervised strategy, (iv) applications to human brain's fMRI map distillation. It was shown that human brain's fMRI data can be handled by a conventional personal computer.

In this paper's ICA, the transferred optimization was the *minimization* of the convex divergence. There is an important relative to the optimization transfer. It is the alpha-EM algorithm. In that case, the likelihood ratio of Equation (8) is

---

[3] The authors are very grateful to Dr. Keiji Tanaka and Dr. R. Allen Waggoner of RIKEN BRI for permitting them to try out their data set.

maximized. This method contains the traditional log-EM algorithm as its special case. Interested readers are requested to refer to [8], [9], [10].

References

1. C. Jutten and J. Herault, Blind separation of sources, Part I: An adaptive algorithm based on neuromimetic architecture, Signal Processing, vol. 24, pp. 1–20, 1991.
2. A.J. Bell and T.J. Sejnowski, An information-maximization approach to blind separation and blind deconvolution, Neural Computation, vol. 7, pp. 1129–1159, 1995.
3. H.H. Yang and S. Amari, Adaptive online learning algorithm for blind separation: Maximum entropy and minimum mutual information, Neural Computation, vol. 9, pp. 1457–1482, 1997.
4. I. Csiszár, Information-type measures of difference of probability distributions and indirect observations, Studia Sci. Math. Hungarica, vol. 2, pp. 299–318, 1967.
5. A. Rényi, On measures of entropy and information, Proc. 4th Berkeley Symp. Math. Stat. and Pr., vol. 1, pp. 547–561, 1960.
6. S. Amari, Differential geometry of statistics, Institute of Mathematical Statistics Lecture Notes, vol. 10, pp. 21–94, 1985.
7. S. Amari and H. Nagaoka, *Methods of Information Geometry*, Iwanami, 1993 (Translation by D. Harada, AMS, 2000).
8. Y. Matsuyama, The α-EM algorithm: A block connectable generalized learning tool for neural networks, Lecture Notes in Computer Science, No. 1240, pp. 483–492, Berlin, Germany: Springer-Verlag, June, 1997.
9. Y. Matsuyama, The α-EM algorithm and its basic properties, Transactions of Institute of Electronics, Information and Communications Engineers, vol. J82-D-I, pp. 1347–1358, 1999.
10. Y. Matsuyama, The α-EM algorithm: Surrogate likelihood optimization using α-logarithmic information measures, IEEE Trans. on Information Theory, vol. 49, no. 3, pp. 692–706, 2003.
11. Y. Matsuyama, S. Imahara and N. Katsumata, Optimization transfer for computational learning, Proc. Int. Joint Conf. on Neural Networks, vol. 3, pp. 1883–1888, 2002.
12. M. Jamshidian and R.I. Jennrich, Conjugate gradient acceleration of the EM algorithm, J. ASA, vol. 88, pp. 221–228, 1993.
13. J.-F. Cardoso and B.H. Laheld, Equivariant adaptive source separation, IEEE Trans. on SP, vol. 44, pp. 3017–3030, 1996.
14. S. Amari, Natural gradient works efficiently in learning, Neural Computation, vol. 10, pp. 252–276, 1998.
15. Y. Matsuyama, N. Katsumata, Y. Suzuki and S. Imahara, The α-ICA algorithm, Proc. Int. Workshop on Independent Component Analysis, pp. 297-302, 2000.
16. Y. Matsuyama and S. Imahara, The α-ICA algorithm and brain map distillation from fMRI images, Proc. Int. Conf. on Neural Information Processing, vol. 2, pp. 708–713, 2000.
17. Y. Matsuyama and R. Kawamura, Supervised map ICA: Applications to brain functional MRI, Proc. Int. Conf. on Neural Information Processing, vol. 5, pp. 2259–2263, 2002.
18. M.J. McKeown, T-P. Jung, S. Makeig, G. Brown, S.S. Kindermann, T-W. Lee and T.J. Sejnowski, Spatially independent activity patterns in functional MRI data during the stroop color-naming task, Proc. National Academy of Sci. USA, vol. 95, pp. 803–810, 1998.

Selecting Salient Features for Classification Committees

Antanas Verikas[1,2], Marija Bacauskiene[2], and Kerstin Malmqvist[1]

[1] Intelligent Systems Laboratory, Halmstad University, Box 823,
S-301 18 Halmstad, Sweden
av@ide.hh.se
[2] Department of Applied Electronics, Kaunas University of Technology, Studentu 50,
LT-3031, Kaunas, Lithuania

Abstract. We present a neural network based approach for identifying salient features for classification in neural network committees. Our approach involves neural network training with an augmented cross-entropy error function. The augmented error function forces the neural network to keep low derivatives of the transfer functions of neurons of the network when learning a classification task. Feature selection is based on two criteria, namely the reaction of the cross-validation data set classification error due to the removal of the individual features and the diversity of neural networks comprising the committee. The algorithm developed removed a large number of features from the original data sets without reducing the classification accuracy of the committees. By contrast, the accuracy of the committees utilizing the reduced feature sets was higher than those exploiting all the original features.

1 Introduction

The pattern recognition problem is traditionally divided into the stages of feature extraction and classification. A large number of features usually can be measured in many pattern recognition applications. Not all of the features, however, are equally important for a specific task. Some of the variables may be redundant or even irrelevant. Usually better performance may be achieved by discarding such variables. Moreover, as the number of features used grows, the number of training samples required grows exponentially. Therefore, in many practical applications we need to reduce the dimensionality of the data.

Feature selection with neural nets can be thought of as a special case of architecture pruning, where input features are pruned, rather than hidden neurons or weights. Pruning procedures extended to the removal of input features have been proposed in [1], where the feature selection process is usually based on some saliency measure aiming to remove less relevant features.

It is well known that a combination of many different neural networks can improve classification accuracy. A variety of schemes have been proposed for combining multiple classifiers. The approaches used most often include the majority vote, averaging, weighted averaging, the fuzzy integral, the Dempster-Shafer theory, the Borda count, aggregation through order statistics, and probabilistic aggregation [2,3]. Numerous previous works on neural network committees have shown that an efficient committee should consist of networks that are not only very accurate, but also diverse in the sense that the network errors occur in different regions of the input space [4]. Bootstrapping [5], Boosting [6], and AdaBoosting [7] are the most often used approaches for data sampling aiming to create diverse committee members. Breiman has recently proposed a very simple algorithm, the so called half & half bagging approach [8]. To create committees comprised of diverse networks, we adopted the half & half bagging technique.

Despite a considerable interest of researchers in neural network based feature selection and neural network committees, to our knowledge, there were no attempts to select features for neural network committees. In this paper, we propose a technique for identifying salient features for classification in neural network committees. Since committee performance depends on both the accuracy and diversity of committee members, feature selection is based on two criteria, namely the reaction of the cross-validation data set classification error due to the removal of the individual features and the diversity of neural networks comprising the committee.

2 Half & Half Bagging and Diversity of Networks

We use fully connected feedforward neural networks. Assume that $o_j^{(q)}$ is the output signal of the jth neuron in the qth layer, $w_{ij}^{(q)}$ is the connection weight coming from the ith neuron in the $(q-1)$ layer to the jth neuron in the qth layer, and let $f(net)$, $net_j^{(q)} = \sum_{i=0}^{n_q-1} w_{ij}^{(q)} o_i^{(q-1)}$, be the sigmoid activation function. Then, given an augmented input vector $\mathbf{x} = [1, x_1, x_2, ..., x_N]^t$, the output signal of the jth neuron in the output (Lth) layer is given by:

$$o_j^{(L)} = f\left(\sum_m w_{mj}^{(L)} f\left(...f\left(\sum_i w_{iq}^{(1)} x_i\right)...\right)\right) \qquad (1)$$

Half & Half Bagging. The basic idea of half & half bagging is very simple. It is assumed that the training set contains P data points. Suppose that k classifiers have been already constructed. To obtain the next training set, randomly select a data point $\mathbf{x}$. Present $\mathbf{x}$ to that subset of k classifiers which did not use $\mathbf{x}$ in their training sets. Use the majority vote to predict the classification result of $\mathbf{x}$ by that subset of classifiers. If $\mathbf{x}$ is misclassified, put it in set MC. Otherwise, put $\mathbf{x}$ in set CC. Stop when the sizes of both MC and CC are equal to K, where $2K \leq P$. Usually, CC is filled first but the sampling continues until MC reaches the same size. In [8], $K = P/4$ has been used. The next training set is given by a union of the sets MC and CC.

An important discrepancy of the *Half & Half* bagging procedure we use from the original one is that the ties occurring in the *Majority Vote* combination rule we break not randomly but in favour of decisions obtained from a group of the most divers networks. Such a modification noticeably improved the classification accuracy. Next, we briefly describe the diversity measure we adopted in this work.

Diversity of networks. To assess the diversity of the obtained neural networks we used the κ-error diagrams [9]. The κ-error diagrams display the accuracy and diversity of the individual networks. For each pair of networks, the accuracy is measured as the average error rate on the test data set, while the diversity is evaluated by computing the so-called *degree-of-agreement* statistic κ. Each point in the diagrams corresponds to a pair of networks and illustrates their diversity and the average accuracy. The κ statistic is computed as

$$\kappa = \frac{\theta_1 - \theta_2}{1 - \theta_2} \qquad (2)$$

with $\theta_1 = \sum_{i=1}^{Q} c_{ii}/P$ and $\theta_2 = \sum_{i=1}^{Q} \{\sum_{j=1}^{Q} \frac{c_{ij}}{P} \sum_{j=1}^{Q} \frac{c_{ji}}{P}\}$, where Q is the number of classes, **C** is a $Q \times Q$ square matrix with c_{ij} containing the number of test data points assigned to class i by the first network and into class j by the second network, and P stands for the total number of test data. The statistic $\kappa = 1$ when two networks agree on every data point, and $\kappa = 0$ when the agreement equals that expected by chance.

3 Related Work

Since we have not found any works attempting to select features for neural network committees, for our comparisons we resorted to neural network based methods developed to select salient features for a single classification network.

Neural-Network Feature Selector [10]. The neural-network feature selector (*NNFS*) is trained by minimizing the cross-entropy error function augmented with the additional term given by Eq. 3. Feature selection is based on the reaction of the cross-validation data set classification error due to the removal of the individual features.

$$R_2(w) = \varepsilon_1 \left\{ \sum_{i=1}^{N} \sum_{j=1}^{n_h} \frac{\beta(w_{ij})^2}{1 + \beta(w_{ij})^2} \right\} + \varepsilon_2 \left\{ \sum_{i=1}^{N} \sum_{j=1}^{n_h} (w_{ij})^2 \right\} \qquad (3)$$

where N is the number of features, w_{ij} is the weight between the ith input feature and the jth hidden node, n_h is the number of the hidden nodes, and the constants ε_1, ε_2 and β have to be chosen experimentally.

Signal-to-Noise Ratio Based Technique [11]. The signal-to-noise ratio (*SNR*) based saliency of feature is determined by comparing it to that of an injected noise feature. The *SNR* saliency measure for feature i is given by:

$$SNR_i = 10 Log_{10} \left(\frac{\sum_{j=1}^{n_h} (w_{ij})^2}{\sum_{j=1}^{n_h} (w_{Ij})^2} \right) \qquad (4)$$

with w_{ij} being the weight between the ith input feature and the jth hidden node, w_{Ij} is the weight from the injected noise feature I to the jth hidden node, and n_h is the number of the hidden nodes. The number of features to be chosen is identified by the `significant` decrease of the classification accuracy of the test data set when eliminating a feature.

4 The Technique Proposed

From Eq. 1 it can be seen that output sensitivity to the input depends on both weight values and derivatives of the transfer functions of the hidden and output layer nodes. To obtain the low sensitivity we have chosen to constrain the derivatives. We train a neural network by minimizing the cross-entropy error function augmented with two additional terms:

$$E = \frac{E_0}{n_L} + \alpha_1 \frac{1}{Pn_h} \sum_{p=1}^{P} \sum_{k=1}^{n_h} f'(net_{kp}^h) + \alpha_2 \frac{1}{Pn_L} \sum_{p=1}^{P} \sum_{j=1}^{n_L} f'(net_{jp}^{(L)}) \quad (5)$$

where α_1 and α_2 are parameters to be chosen experimentally, P is the number of training samples, n_L is the number of the output layer nodes, $f'(net_{kp}^h)$ and $f'(net_{jp}^{(L)})$ are derivatives of the transfer functions of the kth hidden and jth output node, respectively, and

$$E_0 = -\frac{1}{2P} \Big[\sum_{p=1}^{P} \sum_{j=1}^{n_L=Q} (d_{jp} log\, o_{jp}^{(L)} + (1 - d_{jp}) log(1 - o_{jp}^{(L)})) \Big] \quad (6)$$

where d_{jp} is the desired output for the pth data point at the jth output node and Q is the number of classes.

The second and third terms of the cost function constrain the derivatives and force the neurons of the hidden and output layers to work in the saturation region. In [12], it was demonstrated that neural networks regularized by constraining derivatives of the transfer functions of the hidden layer nodes possess good generalization properties. The feature selection procedure proposed is summarized in the following steps.

4.1 The Feature Selection Procedure

1. Choose the number of initializations I and the accuracy increase threshold ΔA_T, which terminates the growing process of the committee—determines the number of neural network committee members L.
2. Randomly divide the data set available into Training, Cross-Validation, and Test data sets. Use half of the Training data set when training the first committee member. Set the committee member index $j = 1$. Set $A_{CMax} = 0$ – the maximum Cross-Validation data set classification accuracy achieved by the committee.
3. Set the actual number of features $k = N$.
4. Starting from random weights train the committee member I times by minimizing the error function given by Eq. 5 and validate the network at each epoch on the Cross-Validation data set. Equip the network with the weights yielding the minimum Cross-Validation error.
5. Compute the Cross-Validation data set classification accuracy A_{jk} for the committee. The committee consists of j members including the one being trained. If $A_{jk} > A_{CMax}$ set $A_{CMax} = A_{jk}$.

6. Eliminate the least salient feature m identified according to the following rules:
$$m = \arg\min_{i \in S} \overline{\kappa}_i \qquad (7)$$
where $\overline{\kappa}_i$ is the average κ statistic calculated for the committee networks when the ith feature is eliminated from the input feature set of the jth network. The feature subset S containing the elimination candidates is given by:
$$i \in S \text{ if } \Delta A_i - \Delta A_q < \Delta A_\alpha, \quad i = 1, ..., k \qquad (8)$$
where
$$q = \arg\min_{p=1,...,k} \Delta A_p \qquad (9)$$
with ΔA_i being the drop of the classification accuracy of the committee for the `Cross-Validation` data set when eliminating the ith feature and ΔA_α is a threshold.
7. Set $k := k - 1$. If the actual number of features $k > 1$, goto Step 4.
8. The selected number M of features for the committee member being trained is given by the minimum value of k satisfying the condition: $A_{CMax} - A_{jk} < \Delta A_0$, where ΔA_0 is the acceptable drop in the classification accuracy. Memorize the set of selected features $F_j = \{f_{j1}, ..., f_{jM}\}$. The feature set contains the remaining and the $M-1$ last eliminated features. Equip the jth member with the $\mathbf{W}_{jM}$ weight matrix.
9. If the increase in A_{CMax}—when adding the last three committee members—is larger than ΔA_T: Set $j := j + 1$. Select, according to the half & half sampling procedure, the `Training` data set for training the next committee member and goto Step 3.
10. Stop. The neural network committee is defined by the weight matrices $\mathbf{W}_{jM}$, $j = 1, ..., L$, where the number of the committee members L is given by the number of networks comprising the committee yielding the maximum classification accuracy A_{CMax}.

5 Experimental Investigations

In all the tests, we run an experiment 10 times with different initial values of weights and different partitioning of the data set into `<Training>`—D_l, `<Test>`—D_t, and `<Cross-Validation>`—D_v sets. The mean values and standard deviations of the correct classification rate presented in this paper were calculated from these 10 trials.

Training Parameters. There are five parameters to be chosen, namely the regularization constants α_1 and α_2, the parameter of the acceptable drop in classification accuracy ΔA_0 when eliminating a feature, and the thresholds ΔA_α and ΔA_T. The parameter ΔA_0 affects the number of features included in the feature subset sought, while the threshold ΔA_α controls the size of the elimination candidates set. The parameter ΔA_T controls the size of the committee.

The values of the parameters α_1 and α_2 have been found by cross validation. The values of the parameters ranged: $\alpha_1 \in [0.001, 0.02]$ and $\alpha_2 \in [0.001, 0.2]$. The value of the parameter ΔA_0 has been set to 0.8%, ΔA_α to 0.4%, and ΔA_T to 0.2%. All the committees consisted of one hidden layer perceptrons.

5.1 Data Used

To test the approach proposed we used three real-world problems. The data used are available at: www.ics.uci.edu/~mlearn/MLRepository.html.

The diabetes diagnosis problem. The Pima Indians Diabetes (*PID*) Data Set contains 768 samples taken from patients who may show signs of diabetes. Each sample is described by eight features. There are 500 samples from patients who do not have diabetes and 268 samples from patients who are known to have diabetes. From the data set, we have randomly selected 345 samples for training, 39 samples for cross-validation, and 384 samples for testing.

US Congressional voting records problem. The (*CV*) data set consists of the voting records of 435 congressman on 16 major issues in the 98th Congress. The votes are categorized into one of the three types of votes: (1) *Yea*, (2) *Nay*, and (3) *Unknown*. The task is to predict the correct political party affiliation of each congressman. We used the same learning and testing conditions as in [11] and [10], namely 197 samples were randomly selected for training, 21 samples were selected for cross-validation, and 217 for testing.

The breast cancer diagnosis problem. The University of Wisconsin Breast Cancer (*UWBC*) Data Set consists of 699 patterns. Each of these patterns consists of nine measurements taken from fine needle aspirates from a patient's breast. To test the approaches we randomly selected 315 samples for training, 35 samples for cross-validation, and 349 for testing.

5.2 Results of the Tests

On average, 3.9, 4.0 and 3.5 features were used by one committee network to solve the *PID*, *CV*, and the *UWBC* problem, respectively. The average number of networks $\widehat{L}$ comprising one committee was equal to 7.4, 4.6 and 3.5, respectively for the *PID*, *CV* and *UWBC* problem. Even least salient features, as deemed by linear discriminant analysis, were used quite often by networks of the committees. Table 1 provides the test data set correct classification rate obtained for the different databases. In the Table we also provide the results taken from references [11] and [10]. In the parentheses, the standard deviations of the correct classification rate are given. The superiority of the approach proposed should be obvious from the Table. As can be seen, committees utilizing the selected feature sets are more accurate than those exploiting all the features available.

Fig 1 presents the κ-error diagrams for the *PID* database displaying the accuracy and diversity of the individual networks comprising committees built using the whole and the selected feature sets. As can be seen from Fig 1, on average, the networks trained on the whole feature set are slightly more accurate, however less diverse than those obtained using the selected feature sets. The

Table 1. Correct Classification Rate for the Different Data Sets

Case	Proposed	SNR	NNFS	Proposed	SNR	NNFS
	All Features			**Selected Features**		
	PIMA INDIANS DIABETES					
# Feat.	8	8	8	3.9(1.37)	1(0.00)	2.03(0.18)
Tr. Set	79.17(1.51)	80.35(0.67)	95.39(0.51)	80.07(1.16)	75.53(1.40)	74.02(1.10)
Test Set	78.01(0.52)	75.91(0.34)	71.03(0.32)	79.98(1.05)	73.53(1.16)	74.29(0.59)
	CONGRESSIONAL VOTING RECORDS					
# Feat.	16	16	16	4.0(1.12)	1(0.00)	2.03(0.18)
Tr. Set	99.06(0.53)	98.92(0.22)	100.0(0.00)	97.72(0.25)	96.62(0.30)	95.63(0.08)
Test Set	95.70(0.57)	95.42(0.18)	92.00(0.18)	97.48(0.97)	94.69(0.20)	94.79(0.29)
	UNIVERSITY OF WISCONSIN BREAST CANCER					
# Feat.	9	9	9	3.5(0.80)	1(0.00)	2.7(1.02)
Tr. Set	98.04(0.83)	97.66(0.18)	100.0(0.00)	98.25(0.62)	94.03(0.97)	98.05(0.24)
Test Set	97.12(0.34)	96.49(0.15)	93.94(0.17)	97.63(0.47)	92.53(0.77)	94.15(0.18)

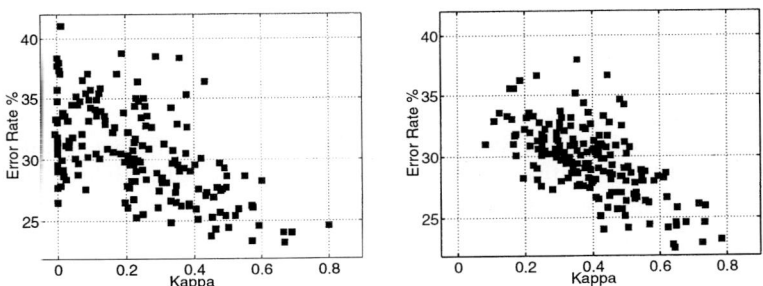

Fig. 1. The κ-error diagram for the *Diabetes* data set. **Left:** networks trained using the selected feature sets and **Right:** networks trained using all the features available.

fact of obtaining more accurate committees when using networks trained on the selected feature sets means that the reduced accuracy is well compensated for by the increased diversity of the networks. We observed the same pattern of the κ-error diagrams for the other data sets—the networks trained on the selected feature sets were less accurate but more diverse than those utilizing all the features available.

6 Conclusions

We presented a neural network based feature selection technique for neural network committees. Committee members are trained on half & half sampled training data sets by minimizing an augmented cross-entropy error function. The augmented error function forces the neural network to keep low derivatives of the transfer functions of neurons when learning a classification task. Such an approach reduces output sensitivity to the input changes. Feature selection is based on the reaction of the cross-validation data set classification error due to the removal of the individual features and on the diversity of neural networks comprising the committee.

We have tested the technique proposed on three real-world problems and demonstrated the ability of the technique to create accurate neural network committees exhibiting good generalization properties. The algorithm developed removed a large number of features from the original data sets without reducing the classification accuracy of the committees. By contrast, the accuracy of committees trained on the reduced feature sets was higher than that obtained exploiting all the features available. On average, neural network committee members trained on the reduced feature sets exhibited higher diversity than members of the committees trained using all the original features.

References

1. LeCun, Y.: Optimal brain damage. In Touretzky, D.S., ed.: Neural Information Processing Systems. Morgan Kaufmann, San Mateo, CA (1990) 598–605
2. Verikas, A., Lipnickas, A., Malmqvist, K., Bacauskiene, M., Gelzinis, A.: Soft combination of neural classifiers: A comparative study. Pattern Recognition Letters **20** (1999) 429–444
3. Verikas, A., Lipnickas, A., Bacauskiene, M., Malmqvist, K.: Fusing neural networks through fuzzy integration. In Bunke, H., Kandel, A., eds.: Hybrid Methods in Pattern Recognition. World Scientific (2002) 227–252
4. Optitz, D.W., Shavlik, J.W.: Generating accurate and diverse members of a neural-network ensemble. In Touretzky, D.S., Mozer, M.C., Hasselmo, M.E., eds.: Advances in Neural Information Processing Systems. Volume 8. MIT Press (1996) 535–541
5. Breiman, L.: Bagging predictors. Technical Report 421, Statistics Departament, University of California, Berkeley (1994)
6. Avnimelech, R., Intrator, N.: Boosting regression estimators. Neural Computation **11** (1999) 499–520
7. Freund, Y., Schapire, R.E.: A decision-theoretic generalization of on-line learning and an application to boosting. Journal of Computer and System Sciences **55** (1997) 119–139
8. Breiman, L.: Half & Half bagging and hard boundary points. Technical Report 534, Statistics Departament, University of California, Berkeley (1998)
9. Margineantu, D., Dietterich, T.G.: Pruning adaptive boosting. In: Proceedings of the 14th Machine Learning Conference, San Francisco, Morgan Kaufmann (1997) 211–218
10. Setiono, R., Liu, H.: Neural-network feature selector. IEEE Transactions on Neural Networks **8** (1997) 654–662
11. Bauer, K.W., Alsing, S.G., Greene, K.A.: Feature screening using signal-to-noise ratios. Neurocomputing **31** (2000) 29–44
12. Jeong, D.G., Lee, S.Y.: Merging back-propagation and hebian learning rules for robust classifications. Neural Networks **9** (1996) 1213–1222

Fast and Efficient Training of RBF Networks

Oliver Buchtala, Alexander Hofmann, and Bernhard Sick

University of Passau, Germany
Chair of Computer Architectures (Prof. Dr.-Ing. W. Grass), 94030 Passau
{buchtala,hofmana,sick}@fmi.uni-passau.de

Abstract. Radial basis function (RBF) networks are used in many applications, e.g. for pattern classification or nonlinear regression. Typically, either stochastic, iterative training algorithms (e.g. gradient-based or second-order techniques) or clustering methods in combination with a linear optimisation technique (e.g. c-means and singular value decomposition for a linear least-squares problem) are applied to find the parameters (centres, radii and weights) of an RBF network. This article points out the advantages of a combination of the two approaches and describes a modification of the standard c-means algorithm that leads to a linear least-squares problem for which solvability can be guaranteed. The first idea may lead to significant improvements concerning the training time as well as the approximation and generalisation properties of the networks. In the particular application problem investigated here (intrusion detection in computer networks), the overall training time could be reduced by about 29% and the error rate could be reduced by about 74%. The second idea rises the reliability of the training procedure at no additional costs (regarding both, run time and quality of results).

1 Introduction

A radial basis function (RBF) network combines a number of different concepts from approximation theory, clustering, and neural network theory [1], making it more than well-suited for many real-world applications. RBF networks can be applied to multi-dimensional function interpolation or approximation as well as to pattern classification, where the outputs of the network are often seen as estimators for the a posteriori probabilities of classes. Detailed descriptions of this network paradigm can be found in [1,2,3], for instance. In contrast to multilayer perceptrons (MLP), RBF networks use a localised representation of information. An important advantage of RBF networks from the viewpoint of practitioners is, therefore, the clear and understandable interpretation of the functionality of basis functions. It is even possible to extract rules from RBF networks for deployment in an expert system, for instance (see, e.g. [4]).

Training algorithms are needed to determine appropriate values for the parameters (centres, radii, and weights) of an RBF network using a given set of training patterns. The RBF architecture allows the application of very different training concepts. Typically, either of the following approaches (or closely related techniques) can be found in the literature (see [5], too):

1. Centres of the basis functions can be selected by means of (unsupervised) clustering algorithms such as c-means. The radii are then determined by using a nearest neighbour algorithm or the empirical variances of the clusters, for instance. Finally, weights in the output layer are given by the solution of a linear least-squares problem (supervised).
2. All network parameters can also be determined by applying an iterative, stochastic training procedure (supervised), for example a gradient-based technique such as backpropagation or resilient propagation (RPROP), or a second-order technique such as Quasi-Newton or Conjugate Gradients.

This article sets out the advantages of a *combination of the two approaches* regarding the computational effort (run time) and the approximation as well as the generalisation capabilities of the networks. I.e., the result of the first training approach is seen as an ideal starting point for the second. We demonstrate the advantages of this training concept with an application example: intrusion detection in computer networks. Here, the Nmap (network mapper) attack will be detected (classified) by means of features extracted from the headers of communication packets (TCP, transmission control protocol).

Initially, a slight *modification of the c-means algorithm* will be introduced which overcomes an inherent problem of many clustering algorithms (including standard c-means) used for the first approach (see Section 2, too). Typically, there is no guarantee that the linear least-squares problem can actually be solved. For the modified c-means algorithm presented here, this guarantee can be given. Moreover, this modification neither requires additional run time nor does it lead to a deterioration of approximation or generalisation capabilities in practical applications. The idea may also be transferred to other clustering algorithms used for RBF training.

2 Definitions and Related Work

In this section, the RBF architecture considered here will be defined and a short overview of different "state-of-the-art" training concepts for this network paradigm will be given.

More or less informally, the RBF networks, which are employed here, may be defined as follows (see Fig. 1 and cf. generalised RBF networks in [3]): The external output vector of the network, $\mathbf{y}(k)$, consists of the activations of output neurons $l \in \mathcal{U}_O$: $y_l^{(O)} \stackrel{def}{=} a_l^{(O)}(k)$. These activations are defined by the weighted sum of activations of hidden and input neurons plus a bias value:

$$a_l^{(O)}(k) \stackrel{def}{=} \sum_{j=1}^{|\mathcal{U}_H|} w_{(j,l)}^{(HO)} \cdot a_j^{(H)}(k) + \sum_{i=1}^{|\mathcal{U}_I|} w_{(i,l)}^{(IO)} \cdot a_i^{(I)}(k) + w_{(B,l)}^{(BO)}. \qquad (1)$$

Shortcut connections are used in order to increase the "smoothness" of the function realised by the network [3]. The activation of each input neuron is $a_i^{(I)}(k) \stackrel{def}{=} x_i(k)$, where $x_i(k)$ is the ith element of the external input vector (pattern) $\mathbf{x}(k)$ ($k = 1, 2, ...$ denotes the number of the pattern). The activation functions in the hidden layer neurons are *radial basis functions* [1,2,3]. Here, Gaussian functions are employed:

$$a_j^{(H)}(k) \stackrel{def}{=} e^{\left(-\frac{s_j^{(H)}(k)^2}{p_j^2}\right)}, \qquad (2)$$

where $s_j^{(H)}(k) \stackrel{def}{=} \|\mathbf{w}_j^{(IH)} - \mathbf{x}(k)\|$ is the Euclidean distance of the weight vector $\mathbf{w}_j^{(IH)} \stackrel{def}{=} \left(w_{(1,j)}^{(IH)}, \cdots, w_{(|\mathcal{U}_I|,j)}^{(IH)}\right)^T$ and the external input vector. The parameter p_j is the *radius* of a basis function; the vector $\mathbf{w}_j^{(IH)}$ its *centre*.

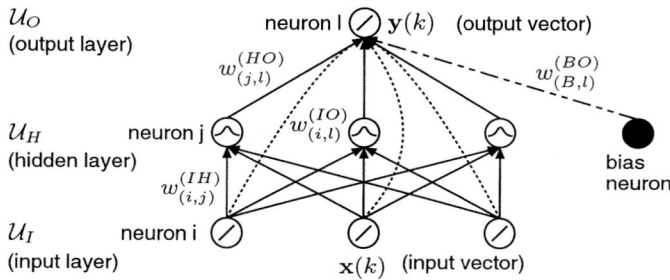

Fig. 1. Example for the Structure of an RBF Network

The activation of a hidden neuron is high, if the current input vector of the network is 'similar' (depending on the value of the radius) to the centre of its basis function. The centre of a basis function can, therefore, be regarded as a prototype of a hyperspherical cluster in the input space of the network. The radius of the basis function depends on the diameter of this cluster.

Any other function which satisfies the (sufficient, but not necessary) conditions derived from theorems of Schoenberg or Micchelli described in [3] can also be used as a basis function. Localised basis functions such as the *Gaussian* or the *inverse multiquadric* are usually preferred. The methods described here can be used in combination with any localised basis function.

Parameters of the network have to be determined by means of a set of training patterns $\mathcal{L} \stackrel{def}{=} \{(\mathbf{x}(k), \mathbf{t}(k))\}$ with $\mathbf{t}(k) \stackrel{def}{=} \left(t_1(k), \cdots, t_{|\mathcal{U}_O|}(k)\right)^T$ and $|\mathcal{L}| \geq |\mathcal{U}_H|$. For a given input $\mathbf{x}(k)$ the network is expected to produce an external output $\mathbf{t}(k)$ (target). The least-squares error (LSE) function will be applied to assess the suitability of network parameters, i.e. the difference between $\mathbf{t}(k)$ and $\mathbf{y}(k)$.

The following algorithms used to determine the different RBF network parameters can be found in the literature:

Centres ($\mathbf{w}_j^{(IH)}$) are selected randomly [1,3,6] or computed using a c-means algorithm or any of its variants such as online c-means, learning vector quantisation, optimal adaptive c-means or probabilistic c-means [1,3,5,6,7,8,9,10]. Examples for other clustering algorithms are DHB, DHF, ABF, AFB or hierarchical clustering [7,11]. Also, algorithms with a graph theoretic background (such as the vertex-chain method, the list-splitting method or the shortest spanning tree method) can be found [8]. Evolutionary (e.g. genetic) algorithms are not only used to optimise RBF network structures, but also to determine centres (and sometimes radii) of basis functions, for example in [12,13,14]. In [9] centres are assigned from a global viewpoint on the basis of a Karhunen-Loève transform.

Radii (p_j) are sometimes set to the same value for all hidden neurons [1,8]. Individual values for each hidden neuron are determined by computing (empirical) variances [7,9] or applying a k-nearest-neighbour algorithm where "neighbour" is either a training pattern or a centre belonging to an other hidden neuron (typically $k = 1, 2$ or 3) [1,5,6,8,11,12]. Radii may also be optimised by evolutionary approaches [13,14].

Output weights ($w_{(j,l)}^{(HO)}$) can be computed in a single step with a linear optimisation technique such as singular value decomposition [3,9,12]. Iterative methods such as the least-mean-squares (LMS) algorithm may also be applied [15,16]. If the linear least-squares problem contains an ill-conditioned or rank-deficient activation matrix, an appropriate regularisation technique such as Tikhonov regularisation may be used (see, e.g. [17,18]). This approach is similar to model-trust region approaches in second-order neural network training [19].

All network parameters may be trained using iterative first-order (such as backpropagation, RPROP or Quickprop) or second-order algorithms (such as Quasi-Newton, Levenberg-Marquardt or conjugate gradient techniques), which can be found in many articles or textbooks [1,2,3,6,19].

Constructive techniques which iteratively add hidden neurons with centres selected from the training data are described in [15,20,21].

3 The Novel Training Concept

We propose the following training concept for RBF networks:
Step 1: A new clustering algorithm is employed for the initialisation of the centres. In substance, this algorithm is a modified c-means approach. The radii depend on the empirical variance of the patterns assigned to a particular cluster.
Step 2: The weights between the hidden and the output layer are determined in a single step, solving a linear least-squares problem. The values of these weights are then optimal (in a least-squares sense) w.r.t. the values of centres and radii.
Step 3: Finally, the remaining parameters (weights of shortcut connections and bias) are initialised with random, small values. An iterative learning algorithm utilises the values of parameters resulting from the precedent steps as a starting point for a weight optimisation using the RPROP algorithm [22]. The training ends, for example, after a certain number of epochs.

Step 1a: Centre Initialisation with Modified c-means Clustering

1. Determine initial cluster prototypes $c_j^{(0)} \in \mathcal{L}$ for all $j \in \mathcal{U}_H$, for example with the Selection Sampling Algorithm [23] or the algorithm described in [24].
2. Let $Q(0) := \infty$, $l := 1$ and $\mathcal{C}_j^{(l)} := \{c_j^{(0)}\}$ for all $j \in \mathcal{U}_H$.

3. Assign each pattern $\mathbf{x}(k) \in \mathcal{L}$ to a set $\mathcal{C}_j^{(l)}$ ($j \in \mathcal{U}_H$) such that for all $i \in \mathcal{U}_H$ with $i \neq j$:
$$\left\|\mathbf{x}(k) - \mathbf{c}_j^{(l-1)}\right\| \leq \left\|\mathbf{x}(k) - \mathbf{c}_i^{(l-1)}\right\|. \tag{3}$$

4. Select new prototypes $\mathbf{c}_j^{(l)} \in \mathcal{C}_j^{(l)}$ for each set $\mathcal{C}_j^{(l)}$ ($j \in \mathcal{U}_H$) such that for all $\mathbf{x}(k') \in \mathcal{C}_j^{(l)}$
$$\sum_{\mathbf{x}(k) \in \mathcal{C}_j^{(l)}} \left\|\mathbf{x}(k) - \mathbf{c}_j^{(l)}\right\| \leq \sum_{\mathbf{x}(k) \in \mathcal{C}_j^{(l)}} \left\|\mathbf{x}(k) - \mathbf{x}(k')\right\|. \tag{4}$$

5. Determine the quality of the current partition of $\mathcal{L}$ by
$$Q(l) := \sum_{j \in \mathcal{U}_H} \sum_{\mathbf{x}(k) \in \mathcal{C}_j^{(l)}} \left\|\mathbf{x}(k) - \mathbf{c}_j^{(l)}\right\|. \tag{5}$$

6. If no reduction of Q could be achieved, then terminate the algorithm with $\mathbf{w}_j^{(IH)} := \mathbf{c}_j^{(l)}$ for all $j \in \mathcal{U}_H$. Otherwise, let $l := l+1$ and goto 3.

Step 1b: Radius Initialisation with Empirical Variances

1. Let $\lambda \in \mathbb{R}^+$ be a user-defined weight (typically $\lambda \in [1,3]$).
2. For all $j \in \mathcal{U}_H$ let
$$p_j^2 := \lambda \cdot \frac{1}{|\mathcal{C}_j^{(l)}| - 1} \cdot \sum_{\mathbf{x}(k) \in \mathcal{C}_j^{(l)}} \left\|\mathbf{x}(k) - \mathbf{w}_j^{(IH)}\right\|^2. \tag{6}$$

Step 2: Computation of Output Weights by the Solution of a Linear Least-Squares Problem

1. Let $\mathbf{t}_l \stackrel{def}{=} (t_l(1), t_l(2), \ldots, t_l(|\mathcal{L}|))^T$ be the vector of desired outputs (targets) and $\mathbf{w}_l^{(HO)} \stackrel{def}{=} \left(w_{(1,l)}^{(HO)}, w_{(2,l)}^{(HO)}, \ldots, w_{(|\mathcal{U}_H|,l)}^{(HO)}\right)^T$ be the output weight vector for all $l \in \mathcal{U}_O$. Let
$$\mathbf{A}^{(H)} \stackrel{def}{=} \begin{pmatrix} a_1^{(H)}(1) & \cdots & a_{|\mathcal{U}_H|}^{(H)}(1) \\ \vdots & \ddots & \vdots \\ a_1^{(H)}(|\mathcal{L}|) & \cdots & a_{|\mathcal{U}_H|}^{(H)}(|\mathcal{L}|) \end{pmatrix} \tag{7}$$
be the matrix of hidden neuron activations for the different input patterns.

2. Solve the linear least-squares problems "minimise $\left\|\mathbf{A}^{(H)} \cdot \mathbf{w}_l^{(HO)} - \mathbf{t}_l\right\|$" for each $l \in \mathcal{U}_O$ by $\mathbf{w}_l^{(HO)} = \left(\mathbf{A}^{(H)}\right)^+ \cdot \mathbf{t}_l$ with $\left(\mathbf{A}^{(H)}\right)^+$ being the Moore-Penrose pseudo inverse of matrix $\mathbf{A}^{(H)}$.

Step 3: Iterative Training of all Network Parameters

1. Initialise all remaining parameters with small, random numbers.
2. Train all parameters (centres, radii, weights, bias) by means of an appropriate first-order or second order technique until a given stopping criterion is met.

Like standard c-means, the modified c-means (step 1a) is globally convergent, as the (always positive) measure Q is reduced in each step until termination. Here, Q is reduced until no further reduction is possible. Alternative stopping criteria, which are based on the quantity of the reduction in subsequent steps, are also applicable. Utilising the modified c-means, the cluster prototypes correspond to training patterns in any cycle, i.e. $\mathbf{c}_j^{(l)} \in \mathcal{L}$ for all $l = 1, 2, \ldots$. Standard c-means and many other clustering algorithms do not have this important property, which will be needed later. The advantages of the novel training concept (see below) are independent from the application of a particular algorithm in step 1b. Therefore, the selection of individual values of λ for each cluster or the initialisation of radii on the basis of nearest-neighbour algorithms, for example, are also possible.

The pseudo inverse of a matrix $\mathbf{X}$, which is needed in step 2, is defined by $\mathbf{X}^+ \stackrel{def}{=} (\mathbf{X}^T\mathbf{X})^{-1}\mathbf{X}^T$ provided that $(\mathbf{X}^T\mathbf{X})^{-1}$ exists. In practice, the linear least-squares problem is solved by means of an efficient, numerically stable algorithm (see, e.g. [18,25]) such as singular value decomposition (SVD). Why *does* the inverse exist here? Consider the interpolation problem $|\mathcal{L}| = |\mathcal{U}_H|$ with $\mathbf{w}_l^{(IH)} \in \mathcal{L}$ and use basis functions $e^{\left(-\frac{s_j^{(H)}(k)^2}{p_j^2}\right)}$. Then, $e^{\left(-\frac{s_j^{(H)}(k)}{p_j^2}\right)}$ is completely monotonic on $(0, \infty)$ and $\mathbf{A}^{(H)}$ is strictly positive definite [3]. If we now transform the interpolation problem into an approximation problem by deleting arbitrary rows of $\mathbf{A}^{(H)}$, then the matrix $((\mathbf{A}^{(H)})^T\mathbf{A}^{(H)})$ is still non-singular. Lumped together: If Gaussian basis functions are used (for other permissible functions see [3]) and the centres are chosen to be a subset of the training data and distinct, the pseudo inverse does exist [3]. These conditions are met here (step 1a); we remark that they are sufficient, but not necessary.

4 Experimental Results

The first three tests show, that run time and results of standard c-means and modified c-means are nearly the same. Here, the two algorithms are applied to the same problem: Three clusters with underlying Gaussian distributions are randomly generated in $\mathbb{R}^2$. The expected values of the distributions are $\mu_1 = (-3; -1)$, $\mu_2 = (-2; 2)$ and $\mu_1 = (3; 1)$. The numbers of patterns are the same for each cluster (100). The variances of the distributions are identical, too (1 in test 1, 2 in test 2, and 3 in test 3). Results are set out in Tab. 1. Each test is repeated 10×10 times, i.e. with 10 different initial cluster prototypes (identical for c-means and modified c-means) for each of 10 random initialisations. The entries in Tab. 1 are average values. The overall run time until termination is at an average of 162 ms for modified c-means and 209 ms for standard c-means (2 GHz Pentium IV). It can be stated, that modified c-means provides advantageous guarantees without requiring additional run time and without yielding worse results.

The following two tests compare a conventional training with RPROP (test 4: step 3 only) to the new training concept (test 5: combination of steps 1, 2 and 3). The application example is intrusion detection in computer networks; here, the Nmap (network mapper) attack will be detected. A detailed description of the application problem and the data can be found in [26]. The network has 6 input, 4 hidden, and 1 output neurons. The results given in Tab. 2 and 3 are average values of 10 repetitions of a 5-fold cross-validation. Tab. 2 (1000 training epochs) shows, that with the new training concept the false alarm rate could be reduced by about 79% for training data (1040 patterns) and by about 74% for

Table 1. Results of the Comparison of Standard c-means and Modified c-means

	Standard c-means		Modified c-means	
	number of steps	avg. distance of centres and expected values	number of steps	avg. distance of centres and expected values
Test 1	4.95	0.1382	4.33	0.1064
Test 2	6.81	0.2771	5.25	0.2167
Test 3	9.07	0.3568	5.55	0.3655

Table 2. Classification Errors in the two Intrusion Detection Tests

	Training Data		Test Data	
	false alarms	undetected attacks	false alarms	undetected attacks
Test 4	0.53%	0.00%	0.66%	0.00%
Test 5	0.11%	0.00%	0.17%	0.00%

Table 3. Run Time in the two Intrusion Detection Tests with a Given Error Threshold

	k-means	least-squares problem	iterative RPROP training	overall run time
Test 4	—	—	50.56 s	50.56 s
Test 5	5.71 s	< 0.005 s	30.33 s	36.04 s

test data (260 patterns). Tab. 3 shows, that for a given error threshold (here: an MSE of 0.001) the overall training time could be reduced by about 29% (results are measured on a AMD-K7 655 MHz). The average number of modified c-means steps was 6.84; the average number of epochs was 382 in Test 4 and 225 in Test 5. It has to be emphasised particularly, that the error threshold could not be reached by executing steps 1 and 2 only!

The advantages of the training concept are also underlined by many additional experiments with other network attacks [26] and by experiments in the area of customer relationship management (prediction of customer behaviour).

5 Conclusion and Outlook

In this article we investigated two ideas that both lead to an improved training of RBF networks. Using a modified c-means to initialise the centres of basis functions, the training is safer. With a combination of two different standard training concepts, the results (regarding approximation and generalisation properties) may be significantly better and the training may even be faster. It has to be mentioned that the modification may also be applied to many other clustering techniques. Our future work particularly deals with improved clustering methods (cf. Section 2), with class-related c-means clustering for RBF networks used in classification applications, with clustering on the basis of the Mahalanobis distance for networks with elliptical basis functions (hyper basis functions), and with second-order training techniques such as scaled conjugate gradients. Also, shortcuts and bias weights will be included into the least-squares problem.

References

1. Bishop, C.M.: Neural Networks for Pattern Recognition. Clarendon Press, Oxford (1995)
2. Haykin, S.: Neural Networks – A Comprehensive Foundation. Macmillan College Publishing Company, New York (1994)
3. Poggio, T., Girosi, F.: A theory of networks for approximation and learning. A.I. Memo No. 1140, C.B.I.P. Paper No. 31, Mass. Inst. of Tech. – Artif. Intell. Lab. & Center for Biol. Information Processing – Whitaker College (1989)
4. Jin, Y., von Seelen, W., Sendhoff, B.: Extracting interpretable fuzzy rules from RBF neural networks. Int. Rep. 2000-02, Institut für Neuroinformatik (INF), Ruhr-Universität Bochum (2000)
5. Moody, J., Darken, C.J.: Fast learning in networks of locally-tuned processing units. In: Neural Computation. Vol. 1. (1989) 281–294
6. Kiernan, I., Mason, J.D., Warwick, K.: Robust initialisation of gaussian radial basis function networks using partitioned k-means clustering. In: Electronics Letters. Vol. 32 (7). (1996) 671–673
7. Brizzotti, M.M., Carvalho, A.C.P.L.F.: The influence of clustering techniques in the RBF networks generalization. In: Proc. of the 7th Int. Conf. on Image Processing and its Applications, Manchester. Vol. 1. (1999) 87–92
8. Hoya, T., Constantinides, A.: An heuristic pattern correction scheme for GRNNs and its application to speech recognition. In: Proc. of the 1998 IEEE Signal Processing Society Workshop Neural Networks for Signal Processing VIII, Cambridge. (1998) 351–359
9. De Castro, M.C.F., De Castro, F.C.C., Arantes, D.S.: RBF neural networks with centers assignment via Karhunen-Loève transform. In: Int. Joint Conf. on Neural Networks (IJCNN '99), Washington. Vol. 2. (1999) 1265–1270
10. Shimoji, S., Lee, S.: Data clustering with entropical scheduling. In: Int. Conf. on Neural Networks, Orlando. Vol. 4. (1994) 2423–2428
11. Musavi, M.T., Ahmed, W., Chan, K.H., Faris, K.B., Hummels, D.M.: On the training of radial basis function classifiers. In: Neural Networks. Vol. 5. (1992) 595–603
12. Mak, M.W., Cho, K.W.: Genetic evolution of radial basis function centers for pattern classification. In: Int. Joint Conf. on Neural Networks (IJCNN '98), Anchorage. Vol. 1. (1998) 669–673
13. Whitehead, B., Choate, T.D.: Cooperative-competitive genetic evolution of radial basis function centers and widths for time series prediction. In: IEEE Trans. on Neural Networks. Vol. 7 (4). (1996) 869–880
14. Billings, S.A., Zheng, G.L.: Radial basis function network configuration using genetic algorithms. In: Neural Networks. Vol. 8 (6). (1998) 877–890
15. Ghinelli, B.M.G., Bennett, J.C.: The application of artificial neural networks and standard statistical methods to SAR image classification. In: IEEE Int. Geoscience and Remote Sensing (IGARSS '97), Singapore. Vol. 3. (1997) 1211–1213
16. Whitehead, B., Choate, T.D.: Evolving space-filling curves to distribute radial basis functions over an input space. In: IEEE Trans. on Neural Networks. Vol. 5 (1). (1994) 15–23

17. Wheeler, K.R., Dhawan, A.P.: Ssme parameter estimation using radial basis function neural networks. In: Int. Conf. on Neural Networks, Orlando. Vol. 5. (1994) 3352–3357
18. Björck, Å.: Numerical Methods for Least Squares Problems. SIAM, Philadelphia (1996)
19. Shepherd, A.J.: Second Order Methods for Neural Networks – Fast and Reliable Training Methods for Multi-Layer Perceptrons. Springer-Verlag, London (1997)
20. Mao, K.Z.: RBF neural network center selection based on Fisher ratio class separability measure. In: IEEE Trans. on Neural Networks. Vol. 13 (5). (2002) 1211–1217
21. Berthold, M.R., Feldbusch, F.: Ein Trainingsverfahren für Radial Basis Function Netzwerke mit dynamischer Selektion der Zentren und Adaption der Radii. In Reusch, B., ed.: Fuzzy Logik – Theorie und Praxis. (1994) 78–85
22. Riedmiller, M.: RPROP – Description and implementation details. Tech. Rep., Univ. Karlsruhe (1994)
23. Knuth, D.E.: The Art of Computer Programming. 3rd edn. Addison Wesley Longman (1998)
24. Cohen, S., Intrator, N.: Global optimization of RBF networks (2000) (submitted to IEEE Trans. on Neural Networks).
25. Golub, G.H., van Loan, C.F.: Matrix Computations. 3 edn. Johns Hopkins studies in the mathematical sciences. Johns Hopkins Univ. Press, Baltimore (1996)
26. Hofmann, A.: Einsatz von Soft-Computing-Verfahren zur Erkennung von Angriffen auf Rechnernetze. Master's thesis, University of Passau (2002)

Loading Temporal Associative Memory Using the Neuronic Equation

Cheng-Yuan Liou[1]* and Un-Cheong Sou[2]**

[1] Dept. of Computer Science and Information Engineering,
cyliou@csie.ntu.edu.tw
[2] Dept. of Physics, National Taiwan University.

Abstract. We discuss the loading capacity of the neuronic equation for temporal associative memory. We show explicitly how to synthesize a perfect temporal associative memory using a network of such neurons, where all non-linear aspects can be linearized in tensorial space.

Keywords: Temporal associative memory, neuronic equation, neural network, inverse problem, music perception

1 Introduction

Usually, a temporal associative memory (AM)[1], any other hetero-AM or a cellular automata can be trained to synthesise a specified sequence of patterns. Many training approaches have been developed with this goal in mind [7][9][10] with various degrees of success. But if the temporal AM we consider is restricted to that defined by a global mapping function, then the direct synthesis method [11] can be used; i.e., this global mapping function can be constructed explicitly from a pre-specified sequence of patterns. We review how to solve this kind of inverse problem using the neuronic equation introduced by Caianiello [2][3][4]. The original neuronic equation was developed to cope with neural networks which indeed share a similar model with cellular automata. In both cases, each unit of the network receives input from its predecessors or neighborhood and then changes its state according to certain functions. These functions are called local transition rules, i.e., $g : \{A_1, A_2, \ldots\}^n \to \{A_1, A_2, \ldots\}$, where $\{A_1, A_2, \ldots\}$ is the alphabet set of the network ($\{A_1, A_2, \ldots\}$ equal to boolean variables $\{+1, -1\}$ in this work) and n is the size of the neighborhood. From this, one can easily construct a global mapping function $G : \{A_1, A_2, \ldots\}^N \to \{A_1, A_2, \ldots\}^N$, where N is the total number of units in a network. This function describes the same transition dynamics as g does, but specifies the changes as a whole.

We will give an example to show how to construct this global function G, and, especially, to show that G can be linearized in extended tensorial space. Then, we will discuss the energy function for the dynamics G and its capacity for loading temporal sequences.

---
* Corresponding author
** Supported by National Science Council NSC 91-2213-E-002-124

2 Review the Neuronic Equation

The state ξ of a network with N-units can be listed in a column as an N-dimensional vector, $\xi = (\xi_1, \xi_2, \ldots, \xi_N)^T$, where $\xi_h = \pm 1$ is the h-th unit's state. Then, the network's transition at iteration (or evolution) time (t) defined by a global mapping function G is

$$\xi^{t+1} = G(\xi^t) \ . \tag{1}$$

Particularly, (1) can be rewritten as

$$\xi^{t+1} = f \cdot \eta^t \quad \text{or} \quad \xi_h^{t+1} = \sum_{\alpha=0}^{2^N-1} f_{h,\alpha} \eta_\alpha^t \ , \tag{2}$$

where

$$\eta = \begin{pmatrix} \eta_0 \\ \eta_1 \\ \vdots \\ \eta_\alpha \\ \vdots \\ \eta_{2^N} \end{pmatrix} = \underbrace{\begin{pmatrix} 1 \\ \xi_N \end{pmatrix} \otimes \cdots \otimes \begin{pmatrix} 1 \\ \xi_2 \end{pmatrix} \otimes \begin{pmatrix} 1 \\ \xi_1 \end{pmatrix}}_{N \text{ times direct product}} = \begin{pmatrix} 1 \\ \xi_1 \\ \xi_2 \\ \xi_1 \xi_2 \\ \xi_3 \\ \xi_1 \xi_3 \\ \vdots \\ \xi_1 \cdots \xi_N \end{pmatrix}$$

is the tensorial expansion of ξ obtained by taking N times the direct product, which includes all the high-order correlations among all units' states. Note that there are only N independent components (the same number as the dimensionality of ξ) in this 2^N-dimensional vector space. The expression in (2) showing that G can be linearized in tensorial form is given in [2], where G can be any boolean function. We may extend the L.H.S. of (2) to retain an even more symmetric equation:

$$\eta^{t+1} = F \cdot \eta^t \quad \text{or} \quad \eta_\beta^{t+1} = \sum_{\alpha=0}^{2^N-1} F_{\beta,\alpha} \eta_\alpha^t \ , \tag{3}$$

where F is now an $2^N \times 2^N$ matrix.

Suppose that a global mapping function G is a linear operation $\mathfrak{L}$, and that $\mathfrak{L}$ is an $N \times N$ matrix operation. The transitions of a temporal pattern sequence under this $\mathfrak{L}$ are $\mathfrak{L}\xi^1 \to \xi^i$, $\mathfrak{L}\xi^2 \to \xi^j$, $\ldots$, $\mathfrak{L}\xi^{2^N} \to \xi^k$. There are 2^N possible network states $(\xi^1, \xi^2, \ldots, \xi^{2^N})$, and all these state vectors can be grouped into a matrix $\varphi_N = (\xi^1, \xi^2, \ldots, \xi^{2^N})$, where each state ξ is a column. Then, we can arrange the dynamics in the form: $\mathfrak{L}\varphi_N = (\mathfrak{L}\xi^1, \mathfrak{L}\xi^2, \ldots, \mathfrak{L}\xi^{2^N})$

$= (\xi^i, \xi^j, \ldots, \xi^k)$. The R.H.S. of this equation is just the permutation of the columns in φ_N, i.e., $\mathfrak{L}\varphi_N = \varphi_N P_N$, where P_N is an $2^N \times 2^N$ permutation matrix, representing the given transition sequence. We then obtain $\mathfrak{L}$ using the equation

$$\mathfrak{L} = \varphi_N P_N \varphi_N^+, \qquad (4)$$

where φ_N^+ is the left (pseudo) inverse of φ_N. The reason for this left inverse is $\mathfrak{L}(\varphi_N) = (\varphi_N P_N \varphi_N^+) \varphi_N = \varphi_N P_N (\varphi_N^+ \varphi_N) \equiv \varphi_N P_N$, which implies that

$$\varphi_N^+ \varphi_N = I. \qquad (5)$$

Since (5) may not have a solution, equation (4) cannot be solved. This is because there are totally $2^N \times 2^N$ equations in the matrix equation (5), but only $N \times 2^N$ variables in the matrix φ_N^+, so in general, it is an overdetermined system, and there is no solution for φ_N^+. That is, generally, one cannot determine the matrix $\mathfrak{L}$ with this linear supposition.

However, the situation is totally different in the case of tensorial expansion. Let us define a new matrix $\Phi_N = (\eta^1, \eta^2, \ldots, \eta^{2^N})$. According to (3), we have $F\Phi_N = (F\eta^1, F\eta^2, \ldots, F\eta^{2^N}) = (\eta^i, \eta^j, \ldots, \eta^k)$. This implies that

$$F = \Phi_N P_N \Phi_N^+ \text{ and } \Phi_N^+ \Phi_N = I, \qquad (6)$$

where Φ_N is an $2^N \times 2^N$ matrix. Actually, if we take a specific form of Φ_N,

$$\Phi_N = \left(\frac{1}{\sqrt{2}}\right)^N \underbrace{\begin{pmatrix} 1 & 1 \\ 1 & -1 \end{pmatrix} \otimes \begin{pmatrix} 1 & 1 \\ 1 & -1 \end{pmatrix} \otimes \ldots \otimes \begin{pmatrix} 1 & 1 \\ 1 & -1 \end{pmatrix}}_{\text{N times direct product}} \qquad (7)$$

then we have $\Phi_N = \Phi_N^+ = (\Phi_N)^T$ and $det(\Phi_N) = 1$. Therefore, Φ_N is a real unitary matrix, and equation (6) can be solved. Then, equation (3) is $\eta^{t+1} = F\eta^t = \Phi_N P_N \Phi_N^+ \eta^t$.

This equation means that η^t first compares itself with the state in each row of Φ_N^+ and finds the corresponding state in the αth row of Φ_N^+. After that, it looks up the transition table in matrix P_N and determines the number β which is the row number of the element with a non-zero value in the αth column of P_N. Then, it picks the state vector in the βth column of Φ_N. This operation determines the transition from η^t to η^{t+1}. Considering the huge size of the matrixes, this is a look up table technique. We will show that it gives huge design capacity.

The energy function for these transitions has the form $E = -\sum_t (\eta^{(t+1)})^T F \eta^t$. It looks like a generalized Hopfield energy function [5][1] with argumented $2^N - N$ neurons (units). It keeps the exact Hebbian outer-product form by including all the high-order correlations among all units' states with (on, off) type synaptic weights. These high-order terms can be constructed by the hierarachy of their low-order terms. So, each high-order term can be represented by a single argumented neuron. This is a design for the Turing's B-type unorganized machine [6]. This is a perfect design for the hidden neurons in Boltzmann machine [8], where each high-order term is represented by a hidden neuron. This is also a deterministic analogue of Boltzmann machine. Various designs can be accomplished by different settings of the high-order terms as the hidden neurons and by exploring the unitary matrix Φ_N and permutation matrix P_N. We omit detailed designs in this work. The Hopfield network gives limited sequences and imperfect recalls while equation (6) accomplishes perfect temporal associative recalls.

Note that when $<\xi^i|\xi^j>=\delta_{i,j}$, $\{\xi^j, j=1,..,N\}$ is a set of N orthogonal vectors in N-D space. This is not true for a general set of $\{\xi^j\}$ with $<\xi^i|\xi^j>\neq \delta_{i,j}$. This suggests that if the set of states undergoing transition are orthogonal, then the linear mapping function g can be obtained by slightly modifying equations (4) and (5) with a different φ_N matrix that includes only those orthogonal states. Note that the number of orthogonal states in N-dimensional space is at most N. The design for orthogonal states is well known in the engineering community [12].

We shown an example. Let $N = 3$,

$$\varphi_3 = \left(\frac{1}{\sqrt{2}}\right)^3 \begin{pmatrix} 1 & -1 & 1 & -1 & 1 & -1 & 1 & -1 \\ 1 & 1 & -1 & -1 & 1 & 1 & -1 & -1 \\ 1 & 1 & 1 & 1 & -1 & -1 & -1 & -1 \end{pmatrix} \begin{matrix} \ldots \xi_1 \\ \ldots \xi_2 \\ \ldots \xi_3, \end{matrix}$$

and

$$\Phi_3 = \left(\frac{1}{\sqrt{2}}\right)^3 \begin{pmatrix} 1 & 1 & 1 & 1 & 1 & 1 & 1 & 1 \\ 1 & -1 & 1 & -1 & 1 & -1 & 1 & -1 \\ 1 & 1 & -1 & -1 & 1 & 1 & -1 & -1 \\ 1 & -1 & -1 & 1 & 1 & -1 & -1 & 1 \\ 1 & 1 & 1 & 1 & -1 & -1 & -1 & -1 \\ 1 & -1 & 1 & -1 & -1 & 1 & -1 & 1 \\ 1 & 1 & -1 & -1 & -1 & -1 & 1 & 1 \\ 1 & -1 & -1 & 1 & -1 & 1 & 1 & -1 \end{pmatrix} \begin{matrix} \ldots 1 \\ \ldots \xi_1 \\ \ldots \xi_2 \\ \ldots \xi_1\xi_2 \\ \ldots \xi_3 \\ \ldots \xi_1\xi_3 \\ \ldots \xi_2\xi_3 \\ \ldots \xi_1\xi_2\xi_3 \end{matrix}.$$

If we want the state transition in the order $1 \to 5 \to 3 \to 2 \to 4 \to 7 \to 6 \to 8 \to 1 \to 5 \to 3 \to 2\ldots$ (loops again), where the states are labeled according to the column index in φ_3 or Φ_3, then

$$P_3 = \begin{pmatrix} 0 & 0 & 0 & 0 & 0 & 0 & 0 & 1 \\ 0 & 0 & 1 & 0 & 0 & 0 & 0 & 0 \\ 0 & 0 & 0 & 0 & 1 & 0 & 0 & 0 \\ 0 & 1 & 0 & 0 & 0 & 0 & 0 & 0 \\ 1 & 0 & 0 & 0 & 0 & 0 & 0 & 0 \\ 0 & 0 & 0 & 0 & 0 & 0 & 1 & 0 \\ 0 & 0 & 0 & 1 & 0 & 0 & 0 & 0 \\ 0 & 0 & 0 & 0 & 0 & 1 & 0 & 0 \end{pmatrix}.$$

This means that for a transition from the jth state to the ith state ("$j \to i$"), the corresponding value in the element $(P_N)_{i,j}$ is set to 1, and that all the other elements in the jth column are set to zero. We show Φ_3 and F in Figure 1, where a white cell = +1, a black cell = −1, and a grey is in between.

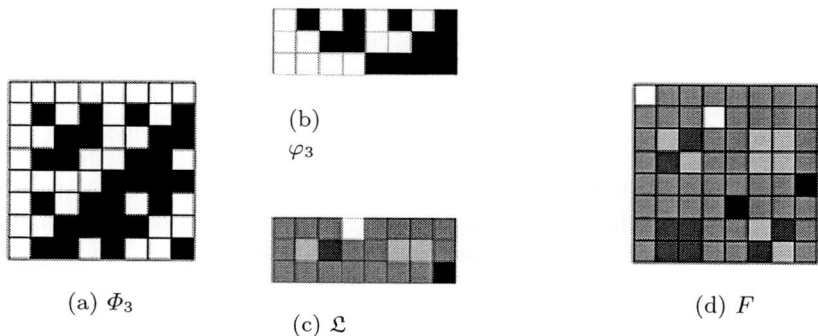

(a) Φ_3

(b) φ_3

(c) $\mathcal{L}$

(d) F

Fig. 1. Diagram representations of matrixes.

As a final step, the state vector ξ can be extracted from the rows of η or using (2) with extraction operation $f = \varphi_N P_N \Phi_N$.

3 Loading Capacity

For a temporal AM with N-units and 2 possible values of each unit, the 2^N possible states can transit to each others according to a specified global mapping function. That is, $S_1 \rightarrow S_2 \rightarrow \ldots S_i \rightarrow S_j \rightarrow S_k \rightarrow \ldots \rightarrow S_i \rightarrow S_j \rightarrow S_k \rightarrow \ldots$. When it encounters a past state (ex. S_i), it will follow the previous transitions and fall into a loop. Furthermore, according to pigeon-hole principle, there must be at least one repeated state after the network iterates 2^N times. Therefore, the sequence structure of the transition will be $\overleftarrow{S_a \rightarrow \ldots S_i}^{n} \overrightarrow{\rightarrow \ldots S_k}^{r}$. Here, 'n' means a non-repeated part and 'r' means a repeated part. Their possible values are $r = 1 \sim 2^N$, $n = 0 \sim (2^N - 1)$, under the condition $n + r = L \leq 2^N$. When we fix the value L, there are $_{2^N}P_L = \frac{2^N!}{(2^N-L)!}$ possible sequences of length L where $_{2^N}P_L$ is the number of permutations containing L objects out of 2^N. For each of this sequence, the repeating length can be different, that is, $r = 1 \sim L$, so there are actually L different ways of transition. The total number is the sum over the all possible lengths of L. Therefore, the capacity is

$$Capacity = \sum_{L=1}^{2^N} L \times {}_{2^N}P_L. \qquad (8)$$

Capacity growth vs size N is plotted in Figure 2. Note the ultra-fast growth. To our knowledge, this is the highest number of capacity. The unrestricted case is also shown by the dashed line, where any sequences of length $\leq 2^N$ are counted (close to $(2^N)^{2^N}$ when N is large).

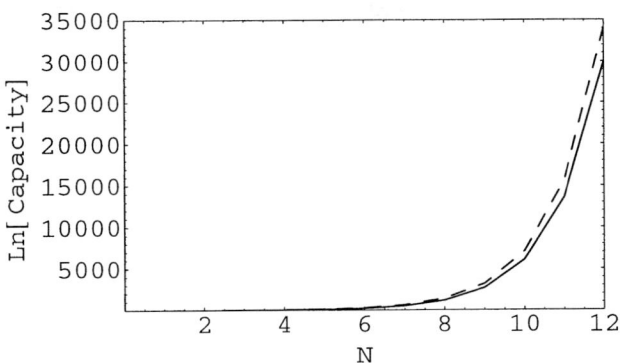

Fig. 2. Loading capacity by the equation (8)

The permutation matrix P_N specifies the all transitions, so it must contain all the information about the process of evolution. Individual transitions can be traced step by step in P_N. On the other hand, the global behavior of the all 2^N state vectors can be obtained by means of its characteristic equation [4]: $\lambda^{n_0} \prod_i (\lambda^{l_i} - 1)^{n_i} = 0$, where the eigenvalues λ can only be zero or roots of the unit. This equation means that all the possible states are either transient states (states which disappear during evolution) or states belonging to a cycle. There are n_0 transient states and an n_i cycle of length l_i. Production covers all the possible cycles. No matter what the initial state is, the network will fall into either a cycle or a stable point (a cycle of length 1). The values n_0, n_i and l_i are related as follows:

$$n_0 + \sum_i n_i l_i = 2^N. \tag{9}$$

This defines a structural capacity within the 2^N states other than the sequential capacity (8). Consider a temporal AM of size $N = 3$; a state transition diagram (STD) can be drawn if P_N is known. An example is shown in Figure 3.

State 1, 2 and 6 are transient states, which will die and never appear again in the process of evolution. There are 2 cycles of length 1 and one cycle of length 3, so $n_0 = 3$, $n_1 = 2$ for $l_1 = 1$, and $n_3 = 1$ for $l_3 = 3$. (For ease of illustration let $n_2 = 0$ for $l_2 = 2$. That is, $l_i \equiv i$ can be omitted. Then only a series of n_i is needed.)

If a state's label is specified and changing it is considered different, then there will totally be $(2^N)^{2^N}$ possible STDs (because any 2^N position in each

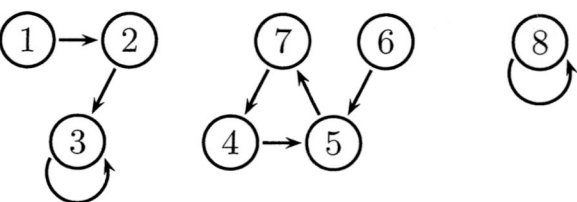

Fig. 3. STD example.

column of matrix P_N can be a non-vanishing element). Otherwise, if we count the structures of STD according to the values $\{n_0, n_1, n_2, n_3 \ldots\}$ only (ignoring the state's label and precedence), then the number of all possible structures is described by (9). This is equal to partitioning the total 2^N states into parts of length 1, 1, 2, 3... with the repetition $n_0, n_1, n_2, n_3 \ldots$. This number can be solved by a generating function:

$$f(x) = \left(1 + x + x^2 + x^3 + \ldots\right)^2 \left(1 + x^2 + x^4 + \ldots\right)\left(1 + x^3 + x^6 + \ldots\right)\ldots$$
$$= \frac{1}{1-x}\left(\prod_{i=1}^{\infty} \frac{1}{1-x^i}\right). \qquad (10)$$

The structural capacity of STD for the network with 2^N possible states is the coefficient of the $(2^N)^{th}$ order term in (10), obtained by expanding the polynomial (see Figure 4).

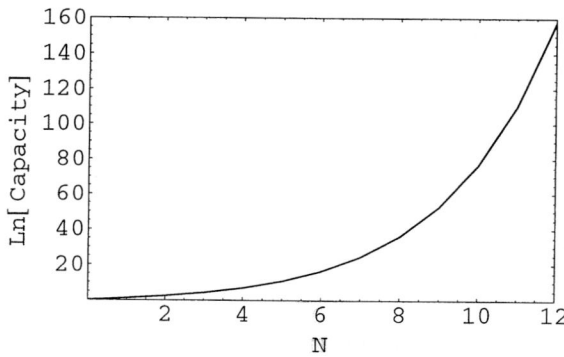

Fig. 4. Structural capacity of the STD by the equation (8).

This capacity grows much more slowly and should not be confused with (8). Equations (9) and (10) produce all the possible structures within the 2^N states, while (8) produces all possible sequences (with the label specified) of the STD.

References

[1] S.I. Amari (1972), Learning patterns and pattern sequences by self-organising nets, IEEE Trans Comput, 21, 1197–1206
[2] E.R. Caianiello (1973), Some remarks on the tensorial linearization of general and l.s. Boolean functions, Kybernetik, 12, 90
[3] E.R. Caianiello (1984), Neuronic equations revisited and completely solved, Proceedings of the First Meeting on Brain Theory, October 1-4, at the International Centre for Theoretical Physics in Trieste, Italy.
[4] E.R. Caianiello and M. Marinaro (1986), Linearization and Synthesis of Cellular Automata: The Additive Case, Physica Scripta, 34, 444–448
[5] J. J. Hopfield (1984), Neurons with graded response have collective computational properties like those of two-state neurons, Proc. Natl. Acad. Sci., 81, 3088–3092
[6] D.C. Ince (1992), Intelligent Machinery, Alan Turing in Collected Works of A.M. Turing: Mechanical Intelligence, Edited by D.C. Ince, Elsevier Science Publishers
[7] Y.C. Lee, S. Qian, R.D. Jones, C.W. Barnes, G.W. Flake, M.K. O'rourke, K. Lee, H.H. Chen, G.Z. Sun, Y.Q. Zhang, D. Chen, C.L. Giles (1990), Adaptive stochastic cellular automata: Theory, Physica D, 45, 159–180
[8] C.-Y. Liou, S.-L. Lin (1989), The Other Variant Boltzmann Machine, International Joint Conference on Neural Networks, Washington D.C., 449–454.
[9] C.-Y. Liou, H.-T. Chen, and Jau-Chi Huang (2000), Separation of internal representations of the hidden layer, Proceedings of the International Computer Symposium, Workshop on Artifical Intelligence, December 6-8, National Chung Cheng University, Chiayi
[10] C.-Y. Liou, S.-L. Yuan (1999), Error Tolerant Associative Memory, Biological Cybernetics, 81, 331–342
[11] F.C. Richards, P. T. Meyer, N. H. Packard (1990), Extracting cellular automaton rules directly from experimental data, Physica D, 45, 189–202.
[12] I. Kanter, H. Sompolinsky (1987), Associative Recall of Memory without Errors, Physical Review A, 35(1), 380–392

Learning Compatibility Functions for Feature Binding and Perceptual Grouping

Sebastian Weng and Jochen J. Steil

Bielefeld University, Neuroinformatics Department, P.O.-Box 100131,
D-33501 Bielefeld, Germany, {sweng,jsteil}@techfak.uni-bielefeld.de,
http://www.TechFak.Uni-Bielefeld.DE/ags/ni/

Abstract. We present and compare data driven learning methods to generate compatibility functions for feature binding and perceptual grouping. As dynamic binding mechanism we use the competitive layer model (CLM), a recurrent neural network with linear threshold neurons. We introduce two new and efficient learning schemes and also show how more traditional standard approaches as MLP or SVM can be employed as well. To compare their performance, we define a measure of grouping quality with respect to the available training data and apply all methods to a set of real world fluorescence cell images.

1 Introduction

One of the essential tasks in image processing on the perceptual level is feature binding and segmentation to obtain image regions containing coherent structures. For human perception, underlying grouping principles have been formulated as Gestalt laws for proximity, connectedness, good continuation, etc. A common approach to incorporate such principles into computational algorithms is to define interactions between the image features, which express the degree of their compatibility with respect to a desired grouping behavior. Based on these interactions a dynamics is defined to obtain temporal synchronization [7,8], or spatial coactivation of neurons for features from the same group.

A representative of the latter class of algorithms is the competitive layer model (*CLM*) [11], which was successfully applied to a variety of tasks like point clustering, contour grouping [11], texture segmentation [5], and cell segmentation [10]. Obviously, the critical issue for all models based on such interactions is to generate an appropriate compatibility interaction.

In [9,10], two learning methods for estimation of a compatibility function from segmented target examples are introduced. The idea is to optimize its parameters based on a set of linear consistency inequalities, which guarantee that the examples are minima of a grouping energy and at the same time stable points of the CLM-dynamics [11]. The main drawback of these methods is their high computational complexity due to the large number of inequalities used.

In this contribution, we show that this learning approach can be drastically simplified at virtually no loss of segmentation quality. We further compare the new methods to [9,10] and the employment of other standard classification algorithms like the multi layer perceptron (*MLP*) or the support vector machine (*SVM*). In Section 2, we formulate the learning problem and the different approaches to solve it including two new efficient methods that are derived in Section 3. We define a statistical measure of grouping quality in Section 4. In Section 5, all methods are applied and compared segmenting a set of real world fluorescence cell images and we discuss the results and conclude in Section 6.

2 Formulation of the Learning Problem

Assume that for a given image there is at every pixel position $r = 1, \ldots, N$ a feature vector $\boldsymbol{m}_r$ encoding the relevant information, for instance position, intensity, color, orientation of local edges or other more sophisticated features. The goal is to assign each feature $\boldsymbol{m}_r$ to one of L groups with labels $\alpha = 1, \ldots, L$.

The CLM describes these assignments by the activation pattern of $N \cdot L$ linear threshold neurons $x_{r\alpha}$. All neurons in the same group α are laterally connected by weights $f_{rr'}$, which yield the compatibilities of features $\boldsymbol{m}_r$ and $\boldsymbol{m}_{r'}$. All neurons sensitive to the same feature $\boldsymbol{m}_r$ are connected by an inhibitive weight that describes the competition between the different groups (details in [11]). An unique and consistent segmentation of the images is given by a target state $x_{r\hat{\alpha}(r)} = 1$ and $x_{r\beta} = 0$ for all $r, \beta \neq \hat{\alpha}(r)$ with

$$\sum_{r'} f_{rr'} x_{r'\beta} < \sum_{r'} f_{rr'} x_{r'\hat{\alpha}(r)} \quad \text{for all} \quad r = 1, \ldots, N, \ \beta \neq \hat{\alpha}(r), \quad (1)$$

where each feature $\boldsymbol{m}_r$ is assigned to the group $\hat{\alpha}(r)$. The inequality (1) expresses that for the target group $\hat{\alpha}(r)$ the overall compatibility with other features $\boldsymbol{m}_{r'}$ in this group is maximal.

The learning problem is to find a suitable compatibility function, which expresses the preference to bind similar or segregate dissimilar features $\boldsymbol{m}_r, \boldsymbol{m}_{r'}$ by positive or negative values of $f_{rr'}$ respectively. From a set of M training images $\mathcal{P}^i, i = 1, \ldots, M$ a subset $\mathcal{R}^i = \{\boldsymbol{m}^i_1, \ldots, \boldsymbol{m}^i_{N^i}\}$ of N^i different features and their corresponding labels $\hat{\alpha}^i(r) = \hat{\alpha}(\boldsymbol{m}^i_r)$ is obtained. We construct from each of these feature patterns a target state $\boldsymbol{y}^i$ by setting the activations of neurons that describe a correct assignment $y^i_{r\hat{\alpha}^i(r)}$ to one and all others to zero.

$$y^i_{r\hat{\alpha}^i(r)} = 1, \quad y^i_{r\beta} = 0 \quad \text{for all} \quad \text{r} \mid \boldsymbol{m}_\text{r} \in \mathcal{R}^\text{i}, \ \beta \neq \hat{\alpha}^\text{i}(\text{r}). \quad (2)$$

In [11] it was shown that stable states of the CLM-dynamics are characterized by the consistency inequalities (1). Therefore we substitute the target states (2) into (1) to obtain $(L-1) \sum_i N^i$ new conditions

$$\sum_{r'} f_{rr'} y^i_{r'\beta} < \sum_{r'} f_{rr'} y^i_{r'\hat{\alpha}^i(r)} \quad \text{for all} \quad i, \ \text{r} \mid \boldsymbol{m}_\text{r} \in \mathcal{R}^\text{i}, \ \beta \neq \hat{\alpha}^\text{i}(\text{r}). \quad (3)$$

To achieve better robustness, it is useful to introduce a positive margin $\kappa > 0$

$$\sum_{r'} f_{rr'} y^i_{r'\beta} + \kappa < \sum_{r'} f_{rr'} y^i_{r'\hat{\alpha}^i(r)} \quad \text{for all i, } r \mid \boldsymbol{m}_r \in \mathcal{R}^i, \; \beta \neq \hat{\alpha}^i(r). \quad (4)$$

If these conditions are fulfilled, the target states correspond to stable states of the CLM dynamics. However, typically not all conditions can be met, and finding $f_{rr'}$ becomes the optimization problem to violate (4) as little as possible.

Superposition of Basis Interactions. To reduce the number of learning parameters in (4) and to achieve a better generalization, we use a set of K basis interactions $g^j_{rr'}, j = 1, \ldots, K$, which are linearly combined such that

$$f_{rr'} = \sum_j c_j g^j_{rr'}. \quad (5)$$

Substituting (5) into (4), we get a compact representation of the learning problem

$$\sum_j c_j Z^k_j + \kappa < 0 \quad \text{for all } k = (i, r \mid \boldsymbol{m}_r \in \mathcal{R}^i, \beta \neq \hat{\alpha}^i(r)) \quad (6)$$

where k is a super-index for the consistency conditions running over all combinations of pattern i, feature r, and label $\beta \neq \hat{\alpha}^i(r)$. Z^k_j describes the information from the training set and the basis interactions by

$$Z^k_j = Z^{ir\beta}_j = \sum_{r' \mid \hat{\alpha}^i(r') = \beta} g^j_{rr'} - \sum_{r' \mid \hat{\alpha}^i(r') = \hat{\alpha}^i(r)} g^j_{rr'}. \quad (7)$$

To generate the basis functions we first transform feature pairs at position (r, r') in a generalized proximity space $\boldsymbol{d}_{rr'} = [d_1(\boldsymbol{m}_r, \boldsymbol{m}_{r'}), \ldots, d_P(\boldsymbol{m}_r, \boldsymbol{m}_{r'})]^T$, and use a variation of Self-Organizing Map, the activity equilibration AEV [1], to reduce the proximity vectors $\boldsymbol{d}_{rr'}$ to a set of K prototypes $\tilde{\boldsymbol{d}}_j$. Then we chose as j-th basis interaction g^j the membership function of the corresponding j-th multidimensional Voronoi cell [9]:

$$g^j_{rr'} = \begin{cases} 1 & : \; \| \boldsymbol{d}_{rr'} - \tilde{\boldsymbol{d}}_j \| \leq \| \boldsymbol{d}_{rr'} - \tilde{\boldsymbol{d}}_i \| \; \text{for all } i \neq j, \; i = 1, \ldots, K \\ 0 & : \; \text{else} \end{cases}. \quad (8)$$

3 Different Learning Approaches

In the following, we describe several approaches to solve the learning problem. Among these are two new and efficient methods which avoid the optimization of coefficients and even the explicit computation of the consistency inequalities. For comparison we also describe how several more traditional classification methods can be applied.

Quadratic Consistency Optimization (QCO). In [9,10], the optimization problem (6) is solved by gradient descend in the quadratic error

$$E_{QCO} = \sum_k \left(\sum_j c_j Z^k_j + \kappa \right)^2. \quad (9)$$

The performance of this approach suffers from the high number of evaluations of the basis functions $g_{rr'}^j$ in (7) due to the number of inequalities, which are highly redundant with respect to the low number of parameters c_j to optimize.

Average Consistency Condition (ACC). In a first approximation, we try to prevent the optimization step (9) by using a geometrical argument. Averaging the consistency inequalities

$$\hat{Z}_j = \frac{\sum_k Z_j^k}{\sum_k 1}, \quad k = 1, \ldots (L-1) \sum_i N^i \qquad (10)$$

yields a "mean" consistency condition. We get an approximate solution for it as

$$c_j = -\hat{Z}_j \Rightarrow \sum_j c_j \hat{Z}_j < 0. \qquad (11)$$

This solution is also a solution for most of the original conditions, while outliers are disregarded.

Averaging of pairwise Interaction within Basis functions (AVBF). The main drawback of the previous aproaches is the explicit calculation of many inequalities, but it can be avoided by further considerations. We assign to all feature-pairs within a training pattern a fixed positive or negative value $Y_{rr'}^i$ according to whether the two features have the same label or not, respectively:

$$Y_{rr'}^i = \begin{cases} 1 & : \quad r \mid \boldsymbol{m}_r \in \mathcal{R}^i, \ r' \mid \boldsymbol{m}_{r'} \in \mathcal{R}^i, \ \hat{\alpha}^i(r) = \hat{\alpha}^i(r') \\ -\frac{1}{L-1} & : \quad r \mid \boldsymbol{m}_r \in \mathcal{R}^i, \ r' \mid \boldsymbol{m}_{r'} \in \mathcal{R}^i, \ \hat{\alpha}^i(r) \neq \hat{\alpha}^i(r') \\ 0 & : \quad \text{else} \end{cases} \qquad (12)$$

We average these pairwise interactions with respect to the basis functions and assign these values to the interaction coefficients c_j as

$$c_j = \frac{\sum_{irr'} Y_{rr'}^i g_{rr'}^j}{\sum_{irr'} g_{rr'}^j}. \qquad (13)$$

This choice for c_j fulfills the mean consistency condition (10). Thus we efficiently obtain a suitable solution for most of the training patterns *without* explicitly calculating the inequalities themselves.

The last result suggests that a good segmentation can be obtained dependent only on the shape of the basis functions rather than by optimization of parameters on which we previously focused in [9]. This motivates to directly train classical classifiers to separate regions of positive and negative examples in the space of feature pairs or the proximity space.

Classificators as Interaction Function (MLP, SVM, MCC). We train standard classification algorithms $C(\boldsymbol{m}_r, \boldsymbol{m}_{r'})$, with the pairwise interactions within the training set and apply these classificators as interaction function $f_{rr'} = C(\boldsymbol{m}_r, \boldsymbol{m}_{r'})$. As adaptive classificator we use the Multi Layer Perceptron (MLP), the Support Vector Machine (SVM) [6], and the Maximum Contrast Classifier (MCC) [2] which employs linearly combined probability density kernels. We test these classificators in two ways: (i) the feature-pairs are presented

Table 1. Average Segmentation Quality

Algorithm	QCO	ACC	AVBF	MLP1	MLP2	SVM1	SVM2	MCC1	MCC2
E_S	0.73	0.98	0.76	0.64	0.95	0.81	0.85	1.71	0.83
E_M	0.65	0.54	0.63	1.50	0.71	1.75	0.54	1.64	0.56

directly as vectors $(m_r, m_{r'})$; (ii) the proximity vectors $\boldsymbol{d}_{rr'}$ are computed as above and the classifiers are trained on these. In this case the interaction function is given by $f_{rr'} = C(\boldsymbol{d}_{rr'})$.

4 Quality Measure

In order to compare the success of the different approaches, we define two measures E_S and E_M to describe the accordance between the desired grouping, given by the labels $\alpha_{tr} = 1, \ldots, L_{tr}$ in the training patterns, and the learned grouping, given by the labels $\alpha_{CLM} = 1, \ldots, L_{CLM}$ from the CLM-answer. E_S describes how much the groups in the input are split to different groups in the output, whereas E_M describes how much different groups in the input are merged to the same group in the output. To this aim, we approximate for each pattern the probabilities $P^i(\alpha_{tr}, \alpha_{CLM})$ from the frequencies, that the label α_{tr} and the label α_{CLM} are assigned to the same feature. Then, for each group in the input we compute it's entropy with respect to the groups in the output and for each group in the output it's entropy with respect to the input. E_S is the mean entropy of all training labels in all patterns, where each group is weighted by it's probability $P^i(\alpha_{tr})$ and E_M is the mean entropy of all CLM labels in all patterns, where each group is weighted by it's probability $P^i(\alpha_{CLM})$.

$$E_S = -\frac{1}{M} \sum_{i=1}^{M} \sum_{\alpha_{tr}=1}^{L_{tr}} P^i(\alpha_{tr}) \sum_{\alpha_{CLM}=1}^{L_{CLM}} P^i(\alpha_{CLM}|\alpha_{tr}) \log P^i(\alpha_{CLM}|\alpha_{tr}). \quad (14)$$

$$E_M = -\frac{1}{M} \sum_{i=1}^{M} \sum_{\alpha_{CLM}=1}^{L_{CLM}} P^i(\alpha_{CLM}) \sum_{\alpha_{tr}=1}^{L_{tr}} P^i(\alpha_{tr}|\alpha_{CLM}) \log P^i(\alpha_{tr}|\alpha_{CLM}). \quad (15)$$

It holds that $E_S = 0$ and $E_M = 0$, whenever the example grouping defines the same partition of the pattern as the CLM-grouping and the values of the two measures increase with the differences between the groupings.

5 Comparison of Segmentation Results

Cell image features: The different approaches were tested by application to the segmentation of fluorescence images shown in the top row of Fig. 1. Cells have a dark cell body and bright irregular corona. As proposed in [3], we obtain suitable feature vectors by combination of position and the direction of the local intensity gradient $\boldsymbol{m}_r = (x_r, y_r, \varphi_r)$, $x_r, y_r \in [1, 45]$, $\varphi_r \in [0, 2\pi]$.

Proximity space: To incorporate the principle of convexity into our interaction function we define a three dimensional input space for the basis functions, that describes the proximity between two edge features. A vector from this space $d_{rr'} = (\| d \|, \theta_1, \theta_2)^T$ consists of the length of the connecting vector d and the relative angles θ_1 and θ_2 between d and the intensity gradients at r, r'.

Basis functions: We compute $K = 30$ basis functions to partition the proximity space as described in Section 2 by means of 10000 clustering steps for randomly chosen proximity vectors $d_{rr'}$ from the training set. This results in ≈ 20000 consistency conditions from which the QCO and ACC algorithms compute 30 parameters only.

Training images: Images and the example labelings are shown in Fig. 1. All described learning approaches were trained with one of the training patterns at a time and tested by application of the CLM with the learned interaction function to all ten patterns. For illustration, Fig. 1 shows the results of all methods trained with the example image number five.

Training parameters: For QCO we employ 10000 gradient descent steps according to function (9), the coefficients for ACC are derived by equation (11), while with the AVBF we use 10000 averaging steps within the basis functions. For training of the classificator MLP, SVM, and MCC, we present 1000 feature-pairs with positive interaction and 1000 with negative interaction. The direct presentation uses the concatenation of local edge features $(x_r, y_r, \varphi_r, x_{r'}, y_{r'}, \varphi_{r'})$, whereas in the second variant the proximity vectors $d_{rr'}$ are presented.

Table 2. E_S/E_M-Values for Results in Fig. 1.

	∅	1	2	3	4	5	6	7	8	9	10
QCO_5	0.67/ 0.64	0.89/ 0.86	0.65/ 0.68	0.53/ 0.77	0.50/ 0.54	0.51/ 0.41	0.69/ 0.75	0.63/ 0.81	0.68/ 0.52	0.93/ 0.50	0.67/ 0.54
ACC_5	1.00/ 0.56	1.03/ 0.72	1.03/ 0.67	0.89/ 0.62	0.89/ 0.52	1.10/ 0.37	1.01/ 0.58	0.85/ 0.59	0.95/ 0.45	1.31/ 0.49	0.92/ 0.58
AVBF_5	0.76/ 0.64	0.83/ 0.94	0.83/ 0.77	0.77/ 0.77	0.58/ 0.58	0.91/ 0.45	0.70/ 0.54	0.68/ 0.65	0.69/ 0.54	1.01/ 0.57	0.60/ 0.56
MLP1_5	0.54/ 1.49	0.51/ 1.67	0.47/ 1.55	0.54/ 1.67	0.53/ 1.59	0.64/ 1.15	0.41/ 1.51	0.59/ 1.74	0.52/ 1.30	0.63/ 1.16	0.58/ 1.59
MLP2_5	0.94/ 0.62	0.92/ 0.80	1.00/ 0.70	0.88/ 0.80	0.72/ 0.52	1.30/ 0.51	0.88/ 0.65	0.79/ 0.63	0.95/ 0.53	1.27/ 0.54	0.71/ 0.58
SVM1_5	0.82/ 1.75	0.80/ 1.74	0.83/ 1.75	0.77/ 1.74	0.81/ 1.76	0.81/ 1.75	0.84/ 1.76	0.83/ 1.75	0.83/ 1.76	0.81/ 1.75	0.82/ 1.75
SVM2_5	0.84/ 0.52	0.91/ 0.72	0.85/ 0.59	0.82/ 0.66	0.65/ 0.42	1.09/ 0.39	0.73/ 0.48	0.72/ 0.56	0.75/ 0.45	1.16/ 0.50	0.69/ 0.47
MCC1_5	1.76/ 1.61	1.78/ 1.84	1.80/ 1.78	1.77/ 1.75	1.75/ 1.71	1.55/ 1.02	1.81/ 1.79	1.71/ 1.75	1.82/ 1.50	1.80/ 1.22	1.78/ 1.74
MCC2_5	0.91/ 0.61	0.99/ 0.95	0.98/ 0.70	0.92/ 0.72	0.74/ 0.51	1.06/ 0.40	0.67/ 0.59	0.66/ 0.62	0.69/ 0.52	1.07/ 0.55	0.60/ 0.56

Table 1 shows for all learning approaches the values of E_S and E_M averaged over all training and test patterns. Table 2 shows the respective quality measure values for all of the results displayed in Fig. 1.

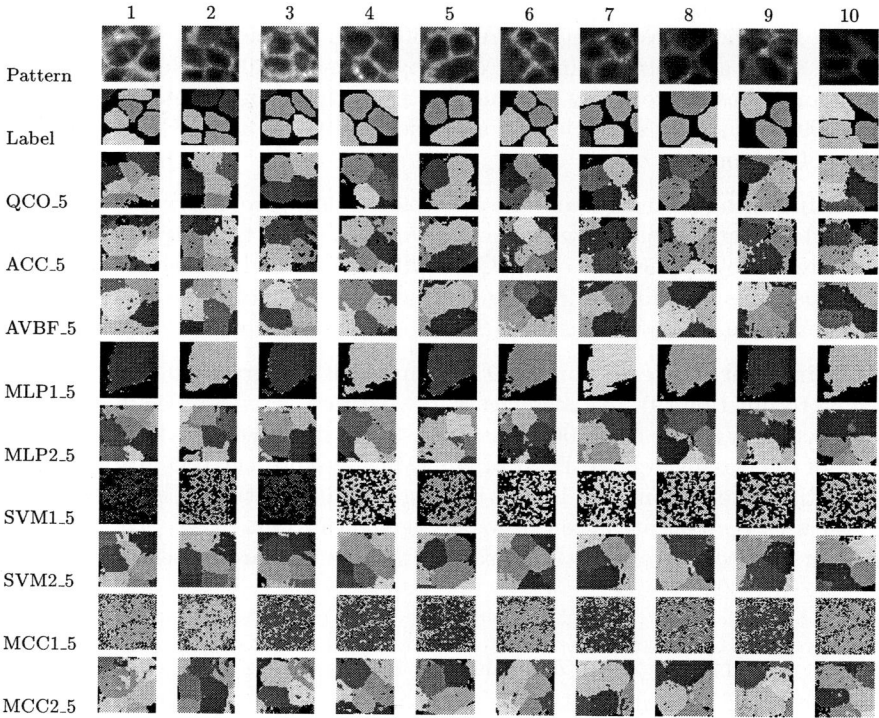

Fig. 1. Segmentation Results.

6 Discussion

The evaluation of segmentation results yields four major important observations: (i) E_M seems to be more discriminative for good segmentation results than E_S, so we focus in or analysis mainly on these values; (ii) the approximative but efficient methods ACC and AVBF show no loss of segmentation quality and are comparable to the earlier proposed QCO-approach; (iii) the standard classificators MLP, SVM, or MCC rely on transformation of the data to a suitable proximity space, because direct application to the raw feature data leads to a total failure. Working with the proximity space, the kernel-based classificators show slightly better results as QCO, ACC, and AVBF while MLP performs worse. (iv) The computationally by far most efficient new method AVBF shows only a slight loss of segmentation quality but the significant smaller training cost compensates this loss such that we prefer this approach for further training experiments.

In summary, we obtain that an suitable interaction for feature grouping can be generated by the direct interpolation of pairwise interactions. In this case, a good segmentation depends essentially on the definition of appropriate proximity measures together with the proposed statistical approximation AVBF to efficiently solve the optimization problem. Thus in future work we will search for strategies of extracting good candidates of such measures directly from the training set. This is a nontrivial problem, because often even human experts do neither agree on what is a correct segmentation of the data [4], nor is the relevance of certain features known beforehand. However, the efficient methods presented here to generate a compatibility function from examples together with the grouping abilities of the CLM yield a means for automatic evaluation of different feature extraction and labeling methods.

Acknowledgments. The authors thank Heiko Wersing for discussion. S. Weng is supported by DFG grant GK-231.

References

1. Heidemann, G., Ritter, H.: Efficient Vector Quantization using the WTA-rule with Activity Equalization, Neural Processing Letters vol. 13, no. 1 (2001), pp. 17–30.
2. Meinicke, P., Twellmann, T., Ritter, H.: Maximum Contrast Classifiers, In Proc. of ICANN (2002), pp. 745–750.
3. Nattkemper, T.W., Wersing, H., Schuber, W., Ritter H.: Fluorescence Micrograph Segmentation by Gestalt-Based Feature Binding Proc. of the Int. Joint Conf. on Neur. Netw. (IJCNN), vol. 1, addr. Como Italy (2000), pp. 248–254.
4. Nattkemper, T.W., Ritter, H., Schubert, W.: A Neural Classificator Enabling High-Throughput Topological Analysis of Lymphocytes in Tissue Sections, IEEE Trans. on Inf. Techn. in Biomed. vol. 5, no. 2 (2001), pp. 138–149
5. Ontrup, J., Ritter, H.: Perceptual Grouping in a Neural Model: Reproducing Human Texture Perception. Technical Report SFB 360 98-6, University of Bielefeld (1998)
6. Smola, A.J., Schölkopf, B.: A Tutorial on Support Vector Regression, NeuroCOLT2 Technical Report Series NC2-TR-1998-030 (1998)
7. Terman, D., Wang, D.L.: Global competition and local cooperation in a network of neural oscillators, Physica D, 81 (1995), pp. 148–176
8. van der Malsburg, C., Buhmann, J.: Sensory Segmentation with Coupled Neural Oscillators, Biol. Cyb. 54 (1992), pp. 29–40
9. Weng, S., Steil, J.J.: Data Driven Generation of Interactions for Feature Binding and Relaxation Labeling, In Proc. of ICANN (2002), pp. 432–437
10. Wersing, H.: Learning Lateral Interactions for Feature Binding and Sensory Segmentation. NIPS (2001)
11. Wersing, H., Steil, J.J., Ritter,H.: A Competitive Layer Model for Feature Binding and Sensory Segmentation, Neural Computation vol. 13 (2001), pp. 357–387.

Differential ICA

Seungjin Choi

Department of Computer Science and Engineering
POSTECH
San 31 Hyoja-dong, Nam-gu
Pohang 790-784, Korea
seungjin@postech.ac.kr

Abstract. As an alternative to the conventional Hebb-type unsupervised learning, differential learning was studied in the domain of Hebb's rule [1] and decorrelation [2]. In this paper we present an ICA algorithm which employs differential learning, thus named as *differential ICA*. We derive a differential ICA algorithm in the framework of maximum likelihood estimation and random walk model. Algorithm derivation using the natural gradient and local stability analysis are provided. Usefulness of the algorithm is emphasized in the case of blind separation of temporally correlated sources and is demonstrated through a simple numerical example.

1 Introduction

Independent component analysis (ICA) is a statistical method, the goal of which is to learn non-orthogonal basis vectors from a set of observation data with basis coefficients being statistically independent. In the framework of linear transform, ICA finds a representation of the form

$$\boldsymbol{x}(t) = \sum_{i=1}^{n} \boldsymbol{a}_i s_i(t)$$
$$= \boldsymbol{A}\boldsymbol{s}(t), \qquad (1)$$

where $\boldsymbol{x} \in \mathbb{R}^n$ is the observation data (which is given) and $\boldsymbol{A} = [\boldsymbol{a}_1 \cdots \boldsymbol{a}_n] \in \mathbb{R}^{n \times n}$ (which is known as a *mixing matrix* in source separation) consists of basis vectors $\{\boldsymbol{a}_i\}$ and $\boldsymbol{s} = [s_1 \cdots s_n]$ is an n-dimensional vector containing basis coefficients $\{s_i\}$ (which are called *independent components* and are also known as *sources*).

It is known that ICA performs source separation, the goal of which is to restore unknowns sources without resorting to any prior knowledge, given only a set of observation data. Source separation is achieved by estimating the mixing matrix $\boldsymbol{A}$ or its inverse $\boldsymbol{W} = \boldsymbol{A}^{-1}$ (which is known as *demixing matrix*).

Let $\boldsymbol{y}(t)$ be the output of demixing transform, i.e.,

$$\boldsymbol{y}(t) = \boldsymbol{W}\boldsymbol{x}(t). \qquad (2)$$

Either maximum likelihood estimation or the minimization of mutual information leads to the well-known natural gradient ICA algorithm [3] whose updating rule has the form

$$\boldsymbol{W}(t+1) = \boldsymbol{W}(t) + \eta \left\{ \boldsymbol{I} - \varphi(\boldsymbol{y}(t))\boldsymbol{y}^T(t) \right\} \boldsymbol{W}(t), \qquad (3)$$

where η is a learning rate and $\varphi(\boldsymbol{y}) = [\varphi_1(y_1) \cdots \varphi_n(y_n)]^T$ is an n-dimensional vector, each element of which corresponds to the negative score function, i.e., $\varphi_i(y_i) = -\frac{d \log p_i(y_i)}{dy_i}$ where $p_i(\cdot)$ is the hypothesized probability density function for s_i. More details on ICA or source separation can be found in [4,5] (and references therein).

In a wide sense, most of ICA algorithms based on unsupervised learning belong to Hebb-type rule or its generalization with adopting nonlinear functions. Motivated from differential Hebb's rule [1] and differential decorrelation [2], we develop an ICA algorithm which employs differential learning where learning resorts to differentiated values (or difference of values in discrete-time counterpart).

Differential Hebb's rule was studied as an alternative to the Hebb's rule The motivation of the differential Hebb's rule is that concurrent change, rather than just concurrent activation, more accurately captures the *concomitant variation*. The differential learning was introduced in the framework of ICA [6] and decorrelation [2] recently. In this paper we derive a differential ICA algorithm in the framework of maximum likelihood estimation and random walk model. In fact, our differential ICA algorithm can be viewed as a simpler form of ICA algorithms which exploit the temporal structure of sources [7,8].

2 Random Walk Model for Latent Variables

Given a set of observation data, $\{\boldsymbol{x}(t)\}$, the task of learning the linear generative model (1) under a constraint that latent variables being statistically independent, is a semiparametric estimation problem. The maximum likelihood estimation of basis vectors $\{\boldsymbol{a}_i\}$ is involved with a probabilistic model for latent variables which are treated as nuisance parameters.

In order to show a link between the differential learning and maximum likelihood estimation, we consider a random walk model for latent variables which is a simple Markov chain, i.e.,

$$s_i(t) = s_i(t-1) + \epsilon_i(t), \qquad (4)$$

where the innovation $\epsilon_i(t)$ is assumed to have zero mean with a density function $q_i(\epsilon_i(t))$. In addition, innovation sequences $\{\epsilon_i(t)\}$ are assumed to be mutually independent.

Let us consider the latent variables $s_i(t)$ over N-point time block. We define the vector $\underline{s}_i$ as

$$\underline{s}_i = [s_i(0), \ldots, s_i(N-1)]^T. \qquad (5)$$

Then the joint probability density function of $\underline{s}_i$ can be written as

$$p_i(\underline{s}_i) = p_i(s_i(0), \ldots, s_i(N-1))$$
$$= \prod_{t=0}^{N-1} p_i(s_i(t)|s_i(t-1)), \quad (6)$$

where $s_i(t) = 0$ for $t < 0$ and the statistical independence of innovation sequences was taken into account.

It follows from the random walk model (4) that the conditional probability density of $s_i(t)$ given its past samples can be written as

$$p_i(s_i(t)|s_i(t-1)) = q_i(\epsilon_i(t)). \quad (7)$$

Combining (6) and (7) leads to

$$p_i(\underline{s}_i) = \prod_{t=0}^{N-1} q_i(\epsilon_i(t))$$
$$= \prod_{t=0}^{N-1} q_i(s'_i(t)), \quad (8)$$

where $s'_i(t) = s_i(t) - s_i(t-1)$ which is the first-order approximation of differentiation.

Take the statistical independence of latent variables and (8) into account, then we can write the joint density $p(\underline{s}_1, \ldots, \underline{s}_n)$ as

$$p(\underline{s}_1, \ldots, \underline{s}_n) = \prod_{i=1}^{n} p_i(\underline{s}_i)$$
$$= \prod_{t=0}^{N-1} \prod_{i=1}^{n} q_i(s'_i(t)). \quad (9)$$

The factorial model given in (9) will be used as a optimization criterion to derive the proposed algorithm.

3 Differential ICA Algorithm

Denote a set of observation data by

$$\mathcal{X} = \{\underline{x}_1, \ldots, \underline{x}_n\}, \quad (10)$$

where

$$\underline{x}_i = \{x_i(0), \ldots, x_i(N-1)\}. \quad (11)$$

Then the normalized log-likelihood is given by

$$\frac{1}{N}\log p(\mathcal{X}|A) = -\log|\det A| + \frac{1}{N}\log p(\underline{s}_1, \ldots, \underline{s}_n)$$
$$= -\log|\det A| + \frac{1}{N} \sum_{t=0}^{N-1} \sum_{i=1}^{n} \log q_i(s'_i(t)). \quad (12)$$

Let us denote the inverse of $\boldsymbol{A}$ by $\boldsymbol{W} = \boldsymbol{A}^{-1}$. The estimate of latent variables is denoted by $\boldsymbol{y}(t) = \boldsymbol{W}\boldsymbol{x}(t)$. With these defined variables, the objective function (that is the negative normalized log-likelihood) is given by

$$\begin{aligned}\mathcal{J}_2 &= -\frac{1}{N}\log p(\mathcal{X}|\boldsymbol{A}) \\ &= -\log|\det \boldsymbol{W}| - \frac{1}{N}\sum_{t=0}^{N-1}\sum_{i=1}^{n}\log q_i(y'_i(t)),\end{aligned} \quad (13)$$

where s_i is replaced by its estimate y_i.

For on-line learning, the sample average is replaced by instantaneous value. Hence the objective function (13) becomes

$$\mathcal{J}_3 = -\log|\det \boldsymbol{W}| - \sum_{i=1}^{n}\log q_i(y'_i(t)), \quad (14)$$

Note that objective function (14) is slightly different from the one used in the conventional ICA based on the minimization of mutual information or the maximum likelihood estimation.

We derive a natural gradient learning algorithm which finds a minimum of (14). To this end, we follow the way that was discussed in [3,9,10]. We calculate the total differential $d\mathcal{J}_3(\boldsymbol{W})$ due to the change $d\boldsymbol{W}$

$$\begin{aligned}d\mathcal{J}_3 &= \mathcal{J}_3(\boldsymbol{W} + d\boldsymbol{W}) - \mathcal{J}_3(\boldsymbol{W}) \\ &= d\{-\log|\det \boldsymbol{W}|\} + d\left\{-\sum_{i=1}^{n}\log q_i(y'_i(t))\right\}.\end{aligned} \quad (15)$$

Define

$$\varphi_i(y'_i) = -\frac{d\log q_i(y'_i)}{dy'_i}. \quad (16)$$

and construct a vector $\varphi(\boldsymbol{y}') = [\varphi_1(y'_1)\cdots\varphi_n(y'_n)]^T$.

With this definition, we have

$$\begin{aligned}d\left\{-\sum_{i=1}^{n}\log q_i(y'_i(t))\right\} &= \sum_{i=1}^{n}\varphi_i(y'_i(t))dy'_i(t) \\ &= \varphi^T(\boldsymbol{y}'(t))d\boldsymbol{y}'(t).\end{aligned} \quad (17)$$

One can easily see that

$$d\{-\log|\det \boldsymbol{W}|\} = \operatorname{tr}\{d\boldsymbol{W}\boldsymbol{W}^{-1}\}. \quad (18)$$

Define a modified differential matrix $d\boldsymbol{V}$ by

$$d\boldsymbol{V} = d\boldsymbol{W}\boldsymbol{W}^{-1}. \quad (19)$$

Then, with this modified differential matrix, the total differential $d\mathcal{J}_3(\boldsymbol{W})$ is computed as

$$d\mathcal{J}_3 = -\text{tr}\{d\boldsymbol{V}\} + \varphi^T(\boldsymbol{y}'(t))d\boldsymbol{V}\boldsymbol{y}'(t). \quad (20)$$

A gradient descent learning algorithm for updating $\boldsymbol{V}$ is given by

$$\begin{aligned}\boldsymbol{V}(t+1) &= \boldsymbol{V}(t) - \eta_t \frac{d\mathcal{J}_3}{d\boldsymbol{V}} \\ &= \eta_t \left\{\boldsymbol{I} - \varphi(\boldsymbol{y}'(t))\boldsymbol{y}'^T(t)\right\}. \end{aligned} \quad (21)$$

Hence, it follows from the relation (19) that the updating rule for $\boldsymbol{W}$ has the form

$$\boldsymbol{W}(t+1) = \boldsymbol{W}(t) + \eta_t \left\{\boldsymbol{I} - \varphi(\boldsymbol{y}'(t))\boldsymbol{y}'^T(t)\right\}\boldsymbol{W}(t). \quad (22)$$

Remarks

- The algorithm (22) was originally derived in an *ad hoc* manner in [6]. Here we show that the algorithm (22) can be derived in the framework of maximum likelihood estimation and a random walk model.
- The algorithm (22) can be viewed as a special case of temporal ICA algorithm [7] where the spatiotemporal generative model was employed.
- In the conventional ICA algorithm, the nonlinear function $\varphi_i(\cdot)$ depends on the probability distribution of source. However, in the differential ICA algorithm, the nonlinear function is chosen, depending on the probability distribution of $\epsilon_i(t) = s_i(t) - s_i(t-1)$, i.e., the difference of adjacent latent variables in time domain. In general, the innovation is more non-Gaussian, compared to the signal itself. In this sense, the differential ICA algorithm works better than the conventional ICA algorithm when source was generated by a linear combination of innovation and its time-delayed replica (e.g., moving average). This is confirmed by a simple numerical example.
- As in the flexible ICA [10], we can adopt a flexible nonlinear function based on the generalized Gaussian distribution.

4 Local Stability Analysis

The differential ICA algorithm (22) can be obtained by replacing $\boldsymbol{y}(t)$ by $\boldsymbol{y}'(t)$ in the conventional ICA algorithm (3). Thus the local stability analysis of the algorithm (22) can be done similarly, following the result in [3]. As in [3], we calculate the expected Hessian $E\{d^2\mathcal{J}_3\}$ (in which the expectation is taken at $\boldsymbol{W} = \boldsymbol{A}^{-1}$) in terms of the modified differential matrix $d\boldsymbol{V}$. For shorthand notation, we omit the time index t in the following analysis.

The expected Hessian $E\{d^2\mathcal{J}_3\}$ is given by

$$\begin{aligned}E\{d^2\mathcal{J}_3\} &= E\left\{\boldsymbol{y}'d\boldsymbol{V}^T\boldsymbol{\Phi}d\boldsymbol{y}' + \varphi^T(\boldsymbol{y}')d\boldsymbol{V}d\boldsymbol{y}'\right\} \\ &= E\left\{\boldsymbol{y}'d\boldsymbol{V}^T\boldsymbol{\Phi}d\boldsymbol{V}\boldsymbol{y}' + \varphi^T(\boldsymbol{y}')d\boldsymbol{V}d\boldsymbol{V}\boldsymbol{y}'\right\} \\ &= \sum_{j\neq i}\left[\sigma_i^2\kappa_j(dv_{ji})^2 + dv_{ij}dv_{ji}\right] + \sum_i(\zeta_i+1)(dv_{ii})^2, \end{aligned} \quad (23)$$

where the statistical expectation is taken at the solution so that $\{y_i\}$ are mutually independent and

$$\boldsymbol{\Phi} = \begin{bmatrix} \dot{\varphi}_1(y_1') & \cdots & 0 \\ \vdots & \ddots & \vdots \\ 0 & \cdots & \dot{\varphi}_n(y_n') \end{bmatrix} \tag{24}$$

$$\dot{\varphi}_i(y_i') = \frac{d\varphi_i(y_i')}{dy_i'} \tag{25}$$

$$\sigma_i^2 = E\{y_i'^2\} \tag{26}$$

$$\kappa_i = E\{\dot{\varphi}_i(y_i')\} \tag{27}$$

$$\zeta_i = E\{y_i'^2 \dot{\varphi}_i(y_i')\}. \tag{28}$$

It follows from (23) that $E\{d^2 \mathcal{J}_3\}$ is positive if and only if

$$\kappa_i > 0 \tag{29}$$

$$\zeta_i + 1 > 0 \tag{30}$$

$$\sigma_i^2 \sigma_j^2 \kappa_i \kappa_j > 1. \tag{31}$$

5 Numerical Example

We present a simple numerical example to show the usefulness of our differential ICA algorithm which is described in (22). Three independent innovation sequences were drawn from Laplacian distribution. Each innovation sequence was convolved with a moving average filter (with exponentially decreasing impulse response) in order to generate colored sources. These sources were linearly mixed via 3×3 mixing matrix $\boldsymbol{A}$

We compare the performance of our differential ICA algorithm with that of the conventional natural gradient ICA algorithm in terms of the performance index (PI) which is defined as

$$\text{PI} = \frac{1}{2(n-1)} \sum_{i=1}^{n} \left\{ \left(\sum_{k=1}^{n} \frac{|g_{ik}|^2}{\max_j |g_{ij}|^2} - 1 \right) + \left(\sum_{k=1}^{n} \frac{|g_{ki}|^2}{\max_j |g_{ji}|^2} - 1 \right) \right\}, \tag{32}$$

where g_{ij} is the (i,j)-element of the global system matrix $\boldsymbol{G} = \boldsymbol{W}\boldsymbol{A}$ and $\max_j g_{ij}$ represents the maximum value among the elements in the ith row vector of $\boldsymbol{G}$, $\max_j g_{ji}$ does the maximum value among the elements in the ith column vector of $\boldsymbol{G}$. The performance index defined in (32) tells us how far the global system matrix $\boldsymbol{G}$ is from a generalized permutation matrix.

It is expected that the conventional ICA algorithm would have difficulty in separating these sources because they are close to Gaussian. The differential ICA algorithm inherently resort to the innovation sequence rather than the source itself (since it is motivated by a simple Markov model). The result of a numerical example is shown in Fig. 1.

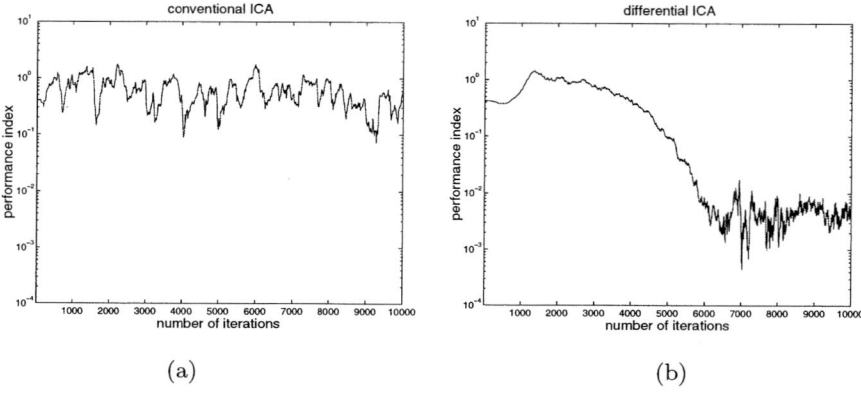

Fig. 1. Evolution of performance index: (a) conventional ICA; (b) differential ICA.

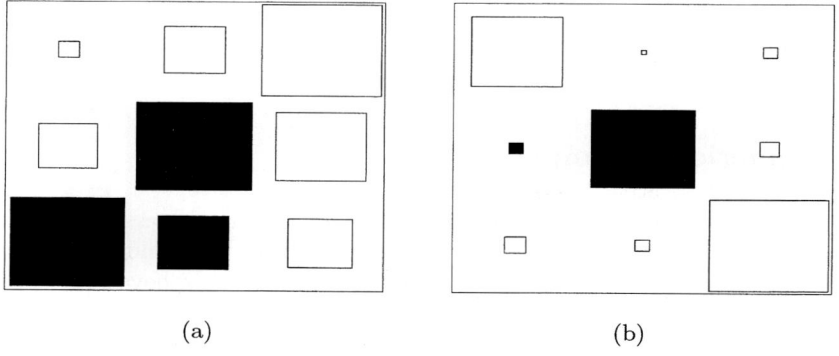

Fig. 2. Hinton's diagram for the global matrix G: (a) conventional ICA; (b) differential ICA. Each square's area represents the magnitude of the element of the matrix G. White square is for positive sign and black square is for negative sign.

6 Discussion

In this paper we have presented a natural gradient learning algorithm for differential decorrelation, the goal of which is to minimize the correlation between differentiated random variables. We showed that the differential decorrelation algorithm could be derived from learning a linear generative model by the maximum likelihood estimation under a random walk model. We also discussed a differential version of the natural gradient ICA algorithm and showed that it could also be derived under the random walk model. The differential correlation algorithm (22) or the differential ICA algorithm (22) could be generalized by adopting higher-order differentiation. This generalization is currently under investigation.

Acknowledgments. This work was supported by Korea Ministry of Science and Technology under Brain Science and Engineering Research Program and an International Cooperative Research Project, by KOSEF 2000-2-20500-009-5, and by Ministry of Education of Korea for its financial support toward the Electrical and Computer Engineering Division at POSTECH through its BK21 program.

References

1. Kosko, B.: Differential Hebbian learning. In: Proc. American Institute of Physics: Neural Networks for Computing. (1986) 277–282
2. Choi, S.: Adaptive differential decorrelation: A natural gradient algorithm. In: Proc. ICANN, Madrid, Spain (2002) 1168–1173
3. Amari, S., Chen, T.P., Cichocki, A.: Stability analysis of learning algorithms for blind source separation. Neural Networks **10** (1997) 1345–1351
4. Hyvärinen, A., Karhunen, J., Oja, E.: Independent Component Analysis. John Wiley & Sons, Inc. (2001)
5. Cichocki, A., Amari, S.: Adaptive Blind Signal and Image Processing: Learning Algorithms and Applications. John Wiley & Sons, Inc. (2002)
6. Choi, S.: Differential Hebbian-type learning algorithms for decorrelation and independent component analysis. Electronics Letters **34** (1998) 900–901
7. Attias, H., Schreiner, C.E.: Blind source separation and deconvolution: The dynamic component analysis algorithms. Neural Computation **10** (1998) 1373–1424
8. Amari, S.: Estimating functions of independent component analysis for temporally correlated signals. Neural Computation **12** (2000) 2083–2107
9. Amari, S.: Natural gradient works efficiently in learning. Neural Computation **10** (1998) 251–276
10. Choi, S., Cichocki, A., Amari, S.: Flexible independent component analysis. Journal of VLSI Signal Processing **26** (2000) 25–38

A Comparison of Model Aggregation Methods for Regression

Zafer Barutçuoğlu and Ethem Alpaydın

Department of Computer Engineering, Boğaziçi University, Istanbul, Turkey
zbarutcu@turk.net, alpaydin@boun.edu.tr

Abstract. Combining machine learning models is a means of improving overall accuracy. Various algorithms have been proposed to create aggregate models from other models, and two popular examples for classification are Bagging and AdaBoost. In this paper we examine their adaptation to regression, and benchmark them on synthetic and real-world data. Our experiments reveal that different types of AdaBoost algorithms require different complexities of base models. They outperform Bagging at their best, but Bagging achieves a consistent level of success with all base models, providing a robust alternative.

1 Introduction

Combining multiple instances of the same model type is a means for increasing robustness to variance, reducing the overall sensitivity to different starting parameters and noise. Two well-known algorithms for this purpose are *Bagging* [1] and *AdaBoost* [2,3]. Both have been analyzed for classification in much more detail than regression, possibly due to the wider availability of real-life applications. Adapting classification algorithms to regression raises some issues in this setting. In this paper we compare the Bagging algorithm and several AdaBoost variants for regression.

2 Bagging

The *Bagging* (Bootstrap Aggregating) algorithm [1] uses *bootstrapping* (equiprobable selection with replacement) on the training set to create many varied but overlapping new sets. The base algorithm is used to create a different base model instance for each bootstrap sample, and the ensemble output is the average of all base model outputs for a given input.

The best enhancement by Bagging is when the model instances are very different from each other, since averaging will not have much effect when the outputs are already close. Hence, the most suitable base models for Bagging are *unstable* models, where small changes in the training set can result in large changes in model parameters. Multilayer perceptrons and regression trees are good candidates.

The particular bootstrap sample size being used has an effect on the performance of Bagging, but the optimal ratio of sample to training set size depends on the data. Instead of manually finetuning this ratio per application, we used validation to automate a coarse adjustment that we named *Best-Ratio Bagging*. It removes a fraction of the training set for validation, performs multiple Bagging instances with different ratios on the remaining training examples, and chooses the Bagging model with the lowest error on the validation set as the final model. Although costly, Best-Ratio Bagging is useful for illustrating the best case performance of Bagging with respect to sample size.

Bagging takes a simple average of outputs, but the evaluation part of AdaBoost can be adopted and a weighted median may be used instead. The weights (confidences) can be calculated as in AdaBoost, using average loss with respect to a loss function. We implemented this variant using linear loss. See Section 3.2 for the computation of confidence and weighted median.

To produce similar but perturbed subsets from one training set, K-*fold cross-validation* is an alternative to bootstrapping. The training set $\mathcal{X}$ is randomly partitioned into K sets $\mathcal{X}_i$ of equal size, and each base model is trained on $\mathcal{X} - \mathcal{X}_i$. We called this algorithm *Cross-Validation Aggregating* (CVA). Evaluation is by averaging outputs, as in Bagging. As opposed to bootstrapping, cross-validation is guaranteed to use all training examples exactly once in exactly $K - 1$ subsets. For small K, this leads to more efficient use of data than bootstrapping. However as K increases, we get increasingly similar subsets, which should decrease the positive effect of combining.

3 The AdaBoost Approach

Since individual bootstrap samples are selected independently, the collective success of the models they produce is through mere redundancy. The *boosting* approach uses the base models in sequential collaboration, where each new model concentrates more on the examples where the previous models had high error. Different ways of realizing this dynamic focus lead to different algorithms. *AdaBoost (Ada*ptive *Boost*ing) [2,3] is an efficient and popular implementation of the boosting principle, applied and analyzed with much deeper interest for classification than regression. Since the latter is a more general problem, the basic concept of AdaBoost can be generalized in more than one way for regression.

3.1 AdaBoost.R

The originally proposed AdaBoost for regression *AdaBoost.R* is based on decomposing regression into infinitely many classification tasks [2]. This construction does allow an implementation, but it involves keeping track of a different updatable and integrable loss function for each example. Furthermore, the base learner must be able to accommodate such dynamic loss functions per example. This *dynamic-loss* approach was also used by Ridgeway *et al.* [4], but their experiments using naive Bayes base learners yielded no significant justification to afford a per-example redefinable loss, seriously constraining the choice of base learners if not time complexity.

3.2 Distribution-Based Algorithms

Drucker's AdaBoost. Drucker's AdaBoost for regression [5] is an *ad hoc* adaption of the classification AdaBoost. Despite the lack of a rigorous derivation, it uses scalar selection probabilities, unlike ADABOOST.R. It works much like classification AdaBoost, favoring examples with high error. The ensemble output is the weighted median of the base model outputs, weighted by the models' training confidences.

The weighted median can be computed by first sorting the outputs in order of magnitude, and then summing their weights until the sum exceeds half the weight total. If the weights were integers, this would be analogous to duplicating the outputs by their weights and taking the regular median.

At each step i, the algorithm minimizes the error function (in rearranged notation)

$$J_i = \sum_{t=1}^{N} \exp(-c_i) \exp\left(c_i L_i^t\right)$$

by minimizing per-example losses L_i^t. c_i is a measure of confidence over all examples, also used as the *combination coefficient* during evaluation. Drucker's AdaBoost chooses $c_i = \ln\left[(1 - \overline{L}_i)/\overline{L}_i\right]$ using $\overline{L}_i = \sum_{t=1}^{N} L_i^t p^t$ to minimize error, but this appears to be an unjustified adoption of the analytical result for classification. In the experiments we used linear loss (absolute difference) $L = |y - r|/D$ in DRUCKER.AD and square loss $L_S = |y - r|^2/D^2$ in DRUCKER.S where $D = \sup_t |y^t - r^t|$.

Zemel & Pitassi's Algorithm. Zemel & Pitassi [6] provide an algorithm similar to Drucker's, but with alternative mathematical particulars. Here the error function is

$$J_i = \sum_{t=1}^{N} c_i^{-1/2} \exp\left(c_i |y_i^t - r^t|^2\right)$$

where the loss function is squared error, and not scaled to $[0, 1]$.

Although the multiplier is now $c_i^{-1/2}$, replacing Drucker's $\exp(-c_i)$, with $0 < c_i \leq 1$ they behave similarly except near zero. Notably Zemel & Pitassi acknowledge that here c_i cannot be analytically determined, and simple line search is used. Finally, this algorithm uses weighted mean instead of weighted median to combine outputs.

We implemented this algorithm as ZEMEL-PITASSI.S and ZEMEL-PITASSI.AD, using the original square loss and linear loss respectively. In ZEMEL-PITASSI.AD we replaced weighted mean by weighted median to match the loss function.

3.3 Relabeling Algorithms

Another group of algorithms [7,8,9], although from different viewpoints, all aim to minimize *residual* error. In these algorithms each new base model learns artificial labels formed using the per-example training errors (*residues*) of the current combined model. After training each model i the residues are updated by subtracting the prediction y_i^t of the new model weighted by its coefficient c_i. Due to the subtractive training, combination is additive, using a weighted sum.

The LS_Boost Algorithm. The algorithm LS_Boost is from Friedman's gradient-based boosting strategy [7], using square loss $L = (y - r)^2/2$ where r is the actual training label and y is the current cumulative output $y_i = c_0 + \sum_{j=1}^{i-1} c_j h_j + c_i h_i = y_{i-1} + c_i h_i$. The new training labels $\hat{r}$ should be set to the direction that minimizes the loss, which is the negative gradient with respect to y evaluated at y_{i-1}. Then $\hat{r} = [-\partial L/\partial y]_{y=y_{i-1}} = r - y_{i-1}$ which is the current residual error. Substituting into the loss, we get the training error

$$E = \sum_{t=1}^{N} [c_i h_i^t - \hat{r}^t]$$

where $\hat{r}^t$ are the current residual labels. The combination coefficients c_i are determined by solving $\partial E/\partial c_i = 0$.

Duffy & Helmbold [8] give an algorithm SQUARELEV.R which is identical in effect. SQUARELEV.C, a variant of SQUARELEV.R, is more interesting in that while also based on residual error, it still uses probabilities. The base learner is fed not the residues $\hat{r}$, but their signs $sign(\hat{r}) \in \{-1, +1\}$, while the distribution weight of each example is made proportional to $|\hat{r}|$, so each example is still "emphasized" in proportion to its residual error. At the cost of handling probabilities, SQUARELEV.C allows using binary classifiers.

The LAD_Boost Algorithm. The LAD_Boost algorithm from [7] is derived from the same gradient-based framework as LS_Boost, but using linear loss (absolute deviation). The gradient of linear loss leads to the sign of the residue, so the base models are trained on $\{-1, +1\}$ labels, which also allows using classifiers. Here the derivation of c_i yields another weighted median computation. See [7] for details.

4 Experiment Design

We tested the algorithms using J-leaf regression trees with constant leaf labels. The learner subdivides the leaf having the greatest total squared deviation from the mean, until a specified node count J is reached or all leaves have a single training element. J is used to control base model complexity. Values of $\{2, 5, 10, 15, 20\}$ were used for the number of base trees to combine.

Bagging used a fixed 50% sample size ratio, while Best-Ratio Bagging compared the ratios $10\%, 20\%, \ldots, 90\%$ of the remaining examples for sample size using 50% of the examples for validation. All experiments were repeated ten times, using 5×2-fold cross-validation to partition the datasets. The algorithms were compared by the *5×2-fold cross-validated F test* [10] at 95% confidence. We used the datasets in Table 1 for our experiments. All of them have one-dimensional continuous output for regression.

syndata was synthetically generated for observing the algorithms visually. It has unidimensional input, and on an output range of $[-15, +15]$ it has Gaussian noise of zero mean and unit variance. abalone, boston and calif1000 are from [11]. prostate and birth are from [12]. votes and kin8 datasets are from the StatLib archive of Carnegie Mellon University. For each dataset, we repeated the experiments using 5×2-fold cross-validation. The error bars in the figures indicate one standard deviation above and below the mean error of the ten runs.

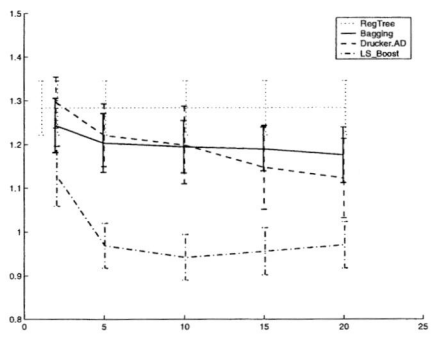

Fig. 1. 5-leaf syndata errors

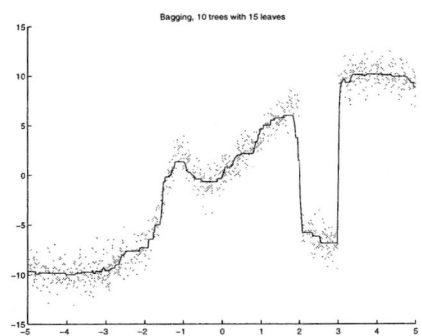

Fig. 4. 15-leaf BAGGING

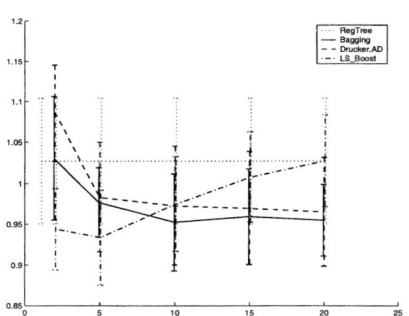

Fig. 2. 10-leaf syndata errors

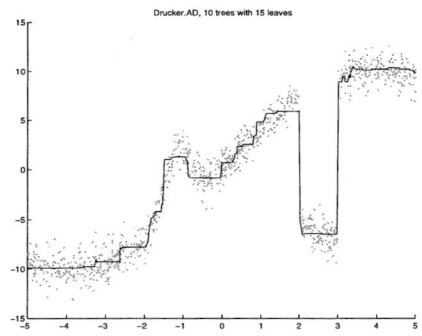

Fig. 5. 15-leaf DRUCKER.AD

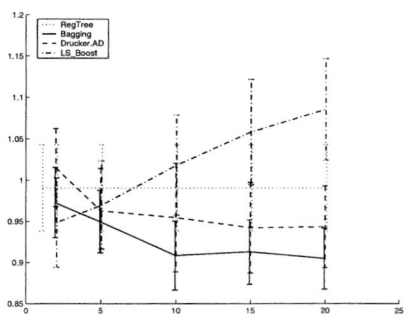

Fig. 3. 15-leaf syndata errors

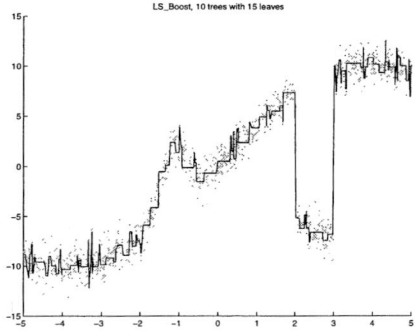

Fig. 6. 15-leaf LS_BOOST

5 Simulation Results

Figures 1 to 3 show the test errors of BAGGING, LS_BOOST and DRUCKER.AD on syndata as the number of trees changes. The unaggregated base algorithm REGTREE is also included, plotted as constant. These figures illustrate typical behaviors, also observed numerically on other datasets. Figures 4, 5 and 6 show example outputs on syndata using 15-leaf regression trees as base models.

The Bagging methods used both small and large trees with consistent success, although they took a large number of large trees to catch up with the relabeling AdaBoost algorithms. CVA was slightly better than Bagging algorithms for very few base models, and fell behind quickly thereafter as the cross-validated training sets became increasingly similar. W-BAGGING never significantly decreased test error beyond Bagging, sometimes even increasing it. Considering that bootstrap samples are selected uniformly, it is not surprising that "confidence" values derived from accidental differences are bound to disrupt Bagging rather than enhance it. Compared to a fixed 50% ratio of sample size with BAGGING, BR-BAGGING did not show significant improvement despite the nine-fold execution time.

ADABOOST.R, despite its unwieldy time complexity, was not able to improve the base model beyond the statistical significance threshold on any of the datasets.

Drucker's and Zemel & Pitassi's algorithms did not perform well using small trees on large datasets. They even increased training error, indicating that this is not due to overfitting, but the base models were too coarse to be useful to them.

LAD_BOOST and LS_BOOST started overfitting at much smaller trees than the base algorithm alone, because their modification of labels reduces the complexity of data. This is especially true of LAD_BOOST which greatly simplifies the problem for the base learners by discretizing pseudo-targets to binary. The rapid overfitting can be observed in Figure 6.

Over the tree sizes used and model counts up to ten, the best instances are reported in Table 2 as average errors and standard deviations over ten runs. The results are compared using the 5×2-fold cross-validated F-test with 95% confidence on each dataset. Some illustrative pairs of algorithms are shown in Table 3, where the column ">" denotes on how many datasets the left-hand algorithm was significantly superior.

6 Conclusion

Bagging proved to be very robust with respect to base model complexity. It was able to reduce test error successfully whether the underlying base models were overfit or underfit. Our variants of Bagging failed to offer any significant improvement over the original BAGGING algorithm, though we did thus verify the integrity of Bagging.

ADABOOST.R as it was originally proposed did not show any improvement over the unaggregated base model, let alone BAGGING, despite its special base model requirements for dynamic loss and prohibitive time complexity.

The distribution-based AdaBoost algorithms needed sufficiently complex base models. Otherwise they failed to reduce even the training error. DRUCKER and ZEMEL-PITASSI

Table 1. Properties of the datasets used

	inputs	size		inputs	size		inputs	size
syndata	1	1,000	prostate	7	376	kin8fh	8	8,192
boston	12	506	birth	5	488	kin8nm	8	8,192
calif1000	8	1,000	votes	6	3,107	kin8nh	8	8,192
abalone	10	4,177	kin8fm	8	8,192			

Table 2. Base model and Bagging results

	RegTree	Bagging	BR-Bagging	W-Bagging	CVA	AdaBoost.R
	avg ± std	avg ± std	avg ± std	avg ± std	avg ± std	avg ± std
syndata	.943± .049	.890±.043	.888± .034	.887±.035	.903±.044	.919± .084
boston	.350± .023	.295±.016	.294± .026	.296±.019	.308±.028	.307± .028
calif1000	.506± .028	.445±.016	.444± .017	.436±.019	.452±.018	.464± .022
votes	.493± .013	.444±.006	.445± .005	.446±.004	.458± .007	
prostate	.668± .072	.635±.042	.642± .035	.605±.044	.627± .053	
birth	.812± .055	.780±.033	.777± .029	.781±.031	.785± .030	
abalone	.545± .005	.521±.018	.513± .011	.483±.008	.523± .015	
kin8fm	.439± .003	.316±.006	.314± .008	.330±.007	.358± .009	
kin8fh	.553± .005	.457±.005	.456± .007	.464±.005	.488± .008	
kin8nm	.595± .012	.523±.004	.523± .003	.511±.007	.546± .006	
kin8nh	.657± .011	.601±.007	.600± .008	.597±.007	.615± .009	
	Drucker.AD	Drucker.S	Z&P.AD	Z&P.S	LAD_Boost	LS_Boost
	avg ± std	avg ± std	avg ± std	avg ± std	avg ± std	avg ± std
syndata	.917± .055	.921±.061	.910± .039	.900±.045	.978± .050	.934± .058
boston	.276± .019	.297±.014	.280± .018	.286±.023	.346± .025	.335± .029
calif1000	.429± .015	.457±.016	.425± .020	.447±.019	.455± .021	.468± .016
votes	.443± .006	.455±.005	.447± .004	.449±.006	.472± .012	.481± .014
prostate	.650± .051	.678±.039	.650± .075	.631±.049	.600± .023	.678± .053
birth	.791± .026	.792±.034	.790± .026	.790±.026	.793± .028	.783± .028
abalone	.514± .015	.544±.029	.497± .011	.544±.039	.497± .005	.520± .008
kin8fm	.288± .005	.279±.006	.294± .005	.295±.007	.316± .012	.296± .011
kin8fh	.444± .006	.438±.004	.446± .004	.446±.005	.481± .005	.485± .004
kin8nm	.502± .004	.523±.007	.510± .005	.523±.004	.531± .009	.528± .012
kin8nh	.597± .011	.600±.012	.601± .009	.604±.012	.627± .011	.624± .010

Table 3. Significant superiority over 11 datasets

		>	=	<			>	=	<
Drucker.AD	ZP.AD	1	10	0	Drucker.S	RegTree	5	6	0
Drucker.S	ZP.S	2	8	1	W-Bagging	Bagging	0	9	2
Drucker.AD	LAD_Boost	4	7	0	BR-Bagging	Bagging	0	11	0
Drucker.S	LS_Boost	2	9	0	LAD_Boost	RegTree	6	5	0
Bagging	RegTree	7	4	0	LS_Boost	RegTree	5	6	0
Bagging	CVA	3	8	0	LAD_Boost	Bagging	0	9	2
Drucker.AD	RegTree	7	4	0	LS_Boost	Bagging	0	7	4

were almost always equal in performance. In that case DRUCKER may be slightly more preferable, considering the inconvenient line search in ZEMEL-PITASSI.

The relabeling AdaBoost algorithms, in contrast, called for very simple models that would normally underfit. With complex base models their performance deteriorated rapidly as they started overfitting the data.

In selecting an aggregation algorithm for a regression task, if the base models are inherently simple or their complexity can be adjusted by some validation method, the relabeling algorithms should be considered, since they can provide the best accuracy using the fewest base models. If the models cannot be prevented from overfitting, one of the distribution-based AdaBoost algorithms can be used. The choice of loss function depends on the data at hand. If one algorithm must be selected to handle both simple and complex base models, Bagging is a safe bet.

Acknowledgments. This work has been supported by Boğaziçi University Scientific Research Project 02A104D and the Turkish Academy of Sciences, in the framework of the Young Scientist Award Program (EA-TÜBA-GEBIP/2001-1-1).

References

1. Breiman, L., "Bagging Predictors", *Machine Learning*, Vol. 24, No. 2, pp. 123–140, 1996.
2. Freund, Y. and R. E. Schapire, "A Decision-Theoretic Generalization of On-line Learning and an Application to Boosting", *European Conf. on Computational Learning Theory*, pp. 23–37, 1995.
3. Freund, Y. and R. E. Schapire, "Experiments with a New Boosting Algorithm", *International Conf. on Machine Learning*, pp. 148–156, 1996.
4. Ridgeway, G., D. Madigan and T. Richardson, "Boosting methodology for regression problems", *Proc. of Artificial Intelligence and Statistics*, pp. 152–161, 1999.
5. Drucker, H., "Improving regressors using boosting techniques", *Proc. 14th International Conf. on Machine Learning*, pp. 107–115, Morgan Kaufmann, San Francisco, CA, 1997.
6. Zemel, R. S. and T. Pitassi, "A Gradient-Based Boosting Algorithm for Regression Problems", *Adv. in Neural Information Processing Systems*, Vol. 13, 2001.
7. Friedman, J. H., *Greedy Function Approximation: a Gradient Boosting Machine*, Tech. Rep. 7, Stanford University, Dept. of Statistics, 1999.
8. Duffy, N. and D. Helmbold, "Leveraging for Regression", *Proc. 13th Annual Conf. on Computational Learning Theory*, pp. 208–219, Morgan Kaufmann, San Francisco, CA, 2000.
9. Rätsch, G., M. Warmuth, S. Mika, T. Onoda, S. Lemm and K.-R. Müller, "Barrier Boosting", *Proc. 13th Annual Conference on Computational Learning Theory*, 2000.
10. Alpaydın, E., "Combined 5×2cv F Test for Comparing Supervised Classification Learning Algorithms", *Neural Computation*, Vol. 11, No. 8, pp. 1885–1992, 1999.
11. Blake, C. and P. M. Murphy, "UCI Repository of Machine Learning Databases", http://www.ics.uci.edu/~mlearn/MLRepository.html.
12. Hosmer, D. and S. Lemeshow, *Applied Logistic Regression*, John Wiley & Sons Inc., 2nd edn., 2000.

Linear Least-Squares Based Methods for Neural Networks Learning

Oscar Fontenla-Romero[1], Deniz Erdogmus[2], J.C. Principe[2],
Amparo Alonso-Betanzos[1], and Enrique Castillo[3]

[1] Laboratory for Research and Development in Artificial Intelligence,
Department of Computer Science, University of A Coruña,
Campus de Elviña s/n, 15071 A Coruña, Spain
[2] Computational NeuroEngineering Laboratory,
Electrical and Computer Engineering Department,
University of Florida, Gainesville, FL 32611, USA
[3] Department of Applied Mathematics and Computational Sciences,
University of Cantabria and University of Castilla-La Mancha,
Avda de Los Castros s/n, 39005 Santander, Spain

Abstract. This paper presents two algorithms to aid the supervised learning of feedforward neural networks. Specifically, an initialization and a learning algorithm are presented. The proposed methods are based on the independent optimization of a subnetwork using linear least squares. An advantage of these methods is that the dimensionality of the effective search space for the non-linear algorithm is reduced, and therefore it decreases the number of training epochs which are required to find a good solution. The performance of the proposed methods is illustrated by simulated examples.

1 Introduction

During the last decade, several techniques have been presented to speed up the convergence of the artificial neural networks learning methods. Among them, some of the most successful are second order methods [1,2]. These techniques have been demonstrated to be significantly faster than gradient based methods. In addition, other algorithms were presented, such as adaptive step size methods. In this last class of methods, Almeida et al. [3] developed a new method for step size adaptation in stochastic gradient optimization. This method uses independent step sizes for all parameters and adapts them employing the estimates of the derivatives available in the gradient optimization procedure. Moreover, a new on line algorithm for local learning rate adaptation was proposed by Schraudolph [4].

Likewise, several solutions have been proposed for the appropriate initialization of weights. Among others, Nguyen and Widrow [5] presented an algorithm that selects initial weights and biases for a layer, so that the active regions of the layer's neurons will be distributed approximately evenly over the input space.

Drago and Ridella [6] proposed a statistical analysis aimed to determine the relationship between a scale factor proportional to the maximum magnitude of the weights and the percentage of paralyzed neurons. These methods were shown to be very useful to improve the convergence speed.

In addition, some least squares applications have been proposed [7,8]. These approaches are based on heuristic assumptions that do not consider the scaling effects of the nonlinear activation function. In this work, new theoretical results are presented that enhance the previous studies. Specifically, two algorithms, based on linear least squares, are presented to aid the current supervised learning methods for neural networks in order to accelerate their convergence speed.

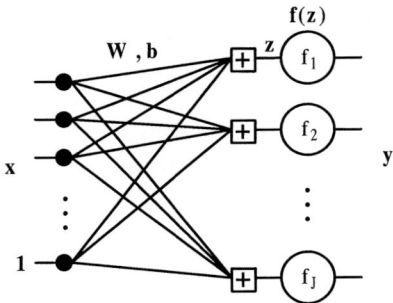

Fig. 1. One-layer neural network and nomenclature employed.

2 Theoretical Background

In this section, previous theoretical results are presented that will be used in the proposed algorithms. Consider the one-layer neural network in figure 1. The input of the network is represented by the vectorial variable $\mathbf{x} = (x_1, x_2, \ldots, x_I)^T$ and the output by the vector $\mathbf{y} = (y_1, y_2, \ldots, y_J)^T$. The outcome of the network is computed as $\mathbf{y} = \mathbf{f}(\mathbf{z})$, where $\mathbf{z} = \mathbf{W}\mathbf{x} + \mathbf{b}$ and $\mathbf{f} \in \mathbb{R}^J$ is a nonlinear function. If the weighted mean squared error (weighted MSE) is employed as cost function then the optimal weights and bias of the network can be obtained by solving the following minimization problem:

$$\min_{\mathbf{W},\mathbf{b}} C = E[(\mathbf{d}-\mathbf{y})^T \mathbf{H}(\mathbf{d}-\mathbf{y})] \qquad (1)$$

where $\mathbf{d} = (d_1, d_2, \ldots, d_J)^T$ is the desired output of the network and $\mathbf{H} = [h_{ij}]$ is a weight matrix (symmetric by definition). However, this problem is, in general, a nonlinear optimization problem and hence it is currently solved using nonlinear methods. In this work a new result is presented that allows to solve this problem using a linear method.

Lemma 1. *Let* **d** *and* **y** *be the desired and actual outputs of a one-layer neural network,* **W** *and* **b** *be the weight matrix and the bias vector, and* $\mathbf{f}, \mathbf{f}^{-1}, \mathbf{f}'$ *be the nonlinear function, its inverse and its derivative. Then the following equivalence holds up to the first order of the Taylor series expansion:*

$$\min_{\mathbf{W},\mathbf{b}} E[(\mathbf{d}-\mathbf{y})^T \mathbf{H}(\mathbf{d}-\mathbf{y})] \approx \min_{\mathbf{W},\mathbf{b}} E[(\mathbf{f}'(\bar{\mathbf{d}}).*\bar{\varepsilon})^T \mathbf{H}(\mathbf{f}'(\bar{\mathbf{d}}).*\bar{\varepsilon})] \qquad (2)$$

where '.' denotes the element-wise product,* $\bar{\mathbf{d}} = \mathbf{f}^{-1}(\mathbf{d})$ *and* $\bar{\varepsilon} = \bar{\mathbf{d}} - \mathbf{z}$.

The proof of this and following lemmas is not included due to space restrictions. Thus, using the previous lemma the initial minimization problem in (1) can be alternatively formulated as:

$$\min_{\mathbf{W},\mathbf{b}} C^* = E[(\mathbf{f}'(\bar{\mathbf{d}}).*\bar{\varepsilon})^T \mathbf{H}(\mathbf{f}'(\bar{\mathbf{d}}).*\bar{\varepsilon})] \qquad (3)$$

If the alternative cost function in (3) is used then the minimization problem is linear in the parameters (weights an biases). This is due to the variable $\bar{\varepsilon}$ depending linearly on **W** and **b**. Let $\{(\mathbf{x}_s, \mathbf{d}_s), s = 1, \ldots, S\}$ be a set of training pairs then the minimization problem in (3) can be rewritten as follows:

$$\min_{\mathbf{W},\mathbf{b}} C^* = \frac{1}{S} \sum_{s=1}^{S} \sum_{i=1}^{J} \sum_{j=1}^{J} h_{ij} f'_i(\bar{d}_{is}) f'_j(\bar{d}_{js}) \bar{\varepsilon}_{is} \bar{\varepsilon}_{js} \qquad (4)$$

where $\bar{d}_{is}$, $\bar{\varepsilon}_{is}$ and f_i are the ith component of the vectors $\bar{\mathbf{d}}_s$, $\bar{\varepsilon}_s$ and **f**, respectively. The optimal solution for the minimization problem in (4) can be obtained taking the derivatives of the cost function with respect to the weights and biases of the system and equating all the derivatives to zero. In this way, the following linear system of equations $((I+1) \times J$ equations and unknowns) is obtained:

$$\sum_{i=1}^{J} b_i h_{ik} \left[\sum_{s=1}^{S} f'_k(\bar{d}_{ks}) f'_i(\bar{d}_{is}) x_{ls} \right] + \sum_{p=1}^{I} \sum_{i=1}^{J} w_{ip} h_{ik} \left[\sum_{s=1}^{S} f'_k(\bar{d}_{ks}) f'_i(\bar{d}_{is}) x_{ls} x_{ps} \right]$$

$$= \sum_{i=1}^{J} h_{ik} \left[\sum_{s=1}^{S} f'_k(\bar{d}_{ks}) f'_i(\bar{d}_{is}) x_{ls} d_{is} \right] ; k = 1, \ldots, J; l = 1, \ldots, I$$

$$\sum_{i=1}^{J} b_i h_{ik} \left[\sum_{s=1}^{S} f'_k(\bar{d}_{ks}) f'_i(\bar{d}_{is}) \right] + \sum_{p=1}^{I} \sum_{i=1}^{J} w_{ip} h_{ik} \left[\sum_{s=1}^{S} f'_k(\bar{d}_{ks}) f'_i(\bar{d}_{is}) x_{ps} \right]$$

$$= \sum_{i=1}^{J} h_{ik} \left[\sum_{s=1}^{S} f'_k(\bar{d}_{ks}) f'_i(\bar{d}_{is}) d_{is} \right] ; k = 1, \ldots, J.$$

(5)

where b_i is the ith component of the bias vector and w_{ip} is the weight connecting the output i and the input p. Therefore, the unique solution (except for degenerated systems) of the proposed minimization problem in (4) can be achieved by solving the system of equations in (5) for the variables w_{ip} and b_i; $i = 1, \ldots, J$; $p = 1, \ldots, I$.

3 Proposed Algorithms

In this work two algorithms for the supervised learning of multilayer feedforward neural networks are proposed. These methods are based on the results obtained in the previous section for one-layer neural networks. Consider the feedforward multilayer neural network in figure 2. It is composed of L layers where each layer l contains N_l neurons. The output of neuron i in layer l, y_i^l, is determined by the activation z_i^l, defined as the weighted sum of the outputs coming from the neurons in the previous layer, and an activation function f_i^l. Specifically, $\mathbf{y}^0 = (y_1^0, \ldots, y_{N_0}^0)^T$ is the input vector of the network.

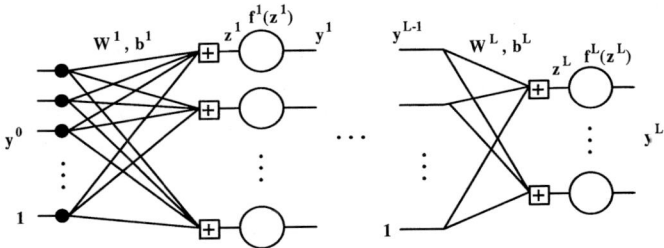

Fig. 2. Feedforward multilayer neural network and nomenclature employed.

3.1 Initialization Method

The result presented in lemma 1 can be used to measure alternatively the error before the nonlinear functions of each layer in the multilayer feedforward neural network presented in figure 2. In this context, the input of the one-layer neural network ($\mathbf{x}$) will correspond to the output of the previous layer. In addition, it is necessary to obtain a result that allows to backpropagate the error from the output (before the activation function) of layer l to the output of the previous layer $(l-1)$. This result is presented in the following lemma.

Lemma 2. *Let $\mathbf{d}^{l-1}, \mathbf{y}^{l-1}, \bar{\mathbf{d}}^l, \mathbf{z}^l$ be the desired signals and corresponding output signals of layers l and $l-1$, $\mathbf{W}^l$ and $\mathbf{b}^l$ be the fixed weight matrix and the bias vector. Minimization of the weighted MSE between $\bar{\mathbf{d}}^l$ and $\mathbf{z}^l$ at the output of the linear layer is equivalent to minimizing a weighted MSE between $\mathbf{d}^{l-1}$ and $\mathbf{y}^{l-1}$, i.e., finding the constrained linear least squares solution for the optimal input vector. Mathematically, this is given by*

$$\min_{\mathbf{y}^{l-1}} E[(\bar{\mathbf{d}}^l - \mathbf{z}^l)^T \mathbf{H}^l (\bar{\mathbf{d}}^l - \mathbf{z}^l)] = \min_{\mathbf{y}^{l-1}} E[(\mathbf{d}^{l-1} - \mathbf{y}^{l-1})^T \mathbf{W}^{lT} \mathbf{H}^l \mathbf{W}^l (\mathbf{d}^{l-1} - \mathbf{y}^{l-1})] \quad (6)$$

There are two different situations in the problem presented in the previous lemma: a) if $N_l \geq N_{l-1}$, then $\mathbf{d}^{l-1} = (\mathbf{W}^{lT}\mathbf{H}^l\mathbf{W}^l)^{-1}\mathbf{W}^{lT}\mathbf{H}^l(\bar{\mathbf{d}}^l - \mathbf{b}^l)$ is the unique weighted least squares solution for the overdetermined system of linear equations $(\mathbf{W}^l\mathbf{d}^{l-1} + \mathbf{b}^l = \bar{\mathbf{d}}^l)$; and b) if $N_l < N_{l-1}$, then the QR factorization may be used to determine the minimum norm least squares solution for this undetermined system of linear equations $(\mathbf{W}^l\mathbf{d}^{l-1} + \mathbf{b}^l = \bar{\mathbf{d}}^l)$.

In both cases, given a desired signal $\bar{\mathbf{d}}^l$, for the linear output $\mathbf{z}^l$ of the layer l^{th}, it can translate as a desired signal $\mathbf{d}^{l-1}$ for the output (after the nonlinearity) of the previous layer. Subsequently, this value can be backpropagate through the nonlinearity as described in lemma 1. Thus, using lemma 1 and 2 the following algorithm is proposed:

1 *Given* $\{(\mathbf{y}^0, \mathbf{d}_s^L), s = 1, \ldots, S\}$, *select random initial values for weights and biases* $\mathbf{W}^l, \mathbf{b}^l; l = 1, \ldots, L$.
2 *Evaluate* $\mathbf{z}_s^l, \mathbf{y}_s^l; s = 1, \ldots, S; l = 1, \ldots, L;$ *using* $\mathbf{y}_s^0$, $\mathbf{W}^l$ *and* $\mathbf{b}^l$; $l = 1, \ldots, L$.
3 *Set* C_{opt} *to the MSE between* $\mathbf{y}_s^L$ *and* $\mathbf{d}_s^L$. *Set* $\mathbf{W}_{opt}^l = \mathbf{W}^l$, $\mathbf{b}_{opt}^l = \mathbf{b}^l$; $l = 1, \ldots, L$.
4 *Compute* $\bar{\mathbf{d}}_s^L = (\mathbf{f}^L)^{-1}(\mathbf{d}_s^L) \forall s$, *as the desired signal for* $\mathbf{z}_s^L$.
5 $n = 1$.
6 **while** $n \leq MaxIterations$
7   **for** $l = L - 1$ *downto* 1
8   *Compute* $\bar{\mathbf{d}}_s^l = (\mathbf{f}^l)^{-1}(\mathbf{d}_s^l) \forall s$, *as the desired signal for* $\mathbf{z}_s^l$.
9   *Compute* $\mathbf{d}_s^{l-1} = (\mathbf{W}^{lT}\mathbf{W}^l)^{-1}\mathbf{W}^{lT}(\bar{\mathbf{d}}_s^l - \mathbf{b}^l)$ *as the desired signal for* $\mathbf{y}_s^{l-1}$ *(this is the case for the overdetermined case, for the undetermined case, the minimum norm solution could be used)*.
10   **end**
11   **for** $l = 1$ *to* L
12   *Optimize* $\mathbf{W}^l$ *and* $\mathbf{b}^l$ *using the linear system of equations in (5), using* $\mathbf{y}_s^{l-1}$ *as input samples and* $\bar{\mathbf{d}}_s^l$ *as desired output samples*.
13   *Evaluate* $\mathbf{z}_s^l$ *and* $\mathbf{y}_s^l$ *using the new values of the weights and bias*.
14   **end**
15   *Evaluate the value of* C *(the MSE between* $\mathbf{y}_s^L$ *and* $\mathbf{d}_s^L$*)*.
16   *If* $C < C_{opt}$ *then set* $C_{opt} = C$, $\mathbf{W}_{opt}^l = \mathbf{W}^l$, $\mathbf{b}_{opt}^l = \mathbf{b}^l$, $l = 1, \ldots, L$.
17     $n = n + 1$.
18 **end**

Finally, an important issue to remark is that this algorithm is proposed as an initialization method and not as a learning method because it has not a smooth convergence to the solution. Instead, it jumps from one region to another of the weight space.

3.2 Learning Method

In this subsection a new learning method based on linear least squares is presented. In this case only the last layer of the network (L) is optimized using linear least squares whereas the other layers are optimized using any standard method. The proposed algorithm for a multilayer feedforward neural network is as follows:

1. Select initial weights $\mathbf{W}_l$, $\mathbf{b}_l$, $\forall l$, using an initialization method or randomly.
2. Evaluate the value of C_0 (MSE between y_s^L and d_s^L) using the initial weights.
3. $n = 1$.
4. **while** $n \leq MaxIterations$ and $(\neg stop\_criterion\_1)$
5. $\mathbf{W}^l = \mathbf{W}^l + \Delta\mathbf{W}^l; l = 1, \ldots, L$.
6. $\mathbf{b}^l = \mathbf{b}^l + \Delta\mathbf{b}^l; l = 1, \ldots, L$.
7.   Evaluate the value of C_n (MSE between y_s^L and d_s^L).
8.   **If** $|C_n - C_{n-1}| < \lambda$ **then**
9.   **while** $(\neg stop\_criterion\_2)$
10. $\mathbf{W}^l = \mathbf{W}^l + \Delta\mathbf{W}^l; l = 1, \ldots, L-1$.
11. $\mathbf{b}^l = \mathbf{b}^l + \Delta\mathbf{b}^l; l = 1, \ldots, L-1$.
12.   Update $\mathbf{W}^L$ and $\mathbf{b}^L$ using the linear system of equations in (5).
13.   **end**
14.   **end_if**
15. **end**

The method works as follows: in the first phase (first epochs of training), all layers of the network are updated using any standard learning rule (steps 5 and 6). In the second stage, when the obtained decrement of the error is small (step 8), then the update procedure switches to the hybrid approach. Thus, $\mathbf{W}_L$ of the network is optimally obtained using linear least squares (step 12) while $\mathbf{W}_l$; $l = 1, \ldots, L - 1$ is still updated using the standard learning method (steps 10 and 11). Finally, it is important to remark that the proposed methods are fast procedures because they are based on a linear system of equations that can easily be solved using a variety of computationally efficient approaches.

4 Results

In this section, a comparative study between the proposed methods and standard algorithms is presented. In order to accomplish the study, several nonlinear system identification data sets were employed. However, due to space restrictions, only the results obtained for one of the data sets are shown. The data employed in this paper is the time series from the K.U. Leuven prediction competition[1] which was part of the International Workshop on Advanced Black-Box Techniques for Nonlinear Modeling in 1998 [9]. The data were generated from a computer simulated 5-scroll attractor, resulting from a generalized Chua's circuit, and it consists of 2000 samples. In this work, the desired signal was normalized in the interval $[0.05, 0.95]$. The time series is shown in figure 3(a). The topology employed in the following experiments was 6-7-1 though other topologies were used to obtain a similar behaviour. Also, logistic and linear functions were used in the processing elements (PEs) of the hidden and output layer, respectively. For all the experiments a Monte Carlo simulation, using 100 different initial random weights sets, was carried out.

---
[1] ftp://ftp.esat.kuleuven.ac.be/pub/sista/suykens/workshop/ datacomp.dat

4.1 Initialization Method

In this subsection, the results for the initialization method (section 3.1) are presented. In this case, the backpropagation method was used to train the network using as initial weights either random values or those obtained by the proposed initialization method (using 3 iterations of the algorithm). In the former case the network was trained during 4000 epochs while in the latter only during 2000 epochs. Figure 3 shows the results obtained in the 100 simulations. Figure 3(b) contains the histogram of the errors using only the initialization method. Moreover, figures 3(c) and 3(d) contain, respectively, the histogram of the errors, in the last epoch of training, for the backpropagation algorithm using random weights and the initial weights obtained by the initialization method (LS).

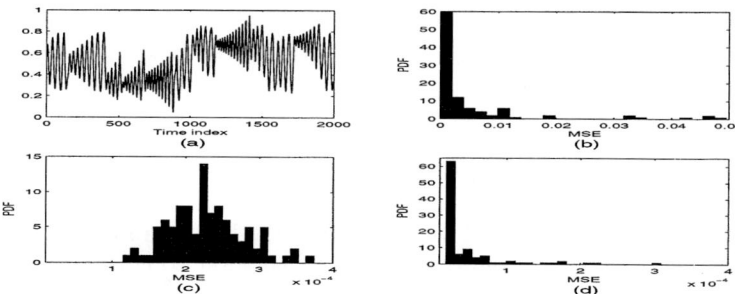

Fig. 3. (a) Time serie of the K.U. Leuven competition and histogram of the final MSE using (b) the initialization method, (c) backpropagation and (d) LS+backpropagation.

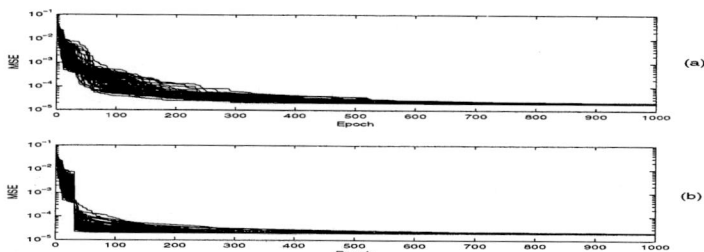

Fig. 4. Learning curves for (a) the SCG algorithm and (b) the proposed hybrid method.

4.2 Learning Method

In this subsection, a comparative study between the proposed hybrid learning method (section 3.2) and the scaled conjugate gradient method (SCG) [10] is presented. In order to accomplish a fair comparison, the hybrid method employed also the SCG for weights and biases update in steps 5, 6, 10 and 11. In all the simulations (100) the initial weights employed by both algorithms (SCG and the hybrid method) were the same, therefore they started at identical initial conditions. The results obtained for this time series are shown in figure 4. Figures 4(a) and 4(b) present the learning curves of the Monte Carlo simulation for the SCG and the proposed method, respectively.

As it can be seen, the proposed learning scheme obtains a faster convergence to the solution than the standard SCG method.

5 Conclusions

In this paper new algorithms for the initialization and supervised learning of the parameters of a feedforward neural network were presented. The proposed algorithms are based on linear least squares for the independent optimization of at least one layer of the network. An advantage of these methods is that the number of epochs needed to achieve a good solution is decreased as a consequence of the dimensionality reduction of the effective search space for the non-linear algorithm. The application to benchmark data confirmed the good performance of the proposed methods.

Acknowledgements. This work is partially supported by NSF grant ECS-9900394 and the Xunta de Galicia (project PGIDT-01PXI10503PR).

References

1. Battiti, R.: First and second order methods for learning: Between steepest descent and newton's method. Neural Computation **4** (1992) 141–166
2. Buntine, W.L., Weigend, A.S.: Computing second derivatives in feed-forward networks: A review. IEEE Trans. on Neural Networks **5** (1993) 480–488
3. Almeida, L.B., Langlois, T., Amaral, J.D., Plakhov, A.: 6. In: Parameter adaptation in stochastic optimization. Cambridge University Press (1999) 111–134
4. Schraudolph, N.N.: Fast curvature matrix-vector products for second order gradient descent. Neural Computation **14** (2002) 1723–1738
5. Nguyen, D., Widrow, B.: Improving the learning speed of 2-layer neural networks by choosing initial values of the adaptive weights. Proc. of the Int. Joint Conference on Neural Networks **3** (1990) 21–26
6. Drago, G., Ridella, S.: Statistically controlled activation weight initialization (SCAWI). IEEE Trans. on Neural Networks **3** (1992) 899–905
7. Biegler-Konig, F., Barnmann, F.: A learning algorithm for multilayered neural networks based on linear least squares problems. Neural Networks **6** (1993) 127–131
8. Yam, Y., Chow, T.: A new method in determining the initial weights of feedforward neural networks. Neurocomputing **16** (1997) 23–32
9. Suykens, J., Vandewalle, J., eds.: Nonlinear Modeling: advanced black-box techniques. Kluwer Academic Publishers, Boston (1998)
10. Moller, M.F.: A scaled conjugate gradient algorithm for fast supervised learning. Neural Networks **6** (1993) 525–533

Optimal Hebbian Learning: A Probabilistic Point of View

Jean-Pascal Pfister[1], David Barber[2], and Wulfram Gerstner[1]

[1] Laboratory of Computational Neuroscience, EPFL
CH-1005 Lausanne, Switzerland
{jean-pascal.pfister, wulfram.gerstner}@epfl.ch,
[2] Institute for Adaptive and Neural Computation, Edinburgh University, 5 Forrest Hill, Edinburgh, EH1 2QL, U.K.
d.barber@anc.ed.ac.uk

Abstract. Many activity dependent learning rules have been proposed in order to model long-term potentiation (LTP). Our aim is to derive a spike time dependent learning rule from a probabilistic optimality criterion. Our approach allows us to obtain quantitative results in terms of a learning window. This is done by maximising a given likelihood function with respect to the synaptic weights. The resulting weight adaptation is compared with experimental results.

1 Introduction

Since synaptic changes are most likely to underly memory and learning processes, it is crucial to determine the causes and underlying laws describing this adaptation process. Among the enormous number of models, there are mainly two categories: rate-based and spike-based learning rule. In this paper, we want to present a new way to derive a spike-time dependent learning rule. Existing models of spike-timing dependent plasticity are either phenomenological [12] or, in contrast, mechanistic [1].

Our model is derived from a probabilistic point of view in the sense that the learning rule should optimise the likelihood of observing a postsynaptic spike train with a desired timing, given the postsynaptic membrane potential at the location of the synapse.

A significant part of the synaptic plasticity models are based on Hebb's postulate [14]:

> When an axon of cell A is near enough to excite cell B or repeatedly or persistently takes part in firing it, some growth process or metabolic change takes place in one or both cells such that A's efficiency, as one of the cells firing B, is increased.

In fact models rephrase this postulate by saying that the adaptation of the synaptic weights is driven by a simultaneous activity of the pre- and the postsynaptic neuron. This simultaneity has to be defined in a time window. Recent

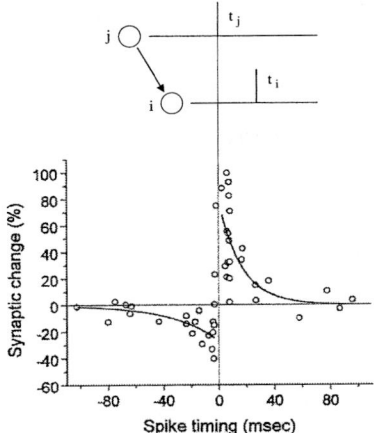

Fig. 1. Critical window for synaptic modifications. Long-term potentiation (LTP)/long-term depression (LTD) were induced by correlated pre- and postsynaptic spiking at synapses between hippocampal glutamatergic neurons in culture. Figure adapted from [4].

experiments [3] have shown the influence of a pair of a single pre- and postsynaptic spike on the synaptic strength (figure 1).

The aim of this paper is to show that it is possible to get a similar learning window as a result from an optimal learning rule. Recently Barber [2] studied this question with neurons discrete in time. Here we want to extend this study to the continuous case and discuss the results in relation with the experiments of Bi and Poo [3].

2 Spike Response Model

For the sake of simplicity, let us consider here a single presynaptic neuron j and a postsynaptic neuron i. Those two neurons are considered as Poisson neurons, i.e their firing times depend only on the present value of the membrane potential. Let w be the synaptic weight between those neurons. Finally, let $\{t_j^{f'}\}$ and $\{t_i^f\}$ denote respectively the pre- and postsynaptic firing times.

The fundamental hypothesis in this article is to assume that the instantaneous firing rate of the postsynaptic neuron is given by an increasing function of the membrane potential $u(t)$:

$$\rho(t) = g(u(t)). \tag{1}$$

This firing rate can be also termed escape rate [11]. The membrane potential model we take is the Spike Response Model (SRM). The simplest SRM is called SRM_0 [9] and defines the membrane potential $u(t)$ as follow:

$$u(t) = u_{\text{rest}} + \eta(t - \hat{t}_i) + w \sum_{f'} \epsilon(t - t_j^{f'}), \qquad (2)$$

where, in our case, $\eta(s)$ is a kernel describing the spike-afterpotential, $\epsilon(s)$ is the kernel representing the excitatory post-synaptic potential (EPSP) and $\hat{t}_i$ is the last firing time of neuron i, i.e. $\hat{t}_i = \max\{t_i^f | t_i^f < t\}$. The goal is now to maximise the probability that the postsynaptic spike train $S_i(t) = \sum_{f'} \delta(t - t_i^{f'})$ has been generated by the firing rate $\rho(t)$.

3 Calculation of the Likelihood $\mathcal{L}$

In order to calculate the likelihood of a spike train given a firing rate, it is useful to first make a time discretization before coming back to the continuous case. Let $\bar{\rho}(t)$ be the discretised version of $\rho(t)$ on the interval $I = [0, T]$ where $\bar{\rho}(t) = \rho(t_n), \forall t \in [t_n, t_n + \Delta t]$ and $t_0 = 0$, $t_N = N\Delta t = T$.

The probability that a neuron produces a spike at time $t \in [\tilde{t}, \tilde{t} + \Delta t]$ given its firing rate $\bar{\rho}(s)$ is simply given by the probability of spiking between $\tilde{t}$ and $\tilde{t} + \Delta t$ multiplied by the probability of not spiking at any other time:

$$\bar{P}(t \in [\tilde{t}, \tilde{t} + \Delta t] | \bar{\rho}(s))\Delta t = \bar{\rho}(\tilde{t})\Delta t \prod_{t_n \neq \tilde{t}} (1 - \bar{\rho}(t_n)\Delta t) \qquad (3)$$

To extend this result to the case of M spikes, we need to define $\mathbf{t} = (t^1, \ldots, t^M)$ a M-dimensional time variable ordered chronologically, i.e. $t^f < t^{f+1}$. Let $\tilde{\mathbf{t}}$ be the M desired firing times and $\Omega(\tilde{\mathbf{t}}) = \prod_n [\tilde{t}_n, \tilde{t}_n + \Delta t]$ a M-dimensional bin. The probability of firing at the M given times $\tilde{\mathbf{t}}$ is

$$\bar{P}(\mathbf{t} \in \Omega(\tilde{\mathbf{t}}) | \bar{\rho}(s))\Delta t^M = \prod_f \bar{\rho}(\tilde{t}^f)\Delta t^M \prod_{t_n \neq \tilde{t}^f} (1 - \bar{\rho}(t_n)\Delta t)$$

$$= \prod_f \frac{\bar{\rho}(\tilde{t}^f)\Delta t^M}{1 - \bar{\rho}(\tilde{t}^f)\Delta t} \prod_n (1 - \bar{\rho}(t_n)\Delta t)$$

$$= \prod_f \frac{\bar{\rho}(\tilde{t}^f)\Delta t^M}{1 - \bar{\rho}(\tilde{t}^f)\Delta t} \exp\left(\sum_n \log(1 - \bar{\rho}(t_n)\Delta t)\right). \qquad (4)$$

Now we can come back to the continuous case. By taking the limit $\Delta t \to 0$, we have $\bar{\rho}(t) \to \rho(t)$, $\bar{P}(\mathbf{t} \in \Omega(\tilde{\mathbf{t}}) | \bar{\rho}(s)) \to P(\mathbf{t} = \mathbf{t}' | \rho(s))$, $\sum_n \log(1 - \bar{\rho}(t_n)\Delta t) \to -\int_0^T \rho(t)dt$ and $1 - \bar{\rho}(\tilde{t}^f)\Delta t \to 1$. Therefore we can define the log-likelihood $\mathcal{L}(\mathbf{t}_i | u(s))$ of the postsynaptic spike train given the membrane potential $u(s)$ by simply taking the logarithm of $P(\mathbf{t} = \mathbf{t}' | \rho(s))$:

$$\mathcal{L}(\mathbf{t}_i | u(s)) = \sum_f \log(g(u(t_i^f))) - \int_0^T g(u(t))dt. \qquad (5)$$

4 Learning Rule

The goal of our study is to find a learning rule which tends to optimise the weight w in order to maximise the likelihood of getting postsynaptic firing times given the firing rate. This means that those weights must evolve in the direction of the gradient of $\mathcal{L}$:

$$w^{\text{new}} = w + \kappa \frac{\partial \mathcal{L}}{\partial w}, \tag{6}$$

with

$$\frac{\partial \mathcal{L}}{\partial w}(\mathbf{t}_i|u(s)) = \sum_f \frac{\frac{dg(u(t_i^f))}{du(t_i^f)} \frac{\partial u(t_i^f)}{\partial w}}{g(u(t_i^f))} - \int_0^T \frac{dg(u(t))}{du(t)} \frac{\partial u(t)}{\partial w} dt$$

$$= \sum_f \sum_{f'} \frac{\epsilon(t_i^f - t_j^{f'})}{g(u(t_i^f))} \frac{dg(u(t_i^f))}{du(t_i^f)} - \int_0^T \frac{dg(u(t))}{du(t)} \sum_{f'} \epsilon(t - t_j^{f'}) dt \tag{7}$$

and κ is the learning rate. Since $g(u(t)) = \exp(\beta(u(t) - \theta))$ is a reasonable choice [11], we can use it to evaluate the gradient of $\mathcal{L}$ for a pre- and a postsynaptic spike train:

$$\frac{\partial \mathcal{L}}{\partial w}(\mathbf{t}_i|u(s)) = \beta \sum_f \sum_{f'} \epsilon(t_i^f - t_j^{f'}) - \beta \int_0^T \exp(\beta(u(t) - \theta)) \sum_{f'} \epsilon(t - t_j^{f'}) dt. \tag{8}$$

Let us now study the restricted case with only one pre- and one postsynaptic spike and $\beta = 1$:

$$\frac{\partial \mathcal{L}}{\partial w}(t_i|u(s)) = \epsilon(t_i - t_j) - \int_0^T \exp(u(t) - \theta) \epsilon(t - t_j) dt. \tag{9}$$

In order to represent the gradient of the log-likelihood function $\mathcal{L}$ (figure 2), it is necessary to choose determine specific kernels for $\eta(s)$ and $\epsilon(s)$. For simplicity sake, we take

$$\eta(s) = \eta_0 e^{-\frac{s}{\tau_\eta}} \Theta(s), \tag{10}$$

$$\epsilon(s) = \epsilon_0 e^{-\frac{s}{\tau_\epsilon}} \Theta(s), \tag{11}$$

where Θ is the usual Heaviside step function with $\Theta(s) = 1$ for $s > 0$ and $\Theta(s) = 0$ else. If $\eta_0 > 0$, the neuron exhibits a depolarizing afterpotential (DAP). In reverse, if $\eta_0 < 0$, is exhibits a hyperpolarizing afterpotential (HAP).

It is interesting to note that the qualitative shape of this learning window is similar to the one obtained by Bi and Poo [3] only in presence of DAP which could be consistent with DAP observed by Connors et al. in neocortical neurons [6].

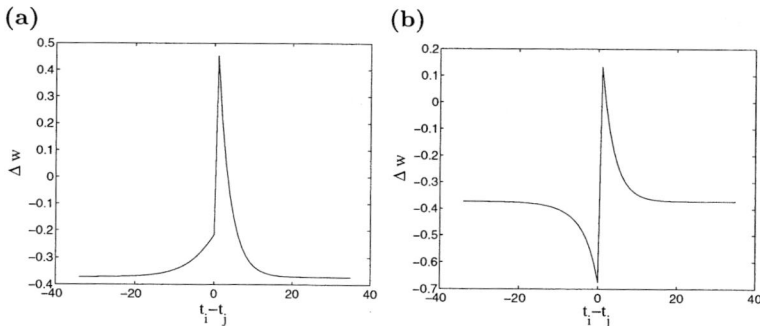

Fig. 2. First step of the adaptation of weights $\Delta w = w^{\text{new}} - w = \frac{\partial \mathcal{L}}{\partial w}$. The parameters for this simulation are : $w = 0.2, \theta - u_{\text{rest}} = -2, \beta = 1, \epsilon_0 = 1, \tau_\epsilon = 3, \tau_\eta = 5$. The amplitude of the spike-afterpotential is given by $\eta_0 = -1$ (HAP) for **(a)** and $\eta_0 = 1$ (DAP) for **(b)**. Note the different vertical scales.

5 Discussion

One can note that a major difference between the result of Bi and Poo and our model is the negative offset. This offset is related to the integral of the kernel $\epsilon(s)$. Indeed, if the postsynaptic spike occurs a long time after the presynaptic spike and if $w \simeq 0$, the first term of equation (9) can be neglected and the membrane potential can be approximated by its resting potential in the range where $\epsilon(t - t_j)$ is significant:

$$\frac{\partial \mathcal{L}}{\partial w} \simeq -\exp(u_{\text{rest}} - \theta) \int_{t_j}^{T} \epsilon(t - t_j) dt$$

$$\simeq -\exp(u_{\text{rest}} - \theta) \int_{0}^{\infty} \epsilon(s) ds. \qquad (12)$$

This is of course valid only if $T \gg t_j$. In fact, this offset is related to the probability of not having a spike at time $t \neq t_i$ (c.f. last term of eq. (3)). In order to increase the likelihood of not having a spike the weight needs to be reduced.

A possible way to solve the problem of negative bias of Δw is to consider a slightly different scenario where we still impose the postsynaptic spike at a given time, but instead of imposing no spike at all the other times, we choose the desired number of spikes that are allowed to occur stochastically over the period T. This number of spikes has to be related to the spontaneous firing rate.

One can also note that the shape of the positive peak on figure 2a is dominated by the kernel $\epsilon(s)$ (c.f. first term of eq. (9)). This is due to the choice of an exponential for the function $g(u)$.

Let us note that the we are looking at the gradient of the likelihood function $\mathcal{L}$ and not at the optimal solution given by $\frac{\partial \mathcal{L}}{\partial w} = 0$. Indeed, it is straightforward to notice that there is no fixed point for w if $t_i < t_j$. For $t_j < t_i$, there is a fixed point and it is stable since $\frac{\partial^2 \mathcal{L}}{\partial w^2} < 0$.

We have shown a new framework for deriving a spike-time dependent learning rule. The interesting feature of this learning rule is the similarity to the one obtained by Bi and Poo. This similarity is valid only in presence of DAP. The duration of the DAP determines the width of the negative phase of the learning window.

As a consequence we could speculate that the form of the learning window changes according to the type of neuron since in this framework the learning window strongly depends on the spike-afterpotential.

It is of course possible to make the model more complex by not using the SRM_0 model but more realistic models. Even if our study was restricted to a single pre- and postsynaptic spike, equation (8) remains totally general for spike trains and is also valid for an entire neural network.

References

1. H.D.I. Abarbanel, R. Huerta and M.I. Rabinovich: Dynamical model of long-term synaptic plasticity. Proc. Natl. Acad. Sci. USA, 2002, Vol. 99, Issue 15, 10132–10137.
2. D. Barber: Learning in Spiking Neural Assemblies. To appear in proceedings of NIPS 2002.
3. G.Q. Bi and M.M. Poo: Synaptic modifications in cultured hippocampal neurons: dependence on spike timing, synaptic strength, and postsynaptic cell type. J. Neurosci., 1998, Vol. 18, 10464–10472.
4. G.Q. Bi and M.M. Poo: Synaptic modifications by correlated activity: Hebb's postulate revisited. Annu. Rev. Neurosci., 2001, Vol. 24, 139–166.
5. G. Bugmann and C. Christodoulou and J.G. Taylor: Role of temporal integration and fluctuation detection in the highly irregular firing of leaky integrator neuron model with partial reset. Neural Computation, 1997, Vol. 9, 985–1000.
6. B.W. Connors, M.J. Gutnick and D.A. Prince: Electrophysiological Properties of Neocortical Neurons in Vitro. J. Neurophysiol. 1982, Vol. 48, 1302–1320.
7. D. Debanne and B.H. Gähwiler and S.M. Thompson: Long-term synaptic plasticity between pairs of individual CA3 pyramidal cells in rat hippocampal slice cultures. J. Physiol., 1998, Vol. 507, 237–247.
8. R. Froemke and Y. Dan: Spike-timing dependent plasticity induced by natural spike trains. Nature, 2002, Vol. 416, 433–438.
9. W. Gerstner: Time Structure of the Activity in Neural Network Models. Phys. Rev. E, 1995, 51, Vol. 1, 738–758.
10. W. Gerstner, R. Kempter, J.L. van Hemmen and H. Wagner: A neuronal learning rule for sub-millisecond temporal coding, Nature, 1996, Vol. 383, 76–78.
11. W. Gerstner and W.M. Kistler: Spiking Neuron Models. Cambridge University Press, 2002.
12. W. Gerstner and W.M. Kistler: Mathematical Formulations of Hebbian Learning. Biological Cybernetics, 2002, 87, 404–415.
13. R. Gütig and R. Aharonov and S. Rotter and H. Sompolinsky: Learning input correlations through non-linear temporally asymmetry Hebbian plasticity. To appear.
14. D.O. Hebb: The Organization of Behavior. Wiley, 1949, New York.

15. R. Kempter and W. Gerstner and J. L. van Hemmen: Hebbian learning and spiking neurons. Phys. Rev. E, 1999, Vol. 59, 4, 4498–4514.
16. W.M. Kistler and J. Leo van Hemmen: Modeling Synaptic Plasticity in Conjunction with the timing of pre- and postsynaptic potentials. Neural Comput. 2000, Vol 12, 385-405.
17. H. Markram and B. Sakmann: Action potentials propagating back into dendrites trigger changes in efficacy of single-axon synapses between layer V pyramidal neurons. Soc. Neurosci. Abstr.", 1995, Vol. 21, 2007.
18. M. Rapp, Y. Yarom and I. Siegev: Modeling back propagating action potential in weakly excitable dendrites of neocortical pyramidal cells. Proc. Natl. Acad. Sci USA, 1996, Vol. 93, 11985–11990.
19. P.D. Roberts and C.C. Bell: Spike timing dependent synaptic plasticity in biological systems. Biol. Cybernetics, 2002, Vol. 87, 392–403.
20. W. Senn, H. Markram and M. Tsodyks: An Algorithm for Modifying Neurotransmitter Release Probability Based on Pre- and Postsynaptic Spike Timing. Neural Comput. 2000, Vol. 13, 35–67.
21. H.Z. Shouval, M.F. Bear and L.N. Cooper: A unified model of NMDA receptor dependent bidirectional synaptic plasticity. Proc. Natl. Acad. Sci. USA, 2002, Vol. 99, 10831–10836.
22. P.J. Sjöström, G.G. Turrigiano and S.B. Nelson; Rate, timing, and cooperativity jointly determine cortical synaptic plasticity. Neuron, 2001, Vol. 32, 1149–1164.
23. S. Song and K.D. Miller and L.F. Abbott: Competitive Hebbian learning through spike-time-dependent synaptic plasticity. Nature Neuroscience, 2000, Vol. 3, 919–926
24. G.J. Stuart and B. Sakmann: Active propagation of somatic action-potentials into neocortical pyramidal cell dendrites. Nature, 1994, Vol. 367, 69–72.
25. T.W. Troyer and K.D. Miller: Physiological gain leads to high ISI variability in a simple model of a cortical regular spiking cell. Neural Computation, 1997, Vol. 9, 971–983.
26. M.C.W. van Rossum and G.Q. Bi and G.G. Turrigiano: table Hebbian learning from spike timing-dependent plasticity. J. Neuroscience, 2000, Vol. 20, 8812–8821.

Competitive Learning by Information Maximization: Eliminating Dead Neurons in Competitive Learning

Ryotaro Kamimura

Information Science Laboratory
and Future Science and Technology Joint Research Center, Tokai University,
1117 Kitakaname Hiratsuka Kanagawa 259-1292, Japan
ryo@cc.u-tokai.ac.jp

Abstract. In this paper, we propose a new information theoretic competitive learning method. In realizing competition, neither the winner-take-all algorithm nor the lateral inhibition is used. Instead, the new method is based upon mutual information maximization between input patterns and competitive units. In maximizing mutual information, the entropy of competitive units is increased as much as possible. This means that all competitive units must equally be used in our framework. Thus, no under-utilized neurons (dead neurons) are generated. We applied our method to a simple artificial data problem and an actual road classification problem. In both cases, experimental results confirmed that the new method can produce the final solutions almost independently of initial conditions, and classification performance is significantly improved.

Keywords: Mutual information maximization, competitive learning, winner-take-all, dead neurons

1 Introduction

In this paper, we propose a new information theoretic method for competitive learning. The new approach is considerably different from conventional competitive learning in that competition is realized by maximizing information. The new method can contribute to neural computing from three perspectives: (1) competition is realized by maximizing mutual information between input patterns and competitive units; (2) we can take into account distance between input patterns and connection weights; and (3) information maximization can solve the serious problem of dead neurons in conventional competitive learning.

First, competition in the new method is realized by maximizing mutual information between competitive units and input patterns. Information theoretic approaches have been used in various aspects of neural computing. For example, Linsker [1], [2] proposed a principle of maximum information preservation in information processing systems. Under the influence of this principle, several attempts have been made to apply information theoretic methods to neural computing. Though Linsker succeeded in formulating information theoretic methods in simple linear models including noisy situations, he did not always succeed in simulating unsupervised learning comparable to that achieved by conventional competitive learning and the self-organizing maps. In contrast to those information theoretic approaches, more practical methods have been developed. That is, information theoretic approaches have been applied to controlling hidden unit activations [3], [4], [5], [6]. Our method is an extension of these practical information theoretic methods. Thus, our method is simple and practical enough to be implemented in neural networks.

Second, we use the distance between input patterns and connection weights as the outputs from the neurons. Our information theoretic methods so far redeveloped are based upon supervised learning, and they could not be applied to the simulation of self-organization processes[3], [4], [5]. Thus, we have tried to extend our methods to cover unsupervised self-organized processes[7],[8]. In previous methods, the outputs from competitive units are a sigmoidal transformation of the weighted sum of input patterns. This is because, by the property of the sigmoid function, negative connections are easily produced. These negative connections are used to turn off the majority of neurons, except some winning neurons. That is, we have focused on introducing negative connections and on maximizing mutual information. Experimental results so far have shown good performance of information theoretic unsupervised learning, compared with the conventional competitive learning methods [7],[8]. However, one problem is that the winning neurons do not always represent typical input patterns. To remedy this shortcoming, we use here as an output the inverse of the Euclidean distance between input patterns and connection weights. As the distance is smaller, the output is larger. This ensures that the winning neurons have a good possibility of representing typical input patterns.

Third, our method can solve the problem of dead neurons in an explicit way. In conventional competitive learning, when initial conditions are far from the final solutions, some neurons tend to be under-utilized, that is, dead neurons. The problem of these dead neurons is one of the serious problems in conventional competitive learning. Therefore, there have been many attempts to solve the dead neuron problem, [9], [10], [11], [12], [13], to cite a few. However, it seems to us that these methods cannot solve the problem directly. In our new model, the problem of dead neurons is explicitly solved in a framework of mutual information maximization. In maximizing mutual information, the entropy of competitive units must be increased as much as possible. This means that all competitive units must be equally used. This property of information maximization ensures that the dead neuron problem is solved in our framework.

2   Information Maximization

We consider information content stored in competitive unit activation patterns. For this purpose, let us define information to be stored in a neural system. Information stored in a system is represented by decrease in uncertainty. Uncertainty decrease, that is, information I, is defined by

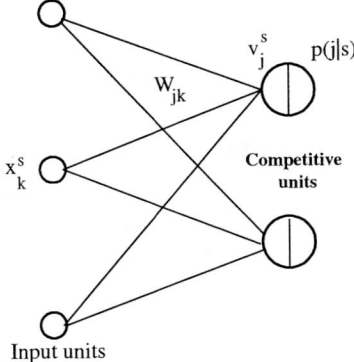

Fig. 1. A network architecture for information maximization.

$$I = -\sum_{\forall j} p(j) \log p(j) + \sum_{\forall s} \sum_{\forall j} p(s) p(j \mid s) \log p(j \mid s), \quad (1)$$

where $p(j)$, $p(s)$ and $p(j|s)$ denote the probability of the jth unit, the probability of the sth input pattern and the conditional probability of the jth unit, given the sth input pattern, respectively.

Let us present update rules to maximize information content. As shown in Figure 1, a network is composed of input units x_k^s and competitive units v_j^s. We use as the output function the inverse of the square of the Euclidean distance between connection weights and outputs for facilitating the derivation. Thus, an output from the jth competitive unit can be computed by

$$v_j^s = \frac{1}{\sum_{k=1}^{L}(x_k^s - w_{jk})^2}, \quad (2)$$

where L is the number of input units, and w_{jk} denote connections from the kth input unit to the jth competitive unit. The output is increased as connection weights are closer to input patterns.

The conditional probability $p(j \mid s)$ is computed by

$$p(j \mid s) = \frac{v_j^s}{\sum_{m=1}^{M} v_m^s}, \quad (3)$$

where M denotes the number of competitive units. Since input patterns are supposed to be uniformly given to networks, the probability of the jth competitive unit is computed by

$$p(j) = \frac{1}{S} \sum_{s=1}^{S} p(j \mid s). \quad (4)$$

Information I is computed by

$$I = -\sum_{j=1}^{M} p(j) \log p(j) + \frac{1}{S} \sum_{s=1}^{S} \sum_{j=1}^{M} p(j \mid s) \log p(j \mid s). \tag{5}$$

Differentiating information with respect to input-competitive connections w_{jk}, we have

$$\Delta w_{jk} = -\beta \sum_{s=1}^{S} \left(\log p(j) - \sum_{m=1}^{M} p(m \mid s) \log p(m) \right) Q_{jk}^{s} \tag{6}$$

$$+\beta \sum_{s=1}^{S} \left(\log p(j \mid s) - \sum_{m=1}^{M} p(m \mid s) \log p(m \mid s) \right) Q_{jk}^{s},$$

where β is the learning parameter, and

$$Q_{jk}^{s} = \frac{2(x_k^s - w_{jk})}{S \sum_{m=1}^{M} v_j^s \left(\sum_{k=1}^{L} (x_k^s - w_{jk})^2 \right)^2}. \tag{7}$$

In mutual information maximization, the first order entropy $-\sum_{j} p(j) \log p(j)$ is simultaneously maximized. This means that all neurons must equally be used. Thus, as mutual information is increased, all neurons tend to respond to different input patterns.

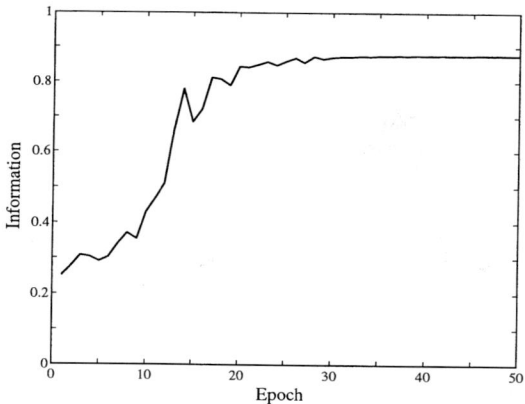

Fig. 2. Information as a function of the number of epochs.

3 Artificial Data

We demonstrate the performance of our information maximization by applying it to the classification of the six vectors represented by "+" in Figure 3. Because this is an extremely easy task, we might imagine that any model could immediately solve this problem. However, if initial conditions are not appropriately given, conventional models cannot give final solutions. The number of input and competitive units are two and three, respectively. In this case, connections into the first competitive units are set to one, while those into the second and the third competitive units are -1. For maximizing mutual information, we need non-uniform connections, and we added small random numbers (with the range:0.001) to all initial conditions. The learning rate was one for all experiments.

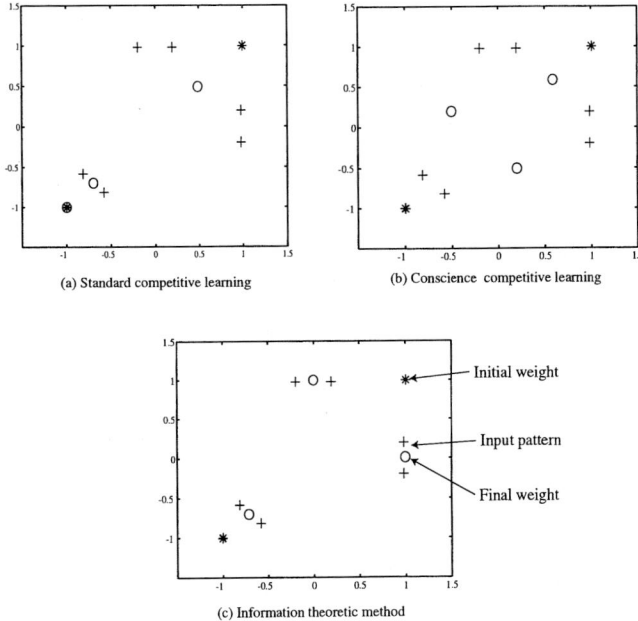

Fig. 3. Input patterns, and initial and final connection weights by three methods.

First, information is increased as much as possible. Figure 2 shows information as a function of the number of epochs. Information is rapidly increased and reaches its stable point of about 84 percent of maximum information in about 30 epochs. Figure 3(a) shows initial and final connection weights by the standard competitive learning method. As can be seen in the figure, one neuron on the lower left-hand side remains at its first position. This neuron becomes a dead neuron. Figure 3(b) shows initial and final connection weights by a conscience method[1]. Though three neurons try to move to the centers of three clusters, they cannot reach the final points. Finally, Figure 3(c) shows initial and final

---

[1] Experiments by a conscience method were performed by using the Matlab Neural Network package with all parameters set to default values

weights by the information maximization method. As shown in the figure, all three neurons move appropriately to the centers of three clusters. We have seen in many experiments that our information maximization can reach the final solutions almost independent of initial conditions. This is because in mutual information maximization, the entropy of competitive units should be increased. This entropy maximization makes all neurons respond appropriately to input patterns.

4 Road Scene Classification

We present here experimental results on a road classification problem. In this problem, networks must infer whether a driver drives in a mixed traffic road or a motor road. In the experiments, we prepared 49 road photographs taken from the drivers' viewpoint. Of the 49 photos, 23 are classified as photos of mixed traffic roads that are relatively narrow. On the other hand, the remaining 26 photos are those of relatively wide motor roads. We carefully examined these photos and made a linguistic checklist composed of 36 features, for example, *walkers*, *bicycles*, *houses*, *road signs* and so on. For the experiment, we examine whether the networks can classify those photos into appropriate classes, and try to see what kinds of features can be extracted by the neural networks. The numbers of input and competitive units are 36 and two, respectively.

Table 1. Comparison of success rates by three methods. In the table, SCL, CCL and IM denote the standard competitive learning, the conscience learning and the mutual information maximization method.

	SCL	CCL	IM
Average	0.531	0.861	0.898
Std Dev	0	0.009	0

First, information is increased as much as possible. Information reaches a steady point of 15 percent of maximum information in about 100 epochs. Table 1 shows the success rates[2] by three methods. As shown in the table, by using the standard competitive learning method, the success rate is very low, that is, 0.531, because one neuron becomes a dead neuron, as shown in Figure 4(a). By using the conscience method, the success rate is increased to 0.861, and by the information maximization method, the rate reaches the best result of 0.898.

To examine why good performance can be obtained by our method, we try to compare connection weights obtained by the standard competitive learning, the conscience learning and the information theoretic method. Figure 4(b) and (c)

---

[2] The success rate is the number of patterns successfully classified by networks. In computing the rate, the outputs from competitive units are rounded to the nearest integer 0 or 1.

show connection weights by the conscience and information theoretic methods. As can be seen in the figure, quite similar weights could be obtained. However, more explicit weights can be obtained by information maximization. We think that the good performance of the information theoretic method is due to this explicit representation. Let us interpret connection weights by information maximization. For the mixed traffic road, three features, such as "residential area,' "telephone pole" and "narrow road," were detected. We observed that these three features are explicitly seen in the photo. For the motor road, about five important features, such as "oncoming car," "guard rail," "bridge," "road sign" and "sidewalk," are detected. We could see that three features-"guard rail," "bridge" and "road sign"-are explicitly detected in the photo. These results suggest that information maximization clearly detects salient features in input patterns.

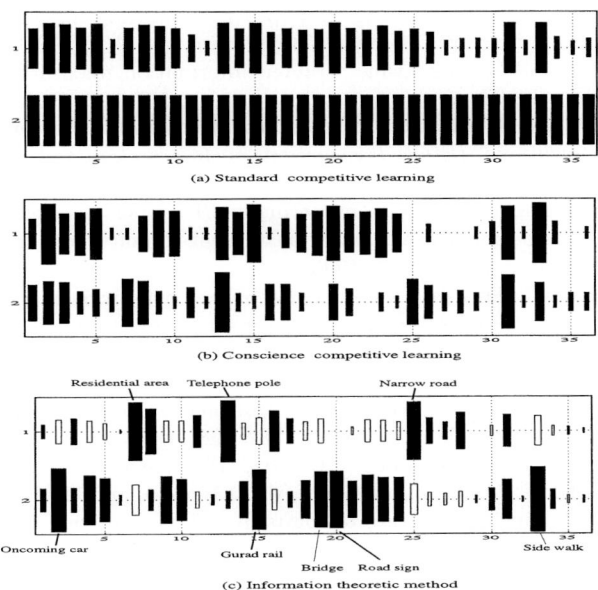

Fig. 4. Connection weights by three methods.

5 Conclusion

In this paper, we proposed a new information theoretic competitive learning method that is completely different from conventional competitive learning. The new method is based upon mutual information maximization between input patterns and competitive units. For the further development of this method, we should consider three points. First, because the computational complexity of the mutual information maximization method is larger than that of the conventional competitive learning methods, elaborated acceleration methods are needed to maximize mutual information, Second, we used the distance function instead of the sigmoidal function. For this reason, it is sometimes difficult to increase mutual information, as shown in the second experiment. We need some methods to facilitate information maximization. Third, we have presented pure competitive learning. The next step is to develop a method to produce self-organizing maps based upon this competitive learning. Finally, though some problems remain to be solved in dealing with more complex problems, it is certain that our method opens up a new perspective in competitive learning.

References

1. R. Linsker, "Self-organization in a perceptual network," *Computer*, vol. 21, pp. 105–117, 1988.
2. R. Linsker, "How to generate ordered maps by maximizing the mutual information between input and output," *Neural Computation*, vol. 1, pp. 402–411, 1989.
3. R. Kamimura and S. Nakanishi, "Hidden information maximization for feature detection and rule discovery," *Network*, vol. 6, pp. 577–622, 1995.
4. R. Kamimura and S. Nakanishi, "Improving generalization performance by information minimization," *IEICE Transactions on Information and Systems*, vol. E78-D, no. 2, pp. 163–173, 1995.
5. G. Deco, W. Finnof, and H. G. Zimmermann, "Unsupervised mutual information criterion for elimination of overtraining in supervised multiplayer networks," *Neural Computation*, vol. 7, pp. 86–107, 1995.
6. Y. Akiyama and T. Furuya, "An extension of the back-propagation learning which performs entropy maximization as well as error minimization," Tech. Rep. NC91-6, IEICE Technical Report, 1991.
7. R. Kamimura, T. Kamimura, and T. R. Shultz, "Information theoretic competitive learning and linguistic rule acquistion," *Transactions of the Japanese Society for Artificial Intelligence*, vol. 16, no. 2, pp. 287–298, 2001.
8. R. Kamimura, T. Kamimura, and O. Uchida, "Flexible feature discovery and structural information," *Connection Science*, vol. 13, no. 4, pp. 323–347, 2001.
9. D. DeSieno, "Adding a conscience to competitive learning," in *Proceedings of IEEE International Conference on Neural Networks*, (San Diego), pp. 117–124, IEEE, 1988.
10. S. C. Ahalt, A. K. Krishnamurthy, P. Chen, and D. E. Melton, "Competitive learning algorithms for vector quantization," *Neural Networks*, vol. 3, pp. 277–290, 1990.
11. L. Xu, "Rival penalized competitive learning for clustering analysis, RBF net, and curve detection," *IEEE Transaction on Neural Networks*, vol. 4, no. 4, pp. 636–649, 1993.
12. A. Luk and S. Lien, "Properties of the generalized lotto-type competitive learning," in *Proceedings of International conference on neural information processing*, (San Mateo: CA), pp. 1180–1185, Morgan Kaufmann Publishers, 2000.
13. M. Marc and M. V. Hulle, *Faithful representations and topographic maps*. New York: John Wiley and Sons, Inc, 2000.

Approximate Learning in Temporal Hidden Hopfield Models

Felix V. Agakov and David Barber

University of Edinburgh, Division of Informatics, Edinburgh EH1 2QL, UK
{felixa, dbarber}@anc.ed.ac.uk
http://anc.ed.ac.uk

Abstract. Many popular probabilistic models for temporal sequences assume simple hidden dynamics or low-dimensionality of discrete variables. For higher dimensional discrete hidden variables, recourse is often made to approximate mean field theories, which to date have been applied to models with only simple hidden unit dynamics. We consider a class of models in which the discrete hidden space is defined by parallel dynamics of densely connected high-dimensional stochastic Hopfield networks. For these Hidden Hopfield Models (HHMs), mean field methods are derived for learning discrete and continuous temporal sequences. We also discuss applications of HHMs to learning of incomplete sequences and reconstruction of 3D occupancy graphs.

1 Markovian Dynamics for Temporal Sequences

Dynamic Bayesian networks are popular tools for modeling temporally correlated patterns. Included in this class of models are Hidden Markov Models (HMMs) and Factorial HMMs [1,2]. These models are special cases of a generalized Markov chain

$$p(\{h\}, \{v\}) = p(h^{(0)})p(v^{(0)}) \prod_{t=0}^{T-1} p(h^{(t+1)}|h^{(t)}, v^{(t)})p(v^{(t+1)}|h^{(t)}, v^{(t)}), \quad (1)$$

where $\{h\} = \{h^{(0)}, \ldots, h^{(T)}\}$ and $\{v\} = \{v^{(0)}, \ldots, v^{(T)}\}$ are hidden and visible variables (see Fig. 1).

A general procedure for learning model parameters Θ is the EM algorithm, which optimizes the lower bound on the log-likelihood

$$\Phi(\{v\}; q, \Theta) = \langle \log p(\{h\}, \{v\}; \Theta) - \log q(\{h\}|\{v\}) \rangle_{q(\{h\}|\{v\})} \quad (2)$$

with respect to the parameters (M-step) and an auxiliary distribution $q(\{h\}|\{v\})$ (E-step). The bound on the log-likelihood $\mathcal{L}$ is exact if and only if $q(\{h\}|\{v\})$ is identical to the true posterior $p(\{h\}|\{v\})$. However, in general, the problem of evaluating the averages over the discrete $p(\{h\}|\{v\})$ is exponential in the dimension of $\{h\}$. This computational intractability of learning is one of the fundamental problems of probabilistic graphical modeling. Many popular models

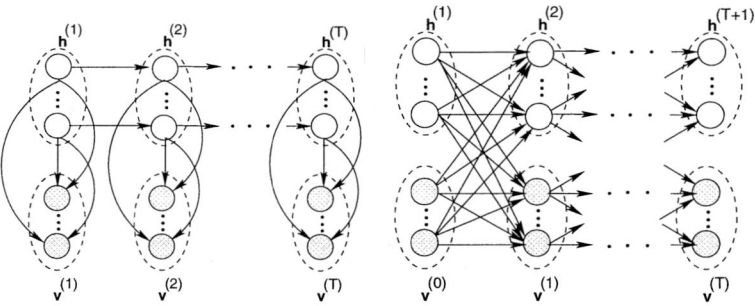

Fig. 1. Graphical models for sequences: *Left:* Factorial HMM; *Right:* a generalized Markov chain with temporally shifted observations.

for temporal sequences therefore assume that the hidden variables are either low-dimensional, in which case $\mathcal{L}$ can be optimized exactly (e.g. HMMs), or have very simple temporal dependencies, so that $p(\{h\}|\{v\})$ is approximately factorized.

Our work here is motivated by the observation that mean field theories succeed in the contrasting limits of extremely sparse connectivity (models are then by construction approximately factorized), and extremely dense connectivity (for conditional distributions dependent on a linear combination of parental states). This raises the possibility of using mean field methods for approximate learning in dynamic networks with *high dimensional, densely connected* discrete hidden spaces. The resulting model with a large discrete hidden dimension can be used for learning highly non-stationary data of coupled dynamical systems. Moreover, as we show in Sect. 5, it yields a fully probabilistic way of addressing some problems of scanning and reconstruction of incomplete temporal sequences.

2 Hidden Hopfield Models

To fully specify the model (1) we need to define the transition probabilities $p(\boldsymbol{h}^{(t+1)}|\boldsymbol{x}^{(t)})$ and $p(\boldsymbol{v}^{(t+1)}|\boldsymbol{x}^{(t)})$, where $\boldsymbol{x} = [\boldsymbol{h}^T \ \boldsymbol{v}^T]^T$. For high-dimensional discrete hidden variables the conditionals $p(h_i^{(t+1)}|\boldsymbol{x}^{(t)})$ cannot be defined by probability tables, and some parameterization needs to be considered. It should be specified in such a form that computationally tractable approximations of $p(\boldsymbol{h}^{(t+1)}|\boldsymbol{x}^{(t)})$ are sufficiently accurate. We consider $h_i^{(t+1)} \in \{-1, +1\}$ and

$$p(h_i^{(t+1)}|\boldsymbol{x}^{(t)}; \boldsymbol{w}_i, b_i) = \sigma\left(h_i^{(t+1)}(\boldsymbol{w}_i^T \boldsymbol{x}^{(t)} + b_i)\right), \text{ where } \sigma(a) \triangleq 1/(1+e^{-a}), \quad (3)$$

$\boldsymbol{w}_i$ is a weight vector connecting node i with the other nodes, and b_i is the bias.

The model has a graphical structure, temporal dynamics, and parameterization of the conditionals $p(h_i|\boldsymbol{x})$ similar to a **synchronous** Hopfield network (e.g. [3]) amended with hidden variables and a full generally non-symmetric weight matrix. This prompts us to refer to a generalized Markov chain (1) with parameterization (3) as a Hidden Hopfield Model (HHM). It is motivated by the observation that, according to the Central Limit Theorem, for large densely connected models without strongly dependent weights, the posteriors (3) are approximately uni-modal. Therefore, the mean field approximation

$$q(\{h\}|\{v\};\lambda) = \prod_k \lambda_k^{(1+h_k)/2}(1-\lambda_k)^{(1-h_k)/2}, \quad \lambda_k \triangleq q(h_k = 1|\{v\}) \quad (4)$$

is expected to be reasonably accurate. During learning we optimize the bound (2) with respect to this factorized approximation q and the model parameters $\Theta = \{W, b, p(h^{(0)})\}$ for two types of visible variables v. In the first case $v \in \{-1, +1\}^n$ and the conditionals $p(v_i|x)$ are defined similarly to (3). This specific case of discrete visible variables is equivalent to sigmoid belief networks [4] with hidden and visible variables in each layer. In the second considered case the observations $v \in \mathbb{R}^n$ with $p(v_i|x) \sim \mathcal{N}(w_i^T x + b_i, s^2)$, where s^2 is the variance of isotropic Gaussian noise.

Previously, [5] used a similar approximation for learning in sigmoid belief networks. Their approach suggests to optimize a variational lower bound on Φ, which is itself a lower bound on $\mathcal{L}$. For HHM learning of discrete time series we adopt a different strategy and exploit approximate Gaussianity of the nodes' fields for numeric evaluation of the gradients, yielding a fast rule for learning incomplete discrete sequences. HHM learning of continuous time series results in a related, but different rule (Sect. 3.1).

Note that although both HMMs and Hidden Hopfield models can be used for learning of non-stationary time series with long temporal dependencies, they fundamentally differ in representations of the hidden spaces. HMMs capture non-stationarities by expanding the number of states of a single multinomial variable. As opposed to HMMs, Hidden Hopfield models have a more efficient, distributed hidden space representation. Moreover, the model allows intra-layer connections between the hidden variables, which yields a richer hidden state structure compared with Factorial HMMs.

3 Learning in Hidden Hopfield Models

Here we outline the variational EM algorithm for HHMs with continuous data. A similar algorithm for discrete-data HHMs and the derivations are given in [6].

3.1 Variational EM Algorithm

Let $H^{(t)}$, $V^{(t)}$ denote sets of hidden and visible variables at time t, and $x_i^{(t)}$ be the ith variable at time t. For each variable we introduce $\lambda_i^{(t)}$, such that

$$\lambda_i^{(t)} \triangleq \begin{cases} q(x_i^{(t)} = 1|v^{(t)}) \in [0,1] & \text{if } i \in H^{(t)}; \\ (x_i^{(t)} + 1)/2 \in \mathbb{R} & \text{if } i \in V^{(t)}. \end{cases} \quad (5)$$

Note that if $x_i^{(t)}$ is hidden then $\lambda_i^{(t)}$ defines its posterior firing rate and must be learned from data. Also, from (5) it is clear that $\langle x_i^{(t)}|v^{(t)}\rangle = 2\lambda_i^{(t)} - 1$.

The M-Step. Let w_{ij} be connecting $x_i^{(t+1)}$ and $x_j^{(t)}$. From (2) we get

$$\frac{\partial \Phi}{\partial w_{ij}} = \sum_{t=0}^{T-1} \left[f_i^{(t+1)} \frac{\partial \Phi_t^v}{\partial w_{ij}} + (1 - f_i^{(t+1)}) \frac{\partial \Phi_t^h}{\partial w_{ij}} \right], \qquad (6)$$

where $f_i^{(t+1)} \in \{0, 1\}$ is an indicator equal to 1 if and only if x_i is visible at time $t+1$ [i.e. $i \in V^{(t+1)}$]. The gradient contributions depend on the units' observability and are given by

$$\frac{\partial \Phi_t^h}{\partial w_{ij}} \approx \lambda_i^{(t+1)}(2\lambda_j^{(t)} - 1) - f_j^{(t)}(2\lambda_j^{(t)} - 1)\langle \sigma(e_i^t) \rangle_{p(e_i^t)}$$
$$- (1 - f_j^{(t)}) \left[\lambda_j^{(t)} \langle \sigma(c_{ij}^t) \rangle_{p(c_{ij}^t)} + (\lambda_j^{(t)} - 1) \langle \sigma(d_{ij}^t) \rangle_{p(d_{ij}^t)} \right], \qquad (7)$$

$$\frac{\partial \Phi_t^v}{\partial w_{ij}} \approx \frac{(2\lambda_j^{(t)} - 1)}{s^2} \left[v_i^{(t+1)} - \boldsymbol{w}_i^T (2\boldsymbol{\lambda}^{(t)} - \mathbf{1}) \right] + (1 - f_j^{(t)}) \frac{4(\lambda_j^{(t)} - 1)\lambda_j^{(t)}}{s^2} w_{ij}. (8)$$

Here $p(c_{ij}^t)$, $p(d_{ij}^t)$, and $p(e_i^t)$ correspond to distributions of the *fields*

$$c_{ij}^t \triangleq \boldsymbol{w}_i^T \boldsymbol{x}^{(t)} + b_i |_{h_j^{(t)}=1}, \quad d_{ij}^t \triangleq \boldsymbol{w}_i^T \boldsymbol{x}^{(t)} + b_i |_{h_j^{(t)}=-1}, \quad e_i^t \triangleq \boldsymbol{w}_i^T \boldsymbol{x}^{(t)} + b_i. \quad (9)$$

Analogously, the gradient for the biases can be expressed as

$$\frac{\partial \Phi}{\partial b_i} \approx \sum_{t=0}^{T-1} \left[\lambda_i^{(t+1)} - \langle \sigma(e_i^t) \rangle_{p(e_i^t)} \right]. \qquad (10)$$

The E-Step. Optimizing (2) for the expected firing rates $\lambda_i^{(t)}|_{t=1,\ldots,T-2}$, we obtain the fixed point equations of the form $\lambda_k^{(t)} = \sigma(l_k^{(t)})$, where

$$l_k^{(t)} = \tilde{l}_k^{(t)} - \frac{2}{s^2} \sum_{i \in V^{(t+1)}} w_{ik} \left[\boldsymbol{w}_i^T(2\boldsymbol{\lambda}^{(t)} - \mathbf{1}) - w_{ik}(2\lambda_k^{(t)} - 1) - v_i^{(t+1)} \right], \quad (11)$$

$$\tilde{l}_k^{(t)} = \langle e_k^{t-1} | \boldsymbol{v}^{(t-1)} \rangle + \sum_{m \in H^{(t+1)}} \left[\left\langle \log \left\{ \sigma(c_{mk}^t)^{\lambda_m^{(t+1)}} \sigma(-c_{mk}^t)^{1-\lambda_m^{(t+1)}} \right\} \right\rangle_{p(c_{mk}^t)}$$
$$- \left\langle \log \left\{ \sigma(d_{mk}^t)^{\lambda_m^{(t+1)}} \sigma(-d_{mk}^t)^{1-\lambda_m^{(t+1)}} \right\} \right\rangle_{p(d_{mk}^t)} \right]. \qquad (12)$$

It can be easily seen that $\lambda_k^{(0)}$ of a starting hidden node can be obtained by replacing contributions of the previous states $\langle e_k^{t-1} | \boldsymbol{v}^{(t-1)} \rangle$ in (12) by the prior term $\log \{ \lambda_k^{(0)} / (1 - \lambda_k^{(0)}) \}$. Finally, since $\boldsymbol{h}^{(T)}$ is unrepresentative of the data, parameters $\lambda_i^{(T-1)}$ are obtained from (11) by setting $\tilde{l}_k^{(T-1)} = \langle e_k^{T-2} | \boldsymbol{v}^{(T-2)} \rangle$.

From (9) it is clear that the fields c_{mk}^t, d_{mk}^t, and e_k^t are given by linear combinations of random variables $x_k^{(t)}$. Then for small and not strongly correlated weights the Central Limit Theorem implies approximate[1] Gaussianity [7] of the

---
[1] This approximation can be made more accurate by training the model from small initializations and applying dilution.

field distributions. Thus $c_{ij}^t \sim \mathcal{N}(\mu_{ij}^c(t), s_{ij}^c(t))$ and $d_{ij}^t \sim \mathcal{N}(\mu_{ij}^d(t), s_{ij}^d(t))$ with

$$\mu_{ij}^c(t) = \boldsymbol{w}_i^T(2\boldsymbol{\lambda}^{(t)} - \mathbf{1}) + 2w_{ij}(1 - \lambda_j^{(t)}) + b_i, \quad \mu_{ij}^d(t) = \mu_{ij}^c(t) - 2w_{ij}, \quad (13)$$

$$s_{ij}^c(t) = s_{ij}^d(t) = 4 \sum_{k \neq j}^{|\boldsymbol{x}^{(t)}|} \lambda_k^{(t)}(1 - \lambda_k^{(t)})w_{ik}^2. \quad (14)$$

Similarly,

$$e_i^t \sim \mathcal{N}\left(\boldsymbol{w}_i^T(2\boldsymbol{\lambda}^{(t)} - \mathbf{1}) + b_i, \; s_{ij}^d(t) + 4\lambda_j^{(t)}(1 - \lambda_j^{(t)})w_{ij}^2\right). \quad (15)$$

Note that the resulting 1-D averages in (7), (10), and (12) may be efficiently evaluated by numerical Gaussian integration, and even crude approximation at the means often leads to accurate approximations (Sect. 5).

3.2 Multiple Sequences

To learn multiple sequences we need to estimate separate parameters $\{\lambda_{ks}^{(t)}\}$ for each node k of sequence s at time $t \geq 0$. This does not change the fixed point equations of the E-step of the algorithm. From (2) it is clear that the gradients $\partial\Phi/\partial w_{ij}$ and $\partial\Phi/\partial b_i$ in the M-step will be expressed according to (7), (8), (10) with an additional summation over the training sequences.

3.3 Constrained Parameterization

Note that the full transition matrix of a n-D HHM contains $O(n^2)$ weights, which may require prohibitively large amounts of training data and result in high computational complexity of learning. In Sect. 5 we impose sparsity constraints on the weight transition and emission matrices so that the number of adaptive parameters is significantly reduced. We also show that while the exact learning and inference in general remain computationally intractable, the Gaussian field approximation remains accurate and results in reasonable performance.

4 Inference

A simple way to approximate the posterior $p(\{\boldsymbol{h}\}|\{\boldsymbol{v}\})$ is by clamping the observed sequence $\{\boldsymbol{v}\}$ on the visible variables, fixing the model parameters $\boldsymbol{\Theta}$, and performing the E-step of the variational EM algorithm (see Sect. 3.1), which yields the mean-field approximation $q(\{\boldsymbol{h}\}|\{\boldsymbol{v}\}; \boldsymbol{\lambda})$.

Alternatively, $p(\{\boldsymbol{h}\}|\{\boldsymbol{v}\})$ can be approximated by sampling. Note that the (generalized) chain structure of temporal HHMs motivates the efficient *red-black* Gibbs sampling scheme, where we first condition on the odd layers of a high-dimensional chain and sample nodes in the even layers in parallel, and then flip the conditioning (all the visible variables are assumed to remain fixed). In general it may be necessary to use another Gibbs sampler for the hidden components of $\boldsymbol{x}^{(t)}$. Indeed, $p(\boldsymbol{x}^{(t)}|\boldsymbol{x}^{(t-1)}, \boldsymbol{x}^{(t+1)}) \propto p(\boldsymbol{x}^{(t)}|\boldsymbol{x}^{(t-1)})p(\boldsymbol{x}^{(t+1)}|\boldsymbol{x}^{(t)})$ is not factorized in $\boldsymbol{x}^{(t)}$ and cannot be easily normalized in large models (see [6] for details).

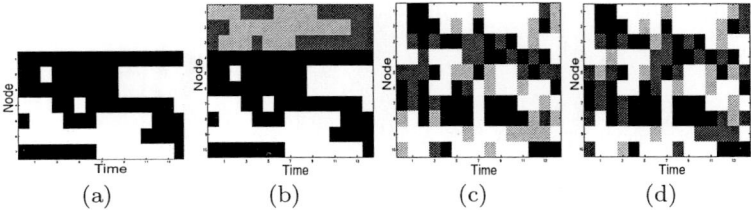

(a) (b) (c) (d)

Fig. 2. Training and retrieved sequences with regular [(a), (b)] and irregular [(c), (d)] observations. *Axes:* time, nodes. Black and white squares correspond to -1 and $+1$ for the visible variables; dark gray and light gray – to -1 and $+1$ for the hidden variables.

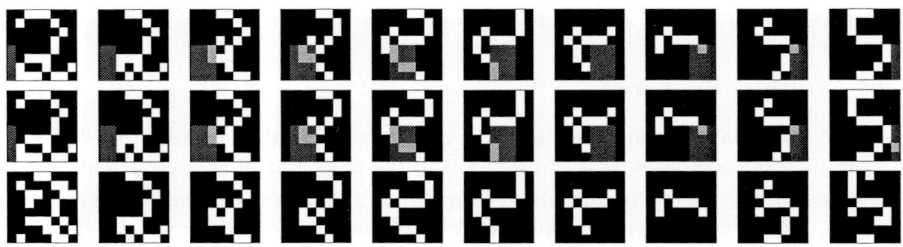

Fig. 3. Reconstruction of incomplete discrete time series. *Top:* true sequence; *Middle:* clamped sequence (black/white) and inferred values of the missing variables (dark/light gray); *Bottom:* reconstruction by forward sampling from a noisy initialization.

5 Experimental Results

Correctness of the HHM learning rule may be validated by deterministically reconstructing learned sequences from noiseless initializations at the starting patterns. For s discrete sequences of length T we expect such reconstructions to be good if the total number of nodes $|\boldsymbol{h}| + |\boldsymbol{v}|$ is of the order of $s \times T$ (for near-deterministic posteriors (3) this follows from the induced linear equations).

Figures 2 (a), (b) illustrate reconstruction of a 7-D discrete sequence of length $T = 15$ by an HHM with $|\{\boldsymbol{v}\}| = 7T$, $|\{\boldsymbol{h}\}| = 3T$. Each subsequent training pattern $\boldsymbol{v}^{(t+1)}$ was generated from $\boldsymbol{v}^{(t)}$ by flipping each bit with probability 0.2, while $\boldsymbol{v}^{(0)}$ was set at random. The HHM was trained by the EM algorithm (Sect. 3). During retrieval, each subsequent pattern $x_i^{(t+1)}$ was set according to $sgn(\sigma(x_i^{(t+1)}(\boldsymbol{w}_i^T \boldsymbol{x} + b_i)) - 1/2)$, while $\boldsymbol{x}^{(0)}$ was sampled from the learned prior $p(\boldsymbol{x}^{(0)})$. Note that $\boldsymbol{v}^{(7)} \equiv \boldsymbol{v}^{(8)}$, and it is only due to the hidden variables that mappings $\boldsymbol{x}^{(7)} \to \boldsymbol{x}^{(8)}$ and $\boldsymbol{x}^{(8)} \to \boldsymbol{x}^{(9)}$ can be distinguished. Figures 2 (c), (d) show a similar experiment for a discrete 10-D sequence with **irregularly** missing data. Note that the model perfectly reproduces the visible patterns.

We also applied HHMs to learning incomplete noisy sequences. The underlying data contained 10 8×8 binary images with an average Hamming distance of

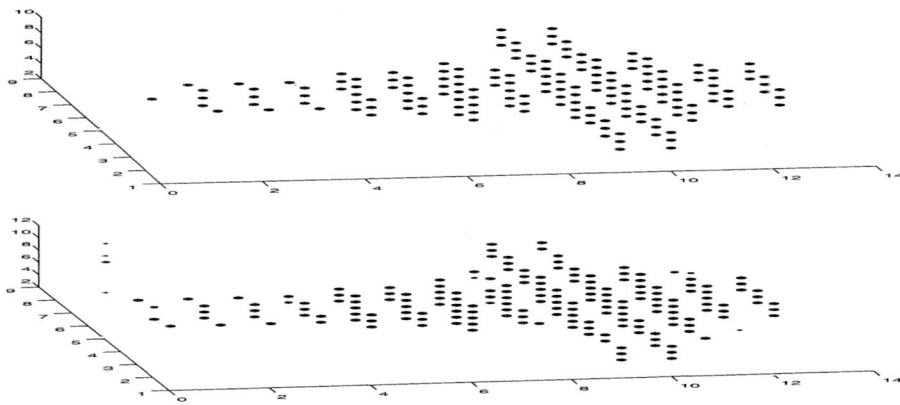

Fig. 4. 3-D graph reconstruction. *Axes*: the scanning plane, time. The disk areas are proportional to $p(h_i^{(t+1)}|v^{(t)})$. *Top:* true shape; *Bottom:* reconstruction [with annealing].

7 bits between the subsequent patterns (see Fig. 3 *top*). The model was trained on 4 sequences obtained from the complete series by randomly omitting about 15% and permuting 10% of each pattern. During reconstruction, the visible part of a sequence with different systematically missing blocks was clamped on $\{v\}$, and the missing bits $\{h\}$ were inferred variationally. As can be seen from Fig. 3 *middle*, the reconstruction is reasonably accurate. Finally, we tried to retrieve the true sequence by deterministic forward sampling from a noisy initialization, perturbing each subsequent pattern with an additional 10% noise (Fig. 3 *bottom*). The results are still accurate, though this reconstruction proves to be sensitive to the noise of the training sequences.

In other experiments we utilized the high-dimensional distributed hidden space representation of HHMs for reconstructing 3D binary occupancy graphs of scanned objects. Each object moved with a constant speed orthogonally to the plane scanned by two mutually perpendicular linear scanners; the measurements were given by the number of filled cells along each planar slice perturbed by the spherical Gaussian noise $\mathcal{N}(0,1)$. For shape reconstruction we applied a **constrained** HHM $p(\{h\},\{v\}|h^{(0)}) = \prod_{t=0}^{T-1} p(h^{(t+1)}|h^{(t)})p(v^{(t+1)}|h^{(t)})$ with $|h^{(t)}| = 12 \times 9$, $|v^{(t)}| = 12 + 9$ and $T = 13$ time frames, where $\{h\}$ and $\{v\}$ correspond to the binary occupancy cells and the noisy measurements respectively. The transition weights were set according to the **local neighborhood** constraints (justified by the presumed smoothness of scanned objects) and fixed at 0.2 (or at 0 outside the region of 9 nearest topological neighbors). The weights connecting $v_i^{(t)}$ with $h^{(t)}$ were set to 0.6 (or 0) to compute sums only along the ith row ($i = 1\ldots 12$) or the ith column ($i = 13\ldots 21$) of the discretized slice of the scanned space at time t. The biases of $p(h^{(t+1)}|h^{(t)})$ were set to 0. From Fig. 4 *bottom* we see that impervious to the constraints and the facts that the scanner data is noisy and the inference task is severely under-determined, the model accurately reconstructs the underlying shape – a hunting knife (Fig. 4 top). The results suggest that constrained versions of HHMs may be practical for inference and learning if the data itself is constrained or inherently smooth. Moreover, the results suggest a possibility for combining exact and approximate methods for sparse HHMs. Finally, note that unlike constrained HMMs [8] or temporal GTMs [9], HHMs feature distributed discrete hidden spaces, suggesting potential applications to half-toning and spiking temporal topographic maps of incomplete sequences under carefully imposed topological constraints [6].

6 Summary

Learning temporal sequences with discrete hidden units is typically achieved using only low dimensional hidden spaces due to the exponential increase in learning complexity with the hidden unit dimension. Motivated by the observation that mean field methods work well in the counter-intuitive limit of a large, densely connected graph with conditional probability tables dependent on a linear combination of parental states, we formulated the Hidden Hopfield Model for which the hidden unit dynamics is specified precisely by a form for which mean field theories may be accurate in large scale systems. For discrete or continuous observations, we derived fast EM-like algorithms exploiting mean and Gaussian field approximations, and demonstrated successful applications to reconstruction of incomplete temporal sequences. We also discussed inference applications of the constrained Hidden Hopfield Models.

References

1. Williams, C.K.I., Hinton, G.E.: Mean field networks that learn to discriminate temporally distorted strings. In: Connectionist models: Proceedings of the 1990 summer school. Morgan Kaufmann (1991)
2. Ghahramani, Z., Jordan, M.: Factorial Hidden Markov Models. In: NIPS. Volume 8., MIT Press (1995)
3. Hertz, J., Krogh, A., Palmer, R.G.: Introduction to the Theory of Neural Computation. MA: Addison-Wesley Publishing Company (1991)
4. Neal, R.M.: Connectionist Learning of Belief Networks. Artificial Intelligence (1992) 71–113
5. Saul, L., Jaakkola, T., Jordan, M.: Mean Field Theory for Sigmoid Belief Networks. Journal of Artificial Intelligence Research **4** (1996)
6. Agakov, F.V., Barber, D.: Temporal Hidden Hopfield Models. Technical Report EDI-INF-RR-0156, Division of Informatics, University of Edinburgh (2002)
7. Barber, D., Sollich, P.: Gaussian Fields for Approximate Inference. In Solla, S.A., Leen, T., Müller, K.R., eds.: Advances in Neural Information Processing Systems 12. MIT Press, Cambridge, MA (2000) 393–399
8. Roweis, S.: Constrained Hidden Markov Models. In: NIPS. Volume 12., MIT Press (1999)
9. Bishop, C.M., Hinton, G.E., Strachan, I.G.D.: GTM Through Time. In: IEE International Conference on Artificial Neural Networks. (1997)

Finite Mixture Model of Bounded Semi-naive Bayesian Networks Classifier

Kaizhu Huang, Irwin King, and Michael R. Lyu

Department of Computer Science and Engineering
The Chinese University of Hong Kong
Shatin, New Territories, Hong Kong
{kzhuang, king, lyu}@cse.cuhk.edu.hk

Abstract. The Semi-Naive Bayesian network (SNB) classifier, a probabilistic model with an assumption of conditional independence among the combined attributes, shows a good performance in classification tasks. However, the traditional SNBs can only combine two attributes into a combined attribute. This inflexibility together with its strong independency assumption may generate inaccurate distributions for some datasets and thus may greatly restrict the classification performance of SNEs. In this paper we develop a Bounded Semi-Naive Bayesian network (B-SNB) model based on direct combinatorial optimization. Our model can join any number of attributes within a given bound and maintains a polynomial time cost at the same time. This improvement expands the expressive ability of the SNB and thus provide potentials to increase accuracy in classification tasks. Further, aiming at relax the strong independency assumption of the SNB, we then propose an algorithm to extend the B-SNB into a finite mixture structure, named Mixture of Bounded Semi-Naive Bayesian network (MBSNB). We give theoretical derivations, outline of the algorithm, analysis of the algorithm and a set of experiments to demonstrate the usefulness of MBSNB in classification tasks. The novel finite MBSNB network shows a better classification performance in comparison with than other types of classifiers in this paper.

1 Introduction

Learning accurate classifiers is one of the basic problems in machine learning. The Naive Bayesian network (NB) [8] shows a good performance in dealing with this problem when compared with the decision tree learner C4.5 [13]. With an independency assumption among the attributes, when given the class label, NB classifies a specific sample into the class with the largest joint probability. This joint probability can be decomposed into a multiplication form based on its independency assumption.

The success of NB is somewhat unexpected since its independency assumption typically does not hold in many cases. Furthermore, the so-called Semi-Naive Bayesian networks are proposed to remedy violations of NB's assumption by joining attributes into several combined attributes based on a conditional independency assumption among the combined attributes. Some performance improvements have been demonstrated in [6,11].

However, two major problems exist for the SNB. First, typically,the traditional SNB can only combine two attributes into a combined attribute or it will be computationally intractable [11]. This inflexibility is obviously a problem, since combining more attributes may generate better results. Second, the conditional independency assumption among the joined attributes is still too strong although it is looser than NB's. These two problems restrict the expressive ability of the SNB and therefore may model inaccurate distributions for some datasets. How to solve these two problems effectively and efficiently becomes an important issue. To handle the first problem, in this paper, we develop a Bounded-SNB model based on direct combinatorial techniques. By transforming a learning problem into an integer programming problem, this model can combine any number of attributes within a given bound and maintain a polynomial time cost at the same time.

To solve the second problem, one possible way is to search an independence or dependence relationship among the attributes rather than impose a strong assumption on the attributes. This is the main idea of so-called unrestricted Bayesian Network (BN) [12]. Unfortunately, empirical results have demonstrated that searching an unrestricted BN structure does not show a better result than NB [3,4]. This is partly because that unrestricted BN structures are prone to incurring overfitting problems [3]. Furthermore, searching an unrestricted BN structure is generally an NP-complete problem [1]. Different from searching unrestricted structures, in this paper, we upgrade the SNB into a mixture structure, where a hidden variable is used to coordinate its components: SNB structures. Mixture approaches have achieved great success in expanding its restricted components expressive power and bringing a better performance.

In summary, in this paper, we use our B-SNB model to deal with the first problem. We then provide an algorithm to perform the mixture structure upgrading on our B-SNB model. On one hand, the B-SNB model enables the mixture a diversity, i.e., it is not necessary to limit the component structure into a SNB with combined attributes consisting of less or equal than two attributes. On the other hand, the mixture model expands the expressive ability for the B-SNB model. This paper is organized as follows. In Section 2, we describe our B-SNB model in detail. Then in Section 3, we discuss the mixture of B-SNB model and give an induction algorithm. Experimental results to show the advantages of our model are demonstrated in Section 4. Finally, we conclude this paper in Section 5.

2 Bounded Semi-naive Bayesian Network

Our Bounded Semi-Naive Bayesian network model is defined as follows:

Definition 1. *B-SNB Model : Given a set of N independent observations $D = \{x^1, \ldots, x^N\}$ and a bound K, where $x^i = (A_1^i, A_2^i, \ldots, A_n^i)$ is an n-*

dimension vector and $A_1, A_2, \ldots, A_n$ are called variables or attributes, B-SNB is a maximum likelihood Bayesian network which satisfies the following conditions:

1. It is composed of m large attributes $B_1, B_2, \ldots, B_m$, $1 \leq m \leq n$, where each large attribute $B_l = \{A_{l_1}, A_{l_2}, \ldots, A_{l_{k_l}}\}$ is a subset of attribute set: $\{A_1, \ldots, A_n\}$.
2. There is no overlap among the large attributes and their union forms the attributes set. That is, (1) $B_i \cap B_j = \phi$, for $i \neq j$, and $1 \leq i, j \leq m$; (2) $B_1 \cup B_2 \cup \ldots \cup B_m = \{A_1, A_2, \ldots, A_n\}$.
3. B_i is independent of B_j, for $i \neq j$, namely, $P(B_i, B_j) = P(B_i)P(B_j)$, for $i \neq j$, and $1 \leq i, j \leq m$.
4. The cardinality of each large attribute $B_l (1 \leq l \leq m)$ is not greater than K. If each large attribute has the same cardinality K, we call the B-SNB K-regular B-SNB.

Except for Item 4, the B-SNB model definition is the definition of the traditional SNB. We argue that this constraint on the cardinality is necessary. K cannot be set as a very large value, or the estimated probability for large attributes will be not reliable. When using B-SNB for classification tasks, we first partition the pre-classified dataset into some sub-datasets by the class label and then train different B-SNB structures for different classes. From this viewpoint, Item 3 is actually a conditional independence formulation, when given the class variable, since this independency is assumed in the sub-database with a uniform class label.

2.1 Learning the Optimal B-SNB from Data

In general, the optimal B-SNB estimated from a dataset D can be achieved in two steps. The first step is to learn an optimal B-SNB structure from D; the second step is to learn the optimal parameters for this optimal structure, where B-SNB parameters are those probabilities of each large attribute, i.e., $P(B_j)$. It is easy to show that the sample frequency of a large attribute B_j is the maximum-likelihood estimator for the probability $P(B_j)$, when a specific B-SNB structure is given (See the Appendix for the proof of Lemma 1). Thus the key problem in learning the optimal B-SNB is the structure learning problem, namely how to find the best m large attributes.

However the combination number for m large attributes in an n-dimension dataset will be $\sum_{\{k_1, k_2, \ldots, k_n\} \in G} C_n^{k_1} C_{n-k_1}^{k_2} \ldots C_{n-\sum_{i=1}^{n-1} k_i}^{k_n}$, $G = \{\{k_1, k_2, \ldots, k_n\} : \sum_{i=1}^{n} k_i = n, 0 \leq k_i \leq K\}$. Such a large searching space for an optimal B-SNB will make it nearly impossible to employ greedy methods especially when K is set to some small values. To solve this problem, we firstly develop the following two lemmas.

Lemma 1. *The maximum log likelihood of a specific B-SNB S for a dataset D, represented by l_S, can be written into the following form $l_S = -\sum_{i=1}^{m} \hat{H}(B_i)$, where $\hat{H}(B_i)$ is the entropy of large attribute B_i based on the empirical distribution of D.*

Lemma 2. *Let μ and μ' be two B-SNBs over dataset D. If μ' is coarser than μ, then μ' provides a better approximation than μ over D.*

The *coarser* concept is defined in this way: If μ' can be obtained by combining the large attributes of μ without splitting the large attribute of μ, then μ' is coarser than μ.

The details of the proof of Lemma 1 and Lemma 2 can be seen in Appendix.

According to Lemma 2, within a reasonable K bound, a higher "order" approximation will be superior to a lower "order" one. For example, it is more accurate using $P(a,b,c)P(d,e,f)$ to approximate $P(a,b,c,d,e,f)$ than using $P(a,b)P(c)P(d,e,f)$ when each subitem probability can be estimated reliably. In a K-B-SNB, K is the possible highest order for any large attributes. Thus we should use as many K-large attributes as possible in constructing B-SNB. Under this consideration, we fix all the large attributes to K large-attributes. On one hand, searching K-regular B-SNBs can reduce the combination number of large attributes to $\frac{n!}{(K!)^{\lceil n/K \rceil}}$. On the other hand, this constraint enables us to transform the optimization into an integer programming (IP) problem easily. Further we can approximate the IP solution via linear programming techniques, which can be solved in a polynomial time cost.

2.2 Transforming into Integer Programming Problem

We first describe our B-SNB optimization problem under Maximum Likelihood Estimation criterion when the cardinality of each large attribute is constrained to be exactly bound K.

B-SNB Optimization Problem: From the attributes set, find $m = \lceil n/K \rceil$ K-cardinality subsets, which satisfy the B-SNB conditions, to maximize the log likelihood $l_S = -\sum_{i=1}^{m} \hat{H}(B_i)$.

We write this B-SNB optimization problem into the following IP problem:

$$\text{Min} \sum_{V_1, V_2, \ldots, V_K} x_{V_1, V_2, \ldots, V_K} \hat{H}(V_1, V_2, \ldots, V_K), \quad \text{where,}$$

$$(\forall V_K) \sum_{V_1, V_2, \ldots, V_{K-1}} x_{V_1, V_2, \ldots, V_K} = 1, \quad x_{V_1, V_2, \ldots, V_K} \in \{0, 1\} \quad (1)$$

Here $V_1, V_2, \ldots, V_k$ represent any K attributes. Equation (1) describes that for any attribute, it can just belong to one large attribute, i.e., when it occurs in one large attribute, it must not be in another large attribute, since there is no overlapping among the large attributes.

We approximate the solution of IP via Linear Programming (LP) method, which can be solved in a polynomial time. By relaxing $x_{V_1, V_2, \ldots, V_K} \in \{0, 1\}$ into $0 \leq x_{V_1, V_2, \ldots, V_K} \leq 1$, the IP problem is transformed into an LP problem. Then a rounding procedure to get the integer solution is conducted on the solution of LP. It should be addressed that direct solving for IP problem is infeasible. It is reported that IP problems with as few as 40 variables can be beyond the abilities of even the most sophisticated computers.

Approximating IP solution by LP may reduce the accuracy of the SNB while it can decrease the computational cost to a polynomial one. Furthermore, shown in our experiments, this approximation achieves a satisfactory prediction accuracy.

3 The Mixture of Bounded Semi-naive Bayesian Network

In this section, we first define the Mixture of Bounded Semi-Naive Bayesian network (MBSNB) model, then we give the optimization problem of the MBSNB model. Finally we conduct theoretical induction to provide the optimization algorithm for this problem under the EM [7] framework.

Definition 2. *Mixture of Bounded Semi-Naive Bayesian network model is defined as a distribution of the form: $Q(x) = \sum_{k=1}^{r} \lambda_k S^k(x)$, where $\lambda_k \geq 0$, $k = 1, \ldots, r$, $\sum_{k=1}^{r} \lambda_k = 1$, r is the number of components in the mixture structure. S^k represents the distribution of the kth component K Bounded Semi-Naive network. λ_k can be called component coefficient.*

Optimization Problem of MBSNB: *Given a set of N independent observations $D = \{x^1, x^2, \ldots, x^N\}$ and a bound K, find the mixture of K-Bounded-SNB model Q, which satisfies $Q = \arg\max_{Q'} \sum_{i=1}^{N} \log Q'(x^i)$.*

We use a modified derivation process as [9] to find the solution of the above optimization problem. According to the EM algorithm, finding the optimal model Q of the above is equal to maximizing the following complete log-likelihood function:

$$l_c(x^{1,\ldots,N}, z^{1,\ldots,N}|Q) = \sum_{i=1}^{N} \log \prod_{k=1}^{r} (\lambda_k S^k(x^i))^{\delta_{k,z^i}}$$

$$= \sum_{i=1}^{N} \sum_{k=1}^{r} \delta_{k,z^i} (\log \lambda_k + \log S^k(x^i)) \quad (2)$$

where z is the choice variable which can be seen as the hidden variable to determine the choice of the component Semi-Naive structure; δ_{k,z^i} is equal to 1 when z^i is equal to the kth value of choice variable and 0 otherwise. We utilize the EM algorithm to find the solution of above log-likelihood formulation. First taking the expectation with respect to z, we will obtain

$$E[l_c(x^{1,\ldots,N}, z^{1,\ldots,N}|Q)] = \sum_{i=1}^{N} \sum_{k=1}^{r} E(\delta_{k,z^i}|D)(\log \lambda_k + \log S^k(x^i)), \quad (3)$$

where $E(\delta_{k,z^i}|D)$ is actually the posterior probability given the ith observation, which can be calculated as: $E(\delta_{k,z^i}|D) = P(z^i|V = x^i) = \frac{\lambda_k S^k(x^i)}{\sum_{k'} \lambda_{k'} S^{k'}(x^i)}$. We define $\gamma_k(i) = E(\delta_{k,z^i}|D)$, $\Gamma_k = \sum_{i=1}^{N} \gamma_k(i)$, $P^k(x^i) = \frac{\gamma_k(i)}{\Gamma_k}$. Thus we obtain the expectation:

$$E[l_c(x^{1,\ldots,N}, z^{1,\ldots,N}|Q)] = \sum_{k=1}^{r} \Gamma_k \log \lambda_k + \sum_{k=1}^{r} \Gamma_k \sum_{i=1}^{N} P^k(x^i) \log S^k(x^i). \quad (4)$$

Then we perform the Maximization step in Equation (4) with respect to the parameters. It is easy to maximize the first part of Equation (4) by Lagrange method with the constraint $\sum_{k=1}^{r} \lambda_k = 1$. We can obtain: $\lambda_k = \frac{\Gamma_k}{N}, k = 1, \ldots, r$.

Table 1. Description of data sets used in the experiments

Dataset	♯Variables	♯Class	♯Train	♯Test
Xor	6	2	2000	CV-5
Vote	15	2	435	CV-5
Tic-tac-toe	9	2	958	CV-5
Segment	19	7	2310	30%

If we consider $P^k(x^i)$ as the probability for each observation over the kth component B-SNB, the latter part of Equation (4) is in fact a B-SNB network optimization problem, which can be solved by our earlier proposed algorithm in Section 2.

4 Experiments

To evaluate the performance of our B-SNB and MBSNB models, we conduct a series of experiments on four databases, among which three come from the UCI Machine learning Repository [10] and the other one dataset called Xor is generated synthetically. In Xor, the class variable C is the result of xor operation between the first two binary attributes and other four binary attributes are created randomly. Table 1 is the detailed information for these four datasets. We use the 5-fold Cross Validation (CV) method [5] to perform testing on these datasets. We train a MBSNB model Q_{C_i} for each class C_i of every dataset. And we use the Bayes formula: $c(x) = \arg\max_{C_i} P(C_i) Q_{C_i}(x)$ to classify a new instance x. We compare B-SNB, MNSNB models with NB, Chow-Liu tree (CLT) algorithm and C4.5 (CLT is a kind of competitive Bayesian classifier [2]). We set the bound K for B-SNB and MBSNB as 2 and 3 to examine their performances. Table 2 summarizes the prediction results of the main approaches in this paper. 2(3)-B-SNB and 2(3)-MBSNB means K is set as 2(3). It is observed that B-SNB can improve the NB's performance. Moreover B-SNB performance can be further improved with the mixture upgrading. Since,B-SNB can be considered as the special case of MBSNB, with mixture number equal to 1. We take the highest accuracy rate as the one of MBSNB from the 2(3)-B-SNB and 2(3)-MBSNB. This result is shown as MBSNB* in the last column of Table 2. We can observe that this column almost demonstrates the best overall performance in comparison with NB, CLT and C4.5.

Table 2. Prediction Accuracy of the Primary Approaches in this paper(%)

Dataset	NB	CLT	C4.5	2-B-SNB	3-B-SNB	2-MBSNB	3-MBSNB	MBSNB*
Xor	54.50	**100**	**100**	100	99.50	99.50	99.50	**100**
Tic-tac-toe	70.77	73.17	84.84	72.65	78.39	88.33	79.38	**88.33**
Vote	90.11	91.26	**94.18**	92.40	92.64	93.10	94.00	94.00
Segment	88.29	91.33	90.61	91.90	89.16	91.47	90.90	**91.90**

5 Conclusion

In this paper, we propose a Bounded Semi-Naive Bayesian network based on direct combinatorial optimization. Different with the traditional SNBs, this model can combine any number of attributes within a given bound and maintain a polynomial time cost at the same time. Furthermore, we upgrade it into a finite mixture model. We designed a serious of experiments to demonstrate our model's advantages. The results show that this mixture model brings in an increase in prediction accuracy.

Acknowledgement. The work described in this paper was fully supported by grants from the Research Grants Council of the Hong Kong Special Administrative Region, China (Project No. CUHK4351/02E and Project No. CUHK4360/02E).

References

1. D. M. Chickering. Learning bayesian networks is NP-complete. In D. Fisher and H.-J. Lenz, editors, *Learning from Data*. Springer-Verlag, 1995.
2. C. K. Chow and C. N. Liu. Approximating discrete probability distributions with dependence trees. *IEEE Trans. on Information Theory*, 14:462–467, 1968.
3. Pedro Domingos and Pazzani Michael. On the optimality of the simple baysian classifier under zero-one loss. *Machine Learning*, 29:103–130, 1997.
4. N. Friedman, D. Geiger, and M. Goldszmidt. Bayesian network classifiers. *Machine Learning*, 29:131–161, 1997.
5. R. Kohavi. A study of cross validation and bootstrap for accuracy estimation and model selection. In *Proceedings of the 14th IJCAI*, pages 338–345. San Francisco, CA:Morgan Kaufmann, 1995.
6. I. Kononenko. Semi-naive bayesian classifier. In *Proceedings of sixth European Working Session on Learning*, pages 206–219. Springer-Verlag, 1991.
7. N. M. Laird, A. P. Dempster, and D.B. Rubin. Maximum likelihood from incomplete data via the EM algorithm. *J. Royal Statist. Society*, B39:1–38, 1977.
8. P. Langley, W. Iba, and K. Thompson. An analysis of bayesian classifiers. *In Proceedings of AAAI-92*, pages 223–228, 1992.
9. M. Meila and M. Jordan. Learning with mixtures of trees. *Journal of Machine Learning Research*, 1:1–48, 2000.
10. Patrick M. Murphy. UCI repository of machine learning databases. In *School of Information and Computer Science, University of California, Irvine*, 2003.

11. M. J. Pazzani. Searching dependency in bayesian classifiers. In D. Fisher and H.-J. Lenz, editors, *Learning from data: Artificial intelligence and statistics V*, pages 239–248. New York, NY:Springer-Verlag, 1996.
12. J. Pearl. *Probabilistic Reasoning in Intelligent Systems: networks of plausible inference*. Morgan Kaufmann, CA, 1988.
13. J. R. Quinlan. *C4.5 : programs for machine learning*. San Mateo, California: Morgan Kaufmann Publishers, 1993.

6 Appendix

Proof for Lemma 1:
Let S is a specific B-SNB with n variables or attributes which are represented respectively by A_i, $1 \leq i \leq n$. And this B-SNB's large attributes are represented by B_i, $1 \leq i \leq m$. We use $(B_1, \ldots, B_m)$ as the short form of $(B_1, B_2, \ldots, B_m)$. The log likelihood over a data set can be written into the following:

$$l_S(x^1, x^2, \ldots, x^s) = \sum_{j=1}^{s} \log P(x^j)$$

$$= \sum_{j=1}^{s} \log(\prod_{i=1}^{m} P(B_i)) = \sum_{i=1}^{m} \sum_{j=1}^{s} \log P(B_i) = \sum_{i=1}^{m} \sum_{B_i} \hat{P}(B_i) \log P(B_i)$$

The above term will be maximized when $P(B_i)$ is estimated by $\hat{P}(B_i)$, the empirical probability for large attribute B_i. This can be easily obtained by maximizing l_S with respect to $P(B_i)$. Thus,

$$l_{S max} = \sum_{i=1}^{m} \sum_{B_i} \hat{P}(B_i) \log \hat{P}(B_i) = -\sum_{i=1}^{m} \hat{H}(B_i)$$

Proof for Lemma 2:
We just consider a simple case, the proof for the general case is much similar. Consider one partition as $\mu = (B_1, B_2, \ldots, B_m)$ and another partition as

$$\mu_1 = (B_1, B_2, \ldots, B_{m-1}, B_{m1}, B_{m2}), \quad \text{where}$$
$$B_{m1} \cap B_{m2} = \phi \quad \text{and} \quad B_{m1} \cup B_{m2} = B_m$$

According to the proof of Lemma 1 above, we have:

$$l_{S_\mu max} = \sum_{i=1}^{m} \hat{H}(B_i) = -\sum_{i=1}^{m-1} \hat{H}(B_i) - \hat{H}(B_m) \qquad (5)$$

According to Entropy theory, $\hat{H}(XY) \leq \hat{H}(X) + \hat{H}(Y)$. We can write Eq. (5) into:

$$l_{S_\mu max} = -\sum_{i=1}^{m-1} \hat{H}(B_i) - \hat{H}(B_m) \geq -\sum_{i=1}^{m-1} \hat{H}(B_i) - \hat{H}(B_{m1}) - \hat{H}(B_{m2})$$

$$= l_{S_{\mu_1} max} \qquad (6)$$

System Identification Based on Online Variational Bayes Method and Its Application to Reinforcement Learning

Junichiro Yoshimoto[1,2], Shin Ishii[2,1], and Masa-aki Sato[3,1]

[1] CREST, Japan Science and Technology Corporation
[2] Nara Institute of Science and Technology
8916-5 Takayama, Ikoma, Nara 630-0192, Japan
{juniti-y, ishii}@is.aist-nara.ac.jp
[3] ATR Human Information Science Laboratories
2-2-2 Hikaridai, Seika, Soraku, Kyoto 619-0237, Japan
masa-aki@atr.co.jp

Abstract. In this article, we present an on-line variational Bayes (VB) method for the identification of linear state space models. The learning algorithm is implemented as alternate maximization of an on-line free energy, which can be used for determining the dimension of the internal state. We also propose a reinforcement learning (RL) method using this system identification method. Our RL method is applied to a simple automatic control problem. The result shows that our method is able to determine correctly the dimension of the internal state and to acquire a good control, even in a partially observable environment.

1 Introduction

A state space model provides a fundamental tool for system identification and control. If state transition and observation are defined by linear systems disturbed by white Gaussian noises, the state space model is formulated as a Gaussian process with internal (hidden) state. This means that the probabilistic generative model belongs to the exponential family with hidden variables and its system parameters can be determined by the expectation-maximization (EM) algorithm [2,6], within the maximum likelihood (ML) estimation.

According to the ML estimation, however, it is difficult to estimate the dimension of the internal state. A Bayesian approach can overcome the difficulty; the marginal likelihood provides the evidence of a model structure [3]. Although actual implementation of Bayes inference is often difficult, the variational Bayes (VB) method [1,4] provides an efficient approximation algorithm as a natural extension of the EM algorithm.

In this article, we present an on-line VB method for the identification of linear state space models with unknown internal dimension. The learning method is implemented as alternate maximization of an on-line free energy [7], which can be used for determining the dimension of the internal state. Using this system identification method, we also propose a belief state reinforcement learning (RL) method. Our RL method is applied to a simple automatic control problem. The result shows that our method is able to estimate correctly the dimension of the internal state and system parameters, and to acquire a good control, even in a partially observable environment.

2   Probabilistic Model for Linear State Space Model

We consider a stationary linear state space model defined by

$$x_{t+1} = Ax_t + Bu_t + v_t; \quad y_t = Cx_t + w_t, \qquad (1)$$

where $x_t \in \Re^N$ is an internal state. $y_t \in \Re^D$ and $u_t \in \Re^M$ denote an observable variable and a control variable, respectively. Suffix t indexes the discrete time. $A \in \Re^{N \times N}$, $B \in \Re^{N \times M}$ and $C \in \Re^{D \times N}$ are system parameters. $v_t \sim \mathcal{N}_N(v_t|0, Q)$ and $w_t \sim \mathcal{N}_D(w_t|0, R)$ are white Gaussian noises[1].

According to equation (1), the likelihood for a sequence of internal states and observation variables $(X_{1:T}, Y_{1:T}) \equiv \{(x_t, y_t) | t = 1, \cdots, T\}$, under a given sequence of control variables $U_{1:T-1} \equiv \{u_t | t = 1, \cdots, T-1\}$, is given by

$$p(X_{1:T}, Y_{1:T} | U_{1:T-1}, \theta) = \prod_{t=1}^{T} p(x_t | \tilde{x}_{t-1}, \theta) p(y_t | x_t, \theta) \qquad (2)$$

$$p(x_t | \tilde{x}_{t-1}, \theta) = \begin{cases} \mathcal{N}_N(x_1 | \mu, S) & \text{(if } t = 1\text{)} \\ \mathcal{N}_N\left(x_t \middle| \tilde{A}\tilde{x}_{t-1}, Q\right) & \text{(otherwise)} \end{cases}$$

$$p(y_t | x_t, \theta) = \mathcal{N}_D(y_t | Cx_t, R),$$

where $\tilde{A} \equiv (A, B)$ and $\tilde{x}_t \equiv (x'_t, u'_t)'$. A prime ($'$) denotes a transpose. μ and S are a mean vector and a precision matrix for the initial state, respectively. $\theta \equiv \{\mu, S, \tilde{A}, Q, C, R\}$ is the set of model parameters. For simplicity, $S \equiv diag(s_1, \cdots, s_N)$ $Q \equiv diag(q_1, \cdots, q_N)$ and $R \equiv diag(r_1, \cdots, r_D)$ are assumed.

We assume that the prior distribution of the model parameter θ is given by

$$p(\theta | \xi) = p(\mu, S | \sigma) p(\tilde{A}, Q | \Phi, \chi) p(C, R | \Psi, \rho) \qquad (3)$$

$$p(\mu, S | \sigma) = \mathcal{N}_N(\mu | 0, \gamma_{\mu 0} S) \prod_{n=1}^{N} \mathcal{G}(s_n | \gamma_{s0}/2, \gamma_{s0}\sigma/2)$$

$$p(\tilde{A}, Q | \Phi, \chi) = \prod_{n=1}^{N} \mathcal{N}_{\tilde{N}}(\tilde{a}_n | 0, \gamma_{a0} q_n \Phi) \mathcal{G}(q_n | \gamma_{q0}/2, \gamma_{q0}\chi/2)$$

$$p(C, R | \Psi, \rho) = \prod_{n=1}^{D} \mathcal{N}_N(c_n | 0, \gamma_{c0} r_n \Psi) \mathcal{G}(r_n | \gamma_{r0}/2, \gamma_{r0}\rho/2),$$

---
[1] $\mathcal{N}_p(x | \mu, S) \equiv (2\pi)^{-p/2} |S|^{-1/2} \exp\left[-\frac{1}{2}(x-\mu)'S(x-\mu)\right]$ denotes the probability density function of the random variable x, which is a p-dimensional normal distribution with a mean vector μ and an precision (inverse covariance) matrix S.

where $\tilde{N} \equiv N+M$, $\tilde{A} \equiv (\tilde{a}_1, \cdots, \tilde{a}_N)'$, $\tilde{a}_n \in \Re^{\tilde{N}}$, $C \equiv (c_1, \cdots, c_D)'$ and $c_n \in \Re^N$. $\mathcal{G}(x|\alpha, \beta)$ denotes the probability density function of the random variable x, which is a gamma distribution with parameters α and β^2. $\xi \equiv \{\sigma, \chi, \rho, \Phi \equiv diag(\phi_1, \cdots, \phi_{\tilde{N}}), \Psi \equiv diag(\psi_1, \cdots, \psi_N)\}$ is the set of variable hyper parameters that parameterize the prior distribution of the model parameter θ.

We also assume a hierarchical prior distribution for the hyper parameter ξ:

$$p(\xi) \equiv p(\sigma)p(\chi)p(\rho)p(\Phi)p(\Psi); \quad p(\sigma) = \mathcal{G}\left(\sigma|\gamma_{\sigma 0}/2, \gamma_{\sigma 0}\tau_{\sigma 0}^{-1}/2\right)$$

$$p(\chi) = \mathcal{G}\left(\chi|\gamma_{\chi 0}/2, \gamma_{\chi 0}\tau_{\chi 0}^{-1}/2\right); \quad p(\rho) = \mathcal{G}\left(\rho|\gamma_{\rho 0}/2, \gamma_{\rho 0}\tau_{\rho 0}^{-1}/2\right)$$

$$p(\Phi) = \prod_{n=1}^{\tilde{N}} \mathcal{G}\left(\phi_n|\gamma_{\phi 0}/2, \gamma_{\phi 0}\tau_{\phi 0}^{-1}/2\right); \quad p(\Psi) = \prod_{n=1}^{N} \mathcal{G}\left(\psi_n|\gamma_{\psi 0}/2, \gamma_{\psi 0}\tau_{\psi 0}^{-1}/2\right).$$

In the above prior distribution, all hyper parameters with suffix '0' are constant.

3 Online Variational Bayes Method

After observing $Y_{1:T}$ by giving $U_{1:T-1}$, the objective of Bayes inference is to obtain the posterior distribution of the unknown variables, $p(X_{1:T}, \theta, \xi|Y_{1:T}, U_{1:T-1})$. According to the Bayes theorem, the posterior distribution is given by

$$p(X_{1:T}, \theta, \xi|Y_{1:T}, U_{1:T-1}) = p(X_{1:T}, Y_{1:T}|U_{1:T-1}, \theta)p(\theta|\xi)p(\xi)/p(Y_{1:T}|U_{1:T-1}).$$

The normalization term $p(Y_{1:T}|U_{1:T-1})^3$ is called the marginal likelihood, which provides the evidence of the model structure[4] [3].

Due to the hierarchical prior distribution, exact calculation of the posterior distribution and the marginal likelihood is difficult; we use an approximation method. In the variational Bayes (VB) method [1], the posterior distribution is approximated by a tractable trial distribution $q(X_{1:T}, \theta, \xi)$. This approximation is executed by maximizing the free energy:

$$F[q] = \log p(Y_{1:T}|U_{1:T-1}) - \mathrm{KL}\left(q(X_{1:T}, \theta, \xi) \| p(X_{1:T}, \theta, \xi|Y_{1:T}, U_{1:T-1})\right). \quad (4)$$

$\mathrm{KL}(\cdot \| \cdot)$ denotes the Kullback-Leibler divergence between two distributions, which becomes minimum at zero when $q(X_{1:T}, \theta, \xi) = p(X_{1:T}, \theta, \xi|Y_{1:T}, U_{1:T-1})$. After the maximization of the free energy, therefore, the trial distribution provides a good approximation for the true posterior distribution. Also, the free energy well approximates the (log) marginal likelihood.

The trial distribution is assumed to be factorized as

$$q(X_{1:T}, \theta, \xi) = q_x(X_{1:T})q_\theta(\theta)q_\xi(\xi), \quad q_x(X_{1:T}) = \prod_{t=1}^{T} q_t(x_t|x_{t-1}),$$

where $q_1(x_1|x_0) \equiv q_1(x_1)$. In this case, the free energy (4) can be rewritten as

---
[2] $\mathcal{G}(x|\alpha, \beta) \equiv \beta^\alpha x^{\alpha-1} e^{-\beta x}/\Gamma(\alpha)$ and $\Gamma(\alpha) \equiv \int_0^\infty t^{\alpha-1} e^{-t} dt$.
[3] $p(Y_{1:T}|U_{1:T-1}) \equiv \int d\theta d\xi dX_{1:T} p(X_{1:T}, Y_{1:T}|U_{1:T-1}, \theta)p(\theta|\xi)p(\xi)$.
[4] Here, the model structure corresponds to the dimension of the internal state, N.

$$F[q] = TL - H^\theta - H^\xi; \quad L = \frac{1}{T}\sum_{t=1}^{T}\left\langle\left\langle \log \frac{p(x_t|\tilde{x}_{t-1},\theta)p(y_t|x_t,\theta)}{q_t(x_t|x_{t-1})}\right\rangle_\theta\right\rangle_x \quad (5)$$

$$H^\theta = \left\langle \log \frac{q(\theta)}{\langle p(\theta|\xi)\rangle_\xi}\right\rangle_\theta ; \quad H^\xi = \left\langle \log \frac{q(\xi)}{p(\xi)}\right\rangle_\xi ,$$

where $\langle f(X_{1:T})\rangle_x = \int dX_{1:T} q_x(X_{1:T}) f(X_{1:T})$, $\langle f(\theta)\rangle_\theta = \int d\theta q_\theta(\theta) f(\theta)$ and $\langle f(\xi)\rangle_\xi = \int d\xi q_\xi(\xi) f(\xi)$. L corresponds to the expected mean log-likelihood. According to a batch VB algorithm [4], the free energy (5) is maximized with respect to q_x, q_θ, and q_ξ, alternately, after observing all times series. Here, we derive an on-line VB algorithm [7], in which the free energy at time τ is redefined by

$$F_\tau^\lambda[q] = T_0 L_\tau^\lambda - H^\theta - H^\xi \quad (6)$$

$$L_\tau^\lambda = \eta(\tau) \sum_{t=1}^{\tau}\left(\prod_{s=t+1}^{\tau}\lambda(s)\right)\left\langle\left\langle \log \frac{p(x_t|\tilde{x}_{t-1},\theta)p(y_t|x_t,\theta)}{q_t(x_t|x_{t-1})}\right\rangle_\theta\right\rangle_x .$$

$\eta(\tau) = \left(\sum_{t=1}^{\tau}\prod_{s=t+1}^{\tau}\lambda(s)\right)^{-1}$ is a normalization term, and T_0 is a constant corresponding to the confidence of the observed time series relative to *a priori* belief of the model parameter. $\lambda(s)$ ($0 < \lambda(s) < 1$) is a time-dependent discount factor for forgetting the effect of early inaccurate inference. By introducing the discount factor, the expected mean log-likelihood is modified into a weighted mean log-likelihood.

The on-line VB algorithm can be implemented as an alternate maximization process of the on-line free energy (6). We here consider the inference at time τ, where $q_{1:\tau-1} \equiv \{q_t|t=1,\cdots,\tau-1\}$, q_θ and q_ξ has been determined from previously observed time series $Y_{1:\tau-1}$. After observing a new output y_τ, the on-line free energy is maximized with respect to q_τ while $q_{1:\tau-1}$, q_θ and q_ξ are fixed. This is the VB-Estep. In the next step, the VB-Mstep, the on-line free energy (6) is maximized with respect to q_θ while $q_{1:\tau}$ and q_ξ are fixed. In the last step, the VB-Hstep, the on-line free energy is maximized with respect to q_ξ while $q_{1:\tau}$ and q_θ are fixed. Although detailed procedure cannot be described for the lack of space, the main part is as follows.

1. VB-Estep

$$\bar{x}_\tau \leftarrow \begin{cases} \langle\mu\rangle_\theta & \text{if } \tau = 1 \\ \langle A\rangle_\theta \hat{x}_{\tau-1} + \langle B\rangle_\theta u_{\tau-1} & \text{otherwise} \end{cases}$$

$$\bar{V}_\tau \leftarrow \begin{cases} \langle S\rangle_\theta^{-1} & \text{if } \tau = 1 \\ \langle Q\rangle_\theta^{-1} + \langle A\rangle_\theta \hat{V}_{\tau-1} \langle A'\rangle_\theta & \text{otherwise} \end{cases}$$

$$K \leftarrow \bar{V}_\tau \langle C'\rangle_\theta \left(\langle R\rangle_\theta^{-1} + \langle C\rangle_\theta \bar{V}_\tau \langle C'\rangle_\theta\right)^{-1}$$

$$\hat{x}_\tau \leftarrow \bar{x}_\tau + K(y_\tau - \langle C\rangle_\theta \bar{x}_\tau); \quad \hat{V}_\tau \leftarrow (I - K\langle C\rangle_\theta)\bar{V}_\tau \quad (7)$$

$$J \leftarrow \hat{V}_{\tau-1}\langle A'\rangle_\theta \bar{V}_\tau^{-1} \quad (8)$$

$$\hat{x}_{\tau-1} \leftarrow \hat{x}_{\tau-1} + J(\hat{x}_\tau - \bar{x}_\tau); \quad \hat{V}_{\tau-1} \leftarrow \hat{V}_{\tau-1} + J(\hat{V}_\tau - \bar{V}_\tau)J' \quad (9)$$

$$\langle\!\langle y_t y_t'\rangle\!\rangle \leftarrow (1-\eta(\tau))\langle\!\langle y_t y_t'\rangle\!\rangle + \eta(\tau) y_\tau y_\tau'$$

$$\langle\!\langle y_t x_t'\rangle\!\rangle \leftarrow (1-\eta(\tau))\langle\!\langle y_t x_t'\rangle\!\rangle + \eta(\tau) y_\tau \hat{x}_\tau'$$

$$\langle\!\langle x_t x_t'\rangle\!\rangle \leftarrow (1-\eta(\tau))\langle\!\langle x_t x_t'\rangle\!\rangle + \eta(\tau)\left(\hat{V}_\tau + \hat{x}_\tau \hat{x}_\tau'\right)$$

$$\langle\!\langle \tilde{x}_{t-1} \tilde{x}_{t-1}'\rangle\!\rangle \leftarrow (1-\eta(\tau))\langle\!\langle \tilde{x}_{t-1} \tilde{x}_{t-1}'\rangle\!\rangle$$

$$+\eta(\tau)\begin{pmatrix} \hat{V}_{\tau-1} + \hat{x}_{\tau-1}\hat{x}_{\tau-1}' & \hat{x}_{\tau-1}u_{\tau-1}' \\ u_{\tau-1}\hat{x}_{\tau-1}' & u_{\tau-1}u_{\tau-1}' \end{pmatrix} \tag{10}$$

$$\langle\!\langle x_t \tilde{x}_{t-1}'\rangle\!\rangle \leftarrow (1-\eta(\tau))\langle\!\langle x_t \tilde{x}_{t-1}'\rangle\!\rangle + \eta(\tau)\begin{pmatrix} \hat{V}_\tau J' + \hat{x}_\tau \hat{x}_{\tau-1}' \\ \hat{x}_\tau u_{\tau-1}' \end{pmatrix}. \tag{11}$$

Equations (8)-(11) are used if $\tau > 1$. I is an identity matrix and $\langle\!\langle \cdot \rangle\!\rangle$ is the weighted mean of sufficient statistics: $\langle\!\langle f(\cdot) \rangle\!\rangle \equiv \eta(\tau)\sum_{t=1}^\tau \left(\prod_{s=t+1}^\tau \lambda(s)\right) \times \int dX_{1:\tau} q_x(X_{1:\tau}) f(\cdot)$.

2. VB-Mstep

$$\Xi \leftarrow \left((T_0-1)\langle\!\langle \tilde{x}_{t-1}\tilde{x}_{t-1}'\rangle\!\rangle + \gamma_{a0}\langle\Phi\rangle_\xi\right)$$

$$\langle \tilde{A}\rangle_\theta \leftarrow \left((T_0-1)\langle\!\langle x_t \tilde{x}_{t-1}'\rangle\!\rangle\right)\Xi^{-1}$$

$$\langle Q\rangle_\theta^{-1} \leftarrow \frac{\mathrm{diag}\left((T_0-1)\langle\!\langle x_t x_t'\rangle\!\rangle - \langle\tilde{A}\rangle_\theta \Xi \langle\tilde{A}'\rangle_\theta + \gamma_{q0}\langle\chi\rangle_\xi\right)}{T_0-1+\gamma_{q0}}$$

$$\Upsilon \leftarrow \left(T_0\langle\!\langle x_t x_t'\rangle\!\rangle + \gamma_{c0}\langle\Psi\rangle_\xi\right); \quad \langle C\rangle_\theta \leftarrow \left(T_0\langle\!\langle y_t x_t'\rangle\!\rangle\right)\Upsilon^{-1}$$

$$\langle R\rangle_\theta^{-1} \leftarrow \frac{\mathrm{diag}\left(T_0\langle\!\langle y_t y_t'\rangle\!\rangle - \langle C\rangle_\theta \Upsilon \langle C'\rangle_\theta + \gamma_{r0}\langle\rho\rangle_\xi\right)}{T_0+\gamma_{r0}}$$

$$\langle \mu\rangle_\theta \leftarrow \hat{x}_1/(1+\gamma_{\mu 0})$$

$$\langle S\rangle_\theta^{-1} \leftarrow \frac{\mathrm{diag}\left(\hat{V}_1 + \hat{x}_1 \hat{x}_1' + \gamma_{s0}\langle\sigma\rangle_\xi - \gamma_{\mu 0}\langle\mu\rangle_\theta\langle\mu\rangle_\theta'\right)}{1+\gamma_{s0}}.$$

3. VB-Hstep

$$\langle\sigma\rangle_\xi \leftarrow \frac{N\gamma_{s0} + \gamma_{\sigma 0}}{\gamma_{s0}\,\mathrm{Tr}\,[\langle S\rangle_\theta] + \gamma_{\sigma 0}\tau_{\sigma 0}^{-1}}$$

$$\langle\Phi\rangle_\xi \leftarrow \left(\frac{\mathrm{diag}\left(\gamma_{a0}\langle\tilde{A}'\rangle_\theta\langle Q\rangle_\theta\langle\tilde{A}\rangle_\theta + N\Xi^{-1} + \gamma_{\phi 0}\tau_{\phi 0}^{-1}I\right)}{N+\gamma_{\phi 0}}\right)^{-1}$$

$$\langle\chi\rangle_\xi \leftarrow \frac{N\gamma_{q0} + \gamma_{\chi 0}}{\gamma_{q0}\,\mathrm{Tr}\,[\langle Q\rangle_\theta] + \gamma_{\chi 0}\tau_{\chi 0}^{-1}}; \quad \langle\rho\rangle_\xi \leftarrow \frac{D\gamma_{r0} + \gamma_{\rho 0}}{\gamma_{r0}\,\mathrm{Tr}\,[\langle R\rangle_\theta] + \gamma_{\rho 0}\tau_{\rho 0}^{-1}}.$$

$$\langle\Psi\rangle_\xi \leftarrow \left(\frac{\mathrm{diag}\left(\gamma_{c0}\langle C'\rangle_\theta\langle R\rangle_\theta\langle C\rangle_\theta + D\Upsilon^{-1} + \gamma_{\psi 0}\tau_{\psi 0}^{-1}I\right)}{D+\gamma_{\psi 0}}\right)^{-1}.$$

4 Belief State Reinforcement Learning

If the true system is consistent with model (1) and we observe the internal state x_τ at every time, we can acquire a good control by applying a reinforcement learning (RL) method, which is formulated as a continuous Markov decision process (MDP). In most of RL methods, mapping from x_τ to u_τ is determined based on rewards received through experiences. In our situation, however, only partial information of the internal state x_τ, i.e., y_τ, is observable. If we try to determine mapping from y_τ to u_τ, which is referred to as a partially observable MDP (POMDP), it is known that the performance is poor [8]. Instead of that, we may consider a control policy that maps a belief state $p(x_\tau | Y_{1:\tau}, U_{1:\tau-1})$ to u_τ. This formulation is a belief state MDP, in which the sequence $\{p(x_\tau | Y_{1:\tau}, U_{1:\tau-1}), u_\tau | \tau = 1, \cdots\}$ becomes a Markov process under a fixed control policy.

Under the formulation of the belief state MDP, our system identification method can be applied to automatic control problems. By applying equation (7) in the VB-Estep, we obtain the trial posterior distribution $q_x(x_\tau)$ as the normal distribution $\mathcal{N}_N \left(x_\tau \middle| \hat{x}_\tau, \hat{V}_\tau^{-1} \right)$, which approximates a current belief state $p(x_\tau | Y_{1:\tau}, U_{1:\tau-1})$. Therefore, the underlying POMDP is regarded as the MDP defined over state $\hat{s}_\tau \equiv (\hat{x}_\tau, \hat{V}_\tau)$ and control u_τ.

In order to solve the decision problem, we apply an actor-critic algorithm proposed by Konda [5]. Although it was derived for the general parameterized families of randomized stationary policies, we employ the following stochastic policy: $\pi_\vartheta(u_\tau | \hat{s}_\tau = \hat{s}) = \prod_{m=1}^{M} \mathcal{N}_1 \left(u_{\tau m} \middle| \sum_{k=1}^{K} \vartheta_{mk} \hat{s}_k, \vartheta_0 \right)$. Here, $u_{\tau m}$ is the m-th element of u_τ and $\hat{s}_k$ ($k = 1, \cdots, K$) is the k-th element of $\hat{s}$. $\vartheta \equiv \{\vartheta_0, \vartheta_{mk} | m = 1, \cdots, M; k = 1, \cdots, K\}$ is the set of parameters that parameterize the control policy π_ϑ. The way to update parameter ϑ is referred to [5].

In the above belief state MDP, the determination of the dimension of the internal state is an important issue because it directly determines the dimension of the belief state $\hat{s}$ and affects the performance. We determine it by the following procedure. We prepare several state space models, which have different dimensions with each other. An RL system is coupled with each state space model. At the beginning of each episode, an RL system corresponding to the model with the largest free energy is selected and trained using experiences in the episode. On the other hand, every state space model is trained using all time series. Figure 1 shows the architecture of our proposed method. Here, the arrow lines denote the stream of signals. The gray rectangle is a couple of the RL system and the state space model selected by maximum free energy criterion.

5 Experiment

Our RL method including the system identification is applied to an automatic control problem for a noisy linear system, which is defined by

$$\ddot{x} = 3u + v; \quad y = x + w; \quad v \sim \mathcal{N}_1(v | 0, 0.1); \quad w \sim \mathcal{N}_1(w | 0, 0.0009),$$

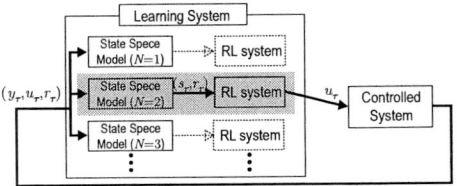

Fig. 1. Architecture of our RL method.

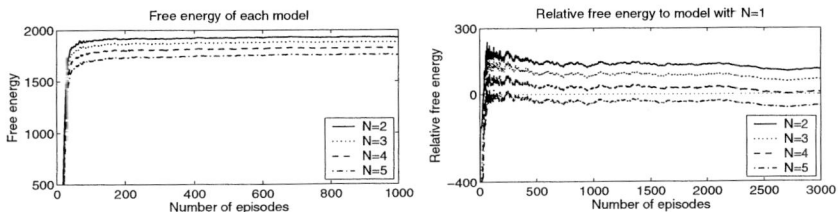

Fig. 2. Time courses of free energy by the five models.

where initial states of x and $\dot{x}$ in each episode are generated from a uniform distribution within ranges of $x \in [-10, 10]$ and $\dot{x} \in [-1, 1]$, respectively. The true dimension of the internal state is $N = 2$. Observation y is given with time interval 0.02 and a single episode consists of 1000 time steps. Control u is bounded within the range of $|u| \leq 1$. The reward function is defined by $r(x, \dot{x}, u) = -0.02x^2 - 0.1\dot{x}^2 - 0.001u^2$, which encourages the state to stay at the origin.

We prepared five state space models, whose dimensions varied from $N = 1$ to $N = 5$. Figure 2 shows the time courses of the free energy for the five state space models. The horizontal axis denotes the number of episodes. The vertical axes of left and right figures denote the absolute and relative free energies to the model structure with $N = 1$, respectively[5]. The free energy of every model structure increases as the learning proceeds. Although the simplest model ($N = 1$) is selected at an early learning stage, the correct model ($N = 2$) has the largest free energy value after 50 episodes. In a later learning stage, the difference between $N = 1$ and $N = 2$ comes to be small because the system is stabilized around the origin, but they were not reversed even if the learning continued. This result shows that our system identification method is able to determine correctly the dimension of the target system.

Figure 3 shows the learning curve of our RL method and a naive actor-critic method without using belief state. The solid and dotted lines denote the time courses of the average cumulative rewards per 20 episodes acquired by our method and the naive method, respectively. Figure 4 shows the test control sequence by our RL system after learning. The left and right figures show the time

---

[5] Although the left figure does not shows the result of $N = 1$, one can know its value easily by seeing the left and right figures.

series of observation y_t and control u_t, respectively. The control policy was gradually improved so that the system is sustained at the origin. This result shows our RL method coupled with the system identification by on-line VB algorithm is able to acquire a good control policy, while the underlying environment is an instance of POMDPs.

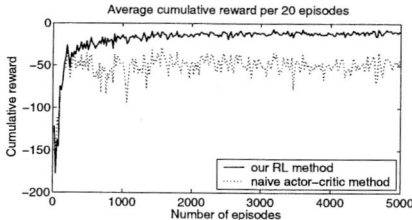

Fig. 3. Learning curve of our RL method and the naive actor-critic method.

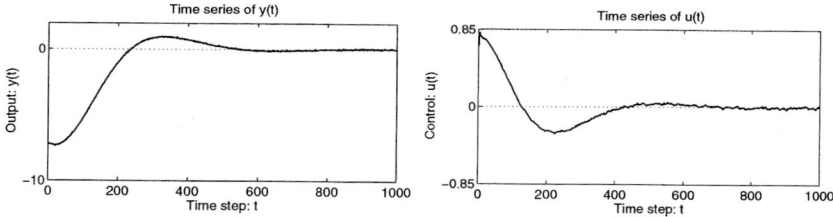

Fig. 4. A test control sequence by the trained system.

6 Conclusion

In this article, we presented an on-line VB algorithm for the identification of linear state space models. The method was able to estimate correctly system parameters, and the dimension of the internal state based on the free energy criterion. We also proposed an RL method using our system identification method, which can be applied to continuous POMDPs. We applied our RL method to a simple control problem. The result showed that our method was able to determine correctly the dimension of the internal state and to acquire a good control. Our near future work is to extend our system identification method to that for non-linear state space models.

Acknowledgement. We would like to thank Dr. Doya for his valuable comments on this research. This research was supported in part by the Telecommunications Advancement Organization of Japan.

References

1. Attias, H.: A variational Bayesian framework for graphical models, *Advances in Neural Information Processing Systems 12*, pp. 206–212 (2000).
2. Dempster, A. P. et al.: Maximum likelihood from incomplete data via the EM algorithm, *Journal of Royal Statistical Society B*, Vol. 39, pp. 1–38 (1977).
3. Früwirth-Schnatter, S.: Bayesian model descrimination and Bayes factors for linear Gaussian state space models, *Journal of Royal Statistical Society B*, Vol. 57, pp. 237–246 (1995).
4. Ghahramani, Z. and Beal, M. J.: Propagation Algorithms for Variational Bayesian Learning, *Advances in Neural Information Processing Systems 13* (2001).
5. Konda, V. R.: *Actor-Critic Algorithms*, PhD Thesis, Department of Electrical Engineering and Computer Science, Massachusetts Institute of Technology (2002).
6. Roweis, S. and Ghahramani, Z.: A Unifying Review of Linear Gaussian Models, *Neural Computation*, Vol. 11, pp. 305–345 (1999).
7. Sato, M.: Online model selection based on the variational Bayes, *Neural Computation*, Vol. 13, No. 7, pp. 1649–1681 (2001).
8. Singh, S. P. et al.: Learning without state-estimation in partially observable Markovian decision processes, *Proceedings of the 11th International Conference on Machine Learning*, pp. 284–292 (1994).

Dimension Reduction Based on Orthogonality – A Decorrelation Method in ICA

Kun Zhang and Lai-Wan Chan

Department of Computer Science and Engineering,
The Chinese University of Hongkong, Hongkong
{kzhang, lwchan}@cse.cuhk.edu.hk

Abstract. In independent component analysis problems, when we use a one-unit objective function to iteratively estimate several independent components, the uncorrelatedness between the independent components prevents them from converging to the same optimum. A simple and popular way of achieving decorrelation between recovered independent components is a deflation scheme based on a Gram-Schmidt-like decorrelation [7]. In this method, after each iteration in estimation of the current independent component, we subtract its 'projections' on previous obtained independent components from it and renormalize the result. Alternatively, we can use the constraints of uncorrelatedness between independent components to reduce the number of unknown parameters of the de-mixing matrix directly. In this paper, we propose to reduce the dimension of the de-mixing matrix to decorrelate different independent components. The advantage of this method is that the dimension reduction of the observations and de-mixing weight vectors makes the computation lower and produces a faster and efficient convergence.

1 Introduction

The objective of this paper is to propose a dimension reduction appoach to achieving decorrelation between independent components. In this section we review the decorrelation method currently used. In Sect. 2 we introduce our method in detail.

Let us denote by $X = (x_1, x_2, ..., x_m)^T$ a zero-mean m-dimensional variable, and $S = (s_1, s_2, ..., s_n)^T$, $n \leq m$, is its linear transform with a constant matrix W:

$$S = WX \qquad (1)$$

Given X as observations, based on different assumptions, principal component analysis (PCA) and independent component analysis (ICA) both aim to estimating W and S. The goal of PCA is to find a new variable S under the orthogonal constraint $W^T W = I$ (I is the unit matrix) such that S becomes uncorrelated in components and accounts for as much as possible of the variance of the variable X [10]. While in ICA, the transformed components s_i are not only uncorrelated with each other, but also statistically as independent of each other as possible [3].

O. Kaynak et al. (Eds.): ICANN/ICONIP 2003, LNCS 2714, pp. 132–139, 2003.
© Springer-Verlag Berlin Heidelberg 2003

Since generally there is no closed-form solution to ICA problems, an ICA algorithm consists of two parts: an objective function (contrast function) and an optimization method used to optimize the objective function [11]. The objective function measures the independence between independent sources with the help of mutual information between them [3], entropy (negentropy) of each independent source [3,6], or their higher-order cumulants [4,9], etc. A multi-unit contrast function treats the problem of estimating all the independent components (the whole data model) at the same time. Or motivated by projection pursuit, we can use a one-unit contrast function whose optimization enables estimation of a single independent component [8,11]. And this procedure can be iterated to find several independent components.

Higher-order cumulants like kurtosis, and approximations of negentropy can provide one-unit contrast functions. The contrast functions used in FastICA [9,5,7] are approximations of negentropy based on the maximum entropy principle [6]. These approximations are often more accurate than the cumulant-based approximations [3], and contrast functions based on approximations of negentropy are more robust than the kurtosis [8,5]. In the simplest case, these approximations are of the form:

$$J_G(y) = [E_y\{G(y)\} - E_v\{G(v)\}]^2 \qquad (2)$$

where G is a non-quadratic, sufficiently smooth function, v a standardized Gaussian random variable, y is zero-mean and normalized to unit variance. As for the optimization method, the convergence of adaptive algorithms based on stochastic gradient descent is often slow and depends crucially on the choice of the learning rate sequence. Batch algorithms based on fixed-point iteration can avoid this problem [9,5,7]. FastICA, a fixed-point algorithm for ICA, was firstly introduced using kurtosis in [9], and it was generalized for general contrast functions (Eq.2) in [5,7]. The following is the FastICA algorithm for whitened data:

$$w(k) = E\{Xg(w(k-1)^T X)\} - E\{g'(w(k-1)^T X)\}w(k-1) \qquad (3)$$

where w^T is a row of W and w is normalized to unit norm after each iteration, the function g is the derivative of the function G used in Eq.2. In this paper, FastICA will be used to extract an independent component from the observations.

In general 'independence' between two variables is a much stronger property than 'uncorrelatedness' between them. When we use a one-unit objective function to iteratively calculate several n independent components, in order to prevent different neurons from converging to the same optimum we must decorrelate the outputs. A simple and common way of achieving decorrelation is the deflation scheme based on Gram-Schmidt-like decorrelation [12,9,5,7]. For whitened data, after we have estimated p independent components, or p weight vectors $w_1, w_2, ..., w_p$, we run the one-unit algorithm to estimate w_{p+1}. In this procedure, after each update iteration step, we subtract from updated w_{p+1} its projections on the previous estimated p vectors, $w_{p+1}^T w_j w_j, j = 1, ..., p$, i.e. let

$$w_{p+1} = w_{p+1} - \sum_{j=1}^{p} w_{p+1}^T w_j w_j, \text{ and then renormalize } w_{p+1}:$$

$$w_{p+1} = w_{p+1}/\sqrt{w_{p+1}^T w_{p+1}}$$

2 Dimension Reduction Based on Orthogonality

In the ICA problem, let n and m be the number of independent components and observations respectively. Generally (but not necessarily), if $n < m$, we first use PCA to extract the n-dimensional 'principal' subspace from the m-dimensional observation space, and then obtain the n independent components in this subspace. So without loss of generality, we extract n independent components given n observations with a positive definite covariance matrix in the following analysis.

In both ICA and PCA, s_i must be mutually uncorrelated, i.e. $E(s_i s_j) = E(w_i^T X X^T w_j^T) = 0$, where $i, j = 1, 2, ..., n, i \neq j$. In PCA, the scaling of each basis vector w_i^T, which is a row of W, is of unit length, i.e. $w_i^T w_i = 1$. In ICA, we can fix the scaling of the independent components to avoid the inherent scaling indeterminacy. Generally we set the variance of s_i to be 1, i.e. $E[s_i^2] = 1$. Now we have $\frac{n(n-1)}{2} + n = \frac{n(n+1)}{2}$ equations for both PCA and ICA problems.

There are n^2 parameters to be determined, which are elements of W. Therefore the PCA or ICA problem can not be solved uniquely with only these restrictions. In PCA, the current PC accounts the maximum variance in current space; and in ICA, IC's should be independent of each other (or they should be as non-Gaussion as possible). These characteristics, together with the $\frac{n(n+1)}{2}$ equations discussed above help to solve the PCA and ICA problems respectively.

The uncorrelatedness between the independent components can help us to obtain multiple independent components with a one-unit objective function. After p independent components have been obtained, we search for the $(p+1)$-th independent component which is uncorrelated with the previous p ones. With the Gram-Schmidt-like decorrelation scheme and whitened data, in each iteration step of estimating w_{p+1} we search for updated w_{p+1} in the original n-dimensional parameter space, and afterwards project the new vector onto the space which is orthogonal to the obtained p weight vectors. Intuitively, since the contrast curve of the objective function may be very complex, this scheme may do harm to the convergence of w_{p+1} to a target in this subspace.

In fact, for whitened data, w_{p+1} lies in the $(n-p)$-dimensional parameter subspace which is orthogonal to the previous p de-mixing weight vectors. Alternatively, we can search w_{p+1} in this space directly, which always guarantees the orthogonality. And in addition, compared to the Gram-Schmidt-like deflation scheme, in this way parameters needed to be estimate become fewer because the parameter dimension used for search becomes lower. Therefore we can lower the computation, and obtain a faster convergence.

2.1 Algorithm

Let's decompose W into two parts:

$$W = \widetilde{W}^{(n)} P \tag{4}$$

where P is the whitening matrix, so that $E(PXX^TP^T) = I$. Since $\widetilde{W}^{(n)}\widetilde{W}^{(n)T} = \widetilde{W}^{(n)}E[PXX^TP^T]\widetilde{W}^{(n)T} = E(SS^T) = I$, $\widetilde{W}^{(n)}$ is an orthonormal matrix. Let $\tilde{w}_i^{(n)T}$ be a row of $\widetilde{W}^{(n)}$.[1] We know:

$$\sum_{k=1}^{n} \tilde{w}_i^{(n)}(k)\tilde{w}_j^{(n)}(k) = 0, i \neq j$$

There exists at least one q such that $\tilde{w}_1^{(n)}(q)$ is not zero, so we have

$$\tilde{w}_2^{(n)}(q) = -\frac{1}{\tilde{w}_1^{(n)}(q)} \sum_{\substack{k=1,\\k\neq q}}^{n} \tilde{w}_1^{(n)}(k)\tilde{w}_2^{(n)}(k), \text{ thus,}$$

$$\tilde{w}_2^{(n)} = \begin{pmatrix} \mathbf{I_{q-1}} & & \mathbf{0_{(q-1)\times(n-q)}} \\ -\frac{\tilde{w}_1^{(n)}(1)}{\tilde{w}_1^{(n)}(q)} \cdots -\frac{\tilde{w}_1^{(n)}(q-1)}{\tilde{w}_1^{(n)}(q)} & -\frac{\tilde{w}_1^{(n)}(q+1)}{\tilde{w}_1^{(n)}(q)} \cdots -\frac{\tilde{w}_1^{(n)}(n)}{\tilde{w}_1^{(n)}(q)} \\ \mathbf{0_{(n-q)\times(q-1)}} & & \mathbf{I_{n-q}} \end{pmatrix}_{n\times(n-1)}$$

$$\cdot \begin{pmatrix} \tilde{w}_2^{(n)}(1) \\ \vdots \\ \tilde{w}_2^{(n)}(q-1) \\ \tilde{w}_2^{(n)}(q+1) \\ \vdots \\ \tilde{w}_2^{(n)}(n) \end{pmatrix} \qquad (5)$$

$$\stackrel{def}{=} Aw_2^{(n-1)}$$

And $s_2 = \tilde{w}_2^{(n)T}PX = w_2^{(n-1)T}A^TPX = w_2^{(n-1)T}X'$, where $X' = A^TPX$. We can see that s_2 can be considered as an independent component of $(n-1)$-dimensional data X'. Let P_1 be the whitening matrix of X', we have $w_2^{(n-1)} = P_1^T\tilde{w}_2^{(n-1)}$, where $\tilde{w}_2^{(n-1)}$ is a de-mixing weight vector of the new data X' after whitening. Obviously the covariance matrix of X' is A^TA, Let $E = (e_1...e_{(n-1)})$ be the orthonormal matrix composed of eigenvectors of A^TA and $D = diag(d_1...d_{(n-1)})$ be the diagonal matrix of its eigenvalues. $P_1 = D^{-1/2}E^T$ is a whitening matrix of X'.

After the estimation of $(n-1)$-dimensional de-mixing weight vector $\tilde{w}_2^{(n-1)}$ given X' as observations with the chosen one-unit contrast function, we can construct $\tilde{w}_2^{(n)}$ and w_2 by Eq.5 and Eq.4, i.e. $\tilde{w}_2^{(n)} = Aw_2^{(n-1)} = AP_1^T\tilde{w}_2^{(n-1)}$, $w_2 = P^T\tilde{w}_2^{(n-1)} = P^T \cdot AP_1^T\tilde{w}_2^{(n-1)}$.

We also have $\tilde{w}_3^{(n)} = Aw_3^{(n-1)}$, and $w_3^{(n-1)} = P_1^T\tilde{w}_3^{(n-1)}$. Since $w_2^{(n-1)}$ and $w_3^{(n-1)}$ are two different de-mixing weight vectors of X', the $(n-1)$-dimensional vectors $\tilde{w}_2^{(n-1)}$ and $\tilde{w}_3^{(n-1)}$ are orthogonal. And there exists r such

---

[1] The superscript n indicates the dimension of de-mixing matrix.

that $\tilde{w}_2^{(n-1)}(r) \neq 0$. In a similar way we can get $\tilde{w}_3^{(n-1)} = A_1 w_3^{(n-2)}$, where $w_3^{(n-2)}$ is $(n-2)$-dimensional and A_1 is a $(n-1) \times (n-2)$ matrix:

$$A_1 = \begin{pmatrix} \mathbf{I_{r-1}} & & \mathbf{0_{(r-1)\times(n-r-1)}} & \\ -\frac{\tilde{w}_2^{(n-1)}(1)}{\tilde{w}_2^{(n-1)}(r)} \cdots -\frac{\tilde{w}_2^{(n-1)}(r-1)}{\tilde{w}_2^{(n-1)}(r)} & -\frac{\tilde{w}_2^{(n-1)}(r+1)}{\tilde{w}_2^{(n-1)}(r)} \cdots -\frac{\tilde{w}_2^{(n-1)}(n-1)}{\tilde{w}_2^{(n-1)}(r)} \\ \mathbf{0_{(n-r-1)\times(r-1)}} & & \mathbf{I_{n-r-1}} & \end{pmatrix}_{(n-1)\times(n-2)}$$
(6)

We can see $s_k = w_3^{(n-1)T} X' = w_3^{(n-2)T} A_1^T P_1 X' = w_3^{(n-2)T} X''$, where $X'' = A_1^T P_1 X' = A_1^T P_1 A^T P X$. s_3 is considered as an independent component as the $(n-2)$-dimensional data X''. Thus the data dimension has been reduced from n to $(n-2)$. Let P_2 be the whitening matrix of X'', which can be constructed easily with the eigenvalues and eigenvectors of $A_2^T A_2$. We have $w_3^{(n-2)} = P_2^T \tilde{w}_3^{(n-2)}$, and $w_3 = P^T \cdot A P_1^T \cdot A_1 P_2^T \tilde{w}_3^{(n-2)}$. In this way after the estimation of $\tilde{w}_3^{(n-2)}$ (from which w_3 is constructed) and some preprocessing, estimation of the next independent component can be performed in $(n-3)$-dimensional parameter space. And so on until the last independent component is recovered.

In practical computation, usually the elements of $\tilde{w}^{(i)}$ are hardly 'strictly' equal to zero. When none of them equals to zero, we can choose its last element as the first non-zero element to construct A (or A_1, etc.).

2.2 Implementation

Using our dimension reduction decorrelation method, the decorrelation step is performed only once for each independent component. While if we use the Gram-Schmidt-like deflation scheme, as we have shown before, we must 'deflate' the weight vector after each update iteration for each independent component.

Based on the analysis above, given n observations, the ICA algorithm for extracting n independent components using a one-unit objective function and our decorrelatin method is formulated as (initially let $k = 1, D = I_n$):

---

for $k = 1$:n

1. If $k = 1$, $A \leftarrow I_n$; otherwise according to Eq.6, use the vector u to construct the $(n-k+2) \times (n-k+1)$ matrix A. $X \leftarrow A^T X$.
2. Preprocess the data X with whitening. Let P be the $(n-k+1) \times (n-k+1)$ whitening matrix. If $k=1$, P is obtained by PCA; otherwise let the eigenvalue decomposition (EVD) of $A^T A$ is EDE^T, and $P \leftarrow D^{-1/2} E^T$. $X \leftarrow PX$, $D \leftarrow PA^T D$.
3. Optimize the chosen one-unit objective function to estimate an independent component s_k from data X: $s_k \leftarrow u^T X$, where u is a $(n-k+1)$-dimensional de-mixing weight vector of X. $w_k \leftarrow D^T u$.

end

The computation load (or time) used for each independent component depends on the number of samples, the iteration steps used for convergence of the chosen contrast function, and the dimension of the observations (or de-mixing weight vectors). If the Gram-Schmidt-like deflation scheme is adopted, without taking computation of decorrelation into account, computation of each update iteration is almost the same in estimating all the independent components. In our method, since the independent components obtained later are extracted from lower dimensional data, computation of each update iteration becomes less.

3 Experiments and Discussion

ICA has been applied in finance to construct factor models [1,2]. We use ICA to extract 22 independent sources with the returns of 22 stocks as observations and compare the performances of our decorrelation method and the Gram-Schmidt-like deflation scheme. There are 2072 samples for each stock. In all experiments, the contrast function is as Eq.2 with $G(u) = \frac{1}{4}u^4$. FastICA (Eq.3) is used to do the optimization. MATLAB is used to do the simulation.

First in order to compare the convergence of these two methods, their termination conditions are set to be the same to guarantee the same quality of the independent components obtained by them. In the Gram-Schmidt-like deflation scheme, the termination condition is $||w(k)-w(k-1)|| < \varepsilon$ or $||w(k)+w(k-1)|| < \varepsilon$. In our dimension reduction method, since $w = D^T u$, the termination condition for $u(k)$ is $||D^T \cdot (u(k) - u(k-1))|| < \varepsilon$ or $||D^T \cdot (u(k) + u(k-1))|| < \varepsilon$. We randomly choose the initial condition for the two methods and repeat them 100 times. The average number of iterations and time needed for convergence of each IC are shown in Fig. 1. Using these two methods, each independent component takes almost the same number of iteration steps for convergence. But our method takes less time, especially for the independent components processed later. However, when the same initialization condition is used, there do exist some cases (about 1%) where our method needs fewer iteration steps, or even our method converges normally (about 50 iteration steps needed) while the Gram-Schmidt-like deflation method does not converge in 1000 steps.

In another experiment we compare the time taken by each iteration step using these two methods. We neglect the termination condition and fix the number of iteration steps used for extracting each independent component as 50, and compare the time taken by these two methods, see Fig. 2. With our dimension reduction method, time taken by each independent component decreases quickly when its sequence number increases. This is encouraging when the number of independent components is large.

4 Conclusion

When a one-unit contrast function is used to estimate the whole ICA transformation, a decorrelation method is needed to prevent the contrast function from converging to the same optimum for different independent components.

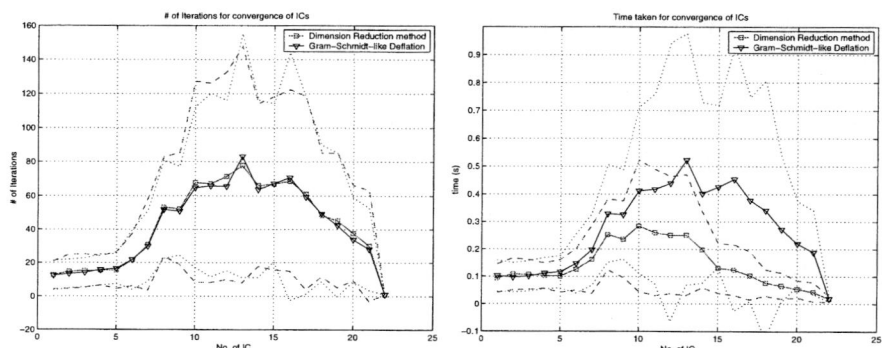

Fig. 1. Average number of iteration steps and time needed for convergence of each independent component Using the deflation scheme and the dimension reduction method respectively. Left and Right are the number of iterations and time used for convergence of each independent component respectively. The dashed and dotted lines indicate standard deviations of the two methods.

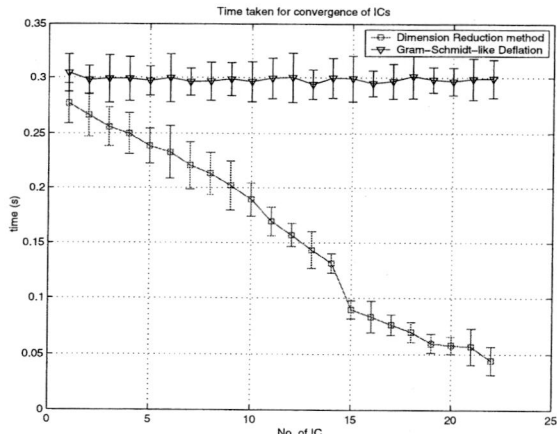

Fig. 2. Average time taken by our decorrelation method and the deflation scheme with the number of iterations used for estimation of each independent component fixed as 50, and each method has been repeated 100 times. Error bar: standard deviation.

Based on the orthogonality of the de-mixing matrix of whitened data, we propose a decorrelation method which lowers the dimension of the observations and de-mixing weight vectors when estimating subsequent independent components. Obviously the Gram-Schmidt-like deflation scheme is easier for comprehension and implementation. However, the dimension reduction method provides better convergence and is more efficient comparing with the popular deflation scheme.

Acknowledgement. The work in this paper was partially supported by a grant from the Research Grants Council of the Hong Kong Special Administration Region, China. We would thank Prof. Hyvärinen and his colleagues for providing free download of FastICA package for MATLAB. Also we are grateful to the reviewers for their helpful comments.

References

1. Siu-Ming Cha and Lai-Wan Chan. Applying independent component analysis to factor model in finance. *Intelligent Data Engineering and Automated Learning-IDEAL 2000, Springer*, pages 538–544, 2000.
2. Lai-Wan Chan and Siu-Ming Cha. Selection of independent factor model in finance. In *proceedings of 3rd International Conference on Independent Component Analysis and blind Signal Separation*, San Diego, California, USA, December 2001.
3. P. Comon. Independent component analysis – a new concept? *Signal Processing*, 36:287–314, 1994.
4. N. Delfosse and P. Loubaton. Adaptive blind separation of independent sources: a deflation approach. *Signal Processing*, 45:59–83, 1995.
5. Aapo Hyvärinen. A family of fixed-point algorithms for independent component analysis. *ICASSP*, pages 3917–3920, 1997.
6. Aapo Hyvärinen. New approximations of differential entropy for independent component analysis and projection pursuit. In *Advances in Neural Information Processing Systems 10*, pages 273–279. MIT Press, 1998.
7. Aapo Hyvärinen. Fast and robust fixed-point algorithms for independent component analysis. *IEEE Transactions on Neural Networks*, 10(3):626–634, 1999.
8. Aapo Hyvärinen. Survey on independent component analysis. *Neural Computing Surveys*, 2:94–128, 1999.
9. Aapo Hyvärinen and Erkki Oja. A fast fixed-point algorithm for independent component analysis. *Neural Computation*, 9(7):1483–1492, 1997.
10. I. J. Jolliffe. *Principal Component Analysis*. Springer series in Statistics. Springer Verlag, 2nd edition, 2002.
11. J. Karhunen, E. Oja, L. Wang, R. Vigario, and J. Joutsensalo. A class of neural networks for independent component analysis. *IEEE Trans. on Neural Networks*, 8(3):486–504, 1997.
12. D. Luenberger. *Optimization by Vector Space Methods*. Wiley, 1969.

Selective Sampling Methods in One-Class Classification Problems

Piotr Juszczak and Robert P.W. Duin

Pattern Recognition Group, Faculty of Applied Sciences,
Delft University of Technology, Lorentzweg 1,
2628 CJ Delft, The Netherlands
{piotr,bob}@ph.tn.tudelft.nl

Abstract. Selective sampling, a part of the active learning method, reduces the cost of labeling supplementary training data by asking only for the labels of the most informative, unlabeled examples. This additional information added to an initial, randomly chosen training set is expected to improve the generalization performance of a learning machine. We investigate some methods for a selection of the most informative examples in the context of one-class classification problems i.e. problems where only (or nearly only) the examples of the so-called target class are available. We applied selective sampling algorithms to a variety of domains, including real-world problems: mine detection and texture segmentation. The goal of this paper is to show why the best or most often used selective sampling methods for two- or multi-class problems are not necessarily the best ones for the one-class classification problem. By modifying the sampling methods, we present a way of selecting a small subset from the unlabeled data to be presented to an expert for labeling such that the performance of the retrained one-class classifier is significantly improved.

1 Introduction

In many classification problems, there can be a large number of unlabeled examples available. To benefit from such examples, one usually exploits either implicitly or explicitly the link between the marginal density $P(x)$ over the examples of a class x and the conditional density $P(y|x)$ representing the decision boundary for the labels y. For example, high density regions or clusters in the data can be expected to fall solely in one or another class. One technique to exploit the marginal density $P(x)$ between classes is selective sampling, which is a part of the active learning method [4]. In this technique the performance of classifiers is improved by adding supplementary information to a training set. In general, there is a small set of labeled data and a large set of unlabeled data. In addition, there exists a possibility of asking an expert (oracle) for labeling additional data. However, this should not be used excessively. The question is: how to select an additional subset of unlabeled data such that by including it in the training set would improve the performance of a particular classifier the most.

These examples are called the most informative patterns. Many methods of selective sampling have already been considered in two- or multi-class problems. They select objects:

- which are close to the description boundary [3] e.g. close to a margin or inside a margin for the support vector classifier [2],
- which have the most evenly split labels over a variation of classifiers:
  - trained on multiple permutations of the labeled data [12],
  - differing by the settings,
  - trained on independent sets of features [8].

These sampling methods are looking for the most informative patterns in the vicinity of a current classifier. It means they select patterns, to be labeled by an oracle, which have a high probability of incorrect classification. The classification performance is improved in small steps. In this paper, we will test a number of selective sampling methods for one-class classification problems [10,6].

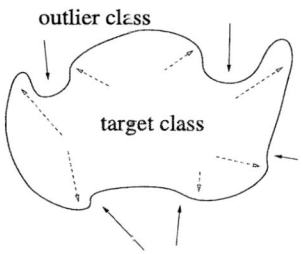

Fig. 1. Influence of the target and the outlier classes on the description boundary.

In the problem of one-class classification, one class of objects, called the target class, has to be distinguished from all the other possible objects, called outliers. The description should be constructed such that the acceptance of objects not originating from the target class should be minimized. The problem of the one-class classification is harder than the standard two-class classification problem. In a two-class classification, when examples of outliers and targets are both available a decision boundary is supported from both sides by examples of each of the classes: see Figure 1. Because in case of a one-class classification only the target class is available, only one side of the boundary is supported. Based on the examples of one class only, it is hard to decide how tight the boundary should fit around the target class. The absence of outlier examples makes it also very hard to estimate the error that the classifier would make. The error of the first kind $\mathcal{E}_\mathcal{I}$, referring to the target objects that are classified as outlier objects, can be estimated on the available data. However, the error of the second kind $\mathcal{E}_{\mathcal{II}}$ referring to the outlier objects that are classified as target objects, cannot be estimated without assumptions on the distribution of the outliers. If no information on the outlier class is given we assume a uniform distribution of the outliers.

In this paper, we will show that the standard selective sampling methods for multi-class problems, which look in the vicinity of the classifier, do not perform well in a one-class classification problem. To justify this, a distance measure to the description boundary defined by the classification confidence [7], will be used.

2 A Formal Framework

In selective sampling algorithms the challenge is to determine which unlabeled examples will be the most informative (e.g. improve the classification performance the most) if they were labeled and added into an existing training set. These are the examples which are presented as a query to an oracle - an expert who can label any new data without error. We begin with a preliminary, weak classifier that has to be first determined by a small set of labeled samples. In particular, in selective sampling algorithms, presented in section 1, the distributions of query patterns will be dense near the final decision boundaries (where examples are informative) rather than at the region of the highest prior probabilities (where patterns are typically less informative). At the beginning, the training set consists of a few randomly selected samples. To reach the desired classification error, we would like to add as few as possible new examples (labeled by the expert) from the unlabeled data using a selective sampling method Table 2.

If a sampling method selects patterns close to the boundary given by the current classifier, then the probability of an incorrect classification is higher for such examples than for examples being far from the description boundary. This approach was proved to work for several multi-class problems [1,2,3,5].

Because it is usually not possible to compute the distance between a pattern and a classifier, we propose to base this distance measure on the preprocessed output of the classifier $f^c(x)$, where c indicates either a target (t) or an outlier (o) class. The raw output of the classifier $f^c(x)$ is converted to the confidence Γ_x^c of the classifier that the

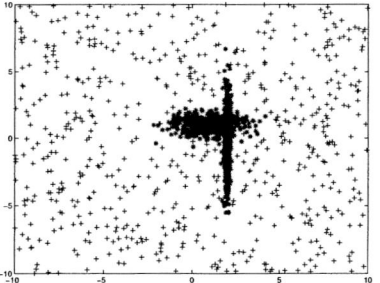

Fig. 2. The merged Higleyman classes {N([1 1],[1 0; 0 0.25]; N([2 0],[0.01 0; 0 4])} with a uniformly distributed outlier class.

object x belongs to one of the classes (target or outlier). Where:

$$\sum_{x \in c}(\Gamma_x^c) = 1;^1 \qquad 0 \leq \Gamma_x^c \leq 1;$$

The confidence Γ_x^c is computed as follows:

$$\Gamma_x^c = \frac{f^c(x)}{\sum_{x \in c}[f^c(x)]} \qquad (1)$$

where $c = target \vee outlier$ class.
For objects classified as targets only the confidences Γ_x^t are computed, for objects classified as outliers only the confidences Γ_x^o are computed.

---

[1] If $f^c(x) > 0$, then x is assigned to the class c. So, the confidences of all objects, within a class (as classified by the actual classifier) sum to one. We realize that this is a nonstandard way of using the 'confidence' concept.

There are two interesting regions of the classification confidences:

1. a high confidence, $\Gamma_x^c \gg 0.5$; the objects are far from the decision boundary,
2. a low confidence, $\Gamma_x^c \ll 0.5$; the objects are close to the decision boundary.

Table 1. The description of selective sampling methods

	ll	lh	hl	hh
target class	$\Gamma_x^t \ll 0.5$	$\Gamma_x^t \ll 0.5$	$\Gamma_x^t \gg 0.5$	$\Gamma_x^t \gg 0.5$
outlier class	$\Gamma_x^o \ll 0.5$	$\Gamma_x^o \gg 0.5$	$\Gamma_x^o \ll 0.5$	$\Gamma_x^o \gg 0.5$

Table 2. Active learning with selective sampling – The algorithm

```
1. assume that a small number of the target objects with true labels is
given constituting an initial training set
2. train a specified classifier on the training set
3. select a number of objects classified as targets and outliers
according to the chosen selective sampling method
4. ask an oracle for labels of these objects and include them in the
training set
5. repeat the steps 2-4 or STOP if e.g. the training set is larger than
a specified size
```

Based on the confidence regions of a classifier, we can describe four selective sampling methods that choose a set of examples (e.g. 5 from each target/outlier class) for an oracle to label them:

ll – a low confidence for both the target and the outlier classes
lh – a low/high confidence for the target/outlier class
hl – a high/low confidence for the target/outlier class
hh – a high confidence for both the target and the outlier classes

We compare these sampling techniques with the two methods that are not dependent on the distance to the description boundary:

hr – a half-random method, which first classifies the unlabeled set of examples and then selects randomly an equal number of examples from each of the two classification sets $rand(x \in t)$ and $rand(x \in o)$. This method selects objects based just on the classification labels; the classification confidences Γ_x^c are not considered during the selection process.
ra – a random selective sampling method, $rand(x \in t \vee o)$. In this method the classification labels as well as the confidences are not considered during the selection process.

To avoid the selection of patterns being 'really far' from the current description boundary we will assume that the class examples in the one-class classification problem are bounded by a box. In our experiments with the artificial data, the lengths of the bounding box edges are set up to 10 times the feature ranges of the initial training set.

In experiments with the artificial data we used the following datasets: banana [10], multidimensional Gaussian and the merged Higleyman classes {N([1 1],[1 0; 0 0.25]; N([2 0],[0.01 0; 0 4])} ; see Figure 2. As the outlier class, we considered objects uniformly distributed in the bounding box. The results for all these datasets were similar. For clarity, in section 3, we present only the outcomes on the merged Higleyman classes.

3 Experiments with the Artificial Data

Now we will present the results of experiments performed on the $2D$ Higleyman classes, using the selective sampling methods described in section 2. A number of different classifiers is taken into account: Support Vector Data Description(SVDD) [11], Autoencoder Neural Network(ANN) and the Parzen classifier. The dataset contains 1000 target objects and 5000 outlier objects chosen in the bounding box. At the beginning, we randomly select 6 patterns from the target class and train a classifier. First, in every sampling step, 5 objects currently classified as targets and 5 objects currently classified as outliers are chosen according to the selective sampling method. Next, the true objects' labels are retrieved and the classifier is retrained. The error of the first kind $\mathcal{E}_\mathcal{I}$ [10] for all the classifiers is set to 0.1 on the training set. The size of the bounding box equals 10. In Table 3 the averaged results over 20 runs are presented. To see how well a classifier fits the data both errors $\mathcal{E}_\mathcal{I}$ and $\mathcal{E}_{\mathcal{II}}$ should be considered.

Support Vector Data Description (SVDD)
In this experiment, the SVDD [11] with kernel whitening [9] is used. From Table 3, it can be seen that:

- the **ll** and **hl** methods are the slowest ones; they require to label more samples than the other methods to reach the same classification error.
- the **lh** method is the fastest one; it requires to label less samples than the other methods. This method allows to evolve the classifier fast by asking for the true labels of highly confident patterns, classified as outliers and supports the description boundary by patterns of a low confidence classified as targets; see Figure 1.
- the **hh** method also allows to evolve the classifier fast by asking for the true labels of highly confident patterns classified as outliers, but the description boundary is not supported by patterns classified as targets close to the boundary. In consequence, the boundary is collapsing around the training size of 50 in Table 3.

Autoencoder Neural Network (ANN)
We train two autoencoder neural networks with 5 hidden units: one for the

Table 3. The classification error $\mathcal{E}_\mathcal{I}$ and $\mathcal{E}_{\mathcal{II}}$ for SVDD, autoencoder (ANN) and Parzen classifier, on merged Higleyman classes for different selective sampling methods. The results were averaged over 20 runs.

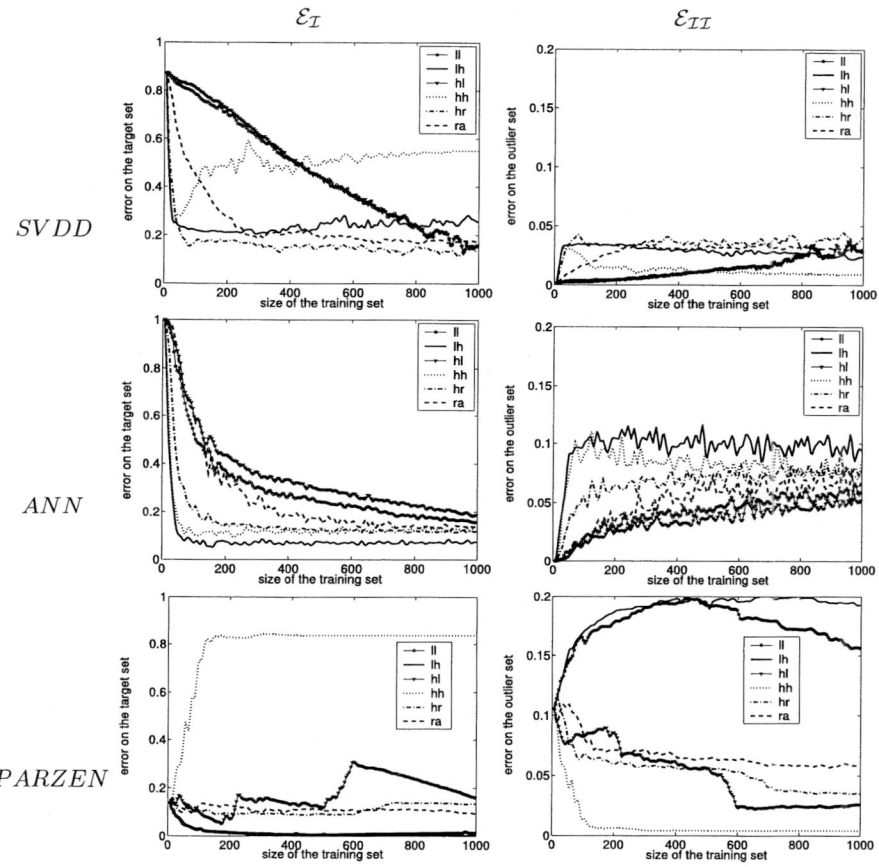

target class and one for the outlier class. For this classifier, both the **lh** and **hh** methods perform almost equally well, since they allow for the fast classification improvement by finding the true labels of the patterns classified as outliers with high confidences. Because the low confidence region $\Gamma_x^t \ll 0.5$, and the high confidence region $\Gamma_x^t \gg 0.5$ for the target class are relatively close to each other compared to the low confidence region $\Gamma_x^o \ll 0.5$ and the high confidence region $\Gamma_x^o \gg 0.5$ for the outlier class, almost no difference between performance of the **lh** and **hh** methods can be observed.

Density Based Classifiers
For density estimation classifiers based on: Parzen, gaussian distribution, mixture of gaussians or for other types like the nearest neighbor classifier, all selective

sampling methods based on distances to a description boundary do not perform well, especially **hh** method; see Table 3. They spoil the density estimation. For this type of classifiers the best sampling algorithm is the random method **ra**, because it uniformly samples the classes over the entire distribution.

4 Experiments with the Real-World Data

Texture Data
This image data contains five different type of textures, where one of them was chosen as the target class and all others become the outlier class. The 7-dimensional data set contains the following features: the outputs of Gabor and Gauss filters and the second derivative estimates. It contains 13231 target examples and 52305 outlier examples.

Mine Data
Mines are hidden in a test bench of different soils: sand, clay, peat and ferruginous. Features are infra-red images taken at different day time (12-dimensional feature space). Only the approximated positions of the mines are known (some mine pixel labels are incorrect). Because the collection of soil samples is easier and safer than the collection of mine samples and some of the mine pixel labels are incorrect, soil was taken as the target class and mines as the outlier class. The data contains 3456 examples of the target class and 23424 examples of outlier class. We built a classifier for each type of soil separately. We did not consider mixtures of soils. In this experiment the SVDD [11] with kernel whitening [9]

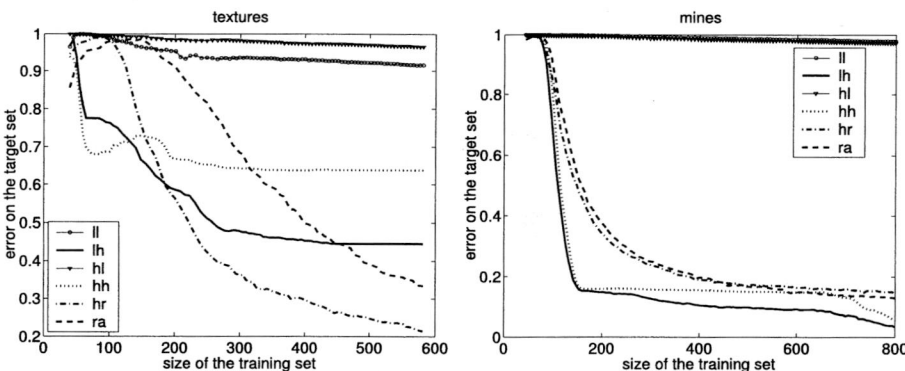

Fig. 3. The classification error $\mathcal{E}_\mathcal{I}$ for the SVDD with kernel whitening, trained on the texture data (top) and the mine data with the sand type of soil (bottom), for different selective sampling methods. The results were averaged over 10 runs.

was used. For each dataset, the initial training sets contain 40 randomly chosen target objects. In each iteration step, 5 objects currently classified as targets and 5 objects currently classified as outliers are added to the training set with their true labels. The classification errors for the selective sampling methods, described in section 2, are shown in Figure 4.

The results for the **hl** and **ll** methods are very bad, because the initial training set might have been too small. The **hl** and **ll** selective sampling methods select mainly those target objects that are close to the actual description boundary. As a result, it can only grow slowly.

5 Conclusions and Open Questions

We have described several methods in which unlabeled data can be used to augment labeled data based on the confidence of classifiers. Many selective sampling methods try to improve the performance of a classifier by adding supplementary patterns from the vicinity of the classifier. These patterns have a high probability to be wrongly classified. Because they are close to the current classifier including them in the training set, with their true labels, will improve the classification performance slightly. One-class classification differs from the standard, half-spaces, two-class problem because of the assumption that the domain of one of the classes, the target class, is limited to a certain area. If in this problem only a small, labeled, target set is available, with the size e.g. twice the data dimensionality and we would like to improve the performance of a classifier by asking an expert for labels of the supplementary data, then the selection of patterns close to the description boundary will build a more dense distribution of the target class.

The choice of a selective sampling method depends on the classifier considered. For some classifiers, like the SVDD or the ANN, selective sampling methods based on the distance to the decision boundary will perform well. Patterns close to the decision boundary influence them the most. For classifiers based on density estimation, like the Parzen classifier, selective sampling methods based on the distance to the decision boundary could spoil the estimation of the density. It could happen that adding more samples to the training set will, in fact, increase the classification error.

In problems where only a small target set is available and the task is to select a small unlabeled set to be labeled by an expert, for reaching the desired classification error, it is worth to base the selection procedure on the confidence of the classifier. Our experiments showed that by selecting objects far from the description boundary it is possible to lower the number of necessary objects to be labeled by the expert. If the classes are not overlapping it is possible to improve further the classifier by changing the selective sampling method to one that chooses the most informative patterns close to the decision boundary.

The performance of the methods, based on the confidence of the classifier, presented in this paper depends on the size of the bounding box. The size of the box has the strongest influence on the random method **ra**. For very large size of the bounding box the best performance will be given by the **ll** selective method.

Acknowledgments. We would like to thank to dr. K. Schutte from FEL-TNO and W.A.C.M. Messelink from TU Delft for providing us with the mine data. This work was partly supported by the Dutch Organization for Scientific Research (NWO).

References

1. A. Blum, T. Mitchell 'Combining labeled and unlabeled data with co-training' Proceedings of the 1998 Conference on Computational Learning Theory
2. C. Cambell, N. Cristianini, A. Smola, 'Query learning with large margin classifiers'
3. D. Cohn, L. Atlas, R. Ladner, 'Improving generalization with active learning', 1992
4. D. Cohn, Z. Ghahramani, M.I. Jordan 'Active learning with statistical models', Journal of artificial intelligence research 4, 1996 129–145
5. Y. Freund, H. S. Seung, E. Shamir, N. Tishby, 'Selective sampling using the query by committee algorithm', Machine Learning, 28, 133–168 (1997)
6. N. Japkowicz, 'Concept-learning in the absence of counter-examples: an autoassociation-based approach to classification', PhD thesis 1999
7. M.J. Kearns, U.V. Vazirani, 'An introduction to computational learning theory', The MIT Press 1994, ISBN 0-262-11193-4
8. Ion Muslea, Steve Minton, Craig Knoblock, 'Selective sampling with redundant views', Proceedings of the 15th National Conference on Artificial Intelligence, 621–626, AAAI-2000.
9. D.M.J. Tax and P. Juszczak, 'Kernel whitening for data description', International Workshop on Pattern Recognition with Support Vector Machines 2002
10. D.M.J. Tax, 'One-class classification', PhD thesis, Delft University of Technology, ISBN:90-75691-05-x, 2001
11. D.M.J. Tax, R.P.W. Duin, 'Support Vector Data Description', Pattern Recognition Letters, December 1999, vol. 20(11-13), pp. 1191–1199
12. M.K. Warmuth, G. Rätsch, M. Mathieson, J. Liao, C. Lemmen, 'Active learning in the drug discovery process'

Learning Distributed Representations of High-Arity Relational Data with Non-linear Relational Embedding

Alberto Paccanaro

Bioinformatics Unit, Dept. of Medical Microbiology,
Queen Mary University of London, UK

Abstract. We summarize Linear Relational Embedding (LRE), a method which has been recently proposed for generalizing over relational data. We show that LRE can represent any binary relations, but that there are relations of arity greater than 2 that it cannot represent. We then introduce Non-Linear Relational Embedding (NLRE) and show that it can learn any relation. Results of NLRE on the Family Tree Problem show that generalization is much better than the one obtained using backpropagation on the same problem.

1 Introduction

Let us imagine a situation in which we have a set of concepts and a set of relations among these concepts, and our data consists of few instances of these relations that hold among the concepts. We want to be able to infer other instances of these relations. For example, if the concepts are the people in a certain family, the relations are kinship relations, and we are given the facts "Alberto has-father Pietro" and "Pietro has-brother Giovanni", we would like to be able to infer "Alberto has-uncle Giovanni". Our ultimate aim is to be able to take a large set of facts about a domain and to be able to infer other "common-sense" facts without having any prior knowledge about the domain. Recently we have introduced a method called Linear Relational Embedding (LRE) [4,5] for solving this kind of problems. The approach is to learn a representation of each concept in terms of its relevant features together with the rules on how such features interact. We then use these representations to infer new instances of the relations. These ideas can be traced back to a paper by Hinton (1981), one of the first attempts to represent relational data in a connectionist network using distributed representations. Hinton chose the distributed representation of each concept to be the set of the semantic features of that concept, and showed that a system can exploit such distributed representations to provide automatic generalization. However he used hand-coded representations and did not provide a satisfactory method for learning them from the data. Few methods for devising such pattern for relational data have been proposed, but are either limited in the type of relations that they can represent, or cannot generalize very well (see for example Hinton, 1986; Miikkulainen & Dyer, 1989). In the next sections we shall present methods to learn distributed representations for concepts and relations that coincide with their semantic features and we shall see that they provide excellent generalization performance.

2   Linear Relational Embedding

Let us consider the case in which all the relations are binary. Our data then consists of triplets ($concept_1, relation, concept_2$), and the problem we are trying to solve is to infer missing triplets when we are given only few of them that is, equivalently, to complete the last element of a triplet, given the first two. LRE represents each concept in the data as a learned vector in a Euclidean space and each relationship between the two concepts as a learned matrix that maps the first concept into an approximation to the second concept. Let us assume that our data consists of C such triplets containing N distinct concepts and M binary relations. We shall call this set of triplets $\mathcal{C}$; $\mathcal{V} = \{\mathbf{v}_1, \ldots, \mathbf{v}_N\}$ will denote the set of n-dimensional vectors corresponding to the N concepts, and $\mathcal{R} = \{R_1, \ldots, R_M\}$ the set of $(n \times n)$ matrices corresponding to the M relations. Often we shall need to indicate the vectors and the matrix which correspond to the concepts and the relation in a certain triplet c. In this case we shall denote the vector corresponding to the first concept with $\mathbf{a}$, the vector corresponding to the second concept with $\mathbf{b}$ and the matrix corresponding to the relation with R. We shall therefore write the triplet c as $(\mathbf{a}^c, R^c, \mathbf{b}^c)$ where $\mathbf{a}^c, \mathbf{b}^c \in \mathcal{V}$ and $R^c \in \mathcal{R}$. The operation that relates a pair $(\mathbf{a}^c, R^c)$ to a vector $\mathbf{b}^c$ is the matrix-vector multiplication, $R^c \cdot \mathbf{a}^c$, which produces an approximation to $\mathbf{b}^c$. If for every triplet $(\mathbf{a}^c, R^c, \mathbf{b}^c)$ we think of $R^c \cdot \mathbf{a}^c$ as a noisy version of one of the concept vectors, then one way to learn an embedding is to maximize the probability that it is a noisy version of the correct completion, $\mathbf{b}^c$. We imagine that a concept has an average location in the space, but that each "observation" of the concept is a noisy realization of this average location. Assuming spherical Gaussian noise with a variance of $1/2$ on each dimension, the discriminative goodness function that corresponds to the log probability of getting the right completion, summed over all training triplets is:

$$D = \sum_{c=1}^{C} \frac{1}{k_c} \log \frac{e^{-\|R^c \cdot \mathbf{a}^c - \mathbf{b}^c\|^2}}{\sum_{\mathbf{v}_i \in \mathcal{V}} e^{-\|R^c \cdot \mathbf{a}^c - \mathbf{v}_i\|^2}} \quad (1)$$

where k_c is the number of triplets in $\mathcal{C}$ having the first two terms equal to the ones of c, but differing in the third term[1].

The distributed representations learned by maximizing D with respect to all the vector and matrix components provide good generalization [4]. However,

---

[1] We would like our system to assign equal probability to each of the correct completions. The discrete probability distribution that we want to approximate is therefore: $\mathsf{P}_\mathbf{x} = \frac{1}{d} \sum_{i=1}^{d} \delta(\mathbf{b}_i - \mathbf{x})$ where δ is the discrete delta function and $\mathbf{x}$ ranges over the vectors in $\mathcal{V}$. Our system implements the discrete probability distribution: $\mathsf{Q}_\mathbf{x} = \frac{1}{Z} \exp(-\|R \cdot \mathbf{a} - \mathbf{x}\|^2)$ where Z is the normalization factor. The $1/k_c$ factor in eq.1 ensures that we are minimizing the Kullback-Leibler divergence between P and Q.

when we learn an embedding by maximizing D, we are not making use of exactly the information that we have in the triplets. For each triplet c, we are making the vector representing the correct completion $\mathbf{b}^c$ *more probable* than any other concept vector given $R^c \cdot \mathbf{a}^c$, while the triplet states that $R^c \cdot \mathbf{a}^c$ must be *equal* to $\mathbf{b}^c$. The numerator of D does exactly this, but we also have the denominator, which is necessary in order to stay away from the trivial $\mathbf{0}$ solution[2]. We noticed however that the denominator is critical at the beginning of the learning, but as the vectors and matrices differentiate we could gradually lift this burden, allowing $\sum_{c=1}^{C} \|R^c \cdot \mathbf{a}^c - \mathbf{b}^c\|^2$ to become the real goal of the learning. To do this we modify the discriminative function to include a parameter α, which is annealed from 1 to 0 during learning[3]:

$$G = \sum_{c=1}^{C} \frac{1}{k_c} \log \frac{e^{-\|R^c \cdot \mathbf{a}^c - \mathbf{b}^c\|^2}}{[\sum_{\mathbf{v}_i \in \mathcal{V}} e^{-\|R^c \cdot \mathbf{a}^c - \mathbf{v}_i\|^2}]^\alpha} \qquad (2)$$

During learning this function G (for Goodness) is maximized with respect to all the vector and matrix components. In our experiments, all the vector and matrix components were updated simultaneously at each iteration. One effective method of performing the optimization is conjugate gradient. Learning was fast, usually requiring only a few hundred updates, and very seldom it got stuck in poor local maxima.

By maximizing G we obtain a set of distributed representations such that for each possible choice of R and $\mathbf{a}$, $R \cdot \mathbf{a} \sim \mathbf{c}_k$ where $\mathbf{c}_k$ is the center of gravity of all the correct completions; or $R \cdot \mathbf{a}$ is "far away" from any concept vectors when no completion is appropriate. Now we need a principled way to use these representations to solve our generalization problem, that is to complete a given triplet. This is made difficult by the fact that for most datasets there exist triplets which cannot be completed using the available data, for which the correct completion should be "don't know"; the system needs a way to indicate when a triplet does not admit a completion. Therefore we embed these representations into a probabilistic model whose parameters are learned. Such model is constituted, for each relation, of a mixture of N identical spherical Gaussians, each centered on a concept vector, and a Uniform distribution. The Uniform distribution will take care of the "don't know" answers, and will be competing with all the other Gaussians, each representing a concept vector. For each relation the Gaussians have different variances and the Uniform a different height. The parameters of this probabilistic model are, for each relation R, the variances of the Gaussians

---

[2] The obvious approach to find an embedding would be to minimize the sum of squared distances between $R^c \cdot \mathbf{a}^c$ and $\mathbf{b}^c$ over all the triplets, with respect to all the vector and matrix components. Unfortunately this minimization (almost) always causes all of the vectors and matrices to collapse to the trivial $\mathbf{0}$ solution.

[3] For one-to-many relations we must not decrease the value of α all the way to 0, because this would cause some concept vectors to become coincident — the only way to make $R^c \cdot \mathbf{a}^c$ equal to k_c different vectors, is by collapsing them onto a unique vector.

152   A. Paccanaro

σ_R and the relative density under the Uniform distribution, which we shall write as $\exp(-r_R^2/2\sigma_R^2)$. These parameters are learned using a validation set, which will be the union of a set of P complete-able triplets and a set of Q pairs which cannot be completed, by maximizing, with respect to the σ_R and r_R parameters:

$$F = \sum_{q=1}^{Q} \log \frac{U}{U + \sum_{\mathbf{v}_i \in \mathcal{V}} \exp(-\frac{\|R^q \cdot \mathbf{a}^q - \mathbf{v}_i\|^2}{2\sigma_R^2})} + \sum_{p=1}^{P} \frac{1}{k_p} \cdot \log \frac{\exp(-\frac{\|R^p \cdot \mathbf{a}^p - \mathbf{b}^p\|^2}{2\sigma_R^2})}{U + \sum_{\mathbf{v}_i \in \mathcal{V}} \exp(-\frac{\|R^p \cdot \mathbf{a}^p - \mathbf{v}_i\|^2}{2\sigma_R^2})} \quad (3)$$

where $U = \exp(-r_R^2/2\sigma_R^2)$. In order to complete any triplet $(R, \mathbf{a}, ?)$ we then compute the probability distribution over each of the Gaussians and the Uniform distribution given $R \cdot \mathbf{a}$. The system then chooses a vector $\mathbf{v}_i$ or the "don't know" answer according to those probabilities, as the completion to the triplet.

Results. One problem on which LRE has been tested is the Family Tree Problem [2]. In this problem, the data consists of people and relations among people belonging to two families, one Italian and one English (Figure 1, left). Using the relations {father, mother, husband, wife, son, daughter, uncle, aunt, brother, sister, nephew, niece} there are 112 triplets of the kind ($person_1$, $relation$, $person_2$). Figure 1 (right) shows the distributed representations for the people obtained after training with LRE using all the 112 triplets. Notice how the Italians are linearly separable from the English people and symmetric to them; the second and third components of the vectors are almost perfect features of generation and nationality respectively. In a dif-

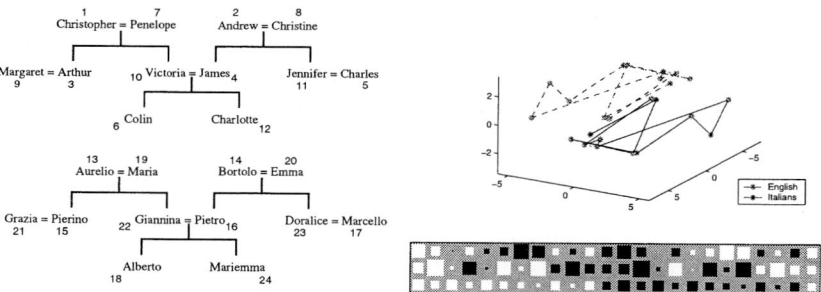

Fig. 1. Left: Two isomorphic family trees. The symbol "=" means "married to". Right Top: layout of the vectors representing the people obtained for the Family Tree Problem in 3D. Vectors end-points are indicated by *, the ones in the same family are connected to each other. Right Bottom: Hinton diagrams of the 3D vectors shown above. The vector of each person is a column, ordered according to the numbering on the tree diagram on the left.

ferent experiment, after learning a distributed representation for the entities in the data by maximizing G using 88 triplets, we learned the parameters of the probabilistic model by maximizing F over a validation set constituted by 12 complete-able and 12 uncomplete-able triplets. The resulting system was able to correctly complete all the 288 possible triplets $(\mathbf{a}, R, ?)$: it assigned a probability close to $1/k$ to each of the k vectors representing a correct answer; or it assigned a probability close to 1 to the "don't know" answer when the triplet was uncomplete-able. The generalization achieved is much better than that obtained by any other method on the same problem: the neural networks of Hinton (1986) and O'Reilly (1996) typically made one or two errors when 4 triplets were held out during training; Quinlan's FOIL [7] could generalize almost perfectly when 4 triplets were omitted from the training set.

LRE seems to scale up well to problems of bigger size. We have used it on the Large Family Tree Problem, a much bigger version of the Family Tree Problem, where the family tree is a branch of the real family tree of the author containing 49 people over 5 generations. Using the same set of 12 relations used in the Family Tree Problem, there is a total of 644 positive triplets. After learning using a training set of 524 positive triplets, and a validation set constituted by 30 positive and 30 negative triplets, the system is able to complete correctly almost all the possible triplets. When many completions are correct, a high probability is always assigned to each one of them. Only in few cases is a non-negligible probability assigned to some wrong completions.

Hierarchical Linear Relational Embedding (HLRE) is an extension of LRE that can be used effectively to find distributed representations for hierarchical structures [5]. The generalization performance obtained by HLRE is much better than the one obtained with RAAMs [6] on similar problems.

3 Non-linear Relational Embedding

In this paper we show that, as long as we consider only *binary* relations, given a sufficient number of dimensions, there always exists an LRE-type of solution that satisfies any set of triplets.

Theorem: *Consider a situation in which we have n concepts $\{\mathfrak{d}_1, \mathfrak{d}_2 \ldots \mathfrak{d}_n\}$ and m binary one-to-one relations $\{\mathfrak{l}_1, \mathfrak{l}_2, \ldots, \mathfrak{l}_m\}$. Suppose that we are given a set of triplets $(\mathfrak{d}_i, \mathfrak{l}_k, \mathfrak{d}_j)$. There always exists a corresponding representation of the concepts as vectors in an n-dimensional space, $\{\mathbf{v}_1, \ldots, \mathbf{v}_n\}$ and of the relations as $(n \times n)$ matrices $\{R_1, \ldots, R_m\}$ such that, for each triplet $(\mathfrak{d}_i, \mathfrak{l}_k, \mathfrak{d}_j)$ we have that $R_k \cdot \mathbf{v}_i = \mathbf{v}_j$.*

Proof: Given n vectors there are $2^{n \times n}$ possible binary relations, and we shall see how each of these relations can be built in order to satisfy every triplet in the data set. We assign each of the n objects to a different vertex of an n-dimensional hyper-cube, by representing object i with a unit vector such that its ith component is 1 and all the other components are 0. In the data set, there can be at the most n triplets involving a certain binary relation $\mathfrak{l}_k$. The desired matrix R_k for that relation will then be such that: $R_k^{(j,i)} = 1$ if there is a triplet (v_i, R_k, v_j) in the data set, and $R_k^{(j,i)} = 0$ otherwise (where $R_k^{(j,i)}$ indicates the (j, i) component of matrix R_k). Q.E.D.

The generalization to one-to-many relations is straightforward: in that case we can show that $R_k \cdot \mathbf{v}_i = \mathbf{v}_c$, where $\mathbf{v}_c$ is the center of gravity of the set of vectors representing the correct completions for the triplet $(\mathfrak{o}_i, \mathfrak{l}_k, ?)$. This means that, no matter how many concepts we have in our data set, and how many binary relations between these concepts hold simultaneously, there will always exist a mapping from the concepts into a space where these binary relations are linear transformations — although the space might need to be very high-dimensional. The extension of LRE to higher arity relations, however, is not straightforward. In this case, for m-arity relations our data consists of $(m+1)$-tuples, of the kind $\{object_1, object_2, \cdots, object_{m-1}, Relation, object_m\}$, and the problem we are trying to solve is again to infer the missing tuples when we are given only few of them, that is to complete the last element of the $(m+1)$-tuples given the m previous ones. We could extend LRE in order to handle m-arity relations simply by concatenating the first $(m-1)$ object vectors in each tuple into a single vector and then maximizing G as before. However, the fact that the transformations between distributed representations are constrained to be linear, carries with it a fundamental limitation when we try to learn relations of arity higher than 2. To see this, we can think of the solutions that LRE finds as a set of one-layer neural networks of linear units, one network for each relation in our problem; during learning we learn both the weights of these networks, and the input and output codes, with the constraint that such codes must be shared by all the networks. Linear neural networks can only represent and learn functions which are linearly separable in the input variables. This limitation transfers to LRE which will only be able to learn a distributed representation for a small class of relations with arity greater than 2. Let us look at some classical examples. We can think of the Boolean functions as two-to-one (ternary) relations, where the Boolean values $[0, 1]$ are the concepts. LRE can find a solution for the *AND* function (see Figure 2top left). However, LRE cannot learn the *XOR* problem, which would require two disjoint regions with a high probability of obtaining concept 1. As it happens for one layer perceptrons, LRE can only capture the pairwise correlation between input and output variables: it will not be able to learn relations for which such correlation is 0 while all the information is of higher order. The standard way to overcome the limitation of one-layer networks, is to add a hidden layer of non-linear units. In a similar way we obtain a non-linear version of LRE, which we have called Non-Linear Relational Embedding (NLRE). For each relation we introduce an extra layer of hidden units with a bias, $\mathbf{h}$, and an extra set of weights, S (see figure 2 bottom left). The hidden units will have a non-linear activation function — we have used the sigmoid function. Equation 2 becomes:

$$G = \sum_{c=1}^{C} \frac{1}{k_c} \log \frac{e^{-\|S^c \cdot \sigma(R^c \cdot \mathbf{A}^c + \mathbf{h}^c) - \mathbf{b}^c\|^2}}{[\sum_{\mathbf{v}_i \in \mathcal{V}} e^{-\|S^c \cdot \sigma(R^c \cdot \mathbf{A}^c + \mathbf{h}^c) - \mathbf{v}_i\|^2}]^\alpha} \qquad (4)$$

where $\mathbf{A}^c$ denotes the vector resulting from concatenating vectors $\mathbf{a}_1, \cdots, \mathbf{a}_{m-1}$ representing the first $(m-1)$ concepts in triplet c, and σ indicates the sigmoid function. During learning we maximize G with respect to the matrices, R^c, S^c, the biases of the hidden units, $\mathbf{h}^c$, and the distributed representation of the

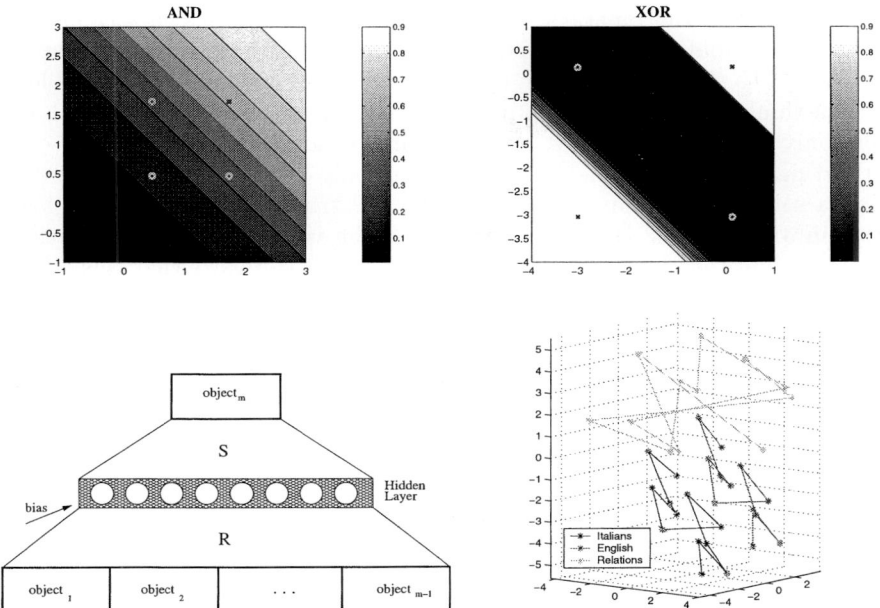

Fig. 2. Top: Probability assigned to concept 1 for the points in a region of the plane for a solution to the *AND* Boolean function using LRE (left) and to the *XOR* Boolean function using NLRE (right). The four points corresponding to (1,1), (0,1) (1,0) and (0,0) are marked by a circles and crosses. Probabilities are computed based on a probabilistic model which has a spherical Gaussian with variance equal to 1/2 centered on each concept. Bottom. Left: the diagram of the neural network corresponding to the implementation of a relation in NLRE. Right: layout of the vectors representing the people and the kinship relations obtained using NLRE for the Family Tree Problem in 3D.

concepts, while annealing α. As for LRE, after optimizing G we can learn the parameters of a probabilistic model, σ_R and r_R, by maximizing:

$$F = \sum_{q=1}^{Q} \log \frac{\exp(-\frac{r_R^2}{2\sigma_R^2})}{\exp(-\frac{r_R^2}{2\sigma_R^2}) + \sum_{\mathbf{v}_i \in \mathcal{V}} G^q_{(\mathbf{A},\mathbf{R},\mathbf{v_i})}} + \sum_{p=1}^{P} \frac{1}{k_p} \cdot \log \frac{\exp(-\frac{\|S^p \cdot \sigma(R^p \cdot \mathbf{A}^p + \mathbf{h}^p) - \mathbf{b}^p\|^2}{2\sigma_R^2})}{\exp(-\frac{r_R^2}{2\sigma_R^2}) + \sum_{\mathbf{v}_i \in \mathcal{V}} G^p_{(\mathbf{A},\mathbf{R},\mathbf{v_i})}}$$

where $G^q_{(\mathbf{A},\mathbf{R},\mathbf{v_i})} = \exp(-\|S^q \cdot \sigma(R^q \cdot \mathbf{A}^q + \mathbf{h}^q) - \mathbf{v}_i\|^2/2\sigma_R^2)$ and $G^p_{(\mathbf{A},\mathbf{R},\mathbf{v_i})} = \exp(-\|S^p \cdot \sigma(R^p \cdot \mathbf{A}^p + \mathbf{h}^p) - \mathbf{v}_i\|^2/2\sigma_R^2)$. NLRE contains LRE as a special case, and with a sufficient number of hidden units is able to represent any relation. Therefore it is able to solve the *XOR* problem (figure 2 top right). Notice that, as α approaches 0 during learning, NLRE becomes the classical backpropagation algorithm. We can see NLRE as a variation of the backpropagation algorithm that allows the neural network to learn the weights and the biases of the units as well as a distributed representation of the input and output vectors. This can lead to a much better generalization performance since the system will be performing a clever, automatic kind of feature extraction, in which it chooses to represents the inputs and the outputs using those features that are relevant to the problem. To show this, we can use NLRE to solve the Family Tree Problem, this time thinking of each person and each kinship relation as an object, and having only one "relation" that maps a pair ($person_1, kinship\text{-}relation$) onto the third person of the triplet. Training using only 100 triplets, NLRE is able to find a solution that can complete all the 112 triplets in the data set using vectors in 3D. Figure 2 (bottom right) shows the vectors representing each of the persons and the kinship relations. It is important to realize that this NLRE architecture is equivalent to the backpropagation architecture used by Hinton (1986) to solve the same problem. However, NLRE can generalize 3 times better: this is due to the fact that, together with the network weights, NLRE also learns a distributed representation of the input and output vectors.

4 Discussion

In this paper we have introduced NLRE, a method that finds distributed representations for the concepts allowing the relations to be non-linear transformations in feature space. NLRE learns an input-output mapping and also suitable distributed representations for the input and output vectors. NLRE can be quite effective for all those tasks in which input and output vectors belong to certain predefined classes. Often this kind of problem is solved training an MLP with backpropagation, after the user has chosen a vector codification for the inputs and the outputs elements in the training pairs. On a small but difficult problem we have shown that if we learn appropriate distributed representations for such elements together with the weights of the network, this leads to much better generalization than using the backpropagation algorithm.

Acknowledgments. The author would like to thank Geoffrey Hinton, Zoubin Ghahramani, Jay McClelland, and Peter Dayan for many useful discussions.

References

1. G. E. Hinton, Implementing Semantic Networks in Parallel Hardware, in *Parallel Models of Associative Memory*, G.E. Hinton and J.A. Anderson eds, Erlbaum, 1981
2. G.E. Hinton, Learning Distributed Representations of Concepts, *Proceedings of the Eighth Annual Conference of the Cognitive Science Society*, Erlbaum, 1–12,1986
3. R. Miikkulainen and M. G. Dyer, Encoding input/output representations in connectionist cognitive systems in *Proc. 1988 Conn. Models Summer School*, 347–356.
4. A. Paccanaro and G. E. Hinton, Learning Distributed Representation of Concepts using Linear Relational Embedding, *IEEE Trans. on Knowledge and Data Engineering*, Vol. 13, N.2, 232–245, 2001
5. A. Paccanaro, G.E. Hinton, Learning Hierarchical Structures with Linear Relational Embedding, *NIPS 14*, MIT Press, Cambridge, MA, 2001
6. J.B. Pollack, Recursive Distributed Representations, *Artificial Intelligence*, vol. 46, 77–105, 1990
7. J.R. Quinlan, Learning logical definitions from relations, *Machine Learning*, 5, 239–266, 1990

Meta-learning for Fast Incremental Learning

Takayuki Oohira, Koichiro Yamauchi, and Takashi Omori

Graduate School of Engineering, Hokkaido University.
Kita ku, Kita 13 Jyou Nishi 8 Chou, Sapporo, 060-8628, Japan.
{o_hira, yamauchi, omori}@complex.eng.hokudai.ac.jp

Abstract. Model based learning systems usually face to a problem of forgetting as a result of the incremental learning of new instances. Normally, the systems have to re-learn past instances to avoid this problem. However, the re-learning process wastes substantial learning time. To reduce learning time, we propose a novel incremental learning system, which consists of two neural networks: a main-learning module and a meta-learning module. The main-learning module approximates a continuous function between input and desired output value, while the meta-learning module predicts an appropriate change in parameters of the main-learning module for incremental learning. The meta-learning module acquires the learning strategy for modifying current parameters not only to adjust the main-learning module's behavior for new instances but also to avoid forgetting past learned skills.

1 Introduction

In our life, we usually acquire a new knowledge incrementally by refining our old knowledge to fit the current new situation. This style of incremental learning reduces the computational complexity for machine learning systems because they do not need to re-learn all previously learned samples. However, if a system learns new instances through conventional learning methods such as a gradient descent learning rule, it will probably forget some learned instances. To prevent the loss of learning with the minimal computational penalty, we usually add a small buffer to the learning module and store some past instances in it [1] [2] [3]. When a new instance is encountered, the system pushes it into the buffer and then uses an off-line learning method to learn all the patterns stored in the buffer. When the buffer becomes full, the system disposes the instance having the smallest error of the learning module. This approach, however, requires the system to spend time performing the off-line learning.

To solve the time requirement problem, Yamauchi et.al. have presented a hybrid learning system which reduces the apparent learning time by introducing sleep phase at fixed interval [4] [5] [6] [7] . The system consists of fast and slow learning modules. The fast learning module records the new instances quickly during daytime (i,e, waking phase), while the slow learning module uses a small number of hidden units to learn the recorded instances during the sleep phase. However, the system does not reduce the actual learning time.

In contrast, this paper presents a new learning system to reduce the actual learning time and is inspired by the model for control and learning of voluntary movement proposed by Kawato et.al. [8](see Fig 1(a)). In classical feed back controller, numerous iterations of calculations must be performed to determine optimal control signal for the plant. The model proposed by Kawato et.al reduces the number of iterations by having the 'inverse dynamics' module approximate the final solution of the feed back controller. Therefore, if the 'inverse dynamics' module knows an appropriate solution to the current desired outputs, the control is achieved quickly.

Similarly, the new proposed system has two learning modules: the main- and the meta-learning. The main-learning module approximates the desired output function, while the meta-learning module predicts appropriate change in the main-learning module's parameters. The main- and meta-learning modules correspond to the plant and the 'inverse dynamics' module of the Kawato's model, respectively (see Fig 1(b)).

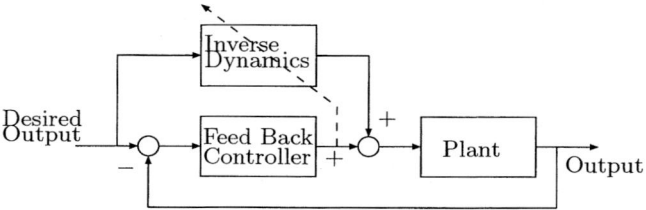

(a) Block Diagram of Feed Back Error Learning (Kawato et.al. 1987)

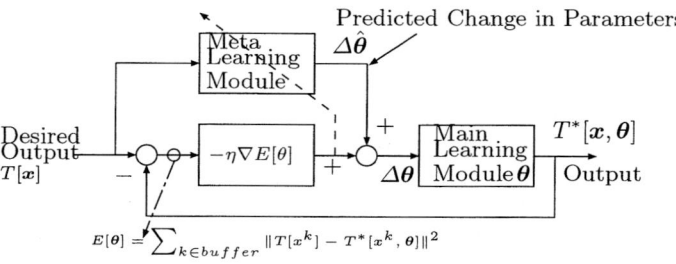

(b) Rough Sketch of Our New System

Fig. 1. Block Diagram of the error feedback learning system and Rough Sketch of our system

Section 2 explains the system structure, while section 3 shows several benchmark tests results.

2 System Structure

2.1 Outline of the System

This system consists of three parts, a pattern buffer, and main- and meta-learning modules. The main-learning module approximates a function between inputs and outputs of instances. In a way similar to the conventional incremental learning systems mentioned in the introduction, this module normally modifies its parameters using gradient descent learning of all instances stored in the pattern buffer. In contrast, the meta-learning module tries to predict appropriate change in parameters of main-learning module according to past experiences of incremental learning. The meta-learning module tries to predict an appropriate change in parameter which makes the output of the main-learning module fit to the new instance with avoiding the loss of previously learned skills. If the meta-learning module is confident about the current prediction, the main-learning module modifies its parameters according to the predicted change and not the gradient descent learning. Thus, the system sometimes finishes the incremental learning with just one modification of the parameters based on the predicted change in parameters. In fact, however, the system usually needs additional gradient descent learning with a small number of iterations to reduce the least error.

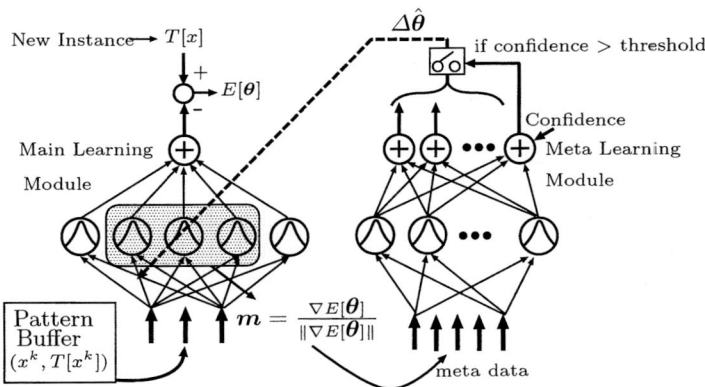

Fig. 2. Structure of the system

The whole learning procedure is summarized as follows.

(1) Store parameter of the main learning network to $\boldsymbol{\theta}^{old}$
(2) Present a new instance $(\boldsymbol{x}, T[\boldsymbol{x}])$ and calculate error $E[\boldsymbol{\theta}]$
(3) Get meta data $\boldsymbol{m}$ (see 2.3) from the current error $E[\boldsymbol{\theta}]$ of the main module.
(4) Calculate output of the meta-learning module.
(5) Modify parameters of the main module using the outputs of step (4)
(6) Push $(\boldsymbol{x}, T[\boldsymbol{x}])$ into the pattern buffer.
(7) Learning of instances stored in the buffer with a gradient descent method.
(8) Have the meta-learning network learn $\boldsymbol{\theta}_m^{new} - \boldsymbol{\theta}_m^{old}$. (see 2.3)

2.2 Neural Network Used

The two learning modules consist of radial basis function (RBF) networks. Let $T^*(x)$ be the output value of the network. Then, $T^*(x)$ is represented as weighted sum of several radial basis functions.

$$T^*(x) = \sum_\alpha h_\alpha \exp\left(-\frac{1}{\sigma_\alpha^2}\|x - u_\alpha\|^2\right) \qquad (1)$$

where h_α denotes the connection strength between the α-th hidden unit and output unit. u_α denotes the centroid of the hidden unit and σ_α is the standard deviation. During the learning, these three parameters are modified. In the following text, we denote the outputs from the main-learning module and the meta-learning module as $T^*(x, \theta)$ and $g^*(m, \xi)$, respectively. Similarly, x and m denote the input vectors for the main-learning network and that of the meta-learning network, respectively. θ and ξ denote the parameter vector of the main- and the meta-learning modules, respectively.

The number of hidden units in the main-learning module is fixed but that of the meta-learning module is adaptively increased. To realize adaptive growth, the meta-learning module employs the Resource Allocating Network (RAN) proposed by J.Platt [9]. In this learning method, a new hidden unit is added when the current error is larger than threshold ϵ_E and the distance between the nearest centroid and the current input is less than threshold ϵ_a. Otherwise, the meta-learning module handles the input with a gradient descent learning method. The centroid of the new hidden unit is set to the current input vector and h_α is set to the current error. The standard deviation of the new one is set as $\sigma_\alpha = \gamma \|m - nearestcenter\|$, where γ denotes the ratio of overlap. Using this growth strategy, the meta-learning module learns inputs very quickly.

2.3 Behavior of Meta-learning Module

The meta-learning module predicts appropriate parameter changes for the main-learning modules. The input vector for the meta-learning module is basically a normalized gradient vector of the main network's least square error of the new instance. However, if the module observes entire dimension of the gradient vector, the module cannot find a rule behind the data because of large-scale variations. To solve the problem, the system extracts a sub-dimension from the gradient vector: the gradient vector of the three hidden units with centroids closest to current input x. Let θ_m be the parameters of the three hidden units:

$$\theta_m \equiv (h_{i1}, \sigma_{i1}, u_{i1}^T, h_{i2}, \sigma_{i2}, u_{i2}^T, h_{i3}, \sigma_{i3}, u_{i3}^T,)^T \qquad (2)$$

where $i1, i2$ and $i3$ denote the indexes of the three hidden units, and 'T' denotes the transportation. $i1, i2$ and $i3$ are arranged in the ascending order of the distance between respective centroid and the current input. We chose the meta-data to be the normalized gradient vector of the main-learning module of the three hidden units:

$$m = D/\|D\| \qquad (3)$$

where

$$D \equiv \nabla_{\boldsymbol{\theta}_m} E[\boldsymbol{\theta}] \,|_{\boldsymbol{\theta}_m = \boldsymbol{\theta}_m^{old}} \tag{4}$$

$E[\boldsymbol{\theta}]$ denotes the current error of the main-learning module:

$$E[\boldsymbol{\theta}] = \|\boldsymbol{T}[\boldsymbol{x}] - \boldsymbol{f}^*(\boldsymbol{x}, \boldsymbol{\theta})\|^2 \tag{5}$$

The met-learning module learns the actual change in parameters of the main-learning module. The changes in parameters are calculated as follows. First of all, the predicted changes in parameters (the output of the meta-learning module) are added to the old parameters.

$$\boldsymbol{\theta}_m' = \boldsymbol{\theta}_m + \|\boldsymbol{D}\| \boldsymbol{g}^*(\boldsymbol{m}, \boldsymbol{\xi}) \tag{6}$$

Note that $\|\boldsymbol{D}\|$ is multiplied to the output vector of the meta-learning network to expand scale of the output vector to an appropriate length. The reason for this adjustment is that the meta-learning network always learns using a normalized vector to avoid the affects of variation in vector length.

Then, the parameter vector of the main-learning module becomes $\boldsymbol{\theta}'$, which is a refrection of $\boldsymbol{\theta}_m'$. The main-learning network learns the instances stored in the pattern buffer until the total error of the main-learning module is less than threshold Err_{min}.

$$\boldsymbol{\theta}_{t+1} = \boldsymbol{\theta}_t - \eta \nabla \left\{ \sum_{k \in buffer} \|\boldsymbol{T}(\boldsymbol{x}^k) - \boldsymbol{T}^*(\boldsymbol{x}^k, \boldsymbol{\theta}_t)\|^2 \right\} \tag{7}$$

where $\eta\ (> 0)$ is the speed of the learning and $\boldsymbol{\theta}_0 = \boldsymbol{\theta}'$.

Then, the parameter vector becomes $\boldsymbol{\theta}^{new}$. The meta-learning module learns the actual change in parameters of the three hidden units: $\boldsymbol{\theta}_m^{new} - \boldsymbol{\theta}_m^{old}$, where $\boldsymbol{\theta}_m^{old}$ denotes the initial parameter vector. Therefore,

$$\boldsymbol{\xi} := \boldsymbol{\xi} - \eta \nabla_{\boldsymbol{\xi}} \left\{ \|\Delta\boldsymbol{\theta}_*/\|\boldsymbol{D}\| - \boldsymbol{g}^*(\boldsymbol{m}, \boldsymbol{\xi})\|^2 + Err_c(\boldsymbol{m}, \boldsymbol{\xi}) \right\} \tag{8}$$

where $\Delta\boldsymbol{\theta}_* \equiv \boldsymbol{\theta}_m^{new} - \boldsymbol{\theta}_m^{old}$. In Eq(8), $Err_c(\boldsymbol{m}, \boldsymbol{\xi})$ denotes the error of the additional unit (see Figure 2), which outputs the 'magnitude of confidence' for the current prediction. The desired output for this additional unit should be large when the current prediction is correct and small when incorrect. So, we defined the desired output of this additional unit T_c as

$$T_c \equiv \exp\left(-\|\Delta\boldsymbol{\theta}_*/\|\boldsymbol{D}\| - \boldsymbol{g}^*(\boldsymbol{m}, \boldsymbol{\xi})\|^2\right) \tag{9}$$

Then, $Err_c(\boldsymbol{m}, \boldsymbol{\xi}) = (T_c - C(\boldsymbol{m}, \boldsymbol{\xi}))^2$ where $C(\boldsymbol{m}, \boldsymbol{\xi})$ denotes the output value of the additional unit. Eq(8) is executed only once every after the learning cycle of the main-learning module.

3 Experiments

We tested the new system with three datasets. The pre-determined parameters for the meta-learning module were $\varepsilon_a = 0.7$, $\eta = 0.1$ and the overlap factor γ was set to 0.65. The size of pattern buffer was set to 20. The initial standard deviation of the hidden units of the main-learning module was set to 0.3. The gradient descent learning of the main-learning module (step (7) in 2.1) was continued until least square error to all instances stored in the pattern buffer was less than 0.00015. The confidence threshold was set to 0.995. In the preliminary simulation study, we empirically found these values of the parameters make the system work appropriately.

Sin curve. The first dataset is $T(x) = \sin(x)$.

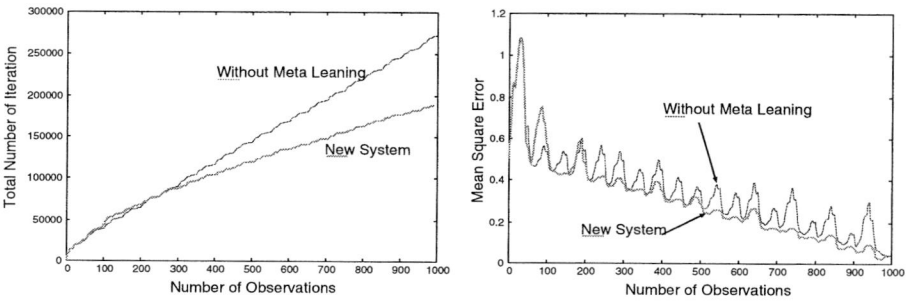

Fig. 3. Total Number of Iterations and Mean Square Error of the sin curve.

The system learned 1000 samples of $(x, T(x))$ from $x = 0$ to $x = 20\pi$ sequentially. 60 centroids of the main-learning module's hidden units were initially positioned equally spaced across the interval of x $[0, 20\pi]$.

Note that, in such cyclic sample patterns, the system encounters homogeneous parameter optimizing tasks repeatedly; consequently, the system can reduce the number of iterations easily. Fig 3 shows the plots the total number of iterations and mean square error of the system. In these figures, the performances of the system without meta-learning is also shown for comparison. We can see that not only the number of iterations but also the mean square error of the new system is less than that of the system without the meta-learning.

Mackey Glass Chaos. The second dataset is the Mackey Glass Chaos of UCI Machine Repository, which is a chaos time series.

This dataset consists of 3000 sets of the four dimensional input pattern and the corresponding desired output value $T[x]$. The centroids of the main-learning

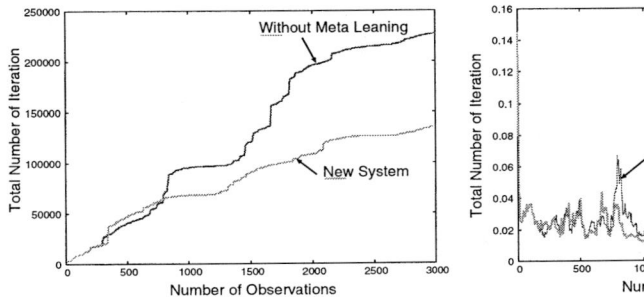
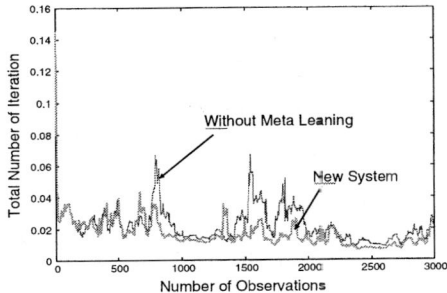

Fig. 4. Total Number of Iterations and Mean Square Error for the Mackey Glass Chaos.

module were initially positioned at lattice points in the cubic area: x_i in the interval $[0.5, 1.2]$ for $i = 1, 2, 3, 4$. The total number of the centroids was 81.

Fig 4 shows the total number of iterations and the mean square error of our new system and the system without the meta-learning module. We also see that the number of iterations of our new system decreases greatly compared with that of the system without meta-learning module.

Sin curve II. The third dataset is almost the same as the first one except for the presentation order of x is random.

The number of iterations is plotted in Fig 5. We can see that the number of iterations is the same as the system without the meta-learning. This result means there are too many variations in the training data $(m, \Delta\theta^*/\|D\|)$ so that the system cannot find any effective law for prediction.

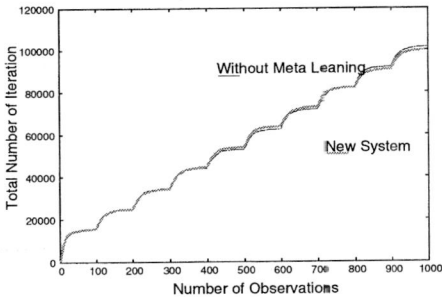

Fig. 5. Total Number of Iterations when x are presented at random

4 Discussion and Conclusion

This paper presents an incremental learning system that improves the learning speed by applying the past learning strategy discovered by the learner.

The meta-learning module in the system tries to predict an optimal change in main-learning module's parameters. If the prediction is correct, the system finishes the incremental learning after only a single iteration. Even if the prediction is not correct, the system finishes the learning with only a small number of iterations to reduce the remaining small error.

In the simulation study, we can see that a condition is needed to make the system work well. The condition is that, during the incremental learning, homogeneous learning situation appears frequently. Therefore, the new incremental learning system works well for both cyclic or chaotic time series.

It is well known that, although the first learning of a foreign language is very hard, the second learning of the another foreign language is easier than that of the first one. There are two possible assumptions for explaining the above phenomena. The first is that we re-use a domain-specific knowledge acquired during the first learning of the foreign language, and the second is that we use a learning technique acquired during the previous learning. There are many models which support the first assumption [10]. In contrast, our system supports the second assumption. We believe that the learning technique is more useful than the domain-specific knowledge for speeding up learning of various problems.

References

1. Takao Yoneda, Masashi Yamanaka, and Yukinori Kakazu. Study on optimization of grinding conditions using neural networks – a method of additional learning –. *Journal of the Japan Society of Precision Engineering/Seimitsu kogakukaishi*, 58(10):1707–1712, October 1992.
2. Hiroshi Yamakawa, Daiki Masumoto, Takashi Kimoto, and Shigemi Nagata. Active data selection and subsequent revision for sequential learning with neural networks. *World congress of neural networks (WCNN'94)*, 3:661–666, 1994.
3. Koichiro Yamauchi, Nobuhiko Yamaguchi, and Naohiro Ishii. Incremental learning methods with retrieving interfered patterns. *IEEE TRANSACTIONS ON NEURAL NETWORKS*, 10(6):1351–1365, November 1999.
4. Koichiro Yamauchi, Sachio Itho, and Naohiro Ishii. Combination of fast and slow learning neural networks for quick adaptation and pruning redundant cells. In *IEEE SMC'99 1999 IEEE System, Man and Cybernetics Conference*, volume III, pages 390–395, October 1999.
5. Koichiro Yamauchi, Sachio Ito, and Naohiro Ishii. Wake-sleep learning method for quick adaptation and reduction of redundant cells. In *ICONIP 2000 7th International Conference on Neural Information Processing*, volume 1, pages 559–564, November 2000.
6. Koichiro Yamauchi. Sequential learning and model selection with sleep. In Liming Zhang and Fanji Gu, editors, *ICONIP 2001 8th International Conference on Neural Information Processing*, volume 1, pages 205–210. Fudan University Press, November 2001.
7. Koichiro Yamauchi and Nobufusa Kobayashi. Incremental learning with sleep – learning of noiseless datasets –. In *International Conference on Neural Information Processing ICONIP2002*, volume 1, pages 398–403, November 2002.
8. M. Kawato, Kazunori Furukawa, and R. Suzuki. A hierarchical neural-network model for control and learning of voluntary movement. *Biological Cybernetics*, 57:169–185, 1987.
9. John Platt. A resource allocating network for function interpolation. *Neural Computation*, 3(2):213–225, 1991.
10. Sebastian Thrun and Lorien Pratt. Learning to learn: Introduction and overview. In Sebastian Thrun and Lorien Pratt, editors, *Learning to Learn*, pages 3–17. Kluwer Academic Publishers, 1998.

Expectation-MiniMax Approach to Clustering Analysis*

Yiu-ming Cheung

Department of Computer Science
Hong Kong Baptist University, Hong Kong
ymc@comp.hkbu.edu.hk

Abstract. This paper proposes a general approach named *Expectation-MiniMax (EMM)* for clustering analysis without knowing the cluster number. It describes the contrast function of Expectation-Maximization (EM) algorithm by an approximate one with a designable error term. Through adaptively minimizing a specific error term meanwhile maximizing the approximate contrast function, the EMM automatically penalizes all rivals during the competitive learning. Subsequently, the EMM not only includes the *Rival Penalized Competitive Learning* algorithm (Xu et al. 1993) and its Type A form (Xu 1997) with the new variants developed, but also provides a better alternative way to optimize the EM contrast function with at least two advantages: (1) faster model parameter learning speed, and (2) automatic model-complexity selection capability. We present the general learning procedures of the EMM, and demonstrate its outstanding performance in comparison with the EM.

1 Introduction

In the literature, the conventional clustering algorithm k-means [4] has been widely used in a variety of applications, which however needs to pre-assign an appropriate cluster number. Otherwise, it often leads to a poor clustering result. Unfortunately, such a setting is an intractable problem from a practical viewpoint. Alternatively, clustering problem has been studied by formulating as a finite mixture of Gaussian densities, in which each density generally describes a cluster in any elliptic shape and in any portion of samples [8]. Subsequently, the Gaussian mixture with the parameters estimated by the Expectation-Maximization (EM) algorithm [3] provides a general solution for clustering in parallel [3,5]. However, in analog with the k-means algorithm, it still needs to pre-assign the correct number of densities.

In the past decades, some works have been done towards determining the correct number of clusters or densities along two major lines. The first one is to formulate the cluster number selection as the choice of component number in a finite mixture model. Consequently, there have been some criteria proposed

---

* This work was supported by the Faculty Research Grant of Hong Kong Baptist University (Project No: FRG/02/03/I-06).

for model selection, such as AIC [1], SIC [6] and so forth. Often, these existing criteria may overestimate or underestimate the cluster number due to the difficulty of choosing an appropriate penalty function. In recent years, a number selection criterion developed from Ying-Yang Machine has been proposed and experimentally verified in [8], whose computing however is laborious.

In contrast, the other line aims to select an appropriate cluster number automatically by algorithms themselves during the competition learning without a large amount of extra computing. In the literature, the typical example is the Rival Penalized Competitive Learning (RPCL) algorithm [9] and its variant RPCL (Type A) [8]. Its basic idea is that for each input, not only the winner of the seed points is updated to adapt to the input, but also its nearest rival (the second winner) is de-learned by a smaller learning rate (also called *de-learning rate* hereafter). Many experiments have shown that the RPCL can perform well in clustering analysis without knowing the cluster number. However, such a penalization scheme is heuristically proposed without any theoretical guidance. In this paper, we propose a general learning approach named *Expectation-MiniMax (EMM)* that describes the contrast function of EM algorithm by an approximate one with a designable error term. Through adaptively minimizing a specific error term meanwhile maximizing the approximate contrast function, we will show that the EMM automatically possesses the penalization scheme to punish all rivals during the competitive learning. Subsequently, the EMM not only includes the RPCL and its Type A form with the new variants proposed, but also shows that such a rival penalized learning actually provides a better alternative way to optimize the EM contrast function with at least two advantages: (1) faster model parameter learning speed, and (2) automatic model-complexity selection capability. We will give out the general learning procedures of the EMM, and show its superior performance in comparison with the EM.

2 Expectation-MiniMax (EMM) Learning Approach

2.1 General Learning Framework

Suppose N observations $\mathbf{x}_1$, $\mathbf{x}_2$, ..., $\mathbf{x}_N$ are independently and identically distributed from an identifiable finite-mixture density population:

$$p^*(\mathbf{x}; \boldsymbol{\Theta}^*) = \sum_{j=1}^{k^*} \alpha_j^* p(\mathbf{x}; \boldsymbol{\theta}_j^*), \qquad \sum_{j=1}^{k^*} \alpha_j^* = 1, \quad \text{and} \qquad \alpha_j^* > 0, \qquad (1)$$

where k^* is the true mixture number of densities, $\boldsymbol{\Theta}^* = \{(\alpha_j^*, \boldsymbol{\theta}_j^*) | 1 \leq j \leq k^*\}$ is the unknown true parameter set. The paper [3] shows that the estimate of $\boldsymbol{\Theta}^*$, written as $\boldsymbol{\Theta}$, can be achieved by maximizing the following contrast function:

$$Q(\mathbf{X}_N; \boldsymbol{\Theta}) = \frac{1}{N} \sum_{t=1}^{N} q_t(\mathbf{x}_t; \boldsymbol{\Theta}), \qquad (2)$$

with

$$q_t(\mathbf{x}_t; \boldsymbol{\Theta}) = \sum_{j=1}^{k} h(j|\mathbf{x}_t) \ln[\alpha_j p(\mathbf{x}_t; \boldsymbol{\theta}_j)], \tag{3}$$

where $\mathbf{X}_N = [\mathbf{x}_1^T, \mathbf{x}_2^T, \dots, \mathbf{x}_N^T]^T$, and the candidate mixture number k measures the model complexity. Furthermore, $h(j|\mathbf{x})$ is the posterior probability of the jth density as given $\mathbf{x}$ with

$$h(j|\mathbf{x}) = \frac{\alpha_j p(\mathbf{x}; \boldsymbol{\theta}_j)}{p(\mathbf{x}_t; \boldsymbol{\Theta})} = \frac{\alpha_j p(\mathbf{x}; \boldsymbol{\theta}_j)}{\sum_{r=1}^{k} p(\mathbf{x}_t; \boldsymbol{\theta}_r)}, \tag{4}$$

and

$$p(\mathbf{x}; \boldsymbol{\Theta}) = \sum_{j=1}^{k} \alpha_j p(\mathbf{x}_t; \boldsymbol{\theta}_j), \quad \sum_{j=1}^{k} \alpha_j = 1, \quad \alpha_j > 0. \tag{5}$$

Hence, with a specific k, minimizing Eq.(2) can be implemented by an adaptive EM algorithm [7]. In Eq.(3), we further replace $h(j|\mathbf{x}_t)$ by

$$I(j|\mathbf{x}_t) = \begin{cases} 1, & \text{if } j = \arg\max_{1 \le r \le k} h(r|\mathbf{x}_t); \\ 0, & \text{otherwise.} \end{cases} \tag{6}$$

Subsequently, the contrast function $Q(\mathbf{x}; \boldsymbol{\Theta})$ in Eq.(2) is approximated by

$$R(\mathbf{X}_N; \boldsymbol{\Theta}) = \frac{1}{N} \sum_{t=1}^{N} J_t(\mathbf{x}_t; \boldsymbol{\Theta}), \quad J_t(\mathbf{x}_t; \boldsymbol{\Theta}) = \sum_{j=1}^{k} I(j|\mathbf{x}_t) \ln[\alpha_j p(\mathbf{x}_t; \boldsymbol{\theta}_j)]. \tag{7}$$

We therefore express $Q(\mathbf{X}_N; \boldsymbol{\Theta})$ by

$$Q(\mathbf{X}_N; \boldsymbol{\Theta}) = R(\mathbf{X}_N; \boldsymbol{\Theta}) - E(\mathbf{X}_N; \boldsymbol{\Theta}) \tag{8}$$

with $E(\mathbf{X}_N; \boldsymbol{\Theta}) = \frac{1}{N} \sum_{t=1}^{N} e(\mathbf{x}_t; \boldsymbol{\Theta})$, $e(\mathbf{x}_t; \boldsymbol{\Theta}) \ge 0$, where $E(\mathbf{X}_N; \boldsymbol{\Theta})$ is the average approximate error, and $e(\mathbf{x}_t; \boldsymbol{\Theta})$ measures an instantaneous error at time step t. In general, $E(\mathbf{X}_N; \boldsymbol{\Theta})$ varies with the change of $\boldsymbol{\Theta}$, thus maximizing $R(\mathbf{X}_N; \boldsymbol{\Theta})$ is not equivalent to maximize $Q(\mathbf{X}_N; \boldsymbol{\Theta})$. That is, we should minimize the approximate error $E(\mathbf{X}_N; \boldsymbol{\Theta})$, meanwhile maximizing $R(\mathbf{X}_N; \boldsymbol{\Theta})$. Subsequently, at each time step t, after calculating $h(j|\mathbf{x}_t)$s by Eq.(4) (also called the *Expectation*-step in the EM), we adjust the parameters with a small step towards minimizing $e(\mathbf{x}_t; \boldsymbol{\Theta})$ meanwhile maximizing $J_t(\mathbf{x}_t; \boldsymbol{\Theta})$. We name such a learning *Expectation-MiniMax (EMM)* approach. It can be seen that EMM degenerates to the EM learning [3] as the error $e(\mathbf{x}_t; \boldsymbol{\Theta}) = \bar{e}(\mathbf{x}_t; \boldsymbol{\Theta}) = J_t(\mathbf{x}_t; \boldsymbol{\Theta}) - q_t(\mathbf{x}_t; \boldsymbol{\Theta})$. In the EMM, we have noticed that replacing $h(j|\mathbf{x}_t)$s by $I(j|\mathbf{x}_t)$s at each time step t eventually brings about $E(\mathbf{X}_N; \boldsymbol{\Theta})$. Hence, we can generally describe the error $e(\mathbf{x}_t; \boldsymbol{\Theta})$ as a function of both $h(j|\mathbf{x})_t$s and $I(j|\mathbf{x}_t)$s so long as each $e(\mathbf{x}_t; \boldsymbol{\Theta}) \ge 0$ holds. Subsequently, we can describe the relationship between it and $\bar{E}(\mathbf{X}_N; \boldsymbol{\Theta}) = \frac{1}{N} \sum_{t=1}^{N} \bar{e}(\mathbf{x}_t; \boldsymbol{\Theta})$ by

$$\bar{E}(\mathbf{X}_N; \boldsymbol{\Theta}) = \lambda(\boldsymbol{\Theta}) E(\mathbf{X}_N; \boldsymbol{\Theta}), \tag{9}$$

where $\lambda(\Theta)$ is a positive scale number, which is generally a function of Θ only, irrelevant to N observations. Hence, estimation of Θ by maximizing $Q(\mathbf{X}_N; \Theta)$ in Eq.(2) is equivalent to maximize

$$Q_m(\mathbf{X}_N; \Theta) = R(\mathbf{X}_N; \Theta) - \lambda_m E(\mathbf{X}_N; \Theta) \qquad (10)$$

where λ_m represents the scale number calculated via Eq.(9) with the value of Θ being the optimal solution of maximizing $Q(\mathbf{X}_N; \Theta)$ in Eq.(2). Under the circumstances, it can be seen that maximizing Eq.(10) via the EMM generally leads to the same solution as the EM. In general, we however need not estimate λ_m. Instead, we simply regard λ_m as a constant during the learning. Subsequently, the EMM provides an approximate, but better way to maximize $Q(\mathbf{X}_N; \Theta)$ of Eq.(2). In the following subsection, we will give out a general EMM learning algorithm under a specific modeling of $E(\mathbf{X}_N; \Theta)$.

2.2 A General EMM Learning Algorithm

We let

$$E(\mathbf{X}_N; \Theta) = \frac{1}{N} \sum_{t=1}^{N} e(\mathbf{x}_t; \Theta) = \frac{1}{N} \sum_{t=1}^{N} \sum_{j=1}^{k} [I(j|\mathbf{x}_t) - h(j|\mathbf{x}_t)]^2. \qquad (11)$$

Eq.(10) can then be specified as

$$Q_m(\mathbf{X}_N; \Theta) = \frac{1}{N} \sum_{t=1}^{N} \sum_{j=1}^{k} J_t(\mathbf{x}_t; \Theta) - \lambda_m \frac{1}{N} \sum_{t=1}^{N} \sum_{j=1}^{k} e(\mathbf{x}_t; \Theta). \qquad (12)$$

Hence, maximizing $Q_m(\mathbf{X}_N; \Theta)$ in Eq.(12) can be realized towards maximizing $R(\mathbf{X}_N; \Theta)$ meanwhile minimizing $E(\mathbf{X}_N; \Theta)$. In adaptive implementation, we have the following EMM learning algorithm:

Step II.B.1 Initialize the parameter set Θ as given a specific k.
Step II.B.2 Given each input $\mathbf{x}_t$, calculate $I(j|\mathbf{x}_t)$ by Eq.(6) with $h(j|\mathbf{x}_t)$ given by Eq.(4) with Θ fixed.
Step II.B.3 Fix $I(j|\mathbf{x}_t)$, update Θ with a small step towards the direction of maximizing $R(\mathbf{X}_N; \Theta)$. To avoid the constraint on α_js during the learning, we let α_js be the soft-max function of k totally-free new variables β_js with

$$\alpha_j = \frac{\exp(\beta_j)}{\sum_{r=1}^{k} \exp(\beta_r)}. \qquad (13)$$

Subsequently, we update

$$\boldsymbol{\beta}_c^{(\text{new})} = \boldsymbol{\beta}_c^{(\text{old})} + \eta_1 \frac{\partial J_t(\mathbf{x}_t; \Theta)}{\partial \boldsymbol{\beta}_c}\Big|_{\boldsymbol{\beta}_c^{(\text{old})}} \qquad (14)$$

$$\boldsymbol{\theta}_c^{(\text{new})} = \boldsymbol{\theta}_c^{(\text{old})} + \eta_1 \frac{\partial J_t(\mathbf{x}_t; \Theta)}{\partial \boldsymbol{\theta}_c}\Big|_{\boldsymbol{\theta}_c^{(\text{old})}}, \qquad (15)$$

where η_1 is a small positive step size. We denote the updating results of **Step II.B.3** as $\Theta^a = \{\beta_j^a, \theta_j^a\}_{j=1}^k$ with

$$\beta_j^a = \begin{cases} \beta_c^{(\text{new})}, & \text{if } j = c, \\ \beta_j^{(\text{old})}, & \text{if } j \neq c \end{cases} \qquad \theta_j^a = \begin{cases} \theta_c^{(\text{new})}, & \text{if } j = c, \\ \theta_j^{(\text{old})}, & \text{if } j \neq c. \end{cases} \quad (16)$$

Step II.B.4 Fix Θ^a, we let

$$h^a(j|\mathbf{x}_t) = \begin{cases} \dfrac{\alpha_c^{(\text{new})} p(\mathbf{x}_t; \theta_c^{(\text{new})})}{p(\mathbf{x}_t; \Theta^a)}, & \text{if } j = c \\ \dfrac{\alpha_j^{(\text{old})} p(\mathbf{x}; \theta_j^{(\text{old})})}{p(\mathbf{x}_t; \Theta^a)}, & \text{otherwise,} \end{cases} \quad (17)$$

with $\alpha_c^{(\text{new})}$ calculated by Eq.(13) based on $\beta_c^{(\text{new})}$ and those $\beta_j^{(\text{old})}$s with $j \neq c$. Then, we adjust $\Theta^{(\text{old})}$ with a small step towards the direction of minimizing $E(\mathbf{X}_N; \Theta)$, where $e(\mathbf{x}_t; \Theta)$ is explicitly given as

$$e(\mathbf{x}_t; \Theta) = (\mathbf{I}_t^a - \mathbf{h}_t^a)^T (\mathbf{I}_t^a - \mathbf{h}_t^a) \quad (18)$$

with

$$\mathbf{I}_t^a = [I^a(1|\mathbf{x}_t), I^a(2|\mathbf{x}_t), \ldots, I^a(k|\mathbf{x}_t)]^T \quad (19)$$

$$\mathbf{h}_t^a = [h^a(1|\mathbf{x}_t), h^a(2|\mathbf{x}_t), \ldots, h^a(k|\mathbf{x}_t)]^T \quad (20)$$

$$I^a(j|\mathbf{x}_t) = \begin{cases} 1, & \text{if } j = \arg\max_{1 \leq r \leq k} h^a(r|\mathbf{x}_t); \\ 0, & \text{otherwise.} \end{cases} \quad (21)$$

It can be shown that $\mathbf{I}_t^a$ must be equal to $\mathbf{I}_t$. Since Θ^a is fixed, it implies that $h^a(c|\mathbf{x}_t)$ is a constant in this step. Hence, we only need to adjust those remaining parameters in Θ except for β_c and θ_c, denoted as $\tilde{\Theta}$ hereafter. Furthermore, we notice that there is a summation constraint on α_js as shown in Eq.(5), the updating of β_c only in Eq.(14) is, in effect, to automatically update those α_js with $j \neq c$ with a small step towards the direction of minimizing $E(\mathbf{X}_N; \Theta)$. Hence, at this step, we need not update those α_js with $j \neq c$. Subsequently, we have, for $\forall 1 \leq j \leq k$ with $j \neq c$,

$$\theta_j^{(\text{new})} = \theta_j^{(\text{old})} - \eta_2 \dfrac{\partial e(\mathbf{x}_t; \Theta^a)}{\partial \theta_j} \bigg|_{\tilde{\Theta}^{(\text{old})}} \quad (22)$$

$$= \theta_j^{(\text{old})} - \eta_2 \dfrac{h^a(j|\mathbf{x}_t)}{p(\mathbf{x}_t; \Theta^a)} \dfrac{\partial}{\partial \theta_j} [\alpha_j p(\mathbf{x}_t; \theta_j)] \bigg|_{\tilde{\Theta}^{(\text{old})}}, \quad (23)$$

where $\eta_2 = \eta_1 \lambda_m$ is the learning step in **Step II.B.4**, and $\mathbf{I}_t^a$ must be equal to $\mathbf{I}_t$ for each time step t. In Eq.(23), extra computing is required to calculate $p(\mathbf{x}_t; \Theta^a)$ and $h^a(j|\mathbf{x}_t)$s with $j \neq c$. For simplicity, we hereafter further approximate $p(\mathbf{x}_t; \Theta^a)$ by $p(\mathbf{x}_t; \Theta^{(\text{old})})$, those $h^a(j|\mathbf{x}_t)$s with $j \neq c$ then become $h(j|\mathbf{x}_t)$s. That is, Eq.(23) is approximated by

$$\theta_j^{(\text{new})} = \theta_j^{(\text{old})} - \eta_2 \dfrac{h(j|\mathbf{x}_t)}{p(\mathbf{x}_t; \Theta^{(\text{old})})} \dfrac{\partial}{\partial \theta_j} [\alpha_j p(\mathbf{x}_t; \theta_j)] \bigg|_{\tilde{\Theta}^{(\text{old})}} \quad (24)$$

for $\forall 1 \leq j \leq k$ with $j \neq c$.

Step II.B.5 **Step II.B.1 – Step II.B.4** are repeated for each input until Θ converges.

If we further let each mixture component $p(\mathbf{x}; \boldsymbol{\theta}_j)$ be a Gaussian density, written as $G(\mathbf{x}; \mathbf{m}_j, \boldsymbol{\Sigma}_j)$, where $\mathbf{m}_j$ and $\boldsymbol{\Sigma}_j$ are the mean and covariance matrix of $\mathbf{x}$, respectively, the previous **Step II.B.3** and **Step II.B.4** can then explicitly become

Step II.B.3 Update $\boldsymbol{\theta}_c$ with $I(c|\mathbf{x}_t) = 1$ only by

$$\beta_c^{(\text{new})} = \beta_c^{(\text{old})} + \eta_1(1 - \alpha_c^{(\text{old})}) \tag{25}$$

$$\mathbf{m}_c^{(\text{new})} = \mathbf{m}_c^{(\text{old})} + \eta_1 \boldsymbol{\Sigma}_c^{-1\,(\text{old})}(\mathbf{x}_t - \mathbf{m}_c^{(\text{old})}) \tag{26}$$

$$\boldsymbol{\Sigma}_c^{-1\,(\text{new})} = (1 + \eta_1)\boldsymbol{\Sigma}_c^{-1\,(\text{old})} - \eta_1 \mathbf{U}_{t,c} \tag{27}$$

with $\mathbf{U}_{t,c} = [\boldsymbol{\Sigma}_c^{-1\,(\text{old})}(\mathbf{x}_t - \mathbf{m}_c^{(\text{old})})(\mathbf{x}_t - \mathbf{m}_c^{(\text{old})})^T \boldsymbol{\Sigma}_c^{-1\,(\text{old})}]$.

Step II.B.4 Update those $\boldsymbol{\theta}_j$s with $j \neq c$ (we call them as *rivals* hereafter). That is,

$$\mathbf{m}_j^{(\text{new})} = \mathbf{m}_j^{(\text{old})} - \eta_2 h^2(j|\mathbf{x}_t) \boldsymbol{\Sigma}_j^{-1\,(\text{old})}(\mathbf{x}_t - \mathbf{m}_j^{(\text{old})}) \tag{28}$$

$$\boldsymbol{\Sigma}_j^{-1\,(\text{new})} = [1 - \eta_2 h^2(j|\mathbf{x}_t)]\boldsymbol{\Sigma}_j^{-1\,(\text{old})} + \eta_2 h^2(j|\mathbf{x}_t)\mathbf{U}_{t,j}. \tag{29}$$

If we fix η_2 at zero and initialize the seed points $\mathbf{m}_j$s such that each true cluster contains at least a seed point, it can be seen that the EMM actually degenerates to the k^*-means algorithm [2]. Otherwise, the EMM not only updates the winner of the component parameters β_c and $\boldsymbol{\theta}_c$ in **Step II.B.3**, but also penalizes all rivals with a de-learning rate η_2 in **Step II.B.4**. In consistence with the updating equations of $\mathbf{m}_c$ and $\boldsymbol{\Sigma}_c$ in Eq.(26) and Eq.(27) respectively, we therefore name $\eta_{j,t} = \eta_2 h^2(j|\mathbf{x}_t)$ with $j \neq c$ as the penalization force rate of the rival with the subscript j. Compared to the exiting RPCL (Type A), the EMM algorithm extends it with the two generalizations:

1. At each time step, the EMM penalizes all rivals rather than the nearest rival of the winner in the RPCL (Type A).
2. The penalization force rate in EMM is dynamically changed, while the RPCL (Type A) set the so-called *de-learning rate* constantly.

Hence, in analog with the RPCL (Type A), the EMM can automatically determine the correct cluster number so long as k in **Step II.B.1** is not less than k^*. If we further simply penalize the nearest rival **only** each time in the same way as the RPCL and its Type A variant, and always fix its penalization force rate at a constant, written as $\bar{\eta}_\tau$, the EMM then degenerates to the RPCL (Type A). Furthermore, during the clustering, if we further fix all $\alpha_j = \frac{1}{k}$, and $\boldsymbol{\Sigma}_j = \mathbf{I}$ for $\forall 1 \leq j \leq k$, where $\mathbf{I}$ is the identity matrix, the learning rule of the seed points $\mathbf{m}_j$s in the EMM is then equivalent to that of the RPCL [9]. That is, either of RPCL or RPCL (Type A) is a special case of the EMM.

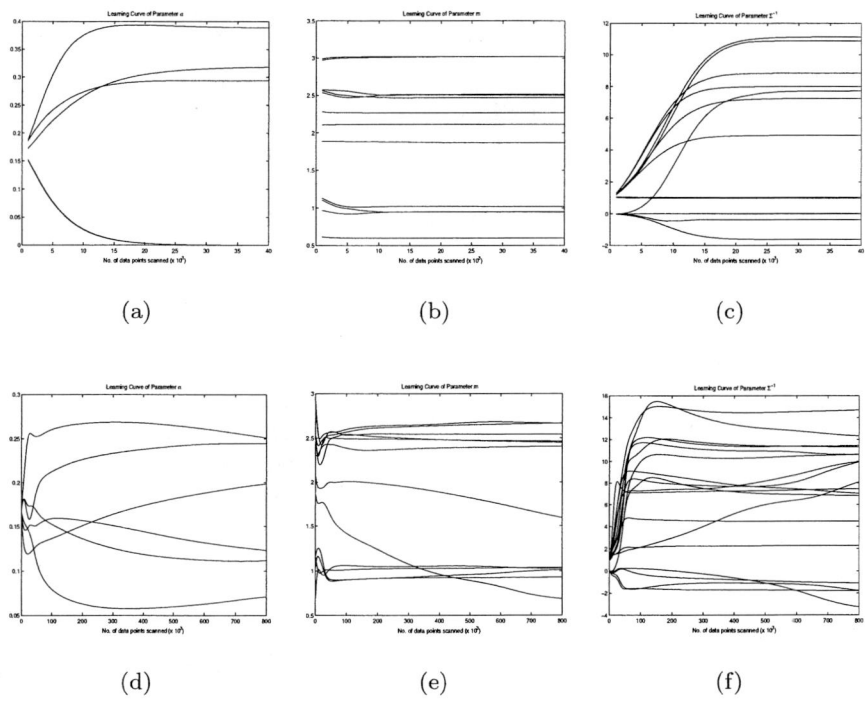

Fig. 1. Sub-figures (a)-(c) show the learning curves of α_js, $\mathbf{m}_j$s and $\boldsymbol{\Sigma}_j^{-1}$s by the EMM, while Sub-figures (d)-(f) show their learning curves by the EM.

3 Experimental Demonstration

To show the performance of the EMM in comparison with the EM, we randomly generated the data points from a mixture of three bivariate Gaussian distributions:

$$p(\mathbf{x}) = 0.3G[\mathbf{x}| \begin{pmatrix} 1 \\ 1 \end{pmatrix}, \begin{pmatrix} 0.15, 0.05 \\ 0.05, 0.25 \end{pmatrix}] + 0.4G[\mathbf{x}| \begin{pmatrix} 1.0 \\ 2.5 \end{pmatrix}, \begin{pmatrix} 0.15, 0.0 \\ 0.0, 0.14 \end{pmatrix}]$$

$$+ 0.3G[\mathbf{x}| \begin{pmatrix} 2.5 \\ 2.5 \end{pmatrix}, \begin{pmatrix} 0.15, -0.1 \\ -0.1, 0.15 \end{pmatrix}] \tag{30}$$

with the sample size $1,000$. We used six seed points, i.e., $k > k^* = 3$, and randomly set the learning rate $\eta_1 = \eta_2 = 0.001$.

Fig. 1 shows the parameter learning curves of the EMM and the EM, respectively. It can be seen that the EM learning speed is much slower than the proposed EMM. Actually, the parameters learned by the EMM have converged after 40 epoches, but the EM not despite 800 epoches. In the EMM, one snapshot at Epoch 40 found that $\{\alpha_i, \boldsymbol{\theta}_i\}$ with $i = 1, 2, 4$ all converged to the correct values, meanwhile $\alpha_3 = \alpha_5 = \alpha_6 = 0$. From the winning rule of Eq.(6), we know that the densities of $3, 5, 6$ have become dead because they have no chance any more to win in the competition learning process. In other words, the data set is recognized to be a mixture of the three densities: $1, 2, 4$. Hence, the EMM has the robust performance without knowing the exact cluster number. In contrast, it was found that the EM leaded six densities to compete each other without making extra densities die. Subsequently, all the parameters were converged to the wrong positions. That is, the EM cannot work in this case.

4 Conclusion

This paper have proposed a general *Expectation-MiniMax* learning approach that not only includes the RPCL and its Type A form with the new variants developed, but also shows that such a penalized learning actually provides an alternative way to optimize the EM contrast function. Compared to the EM, the EMM converges much faster with the robust performance in clustering analysis without knowing the cluster number. We have presented the general learning procedures of the EMM, and successfully demonstrated its superior performance in comparison with the EM.

References

1. H. Akaike, "A New Look at the Statistical Model Identfication", *IEEE Transactions on Automatic Control AC-19*, pp. 716–723, 1974.
2. Y.M. Cheung, "k^*-means — A Generalized k-means Clustering Algorithm with Unknown Cluster Number", *Proceedings of Third International Conference on Intelligent Data Engineering and Automated Learning* (IDEAL'02), pp. 307-317, 2002.
3. A.P. Dempster, N.M. Laird and D.B. Rubin, "Maximum Likelihood from Incomplete Data via The EM Algorithm", *Journal of Royal Statistical Society*, Vol. 39, pp. 1–38, 1977.
4. J.B. MacQueen, "Some Methods for Classification and Analysis of Multivariate Observations", *Proceedings of 5nd Berkeley Symposium on Mathematical Statistics and Probability*, 1, Berkeley, University of California Press, pp. 281–297, 1967.
5. G.J. McLachlan and K.E. Basford, "Mixture Models: Inference and Application to Clustering", Dekker, 1988.
6. G. Schwarz, "Estimating the Dimension of a Model", *The Annals of Statistics*, Vol. 6, No. 2, pp. 461–464, 1978.
7. L. Xu, "A Unified Learning Scheme: Bayesian-Kullback Ying-Yang Machine", *Advances in Neural Information Processing Systems*, Vol. 8, pp. 444–450, 1996.
8. L. Xu, "Bayesian Ying-Yang Machine, Clustering and Number of Clusters", *Pattern Recognition Letters*, Vol. 18, No. 11-13, pp. 1167–1178, 1997.
9. L. Xu, A. Krzyżak and E. Oja, "Rival Penalized Competitive Learning for Clustering Analysis, RBF Net, and Curve Detection", *IEEE Transaction on Neural Networks*, Vol. 4, pp. 636–648, 1993.

Formal Determination of Context in Contextual Recursive Cascade Correlation Networks

Alessio Micheli[1], Diego Sona[2], and Alessandro Sperduti[3]

[1] Dipartimento di Informatica, Università di Pisa, Italy
[2] SRA division, ITC-IRST, Trento, Italy
[3] Dipartimento di Matematica Pura ed Applicata, Università di Padova, Italy

Abstract. We consider the Contextual Recursive Cascade Correlation model (CRCC), a model able to learn contextual mappings in structured domains. We propose a formal characterization of the "context window", i.e., given a state variable, the "context window" is the set of state variables that directly or indirectly contribute to its determination. On the basis of this definition, a formal and compact expression describing the "context windows" for the CRCC, and RCC model, are derived.

1 Introduction

In recent years, neural network models for processing of structured data have been developed and studied (see for example [6,3,7,2]). Almost all these models assume causality and stationarity. Unfortunately, in several real-world applications, such as language understanding, and DNA and proteins analysis, these assumptions do not hold. For this reason some authors are starting to propose models that try to exploit contextual information within recurrent and recursive models. Examples of these models for the processing of sequences are described in [1,4,8], while in [5] the *Contextual Recursive Cascade Correlation* model (CRCC), able to process structured data, i.e., directed positional acyclic graphs, using contextual information in a incremental way has been proposed.

In CRCC, which combines both structured data and contextual information, the adoption of an incremental learning strategy makes it hard to relate the insertion of new state variables (i.e., hidden units) with the "shape" of the contextual information taken into account during learning and computation.

The aim of this paper is to formally elucidate how the "shape" of the contextual information evolves by inserting new state variables. Specifically, we abstract from any specific neural realization of the CRCC model, and we propose the definition of the "context window" of a given state variable as the set of (already defined) state variables that directly or indirectly contribute to the determination of the considered state variable. Starting from this definition, we are able to define a compact expression of context window for a given vertex computation, described as a function of the state variables in the model, computed for the current vertex and all vertexes in the neighborhood. The "context window" for the non-contextual Recursive Cascade Correlation (RCC) [6] is computed as well. These context windows can be exploited to characterize the computational power of CRCC versus RCC.

2 Structured Domains

Given a directed acyclic graph $\mathcal{D}$ we denote the vertexes set with vert($\mathcal{D}$) and the edges set with egd($\mathcal{D}$). Given a vertex $v \in$ vert($\mathcal{D}$) we denote the set of edges entering and leaving from v with egd(v). Moreover, we define: out_set(v) = $\{u|(v,u) \in$ egd(v)$\}$, and in_set(v) = $\{u|(u,v) \in$ egd(v)$\}$. We assume that instances in the learning domain are DPAGs (directed positional acyclic graphs) with bounded outdegree (out) and indegree (in), and with all vertexes $v \in$ vert($\mathcal{D}$) labelled by vectors of real numbers $l(v)$. An instance of DPAG is a DAG where we assume that for each vertex $v \in$ vert($\mathcal{D}$), two injective functions P_v : egd(v) $\rightarrow$ $[1, 2, ..., in]$ and S_v : egd(v) $\rightarrow$ $[1, 2, ..., out]$ are defined on the edges entering and leaving from v respectively. In this way, a positional index is assigned to each entering and leaving edge from a vertex v. Moreover, $\forall u \in$ vert($\mathcal{D}$), and let define $\forall j \in [1, \ldots, in]$ in_set$_j(u)$ = v if $\exists v \in$ vert($\mathcal{D}$) such that $P_u((v,u))$ = j; nil otherwise, and similarly, $\forall j \in [1, \ldots, out]$ out_set$_j(u)$ = v if $\exists v \in$ vert($\mathcal{D}$) such that $S_u((u,v))$ = j; nil otherwise. We shall require the DPAGs to possess a supersource, i.e. a vertex $s \in$ vert($\mathcal{D}$) such that every vertex in vert($\mathcal{D}$) can be reached by a directed path starting from s. With dist(u,v), where $u,v \in \mathcal{D}$, we denote the shortest (directed) path in $\mathcal{D}$ from the vertex u to the vertex v.

3 Recursive Models

Recursive Neural Networks [3,7] possess, in principle, the ability to memorize "past" information to perform structural mappings. The state transition function $\tau()$ and the output function $g()$, in this case, prescribe how the state vector $\boldsymbol{x}(v)$ associated to a vertex v is used to obtain the state and output vectors corresponding to other vertexes. Specifically, given a state vector $\boldsymbol{x}(v) \equiv [x_1(v), \ldots, x_m(v)]^t$, we define the extended shift operators $q_j^{-1} x_k(v) \equiv x_k(\text{out\_set}_j(v))$ and $q_j^{+1} x_k(v) \equiv x_k(\text{in\_set}_j(v))$. If out_set$_j(v)$ = nil then $q_j^{-1} x_k(v) \equiv x_0$, the null state. Similarly, if in_set$_j(v)$ = nil then $q_j^{+1} x_k(v) \equiv x_0$. Moreover, we define $\boldsymbol{q}^{-1} x_k(v) = [q_1^{-1} x_k(v), \ldots, q_{out}^{-1} x_k(v)]^t$, and $\boldsymbol{q}^{+1} x_k(v) = [q_1^{+1} x_k(v), \ldots, q_{in}^{+1} x_k(v)]^t$ and, given $e \in \{-1, +1\}, \boldsymbol{q}^e \boldsymbol{x}(v) = [\boldsymbol{q}^e x_1(v), \ldots, \boldsymbol{q}^e x_m(v)]$.

On the basis of these definitions, the mapping implemented by a Recursive Neural Network can be described by the following equations:

$$\begin{cases} \boldsymbol{x}(v) = \tau(\boldsymbol{l}(v), \boldsymbol{q}^{-1}\boldsymbol{x}(v)) \\ \boldsymbol{y}(v) = g(\boldsymbol{l}(v), \boldsymbol{x}(v)) \end{cases} \quad (1)$$

where $\boldsymbol{x}(v)$ and $\boldsymbol{y}(v)$ are respectively the network state and the network output associated to vertex v. This formulation is based on a structural version of the *causality* assumption, i.e., the output $\boldsymbol{y}(v)$ of the network at vertex v only depends on labels of v and of its descendants. Specifically, RCC equations, where we disregard direct connections between hidden units, can be written as ($j = 1, \ldots, m$)

$$x_j(v) = \tau_j(\boldsymbol{l}(v), \boldsymbol{q}^{-1}[x_1(v), \ldots, x_j(v)]), \tag{2}$$

where $x_i(v)$ is the output of the i-th hidden unit in the network when processing vertex v. Since RCC is a constructive algorithm, training of a new hidden unit is based on already frozen units. Thus, when training hidden unit k, the state variables $x_1, \ldots, x_{k-1}$ for *all* the vertexes of all the DPAGs in the training set are already available, and can be used in the definition of x_k. This observation is very important since it yields to the realization that *contextual* information is already available in RCC, but it is not exploited. The *Contextual Recursive Cascade Correlation* network [5] exploits this information. Specifically, eqs. (2) can be expanded in a contextual fashion by using, where possible, the shift operator $\boldsymbol{q}^{+1}$:

$$x_1(v) = \tau_1(\boldsymbol{l}(v), \boldsymbol{q}^{-1} x_1(v)), \tag{3}$$
$$x_j(v) = \tau_j(\boldsymbol{l}(v), \boldsymbol{q}^{-1}[x_1(v), .., x_j(v)], \boldsymbol{q}^{+1}[x_1(v), .., x_{j-1}(v)]), \ j = 2, \ldots, m. \tag{4}$$

4 Formal Determination of Context

In this section, we characterize the "shape" of the context exploited by a state variable in terms of the set of state variables directly or indirectly contributing to its determination. Specifically, we propose a definition of "contextual window" and elucidate how its "shape" evolves adding hidden units, both in the CRCC model and in the RCC model. In order to formalize the above concepts, given a subset $V \subseteq \text{vert}(\mathcal{D})$ let us define the "descendants" operator $\downarrow$ as $\downarrow V = V \cup \downarrow \text{out\_set}(V) = V \cup \{u | v \in V \ \wedge \exists \ path(v, u)\}$, where the descendants set of an empty set is still an empty set, i.e., $\downarrow \emptyset = \emptyset$.

Let the set functions in_set($\cdot$) and out_set($\cdot$) be defined also for sets of vertexes as argument (e.g., in_set(V) = $\bigcup_{v \in V}$ in_set(v)) and let denote with $(\downarrow \text{in\_set})^p(V)$ the repeated application (p times) of the in_set function composed with the "descendants" operator $\downarrow$. Moreover, given a subset of vertexes V, with the notation $x_j.V$ we refer to the set of state variables $\{x_j(v) | v \in V\}$, where for an empty subset of vertexes we define $x_j.\emptyset = \{x_0\}$. Note that for any couple of vertexes sets $V, Z \subseteq \text{vert}(\mathcal{D})$, $\downarrow V \cup \downarrow Z = \downarrow (V \cup Z)$ and $x_j.V \cup x_j.Z = x_j.(V \cup Z)$. Finally, let formally define the concept of *context window*, i.e. the set of internal states which may contribute to the computation of a new internal state

Definition 1 (Context Window). *The context window of a state variable $x_k(v)$, denoted by $\mathcal{C}(x_k(v))$, is defined as the set of* all *state variables (directly or indirectly) contributing to its determination.*

Note that, by definition, $\mathcal{C}(x_0) = \emptyset$. In the following we will use the above definition to characterize the context window of the CRCC and RCC models.

First of all, let us state some basic results that will be used to derive the main theorems.

All the results reported in the following will concern the CRCC model. Referring to eq. (3) it is possible to derive the following

Lemma 1. *Given a DPAG $\mathcal{D}$, for any vertex $v \in \text{vert}(\mathcal{D})$*

$$\mathcal{C}(x_1(v)) = x_1 . \downarrow\text{out\_set}(v). \tag{5}$$

Proof. It can be proved by induction on the partial order of vertexes.
By definition of context window, and by eq. (3) for any v in $\text{vert}(\mathcal{D})$, the context window for the state variable $x_1(v)$ can be expressed as follows

$$\mathcal{C}(x_1(v)) = \underbrace{\bigcup_{i=1}^{\text{out}} q_i^{-1} x_1(v)}_{\text{direct}} \cup \underbrace{\bigcup_{i=1}^{\text{out}} \mathcal{C}(q_i^{-1} x_1(v))}_{\text{indirect}}$$

Base Case: v is a leaf of $\mathcal{D}$.
By definition of out_set, $\forall i \in [1,\ldots,\text{out}]$ out_set$_i(v) = \emptyset$, thus by definition of "descendants" operator $x_1 . \downarrow\text{out\_set}(v) = x_1.\emptyset = \{x_0\}$.
Moreover, by definition of extended shift operator, $\forall i \in [1,\ldots,\text{out}]\ q_i^{-1} x_1(v) = x_0$, and $\mathcal{C}(q_i^{-1} x_1(v)) = \mathcal{C}(x_0) = \emptyset$. This proves that

$$\mathcal{C}(x_1(v)) = x_1 . \downarrow\text{out\_set}(v) = \{x_0\}$$

for any leaf v of the data structure $\mathcal{D}$.
Inductive Step: v is an internal vertex of $\mathcal{D}$.
Assume that eq. (5) holds $\forall u \in \text{out\_set}(v)$ (Inductive Hyp.).
By definition of generalized shift operator, and because of the inductive hypothesis,

$$\mathcal{C}(x_1(v)) = \bigcup_{u \in \text{out\_set}(v)} [x_1(u) \cup x_1 . \downarrow\text{out\_set}(u)] = \bigcup_{u \in \text{out\_set}(v)} x_1 . \downarrow u = x_1 . \downarrow\text{out\_set}(v)$$

□

Referring to eq. (4) it is now possible to derive the following results, which are then used to prove Theorem 1.

Lemma 2. *Given a DPAG $\mathcal{D}$, for any vertex $v \in \text{vert}(\mathcal{D})$ the following equation holds*

$$\mathcal{C}(x_2(v)) = x_1 . \downarrow\text{in\_set}(\downarrow v) \cup x_2 . \downarrow\text{out\_set}(v). \tag{6}$$

Proof. It can be proved by induction on the partial order of vertexes.
By definition of context window, and by eq. (4) for any v in $\text{vert}(\mathcal{D})$ the context window for the state variable $x_2(v)$ can be expressed by

$$\mathcal{C}(x_2(v)) = \bigcup_{i=1}^{\text{out}} [q_i^{-1} x_2(v) \cup \mathcal{C}(q_i^{-1} x_2(v))] \cup \bigcup_{i=1}^{\text{out}} [q_i^{-1} x_1(v) \cup \mathcal{C}(q_i^{-1} x_1(v))]$$

$$\cup \bigcup_{i=1}^{\text{in}} [q_i^{+1} x_1(v) \cup \mathcal{C}(q_i^{+1} x_1(v))] \tag{7}$$

Base Case: v is a leaf of $\mathcal{D}$.

By the definitions of out_set, in_set, and "descendants" operator it follows that $x_2.{\downarrow}\text{out\_set}(v) = x_2.\emptyset = \{x_0\}$, and $x_1.{\downarrow}\text{in\_set}({\downarrow}v) = x_1.{\downarrow}\text{in\_set}(v)$. Thus eq. (6) becomes $\mathcal{C}(x_2(v)) = x_1.{\downarrow}\text{in\_set}(v) \cup \{x_0\}$.

By definition of generalized shift operators, $q_i^{-1}x_2(v) = x_2.\text{out\_set}_i(v) = \{x_0\}$ and $q_i^{+1}x_1(v) = x_1.\text{in\_set}_i(v)$. Moreover, $\mathcal{C}(q_i^{-1}x_2(v)) = \mathcal{C}(x_2.\text{out\_set}_i(v)) = \mathcal{C}(\{x_0\}) = \emptyset$, and by Lemma 1,

$$\mathcal{C}(q_i^{+1}x_1(v)) = \mathcal{C}(x_1(\text{in\_set}_i(v))) = x_1.{\downarrow}\text{out\_set}(\text{in\_set}_i(v)).$$

Thus, by the associative rule on "dot" operator and by definition of "descendants" operator, eq. (7) becomes

$$\mathcal{C}(x_2(v)) = \{x_0\} \cup x_1.\text{in\_set}(v) \cup x_1.{\downarrow}\text{out\_set}(\text{in\_set}(u)) = x_1.{\downarrow}\text{in\_set}(v).$$

The thesis follows for all leaves of $\mathcal{D}$.

Inductive Step: v is an internal vertex of $\mathcal{D}$.

Assume that eq. (6) holds for all $u \in \text{out\_set}(v)$ (Inductive Hyp.).
By definition of generalized shift operator, associative rule for "dot" definition of "descendants" operator, and by Lemma 1, eq. (7) becomes

$$\mathcal{C}(x_2(v)) = \bigcup_{u \in \text{out\_set}(v)} [x_2(u) \cup \mathcal{C}(x_2(u))] \cup x_1.{\downarrow}\text{out\_set}(v) \cup x_1.{\downarrow}\text{in\_set}(v)$$

By the inductive hypothesis and by the definition of "descendants" operator

$$\mathcal{C}(x_2(v)) = x_2.{\downarrow}\text{out\_set}(v) \cup x_1.{\downarrow}\text{in\_set}({\downarrow}\text{out\_set}(v))$$
$$= \cup x_1.{\downarrow}\text{out\_set}(v) \cup x_1.{\downarrow}\text{in\_set}(v)$$

By the associative rules and by definition of in_set

$$\mathcal{C}(x_2(v)) = x_2.{\downarrow}\text{out\_set}(v) \cup x_1.{\downarrow}\text{in\_set}({\downarrow}v) \cup x_1.{\downarrow}\text{out\_set}(v).$$

Since $\forall v \in \text{vert}(\mathcal{D})$, ${\downarrow}\text{out\_set}(v) \subset {\downarrow}v \subseteq {\downarrow}\text{in\_set}({\downarrow}v)$, the thesis follows. $\square$

Theorem 1. *Given a DPAG $\mathcal{D}$, $\forall v \in \text{vert}(\mathcal{D})$, and $k \geq 2$*

$$\mathcal{C}(x_k(v)) = \bigcup_{i=1}^{k-1} x_i.({\downarrow}\text{in\_set})^{k-i}({\downarrow}v) \cup x_k.{\downarrow}\text{out\_set}(v). \tag{8}$$

Proof sketch. The theorem can be proved by induction on the partial order of vertexes, and on the order of indexes of variables.

By definition of context window and generalized shift operator, by eq. (4), and by the fact that $\forall v \in \text{vert}(\mathcal{D})$ and $\forall k \geq 2$, $\mathcal{C}(x_k(v)) \supseteq \mathcal{C}(x_{k-1}(v))$ (which is not hard to prove), the context window for the state variable $x_k(v)$ can be expressed as

$$\mathcal{C}(x_k(v)) = \bigcup_{i=1}^{k} x_i.\text{out\_set}(v) \cup \mathcal{C}(x_k.\text{out\_set}(v)) \cup \tag{9}$$

$$= \bigcup_{i=1}^{k-1} x_i.\text{in\_set}(v) \cup \mathcal{C}(x_{k-1}.\text{in\_set}(v))$$

Base Case: v is a leaf of $\mathcal{D}$.

For $k = 2$, eq. (8) reduces to eq. (6).

Now, let assume that eq. (8) holds for all j, $2 \leq j \leq k-1$ (Inductive Hyp.). Since v is a leaf, eq. (9) can be reduced to $\mathcal{C}(x_k(v)) = \{x_0\} \cup \bigcup_{i=1}^{k-1} x_i.\text{in\_set}(v) \cup \mathcal{C}(x_{k-1}.\text{in\_set}(v))$ and, applying the inductive hypothesis, it becomes

$$\mathcal{C}(x_k(v)) = x_{k-1}.\text{in\_set}(v) \cup x_{k-1}.\downarrow\text{out\_set}(\text{in\_set}(v)) \cup \bigcup_{i=1}^{k-2} [x_i.\text{in\_set}(v) \cup x_i.(\downarrow\text{in\_set})^{k-i}(v)]$$

By definition of "descendants" operator, and because of the fact that $\forall v \in \text{vert}(\mathcal{D})$ and $\forall j \geq 1$, $\text{in\_set}(v) \subseteq \downarrow\text{in\_set}(v) \subseteq (\downarrow\text{in\_set})^j(v)$, it follows that

$$\mathcal{C}(x_k(v)) = x_{k-1}.\downarrow\text{in\_set}(v) \cup \bigcup_{i=1}^{k-2} x_i.(\downarrow\text{in\_set})^{k-i}(v) = \bigcup_{i=1}^{k-1} x_i.(\downarrow\text{in\_set})^{k-i}(v)$$

which is equivalent to eq. (8) since $v =\downarrow v$ and $x_k.\downarrow\text{out\_set}(v) = \{x_0\}$. This proves the correctness of the assertion for all leaves of $\mathcal{D}$ and for any $k \geq 2$.

Inductive Step: v is an internal vertex of $\mathcal{D}$.

Assume that eq. (8) holds $\forall u \in \text{vert}(\mathcal{D})$ if $2 \leq j \leq k-1$, and $\forall u \in \text{out\_set}(v)$ if $j = k$ (Inductive Hyp.).

Applying the induction hypotheses and by the associative properties of "dot" and "descendants" operators, eq. (9) becomes

$$\mathcal{C}(x_k(v)) = \bigcup_{i=1}^{k-1} x_i.\text{out\_set}(v) \cup \bigcup_{i=1}^{k-2} x_i.\text{in\_set}(v) \cup$$

$$= \bigcup_{i=1}^{k-1} x_i.(\downarrow\text{in\_set})^{k-i}(\downarrow v) \cup x_k.\downarrow\text{out\_set}(v)$$

Since for any $v \in \text{vert}(\mathcal{D})$ and for any $j \geq 1$ it trivially holds that $\text{out\_set}(v) \subseteq \downarrow\text{in\_set}(v) \subseteq (\downarrow\text{in\_set})^j(v) \subseteq (\downarrow\text{in\_set})^j(\downarrow v)$, and similarly $\text{in\_set}(v) \subseteq \downarrow\text{in\_set}(v) \subseteq (\downarrow\text{in\_set})^j(v) \subseteq (\downarrow\text{in\_set})^j(\downarrow v)$ the thesis follows. □

In general, for CRCC, the evolution of the context with respect to the addition of hidden units is characterized by the following property.

Proposition 1. *Given a vertex v in a DPAG $\mathcal{D}$ with supersource s, such that $\text{dist}(s, v) = d$, the contexts $\mathcal{C}(x_h(v))$, with $h > d$ involve all the vertexes of $\mathcal{D}$.*

Proof. According to eq. (8), when computing $\mathcal{C}(x_{d+1}(v))$, in_set is recursively applied d times. Thus the shortest path from s to v is fully followed in a backward fashion starting from v, so that $x_1(s)$ is included in $\mathcal{C}(x_{d+1}(v))$. Moreover, since $x_1(s)$ is included in $\mathcal{C}(x_{d+1}(v))$, by definition of eq. (8), also the state variables $x_1(u)$ for each $u \in \text{vert}(\mathcal{D})$ are included in $\mathcal{C}(x_{d+1}(v))$. The statement follows from the fact that $\mathcal{C}(x_{d+1}(v)) \subset \mathcal{C}(x_h(v))$. □

When considering a transduction whose output for each vertex v depends on the whole structure, the following proposition suggests that such information is available to a CRCC model with "enough" hidden units.

Proposition 2. *Given a DPAG $\mathcal{D}$ there exists a finite number h of hidden units such that for each $v \in \text{vert}(\mathcal{D})$ the context $\mathcal{C}(x_h(v))$ involves all the vertexes of $\mathcal{D}$. In particular, given $r = \max_{v \in \text{vert}(\mathcal{D})} \text{dist}(s,v)$, any $h > r$ satisfies the proposition.*

Proof. Let consider $h = r + 1$. The proposition follows immediately by the application of Proposition 1 for each v since $h > \text{dist}(s,v)$. □

For the sake of comparison, let us now consider the "context window" for the RCC model (eq. 2). The following theorem holds:

Theorem 2. *Given a DPAG $\mathcal{D}$, $\forall v \in \text{vert}(\mathcal{D})$, and $k \geq 1$*

$$\mathcal{C}_{RCC}(x_k(v)) = \bigcup_{i=1}^{k} x_i . \downarrow \text{out\_set}(v). \qquad (10)$$

Proof. For $k = 1$ the proof is given by Lemma 1, since eq. 2 is equivalent to eq. 3. For $k > 1$ the proof is similar to the proof given for Theorem 1. □

The above result formally show that RCC is unable to perform contextual transductions, since only information on the descendants of a vertex is available.

The devised properties can be exploited to show the relevance of the CRCC model in terms of computational power with respect to the RCC model.

From Theorems 1 and 2, and Proposition 2, it follows that all the computational tasks characterized by a target that is a function of a context including the whole structure, as expressed for CRCC model, are not computable by RCC. Examples of such functions can be found in tasks where the target is not strictly causal and it is function of the "future" information with respect to the partial order of the DPAG. The formal description of the context expressed in Theorems 1 and 2 allows to highlight the explicit dependences of the functions computed by CRCC from information that RCC cannot capture.

Besides contextual transductions, the above results can also be exploited to study supersource transductions that involve DPAGs. The aim is to show that RCC can compute only supersource transductions (thus, non-contextual transductions) involving *tree structures* while CRCC allows to extend the computational power also to supersource and contextual transductions that involves DPAGs.

5 Conclusion

We have considered the problem to give a formal characterization of the functional dependencies between state variables in recursive models based on Cascade

Correlation for the processing of structured data. Specifically, we have defined the "context window" for a state variable as the set of state variables that contribute, directly or indirectly, to the determination of the considered state variable. Then, on the basis of this definition, we have been able to define a compact expression which describes the "context window" as a function of the state variables in the model associated to specific sets of ancestors and descendants belonging to the vertex taken in consideration. This expression has been devised both for the *Recursive Cascade Correlation* model and the *Contextual Recursive Cascade Correlation* model.

The relevance of the results obtained in this paper is due to the possibility to use them in order to characterize the computational power of the above models. Moreover, the approach used in this paper, which is independent from the specific neural implementation, can easily be applied to other recurrent and recursive models in order to compare them from a computational point of view.

References

1. P. Baldi, S. Brunak, P. Frasconi, G. Pollastri, and G. Soda. Exploiting the past and the future in protein secondary structure prediction. *Bioinformatics*, 15(11):937–946, 1999.
2. P. Frasconi, M. Gori, and A. Sperduti. A general framework for adaptive processing of data structures. *IEEE Transactions on Neural Networks*, 9(5):768–786, 1998.
3. C. Goller and A. Küchler. Learning task-dependent distributed structure-representations by backpropagation through structure. In *IEEE International Conference on Neural Networks*, pages 347–352, 1996.
4. A. Micheli, D. Sona, and A. Sperduti. Bi-causal recurrent cascade correlation. In *Proc. of the Int. Joint Conf. on Neural Networks – IJCNN'2000*, volume 3, pages 3–8, 2000.
5. A. Micheli, D. Sona, and A. Sperduti. Recursive cascade correlation for contextual processing of structured data. In *Proc. of the Int. Joint Conf. on Neural Networks – WCCI-IJCNN'2002*, volume 1, pages 268–273, 2002.
6. A. Sperduti, D. Majidi, and A. Starita. Extended cascade-correlation for syntactic and structural pattern recognition. In P. Perner, P. Wang, and A. Rosenfeld, editors, *Advances in Structural and Syntactical Pattern Recognition*, volume 1121 of *Lecture notes in Computer Science*, pages 90–99. Springer-Verlag, 1996.
7. A. Sperduti and A. Starita. Supervised neural networks for the classification of structures. *IEEE Transactions on Neural Networks*, 8(3):714–735, 1997.
8. H. Wakuya and J. Zurada. Bi-directional computing architectures for time series prediction. *Neural Network*, 14:1307–1321, 2001.

Confidence Estimation Using the Incremental Learning Algorithm, Learn++

Jeffrey Byorick and Robi Polikar

Electrical and Computer Engineering, Rowan University,
136 Rowan Hall, Glassboro, NJ 08028, USA.
byor4610@students.rowan.edu, polikar@rowan.edu

Abstract. Pattern recognition problems span a broad range of applications, where each application has its own tolerance on classification error. The varying levels of risk associated with many pattern recognition applications indicate the need for an algorithm with the ability to measure its own confidence. In this work, the supervised incremental learning algorithm Learn++ [1], which exploits the synergistic power of an ensemble of classifiers, is further developed to add the capability of assessing its own confidence using a weighted exponential majority voting technique.

1 Introduction

1.1 Incremental Learning

It is widely recognized that the recognition accuracy of a classifier is heavily incumbent on the availability of an adequate and representative training dataset. Acquiring such data is often tedious, time-consuming, and expensive. In practice, it is not uncommon for such data to be acquired in small batches over a period of time. A typical approach in such cases is combining new data with all previous data, and training a new classifier from scratch. This approach results in loss of all previously learned knowledge, a phenomenon known as catastrophic forgetting. Furthermore, the combination of old and new datasets is not even always a viable option if previous datasets are lost, discarded, corrupted, inaccessible, or otherwise unavailable.

Incremental learning is the solution to such scenarios, which can be defined as the process of extracting new information without losing prior knowledge from an additional dataset that later becomes available. Various definitions and interpretations of incremental learning can be found in literature, including online learning [2,3], re-learning of previously misclassified instances [4,5], and growing and pruning of classifier architectures [6,7]. For the purposes of this work, an algorithm possesses incremental learning capabilities, if it meets the following criteria: (1) ability to acquire additional knowledge when new datasets are introduced; (2) ability to retain previously learned information; (3) ability to learn new classes if introduced by new data.

1.2 Ensemble of Classifiers

Ensemble systems have attracted a great deal of attention over the last decade due to their empirical success over single classifier systems on a variety of applications. Such systems combine an ensemble of generally weak classifiers to take advantage of the so-called *instability* of the weak classifier, which causes the classifiers to construct sufficiently different decision boundaries for minor modifications in their training parameters, causing each classifier to make different errors on any given instance. A strategic combination of these classifiers, such as weighted majority voting [8], then eliminates the individual errors, generating a strong classifier. A rich collection of algorithms have been developed using multiple classifiers, such as AdaBoost [9], with the general goal of improving the generalization performance of the classification system. Using multiple classifiers for incremental learning, however, has been largely unexplored. Learn++, in part inspired by AdaBoost, was developed in response to recognizing the potential feasibility of ensemble of classifiers in solving the incremental learning problem. Learn++ was initially introduced in [1] as an incremental learning algorithm for MLP type networks. A more versatile form of the algorithm was presented in [10] for all supervised classifiers. We have recently recognized that inherent voting mechanism of the algorithm can also be used in effectively determining the confidence of the classification system in its own decision. In this work, we describe the algorithm Learn++, along with representative results on incremental learning and confidence estimation obtained on one real world and one benchmark database from the Univ. of California, Irvine (UCI) machine learning repository [11].

2 Learn++

The Learn++ algorithm, given in Fig. 1, exploits the synergistic power of an ensemble of classifiers to incrementally learn new information that may later become available. Learn++ generates multiple weak classifiers, each trained with different subsets of the data. For each database $\mathcal{D}_k$, $k=1,...,K$ that becomes available, the inputs to Learn++ are (i) $S_k = \{(x_i, y_i) | i = 1,\cdots,m_k\}$, a sequence of m_k training data instances x_i, along with their correct labels y_i, (ii) a weak classification algorithm **BaseClassifier** to generate weak classifiers, and (iii) an integer T_k specifying the number of classifiers (hypotheses) to be generated for that database. We require that **BaseClassifier** obtain at least 50% correct classification performance on its own training dataset, to ensure a meaningful classification performance for each classifier.

Learn++ starts by initializing a set of weights for the training data, w, and a distribution D obtained from w, according to which a training subset TR_t and a test subset TE_t are drawn at the tth iteration of the algorithm, $t=1,...,T_k$, where $S_k = TR_t \cup TE_t$. Unless *a priori* information indicates otherwise, this distribution is initially set to be uniform, giving equal probability to each instance to be selected into the first training subset. The variation of instances within the training data subsets is achieved by iteratively updating the distribution of weights D. At each iteration t, the weights adjusted at iteration t-1 are normalized to ensure that a legitimate distribution, D_t, is obtained. TR_t and TE_t are then drawn according to D_t and **BaseClassifier** is trained with the training subset. A hypothesis h_t is obtained as the tth classifier, whose error ε_t is computed on the entire (current) database S_k simply by adding the distribution weights of the misclassified instances

$$\varepsilon_t = \sum_{i:h_t(x_i)\neq y_i} D_t(i) \qquad (1)$$

If $\varepsilon_t > \tfrac{1}{2}$, h_t is discarded and a new TR_t and TE_t are selected. If the error is less then half, then the error is normalized and computed as

$$\beta_t = \varepsilon_t/(1-\varepsilon_t), \qquad 0 \leq \beta_t \leq 1 \qquad (2)$$

Hypotheses generated in all previous iterations are then combined using weighted majority voting to form a *composite hypothesis* H_t using

$$H_t = \arg\max_{y \in Y} \sum_{t:h_t(x)=y} \log\frac{1}{\beta_t} \qquad (3)$$

where the sum of weights associated with each classifier is computed for every class present in the classification task. A higher weight is given to classifiers that perform better on their specific training sets. The composite hypothesis H_t is obtained by assigning the class label to an instance x_i that receives the largest total vote. The composite error made by H_t is then computed as

$$E_t = \sum_{i:H_t(x_i)\neq y_i} D_t(i) = \sum_{i=1}^{m} D_t(i)[\![H_t(x_i)\neq y_i]\!] \qquad (4)$$

where $[\![\cdot]\!]$ evaluates to 1, if the predicate holds true. Similar to the calculation of β_t, a normalized composite error B_t is computed as

$$B_t = E_t/(1-E_t), \qquad 0 \leq B_t \leq 1 \qquad (5)$$

The weights $w_t(i)$ are then updated to obtain D_{t+1}, which is used for the selection of the next training and testing subsets, TR_{t+1} and TE_{t+1}, respectively. The distribution update rule which comprises the heart of the algorithm is given by

$$w_{t+1}(i) = w_t(i) \times \begin{cases} B_t, & \text{if } H_t(x_i) = y_i \\ 1, & \text{otherwise} \end{cases} = w_t(i) \times B_t^{1-[\![H_t(x_i)\neq y_i]\!]}. \qquad (6)$$

This rule reduces the weights of those instances that are correctly classified by the composite hypothesis H_t, so that their probability of being selected into the next training subset is reduced. When normalized during iteration $t+1$, the weights of misclassified instances are increased relative to the rest of the dataset. We emphasize that unlike AdaBoost and its variations, the weight update rule in Learn++ looks at the classification output of the composite hypothesis, not to that of a specific hypothesis. This weight update procedure forces the algorithm to focus more on instances that have not been properly learned by the ensemble. When Learn++ is learning incrementally, the instances introduced by the new database are precisely those not learned by the ensemble. After T_k hypotheses are generated for each database $\mathcal{D}_k$, the final hypothesis is obtained by the weighted majority voting of all composite hypotheses:

$$H_{final} = \arg\max_{y \in Y} \sum_{k=1}^{K} \sum_{t:H_t(x)=y} \log\frac{1}{B_t} \qquad (7)$$

Input: For each dataset drawn from $\mathcal{D}_k$ $k=1,2,...,K$
- Sequence of m_k examples $S_k = \{(x_i, y_i) | i = 1,\cdots,m_k\}$
- Weak learning algorithm **BaseClassifier**
- Integer T_k, specifying the number of iterations

Initialize $w_1(i) = D_1(i) = 1/m_k, \forall i, i=1,2,...,m_k$
Do for each $k=1,2,...,K$:
  Do for $t= 1,2,...,T_k$:
  1. Set $D_t = \mathbf{w_t} \bigg/ \sum_{i=1}^{m} w_t(i)$ so that D_t is a distribution
  2. Draw training TR_t and testing TE_t subsets from D_t.
  3. Call **BaseClassifier** to be trained with TR_t.
  4. Obtain a hypothesis $h_t: X \rightarrow Y$, and calculate the error of h_t: $\varepsilon_t = \sum_{i:h_t(x_i) \neq y_i} D_t(i)$
     on $TR_t + TE_t$. If $\varepsilon_t > \frac{1}{2}$, discard h_t and go to step 2. Otherwise, compute normalized error as $\beta_t = \varepsilon_t/(1-\varepsilon_t)$.
  5. Call weighed majority voting and obtain the composite hypothesis
     $H_t = \arg\max_{y \in Y} \sum_{t:h_t(x)=y} \log(1/\beta_t)$
  6. Compute the error of the composite hypothesis
     $E_t = \sum_{i:H_t(x_i) \neq y_i} D_t(i) = \sum_{i=1}^{m} D_t(i) [\![H_t(x_i) \neq y_i]\!]$
  7. Set $B_t = E_t/(1-E_t)$, and update the weights: $w_{t+1}(i) = w_t(i) \times B_t^{1-[\![H_t(x_i) \neq y_i]\!]}$

Call Weighted majority voting and **Output** the final hypothesis:
$$H_{final}(x) = \arg\max_{y \in Y} \sum_{k=1}^{K} \sum_{t:h_t(x)=y} \log(1/\beta_t)$$

Fig. 1. Learn++ Algorithm

3 Confidence Estimation

An intimately relevant issue is the confidence of the classifier in its decision, with particular interest in whether the confidence of the algorithm improves as new data becomes available. The voting mechanism inherent in Learn++ hints to a practical approach for estimating confidence: decisions made with a vast majority of votes have better confidence then those made by a slight majority. We have implemented McIver and Friedl's weighted exponential voting based confidence metric [12] with Learn++ as

$$C_j(x) = P(y = j \mid x) = \frac{e^{F_j(x)}}{\sum_{k=1}^{N} e^{F_k(x)}}, \quad 0 \leq C_j(x) \leq 1 \tag{8}$$

where $C_j(x)$ is the confidence assigned to instance x when classified as class j, $F_j(x)$ is the total vote associated with the jth class for the instance x, and N is the total number of classes. The total vote $F_j(x)$ class j receives for any given instance is computed as

$$F_j(x) = \sum_{t=1}^{N} \begin{pmatrix} \log \frac{1}{\beta_t} & h_t(x) = j \\ 0 & otherwise \end{pmatrix} \tag{9}$$

The confidence of winning class is then considered as the confidence of the algorithm in making the decision with respect to the winning class. Since $C_j(x)$ is between 0 and 1, the confidences can be translated into linguistic indicators, such as those shown in Table 1. These indicators are adopted and used in tabulating the results.

Table 1. Confidence percentages represented by linguistic indicators

Confidence Percentage Range	Confidence Level
$90 \leq C \leq 100$	Very High (VH)
$80 \leq C < 90$	High (H)
$70 \leq C < 80$	Medium (M)
$60 \leq C < 70$	Low (L)
$C < 60$	Very Low (VL)

Equations (8) and (9) allow Learn++ to determine its own confidence in any classification it makes. The desired outcome of the confidence analysis is to observe a high confidence on correctly classified instances, and a low confidence on misclassified instances, so that the low confidence can be used to flag those instances that are being misclassified by the algorithm. A second desired outcome is to observe improved confidences on correctly classified instances and reduced confidence on misclassified instances, as new data becomes available, so that the incremental learning ability of the algorithm can be further confirmed.

4 Simulation Results on Learn++

Learn++ has been tested on a diverse set of benchmark databases acquired from the UCI Machine Learning Repository, as well as a few real-world applications, both for incremental learning – where new datasets included new classes – and for estimating the confidence of Learn++ in its own decisions. The incremental learning results with new classes are presented in [1]. In this paper, we present the results on confidence estimation, and we use two databases, one benchmark database from UCI, and one real world on gas sensing, as representative simulations.

4.1 Volatile Organic Compound (VOC) Database

The VOC database is a real world database for the odorant identification problem. The instances are responses of six quartz crystal microbalances to five volatile organic compounds, including ethanol (ET), octane (OC), toluene (TL), trichloroethelene (TCE), and xylene (XL), constituting a five class, six feature database.

Three datasets S_1, S_2 and S_3, where each dataset included approximately one third of the entire training data, were provided to Learn++ in three training sessions for incremental learning. The data distribution and the percent classification performance are given in Table 2. The performances listed are on the validation data, *TEST*, following each training session. Table 3 provides an actual breakdown of correctly classified and misclassified instances falling into each confidence range after each training session. The trends of the confidence estimates after subsequent training sessions are given in Table 4. The desired outcome on the actual confidences is high to very high confidences on correctly classified instances, and low to very low confidences on misclassified instances. The desired outcome on confidence trends is increasing or steady confidences on correctly classified instances, and decreasing confidences on misclassified instances, as new data is introduced.

Table 2. Data distribution and performance on VOC database

	Ethanol	Octane	Toluene	TCE	Xylene	Test Perf. (%)
S_1	13	11	12	9	15	84.3
S_2	9	10	14	11	16	85.8
S_3	8	9	24	10	9	87.7
TEST	34	34	62	34	40	-------

Table 3. Confidence results on VOC database

		VH	H	M	L	VL
Correctly Classified	S_1	149	9	3	8	3
	S_2	163	6	2	4	0
	S_3	172	0	2	0	5
Misclassified	S_1	16	4	3	6	3
	S_2	25	2	0	0	2
	S_3	23	0	1	0	1

Table 4. Confidence trends for the VOC database.

	Increasing/Steady	Decreasing
Correctly Classified	172	7
Misclassified	9	16

The performance figures in Table 2 indicate that the algorithm is improving its generalization performance as new data becomes available. The improvement is modest, however, as majority of the new information is already learned in the first training session. Other experiments, where new data introduced new classes, showed remarkable performance increase as reported in [1]. Table 3 indicates that the vast majority of correctly classified instances tend to have very high confidences, with continually improved confidences at consecutive training sessions. While a considerable portion of misclassified instances also had high confidence for this database, the general desired trends of increased confidence on correctly classified instances and decreasing confidence on misclassified ones were notable and dominant, as shown in Table 4.

4.2 Glass Database

The glass database, retrieved from UCI repository, is a 10-feature, 6-class database with samples of glass from buildings, vehicles, containers, tableware, and headlamps. The buildings include two types of glass, which are float processed and non-float processed. This database was also provided incrementally in three training sessions, with each session using one of the datasets, $S_1 \sim S_3$. The distribution of data, as well as the performance on the validation dataset, is shown in Table 5. The confidence results are shown in Table 6, while the confidence trends are provided in Table 7.

Table 5. Data distribution and generalization performance on glass database

	Float	Non-Float	Vehicle	Container	Table	Lamp	Test Perf. (%)
S_1	14	22	3	1	2	6	84.0
S_2	14	17	4	3	2	9	85.5
S_3	17	13	6	3	2	7	92.8
TEST	25	24	4	6	3	7	------

Table 6. % Confidence Results on Glass Database

		VH	H	M	L	VL
	S_1	0	0	17	6	35
Correctly Classified	S_2	47	1	5	2	5
	S_3	57	4	2	2	3
	S_1	0	0	0	0	11
Misclassified	S_2	0	0	0	1	9
	S_3	1	0	0	2	2

Table 7. Confidence trends for glass database

	Increasing/Steady	Decreasing
Correctly classified	63	1
Misclassified	3	2

For the glass database, the above-mentioned desirable traits are even more remarkable. The majority of correctly classified instances fell into a very high confidence range, while the misclassified instances fell into the very low confidence range. Positive attributes were also seen in the confidence trends where the majority of correctly classified instances had an increasing or steady confidence through consecutive training sessions. Furthermore, the incremental learning ability of the algorithm is also demonstrated through the improved generalization performance (from 83% to 93%) on the TEST dataset with availability of additional data.

5 Discussion and Conclusions

Apart from the incremental learning ability of Learn++, it was found that the algorithm can also assess the confidence of its own decisions. In general, majority of correctly classified instances had very high confidence estimates while lower confidence values were associated with misclassified instances. Therefore, classifications with low confidences can be used as a flag to further evaluate those instances. Furthermore, the algorithm also showed increasing confidences in correctly classified instances and decreasing confidences in misclassified instances after subsequent training sessions. This is a very comforting outcome, which further indicates that algorithm can incrementally acquire new and novel information from additional data. Work is in progress to further test the algorithm's capabilities on a more diverse set of real world and benchmark databases.

Acknowledgement. This material is based upon work supported by the National Science Foundation under Grant No. 0239090.

References

[1]   R. Polikar, L. Udpa, S. Udpa, V. Honavar. Learn++: An incremental learning algorithm for supervised neural networks. *IEEE Tran. on Systems, Man, and Cybernetics(C).*, Vol. 31, no. 4, November 2001.
[2]   P. Winston, "Learning structural descriptions from examples," In *The Psychology of Computer Vision* P. Winston (ed.), pp. 157–209, McGraw-Hill: New York, NY, 1975.
[3]   N. Littlestone, "Learning quickly when irrelevant attributes abound," *Machine Learning*, vol. 2, pp. 285–318, 1988.
[4]   P. Jantke, "Types of incremental learning," *Training Issues in Incremental Learning*, A. Cornuejos (ed.) pp.26-32, The AAAI Press: Menlo Park, CA 1993.
[5]   M.A. Maloof and R.S. Michalski," Selecting examples for partial memory learning," *Machine Learning*, vol. 41, pp. 27–52, 2000.
[6]   F.S. Osario and B. Amy," INSS: A hybrid system for constructive machine learning," *Neurocomputing*, vol. 28, pp. 191–205, 1999.
[7]   J. Ghosh and A,c, Nag," Knowledge enhancement and reuse with radial basis function networks," *Proceeding of International Joint Conference on Neural Networks*, vol. 9, no. 2, pp. 1322–1327, 2002.
[8]   N. Littlestone and M. Warmuth, "Weighted Majority Algorithm," *Information and Computation*, vol. 108, pp. 212-261, 1994.
[9]   Y. Freund and R. Schapire, "A decision-theoretic generalization of on-line learning and an application to boosting," *Journal of Computer and System Sciences*, 1997.
[10] R. Polikar, J. Byorick, S. Krause, A. Marino, and M. Moreton, "Learn++: A classifier independent incremental learning algorithm," *Proceedings of International Joint Conference on Neural Networks*, May 2002.
[11] C. L. Blake and C. J. Merz. (1998) UCI repository of machine learning databases. Dept. Inform. and Comput. Sci., University of California, Irvine. [Online]. Available: http://www.ics.uci.edu/~mlearn/MLRepository.html.
[12] D. McIver and M. Friedl, "Estimating Pixel-Scale Land Cover Classification Confidence Using Nonparametric Machine Learning Methods," *IEEE Transactions on Geoscience and Remote Sensing*, Vol. 39, No. 9, September 2001.

Stability and Convergence Analysis of a Neural Model Applied in Nonlinear Systems Optimization

Ivan Nunes da Silva

State University of São Paulo, UNESP, Department of Electrical Engineering
CP 473, CEP 17033.360, Bauru/SP, Brazil
ivan@feb.unesp.br

Abstract. A neural model for solving nonlinear optimization problems is presented in this paper. More specifically, a modified Hopfield network is developed and its internal parameters are computed using the valid-subspace technique. These parameters guarantee the convergence of the network to the equilibrium points that represent an optimal feasible solution. The network is shown to be completely stable and globally convergent to the solutions of nonlinear optimization problems. A study of the modified Hopfield model is also developed to analyze its stability and convergence. Simulation results are presented to validate the developed methodology.

1 Introduction

Artificial neural networks are richly connected networks of simple computational elements modeled on biological processes. These networks have been applied to several classes of optimization problems and have shown promise for solving such problems efficiently.

Nonlinear optimization problems have a fundamental role in many areas of sciences and engineering, where a set of design parameters is optimized subject to inequality and/or equality constraints [1]. Basically, all of the neural networks [2][3][4] used in nonlinear optimization contain some penalty parameters. The stable equilibrium points of these networks are obtained only when the penalty parameters are sufficiently large [5]; and in this case, the accuracy can be affected. Hence, we have developed a modified Hopfield network not depending on the penalties.

For this purpose, the organization of the present paper is as follows. In Section 2, the modified Hopfield network is presented. Section 3 contains a linearized analysis of the network dynamics in the context of the valid subspace. In Section 4, a mapping of nonlinear optimization problems is formulated using the modified Hopfield network. In Section 5, the key issues raised in the paper are summarized.

2 The Modified Hopfield Network

An artificial neural network (ANN) is a dynamic system that consists of highly interconnected and parallel non-linear processing elements that shows extreme efficiency in computation. In this paper, a modified Hopfield network with equilibrium points representing the problem solution has been developed. As introduced in [6], Hopfield networks are single-layer networks with feedback connections between nodes. In the standard case, the nodes are fully connected, i.e., every node is connected to all others nodes, including itself. The node equation for the continuous-time network with n-neurons is given by:

$$\dot{u}_i(t) = -\eta . u_i(t) + \sum_{j=1}^{n} T_{ij} . v_j(t) + i_i^b . \quad (1)$$

$$v_i(t) = g(u_i(t)) . \quad (2)$$

where $u_i(t)$ is the current state of the i-th neuron, $v_j(t)$ is the output of the j-th neuron, i_i^b is the offset bias of the i-th neuron, $\eta . u_i(t)$ is a passive decay term, and T_{ij} is the weight connecting the j-th neuron to i-th neuron.

In Equation (2), $g(u_i(t))$ is a monotonically increasing threshold function that limits the output of each neuron to ensure that network output always lies in or within a hypercube. It is shown in [6] that the equilibrium points of the network correspond to values $v(t)$ for which the energy function (3) associated to the network is minimized:

$$E(t) = -\frac{1}{2} v(t)^T . T . v(t) - v(t)^T . i^b . \quad (3)$$

The mapping of constrained nonlinear optimization problems using a Hopfield network consists of determining the weight matrix T and the bias vector i^b to compute equilibrium points. A modified energy function $E^m(t)$ is used here, defined as follows:

$$E^m(t) = E^{conf}(t) + E^{op}(t) . \quad (4)$$

where $E^{conf}(t)$ is a confinement term that groups all the constraints imposed by the problem, and $E^{op}(t)$ is an optimization term that conducts the network output to the equilibrium points. Thus, the minimization of $E^m(t)$ of the modified Hopfield network is conducted in two stages:

i) minimization of the term $E^{conf}(t)$:

$$E^{conf}(t) = -\frac{1}{2} v(t)^T . T^{conf} . v(t) - v(t)^T . i^{conf} . \quad (5)$$

where: $v(t)$ is the network output, T^{conf} is weight matrix and i^{conf} is bias vector belonging to E^{conf}. This corresponds to confinement of $v(t)$ into a valid subspace that confines the inequality constraints imposed by the problem.

ii) minimization of the term $E^{op}(t)$:

$$E^{op}(t) = -\frac{1}{2} v(t)^T . T^{op} . v(t) - v(t)^T . i^{op} . \quad (6)$$

where: T^{op} is weight matrix and i^{op} is bias vector belonging to E^{op}. This move $v(t)$ towards an optimal solution (the equilibrium points).

Thus, the operation of the modified Hopfield network consists of three main steps, as shown in Figure 1:

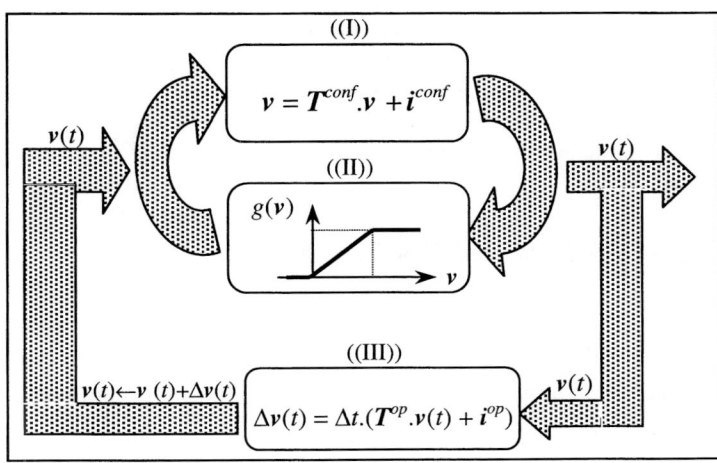

Fig. 1. Modified Hopfield network.

Step ((I)): Minimization of E^{conf}, corresponding to the projection of $v(t)$ in the valid subspace defined by [7][8]:

$$v(t+1) = T^{conf}.v(t) + i^{conf}. \tag{7}$$

where: T^{conf} is a projection matrix ($T^{conf}.T^{conf} = T^{conf}$) and $T^{conf}.i^{conf} = \mathbf{0}$. This operation corresponds to an indirect minimization of $E^{conf}(t)$.

Step ((II)): Application of a 'symmetric ramp' activation function constraining $v(t)$ in a hypercube:

$$g(v_i) = \begin{cases} lim^{inf}, & \text{if } lim^{inf} > v_i \\ v_i, & \text{if } lim^{inf} \leq v_i \leq lim^{sup} \\ lim^{sup}, & \text{if } v_i > lim^{sup} \end{cases} \tag{8}$$

where $v_i(t) \in [lim^{inf}, lim^{sup}]$.

Step ((III)): Minimization of E^{op}, which involves updating of $v(t)$ in direction to an optimal solution (defined by T^{op} and i^{op}) corresponding to network equilibrium points, which are the solutions for the constrained optimization problems, by applying the gradient in relation to the energy term E^{op}.

$$\frac{dv(t)}{dt} = \dot{v} = -\frac{\partial E^{op}(t)}{\partial v}$$

$$\Delta v = -\Delta t. \nabla E^{op}(v) = \Delta t.(T^{op}.v + i^{op}). \tag{9}$$

Therefore, minimization of E^{op} consists of updating $v(t)$ in the opposite direction of the gradient of E^{op}. These results are also valid when a 'hyperbolic tangent' activation function is used.

As seen in Figure 1, each iteration represented by the above steps has two distinct stages. First, as described in Step (II), v is updated using the gradient of the term E^{op}

alone. Second, after each updating, v is projected directly in the valid subspace. This is an iterative process, in which v is first orthogonally projected in the valid subspace (7) and then thresholded so that its elements lie in the range $[lim^{inf}, lim^{sup}]$. Thus, the mapping of constrained nonlinear optimization problems using a modified Hopfield network consists of determining the matrices T^{conf} and T^{op}, and the vectors i^{conf} and i^{op}.

3 Analysis of the Modified Hopfield Network Dynamics

The operation of the modified Hopfield network in the early stages of convergence is analyzed in this section. Initially, the component of $\dot{v}$ {defined in equation (9)}, which lies in the valid subspace, is defined as $\dot{v}^{conf}$. Since v is confined to the valid subspace (i.e. $v = T^{conf}.v + i^{conf}$), any component of $\dot{v}$ orthogonal to $\dot{v}^{conf}$ is continually suppressed [9]; hence it is $\dot{v}^{conf}$, not $\dot{v}$, which best characterizes the overall dynamics of the network. Thus:

$$\dot{v}^{conf} = T^{conf}.\dot{v} = T^{conf}(T^{op}.v + i^{op})$$
$$= T^{conf}(T^{op}(T^{conf}.v + i^{conf}) + i^{op})$$
$$= T^{conf}T^{op}T^{conf}.v + T^{conf}(T^{op}.i^{conf} + i^{op}). \tag{10}$$

The component $\dot{v}^{conf}$ consists of two parts, a constant term, $T^{conf}(T^{op}.i^{conf} + i^{op})$, and a term which depends on v, $T^{conf}T^{op}T^{conf}v$. These expressions can be simplified by:

$$T^{conf}T^{op}T^{conf} = A. \tag{11}$$

$$T^{conf}(T^{op}.i^{conf} + i^{op}) = b. \tag{12}$$

which gives:

$$\dot{v}^{conf} = A.v + b = A.v^{conf} + b. \tag{13}$$

where $v^{conf} = T^{conf}.v$ and $T^{conf}.T^{conf} = T^{conf}$.

With v confined to the valid subspace (i.e. $v=T^{conf}.v+i^{conf}$ and $T^{conf}.i^{conf} = 0$), E^{op} can be expressed as:

$$E^{op} = -\frac{1}{2}v^T.A.v - b^T.v. \tag{14}$$

It is thus apparent, that the dynamics of $\{\dot{v} = \dot{v}^{conf} = A.v+b\}$ simply results in the steepest descent in relation to E^{op} within the valid subspace, which is consistent with the goal of finding a valid solution which minimizes E^{op}. The general solution of (13) can be expressed by means of the matrix exponential [10]:

$$v^{conf}(t) = e^{At}v_0^{conf} + \int_0^t e^{A(t-\tau)}b.d\tau. \tag{15}$$

where v_0^{conf} is the value of v^{conf} at time $t = 0$, usually set to be a small random vector. Rewriting the matrix exponentials as power series gives:

$$v^{conf}(t) = \sum_{k=0}^{\infty} \frac{t^k}{k!} A^k v_0^{conf} + \int_0^t \sum_{k=0}^{\infty} \frac{(t-\tau)^k}{k!} A^k b \, d\tau$$

$$= \sum_{k=0}^{\infty} \frac{t^k}{k!} A^k v_0^{conf} + \sum_{k=0}^{\infty} \frac{A^k b}{k!} \int_0^t (t-\tau)^k \, d\tau$$

$$= \sum_{k=0}^{\infty} \frac{t^k}{k!} A^k v_0^{conf} + \sum_{k=0}^{\infty} \frac{t^{k+1}}{(k+1)!} A^k b \, . \tag{16}$$

Suppose A has eigenvalues $\lambda_1, \lambda_2, ..., \lambda_n$, with associated normalized eigenvectors $u_1, u_2, ..., u_n$. It is necessary to distinguish between the zero and non-zero eigenvalues of A, so the set Z is defined, such as $\lambda_i = 0$ for $i \in Z$ and $\lambda_i \neq 0$ for $i \notin Z$. Let v^{conf}, v_0^{conf} and b be decomposed along the eigenvectors of A as follows:

$$v^{conf} = \sum_{i=1}^{n} v_i u_i \, , \quad v_0^{conf} = \sum_{i=1}^{n} o_i u_i \, , \quad b = \sum_{i=1}^{n} b_i u_i \tag{17}$$

giving

$$A^k v_0^{conf} = \sum_{i=1}^{n} o_i \lambda_i^k u_i \, , \quad A^k b = \sum_{i=1}^{n} b_i \lambda_i^k u_i$$

Inserting the above equations in (16) results in:

$$v^{conf}(t) = \sum_{k=0}^{\infty} \frac{t^k}{k!} \sum_{i=1}^{n} o_i \lambda_i^k u_i + \sum_{k=0}^{\infty} \frac{t^{k+1}}{(k+1)!} \sum_{i=1}^{n} b_i \lambda_i^k u_i$$

$$= \sum_{i=1}^{n} o_i u_i \sum_{k=0}^{\infty} \frac{t^k \lambda_i^k}{k!} + \sum_{i \notin Z} \frac{b_i u_i}{\lambda_i} \sum_{k=0}^{\infty} \frac{t^{k+1} \lambda_i^{k+1}}{(k+1)!} + \sum_{i \in Z} b_i u_i \sum_{k=0}^{\infty} \frac{t^{k+1} 0^k}{(k+1)!}$$

$$= \sum_{i=1}^{n} e^{\lambda_i t} o_i u_i + \sum_{i \notin Z} \frac{b_i u_i}{\lambda_i} \left(\sum_{k=0}^{\infty} \frac{t^k \lambda_i^k}{k!} - 1 \right) + \sum_{i \in Z} b_i u_i t$$

$$= \sum_{i=1}^{n} e^{\lambda_i t} o_i u_i + \sum_{i \notin Z} \frac{b_i u_i}{\lambda_i} (e^{\lambda_i t} - 1) + \sum_{i \in Z} b_i u_i t \, . \tag{18}$$

Equation (18) is completely general in that it holds for any arbitrary A, b and v_0^{conf}. However, the expression can be simplified if A and b are defined as in equations (11) and (12). In this case the eigenvectors of A with corresponding zero eigenvalues are confined to spanning the invalid subspace, whilst b lies wholly within the valid subspace, so $b_i = 0$ for $i \in Z$. Equation (18) can sequentially becomes

$$v^{conf}(t) = \sum_{i=1}^{n} e^{\lambda_i t} o_i u_i + \sum_{i \notin Z} \frac{b_i u_i}{\lambda_i} (e^{\lambda_i t} - 1) \, . \tag{19}$$

It is important to examine the expression for $v^{conf}(t)$ given by equation (19) in the limits of small and large t. For small t, we make the approximation following:

which gives:
$$e^{\lambda_i t} \approx 1 + \lambda_i t.$$

$$v^{conf}(t) \approx \sum_{i=1}^{n} [o_i(1+\lambda_i t) + b_i t].u_i. \qquad (20)$$

Further noting that for a small random v_0^{conf} the terms o_i are often small in comparison with the b_i. Thus, equation (20) transforms in

$$v^{conf}(t) \approx t \sum_{i=1}^{n} b_i u_i = t.b. \qquad (21)$$

So it is apparent that v^{conf} initially takes off in the direction of the vector b. In the limit of large t, equation (19) indicates that v^{conf} will tend towards the eigenvector of A corresponding to the largest positive eigenvalue. In this case, the equilibrium point of the network may be iteratively computed, since the state of the network starting from an arbitrary initial position will converge to the equilibrium point, which is bounded by the hypercube defined by the 'symmetric ramp' activation function in (8).

4 Formulation of Constrained Nonlinear Optimization Problems Through Modified Hopfield Architecture

Consider the following general nonlinear optimization problem, with m-constraints and n-variables, given by the following equations:

$$\text{Minimize } E^{op}(v) = f(v). \qquad (22)$$

$$\text{subject to } E^{conf}(v): h_i(v) \leq 0, \quad i \in \{1..m\} \qquad (23)$$

$$z^{min} \leq v \leq z^{max} \qquad (24)$$

where v, z^{min}, $z^{max} \in \Re^n$; $f(v)$ and $h_i(v)$ are continuous, and all first and second order partial derivatives of $f(v)$ and $h_i(v)$ exist and are continuous. The vectors z^{min} and z^{max} define the bounds on the variables belonging to the vector v. The conditions in (23) and (24) define a bounded convex polyhedron. The vector v must remain within this polyhedron if it is to represent a valid solution for the optimization problem (22). A solution can be obtained by a modified Hopfield network, whose valid subspace guarantees the satisfaction of condition (23). Moreover, the initial hypercube represented by the inequality constraints in (24) is directly defined by the 'symmetric ramp' function given in (8), which is used as neural activation function.

Defining Equations to T^{conf}, i^{conf}, T^{op} and i^{op}

The parameters T^{conf} and i^{conf} are calculated by transforming the inequality constraints in (23) into equality constraints by introducing a slack variable $w \in \Re^n$ for each inequality constraint:

$$g_i(v) + \sum_{j=1}^{q} \delta_{ij}.w_j = 0. \tag{25}$$

where w_j are slack variables, treated as the variables v_i, and δ_{ij} is defined by:

$$\delta_{ij} = \begin{cases} 1, & \text{if } i = j \\ 0, & \text{if } i \neq j \end{cases} \tag{26}$$

After this transformation, the problem defined by equations (22), (23) and (24) can be rewritten as:

$$\text{Minimize } E^{op}(v^+) = f(v^+). \tag{27}$$

$$\text{subject to } E^{conf}(v): h^+(v^+) = 0. \tag{28}$$

$$z^{min} \leq v^+ \leq z^{max}, i \in \{1..n\} \tag{29}$$

$$0 \leq v^+ \leq z^{max}, i \in \{n+1..N^+\} \tag{30}$$

where $N^+ = n + m$, and $v^{+T} = [v^T \ w^T] \in \Re^{N+}$ is a vector of extended variables. Note that E^{op} does not depend on the slack variables w. In [11] has been shown that a projection matrix to the system defined in (28) is given by:

$$T^{conf} = I - \nabla h(v)^T.(\nabla h(v).\nabla h(v)^T)^{-1}.\nabla h(v). \tag{31}$$

where:

$$\nabla h(v) = \begin{bmatrix} \frac{\partial h_1(v)}{\partial v_1} & \frac{\partial h_1(v)}{\partial v_2} & \cdots & \frac{\partial h_1(v)}{\partial v_N} \\ \frac{\partial h_2(v)}{\partial v_1} & \frac{\partial h_2(v)}{\partial v_2} & \cdots & \frac{\partial h_2(v)}{\partial x_N} \\ \vdots & \vdots & \ddots & \\ \frac{\partial h_p(v)}{\partial v_1} & \frac{\partial h_p(v)}{\partial v_2} & \frac{\partial h_p(v)}{\partial v_N} \end{bmatrix} = \begin{bmatrix} \nabla h_1(v)^T \\ \nabla h_2(v)^T \\ \vdots \\ \nabla h_m(v)^T \end{bmatrix}. \tag{32}$$

Inserting the value of (31) in the expression of the valid subspace in (7), we have:

$$v = [I - \nabla h(v)^T.(\nabla h(v).\nabla h(v)^T)^{-1}.\nabla h(v)].v + i^{conf}. \tag{33}$$

Results of the Lyapunov stability theory [10] can be used in order to develop a deeper understanding of the equilibrium condition. By the definition of the Jacobean, when v leads to equilibrium point $v^e = 0$ ($\|i^{conf}\| \to 0$), we may approximate $h(v)$ as follows:

$$h(v) \approx h(v^e) + J.(v - v^e). \tag{34}$$

where $J = \nabla h(v)$.

In the proximity of the equilibrium point $v^e = 0$, we obtain the following equation:

$$\lim_{v \to v^e} \frac{\|h(v)\|}{\|v\|} = 0. \tag{35}$$

Finally, introducing (34) and (35) in equation given by (33), we obtain:

$$v = v - \nabla h(v)^T.(\nabla h(v).\nabla h(v)^T)^{-1}.h(v). \quad (36)$$

The parameters T^{op} and i^{op} in this case are such that the vector v^+ is updated in the opposite gradient direction that of the energy function E^{op}. Since conditions (23) and (24) define a bounded convex polyhedron, the objective function (22) has a unique global minimum. Thus, the equilibrium points of the network can be calculated by assuming the following values to T^{op} and i^{op}:

$$i^{op} = -\left[\frac{\partial f(v)}{\partial v_1} \frac{\partial f(v)}{\partial v_2} \cdots \frac{\partial f(v)}{\partial v_N}\right]. \quad (37)$$

$$T^{op} = \mathbf{0}. \quad (38)$$

Several simulation results have confirmed the validity of this proposed approach.

5 Conclusions

In this paper, we have developed a modified Hopfield network for solving constrained nonlinear optimization problems. The simulation results demonstrate that the network is an alternative method to solve these problems efficiently. All simulation results show that the proposed network is completely stable and globally convergent to the solutions of the nonlinear optimization problem. Some particularities of the neural approach in relation to primal methods normally used in nonlinear optimization are: i) it is not necessary the computation, in each iteration, of the active set of constraints; ii) the neural approach does not compute Lagrange's multipliers; and iii) the initial solution used to initialize the network can be outside of the feasible set defined from the constraints.

References

1. Bazaraa, M. S., Shetty, C. M.: Nonlinear Programming. John Wiley & Sons (1979)
2. Kennedy, M. P., Chua, L. O.: Neural Networks for Nonlinear Programming. IEEE Trans. Circuits Syst., Vol. 35 (1988) 554–562
3. Rodriguez-Vazquez, A., et al.: Nonlinear Switched-Capacitor Neural Network for Optimization Problems. IEEE Trans. Circuits Syst., Vol. 37 (1990) 384–398
4. Tank, D. W., Hopfield, J. J.: Simple Neural Optimization Networks: An A/D Converter, Signal Decision Network, and a Linear Programming Circuit. IEEE Trans. Circuits Syst., Vol. 33 (1986) 533–541
5. Wu, X.-Y., et al.: A High-Performance Neural Network for Solving Linear and Quadratic Programming Problems. IEEE Trans. Neural Networks, Vol. 7 (1996)
6. Hopfield, J. J.: Neurons with a Graded Response Have Collective Computational Properties Like Those of Two-State Neurons. Proc. of Nat. Acad. of Science, Vol. 81 (1984) 3088–3092
7. Aiyer, S. V. B., Niranjan, M., Fallside, F.: A Theoretical Investigation into the Performance of the Hopfield Model. IEEE Trans. Neural Networks, Vol. 1 (1990) 53–60

8. Silva, I. N., Arruda, L. V. R., Amaral, W. C.: Robust Estimation of Parametric Membership Regions Using Artificial Neural Networks. International Journal of Systems Sciences, Vol. 28 (1997) 447–455
9. Gee, A. H., Aiyer, S. V. B., Prager, R. W.: Analytical Framework for Optimization Neural Networks. Neural Networks, Vol. 6 (1993) 79–97
10. Vidyasagar, M.: Nonlinear Systems Analysis. Prentice-Hall (1988)
11. Luenberger, D. G.: Linear and Nonlinear Programming. Addison-Wesley (1984)

SVM and Kernel Methods

Generalization Error Analysis for Polynomial Kernel Methods – Algebraic Geometrical Approach

Kazushi Ikeda

Graduate School of Informatics, Kyoto University, Kyoto 606-8501 Japan
kazushi@i.kyoto-u.ac.jp

Abstract. The generalization properties of learning classifiers with a polynomial kernel function are examined here. We first show that the generalization error of the learning machine depends on the properties of the separating curve, that is, the intersection of the input surface and the true separating hyperplane in the feature space. When the input space is one-dimensional, the problem is decomposed to as many one-dimensional problems as the number of the intersecting points. Otherwise, the generalization error is determined by the class of the separating curve. Next, we consider how the class of the separating curve depends on the true separating function. The class is maximum when the true separating polynomial function is irreducible and smaller otherwise. In either case, the class depends only on the true function and does not on the dimension of the feature space. The results imply that the generalization error does not increase even when the dimension of the feature space gets larger and that the so-called overmodeling does not occur in the kernel learning.

1 Introduction

Kernel classifiers, such as the Support Vector Machine (SVM) and the Kernel Perceptron Learning Algorithm, have been paid much attention in recent years as new successful pattern classification techniques [7,13,14,17]. A kernel classifier maps the input vector $x \in X$ to a feature vector $f(x)$ in a high-dimensional feature space F and discriminates it linearly, that is, outputs the sign of the inner product of the feature vector and a parameter vector w [1].

An SVM has a good generalization performance and many of its theoretical analyses [17] are based on the probably approximately correct (PAC) learning approach, that is, the sufficient number of examples is given as a function of δ and ϵ such that the probability the generalization error becomes more than ϵ is less than δ [16]. This framework considers the worst case in a sense where the VC dimension plays an essential role representing the complexity of the learning machines [18].

Another criterion to evaluate generalization ability is to analyze the average generalization error, which is defined as the average of the probability that a learning machine given some examples mispredicts the output of a new input. The average generalization error as a function of the number of given examples is called a learning curve. One tool to derive the learning curve is statistical mechanics [5,12] and it has been applied to SVM in [8]. Another approach is asymptotic statistics [2,3,4,11] which is based on the Taylor expansion of the probablity density function by parameters. When the learning machine is not differentible, like a linear dichotomy, a stochastic geometrical method is also useful [10]. The analyses above have shown that the generalization error is proportional to the number of parameters and inversely proportional to the number of given examples.

Kernel classifiers are essentially linear dichotomies in a high-dimensional feature space F. How are their learning curves? For linear discrimination problems, in general, the generalization errors are proportional to the dimension of the space F. In kernel methods, however, the input vector $\boldsymbol{f}(\boldsymbol{x})$ in F is the mapped one from a low-dimensional input space X and lies on a low-dimensional subset in F. If the generalization error would be proportional to the dimension of the space F even in kernel methods they have little generalization ability since the feature space is of very high dimensions in usual. However, they are known to have a good generalization performance in a lot of applications and an analysis in the PAC learning framework has shown that the generalization error does not depend on the apparent high dimension of the feature space [17].

The purpose of this paper is to derive the learning curves of kernel methods and to clarify why kernel methods have good generalization ability. We employ the average prediction error as the criterion for the generalizaiton ability and the polynomial kernel as the kernel function. When the input space is one-dimensional, the average prediction error can be derived. The results in [9] showed that the average prediction error depends only on the complexity of the true separating function and does not increase even if the order of the polynomial kernel becomes larger, however, the method for analysis was based on the fact that the input space is one-dimensional. In this paper, we will show that the results can be extended to cases of general dimensions from algebraic geometrical approach.

The rest of the paper is organized as follows: Section II contains the mathematical formulation of deterministic dichotomy machines with polynomial kernel methods; Input surface in the feature space is introduced in Section III; Section IV is devoted to the relationship between reducibility and the class of a separating polynomial; Conclusions and discussions are given in Section V.

2 Formulation

This paper considers a deterministic dichotomy, which outputs $y = \pm 1$ for the input vector $\boldsymbol{x} = (x_0, x_1, \ldots, x_m)^T$ in an $(m+1)$-dimensional space $X = \boldsymbol{R}^{m+1}$ by calculating $\text{sgn}[\boldsymbol{w}^T \boldsymbol{f}(\boldsymbol{x})]$. Here $\boldsymbol{f}(\boldsymbol{x})$ is an $(M+1)$-dimensional vector, called the feature vector, which consists of $(M+1)$ monomials of degree p where $M = {}_{m+p}C_m - 1$, that is, each component of the feature vector $\boldsymbol{f}(\boldsymbol{x})$ is of the form

$$(f(x))_{d_0 d_1 \cdots d_m} = x_0^{d_0} x_1^{d_1} \cdots x_m^{d_m} \tag{1}$$

where $\sum_{i=0}^{m} d_i = p$. Note that the coefficient of each component is not necessarily unity when the polynomial kernel $K(x, x') = (x^T x')^p$ is employed. However, we define the map function as (1) for simplicity since the coefficients do not affect the result when the number of given examples is large.

A given example consists of an input x drawn from a certain probability distribution having a density $q(x) > 0$ and the corresponding output $y = \text{sgn}[w_o^T f(x)]$ where w_o is the true parameter vector the teacher machine has. Given N examples denoted by $D^{(N)} = \{(x_n, y_n), n = 1, \ldots, N\}$, a machine is trained so that the machine can reproduce y_n for any x_n in the example set $D^{(N)}$. Let $\hat{w}$ be such a parameter vector of the learning machine. The learning machine with the parameter vector $\hat{w}$ predicts the output y_{N+1} for a test input vector x_{N+1} which is independently chosen from the same density $q(x)$. The prediction error $\varepsilon(D^{(N)})$ of the trained machine for the example set $D^{(N)}$ is defined as the probability that the predicted output $\hat{y}$ is false. The average prediction error is a function of N defined as the average of the prediction errors over all example sets and is denoted by

$$\varepsilon_N = \langle \varepsilon(D^{(N)}) \rangle_{D^{(N)}}.$$

The average prediction error depends on how the estimator $\hat{w}$ is chosen. We choose an estimator according to the posterior distribution $q_{\text{po}}(w)$ in the Bayesian framework assuming a prior distribution $q_{\text{pr}}(w)$ of the true parameter vector w_o. In the case of deterministic dichotomies, the posterior distribution is written as $q_{\text{po}}(w) = q_{\text{pr}}(w)/Z_N$ where $Z_N = \int_{A_N} q_{\text{pr}}(w) dw$ is the partition function and

$$A_N = \{w | w^T f(x_n) y_n > 0, n = 1, \ldots, N\}$$

is the version space since $q_{\text{po}}(w) \propto q_{\text{pr}}(w)$ when $w \in A_N$ and $q_{\text{po}}(w) = 0$ otherwise (Figure 1). This method is called the Gibbs algorithm.

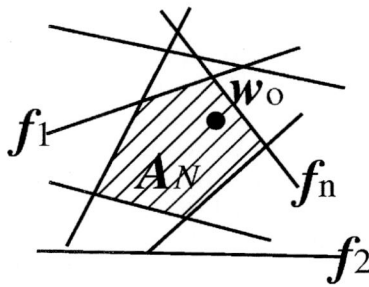

Fig. 1. Examples and version space in the parameter space.

Several other algorithms, such as the Bayes algorithm and the Support Vector Machine, have been considered in the statistical learning theory, however, we consider only the Gibbs algorithm in this paper since our analysis given later show that kernel methods can be decomposed to a combination of ordinary problems in learning properties and it does not depend on which algorithm is employed as long as the algorithm chooses an estimator $\hat{\boldsymbol{w}}$ within the version space.

3 Input Surface and Prediction Error

A separating function in the feature space is a hyperplane which includes the origin

$$\boldsymbol{w}^T \boldsymbol{f}(\boldsymbol{x}) = 0$$

and a polynomial of $\boldsymbol{x}$ of degree p. This is denoted by $\psi(\boldsymbol{x};\boldsymbol{w})$ when it should be emphasized that the polynomial is a function of $\boldsymbol{x}$ with a parameter vector $\boldsymbol{w}$. Since $\boldsymbol{x}$ and $c\boldsymbol{x}$ have the same output when $c > 0$, $\boldsymbol{x}$ essentially lies on an m-dimensional hypersphere $\boldsymbol{S}^m$, and $\boldsymbol{f}(\boldsymbol{x}) \in \boldsymbol{S}^M$ in the same way.

The set of all $\boldsymbol{f}(\boldsymbol{x})$ constitutes an m-dimensional submanifold in $\boldsymbol{S}^M$, called the input surface. The input surface intersects the true separating hyperplane $\psi(\boldsymbol{x};\boldsymbol{w}_\mathrm{o}) = \boldsymbol{w}_\mathrm{o}^T \boldsymbol{f}(\boldsymbol{x}) = 0$ at $(m-1)$-dimensional surface in $\boldsymbol{S}^M$, called the separating curve. Hence, the task of the learning machine is to find a separating curve from given examples. Note that the terms are named assuming $m = 2$ for clarity, the input surface and the separating curve for example, but the analysis is applicable to general cases.

In the case of $m = 1$, the input surface becomes a closed curve called the input curve and the separating curve consists of distinct points called the separating points. Therefore, the problem of estimating the true separating hyperplane is decomposed to estimating the true separating points using positive and negative examples in the input curve. In other words, the problem is equivalent to as many one-dimensional problems as the number of the separating points [9]. This means that the generalization error does not increase even if the degree of the polynomial kernel becomes larger since the number of the separating points is determined only by the complexity of the true separating function.

Let us consider general cases with $m \geq 2$. The input surface and the separating hyperplane are respectively shown in Figure 2 by a mesh surface and a flat plane in the case of $m = 2$. Since the separating curve consists of several closed loops, the problem seems to be decomposed to as many two-dimensional problems as the number of the loops. However, this is not true as shown in the following. Since the problem is to find the separating curve $\psi(\boldsymbol{x};\boldsymbol{w}_\mathrm{o}) = 0$ using positive and negative examples in its neighborhood, it is important what information such examples have. In other words, we should consider the dimension of the space $\Delta\boldsymbol{w}$ spans which satisfies $\psi(\boldsymbol{x} + \Delta\boldsymbol{x};\boldsymbol{w}_\mathrm{o} + \Delta\boldsymbol{w}) = 0$ for an input $\boldsymbol{x} + \Delta\boldsymbol{x}$ s.t. $\psi(\boldsymbol{x};\boldsymbol{w}_\mathrm{o}) = 0$, assuming that $\Delta\boldsymbol{w}$ and $\Delta\boldsymbol{x}$ are small in the asymptotic limit. The dimension of the space all such $\Delta\boldsymbol{w}$ span is called the class of

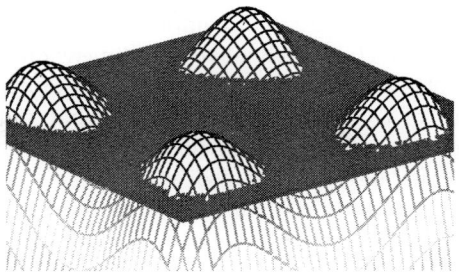

Fig. 2. Input surface and the separating hyperplane.

$\psi(\boldsymbol{x};\boldsymbol{w}_o)$ since this is based on a similar (but different) idea to the dual curve of Plücker in algebraic geometry [15].

Let us consider an intuitive example. Figure 3 shows the two cases where the cylinder and the cone represent the input curve in each. Although they have the same separating curve, examples in the cone have two-dimensional components while one-dimensional in the cylinder since all of $\Delta \boldsymbol{x}$ in the cylinder are parallel to each other. Note that we shold consider only the components orthogonal to the separating curve since the component in the direction of the separating curve must be considered as the change of $\boldsymbol{x}$ itself. This example implies that the difficulty of estimating the separating curve depends not only on the shape of the separating curve but also on the input surface around it.

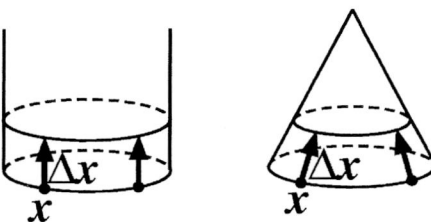

Fig. 3. Geometrical meaning of the class of the separating function.

Now let us show how to evaluate the class of the separating function. Since both of $\psi(\boldsymbol{x};\boldsymbol{w}_o) = 0$ and $\psi(\boldsymbol{x}+\Delta\boldsymbol{x};\boldsymbol{w}_o+\Delta\boldsymbol{w}) = 0$ hold for small $\Delta \boldsymbol{w}$ and $\Delta \boldsymbol{x}$,

$$\psi_{\boldsymbol{w}} \cdot \Delta\boldsymbol{w} + \psi_{\boldsymbol{x}} \cdot \Delta\boldsymbol{x} = 0 \qquad (2)$$

must be satisfiede for any $\boldsymbol{x}$ s.t. $\psi(\boldsymbol{x};\boldsymbol{w}_o) = 0$ where $\psi_{\boldsymbol{w}} = \partial\psi/\partial\boldsymbol{w}$ and $\psi_{\boldsymbol{x}} = \partial\psi/\partial\boldsymbol{x}$. In other words, $\psi_{\boldsymbol{w}} \cdot \Delta\boldsymbol{w} + \psi_{\boldsymbol{x}} \cdot \Delta\boldsymbol{x}$ is zero as a polynomial of $\boldsymbol{x}$. The first term $\psi_{\boldsymbol{w}} \cdot \Delta\boldsymbol{w}$ represents a polynomial of degree p due to $\psi_{\boldsymbol{w}} = \boldsymbol{f}(\boldsymbol{x})$ while the second term $\psi_x \cdot \Delta x$ represents a linear combination of $m+1$ polynomials ψ_x of degree $(p-1)$. Hence, the class is equal to the dimension of the space that the coefficient vectors of pth-order polynomials span each of which is represented as a linear combinations of ψ_x. Taking into account that multiplying a constant or a polynomial does not affect the dimension in (2), we should consider the ideal[1] $I = \langle \psi_x \rangle^2$ from the algebraic point of view.

When the class is equal to C, the parameter vector w essentially has C effective components around the true parameter vector w_o in the point of separating input vectors. Hence, its learning properties are equivalent to a linear dichotomy with C parameters. Strict analysis of the average prediction error $\langle \varepsilon(D^{(N)}) \rangle_{D^{(N)}}$ for a linear dichotomy is still open however an upper bound $\langle \log[1-\varepsilon(D^{(N)})] \rangle_{D^{(N)}}$ called the average prediction entropy is found to be C/N. So, the average prediction error of kernel methods has an upper bound C/N where C is the class of the true separating function and N is the number of given examples. See [2] for the detail.

4 Factorability and Class

We show the relationship between factorability or reducibility of the true separating function and its class by considering the ideal $I = \langle \psi_x \rangle$.

We first consider the case that the separating function $\psi(x; w_o)$ is an irreducible polynomial. The $(m+1)$ polynomials, ψ_{x_i}, $i = 0, \ldots, m$, have no common factors since a linear combination of them, $\sum x_i \psi_{x_i} = p\psi$, is irreducible. Hence, the ideal $I = \langle \psi_x \rangle$ includes any polynomials of degree p and Δw spans an $(M+1)$-dimensional space. However, since a polynomial has to be regarded as the same when a constant is multiplied, the dimension is equal to M. This can also be derived from the fact that $f(x) \cdot \Delta w = 0$ has to hold true when $\Delta w \propto w$. Anyway, the class C of $\psi(x; w_o)$ is equal to M.

We next consider the case that the $\psi(x; w_o)$ is decomposed to n irreducible polynomials $\psi_i(x; w_o)$ of degree p_i where $p = \sum_i p_i$, that is,

$$\psi(x; w_o) = \prod_i^n \psi_i(x; w_o).$$

Since the ideal of $\psi(x; w_o)$, $I = \langle \psi_x \rangle$, is written as

$$I = \sum_i \psi_1 \ldots \psi_{i-1} \psi_{i+1} \cdots \psi_n I_i$$

where $I_i = \langle \psi_{i x} \rangle$, the class C of $\psi(x; w_o)$ is more than or equal to $\sum M_i$ where $M_i = {}_{m+p_i}C_m - 1$ is the class of $\psi_i(x; w_o)$. It should be noted that $\sum M_i \leq M = {}_{m+p}C_m - 1$ due to $p = \sum p_i$ and convexity of $({}_{m+p}C_m - 1)$. This means that a

---
[1] A subset I of polynomials $k[x_0, \ldots, x_m]$ is called an ideal when (i) $0 \in I$, (ii) $f, g \in I \to f+g \in I$ and (iii) $f \in I, h \in k[x_0, \ldots, x_m] \to hf \in I$ are satisfied [6].
[2] $\langle f_1, \ldots, f_s \rangle = \{\Sigma_{i=1}^s h_i f_i : h_1, \ldots, h_s \in k[x_0, \ldots, x_m]\}$.

reducible problem may have a smaller generalization error than an irreducible one when they have the same degree.

We last consider the case that the true separating function is essentially a polynomial of degree p_o less than p. This means that $\psi(\boldsymbol{x};\boldsymbol{w}_o)$ is decomposed to a polynomial $\psi'(\boldsymbol{x};\boldsymbol{w}_o)$ of degree p_o and a non-negative polynomial $\phi(\boldsymbol{x};\boldsymbol{w}_o)$ of degree $(p-p_o)$. From $\psi(\boldsymbol{x};\boldsymbol{w}_o) = \phi(\boldsymbol{x};\boldsymbol{w}_o)\psi'(\boldsymbol{x};\boldsymbol{w}_o)$, the ideal $I = \langle \psi_x \rangle$ is expressed as $I = \phi I_o$ where $I_o = \langle \psi'_x \rangle$ since $\psi'(\boldsymbol{x};\boldsymbol{w}_o)$ is null for any $\boldsymbol{x}$ s.t. $\psi(\boldsymbol{x};\boldsymbol{w}_o) = 0$. Hence, the class C of $\psi(\boldsymbol{x};\boldsymbol{w}_o)$ is more than or equal to the class of $\psi'(\boldsymbol{x};\boldsymbol{w}_o)$, which is $M' = {}_{m+p'}C_m - 1$ at most and smaller than M.

In total, the class C of a separating function $\psi(\boldsymbol{x};\boldsymbol{w}_o)$ depends on its factorability and is maximum when the polynomial is irreducible. When it can be decomposed to polynomials of smaller degrees, an lower bound of the class is expressed as the sum of the classes of the polynomials. Non-negative components also reduce the class.

When $m = 1$, for example, $\psi(\boldsymbol{x};\boldsymbol{w}_o)$ can be decomposed to p_o polynomials of degree one and a non-negative polynomial $\phi(\boldsymbol{x};\boldsymbol{w}_o)$ of degree $(p-p_o)$ and the class C of $\psi(\boldsymbol{x};\boldsymbol{w}_o)$ is equal to p_o since $M_1 = M_2 = \cdots = M_{p_o} = 1$. This agrees with the result derived in [9].

5 Conclusions

The generalization properties of polynomial kernel classifiers have been examined. First, It was shown that the generalization error of a kernel method is determined not by the dimensions of the input space or the feature space themselves but by how the input space is embedded into the feature space, more precisely, by the class defined as the dimension of the space the parameter vectors span around the separating curve.

Second, the relation between factorability of the true separating function and its class was shown by considering the ideal and it was found that the generalization error can be smaller when the true model is smaller than the model of the learning machine. The generalization error can decrease even when the true model is the same size but can be decomposed to smaller models.

Let us discuss the relationship between our result and the statistical mechanical analyses in [8], where, assuming $\boldsymbol{x} \in \{\pm 1\}^m$ and $m^p/N = O(1)$, it was shown in our notation that the average prediction error ε_N converges to a nonzero plateau when p is smaller than p_o and that the average prediction error obeys $\varepsilon_N \approx cm^p/N$ when enough examples are given and $p = p_o$. This is consistent with our result since ${}_{p+m}C_p \approx m^p$ when p is fixed and $N, m \to \infty$, assuming the irreducibility of the true separating function.

References

1. Aizerman, M.A., Braverman, E.M., Rozonoer, L.I.: Theoretical foundations of the potential function method in pattern recognition learning. Automation and Remote Control, **25** (1964) 821–837

2. Amari, S.: A universal theorem on learning curves. Neural Networks, **6** (1993) 161–166
3. Amari, S., Fujita, N., Shinomoto, S.: Four Types of Learning Curves. Neural Computation, **4** (1992) 605–618
4. Amari, S., Murata, N.: Statistical Theory of Learning Curves under Entropic Loss Criterion. Neural Computation, **5** (1993) 140–153
5. Baum, E.B., Haussler, D.: What Size Net Gives Valid Generalization? Neural Computation, **1** (1989) 151–160
6. Cox, D.: Ideals, Varieties, and Algorithms. Springer-Verlag, New York, NY (1997)
7. Cristianini, N., Shawe-Taylor, J.: An Introduction to Support Vector Machines. Cambridge Univ. Press, Cambridge, UK (2000)
8. Dietrich, R., Opper, M., Sompolinsky, H.: Statistical Mechanics of Support Vector Networks. Physical Review Letters, **82** (1999) 2975–2978
9. Ikeda, K.: Geometry and Learning Curves of Kernel Methods with Polynomial Kernels. Trans. of IEICE, **J86-D-II** (2003) in press (in Japanese).
10. Ikeda, K., Amari, S.: Geometry of Admissible Parameter Region in Neural Learning. IEICE Trans. Fundamentals, **E79-A** (1996) 409–414
11. Murata, N., Yoshizawa, S., Amari, S.: Network Information Criterions — Determining the Number of Parameters for an Artifcial Neural Network Model. IEEE Trans. Neural Networks, **5** (1994) 865–872
12. Opper, M., Haussler, D.: Calculation of the Learning Curve of Bayes Optimal Classification on Algorithm for Learning a Perceptron with Noise. Proc. 4th Ann. Workshop Comp. Learning Theory (1991) 75–87
13. Schölkopf, B., Burges, C., Smola, A.J.: Advances in Kernel Methods: Support Vector Learning. Cambridge Univ. Press, Cambridge, UK (1998)
14. Smola, A.J. et al. (eds.): Advances in Large Margin Classifiers. MIT Press, Cambridge, MA (2000)
15. Ueno, K.: Introduction to Algebraic Geometry. Iwanami-Shoten, Tokyo (1995) (in Japanese)
16. Valiant, L.G.: A Theory of the Learnable. Communications of ACM, **27** (1984) 1134–1142
17. Vapnik, V.N.: Statistical Learning Theory. John Wiley and Sons, New York, NY (1998)
18. Vapnik, V.N., Chervonenkis, A.Y.: On the Uniform Convergence of Relative Frequencies of Events to Their Probabilities. Theory of Probability and its Applications, **16** (1971) 264–280

Regularized Kriging: The Support Vectors Method Applied to Kriging

José M. Matías[1] and Wenceslao González-Manteiga[2]

[1] Dpt. de Estadística, Univ. de Vigo, 36200 Vigo, Spain, `jmmatias@uvigo.es`
[2] Dpt. de Estadística, Univ. de Santiago de Compostela
15782 Santiago de Compostela, Spain, `wences@zmat.usc.es`

Abstract. We explore the possible advantages of relaxing the universal kriging non-bias condition using the Support Vectors methodology. This leads to a regularized problem with restrictions, in which the objective function is the traditional variance term plus a term that penalises the bias, and whose resolution gives rise to a continuum of solutions for different values of the regularizer, including simple kriging and universal kriging as specific cases.

The analysis also permits the identification of prediction points that will admit slack in the non-bias condition without adversely affecting the prediction.

The simulations conducted demonstrate that when the process mean function is poorly specified and when there is a significant percentage of outliers, regularized kriging tends to improve the results of ordinary kriging. Given the relationship between kriging, regularization networks and Gaussian processes, the same considerations also apply to both the latter techniques.

1 Introduction

Kriging is a well-entrenched estimation method traditionally used in the spatial statistics field ([1] and references therein). Nonetheless, it has, perhaps, been somewhat neglected in other areas such as machine learning or signal processing.

At first glance, it may seem that kriging does not derive from a regularization problem. However, imposing a non-bias condition in the minimisation of the estimator variance is, as we shall see, a regularization method with a regularizing parameter that is implicitly chosen *a priori*.

This paper seeks to explore the possible advantages of relaxing this non-bias condition. For this purpose, we have used the support vectors method, [2], [3], applied to the components of the mean assumed as a hypothesis in the process.

The first section includes a brief overview of universal kriging. Next, regularized kriging is formulated and its relationship to universal and simple kriging demonstrated. The different types of prediction points will be analysed according to their behaviour in the problem restrictions. The two last sections will describe the results of the simulations and our conclusions.

2 Universal Kriging

For reference purposes this section will briefly describe the universal kriging estimator. We consider the model:

$$F(\mathbf{x}) = \sum_{j=1}^{r} \mu_j q_j(\mathbf{x}) + Z(\mathbf{x}) \tag{1}$$

where $\mathbf{x} \in S \subset \mathbb{R}^d$, $\mu = (\mu_1, ..., \mu_r) \in \mathbb{R}^r$ is an unknown, $q_j : S \to \mathbb{R}$, $j = 1, ..., r$ are known functions and $Z(\mathbf{x})$ is a second order zero mean stochastic stationary process with a covariance function $k(\mathbf{x}_1, \mathbf{x}_2) = \text{Cov}(Z(\mathbf{x}_1), Z(\mathbf{x}_2))$. We consider the general case, where the observation of the process $F(\mathbf{x})$ is subject to random noise ν independent of F with $E(\nu) = 0$ and $\text{Var}(\nu) = \sigma^2$:

$$Y(\mathbf{x}) = F(\mathbf{x}) + \nu$$

From this, $\text{Var}(Y(\mathbf{x})) = \text{Var}(F(\mathbf{x})) + \sigma^2 = \text{Var}(Z(\mathbf{x})) + \sigma^2 = k(\mathbf{x}, \mathbf{x}) + \sigma^2$.

The aim is to obtain an estimator $\hat{F}(\mathbf{x})$ for the subjacent process $F(\mathbf{x})$, from the n observations $\{Y(\mathbf{x}_i) = y_i\}_{i=1}^n$ where: $Y(\mathbf{x}_i) = F(\mathbf{x}_i) + \nu_i$, $i = 1, ..., n$, where $\nu = (\nu_1, ..., \nu_n)^t$ with $E(\nu) = \mathbf{0}$ and $\text{Var}(\nu) = \sigma^2 I$.

The universal kriging estimator of F in $\mathbf{x}_0 \in S$ is the minimum-variance unbiased linear estimator $\hat{F}(\mathbf{x}_0) = \lambda^t(\mathbf{x}_0)\mathbf{Y}$, i.e. the solution to the following Lagrange problem:

$$\min_{\lambda, \beta} \{\tfrac{1}{2}[k(\mathbf{x}_0, \mathbf{x}_0) + \lambda^t(K + \sigma^2 I)\lambda - 2\lambda^t \mathbf{k_0}] + \beta^t(Q^t \lambda - \mathbf{q}_0)\} \tag{2}$$

where $\mathbf{Y}^t = (Y_1, ..., Y_n)$, K matrix with $K_{ij} = k(\mathbf{x}_i, \mathbf{x}_j)$, $(\mathbf{k}_0)_i = k(\mathbf{x}_0, \mathbf{x}_i)$, $(\mathbf{q}_0)_l = q_l(\mathbf{x}_0)$, Q matrix with $Q_{il} = q_l(\mathbf{x}_i)$ with $i, j = 1, ..., n$, $l = 1, ..., r$, and $\beta \in \mathbb{R}^r$ is a Lagrange multiplier vector. The optimality conditions are:

$$\begin{cases} (K + \sigma^2 I)\lambda + Q\beta = \mathbf{k}_0 \\ Q^t \lambda - \mathbf{q}_0 = 0 \end{cases} \equiv \begin{bmatrix} K + \sigma^2 I & Q \\ Q^t & 0 \end{bmatrix} \begin{bmatrix} \lambda \\ \beta \end{bmatrix} = \begin{bmatrix} \mathbf{k}_0 \\ \mathbf{q}_0 \end{bmatrix}$$

which we denote in brief as $\bar{K}\bar{\lambda} = \bar{\mathbf{k}}_0$. The solution for problem (2) is $\bar{\lambda} = \bar{K}^{-1}\bar{\mathbf{k}}_0$, and so we can write the universal kriging estimation as follows:

$$\hat{F}_0 = \lambda^t \mathbf{y} = \bar{\lambda}^t \bar{\mathbf{y}} = \bar{\mathbf{k}}_0^t \bar{K}^{-1} \bar{\mathbf{y}} = \sum_{i=1}^n \lambda_i y_i \tag{3}$$
$$= \bar{\mathbf{k}}_0^t \bar{\mathbf{c}} = \sum_{i=1}^n c_i k(\mathbf{x}_0, \mathbf{x}_i) + \sum_{j=1}^r d_j q_j(\mathbf{x}_0)$$

where $\bar{\mathbf{c}} = \bar{K}^{-1}\bar{\mathbf{y}}$ with $\bar{\mathbf{y}} = (\mathbf{y}^t, \mathbf{0}_{1\times r})^t$, and $\bar{\mathbf{c}}^t = (\mathbf{c}^t, \mathbf{d}^t)$ with $\mathbf{c} \in \mathbb{R}^n$, $\mathbf{d} \in \mathbb{R}^r$. The expression of the estimator (3) in terms of $\bar{\lambda}$ and with the previous optimality conditions is known as the primal kriging formulation, whilst its expression in terms of $\bar{\mathbf{c}} = \bar{K}^{-1}\bar{\mathbf{y}}$ is known as its dual formulation[1].

Specific cases of the model described are **ordinary kriging**, when $q_1(\mathbf{x}) = q(\mathbf{x}) = 1 \ \forall \mathbf{x} \in S$, $\mu_1 = \mu$, $\mu_j = 0$, $j = 2, ..., r$, $Q = (1, ..., 1)^t = \mathbf{1}^t$, with optimum $\lambda = (K + \sigma^2 I)^{-1}(\mathbf{k}_0 - \mathbf{1}\beta)$, and **simple kriging** when $\mu = 0$, which gives $\lambda = (K + \sigma^2 I)^{-1}\mathbf{k}_0$ and $\hat{y}_0 = \lambda^t \mathbf{y} = \mathbf{k}_0^t(K + \sigma^2 I)^{-1}\mathbf{y} = \mathbf{k}_0^t \mathbf{c}$, with $\mathbf{c} = (K + \sigma^2 I)^{-1}\mathbf{y}$.

---
[1] This makes clear the relationship between kriging, regulariztion networks [4], and gaussian processes for regression, [5].

3 Kriging from a Regularization Perspective

The universal kriging estimator assumes a parametric model for the process mean. However, this assumption can be false and, even if true, would not guarantee a minimum mean squared error:

$$\mathrm{MSE}(\hat{F}_0) = E[(\hat{F}_0 - F_0)^2] = E[R_0^2] = \mathrm{Var}(R_0) + [E(R_0)]^2$$
$$= \mathrm{Var}(\hat{F}_0 - F_0) + [\mathrm{Bias}(\hat{F}_0)]^2$$

where $R_0 = R(\mathbf{x}_0) = \hat{F}(\mathbf{x}_0) - F(\mathbf{x}_0)$ is the error. The universal kriging estimator imposes $E(R_0) = \mathrm{Bias}(\hat{F}_0) = 0$ and, in these conditions, minimises the variance.

With a view to evaluating the possible benefits of admitting a certain degree of bias, we formulate the following regularized estimation problem:

$$\hat{F}'(\mathbf{x}_0) = \arg \min_{G(\mathbf{x}_0) \in \mathcal{F}} \{\mathrm{Var}[G(\mathbf{x}_0) - F_0] + C \cdot [\mathrm{Bias}(G(\mathbf{x}_0))]^2\}$$

with $\mathcal{F}$ the set of linear estimators and C a regularizing constant such that: if $C = 1$, the mean squared error of the estimator is a specific case; if $C = 0$, the problem is reduced to a determination of the minimum variance linear estimator (with no non-bias restrictions); and finally, if $C = \infty$, then obtaining an unbiased linear estimator becomes a priority.

Let us assume the process mean as in (1), with $\mu_j \neq 0$, $j = 1, ..., r$, unknown constants. Since the non-bias condition is given by: $\mu_j[\langle \lambda, \mathbf{q}_j \rangle - q_j(\mathbf{x}_0)] = 0$, $j = 1, ..., r$, we can formulate the optimisation problem as follows:

$$\min_{\lambda, \xi, \xi'} \tfrac{1}{2}\{k(\mathbf{x}_0, \mathbf{x}_0) + \lambda^t(K + \sigma^2 I)\lambda - 2\lambda^t \mathbf{k}_0 + C\sum_{j=1}^{r}(\xi_j^2 + \xi_j'^2)\}$$

$$\text{subject to: } \begin{cases} \mu_j[q_j(\mathbf{x}_0) - \langle \lambda, \mathbf{q}_j \rangle] \leq \varepsilon + \xi_j \\ \mu_j[\langle \lambda, \mathbf{q}_j \rangle - q_j(\mathbf{x}_0)] \leq \varepsilon + \xi_j' \\ \xi_j, \xi_j' \geq 0 \end{cases}, j = 1, ..., r$$

where $\varepsilon \geq 0$ is a constant, $\xi, \xi' \in (\mathbb{R}^+ \cup \{0\})^r$, with its components the slack variables ξ_j, ξ_j', $j = 1, ..., r$, and $\mathbf{q}_j = (q_j(\mathbf{x}_1), ..., q_j(\mathbf{x}_n))^t$.

With respect to this formulation, we make the following observations:

1. The preceding restrictions allow for violation of non-bias conditions in each component of the mean function if this results in an improvement to the objective function. The slack variables capture the bias, whether positive or negative, in each component. Consequently, the sum of their squares, $\sum_{j=1}^{r}(\xi_j^2 + \xi_j'^2)$, is an approximation to the square of the bias given that crossed products are not considered.
2. The constant $\varepsilon \geq 0$ is maintained for greater generality and makes it possible to counteract the approximation of the square of the bias due to the absence of crossed products. This constant could reflect the degree of distrust in the hypotheses as to the process mean.

The unknowns μ_j appear in the restrictions but, regardless of their signs, we can include them in new constants $\varepsilon_j \geq 0$, and slack variables $\xi_j, \xi'_j \geq 0$, and approximate the bias term in the objective function:

$$C\sum_{j=1}^{r}\mu_j^2(\xi_j^2 + \xi_j'^2) \leq C \max_{j \in \{1,r\}}\{\mu_j^2\}\sum_{j=1}^{r}(\xi_j^2 + \xi_j'^2) = \bar{C}\sum_{j=1}^{r}(\xi_j^2 + \xi_j'^2)$$

This approximation is exact in the case of $r = 1$ (ordinary kriging) so, if the mean quadratic error is to be represented by the objective function, $\bar{C}$ can be estimated by means of $\bar{y}^2 = [\sum_{i=1}^{n} y_i/n]^2$.

In this way, denoting $\bar{C}$ by C, we can formulate the following final optimisation problem[2]:

$$\min_{\lambda,\xi,\xi'} \tfrac{1}{2}\{\lambda^t(K + \sigma^2 I)\lambda - 2\lambda^t \mathbf{k}_0 + C\sum_{j=1}^{r}(\xi_j^2 + \xi_j'^2)\} \qquad (4)$$

subject to: $\begin{cases} q_j(\mathbf{x}_0) - \langle \lambda, \mathbf{q}_j \rangle \leq \varepsilon_j + \xi_j \\ \langle \lambda, \mathbf{q}_j \rangle - q_j(\mathbf{x}_0) \leq \varepsilon_j + \xi'_j \end{cases}, j = 1, ..., r$

Note that one and only one of each pair of restrictions j can be saturated (if $\varepsilon_j > 0$), which means that the corresponding slack variables verify $\xi_j \xi'_j = 0$. The problem of optimisation (4) is a quadratic problem with linear restrictions. Substituing the optimality conditions for the primal variables in the Lagrangian, defining $\beta = \alpha' - \alpha$ and using $\alpha_j \alpha'_j = 0$, the following problem is obtained[3]:

---

[2] With quadratic loss, the restrictions $\xi_j, \xi'_j \geq 0$, $j = 1, ..., r$ are not necessary because if the above restrictions are true for $\xi_j < 0$ ($\xi'_j < 0$) they are also true for $\xi_j = 0$ ($\xi'_j = 0$) with these values improving the objective function.

[3] This problem is very similar to that posed by [6] in the semi-parametric formulation of the SVMs. In fact, both problems apply a similar strategy, i.e. they admit a certain level of bias with a view to reducing the variance and improve, if at all possible, the generalisation ability of the corresponding estimator.

However, there are important differences. First of all, whereas the problem posed here is developed on the primal side in the context of a random function, that posed by [6] is formulated on the dual side in the context of a regression function ([7]) and both are governed by different hypotheses (the mean and the structure of dependence are diferent for both problems).

Secondly, whilst our approach admits bias by endeavouring to correct the poorly specified mean, the inverse of the constant C in the formulation of the SVMs plays the same role as σ^2 in our problem; in other words, it fundamentally acts to counteract noise in the data. Nonetheless, the ε-insensitive loss also permits the SVMs to handle outliers produced for other reasons (such as alterations in the process for generating data) and in this respect, both approaches are similar. As we shall see in fact, the benefits of regularized kriging (RK) increase when used in this kind of context. In this respect, RK incorporates a complementary mechanism for handling the outliers that it is unable to deal with adequately using the quadratic loss function that it uses on the dual side (splines, regularization networks) and that causes its lack of sparsity.

$$\max_{\beta}\{W(\beta) = -\tfrac{1}{2}\beta^t Q^t (K+\sigma^2 I)^{-1} Q\beta + \beta^t Q^t (K+\sigma^2 I)^{-1} \mathbf{k_0}$$
$$- \sum_{j=1}^{r} \varepsilon_j |\beta_j| - \beta^t \mathbf{q}(\mathbf{x}_0) - \tfrac{1}{2C}\beta^t \beta\}$$

where β now has no restrictions. (It can be shown that if 1-norm is used for the slack variables, it will be necessary to add the restrictions $-C\mathbf{1} \leq \beta \leq C\mathbf{1}$). The solution is given by[4]:

$$\tfrac{\partial W}{\partial \beta} = -Q^t(K+\sigma^2 I)^{-1} Q\beta + Q^t(K+\sigma^2 I)^{-1}\mathbf{k_0} - \mathbf{q}(\mathbf{x}_0) - \varepsilon \cdot \mathrm{sgn}(\beta) - \tfrac{1}{C}\beta = 0$$
$$\Rightarrow \beta = (Q^t(K+\sigma^2 I)^{-1} Q + \tfrac{1}{C} I)^{-1} [Q^t(K+\sigma^2 I)^{-1}\mathbf{k_0} - \mathbf{q}(\mathbf{x}_0) - \varepsilon \cdot \mathrm{sgn}(\beta)]$$

where $\varepsilon = (\varepsilon_1, ..., \varepsilon_r)^t$, and $\varepsilon \cdot \mathrm{sgn}(\beta)$ is the vector with components $\varepsilon_j \, \mathrm{sgn}(\beta_j)$. In the above expression for β we can observe two actions of regularisation: one to counteract the noise ($\sigma^2 I$) and a new one to allow for some bias ($\tfrac{1}{C} I$).

For $\varepsilon_j = \varepsilon = 0$, $j = 1, ..., r$, the following are specific cases of the above, [8]:

1. **Simple Kriging (SK)**. If $C = 0$, i.e., if the bias is irrelevant for our purposes, we have $\beta = \mathbf{0}$ and obtain the solution provided by simple kriging.
2. **Universal Kriging (UK)**. If $C = \infty$, i.e., if the priority is to obtain an unbiased estimator, we obtain the universal kriging solution:

$$\beta = (Q^t(K+\sigma^2 I)^{-1} Q)^{-1} [Q^t(K+\sigma^2 I)^{-1}\mathbf{k_0} - \mathbf{q}(\mathbf{x}_0)]$$

Therefore, UK and SK can be viewed as extreme solutions to a regularization problem whose objective function contains a variance term and a penalised bias term, reflecting the typical and necessary trade-off between bias and variance (unavoidable in any estimation task based on a finite set of data).

It should be noted that, in all of the above, there is a problem of optimisation for each prediction point $\mathbf{x}_0$, (vector β should actually be denoted $\beta(\mathbf{x}_0)$, which we have avoided for the sake of simplicity). This is standard in the derivation of (primal) kriging which does not generate problems in practice, given that there is an exact formula for calculating $\lambda_0 = \lambda(\mathbf{x}_0)$. (The dual form of the regularized kriging can also be derived, [8]).

Finally, points $\mathbf{x}_0 \in S \subset \mathbb{R}^d$ can be divided into two groups according to their behaviour in the restrictions on their respective optimisation problems, (for simplicity, let us suppose that $r = 1$ and $\varepsilon > 0$):

1. Points which saturate the restrictions. These are points for which $q(\mathbf{x}_0) - \langle \lambda, \mathbf{q} \rangle = 1 - \sum_{i=1}^{n} \lambda_i = \varepsilon + \xi$ (or alternatively, $\langle \lambda, \mathbf{q} \rangle - q(\mathbf{x}_0) = \sum_{i=1}^{n} \lambda_i - 1 = \varepsilon + \xi'$). As per the Kuhn-Tucker complementarity conditions, these points verify $\alpha = C\xi > 0$ (or alternatively, $\alpha' = C\xi' > 0$), i.e. they admit a small degree of bias (above the threshold ε), which benefits the objective function.

---

[4] For $r = 1$, there exists a simple rule for the solution of this problem. For $r > 1$, we are unaware of any direct method; the solution may be determined, for example, by means of an evaluation of the possible solutions (for $\pm \varepsilon_j$) in the objective function.

2. Points which do not saturate the restrictions. In this case, $\alpha = \xi = 0$ and $\alpha' = \xi' = 0$, which means that these points do not admit a relaxation of the non-bias hypothesis (greater than or equal to the threshold ε) which would improve the objective function.

4 Simulations

The following estimators were compared: simple kriging (SK), regularized kriging (RK) with $r = 1$ ($q(\mathbf{x}) = 1$), ordinary kriging (OK), universal kriging (UK) with a linear mean hypothesis, and regularized kriging with an identical trend component (LRK). Here, we compare only RK and OK, [8].

Four Gaussian processes with different hypotheses for the mean were considered: constant ($m(\mathbf{x}) = 100$), linear (with a marked slope, $m(\mathbf{x}) = 100x_1 + 100x_2 + 100$), quadratic ($m(\mathbf{x}) = 0.5x_1^2 + 0.5x_2^2 + 2x_1x_2 + 10$), and finally, additive:

$$m(\mathbf{x}) = 100 + [1.5(1 - x_1) + e^{2x_1 - 1}\sin(3\pi(x_1 - 0.6)^2) + e^{3(x_2 - 0.5)}\sin(4\pi(x_2 - 0.9)^2)]$$

Two-hundred different realizations were generated for each process, in which the five previously mentioned estimators were compared in different circumstances that were common to all, whether using the true covariogram (of various kinds) or estimating the covariogram using different models.

Each realization consisted of 400 observations of the process at points distributed uniformly in $[0, 1] \times [0, 1]$. The observations were subject to Gaussian noise (we experimented with different levels of noise). From these observations, training samples of different sizes were randomly chosen. The remaining observations were used as test samples for comparing the predictive capacity of the estimators for each situation. As goodness-of-fit criteria in test sample, we used the average of squared residuals (ASR) and the absolute relative deviation:

$$\text{ARD} = \frac{1}{n_{test}} \sum_{i=1}^{n_{test}} \left| \frac{F(\mathbf{x}_i) - \hat{F}(\mathbf{x}_i)}{F(\mathbf{x}_i)} \right|$$

Given that the results obtained were very similar for all the tests carried out, we show the results when a true Gaussian covariogram (width $\sigma_k = 0.3$) was used in the estimation. Training and test samples were sized 100 and 300, respectively, subject to Gaussian noise with $\sigma = 1$. The C parameter for the RK was selected by squaring the mean of the data and ε was selected via cross-validation techniques from among the values 0, 10^{-5}, 10^{-4} and 10^{-3}.

Figure 1 shows the box plots displaying the $ARD_{OK} - ARD_{RK}$ differences obtained for the 200 simulations for each process (similar results are obtained for ASR). The results can be summarised as follows: when the estimator assumes the correct mean the difference between ordinary kriging and its regularized version is random and small in quantity. Nonetheless, when the mean is poorly identified then the regularized version produces more frequent improvements.

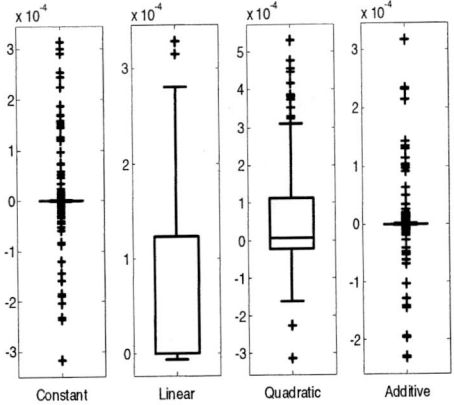

Fig. 1. $ARD_{OK} - ARD_{RK}$ for no outliers.

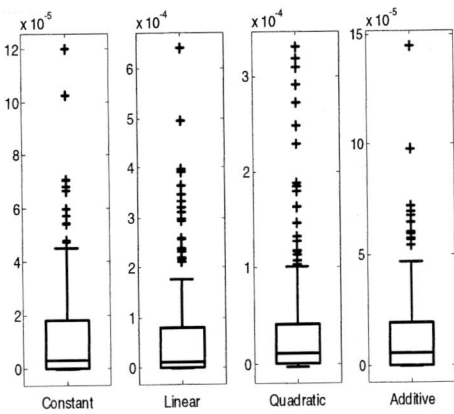

Fig. 2. $ARD_{OK} - ARD_{RK}$ for 10% outliers.

Further tests were designed in which artificial outliers were included in the training sample, replacing a pre-established number of observations (now not subject to noise) with values generated using: $y_i \leftarrow \bar{y} + u_i$ where $\bar{y}$ is the mean of the initial observations and $u_i \sim N(0,1)$. Similar situations to this are relatively frequent in many application areas, where a percentage of the data may not be sufficiently reliable.

Figure 2 show the box plots of $ARD_{OK} - ARD_{RK}$, for the 10% outlier cases in the training data . The results shown indicate that the RK produces consistently more satisfactory results that the OK[5]; moreover, as the percentage of atypical data in the sample increases, the results improve even further.

5 Conclusions

This paper has explored the possible advantages associated with relaxing the non-bias condition in universal kriging through the methodology of support vectors. From within this approach, simple kriging and universal kriging appear as extreme solutions in a general class of regularized kriging estimators.

The simulations that compared ordinary kriging with regularized kriging using simulated Gaussian processes demonstrate that, when the observations are reliable, the relaxation of the non-bias condition does not bring significant advantages. Nonetheless, faced with a significant percentage of atypical observations, regularized kriging consistently improved the results of ordinary kriging.

One of our aims was to determine the primal form of the semiparametric SVM and its significance (and that of the support vectors), under the primal hypotheses of a random function within the framework of which kriging is developed. This remains an open question that requires further research.

References

1. Cressie, N.: Statistics for Spatial Data. John Wiley (1993)
2. Vapnik, V.N.: Statistical Learning Theory. John Wiley (1998)
3. Schölkopff, B., Smola, A.J.: Learning with Kernels. The MIT Press (2002)
4. Girosi, F., Jones, M., Poggio, T.: Regularization theory and neural networks architectures. Neural Computation **7** (1995) 219–269
5. Williams, C.K.I.: Prediction with gaussian processes: From linear regression to linear prediction and beyond. In Jordan, M.I., ed.: Learning and Inference in Graphical Models, Kluwer (1998)
6. Smola, A., Frieß, J., Scholköpf, B.: Semiparametric support vector and linear programming machines, MIT Press (1999) 585–591
7. Matías, J.M., Vaamonde, A., Taboada, J., González-Manteiga, W.: SVM versus kriging and neural networks in a slate mine. Technical report, Dpto. de Estadística, Universidad de Vigo (2002)
8. Matías, J.M., González-Manteiga, W.: Regularised kriging as a generalization of simple and universal kriging. Technical report, Dpto. de Estadística, Universidad de Vigo (2003)

---

[5] The scale of *ARD* values obtained by both estimators was of the order 10^{-3} or 10^{-2} depending on the mean hypothesis, which resulted in RK improvements of about 1% in *ARD*. Apart from the excellent predictive capacity of kriging (it is the MSE optimum estimator for Gaussian processes with known mean), this is also due to the fact that RK admits bias by reference to the hypothesis of the mean (this hypothesis –constant mean– is relaxed but this does not establish a new more complex parametric hypothesis), which limits the range of permitted bias.

Support Vector Machine Classifiers for Asymmetric Proximities

Alberto Muñoz[1], Isaac Martín de Diego[1], and Javier M. Moguerza[2]

[1] University Carlos III de Madrid, c/ Madrid 126, 28903 Getafe, Spain
{albmun,ismdiego}@est-econ.uc3m.es
[2] University Rey Juan Carlos, c/ Tulipán s/n, 28933 Móstoles, Spain
j.moguerza@escet.urjc.es

Abstract. The aim of this paper is to afford classification tasks on asymmetric kernel matrices using Support Vector Machines (SVMs). Ordinary theory for SVMs requires to work with symmetric proximity matrices. In this work we examine the performance of several symmetrization methods in classification tasks. In addition we propose a new method that specifically takes classification labels into account to build the proximity matrix. The performance of the considered method is evaluated on a variety of artificial and real data sets.

1 Introduction

Let X be an $n \times p$ data matrix representing n objects in $\mathbb{R}^p$. Let S be the $n \times n$ matrix made up of object similarities using some similarity measure. Assume that S is asymmetric, that is, $s_{ij} \neq s_{ji}$. Examples of such matrices arise when considering citations among journals or authors, sociometric data, or word association strengths [11]. In the first case, suppose a paper (Web page) i cites (links to) a paper (Web page) j, but the opposite is not true. In the second example, a child i may select another child j to sit next in their classroom, but not reciprocally. In the third case, word i may appear in documents where word j occurs, but not conversely.

Often classification tasks on such data sets arise. For instance, we can have an asymmetric link matrix among Web pages, together with topic labels for some of the pages ('computer sicence', 'sports', etc). Note that there exists no Euclidean representation for Web pages in this problem, and classification must be done using solely the cocitation matrix: we are given the S matrix, but there is no X matrix in this case. SVM parametrization [1,2] of the classification problem is well suited for this case. By the representer theorem (see for instance [3,8]), SVM classifiers will always take the form $f(x) = \sum_i \alpha_i K(x, x_i)$, where K is a positively definite matrix. Thus, if we are given the similarity matrix $K = (s_{ik})$ and this matrix admits an Euclidean representation (via classical scaling), this is all we need to classify data using a SVM. In the case of asymmetric $K = S$, Schölkopf et al [9] suggest to work with the symmetric matrix $S^T S$. Tsuda [10] elaborates on the SVD of S, producing a new symmetric similarity matrix, that serves as input for the SVM.

A standard way to achieve symmetrization is to define $K_{ij} = \dfrac{s_{ij} + s_{ji}}{2}$, taking the symmetric part in the decomposition $S = \frac{1}{2}(S+S^T) + \frac{1}{2}(S-S^T)$. This choice can be interpreted in a classification setting as follows: we assign the same weight (one half) to s_{ij} and s_{ji} before applying the classifier. However, note that this choice is wasting the information provided by classification labels. In addition, ignoring the skew-symmetric part implies a loss of information.

In next section we elaborate on an interpretation of asymmetry that could explain why and when some symmetrization methods may success. In addition we show the existing relation between the methods of Tsuda and Schölkopf and his coworkers. In section 3 we propose a new method to build a symmetric Gram matrix from an asymmetric proximity matrix. The proposed method specifically takes into account the labels of data points to build the Gram matrix. The different methods are tested in section 4 on a collection of both artificial and real data sets. Finally, section 5 summarizes.

2   A Useful Interpretation of Asymmetry

There is a particular choice of s_{ij} that makes sense in a number of interesting cases. Denote by $\wedge$ the fuzzy 'and' operator, and define:

$$s_{ij} = \frac{|x_i \wedge x_j|}{|x_i|} = \frac{\sum_k |\min(x_{ik}, x_{jk})|}{\sum_k |x_{ik}|} \qquad (1)$$

where the existence of a data matrix X is assumed. Suppose X corresponds to a *terms* × *documents* matrix. $|x_i|$ measures the number of documents indexed by term i, and $|x_i \wedge x_j|$ the number of documents indexed by both i and j terms. Therefore, s_{ij} may be interpreted as the degree in which topic represented by term i is a subset of topic represented by term j. This numeric measure of subsethood is due to Kosko [4]. In the case of a cocitation matrix, $|x_i|$ is the number of cites received by author (or Web page) i, and $|x_i \wedge x_j|$ measures the number of authors (or Web pages) that simultaneously cite authors i and j. All these problems have in common that the norms of individuals (computed by the $|x_i|$'s) follow a Zipf's law [6]: there are a few individuals with very large norms (very cited), and in the opposite side of the distribution, there are a lot of individuals with very small norms. This asymmetry can be interpreted as a particular type of hierarchy. Individuals organize in a kind of tree: in the top lie words with large norms, corresponding to broad topics (authorities in the case of Web pages). In the base would lie words with small norms, corresponding to rare topics.

We are going next to relate norms with asymmetry. In the decomposition $s_{ij} = \frac{1}{2}(s_{ij} + s_{ji}) + \frac{1}{2}(s_{ij} - s_{ji})$, the second term conveys the information provided by asymmetry (it equals to zero if S is symmetric). This skew-symmetric term can be written as follows:

$$\frac{1}{2}(s_{ij} - s_{ji}) = \frac{1}{2}(\frac{|x_i \wedge x_j|}{|x_i|} - \frac{|x_i \wedge x_j|}{|x_j|}) = \frac{|x_i \wedge x_j|}{|x_i||x_j|}(|x_j| - |x_i|) \propto (|x_j| - |x_i|) \quad (2)$$

Thus asymmetry is directly related to difference in norms, and will naturally arise when the norms of data points follow Zipf's law.

The method suggested by Schölkopf et al in [9] consists in taking $K = S^T S$ as kernel matrix. This method makes sense for the case of cocitation matrices, because $K_{ij} = 1$ when there is a k such that $s_{ki} = s_{kj} = 1$: there exists an author that simultaneously cites both i and j. However, we will loose a case of similarity that happens when two authors both cite a third (this information is conveyed by SS^T).

The method proposed by Tsuda [10] builds a symmetric kernel matrix as follows: a transformation WH is defined, where $H(x) = (s_{(x,x_1)}, \ldots, s_{(x,x_n)})$, and $W = L^{-1/2}U^T$. Here L and U come from the SVD of the data matrix HX, whose i-th column vector is $H(x_i)$: $HX = ULV^T$. The new similarity matrix is now symmetric: $K_{ij} = (WH(x_i))^T(WH(x_j)) = (H(x_i))^T UL^{-1}U^T H(x_j)$.
Tsuda's method produces a kernel matrix close to $S^T S$. Consider the SVD of the original asymmetric similarity matrix $S = (s_{ij})$: $S = HX = ULV^T$. It is straightforward to show that the corresponding kernel matrix is VLV^T. To conclude, note that the kernel matrix $S^T S = VL^2V^T$.

3 Combining Kernels for Asymmetric Proximities

Following the notation of section 1, let X and S be respectively, the data matrix and the asymmetric proximity matrix. For the sake of clarity, in this paper we will focus on binary classification problems. Let C_1 and C_2 denote the two classes. To use SVM classifiers on X, S needs to be a positively definite symmetric matrix. Thus we are faced to transform S in order to match SVM conditions.

From a geometric point of view, the solution of a binary classification problem is given by a hyperplane or some type of decision surface. If it is possible to solve a classification problem in this way, then the following topologic assumption must be true: given a single datum, points in a sufficiently small neighborhood should belong to the same class (excluding points lying on the decision surface). As a consequence, if we are going to classify a data set relying on a given proximity matrix, points close each other using such proximities should in general belong to the same class.

Therefore, K_{ij} should be large for i and j in the same class, and small for i and j in different classes. We have two possibly contradictory sources of information: s_{ij} and s_{ji}. We should define K_{ij} as a function $f(s_{ij}, s_{ji})$ that conforms to the preceding rule. In this work we will adopt a simple and intuitive choice:

$$K_{ij} = \begin{cases} \max(s_{ij}, s_{ji}), & \text{if } i \text{ and } j \text{ belong to the same class} \\ \min(s_{ij}, s_{ji}), & \text{if } i \text{ and } j \text{ belong to different classes} \end{cases} \quad (3)$$

In this way, if i and j are in the same class, it is guaranteed that K_{ij} will be the largest possible, according to the available information. If i and j belong to different classes, we can expect a low similarity between them, and this is achieved by the choice $K_{ij} = \min(s_{ij}, s_{ji})$. This kernel matrix K is now symmetric and reduces to the usual case when S is symmetric. However, positive definiteness is not assured. In this case, K should be replaced by $K + \lambda I$, for $\lambda > 0$ large enough to make all the eigenvalues of the kernel matrix positive. We will call this method the **pick-out** method.

Note that this kernel makes sense only for classification tasks, since we need class labels to build it.

4 Experiments

In this section we show the performance of the preceding methods on both artificial and real data sets. The testing methodology will follow the next scheme: After building the K matrix, we have a representation for point x_i given by $(K(x_i, x_1), \ldots, K(x_i, x_n))$. Consider the X matrix defined as $(K(x_i, x_j))_{ij}$. Next, we produce Euclidean coordinates for data points from matrix X by a classic scaling process. The embedding in a Euclidean space is convenient to make the notion of separating surface meaningful, and allows data visualization. Next, we use a linear SVM on the resulting data set and finally, classification errors are computed. For all the methods, we use 70% of the data for training and 30% for testing.

Regarding the pick-out method, we need a wise to calculate $K(x, x_i)$ for non-labelled data points x. Given a point x, we will build two different sets of $K_{xi} = K(x, x_i)$. The first, assuming x belongs to class C_1, and the second assuming x belongs to class C_2. Suppose you have trained a SVM classifier with labelled data points. Now, calculate the distance of the two Euclidean representations of x to the SVM hyperplane. Decide x to belong to class C_1 if the second representation is the closest to this hyperplane, and to belong to C_2 in the other case.

4.1 Artificial Data Sets

The two-servers data base. This data set contains 300 data points in $\mathbb{R}^2$. There are two groups linearly separable. At the beginning, there is a kernel matrix defined by: $s_{ij} = 1 - d_{ij}/\max\{d_{ij}\}$, where d_{ij} denotes Euclidean distance. Suppose that entries of the matrix are corrupted at random: for each pair (i, j), one element of the pair (s_{ij}, s_{ji}) is substituted by a random number in $[0, 1]$. This data set illustrates the situation that happens when there are two groups of computers (depending on two servers) sending e-mails among them: d_{ij} corresponds to the time that a message takes to travel from computer i to computer j. The asymmetry between d_{ij} and d_{ji} is explained by two different ways of travelling information between i and j. The randomness is introduced because it is not always true that $d_{ij} < d_{ji}$ or conversely. Therefore, it is not possible to find kernels K_1 and K_2 that allow to express the kernel in the form $K = \lambda_1 K_1 + \lambda_2 K_2$.

We run the four methods and the average results are shown in table 1.

Table 1. Classification errors for the two-servers database.

Method	Train error	Test error
Pick-out	6.6 %	8.0 %
$1/2(S + S^T)$	10.0 %	11.5 %
$S^T S$	21.3 %	23.1 %
Tsuda	14.0 %	15.9 %

The pick-out method achieves the best performance. Since we are introducing information about labels in the pick-out kernel, we expect this kernel will be more useful than the others for data visualization. To check this conjecture, we represent the two first coordinates obtained by multidimensional scaling for each of the methods. The result is shown in figure 1, and confirms our supposition.

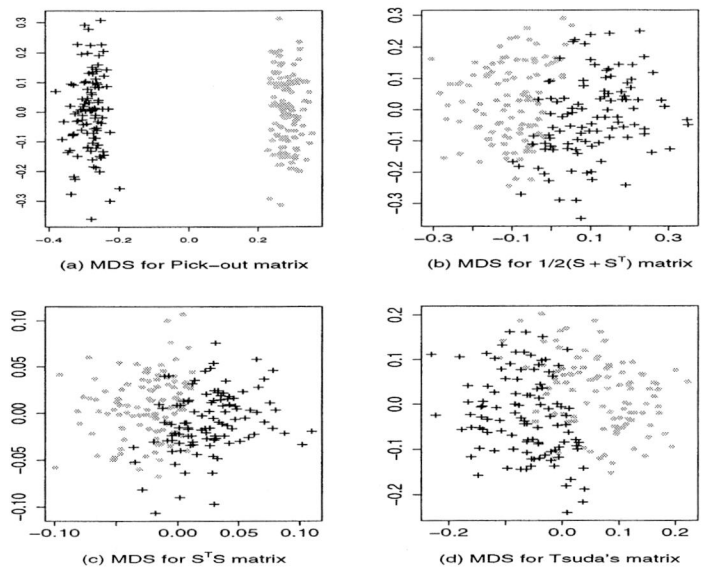

Fig. 1. Multidimensional scaling (MDS) representation of symmetrized kernels.

Two groups with different scattering matrices. In this data set there are 350 points in $\mathbb{R}^2$, divided in two groups (175 of each class). Each group C_i correspond to a normal cloud with diagonal covariance matrix $\sigma_i^2 I$. Here $\sigma_2 = 5\sigma_1$. The overlap in the data set amounts to about 5%. We will define $s_{ij} = e^{-d_{ij}^2/\sigma_j^{*2}}$, where σ_j^{*2} denotes the variance in the vicinity of point j, estimated as the sample variance using the k-nearest neighbors of point j. Here we will take $k = 3$. The underlying idea is to use a local-normalized distance: if distance of point i to point j is large relative to the average of distances in the neighborhood of j, then s_{ij} will be small.

Results for this data set are shown in table 2.

Table 2. Classification errors for the two groups with different scattering matrices.

Method	Train error	Test error
Pick-out	5.1 %	8.0 %
$1/2(S + S^T)$	6.4 %	11.5 %
$S^T S$	7.1 %	8.5 %
Tsuda	6.9 %	9.2 %

Again the pick-out method attains the best results. The MDS representations of the symmetrized kernel matrices are very similar to the preceding case, and will not be displayed.

A false two-groups classification problem. A natural question is whether the pick-out method will separate any data set with arbitrary labels. It should not. To test this hypothesis we have generated a normal spherical cloud in $\mathbb{R}^2$, and assigned random labels to data points. In this case there is no continuous classification surface able to separate the data in two classes. As expected, the classification error rates are close to 50% for each of the proposed methods.

4.2 A Text Data Base

Next we will work on a small text data base, to check the methods in a high dimensional setting. The first class is made up of 296 records from the LISA data base, with the common topic "library science". The second class contains 394 records on "pattern recognition" from the INSPEC data base. There is a mild overlap between the two classes, due to records dealing with automatic abstracting. We select terms that occur in at least 10 documents; there are 982. Labels are assigned to terms by voting on the classes of documents in which these terms appear. The similarity coefficient defined by eq. (1) is used, and therefore we are in the asymmetry situation described in section 2. The overlap in the term data set comes form words common to both topics and also from common words present in records of the two classes. The task is to classify database terms using the information provided by the matrix (s_{ij}). Note that we are dealing with about 1000 points in 600 dimensions, and this is a near empty set. This means that it will be very easy to find a hyperplane that divides the two classes. Notwithstanding, the example is still useful to guess the relative performance of the proposed methods.

Following the same scheme of the preceding examples, table 3 shows the result of classifying terms using the SVM with the symmetrized matrices returned by the four studied methods.

Table 3. Classification errors for the term data base.

Method	Train error	Test error
Pick-out	2.0 %	2.2 %
$1/2(S + S^T)$	2.1 %	2.4 %
$S^T S$	3.8 %	4.2 %
Tsuda	3.3 %	3.6 %

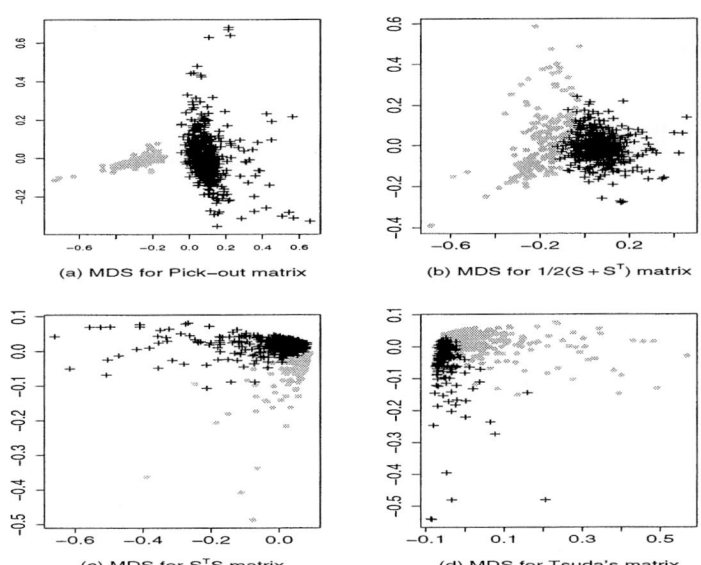

Fig. 2. MDS representation of symmetrized kernels.

The best results are obtained for the pick-out method. The MDS representation of the symmetrized kernel matrix for each method is shown in figure 2. The symmetrization methods achieves a similar performance for this data set. This fact is due to the high sparseness of the data set, as explained above. The best visualization is obtained when using the pick-out kernel matrix. Working with larger textual data sets [5,7], the method using $K = 1/2(S + S^T)$ seems to give poor results, due to the loss of the skew-symmetric part of the similarity matrix.

5 Conclusions

In this work on asymmetric kernels we propose a new technique to build a symmetric kernel matrix from an asymmetric similarity matrix in classification problems. The proposed method compares favorably to other symmetrization methods proposed in the classification literature. In addition, the proposed scheme seems appropriate for data structure visualization. Further research will focus on theoretical properties of the method and extensions.

Acknowledgments. This work was partially supported by DGICYT grant BEC2000-0167 and grant TIC2000-1750-C06-04 (Spain).

References

1. C. Cortes and V. Vapnik. *Support Vector Networks*. Machine Learning, 20:1–25, 1995.
2. N. Cristianini and J. Shawe-Taylor. *An Introduction to Support Vector Machines*. Cambridge University Press, 2000.
3. T. Evgeniou and M. Pontil and T. Poggio. *Statistical Learning Theory: A Primer*. International Journal of Computer Vision, vol. 38, no. 1, 2000, pages 9–13.
4. B. Kosko. *Neural Networks and Fuzzy Systems: A Dynamical Approach to Machine Intelligence*. Prentice Hall, 1991.
5. M. Martin-Merino and A. Muñoz. *Self Organizing Map and Sammon Mapping for Asymmetric Proximities*. Proc. ICANN (2001), LNCS, Springer, 429–435.
6. A. Muñoz. *Compound Key Words Generation from Document Data Bases using a Hierarchical Clustering ART Model*. Journal of Intelligent Data Analysis, vol. 1, no. 1, 1997.
7. A. Muñoz and M. Martin-Merino. *New Asymmetric Iterative Scaling Models for the Generation of Textual Word Maps*. Proc. JADT (2002), INRIA, 593–603. Available from Lexicometrica Journal at www.cavi.univ-paris3.fr/lexicometrica/index-gb.htm.
8. B. Schölkopf, R. Herbrich, A. Smola and R. Williamson. *A Generalized Representer Theorem*. NeuroCOLT2 TR Series, NC2-TR2000-81, 2000.
9. B. Schölkopf, S. Mika, C. Burges, P. Knirsch, K. Müller, G. Rätsch and A. Smola. *Input Space versus Feature Space in Kernel-based Methods*. IEEE Transactions on Neural Networks 10 (5) (1999) 1000–1017.
10. K. Tsuda. *Support Vector Classifier with Asymmetric Kernel Function*. Proc. ESANN (1999), D-Facto public., 183–188.
11. B. Zielman and W.J. Heiser. *Models for Asymmetric Proximities*. British Journal of Mathematical and Statistical Psychology, 49:127–146, 1996.

Fuzzy Model Identification Using Support Vector Clustering Method

Ayşegül Uçar[1], Yakup Demir[1], and Cüneyt Güzeliş[2]

[1] Electrical and Electronics Engineering Department,
Engineering Faculty, Fırat University, Elazig, Turkey
agulucar@ieee.org, ydemir@firat.edu.tr
[2] Electrical and Electronics Engineering Department,
Dokuz Eylül University, Kaynaklar Campus, İzmir, Turkey
guzelis@eee.deu.edu.tr

Abstract. We have observed that the support vector clustering method proposed by Asa Ben Hur, David Horn, Hava T. Siegelmann, Vladimir Vapnik, (Journal of Machine Learning Research, (2001), 125–137) can provide cluster boundaries of arbitrary shape based on a Gaussian kernel abstaining from explicit calculations in the high-dimensional feature space. This allows us to apply the method to the training set for building a fuzzy model. In this paper, we suggested a novel method for fuzzy model identification. The premise parameters of rules of the model are identified by the support vector clustering method while the consequent ones are tuned by the least squares method. Our model does not employ any additional method for parameter optimization after the initial model parameters are generated. It gives also promising performances in terms of a large number of rules. We compared the effectiveness and efficiency of our model to the fuzzy neural networks generated by various input space-partition techniques and some other networks.

1 Introduction

In recent years, fuzzy models have successfully appeared on a lot of applications in system identification, control, prediction and inference. An important property of fuzzy models is their ability to represent highly nonlinear systems. In comparison with other nonlinear black-box modeling techniques, fuzzy models have the advantage of giving insight into the relations between model variables and combining prior knowledge with the information identified from numerical data.

The fuzzy models are accomplished by structure identification and parameter adjustment procedures. Generally, these models are built from two learning phases, the structure learning phase and the parameter learning phase. These two phases are usually done sequentially; the structure learning phase is employed to decide the structure of fuzzy rules first and then the parameter learning phase is used to fine tune the coefficients of each rule obtained from the first one. Various methods have been proposed to solve these problems separately or in a combinatorial way [1–3].

In this paper, we deal with the support vector clustering method suggested by Asa Ben Hur and co-workers [4] for the structure identification of fuzzy model. In contrast to some graph theoretic and parametric clustering methods [5], a non-parametric clustering method based on the support vector approach provides a set of contours which enclose the data points without imposing any assumptions on the cluster number and shape. For the first time in this paper, the method is proposed to partition the sample data into clusters and simultaneously estimate the parameter, which define the best-affine fuzzy models without an additional parameter identification cost. The method performs better than other neural and fuzzy neural networks and those generated by partition techniques in the literature. If the training set were large, the method would result in a large amount of rules. To eliminate some of these rules, reducing the measure of the training set could be considered as an alternative solution. We considered the technique developed for pruning the Least Squares version of Support Vector Machines (LS-SVM) in [6] at the problems exhibiting too many rules. This technique is based upon simply applicable methods in the neural networks literature. In these methods, the pruning process is made starting from the huge network and canceling interconnection weights that are less relevant so as to be obtained a better generalization performance. Similarly, it is dismissed data with the smallest support values having the least important for the construction of the LS-SVM model. We gradually removed useless samples from the training set by the technique, and then applied to this reduced training set the support vector clustering technique.

The paper is organized into four sections. In Section 2, the support vector clustering method is introduced. Adaptive Network based Fuzzy Inference System (ANFIS) and its initialization techniques are briefly reviewed in Section 3. In Section 4, simulation tests in fuzzy modeling are conducted to assess the effectiveness of the proposed method and the results are demonstrated in Section 5. These results are also compared with the ones obtained by the Multilayer Perceptron (MLP) [7], the Radial Basis Function (RBF) [8], the self-organized fuzzy rule generation (SOFRG) [9], and LS-SVM [6].

2 Support Vector Clustering

Given a data set $\{x_i\}_{i=1}^N$ with $x_i \in \Re^d$, the support vector-clustering algorithm searches the smallest enclosing sphere of radius R. The problem can be defined by the following constraints:

$$\|\Phi(x_j) - a\|^2 \leq R^2 \quad \forall_j, \tag{1}$$

where $\Phi(x_j): \Re^m \to \Re^{m_h}$ nonlinearly maps the input space to the high dimensional feature space, $\|\cdot\|$ is the Euclidean norm, and a is the centre of the sphere. To satisfy (1) the slack variables ξ_j is introduced such that

$$\|\Phi(x_j) - a\|^2 \leq R^2 + \xi_j \qquad (2)$$
$$\xi_j \geq 0$$

and the following Lagrangian augmented minimization problem is considered:

$$L = R^2 - \sum_j \left(R^2 + \xi_j - \|\Phi(x_j) - a\|^2\right)\beta_j - \sum \xi_j \mu_j + C \sum \xi_j \qquad (3)$$

$$\sum_j \beta_j = 1$$
$$a = \sum_j \beta_j \Phi(x_j) = 1 \qquad (4)$$
$$\beta_j = C - \mu_j.$$

where $\beta_j \geq 0$ and $\mu_j \geq 0$ are Lagrange multipliers, C is a constant, and $C\sum \xi_j$ is a penalty term. Applying the Karush-Kuhn Tucker conditions we obtain

$$\xi_j \mu_j = 0, \qquad (5)$$

$$\sum_j \left(R^2 + \xi_j - \|\Phi(x_j) - a\|^2\right)\beta_j = 0. \qquad (6)$$

For $\xi_i > 0$ and $\beta_i > 0$ the points x_i lies outside the feature space sphere. If $\mu_j = 0$, $\xi_i > 0$ and $\beta_i = C$, the points are called as a Bounded Support Vectors (BSVs). A point x_i with $\xi_i = 0$ is mapped to the inside or the surface of the feature space sphere. For $0 < \beta_i < C$, $\Phi(x_i)$ lies on the surface of the feature boundaries and they are called support vector (SV). As a result, BSVs lie outside the boundaries, and all other points lie inside them.

By constructing the Lagrangian in the Wolfe dual form, the variables R, a, and μ_j are eliminated:

$$W = \sum_j \Phi(x_j)^2 \beta_j - \sum_{i,j} \beta_i \beta_j \Phi(x_i)\Phi(x_j) \qquad (7)$$

$$0 \leq \beta_j \leq C, \; j = 1, \ldots, N. \qquad (8)$$

If Mercer's theorem [10] is applied to the kernel matrix of Gaussian with width parameter q,

$$K(x_i, x_j) = \exp(-q\|x_i - x_j\|^2) = \Phi(x_i).\Phi(x_j), \qquad (9)$$

then the Lagrangian W and the definition kernel are rewritten as:

$$W = \sum_j K(x_j, x_j)\beta_j - \sum_{i,j} \beta_i \beta_j K(x_i, x_j) \qquad (10)$$

$$R(x)^2 = K(x,x) - 2\sum_j \beta_j K(x_j, x_j) + \sum_{i,j} \beta_i \beta_j K(x_i, x_j). \qquad (11)$$

The contours that enclose the points in data space are defined by the set

$$\{x | R(x) = R_i\}.$$

3 Fuzzy Inference System

The fuzzy inference system under consideration is ANFIS [3]. ANFIS consist of five layers and the basis functions of each layer are the input, fuzzification, rule inference, normalization, and defuzzification. A detailed description of ANFIS can be found in [3]. An ANFIS architecture with two inputs, two rules and one output is shown in Fig. 1.

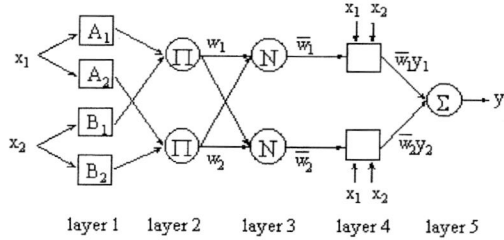

Fig 1. ANFIS architecture for the two-input two-rule Sugeno fuzzy model.

A typical fuzzy rule set has the form

IF x_1 is A_1 and x_2 is B_1 THEN $y_1 = p_1 x_1 + q_1 x_2 + r_1$,
IF x_1 is A_2 and x_2 is B_2 THEN $y_2 = p_2 x_1 + q_2 x_2 + r_2$.

where x_1 and x_2 are the inputs relating to the node, A and B are Membership Functions (MFs) associated with this node. The parameters of the MFs and the coefficients of the linear equations are called as the premise and the consequent parameters, respectively. In order to tune the premise parameters, several methods are available in the literature [1-3]. The most direct way is to partition the input space into grid types with each grid representing a fuzzy if-then rule. The major problem of such kind of partition is that the number of fuzzy rules increases exponentially as the dimension of the input space increases. Another frequently used method for input space partitioning is to cluster the input training vectors in the input space. Such the methods provide a more flexible partition. In this paper, the grid partition, subtractive clustering and hyperplane fuzzy clustering algorithms are considered in comparison to the proposed method [3]. On the other hand, the consequent parameters are adjusted by the least squares method and in order to optimize all the parameters of the ANFIS network, the backpropagation and the least squares algorithms are used simultaneously [3].

We used the support vector clustering method to obtain the number, centers, and widths of the MFs in this paper. We assign the obtained support vectors as the centers of the Gaussian MFs that are radially symmetric with kernel width 1/q and also accept their number as the rule number. Similar to the ANFIS architectures initialized by the above mentioned methods, we used a least squares technique to find the consequent parameters. The only difference is that our model has a better performance than the other ANFIS architectures in function approximation without requiring any additional optimization method, i.e., without the parameter learning processes.

In this paper, ANFIS-1, ANFIS-2, and ANFIS-3 indicate the ANFIS architectures generated by the grid partition, subtractive and hyperplane fuzzy clustering methods, respectively.

4 Simulation Results

To illustrate the validity of the proposed method, two sets of examples are carried out. Comparing with the ANFIS architectures generated by partitioning the input space is shown in the first example. In another example, the obtained results from other neural and fuzzy neural networks are cited from the relevant references so as to be able to compare performance on the same functions.

Example 1

In this example, a 2D Sinc function which is a typical benchmark of functional approximation is examined due to its highly varying characteristic. From evenly distributed grid points of the input space [-10,10] x [-10,10], 121 training data pairs were obtained. The performance of the architecture generated by support vector clustering method (SVCM) was evaluated changing C and q parameters. The accuracy of model was assessed as mean squared error (MSE). The particular values for C and q parameters were chosen as the results of the smallest MSE search taking into consideration the number of both SV and BSV as in [4]. As can be seen from some results given in Table 1, the best results were obtained by small BSV and large SV number. Without using any pruning to reduce the training set, good performances were obtained by approximately 40 support vectors. When the number of the training samples was reduced to 71 by pruning the training set, the promising performances with respect to the previous case were exposed by approximately 16 support vectors. The results obtained by pruning are listed in the last six line of the Table 1. On the other hand, all the

ANFIS architectures were trained for 300 epochs. Their performances were evaluated for the number of rules ranging from 2 to 50. As the rule number increases, the performances of all ANFISs decrease, however that of the SVCM increases. In order to show the generalization capability, other 2500

Table 1. The performance of SVCM in contrast to C and q parameters.

C	q	SV	BSV	MSE
0.0556	2	29	3	1e-2
0.2	3.333	36	0	1.3e-2
0.05	3.33	41	3	1.4e-4
0.055	3.333	42	2	1.3e-4
0.0555	3.3	46	2	6.7se-6
0.02	3.3	15	37	1.2e-2
0.0556	5	44	21	6.33e-7
0.0556	1	18	7	4.7e-2
0.0556	5	44	21	6.3e-7
0.0556	6	50	2	7.2e-7
0.0556	10	81	0	6.85e-9
0.0556	48	121	0	1.9e-31
0.0018	7	19	03	5.6e-5
0.0238	2	27	22	5.8e-4
0.06	2	25	7	8.88e-4
0.0083	2	29	0	2e-3
0.0167	2.9	11	2	5.1-5
0.0658	2	16	0	1.1e-5

checking data was uniformly sampled in the input space. Fig. 2 illustrates the reconstructed surface of the original function and the networks. It is clearly seen that the reconstructed surfaces looks similar to the original function except at the surfaces around the peaks and at valleys with highly varying nonlinear characteristics.

Table 2. Comparison of the performances of SVCM architecture and the ANFIS architectures.

Rule Number	MSE			
	SVCM	ANFIS1	ANFIS2	ANFIS3
16	1.1e-5	4.1e-4	5.7e-5	9.4e-4
18	4.1e-5	1.7e-3	3.9e-4	1.8e-3
42	6.1e-6	5.1e-4	1.2e-3	2.4e-2

Example 2
SVC procedure is compared with respect to LS-SVM and the fuzzy neural networks obtained by using SOFRG method proposed in [9], where the results of RBF and MLP were also considered. Therefore three functions considered in [9] are used.

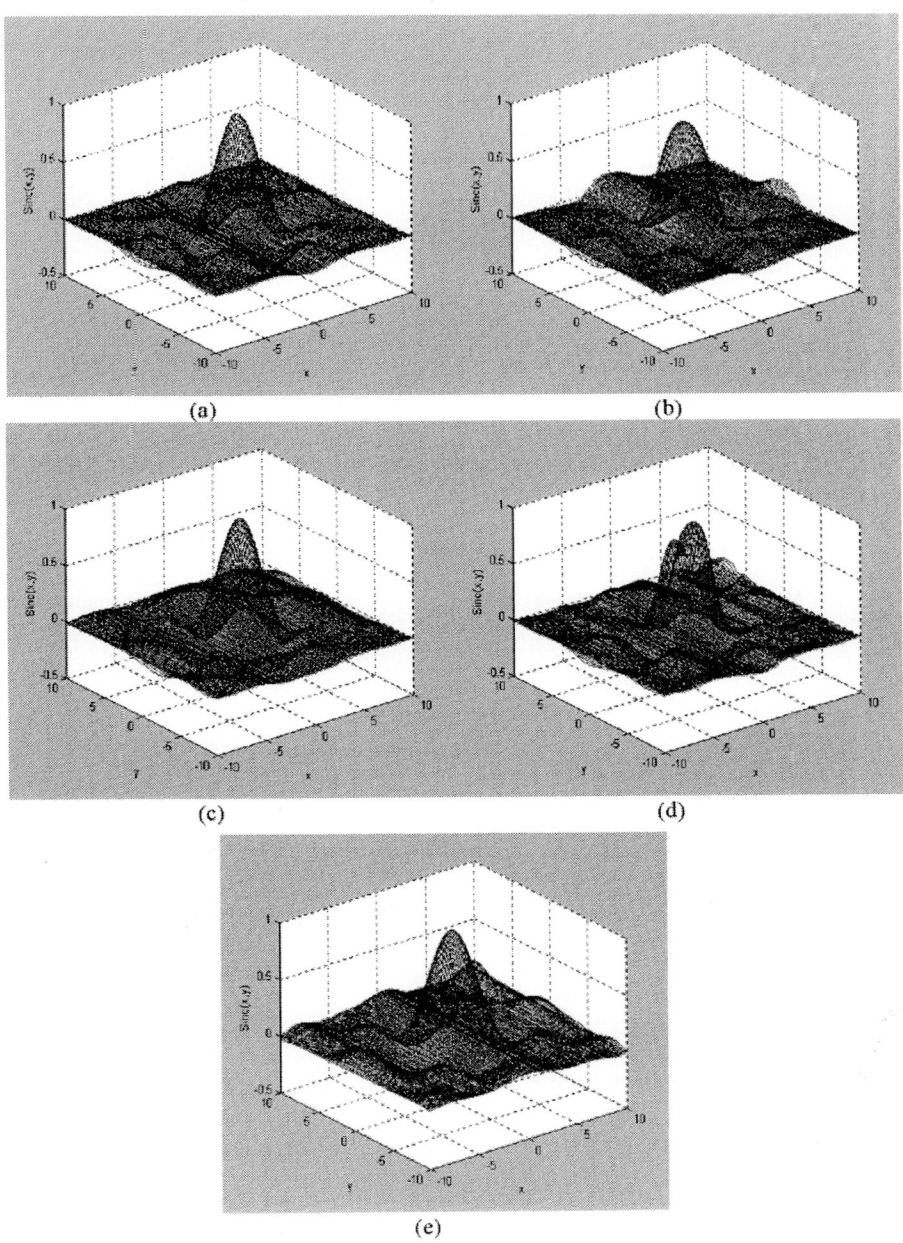

Fig. 2. Fuzzy identification of a 2D-Sinc function (a) Original function and reconstructed surfaces with (b) ANFIS-1 (c) ANFIS-2 (d) ANFIS-3, and (e) SVCM.

$$f_1(x_1, x_2) = \frac{D_a}{1+e^{-D_b x_2}} + \Theta(x_1),$$

$$f_2(x_1, x_2) = D_c \sin^2\left(2\pi\sqrt{\frac{(5-x_1)^2 + (5-x_2)^2}{10}}\right), \quad (12)$$

$$f_3(x_1, x_2) = D_d \frac{(5-x_2)^2}{3.(5-x_1)^2 + (5-x_2)^2}.$$

with $x_1, x_2 \in [0,10]$ and a small perturbation $\Theta(x_1)$ introduced on a specific region of the output surface. Here, D is adjusted to ensure that the input and output domains will be the interval [0,10]. A training set of 400 samples for each function was generated by a uniform spiral distribution produced.

Table 3. Comparison of the identification performances.

Model			MSE			Number of Parameters			Computational Complexity	
			f_1	f_2	f_3	f_1	f_2	f_3	Mean Number of Iterations	Mean time
SVCM	C=0.0025	q=34	2.3e-5	4.1e-5	1.58-5	312	300	317	-	120s
SVCM	C=0.039	q=8.65	4.2e-4	1.16e-5	6.56e-4	200	210	200	-	120s
SVCM	C=0.039	q=7	1.1e-4	9.8e-4	7.7e-4	200	200	200	-	120s
SVCM	C=0.006	q=3	2.5e-3	5.1e-2	1.6e-2	23	56	71	-	100s
SVCM	C=0.083	q=2	6e-3	5e-6	2e-3	13	21	29	-	35s
SVCM	C=0.083	q=1	1.7e-3	3.7e-3	3.7e-3	25	19	18	-	35s
SVCM	C=0.083	q=1.2	3.4e-3	1.8e-3	3.4e-3	19	28	19	-	35s
SOFRG			4.9e-2	3.8e-2	1.2e-2	19	59	44	5	4.5s
RBF			3.1e-2	9.8e-2	1.9e-2	101			-	86s
MLP			2.6e-2	1.73e-1	2.1e-2	101			2000	310s
LS-SVM			1.1e-3	9.3e-5	5e-3	400			-	160s

Fuzzy models determined by the SVCM outperform the other neural and fuzzy networks methods under consideration in approximation accuracy in terms of MSE, as reported in Table 3. Besides, one can verify that the computational complexity is similar to that of SOFRG.

5 Conclusions

In this paper, we have proposed a novel automatic design method for identifying fuzzy models from data. The reason is that the premise parameters are first identified by the support vector clustering method and then the consequent parameters is defined by the least squares method. Perhaps the greatest advantage of the proposed method is that there is no need to any optimization technique different than those in literature after the initial architecture is constructed.

The generation of the fuzzy model by applying support vector clustering method to the pruned training set results in a good performance and less rule. Different pruning techniques and alternatively solutions with the objective of reducing the rule number can be experimented. This seems as an interesting point to be improved by further study.

The validity of the fuzzy model generated by support vector clustering method is demonstrated on several tests. The performance of the resulting network is compared with the best performances obtained by different neural and fuzzy neural network architectures and the partition approaches reported in the literature. The main conclusion of this comparison is that the proposed SCVM provides high modeling accuracy with a reasonable computational complexity.

References

1. Linkens, D.A., Min-You, C.: Input Selection and Partition Validation for Fuzzy Modelling Using Neural Network, Fuzzy Sets and Systems, Vol. 107. (1999) 299–308
2. Mu-Song, C., Shinn-Wen, W.: Fuzzy Clustering Analysis for Optimizing Fuzzy Membership Functions, Fuzzy Sets and Systems, Vol. 103. (1999) 239–254
3. Jang, J.S.R., Sun, C.T., Mizutani, E.: Neuro-Fuzzy and Soft Computing: A Computational Approach to Learning and Machine Intelligence, Prentice-Hall 1997
4. Ben-Hur, A., Hor, D., Siegelmann, H.T., Vapnik, V.: Support Vector Clustering, Journal of Machine Learning Research, Vol. 2. (2001) 125–137
5. Duda, R.O., Hart, E.P., Stork, D.G.: Pattern Classification, John Wiley, New York 2001
6. Suykens, J.A.K., Gestel, T.V., Brabanter, J.D., Moor, D.B., Vandewalle J.: Least Squares Support Vector Machine, World Scientific 2002
7. Rumelhart, D.E., Hinton, G.E., Williams, R.J.: Learning Internal Representations by Error Propagation, Parallel Data Processing, Cambridge, MA: MIT Press, Vol. 1. (1986)
8. Bors, A.G., Pitas, I.: Median Radial Basis Function Neural Network, IEEE Trans. Neural Networks, Vol. 7. (1996) 1351–1364
9. Ignacio, R., Hector, P., Julio, O., Alberto, P.: Self-Organized Fuzzy System Generation from Training Examples, IEEE Trans. Fuzzy Systems, Vol. 8. (2000) 23–36
10. Cristianini, N., Shawe-Taylor, J.: An Introduction to Support Vector Machines, Cambridge University Press 2000

Human Splice Site Identification with Multiclass Support Vector Machines and Bagging

Ana Carolina Lorena and André C.P.L.F. de Carvalho

Laboratório de Inteligência Computacional (LABIC),
Instituto de Ciências Matemáticas e de Computação (ICMC),
Universidade de São Paulo (USP),
Av. do Trabalhador São-Carlense, 400 – Centro – Cx. Postal 668
São Carlos – São Paulo – Brasil
{aclorena, andre@icmc.usp.br}

Abstract. The complete identification of human genes involves determining parts that generates proteins, named *exons*, and those that do not code for proteins, known as *introns*. The splice site identification problem is concerned with the recognition of the boundaries between these regions. This work investigates the use of Support Vector Machines (SVMs) in human splice site identification. Two methods employed for building multiclass SVMs, one-against-all and all-against-all, were compared. For this application, the all-against-all method obtained lower classification error rates. Ensembles of multiclass SVMs with Bagging were also evaluated. Against the expected, the use of ensembles did not improve the performance obtained.

1 Introduction

One of the main goals of the Human Genome Project is the analysis of the data produced by sequencing efforts, looking for information like the localization and structure of genes [5].

Human genes are composed of intercalated segments of regions that code for proteins, named *exons*, and regions that do not code for proteins, known as *introns*. The complete determination of human genes' structure involves the accurate identification of these regions. Splice sites are the boundaries between *exons* and *introns*. For identifying these frontiers, several works have employed Machine Learning techniques [3,9,13,16].

This work investigates the recognition of splice sites on human genetic data using Support Vector Machines (SVMs). Since SVMs are originally binary classifiers[1], another issue considered was the method employed for building multiclass SVMs.

Motivated by the fact that the combination of multiple predictors can improve the overall recognition performance, ensembles of SVMs with Bagging are also investigated.

---

[1] Binary classifiers are predictors that deal with two classes only.

This work is organized as follows: Section 2 presents concepts from Molecular Biology, necessary for the understanding of splice site recognition, which is described on Section 3. Section 4 presents the materials and methods employed. Section 5 describes the experiments conducted and presents the results achieved. Section 6 concludes this paper.

2 Concepts from Molecular Biology

Molecular Biology is concerned with the study of cells and molecules, basic blocks of all living beings. In particular, it studies the organisms' genomes, defined as their set of genetic information. This information is coded on genes along DNA (*Deoxyribonucleic Acid*) molecules. The DNA is composed of structures named nucleotides, which can be of four types: Adenine (A), Cytosine (C), Guanine (G) and Thymine (T). A single DNA molecule has typically thousands of genes.

The main process that occurs in all organisms' cells is the *gene expression*, in which proteins are produced from the gene sequence information. The gene expression is composed of two stages: *transcription* and *translation* (Figure 1). In the transcription stage, a mRNA (*messenger Ribonucleic Acid*) is produced from a DNA strand. In the translation stage, this mRNA molecule codes for the final protein. The mRNA is similar to the DNA, being also composed of nucleotides, except for an Uracil (U) in the place of the Thymine.

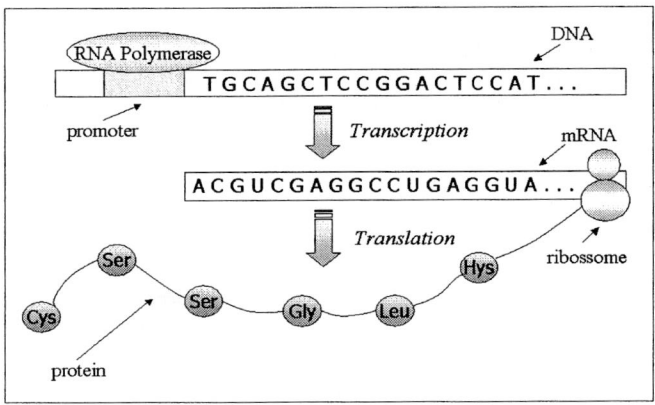

Fig. 1. Gene expression process.

The understanding of the gene expression process is a great source of knowledge. Researches in this field can benefit several areas, such as Medicine, Agriculture and Pharmacy, auxiliating, for example, the identification of the causes of some diseases. In this sense, an important issue is the gene identification in a DNA sequence. Next Section describes one particular characteristic of human DNA, the presence of splice sites.

3 Splice Site Identification

There are some differences on gene expression between eukaryote organisms (complex beings, like humans), which have most of the genetic material delimited in a nucleus, and prokaryote organisms (like bacterias), that have the genetic material dispersed in the cell.

Eukaryote genes are composed of alternate segments of *exons* and *introns*. Exons are regions that code for the final protein. Introns intermediate exons and do not code for proteins. The eukaryotic gene expression process includes an additional step, the elimination of introns from the mRNA molecule (Figure 2). This process is known as *splicing*. The frontiers between exons and introns are named *splice junctions* (or *splice sites*).

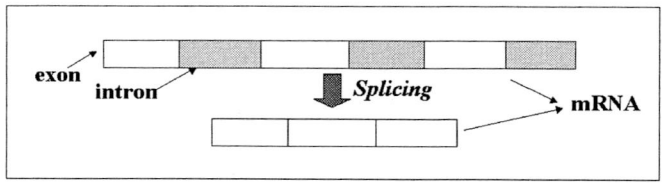

Fig. 2. Splicing in mRNA molecule.

The splice junction recognition problem involves identifying if a sequence of a fixed size has an intron/exon (IE) site, an exon/intron (EI) site, or if it does not have a splice site (N). The complete structure determination of eukaryotic genes includes the accurate identification of these sites.

Machine Learning (ML) techniques have been successfully used in primate splice junction recognition. In [13] propositional rules from the biological domain are used to initialize an Artificial Neural Network (ANN). The Statlog Project [9] also reports the use of various ML techniques for primate splice site identification. Another work based on ANNs was proposed in [16], in which Boolean formulaes inferred from data were refined by an ANN.

4 Materials and Methods

This section describes the materials and methods used in this work, including a description of the dataset and learning technique employed.

4.1 Dataset

The dataset used in this work was extracted from HS3D (*Homo Sapiens Splice Site Dataset*), which contains 5947 sequences of human DNA with known splice sites (IE or EI) and 635666 sequences that do not contain a splice site (false splice sites), collected from GenBank Primate Sequences release 123 [14].

From this data, 5000 examples were randomly chosen, 25 % of the IE type, 25 % of the EI type and 50 % of the N type, as a final dataset for performing the experiments. A higher proportion of N samples was chosen because these are the most common cases in the splice site domain.

Table 1 summarizes this dataset, showing the total number of instances (♯ Instances), the number of continuous and nominal attributes (♯ Attributes), the class distribution (Class %), the majority error (ME) and if there are missing values (MV).

Table 1. Dataset summary description.

♯ Instances	♯ Attributes (cont., nom.)	Class	%	ME	MV
5000	140 (0, 140)	IE	25%	50%	no
		EI	25%		
		N	50%		

4.2 Learning Technique

This work investigates the use of Support Vector Machines (SVMs), a ML technique following a statistical approach [6]. The SVMs principle lies on mapping data to a high dimensional space, named feature space, where the classes become linearly separable. The optimal hyperplane in this space is defined as the one that maximizes the separation margin between the classes. The migration of data to the feature space is performed with the use of *Kernel* functions [12]. The Kernels allow access to spaces of high dimensions (in some cases infinite) without the need of knowing the mapping function explicitly, which usually is very complex.

The problem investigated has three classes. SVMs are originally binary classifiers. To build multiclass predictors with SVMs, one may follow two strategies: one-against-all (1-a-a) and all-agains-all (a-a-a) [11].

Given a problem with C classes, the 1-a-a method builds C SVMS, each one responsible to differentiate a class C_i ($i = 1, \ldots, C$) from the others. The final prediction is given by the SVM with higher output.

In the case of the a-a-a technique, $C(C-1)/2$ SVMs are induced, one for each pair of classes C_i, C_j ($i, j = 1, \ldots, n; i \neq j$). The final result is then obtained by a majority voting among the individual SVMs.

4.3 Bagging SVMs

Many studies have shown that aggregating the prediction of multiple classifiers can improve the performance achieved by a single classifier [2,7,17]. This is the motivation of generating ensembles of classifiers. The key to successful ensemble methods is to have individual classifiers with error rates above 0.5 and as uncorrelated as possible [7].

There are several techniques for constructing ensembles of classifiers. The technique used in this work was Bagging [2]. In Bagging, several classifiers are trained independently over different training sets, sampled through a bootstrap method [2]. Following the bootstrap resampling technique, k training sets T_i are generated from a common set T, one for each base classifier of the final ensemble. The examples in these sets are chosen randomly from T, with replacement. This procedure seeks to make training sets as different as possible in order to obtain higher improvement performance on the aggregation result.

In [8] two approaches to build SVMs ensembles with Bagging are proposed, exploring the fact that SVMs are binary classifiers.

The first one, named *multiclass classifier level SVM ensemble*, consists of constructing k multiclass SVMs (following the 1-a-a or a-a-a strategies) and aggregating their response. This corresponds to the usual Bagging procedure.

The second strategy is named *binary classifier level SVM ensemble*. Following the 1-a-a methodology, given a problem with C possible classifications, C ensembles of k binary SVMs are built, each responsible to distinguish the class C_i from the others. In the a-a-a case, $C(C-1)/2$ ensembles of k classifiers are constructed, discriminating a class C_i from another class C_j.

Having the trained classifiers, their responses were aggregated with four methodologies:

- **Majority voting:** attributes to pattern **x** the class produced by the majority of the SVMs in the ensemble.
- **Sum of responses:** consists of summing up the responses of all SVMs in the ensemble [15]. This procedure was applied to binary level ensembles only, since the binary SVM outputs for each sample a value indicating its position in relation to the optimal hyperplane.
- **LSE-based weighting:** this combination strategy is also applied only in the case of binary level ensembles. Each SVM in the C_i ensemble has different weights in the final aggregation. The weight vector is calculated as $w = A^{-1}y$, where $A = (h_i(\mathbf{x}_j))$. The matrix A contains the predictions of each SVM h_i in the ensemble for every data sample x_j. The final decision function is given by Equation 1, where sign(v) is equal to +1 if $v > 0$ and -1 if $v < 0$.

$$f(\mathbf{x}) = \text{sign}(\mathbf{w} \cdot f_i(\mathbf{x})) \tag{1}$$

- **Double-layer hierarchical combining:** in this case, the responses of the SVMs in the ensemble are aggregated by another SVM.

5 Experimental Results

In order to obtain a better estimative of the error rates of the induced classifiers in the experiments conducted, the dataset described in Section 4 was divided following the *Random Subsampling* methodology [10]. According to this method, the original dataset was divided in two subsets: training set and test set (in this work 75% of the original examples were chosen for training and the 25% remaining for testing). The training set was used in the classifier induction. The test set is presented to the trained classifier and evaluates its precision with unknown data, that is, its generality. These subsets are generated three times, randomly, making a total of three partitions for training and testing.

SVMs require data to be in numerical format. Since the attributes in the investigated application are in a symbolic format each feature was coded by four bits using the orthogonal encoding.

The software applied for SVMs induction was SVMTorch II [4]. A Gaussian Kernel with standard deviation parameter of 10 was used for the individual SVM and the SVMs in the ensembles induction.

Section 5.1 and 5.2 presents the experimental results for the multiclass SVM experiments and for the SVM ensemble with Bagging, respectively.

5.1 Multiclass Results

Here the results achieved by multiclass SVMs using the 1-a-a and a-a-a approaches are compared. Table 2 shows the precision obtained in these experiments. It shows the overall classification precision (Total), as well as the precision observed in each class (IE, EI and N).

Table 2. Multiclass precision.

Technique	Total	IE	EI	N
1-a-a SVM	86.8 ± 0.7	88.5 ± 1.2	84.7 ± 2.6	87.2 ± 1.5
a-a-a SVM	88.1 ± 0.7	88.3 ± 0.7	87.2 ± 3.5	88.5 ± 1.9

Performing statistical tests [1] to these results, it can be verified that the a-a-a SVM outperforms the 1-a-a SVM in this application, with 90% of confidence level. It must be observed that some of the patterns were classified as unknown by the a-a-a approach. If only the classifier error rates are considered, the a-a-a strategy outperforms the 1-a-a one with 95% of confidence level.

5.2 Bagging Results

For generating the resampled datasets for Bagging SVMs, 3000 examples were randomly selected with replacement from the original training datasets for each partition. Each ensemble was composed of five SVM classifiers. The goal was to study how the multiclass approach influences the results obtained in ensembles of SVMs.

Similarly to Table 2, Table 3 presents the precision achieved in the Bagging experiments. Multiclass and binary level SVM ensembles were generated following the 1-a-a and a-a-a strategies. The results obtained with the different alternatives of combination presented on Section 4.3 are shown.

Table 3. Ensembles precision.

Technique	Total	IE	EI	N
1-a-a multiclass (majority voting)	85.5 ± 0.3	86.1 ± 2.2	81.9 ± 2.6	87.2 ± 1.4
1-a-a multiclass (hierarchical)	85.5 ± 0.1	87.6 ± 4.6	82.1 ± 2.3	87.0 ± 1.8
1-a-a binary (majority voting)	86.0 ± 0.3	86.2 ± 1.8	82.9 ± 2.4	87.7 ± 1.2
1-a-a binary (sum of responses)	86.2 ± 0.2	86.4 ± 1.9	83.4 ± 2.4	87.8 ± 1.5
1-a-a binary (LSE weighting)	86.8 ± 0.8	86.4 ± 0.9	82.2 ± 2.3	89.6 ± 2.5
1-a-a binary (hierarchical)	86.1 ± 0.6	87.2 ± 1.4	85.0 ± 3.4	86.2 ± 1.0
a-a-a multiclass (majority voting)	87.0 ± 0.5	86.7 ± 0.8	85.0 ± 4.0	88.3 ± 1.4
a-a-a multiclass (hierarchical)	86.9 ± 0.5	87.2 ± 1.4	84.9 ± 3.4	88.2 ± 1.5
a-a-a binary (majority voting)	87.1 ± 0.4	85.7 ± 2.3	87.6 ± 2.9	87.6 ± 1.2
a-a-a binary (sum of responses)	87.2 ± 0.5	87.2 ± 1.6	84.6 ± 3.8	88.6 ± 1.3
a-a-a binary (LSE weighting)	87.1 ± 0.4	87.2 ± 0.9	84.5 ± 3.4	88.6 ± 1.3
a-a-a binary (hierarchical)	87.2 ± 0.4	87.3 ± 2.1	84.7 ± 3.0	88.7 ± 1.6

As in the single multiclass SVMs case, the a-a-a SVM ensembles outperform the 1-a-a ensembles.

The use of SVM ensembles through Bagging did not improve the results obtained by the individual classifier in this application. Its precisions rates are, in the best case, statistically similar to the one obtained by a single SVM. This may be due to the fact that the SVMs alone are very stable techniques, generating somewhat correlated errors on the individual predictors of the ensembles. Another possibility is the occurrence of overfitting on training data with the combination of multiple SVM predictors. Further experiments shall investigate the reason of this result.

There are other works that employed ML techniques in splice site recognition. Some of them were briefly described on Section 3 [3,9,13,16]. However, the datasets used in these works were different, making a comparison difficult.

6 Conclusion

This work investigated the use of multiclass SVMs in human splice site identification. Results indicate that the use of an all-against-all approach to construct the multiclass classifier outperforms an one-against-all strategy.

In a parallel study, multiclass ensembles of SVMs with Bagging were also generated. Although the performance did not improve with the combination of multiple SVMs, the superiority of the a-a-a methodology over the 1-a-a approach, in the investigated application, was confirmed.

Acknowledgements. The authors would like to thank the Brazilian research agencies CNPq and Fapesp for the financial support provided and Pollastro and Rampone for the database.

References

1. Baranauskas, J. A., Monard, M. C.: Reviewing some Machine Learning Concepts and Methods. Technical Report 102, Istituto de Ciências Matemáticas e de Computação, Universidade de São Paulo, São Carlos, Brazil (2000)
2. Breiman, L.: Bagging Predictors. Technical Report 421, Department of Statistics, University of California, Berkley (1994)
3. Brunak, S., Engelbrecht, J., Knudsen, S.: Prediction of Human mRNA Donor and Acceptor Sites from the DNA Sequence. Journal of Molecular Biology, Vol. 220 (1991) 49–65
4. Collobert, R., Bengio, S.: SVMTorch: Support vector machines for large scale regression problems. Journal of Machine Learning Research, Vol. 1 (2001) 143–160
5. Cravem, M. W., Shavlik, J. W.: Machine Learning Approaches to Gene Recognition. IEEE Expert, Vol. 9, N. 2 (1994) 2–10
6. Cristianini, N., Taylor, J. S.: An Introduction to Support Vector Machines. Cambridge University Press (2000)
7. Dietterich, T. G.: Machine Learning Research: Four Current Directions. The AI Magazine, Vol. 18, N. 4 (1998) 97–136
8. Kim, H.-C., Pang, S., Je, H.-M., Kim, D., Bang, S.-Y.: Support Vector Machine Ensemble with Bagging. Pattern Recognition with Support Vector Machines, First International Workshop on SVMs, Springer-Verlag (2002)
9. Michie, D., Spiegelhalter, D. J., Taylor, C. C.: Machine Learning, Neural and Statistical Classification. Ellis Horwood (1994)
10. Mitchell, T.: Machine Learning. McGraw Hill (1997)
11. Mayoraz, E., Alpaydm, E.: Support Vector Machines for Multi-Class Classification. Research Report IDIAP-RR-98-06, Dalle Molle Institute for Perceptual Artificial Intelligence, Martigny, Switzerland (1998)
12. Müller, K. R., Mika, S., Rätsch, G., Tsuda, K., Schölkopf, B.: An Introduction to Kernel-based Learning Algorithms. IEEE Transactions on Neural Networks, Vol. 12, N. 2 (2001) 181–201
13. Noordewier, O., Rowell, G. G., Shavlik, J. W.: Training Knowledge-Based Neural Networks to Recognize Genes in DNA Sequences. Advances in Neural Information Processing Systems, Vol. 3. Morgan Kaufmann (1991)
14. Pollastro, P., Rampone, S.: HS3D: Homo Sapiens Splice Site Dataset. Nucleic Acids Research, Annual Database Issue (2002)
15. Prampero, P. S.: Combination of Classifiers for Pattern Recognition (in Portuguese). Msc. degree dissertation, Instituto de Ciências Matemáticas e de Computação, Universidade de São Paulo, São Carlos, Brazil (1998)
16. Rampone, S.: Recognition of Splice Junctions on DNA Sequences by BRAIN Learning Algorithm. Bioinformatics, Vol. 14, N. 8 (1998) 676–684
17. Schapire, R., Freund, Y., Barlett, P., Lee, W. S.: Boosting the margin: a new explanation for the effectiveness of voting methods. In Proceedings of the International Conference on Machine Learning (ICML97), Morgan Kaufmann (1997)

Statistical Data Analysis

Optimizing Property Codes in Protein Data Reveals Structural Characteristics

Olaf Weiss[1]*, Andreas Ziehe[1], and Hanspeter Herzel[2]

[1] Fraunhofer FIRST.IDA, Kekuléstr. 7, 12489 Berlin, Germany
olaf.weiss@first.fraunhofer.de
[2] Institute for Theoretical Biology, Humboldt-University Berlin Invalidenstr. 43, 10115 Berlin, Germany

Abstract. We search for assignments of numbers to the amino acids (property codes) that maximize the autocorrelation function signal in given protein sequence data by an iterative method. Our method yields similar results to optimization with the related extended Jacobi method for joint diagonalization and standard optimization tools.

In nonhomologous sets representative of all proteins we find optimal property codes that are similar to hydrophobicity but yield much clearer correlations. Another property code related to α-helix propensity plays a less prominent role representing a local optimum. We also apply our method to sets of proteins known to have a high content of α- or β-structures and find property codes reflecting the specific correlations in these structures.

1 Introduction

Property codes such as hydrophobicities are used in a wide range of bioinformatical applications such as prediction of transmembrane regions [1], secondary structure prediction [2], or derivation of contact potentials for protein 3D structure modeling [3]. Furthermore, property codes are necessary to translate protein sequences into time series which can be analyzed by artificial neural networks [4,5], correlation functions [6] and other methods.

The AAindex database [7] currently contains 437 property codes, many of which are related. The choice of which property code to use is rather arbitrary.

A few studies have been aimed at optimizing property codes from mutation matrices [8,9] or 3D-structure modelling [3,5].

In this study we aim at finding property codes leading to a large autocorrelation function signal strength in given protein sequence data. We have already addressed this question in [10] by brute force random search. In this study, we present a fast iterative method based on matrix diagonalization. Furthermore, the similar concept of joint Matrix diagonalization with Jacobi methods [11] is also applied. To our knowledge, this is the first use of this method in a bioinformatics context. We compare our results to off-the-shelf optimizers and get

---

* Corresponding author

similar results. However, our method has the advantage of discovering additional biologically relevant property codes from local optima.

Finally we show how our method can be applied to sets of protein sequences rich in specific secondary structure. We find property codes and autocorrelation patterns specific to α-helices and β-strands.

2 Methods

We consider property codes as a translation of the 20 amino acids to numbers. We write a property code as a vector **a**, whose elements are the values that the code assigns to the amino acids. A property code represents one possible mapping of protein sequences to numerical series upon which time series analysis tools can be applied. We denote such a resulting numerical series by $(x_l^{(a)})$.

2.1 The Autocorrelation Function in Symbol Sequences

The autocorrelation function (acf) of a protein sequence using the property code **a**

$$C_a(k) = < x_l^{(a)} x_{l+k}^{(a)} > - < x_l^{(a)} >< x_{l+k}^{(a)} > \tag{1}$$

can also be written as a quadratic form

$$C_a(k) = \mathbf{a}^t \mathbf{D}(k) \mathbf{a} \tag{2}$$

of the matrix $\mathbf{D}(k)$ whose elements are defined by

$$D_{ij}(k) = P_{ij}(k) - p_i q_j \tag{3}$$

where $P_{ij}(k)$ is the joint probability of finding residues i and j separated by $k-1$ positions, $p_i = \sum_j P_{ij}(k)$, and $q_j = \sum_i P_{ij}(k)$ [12]. Thus, the contribution of the sequence to the acf is captured in $\mathbf{D}(k)$. Note that the natural estimator of the $D_{ij}(k)$ is biased and needs to be corrected [10]. A plot of the Kyte-Doolittle hydrophobicity [13] acf using (2) averaged over the pdb_select set of protein sequences [14] is plotted as the black line in Fig. 1.

As already done in [10], we define the signal strength

$$S_a := \sum_{k=1}^{k_{\max}} (C_a(k))^2 \tag{4}$$

as a quantity that we want to maximize by varying **a** to find optimal property codes. As constraint we fix

$$\mathbf{a}^t \mathbf{a} = \sum_i a_i^2 = 1. \tag{5}$$

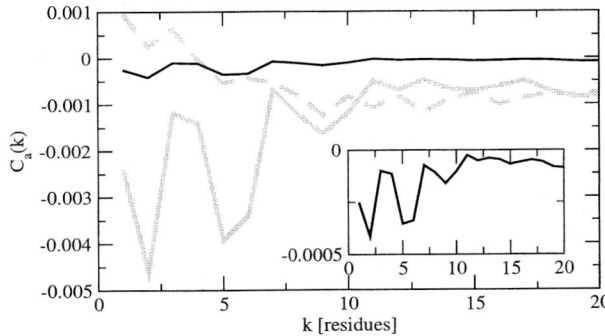

Fig. 1. Acfs in the `pdb_select` data: Kyte-Doolittle hydrophobicity-acf (*black line, also enlarged in the insert*) and optimized acfs with signal strength $S = 68 \cdot 10^{-6}$ (*grey solid*) and $S = 13 \cdot 10^{-6}$ (*grey dashed*)

2.2 The Eigenvector Iteration

Maximizing $C_a(k)$ for one single k with constraint (5) leads to the eigenvalue equation

$$\mu \mathbf{a} = \mathbf{D}^{sym}(k)\mathbf{a} \tag{6}$$

where $\mathbf{D}^{sym} = \frac{1}{2}(\mathbf{D} + \mathbf{D}^t)$. The eigenvalues $\mu^i = C_{a^i}(k)$ are the acf of the eigenvectors $\mathbf{a}^i$. This can also be applied to maximize a linear combination $\sum_k \xi_k C_a(k) = \mathbf{a}^t \boldsymbol{\Delta} \mathbf{a}$ with

$$\boldsymbol{\Delta} = \sum_{k=1}^{k_{max}} \xi_k \mathbf{D}^{sym}(k), \tag{7}$$

because C_a is linear in the $\mathbf{D}(k)$.

From this we derived the following iteration which puts emphasis on those k where the acf $C_a(k)$ is far away from zero:

1. Estimate the corrected covariance matrices $\mathbf{D}(k)$ from sequence data.
2. Set ξ_k as an initialization.
3. Calculate the matrix $\boldsymbol{\Delta}$ as in (7) using the current ξ_k.
4. Maximize $\mathbf{a}^t \boldsymbol{\Delta} \mathbf{a}$ by finding the eigenvector corresponding to the largest eigenvalue of the symmetric part of $\boldsymbol{\Delta}$.
5. Change the ξ_k to $\xi_k = C_{aa}(k)$ with the property code $\mathbf{a}$ obtained in step 4.
6. Return to step 3 with the new ξ_k.

A mathematical analysis of this iteration procedure shows that it *i)* finds a local maximum of S, and *ii)* is closely related to gradient methods for optimization (see [15, appendix A]). We termed this iteration *eigenvector iteration*. It usually converges after 15–25 steps.

To ensure that we find all relevant local maxima, we perform the iteration with 1000 random initial conditions. This takes a few minutes on a PC. In Fig. 1

the effect of the optimization can be seen: the solid grey line shows the acf of an optimized hydrophobicity which has a much larger signal of similar structure to that of the Kyte-Doolittle hydrophobicity acf (black line and insert).

2.3 Extended Jacobi Method for Joint Diagonalization

An alternative method to determine an eigenvector (property code) corresponding to the maximal (average) eigenvalue is based on joint diagonalization of the correlation matrices $\mathbf{D}(k)$ as defined in eq. (3). Instead of forming the weighted sum of $\mathbf{D}(k)$ as in (7) and solving the eigenvalue equation we propose using a simultaneous diagonalization method by Cardoso and Souloumiac (1996)[11]. Exact joint diagonalization is formally defined for a set of normal matrices $\mathbf{M}_1, \ldots, \mathbf{M}_n$ which commute and means that an orthogonal matrix $\mathbf{V}$ exists, such that $\mathbf{V}^T \mathbf{M}_1 \mathbf{V}, \ldots, \mathbf{V}^T \mathbf{M}_n \mathbf{V}$ are all diagonal.

In practical applications an exact diagonalization is not possible, but one can still try to minimize the deviation from diagonality. Using the common diagonality measure

$$\text{off}(\mathbf{M}) := \sum_{i \neq j} (M_{ij})^2,$$

leads to the following constrained optimization problem:

$$\min_{\mathbf{V}:\mathbf{V}^T\mathbf{V}=\mathbf{I}} \sum_{k=1}^{k_{max}} \text{off}(\mathbf{V}^T \mathbf{M}_k \mathbf{V}).$$

The basic idea of the extended Jacobi technique is to approximate the orthogonal matrix $\mathbf{V}$ by applying a sequence of elementary rotations $\mathbf{R}_n(\phi_n)$ which minimize the off-diagonal elements at position (i,j) of the respective $\mathbf{M}_k$ matrices. One obtains the final solution by forming the product of all elementary rotations, i.e. $\mathbf{V} = \prod_n \mathbf{R}_n(\phi_n)$. It has been shown that the optimal rotation angle ϕ_n can be calculated in closed form, which leads to a highly efficient numerical algorithm[1] (for details see [11]).

For our application, we jointly diagonalize symmetrized $\mathbf{D}(k)$ matrices $\mathbf{D}^{sym}(k)$. Then we choose the eigenvector with the highest average eigenvalues of the $\mathbf{D}^{sym}(k)$.

While this method has been applied successfully to real world problems such as blind source separation [16,17], this represents – to the best of our knowledge – the first application of joint diagonalization in bioinformatics.

2.4 Optimization with Standard Tools

We also numerically optimized S_a as a function of the a_i using the MATLAB optimization toolbox. The off-the-shelf method applied – `fmincon()` with medium-scale optimization – is based on Sequential Quadratic Programming and line search as described in [18]. The results obtained confirm the maxima found with the other algorithms described above.

---
[1] see http://tsi.enst.fr/~cardoso/jointdiag.html for MATLAB code

3 Results

We applied the different methods described above to several sets of protein sequences. The resulting optimized property codes are listed in Tab. 1.

Table 1. Property Codes: The amino acids are ordered according to the optimized hydrophobicity in the pdb_select set. S_a $[10^{-6}]$ gives the signal strength of the property code in the data it was optimized with.

	p_s 1	p_s 2	jdiag	matl.	α 1	α 2	β 1	β 2	β 3
L	-0.63	-0.19	0.68	-0.64	-0.16	-0.62	-0.41	0.20	0.25
I	-0.34	0.00	0.34	-0.35	0.14	-0.26	-0.21	0.09	-0.08
V	-0.28	0.04	0.18	-0.27	-0.13	-0.31	-0.48	0.13	-0.15
F	-0.19	0.13	0.20	-0.20	0.03	-0.21	-0.19	0.16	-0.02
Y	-0.09	0.07	0.09	-0.09	0.09	-0.11	-0.08	0.06	-0.25
W	-0.07	-0.01	0.07	-0.07	-0.01	-0.03	-0.05	0.06	-0.04
M	-0.06	-0.11	0.06	-0.06	0.00	-0.09	-0.06	0.06	-0.02
C	-0.02	0.04	0.01	-0.01	0.09	-0.09	-0.01	0.03	-0.03
A	-0.01	-0.56	-0.01	0.00	-0.82	0.12	0.14	0.24	0.82
H	0.03	0.21	-0.04	0.03	0.04	-0.04	0.01	-0.12	-0.08
T	0.04	0.09	-0.03	0.04	0.06	0.09	-0.16	-0.26	-0.07
P	0.08	0.32	-0.07	0.08	0.08	0.05	0.11	0.02	-0.03
R	0.10	-0.10	-0.15	0.11	0.08	0.16	0.02	-0.03	0.06
Q	0.12	-0.13	-0.15	0.13	-0.10	0.18	-0.01	-0.23	-0.08
S	0.13	0.44	-0.11	0.12	0.17	0.10	0.16	-0.45	0.14
N	0.17	0.03	-0.15	0.17	0.08	0.12	0.19	-0.16	-0.25
K	0.19	-0.23	-0.21	0.20	-0.22	0.31	0.00	0.06	0.08
G	0.20	0.25	-0.11	0.18	0.31	0.06	0.46	0.61	-0.21
D	0.30	0.07	-0.25	0.29	0.20	0.24	0.39	-0.22	-0.11
E	0.32	-0.36	-0.35	0.32	0.07	0.33	0.18	-0.23	0.08
S_a $[10^{-6}]$	68	13	67	68	49	74	49	30	38

3.1 Application to the pdb_select Data

As a representative set of proteins we took the current version (Apr. 2002) of the pdb_select list [14], which comprises 1771 proteins of less than 25% sequence identity from the Brookhaven Protein Database. We computed $\mathbf{D}(k)$ in the 1414 sequences longer than 70 residues after randomly assigning one of the 20 amino acids to the undetermined positions marked by X in the sequence.

The eigenvector iteration gives an optimized correlation function (grey, solid line in Fig. 1) with a similar shape as the hydrophobicity acf, but with an amplitude that is an order of magnitude larger. The corresponding property code (Tab. 1, col. 'p_s 1') has some similarity to hydrophobicities, the correlation coefficient ρ with the Kyte-Doolittle hydrophobicity is 0.46, that with the Goldmann-Engelmann-Steitz (GES) hydrophobicity [19] is 0.66. This property code can be seen as an optimized hydrophobicity. The oscillation in the acf corresponds to amphiphilic α-helices with the hydrophobic side facing to the core of the protein and the polar side exposed to the solvent [6]. This optimum is also found using the joint diagonalization method (Tab. 1, col. 'jdiag') and the MATLAB optimization toolbox (col. 'matl.').

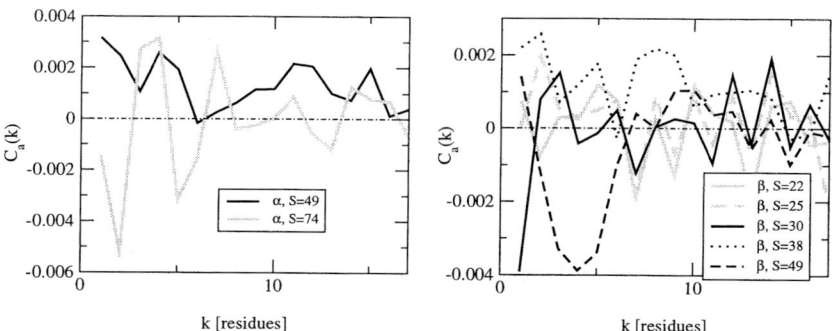

Fig. 2. The acfs using property codes optimized in the sets of α-helix (*left*) and β-strand rich proteins (*right*) in the respective sets

With some initializations the eigenvector optimization finds another local maximum of S_a which is related to α-helix propensity (Tab. 1, col. 'p_s 2'). The corresponding acf (dashed grey line, Fig. 1) shows a nonoscillating decay with the same length scale as α-helices, as described in [10]. This local optimum is reached from only about 0.05% of the initial conditions. It is one of the advantages of the eigenvector iteration that it is capable of finding other local optima than the highest one. As shown for this data, additional local maxima are also of biological relevance as α-helix-propensity is a helpful property for secondary structure prediction [20].

3.2 Secondary Structure

We also performed the eigenvector iteration in sets of sequences of proteins having mainly one type of secondary structure. We use the α-helix- and β-strand-rich datasets introduced in [10] comprising less than 100 sequences each. Therefore, all correlation functions estimated in these sets have a high level of noise. Still, correlation signals can be measured in these sets. However, the optimization procedures are facing rather rough landscapes where multiple local maxima are to be expected.

There are two local optima in the set of sequences from α-helix rich proteins. The corresponding acfs are plotted in the left graph of Figure 2. The more weakly correlated property causes a signal strength of $S = 49 \cdot 10^{-6}$ in the autocorrelation function (black line, col. α 1 in Tab. 1). Although the acf is heavily affected by fluctuations it shows a clear tendency towards positive correlations, especially for $k < 5$. Indeed, this property is weakly related to α-helix propensity ($\rho = -0.55$) while it is uncorrelated to the GES hydrophobicity scale ($\rho = 0.10$). Thus this property constitutes an optimized α-helix propensity. The other optimized property code in the α-helical protein sequence set is clearly correlated to hydrophobicity ($\rho = 0.71$). It is therefore not surprising to see that the corresponding acf strongly oscillates. It could be termed α-helix specific hydrophobicity as it is optimized to detect the oscillations caused by α-helices.

The picture in the set of β-strand rich proteins is more confusing as there are as many as five local optima. The two optimized property codes that cause the weakest signal ($S = 22 \cdot 10^{-6}$ and $S = 24 \cdot 10^{-6}$) are only reached by very few initial conditions. The corresponding acfs look very noisy (grey lines in the right graph of Fig. 2). We consider that these property codes are results of optimizing the noise rather than true (i.e. biological) signals.

The three other optimized property codes show weak correlations to hydrophobicity (those with $S = 49 \cdot 10^{-6}$ and $30 \cdot 10^{-6}$) or α-helix propensity (the one with $S = 38 \cdot 10^{-6}$, cols. β 1–3 in Tab. 1). There are two prominent features visible in the corresponding acfs. The property with $S = 30 \cdot 10^{-6}$ shows a clear anticorrelation at $k = 1$. This means that the corresponding property has the tendency to be concentrated on one side of the β-sheet. An even clearer signal can be seen in the acf of the property with $S = 49 \cdot 10^{-6}$: a pronounced negative peak at $k = 3, 4, 5$. The exact biochemical explanation for this is still unclear, but the distance is in the typical range of short loops connecting antiparallel β-strands. Thus, this signal could be caused by residues that actually have physical contact in the protein. Presumably certain residue combinations are selected to stabilize short loops (i.e. turns) in β-sheets.

4 Discussion

For given sets of protein sequences, we have maximized the correlation function signal by varying the property code, i.e. translation of the sequences to numerical series. We have done this using our eigenvector iteration, extended Jacobi method for joint diagonalization – introduced here for the first time in bioinformatics – and an off-the-shelf MATLAB optimization. All methods yielded similar results, the eigenvector iteration can find additional local optima which often hold additional biological significance.

Hydrophobicity- and α-helix propensity-related properties are found in the pdb_select dataset representing all proteins. These types of properties are found to be more pronounced in a set of α-helix-rich proteins. The optimized properties in β-strand-rich proteins include a novel correlation pattern with anticorrelations at $k = 3\ldots 5$.

Our methods are applicable to other sets of proteins as well, e.g. comparisons of optimized property codes in proteomes of different organisms will be done in forthcoming studies.

Acknowledgements. We thank the EU for funding via project IST-1999-14190 – BLISS and the DFG for funding via SFB 618. Furthermore, we gratefully acknowledge Johannes Schuchhardt, Sebastian Mika, and David Tax for help- and fruitful discussions, as well as Caspar van Wrede and Klaus-Robert Müller for proofreading.

References

1. Eisenberg, D., Schwarz, E., Komaromy, M., Wall, R.: Analysis of membrane and surface protein sequences with the hydrophobic moment plot. J. Mol. Biol. **179** (1984) 125–142
2. Frishman, D., Argos, P.: Seventy-five percent accuracy in protein secondary structure prediction. Proteins **27** (1997) 329–335
3. Casari, G., Sippl, M.J.: Structure-derived hydrophobic potential. J. Mol. Biol. **224** (1991) 725–732
4. Jagla, B., Schuchhardt, J.: Adaptive encoding neural networks for the recognition of human signal peptide cleavage sites. Bioinformatics **16** (2000) 245–250
5. Lin, K., May, A.C.W., Taylor, W.: Amino acid encoding schemes from protein structure alignments: Multi-dimensional vectors to describe residue types. J. theor. Biol. **216** (2002) 361–365
6. Kanehisa, M.I., Tsong, T.Y.: Hydrophobicity and protein structure. Biopolymers **19** (1980) 1617–1628
7. Kawashima, S., Kanehisa, M.: AAindex: Amino acid index database. Nucleic Acids Res. **28** (2000) 374
8. Sneath, P.H.A.: Relations between chemical and biological activity in peptides. J. theor. Biol **12** (1966) 157–195
9. Stanfel, L.E.: A new approach to clustering the amio acids. J. theor. Biol. **183** (1996) 195–205
10. Weiss, O., Herzel, H.: Correlations in protein sequences and property codes. J. theor. Biol. **190** (1998) 341–353
11. Cardoso, J.F., Souloumiac, A.: Jacobi angles for simultaneous diagonalization. SIAM J. Mat. Anal. Appl. **17** (1996) 161–164
12. Herzel, H., Große, I.: Measuring correlations in symbol sequences. Physica A **216** (1995) 518–542
13. Kyte, J., Doolittle, R.F.: A simple method for displaying the hydropathic character of a protein. J. Mol. Biol. **157** (1982) 105–132
14. Hobohm, U., Sander, C.: Enlarged representative set of protein structures. Protein Sci. **3** (1994) 552–554
15. Weiss, O.: Korrelationen und Eigenschaftscodes in Proteinsequenzen (Correlations and Property Codes in Protein Sequences). Logos, Berlin (2001) PhD Thesis, english.
16. Ziehe, A., Müller, K.R.: TDSEP – an efficient algorithm for blind separation using time structure. In Niklasson, L., Bodén, M., Ziemke, T., eds.: Proceedings of the 8th International Conference on Artificial Neural Networks, ICANN'98. Perspectives in Neural Computing, Berlin, Springer Verlag (1998) 675–680
17. Ziehe, A., Müller, K.R., Nolte, G., Mackert, B.M., Curio, G.: Artifact reduction in magnetoneurography based on time-delayed second-order correlations. IEEE Trans Biomed Eng. **47** (2000) 75–87
18. Nocedal, J., Wright, S.J.: Numerical Optimization. Springer (1999)
19. Engelmann, D.M., Steitz, T.A., Goldmann, A.: Identifying nonpolar transbilayer helices in amino acid sequences of membrane proteins. Annu. Rev. Biophys. Chem. **115** (1986) 321–353
20. Chou, P., Fasman, G.: Prediction of the secondary structure of proteins from their amino acid sequence. Adv. Enzymol. **47** (1978) 45–148

Multicategory Bayesian Decision Using a Three-Layer Neural Network

Yoshifusa Ito[1] and Cidambi Srinivasan[2]

[1] Department of Information and Policy Studies,
Aichi-Gakuin University,
Iwasaki, Nisshin-shi, Aichi-ken 470-0195, Japan,
ito@psis.aichi-gakuin.ac.jp
[2] Department of Statistics, Patterson office tower,
University of Kentucky,
Lexington, Kentucky 40506, USA
srini@ms.uky.edu

Abstract. We realize a multicategory Bayesian classifier by a three-layer neural network having rather a small number of hidden layer units. The state-conditional probability distributions are supposed to be multivariate normal distributions. The network has direct connections between the input and output layers. Its outputs are monotone mappings of posterior probabilities. Hence, they can be used as discriminant functions and, in addition, the posterior probabilities can be easily retrieved from the outputs.

1 Introduction

Funahashi (1989) has realized a two-category Bayesian classifier by a feedforward three-layer neural network having rather a small number, $2d$, of hidden layer units in the case where the state-conditional probability distributions of observable x are d-dimensional normal distributions [2]. The log ratio

$$\log(P(\theta_1|x)/P(\theta_2|x)) \tag{1}$$

of posterior probabilities of the categories is a quadratic function, where log stands for the natural logarithm and θ_1 and θ_2 are indeces of the respective categories. The output of the network can approximate the posterior probability $P(\theta_1|x)$, which can be used as a discriminant function. The point of his proof of the main theorem is to remark that any quadratic function can be approximated by a linear sum of outputs of $2d$ nonlinear hidden layer units and a constant uniformly on compact sets [2]. We have later decreased the number to $d+1$ by improving the method of approximating quadratic forms in x [4].

The logistic transform of the log ratio is the posterior probability:

$$P(\theta_1|x) = \sigma(\log(P(\theta_1|x)/P(\theta_2|x))), \tag{2}$$

where σ is the logistic function and log stands for the natural logarithm. Since the output unit of Funahashi's network has the logistic activation function, the output can approximate the posterior probability. To prove that the approximation is in the sense of $L^2(\mathbf{R}^d, p)$, he relied on the fact that the logistic transform is a mapping of the whole line $\mathbf{R}$ onto a finite interval (0,1) [2]. However, we have proved that the log ratio (1) itself can be approximated by a linear sum of outputs of $d+1$ hidden layer units and a constant not only uniformly on compact sets but also on the whole space in the sense of $L^p(\mathbf{R}^d, p)$ [4], where the result of [3] was applied. This is a meaningful result because the log ratio is also a discriminant function. Since the mapping by σ is a contraction, the approximation of the posterior probability (2) automatically follows.

In this paper we extend the result of [4] to multicategory cases, carrying on the policy of constructing a neural network with rather a small number of units. The number of the hidden layer units of our network is fixed to $\frac{1}{2}d(d+1)$, regardless of the number of the categories. A Bayesian classifier in the multicategory case can be represented in terms of a set of discriminant functions, as is detailed in [1]. If the value of a discriminant function indexed by one of the categories is greater than others for an observable, it is assigned to the category.

However, a simple extension of [4] is impossible because the posterior probabilities are not logistic transforms of quadratic forms in the multicategory case. Nevertheless, the method use in [4] can be applied to multicategory cases with an idea of using one of the categories, say θ_m, as a reference. The log ratios

$$\log(P(\theta_k|x)/P(\theta_m|x)), \quad k = 1, \cdots, m, \qquad (3)$$

are monotone mappings of the posterior probabilities $P(\theta_k|x)$ respectively. Hence, these as well as their logistic transforms can be used as discriminant functions. Since (3) are quadratic functions, the method used in [4] can be used. Moreover, the posterior probabilities $P(\theta_k|x)$, $k = 1, \cdots, m$, can be easily retrieved from the logistic transforms of the log ratio (3) for $k = 1, \cdots, m-1$ by a simple calculation. We do not need to approximate (3) for $k = m$ because it is zero.

We use a three layer neural network having direct connections between the input and output layers. This decreases the number of hidden layer units and prevents the linear term in the approximation formula from distortion. If it does not have the direct connections, the number of the hidden layer units is $\frac{1}{2}d(d+3)$.

2 Mean Square Learning

Let $x \in \mathbf{R}^d$ be observables and θ_k, $k = 1, \cdots, m$, be indices of categories, from one of which x comes out. Setting $\Theta = \{\theta_1, \cdots, \theta_m\}$, we denote by $(x, \theta) \in \mathbf{R}^d \times \Theta$ a pair of an observable and its category. We treat the case where the state-conditioned probability $p(x|\theta_k)$ is normal:

$$p(x|\theta_k) = (2\pi|\Sigma_k|)^{-\frac{1}{2}} \exp\left(-\frac{(x-\mu_k)^2}{2|\Sigma_k|}\right), \quad k = 1, \cdots, m,$$

where μ_k and Σ_k are the mean vectors and covariance matrices of the respective distributions. Let $P(\theta_k)$, $k = 1, \cdots, m$, be the prior probabilities. Then,

$p(x, \theta) = P(\theta)p(x|\theta)$ is a probability measure over $\mathbf{R}^d \times \Theta$, $p(x) = \sum_\Theta p(x, \theta) = \sum_{k=1}^m p(x, \theta_k)$ is the probability measure over $\mathbf{R}^d$, and $P(\theta|x) = p(x, \theta)/p(x)$ is the posterior probability over Θ.

We further set

$$P_k(\theta_i|x) = \frac{P(\theta_i|x)}{P(\theta_k|x) + P(\theta_m|x)} \quad \text{for} \quad i = k, m, \quad P_k(\theta_i|x) = 0 \quad \text{for} \quad i \neq k, m.$$

Then, $P_k(\theta|x)$ is a probability measure on Θ supported by $\{\theta_k, \theta_m\}$. We write $p_k(x, \theta_i) = P_k(\theta_i|x)p(x)$, $p_k(x) = p_k(x, \theta_k) + p_k(x, \theta_m)$. Then, $p_k(x, \theta)$ is a probability distribution over $\mathbf{R}^d \times \Theta$ supported by $\mathbf{R}^d \times \{\theta_m, \theta_k\}$ and $p_k(x)$ is that over $\mathbf{R}^d$.

Since $\sum_{k=1}^m p(\theta_i|x) = 1$, it is sufficient for our network to have $m - 1$ output units. Let $F_k(x, w)$ be the output of the k-th output unit, let $\xi_k(x, \theta)$ be a function on $\mathbf{R}^d \times \Theta$ and set

$$E(w) = \int_{\mathbf{R}^d} \sum_{k=1}^{m-1} \sum_\Theta (F_k(x, w) - \xi_k(x, \theta))^2 p_k(x, \theta) dx.$$

The training of the network is carried out by minimizing

$$E_n(w) = \frac{1}{n} \sum_{i=1}^n \sum_{k=1}^{m-1} \sum_\Theta (F_k(x^{(i)}, w) - \xi_k(x^{(i)}, \theta^{(i)}))^2,$$

with respect to w, where $\{(x^{(i)}, \theta^{(i)})\}_{i=1}^n$ is a segment of the training sequence. We obtain

$$E(w) = \sum_{k=1}^{m-1} \int_{\mathbf{R}^d} (F_k(x, w) - E_k[\xi_k(x, \cdot)|x])^2 p_k(x) dx$$

$$+ \int_{\mathbf{R}^d} V_k[\xi_k(x, \cdot)|x] p_k(x) dx, \qquad (4)$$

where

$$E_k[\xi_k(x, \cdot)|x] = \xi_k(x, \theta_k) P_k(\theta_k|x) + \xi_m(x, \theta_k) P_k(\theta_m|x)$$

and

$$V_k[\xi(x, \cdot)|x] = E_k[\xi(x, \cdot)^2|x] - E_k[\xi(x, \cdot)|x]^2$$

are the conditional expectation and variance of $\xi_k(x, \theta)$ respectively. The same calculation as this with details is found in [5], [6] or [8]. Setting $\xi_k(x, \theta_k) = 1$ and $\xi_k(x, \theta_i) = 0$ for $i \neq k$, we obtain $E_k[\xi_k(x, \cdot)|x] = P_k(\theta_k|x)$. Since the second term of the right hand side of (4) does not include w, minimization of (4) implies that of the first term. Hence, when (4) is minimized, we expect that $F_k(x, w)$ approximate $P_k(\theta_k|x)$ respectively as long as the network has a capability of approximating the posterior probabilities.

3 An Approximation Theorem

Funahashi [2] has proved that the logistic transform (2) can be approximated in the sense of $L^2(\mathbf{R}^d, p)$ by a neural network having $2d$ hidden layer units, whereas we have proved that the log ratio (1) itself can be approximated in $L^p(\mathbf{R}^d, p)$ by a network with almost half a number of the units [4]. Both the paper [4] and this paper are based on [3]. Though Theorem 3 below can be regarded as a corollary to the main theorem in [3], we include it here for completeness in the form adapted to our present use.

The $L^p(\mathbf{R}^d, p)$-norm with respect to the probability distribution p is defined by $\|f\|_{L^p(\mathbf{R}^d,p)} = \left[\int_{\mathbf{R}^d} |f(x)|^p dp(x)\right]^{\frac{1}{p}}$, where the power p is greater than or equal to 1. The lemma below is a special case of a theorem in [3].

Lemma 1. *Let p be a probability measure on $\mathbf{R}$ and let $g \in C^2(\mathbf{R})$. If $t^2 \in L^p(\mathbf{R}, p)$, g'' is bounded and $g''(0) \neq 0$, then, for any $\varepsilon > 0$, there is a constant $\gamma > 0$ such that for any δ, $0 < |\delta| < \gamma$,*

$$\left\|t^2 - \frac{2}{\delta^2 g''(0)}(g(\delta t) - \delta g'(0)t - g(0))\right\|_{L^p(\mathbf{R},p)} < \varepsilon. \tag{5}$$

Proof. By Maclaurin's theorem,

$$t^2 - \frac{2}{\delta^2 g''(0)}(g(\delta t) - \delta g'(0)t - g(0)) = \frac{1}{g''(0)}(g''(0) - g''(\theta \delta t))t^2.$$

By assumption, the right hand side converges to zero uniformly as $\delta \to 0$ on any bounded interval and its L^2-norm outside $[-T, T]$ can be arbitrarily small for a sufficiently large T. Hence, the lemma follows.

We use Lemma 1 in a modified form. Let $v \in \mathbf{S}^{d-1}$ and let p be a probability on $\mathbf{R}^d$. Suppose that $(v \cdot x)^2 \in L^p(\mathbf{R}^d, p)$ and $g \in C^2(\mathbf{R})$ satisfies the condition of Lemma 1. Then, for any $\varepsilon > 0$, there is a constant $\gamma > 0$ such that for any δ, $0 < |\delta| < \gamma$,

$$\left\|(v \cdot x)^2 - \frac{2}{\delta^2 g''(0)}(g(\delta v \cdot x) - \delta g'(0)(v \cdot x) - g(0))\right\|_{L^p(\mathbf{R}^d,p)} < \varepsilon. \tag{6}$$

In fact, let $t = x \cdot v$, let $\mathbf{L}_v = \{sv| -\infty < s < \infty\}$ and replace p by its projection onto $\mathbf{L}_v$. Then, Lemma 1 implies (6).

Lemma 2. *There are unit vectors $v_1, \cdots, v_{\frac{1}{2}d(d+1)} \in \mathbf{S}^{d-1}$ such that any homogenous quadratic form in $x \in \mathbf{R}^d$ can be expressed as a linear sum of $(v_1 \cdot x)^2, \cdots, (v_{\frac{1}{2}d(d+1)} \cdot x)^2$.*

Proof. For $t \neq 0, 1$, set $w_i = (t^{i-1}, t^{3(i-1)}, \cdots, t^{3^{d-1}(i-1)})$, $i = 1, \cdots, \frac{1}{2}d(d+1)$. Let α be the multi-index: $\alpha! = \alpha_1!, \cdots, \alpha_d!$, $|\alpha| = \alpha_1 + \cdots + \alpha_d$ and $x^\alpha = x_1^{\alpha_1}, \cdots, x^{\alpha_d}$. Then,

$$(w_i \cdot x)^2 = \left(\sum_{j=1}^d t^{3^{j-1}(i-1)} x_j\right)^2 = \sum_{|\alpha|=2} \frac{|\alpha|!}{\alpha!} t^{(\alpha_1 + 3\alpha_2 + \cdots + 3^{d-1}\alpha_d)(i-1)} x^\alpha.$$

If $\alpha \neq \beta$ and $|\alpha| = |\beta| = 2$, $\alpha_1 + 3\alpha_2 + \cdots + 3^{d-1}\alpha_d \neq \beta_1 + 3\beta_2 + \cdots + 3^{d-1}\beta_d$. In fact, let j be the greatest suffix for which $\alpha_j \neq \beta_j$. We may suppose that $\alpha_j < \beta_j$. Then, $\alpha_1 + 3\alpha_2 + \cdots + 3^{j-1}\alpha_j < 3^{j-1}(1+\alpha_j) \leq \beta_1 + 3\beta_2 + \cdots + 3^{j-1}\beta_j$ because $\alpha_1, \cdots, \alpha_j \leq 3$.

Let A be a $\frac{1}{2}d(d+1) \times \frac{1}{2}d(d+1)$ matrix whose i-th row is a vector having elements $t^{(\alpha_1 + 3\alpha_2 + \cdots + 3^{d-1}\alpha_d)(i-1)}$, $|\alpha| = 2$, ordered lexicographically in α. Note that the number of α, $|\alpha| = 2$, is $\frac{1}{2}d(d+1)$. We have that $|A| \neq 0$ because it is a Vandermond matrix with respect to $t^{(\alpha_1 + 3\alpha_2 + \cdots + 3^{d-1}\alpha_d)}$, $|\alpha| = 2$, which are mutually distinct. This implies that the vectors

$$w_i = (t^{(\alpha_1 + 3\alpha_2 + \cdots + 3^{d-1}\alpha_d)(i-1)}||\alpha| = 2), \qquad i = 1, \cdots, \frac{1}{2}d(d+1),$$

are linearly independent, which in turn implies that the homogeneous polynomials $(w_i \cdot x)^2$, $i = 1, \cdots, \frac{1}{2}d(d+1)$, are linearly independent. Setting $v_i = \frac{w_i}{|w_i|}$, $i = 1, \cdots, \frac{1}{2}d(d+1)$, we conclude the proof.

In the theorem below the quadratic forms in x are not necessarily homogeneous.

Theorem 3. *Let $g \in C^2(\mathbf{R}^d)$ and let p be a probability measure on $\mathbf{R}^d$. If $|x|^2 \in L^p(\mathbf{R}^d, p)$, g'' is bounded and $g''(0) \neq 0$, then, there are unit vectors $v_i \in \mathbf{S}^{d-1}$, $i = 1, \cdots, \frac{1}{2}d(d+1)$, such that, for any number n of any quadratic functions $Q_1, \cdots, Q_n$ in $x \in \mathbf{R}^d$ and any $\varepsilon > 0$, there are a constant δ, coefficients a_{ki}, b_{kj} and constants c_k, $k = 1, \cdots, n$, $i = 1, \cdots, \frac{1}{2}d(d+1)$, b_{kj}, $j = 1, \cdots, d$, for which*

$$\|Q_k - \bar{Q}_k\|_{L^p(\mathbf{R}^d, p)} < \varepsilon, \qquad k = 1, \cdots, n, \qquad (7)$$

where $\bar{Q}_k$ are defined by

$$\bar{Q}_k(x) = \sum_{i=1}^{\frac{1}{2}d(d+1)} a_{ki} g(\delta v_i \cdot x) + \sum_{j=1}^{d} b_{kj} x_j + c_k. \qquad (8)$$

Proof. There are $\frac{1}{2}d(d+1)$ monomials of order 2 in $x \in \mathbf{R}^d$ and, by Lemma 2, there are the same number of vectors $v_i \in \mathbf{S}^{d-1}$, $k = 1, \cdots, \frac{1}{2}d(d+1)$, for which $\{(v_i \cdot x)^2\}_{i=1}^{\frac{1}{2}d(d+1)}$ are linearly independent. Hence, any homogeneous polynomial of order 2 in $x \in \mathbf{R}^d$ can be expressed as a linear sum of the squares $(v_i \cdot x)^2$. Using them, we have that

$$Q_k(x) = \sum_{i=1}^{\frac{1}{2}d(d+1)} a'_{ki}(v_i \cdot x)^2 + \sum_{j=1}^{d} b'_{kj} x_j + c'_k, \qquad k = 1, \cdots, n,$$

where a'_{ki} and b'_{kj} are coefficients and c'_k are constant. We have, by Lemma 1, that

$$Q_k(x) \simeq \sum_{i=1}^{\frac{1}{2}d(d+1)} a'_{ki} \frac{1}{h''(0)\delta^2} \left(g(\delta v_i \cdot x) - \delta g'(0) v_i \cdot x - g(0)\right) + \sum_{j=1}^{d} b'_{kj} x_j + c'_k$$

$$\simeq \sum_{i=1}^{\frac{1}{2}d(d+1)} a_{ki} g(\delta v_i \cdot x) + \sum_{j=1}^{d} b_{kj} x_j + c_k, \tag{9}$$

where $\simeq$ stands for an approximation with any accuracy in the sense of $L^p(\mathbf{R}, p)$,

$$a_{ki} = a'_{ki} \frac{1}{g''(0)\delta^2}, \qquad b_{kj} = -\sum_{i=1}^{\frac{1}{2}d(d+1)} a'_{ki} \frac{1}{g''(0)\delta} g'(0) v_{kj} + b'_{kj}$$

and

$$c_k = -\sum_{i=1}^{\frac{1}{2}d(d+1)} a'_{ki} \frac{1}{h''(0)\delta^2} g(0) + c'_k.$$

This concludes the proof.

In this proof, the linear terms originally included in the polynomial Q_k and those included in the the approximation formulae of $(v_i \cdot x)^2$ are put together. This method was used in [4].

4 A Neural Network for Bayesian Decision Problems

In order to approximate a set of discriminant functions, we construct a three-layer neural network having direct connections between the input and output layers. The approximation formulae (8) are realized as inner potentials of the output units. The network has d linear input layer units, $\frac{1}{2}d(d+1)$ hidden layer units with an activation function satisfying the condition of Theorem 3, and $m-1$ output units with the logistic activation function, where m is the number of categories.

Existence of $\frac{1}{2}d(d+1)$ unit vectors $v_i = (v_{i1}, \cdots, v_{id})$, $i = 1, \cdots, \frac{1}{2}d(d+1)$, for which $(v_i \cdot x)^2$ are linearly independent, is guaranteed by Lemma 2. We fix a set of such vectors v_i. Choosing a sufficiently small constant $\delta \neq 0$, we let δv_{ij} be the connection weight between the j-th input unit and i-th hidden layer unit. If necessary, the constant δ may be chosen again, but it is not a constant to be adjusted by training. The coefficient a_{ki} is the connection weight between the i-th hidden layer unit and k-th output unit, b_{kj} is the connection weight between the j-th input layer unit and k-th output unit, and c_k is the bias of the k-th output units. Only the constants a_{ki}, b_{kj} and c_k are to be adjusted by training in our network. Since they are outer coefficients of the respective nonlinear terms or a constant term in (8), partial derivatives of the approximation formula with respect to these constants are respectively the terms themselves or a constant 1. Hence, the training algorithm based on the gradient descent method is simple. This is a merit of the network. The numbers of the weights a_{ki}, b_{kj} and c_k are respectively $(m-1)\frac{1}{2}d(d+1)$, $(m-1)d$ and $(m-1)$. Hence, their total number is $(m-1)\frac{1}{2}(d+1)(d+2)$.

The log ratios, $\log(P(\theta_k|x)/P(\theta_m|x))$, $k = 1, \cdots, m-1$, are quadratic forms. Hence, by Theorem 3, a linear sum of the outputs of hidden units, those of input units and a constant can approximate them in $L^p(\mathbf{R}^d, p)$. Accordingly, when training is completed, the inner potentials of the output units are expected to realize approximately the formulae (8) respectively for $k = 1, \cdots, n-1$. The mapping by σ is a contraction:

$$\|\sigma(f) - \sigma(\bar{f})\|_{L^p(\mathbf{R},p)} < \|f - \bar{f}\|_{L^p(\mathbf{R},p)}.$$

Hence, if the training goes well, the outputs $F_k(x, w)$ of the network approximate the logistic transforms

$$\sigma\left(\log \frac{P(\theta_k|x)}{P(\theta_m|x)}\right) = \frac{P(\theta_k|x)}{P(\theta_k|x) + P(\theta_m|x)} = P_k(\theta_k|x), \quad k = 1, \cdots, m-1,$$

in $L^p(\mathbf{R}^d, p)$ respectively. For $k = m$, we set

$$P_m(\theta_m|x) = \frac{P(\theta_m|x)}{P(\theta_m|x) + P(\theta_m|x)} = \frac{1}{2}.$$

These are not the posterior probabilities $P(\theta_k|x)$ of the respective categories θ_k for $m > 2$. Nevertheless, they can be used as discriminant functions, because they are monotone mappings of the posterior probabilities: $P_{k_1}(\theta_{k_1}|x) > P_{k_2}(\theta_{k_2}|x)$ implies $p(x, \theta_{k_1}) > p(x, \theta_{k_2})$ and vice versa. Hence, an observable x is allocated to the category θ_k if $F_k(x, w) > F_i(x, k)$ for all $i \neq k$.

Moreover, the posterior probabilities $P(\theta_k|x)$, $k = 1, \cdots, m$, can be easily obtained from the probabilities $P_k(\theta_k|x)$, $k = 1, \cdots, m-1$. Set

$$q_k(x) = \frac{P_k(\theta_k|x)}{1 - P_k(\theta_k|x)}, \quad k = 1, \cdots, m-1,$$

Then, $q_k(x) = P(\theta_k|x)/P(\theta_m|x)$. Hence,

$$P(\theta_k|x) = \frac{q_k(x)}{1 + \sum_{i=1}^{m-1} q_i(x)}, \quad k = 1, \cdots, m-1,$$

$$P(\theta_m|x) = \frac{1}{1 + \sum_{i=1}^{m-1} q_i(x)}.$$

Conversely, we can obtain $P_k(\theta_k|x)$, $k = 1, \cdots, m-1$, from the posterior probabilities. Hence, when the learning is completed, we can easily obtain approximations of the respective posterior probabilities from the set of outputs $F_k(x, w)$. This calculation is irrelevant to learning and can be done by a simple additional calculator.

5 Discussions

The network has direct connections between the input and output layers. The connections actually save d hidden layer units and, moreover, prevent the inner potentials of output units from additional distortion caused by approximation.

The network has $\frac{1}{2}d(d+1)$ hidden layer units. If the dimension d is large, this number is large. Otherwise, it is not particularly large, compared to the case of the two-category classifiers. Recalling that Funahashi's network [2] and ours [4] have $2d$ and $d+1$ hidden layer units respectively, note that for $d = 1, 2, 3$, $\frac{1}{2}d(d+1) \leq 2d$ and, for $d = 1, 2$, $\frac{1}{2}d(d+1) \leq d+1$.

Since δ and v_i in (8) can be fixed beforehand, the connection weights to be trained are those corresponding to the constants a_{ki}, b_{kj} and c_k in (8). The total number of these weights is $(m-1)\frac{1}{2}(d^2 + 3d + 2)$. In the case of Funahashi's network [2], the number is $2d^2 + 4d + 1$. This is greater than $(m-1)\frac{1}{2}(d^2 + 3d + 2)$ for $m = 2, 3, 4$. In the case of our previous network [4], the number is $d^2 + 3d + 3$. Even this number is greater than $(m-1)\frac{1}{2}(d^2 + 3d + 2)$ for $m = 2, 3$. The weights to be trained are simply coefficients and constants, and are not incorporated into the inner variables of the activation function in our network. This is advantageous because it makes the learning algorithm simpler.

While Funahashi has proved that the logistic transform of the log ratio is approximated in $L^2(\mathbf{R}^d, p)$ relying on the logistic transform [2], we have proved that the log ratios $\sigma(\log(P(\theta_k|x)/P(\theta_m|x))$ themselves can be approximated in $L^p(\mathbf{R}^d, p)$. This implies that even if the output units are linear, the outputs can approximate a set of discriminant functions in $L^p(\mathbf{R}^d, p)$. In this case, training must be carried out with the logistic transforms of the outputs.

We have to carefully index the categories in applications. The category from which observables come out less frequently should not be chosen as the m-th category, because it may cause more statistical errors. The category generating observables reasonably frequently all over the domain may be the reference category.

In conclusion: we have extended the classifier for the two-category case in [4] to the multicategory case, carrying on the policy of using rather a small number of units. However large is the number of categories, the hidden layer units is fixed at $\frac{1}{2}d(d+1)$. Approximation of discriminant functions in $L^p(\mathbf{R}^d, p)$ is realized at the level of inner potentials of the output units in our network. The weights to be trained are only coefficients of the respective terms and biases in the approximation formulae (8), which makes the training algorithm simpler. Hence, we expect that the problems of local minima and over-fitting are not serious to our networks. Details of this paper with related topics will appear somewhere.

References

1. R.O. Duda and P.E. Hart, Pattern classification and scene analysis (John Wiley & Sons, New York, 1973).
2. K. Funahashi, Multilayer neural networks and Bayes decision theory, Neural Networks, 11(1998)209–213.
3. Y. Ito, Simultaneous L^p-approximations of polynomials and derivatives on $\mathbf{R}^d$ and their applications to neural networks. (in preparation)
4. Y. Ito and C. Srinivasan, Bayesian decision thoery on three layered neural networks, in: Proc. ESANN2001(2001)377–382.

5. M.D. Richard and R.P. Lipmann: Neural network classifiers estimate Basian *a posteriori* probabilities, Neural Computation, 3(1991)461–483.
6. D.W. Ruck, S. Rogers, M. Kabrisky, H. Oxley, B. Sutter, The multilayer perceptron as an approximator to a Bayes optimal discriminant function, IEEE Transactions on Neural Networks, 1(1990) 296–298.
7. D.E. Rumelhart, G.E. Hinton and R.J. Williams, Learning internal representations by error propagation. In Parallel distributed processing ed. D.E. Rumelhart and J.L. McClelland, vol. 1(1986) 318–362.
8. H. White, Learning in artificial neural networks: A statistical perspective. Neural Computation, 1(1989)425–464.

Integrating Supervised and Unsupervised Learning in Self Organizing Maps for Gene Expression Data Analysis

Seferina Mavroudi[1], Andrei Dragomir[1], Stergios Papadimitriou[2], and Anastasios Bezerianos[1]

[1] Department of Medical Physics, School of Medicine, University of Patras,
26500 Patras, Greece
{severina,adragomir}@heart.med.upatras.gr,
bezer@patreas.upatras.gr

[2] Department of Information Management, Technological Educational Institute,
65404 Kavala, Greece
sterg@teikav.edu.gr

Abstract. Recently, Self Organizing Maps have been a popular approach to analyze gene expression data. Our paper presents an improved SOM-based algorithm called Supervised Network Self Organizing Map (sNet-SOM), which overcomes the main drawbacks of existing techniques by adaptively determining the number of clusters with a dynamic extension process and integrating unsupervised and supervised learning in an effort to make use of prior knowledge on data. The process is driven by an inhomogeneous measure that balances unsupervised/supervised learning and model complexity criteria. Multiple models are dynamically constructed by the algorithm, each corresponding to an unsupervised/supervised balance, model selection criteria being used to select the optimum one. The design allows us to effectively utilize multiple functional class labeling.

1 Introduction

Clustering is a core task in data mining being successfully used to systematically analyze large sets of high dimensional data in order to partition it into groups exhibiting similar variation patterns. It provides a meaningful representation of data, thus enabling further processing. However, there are major drawbacks of existing clustering methods, as the need to specify a priori the number of clusters, which can be annoying when we handle data without having information on its intrinsic structure. Furthermore, when partial class information is available, pure unsupervised approaches are not suitable tools.

Current clustering approaches used in gene expression data analysis [1,2], like hierarchical clustering [1], K-means clustering, Bayesian clustering [3] and self-organizing maps (SOM)[4] stumble upon using existing class information and do not incorporate flexible means for coupling effectively the unsupervised phase with a supervised complementary one. In spite of that, the easy implementation, fast and robust scaling to large data sets and the visualization and interpretation benefits, make SOM a candidate of particular interest. There have been previous efforts to surpass the limitation of fixed non-adaptable architecture of SOM by developing dynamically extendable maps [5,6].

Our approach, besides tackling the fixed grid structure problem (and thus the pre-determination on the number of clusters), proposes an elegant solution of integrating unsupervised and supervised learning components. While still retaining the benefits of the SOM and of previous more complex dynamical extension schemes, we built simple algorithms that through the restriction of growing on a rectangular grid can be implemented easily and significantly reduce the computational time.

2 Methods

We have used our model on analyzing gene expression data as, it is known, recent developments in molecular biology produced tremendous amounts of data, especially from microarray experiments [7,8]. Such an experiment yields expression patterns of thousands of genes, partially annotated until now. There is a real need for getting an insight into their structure, as well as deducing their biological role, which finally could lead to unveiling diseases mechanisms. This can be obtained by a reliable clustering of patterns, as it was experimentally proved that correlated genes are acting together when they belong to similar or at least related functional categories.

The driving force behind our work was to take into account prior partial knowledge on data. Conceptually, the input space is "divided" into unambiguous regions where the classification task is trivial and upon which sole unsupervised learning is sufficient to decide over classes separation and ambiguous regions where classification decisions are difficult to perform and additional supervised information is needed. The unambiguous regions usually account for most of the state space and are managed with low computational costs, having as result the decrease of the total computational requirements of the algorithm.

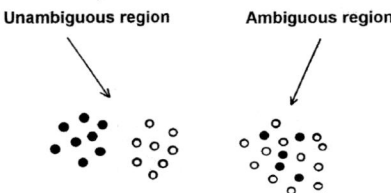

Fig. 1. Complex decision boundaries, which cannot be separated due to SOM distance metric mechanisms, are subjected to a supervised approach; unsupervised learning is used upon regions where classes can be well separated

2.1 The SNet-SOM Model

Called sNet-SOM (from Supervised Network SOM), our neural model adaptively determines the number of clusters with a properly defined measure based on the algorithm itself and is able to successfully deal with multi-labeled data. Although it is SOM based, it includes prior knowledge on data, without discarding benefits of pure unsupervised clustering i.e. exploratory analysis and structure insight of the data.

The map is initialized with four nodes arranged in a 2X2 rectangular grid and grows to represent the input data. New nodes are inserted either from boundary nodes, or by inserting whole columns of new units. Weight values of the nodes are initialized with random numbers within the domain of feature values and the self organization performed according to a new method inspired by the SOM algorithm.

2.2 Expansion Mechanisms

Specifically, our clustering algorithm modifies the original SOM algorithm with a dynamic expansion process controlled by a learning process that aims to minimize an inhomogeneous measure of the form:

$$\Im_E = \min\left\{\sum_{i=1}^{K}(\text{AverageLocalError}_i + r_{su} \cdot \text{Entropy}_i)\right\} \quad (1)$$

Where K is the number of nodes.

We call the aggregate term, consisting of a *local error* and an *entropy* component, the *Growth Parameter (GP)* on which the direction of expansion is based. Neurons with large *GP* are referred to as the *unresolved* neurons. The node i with the largest GP_i becomes the current focus of map expansion. If i is a boundary node then the algorithm smoothly joins neighbors in all the free neighboring positions. If it is located near a boundary node then the algorithm ripples weights towards the neighbors and finally, if the unresolved node is located far from the map borders, a whole column is inserted. The weights of the new nodes are computed by averaging the weights of nearby nodes, in the direction of the largest total error, such that the 'weight flow' is retained. In the end, nodes that are selected as winners for few (usually one or two) or no training patterns are deleted.

Unsupervised Contribution. Dynamically growing schemes usually employ a local error term [5]. Instead, we used an average local error ale_i given by :

$$ale_i = \frac{\sum_{x \in S_i} d(x, w_i)}{S_i} \quad (2)$$

Where we denote by S_i the set of patterns x mapped to node i, w_j the weight vector of node i and the d operator denotes the corresponding distance metric. The choice was driven by the fact that this measure does not increase when many similar patterns are mapped to the same node, making the objective of assigning all the similar patterns to the same node easier to achieve.

The unsupervised contribution *Local Error$_i$* can deal with the lack of class information and accounts for the unsupervised ("quantization") error corresponding to node *i*. It disperses patterns that are different according to some similarity metric, to different clusters, even if they have the same class label. The unsupervised dynamic expansion is controlled by local variance, resource counts or similarity metrics (e.g. Bayesian, correlation) criteria.

Supervised Contribution. The supervised contribution to the inhomogeneous error of (1) is based on characterizing the entropy of the class assignment content of each node *i*. An advantage of the entropy is that it is relatively insensitive to the overrepresentation of classes. This means that independently of how many patterns of a class are mapped to the same node, if the node does not represent significantly other classes, its entropy is very small.

The simple case of each pattern belonging only to one class is considered first. A majority-voting scheme [4] is employed for the assignment of a class label to each neuron of the sNet-SOM. The entropy parameter that quantifies the uncertainty of the class label of neuron *m* can be directly evaluated by counting the votes at each SOM neuron for every class as [9]:

$$HN(m) = -\sum_{k=1}^{N_c} p_k \log p_k \quad (3)$$

where N_c denotes the number of classes and p_k, is the ratio of votes V_k for class k to the total number of patterns $V_{pattern}$ that vote to neuron *m*. For the single label case, the number of labeled patterns $V_{pattern}$ is also equal to the number of votes.

For the multi-label case, the voting scheme remains the same, but each pattern is in this case voting for more than one class. A quantity *HR(m)* is defined similarly as above. However, in this case:

$$\sum_k V_k > V_{pattern} \text{ and therefore } \sum_{k=1}^{N_c} p_k > 1.$$

HR(m) retains properties similar to the entropy, while it is able to deal effectively with the similarity of multiple class labeling, although mathematically, *HR(m)* is not an entropy of a probability distribution. We consider an example in order to explain the handling of multiple labeling: let N_c=3 and suppose that 30 patterns are assigned to node m_1, all of them having as a label all three classes and that 90 patterns are assigned to node m_2, each third of them having as a label a different class. Although in each case there are 30 genes voting for each class, the quantity *HR* will be high in the former case (i.e. log(3)) and zero in the latter.

Entropy$_i$ considers the available a priori information for the class of the patterns, quantifying the accuracy of class representation of a gene by the winning sNet-SOM node. This measure tends to force similar labels onto the same clusters Accordingly, the model is adapted dynamically in order to minimize the entropy within the generated clusters. The entropy criterion concentrates on the resolution of the regions characterized by class ambiguity.

The supervision weighting parameter r_{su} balances the model's supervised / unsupervised ratio, each r_{su} value constructing an sNet-SOM model, the one that provides best classification results being chosen by means of model selection criteria. The heuristic criteria used for model selection require that a steep increase in the classification performance is obtained for the selected r_{su} value and the number of nodes that grow for that value is relatively small (small model complexity). With $r_{su} = 0$ we have pure unsupervised learning, as r_{su} increases, the cost $\Im_E$ is minimized for configurations that fit better to the a priori classification.

2.3 Algorithm Outline

As stated before, the map is initialized with a small number of nodes, the growing structure taking the form of a nonuniform rectangular grid. An outline of the whole process is described below:

    1. \<Initialization phase\> $r_{su} = 0$
  Repeat   // model selection
    Repeat
        2. \<Training Run Adaptation phase\>
        3. \<Expansion phase\>
    until \< criteria for stopping map expansion are satisfied\>
    4. \<Fine Tuning Adaptation phase\>
    5. Save configuration of the map for the current supervised/unsupervised ratio r_{su}.
    6. \<Compute classification performance for the current r_{su} parameter\>
    7. Increment the significance of the supervised part, i.e. increase ratio r_{su}.
  until \<classification performance ≈ 1\>
    8.   \<Model Selection Step\>

The aim of the training run adaptation is to stabilize the current map configuration in order to evaluate its effectiveness and requirements for further expansion. During this phase the input patterns are repeatedly presented and corresponding self organization actions are performed. The convergence is quantified in terms of decrease of the total growth parameters between successive training epochs and is thus independent on the cluster size. Each time the map is expanded, the map adaptation is executed until convergence criteria are met.

Opposed to the classic SOM algorithm, the neighborhood does not need to shrink with time since initially it is large enough to include the whole map and as training proceeds, the neighborhood confines itself to the winning neuron, not by decreasing the vicinity radius but rather by enlarging the map. The learning rate starts from a value of 0.1 and decreases gradually to 0.02, producing a relatively fast convergence without sacrificing the stability of the map.

The fine tuning phase tries to optimize the final map configuration in a similar manner with the training run adaptation, just that in this case a much smaller change of the total growth parameter is required, while the learning rate is decreased to a smaller value (0.01).

For each r_{su} (sNet-SOM model) value a classification performance is computed. The classification is a soft one and is inspired by a metric proposed by [10]. Nodes of the current grid structure are assigned classification vectors $cl_i = p_i$ representing the probability that the respective node, together with its mapped patterns, is assigned a label i. Each data pattern j is then assigned a score for each of its class labels i, which is equal either to p_i, if the corresponding label is included in the original class assignment, or to $q_i = 1 - p_i$ if the reverse is true. A total score for each pattern is computed, representing the sum over the number of classes of p_i or q_i, respectively:

$$TotalScore_j = \sum_{i=1}^{N_c} score_i, \text{ where } score_i = \begin{cases} p_i & \text{if } c_i = 1 \\ q_i = 1 - p_i & \text{if } c_i = 0 \end{cases} \quad (4)$$

Averaging this score over the total number of classes derives the performance of each pattern. Straightforward, a global measure of classification performance for the whole map is computed by summing the performances of all patterns and dividing the result with the number of patterns in the data set.

We have extensively presented the expansion process of the map above but we should mention at this point that the dynamic growing of the map is controlled by a statistically derived randomness level for the distance between patterns assigned to a node [11]. Using the distribution of these distances we set a confidence level (a statistically common value of 0.05 was used) from which we derive a threshold below which we consider patterns are similar. The maximum percentage of random patterns allowed in a node is 2%, which produces a well-behaved extension of the map.

3 Results

In one of the experiments we performed, we applied the sNet-SOM to analyze a set of gene expression data from budding yeast *Saccharomyces cerevisiae* microarray experiments, including essentially every Open Reading Frame (ORF) and publicly available on the Stanford University website. The whole data set consists of 6221 genes with samples collected at different time points during diauxic shift, mitotic cell division cycle and sporulation, 80-element gene expression patterns resulted. Selected annotations obtained from Munich Information Center for Protein Sequences (MIPS) Comprehensive Yeast Genome Database included 19 functional categories.

For this data set an appropriate model for the sNet-SOM is selected as the one corresponding to supervision parameter value $r_{su} = 10$ (See Table 1 above). The model selection is accomplished according to heuristic criteria.

Table 1. Model Selection process

r_{su}	Number of nodes K	Classification perf.
0	71	0.17
4	96	0.32
6	91	0.43
8	87	0.6
10	80	0.71
12	65	0.73
14	82	0.87
16	91	0.92
20	98	0.96
24	111	0.99

We require acceptable classification performance, small number of nodes (model complexity control) while the classification peformance to steeply increase for the respective r_{su} value and to be followed by a relatively slower increase. A tradeoff classification performance versus possibility of further analyzing subclasses of genes is also considered when choosing an appropriate sNet-SOM model.

In another experiment we trained the sNET-SOM with the same functional classes as in [6]. Gene expression data from 2467 genes from budding yeast *Saccharomyces cerevisiae* measured in 79 time points (i.e. 79-element vector patterns) were used. The functional classifications were obtained from the Munich Information Center for Protein Sequences (MIPS). We used six functional classes, namely tricarboxylic acid (TCA) cycle, respiration, cytoplasmic ribosomes, proteasome, histones and helix-turn-helix (HTH) proteins. The first five are valid categories of genes that are expected to induce similar expression characteristics, while the HTH proteins is used as a control group as there are no biological reasons for members of this class to be clustered together.

The entropy is evaluated over the nodes in order to quantify the dispersion of class representation. We expect this measure to be large in the case of HTH patterns, which indeed is verified. An entropy value of 2.78 was obtained for HTH class representation, while for example the Proteasome class had entropy of 0.51.

An initial form of the sNet-SOM was developed within the context of an ischiemic episodes detection application [12]. However, the peculiarities of gene expression data made mandatory the radical redesign of the algorithms. The implementation was made in Borland C++ Builder 5.0. Figure 2 presents a snapshot of the program displaying the progress of the learning process for the 2467 gene patterns of 79-elements.

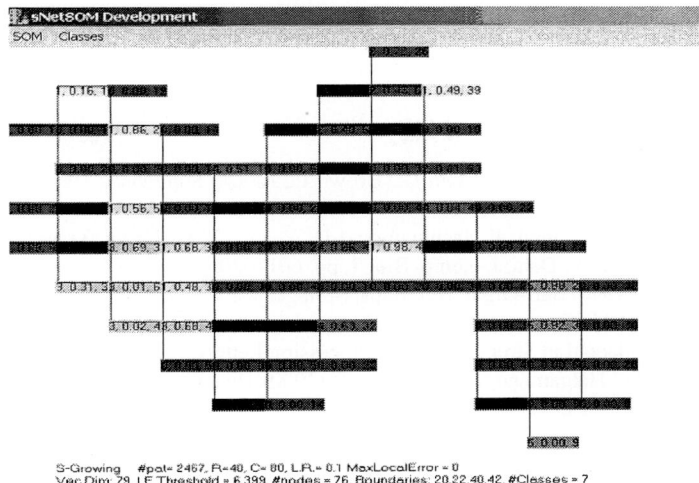

Fig. 2. sNet-SOM snapshot. At each node there are 3 parameters displayed: the class, the entropy and the number of patterns currently mapped.

4 Conclusions

Particularities of gene expression data require improved computational methods for analysis. Our approach proves to be a relying tool, yielding results competitive to the current supervised efforts, while significantly reducing the computational costs. Especially, the implementation of the column insertion, when the expansion focus is placed deep inside the map, has significantly accelerated the training of large maps. In addition, we elegantly incorporate existing class information in the process and successfully handle multi-labeled data.

The benefits of current unsupervised methods such as exploratory analysis and data structure insight are retained, while we overcome the main drawback of clustering methods (a priori specification of number of clusters). Multiple models are dynamically constructed, each corresponding to a different unsupervised / supervised balance. Model selection criteria are used to select a sNet-SOM model that optimizes the contribution of the unsupervised part of the gene expression data with the a priori knowledge (supervised part).

Further use of the sNet-SOM could come the coupling of our model as a front-end processing within a Bayesian network structure learning algorithm (capable of determining gene regulatory networks), while from the incorporation of more advanced distance metrics in the clustering algorithm, such as Bayesian ones could provide interesting results.

References

1. Eisen, M. B., Spellman P. T., Brown, P., Botstein D., (1998) Cluster Analysis and Display of Genome-wide Expression Patterns, Proc. Natl. Acad. Science, Vol. 95, pp. 14863–14868.
2. Hastie T., Tibshirani R., Botstein D., Brown P., (2001) Supervised Harvesting of expression trees, Genome Biology, 2 (1).
3. Friedman, N., M. Linial, I. Nachman, and D' Pe'er, (2000) Using Bayesian Networks to Analyze Expression Data, J. Comp. Bio. 7, pp. 601–620.
4. Kohonen T.,(1997) Self-Organized Maps, Springer-Verlag, Second Edition.
5. Fritzke B., (1995) Growing Grid - a Self Organizing Network with Constant Neighborhood Range and Adaptation Strength, Neural Processing Letters, Vol. 2, No. 5, pp. 9–13.
6. Alakahoon D., Halgamuge S., Srinivasan B.(2000) Dyamic SOM with Controlled Growth for Knowledge Discovery, IEEE Trans. on Neural Networks, Vol.11, No.3, pp 601–614.
7. Brown M., Grundy W. N., Lin D., Cristianini N., Sugnet C. W., Furey T., Ares M., Haussler D., (1997) Knowledge-based Analysis of Microarray Gene Expression Data By Using Support Vector Machines, Proc. Natl. Acad. Science, Vol 97, No 1, pp. 262–267.
8. Brazma A., Jaak V., (2000) Gene Expression Data Analysis, FEBS Letters, 480, pp. 17–24.
9. Haykin S,(1999) Neural Networks, Prentice Hall International, Second Edition.
10. Sable, C. L., Hatzivassiloglou, V., (1999) Text-Based Approaches for the Categorization of Images, 3rd Annual Conf. on Research and Advanced Techn. for Digital Libraries, Paris.
11. Herrero J., Valencia A., and Dopazo J. (2001) A Hierarchical Unsupervised Growing Neural Network for Clustering Gene Expression Patterns. Bioinformatics,17, 126–136.
12. Papadimitriou S., Mavroudi S., Vladutu L., Bezerianos A.(2001) Ischemia detection with a Self Organizing Map Supplemented by Supervised Learning, IEEE Trans. On Neural Networks, Vol.12, No.3, pp. 503–515.

Prior Hyperparameters in Bayesian PCA

Shigeyuki Oba[1], Masa-aki Sato[2,3], and Shin Ishii[1,3]

[1] Nara Institute of Science and Technology, Japan.
shige-o@is.aist-nara.ac.jp
[2] ATR Human Information Science Laboratories, Japan.
[3] CREST, JST.

Abstract. Bayesian PCA (BPCA) provides a Bayes inference for probabilistic PCA, in which several prior distributions have been devised for example, automatic relevance determination (ARD) is used for determining the dimensionality. However, there is arbitrariness in prior setting; different prior settings result in different estimations. This article aims at presenting a standard setting of prior distribution for BPCA. We first define a general hierarchical prior for BPCA and show an exact predictive distribution. We show that several of the already proposed priors can be regarded as special cases of the general prior. By comparing various priors, we show that BPCA with nearly non-informative hierarchical priors exhibits the best performance.

1 Introduction

Probabilistic principal component analysis (PPCA) [1] provides a probabilistic reformulation of principal component analysis (PCA); its maximum likelihood (ML) inference is equivalent to PCA. Bishop [2] showed that maximum a posteriori (MAP) estimation for PPCA with an automatic relevance determination (ARD) prior can determine an appropriate dimension of principal components. In such a Bayesian PCA (BPCA), the prior distribution makes the result not the same as that in usual PCA. In many cases, this difference produces improvement in the generalization ability. We proposed a full Bayes estimation algorithm for BPCA, based on the variational Bayes (VB) approximation, and obtained high generalization ability in a missing value estimation problem [3].

Determination of prior distribution is important, because different priors produce different results. In data analyses, BPCA with nearly non-informative hierarchical priors have been used [3,4,5].

This article aims at presenting a standard setting of prior distribution for BPCA. We first define a general hierarchical prior for BPCA. Using such a hierarchical prior, we show an exact predictive distribution; this is a new result as far as we know. After that, we show that several of the already proposed priors can be regarded as special cases of the general prior. By comparing various priors, we show that BPCA with nearly non-informative hierarchical priors exhibits the best performance. We also examine the effect of various priors in detail using a simplified estimation situation.

2 BPCA and Generalization Ability

2.1 PPCA

For an observed data set $\mathcal{D} = \{y(n) \in \mathbb{R}^{m \times 1} | n = 1, ..., N\}$, the sample covariance matrix is defined by $S \stackrel{\text{def}}{=} (1/N) \sum_{n=1}^{N} (y(n) - \overline{y})(y(n) - \overline{y})^{\mathsf{T}}$, where $\overline{y} \stackrel{\text{def}}{=} (1/N) \sum_{n=1}^{N} y(n)$ is the sample mean. Let $\lambda_1 \geq ... \geq \lambda_N$ be the eigenvalues of S, and $u_1, ..., u_N$ be the corresponding eigenvectors.

In PPCA, each datum y is assumed to be generated from a noisy linear transformation $y = Wx + \mu + \epsilon$ from a hidden variable $x \in \mathbb{R}^{l \times 1}$ ($l \leq m$). Noise ϵ is assumed to obey an isotropic m-dimensional Gaussian distribution. Under that formulation, the likelihood for the complete data, (y, x), is given by[1]

$$p(y, x | \theta) = \mathcal{N}(y | Wx + \mu, \tau^{-1} I_m) \mathcal{N}(x | 0, I_l). \quad (1)$$

Utilizing the ML solution θ_{ML} for the observed data $\mathcal{D}$, equation (1) is marginalized with respect to the hidden variable, and hence a PPCA predictive distribution is obtained: $p(y | \theta_{\text{ML}}) = \mathcal{N}(y | \mu_{\text{ML}}, (\tau_{\text{ML}}^{-1} I_m + W_{\text{ML}} W_{\text{ML}}^{\mathsf{T}}))$. The covariance in the predictive distribution is called predictive covariance, and its eigenvalues $\overline{\lambda}_1 \geq ... \geq \overline{\lambda}_m$ are called reconstructed eigenvalues:

$$\overline{\lambda}_j = \begin{cases} w_j^{\mathsf{T}} w_j + 1/\tau_{\text{ML}} & (1 \leq j \leq l) \\ 1/\tau_{\text{ML}} & (l < j \leq m) \end{cases}, \quad (2)$$

where w_j is the jth column vector of W_{ML}.

2.2 BPCA

In a Bayes inference, all or a part of parameters are treated as random variables with prior distributions. We here present a Bayesian prior for θ, introducing a hierarchical prior. In order to estimate the posterior distribution, we use a variational Bayes (VB) approximation [6,7].

We assume conjugate priors for τ and μ, and an ARD prior for W. They are parameterized by hyperparameter $\xi = (\xi \in \mathbb{R}, \alpha \in \mathbb{R}^{l \times 1})$. We also assume a hierarchical prior for the hyperparameter.[2]

$$
\begin{aligned}
p(\theta | \xi) &= p(\mu, W, \tau | \alpha, \xi) = p(\mu | \tau) p(\tau | \xi) \prod_{j=1}^{l} p(w_j | \tau, \alpha_j), \\
p(\mu | \tau) &= \mathcal{N}(\mu | \overline{\mu}_0, (\gamma_{\mu_0} \tau)^{-1} I_m), \; p(w_j | \tau, \alpha_j) = \mathcal{N}(w_j | 0, (\alpha_j \tau)^{-1} I_m), \\
p(\tau | \xi) &= \text{Ga}(\tau | \xi, \gamma_{\tau 0}), \; p(\xi) = \text{Ga}(\xi | \overline{\xi}_0, \gamma_{\xi 0}), \; p(\alpha) = \prod_{j=1}^{l} \text{Ga}(\alpha_j | \overline{\alpha}_0, \gamma_{\alpha 0}).
\end{aligned} \quad (3)
$$

---

[1] $\mathcal{N}(y | \mu, \Sigma)$ denotes a Gaussian density function of y, with center μ and covariance Σ. $\theta \stackrel{\text{def}}{=} (W \in \mathbb{R}^{m \times l}, \mu \in \mathbb{R}^{m \times 1}, \tau \in \mathbb{R})$ is a set of model parameters.

[2] $\text{Ga}(\tau | \overline{\tau}, \gamma_\tau)$ denotes a Gamma distribution with hyperparameters $\overline{\tau}$ and γ_τ: $\text{Ga}(\tau | \overline{\tau}, \gamma_\tau) \stackrel{\text{def}}{=} \frac{(\gamma_\tau \overline{\tau}^{-1})^{\gamma_\tau}}{\Gamma(\gamma_\tau)} \exp\left[-\gamma_\tau \overline{\tau}^{-1} \tau + (\gamma_\tau - 1) \ln \tau\right]$, where $\Gamma(\cdot)$ is a Gamma function.

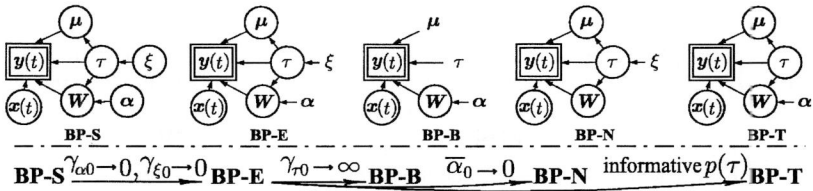

Fig. 1. Variations of BPCA and their relationship. Each circled node denotes a random variable. Each not-circled node denotes a hyperparameter which is determined by the type-II ML.

The variables used in the above prior, $\gamma_{\mu_0}, \overline{\mu}_0, \gamma_{\tau_0}, \gamma_{\xi_0}, \overline{\xi}_0, \gamma_{\alpha_0}$ and $\overline{\alpha}_0$, are constant hyperparameters that define the prior. Their actual values should be given before the estimation. Let **BP-S** denote an estimation using the prior (3) based on the standard hyperparameter setting:

$$\overline{\mu}_0 = \mathbf{0}, \ \gamma_{\mu_0} = \gamma_{\tau_0} = \gamma_{\alpha_0} = 10^{-10}, \ \gamma_{\xi_0} = \overline{\xi}_0 = \overline{\alpha}_0 = 1. \tag{4}$$

Here, we define variations of priors for BPCA (Fig. 1). **BP-E** assumes ξ and α are hyperparameters without their priors and they are determined by the type-II ML. **BP-B** assumes μ, τ and α are hyperparameters without their priors and they are determined by the type-II ML. **BP-B** is the same as that Bishop introduced in [2]. **BP-N** assumes $p(\boldsymbol{W})$ is a nearly uniform prior that is independent of α, which disables ARD effects. **BP-T** assumes $p(\tau)$ is an informative prior that reflects *a priori* knowledge on τ explicitly, and it is independent of ξ. Each of the variations can be obtained by an extreme setting of the constant hyperparameters in **BP-S** (Fig. 1, lower; details are discussed in section 3).

We first show a Bayes inference with a hierarchical prior (3). Random parameter $\boldsymbol{\theta}$, random hyperparameter $\boldsymbol{\xi}$, and hidden variable $X \stackrel{\text{def}}{=} \{\boldsymbol{x}(n) \in \mathbb{R}^l | n = 1, ..., N\}$ are estimated as a posterior $p(\boldsymbol{\theta}, \boldsymbol{\xi}, X | Y)$. According to the VB approximation, $p(\boldsymbol{\theta}, \boldsymbol{\xi}, X | Y)$ is approximated by a trial posterior $q(X, \boldsymbol{\theta}, \boldsymbol{\xi})$, in which independence among three constituents is assumed:

$$q(X, \boldsymbol{\theta}, \boldsymbol{\xi}) = q(X) q(\boldsymbol{\theta}) q(\boldsymbol{\xi}). \tag{5}$$

The lower bound of the log marginal likelihood is then given by

$$\ln p(Y) \geq \mathcal{F} \stackrel{\text{def}}{=} \langle \ln p(Y, X, \boldsymbol{\theta}, \boldsymbol{\xi}) \rangle_{X, \boldsymbol{\theta}, \boldsymbol{\xi}} - \langle \ln q(X, \boldsymbol{\theta}, \boldsymbol{\xi}) \rangle_{X, \boldsymbol{\theta}, \boldsymbol{\xi}} \tag{6}$$
$$= \langle \ln p(X, Y | \boldsymbol{\theta}) \rangle_{X, \boldsymbol{\theta}} + \langle \ln p(\boldsymbol{\theta} | \boldsymbol{\xi}) \rangle_{\boldsymbol{\theta}, \boldsymbol{\xi}} - \langle \ln q(\boldsymbol{\theta}) \rangle_{\boldsymbol{\theta}} + \langle \ln p(\boldsymbol{\xi}) \rangle_{\boldsymbol{\xi}} - \langle \ln q(\boldsymbol{\xi}) \rangle_{\boldsymbol{\xi}},$$

where $\langle f(\theta) \rangle_\theta \stackrel{\text{def}}{=} \int d\theta q(\theta) f(\theta)$ denotes an ensemble average of function $f(\theta)$ with respect to $q(\theta)$.[3] When $\mathcal{F}$ is maximized with respect to the trial posterior, the

---
[3] Similarly, $\langle f(\boldsymbol{\xi}) \rangle_{\boldsymbol{\xi}}$ and $\langle f(X) \rangle_X$ are defined.

trial posterior approaches the true posterior under the independence constraint (5), and $\mathcal{F}$ approaches the true log marginal likelihood from beneath.

From the variational conditions: $\delta\mathcal{F}/\delta q(X) = 0, \delta\mathcal{F}/\delta q(\theta) = 0$ and $\delta\mathcal{F}/\delta q(\xi) = 0$, the trial posterior is obtained as

$$q(X) = \prod_{n=1}^{N} q(\boldsymbol{x}(n)) = \prod_{n=1}^{N} \mathcal{N}(\boldsymbol{x}(n)|\overline{\boldsymbol{x}}(n), \overline{\boldsymbol{R}_x}), \quad q(\boldsymbol{\theta}) = q(\boldsymbol{\mu}|\tau)q(\boldsymbol{W}|\tau)q(\tau),$$
$$q(\boldsymbol{\mu}|\tau) = \mathcal{N}(\boldsymbol{\mu}|\overline{\boldsymbol{\mu}}, (\gamma_\mu \tau)^{-1}\mathbf{I}_m),$$
$$q(\boldsymbol{W}|\tau) = \exp\left[-\frac{1}{2}\tau \mathrm{Tr}\,(\boldsymbol{W} - \overline{\boldsymbol{W}})\Delta_{\boldsymbol{W}}(\boldsymbol{W} - \overline{\boldsymbol{W}})^\mathsf{T} + \frac{d}{2}\ln|\Delta_{\boldsymbol{W}}| + \frac{dl}{2}\ln(\tau/2\pi)\right],$$
$$q(\tau) = \mathrm{Ga}(\tau|\overline{\tau}, \gamma_\tau), \quad q(\xi) = \mathrm{Ga}(\xi|\overline{\xi}, \gamma_\xi), \quad q(\boldsymbol{\alpha}) = \prod_{j=1}^{l} \mathrm{Ga}(\alpha_j|\overline{\alpha}_j, \gamma_\alpha),$$

where $\overline{\boldsymbol{x}}(n), \overline{\boldsymbol{R}_x}, \overline{\boldsymbol{\mu}}, \gamma_\mu, \overline{\tau}, \gamma_\tau, \overline{\boldsymbol{W}}, \Delta_{\boldsymbol{W}}, \overline{\xi}, \gamma_\xi, \overline{\alpha}_j$ and γ_α are deterministic hyperparameters that determine the trial posterior. $\mathcal{F}$ is maximized with respect to the deterministic hyperparameters by using an EM-like iterative optimization algorithm [3], which results in a locally optimal trial posterior.

Using the trial posterior $q(\boldsymbol{\theta})$ after the convergence, the predictive distribution is given by $p_{\mathrm{pred}}(\boldsymbol{y}) = \int d\boldsymbol{\theta} d\boldsymbol{x} p(\boldsymbol{x}, \boldsymbol{y}|\boldsymbol{\theta})q(\boldsymbol{\theta})$. By integrating first over $\boldsymbol{\theta}$ and then over $\boldsymbol{x}$, the predictive distribution is calculated as

$$p_{\mathrm{pred}}(\boldsymbol{y}) = \int d\boldsymbol{x}\, \mathrm{St}_m\left(\boldsymbol{y} \mid \overline{\boldsymbol{W}}\boldsymbol{x} + \overline{\boldsymbol{\mu}}, \tilde{\tau}\mathbf{I}_m, 2\gamma_\tau\right) \mathcal{N}(\boldsymbol{x}|\mathbf{0}, \mathbf{I}_l), \quad (7)$$
$$\tilde{\tau} \stackrel{\mathrm{def}}{=} \overline{\tau}\left(1 + (1/\gamma_\mu) + \boldsymbol{x}^\mathsf{T}(\Delta_{\boldsymbol{W}})^{-1}\boldsymbol{x}\right)^{-1}.$$

$\mathrm{St}_k(\cdot)$ denotes a k-dimensional Student's t-distribution[4]. Note that the predictive distribution (7) is not a t-distribution. Using this result, the predictive covariance $\boldsymbol{C}_{\mathrm{pred}}$ of $p_{\mathrm{pred}}(\boldsymbol{y})$ is exactly obtained:

$$\boldsymbol{C}_{\mathrm{pred}} = \tau_B^{-1}\mathbf{I}_d + \overline{\boldsymbol{W}}\,\overline{\boldsymbol{W}}^\mathsf{T}, \quad \tau_B^{-1} \stackrel{\mathrm{def}}{=} \frac{\gamma_\tau}{\gamma_\tau - 1}\left(1 + \gamma_\mu^{-1} + \mathrm{Tr}\,(\Delta_{\boldsymbol{W}}^{-1})\right)\overline{\tau}^{-1}. \quad (8)$$

Since $q(\xi)$ does not appear in the calculation of the predictive distribution, the above result holds even when a hierarchical prior is not used.

From $\boldsymbol{C}_{\mathrm{pred}}$, we find that the reconstructed eigenvalues are given by

$$\overline{\lambda}_j = \begin{cases} \overline{\boldsymbol{w}}_j{}^\mathsf{T}\overline{\boldsymbol{w}}_j + \tau_B^{-1} & (1 \leq j \leq l) \\ \tau_B^{-1} & (l < j \leq m) \end{cases}, \quad (9)$$

where $\overline{\boldsymbol{w}}_j$ is the jth column vector of $\overline{\boldsymbol{W}}$.

2.3 Generalization Ability

In order to compare BPCA variations, we prepare a gene expression data set D_{org} consisting of 758 genes × 50 samples [3]. Note that D_{org} does not necessarily

---

[4] $\mathrm{St}_k(\boldsymbol{x}|\boldsymbol{\mu}, \boldsymbol{S}, \gamma) \stackrel{\mathrm{def}}{=} \frac{\Gamma((\gamma+k)/2)|\boldsymbol{S}|^{1/2}}{\Gamma(\gamma/2)(\gamma\pi)^{k/2}}\left[1 + \frac{1}{\gamma}(\boldsymbol{x} - \boldsymbol{\mu})^\mathsf{T}\boldsymbol{S}(\boldsymbol{x} - \boldsymbol{\mu})\right]^{\frac{\gamma+k}{2}}$.

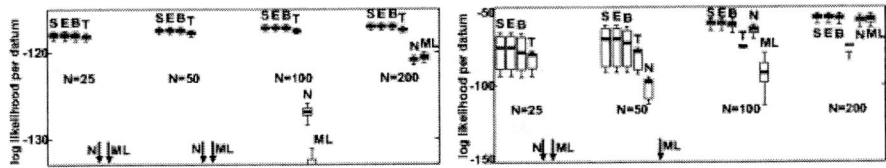

Fig. 2. Generalization ability of BPCA variations and ML. Left: Gaussian data (D_{gauss}). Right: original data (D_{org}). Each bar denotes 5, 25, 50, 75 or 95 percentile in 100 trials.

obey a Gaussian distribution. We also prepare another data set D_{gauss} generated from a mean zero Gaussian with covariance S of the data set D_{org}.

Figure 2 shows comparison of the generalization ability of BPCA variations and ML. Parameters are estimated by using N points randomly selected from the data set, and the generalization ability is evaluated by using other 500 points. For **BP-T**, we set $\gamma_{\tau 0}$ and $\bar{\tau}_0$ such that τ_{MAX} (see Eq.(15)) becomes 10^0.

BP-S and **BP-E** exhibit the best performance in average. ML is bad especially when the data number is small. When the data number becomes large, the difference among the variations becomes small. **BP-B** is a little inferior to **BP-S**. Since the difference between **BP-B** and **BP-S** is mainly in the predictive distribution, the improvement by **BP-S** is owing to the fully Bayesian predictive distribution. **BP-N** is much worse than **BP-S**, indicating that the ARD effects are important for the generalization ability. **BP-T** is not good implying that the informative prior for τ is harmful for the generalization ability.

3 Analytic Comparison among BPCA Variations

In order to examine the roles of BPCA hyperparameters, we introduce a simplified situation. Assume y is normalized so that the mean is $\mathbf{0}$ and hyperparameter $\overline{\mu}$ is fixed at $\mathbf{0}$. Assume also that eigenvalues λ_i and eigenvectors u_i of the covariance are known. Since eigenvalues and eigenvectors are known, each single datum is not necessary any more and only the data number N is used for the estimation. In this case, each column vector in $\overline{W}$ has a form $\overline{w}_j \stackrel{\text{def}}{=} w_j u_j$, where a factor w_j is unknown. Under these assumptions, matrices $\overline{R}_x$ and Δ_W become diagonal: $r_j \stackrel{\text{def}}{=} [\overline{R}_x]_{jj}$ and $\Delta_j \stackrel{\text{def}}{=} [\Delta_W]_{jj}$. The VB algorithm then becomes as simple as follows.
1. Some deterministic hyperparameters are obtained without any iterative procedure.

$\overline{\mu} = \mathbf{0}, \gamma_\tau = \frac{mN}{2} + \gamma_{\tau 0}, \gamma_\mu = N + \gamma_{\mu 0}, \gamma_\xi = \gamma_{\tau 0} + \gamma_{\xi 0}, \gamma_\alpha = \frac{m}{2} + \gamma_{\alpha 0}, \operatorname{Tr} S = \sum_{i=1}^m \lambda_i.$

2. Repeat the followings until convergence.

$t_j \leftarrow \overline{\tau} \lambda_j w_j / r_j, \quad \Delta_j \leftarrow (1/r_j) + \overline{\tau} w_j t_j / r_j + \overline{\alpha}_j / N, \quad w_j \leftarrow t_j / \Delta_j,$

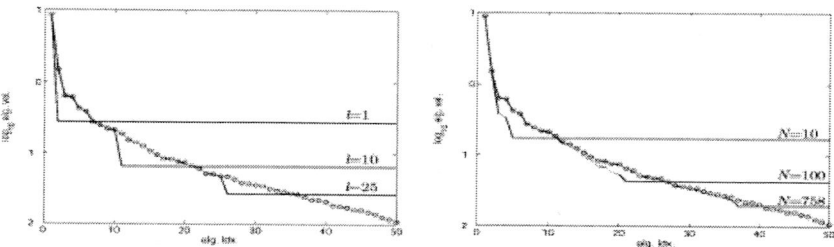

Fig. 3. Horizontal and vertical axes denote eigenvalue indices and $\log_{10}$ of eigenvalues, respectively. Lines denote reconstructed spectrums.

$$\bar{\tau}^{-1} \leftarrow \gamma_\tau^{-1}\left\{\frac{N}{2}(\text{Tr}\, S - \sum_{j=1}^l t_j w_j) + \gamma_{\tau 0}\bar{\xi}\right\}, \tag{10}$$

$$\bar{\xi}^{-1} \leftarrow \gamma_\xi^{-1}(\gamma_{\tau 0}\bar{\tau} + \gamma_{\xi 0}/\bar{\xi}_0), \tag{11}$$

$$r_j \leftarrow 1 + \bar{\tau}w_j^2 + (m/N)\Delta_j^{-1}, \tag{12}$$

$$\bar{\alpha}_j^{-1} \leftarrow \gamma_\alpha^{-1}\left\{\frac{1}{2}(\bar{\tau}w_j^2 + (m/N)\Delta_j^{-1}) + \gamma_{\alpha 0}/\bar{\alpha}_0\right\}. \tag{13}$$

3.1 Comparison between ML and VB

Figure 3(left) shows spectrums of reconstructed eigenvalues in ML, given by (2), for three l values. This ML estimation is equivalent to usual PCA ('o' marks), for component indices from 1 to l. It is also equivalent to the infinite limit of the data number in **BP-S**. On the other hand, **BP-S**'s results depend on the data number N. Figure 3(right) shows Bayesian reconstructed spectrums, given by (9), for three N values. In **BP-S**, l is set at the maximum value $m-1$ at the beginning of the estimation, and is automatically controlled by ARD.

The effect of ARD depends on the data number N; when N is small, a large number of minor eigenvalues shrink to the same value. Eigenvalues that do not shrink also become smaller than their original values.

3.2 Controlling $p(\alpha)$ and ARD

In **BP-B**, which first introduced ARD to PPCA [2], the prior of W depended on α and hyperparameters α, τ and μ were determined by the type-II ML. Faul et al. studied analytically the marginal likelihood as a function of α [8]. When w_i shrinks to zero due to the ARD effect, the marginal likelihood increases monotonically as a function of α_i and converges as $\alpha_i \to \infty$. Although they dealt with a relevance vector machine, their theoretical result holds also in **BP-B**. On the other hand, **BP-S** assumes α as a random variable with a Gamma prior $p(\alpha)$. Then, there is an upper bound of $\bar{\alpha}$:

$$\alpha_{\text{MAX}} = \bar{\alpha}_0(d/2 + \gamma_{\alpha 0})/\gamma_{\alpha 0}, \tag{14}$$

which can be confirmed from the update rule (13).

We consider two special cases for the hyperparameters in $p(\alpha)$.

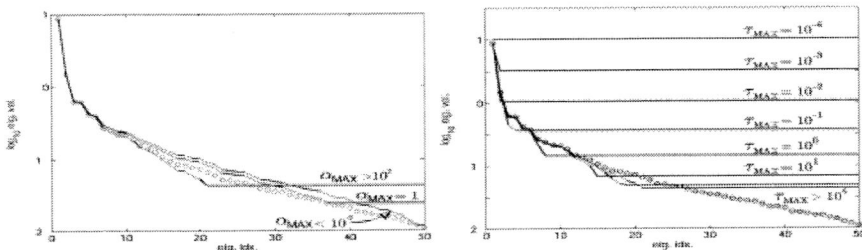

Fig. 4. Left figure shows the relationship between α_{MAX} and reconstructed spectrums. Right figure shows the relationship between τ_{MAX} and reconstructed spectrums. In both figures, unspecified parameters are set at their default values (4) and $N = 100$.

Non-informative limit of α. When $\gamma_{\alpha_0} \to 0$, $\overline{\alpha}$ is obtained from the update rule (13) as $\overline{\alpha}_j^{-1} \leftarrow \frac{1}{m}(\overline{\tau} w_j^2 + (m/N)\Delta_j^{-1})$, which is independent of $\overline{\alpha}_0$. This estimation for $\overline{\alpha}$ is equivalent to that by the type-II ML used in **BP-B** and **BP-E**.

ARD disabled limit. When $\gamma_{\alpha_0} \ll \infty$ and $\overline{\alpha}_0 \to 0$, $p(\boldsymbol{W}|\boldsymbol{\alpha})$ becomes a uniform prior. In this case, ARD is inhibited completely, which is equivalent to **BP-N**.

In order to see variations among the two special cases above, reconstructed spectrums with various γ_{α_0} and $\overline{\alpha}_0$ values are shown in Figure 4 (left). It is found that the spectrum depends only on α_{MAX} in the area $\gamma_{\alpha_0} < 1$. When $\alpha_{\text{MAX}} \to \infty$, i.e., the non-informative limit, the spectrum is almost the same as that in **BP-S**. When $\alpha_{\text{MAX}} \to 0$, the eigenvalues are a little larger than those in ML; this is equivalent to **BP-N**. A medium value, e.g., $\alpha_{\text{MAX}} = 1.0$, results in a spectrum within those of the two extremes.

3.3 $p(\tau)$ and ARD Control

Effect of the hierarchical prior. In **BP-S**, the prior for τ is defined by a parametric prior $p(\tau|\xi)$ and a hyper-prior $p(\xi)$. When $\gamma_{\xi_0} \to \infty$, $\overline{\xi}$ becomes a constant at $\overline{\xi}_0$ and $p(\tau|\xi)$ is equivalent to a Gamma prior $p(\tau) = \text{Ga}(\tau|\overline{\tau}_0, \gamma_{\tau_0})$ with the mean $\overline{\tau}_0 \stackrel{\text{def}}{=} \overline{\xi}_0^{-1}$. This is equivalent to **BP-T**. In this case, $\overline{\tau}$ has its upper bound:

$$\tau_{\text{MAX}} = \gamma_\tau / (\gamma_{\tau_0} \overline{\xi}) = (Nm/2 + \gamma_{\tau_0})/(\gamma_{\tau_0} \overline{\xi}_0). \tag{15}$$

Figure 4(right) shows reconstructed spectrums with various values of prior hyperparameters γ_{τ_0} and $\overline{\xi}_0$. It is found that the spectrum depends only on $\overline{\tau}_{\text{MAX}}$. When $\overline{\tau}_{\text{MAX}} > 10^4$, the spectrum is almost the same as that in **BP-S**. When $\overline{\tau}_{\text{MAX}} \to 0$, the eigenvalues diverge to infinity.

By using a hierachical prior with $\gamma_{\xi_0} \ll \infty$, the reconstructed spectrums are almost the same as that in **BP-S**, even when $\gamma_{\tau_0}, \gamma_{\xi_0}$ and $\overline{\xi}_0$ vary within from

10^{-5} to 10^5. Accordingly, the hierarchical setting in the form of $p(\tau|\xi)p(\xi)$ is robust with respect to $p(\xi)$. This robustness validates the type-II ML estimation of hyperparameters in **BP-E**.

Figure 4(right) shows that the ARD effect is strong when τ_{MAX} is small, implying that τ_{MAX} can be set small when sparse representation is required due to, for example, the constraint of computation cost.

Non-informative limit of $p(\tau)$. When $\gamma_{\xi_0} = 0$, $\overline{\xi}$ is obtained as $\overline{\tau}^{-1}$ from the update rule (11), which is independent of $\overline{\xi}_0$. The update rule of $\overline{\tau}$, (10), becomes $\overline{\tau}^{-1} \leftarrow \gamma_\tau^{-1}\{\frac{N}{2}(\text{Tr }\boldsymbol{S} - \sum_{j=1}^{l} t_j w_j) + \gamma_{\tau_0}\overline{\tau}^{-1}\}$. Since $\gamma_\tau = N/2 + \gamma_{\tau_0}$ holds, the solution of the update rule converges to $\overline{\tau}^{-1} = \text{Tr }\boldsymbol{S} - \sum_{j=1}^{l} t_j w_j$, which is independent of the prior. This update rule of $\overline{\tau}$ is the same as those in **BP-B** and **BP-E**. Concerning the predictive distribution, this limit is identical to **BP-E**, but different from **BP-B** due to the remaining finite variance $\overline{\tau}^2/\gamma_\tau$ of the posterior $q(\tau)$. This situation is different from the non-informative limit of $p(\boldsymbol{\alpha})$.

4 Conclusion

We examined prior variations for BPCA and found the following results. (a) **BP-S** was better than **BP-B**, i.e., by regarding τ as a random variable, the generalization ability is improved. (b) The performance of **BP-S** is robust with respect to variety in hyper-priors $p(\boldsymbol{\alpha})$ and $p(\xi)$. There is no significant disadvantage in performance when $\boldsymbol{\alpha}$ and ξ are determined simply by the type-II ML, like in **BP-E**. (c) τ_{MAX} or α_{MAX} controls the strength of the ARD effect. However, the generalization ability degrades if ARD is disabled.

Acknowledgement. The second author is supported in part by the Telecommunications Advancement Organization of Japan.

References

1. M. E. Tipping and C. M. Bishop: "Mixtures of probabilistic principal component analysers", Neural Computation, **11**, pp. 443–482 (1999).
2. C. M. Bishop: "Bayesian PCA", Proceedings of Advances in Neural Information Processing Systems, Vol. 11, pp. 509–514 (1999).
3. S. Oba, M. Sato, I. Takemasa, M. Monden, K. Matsubara and S. Ishii: "Missing value estimation using mixture of PCAs", International Conference on Artificial Neural Networks (ICANN2002), Vol. LNCS2415, Springer-Verlag, New York, NY, pp. 492–497 (2002).
4. S. Oba, M. Sato and S. Ishii: "Variational bayes method for mixture of principal component analyzers", 7th International Conference on Neural Information Processing (ICONIP2000), Vol. 2, pp. 1416–1421 (2000).
5. M. E. Tipping: "Sparse kernel principal component analysis", Advances in Neural Information Processing Systems, Vol. 13, MIT Press (2001).

6. H. Attias: "Inferring parameters and structure of latent variable models by variational bayes", Proceedings of Uncertainty in Artificial Intelligence, pp. 21–30 (1999).
7. M. Sato: "On-Line Model Selection Based on the Variational Bayes", Neural Computation, Vol. 13, pp. 1649–1681 (2001).
8. A. C. Faul and M. E. Tipping: "Analysis of sparse bayesian learning', T. G. Dietterich, S. Becker, and Z. Ghahramani (Eds.), Advances in Neural Information Processing Systems, pp. 383–389 (2002).

Relevance and Kernel Self-Organising Maps

Emilio Corchado and Colin Fyfe

School of Information and Communication Technologies,
The University of Paisley,
Scotland.

Abstract. We review the recently proposed method of Kernel Self-organising maps (KSOM) which has been shown to exhibit very fast convergence. We show that this is due to an interaction between the fact that we are working in an overcomplete basis and the fact that we are using a mixture of one-shot and incremental learning. We then review Relevance Vector Machines which is a supervised training method related to Support Vector Machines and apply it to creating the Relevance Self-Organising Map, RSOM. We show results on artificial data and on the iris data set.

1 Introduction

Kernel methods were introduced in the context of supervised learning and Support Vector Machines. [4] extended their use to unsupervised methods. We [1] have recently developed a method of creating a Self-organising Feature Map in Feature space using these methods. The concept of Relevance Vectors was introduced by Tipping [6] in acknowledgement of McKay and Neal's contribution to the concept of Automatic Relevance Detection (ARD). The vectors found by the RVM method are prototypical vectors of the class types which is a very different concept from the Support Vectors whose positions are always at the edges of clusters, thereby helping to delimit one cluster from another.

In this paper, we first review the Kernel SOM and show that its speed of convergence is due to an interaction between the overcomplete basis in which it works and the mixed learning methods which it employs. We then review Relevance Vector Regression and apply the concepts from this to create a new method of performing topology preserving mappings in feature space. We illustrate the mapping found on artificial data and then show the sparse representation found on the well-known iris data set.

2 Kernel K-Means Clustering

Kernel methods [4] are based on a mapping of the input data space onto a Kernel or Feature space; generally the mapping is nonlinear and the expectation is that, when we perform a linear operation in Kernel space, we are equivalently performing a nonlinear operation in the original data space. We will follow the derivation of [3] who have shown that the k means algorithm can be performed in Kernel space. The aim is to find k means, $\mathbf{m}_\mu$ so that each point is close to one of the means. Now as with KPCA, each mean may be described as lying in the manifold spanned by the observations, $\phi(\mathbf{x}_i)$ i.e. $\mathbf{m}_\mu = \sum_i w_{\mu i} \phi(\mathbf{x}_i)$. Now the k means algorithm choses the means, $\mathbf{m}_\mu$, to minimise the Euclidean distance between the points and the closest mean

$$||\phi(\mathbf{x}) - \mathbf{m}_\mu||^2 = ||\phi(\mathbf{x}) - \sum_i w_{\mu i} \phi(\mathbf{x}_i)||^2$$

$$= k(\mathbf{x}, \mathbf{x}) - 2 \sum_i w_{\mu i} k(\mathbf{x}, \mathbf{x}_i) + \sum_{i,j} w_{\mu i} w_{\mu j} k(\mathbf{x}_i, \mathbf{x}_j)$$

i.e. the distance calculation can be accompised in Kernel space by means of the K matrix alone.

Let $M_{i\mu}$ be the cluster assignment variable. i.e. $M_{i\mu} = 1$ if $\phi(\mathbf{x}_i)$ is in the μth cluster and is 0 otherwise. [4] initialise the means to the first training patterns and then each new training point, $\phi(\mathbf{x}_{t+1}), t+1 > k$, is assigned to the closest mean and its cluster assignment variable calculated using

$$M_{t+1,\alpha} = \begin{cases} 1 & \text{if } ||\phi(\mathbf{x}_{t+1}) - \mathbf{m}_\alpha|| < ||\phi(\mathbf{x}_{t+1}) - \mathbf{m}_\mu||, \forall \mu \neq \alpha \\ 0 & \text{otherwise} \end{cases} \quad (1)$$

In terms of the kernel function (noting that $k(\mathbf{x}, \mathbf{x})$ is common to all calculations) we have

$$M_{t+1,\alpha} = \begin{cases} 1 & \text{if } \sum_{i,j} w_{\alpha i} w_{\alpha j} k(\mathbf{x}_i, \mathbf{x}_j) - 2 \sum_i w_{\alpha i} k(\mathbf{x}, \mathbf{x}_i) \\ & < \sum_{i,j} w_{\mu i} w_{\mu j} k(\mathbf{x}_i, \mathbf{x}_j) - 2 \sum_i w_{\mu i} k(\mathbf{x}, \mathbf{x}_i), \forall \mu \neq \alpha \\ 0 & \text{otherwise} \end{cases} \quad (2)$$

We must then update the mean, $\mathbf{m}_\alpha$ to take account of the $(t+1)^{th}$ data point

$$\mathbf{m}_\alpha^{t+1} = \mathbf{m}_\alpha^t + \zeta(\phi(\mathbf{x}_{t+1}) - \mathbf{m}_\alpha^t) \quad (3)$$

where we have used the term $\mathbf{m}_\alpha^{t+1}$ to designate the updated mean which takes into account the new data point and

$$\zeta = \frac{M_{t+1,\alpha}}{\sum_{i=1}^{t+1} M_{i,\alpha}} \quad (4)$$

Now (3) may be written as

$$\sum_i w_{\alpha i}^{t+1} \phi(\mathbf{x}_i) = \sum_i w_{\alpha i}^t \phi(\mathbf{x}_i) + \zeta(\phi(\mathbf{x}_{t+1}) - \sum_i w_{\alpha i}^t \phi(\mathbf{x}_i))$$

which leads to an update equation of

$$w_{\alpha i}^{t+1} = \begin{cases} w_{\alpha i}^t (1 - \zeta) & \text{for } i \neq t+1 \\ \zeta & \text{for } i = t+1 \end{cases} \quad (5)$$

2.1 The Kernel Self Organising Map, KSOM

We have previously used the above analysis to derive a Self Organising Map [1] in Kernel space. The SOM algorithm is a k means algorithm with an attempt to distribute the means in an organised manner and so the first change to the above algorithm is to update the closest neuron's weights and those of its neighbours. Thus we find the winning neuron (the closest in feature space) as above but now instead of (2), we use

$$M_{t+1,\mu} = \Lambda(\alpha, \mu), \forall \mu \quad (6)$$

where α is the identifier of the closest neuron and $\Lambda(\alpha, \mu)$ is a neighbourhood function which in the experiments reported herein was a gaussian. Thus the winning neuron has a value of M=1 while the value of M for other neurons decreases monotonically with distance (in neuron space) away from the winning neuron. For the experiments reported in this paper, we used a one dimensional vector of output neurons numbered 1 to 20 or 30. The remainder of the algorithm is exactly as reported in the previous section. However there may appear to be a difficulty with this: the SOM requires a great number of iterations for convergence and since $\zeta = \frac{M_{t+1,\alpha}}{\sum_{i=1}^{t+1} M_{i,\alpha}}$, this leads naturally to $\zeta \to 0$ over time. In fact, since the method learns so quickly, we only need one pass through the data set for convergence. If we wish to use more, we may initially select a number of centres, k and train the centres with one pass through the data set in a random order. We then have a partially ordered set of centres. We now reset all values of $M_{i,\alpha}$ to zero and perform a second pass through the data set, typically also decreasing the width of the neighbourhood function as with the normal Kohonen SOM.

However this algorithm typically uses all data points in constructing the map. In this paper, we will use the concepts from the Relevance Vector Machine to achieve a sparse representation of the map.

2.2 The Linear Map

In this section we will consider the linear Kernel SOM in order to investigate its very fast convergence. Note that the learning

$$w_{\alpha i}^{t+1} = \begin{cases} \zeta & \text{for } i = t+1 \\ w_{\alpha i}^{t}(1-\zeta) & \text{for } i \neq t+1 \end{cases} \quad (7)$$

has two modes:

1. The first mode is one shot learning for the current input; the weights from all outputs to the current input are set to the exponential of the negative squared distance in output space of the output neurons from the winning neuron.
2. The second mode is decay from the values set in the first mode; note that we need only consider this decay subsequent to the one shot learning because the one shot learning removes any previously learned values and the algorithm ensures that each node is selected exactly once for the one shot learning.

The second thing to emphasise is that while we are working in the space of input variables we are using an unusual basis in treating every data point as the end point of a basis vector. This will typically give us a very overcomplete representation.

Let the first time neuron α wins a competition be the competition for the ith input, $\mathbf{x}_i$. Then the weight $w_{\alpha i}$ is set to $\frac{e^0}{e^0} = 1$ where the denominator is the history to date of its winnings to date. For the time being, we will ignore the interaction with other neurons in the environment of α. Let the neuron c now win the competition for the input, $\mathbf{x}_j$. Then the weight $w_{\alpha j}$ is set to $\frac{e^0}{\sum_{i,j} e^0} = \frac{1}{2}$. Also the weight $w_{\alpha i}$ decays to $w_{\alpha i} * (1 - \frac{1}{2})$, so that now the neuron's centre is the mean of the two data points for which it has won the competition. Similarly if the same neuron wins the competition to represent $\mathbf{x}_k$, the weight $w_{\alpha k}$ is set to $\frac{e^0}{\sum_{i,j,k} e^0} = \frac{1}{3}$, and the weights $w_{\alpha i}$ and $w_{\alpha j}$ decay to $\frac{1}{3}$, which again means the centre of the neuron is the mean of the three data points for which it has won the competition. A recursive argument shows that this will always be the case.

Now consider the effect of these three competitions on a neuron, μ in the neighbourhood of α. When neuron α wins the competition for the ith input, $\mathbf{x}_i$, the weight, $w_{\mu i}$ is set to $\frac{\Lambda(\alpha,\mu)}{\Lambda(\alpha,\mu)} = 1$. When neuron α wins the competition for the input, $\mathbf{x}_j$, the weight, $w_{\mu j}$ is set to $\frac{\Lambda(\alpha,\mu)}{\sum_{i,j} \Lambda(\alpha,\mu)} = \frac{1}{2}$ and the weight $w_{\mu i}$ decays to $\frac{1}{2}$. Note the strength of the effect of the neighbourhood function which explains the strong grouping effect of the method.

Thus initially all neurons will respond to the first inputs met during training. But the above argument ignores the interaction between different responses. Consider the effect on neuron α's weight vector when neuron μ wins the competition for the lth, input, $\mathbf{x}_l$. Now

$$\zeta_\mu = \frac{\Lambda(\mu,\alpha)}{\Lambda(\mu,\alpha) + \sum_{i,j,k} e^0} = \frac{\Lambda(\mu,\alpha)}{\Lambda(\mu,\alpha) + 3} \tag{8}$$

where we have used ζ_μ to designate that part of the ζ vector devoted to μ. For μ sufficiently far from α, this will be rather small and both of the learning effects will be negligible as a response to this input. Note that quite the opposite effect happens at μ and vectors close to it. Their previous history has given very small values of $\sum \Lambda(\alpha,\mu)$ and so now a value of $\Lambda(\mu,\mu) = 1$ will easily dominate the learning of these neurons and a type of phase change will take place as these neurons respond to a new input region due to the one-shot learning.

3 Relevance Vector Regression

Relevance Vector Regression uses a dataset of input-target pairs $\{\mathbf{x}_i, t_i\}_{i=1}^{N}$. It assumes that the machine can form an output y from

$$y(\mathbf{x}) = \sum_{i=1}^{N} w_i K(\mathbf{x}, \mathbf{x}_i) + w_0 \qquad (9)$$

and $p(t|\mathbf{x})$ is Gaussian $N(y(\mathbf{x}), \sigma^2)$. The likelihood of the model is given by

$$p(\mathbf{t}|\mathbf{w}, \sigma) = \frac{1}{(2\pi\sigma^2)^{-\frac{N}{2}}} \exp\{-\frac{1}{2\sigma^2}||\mathbf{t} - K\mathbf{w}||^2\} \qquad (10)$$

where $\mathbf{t} = \{t_1, t_2, ..., t_N\}$, $\mathbf{w} = \{w_0, w_1, ..., w_N\}$, and K is the $N*(N+1)$ design matrix. To prevent overfitting, an ARD prior is set over the weights

$$p(\mathbf{w}|\alpha) = \prod_{i=0}^{N} N(0, \alpha^{-1}) \qquad (11)$$

To find the maximum likelihood of the data set with respect to α and σ^2, we iterate between finding the mean and variance of the weight vector and then calculating new values for α and σ^2 using these statistics. We find that many of the α_i tend to infinity which means that the corresponding weights tend to 0. In detail, we have that the posterior of the weights is given by

$$p(\mathbf{w}|\mathbf{t}, \alpha, \sigma^2) \propto |\Sigma|^{-\frac{1}{2}} \exp\{-\frac{1}{2}(\mathbf{w} - \mu)^T \Sigma^{-1}(\mathbf{w} - \mu)\} \qquad (12)$$

where

$$\Sigma = (K^T B K + A)^{-1}$$
$$\mu = \Sigma K^T B \mathbf{t} \qquad (13)$$

with $A = diag(\alpha_0, \alpha_1, ..., \alpha_N)$ and $B = \sigma^{-2} I_N$.

If we integrate out the weights, we obtain the marginal likelihood

$$p(\mathbf{t}|\alpha, \sigma^2) \propto |B^{-1} + KA^{-1}K^T|^{-\frac{1}{2}} \exp\{-\frac{1}{2}\mathbf{t}^T (B^{-1} + KA^{-1}K^T)^{-1}\mathbf{t}\} \qquad (14)$$

which can be differentiated to give at the optimum,

$$\alpha_i^{new} = \frac{\gamma_i}{\mu_i^2} \qquad (15)$$

$$(\sigma^2)^{new} = \frac{||\mathbf{t} - K\mu||^2}{(N - \sum_i \gamma_i)} \qquad (16)$$

where $\gamma_i = 1 - \alpha_i \Sigma_{ii}$.

3.1 The Relevance Self-Organising Map, RSOM

To create a sparse SOM, we use the KSOM algorithm as above but, having selected the winner, use the neighbourhood function values as the target values, **t**, for that data point in (13). The algorithm iterates between using the current values of the weights to find the winning centres and then using the neighbourhood functions determined by the winning centres to update the means and variances of the weights at which point the new maximum likelihood value of the weights will be chosen.

The algorithm is rather similar in operation to that suggested by [5] in that it iterates between two phases

Phase 1. In this phase, the Kernel SOM method of Section 2.1 is used to find the centres closest to the current data point and to update the parameters which define these centres, $\gamma_{\mu i}$. We also in this phase, take note of the neighbourhood function values *for each data point*.

Phase 2. Now we use these neighbourhood values for each data point as targets which we use exactly as they are in the Relevance Vector Method. We iterate through each centre of the SOM in turn, updating all $\gamma_{\mu i}$ using the RVM method as before. The updating of the $\gamma_{\mu i}$ in this part of the method uses the neighbourhood values as targets **t** in (13) and (16).

Since the algorithm cuts down the number of data points determining a manifold, it will also have a regularisation effect which was the effect of amending the quantisation functional in [5].

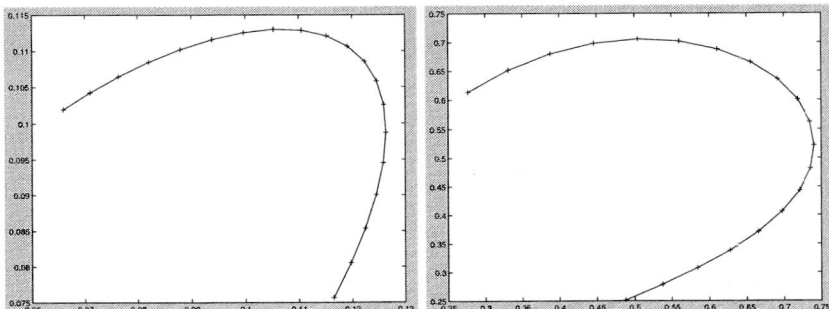

Fig. 1. The left diagram shows the converged weights after 3 iterations of the KSOM algorithm. The right diagram shows the converged weights after 3 iterations of the RSOM algorithm.

4 Simulation

We perform a simulation on the standard data set for topology preserving mappings - points are drawn iid from the unit square in two dimensions. This data

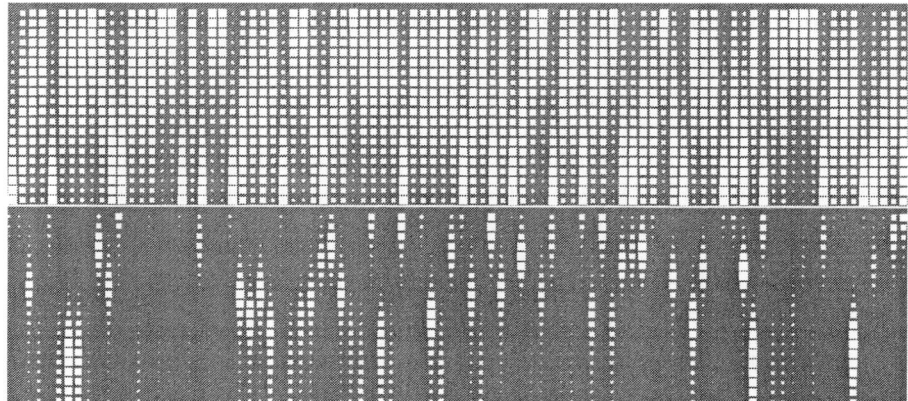

Fig. 2. The top diagram is a Hinton map of the converged weights of the KSOM algrorithm. It is 90 (the number of data points) by 20 (the number of centres). We see that nearly every centre uses quite a few data points. The bottom diagram shows the same map for the RSOM; we see that it is a much sparser representation.

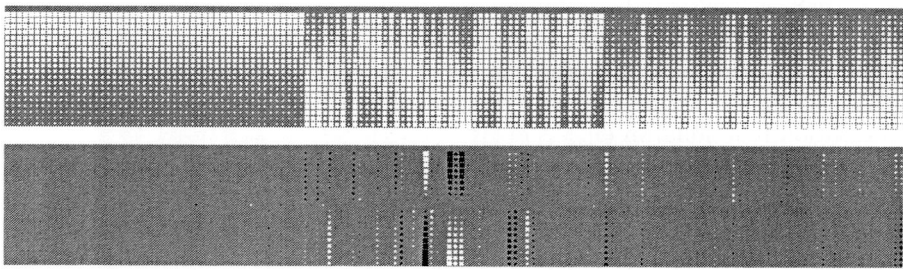

Fig. 3. The top diagram shows the weights in data space of the KSOM algorithm after 1 pass through the data. The figure is 150 (the number of data points) by 20 (the number of centres). The bottom diagram shows the corresponding weights from the RSOM. We see that the weights are much sparser, particularly so for the first and third types of iris.

set is chosen since it is very easy to interpret the results. We randomly select 90 points from the unit square $[0,1)^2$ and use the linear KSOM and linear RSOM algorithm for only 3 iterations. In Figure 1, we have mapped the centres back into data space. The left diagram shows the converged weights after 3 iterations of the KSOM algorithm. The right diagram shows the converged weights after 3 iterations of the RSOM algorithm. In Figure 2 we show the contribution of each data point to the position of the centre; clearly the RSOM centres are much sparser.

We now apply the method to the well known iris data set [2]. The resulting weight vectors are shown in Figure 3: the top diagram is the set of weights found by the linear KSOM algorithm after 1 iteration while the bottom weights are those from the linear RSOM after 1 iteration. We see that the first type of iris is categorised using very few data points by the RSOM and very few centres. The third type of iris requires more data points to categorise it but still less than the second data type though this still rather fewer than used by the KSOM.

5 Conclusion

We have reviewed the Kernel Self-organising Map and shown that its fast convergence is due to an interaction between the fact that we are working in an overcomplete basis and the two learning methods employed. Using the methods of Relevance Vectors, we have derived a new SOM in feature space which we have called the Relevance Self Organising Map (RSOM) and which has the property that it is extremely sparse in the data points which it uses.

Now a regression which has a sparse representation in terms of the data points by which it is defined is liable to be rather better at generalisation. Similarly, it is reasonable to suggest that a quantisation like the SOM may be better if it is built on a smaller number of data points. Future work will investigate this feature.

References

1. D. MacDonald and C. Fyfe. The kernel self-organising map. In R.J. Howlett and L. C. Jain, editors, *Fourth International Conference on Knowledge-based Intelligent Engineering Systems and Allied Technologies, KES2000*, 2000.
2. D. Michie, D. J. Spiegelhalter, and C. C. Taylor, editors. *Machine learning, neural and statistical classification*. Ellis Horwood, 1994.
3. B. Schölkopf. The kernel trick for distances. Technical report, Microsoft Research, May 2000.
4. B. Schölkopf, A. Smola, and K.-R. Muller. Nonlinear component analysis as a kernel eigenvalue problem. *Neural Computation*, 10:1299–1319, 1998.
5. A. J. Smola, S. Mika, B. Schölkopf, and R. C. Williamson. Regularized principal maniforlds. *Machine Learning*, pages 1–28, 2000.
6. M. Tipping. The relevance vector machine. In S. A. Solla, T. K. Leen and K.-R. Muller, editors, *Advances in Neural Information Processing Systems, 12*. MIT Press, 2000.

Pattern Recognition

Hierarchical Bayesian Network for Handwritten Digit Recognition

JaeMo Sung and Sung-Yang Bang

Department of Computer Science and Engineering,
Pohang University of Science and Technology,
San 31, Hyoja-Dong, Nam-Gu, Pohang, 790-784, Korea
{emtidi, sybang}@postech.ac.kr

Abstract. This paper introduces a hierarchical Gabor features(HGFs) and hierarchical bayesian network(HBN) for handwritten digit recognition. The HGFs represent a different level of information which is structured such that the higher the level, the more global information they represent, and the lower the level, the more localized information they represent. The HGFs are extracted by the Gabor filters selected using a discriminant measure. The HBN is a statistical model to represent a joint probability which encodes hierarchical dependencies among the HGFs. We simulated our method about a handwritten digit data set for recognition and compared it with the naive bayesian classifier, the backpropagation neural network and the k-nearest neighbor classifier. The efficiency of our proposed method was shown in that our method outperformed all other methods in the experiments.

1 Introduction

We believe that human beings exploit structured information rather than non-structured information and use the relations among the structured information by some mechanism for recognition. We assume that this structured information is hierarchical and that the relations are limited by hierarchical dependencies. With above assumption, we propose a hierarchical Gabor features(HGFs) and hierarchical bayesian network(HBN) for a recognition mechanism.

2 Hierarchical Gabor Features Extraction

2.1 Gabor Filter

The Gabor filter which is represented in the spatial-frequency domain is defined as

$$G(x,y,\omega_0,\sigma,r,\theta) = \frac{1}{\sqrt{\pi r \sigma}} e^{-\frac{1}{2}\left[\frac{(rR_1)^2 + R_2^2}{(r\sigma)^2}\right]} e^{i\omega_0 R_1}, \tag{1}$$

where $R_1 = x\cos\theta + y\sin\theta$, $R_2 = -x\sin\theta + y\cos\theta$, ω_0 is the radial frequency in radians per unit length, θ is the orientation in radians and σ is the standard

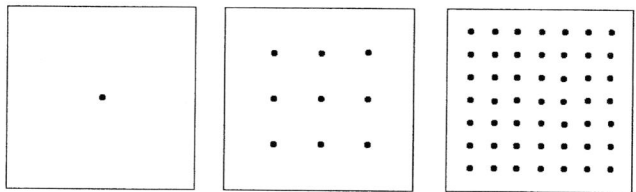

Fig. 1. Sampling points of each level, with level, 1, 2, 3 from left to right

deviation of the elliptical gaussian envelope along the x axes. The Gabor filter is centered at $(x = 0, y = 0)$ in the spatial domain. Also, the elliptical gaussian envelope of the Gabor filter has the aspect ratio $\sigma_y/\sigma_x = r$ and the plane wave's propagating direction along the short axis, where σ_x, σ_y are the standard deviations of elliptical gaussian envelope along the x, y axes[1].

2.2 Hierarchical Gabor Features Extraction

To structure features hierarchically, the features must be able to represent different level information such that the features in the higher level represent more global information and the features in the lower level represent more localized information. First, the Gabor filter banks whose Gabor filters can represent the global or the localized information are defined. Next, the optimal Gabor filters are selected from the Gabor filter banks using a discriminant measure, and the HGFs are then extracted from the optimal Gabor filters.

To define the Gabor filter banks, recursively from the highest level which has only one sampling point, a sampling point is decomposed into nine sub-sampling points in the lower level. This sub-sampling decomposition is shown in Fig.1. The position of a sampling point is the center of a Gabor filter in the spatial domain.

In order to extract information having the global property at a high level and the localized property at a low level from the Gabor filters(See the Fig.2(a)), the standard deviation σ^{ls} must be restricted according to level such that the contour's radius having half of max of the circular gaussian envelope becomes k. From the equation (1), σ^{ls} becomes

$$\sigma^{ls} = \frac{k}{\sqrt{ln2}}, \qquad (2)$$

where ls is the index for a sampling point s at level l, $l = 1, \ldots, N_L$ and $s = 1, \ldots, N_{lS}$. N_L is a level size and N_{lS} is the number of sampling points at level l. To extract the localized information which is not represented in the higher level, k is selected as a half mean of distances, $d1, d2, d3, d4$, where d_1, d_2, d_3, d_4 are distances from a sampling point to its four neighbor sampling points, n_1, n_2, n_3, n_4(See Fig.2(b)).

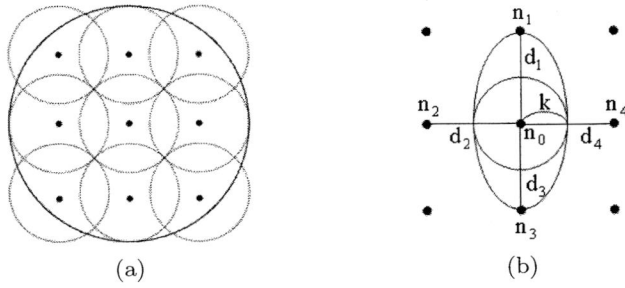

Fig. 2. (a) A big circle shows a region covered by gaussian envelope of the upper sampling point. The smaller nine circles show regions covered by gaussian envelopes of the sub-sampling points (b) A Circle is a contour having half of the max of the circular gaussian envelope with $k = \text{mean}(d_1, d_2, d_3, d_4)/2$. In the case of ellipse, aspect ratio $r = 2$

After the standard deviation σ^{ls} and the aspect ratio r of the Gabor filter are determined, the Gabor filter bank $\mathbf{GB}_j^{ls}$ is defined as

$$\mathbf{GB}_j^{ls} = \{G_{j1}^{ls}, \ldots, G_{jN_\omega}^{ls}\}, \; G_{ji}^{ls}(x,y) = G(x^{ls} - x, y^{ls} - y, \omega_i, \sigma^{ls}, r, \theta_j), \quad (3)$$
$$\omega_i \in \Omega \quad \text{and} \quad \Omega = \{\omega_1, \ldots, \omega_{N_\omega}\}, \quad i = 1, \ldots, N_\omega,$$
$$\theta_j \in \Theta \quad \text{and} \quad \Theta = \{\theta_1, \ldots, \theta_{N_\theta}\}, \quad j = 1, \ldots, N_\theta,$$

where Ω is a set of spatial frequencies, Θ is a set of the orientations, and G_{ji}^{ls} is a Gabor filter centered at (x^{ls}, y^{ls}) from the equation (1). (x^{ls}, y^{ls}) is xy-coordinates of the sampling point in an image plane. Thus, for each sampling point and orientation, the Gabor filter bank $\mathbf{GB}_j^{ls}$ is a set of Gabor filters which have different frequencies in the Ω.

An optimal Gabor filter OG_j^{ls} is selected from $\mathbf{GB}_j^{ls}$ using a discriminant measure. The discriminant measure is a measure of how certain information is efficient for discrimination(See the Appendix). Using the discriminant measure is reasonable because our ultimate goal is classification. Let (h_d, I_d) be a preclassified training image, where $h_d \in \mathbf{C}$ and $I_d \in \mathbf{I}$. $\mathbf{C} = \{c_i: i = 1, \cdots, N_c, N_c : \text{the number of classes}\}$ is a set of class hypotheses and $\mathbf{I}$ is a set of training images. An optimal Gabor filter OG_j^{ls} is selected such as

$$OG_j^{ls} = \underset{G_{ji}^{ls}}{\arg\max}\; (DM_i), \quad DM_i = Discriminant\; Measure\,(\mathcal{X}_i), \quad (4)$$
$$\mathcal{X}_i = \{(h_1, g_1), \ldots, (h_{N_I}, g_{N_I})\}, \quad g_d = \sum_{\{x\}}\sum_{\{y\}} I_d(x,y)\, G_{ji}^{ls}(x,y),$$
$$G_{ji}^{ls} \in \mathbf{GB}_j^{ls}, \quad i = 1, \ldots, N_\omega,$$

where g_d is a Gabor filter response of an image and N_I is the number of training images. For each Gabor filter G_{ji}^{ls} in $\mathbf{GB}_j^{ls}$, the Gabor filter responses of all the training images are calculated. Next, the Gabor filter whose frequency gives the highest discriminant measure for the training data set is selected as the optimal Gabor filter OG_j^{ls}.

After obtaining every OG_j^{ls}, the Gabor feature of a sampling point about an image I is defined as

$$\mathbf{a}^{ls} = [a_1^{ls}\ a_2^{ls}\ \ldots\ a_{N_\theta}^{ls}]^T, \quad a_j^{ls} = \sum_{\{x\}}\sum_{\{y\}} I(x,y)\, OG_j^{ls}(x,y) \qquad (5)$$

The Gabor feature $\mathbf{a}^{ls}$ of a sampling point s at level l becomes an N_θ-dimensional vector whose elements are responses of optimal Gabor filters on an image I for all orientations. Finally the HGFs $\mathbf{a}$ of an image I consists of Gabor features of all the sampling points.

$$\mathbf{a} = \{\mathbf{a}^1, \mathbf{a}^2, \ldots, \mathbf{a}^{N_L}\}, \quad \mathbf{a}^l = \{\mathbf{a}^{l1}, \mathbf{a}^{l2}, \ldots, \mathbf{a}^{lN_{lS}}\}, \qquad (6)$$

where $\mathbf{a}^l$ is a set of Gabor features of level l.

3 Hierarchical Bayesian Network

3.1 Bayesian Network

About a finite set of random variables, $\mathbf{U} = \{A_1, \ldots, A_n\}$, a bayesian network[2][3] is generally defined by $<DAG, \mathbf{CP}>$. The $DAG = (\mathbf{V}, \mathbf{E})$, that is, a directed acyclic graph defines the structure of a bayesian network. $\mathbf{V} = \{A_1, \ldots, A_n\}$ is a set of nodes and $\mathbf{E} = \{(A_i, A_j) : A_i, A_j \in \mathbf{V}, \text{where } i \neq j\}$ is a set of direct edges, where (A_i, A_j) denotes directed edge from A_i to A_j which implies that the node A_i affects the node A_j directly. There is a one-to-one correspondence between elements of $\mathbf{V}$ and $\mathbf{U}$. A directed edge set $\mathbf{E}$ represents directed dependencies between the random variables in $\mathbf{U}$. $\mathbf{CP}$ is a set of conditional probability distributions of nodes. The conditional probability distribution of a node A_i is defined by $P(A_i|\, \mathbf{\Pi}_{A_i})$ where $\mathbf{\Pi}_{A_i}$ is the parent node set of A_i in DAG. Also, the joint probability distribution $P(\mathbf{U})$ explained by a bayesian network can be factorized by conditional probability distributions in the $\mathbf{CP}$ and is followed as

$$P(A_1, \ldots, A_n) = \prod_{i=1}^{n} P(A_i|\, \mathbf{\Pi}_{A_i}) \qquad (7)$$

For example, the structure of the naive bayesian classifier[4], which does not represent any dependencies among the feature nodes, is shown in Fig.3.(a) and the joint probability explained by the naive bayesian classifier can be factorized such as $P(A_1, \ldots, A_N, C) = \prod_{i=1}^{N} P(A_i|\, C) P(C)$.

3.2 Hierarchical Bayesian Network

The HBN is constructed to the hierarchical structure so that the Gabor features at a certain level affect the Gabor features at its lower level with the more local property.

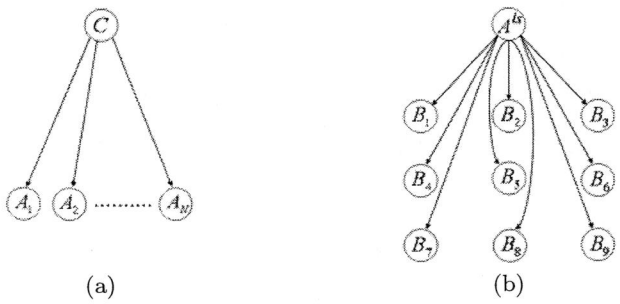

Fig. 3. (a) Structure of bayesian network for naive bayesian classifier (b) Sub-structure of HBN

The structure of HBN, excluding a class node, is defined as the $DAG_H = < \mathbf{V}_H, \mathbf{E}_H >$. Let A^{ls} be a node in $\mathbf{V}_H$ or a random variable in $\mathbf{U}_H$. There is a one-to-one correspondence between a sampling point s at level l in section.2.2 and a node A^{ls}, that is, a random variable A^{ls} has a value as the Gabor feature $\mathbf{a}^{ls}$. Thus, the node set $\mathbf{V}_H$, for the HGFs, becomes

$$\mathbf{V}_H = \mathbf{A}^1 \cup \cdots \cup \mathbf{A}^{N_L}, \quad \mathbf{A}^l = \{A^{l1}, \ldots, A^{lN_{ls}}\}, \qquad (8)$$

where $\mathbf{A}^l$ is a set of nodes at level l. A node set $\mathbf{\Phi}^{ls}$, nodes for nine subsampling points of A^{ls}, is defined as

$$\mathbf{\Phi}^{ls} = \{B_1^{ls}, \ldots, B_9^{ls}\}, \quad B_i^{ls} \in \mathbf{A}^{l+1}, \qquad (9)$$

where $l = 1, \ldots, N_L - 1$. Thus, a directed edge set $\mathbf{E}_H$ is defined as

$$\begin{aligned} \mathbf{E}_H &= \mathbf{E}^1 \cup \cdots \cup \mathbf{E}^{N_L - 1}, \\ \mathbf{E}^l &= \mathbf{E}^{l1} \cup \ldots \cup \mathbf{E}^{lN_{ls}}, \\ \mathbf{E}^{ls} &= \{(A^{ls}, B_1^{ls}), \ldots, (A^{ls}, B_9^{ls})\}, \end{aligned} \qquad (10)$$

where (A^{ls}, B_i^{ls}) is a directed edge from A^{ls} to B_i^{ls}, $B_i^{ls} \in \mathbf{\Phi}^{ls}$ and level $l = 1, \ldots, N_L - 1$.

In the hierarchical structure DAG_H of HBN, the node A^{ls} affects the nodes in $\mathbf{\Phi}^{ls}$ corresponding to its nine sub-sampling points at level $l+1$ (See Fig.3(b)). Thus, directed dependencies from a node to nodes in the lower level are limited to the nodes of nine sub-sampling points.

For classification, the hierarchical structure DAG_H must be modified to DAG_H' for including the class node C. $DAG_H' = < \mathbf{V}_H', \mathbf{E}_H' >$ is defined as

$$\begin{aligned} \mathbf{V}_H' &= \mathbf{U}_H' = \mathbf{V}_H \cup \{C\}, \\ \mathbf{E}_H' &= \mathbf{E}_H \cup \mathbf{E}_c, \quad \mathbf{E}_c = \{(C, A^{ls}) : \text{for all } A^{ls} \in \mathbf{V}_H\}, \end{aligned} \qquad (11)$$

where $\mathbf{E}_c$ is a set of directed edges from the class node C to all nodes in the set $\mathbf{V}_H$. All nodes excepting node C in DAG_H' have node C as its parent.

Table 1. The number of testing data per class

Class	0	1	2	3	4	5	6	7	8	9	Total
N_{class}	189	198	195	199	186	187	195	201	180	204	1934

For the complete definition of HBN with hierarchical structure DAG_H', a set of conditional probability distributions, denoted by **CP**, must be defined. HBN has mixed types of continuous and discrete variables. The variables in $\mathbf{U}_H$ for HGFs are continuous and only the class variable C is discrete. Thus, for each continuous Gabor feature variable A^{ls}, the conditional probability distribution $P(A^{ls}|\mathbf{\Pi}_{ls}')$ is defined as a conditional multivariate gaussian[3], where $\mathbf{\Pi}^{ls'}$ is a set of parents of A^{ls} in DAG_H'. Also, for the discrete class variable C which does not have any parents, the conditional probability distribution $P(C)$ is defined as a multinomial distribution[3]. The joint probability distribution of $\mathbf{U}_H'$ can be factorized by the conditional probability distributions such as equation (7).

With the HBN defined as $< DAG_H', \mathbf{CP} >$, an inference can be made by a belief propagation algorithm in [2][3]. As the interesting variable is the class variable C for classification, inference is performed for $P(C|\mathbf{U}_H = \mathbf{a})$, where $\mathbf{a}$ is an instance of the HGFs of an image from (6). Afterwards, the instance $\mathbf{a}$ is assigned to a class label maximizing $P(C|\mathbf{U}_H = \mathbf{a})$ for classification.

4 Experimental Results

Our HBN was simulated about binary handwritten numerical data set for recognition[5]. This numerical data set was obtained from the UCI(University of California, Irvine) databases[6].

The experiments were conducted with the following conditions for comparison with other methods. The training data set consisted of randomly chosen 500 samples(50 per class) and the testing data set consisted of the remaining 1,943 samples. The number of testing data set per class is shown in Table.1. The training and testing data set were not overlapped. For extracting the HGFs, the imaginary part of Gabor filter was used. The parameters of Gabor filter banks were set up such as $\mathbf{\Omega} = \{0.025, 0.05, 0.075, 0.1, 0.15, 0.2, 0.4, 0.6, 0.8, 1\}$ for frequencies, $\mathbf{\Theta} = \{0, \frac{1}{4}\pi, \frac{1}{2}\pi, \frac{3}{4}\pi\}$ for orientations, aspect ratio $r = 2$, and the level size $N_L = 3$.

Experiment 1: Our proposed HBN was simulated. From the training handwritten numerical character images, the HGFs were extracted such as in section 2.2. After constructing the hierarchical structure of HBN, the parameters of the conditional probability distributions of the HBN were learned by the maximum likelihood(ML) method from the HGFs of training images[2][3].

Experiment 2: The naive bayesian classifier[4](See Fig.3(a)), which had exactly the same nodes of the HBN and the HGFs in the experiment 1, was simulated.

Table 2. Recognition results with 90% confidence interval. HBN: hierarchical bayesian network, NBC: naive bayesian classifier, KNN: k-nearest neighbor classifier, NN: backpropagation neural network

Experiment 1	Experiment 2	Experiment 3	Experiment 4
HBN	NBC	KNN with $k = 1$	NN
0.9675 ± 0.0031	0.9567 ± 0.0031	0.9565 ± 0.0040	0.9451 ± 0.0048

Experiment 3: For the inputs of the k-nearest neighbor classifier[7][8], the HGFs in the experiment 1 were modified to a $236(=59 \times 4)$ dimensional feature vector, where 59 was the number of the Gabor features in the HGFs and 4 was the dimension of a Gabor feature. In these experiments the k-nearest neighbor classifiers with $k = 1, 3, 5$ were simulated. In this experiment, the case of the $k = 1$ showed the best recognition result.

Experiment 4: The number of input nodes of backpropagation neural network[7][8] were set up to $236(=59 \times 4)$ to accept the same HGFs in experiment 1. Also, the parameters of the backpropagation neural network were set up such as 150 hidden units, learning rate $\eta = 0.01$, momentum rate $\alpha = 0.5$, number of learning iteration = 10,000.

The results of the experiments are shown in Table.2. From the results, it is reliable that the HGFs are efficient for recognition in spite of relatively small training data set. That the hierarchical dependencies within the HBN for the HGFs more improve the recognition is explained from that the HBN outperformed over all other methods which do not represent any hierarchical dependencies.

5 Conclusion

In this paper we have proposed a HGFs and HBN for a recognition mechanism. To represent the hierarchical property with the HGFs, we decomposed a sampling point into nine sub-sampling points and adjusted covered regions of Gabor filters with levels. And the optimal Gabor filters were selected using the discriminant measure. To represent dependencies within the HGFs, we constructed a bayesian network structure to be hierarchical by analogy of the HGFs extraction method.

Our proposed method was applied to the problem of handwritten digit recognition and compared it with other methods, such as the naive classifier, k-nearest neighbor classifier, and backpropagation neural network. The results confirmed the useful behavior of our method in which the HGFs are well structured information and the hierarchical dependencies in the HBN improve recognition.

Although we only applied this approach to the problem of the handwritten digit recognition, we believe our method can be extended to a general recognition system.

References

1. Tai Sing Lee: Image Representation Using 2D Gabor Wavelets. IEEE trans. PAMI, vol. 18. no. 10. (1996) 959–971
2. Pearl, J. : Probabilistic Inference in Intelligent Systems. Morgan Kaufmann, San Mateo, California, (1988)
3. Robert G. Cowell, A. Philip Dawid, Steffen L. Lauritzen, David J, Spiegelhalter: Probabilistic Networks and Expert Systems. Springer (1999)
4. N. Friedman, D. Geiger, M Goldszmidt: Bayesian network classifiers. Mach. Learn 29 (1997) 131–163
5. Daijin Kim, Sung-Yang Bang: A Handwritten Numeral Character Classification Using Tolerant Rough Set. IEEE trans. PAMI, vol. 22. no. 9. (2000) 923–937
6. C. L. Blake and C. J. Merz: UCI Repository of Machine Learning Databases. Dept. of Information and Computer Science, Uive. of California, Irvine, (1998)
7. Chistopher M. Bishop: Neural Networks for Pattern Recognition. Oxford University Press (1995)
8. Richard O. Duda, Peter E. Hart, David G. Strok: Pattern Classification. John Wiley and Sons. (2001)

Appendix: Discriminant Measure

A discriminant measure is a measure to how certain information is efficient for discrimination. The discriminant measure is defined by a within-class scatter matrix and a between-class scatter matrix. If within the one class, scatter of information are smaller and among the classes, the scatter of information are larger[8], this discriminant measure gives a higher output.

For the c-class problem, suppose that a set of n d-dimensional instances, $\mathcal{X}$, have its elements such as $\mathbf{x}_1, \ldots, \mathbf{x}_n$, n_i in the subset $\mathcal{X}_i$ labeled c_i. Thus within-class scatter matrix $\mathbf{S}_W$ is defined by

$$\mathbf{S}_i = \sum_{\mathbf{x} \in \mathcal{X}_i} (\mathbf{x} - \mathbf{m}_i)(\mathbf{x} - \mathbf{m}_i)^T, \qquad \mathbf{m}_i = \frac{1}{n_i} \sum_{\mathbf{x} \in \mathcal{X}_i} \mathbf{x} \qquad \mathbf{S}_W = \sum_{i=1}^{c} \mathbf{S}_i,$$

where T is matrix transpose. After defining a total mean vector $\mathbf{m}$, between-class scatter matrix $\mathbf{S}_B$ is defined as

$$\mathbf{m} = \frac{1}{n} \sum_{\mathbf{x} \in \mathcal{X}} \mathbf{x} = \frac{1}{n} \sum_{i=1}^{c} n_i \mathbf{m}_i, \qquad \mathbf{S}_B = \sum_{i=1}^{c} n_i (\mathbf{m}_i - \mathbf{m})(\mathbf{m}_i - \mathbf{m})^T$$

A simple scalar measure of scatter is the determinant of the scatter matrix. From this scatter measure, *Discriminant Measure* is

$$Discriminant\ Measure = \frac{|\mathbf{S}_B|}{|\mathbf{S}_W|}, \text{ where } |\cdot| \text{ denotes determinant.}$$

In our approach, an instance $\mathbf{x}$ is a scalar.

A Novel Neural Network Approach to Solve Exact and Inexact Graph Isomorphism Problems

Brijnesh J. Jain and Fritz Wysotzki

Dept. of Electrical Engineering and Computer Science, TU Berlin
Franklinstr. 28/29, D-10587 Berlin, Germany

Abstract. We present a neural network approach to solve exact and inexact graph isomorphism problems for weighted graphs. In contrast to other neural heuristics or related methods our approach is based on approximating the automorphism partition of a graph to reduce the search space followed by an energy-minimizing matching process. Experiments on random graphs with 100–5000 vertices are presented and discussed.

1 Introduction

Given two graphs G and H the *graph isomorphism problem* (GIP) is the problem of deciding whether G and H are structurally equivalent. The problem is of practical as well as theoretical importance. Applications include the identification of isomorphic molecular structures in chemistry, the recognition of protein molecules, the detection of kinematic chains, or optimal routing of messages in multistage interconnecting networks (see [1] and references therein). The theoretical interest in the GIP is based on the persistent difficulty in characterizing its computational complexity. The GIP is still unsolved in the sense that there is neither an NP-completeness proof, nor an efficient algorithm with polynomial complexity has yet been found.

Despite the practical and theoretical importance of the GIP no neural network approach and related heuristics can be used unmodified in a practical setting. Even the most powerful approaches by Pelillo [7] and Rangarajan et al. [9], [10] require a prohibitive amount of time and are too erroneous on random graphs with only 100 vertices, although the GIP is considered to be trivial for almost all random graphs [3]. The main reason that neural networks or related methods are not competitive with efficient graph isomorphism algorithms is that they solely rely on powerful energy minimization procedures and neglect graph-theoretical properties that are preserved under isomorphism.

In this paper we devise a neural graph isomorphism (NGI) algorithm, which can also cope with noisy data. In a preprocessing step a neural stabilization procedure partitions the vertex sets of both graphs into equivalence classes. In a second step the information about the vertex partitions is used to match the graphs with a special Hopfield network. The effectiveness of the proposed NGI approach is tested on weighted graphs with 100–5000 vertices.

The rest of this paper is organized as follows: We conclude this section by introducing the basic definitions and the statement of the problem. Section 3 introduces vertex ε-invariants. In Section 4 we propose the NGI algorithm. Section 5 presents the experimental results and Section 6 concludes this contribution.

Terminologies and Definitions: Let V be a set. With $[V]^2$ we denote the set of all 2-element subsets $\{i, j\} \subseteq V$. A *partition* $P = \{V_1, \ldots, V_k\}$ of a set V is a set of disjoint non-empty subsets $V_i \subseteq V$ whose union is V. Let $\mathcal{P}(V)$ be the set of all partitions of V. The elements V_i of a partition $P \in \mathcal{P}(V)$ are usually called its *cells*. If $P, P' \in \mathcal{P}(V)$, we say P is *finer* than P', if every cell of P is a subset of some cell P'. Under this conditions, P' is *coarser* than P.

A *weighted graph* is a pair $G = (V, \mu)$ consisting of a finite set $V \neq \emptyset$ of *vertices* and a mapping $\mu : [V]^2 \to \mathbb{R}_+$ assigning each pair $\{i, j\} \in V^2$ a non-negative real valued weight. The elements $\{i, j\} \in [V]^2$ with positive weight $\mu(\{i, j\}) > 0$ are the *edges* of G. The vertex set of a graph G is referred to as $V(G)$, its edge set as $E(G)$, and its weight mapping as μ_G. A *binary graph* is a weighted graph $G = (V, \mu)$ with $\mu([V]^2) \subseteq \{0, 1\}$. A binary graph assigns the weight 1 for its edges and the weight 0 for non-edges. The *structure graph* S_G of a weighted graph G is a binary graph with $E(S_G) = E(G)$. The *adjacency matrix* of a graph G is a matrix $A(G) = (a_{ij})$ with entries $g_{ij} = \mu_G(\{i, j\})$.

A subset C_m of $V(G)$ consisting of m vertices is called *clique* of G if $[C]^2 \subseteq E(G)$. A *maximum clique* is a clique with maximum cardinality of vertices. A *maximal clique* is a clique which is not contained in any larger clique. The *clique number* $\omega(G)$ of a graph G is the number of vertices of a maximum clique in G.

Let G and H be graphs with adjacency matrix $A(G) = (g_{ij})$ and $A(H) = (h_{ij})$, respectively. An *isomorphism* from G to H is a bijective mapping $\phi : V(G) \to V(H)$, $i \mapsto i^\phi$ with $g_{ij} = h_{i^\phi j^\phi}$ for all $i, j \in V$. An *automorphism* of G is an isomorphism from G to itself. Let Aut_G denote the set of all automorphisms of G. Two vertices $i, j \in V$ are *similar* $(i \sim j)$ if there exists an automorphism $\phi \in \text{Aut}_G$ with $i^\phi = j$. The *automorphism partition* Π_G of G is the partition of V induced by the equivalence relation $\sim$. A cell of Π_G is called *orbit*.

STATEMENT OF THE PROBLEM: Throughout this contribution let G and H be graphs with n vertices and adjacency matrices $A(G) = (g_{ij})$ and $A(H) = (h_{ij})$, respectively. With $\varepsilon \geq 0$ we denote a threshold.

An ε-*isomorphism* of G to H is a bijective mapping $\phi : V(G) \to V(H)$, $i \mapsto i^\phi$ with $|g_{ij} - h_{i^\phi j^\phi}| \leq \varepsilon$ for all $i, j \in V(G)$. If there is an ε-isomorphism between two graphs then the graphs are ε-*isomorphic*. If $\varepsilon = 0$ an ε-isomorphism ϕ is an (*exact*) *isomorphism*[1]. Otherwise, if $\varepsilon > 0$, we call ϕ an *inexact isomorphism*. The ε-*graph isomorphism problem* (ε-GIP) is the problem of deciding whether two graphs are ε-isomorphic.

2 Exact and Inexact Local Invariants

To solve the GIP for G and H, any algorithm has to search for an isomorphism between G and H among $n!$ possible bijections $\phi : V(G) \to V(H)$. A very

---
[1] If we refer to exact concepts, i.e. if $\varepsilon = 0$, we simply write isomorphism, GIP, etc. instead of ε-isomorphism, ε-GIP, etc.

practical and commonly applied technique to restrict the search space consisting of $n!$ possible candidates, is the use of *vertex invariants* [4]. A vertex invariant is a property of a vertex, which is preserved under isomorphism. Thus only vertices with the same invariants must be mapped onto each other under any isomorphism. In the following we describe this approach, which is independent of the algorithm used to actually solve the GIP, and extend it to the ε-GIP.

Let $\mathcal{G}_V = \{(G,i) : G \in \mathcal{G}, i \in V(G)\}$, where $\mathcal{G}$ denotes the set of all weighted graphs G. A function $f_\varepsilon : \mathcal{G}_V \to \mathbb{R}$ is a *vertex ε-invariant*, if $|f(G,i) - f(H,i^\phi)| \leq \varepsilon$ for any ε-isomorphism $\phi : G \to H$.

To restrict the search space by using vertex ε-invariant, we first inspect the underlying structure graphs S_G and S_H of G and H, respectively. In a second step, further restriction of the search space is imposed by taking the weights g_{ij}, h_{ij} into account.

Step 1 ($\varepsilon = 0$): Let $S = S_G$ be the structure graphs of G. By $f(G, V(G)) = \{v_1, \ldots, v_k\}$ we denote the image of f. Since $V(G)$ has n elements, $f(G, V(G))$ consists of at most n distinct values. Without loss of generality, we can assume a numbering of the values v_c in such a way that $v_1 < \ldots < v_k$. Then f induces a partition $P_f(G) = \{V_1(G), \ldots, V_k(G)\}$ of $V(G)$ with $i, j \in V_c$ if and only if $f(G,i) = f(G,j) = v_c$. Since f is constant on the orbits of Aut_G, the partition P_f is coarser than or equal to the automorphism partition $\Pi(G)$ of G.

To preserve the structure, any isomorphism from G to H must map vertices of cell $V_c(G)$ to vertices of cell $V_c(H)$. This restricts the search space from $n!$ possible candidates to $\prod n_c!$ possible candidates, where $n_c = |V_c(G)| = |V_c(H)|$.

The best known and most frequently used vertex invariant is the degree of a vertex. Further examples assign a vertex i the number of vertices reachable along a path of length k, the number of different cliques of size k, etc.

Step 2 $\varepsilon > 0$: Let $P_f(G)$ and $P_f(H)$ be the partitions obtained in Step 1. As opposed to (exact) vertex invariants a vertex ε-invariant does not in general induce a partition. Nevertheless, vertex ε-invariants further restrict the search space, since they only allow mappings between vertices $i \in V_c(G)$ and $j \in V_c(H)$ that satisfy $|f_\varepsilon(G,i) - f_\varepsilon(H,j)| \leq \varepsilon$.

Examples of vertex ε-invariants are the mean weight $\bar{f}(G,i) = \frac{1}{n} \cdot \sum_{j \neq i} g_{ij}$, the minimum weight $f_*(G,i) = \min_j\{g_{ij}\}$, or the maximum weight $f^*(G,i) = \max_j\{g_{ij}\}$ of all edges incident to vertex i, where non-edges are regarded as edges with weight 0.

Theorem 1. *For any $\varepsilon \geq 0$ the functions $\bar{f}$, f_*, and f^* are vertex ε-invariants.*

Proof. We sketch the proof only for $\bar{g}(i)$. The other proofs are similar. Let $\phi : G \to H$ be an ε-isomorphism and $i \in V(G)$ with $j = i^\phi \in V(H)$. Since ϕ is an ε-isomorphism, we have $|g_{ik} - h_{jk^\phi}| \leq \varepsilon$ for all $k \neq i$. This yields

$$\left|\bar{f}(G,i) - \bar{f}(H,j)\right| = \left|\frac{1}{n-1}\sum_{k \neq i} g_{ik} - \frac{1}{n-1}\sum_{l \neq j} h_{jl}\right| \leq \frac{1}{n-1}\sum_{k \neq i}|g_{ik} - h_{jk^\phi}| \leq \varepsilon.$$

3 A Neural ε-GIP Solver

In practice, most algorithms adopt the same basic approach to the exact GIP, though the details may vary. To reduce the search space this approach first approximates the automorphism partition of each graph using a vertex classification procedure which is based on a set of vertex invariants. In a second step an isomorphism is constructed or non-isomorphism is established by applying a breadth-first search, depth-first search, or a mixture of both methods. The NGI algorithm follows a similar approach for the GIP and extends it to the ε-GIP:

OUTLINE OF THE NGI ALGORITHM: Let G and H be graphs with n vertices.
1. Classify vertices of G and H by using a neural stabilization procedure. The outputs are vertex partitions $P_f(G)$ and $P_f(H)$ of G and H, resp., which are coarser than or equal to their automorphism partitions.
2. Use the vertex partitions $P_f(G)$ and $P_f(H)$ to construct an ε-association graph $G \diamond_\varepsilon H$ of G and H. This maps the ε-GIP to the problem of finding a maximum clique in $G \diamond_\varepsilon H$.
3. Search for a maximum clique C_m in $G \diamond_\varepsilon H$ by using a special Hopfield network.
4. G and H are ε-isomorphic if and only if $m = n$.

In the following we describe Step 1–3 of the NGI algorithm. For convenience of presentation we precede with a general remark. All neural networks involved in the NGI algorithm are associated with a specific graph. Networks for approximating the automorphism partition are associated with the given graphs to test for isomorphism and the network for solving the maximum clique problem is associated with their association graph. A neural network N_G associated with G consists of n fully connected units. For any vertex $i \in V(G)$ let $N(i)$ be the set of all vertices j adjacent to i. Then the dynamics of the network is given by

$$x_i(t+1) = x_i(t) + w_E \cdot \sum_{j \in N(i)} o_i(t) + w_I \cdot \sum_{j \notin N(i)} o_i(t) \qquad (1)$$

where $x_i(t)$ denotes the activity of unit i. The synaptic weight between unit i and unit j is $w_E > 0$, if the corresponding vertices are connected by an edge $\{i,j\} \in E$ and $w_I \leq 0$, if $\{i,j\} \notin E$. The output function $o_i(t)$ of unit i is a non-decreasing function applied on its activation $x_i(t)$.

Step 1 – Approximating the ε-Automorphism Partition: For any graph G, a stabilization procedure starts with an initial partition P of $V(G)$, which is coarser than the (exact) automorphism partition. The partition P is iteratively refined using a set of vertex invariants. If no further refinement is possible, then the current partition is said to be stabilized. A stabilization procedure always stabilizes in a partition which is coarser than or equal to the automorphism partition.

Let N_G be a neural network associated with G. Suppose the initial activation is identical for all units. Then N_G together with the update rule (1) is a stabilization procedure, which approximates the (exact) automorphism partition of

G: At each time instance t the activation vector $\mathbf{x}(t)$ of N_G induces a partition $P_t(G)$ of the vertex set $V(G)$. Two vertices i and j are members of the same cell $V_k(t) \in P_G(t)$ if and only if $x_i(t) = x_j(t)$. Since the initial activation is identical for all units, the neural stabilizer starts with the coarsest partition $P_0(G)$ consisting of the single cell $V(G)$ and iteratively refines that partition according to its dynamical rule (1). The network has stabilized if the current partition $P_t(G)$ is not finer than $P_{t-1}(G)$. Theorem 2 and its implications summarize and prove the statements of this paragraph.

Theorem 2. *Let N_G be the neural network associated with G and $x_i(0) = \alpha$ for all $i \in V(G)$. Then for all $i, j \in V(G)$ and $t \geq 0$ we have*

$$i \sim j \quad \Rightarrow \quad x_i(t) = x_j(t).$$

Proof. The assertion holds for $t = 0$, since $x_i(t) = x_j(t) = \alpha$ for all $i, j \in V(G)$ irrespective of the similarity relation $\sim$. Now assume that $i \sim j \Rightarrow x_i(t) = x_j(t)$ holds for a $t > 0$. Since $i \sim j$ there exists an automorphism $\phi \in \mathrm{Aut}_G$ with $i^\phi = j$. By construction of N_G all self-coupling weights w_{ii} are identical. Furthermore from the definition of N_G together with the edge preserving property of an automorphism follows that $w_{ik} = w_{jk^\phi}$ where $w_{ik} \in \{1, w_E, w_I\}$. Then by induction we have

$$x_i(t+1) = \sum_k w_{ik} o_k(t) = \sum_k w_{jk^\phi} o_{k^\phi}(t) = x_j(t+1) \ .$$

From Theorem 2 directly follows, that for all $t \geq 0$ the partitions $P_t(G)$ are coarser than or equal to the automorphism partition $\Pi(G)$ of G. Thus it is left to show, that the neural stabilizer N_G stabilizes within finite time. Since $V(G)$ is finite, there are only finitely many partitions $V(G)$ which are coarser than $\Pi(G)$. Thus any sequence of refinements is finite.

Note that stabilization and convergence to a stable state are different concepts. The first notion corresponds to stability of a partition, the latter to stability of the the dynamical system (1). For $w_E = 1$ and $w_I = 0$ we obtain Morgan's procedure [6].

Step 2 – Construction of an ε-Association Graph: Given two graphs G and H we map the ε-GIP to the problem of finding a maximum clique in an ε-association graph of G and H. The ε-association graph is an extension of the well-known original term of an association graph [2], which has been employed with varied success not only to the graph isomorphism, but also to the more general graph matching problem [7], [8].

Let f_ε be a vertex ε-invariant. The ε-association graph $G \diamond_\varepsilon H$ of graphs G and H is a graph with

$$V(G \diamond_\varepsilon H) = \left\{ (i,j) \in V(G) \times V(H) \ : \ |f_\varepsilon(i) - f_\varepsilon(j)| \leq \varepsilon \right\}$$

$$E(G \diamond_\varepsilon H) = \left\{ \{(i,k),(j,l)\} \in [V(G \diamond_\varepsilon H)]^2 \ : \ |g_{ij} - h_{kl}| \leq \varepsilon, i \neq j, k \neq l \right\}$$

Since G and H are isomorphic if and only if $\omega(G \diamond_\varepsilon H) = n$, we can cast the ε-GIP to the maximum clique problem in an ε-association graph.

Theorem 3. Let $G \diamond_\varepsilon H$ be the ε-association graph of graphs G and H with n vertices. Then there exists a bijection $\chi : \mathcal{I}_\varepsilon(G, H) \to \mathcal{C}(G \diamond_\varepsilon H)$ from the set of all ε-isomorphism $\mathcal{I}_\varepsilon(G, H)$ between G and H and the set of all maximum cliques $\mathcal{C}(G \diamond_\varepsilon H)$.

Proof. (Sketch) Define $\chi(\phi) = C_\phi = \{(i, i^\phi) : i \in G(V)\}$ for all $\phi \in \mathcal{I}_\varepsilon(G, H)$. Then C_ϕ is a clique with n vertices by construction of $G \diamond_\varepsilon H$. But then C_ϕ is a maximum clique by definition of $G \diamond_\varepsilon H$. In addition, χ is well-defined. The mapping χ is bijective by construction of $\chi(\phi)$ and $G \diamond_\varepsilon H$.

Step 3 – A Neural Maximum Clique Solver: For finding the maximum clique in $G \diamond_\varepsilon H$ we use the winner-takes-all (WTA) network as described in [5]. This WTA algorithm is extremely fast and outperforms greedy heuristics with respect to both speed and solution quality. The performance of the WTA network is based on an optimal parameter setting which is theoretically justified in [5].

The topology of the WTA net is associated with the graph $G \diamond_\varepsilon H$, where the connective weights w_E and w_I depend on the structure of $G \diamond_\varepsilon H$. The WTA algorithm operates as follows: An initial activation is imposed on the network. Finding a maximum clique then proceeds in accordance with (1) until the system reaches a stable state. During evolution of the network any unit is excited by all active units with which it can form a clique and inhibits all other units. After convergence the stable state corresponds to a maximal clique of $G \diamond_\varepsilon H$. The size of a maximal clique can be read out by counting all units with output $o_i(t) = 1$.

4 Experimental Results

We tested the NGI algorithm on random binary and random weighted graphs. The algorithm is implemented in Java using JDK 1.2. All experiments were run on a Sparc SUNW Ultra-4.

Random binary graphs: For each isomorphism test we considered pairs of graphs (G, H) where G is a randomly generated graph with n vertices and edge probability p and H is a randomly permuted version of G. The chosen parameters were $n = 100, 500, 1000, 2500, 5000$ and $p = 0.01, 0.05, 0.1, 0.2, 0.3, 0.4, 0.5$. We generated 100 examples for each pair (n, p) giving a total of 3500 isomorphism tests. Note, that the GIP of graphs with $p > 0.5$ is equivalent to the GIP of the complementary graphs. We use random graphs for the purpose of comparing the proposed NGI algorithm with the best methods applied to the GIP within the neural network community. In particular, we shall compare our results with the Lagrangian Relaxation Network (LRN) by Rangarajan and Mjolsness [10], the Optimizing Network Architecture (ONA) by Rangarajan, Gold, and Mjolness [9], and the Exponential Replicator Equations (REP) by Pelillo [7].

NGI significantly outperforms LRN, ONA, and REP with respect to both, accuracy and speed. Due to their high computational effort LRN, ONA, and REP were tested on 100-vertex random graphs only. Accuracy of LRN, ONA, REP degrades for sparse graphs. The LRN algorithm terminated with a correct solution for all test runs except for 5% failures at $p = 0.01$. ONA and REP performed poorly on

Table 1. Binary graphs.

size n	edge probability p						
	0.01	0.05	0.1	0.2	0.3	0.4	0.5
100	6	3	2	3	3	3	5
500	72	49	57	55	53	55	58
1000	239	181	207	195	204	217	231
2500	1321	1140	1206	1150	1217	1360	1402
5000	5133	5080	4767	4740	5334	5594	6046

Table 2. Weighted graphs.

size n	noise factor α			
	1.0	0.5	0.25	0.1
100	76	24	20	17
250	488	152	128	122
500	2064	662	549	535
750	4888	1575	1305	1314
1000	9491	2802	2376	2321

Average computational time in *msec* required by the NGI algorithm.

100-vertex random graphs with $p < 0.05$. As an example for $p = 0.01$ the percentage of correct solutions is about 0.11 for REP and 0.0 for ONA. In contrast NGI gave exact results on all 3500 trials. But even if we are willing to live with a small degree of uncertainty, LRN, ONA, and REP are prohibitively slow. The average times to match two 100-vertex random graphs were about 600 - 1800 seconds for LRN on a SGI workstation, about 80 seconds for ONA on the same SGI workstation, and about 3-2000 seconds for REP on a SPARC-20 workstation. In contrast, the average time required by NGI is about 0.002 - 0.006 seconds for 100-vertex graphs and 5-6 seconds for 5000-vertex graphs. Table 1 shows the average computational time in milliseconds (*msec*) required by NGI for an isomorphism test on random graphs with the specified parameters n and p.

Random weighted graphs: For each ε-isomorphism test we generate pairs of graphs (G, H) as follows: G is a randomly generated graph with n fully connected vertices. To each edge $\{i, j\}$ of G we assign a randomly chosen weight $w_{ij} \in [0, 1]$. To construct H we randomly permute G and add uniform noise in the interval $[-\varepsilon, +\varepsilon]$ to all edges of H. The chosen parameters were $n = 100, 250, 500, 750, 1000$ and $\varepsilon = \alpha/n$ with $\alpha = 1.0, 0.5, 0.25, 0.1$. We generated 100 examples for each pair (n, α) giving a total of 2000 isomorphism tests. We have chosen fully connected graph to facilitate comparison with other neural network methods, namely LRN and ONA, both tested on 100-vertex graphs.

Again NGI terminated with the correct solution on all 2000 trials. Table 2 shows the computational times in *msec* required of NGI for an ε-isomorphism test of random weighted graphs with the specified parameters n and α. If the noise is sufficiently small such that it does not disrupt the structure of a graph, NGI is clearly superior than LRN and ONA. The faster of both other approaches (ONA) takes about 80 seconds to match two 100-vertex graphs, while NGI requires about 0.017 - 0.076 seconds for matching 100-vertex graphs and about 2-9 seconds to match 1000-vertex graphs. If the noise level becomes too large ($\varepsilon > 1/n$ for uniformly distributed weights) and disrupts the structure of the graph, then the ε-GIP turns into a general graph matching problem. In this case LRN and ONA outperform NGI with respect to both accuracy and speed.

5 Conclusion

We have formulated and tested a neural approach to solve the ε-GIP based on using vertex ε-invariants, which can be recognized by a neural network. Experimental results on random weighted graphs yield exact results on all 5500 test instances within impressive time limits. The results suggest testing NGI on classes of graphs which are known to be *harder* for the ε-GIP than random graphs and to applications in pattern recognition and computer vision. The results demonstrate that (1) neural networks are capable of discovering structural properties in a preprocessing step, (2) the further neural processing of the discovered structural properties to solve a given problem is of greater impact than sophisticated energy minimization methods. The authors believe that this two stage approach *neural preprocessing – neural assembling* can be applied to other graph matching problems similarly.

References

1. M. Abdulrahim and M. Misra. A graph isomorphism algorithm for object recognition. *Pattern Analysis and Application*, 1(3):189–201, 1998.
2. A.P. Ambler, H.G. Barrow, C.M. Brown, R.M. Burstall, and R. J. Popplestone. A versatile computer-controlled assembly system. In *International Joint Conference on Artificial Intelligence*, pages 298–307. Stanford University, California, 1973.
3. L. Babai, P. Erdös, and S. Selkow. Random graph isomorphism. *SIAM Journal on Computing*, 9:628–635, 1980.
4. D.G. Corneil and D.G. Kirkpatrick. A theoretical analysis of various heuristics for the graph isomorphism problem. *SIAM Journal of Computing*, 9(2):281–297, 1980.
5. B.J. Jain and F. Wysotzki. Fast winner-takes-all networks for the maximum clique problem. In *25th German Conference on Artificial Intelligence*, pages 163–173. Springer, 2002.
6. H.L. Morgan. The generation of a unique machine description for chemical structures. *Journal of Chemical Documentation*, 5:107–112, 1965.
7. M. Pelillo. Replicator equations, maximal cliques, and graph isomorphism. *Neural Computation*, 11(8):1933–1955, 1999.
8. M. Pelillo, K. Siddiqi, and S.W. Zucker. Matching hierarchical structures using association graphs. *IEEE Transactions on Pattern Analysis and Machine Intelligence*, 21(11):1105–1120, 1999.
9. A. Rangarajan, S. Gold, and E. Mjolsness. A novel optimizing network architecture with applications. *Neural Computation*, 8(5):1041–1060, 1996.
10. A. Rangarajan and E. Mjolsness. A Lagrangian relaxation network for graph matching. *IEEE Transactions on Neural Networks*, 7(6):1365–1381, 1996.

Evolutionary Optimisation of RBF Network Architectures in a Direct Marketing Application

Peter Neumann[1], Bernhard Sick[1], Dirk Arndt[2], and Wendy Gersten[2]

[1] University of Passau, Chair of Computer Architectures (Prof. Dr.-Ing. W. Grass),
Innstrasse 33, D-94032 Passau (neumann.p@pg.com, sick@fmi.uni-passau.de)
[2] DaimlerChrysler AG, Research & Technology, Information Mining (RIC/AM),
PO Box 2360, D-89013 Ulm ({dirk.arndt,wendy.gersten}@daimlerchrysler.com)

Abstract. Feature selection and structure optimisation are two key tasks in many neural network applications. This article sets out an evolutionary algorithm (EA) that performs the two tasks simultaneously for radial basis function (RBF) networks. The algorithm selects appropriate input features from a given set of possible features and adapts the number of basis functions (hidden neurons). The feasibility and the benefits of this approach are demonstrated in a direct marketing application in the automotive industry: the selection of promising targets for a direct mailing campaign, i.e. people who are likely to buy a certain product (here: car of a certain make). The method is independent from the application example given so that the ideas and solutions may easily be transferred to other neural network paradigms.

1 Introduction

In a large number of neural network applications, the most appropriate input features must be selected from a given set of possible input features. Also, the network structure (e.g. number of hidden layers, number of hidden neurons, existence of connections between any two neurons) must be optimised with respect to a particular application. Radial basis function (RBF) networks (see [1,2,3]) are considered here, as they employ a localised representation of information, facilitating interpretation of results (and classification results in particular). RBF networks, which are trained by a supervised algorithm, combine various concepts from approximation theory, clustering, and neural network theory [1]. The two tasks cited are addressed by an evolutionary algorithm (EA) that selects appropriate input features and derives optimal values for the number of hidden neurons. While other network parameters are not optimised here, the algorithm can easily be extended. An appropriate representation (coding) scheme for RBF networks, suitable selection mechanisms, and reproduction operators for mutation and recombination are provided. An evolutionary approach was chosen since it allows smooth combination with RBF networks to build a *wrapper* for feature selection. Such a combination of evolutionary and neural techniques is called a *hybrid* approach.

The benefits of this approach are shown in an application example from the field of *direct marketing (customer relationship management)*. Within the framework of a *direct marketing campaign* in the automotive industry, promising addressees are to be selected, i.e. those likely to show a desired behaviour (here: to buy a car of a specific make). Selection is to be done by utilising so-called *micro-geographical* information. Typical examples for micro-geographical information are the average degree of education and income of the inhabitants of a certain geographical unit, their average purchasing power, or the percentage of cars of a certain make. The task is to choose suitable micro-geographical features from a large set of possible features and utilise them to build a prediction model for the behaviour of a potential customer on the basis of RBF networks. This task may also be regarded as a *data mining* and *knowledge discovery* problem.

This article introduces the two key contributions of our work. Firstly, a new evolutionary technique for the optimisation of RBF network architectures (features and structure) was developed. Secondly, this approach yields best results for the marketing application described compared to other techniques such as regression approaches, decision trees, or MLP networks.

2 The Marketing Application

The particular business application arose in the Sales Department of DaimlerChrysler AG, when a direct mailing campaign slated for the launch of the new Mercedes Benz E-Class was planned. In a direct mailing campaign, target individuals receive post in the form of personalised letters and brochures promoting a product or service. Here, promising adressees had to be selected on the basis of so-called *micro-geographical* data, i.e. aggregated information on small geographical units (micro-cells) where target individuals reside. Some of the micro-geographical features used are set out in Tab. 1.

Table 1. Examples for micro-geographical features

Feature name	Explanation
STATUS	status of the residents w.r.t. education and income
ALTERSTD	average age of the heads of the households
RISIKO	credit risk information
MERCEDES	proportion of MERCEDES-brand cars
PROHH	average purchasing power per household
FLUKT	fluctuation in the micro-geographical unit

The objective was to set up a model that describes the non-linear functional relationship between certain micro-geographical features (a subset of the possible features) and an output feature indicating whether a person receiving a direct mail will buy a Mercedes Benz automobile. Binary output data ('buyer' or 'nonbuyer') gained from past promotions was available, allowing supervised set-up of the model. These data consisted of approximately 18 000 samples with 47 micro-geographical features. The trained model was then employed to assess all German micro-cells. This evaluation, called *scoring*, regards only the micro-cells in the top percentile of the scores (defined by the so-called *cut-off point*) as promising with respect to the target variable. Finally, addresses were acquired for the selected micro-cells and mails were sent.

A typical measure that may be employed to assess the suitability of a model for an application is the *lift factor* [4,5]. To evaluate the performance of a certain model, the percentage of 'buyers' among the recipients of the mails for this model (*Percentage_Buyers_Model*) and the percentage for a model where the recipients are chosen randomly (*Percentage_Buyers_Random*) are compared for a specified cut-off point (*cut*). Thus, in our case the lift factor is given by [6,7]:

$$Lift(cut) \stackrel{def}{=} \frac{Percentage\_Buyers\_Model(cut)}{Percentage\_Buyers\_Random(cut)}.$$

3 The State of the Art

In this article, we focus on two tasks "feature selection" and "structure optimisation" for neural networks (here, for RBF networks). Possible feature selection algorithms are characterised in [8,9]. As a rule, *filter* and *wrapper* approaches are distinguished. The issue of structure optimisation for neural networks is discussed in [1,10,11] in greater detail. Usually, these techniques are categorised as being either *constructive*, *destructive* (pruning techniques), or *hybrid*. The topic of data mining and knowledge discovery with an EA is addressed in [12], for instance. The combination of EAs and neural networks in general is investigated in [13,14]. Here, we will discuss some examples where an EA is combined with RBF networks (also see [15]):

– The *computation of weights* (in particular, centres and radii) with genetic methods is proposed in [16,17,18,19], for example. Individuals are either complete networks or basis functions (sets or single functions), which together constitute a network. The networks are evaluated either in each cycle or at the end of the evolution.
– Closely related to the former is the notion of *structure* or *architecture* evolution. This issue is addressed in [20], for example, where the number of hidden neurons is subject to optimisation. Alternative approaches are set out in [15, 21], for instance.
– Examples of *feature selection* for RBF networks by means of an EA could not be found, yet many approaches for other network paradigms could be adapted (see [14]). *Rule extraction* from trained networks, which is closely related to feature selection, is elaborated in [22,23], for instance.

4 The New, Hybrid Solution

An optimal classification or approximation result hinges not only on appropriate input features but also an optimal (i.e. for the features selected) number of hidden neurons. Thus, we combine the two tasks of feature selection and structure optimisation within a single evolutionary approach. From the viewpoint of feature selection this approach may be regarded as a "wrapper" technique; from the viewpoint of structure optimisation it is "hybrid" (see above). Training of parameters is effected using conventional techniques. Rules for deployment in an expert system could be extracted by means of the methods cited in [24], for instance.

RBF networks are employed in our case to model the functional relationship between micro-geographical parameters (input features) and customer behaviour (output feature). For an in-depth description of the network paradigm and suitable learning algorithms, see [1,2,3]. Here, we use networks with Gaussian basis functions and shortcut connections (see Fig. 1) which are trained with a combination of k-means clustering, singular value decomposition and backpropagation.

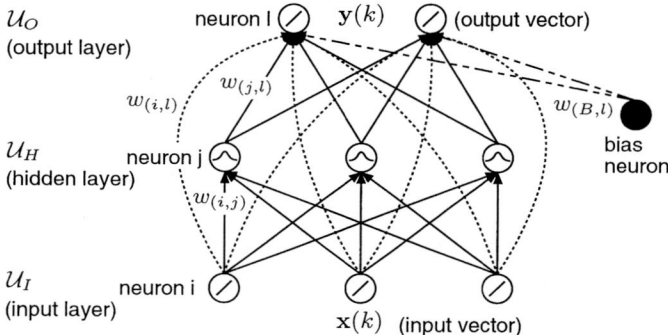

Fig. 1. Example for the structure of an RBF network

From an algorithmic perspective, evolution is a stochastic search strategy based on multiple solutions that can be used in solving a wide range of optimisation tasks including architecture optimisation of neural networks. Different classes of techniques such as genetic algorithms, genetic programming, evolution strategies, or evolutionary programming are described in [25,26] in depth. Fig. 2 provides an overview of the EA employed here.

Representation of individuals: The set of possible features is represented by a vector (or string) of bits, with each bit representing the presence or absence of one of the features in the currently chosen subset. To represent the number of hidden neurons in the RBF network, a positive integer variable is appended to the binary vector. This representation scheme may be viewed as a *high-level specification scheme* (*weak encoding scheme*, see [27]).

Initialisation of the population: In a random initialisation, the value of each element in the string representation of an individual is determined by means of a random variable, taking the possible range of the values into account.

Fitness evaluation: To eliminate stochastic influences and arrive at a more realistic estimate of an individual's fitness (i.e. to assess its *phenotype*), several instances of an individual (i.e. an RBF network with a specific architecture) are created and trained independently in accordance with a k-fold cross-validation technique [1,10]. The various instances are trained with respect to the least-squares error (LSE), whereas the fitness is determined using the lift factor (see Section 2) computed for 'unknown' data, i.e. data not used for training purposes. A specific fitness value is assigned, corresponding to the rank of an individual in the current population. Hence, absolute differences between individuals are neglected.

Selection: Selecting parents for reproduction is effected using *stochastic universal sampling* [28]. After recombination and mutation, a new generation of individuals must be established (next cycle). Here, the fittest individuals 'survive' (*elitist selection*; see [29]).

Pairing and recombination: Recombination produces descendants of a set of parents by combining the *genotypes* of parents. In a first step, pairs of individuals are chosen from the set of parents obtained by stochastic universal sampling using a distance-based approach to prevent *inbreeding* as far as possible. In a second step, the pairs of individuals selected recombine their representation vectors, producing two descendants each. For the bit vector (input features), a *uniform crossover* operator [26] was chosen and, for the integer value (number of hidden neurons), an *intermediate recombination* [26] is carried out.

Mutation: For the binary string describing the input features of a network, mutation is the random change (*switch*) of a bit by means of two variable mutation probabilities: one for the mutation from "0" to "1" and one for the mutation from "1" to "0" in order to avoid a drift of the number of features. The number of hidden neurons is mutated by adding discrete white noise with a mean of zero and a certain standard deviation.

Stopping criterion: The number of evolution cycles serves as a stopping criterion for reasons of its simplicity.

5 Results

In the following, the EA introduced in Section 4 is applied to the marketing problem set out in Section 2 and principal experimental results are presented. It is essential to note that a large number of additional experiments were carried out. Results of the evaluation of these experiments and a more detailed description of the experimental conditions can be found in [29]. As stated in Section 2, a cut-off point must be selected (here, 5%): hence, the response rate of the network (*Percentage_Buyers_Model*) and the lift are determined solely for the inputs yielding the top 5% of the network outputs. Evaluation of each network is performed by applying a 5-fold cross-validation method. Roughly 4 000 samples were available for training of the networks and an additional 8 000 samples for testing. The proportion of 'buyers' to 'non-buyers' in the test sets reflects the real-world ratio, whereas a 50:50 ratio was selected for the training sets.

Fig. 3 depicts an example of an evolution experiment and some parameters utilised. The lift factor (measured at the beginning of each cycle) starts at a

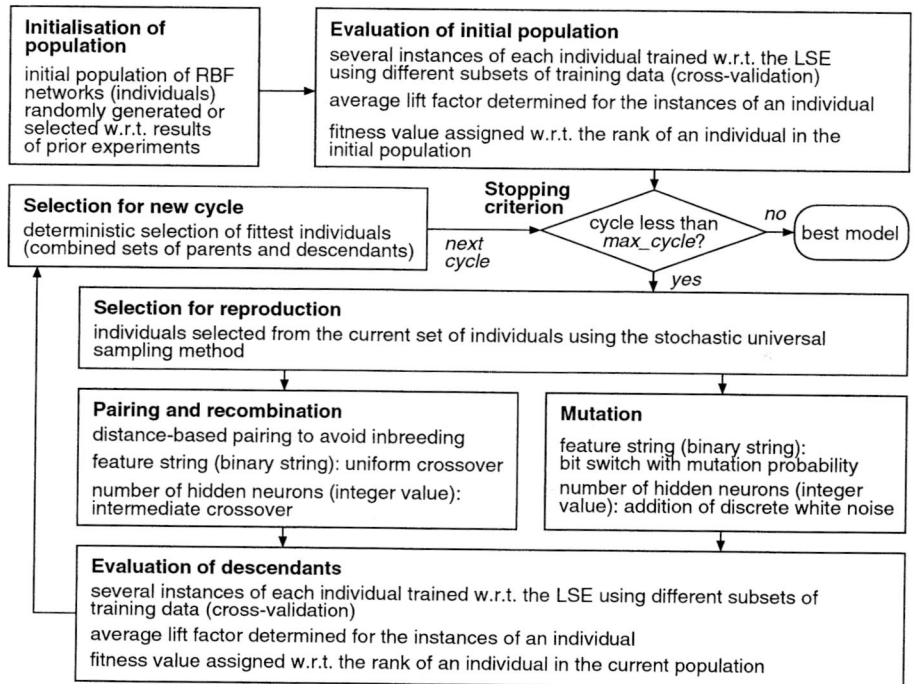

Fig. 2. Overview of the evolutionary algorithm for RBF architecture optimisation

value of ca. 1.2, finally converging to a value of ca. 2.4. During these 100 cycles, the MSE for training data (not shown) decreases from about 0.28 to 0.25. The network structure converges towards 10 features and 9 hidden neurons. A more detailed analysis of the results illustrates that key improvements are typically driven by feature selection. It can also be noted, that the variance of all parameters decreases significantly during the second half of the evolution.

6 Summary and Outlook

The article presented an evolutionary algorithm for feature selection and structure optimisation of RBF networks. The successful application of this combination of two soft-computing approaches to a problem in the area of direct marketing has been demonstrated. Using all available features and the commercial algorithms CHAID and C5, average lift factors of about 1.5 and 1.6 could be achieved. With MLP networks (as implemented in the software Clementine) average lift factors of about 1.7 could be obtained. The method introduced here led to a lift factor of about 2.4 on the test data utilized. From a business perspective, the EA turned out to be a breakthrough, enabling greater impact and higher efficiency of direct mailings. In fact, the EA as set out here may also be applied to comparable data mining and knowledge discovery problems. A com-

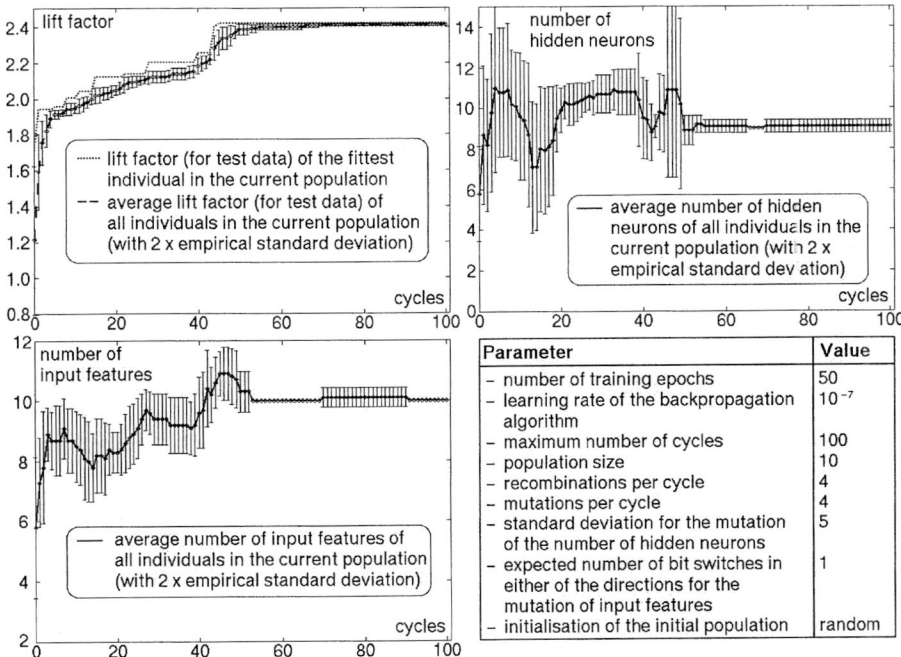

Fig. 3. Development of the evolution (example run)

bination with other network paradigms is feasible as well. Currently, we employ similar methods to address the issue of feature selection and model architecture optimisation for intrusion detection in computer networks [30].

It must be mentioned that the runtime of the EA is relatively high compared to other data mining and knowledge discovery methods (ca. eight days on a 1.3 GHz Pentium IV for an evolution as described in Section 5). Thus, our future work deals with a variety of ideas showing promise of accelerating the EA: in particular, centres and radii of basis functions will be handed down to descendants, the stochastic search will be supported by additional hard-computing optimisation concepts, and filter techniques will be applied to rank possible input features in advance.

References

1. Bishop, C.M.: Neural Networks for Pattern Recognition. Clarendon Press, Oxford (1995)
2. Haykin, S.: Neural Networks – A Comprehensive Foundation. Macmillan College Publishing Company, New York (1994)
3. Poggio, T., Girosi, F.: A theory of networks for approximation and learning. A.I. Memo No. 1140, C.B.I.P. Paper No. 31, Massachusetts Institute of Technology – Artificial Intelligence Laboratory & Center for Biological Information Procesing – Whitaker College (1989)

4. Arndt, D., Gersten, W.: Lift – a leading measure for predictive modeling. In: Proc. of the Int. Conf. on Machine Learning and Applications ICMLA. (2002) 249–255
5. Piatetsky-Shapiro, G., Steingold, S.: Measuring lift quality in database marketing. ACM SIGKDD – Explorations (Association for Computer Machinery, Special Interest Group on Knowledge Discovery and Data Mining) **2** (2000) 76–80
6. Gersten, W., Arndt, D.: Effective target variable selection from multiple customer touchpoints. In: Workshop on Mining Data Across Multiple Customer Touchpoints for CRM (MDCRM02) at the Sixth Pacific-Asia Conf. on Knowledge Discovery and Data Mining (PAKDD-02). (2002) 1–13
7. Arndt, D., Gersten, W.: External data selection for data mining in direct marketing. In: Proc. of the Int. Conf. on Information Quality. (2001) 44–61
8. Liu, H., Motoda, H.: Feature Selection for Knowledge Discovery and Data Mining. Kluwer Academic Publishers, Boston (1998)
9. Liu, H., Motoda, H., eds.: Feature Extraction, Construction, and Selection: A Data Mining Perspective. Kluwer Academic Publishers, Boston (1998)
10. Sick, B.: Technische Anwendungen von Soft-Computing Methoden. Lecture Notes, University of Passau, Faculty of Mathematics and Computer Science (2001)
11. Reed, R.: Pruning algorithms – a survey. IEEE Trans. on Neural Networks **4** (1993) 740–747
12. Freitas, A.A., ed.: Data Mining and Knowledge Discovery with Evolutionary Algorithms. Springer-Verlag, Berlin, Heidelberg, New York (2002)
13. Schaffer, J.D., Whitley, D., Eshelman, L.J.: Combinations of genetic algorithms and neural networks: A survey of the state of the art. In: Int. Workshop on Comb. of Genetic Algorithms and Neural Networks (COGANN-92). (1992) 1–37
14. Yao, X.: Evolving artificial neural networks. Proc. of the IEEE **87** (1999) 1423–1447
15. Lacerda, E., de Carvalho, A., Ludermir, T.: Evolutionary optimization of RBF networks. In Howlett, R.J., Jain, L.C., eds.: Radial Basis Function Networks 1. Physica Verlag, Heidelberg, New York (2001)
16. Mak, M.W., Cho, K.W.: Genetic evolution of radial basis function centers for pattern classification. In: Int. Joint Conf. on Neural Networks (IJCNN '98). Volume 1. (1998) 669–673
17. Whitehead, B., Choate, T.D.: Cooperative-competitive genetic evolution of radial basis function centers and widths for time series prediction. IEEE Tr. on Neural Networks **7** (1996) 869–880
18. Whitehead, B., Choate, T.D.: Evolving space-filling curves to distribute radial basis functions over an input space. IEEE Tr. on Neural Networks **5** (1994) 15–23
19. Billings, S.A., Zheng, G.L.: Radial basis function network configuration using genetic algorithms. Neural Networks **8** (1998) 877–890
20. Leung, H., Dubash, N., Xie, N.: Detection of small objects in clutter using a GA-RBF neural network. IEEE Tr. on Aerospace and Electronic Systems **38** (2002) 98–118
21. Zhao, W., Huang, D.S., Yunjian, G.: The structure optimization of radial basis probabilistic neural networks based on genetic algorithms. In: Proc. of the 2002 Int. Joint Conf. on Neural Networks (IJCNN '02). Volume 2. (2002) 1086–1091
22. Fu, X., Wang, L.: A GA-based RBF classifier with class-dependent features. In: Proc. of the 2002 Congr. on Evolutionary Comp. (CEC '02). Volume 2. (2002) 1890–1894
23. Fu, X., Wang, L.: Rule extraction from an RBF classifier based on class-dependent features. In: Proc. of the 2002 Congr. on Evolutionary Comp. (CEC '02). Volume 2. (2002) 1916–1921

24. Jin, Y., von Seelen, W., Sendhoff, B.: Extracting interpretable fuzzy rules from RBF neural networks. Int. Rep. 2000-02, Inst. für Neuroinformatik (INF), Ruhr-Universität Bochum (2000)
25. Michalewicz, Z.: Genetic Algorithms + Data Structures = Evolution Programs. 3rd edn. Springer-Verlag, Berlin, Heidelberg, New York (1996)
26. Bäck, T.: Evolutionary Algorithms in Theory and Practice. PhD thesis Universität Dortmund, Fachbereich Informatik (1994)
27. Roberts, S.G., Turega, M.: Evolving neural network structures: An evaluation of encoding techniques. In Pearson, D.W., Steele, N.C., Albrecht, R.F., eds.: Artificial Neural Nets and Genetic Algorithms, Springer Verlag, Wien, New York (1995) 96–99
28. Pohlheim, H.: Evolutionäre Algorithmen: Verfahren, Operatoren und Hinweise für die Praxis. Springer-Verlag, Berlin (2000)
29. Neumann, P.: Soft-computing methods for the identification of relevant features and the prediction of customer behaviour in the automotive industry. Master's thesis, University of Passau (2002)
30. Hofmann, A., Sick, B.: Evolutionary optimization of radial basis function networks for intrusion detection. In: IJCNN 2003: Proc. of the IEEE-INNS-ENNS Int. Joint Conf. on Neural Networks. (2003) (to appear).

Intrusion Detection in Computer Networks with Neural and Fuzzy Classifiers

Alexander Hofmann, Carsten Schmitz, and Bernhard Sick

University of Passau, Germany
Chair of Computer Architectures (Prof. Dr.-Ing. W. Grass), 94030 Passau
{hofmana,schmitzc,sick}@fmi.uni-passau.de

Abstract. With the rapidly increasing impact of the Internet, the development of appropriate intrusion detection systems (IDS) gains more and more importance. This article presents a performance comparison of four neural and fuzzy paradigms (multilayer perceptrons, radial basis function networks, NEFCLASS systems, and classifying fuzzy-k-means) applied to misuse detection on the basis of TCP and IP header information. As an example, four different attacks (Nmap, Portsweep, Dict, Back) will be detected utilising evaluation data provided by the Defense Advanced Research Projects Agency (DARPA). The best overall classification results (99.42%) can be achieved with radial basis function networks, which model hyperspherical clusters in the feature space.

1 Introduction

With the increasing number of computers being connected to the Internet, the security of network systems becomes more and more important. The recent attack (October, 2002) against the 13 official DNS root servers, which provide the primary road map for almost all Internet communications, underlined this statement once again. Even though 4 of them could resist the attack, this was probably the most concerted attack against the Internet infrastructure ever seen. Especially where sensitive and confidential information (e.g. for Internet banking or online shopping) is being stored and processed, there is a vital importance of security. Among other techniques such as authentication methods, data encryption, or firewalls, the use of *intrusion detection systems (IDS)* is essential to protect against attacks.

Since about a decade, the utilisation of soft-computing (SC) techniques has been investigated for different kinds of intrusion detection (misuse detection, anomaly detection). SC – with its principal constituents neural networks, fuzzy logic and probabilistic reasoning (e.g. evolutionary algorithms) – is, unlike conventional hard-computing (e.g. decision trees, linear regression techniques, "classical" pattern recognition algorithms), tolerant of imprecise data, uncertain information, and partial truth. Neural networks and neuro-fuzzy-systems with their learning capabilities seem to be the most appropriate SC approach for intrusion detection. Consequently, publications dealing with such approaches can be found regularly in journals and proceedings. However, the advantages of different model paradigms still seem to be the subject of a never-ending discussion. Actual experimental comparisons of different paradigms have been limited to very few cases.

The aim of this article is to compare the intrusion detection performance of four different neural and neuro-fuzzy paradigms (multilayer perceptrons, radial basis function networks, NEFCLASS systems, and classifying fuzzy-k-means) by means of data provided in the context of the first DARPA off-line intrusion detection evaluation in 1998. Here, the four attacks Nmap, Portsweep, Dict and Back will be detected. The generalisation capabilities of the paradigms will be evaluated in detail. The IDS presented here (which is still uncomplete, of course), can be regarded as a network-based system for offline misuse detection with central data collection according to the taxonomy of Axelsson described in [1]. Additionally, the combination of different paradigms will be investigated.

2 Related Work

Since the first steps in intrusion detection research were made in 1972 by Anderson [2], various IDS were developed and introduced. Especially in the last few years, with the vast growing of the Internet, a lot of new and sophisticated systems were made available. [3] provides a good overview over the evolution of research in intrusion detection. More recent efforts are described in [4,5]. The most comprehensive evaluations of IDS performed to date were supported by the Defense Advanced Research Projects Agency (DARPA) in 1998 and 1999 [6, 7,8].

Intrusion detection can be divided into two main categories: *misuse detection* and *anomaly detection*. Misuse detection is trying to discover intrusions by searching for distinguishing patterns or signatures of known attacks, whereas anomaly detection is based on the assumption that intrusive behaviour deviates significantly from a previously learned normal behaviour. Lots of other distinguishing features for IDS, for example the classification into *host-based* and *network-based* systems, are set out in [1,9].

The number of publications where neural network based IDS are proposed is rapidly increasing since about three years. Network paradigms which are trained with a supervised training algorithm are often (but not only) used for misuse detection. In more than a half of the publications, multilayer perceptrons (MLP) are taken, for example in [10,11,12,13]. Radial basis function networks (RBF) are applied in [10], for instance. Other examples are recurrent neural networks (RNN, e.g. Elman networks) [14], the cerebellar model articulation controller (CMAC) [15], FuzzyARTMAP [16], support vector machines (SVM) [12] or learning vector quantisation (LVQ) [10]. Network paradigms which are trained with unsupervised learning algorithms are often used for anomaly detection. Typical examples are the self-organising map (SOM) utilised in [17,18] or the ART-2 (adaptive resonance theory) networks applied in [19].

A comparison of different network paradigms can only be found in two recent articles: MLP, RBF and SOM+LVQ in [10] and MLP and SVM in [12]. However, a detailed analysis of the objectives (detection of 22 different attacks with a single model in [12]) and the experimental conditions (huge network structures with thousands of weights in some experiments and relatively small numbers of training patterns in both articles) shows, that reliable conclusions concerning a comparison of network paradigms cannot be drawn up to now.

3 Intrusion Data, Attack Types, and Features

The data of the first DARPA IDS evaluation in 1998 was used here. For this evaluation, seven weeks of training data and two weeks of test data have been generated on a test bed that emulates a small government site. A relatively simple network architecture and background traffic, designed to be similar to traffic on an Air Force base, have been used. More than 300 instances of 38 attack types have been launched against UNIX and Linux hosts. Here, the original training data are used for training, test and validation, because the original test data are not provided with labels that allow the identification of attacks.

Table 1. Features extracted for attack detection

Feature	Attacks
source port of TCP connection	Nmap
avg. TTL (Time To Life) value for packets sent by client	Nmap
avg. number of packets sent by client containing the FIN (FINISH) Flag	Nmap
avg. number of packets in the connection containing the FIN Flag	Nmap
avg. number of packets in the connection containing the RST (RESET) Flag	Portsweep
avg. number of packets sent by client containing the TCP options	Portsweep
maximum data length for TCP packets in the connection	Portsweep
number of packets in the connection	Dict
number of packets sent by client containing the TOS (Type Of Service) "Minimize Delay"	Dict
avg. TCP segment length for TCP packets sent by client	Dict
max. TTL value for packets sent by server	Back
number of packets sent by server containing the TOS (Type Of Service) "Normal Service"	Back
number of packets in the connection containing the ACK (ACKNOWLEDGE) Flag	Back
number of packets in the connection containing the SYN (SYNCHRONIZE) Flag	Back

Four attack types (Nmap, Portsweep, Dict, Back) were selected for our performance comparison. Nmap is a very sophisticated and extensive open source utility for performing network scans on several hosts or whole networks. It can be used to scan for open ports (normal and stealth portscans), to determine the running services on a machine, and even to identify the operating system running on a victim host (OS fingerprinting). In comparison to Nmap, Portsweep is a very simple tool for probing networks. It performs simple network scans and is able to search for ports and hosts listening on a specific network. Back is a Denial of Service attack launched against the Apache web server. An attacker sends requests to the web server containing up to thousands of leading slashes. With the servers attempt to process these requests, it will dramatically slow down and be unable to process any further requests. With the Dict attack, an attacker tries to gain access to a victims machine by guessing different username/password combinations. This process is usually automated and uses – beside a brute force method (try all possible combinations) – large predefined dictionaries. Further information on these and other attacks is available in [20].

In order to recognise attacks and to distinguish between normal and intrusive behaviour, features are needed. Therefore, pre-processing algorithms have been applied to construct statistical connection records from a raw tcpdump output. Here, only protocol information, i.e. TCP and IP header information, and not the transmitted data have been used for feature extraction (see Tab. 1).

4 Model Paradigms

The paradigms selected here will now be described in some more detail:
Multilayer perceptrons (MLP) [21,22] form the basis of our comparison as they are used in a major part of other publications addressing the use of neural networks for intrusion detection. MLPs separate clusters in the input (feature) space by means of a hierarchical combination of smooth hyperplanes. Here, MLPs are trained using a combination of resilient backpropagation (RPROP) and backpropagation with momentum.
Radial basis function networks (RBF) [21,22] typically use – in contrast to MLPs – a localised representation of information. With Gaussian basis functions, for example, clusters in the input space are modelled by means of hyperspheres. The activation of a hidden neuron is high, if the current input vector of the network is "similar" to the centre of its basis function. The centre of a basis function can, therefore, be seen as a prototype of a hyperspherical cluster in the feature space. The radius of the basis function depends on the diameter of the cluster. Here, the RBF networks are trained by means of a combination of k-means clustering, singular value decomposition and RPROP.
NEFCLASS (neuro-fuzzy classification) is a system for the classification of data based on a generic model of a 3-layer fuzzy perceptron [23]. Rules (neurons in the rule layer) are created in a first run through the training data (rule learning). In a second, supervised step (fuzzy set learning) NEFCLASS adapts the parameters of membership functions. The fuzzy rules have the form "if $[x_1$ is $\mu_1^{(s)}]$ and ... and $[x_n$ is $\mu_n^{(t)}]$ then pattern x belongs to class c_i", where $\mathbf{x} = (x_1, x_2, \ldots, x_n)$ is the feature vector, $\mu_1^{(s)}, \mu_n^{(t)}, \ldots$ are fuzzy sets and $c_1, \ldots, c_c$ are classes. NEFCLASS systems model clusters in the feature space by means of fuzzy hypercuboids.

Classifying fuzzy-k-means (CFKM): The k-means algorithm is a clustering method which assigns sample vectors to clusters using a minimum distance assignment principle (e.g. based on an Euclidean distance measure). The fuzzy-k-means algorithm was introduced by Bezdek [24]. Here, a fuzzy version of the ISODATA algorithm is applied [25]. It allows each sample vector to belong to each cluster with a certain fuzzy membership degree between 0 and 1. Fuzzy-k-means results in a matrix $U \in \mathbb{R}^{k \times m}$ which contains the membership degree of each sample vector $\mathbf{x}_1, \mathbf{x}_2, \ldots, \mathbf{x}_m$ w.r.t. each cluster $c_1, c_2, \ldots, c_k$. In addition to fuzzy-k-means, we use a method to derive rules from fuzzy clusters. The principal idea is that each cluster implies an if-then rule by projecting the cluster onto the corresponding axes of the feature space [26].

5 Experimental Results

In the following, an individual model will be set up (trained and evaluated) for each combination of attack type and model paradigm. The models use the input features given in Tab. 1 (i.e. 3 – 4 inputs only). The number of training and test patterns is 1300 (**Nmap** and **Dict**), 2900 (**Back**) and 7400 (**Portsweep**), respectively. These patterns will be used following a 5-fold cross-validation approach, i.e. $\frac{4}{5}$ are applied for training and $\frac{1}{5}$ for tests. The ratio of attacks and non-attacks (including data of other attack types) in each data set is 50:50.

The MLPs use one hidden layer with 3 neurons; activation function is the tanh. Depending on the attack type the MLPs are trained between 20 and 300 epochs. The RBF networks use between 2 and 4 hidden neurons with Gaussian basis functions and they are trained either 500 or 1000 epochs. The NEFCLASS systems extract all possible rules which typically results in a set of 40 – 50 rules, about 3 – 5 of them being necessary to classify the attacks. The membership functions are triangular and trapezoid. The CFKM utilise – again depending on the attack type – 10 up to 30 clusters. Typically only one of these clusters is necessary to classify the attacks. The number of epochs is 50.

The results in Tab. 2 (average results of 5 test data sets in the cross-validation) show that the overall classification rate is high for all combinations of paradigms and attack types (97.46% – 100.00%). RBF networks, however, yield better results than the other network paradigms. The first runner-up is – apart from the **Dict** attack – NEFCLASS. An analysis of the results for **Dict** shows that NEFCLASS has serious problems with the specific size and the distribution of the clusters in the feature space.

As the network structures (e.g. number of hidden neurons) and certain learning parameters (e.g. number of epochs) were optimised with respect to test patterns in the cross-validation, another, independent data set is needed for the validation of results. This validation set contains 60 000 patterns (59 400 non-attacks and 4 × 150 attacks). Results achieved for this data set, which is closer to the real-world ratio of attacks and non-attacks, are set out in Tab. 3. Here, trained models for the four different attack types are combined to distinguish

Table 2. Results achieved for different attacks with different model paradigms

intrusion type	misidentified normal behaviour (false alarms)	misidentified attacks (missing alarms)	overall result
Multilayer Perceptron (MLP)			
Nmap	0.00%	0.00%	100.00%
Portsweep	1.68%	1.10%	98.59%
Dict	0.86%	0.17%	99.46%
Back	2.53%	1.14%	98.14%
Radial Basis Function Network (RBF)			
Nmap	0.00%	0.00%	100.00%
Portsweep	1.61%	1.15%	98.61%
Dict	0.00%	0.00%	100.00%
Back	0.20%	0.64%	99.41%
NEFCLASS			
Nmap	0.00%	0.00%	100.00%
Portsweep	1.66%	1.10%	98.61%
Dict	4.57%	0.17%	97.46%
Back	0.80%	0.43%	99.38%
Classifying Fuzzy-k-means (CFKM)			
Nmap	1.14%	0.00%	99.39%
Portsweep	1.66%	2.20%	98.08%
Dict	2.14%	0.17%	98.77%
Back	1.07%	0.57%	99.17%

"attacs" and "normal behaviour". Again, it can be noted that RBF networks clearly outperform the other paradigms (false alarm rate and overall result).

Tab. 3 also sets out the results of two experiments, where the different model paradigms classifying the same attack type are combined in order to improve the results further ("ensemble" appoach). In the first experiment (3 of 4), an attack will be detected only if at least 3 out of the 4 different paradigms detect this attack. Compared to the results for RBF networks, the rate of false alarms can be reduced slightly, while the rate of missing alarms remains unchanged. If all four networks have to agree in detecting an attack (4 of 4), the overall classification rate is increased again, because the false alarm rate is reduced significantly. In this case, however, a higher number of attacks is not detected.

6 Conclusion and Outlook

The article presented a performance comparison of four different standard model paradigms (multilayer perceptrons, radial basis function networks, NEFCLASS systems, classifying fuzzy-k-means) applied for intrusion detection in computer networks. Only TCP and IP header information has been used for the detection. As a general result, it can be stated that all paradigms are able to detect the

Table 3. Results on validation data achieved with different model paradigms

model paradigm	misidentified normal behaviour (false alarms)	misidentified attacks (missing alarms)	overall result
MLP	3.92%	0.33%	96.11%
RBF	0.58%	0.33%	99.42%
NEFCLASS	1.65%	0.33%	98.36%
CFKM	5.62%	2.00%	94.41%
ensemble 3 of 4	0.55%	0.33%	99.45%
ensemble 4 of 4	0.21%	2.17%	99.77%

attacks (Nmap, Portsweep, Dict, Back). However, further efforts are necessary to reduce the false alarm rate which is still to high for practical applications.

RBF networks led to better results than the other paradigms. In contrast to other paradigms, RBF networks are able to model hyperspherical clusters in the feature space by means of localised radial basis functions. It must be emphasised, that only a few input features (3 – 4, depending on the attack type) were necessary to achieve overall classification rates between 98.61% (Portsweep) and 100.00% (Nmap and Dict). This approach offers the opportunity to extract rules which may be deployed in an expert system (see, e.g. [27]) and may help to improve the understanding of the functional relationship between certain features and attack types. This analysis will be possible because the network structures investigated here are very small (3 – 4 inputs, 2 – 4 hidden neurons).

Further improvements of the intrusion detection can be expected. Possible starting points for refinements are: Evaluation of the transmitted data (not only utilisation of header information), consideration of the temporal behaviour of intrusions, automated feature selection and structure optimisation for neural networks, improved and accelerated training methods for neural networks etc.

Our current and future research deals with automated architecture optimisation of RBF networks by means of evolutionary algorithms [28] and with rule extraction from trained neural networks [26]. Also, the temporal behaviour of attacks will be investigated in greater detail.

References

1. Axelsson, S.: Intrusion detection systems: A survey and taxonomy. Tech. Rep. 99-15, Department of Computer Engineering, Chalmers University of Technology, Göteborg (2000)
2. Anderson, J.P.: Computer security threat monitoring and surveillance. Tech. Rep., James P. Anderson Co., Fort Washington (1980)
3. Lunt, T.F.: A survey of intrusion detection techniques. Computers and Security **12** (1993) 405–418
4. Wespi, A., Vigna, G., Deri, L., eds.: Recent Advances in Intrusion Detection. LNCS 2516. Springer Verlag, Berlin, Heidelberg, New York (2002) (Proc. of the 5th Int. Symp. RAID 2002, Zurich).

5. Northcutt, S., Novak, J.: Network Intrusion Detection. 3 edn. New Riders, Indianapolis (2002)
6. Durst, R., Champion, T., Witten, B., Miller, E., Spagnuolo, L.: Testing and evaluating computer intrusion detection systems. Comm. of the ACM **42** (1999) 53–61
7. Lippmann, R.P., Haines, J.W., Fried, D.J., Korba, J., Das, K.: The 1999 DARPA off-line intrusion detection evaluation. Computer Networks **34** (2000) 579–595
8. Lippmann, R.P., Fried, D.J., Graf, I., Haines, J.W., Kendall, K.R., McClung, D., Weber, D., Webster, S.E., Wyschogrod, D., Cunningham, R.K., Zissman, M.A.: Evaluating intrusion detection systems: the 1998 DARPA off-line intrusion detection evaluation. In: Proc. of the 2000 DARPA Information Survivability Conf. and Exposition (DISCEX), Hilton Head. Vol. 2., IEEE Press (1999) 12–26
9. Axelsson, S.: Research in intrusion detection systems: A survey. Tech. Rep. 98-17, Department of Computer Engineering, Chalmers University of Technology, Göteborg (1999) (revised version).
10. Liu, Z., Florez, G., Bridges, S.: A comparison of input representations in neural networks: a case study in intrusion detection. In: Proc. of the Int. Joint Conf. on Neural Networks (IJCNN 2002), Honolulu. Vol. 2. (2002) 1708–1713
11. Lee, S., Heinbuch, D.: Training a neural-network based intrusion detector to recognize novel attacks. IEEE Tr. on Systems, Man and Cybernetics, Part A **31** (2001) 294 – 299
12. Mukkamala, S., Janoski, G., Sung, A.: Intrusion detection using neural networks and support vector machines. In: Proc. of the Int. Joint Conf. on Neural Networks (IJCNN 2002), Honolulu. Vol. 2. (2002) 1702–1707
13. Wang, L., Yu, G., Wang, G., Wang, D.: Method of evolutionary neural network-based intrusion detection. In Zhong, Y., Cui, S., Wang, Y., eds.: Int. Conf. on Info-tech and Info-net (ICII 2001), Beijing. Vol. 5. (2001) 13–18
14. Debar, H., Dorizzi, B.: An application of a recurrent network to an intrusion detection. In: Proc. of the Int. Joint Conf. on Neural Networks (IJCNN 1992), Baltimore. Vol. 2. (1992) 478–483
15. Cannady, J.: Applying CMAC-based online learning to intrusion detection. In: Proc. of the IEEE-INNS-ENNS Int. Joint Conf. on Neural Networks (IJCNN 2000), Como. Vol. 5. (2000) 405–410
16. Cannady, J., Garcia, R.C.: The application of fuzzy ARTMAP in the detection of computer network attacks. In Dorffner, G., Bischof, H., Hornik, K., eds.: Artificial Neural Networks – ICANN 2001 (Proc. of the 11th Int. Conf. on Artificial Neural Networks), Vienna. (Number 2130 in Lecture Notes in Computer Science, Springer Verlag, Berlin, Heidelberg, New York) (2001) 225–230
17. Hoglund, A., Hatonen, K., Sorvari, A.: A computer host-based user anomaly detection system using the self-organizing map. In: Proc. of the IEEE-INNS-ENNS Int. Joint Conf. on Neural Networks (IJCNN 2000), Como. Vol. 5. (2000) 411–416
18. Rhodes, B.C., Mahaffey, J.A., Cannady, J.D.: Multiple self-organizing maps for intrusion detection. In: Proc. of the 23rd National Information Systems Security Conf. (NISSC 2000), Baltimore. (2000)
19. Dasgupta, D., Brian, H.: Mobile security agents for network traffic analysis. In: Proc. of DARPA Information Survivability Conference & Exposition II (DISCEX '01), Anaheim. Vol. 2. (2001) 332–340
20. Kendall, K.: A database of computer attacks for the evaluation of intrusion detection systems. Master's thesis, MIT, Department of Electrical Engineering and Computer Science (1999)
21. Haykin, S.: Neural Networks – A Comprehensive Foundation. Macmillan College Publishing Company, New York (1994)

22. Bishop, C.M.: Neural Networks for Pattern Recognition. Clarendon Press, Oxford (1995)
23. Nauck, D., Kruse, R.: Nefclass – a neuro-fuzzy approach for the classification of data. In George, K.M., Carrol, J.H., Deaton, E., Oppenheim, D., Hightower, J., eds.: Applied Computing, ACM Press (1995) 461–465 (Proc. of the 1995 ACM Symp. on Applied Computing, Nashville).
24. Bezdek, J.C.: Pattern Recognition with Fuzzy Objective Algorithms. Plenum Press, New York (1981)
25. Dunn, J.C.: A fuzzy relative of the ISODATA process and its use in detecting compact, well separated clusters. Journal on Cybernetics **3** (1973) 32–57
26. Schmitz, C.: Regelbasierte Klassifikation von Angriffen in Rechnernetzen mit lernenden Verfahren. Master's thesis, University of Passau (2002)
27. Jin, Y., von Seelen, W., Sendhoff, B.: Extracting interpretable fuzzy rules from RBF neural networks. Internal Rep. 2000-02, Institut für Neuroinformatik (INF), Ruhr-Universität Bochum (2000)
28. Hofmann, A.: Einsatz von Soft-Computing-Verfahren zur Erkennung von Angriffen auf Rechnernetze. Master's thesis, University of Passau (2002)

Optimal Matrix Compression Yields Storage Capacity 1 for Binary Willshaw Associative Memory

Andreas Knoblauch

Abteilung Neuroinformatik, Fakultät für Informatik, Universität Ulm,
Oberer Eselsberg, D-89069 Ulm, Germany
Tel: (+49)-731-50-24151; Fax: (+49)-731-50-24156
knoblauch@neuro.informatik.uni-ulm.de

Abstract. The classical binary Willshaw model of associative memory has an asymptotic storage capacity of $\ln 2 \approx 0.7$ which exceeds the capacities of other (e.g., Hopfield-like) models by far. However, its practical use is severely limited, since the asymptotic capacity is reached only for very large numbers n of neurons and for sparse patterns where the number k of one-entries must match a certain optimal value $k_{\mathrm{opt}}(n)$ (typically $k_{\mathrm{opt}} = \log n$). In this work I demonstrate that optimal compression of the binary memory matrix by a Huffman or Golomb code can increase the asymptotic storage capacity to 1. Moreover, it turns out that this happens for a very broad range of k being either ultra-sparse (e.g., k constant) or moderately-sparse (e.g., $k = \sqrt{n}$). A storage capacity in the range of $\ln 2$ is already achieved for practical numbers of neurons.

1 Introduction

Associative memories are systems that contain information about a finite set of associations between pattern pairs $\{(x^\mu \to y^\mu) : \mu = 1, ..., M\}$. A possibly noisy address pattern $\tilde{x}^\mu$ can be used to retrieve an associated pattern $\hat{y}^\mu$ that ideally will equal y^μ.

In *neural implementations* the information about the associations is stored in the synaptic connectivity of one or more neuron populations. Neural implementations can be advantageous over hash-tables or simple look-up-tables if the number of patterns is large, if parallel implementation is possible, or if fault-tolerance is required, i.e., if the address patterns $\tilde{x}^\mu$ may differ from the original patterns x^μ used for storing the associations.

The so-called *storage capacity* of an associative memory can be measured information-theoretically by maximizing the transinformation between the stored patterns y^μ and the retrieved patterns $\hat{y}^\mu$. A valid quality measure is the storage capacity *normalized* to the required *physical memory* (or, less valid, normalized to the number of required synapses).

In 1969 Willshaw et al. [17] discovered that a high (normalized) storage capacity of $\ln 2 \approx 0.7$ is possible for Steinbuch's neural implementation of associative memory using binary patterns and synapses [16]. These results were refined by Palm in 1980 [11]. The analysis showed that the upper bound $\ln 2$ is only approached asymptotically for very large (i.e., not practical) numbers n of neurons. Even worse, high capacities are only possible for sparse patterns ,i.e., if the number k of one-entries is much smaller than the pattern size n, typically $k = c \log n$ for a constant c (cf. Fig. 1). For k smaller or larger than required for the optimum, the capacity usually decreases rapidly to small values. These requirements imposed a severe limitation to the practical use of the *Willshaw (or Steinbuch) model* since it turned out to be difficult to find adequate codes that match the strict requirements for the pattern activity k. Another severe limitation is that high capacities can only be achieved for random patterns, i.e., if the stored patterns are uncorrelated.

In the mid eighties alternative neural implementations were proposed [4,5]. But it turned out that the capacity of the Willshaw model exceeds the capacities of other models by far [12]. From the late eighties on methods were developed to improve the retrieval results under noisy conditions, e.g., by bidirectional, iterative, or spiking retrievals [10,14,15,7], and an early attempt to use sparse matrices efficiently was not very promising [1] (cf. [9]).

Although it was possible to slightly extend the upper theoretical bound for the storage capacity (per synapse) to $1/(2 \ln 2) \approx 0.72$ for non-binary synapses [12], the bound of $\ln 2$ for the storage capacity normalized to the required physical memory was never exceeded for non-trivial models. It was even believed that it would be impossible to reach capacity 1 (or at least exceed $\ln 2$) for really distributed storage [12].

In this work we will see that it is indeed possible to reach capacity 1 asymptotically for really distributed storage. This can be achieved for the Willshaw model if the patterns are *not* optimally sparse in the sense of the classical analysis ($k \neq c \log n$). Then the memory matrix contains sparsely either one-entries (for $k < c \log n$) or zero-entries (for $k > c \log n$). It turns out that optimal compression of the memory matrix (e.g., by a Huffman or Golomb code [6,3]) leads to capacities exceeding the classical optimum. Although capacity 1 is approached only for unrealistically large n, values in the range of $\ln 2$ (the classical upper bound) can already be reached for practical n. Even more relevant for real applications with finite n is the fact that high capacities on the order of or above the classical optimum are obtained for a very broad range of k, including ultra-sparse patterns (e.g., k constant) and moderately-sparse patterns (e.g., $k = \sqrt{n}$).

In section 2 we will briefly review the classical analysis of the basic storing and retrieval algorithms used in the Willshaw model. These classical results are applied in section 3 to analyze optimal compression of the memory matrix. The main results, some open problems, and the prospects for future work are discussed in the concluding section.

2 Classical Analysis of the Willshaw Model

In this section we will briefly review the classical analysis of the basic storing and retrieving procedures used in the Willshaw model [16,17,11,12,15].

2.1 Storing and Retrieving Patterns

Consider the set of *associations* between M pattern pairs $\{(x^\mu \to y^\mu) : \mu = 1, ..., M\}$ where all patterns are *binary vectors* of length n containing exactly k ones.

We *store* the patterns hetero-associatively in the *binary memory matrix* $A \in \{0,1\}^{n \times n}$ corresponding to synaptic connections between two neuron populations, the *address population* corresponding to the x^μ patterns, and the *addressed* or *retrieval population* corresponding to the y^μ-patterns. Matrix entry A_{ij} corresponds to the synaptic weight of the connection from neuron i in the address population to neuron j in the retrieval population, and is obtained from the superposition of outer products of corresponding pattern vectors as

$$A_{ij} = \min\left(1, \sum_{\mu=1}^{M} x_i^\mu \cdot y_j^\mu\right) \in \{0,1\}. \tag{1}$$

For pattern *retrieval* we address the associative memory by an address pattern $\tilde{x}$ which may (for example) be the noisy version of one of the original address patterns x^μ. By vector-matrix-multiplication $\tilde{x}A$ we obtain neuron potentials which can be transformed to the retrieval result $\hat{y}$ by applying a threshold Θ,

$$\hat{y}_j = \begin{cases} 1, & (\sum_{i=1}^{n} \tilde{x}_i A_{ij}) \geq \Theta \\ 0, & \text{otherwise} \end{cases}. \tag{2}$$

The choice of the threshold Θ is important for good retrieval results. One possibility which is referred to as the *Willshaw-retrieval-strategy* is simply setting the threshold equal to the number of one-entries in the address pattern $\tilde{x}$,

$$\Theta = \sum_{i=1}^{n} \tilde{x}_i \tag{3}$$

If all the one-entries in the address pattern $\tilde{x}$ occur also in one of the original patterns, x^μ, then the one-entries in the retrieval result $\hat{y}$ will be a superset of the ones in the associated pattern, y^μ. Indeed, this strategy is the only possible choice if one assumes that the address pattern contains no 'false alarms', and it plays also an important role for pattern separation in spiking associative memories with time-continuous retrievals [7,8]. In the following we will investigate the storage capacity of the Willshaw model for this simple one-step retrieval algorithm.

2.2 Classical Analysis of One-Step Retrieval

Consider storing hetero-associatively M random pattern pairs (x^μ, y^μ) as described in section 2.1. All patterns have size n and contain exactly k ones. The probability that a given synapse is *not* set by the association of one pattern pair is approximately $1 - k^2/n^2$. Therefore the probability p_1 of a one-entry in the resulting binary $n \times n$-matrix A after association of all M pattern pairs can be approximated by

$$p_1 \approx 1 - (1 - k^2/n^2)^M \approx 1 - e^{-Mk^2/n^2} \qquad (4)$$

After storing the patterns we can use the address patterns x^μ to retrieve the associated patterns y^μ. Applying the Willshaw strategy $\Theta = k$ (see sect. 2.1) we obtain a retrieved pattern $\hat{y}^\mu$ that contains all the one-entries of y^μ, but possibly also false one-entries. The probability p_{01} of a false one can be approximated by

$$p_{01} \approx p_1^k. \qquad (5)$$

To obtain good retrieval results we demand similarly as in [12] a *high-fidelity-requirement* $p_{01}/(k/n) \approx 0$ and $p_{01} \to 0$ for $n \to \infty$ which states that the relative number of false ones is near zero. *High-fidelity* can be obtained by requiring $p_{01} \leq \epsilon k/n$ for a small positive ϵ and $k/n \to 0$ which is true for (sublinearly) sparse patterns. From eq. 5 we obtain a minimal address pattern size of

$$k_{\text{HiFi}} := \frac{\ln(n/k) - \ln \epsilon}{- \ln p_1}. \qquad (6)$$

The storing and retrieving of the M pattern pairs as described can approximately be thought of as the transmission of Mn binary digits (of the y^μ patterns) over a binary channel. For small k/n the information per digit is approximately $-k/n \log k/n$ and for small ϵ the stored information is about

$$T(n, k; M) \approx M k \log(n/k) \qquad (7)$$

To *maximize* T for given n and k we store as much patterns as possible so that we still fulfill the *hifi-requirement*. This means we can increase the memory load p_1 by storing patterns until $k_{\text{HiFi}}(p_1) = k$. From the hifi-requirement and eq. 5 it follows the *maximal* matrix load

$$p_{1,\max} = (\epsilon k/n)^{1/k}, \qquad (8)$$

and with eq. 4 we get the *maximal* number of stored patterns

$$M_{\max} = \frac{\ln(1 - p_{1,\max})}{\ln(1 - k^2/n^2)} \approx -\frac{n^2}{k^2} \ln(1 - p_{1,\max}), \qquad (9)$$

and therefore we obtain for the *storage capacity* $C(n, k)$ as the *maximal* stored information per physical memory unit (bit for $\log = \log_2$)

$$C(n, k) := \frac{T(n, k; M_{\max})}{n^2} \approx -\ln(1 - p_{1,\max}) \frac{\log(n/k)}{k}. \qquad (10)$$

To compute the *storage capacity* $C(n) := C(n, k_{\text{opt}})$ of an associative memory with n neurons, we still have to *maximize* $C(n, k)$ with respect to k. From eq. 6 we obtain $k_{\text{opt}} = -\log n / \log p_{1,\max}$ for large $n \to \infty$, and with eq. 10

$$C(n) \approx \log p_{1,\max} \ln(1 - p_{1,\max}). \qquad (11)$$

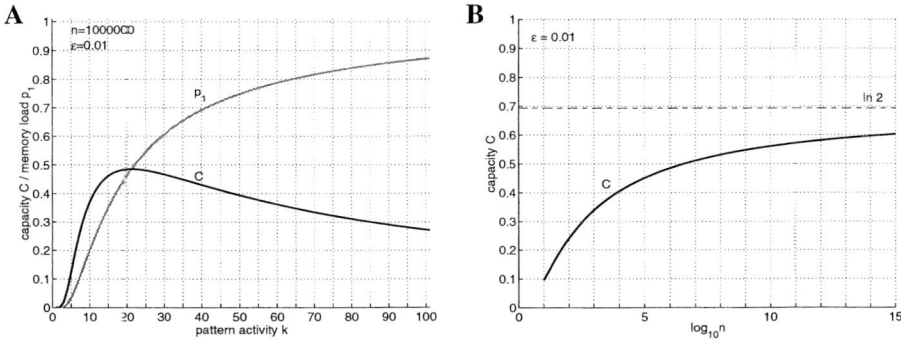

Fig. 1. Some results from the classical analysis of the Willshaw model (hifi-parameter $\epsilon = 0.01$, see text). **A** : Dependence of the storage capacity $C(n,k)$ (black) and memory load $p_1(n,k)$ on the pattern activity k (number of one-entries in a pattern) for pattern size $n = 10^6$. The optimal capacity $C \approx 0.49$ is reached for $k = 21$. For larger or smaller k the capacity decreases rapidly. The memory load p_1 increases with k monotonously from 0 to 1. p_1 is near 0.5 for optimal k. **B** : For $n \to \infty$ we have $C(n) \to \ln 2$. Unfortunately, the convergence is rather slow.

This is maximal for $p_{1,\max} = 0.5$ and therefore $C(n) \to \ln 2$ for $n \to \infty$. In the following we will simply write p_1 for $p_{1,\max}$. Fig. 1 illustrates some results of the classical analysis. Unfortunately, the convergence of C towards $\ln 2$ is very slow.

For a given n, high capacities C are obtained only for a very narrow range of k around an optimum k_{opt} ($\epsilon = 0.01$, $n = 1000000$, $k_{\mathrm{opt}} = 21$, and $C \approx 0.49$ in Fig.1A). For larger or smaller k the capacity decreases rapidly. The memory load p_1 increases with k monotonously from 0 to 1. For $k = k_{\mathrm{opt}}$ the memory matrix is not sparse with $p_1 \approx 0.5$. and compression is not possible. However, for k smaller and larger the memory load approaches 0 and 1, respectively, and we can hope to improve the storage capacity by compressing the memory matrix. This is investigated in the next section.

3 Compressing the Binary Memory Matrix

As a result from the analysis above, the storage capacity *per synapse* is limited to $\ln 2$, and even this value is achieved only for infinite large numbers of neurons $n \to \infty$ and a certain $k(n)$. Nevertheless what we can do is making use of the *physical memory* in an optimal way by compressing the memory matrix A by applying Huffman or Golomb coding [6,3]. However, compressing the matrix for the classical maximum C(n) is useless since it is obtained at a memory load $p_1 = 0.5$. On the other hand, for (classical) non-optimal k we will obtain $p_1 \neq 0.5$, and by *optimal* compression of the memory matrix (which requires $p_1 \to 0$ or $p_1 \to 1$ for Golomb coding) we can decrease the required physical memory by a factor of $I(p_1) := -p_1 \log p_1 - (1-p_1) \log(1-p_1)$ [2,9].

Fig.2A,B shows the dependence of C and the improved storage capacity $C^{\text{cmpr}} := C/I(p_1)$ on k for $n = 10^6$, $\epsilon = 0.01$. While p_1 increases monotonously with k from 0 to 1 (cf. Fig.1A), surprisingly, for $k \neq k_{\text{opt}}$ we have not only $C^{\text{cmpr}}(k) > C(k)$, but also $C^{\text{cmpr}}(k) > C(k_{\text{opt}})$. Indeed it turns out that $C(k_{\text{opt}})$, the classical maximum of C, is rather a local minimum of C^{cmpr} (Fig.2B,C):

From eq. 11 we obtain for large n an improved storage capacity C^{cmpr} of

$$C^{\text{cmpr}}(n) \approx \frac{\ln p_1 \ln(1-p_1)}{-p_1 \ln p_1 - (1-p_1)\ln(1-p_1)}. \tag{12}$$

For small $p_1 \to 0$ we have $I(p_1) \approx -p_1 \log p_1$ and $\ln(1-p_1) \approx -p_1$ and therefore $C^{\text{cmpr}} \to 1$. Similarly for large $p_1 \to 1$ we have $I(p_1) \approx -(1-p_1)\log(1-p_1)$ and therefore also $C^{\text{cmpr}} \approx (\ln p_1)/(1-p_1) \to 1$.

Together, we obtain an asymptotic storage capacity of 1 as soon as $p_1 \to 0$ or $p_1 \to 1$ for $n \to \infty$. From eq. 8 we see that this can be fulfilled for almost all sublinear functions $k(n)$. For $c > 0$ and logarithmic $k = c \ln n$ we obtain from eq. 8

$$\ln p_1 = \frac{\ln(\epsilon c \ln n) - \ln n}{c \ln n} \to -\frac{1}{c}, \tag{13}$$

and therefore $p_1 \to \exp(-1/c)$ for $n \to \infty$. So varying c one can obtain all possible values in $(0;1)$ for asymptotic p_1 and correspondingly all values in $[\ln 2; 1)$ for asymptotic C^{cmpr} (see Fig. 2C). Since p_1 is monotonously increasing in k we conclude that $C^{\text{cmpr}} \to 1$ for all sublinear, but non-logarithmic functions $k(n)$.

Fig.2D shows the convergence of C^{cmpr} for $k = 3$, $k = 30$, and $k = \sqrt{n}$ in comparison to the classical C. All the C^{cmpr} functions slowly approach 1. Values in the range of $\ln 2$, the classical maximum, are already approached for relatively small n at least for ultra-sparse patterns (e.g., $n = 10^8$ for $k = 3$).

Although the convergence of C^{cmpr} is fastest for ultra-sparse patterns ($k < k_{\text{opt}}$), the results for the moderately-sparse patterns ($k > k_{\text{opt}}$) are also relevant for applications because the broad range of k with $C^{\text{cmpr}}(k) \geq C(k_{\text{opt}})$ makes it much easier to find adequate codes.

4 Conclusions

We have demonstrated that optimal matrix compression by Huffman or Golomb coding [6,3] yields storage capacity $C^{\text{cmpr}} = 1$ asymptotically. Surprisingly, this happens for almost all sublinear functions $k(n)$. Indeed, it is somewhat ironic that choosing $k = c \log n$, which was widely analyzed so far and thought to be optimal, is the *only* possible choice of a (sublinearly) sparse code where $C^{\text{cmpr}} \to 1$ is *not* possible.

Similarly as for the classical capacity C the convergence of C^{cmpr} is rather slow, and values near 1 are obtained only for n too large for real implementations (Fig. 2D). However, at least for ultra-sparse patterns (e.g., constant k with still $M = O(n^{2-1/k})$) values $C^{\text{cmpr}} \approx \ln 2$, the classical upper bound, can be achieved already for practical n (e.g., $C^{\text{cmpr}}(n) \approx 0.7$ for $k = 3$ and $n = 10^8$ in Fig.2D).

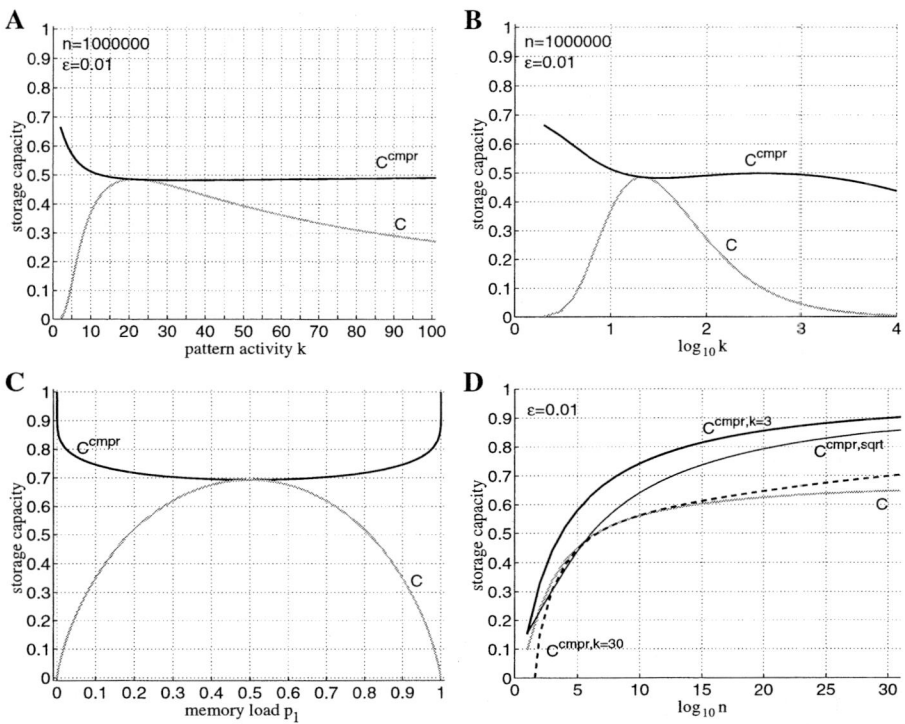

Fig. 2. Comparison of the classical storage capacity C per synapse (gray) and the storage capacity C^{cmpr} per bit of physical memory after optimal compression of the memory matrix (black). **A** : Comparison of $C(n,k)$ and $C^{\mathrm{cmpr}}(n,k) := C/I(p_1)$ for $n = 10^6$, $\epsilon = 0.01$ (cf. Fig.1A). **B** : Same as A but with logarithmic scale for k. While C reaches high values only for a narrow range of k around the optimum $k_{\mathrm{opt}} = 21$, $C^{\mathrm{cmpr}}(n,k) > C(n,k_{\mathrm{opt}})$ is possible for a very broad range of k. **C** : Asymptotic storage capacities C and C^{cmpr} over memory load p_1 for $n \to \infty$. The maximum $\ln 2$ of C at $p_1 = 0.5$ turns out to be the minimum of C^{cmpr}. $C^{\mathrm{cmpr}} \to 1$ for $p_1 \to 0$ or $p_1 \to 1$. **D** : $C^{\mathrm{cmpr}}(n)$ for different functions $k(n)$ (and $\epsilon = 0.01$). In contrast to classical C (gray) which reaches $\ln 2 \approx 0.7$ asymptotically for $k = c \log n$, optimal compression yields storage capacity 1 asymptotically for constant $k = 3$ ($C^{\mathrm{cmpr},k=3}$, thick), constant $k = 30$ ($C^{\mathrm{cmpr},k=30}$, dashed), and $k = \sqrt{n}$ ($C^{\mathrm{cmpr,sqrt}}$, thin) as well as for all sublinear but non-logarithmic functions (see text).

The fact that high storage capacities of the order of or above the classical optimum occur for *all* sublinear pattern activities $k(n)$ (and not only for $k = \log n$, cf. Fig.2B) is a big relief for finding adequate codes. For certain applications $k = \log n$ is simply too small for practical n to express complex hierarchical relations between the patterns [13], and one would prefer $k = \sqrt{n}$ where still a large number of (random) patterns $M = O(n \ln n)$ can safely be retrieved.

There are still a number of issues that have to be addressed. For example it would be interesting to compare efficient implementations of Huffman or Golomb decompression with classical retrievals. At least Golomb coding should be almost as efficient as explicitly storing the indices of sparse matrix entries. It would also be interesting to compute the local maximum of $C^{\mathrm{cmpr}}(n,k)$ for $k > k_{\mathrm{opt}}$ (see Fig.2B) analytically. Another question is how this local optimum could be used for real applications, and if emerging problems concerning the trade-off between the number of stored patterns, fault-tolerance, memory load and compressibility can be solved. These and other issues will be discussed in future work [9].

Acknowledgements. I am grateful to Günther Palm, Friedrich T. Sommer, and Thomas Wennekers for ongoing support and valuable discussions. This work was partially sponsored by the MirrorBot project of the European Union.

References

1. Bentz, H.J., Hagstroem, M., Palm, G.: Information storage and effective data retrieval in sparse matrices. Neural Networks **2** (1989) 289–293
2. Cover, T.M, Thomas, J.A.: Elements of information theory. Wiley, New York, 1991
3. Golomb, S.W.: Run-length encodings. IEEE Transactions on Information Theory **12** (1966) 399–401
4. Hopfield, J.J.: Neural networks and physical systems with emergent collective computational abilities. Proc. Natl. Acad. Sci. USA **79** (1982) 2554–2558
5. Hopfield, J.J., Tank, D.W.: Computing with neural circuits. Science **233** (1986) 625–633
6. Huffman, D.A.: A method for the construction of minimum redundancy codes. Proceedings of the Institute of Radio Engineers **40** (1952) 1098–1101
7. Knoblauch, A., Palm, G.: Pattern separation and synchronization in spiking associative memories and visual areas. Neural Networks **14** (2001) 763–780
8. Knoblauch, A., Palm, G.: Scene segmentation by spike synchronization in reciprocally connected visual areas. II. Global assemblies and synchronization on larger space and time scales. Biological Cybernetics **87** (2002) 168–184
9. Knoblauch, A., Sommer, F.T., Palm, G.: Willshaw associative memory and matrix compression. in preparation
10. Kosko, B.: Bidirectional associative memories. IEEE Transactions on Systems, Man, and Cybernetics **18** (1988) 49–60
11. Palm, G.: On associative memories. Biological Cybernetics **36** (1980) 19–31
12. Palm, G.: Memory capacities of local rules for synaptic modification. A comparative review. Concepts in Neuroscience **2** (1991) 97–128
13. Rachkovskij, D.A., Kussul, E.M.: Binding and normalization of binary sparse distributed representations by context-dependent thinning. Neural Computation **13** (2001) 411–452
14. Schwenker, F., Sommer, F.T., Palm, G.: Iterative retrieval of sparsely coded associative memory patterns. Neural Networks **9** (1996) 445–455
15. Sommer, F.T., Palm, G.: Improved bidirectional retrieval of sparse patterns stored by Hebbian learning. Neural Networks **12** (1999) 281–297
16. Steinbuch, K.: Die Lernmatrix. Kybernetik **1** (1961) 36–45
17. Willshaw, D.J., Buneman, O.P., Longuet-Higgins, H.C.: Non-holographic associative memory. Nature **222** (1969) 960–962

Supervised Locally Linear Embedding

Dick de Ridder[1], Olga Kouropteva[2], Oleg Okun[2], Matti Pietikäinen[2], and Robert P.W. Duin[1]*

[1] Pattern Recognition Group, Department of Imaging Science and Technology, Delft University of Technology, Lorentzweg 1, 2628 CJ Delft, The Netherlands
{dick,bob}@ph.tn.tudelft.nl, http://www.ph.tn.tudelft.nl
[2] Machine Vision Group, Infotech Oulu and Department of Electrical and Information Engineering, P.O.Box 4500, FIN-90014 University of Oulu, Finland
{kouropte,oleg,mkp}@ee.oulu.fi, http://www.ee.oulu.fi/mvg/mvg.php

Abstract. Locally linear embedding (LLE) is a recently proposed method for unsupervised nonlinear dimensionality reduction. It has a number of attractive features: it does not require an iterative algorithm, and just a few parameters need to be set. Two extensions of LLE to supervised feature extraction were independently proposed by the authors of this paper. Here, both methods are unified in a common framework and applied to a number of benchmark data sets. Results show that they perform very well on high-dimensional data which exhibits a manifold structure.

1 Introduction

In many real-world classification problems, high-dimensional data sets are collected, e.g. from sensors. Often, the ideal decision boundary between different classes in such sets is highly nonlinear. A classifier should therefore have many degrees of freedom, and consequently a large number of parameters. As a result, training a classifier on such data sets is quite complicated: a large number of parameters has to be estimated using a limited number of samples. This is the well-known *curse of dimensionality*.

One can overcome this problem by first mapping the data to a high-dimensional space in which the classes become (approximately) linearly separable. Kernel-based techniques, such as support vector machines (SVMs), are typical examples of this approach. An alternative is to *lower* the data dimensionality, rather than increase it. Although it might seem information is lost, the reduction in the number of parameters one needs to estimate can result in better performance. Many linear methods for performing dimensionality reduction, such as principal component analysis (PCA) and linear discriminant analysis (LDA) are well-established in literature.

---

* The financial support of the Infotech Oulu graduate school is gratefully acknowledged. This work was partly sponsored by the Dutch Foundation for Applied Sciences (STW) under project number AIF.4997.

Here, a nonlinear dimensionality reduction method called locally linear embedding (LLE, [9]) is considered. The main assumption behind LLE is that the data set is sampled from a (possibly nonlinear) manifold, embedded in the high-dimensional space. LLE is an unsupervised, non-iterative method, which avoids the local minima problems plaguing many competing methods (e.g. those based on the EM algorithm). Some other advantages of LLE are that few parameters need to be set (selecting optimal values for these is discussed in [3,7]) and that the local geometry of high-dimensional data is preserved in the embedded space.

To extend the concept of LLE to multiple manifolds, each representing data of one specific class, two supervised variants of LLE were independently proposed in [3,6]. In this paper, a framework unifying the unsupervised and both supervised methods is given. Supervised LLE is then applied as a feature extractor on a number of benchmark data sets, and is shown to be useful for high-dimensional data with a clear manifold structure.

2 LLE Framework

2.1 LLE

As input, LLE takes a set of N D-dimensional vectors assembled in a matrix $\boldsymbol{X}$ of size $D \times N$. Its output is a set of N M-dimensional vectors ($M \ll D$) assembled in a matrix $\boldsymbol{Y}$ of size $M \times N$, where the kth column vector of $\boldsymbol{Y}$ corresponds to the kth column vector of $\boldsymbol{X}$. First, the $N \times N$ squared distance matrix $\boldsymbol{\Delta}$ between all samples is constructed. For each sample $\boldsymbol{x}_i$, $i = 1, \ldots, N$, its K nearest neighbours are then sought; their indices are stored in an $N \times K$ matrix $\boldsymbol{\Gamma}$, such that Γ_{ij} is the index of the j-nearest neighbour of sample $\boldsymbol{x}_i$.

In the first step, each sample $\boldsymbol{x}_i$ is approximated by a weighted linear combination of its K nearest neighbours, making use of the assumption that neighbouring samples will lie on a locally linear patch of the nonlinear manifold. To find the reconstruction weight matrix $\boldsymbol{W}$, where $W_{i\Gamma_{ij}}$ contains the weight of neighbour j in the reconstruction of sample $\boldsymbol{x}_i$, the following expression has to be minimised w.r.t. $\boldsymbol{W}$ [9]:

$$\varepsilon_I(\boldsymbol{W}) = \sum_{i=1}^{N} \| \boldsymbol{x}_i - \sum_{j=1}^{K} W_{i\Gamma_{ij}} \boldsymbol{x}_{\Gamma_{ij}} \|^2, \qquad (1)$$

subject to the constraint $\sum_{j=1}^{K} W_{i\Gamma_{ij}} = 1$. It is easy to show that each weight can be calculated individually [9]. For each sample $\boldsymbol{x}_i$, construct a matrix $\boldsymbol{Q}$ with $Q_{jm} = \frac{1}{2}(\Delta_{i\Gamma_{ij}} + \Delta_{i\Gamma_{im}} - \Delta_{\Gamma_{ij}\Gamma_{im}})$. Let $\boldsymbol{R} = (\boldsymbol{Q} + r\boldsymbol{I})^{-1}$, where r is a suitably chosen regularisation constant (see [3]). Then $W_{i\Gamma_{ij}} = (\sum_{m=1}^{K} R_{jm})/(\sum_{p,q=1}^{K} R_{pq})$.

In the second and final step, the weights stored in $\boldsymbol{W}$ are kept fixed and an embedding in $\mathbb{R}^M$ is found by minimising w.r.t. $\boldsymbol{Y}$:

$$\varepsilon_{II}(\boldsymbol{Y}) = \sum_{i=1}^{N} \| \boldsymbol{y}_i - \sum_{j=1}^{K} W_{i\Gamma_{ij}} \boldsymbol{y}_{\Gamma_{ij}} \|^2 . \qquad (2)$$

This minimisation problem can be solved by introducing the constraint that the embedded data should have unit covariance, i.e. $\frac{1}{n}YY^T = I$ (otherwise, $Y = 0$ would minimise (2)). As a result, (2) is minimised by carrying out an eigen-decomposition of the matrix $M = (I - W)^T(I - W)$ [9]. The eigenvectors corresponding to the 2nd to $(M+1)^{st}$ smallest eigenvalues then form the final embedding Y; the eigenvector corresponding to the smallest eigenvalue corresponds to the mean of the embedded data, and can be discarded to obtain an embedding centered at the origin.

After embedding, a new sample can be mapped quickly by calculating the weights for reconstructing it by its K nearest neighbours in the training set, as in the first step of LLE. Its embedding is then found by taking a weighted combination of the embeddings of these neighbours [3,10].

LLE has been shown to be useful for analysis of high-dimensional data sets [3, 6,7,9]. A typical example is visualisation of a sequence of images, e.g. showing a person's face slowly rotating from left to right. For such data sets, LLE finds embeddings in which the individual axes correspond (roughly) to the small number of degrees of freedom present in the data.

2.2 Supervised LLE

Supervised LLE (SLLE, [3,6]) was introduced to deal with data sets containing multiple (often disjoint) manifolds, corresponding to classes. For fully disjoint manifolds, the local neighbourhood of a sample x_i from class c ($1 \leq c \leq C$) should be composed of samples belonging to the same class only. This can be achieved by artificially increasing the pre-calculated distances between samples belonging to different classes, but leaving them unchanged if samples are from the same class:

$$\Delta' = \Delta + \alpha \max(\Delta)\Lambda, \ \alpha \in [0,1], \quad (3)$$

where $\max(\Delta)$ is the maximum entry of Δ and $\Lambda_{ij} = 1$ if x_i and x_j belong to the same class, and 0 otherwise. When $\alpha = 0$, one obtains unsupervised LLE; when $\alpha = 1$, the result is the fully supervised LLE introduced in [6] (called 1-SLLE). Varying α between 0 and 1 gives a partially supervised LLE (α-SLLE) [3].

For 1-SLLE, distances between samples in different classes will be as large as the maximum distance in the entire data set. This means neighbours of a sample in class c will always be picked from that same class. In practice, one therefore does not have to compute (3), but instead one can just select nearest neighbours for a certain sample from its class only. 1-SLLE is thereby a nonparameterised supervised LLE. In contrast, α-SLLE introduces an additional parameter α which controls the amount of supervision. For $0 < \alpha < 1$, a mapping is found which preserves some of the manifold structure but introduces separation between classes. This allows supervised data analysis, but may also lead to better generalisation than 1-SLLE on previously unseen samples.

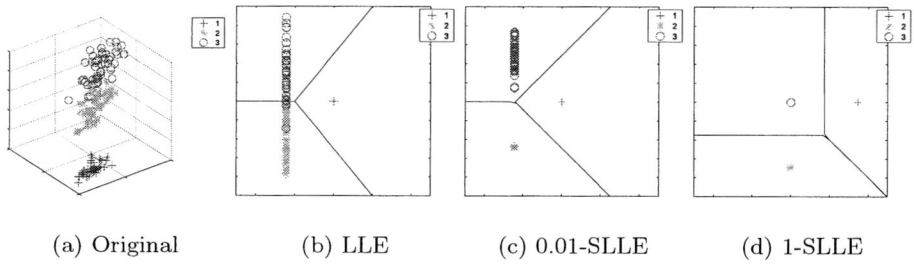

(a) Original   (b) LLE   (c) 0.01-SLLE   (d) 1-SLLE

Fig. 1. (a) First, third and fourth feature of the **iris** set ($N = 150$, $D = 4$, $C = 3$). (b)-(d) (S)LLE embeddings ($M = 2$), with trained nearest mean classifier.

2.3 Feature Extraction

For $\alpha = 1$, the distance matrix represents C fully disconnected classes, each of which should be mapped fairly by LLE. These added degrees of freedom are used in the second step (2) to separate the classes, using the eigenvectors corresponding to the 2nd to C^{th} smallest eigenvalues, just as the first one was used to discard the mean of the data. Mapped classes are separated due to the constraint $\frac{1}{n}\boldsymbol{Y}\boldsymbol{Y}^T = \boldsymbol{I}$, and all samples in a certain class are mapped on a single point in $\mathbb{R}^{C-1}$. The optimal embedding dimensionality M therefore is $C-1$. For α-SLLE, this is not necessarily optimal, as this method is a trade-off between LLE and 1-SLLE. An automatic setting for M can be found by demanding that locally, on average, 90% of the variance is retained in the remaining M dimensions [3]. This local intrinsic dimensionality estimate is denoted by M_L.

The feature extraction process is illustrated in Figure 1: the $C = 3$ classes in the **iris** data set [1] are mapped onto single points by 1-SLLE. α-SLLE retains some of the class structure, but reduces within-class dispersion compared to LLE. Clearly, SLLE is suitable as a feature extraction step prior to classification. And, although internal structure of each class is (partially) lost during mapping, class overlap can easily be visualised in the $C-1$ dimensional space.

The idea behind SLLE is related to that of spectral clustering [11]. There, first an affinity matrix between all samples is calculated. If clusters are present, this matrix will have a block-diagonal structure. An eigen-decomposition of the (normalised) affinity matrix then gives an embedding in a small number of dimensions, in which clusters are more clearly separated than in the original space. SLLE uses class label information to construct an artificial off-diagonal block matrix $\boldsymbol{\Lambda}$, and applies this to change the distance matrix used as the basis for LLE. The resulting matrix $\boldsymbol{W}$, which is already sparse (containing only K non-zero entries in each row), is changed towards a block-diagonal matrix. As a result, a mixture between unsupervised LLE and supervised spectral clustering is obtained.

3 Experiments

3.1 Setup

To verify the feature extraction capabilities of SLLE, it was applied to a number of data sets varying in number of samples N, dimensions D and classes C. The sets, together with the experimental results, are given in Tables 1 ($D \leq 30$) and 2 ($D > 30$). For later comparison, the number of dimensions needed by global PCA to retain 90% of the variance, the global intrinsic dimensionality M_G, is shown in the tables as well. Most of the sets were obtained from the UCI repository [1], some were used in our earlier work. The **chromosomes** set contains 30 gray-values sampled from chromosome banding profiles. The two **textures** sets contain 12 × 12-pixel gray-value image patches of either natural (i.e. unstructured) or structured (i.e. regular) Brodatz textures [2]. The **nist digits** set consists of 16 × 16-pixel gray-value images of pre-processed handwritten digits, taken from the NIST database [2]. Finally, the **paper** set contains 857 multiresolution local binary patterns, calculated on images of different types of paper [8].

The experiments were set up as follows: a set was randomly split 10 times into a training set (80%) and a test set (20%). Four classifiers were used: nmc, the nearest mean classifier; ldc and qdc, the Bayes plug-in linear and quadratic classifiers; and knnc, the K-NN classifier, with K optimised by the leave-one-out procedure on the training set [5]. This was repeated on data mapped by LLE and α-SLLE to M_L dimensions (see section 2.3) and by 1-SLLE to $C-1$ dimensions. Mappings were calculated for a range of values of K, the neighbourhood size parameter, and α (if applicable).

To compare the (S)LLE methods to more traditional feature extraction techniques, the classifiers were also trained on data mapped to M_L dimensions by principal component analysis (PCA), linear discriminant analysis (LDA) and multidimensional scaling (MDS) (see e.g. [4] for an overview of these methods).

3.2 Results

Tables 1 and 2 present average errors on the test set (in %) over the 10 random set splits, with the standard deviation given between brackets. The best result is shown in bold and underlined; all results not significantly worse (paired t-test with 9 d.o.f., $p = 0.95$) are shown in bold as well. For 1-SLLE and α-SLLE, only the best result found in the range of values for K and α is shown. Ideally, these optimal values should be found on an independent validation set, but the size of many of the data sets did not permit setting aside samples for this.

The results confirm that SLLE generally leads to better classification performance than LLE and, usually, any other mapping technique. This is to be expected, as SLLE can extract nonlinear manifolds in a supervised way, and is thereby the most general of the feature extraction methods. Besides this, there are a number of interesting observations:

Table 1. Test error (in %), low-dimensional data sets.

	Original	PCA	Fisher	MDS	LLE	1-SLLE	α-SLLE
iris [1]				$N=150, C=3, D=4, M_G=1, M_L=3$			
nmc	7.7 (2.7)	9.3 (4.1)	**1.7** (2.4)	8.7 (4.5)	4.7 (3.9)	3.3 (3.1)	**1.7** (2.4)
ldc	1.7 (2.4)	4.0 (3.1)	**1.7** (2.4)	4.7 (3.6)	**1.0** (1.6)	12.0 (6.1)	**1.0** (1.6)
qdc	3.3 (3.1)	4.3 (3.5)	3.3 (3.5)	5.0 (3.6)	**2.3** (2.2)	23.0 (27.7)	**2.3** (2.2)
knnc	2.3 (1.6)	3.3 (3.1)	**3.0** (3.3)	3.7 (1.9)	**2.3** (2.7)	3.3 (3.1)	**2.3** (2.2)
wine [1]				$N=178, C=3, D=13, M_G=1, M_L=2$			
nmc	25.3 (5.3)	27.2 (7.9)	**1.1** (1.4)	27.2 (7.9)	25.3 (5.3)	4.7 (3.2)	5.8 (3.6)
ldc	1.1 (1.4)	32.8 (6.1)	**1.1** (1.4)	34.2 (6.1)	26.7 (5.3)	41.1 (17.2)	15.6 (5.1)
qdc	**1.1** (1.4)	27.8 (8.5)	**1.4** (1.5)	28.1 (8.1)	25.8 (6.4)	46.4 (11.0)	16.4 (5.1)
knnc	24.4 (5.4)	34.2 (6.3)	**1.1** (1.4)	34.7 (5.9)	24.7 (6.2)	4.7 (3.2)	11.4 (3.8)
diabetes [1]				$N=768, C=2, D=8, M_G=2, M_L=4$			
nmc	34.5 (4.0)	39.2 (2.2)	24.2 (2.9)	34.5 (4.4)	27.1 (2.9)	25.1 (2.4)	25.5 (2.9)
ldc	**22.2** (1.9)	34.5 (1.2)	**22.8** (2.3)	34.2 (1.2)	24.5 (1.8)	31.6 (4.6)	24.5 (1.8)
qdc	24.9 (1.9)	34.3 (2.0)	**22.5** (2.1)	34.5 (1.8)	28.1 (2.6)	35.1 (0.0)	27.5 (3.0)
knnc	24.4 (2.6)	32.9 (2.9)	**23.1** (2.5)	34.8 (1.5)	24.9 (2.9)	25.1 (2.4)	24.9 (2.9)
glass [1]				$N=214, C=6, D=9, M_G=4, M_L=3$			
nmc	57.0 (6.8)	51.2 (5.3)	40.7 (9.8)	50.7 (5.1)	61.2 (5.7)	29.5 (4.8)	36.5 (6.5)
ldc	36.0 (5.7)	45.8 (11.0)	37.0 (10.0)	44.4 (8.9)	44.0 (8.1)	48.1 (6.2)	39.5 (7.4)
qdc	83.5 (7.2)	47.0 (4.5)	47.2 (5.9)	47.2 (6.8)	50.2 (6.5)	59.8 (5.3)	41.2 (6.1)
knnc	**28.4** (4.5)	**22.8** (6.7)	38.1 (7.7)	**24.4** (8.3)	33.0 (7.0)	30.0 (4.7)	33.0 (7.0)
vehicle [1]				$N=846, C=4, D=18, M_G=1, M_L=5$			
nmc	61.7 (1.7)	60.1 (1.6)	20.6 (2.4)	60.6 (2.1)	50.9 (3.4)	26.6 (4.6)	23.5 (3.3)
ldc	22.0 (3.9)	63.5 (3.9)	20.7 (2.6)	62.6 (2.9)	50.8 (3.4)	59.5 (1.3)	24.6 (3.7)
qdc	**14.4** (2.1)	57.2 (2.6)	19.8 (1.9)	57.5 (4.0)	47.7 (2.9)	59.5 (1.3)	47.7 (2.9)
knnc	36.9 (2.8)	46.4 (2.3)	20.9 (2.2)	45.7 (2.0)	44.9 (3.7)	26.6 (4.6)	22.0 (3.2)
hepatitis [1]				$N=80, C=2, D=19, M_G=2, M_L=3$			
nmc	**29.4** (9.8)	39.4 (10.6)	**29.4** (11.0)	38.8 (10.5)	**25.0** (10.6)	**29.4** (7.2)	**25.0** (10.6)
ldc	**22.5** (13.9)	46.2 (6.0)	**29.4** (11.4)	45.6 (7.2)	31.2 (5.1)	**33.8** (9.4)	**25.0** (13.5)
qdc	**32.5** (17.1)	46.2 (6.0)	**29.4** (11.4)	45.6 (6.6)	30.0 (7.1)	36.2 (9.2)	**25.6** (13.3)
knnc	39.4 (10.6)	48.1 (7.2)	**30.0** (14.7)	46.9 (6.8)	34.4 (13.3)	**29.4** (7.2)	**24.4** (10.0)
chromosomes				$N=2520, C=24, D=30, M_G=8, M_L=8$			
nmc	33.2 (2.0)	33.0 (1.8)	24.9 (1.4)	33.1 (1.7)	31.4 (1.7)	37.4 (1.5)	28.2 (1.7)
ldc	25.1 (2.5)	24.1 (1.0)	24.9 (1.4)	23.8 (1.0)	28.4 (1.0)	93.5 (0.5)	27.6 (1.8)
qdc	27.1 (1.4)	21.4 (1.3)	21.7 (1.9)	**19.3** (1.7)	22.2 (2.2)	94.1 (1.4)	22.2 (2.2)
knnc	23.6 (1.7)	23.3 (1.5)	24.5 (1.9)	23.1 (1.2)	25.2 (2.0)	37.4 (1.5)	24.3 (1.7)

- **SLLE does not work on low-dimensional data.** For the low-dimensional sets shown in Table 1, the Bayes plug-in classifiers, ldc and qdc, often work well on the original data, as the number of parameters that need to be estimated is still reasonably low. In these cases, SLLE will not improve classification to the point where it is better than on the original data.
- **SLLE works well on high-dimensional data.** In some cases, performance is (nearly) as good as on the original data, but in others it is significantly better (**ionosphere**, **sonar**, the **textures** sets). The **splice** set is the exception: the quadratic classifier qdc performs surprisingly well and cannot be improved upon.

Table 2. Test error (in %), high-dimensional data sets.

	Original	PCA	Fisher	MDS	LLE	1-SLLE	α-SLLE
ionosphere [1]			$N = 351, C = 2, D = 34, M_G = 18, M_L = 4$				
nmc	29.9 (5.5)	28.9 (7.6)	12.1 (2.7)	28.4 (7.6)	21.6 (3.8)	**7.7** (3.1)	**7.0** (2.5)
ldc	16.4 (7.2)	44.3 (5.9)	13.9 (2.9)	34.9 (6.9)	19.4 (4.5)	31.9 (5.7)	**7.0** (2.5)
qdc	11.4 (3.8)	38.0 (4.8)	12.6 (2.7)	35.4 (7.1)	19.0 (5.5)	26.9 (2.4)	**7.3** (2.1)
knnc	16.3 (3.1)	20.9 (3.4)	13.0 (2.7)	25.0 (5.1)	13.0 (2.2)	**7.7** (3.1)	**7.4** (1.8)
splice [1]			$N = 3188, C = 3, D = 60, M_G = 51, M_L = 18$				
nmc	23.9 (2.0)	44.1 (1.1)	21.2 (1.4)	37.3 (3.7)	36.2 (2.0)	19.5 (2.3)	**17.2** (2.2)
ldc	19.0 (1.4)	33.2 (0.8)	19.3 (1.7)	30.9 (1.3)	35.6 (1.4)	75.9 (0.1)	**17.6** (1.5)
qdc	**7.0** (1.2)	32.1 (1.2)	19.0 (1.4)	30.5 (1.7)	42.5 (1.8)	75.9 (0.1)	27.1 (1.9)
knnc	20.5 (1.4)	32.8 (1.3)	18.9 (1.6)	32.8 (3.8)	32.8 (2.0)	19.5 (2.3)	**18.6** (2.1)
sonar [1]			$N = 208, C = 2, D = 60, M_G = 12, M_L = 8$				
nmc	32.4 (7.0)	46.8 (5.6)	25.4 (10.0)	46.8 (6.3)	23.4 (6.1)	**11.7** (3.0)	**13.7** (4.5)
ldc	25.4 (5.2)	44.6 (6.7)	25.6 (10.6)	45.4 (4.0)	22.0 (5.7)	53.7 (0.0)	**14.4** (4.8)
qdc	27.8 (5.9)	43.4 (5.6)	25.4 (10.9)	44.9 (4.9)	26.1 (5.4)	53.7 (0.0)	**14.6** (3.3)
knnc	18.5 (5.3)	51.7 (3.9)	24.6 (10.1)	49.3 (5.1)	18.8 (7.4)	**11.7** (3.0)	**12.9** (2.3)
optdigits [1]			$N = 5620, C = 10, D = 64, M_G = 21, M_L = 10$				
nmc	8.6 (0.7)	10.1 (0.8)	4.7 (0.7)	10.1 (0.6)	15.6 (1.5)	**1.4** (0.4)	**1.4** (0.4)
ldc	55.8 (44.3)	8.4 (1.0)	4.7 (0.7)	8.8 (0.6)	10.4 (1.2)	31.0 (1.0)	**2.0** (0.4)
qdc	90.1 (0.0)	4.2 (0.5)	3.1 (0.5)	4.2 (0.4)	5.1 (1.0)	31.0 (1.0)	**3.4** (0.6)
knnc	**1.2** (0.4)	2.8 (0.5)	2.9 (0.3)	3.0 (0.4)	3.2 (0.5)	**1.4** (0.4)	**1.3** (0.2)
natural textures [2]			$N = 3000, C = 6, D = 144, M_G = 33, M_L = 6$				
nmc	54.5 (2.1)	54.5 (1.2)	55.2 (1.7)	55.1 (1.7)	56.0 (2.0)	**30.6** (2.9)	33.7 (2.6)
ldc	54.9 (1.5)	53.9 (1.4)	55.2 (1.7)	54.9 (1.5)	55.6 (1.7)	79.7 (0.9)	**38.1** (2.6)
qdc	46.0 (1.8)	41.2 (2.2)	52.4 (2.1)	43.9 (2.0)	58.3 (3.3)	79.7 (0.9)	**37.5** (2.3)
knnc	34.2 (1.0)	40.9 (2.7)	53.6 (1.4)	43.2 (2.2)	49.4 (2.4)	**30.6** (2.9)	**30.6** (3.1)
structured textures [2]			$N = 3000, C = 6, D = 144, M_G = 39, M_L = 17$				
nmc	51.3 (1.4)	52.0 (1.5)	55.8 (1.9)	52.7 (1.7)	27.9 (2.1)	9.5 (0.9)	**8.2** (0.8)
ldc	55.1 (1.7)	52.0 (1.5)	55.8 (1.9)	53.6 (1.2)	27.8 (1.7)	49.3 (1.9)	**8.2** (0.7)
qdc	24.4 (0.8)	30.2 (1.2)	50.4 (1.6)	36.3 (1.2)	**13.4** (1.3)	49.3 (1.9)	11.7 (1.2)
knnc	13.7 (1.3)	30.0 (1.9)	52.9 (1.7)	37.6 (1.0)	14.5 (1.4)	9.5 (0.9)	**7.5** (1.0)
nist digits [2]			$N = 6250, C = 10, D = 256, M_G = 52, M_L = 12$				
nmc	16.5 (0.9)	21.5 (0.9)	10.3 (0.9)	20.1 (0.7)	17.1 (0.7)	3.4 (0.5)	**2.3** (0.3)
ldc	10.8 (0.4)	17.0 (1.0)	10.3 (0.9)	17.4 (0.7)	16.1 (0.8)	40.0 (1.1)	**3.2** (0.7)
qdc	89.8 (0.4)	9.3 (1.0)	**7.9** (0.8)	8.8 (0.9)	10.7 (0.6)	40.0 (1.1)	10.7 (0.6)
knnc	**2.5** (0.2)	6.7 (0.7)	7.0 (0.8)	7.1 (1.0)	6.7 (0.5)	3.4 (0.5)	**2.5** (0.4)
paper [8]			$N = 1004, C = 4, D = 857, M_G = 2, M_L = 7$				
nmc	3.3 (1.2)	2.8 (1.2)	26.7 (4.1)	1.4 (0.9)	0.3 (0.3)	**0.1** (0.2)	**0.2** (0.3)
ldc	75.1 (0.0)	1.2 (0.9)	75.1 (0.0)	**0.1** (0.2)	**0.2** (0.3)	2.9 (0.8)	**0.2** (0.3)
qdc	75.1 (0.0)	0.5 (0.5)	75.1 (0.0)	**0.1** (0.2)	21.3 (29.4)	2.9 (0.8)	21.3 (29.4)
knnc	**0.2** (0.3)	**0.1** (0.2)	26.7 (4.1)	**0.1** (0.2)	**0.2** (0.3)	**0.1** (0.2)	**0.1** (0.2)

- **SLLE works well where K-NN works well on the original data.**
  SLLE is a neighbourhood-based method, like the K-NN classifier. In fact, SLLE can be seen as a generalised K-NN method, where not only the neighbours' labels play a role, but also the distances to these neighbours.

- **1-SLLE vs. α-SLLE: neither consistently outperforms the other.** Although α-SLLE was expected to generalise better, there are two extra parameters to be estimated: α and the embedding dimensionality, M_L. The performance of α-SLLE is especially sensitive to the latter. Bayes plug-in classifiers trained on 1-SLLE mapped data perform poorly: as all samples are mapped onto a single point, there is no covariance structure left.
- **The nearest mean classifier performs well.** SLLE maps the data non-linearly such that this simple classifier can do well. This is analogous to SVMs: after the kernel function performs the desired nonlinear mapping, a simple linear classifier suffices.
- **Local vs. global intrinsic dimensionality.** A priori one would expect SLLE to work well for sets which contain curved manifolds. Such sets would exhibit a high global intrinsic dimensionality (M_G) coupled with a low local one (M_L). Indeed, for all sets on which SLLE performs well (except **splice**), $M_L \ll M_G$.

The latter observation means that a simple test for the applicability of SLLE would be to quickly estimate M_L on a subset of samples and compare it to M_G. A significant difference indicates that good performance of SLLE is highly likely.

4 Conclusions

A common framework for unsupervised and supervised LLE was proposed. Experiments on a number of benchmark data sets demonstrated that SLLE is a powerful feature extraction method, which when coupled with simple classifiers can yield very promising recognition results. SLLE seems to be mainly applicable to high-dimensional data sets which clearly exhibit manifold structure.

Further research will address the problems of choosing α and M_L in a more well-founded way for α-SLLE. Computational and storage complexity is also still a concern: as the whole data set needs to be retained and is used in mapping new data, application to large data sets ($N \geq 10^4$) is still infeasible. Subset selection [3] may alleviate this problem.

References

1. C.L. Blake and C.J. Merz. UCI repository of machine learning databases, 1998.
2. D. de Ridder. *Adaptive methods of image processing*. PhD thesis, Delft University of Technology, Delft, 2001.
3. D. de Ridder and R.P.W. Duin. Locally linear embedding for classification. Technical Report PH-2002-01, Pattern Recognition Group, Dept. of Imaging Science & Technology, Delft University of Technology, Delft, The Netherlands, 2002.
4. R.O. Duda, P.E. Hart, and D.G. Stork. *Pattern classification*. John Wiley & Sons, New York, NY, 2nd edition, 2001.
5. R.P.W. Duin. PRTOOLS, a pattern recognition toolbox for MATLAB, 2003. Download from http://www.ph.tn.tudelft.nl/~duin.

6. O. Kouropteva, O. Okun, A. Hadid, M. Soriano, S. Marcos, and M. Pietikäinen. Beyond locally linear embedding algorithm. Technical Report MVG-01-2002, Machine Vision Group, University of Oulu, Finland, 2002.
7. O. Kouropteva, O. Okun, and M. Pietikäinen. Selection of the optimal parameter value for the locally linear embedding algorithm. In *Proc. of the 1st Int. Conf. on Fuzzy Systems and Knowledge Discovery, Singapore*, pages 359–363, 2002.
8. T. Ojala, M. Pietikäinen, and T. Mäenpää. Multiresolution gray-scale and rotation invariant texture classification with local binary patterns. *IEEE Transactions on Pattern Analysis and Machine Intelligence*, 24(7):971–987, 2002.
9. S.T. Roweis and L.K. Saul. Nonlinear dimensionality reduction by locally linear embedding. *Science*, 290(5500):2323–2326, 2000.
10. L.K. Saul and S.T. Roweis. Think globally, fit locally: unsupervised learning of nonlinear manifolds. Technical Report MS CIS-02-18, Univ. of Pennsylvania, 2002.
11. Y. Weiss. Segmentation using eigenvectors: a unifying view. In *Proc. of the IEEE Int. Conf. on Computer Vision (ICVV'99)*, pages 975–982, 1999.

Feature Extraction for One-Class Classification

David M.J. Tax and Klaus-R. Müller

Fraunhofer FIRST.IDA, Kekuléstr.7, D-12489 Berlin, Germany
davidt@first.fhg.de

Abstract. Feature reduction is often an essential part of solving a classification task. One common approach for doing this, is Principal Component Analysis. There the low variance directions in the data are removed and the high variance directions are retained. It is hoped that these high variance directions contain information about the class differences. For one-class classification or novelty detection, the classification task contains one ill-determined class, for which (almost) no information is available. In this paper we show that for one-class classification, the low-variance directions are most informative, and that in the feature reduction a bias-variance trade-off has to be considered which causes that retaining the high variance directions is often not optimal.

1 Introduction

Feature reduction is important when we want to fit a classifier using finite sample sizes. Using too many features will introduce too much noise, and classifiers can easily overfit. To avoid this, the data is preprocessed to remove as many noisy or redundant features as possible. A typical preprocessing is Principal Component Analysis (PCA), where the directions with high variance in the data are retained [Jol86]. However this heuristic does not directly guarantee that the best classification performance can be obtained.

When we are interested in the problem of novelty detection, or one-class classification [MH96,RGG95,SPST+99,JMG95,Tax01], just one class is sampled well: the target class. A classifier should be trained such that it distinguishes this class from all other possible objects, the outlier objects. To avoid the trivial solution to classify all objects as target objects, one has to assume an outlier distribution. In this paper we will assume a uniform distribution (where in practice some upper and lower bounds on the outlier domain have to be defined). In that case, the classifier should capture all (or a pre-specified fraction) of the target data, while it covers a minimum volume in the feature space.

In this paper we want discuss PCA preprocessing for this one-class classification (OCC) problem. We found that there is a bias-variance trade-off [GBD92, Hes98] in feature extraction which can cause that the low-variance directions are more useful than the high-variance directions. Removing these low-variance directions is then counter-productive. In sections 2 and 3 we look how OCC behaves on a Gaussian target distribution, and what happens when PCA is applied. In sections 4 and 5 some experiments are shown and conclusions are given.

2 OCC for Gaussian Target Distribution

Assume that we are given a p-dimensional dataset $\mathcal{X}^{tr} = \{\mathbf{x}_i, i = 1,..,n\}$, drawn from a Gaussian distribution $N(\mu, \Sigma)$. Assume further that the outliers are uniformly distributed in a box with the center at μ and edges of length M, where M is much larger than any of the eigenvalues of Σ. A Gaussian one-class classifier estimates the mean and covariance matrix, $\bar{\mathbf{x}}$ and S_n respectively, and uses the Mahalanobis distance $(\mathbf{x} - \mu_n)^T S_n^{-1} (\mathbf{x} - \mu_n)$ as the fit to the target class. A threshold $\theta_{p,n}$ is defined, such that the empirical target acceptance rate equals a predefined fraction, for instance $f = 90\%$. New instances $\mathbf{z}$ are evaluated by:

$$\text{accept } \mathbf{x} \quad \text{if} \quad (\mathbf{x} - \mu_n)^T S_n^{-1} (\mathbf{x} - \mu_n) \leq \theta_{p,n} \tag{1}$$

To evaluate the dependence of the performance on the dimensionality p and the sample size n, the error on the outliers or the volume captured by the classifier (false acceptance rate, f_o) and the error on the target objects (false rejection rate, f_t) have to be considered.

The captured volume f_o is determined by the ellipsoid, characterized by the (estimated) covariance matrix and the threshold $\theta_{p,n}$. From geometry we know that the volume of the ellipsoid is the volume of the sphere times the absolute value of the determinant of the transformation matrix. In total, the volume of the captured space is computed by:

$$V = \sqrt{|S_n|}\, \theta_{p,n}^{p/2} V_p \tag{2}$$

where V_p is the volume of a p-dimensional unit ball: $V_p = \frac{2\pi^{p/2}}{p\Gamma(p/2)}$ and $|S_n|$ the determinant of the (estimated) covariance matrix $S_n = \frac{1}{n}\sum_i (\mathbf{x} - \bar{\mathbf{x}})'(\mathbf{x} - \bar{\mathbf{x}})$. The distribution of the determinant $|S_n|$ is the same as $|A|/(n-1)^p$, where $A = \sum_{i=1}^{n-1} \mathbf{z}_i' \mathbf{z}_i$ and $\mathbf{z}_i, i = 1,..,n-1$ are all distributed independently according to $N(0, \Sigma)$. The hth moment of $|A|$ is given by [And84]:

$$2^{hp} |\Sigma|^h \frac{\prod_{i=1}^{p} \Gamma[\frac{1}{2}(N-i) + h]}{\prod_{i=1}^{p} \Gamma[\frac{1}{2}(N-i)]} \tag{3}$$

Thus the first moment is $E(|A|) = |\Sigma| \prod_{i=1}^{p}(n + 1 - i)$.

The threshold $\theta_{p,n}$ can be derived from the (Mahalanobis) distance distribution of objects $\mathbf{x}_i$ to the estimated mean $\bar{\mathbf{x}}$, assuming that the objects are drawn from a Gaussian distribution. The (scaled) distances are distributed as a beta distribution [Wil62,HR99]: $\frac{(n-1)^2}{n} d_S^2(\mathbf{x}_i, \bar{\mathbf{x}}) \sim \text{Beta}\left(\frac{p}{2}, \frac{(n-p-1)}{2}\right)$. The threshold $\theta_{p,n}$ is set such that a certain fraction f (say $f = 0.9$) of the data is accepted. This means:

$$\frac{(n-1)^2}{n} \int_0^{\theta_{p,n}} \text{Beta}\left(\frac{p}{2}, \frac{(n-p-1)}{2}\right) = f \tag{4}$$

When we are interested in the *fraction* of the outliers which is accepted (f_o, the fraction false positive), this volume has to be compared with the volume covered by the outlier objects M^p:

$$f_o = \frac{V}{M^p} = \sqrt{|S_n|} V_p \left(\frac{\sqrt{\theta_{p,n}}}{M}\right)^p = V_p \prod_{i=1}^{p} \frac{\sqrt{\hat{\lambda}_i \theta_{p,n}}}{M} \qquad (5)$$

where $\hat{\lambda}_i$ are the eigenvalues of S_n.

Note that by the assumption that the outliers cover the whole target distribution, $\sqrt{\theta_{p,n}} < M$ and thus $\left(\frac{\sqrt{\theta_{p,n}}}{M}\right)^p$ vanishes for increasing dimensionality p. Thus the volume of the captured volume (the area for which $\mathbf{x}' S^{-1} \mathbf{x} \leq \theta_{p,n}$) and the error on the outliers will decrease.

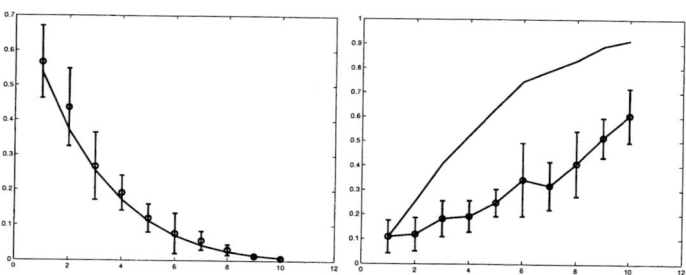

Fig. 1. Left, the relative space captured by the Gaussian one-class classifier for varying dimensionalities, $n = 25$. Right, the probability mass missed by the classifier.

In the left subplot of figure 1 the relative volumes captured by the Gaussian one-class classifier is plotted for varying p. The target class is distributed as a standard Gaussian distribution with $n = 25$ objects. The outlier objects are uniformly distributed in a box with edges of length 8. The solid line shows the theoretical fraction of accepted outlier objects (by equation (5)). The circles show the results obtained by simulation.

To estimate the error on the target set f_t, we have to compute the probability mass captured by the estimated classifier:

$$1 - f_t = \int_{(\mathbf{x}-\bar{\mathbf{x}})' S_n^{-1} (\mathbf{x}-\bar{\mathbf{x}}) \leq \theta} \frac{1}{Z} \exp\left(-\frac{1}{2}(\mathbf{x}-\boldsymbol{\mu})^T \Sigma^{-1} (\mathbf{x}-\boldsymbol{\mu})\right) d\mathbf{x} \qquad (6)$$

To simplify this integration, we assume that that the means are estimated well and that they are at the origin, i.e. $\boldsymbol{\mu} = \bar{\mathbf{x}} = \mathbf{0}$.[1] By transforming $\mathbf{y} = S_n^{-1/2} \mathbf{x}$ the integration area becomes circular, and we can write:

$$1 - f_t = \int_{\mathbf{y}' \mathbf{y} \leq \theta} \frac{1}{Z'} \exp\left(-\frac{1}{2} \mathbf{y}^T (S_n^{T/2} \Sigma^{-1} S_n^{1/2}) \mathbf{y}\right) d\mathbf{y} \qquad (7)$$

where the Jacobian $|\det(S_n)|$ is absorbed in Z'.

---

[1] In practice this does not completely hold, but it appears that the errors introduced by poor estimates of $|S_n|$ are much more important.

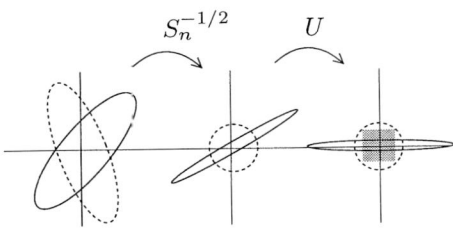

Fig. 2. Transformation of the integral (6).

Finally, we can rotate such that the main axes of $\tilde{\Sigma} = S^{T/2} \Sigma^{-1} S^{1/2}$ are aligned with the coordinate axes, by observing that we can factorize $\tilde{\Sigma} = U^T D U$ where U is an orthogonal matrix (containing the eigenvectors of $\tilde{\Sigma}$ and D is a diagonal matrix (containing the eigenvalues $\lambda_1, ..., \lambda_p$), see also figure 2 for a visualization:

$$1 - f_t = \int_{\mathbf{z}'\mathbf{z} \leq \theta_{p,n}} \frac{1}{Z''} \exp\left(-\frac{1}{2}\mathbf{z}^T D \mathbf{z}\right) d\mathbf{z}$$

Unfortunately, this integral is also not analytically solvable (due to the fact that $\exp\left(-\frac{1}{2}\mathbf{z}^T D \mathbf{z}\right)$ is not rotational symmetric). We approximate this integral by integrating over a box which is within the sphere. The edges of this box have size $2a = \sqrt{\theta_{p,n}/p}$.[2] Integrating over the box, yields:

$$1 - f_t = \int_{-\sqrt{\theta_{p,n}/p}}^{\sqrt{\theta_{p,n}/p}} \frac{1}{Z''} \exp\left(-\frac{1}{2}\mathbf{z}^T D \mathbf{z}\right) d\mathbf{z} \tag{8}$$

$$= \prod_{i=1}^{p} \left(\text{erf}(\sqrt{\theta_{p,n}/(p\lambda_i)}) - \text{erf}(-\sqrt{\theta_{p,n}/(p\lambda_i)}) \right) \tag{9}$$

In the right subplot of figure 1 f_t and the simulation results are shown for varying dimensions. It is clear that equation (9) is a crude approximation to (6), but it shows a similar trend. The target error depends on the threshold $\theta_{F,n}$ and the eigenvalues of $S_n^{T/2} \Sigma^{-1} S_n^{1/2}$, $\lambda_1, ..., \lambda_p$. When one of the eigenvalues λ_i is large, one element in the product of (9) becomes small and the $1 - f_t$ becomes small.

The total error is thus a combination of f_o, (5) and f_t, (9). Note that for the computation of (9) both the estimated as the true covariance matrix of the target class is required. This means that these equations cannot be used to find the generalization error for a given dataset.

3 Feature Extraction

When the dimensionality is reduced using PCA, both high or low variance directions can be removed, effectively removing high or low eigenvalues λ_i from S_n. Equation (2) shows that $(\sqrt{\theta_{p,n}}/M)^p$ is an important factor for f_o (directly depending on p). But the actual value does not change when the difference between using the high- or low-variance directions is considered. For that, $|S_n|$ (using equation (3)) should be considered. When low variance directions are removed from $|S_n|$, $|S_n|$ basically increases, and thus f_o increases. On the other hand, when high variance directions are removed, $|S_n|$ is still mainly determined by the smallest eigenvalues, and thus the error stays constant.

---

[2] Integrating over the box around the sphere is also possible, but this approximation is much worse.

When we assume that S_n approximates Σ, equation (9) shows that removing high-variance directions from $|S_n|$ will remove terms with large λ_i from $|S_n\Sigma|$ and thus small value of $\text{erf}(\sqrt{\theta/(p\lambda_i)}) - \text{erf}(-\sqrt{\theta/(p\lambda_i)})$. Effectively, $1 - f_t$ will increase and thus the error decrease. When low-variance directions are removed, the change of the product is very small. When S_n does not approximate Σ very well, removing a high- or low-variance direction gives a random result for $|S_n\Sigma|$, and so the improvement for removing high-variance directions will disappear.

In figure 3 a schematic picture for a two dimensional case is shown. The target data is distributed in the ellipsoidal area. When the data is mapped onto the largest eigenvector (direction λ_1), essentially all data between the dashed lines will be labeled target object. All outlier objects in A_1 will therefore be misclassified. When the data is mapped onto the smallest eigenvector (λ_2), all data between the solid lines (A_2) will be labeled target. Because the volume of A_2 is much smaller than that of A_1, f_o will be smaller in the second case. The f_t will be the same in both cases, so the total error decreases.

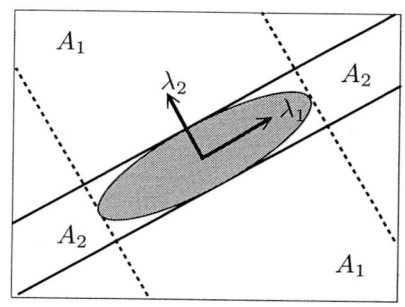

Fig. 3. Feature reduction for a two dimensional dataset.

For low sample sizes, the estimates of the low and high variance directions become noisy. In that case, not only the volume difference between A_1 and A_2 becomes smaller, also the error on the target set will in both cases increase. In figure 4 the total error is shown when the dimensionality is reduced. It shows that when data is reduced to low dimensionalities (1D, 2D), it is always better to remove the high variance directions. To determine the optimal dimensionality and which

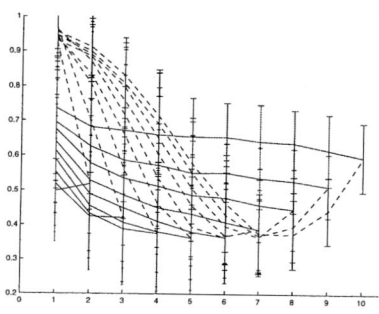

Fig. 4. The total error $f_t + f_o$.

directions to use, the basic bias-variance dilemma has to be considered: how well can the different variance directions be estimated from a finite sample, and how well do these directions distinguish between the targets and outliers? We just saw that for one-class classification, the low-variance directions in the data have lowest average error (low bias). When the sample size is sufficiently high and the eigenvectors of S_n can be estimated well, the best approach is thus to reduce the dimensionality by removing high variance directions. In these cases the effect of removing a large eigenvalue from $S_n\Sigma^{-1}$ dominates the effect of removing a large eigenvalue of S_n. On the other hand, when the matrix S_n is a poor approximation to Σ, then $S_n\Sigma^{-1}$ is far from identity. Removing small eigenvalues from S_n does not mean removing small eigenvalues from $S_n\Sigma$ and the removal of a low-variance direction will still result in a large increase of f_o in equation (9).

Unfortunately, the (approximation to the) target error estimation still depends on both the estimated and 'true' covariance matrix, S_n and Σ. To estimate the dependence to the dimensionality and the sample size, datasets with known Σ and simulated S_n are generated. We use a Gaussian distributed target class, where Σ has eigenvalues between 2 and $\frac{1}{2}$, and $|\Sigma| = 1$. From each generated dataset S_n is estimated, and both f_t and f_o are computed.

Table 1. Optimal dimensionality p^* for varying sample sizes n and starting dimensionalities ($p = 2 - 10$), for both removing the high variance directions (high) and low-variance directions (low). Underlined dimensionalities give superior performance.

	Variance between 1.5 and 0.66									Variance between 2 and 0.5							
n	10		25		50		100		n	10		25		50		100	
p	high	low	high	low	high	low	high	low	p	high	low	high	low	high	low	high	low
2	2	2	<u>1</u>	2	<u>1</u>	2	<u>1</u>	2	2	<u>1</u>	2	<u>1</u>	2	<u>1</u>	2	<u>1</u>	2
3	3	3	3	3	<u>2</u>	3	<u>2</u>	3	3	<u>2</u>	3	<u>2</u>	3	<u>2</u>	3	<u>2</u>	3
4	4	<u>3</u>	4	4	4	4	<u>3</u>	4	4	<u>2</u>	4	<u>2</u>	4	<u>3</u>	4	<u>3</u>	4
5	5	<u>4</u>	5	5	5	5	<u>5</u>	5	5	<u>2</u>	<u>4</u>	<u>2</u>	5	<u>4</u>	5	<u>3</u>	5
6	6	<u>4</u>	6	6	6	6	6	6	6	1	<u>5</u>	<u>2</u>	6	<u>4</u>	6	<u>4</u>	6
7	7	<u>5</u>	7	<u>6</u>	7	7	7	7	7	1	<u>5</u>	<u>2</u>	<u>6</u>	4	7	<u>5</u>	7
8	8	<u>5</u>	8	<u>7</u>	8	8	8	8	8	1	<u>5</u>	<u>2</u>	<u>7</u>	5	8	<u>5</u>	8
9	8	<u>5</u>	9	<u>7</u>	9	<u>8</u>	9	9	9	1	<u>5</u>	<u>2</u>	<u>7</u>	4	8	<u>5</u>	9
10			10	<u>8</u>	10	<u>9</u>	10	10	10			<u>2</u>	<u>7</u>	4	8	<u>5</u>	10

In table 1 the optimal dimensionality p^* for varying sample sizes n and starting dimensionalities ($p = 2 - 10$) for both removing the high variance directions (high) and low-variance directions (low) are shown. The left table shows the results when the eigenvalues are distributed between 1.5 and 0.666, in the right table the eigenvalues are between 2 and 0.5. The result for $n = 10, p = 10$ cannot be shown, because $n = 10$ objects can maximally span a 9-dimensional space. Note, that for high sample sizes it is in general bad to remove low-variance directions. Then the optimal dimensionality is always the original dimensionality. By removing high-variance directions, the performance stays constant but the dimensionality can be reduced significantly. For small sample sizes and small differences in eigenvalues, the estimates of the low variance directions become inaccurate. In that case, the performance of retaining the high-variance directions is higher.

4 Experiments

This difference in performance can also be observed in real world datasets. Here we consider two datasets. The first is the face database [HTP00,Sun96], containing 19×19 gray value images of faces and non-faces. The training set consist of 2429 target objects (faces) and the testing set contains 472 face and 23573 non-face objects. The second dataset is the standard Concordia dataset [Cho96] containing 32×32 black-and-white images of handwritten digits. For each class,

400 objects were available for training and testing. In this experiment, objects of class '7' were considered target objects, all other objects are outliers. In figure 5 the area under the ROC curve (AUC, a more robust error measure for one-class classification than standard classification error [Met78]) for varying dimensionalities is shown. When few dimensions are removed, using the high variance directions is often better, but at the very low dimensionalities, *removing* high-variance directions is best. This is according to the previous experiments.

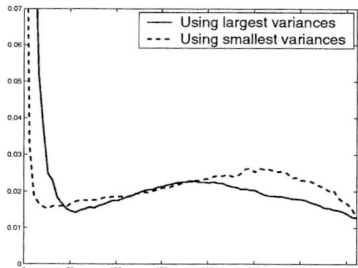
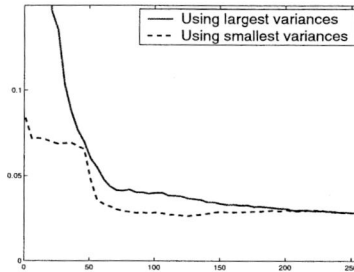

Fig. 5. The AUC of the face dataset (left) and the Concordia handwritten digits (right) for varying dimensionality, by removing the high and low variance directions.

5 Conclusions and Discussion

We showed that reducing the dimensionality by PCA and retaining the high variance directions, is not always the best option for one-class classification. For high sample sizes and large differences in variances of the target distribution, retaining the low variance directions has smaller error. This is caused by the fact that the error on the outliers mainly depends on the eigenvalues of the estimated target covariance matrix S_n, and the error on the target class on the eigenvalues of $S_n \Sigma^{-1}$, where Σ is the true target covariance matrix.

Which approach is best depends on the basic bias-variance dilemma: how well can the different variance directions be estimated from a finite sample, and how well does this direction distinguish between the classes? These basic characteristics will be observed in other feature reduction methods, as Kernel PCA, Independent Component Analysis, Local Linear Embedding, etc.

Finally, it might seem that the OCC problem is now very simple. We can always transform the data, such that one, or a few directions have zero variance. This direction should then be used to get very good classification results (by equations (5) and (9)). Unfortunately, in practice the data cannot be scaled at will, because it is assumed that the outlier distribution is uniform. Transforming the data will therefore also transform the outlier distribution, and invalidate the results shown above.

Acknowledgements. This research was supported through a European Community Marie Curie Fellowship. The author is solely responsible for information communicated and the European Commission is not responsible for any views or results expressed. I would like to thank Klaus Müller for the useful discussions.

References

[And84]   T.W. Anderson. *An introduction to multivariate statistical analysis.* John Wiley & Sons, 2nd edition, 1984.

[Cho96]   Sung-Bae Cho. Recognition of unconstrained handwritten numerals by doubly self-organizing neural network. In *International Cconference on Pattern Recognition*, 1996.

[GBD92]   S. Geman, E. Bienenstock, and R. Doursat. Neural networks and the bias/variance dilemma. *Neural Computation*, 4:1–58, 1992.

[Hes98]   T. Heskes. Bias/variance decomposition for likelihood-based estimators. *Neural Computation*, 10:1425–1433, 1998.

[HR99]   J. Hardin and D.M. Rocke. The distribution of robust distances. Technical report, University of California at Davis, 1999.

[HTP00]   B. Heisele, Poggio. T., and M. Pontil. Face detection in still gray images. A.I. memo 1687, Center for Biological and Computational Learning, MIT, Cambridge, MA, 2000.

[JMG95]   N Japkowicz, C. Myers, and M. Gluck. A novelty detection approach to classification. In *Proceedings of the Fourteenth International Joint Conference on Artificial Intelligence*, pages 518–523, 1995.

[Jol86]   I.T. Jollife. *Principal Component Analysis.* Springer-Verlag, New York, 1986.

[Met78]   C.E. Metz. Basic principles of ROC analysis. *Seminars in Nuclear Medicine*, VIII(4), October 1978.

[MH96]   M.M. Moya and D.R. Hush. Network contraints and multi-objective optimization for one-class classification. *Neural Networks*, 9(3):463–474, 1996.

[RGG95]   G. Ritter, M.T. Gallegos, and K. Gaggermeier. Automatic context-sensitive karyotyping of human elliptical symmetric statistical distributions. *Pattern Recognition*, 28(6):823–831, December 1995.

[SPST$^+$99]   B Schölkopf, J. Platt, J. Shawe-Taylor, Smola A., and R. Williamson. Estimating the support of a high-dimensional distribution. *Neural Computation*, 13(7), 1999.

[Sun96]   K.-K. Sung. *Learning and Example Selection for Object and Pattern Recognition.* PhD thesis, MIT, Artificial Intelligence Laboratory and Center for Biological and Computational Learning, Cambridge, MA, 1996.

[Tax01]   D.M.J. Tax. *One-class classification.* PhD thesis, Delft University of Technology, http://www.ph.tn.tudelft.nl/~davidt/thesis.pdf, June 2001.

[Wil62]   S. Wilks. *Mathematical statistics.* John Wiley, 1962.

Auto-adaptive and Dynamical Clustering Neural Network

Stéphane Lecoeuche[1,2] and Christophe Lurette[2]

[1] Département Génie Informatique et Productique,
École des Mines de Douai, 941, rue Charles Bourseul, BP838,
59508 Douai, France
lecoeuche@ensm-douai.fr
http://www.ensm-douai.fr/

[2] Laboratoire Intéraction Image et Ingénerie de la décision,
Université des Sciences et Technologies de Lille,
59655 Villeneuve d'Ascq, France
christophe.lurette@univ-lille1.fr

Abstract. In the context of pattern recognition area, a small number of clustering techniques are dedicated to the on-line classification of non-stationary data. This paper presents a new algorithm designed with specific properties for the dynamical modeling of classes. This algorithm, called AUDyC (Auto-adaptive and Dynamical Clustering), is based on an unsupervised neural network with full auto-adaptive abilities. The classes modeling is obtained using Gaussian prototypes. Thanks to specific learning strategies, prototypes and classes are created, adapted or eliminated in order to incorporate new knowledge from on-line data. To do that, new learning rules have been developed into three stages: "Classification", "Fusion" and "Evaluation". The results show the real abilities of the AUDyC network to track classes and then to model their evolutions thanks to the adaptation of the prototypes parameters.

1 Introduction

Numerous kinds of clustering techniques have been developed for Pattern Recognition. The goal of any clustering technique is to correctly define class models from datasets using learning processes. This being achieved, the classification task consists in labeling new unknown data using models resulting from these previous learning processes. But, in many real-life applications, the initial class models have to evolve with time. For example, in face or voice recognition, it will be necessary to refine the known models for taking into account the changes introduced by ageing. In these particular cases, the deviations are slight and the classes adaptation can be achieved by carrying out periodic learning processes. In many other applications such as time series classification, where the classes evolve faster, it will be a real benefit to use dynamical models of classes. For example, in particular applications like monitoring of systems, the region labeled "good state" will evolve during the system life, it is useful to get a dynamical model to characterize and to track this class in order to take account of running in periods, drifts, wears,... As the data will evolve, new information have to be incorporated and old information might be forgotten. So, an unsupervised dynamical classifier has to modify the classification space by creating, adapting or eliminating clusters of data without any supervisor knowledge.

Most of the techniques that are dedicated to on-line classification of data, are neural networks techniques. For example, the first neural networks that have been developed for pattern recognition like Neocognitron and ART have real self-organizing abilities by adapting the weights connections and by creating new neurons. Some evolutionary neural architectures with supervised learning have been proposed for on-line classification by not-only using creation and adaptation but also elimination abilities during the learning phase [1] [2] [3]. Their motivations were to optimize the use of the hidden neurons by introducing a dynamical reallocation of nodes. In fact, neural architectures fit well to online adaptation thanks to their self-organizing properties and their learning abilities but several studies (see [4] for a review) have proved that classical neural networks are not suitable and need adaptive learning. Then, numerous neural networks algorithms have been developed in order to adapt on-line their structure and their connections thanks to specific learning strategies like Incremental and Active Learning. Generally, the goal is to optimize the size of the neural structure (*constructivism* and *selectivism*) and to reduce the cost of the learning process [5] [6] [7] [8] [9]. In fact, adaptive learning is useful when the initial learning set contains incomplete information (huge sets where some cases might have been forgotten or on-line learning where some cases might have not been already met). Even if knowledge evolution seems to be possible (new classes are created or are refined by incorporating new information), most of these algorithms can not model real dynamical models of classes without the help of a supervisor.

Although it seems a priori obvious to achieve dynamical classification using techniques that have self-organizing abilities, unsupervised learning strategies, constructive architectures or fully auto-adaptive structures, there is a very small number of algorithms that have all the previous properties and generally their clustering model is very coarse [10] [11] [12]. This paper proposes a new approach for clustering applications by presenting a new concept called AUDyC : AUto-adaptive and Dynamical Clustering Neural Network that consists of an unsupervised neural network with a complete auto-adaptive structure. This algorithm has been developed for classification of temporal data using on-line dynamical class models.

2 Description of the AUDyC Neural Network

2.1 Overall Description

The technique developed here is based on a complete auto-adaptive architecture with unsupervised learning rules. In non-stationary environnement, this new neural network has the abilities to dynamically learn prototypes and classes from on-line data. Its structure is very common in Pattern Recognition area:

one input layer, one prototype layer and one output layer are used. The input layer is fixed and its size (D) equals the dimension of the data. For the two last layers, the number of neurons and their connections could be modified thanks to a continuous learning.

The (J) nodes on the hidden layer are called the prototypes. Their connections (W^P) with the input layer memorize the prototypes centers. Each prototype (P_j) represents a Gaussian model for a local data distribution. So, its parameters are a center M_{P_j} and an neighborhood (Σ_{P_j}). The output of each hidden node represents the membership degree of the input example (X_i) to one known prototype and is defined by (1).

$$\mu_i^j = \mu(P_j, X_i) = \exp(-\frac{1}{2}(((X_i - M_{P_j})^T \Sigma_{P_j}^{-1}(X_i - M_{P_j}))^2)) \qquad (1)$$

The (K) nodes on the output layer represent the classes. Their connections (W^C) with the hidden layer memorize the membership of prototypes to classes. Each class is defined thanks to a set of prototypes and, then, any complex class could be represented by an assembly of Hyper-elliptic Gaussian models. The output of each output layer neuron defines the membership degree of the example X_i to the corresponding class C_k. Their activation function is defined as:

$$\Psi(C_k, X_i) = \min(1, \sum_{P_j \in C_k} W_{jk}^C . \mu(P_j, X_i)) \qquad (2)$$

From the architecture point of view, the AUDyC network is very similar to many networks with constructive structure. To ensure a continuous adaptation of the structure, the learning is achieved on-line. So, its main feature is to have learning rules that are dedicated to on-line learning and to classification of non-stationary data. From temporal data, datasets are extracted as time goes on using a sliding window χ_s^{Nswn}. Its specific learning strategy allows to use these sets to adapt the architecture in order to accommodate new information and then to take into account evolutions of data distributions and so evolutions of classes. Figure 1 illustrates the overall schema of the on-line adaptation.

2.2 Learning Phase

From each new set χ_s^{Nswn}, the learning stages allow to construct and to adapt the structure of the neural network. The principle of the learning has been inspired form the CDL network [10]. Three stages, illustrated on fig.1, are used in a cyclic manner. The first stage "Classification" allows the creation and the adaptation of prototypes and of classes. The second "Fusion" allows the fusion of prototypes and of classes. The last stage "Evaluation" is used to eliminate prototypes and classes that have been created with a too small number of data.

No initialisation structure is needed. The initial structure is empty and then the first example X_1 creates the first prototype P_1 ($J = 1$) with $M_{P_1} = X_1$ and $\Sigma_{P_1} = \Sigma_{ini} = \sigma_{ini}^2.I$ and the class C_1 ($K = 1$) is created. When new data are presented, new knowledge is incorporated into the network by a constructive way thanks to different rules, described in the next three sections.

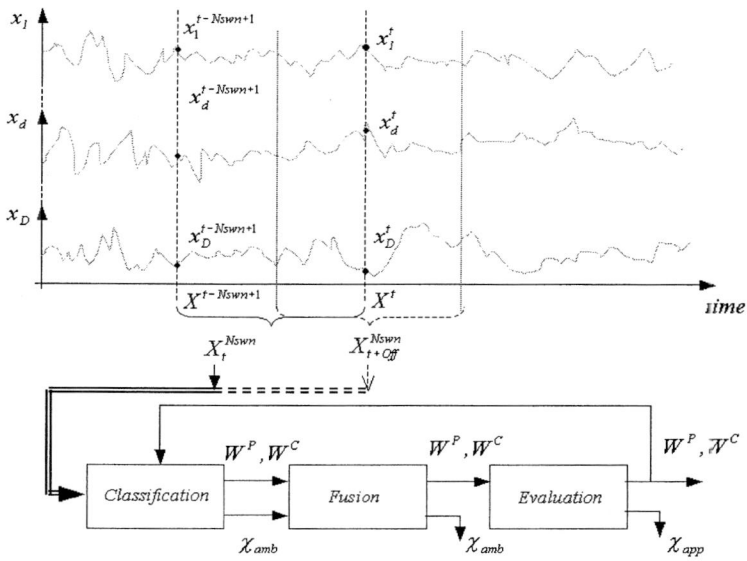

Fig. 1. Illustrations of the on-line learning

2.3 First Stage: Classification

The particularity of this first stage is to make possible the creation of new prototypes and new classes, and the parameters adaptation of existing prototypes. This corresponds to the creation of the new nodes and to the modification of the connection weights. When a new vector is presented to the input layer, the membership degree (1) of this example X_i to each known prototype P_j is compared to two thresholds μ_{min} and μ_{max} which are identical for all prototypes, and fixed for all iterations. μ_{min} is the lower level for **class membership** and μ_{max} is the lower level for **prototype membership**. From the comparison of μ_i^j with these two thresholds, the table 1 gives the four cases.

Table 1. Different cases for the "classification" stage.

	If	Then
1st Case	$\mu_i^j < \mu_{min}$ $\forall j \in \{1..J\}$	New prototype. $P_{J+1}=X_i$; New class C_{K+1}; $X_i \in \chi_{cl}$
2nd Case	$\mu_{min} < \mu_i^j < \mu_{max}$ for 1 or several j with all $P_j \in$ to a unique class C_k	New prototype. $P_{J+1} = X_i$; X_i belongs to C_k; $X_i \in \chi_{cl}$
3rd Case	$\mu_{max} < \mu_i^j$ for 1 or several j with $P_j \in$ to a unique class C_k	Adaptation of prototypes (j); X_i belongs to C_k; $X_i \in \chi_{cl}$
4th Case	$\mu_{min} < \mu_i^j$ for several j with $P_j \in$ to several classes C_k	New prototype. $P_{J+1} = X_i$; Ambiguity; $X_i \in \chi_{amb}$ and $X_i \in C_{k_1,n,..}$

1st case: For all P_j, the membership degree of the example X_i to any known prototype is smaller than the first threshold, that is to say the example is not close enough to any prototype. Hence, it is necessary to create a new prototype with X_i as center and $\Sigma_{ini} = \sigma_{ini}^2 . I$ as the initialization of the covariance matrix and a new class. The structure grows with a new neuron on the hidden layer: $J = J + 1$ and on the output layer : $K = K + 1$.

2nd case: For several P_j belonging to the same class, the membership degree is larger than the lower threshold but smaller than the second threshold. The example is close to these P_j prototypes, but not enough to be associated with one of them. It is necessary to create a prototype (as in 1st case). This new one belongs to the class of P_j prototypes.

3rd case: For several P_j belonging to the same class, the membership degree is larger than the two thresholds. Then, the example is associated to the nearest prototype in terms of membership degree and the adaptation of this prototype is done in a recursive manner. As the goal of this network is to obtain dynamical models of classes, it is necessary to allow the forgetting of old data [13]. To do that, a window of size (N) is defined for each prototype. So, the center and covariance matrix of the prototype are iteratively computed by these two equations:

$$M_{P_j}^i = M_{P_j}^{i-1} + \frac{1}{N}(X_i - X_{i-N+1}) \qquad (3)$$

$$\Sigma_{P_j}^i = \Sigma_{P_j}^{i-1} + \Delta X \begin{pmatrix} \frac{1}{N} & \frac{1}{N(N-1)} \\ \frac{1}{N(N-1)} & \frac{-(N+1)}{N(N-1)} \end{pmatrix} \Delta X^T \qquad (4)$$

$$\text{with} \quad \Delta X = \begin{bmatrix} X_i - M_{P_J}^{i-1} & X_{i-N+1} - M_{P_J}^{i-1} \end{bmatrix}$$

So, as a minimum number (N) of examples assigned to the prototype has to be reached to use these relations, before this value, the center and the covariance matrix are recursively adapted with only new data X_i [11].

In order to define significance of existing prototypes, their connections W_{jk}^C with the output layer are weighted in order to define the representativeness of a prototype P_j to a class C_k:

$$W_{jk}^C = \frac{Card(P_j^{C_k})}{N} \qquad (5)$$

4th case: For several P_j belonging to different classes, the membership degree of X_i is larger than the first threshold for multiple prototypes. So, $\chi_{amb} = \{\chi_{amb} \cup X_i\}$ and this ambiguity set will be analyzed during the next stage of the learning procedure (See §2.4).

At the end of this first stage, one part of the learning set has already been classified and stored in χ_{Cl}, and another part (χ_{amb}) has been rejected according to this 4th case.

2.4 Second Stage: "Fusion"

This stage puts together classes that are close in the representation space. Each time an ambiguity is detected (§2.3: Case 4), the corresponding classes are merged into a new one. To be noise-insensitive, a n_{amb} threshold is fixed. So, the merging between two classes C_{k1} and C_{k2} and between prototypes is performed when:

$$Card(\{X_i \in \chi_{amb}/X_i \in C_{k1} \ AND \ X_i \in C_{k2}\}) \geq n_{amb} \qquad (6)$$

Then, the output layer is modified by eliminating neurons that defined the ambiguous classes. A unique neuron resulting from the classes merging process remains for each detected ambiguity. A new prototype, which is created by X_i ($\in \chi_{amb}$), and ambiguous prototypes are associated to this new class. If $\mu_{max} < \mu_i^j$, former prototypes are merged into a unique as shown in Figure 2.

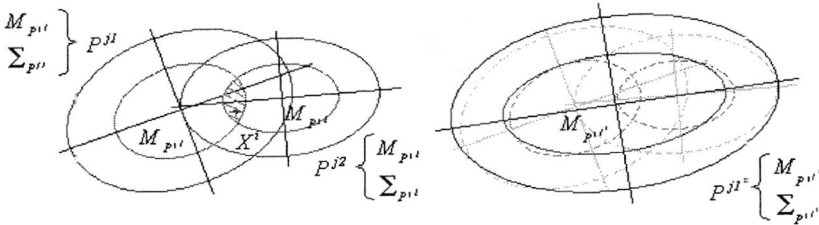

Fig. 2. Illustrations of prototypes fusion

2.5 Third Stage: "Evaluation"

This stage makes possible the evaluation of different prototypes and classes. A fixed threshold $N_{P_{min}}$ is used to eliminate prototypes defined by too few assigned examples. These examples are marked as "unclassified" and stored in χ_{app} and will be again presented at the next iteration. In a same way, $N_{C_{min}}$ is used to impose a minimal cardinality to classes and so to eliminate output neurons.

2.6 Cycle Description

At the output of the evaluation stage, the non-classified data, memorized in χ_{app} and χ_{amb}, are again presented to the neural network. As this process is cyclic, the stop criterion is to classify all the data (or a fixed percentage) or to have a stabilisation of the χ_{app} and χ_{amb} sets. To improve the quality of modeling, it is also possible to present again the whole set of data. In this case, even if the learning is longer, the results could be optimal with less than 3 cycles. For on-line data, a new set χ_{s+1}^{Nswn} is presented at the entry of the previous stabilized network, used as initialisation structure.

3 Simulation Results

In order to illustrate the AUDyC network abilities for the classification of non-stationary data, synthetic data of Gaussian distributions have been created. Figure 3 represents the results for two clusters of data at different time (t).

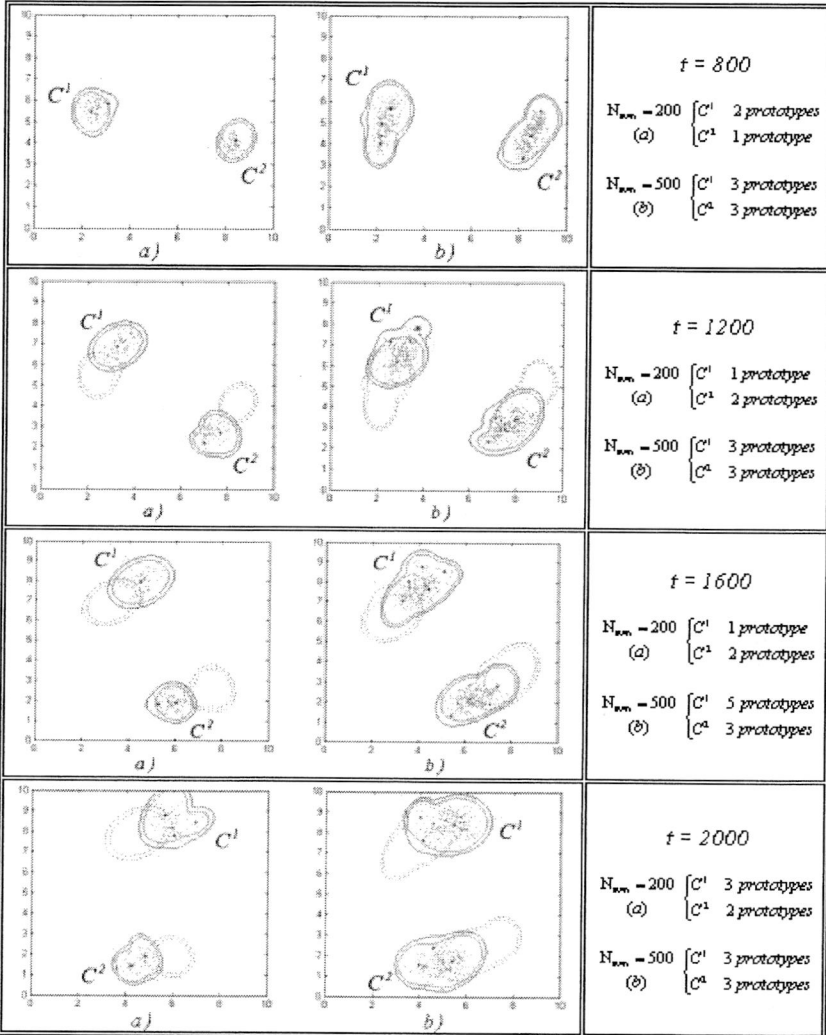

Fig. 3. Illustration of the on-line prototypes adaptation

As time goes on, the data evolve following specific shapes and trajectories. Each evolutionary class is represented by 1000 samples. Each χ_s^{Nswn} dataset is built equally with data that belong to C_1 or C_2. An offset of 4 data is used between each dataset (Fig 1). Hence, no cycle is needed to achieve the learning process. In order to appreciate the influence of the window width ($Nswn$), two values are used: 200 (case a) and 500 (case b). In both cases, the AUDyC network is initialized with: $\mu_{min} = 0.1$; $\mu_{max} = 0.3$; $\sigma_{ini} = 0.5$; $n_{amb} = 2$; $N_{min}^P = 7$; $N_{min}^C = 10$ and $N = 100$. The results, where the two boundaries correspond to membership degrees higher than μ_{min} and μ_{max}, show the abilities to correctly follow classes evolution thanks to a right adaptation of the prototypes.

4 Conclusion

A new neural network for dynamical classification of non-stationary data has been presented. The AUDyC network is built with unsupervised learning abilities and a full-adaptive structure in order to take into account classes evolutions. Each complex class is correctly and finely defined thanks to a set of Hyperelliptic Gaussian prototypes. Due to the learning stages, prototypes and classes are continuously adapted in order to take into account most recent informations of the data. From this point and in practice, the AUDyC network need to be adapted in accordance with the application requirements and particularly by taking care of its forgetting capacity. In many cases, it will be necessary to chose $Nswn$ specifically for each class depending on their dynamics.

References

1. Platt, J.: A resource-allocating network for function interpolation. Neural Computation **3** (1991) 213–225
2. J. Gomm: Process fault diagnosis using self-adaptative neural network with on-line learning capabilities. In: Online fault detection and supervision in the chemical process industries. Volume 1., IFAC (1995) 69–74
3. Fritzke, B.: A self-organizing network that can follow non-stationary distributions. In: International Conference on Artificial Neural Networks – ICANN'97, Lausane (1997) 613–618
4. Kasabov, N.: Evolving connectionist systems for on-line, knowledge-based learning: Principles and applications. Technical report, Departement of Information Science, University of Otago, New Zealand (1999)
5. Hassibi, B., Stork, D.: Second order derivatives for network pruning: Optimal brain surgeon. Advances in Neural Information Processing Systems **5** (1993) 164–171
6. Castellano, G., Fanelli, A.M., Pelillo, M.: An iterative pruning algorithm for feed-forward neural networks. IEEE Trans on, Neural Networks **8** (1997) 519–531
7. Polikar, R., Udpa, L., Udpa, S., Honavar, V.: Learn ++: An incremental learning algorithm for supervised neural networks. IEEE trans on Systems, Mans and Cybernetics **31** (2001) 497–508
8. Engelbrecht, A., Brits, R.: Supervised training using an unsupervised approach to active learning. Neural processing letters **15** (2002) 247–260
9. Mouchaweh, M., Devillez, A., Villermain, G., Billaudel, P.: Incremental learning in fuzzy pattern matching. Fuzzy Sets and Systems **132** (2002) 49–62

10. Eltoft, T., deFigueiredo, R.: A new neural network for cluster-detection-and-labeling. IEEE Trans. on Neural Networks **9** (1998) 1021–1035
11. Lurette, C., Lecoeuche, S.: Improvement of cluster detection and labeling neural network by introducing elliptical basis functions. In Dorffner, G., Bischof, H., Hornik, K., eds.: International Conference on Artificial Neural Networks – ICANN 01, Vienna, Austria, Springer (2001) 196–202
12. Deng, D., Kasabov, N.: On-line pattern analysis by evolving self-organizing maps. Neurocomputing **51** (2003) 87–103
13. Lecoeuche, S., Lurette, C.: Classification non supervisée de données évolutives par architecture neuronale autoadaptative. In SFC2002, ed.: 9ème rencontres de la Société Francophone de Classification, Toulouse, France (2002)

Transformations of Symbolic Data for Continuous Data Oriented Models

Krzysztof Grąbczewski and Norbert Jankowski

Department of Informatics, Nicolaus Copernicus University
ul. Grudziąadzka 5, 87-100 Toruń, Poland
{kgrabcze|norbert}@phys.uni.torun.pl, http://www.phys.uni.torun.pl/kmk

Abstract. Most of Computational Intelligence models (e.g. neural networks or distance based methods) are designed to operate on continuous data and provide no tools to adapt their parameters to data described by symbolic values. Two new conversion methods which replace symbolic by continuous attributes are presented and compared to two commonly known ones. The advantages of the continuousification are illustrated with the results obtained with a neural network, SVM and a kNN systems for the converted data.

1 Introduction

The majority of the Computational Intelligence (CI) systems are designed to deal with continuous data. The adaptive processes of neural networks and most of similarity based models operate in R^n space to perform their approximation or distance calculation tasks. Building such models for data described by symbolic attributes requires an embedding of the sets of symbols into some sets of real numbers. The simplest (and most commonly used) mapping arbitrarily replaces subsequent symbolic values with subsequent natural numbers. The order of the symbols is random and different randomizations may lead to significantly different results obtained with CI systems, so finding an appropriate mapping from symbols to real numbers is mostly advisable.

A simple way to get rid of symbolic features is to replace each of them by a number of binary features.

Distance based systems may use some similarity measures which are designed for symbolic data like Value Difference Metric (VDM), Heterogeneous Euclidean-Overlap Metric [13] or Minimum Risk Metric [2].

A simple observation that instead of using VDM metric, one can replace each symbolic value with a number of probabilities and use Minkovski measure on the converted data, leads to a conclusion that thanks to the data conversion any system designed for continuous data may also take advantage of the VDM measure [7].

Using another conditional probability yields very similar (but of different behavior in applications) MDV continuousification scheme.

A conversion from symbolic to continuous data can also be done with the usage of a separability criterion dedicated for decision tree systems.

CI systems augmented by some continuousification methods become yet more powerful tools, which take advantage of different methods of information extraction and

2 Continuousification Methods

The arbitrary coding of symbols may lead to very different orders and distances between attribute values. As a consequence of that the placement of the training data in the feature space is different for each mapping and this significantly affects the distances between the data vectors. The goal of continuousification is to find such a representation of symbols in the set of real numbers, that makes the classification or approximation problem easier.

NBF continuousification. Some of CI systems convert symbolic features consisting of n symbols with n binary features (NBF). For each $i = 1, \ldots, n$ the i'th new feature indicates whether the value of the original feature of given vector is the i'th symbol or not. Such data conversion results in a dataset of dimensionality strongly dependent on the numbers of symbols representing the features and does not depend on the number of classes (in opposition to the VDM and MDV methods presented below).

VDM continuousification. In the space of symbolic features $X = X_1 \times \cdots, X_n$, for the set of classes $C = \{c_1, \ldots, c_k\}$ the Value Difference Metric (VDM) for $x, y \in X \times C$ and a parameter q is defined as:

$$D^q_{\text{VDM}}(x,y) = \sum_{i=1}^{n} \sum_{j=1}^{k} |P(c_j|X_i = x_i) - P(c_j|X_i = y_i)|^q \quad (1)$$

where $P(c_j|X_i = z_i)$ is a shortened form of $P(C(u) = c_j | u_i = z_i \wedge u \in X \times C)$. In the tests presented in section 5 the probabilities $P(c_j|X_i = z_i)$ were estimated by $|\{x \in T : x_i = z_i \wedge C(x) = c_j\}| / |\{x \in T : x_i = z_i\}|$, where T is the training data set.

Duch et al. [7] presented the idea of mapping each of the x_i symbolic values of a vector x with k real numbers $P(c_1|X_i = x_i), \ldots, P(c_k|X_i = x_i)$.

In two class problems the dimensionality of the space may remain unchanged, since only one probability may be used without any change of the relative distances between data vectors (using two probabilities instead of one would just double each distance).

MDV continuousification. A natural alternative to VDM continuousification is to use the other conditional probability binding the feature values with class labels. Replacing $P(c_j|X_i = x_i)$ by $P(X_i = x_i|c_j)$ we obtain a mapping of an idea similar to VDM (hence we call it MDV), but with several important differences.

The main dissimilarity is that in the case of VDM the feature values are ordered according to how specific they are for given class and in the case of MDV according to the frequency of given value among the vectors belonging to the class.

The nature of VDM causes that in two class tasks, only one of the probabilities is necessary to preserve the whole information of two values. MDV's nature is different -

both probabilities are not so closely related – they are different sources of information, however assuming some similarity one can use probabilities for one of the classes to reduce the dimensionality of the resulting data.

SSV criterion and SSV based continuousification. The SSV criterion is one of the most efficient among criteria used for decision tree construction [8,9]. It's basic advantage is that it can be applied to both continuous and discrete features. The *split value* (or *cut-off point*) is defined differently for continuous and symbolic features. For continuous features it is a real number and for symbolic ones it is a subset of the set of alternative values of the feature. The *left side* (LS) and *right side* (RS) of a split value s of feature f for a given dataset D is defined as:

$$\text{LS}(s, f, D) = \begin{cases} \{x \in D : f(x) < s\} & \text{if } f \text{ is continuous} \\ \{x \in D : f(x) \notin s\} & \text{otherwise} \end{cases} \quad (2)$$

$$\text{RS}(s, f, D) = D - \text{LS}(s, f, D)$$

where $f(x)$ is the f's feature value for the data vector x. The definition of the *separability of a split value* s is:

$$\text{SSV}(s) = 2 * \sum_{c \in C} |\text{LS}(s, f, D) \cap D_c| * |\text{RS}(s, f, D) \cap (D - D_c)| \\ - \sum_{c \in C} \min(|\text{LS}(s, f, D) \cap D_c|, |\text{RS}(s, f, D) \cap D_c|) \quad (3)$$

where C is the set of classes and D_c is the set of data vectors from D which belong to class $c \in C$. A similar criterion has been used for design of neural networks by Bobrowski et al. [3].

Decision trees are constructed recursively by searching for best splits (with the largest SSV value) among all the splits for all the features. At each stage when the best split is found and the subsets of data resulting from the split are not completely pure (i.e. contain data belonging to more than one class) each of the subsets is being analyzed in the same way as the whole data. The decision tree built this way gives maximal possible accuracy (100% if there are no contradictory examples in the data) which usually means that the created model overfits the data. To remedy this a cross validation training is performed to find the optimal parameters for pruning the tree. Optimal pruning produces a tree capable of good generalization of the patterns used in the tree construction process.

SSV based continuousification. The SSV criterion can also be a successful tool for symbolic to real-valued feature mapping. It can be used to determine the order of the leaves of the SSV-based decision tree and to project them to $[0, 1]$ interval, as shown in the following algorithm:

Algorithm 1 (SSV based continuousification)
  Input: *The classification space X, set of classes C, training set $T \subseteq X \times C$, symbolic feature F (of space X).*
  Output: *Mapping $F \to R$.*

1. Build a decision tree D using $T' = \{(x_F, c) \in F \times C : (x, c) \in T\}$ where x_F is the value of the feature F for vector x.

2. *For each node W of the tree D, such that W is not the root or a direct subnode of the root, calculate SSV_W as the SSV criterion value for the split between W and the sibling of it's parent (the split of the set of vectors belonging to the two nodes, to the two sets determined by the nodes).*
3. *For each node W of the tree D, such that W is not the root or a leaf (starting with the root's direct subnodes, through their subnodes to the parents of the leaves) order the children W_i of W:*
   - *with decreasing (from left to right) values of SSV_{W_i} if W is the left child of it's parent.*
   - *with increasing (from left to right) values of SSV_{W_i} if W is the right child of it's parent.*
4. *Create the list $L_1, \ldots, L_n$ of all the leaves of the tree D with the order of visiting them with the depth first search (where the left child is visited before the right one).*
5. *Calculate the criterion values $SSV_{i,i+1}$ for $i = 1, \ldots, n-1$ for the pairs of leaves that are neighbors in the list.*
6. *For each $i = 1, \ldots, n$ assign to the L_i leave the real value*

$$\frac{\sum_{j=1}^{i-1} SSV_{j,j+1}}{\sum_{j=1}^{n-1} SSV_{j,j+1}}. \qquad (4)$$

7. *The output is the mapping which maps each possible value f of the F feature to the real number calculated in the preceding step for the leave which contains the vectors with f value of the F feature.*

The algorithm takes advantage of the fact, that SSV tree usually puts each symbolic value of the feature into a separate leave. Two different values may end up in a single leave only if all the vectors with any of that values belong to the same class – in such a case the two values (from the classification point of view) need not be distinguished and the above algorithm maps them to the same real value.

3 Adaptive Models Tested

We have tested the algorithms with three different kinds of adaptive models: a neural network (FSM), an SVM and a minimal distance system (kNN).

FSM neural network. Feature Space Mapping (FSM) is a neural network system based on modelling probability distribution of the input/output data vectors [6,1]. The learning algorithm facilitates growing and shrinking of the network structure, which makes the method flexible and applicable to classification problems of miscellaneous domains.

SVM method. The SVM algorithm we have used is the Platt's Sequential Minimal Optimization (SMO) [12] augmented by the ideas presented in [10]. Such version (with Gaussian kernels) yields very fast and accurate solutions.

Table 1. Results for Promoters (106 instances, 57 attributes, 2 classes).

FSM	Acc.	Std.dev.	P_1	P_2	P_3	P_4	P_5
1: None	0.673	0.034	—	0.000	0.000	0.000	0.000
2: SSV	0.878	0.029	**1.000**	—	0.175	0.308	0.540
3: NBF	0.912	0.013	**1.000**	0.825	—	0.734	**0.968**
4: VDM	0.893	0.024	**1.000**	0.692	0.266	—	0.706
5: MDV	0.874	0.017	**1.000**	0.460	0.032	0.294	—
SVM	Acc.	Std.dev.	P_1	P_2	P_3	P_4	P_5
1: None	0.478	0.014	—	0.000	0.000	0.000	0.000
2: SSV	0.903	0.015	**1.000**	—	**1.000**	0.091	0.045
3: NBF	0.695	0.040	**1.000**	0.000	—	0.000	0.000
4: VDM	0.930	0.016	**1.000**	0.909	**1.000**	—	0.376
5: MDV	0.936	0.006	**1.000**	**0.955**	**1.000**	0.624	—
kNN	Acc.	Std.dev.	P_1	P_2	P_3	P_4	P_5
1: None	0.725	0.026	—	0.001	0.069	0.000	0.000
2: SSV	0.860	0.020	**0.999**	—	**0.992**	0.008	0.014
3: NBF	0.771	0.022	0.931	0.008	—	0.000	0.000
4: VDM	0.929	0.019	**1.000**	**0.992**	**1.000**	—	0.587
5: MDV	0.924	0.011	**1.000**	**0.986**	**1.000**	0.413	—

kNN method. The *k Nearest Neighbours (kNN)* algorithm we used is a method with automated selection of the k parameter. For given training dataset the k is determined by means of cross validation training performed inside the training set (the winner k is the one that gives the smallest average validation error). The distances were calculated with the Euclidean metric.

4 Statistical Significance Test

When comparing the performances of different classification systems it is important not only to see the average accuracies, but to answer the question of the probability, that the average accuracy of a number of tests for one system will be higher than the average for the other. Assuming normal distribution of the accuracies, we estimate the probability with Student's t test [4,5].

In our experiments we repeated a cross validation (CV) test 10 times. Each competing system was run for the same data sample, so we are justified to estimate the statistical significance with paired t test with 10 degrees of freedom. The estimation of the variance of the CV mean is done on the basis of the 10 results.

5 Results

There is no point in continuousification of binary features, so the datasets containing continuous and binary features only are not eligible for the test. Also the results obtained for a dataset containing just one or two symbolic features do not allow for any conclusions.

Table 2. Results for Soybean (290 instances, 35 attributes, 15 classes).

FSM	Acc.	Std.dev.	P_1	P_2	P_3	P_4	P_5		
1: None	0.868	0.010	—	0.539	0.012	0.434	0.261		
2: SSV	0.867	0.007	0.461	—	0.000	0.407	0.198		
3: NBF	0.894	0.006	**0.988**	**1.000**	—	**0.987**	0.926		
4: VDM	0.870	0.010	0.566	0.593	0.013	—	0.320		
5: MDV	0.877	0.013	0.739	0.802	0.074	0.680	—		
SVM	**Acc.**	**Std.dev.**	P_1	P_2	P_3	P_4	P_5	P_6	P_7
1: None	0.664	0.007	—	0.000	0.000	0.000	0.845	**1.000**	0.000
2: SSV	0.762	0.007	**1.000**	—	0.001	**0.999**	**1.000**	**1.000**	0.001
3: NBF	0.787	0.007	**1.000**	**0.999**	—	**1.000**	**1.000**	**1.000**	0.134
4: VDM	0.729	0.007	**1.000**	0.001	0.000	—	**1.000**	**1.000**	0.000
5: MDV	0.656	0.005	0.155	0.000	0.000	0.000	—	**1.000**	0.000
6: k VDM	0.487	0.007	0.000	0.000	0.000	0.000	0.000	—	0.000
7: k MDV	0.796	0.005	**1.000**	**0.999**	0.866	**1.000**	**1.000**	**1.000**	—
kNN	**Acc.**	**Std.dev.**	P_1	P_2	P_3	P_4	P_5	P_6	P_7
1: None	0.831	0.006	—	0.000	0.000	0.000	0.000	0.000	0.000
2: SSV	0.894	0.005	**1.000**	—	0.039	0.003	0.011	**0.953**	0.517
3: NBF	0.909	0.005	**1.000**	**0.961**	—	0.059	0.415	**0.992**	0.942
4: VDM	0.923	0.007	**1.000**	**0.997**	0.941	—	0.938	**0.999**	**0.999**
5: MDV	0.910	0.004	**1.000**	**0.989**	0.585	0.062	—	**0.991**	**0.958**
6: k VDM	0.878	0.008	**1.000**	0.047	0.008	0.001	0.009	—	0.086
7: k MDV	0.894	0.008	**1.000**	0.483	0.058	0.001	0.042	0.914	—

We have tested the continuousification algorithms on three datasets from the UCI repository [11], defined in spaces consisting of symbolic features only: *Promoters*, *Soybean* and *DNA*. The tables 1 and 2 present the results of the 10 repetitions of 10 fold CV for each of the tested models, and table 3 shows average results for 10 training and test runs (the data is divided into training and test parts). The first row of each table shows the result obtained on raw data (arbitrary coding of symbols) while the other rows show the results with continuousification noted in the first column. A "k" before the method's name means that *one-against-rest* technique was used, i.e. the data was classified by a committee of k experts (where k is the number of classes) – each specializing in the recognition of one of the classes against all the others. For each continuousifier the columns $P_1, P_2, \ldots$ show the probabilities (calculated with the t test) that it's averaged test accuracy is higher then that of method 1, 2, etc.

6 Conclusions

The presented results clearly show that commonly used continuousification methods do not perform very well. Whether the results are good is the matter of luck. The VDM method as well as the new MDV and SSV methods are significantly more reliable. The need for appropriate data preparation confirms, that combinations of different kinds of information retrieval (hybrid methods) are necessary to obtain good results.

Table 3. Results for DNA (2000 instances for training, 1186 for test, 60 attributes, 3 classes).

FSM	Acc.	Std.dev.	P_1	P_2	P_3	P_4	P_5	P_6	P_7
1: None	0.906	0.007	—	0.001	0.000	0.000	0.000	0.000	0.000
2: SSV	0.936	0.004	**0.999**	—	0.058	0.007	0.060	0.005	0.099
3: NBF	0.948	0.005	1.000	0.942	—	0.620	0.715	0.238	0.500
4: VDM	0.946	0.002	1.000	0.993	0.380	—	0.699	0.052	0.405
5: MDV	0.944	0.003	1.000	0.940	0.285	0.301	—	0.032	0.282
6: k VDM	0.953	0.003	1.000	0.995	0.762	0.948	**0.968**	—	0.721
7: k MDV	0.948	0.007	1.000	0.901	0.500	0.595	0.718	0.279	—

SVM	Acc.	Std.dev.	P_1	P_2	P_3	P_4	P_5	P_6	P_7
1: None	0.611	0.000	—	0.000	0.000	0.000	0.000	0.000	0.000
2: SSV	0.927	0.000	1.000	—	1.000	0.000	0.000	0.000	1.000
3: NBF	0.633	0.000	1.000	0.000	—	0.000	0.000	0.000	0.000
4: VDM	0.948	0.000	1.000	1.000	1.000	—	1.000	1.000	1.000
5: MDV	0.947	0.000	1.000	1.000	1.000	0.000	—	1.000	1.000
6: k VDM	0.935	0.000	1.000	1.000	1.000	0.000	0.000	—	1.000
7: k MDV	0.895	0.000	1.000	0.000	1.000	0.000	0.000	0.000	—

kNN	Acc.	Std.dev.	P_1	P_2	P_3	P_4	P_5	P_6	P_7
1: None	0.676	0.001	—	0.000	0.000	0.000	0.000	0.000	0.000
2: SSV	0.876	0.003	1.000	—	1.000	0.000	0.000	0.000	0.000
3: NBF	0.827	0.004	1.000	0.000	—	0.000	0.000	0.000	0.000
4: VDM	0.949	0.001	1.000	1.000	1.000	—	0.883	0.000	0.889
5: MDV	0.947	0.003	1.000	1.000	1.000	0.117	—	0.001	0.822
6: k VDM	0.958	0.001	1.000	1.000	1.000	1.000	0.999	—	**0.991**
7: k MDV	0.941	0.006	1.000	1.000	1.000	0.111	0.178	0.009	—

All the presented algorithms are fast, however NBF, VDM and MDV may produce high dimensional data, which may significantly slow down the learning of the final models. In the case of Soybean data consisting of 35 features NBF produced 97 new features and both VDM and MDV 525 features. For DNA data (60 features) NBF gave 240 features and both VDM and MDV 180 features.

Instead of producing large spaces with VDM or MDV, sometimes it is reasonable to use the *one-against-rest* technique - although it requires the final classifier to be trained several times, it may be faster than training a single final model – it depends on how efficient the model is in high dimensional spaces.

The SSV method does not enlarge the dataset by features multiplication, regardless the number of classes and feature values. Hence it is very efficient for complex data. Although some other continuousification methods may give higher accuracies, the difference is usually small in comparison to the difference between SSV and an arbitrary symbols coding.

In general, if f is the number of features, k – the number of classes and v is the expected number of values per feature, then the dimensionality of the target space and the number of models that must be trained are presented in the following table:

	NBF	VDM/MDV	k-VDM/k-MDV	SSV
Dim	vf	kf	f	f
Models	1	1	k	1

It must be pointed out, that the VDM, MDV and SSV methods use the information about the classes of the vectors, so in the case of the tests like cross validation it should not be used at the stage of data preprocessing. It must be run separately for each fold of the test. Used at the preprocessing stage they yield overoptimistic results.

References

1. R. Adamczak, W. Duch, and N. Jankowski. New developments in the feature space mapping model. In *Third Conference on Neural Networks and Their Applications*, pages 65–70, Kule, Poland, October 1997.
2. E. Blanzieri and F. Ricci. Advanced metrics for class-driven similarity search. In *Proceedings of the International Workshop on Similarity Search*, Firenze, Italy, September 1999.
3. L. Bobrowski, M. Krętowska, and M. Krętowski. Design of neural classifying networks by using dipolar criterions. In *Third Conference on Neural Networks and Their Applications*, Kule, Poland, October 1997.
4. S. Brandt. *Data Analysis*. Springer, New York, 1999.
5. T. G. Dietterich. Approximate statistical tests for comparing supervised classification learning algorithms. *Neural Computation*, 10(7):1895–1924, 1998.
6. W. Duch and G. H. F. Diercksen. Feature space mapping as a universal adaptive system. *Computer Physics Communications*, 87:341–371, 1995.
7. W. Duch, K. Grudziński, and G. Stawski. Symbolic features in neural networks. In *Proceedings of the 5th Conference on Neural Networks and Their Applications*, pages 180–185, Zakopane, Poland, June 2000.
8. K. Grąbczewski and W. Duch. A general purpose separability criterion for classification systems. In *Proceedings of the 4th Conference on Neural Networks and Their Applications*, pages 203–208, Zakopane, Poland, June 1999.
9. K. Grąbczewski and W. Duch. The separability of split value criterion. In *Proceedings of the 5th Conference on Neural Networks and Their Applications*, pages 201–208, Zakopane, Poland, June 2000.
10. S. S. Keerthi, S. K. Shevade, C. Bhattacharyya, and K. R. K. Murthy. Improvements to Platt's SMO algorithm for SVM classifier design. *Neural Computation*, 13:637–649, 2001.
11. C. J. Merz and P. M. Murphy. UCI repository of machine learning databases, 1998. http://www.ics.uci.edu/~mlearn/MLRepository.html.
12. J. C. Platt. Fast training of support vector machines using sequential minimal optimization. In B. Schölkopf, C. J. C. Burges, and A. J. Smola, editors, *Advances in Kernel Methods - Support Vector Learning*. MIT Press, Cambridge, MA., 1998.
13. D. R. Wilson and T. R. Martinez. Improved heterogeneous distance functions. *Journal of Artificial Intelligence Research*, 11:1–34, 1997.

Comparing Fuzzy Data Sets by Means of Graph Matching Technique

Giuseppe Acciani, Girolamo Fornarelli, and Luciano Liturri

D.E.E.-Electro-technology and Electronics Department
Politecnico di Bari, Via E. Orabona, 4
I-70125, Bari-Italy
{acciani, fornarelli, liturri}@deemail.poliba.it

Abstract. In several applications it is necessary to compare two or more data sets. In this paper we describe a new technique to compare two data partitions of two different data sets with a quite similar structure as frequently occurs in defect detection. The comparison is obtained dividing each data set in partitions by means of a supervised fuzzy clustering algorithm and associating an undirected complete weighted graph structure to these partitions. Then, a graph matching operation returns an estimation of the level of similarity between the data sets.

1 Introduction

Often, data sets have to be compared. This is a very important task in various methods to perform the comparison between data coming from images, like in image retrieval or in detecting flaws, where the level of similarity between two data sets have to be evaluated. The most common data-comparing methods are based on the search of eigenvalues in appropriate matrix, the search of recurrences by the use of filters and on the definition of proper metrics on the whole data set (e.g. single pixel classification in comparing images) [1], [2], [3]. In methods that perform the comparison by data filtering is very difficult to set the optimal filter parameters. Moreover, the search eigenvalues-based methods and the ones operating on the whole data sets are both computational expensive. In fact, the inversion of large sized matrixes or the two-by-two comparisons of each single datum of large sets are needed. To overcome these drawbacks we propose a technique that requires only the minimization of a simple function and simple operations on little sized matrices. This technique is based on the Fuzzy C-Means clustering algorithm (FCM) and a subsequent graph matching operation (GM). The FCM is performed using a standard validation algorithm (Xie-Beni validation index) [4] in order to evaluate the correct number of clusters. Then a weighted graph is associated with the representation of data set obtained from FCM analysis. The last operation is able to compute the level of similarity between two data sets. The weighted graphs are very compact instruments to represent the whole data set and to compare two data sets through a graph matching operation. For this reason graph theory has been often used in pattern recognition [5], [6]. In this paper we want to compare two data sets with few differences, a frequently recurring problem in defect detection. This paper is organized as follows. In Section 2 and 3 we describe the FCM algorithm and the adopted validity index and define the graph associated with a fuzzy partition. A graph matching technique and a matching coefficient are introduced in Section 4. In Section 5 we show the results of a test performed on a reference data set and some data sets affected by increasing Gaussian noise. Finally we summarize our findings and outline our future works.

2 The Fuzzy Partitioning Algorithm

FCM is a supervised fuzzy partitioning algorithm which gives a representation of the whole data set in terms of centers (belonging to the same space of the data) and of values of a membership function for each datum in the set. Supervised algorithms need an a priori knowledge about the number of clusters. To overcome this problem is possible to use a validation index. In this work Xie-Beni validation index (XB) is adopted as described in 2.2.

2.1 The FCM Algorithm

The Fuzzy C-Means [7], [8] clustering algorithm is a clustering algorithm based on the minimization of the following objective function with respect to the fuzzy membership u_{ij} and the cluster center C_i:

$$J_m(U,C) = \sum_{j=1}^{n}\sum_{i=1}^{k}(u_{ij})^m d^2(X_j, C_i) , \qquad (1)$$

where $d(X_j, C_i)$ is a distance in a generic metric between the data point X_j and the center C_i, k is the number of centers, n is the number of data points and $m>1$ is the fuzziness index (in this work the Euclidean distance and $m=2$ have been used). The FCM algorithm is executed in the following steps:

1) Initialize membership u_{ij} of X_j belonging to cluster i so that

$$\sum_{i=1}^{k} u_{ij} = 1 . \qquad (2)$$

2) Compute the fuzzy center C_i for $I=1,2....,k$ using:

$$C_i = \frac{\sum_{j=1}^{n}(u_{ij})^m X_j}{\sum_{j=1}^{n}(u_{ij})^m} . \qquad (3)$$

3) Update the fuzzy membership u_{ij} using:

$$u_{ij} = \frac{\left[\dfrac{1}{d^2(X_j,C_i)}\right]^{1/(m-1)}}{\sum_{i=1}^{k}\left[\dfrac{1}{d^2(X_j,C_i)}\right]^{1/(m-1)}} \quad . \tag{4}$$

4) Repeat steps 2) and 3) until the value of J_m is no longer decreasing.

2.2 The XB Validity Index

The best number of partitions (the number of centers k) to perform the FCM is evaluated using the Xie-Beni validity index [4]. This validation index has been chosen because it shows a more stable behavior with respect to other indexes which search the best fuzzy partition. XB is defined as:

$$XB(f) = \frac{\sum_{x \in X}\sum_{k \in K} u_{ij}^2 \cdot d^2(X_i,C_j)}{n \min_{i,j} d^2(C_i,C_j)} \quad . \tag{5}$$

For the FCM algorithm with $m=2$ [8], [9], XB can be shown to be:

$$XB = \frac{J_2}{n \min_{i,j} d^2(C_i,C_j)} \quad . \tag{6}$$

The optimal number of clusters to initialize the FCM algorithm can be found with the following procedure:
1) Run the FCM with $k^*=2$;
2) Evaluate Xie-Beni index, XB*, as in (6) using the objective function calculated in step 1;
3) Run the FCM with $k=k^*+1$;
4) Evaluate Xie-Beni index, XB, as in (6) using the objective function calculated in step 3. If XB>XB*, k^* is the optimal partition else go to step 3 with $k^*=k$.

This procedure minimizes the Xie-Beni index. Minimizing XB corresponds to minimizing J_2, which is the goal of FCM. The additional factor $min_{i,j} d^2(C_i, C_j)$ in XB, is the separation measurement between i and j clusters. The more separated the clusters are, the larger $min_{i,j} d^2(C_i, C_j)$, and the smaller XB are. Thus, the smallest XB, indeed indicates a valid optimal partition with clusters well distinguishable.

3 Weighted Graph Associated with a Data Partition (WAG)

Let $\Pi(X)$ be a partition of the $n \times p$ dimensional data set X ($X_i=x_{i1}$, x_{i2}, ..., x_{ip} $i=1,2,...n$) represented by the k centers C ($C_j=c_{j1}$, c_{j2},......, c_{jp} $j=1,2,...k$) and the $k \times n$ dimension membership function matrix U. Let $G(V,W)$ be a complete undirected weighted graph with the vertexes V and the weight function W which returns a real nonnegative value for each pair of vertexes (i.e. the branch weight). Let $A(V,W)$ be the adjacency matrix associated with the graph G. We define as WAG the weighted graph $G(C,W)$, where C are the centers of the data set (given by the FCM algorithm) and W is the following weight function:

$$W = w_{ij}(C_i, C_j) = \frac{1}{n}\sum_{k=1}^{n} u_{ik} \cdot u_{jk} \quad \forall C_i, C_j \in C, \tag{7}$$

the adjacency matrix associated with WAG is:

$$A(C,W) = [a_{ij}] = w_{ij}(C_i, C_j), \tag{8}$$

this very simple choice for W allows to link each vertex (center) of the graph with a branch whose weight depends on where the data points are with respect to the position of the centers (vertexes). If a data point X_k is near to the center C_i but far from the center C_j the contribution to the weight of the branch is poor, on the contrary if it is near to both vertexes, the contribution is high, according to the definition of the membership function U whose value decreases when the distance increases [7]. In other words, the graph built in this way respect the internal structure of data set.

4   The Weighted Graph Matching

Let $\Pi_1(X_1)$ be the fuzzy partition of the n_1 x p dimensional data X_1 represented by the k_1 centers C_1 and the membership matrix U_1 (k_1 x n_1) and $\Pi_2(X_2)$ be the fuzzy partition of the n_2 x p dimensional data X_2 represented by the k_2 centers C_2 and the membership matrix U_2 (k_2 x n_2). Let G_1 be the WAG associated with the partition $\Pi_1(X_1)$ and G_2 be the WAG associated with the partition $\Pi_2(X_2)$. A graph matching operation is a method to match two isomorphic graphs. Two graphs are isomorphic if there exists a one to one correspondence between their vertex sets, which preserves adjacency. Therefore, we have two tasks to operate a graph matching. The first is to generate the isomorphism between the two WAG, the second is to evaluate the level of similarity of two isomorphic graphs.

4.1   The Isomorphism

The $G_1(C_1,W_1)$ and $G_2(C_2,W_2)$ might have a different number of vertexes. To build an isomorphism we have to associate uniquely each vertex of the set C_1 with each vertex of the set C_2. For this purpose we adopted a hierarchical cluster tree algorithm [7].
It consists of the following steps:
1) Find the similarity between every pair of objects in the data set. In this step, we calculate the Euclidean distances between the objects of the data set (the centers C_1 and C_2).
2) Group the objects into a binary, hierarchical cluster tree. In this step, we link together pairs of objects that are in close proximity, that is the distance calculated in

step 1. As objects are paired into binary clusters, the newly formed clusters are grouped into larger clusters until a hierarchical tree is formed.
3) Determine where to divide the hierarchical tree into clusters. In this step, we divide the objects in the hierarchical tree into clusters. The cluster can be created by detecting natural groupings in the hierarchical tree or by cutting off the hierarchical tree at an arbitrary point.

We "cut" the tree at the first level of association as we want a binary association. Let now be n_a the number of associated vertex of G_1 and G_2. The number of unassociated vertexes is $n_{u1}= k_1-n_a$ for G_1 and $n_{u2}=k_2-n_a$ for G_2. As seen before the two data sets are different but similar, so the different number of centers is already a key for a similarity measure. To keep the information about the unassociated vertexes we use $n_d = n_{u1}+ n_{u2}$ dummy vertexes [12]. The vertex i is a dummy vertex if it has $w_{ij}=0$ for each j. It is interesting to note that the introduction of dummy vertexes generates n_{u1} rows and columns in adjacency matrix of G_2 and n_{u2} rows and columns in adjacency matrix of G_1. The adjacency matrixes associated with G_1 and G_2 become n x n matrixes with:

$$n = k_1 + n_{u2} = k_1 + k_2 - n_a = k_2 + n_{u1}. \qquad (9)$$

The correspondences find above constitute the isomorphism. It can be represented through an orthogonal permutation matrix P [10], [11], in fact, the matrix P will be useful to evaluate the level of similarity of two isomorphic graphs.
An orthogonal permutation matrix P, is defined as:

$$P \cdot P^T = P^T \cdot P = I, \qquad (10)$$

where P is a square matrix (n x n) and defines uniquely the isomorphism Φ between the pair of graphs. Each row and each column of the P matrix has only one non singular element, $P(i,j)$, that is equal to 1 if the i-th vertex of the vertex set C_1 is associated with the j-th vertex C_2, and vice versa, while the unassociated vertexes of G_1 and G_2 are associated with dummy vertexes. In Fig. 1 are shown only vertexes of sample graphs G_1 and G_2 and a possible association can be seen.

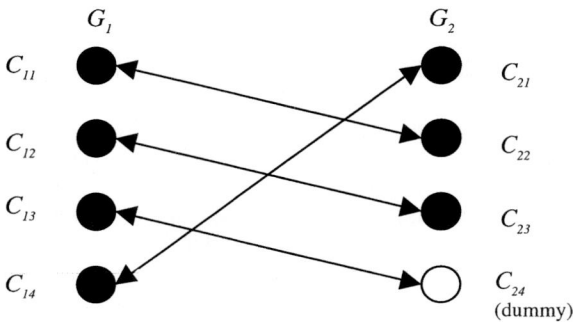

Fig. 1. Three vertexes of G_1 are associated with every vertex of G_2. The fourth vertex (C_{13}) is associated with the dummy vertex generated in G_2 (C_{24}).

4.2 The Matching Coefficient (MC)

Let Φ be the isomorphism between the graphs G_1 and G_2, and let A_1 and A_2 the corresponding adjacency matrixes as in (8). We define the Matching Coefficient (*MC*) as [5]:

$$MC = \|A_1 - A_2(\Phi)\|, \qquad (11)$$

where $\| X \|$ is the Frobenius norm defined as:

$$\|X\| = \sqrt{\sum_{i=1}^{n} X_1(i,i)} \quad \text{where} \quad X_1 = X^T \cdot X. \qquad (12)$$

Let P be the permutation matrix that defines the isomorphism Φ as in 4.1. The Matching Coefficient can be shown to be:

$$MC = \|A_1 - PA_2 P^T\|. \qquad (13)$$

The matching coefficient *MC* evaluates the level of similarity of two isomorphic graphs. Different values of *MC* are due to different weights of branches weighing upon associated vertexes.

5 The Testing Procedure

The method has been performed on nine data sets obtained from nine images. Each image is 164 x 311 pixel sized in RGB color space and is represented by a three dimensional matrix (164 x 311 x 3). The first image is the reference data set, while the other eight images are obtained from the first overlapping an increasing value of the variance of zero-mean Gaussian noise. In Fig. 2 we can see the reference image and the image with the higher value of noise variance in Fig. 3. The comparison is made between the reference data set and each data set originated from noisy images. The measure of the comparison, that is the level of similarity, between data sets can be immediately pointed out by the coefficient *MC* shown in Table 1. In this table, the results of the test are returned. Each row is related to a different data sets. The first and second column in the table indicate the values of the variance of the Gaussian noise and the number of centers found by FCM respectively. In the third column the number of the associated centers between the reference image and the noisy image can be seen. The size of the adjacency matrix (number of vertexes of the associated graphs in the isomorphism) and, in brackets, the number of dummy vertexes are in column four. Last column reports the value of *MC*. As expected, the value of the matching coefficient increases as the value of the variance increases. As matter of fact a little value of *MC* indicates a good match between two data sets. In fact, in the first row *MC* is zero because the data set matches perfectly itself. It can be pointed out that, as the noise increases, some dummy vertexes appear, because they are a qualitative measure for the comparison. The appearing of the dummy vertexes and the variations of branches weight in the adjacency matrix of the graphs are the cause of the increasing of the matching coefficient *MC*.

Comparing Fuzzy Data Sets by Means of Graph Matching Technique 373

Fig. 2. Reference image (reference data set).

Fig. 3. Noisy image with Gaussian noise of variance 5×10^{-1}.

Table 1. Testing procedure result.

Noise Variance (10^{-5})	No. of centers	No. of associated centers (n_a)	Total No. of vertex (n)	MC (10^{-3})
0	7	7	7(0 dummy)	0
0.01	7	7	7(0dummy)	5.0
0.05	7	7	7(0dummy)	22.1
0.1	7	7	7(0dummy)	37.9
0.5	6	6	7(1dummy)	97.7
0.7	6	6	7(1dummy)	116.6
1	6	6	7(1dummy)	131.6
3	6	6	7(1dummy)	164.8
5	6	4	9(5dummy)	277.3

6 Conclusions

In this paper we present a new technique based on the Fuzzy C-Means clustering algorithm and a subsequent graph matching operation to compare quite similar data sets. This new technique was shown to be very useful to compare two similar data sets. In fact, the value of the matching coefficient immediately gives the level of similarity between the analyzed data as it can be seen by the results of the test procedure. This method uses only the information about the centers of Fuzzy C-Means and does not need to work with the whole data set. Moreover, the graph is represented by small size matrixes and it is a very simple and computationally light instrument. The aim of our future work is to perform some additional experiments on real data sets coming from some different variety in images like shifts or occlusions.

References

1. Bodnarova, A., Bennamoun, M., Latham, S.: Optimal Gabor Filter for Textile Flaw Detection. *Elsevier, Pattern recognition*, n°35, 2002, pp. 2973–2991.
2. Aksoy, S., Haralick, R. M.: Graph Theoretic Clustering for Image Grouping and Retrieval. *IEEE, Conference on Computer Vision and Pattern Recognition*, June 1999, pp. 63–68.
3. Sahasrabudhe, N., West, J.E., Machiraju, R., Janus, M: Structured Spatial Domain Image and Data Comparison Metrics. *Visualization '99, Proceedings*, October 1999 pp. 97–105.
4. Pal, N. R., Bezdek, J. C.: On Cluster Validity for the Fuzzy c-Means Model. *IEEE, Transaction on Fuzzy Systems*, Vol. 3, n°3, August 1995, pp. 370–379.
5. Wang, J., Rau, D.: VQ-Agglomeration: a Novel Approach to Clustering. *IEE proceedings-Visual Image Signal Processing*. Vol 148, n° 1, February 2001, pp. 36–44.
6. Wu, Z., Leahy, R.: An optimal Graph Theoretic Approach to Data Clustering: Theory and Its Application to image segmentation. *IEEE, Transaction on Pattern Analysis and Machine Intelligence*, Vol 15, n° 11, November 1993, pp. 1101–1113.
7. Hoppner, F., Klawonn, F., Kruse, R., Runkler, T.: Fuzzy Cluster Analysis. *John Wiley & Sons, LTD*, Chichester, New York, Weinheim, Brisbane, Singapore, Toronto, 2000.
8. Gath, V. A., Geva, B.: Unsupervised Optimal Fuzzy Clustering. *IEEE, Transaction on Pattern Analysis and Machine Intelligence*, Vol 11, n° 7, July 1989, pp. 773–781.
9. Babuska, R.: Fuzzy and Neural Control. *Disc Course Lecture Notes*, October 2001.
10. Umeyama, S.: An Eigendecomposition Approach to Weighted Graph Matching Problems. *IEEE, Transaction on Pattern Analysis and Machine Intelligence*, Vol 10, n° 5, September 1988, pp. 695–703.
11. Almohamad, H. A., Dufuaa, S. O.: A Linear Programming Approach for the Weighted Graph Matching Problem. *IEEE, Transaction on Pattern Analysis and Machine Intelligence*, Vol 15, n° 5, May 1993, pp. 522–525.
12. Papadimitiou, C. H., Steiglitz, K.: Combinatorial Optimization: Algorithm and Complexity. Englewood Cliffs, NJ: Prentice-Hall 1982.

How to Do Multi-way Classification with Two-Way Classifiers

Florin Cutzu

Dept. of Computer Science
Indiana University
Bloomington, IN 47405
USA
`florin@indiana.edu`

Abstract. A new principle for performing polychotomous classification with pairwise classifiers is introduced: if pairwise classifier $\mathcal{N}_{ij}$, trained to discriminate between classes i and j, responds "i" for an input $\boldsymbol{x}$ from an unknown class (not necessarily i or j), one can at best conclude that $\boldsymbol{x} \notin j$. Thus, the output of pairwise classifier $\mathcal{N}_{ij}$ can be interpreted as a vote against the losing class j, and not, as existing methods propose, as a vote for the winning class i. Both a discrete and a continuous classification model derived from this principle are introduced.

1 Introduction

Consider the problem of m-way classification ($m \geq 2$) of the random variable $\boldsymbol{x} \in \mathcal{R}^d$. The probability density function of $\boldsymbol{x}$ is a mixture of m partially overlapping components corresponding to the classes of interest in the classification problem: $p(\boldsymbol{x}) = \sum_1^m w_k p(\boldsymbol{x} \mid k)$ where the weights are the prior class probabilities: $w_k = P(k)$, $\sum_1^m w_k = 1$. The training data consists of n input vectors $\boldsymbol{x}_i$, which usually are typical representatives of the classes, and the corresponding class labels $y_i \in \{1, \ldots, m\}$. The goal is to assign class labels to novel inputs. The direct approach is to use a single m-way classifier; an alternative approach is to employ several k-way classifiers ($k < m$) and combine their outputs in a m-way classification decision. In this paper the case $k = 2$ (pairwise classifiers) is explored. The idea of performing complex multi-way classification tasks by combining multiple simpler, specialized classifiers is not new and various approaches based on this principle have been presented in the research literature as well as in pattern recognition textbooks such as [6]. Of particular interest in the context of this paper are Friedman's method [2], the pairwise coupling model of Hastie & Tibshirani [3] and the related approach presented in [6].

Friedman's Voting Method. The Bayesian solution to the classification of $\boldsymbol{x}$ requires that estimates of the m class posterior probability densities $P(k \mid \boldsymbol{x})$ be obtained in the training stage. Friedman's approach reformulates the Bayesian solution to reduce the m-way classification problem to $m(m-1)/2$ pairwise discrimination problems, as follows. During training, possibly using neural network techniques, estimates of the following ratios of probability densities are obtained:

$$r_{ij}(\boldsymbol{x}) = \frac{P(i \mid \boldsymbol{x})}{P(j \mid \boldsymbol{x}) + P(i \mid \boldsymbol{x})} \quad (i, j = 1, \ldots, m) \tag{1.1}$$

The functions r_{ij} learned in the training phase are then used in the testing phase. If for input vector $\boldsymbol{x}$, $r_{ij}(\boldsymbol{x}) > 0.5$ then $P(i \mid \boldsymbol{x}) > P(j \mid \boldsymbol{x})$, and class i is the "winner" of the $i-j$ comparison. Thus, the output of pairwise estimator (i,j) can be interpreted as a vote for either class i or for class j. There are $m(m-1)/2$ non-trivially distinct functions r_{ij}, one for each pair of classes. Input vector $\boldsymbol{x}$ is assigned to class k if class k wins the most votes, or two-class classifier decisions $k - i$ $(i = 1, \ldots, m)$.

Pairwise Coupling and Similar Models. The pairwise coupling model [3] assumes that, for input $\boldsymbol{x}$, the output of pairwise classifier (i, j) is given by:

$$s_{ij}(\boldsymbol{x}) = P(i \mid \boldsymbol{x}, i \vee j) \tag{1.2}$$

and that

$$s_{ij}(\boldsymbol{x}) = \frac{P(i \mid \boldsymbol{x})}{P(i \mid \boldsymbol{x}) + P(j \mid \boldsymbol{x})} \tag{1.3}$$

which is the same relation as in Eq. 1.1. The authors then proceed to find the set of probabilities $P(i \mid \boldsymbol{x})$ that best fit the set of classier outputs s_{ij} via Eq. 1.3. Thus, while Friedman determines only the class with maximum posterior probability, the pairwise coupling model estimates the class posterior probabilities of all classes. A similar model is given in [6]. For input $\boldsymbol{x}$, the output of pairwise classifier (i, j) is given, as in the pairwise coupling model, by:

$$s_{ij}(\boldsymbol{x}) = P(i \mid \boldsymbol{x}, i \vee j)$$

By Bayes law

$$s_{ij}(\boldsymbol{x}) = \frac{w_i P(\boldsymbol{x} \mid i)}{w_i P(\boldsymbol{x} \mid i) + w_j P(\boldsymbol{x} \mid j)} \tag{1.4}$$

where w_i is the prior probability of class i. Note that, as opposed to Eq. 1.3 of the pairwise coupling model, this is an exact relation. Given the classifier outputs s_{ij}, using Eq. 1.4 and Bayes' law

$$P(i \mid \boldsymbol{x}) = \frac{w_i P(\boldsymbol{x} \mid i)}{\sum_{j=1}^{m} w_j P(\boldsymbol{x} \mid j)}$$

one can compute all class posterior probabilities. The literature contains a relatively large number of papers on the problem of combining simpler classifiers into multi-way classifiers: [1,4,5,7]. These papers will not be discussed any further, since they generalize the problem and its solution in various ways, but, as far as the focus of the present paper is concerned, do not fundamentally change the principles introduced by Friedman.

2 The Proposed Approach

Friedman's method, being a form of Bayesian classification, requires estimates of the probabilities of the various classes at the input vector. Unfortunately, class probability estimation is a difficult problem. Thus, it is desirable to design a classification method that retains the advantage of reducing the multi-way problem to a set of two-way decisions but does not require pairwise class density comparison. The problem with with the pairwise coupling and related models is more basic. According to these models, the output of classifier (i, j) for input vector x is given by $s_{ij}(x) = P(i \mid x, i \vee j)$. In other words, the input vector is assumed to belong to class i or to class j. However, in the testing phase, it is impossible to ensure that input vector x fed to classifier (i, j) belongs to either class i or j. If the input belongs to some other class, $x \in k \neq i, j$, then the output of classifier (i, j) can no longer be interpreted as in Eqs 1.2, 1.3, 1.4, and these models cannot be applied.

The goal of this paper is to formulate a multi-way classification scheme based on pairwise classifiers that do not estimate the pairwise class probability ratios of the type 1.1 for the input vector. Such classifiers will be hereafter termed "non-probabilistic". A typical example of such a classifier is the multilayer perceptron. A non-probabilistic classifier performs certain calculations on the components of the input vector. For example, such a pairwise classifier may discriminate between two classes by comparing a certain continuous feature with a threshold, or by detecting the presence of one of two distinguishing features, or by performing more complex calculations on the vector components in the case of the neural networks. In vision application, one may differentiate between two image classes by detecting one or two image templates at certain positions in the image. In the training stage, using neural networks or related techniques as pairwise classifiers is attractive because, in general, learning one m-way classification is more expensive computationally than learning $m(m-1)/2$ two-way classifications. For input $x \in i \vee j$, the output of a pairwise neural network $\mathcal{N}_{i,j}$ trained to discriminate between classes i and j (by outputting 0 for class i and 1 for class j) can be *interpreted* as deciding whether $p_i(x) > p_j(x)$ (despite the fact that such networks do not actually estimate class probabilities). One is therefore tempted to try to apply Friedman's voting method to the outputs of neural, non-probabilistic pairwise classifiers. However, the output of pairwise network $\mathcal{N}_{ij}(x)$ has the same meaning as $r_{ij}(x)$ in Eq. 1.1 only if the input $x \in i \vee j$, condition that can be verified only for the training set. This is a problem, since in practical classification problems the different classes have finite extents and overlap only partially in input space. Consequently, there usually exist regions in input space where only one single class is present, and consequently the ratio $r_{ij}(x)$ may be undefined, since both $P_i(x)$ and $P_j(x)$ may be 0. At these locations the neural network pairwise classifier $\mathcal{N}_{i,j}$ will have some output in $[0, 1]$; however, comparing this output to 0.5 to determine whether $p_i > p_j$ is no longer legitimate. The meaning of the output of $\mathcal{N}_{ij}(x)$ for $x \notin i \vee j$ is not obvious, and applying Friedman's voting scheme is not justified. To correctly use the pairwise non-probabilistic classifiers $\mathcal{N}_{ij}$ for classification of novel inputs one must interpret the outputs of these classifiers for inputs from untrained-for classes $k \neq i,j$. The problem with directly applying the Friedman [2] or Hastie-Tibshirani [3] approaches to non-probabilistic pairwise classifiers is the following. Consider classifier $\mathcal{N}_{ij}$, trained to discriminate between classes i and j. If, for input x of unknown class membership, the output of the classifier is "i", applying the Friedman algorithm results in a vote for class i. Similarly, the Hastie-Tibshirani algorithm increases the probability of class i. However, since the true class of x can be other than i or j, such an interpretation of the output of classifier $\mathcal{N}_{ij}$ can result in *false positive* errors—i.e., falsely attributing $x \notin i \cup j$ to class i or j. On the other hand, one can expect that, if properly trained, the pairwise classifiers do not make (many) *false negative* errors—i.e., give the wrong response to inputs from trained-for classes. Thus, false positive errors are much more likely than false negative errors. This observation leads to the following classification rule. If, for input x of unknown class membership, classifier $\mathcal{N}_{ij}$ responds "i", one can *not* conclude that $x \in i$. Due to the possibility of false positive errors, one can only conclude that $x \notin j$, because, if the input was from class j, the classifier $\mathcal{N}_{ij}$ would have responded "j" (assuming no false negative errors). In other words, one votes *against* j, not *for* i. Formally, $(x \in i \rightarrow \mathcal{N}_{ij}$ responds "i") $\equiv (x \notin i \rightarrow \mathcal{N}_{ij}$ does not respond "i") $\not\equiv (\mathcal{N}_{ij}$ responds "i" $\rightarrow x \in i)$.

Let y_{ij} denote the output of non-probabilistic pairwise classifier $\mathcal{N}_{ij}$ for an input x from an arbitrary class. y_{ij} is a random variable. Using solely the principle formulated above, a model for the class posterior probabilities $P(k \mid y_{ij})$ can be formulated, as follows. This model represents a conservative (maximum ignorance) interpretation of the outputs of the classifiers when nothing is known about the class membership of the input. To simplify, assume first the classifiers $\mathcal{N}_{ij}$, $i,j = 1, \ldots, m$ output binary decisions: either i or j. Given that classifier $\mathcal{N}_{ij}$ outputs j, what are the probabilities of each of the m classes? It can reasonably be assumed that the classifiers are properly trained, and thus very few false negative errors occur. Therefore, if classifier $\mathcal{N}_{ij}$ outputs j, the posterior probability of class i is reduced to zero, or more generally, to a very small fraction ϵ_{ji} of its prior probability w_i, that is, $P(i \mid y_{ij} = j) = \epsilon_{ji} w_i$. All the other classes $k \neq i$ (not only class j!) are possible, it is hypothesized, with probabilities that sum up to $1 - \epsilon_{ji} w_i$ and are in ratios equal to the ratios of their prior probabilities w_k. Therefore:

$$P(i \mid y_{ij} = j) = \epsilon_{ji} w_i; \tag{2.1}$$

$$P(j \mid y_{ij} = j) = \frac{w_j(1 - \epsilon_{ji} w_i)}{1 - w_i}; \tag{2.2}$$

$$\text{Generally, } \forall k \neq i : P(k \mid y_{ij} = j) = \frac{w_k(1 - \epsilon_{ji} w_i)}{1 - w_i}; \tag{2.3}$$

As desired, $\forall k, h \neq i$, $P(k \mid y_{ij} = j)/P(h \mid y_{ij} = j) = w_k/w_h$. As required, $\sum_{k=1}^{m} P(k \mid \mathcal{N}_{ij} = j) = 1$. The factor ϵ_{ji} determines the probability that classifier $\mathcal{N}_{ij}$ outputs "i" for an input of class j, and it can be estimated in the training stage. Similarly, ϵ_{ij} measures the probability that classifier $\mathcal{N}_{ij}$ outputs "j" for an input of class i. If ϵ_{ji} is sufficiently small, $\forall k \neq i, P(k \mid y_{ij} = j) > w_k$. Note that if w_i increases for w_j constant $P(j \mid y_{ij} = j)$ increases nonlinearly. This is a consequence of the fact that class i is excluded and the "missing probability" is made up for in part by class j. If $w_i + w_j = $ constant then $P(j \mid y_{ij} = j)$ decreases with increasing w_i. It will be shown later that if the prior probabilities w_i are equal, and all ϵ_{ij} are equal, the voting-against method is equivalent to Friedman's voting-for method. Intuitively, voting against class j is equivalent to voting equally for each of the other classes $j \neq i$ — in other words, if $\mathcal{N}_{ij}$ classifier responds "i", the true class can be any class except j, with the same probability. If classifier outputs y_{ij} are not binary but continuous in $[0, 1]$ a simple possibility is to interpolate between the limiting cases $P(k \mid y_{ij} = 0)$ and $P(k \mid y_{ij} = 1)$ to obtain $P(k \mid y_{ij} \in (0, 1))$. Assuming that for classifier $\mathcal{N}_{ij}$, $y_{ij} = 0$ corresponds to $y_{ij} = j$ and $y_{ij} = 1$ corresponds to $y_{ij} = i$, these limiting probabilities are given, for the various values of k, by Eqs 2.1, 2.2, 2.3. By linear interpolation:

$$P(k \mid y_{ij}) = (1 - y_{ij}) \frac{w_k(1 - \epsilon_{ji} w_i)}{1 - w_i} + y_{ij} \frac{w_k(1 - \epsilon_{ij} w_j)}{1 - w_j}, \quad k \neq i, j \quad (2.4)$$

$$P(i \mid y_{ij}) = (1 - y_{ij}) \epsilon_{ji} w_i + y_{ij} \frac{w_i(1 - \epsilon_{ij} w_j)}{1 - w_j},$$

$$P(j \mid y_{ij}) = (1 - y_{ij}) \frac{w_j(1 - \epsilon_{ji} w_i)}{1 - w_i} + y_{ij} \epsilon_{ij} w_j.$$

It can be verified that $\sum_{k=1}^{m} P(k \mid y_{ij}) = 1$. The next step is to determine the joint $P(i \; \boldsymbol{y})$, where $\boldsymbol{y} = [y_{1,2}, \ldots, y_{m-1,m}]$. By Bayes

$$p(y_{ij} \mid i) = \frac{P(i \mid p_{ij}) p(y_{ij})}{w_i}$$

If the assumption is made that the outputs of the classifiers in the classifier bank are (conditionally) independent, the conditional joint probability $p(\boldsymbol{y} \mid i)$ of the output of the full classifier bank is:

$$p(\boldsymbol{y} \mid i) = \prod_{k,j} p(y_{kj} \mid i) = w_i^{-m(m-1)/2} \prod_{k,j} P(i \mid y_{kj}) p(y_{kj}).$$

By Bayes, the desired class posterior probability is:

$$P(i \mid \boldsymbol{y}) = \frac{p(\boldsymbol{y} \mid i) w_i}{p(\boldsymbol{y})} = w_i^{1 - m(m-1)/2} \frac{\prod_{k,j} P(i \mid y_{kj}) p(y_{kj})}{p(\boldsymbol{y})} \quad (2.5)$$

Given that $p(\boldsymbol{y})$ and $\prod_{k,j} p(y_{kj})$ are the same for all class posterior probabilities $P(i \mid \boldsymbol{y})$, $i = 1, \ldots, m$, they can be ignored. Therefore

$$P(i \mid \boldsymbol{y}) \sim w_i^{1 - m(m-1)/2} \prod_{k,j} P(i \mid y_{kj}) \quad (2.6)$$

Taking logarithm:

$$\log P(i \mid \boldsymbol{y}) = c + (1 - m(m-1)/2) \log w_i + \sum_{k,j} \log P(i \mid y_{kj}) \quad (2.7)$$

where c is a constant that is the same for all classes i. The logarithm exists for $P(i \mid y_{kj}) > 0$, and this requires that $\epsilon_{ij} > 0$, condition which can always be met.

For classifiers with *binary outputs* $y_{ij} = i$ or j, replacing the probabilities $P(i \mid y_{kj})$ with the expressions given in Eq. 2.1, 2.2, 2.3, gives:

$$\log P(i \mid \boldsymbol{y}) = c + \log w_i + \qquad (2.8)$$
$$\sum_{j \neq i} \log \left(\epsilon_{ji}, \text{ if } y_{ij} = j \; ; \; \frac{1-\epsilon_{ij}w_j}{1-w_j}, \text{ if } y_{ij} = i \right) +$$
$$\sum_{k, j \neq i} \log \left(\frac{1-\epsilon_{kj}w_j}{1-w_j}, \text{ if } y_{kj} = k \; ; \; \frac{1-\epsilon_{jk}w_k}{1-w_k}, \text{ if } y_{kj} = j \right)$$

This equation indicates that each pairwise classifier contributes "votes" for class i. If a classifier of type $\mathcal{N}_{ij}$ outputs j, its vote is negative ($\epsilon < 1$); otherwise the votes are positive $((1-\epsilon w_j)/(1-w_j) > 1)$, the strength of the vote depending on the network output, prior class probabilities, and the false negative error rates ϵ_{ij}.

If all classes have the same prior probability $w_i = 1/m$ and if all ϵ_{ij} are equal, then the classifiers of type $\mathcal{N}_{kj}$, $k, j \neq i$ become irrelevant to classifying class i, and the relation above is equivalent to Friedman's voting formula, which thus obtains as a special case:

$$\log P(i \mid \boldsymbol{y}) = c + \sum_{j \neq i} \log \left(\epsilon, \text{ if } y_{ij} = j \; ; \; \frac{m-\epsilon}{m-1}, \text{ if } y_{ij} = i \right) \qquad (2.9)$$

Since $\log \frac{m-\epsilon}{m-1} > \log \epsilon$, the probability of class i increases with the proportion of the $m-1$ classifiers of type $\mathcal{N}_{ij}$ that respond i (as opposed to j).

For continuous-output classifiers, using Eq. 2.4, and assuming that classifier $\mathcal{N}_{ij}$ outputs 1 for class i and 0 for class j:

$$\log P(i \mid \boldsymbol{y}) = c + \log w_i + \qquad (2.10)$$
$$\sum_{j \neq i} \log \left(\epsilon_{ji}(1 - y_{ij}) + \frac{1-\epsilon_{ij}w_j}{1-w_j} y_{ij} \right) +$$
$$\sum_{k, j \neq i} \log \left(\frac{1-\epsilon_{kj}w_j}{1-w_j} y_{kj} + \frac{1-\epsilon_{jk}w_k}{1-w_k}(1 - y_{kj}) \right).$$

This equation is the one of the main results of this paper.

If all classes have the same prior probability $w_i = 1/m$ and if all ϵ_{ij} are equal, then the classifiers of type $\mathcal{N}_{kj}$, $k, j \neq i$ become irrelevant to classifying class i:

$$\log P(i \mid \boldsymbol{y}) = c + \sum_{j \neq i} \log \left(\epsilon(1 - y_{ij}) + \frac{m-\epsilon}{m-1} y_{ij} \right) \qquad (2.11)$$

which is a continuous analogue of the Friedman voting rule (soft voting).

Classifying with an incomplete pairwise classifier set. From a computational standpoint it is important to study the situation in which only a subset of all $m(m-1)/2$ pairwise classifiers are used.

Here only the simplest situation is considered, namely, binary output pairwise classifiers that do not make false negative errors ($\epsilon = 0$).

Consider a subset of the complete classifier set consisting of $b \leq m(m-1)/2$ classifiers, and consider class i. Assume there are $n(i) \leq (m-1)$ classifiers of type $\mathcal{N}_{i*}$, trained to discriminate class i from other classes ($*$). Assume that for input $\boldsymbol{x}$ of indeterminate class membership, a number $v(i) \leq n(i)$ of these classifiers will respond "i". Because voting against class $j \neq i$ is equivalent to voting for all classes $k \neq j$, including i, the number of votes *for* class i resulting from the votes *against* classes $j \neq i$ is, for input $\boldsymbol{x}$:

$$f(i) = b - n(i) + v(i) \qquad (2.12)$$

Therefore, the vote-against method results in $f(i)$ votes for class i; under usual voting-for method class i receives $v(i)$ votes. The voting-against and the voting-for methods are equivalent if $n(i)$ does not depend on i, and in particular if all $m(m-1)/2$ pairwise classifiers are used in the classification process.

The voting-against method is superior if not all classifiers are used. Unlike the voting-for method, regardless of the number of pairwise classifiers employed, the voting-against method never selects the wrong class: it never casts a vote against the true class (assuming no false negative errors occur). If $\boldsymbol{x} \in i$ is input to classifier $\mathcal{N}_{ij}$, the vote-for method will correctly vote for class i; the vote-against method will, also correctly, vote against class j. However, if $\boldsymbol{x} \in i$ is input to classifier $\mathcal{N}_{kj}$, the vote-for method will incorrectly vote for either class k or j; the vote-against method will correctly vote against either class j or k. The vote-for method fails if the classifiers trained on the true class are not used in the classification process; the vote-against method correctly selects the true class even if none of these are used. Both methods give the same, correct results if only the classifiers trained on the true class are used. The vote-against method, while never voting against the true class i, can however fail to cast votes against some classes $j \neq i$, resulting in a non-unique solution. However, this happens if the only classifiers used are a subset of the classifiers $\mathcal{N}_{ij}$ trained on the true class, i.

3 Summary and Conclusions

This paper addresses the problem of polychotomous classification with pairwise classifiers. The essential difference from previous methods such as [2] and [3] is that the pairwise classifiers considered in the present paper are common classifiers such as the multilayer perceptron which do not require class probability estimation to perform classification. To handle such classifiers the paper introduces a new, conservative interpretation of the output of a pairwise classifier for inputs of unknown class membership. The observation at the basis of the proposed method is that, while an adequately-trained classifier will inevitably falsely recognize inputs from unknown classes, it will not fail to recognize inputs from trained-for classes. This approach has not only the theoretical advantage of being logically correct, but is also, unlike other methods, robust to reducing the number of pairwise classifiers used in the classification process. Interpreting the output of a pairwise, or more generally, n-way classifier as evidence against (rather than for) a trained-for class has the advantage that it allows, conceptually, the classification of an input in an "unknown" class if there is evidence against all known classes. Two practical classification models based on this principle were proposed: one for discrete-output pairwise classifiers, in Equation 2.8 and another for continuous-output classifiers, in Equation 2.10. The Friedman voting scheme is as a particular case of the proposed model. In practice it should be possible to use a less conservative interpretation of the outputs of the pairwise classifiers. The idea is to use the training data not only for training the pairwise classifiers, but also for testing them and getting an idea, in probabilistic terms, of their behavior for inputs from untrained-for classes.

References

1. Erin L. Allwein, Robert E. Schapire, and Yoram Singer. Reducing multiclass to binary: A unifying approach for margin classifiers. In *Proc. 17th International Conf. on Machine Learning*, pages 9–16. Morgan Kaufmann, San Francisco, CA, 2000.
2. Jerome H. Friedman. Another approach to polychotomous classification. Technical report, Stanford University, 1996.
3. Trevor Hastie and Robert Tibshirani. Classification by pairwise coupling. In Michael I. Jordan, Michael J. Kearns, and Sara A. Solla, editors, *Advances in Neural Information Processing Systems*, volume 10. The MIT Press, 1998.
4. Eddy Mayoraz and Ethem Alpaydin. Support vector machines for multi-class classification. In *IWANN (2)*, pages 833–842, 1999.
5. Volker Roth. Probabilistic discriminative kernel classifiers for multi-class problems. *Lecture Notes in Computer Science*, 2191:246–266, 2001.
6. Jürgen Schürmann. *Patern Classification. A Unified View of Statistical and Neural Principles.* John Wiley & Sons, Inc, New York, NA, 1996.
7. B. Zadrozny. Reducing multiclass to binary by coupling probability estimates, 2001.

Vision

Sparse Coding with Invariance Constraints

Heiko Wersing, Julian Eggert, and Edgar Körner

HONDA Research Institute Europe GmbH
Carl-Legien-Str. 30, 63073 Offenbach/Main, Germany
{heiko.wersing,julian.eggert,edgar.koerner}@honda-ri.de

Abstract. We suggest a new approach to optimize the learning of sparse features under the constraints of explicit transformation symmetries imposed on the set of feature vectors. Given a set of basis feature vectors and invariance transformations, from each basis feature a family of transformed features is generated. We then optimize the basis features for optimal sparse reconstruction of the input pattern ensemble using the whole transformed feature family. If the predefined transformation invariance coincides with an invariance in the input data, we obtain a less redundant basis feature set, compared to sparse coding approaches without invariances. We demonstrate the application to a test scenario of overlapping bars and the learning of receptive fields in hierarchical visual cortex models.

1 Introduction

Redundancy reduction has been proposed as an important processing principle in hierarchical cortical networks [1]. Following this concept, wavelet-like features resembling the receptive fields of V1 cells have been derived either by imposing sparse overcomplete representations [9] or statistical independence as in independent component analysis [2]. Extensions for complex cells [7,6] and spatiotemporal receptive fields were shown [5]. Lee & Seung [8] suggested the principle of nonnegative matrix factorizations to obtain sparse distributed representations. Simple-cell-like receptive fields and end-stopping cells were also found using a predictive coding scheme [10]. Learning algorithms used in these approaches normally get their input from local, isolated regions, and perform a local reconstruction using the gained representation from a single group of feature vectors. As a consequence of invariances in the input ensembles, the obtained feature sets are usually redundant with respect to translation, rotation or scale. In certain architectures like e.g. convolutional networks, it is, however, highly desirable to obtain only a single representative for each structurally different feature.

Here, we consider a setting with several families of feature vector sets, where each family is obtained from one feature of a basis set of feature vectors via invariance transformations. Reconstruction of an input vector is achieved by overlapping contributions of each of these transformation-dependent groups of feature vectors. We illustrate the approach with the example of 2-dimensional inputs and translation in the 2D plane. In this case the feature vectors within a family are translated versions of each other, so that we may sample a large input space by repeating the "same" feature vectors at every position, imposing a translational symmetry on the feature vector set. (This is similar to weight-sharing architectures, however, the approach presented here can be used with any type of transformations and we are using the weight-shared representation for the unsupervised learning of the feature vectors instead of being a processing constraint.) This has a series of consequences. First, the input reconstruction is achieved by considering the contributions of feature vector groups anchored at different positions in an overlapping manner. Second, after learning we have gained a translation-independent common set of feature vectors, and third, every input image is reconstructed independently of its position, i.e., in a translationally invariant way. The result is a compact representation of encoding feature vectors that reflect transformation-invariant properties of the input. The work thus addresses two problem domains. On the one hand, it proposes a learning and encoding scheme for feature vectors in the case of a "patchy" reconstruction scheme that uses not only a single local input region but several regions that interact with each other. On the other hand, it takes advantage of specific transformation properties of the input (that may be known in advance, e.g. for a neural network that is supposed to detect input vectors at various degrees of translation, scaling, rotation, etc.) to select the best representation subject to the transformation constraints, which can be used afterwards for a transformation invariant postprocessing stage.

In Section 2 we introduce the standard sparse coding approaches and formulate our extension to transformation-invariant encodings. In Section 3 we derive an explicit learning algorithm for the case of nonnegative signals and basis vectors. We give two application examples in Sections 4 and 5 and discuss our results in Section 6.

2 Transformation-Invariant Sparse Coding

Olshausen & Field [9] demonstrated that by imposing the properties of input reconstruction and sparse activation a low-level feature representation of images can be obtained that resembles the receptive field profiles of simple cells in the V1 area of the visual cortex. The feature set was determined from a collection of local image patches $\mathbf{I}^p$, where p runs over patches and $\mathbf{I}^p$ is a vectorial representation of the array of image pixels. A set of sparsely representing features can then be obtained from minimizing

$$E_1 = \frac{1}{2} \sum_p ||\mathbf{I}^p - \sum_i s_i^p \mathbf{w}_i||^2 + \sum_p \sum_i \Phi(s_i^p), \qquad (1)$$

where $\mathbf{w}_i, i = 1, \ldots, B$ is a set of B basis representatives, s_i^p is the activation of feature $\mathbf{w}_i$ for reconstructing patch p, and Φ is a sparsity enforcing function. Feasible choices for $\Phi(x)$ are $\log(1+x^2)$, and $|x|$ [9]. The joint minimization in $\mathbf{w}_i$ and s_i^p can be performed by gradient descent in the cost function (1).

Symmetries that are present in the sensory input are also represented implicitly in the obtained sparse feature sets from the abovementioned approach. Therefore, the derived features contain large subsets of features which are rotated, scaled or translated versions of a single basis feature. In order to avoid this redundancy, it may be desirable to represent the symmetries explicitly by using only a single representative for each family of transformations. For example in a translational weight-sharing architecture which pools over degrees of freedom in space only a single representative is needed for all positions. From this representative, a complete set of features can be derived by

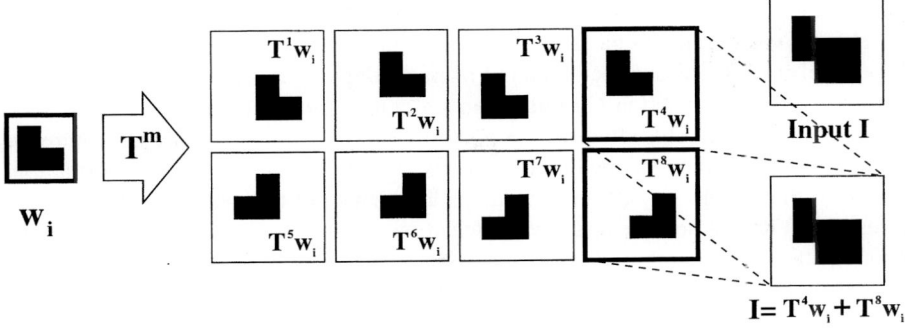

Fig. 1. Transformation-invariant sparse coding. From a single feature representative $\mathbf{w}_i$ a feature family is generated using a set of invariance transformations T^m. From this feature set, a complex input pattern can be sparsely represented using only few of the transformed features.

applying a set of invariance transformations. To deal with shift invariance, nonlinear generative models with steerable shift parameters were proposed [9]. Using this concept as a direct coding model for natural images, Hashimoto & Kurata [4] obtained complex-patterned feature representations which were, however, difficult to interpret.

In the following we formulate the proposed invariant generative model in a linear framework. For a better understanding, we will consider the case of 2D images so that the model works using ensembles of local image patches. Let $\mathbf{I}^p \in R^{MN}$ be a large image patch of pixel dimensions $M \times N$. Let $\mathbf{w}_i \in R^{M'N'}$ (usually with $N' \leq N$ and $M' \leq M$) be a reference feature. We can now use a transformation matrix $T^m \in R^{MN \times M'N'}$, which performs an invariance transform like e.g. shift or rotation and maps the representative $\mathbf{w}_i$ into the larger patch $\mathbf{I}^p$ as visualized in Figure 1 (departing from the notation in Eq. 1 now $\mathbf{w}_i$ and $\mathbf{I}^p$ have a different dimensionality). For example, by applying all possible shift transformations, we obtain a collection of features with differently placed receptive field centers, which are, however, characterized by a single representative $\mathbf{w}_i$. We can now reconstruct the larger local image patch from the whole set of transformed basis representatives by minimizing

$$E_2 = \frac{1}{2}\sum_p \|\mathbf{I}^p - \sum_i \sum_m s_{im}^p T^m \mathbf{w}_i\|^2 + \sum_p \sum_i \sum_m \Phi(s_{im}^p), \quad (2)$$

where s_{im}^p is the activation of the representative $\mathbf{w}_i$ transformed by T^m, with $m = 1,\ldots,C$ indicating the C chosen transformations. The task of the combined minimization of (2) in s_{im}^p and $\mathbf{w}_i$ is to reconstruct the input from the constructed transforms under the constraint of sparse combined activation. For a given ensemble of patches the optimization can be carried out by gradient descent, where first a local solution in s_{im}^p with $\mathbf{w}_i$ fixed is obtained. Secondly, a gradient step is done in the $\mathbf{w}_i$'s, with s_{im}^p fixed and averaging over all patches p. For a detailed discussion of the algorithm see Section 3. Although the presented approach can be applied to any symmetry transformation, we restrict ourselves to spatial translation in the examples. The reduction in feature complexity results in a tradeoff for the optimization effort in finding the feature basis. Whereas in the simpler case of equation (1) a local image patch was reconstructed from a set of B basis vectors, in our invariant decomposition setting, the patch must be reconstructed from $C \cdot B$ basis vectors (the B basis vectors, each considered at C displacement positions, respectively) which reconstruct the input from overlapping receptive fields. The second term in the quality function (2) implements a competition between the activations of the entire input field. This effectively suppresses the formation of redundant features $\mathbf{w}_i$ and $\mathbf{w}_j$ which could be mapped onto each other via one of the chosen transformations. Note also that, if the set of transformations T^m maps out the whole input space, it is necessary to have a positive sparsity contribution. Otherwise, the input can be trivially reconstructed from a simple "delta-peak" feature that can be used to represent the activity independently at each point of the input.

There exist different approaches for the general sparse coding model as expressed by the cost function (1). Due to the multiplicative coupling of the $\mathbf{w}_i$ and s_i^p either the norms of the $\mathbf{w}_i$ or the s_i^p must be held constant. If the $\mathbf{w}_i$ and s_i^p have no sign restriction, the minimization of (1) can be rephrased in the standard independent component analysis framework. If the basis vectors and activations are constrained to be nonnegative, one obtains the NMF framework for $\Phi(x) = 0$ for all x or the nonnegative sparse coding framework for $\Phi(x) > 0$ for $x > 0$. The general invariant sparse coding approach outlined in (2) is applicable to all these models. In the following examples we will, however, concentrate on nonnegative sparse coding.

3 Sparse Decomposition Algorithm

The invariant sparse decomposition is formulated as minimizing (2) where $\mathbf{I}^p, p = 1, \ldots, P$ is an ensemble of P image patches to be reconstructed, $\mathrm{T}^m, m = 1, \ldots, C$ is a set of invariance transformation matrices applied to the B feature representatives $\mathbf{w}_i, i = 1, \ldots, B$ which are the target of the optimization. We assume nonnegativity for the $\mathbf{w}_i$, i.e. $\mathbf{w}_i = 0$ componentwise. We choose the sparsity enforcing function as $\Phi(x) = \lambda x$, with $\lambda = 0.5$ as strength of the sparsity term [6]. We use $*$ to denote the inner product between two vectorially represented image patches. The algorithm consists of two steps [9]. First for fixed $\mathbf{w}_i$'s a local solution for the s_{im}^p for all patches is found by performing gradient descent. In the second step a gradient descent step with fixed stepsize is performed in the $\mathbf{w}_i$'s with the s_{im}^p fixed. The first gradient is given by

$$\frac{\partial E_2}{\partial s_{im}^p} = b_{im}^p - \sum_{jm'} c_{jm'}^{im} s_{jm'}^p - \lambda, \qquad (3)$$

where $b_{im}^p = (\mathrm{T}^m \mathbf{w}_i) * \mathbf{I}^p$ and $c_{jm'}^{im} = (\mathrm{T}^m \mathbf{w}_i) * (\mathrm{T}^{m'} \mathbf{w}_j)$. A local solution to $\frac{\partial E_2}{\partial s_{im}^p} = 0$ subject to of $s_{im}^p \geq 0$ can be found by the following asynchronous update algorithm:

1. Choose i, p, m randomly.
2. Update $s_{im}^p = \sigma\left(b_{im}^p - \sum_{(jm') \neq (im)} c_{jm'}^{im} s_{jm'}^p - \lambda\right)/c_{im}^{im}$. Goto 1 till convergence.

Let $\sigma(x) = \max(x, 0)$. This update converges to a local minimum of (3) according to a general convergence result on asynchronous updates by Feng [3] and exhibits fast convergence properties in related applications [11].

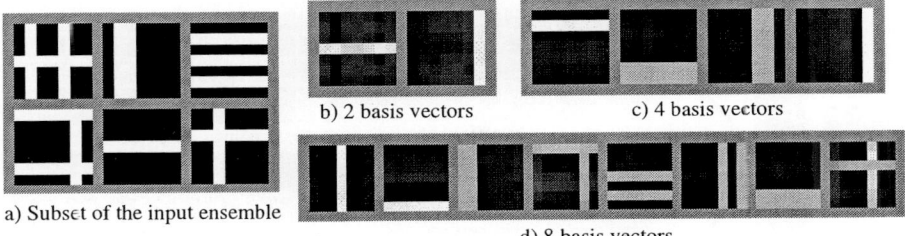

Fig. 2. Bar example. In a), 7 out of 1000 input images generated by overlaying 1-4 bars (randomly horizontal/vertical) are shown. The overlapping coding scheme was used to extract the basis vectors that best encode the input set under consideration of translational invariance. The result for 2 basis vectors are single bars at horizontal and vertical orientations as shown in b). In c) and d) 4 and 8 basis vectors were used, resulting in increasingly complex basis vectors. The basis vectors form an efficient sparse code for the ensemble using translations.

The second step is done performing a single synchronous Euler gradient step in the $\mathbf{w}_i$'s with a fixed stepsize η. For all $\mathbf{w}_i$ set

$$\mathbf{w}_i(t+1) = \sigma\bigg(\mathbf{w}_i(t) + \eta \sum_{pm}\Big(s^p_{im}\mathbf{I}^p\mathbf{T}^m + \sum_{jm'}s^p_{im}s^p_{jm'}(\mathbf{T}^m * \mathbf{w}_j(t))\mathbf{T}^{m'}\Big)\bigg), \quad (4)$$

where σ is applied componentwise. The stepsize was set to $\eta = 0.0001$. After each update step the $\mathbf{w}_i$ are normalized to unit norm.

4 Example: Translationally Invariant Bar Decomposition

We applied the algorithm of Section 3 to an input image set that was gained by combining horizontal and vertical bars at different positions, thus containing translational symmetries in its components. The expected outcome would be a compact set of basis vectors (the representative set of underlying feature vectors from which the transformed feature vectors for the reconstruction are ultimately gained) that, together with the transformations, encodes the input. The entire input set can be described fairly well with only two basis vectors, and their superposition at different positions.

The input images and feature vectors were images of size 7×7 pixels. We used 1000 input images containing between 1 and 4 bars each, with pixel values 0 (background) and 1 (bar parts), such that the bars do not add linearly at intersections. A subset of the input images is shown in Fig. 2 (a). The transformation set $\mathbf{T}^m$ was composed of all possible translations of the basis vectors that influenced the 7×7 input/reconstruction image region. Contributions of the transformed basis vectors were considered only for pixels inside of the input image patch, resulting in a well-defined transformation set $\mathbf{T}^m$: $R^{M' \times N'} \to R^{M \times N}$ where pixels outside of the input image region do not contribute to measuring the reconstruction error in (2). Effectively, this means that $C = (7+6)^2$ transformations had to be taken into account for full translation invariance.

The simulations were run for 100 steps and with different numbers of basis vectors $B = \{2, 4, 8\}$. In Fig. 2 (b), the result for 2 basis vectors is shown. The outcome are

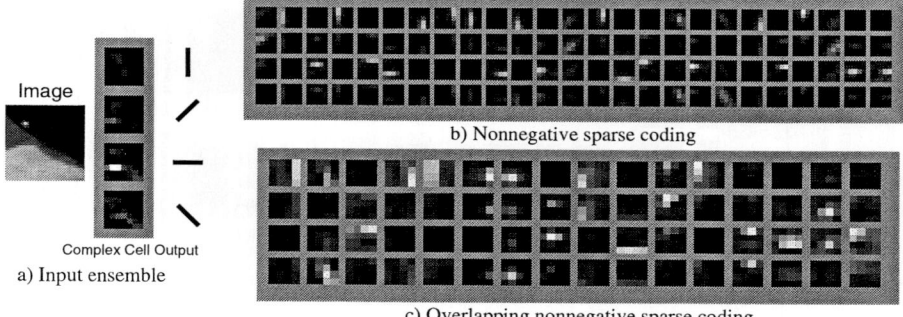

Fig. 3. Learning of receptive fields for complex-cell-integrating neurons. a) shows two examples from the natural image input patch ensemble with the obtained complex cell output, which is aligned vertically for the four considered orientations. In b) we show a subset of 25 features from a set of 144 features learned using the nonnegative sparse coding approach suggested by Hoyer & Hyvärinen. Each column characterizes the weights from the 4 complex cell output patches to the integrating cell. Features are collinear with different lengths and anchor positions. In c) we show the result of applying the invariant sparse coding approach with translation invariance. We optimized a set of 16 features with 4 × 4 receptive field dimensions. The feature set contains collinear features, but with more structural than positional variation as in b).

the two expected horizontal and vertical bar representatives. When we expand the basis vector set to 4 (see Fig. 2c), the same result is obtained for two of the basis vectors, while the remaining two converge to basis vectors that efficiently describe larger components of the input images, in our example double bars (here the encoding is efficient because the activation is sparser when using a single basis vector for describing an input image with double bars, than when using two horizontal or vertical basis vectors). For 8 basis vectors, yet other statistically frequent components appear, such as 2 aligned bars with a gap and two perpendicular bars forming crosses, as shown in Fig. 2 (d). Note that without the overlapping encoding scheme, the resulting feature vectors are first bars at all different horizontal and vertical positions (i.e., 14 in total), and then the more complex features such as double bars and crosses, again at all different positions.

5 Learning of Visual Cortex Receptive Fields

Recently Hoyer & Hyvärinen [6] applied a nonnegative sparse coding framework to the learning of combination cells driven by orientation selective complex cell outputs. To take into account the nonnegativity of the complex cell activations, the optimization was subject to the constraints of both coefficients s_i^p and vector entries of the basis representatives $\mathbf{w}_i$ being nonnegative. These nonnegativity constraints are similar to the method of nonnegative matrix factorization (NMF), as proposed by [8]. Differing from the NMF approach they also added a sparsity enforcing term like in (1). The optimization of (1) under combined nonnegativity and sparsity constraints gives rise to short and elongated collinear receptive fields, which implement combination cells being sensitive to collinear structure in the visual input. As Hoyer and Hyvärinen noted, the approach does not produce curved or corner-like receptive fields.

We repeated the experiments with the non-overlapping setup as was done by Hoyer & Hyvärinen and compared this with results gained from our overlapping sparse reconstruction approach for translation invariance. The patch ensemble was generated in the following way (see also [6]). First a set of 24×24 pixel patches was collected from images containing natural scenes. On each patch the response of a simple cell pair which consisted of an even and an odd Gabor filter was computed on a 6×6 grid (see Figure 3). The complex cell output was obtained by a simple sum of squares of a quadrature filter pair. At each grid position, four Gabor orientations were considered. Therefore a total patch activation vector $\mathbf{I}_p$ consisted of $6 \times 6 \times 4 = 144$ components. We generated a set of 10000 patches and applied the nonnegative sparse coding learning rule as described in [6] for a set of 144 feature vectors using the gradient-based relaxation as described in Section 3, but without overlaps. As shown in Figure 3 we could essentially reproduce the results in [6], consisting of collinear features of differing lengths and positions.

We then investigated the invariant sparse coding scheme by considering all possible translations of the features on the complex cell output patches for a basis of 16 features. Due to computational performance constraints we reduced the patch size to 4×4 pixels (resulting in $C = (4 + 3)^2 = 49$) and reduced the number of patches to 2000. In this setting the optimizations takes about 1-2 days on a standard 1 GHz CPU. The result shows that we obtained a less redundant feature set with respect to translations. The set contains collinear features of differing lengths (or width), with a greater emphasis on the vertical and horizontal directions for long edges. There are some rather local features which combine two local neighboring orientations, and which may be used to capture a local residual that is not covered by the other features.

6 Summary and Discussion

We have demonstrated how to exploit explicitly formulated transformation symmetries for the overlapping reconstruction of input vectors and the learning of an optimal encoding scheme subject to given transformation constraints. Although we have shown these capabilities using an example with translational symmetries and transforms only, the presented algorithm can be used for any transformation set $\mathbf{T}^m$. One could think of rotational, scaling and other transforms in addition to the translational transform. This would result (after learning) in a network that is able to reconstruct an input stimulus equally well for different translations, rotations and scaling operations. Such a transformation invariant preprocessing could well be a necessary step to achieve transformation invariant classification/detection in a hierarchical system. Posterior stages could take advantage of the known transformation properties to achieve a transformation invariant response, like e.g. pooling over transformed variants of the same feature. Future work on the subject may therefore include the extension of the shown principle to incorporate additional transforms and its application in a larger, hierarchical network.

We have shown in the two examples that the invariant sparse coding approach allows to describe an input ensemble using fewer features than a direct sparse encoding. This reduction of free parameters is achieved by using a more powerful representational architecture, which in turn is paid by a greater effort of estimating the model. For the receptive-field learning example the representational effort scales linearly with the number of pixels in the input patches. The same scaling, however, also holds for the direct sparse encoding, since the number of representing features must be large enough to carry all possible translated versions of a particular local feature.

Could the implemented encoding scheme be part of a biological neural system, e.g. for feature learning and input representation in the early visual pathway? On a first glance, the spread of receptive field profiles suggests a sampling of the visual input with inhomogeneous "feature" vectors, conflicting with the idea of general basis vectors from which the individual feature vectors are drawn. Nevertheless, on a semi-local basis, the brain has to deal with transformation symmetries that could be exploited in the proposed way. There is no reason to specifically learn all feature vectors at every position anew, if they turn out to be translated/transformed versions of each other. The biological feasibility of the basis vector learning rule (4) is, therefore, a matter of debate. On the other hand, one could certainly devise neural-like mechanisms for the activity adjustment rule (3), since the equation for the s_{im}^p can be seen as a shortcut of a relaxation dynamics of graded-response type with a positive rectifying nonlinearity. The constraint of the activations to positive values even adds to the biological plausibility of this rule, since a biologically plausible rate coding implies positive activation variables.

Acknowledgments. This work was partially supported by the Bundesministerium für Bildung und Forschung under LOKI project grant 01IB001E.

References

1. H. B. Barlow. The twelfth Bartlett memorial lecture: The role of single neurons in the psychology of perception. *Quart. J. Exp. Psychol.*, 37:121–145, 1985.
2. A. J. Bell and T. J. Sejnowski. The 'independent components' of natural scenes are edge filters. *Vision Research*, 37:3327–3338, 1997.
3. J. Feng. Lyapunov functions for neural nets with nondifferentiable input-output characteristics. *Neural Computation*, 9(1):43–49, 1997.
4. W. Hashimoto and K. Kurata. Properties of basis functions generated by shift invariant sparse representations of natural images. *Biological Cybernetics*, 83:111–118, 2000.
5. J. H. Van Hateren and D. L. Ruderman. Independent component analysis of natural image sequences yields spatio-temporal filters similar to simple cells in primary visual cortex. *Proc. R. Soc. London B*, 265:2315–2320, 1998.
6. P. O. Hoyer and A. Hyvärinen. A multi-layer sparse coding network learns contour coding from natural images. *Vision Research*, 42(12):1593–1605, 2002.
7. A. Hyvärinen and P. O. Hoyer. Emergence of phase and shift invariant features by decomposition of natural images into independent feature subspaces. *Neur. Comp.*, 12(7):1705–1720, 2000.
8. D. L. Lee and S. Seung. Learning the parts of objects by non-negative matrix factorization. *Nature*, 401:788–791, 1999.
9. B. A. Olshausen and D. J. Field. Sparse coding with an overcomplete basis set: A strategy employed by V1 ? *Vision Research*, 37:3311–3325, 1997.
10. R. P. N. Rao and D. H. Ballard. Predictive coding in the visual cortex: a functional interpretation of some extra-classical receptive-field effects. *Nat. Neurosc.*, 2(1):79–87, 1999.
11. H. Wersing, J. J. Steil, and H. Ritter. A competitive layer model for feature binding and sensory segmentation. *Neural Computation*, 13(2):357–387, 2001.

Restoring Partly Occluded Patterns: A Neural Network Model with Backward Paths

Kunihiko Fukushima

Tokyo University of Technology, Hachioji, Tokyo 192-0982, Japan
fukushima@media.teu.ac.jp

Abstract. This paper proposes a neural network model that has an ability to restore the missing portions of partly occluded patterns. It is a multi-layered hierarchical neural network, in which visual information is processed by interaction of bottom-up and top-down signals. Occluded parts of a pattern are reconstructed mainly by feedback signals from the highest stage of the network, while the unoccluded parts are reproduced mainly by signals from lower stages. The model does not use a simple template matching method. It can restore even deformed versions of learned patterns.

1 Introduction

When we human beings watch a pattern that is partly occluded by other objects, we often can perceive the original shape of the occluded pattern. If the pattern is unfamiliar to us, we imagine the original shape using the geometry of the unoccluded part of the pattern. If the occluded pattern is already familiar to us, like an alphabetical character, we can perceive a complete shape of the original pattern even if the occluded portion of the pattern has a complicated shape.

This paper proposes a neural network model that has such a human-like ability. The model is a multi-layered network that has top-down as well as bottom-up signal paths. Interaction of bottom-up and top-down signals in the hierarchical network plays an important role for restoring occluded patterns.

The author proposed previously a neural network model that can recognize partly occluded patterns [1]. The model is an extended version of the *neocognitron* model [2]. Figure 1(a) shows some examples of partly occluded patterns, which were used to test the model. These patterns were all recognized correctly by the model. The model detects occluding object first, and then the activity of the feature-extracting cells whose receptive fields cover the occluding objects is suppressed in an early stage of the hierarchical network. When a pattern is partly occluded, a number of new features, which did not exist in the original pattern, are generated near the contour of the occluding objects. Since the irrelevant features generated by the occlusion are thus eliminated, the model can recognize occluded patterns correctly. This process of eliminating irrelevant features is useful because the correct recognition of the pattern by the model, as well as by human beings, is largely disturbed by irrelevant features but not so much by partial absence of relevant features.

It should be noted here that elimination of occluding objects is not enough for correct recognition. This can be seen by the fact that patterns in Fig. 1(b), in which occluding

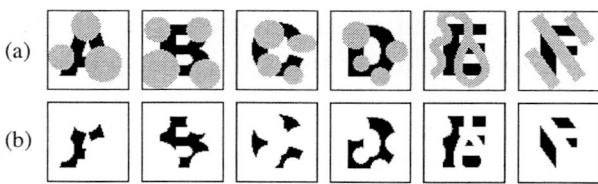

Fig. 1. (a) Partly occluded patterns that were recognized correctly by the previous model [1]. (b) The same patterns as (a), but the occluding objects are not visible. These patterns are much more difficult to recognize than patterns in (a).

objects are not visible, are much more difficult to recognize than patterns in (a), in which occluding objects are visible.

Although this previous model can thus recognize partly occluded patterns correctly, it cannot reconstruct the shape of missing portions of the occluded pattern because it lacks top-down signal paths.

The author also proposed previously another neural network model called *Selective Attention Model* [3], which can emulate the mechanism of visual attention. It is a multilayered hierarchical network having not only forward (bottom-up) but also backward (top-down) signal paths. The forward paths work mainly for recognizing patterns, while the backward paths are mainly for segmenting the recognized patterns. When a composite stimulus, consisting of two patterns or more, is presented, the model focuses its attention selectively to one of the patterns, segments it from the rest, and recognizes it. After the identification of the first segment, the model switches its attention to recognize another pattern. The model also has the function of restoring damaged patterns: Even if noise or defects affect the stimulus pattern, the model can recognize it and recall the complete pattern from which the noise has been eliminated and defects corrected. These functions can be successfully performed even for deformed versions of training patterns, which have not been presented during the learning phase.

In this previous model, however, the backward signals are fed back only from the cells of the highest stage of the hierarchical network. If an unlearned pattern is presented to the input layer of the network, however, no recognition cell will respond at the highest stage, hence backward signals cannot start flowing.

This paper proposes an extended neural network model, combining these two models. It is a multi-layered hierarchical neural network and has forward (bottom-up) and backward (top-down) signal paths. The feedback signals come down to lower stages, not only from the highest stage, but also from every stages of the hierarchy.

The author proposed recently another model expecting these abilities, but this old model had some problems in restoring curved shapes in occluded parts [4]. The new model that will be discussed in this paper has backward paths designed with a different principle.

The new model can reconstruct a complete shape of a partly occluded pattern, if the pattern has been shown to the model during the learning phase. It should be noted here that the model does not use a simple template matching method to recognize and restore an occluded pattern. The model can accept some amount of deformation of the input pattern, and can restore the occluded portion of the pattern even if the pattern is

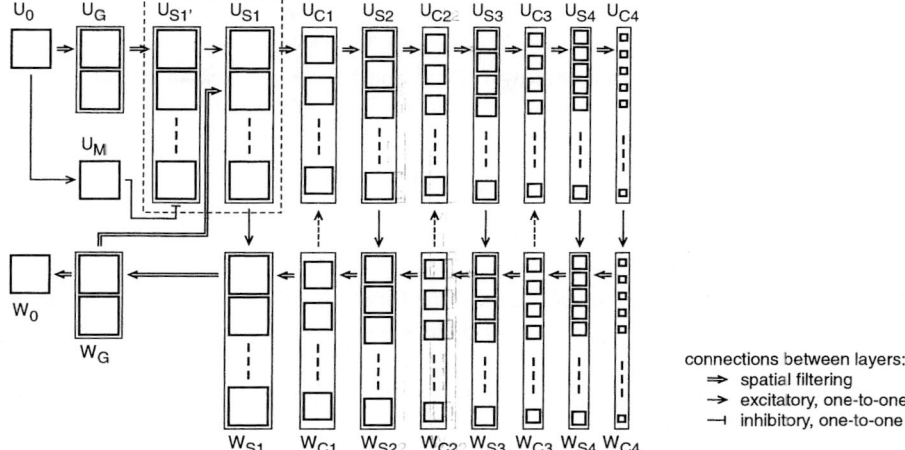

Fig. 2. The architecture of the proposed network.

a deformed version of a learned pattern. Occluded parts of a pattern are reconstructed mainly by feedback signals from the highest stage of the network, while the unoccluded parts are reproduced mainly by signals from lower stages.

2 Network Architecture

Figure 2 illustrates the network architecture of the proposed model, showing how the information flows between layers. The architecture resembles that of the selective attention model. U represents a layer of cells in the forward paths, and W in the backward paths. Each layer consists of cell-planes, in a similar way as in the neocognitron. In the figure, $\Rightarrow$ represents connections that make a kind of spatial filtering operation. Arrow $\rightarrow$ shows that there are one-to-one excitatory connections between cells of the layers, and $\dashv$ represents inhibitory connections.

The architecture and the function of the forward paths (from U_0 through U_{C4}) is almost the same as that of the neocognitron [5]. Layer U_0 is the input layer consisting of photoreceptor cells, to which visual pattern is presented.

A layer of contrast-extracting cells (U_G), which corresponds to lateral geniculate nucleus cells (or retinal ganglion cells), follows layer U_0. The contrast-extracting layer U_G consists of two cell-planes: one cell-plane consisting of cells with concentric on-center receptive fields, and one cell-plane consisting of cells with off-center receptive fields. The former cells extract positive contrast in brightness, whereas the latter extract negative contrast from the images presented to the input layer.

The output of layer U_G is sent to the S-cell layer of the first stage (U_{S1}). The S-cells of layer U_{S1} correspond to simple cells in the primary visual cortex. They have been trained using supervised learning [2] to extract edge components of various orientations from the input image. To be more precise, layer U_{S1} is divided into two sub-layers $U_{S1'}$

and U_{S1}. Sub-layer $U_{S1'}$ receives inhibitory signals from masker layer U_M, as will be discussed below.

The present model has four stages of S-cell and C-cell layers. The output of layer U_{Sl} (S-cell layer of the lth stage) is fed to layer U_{Cl}, where a blurred version of the response of layer U_{Sl} is generated.

The S-cells of layers U_{S2} and U_{S3} are self-organized using unsupervised competitive learning, and layer U_{S4} by supervised competitive learning, similar to the method used by the conventional neocognitron [5]. The S-cells in higher stages come to extract global features of the training patterns.

Layer U_{C4}, which is the highest stage of the forward paths, is the recognition layer, whose response shows the final result of pattern recognition by the network. There is a mechanism of lateral inhibition among cells of U_{S4}, and only one cell that would respond most strongly can be active. In other words, a kind of winner-take-all process takes place in this layer.

The model has a layer (U_M) that detects and responds only to occluding objects [1]. This layer, which has only one cell-plane, is called the *masker layer*. The shape of the occluding objects is detected and appears in layer U_M, in the same shape and at the same location as in the input layer U_0. (Segmentation of occluding objects is another problem to be solved in the future. In the computer simulation discussed later, occluding objects are detected based on the difference in brightness between occluding objects and occluded patterns.)

There are topographically ordered and slightly diverging inhibitory connections from layer U_M to all cell-planes of layer $U_{S1'}$. The responses to features irrelevant to the occluded pattern are suppressed by the inhibitory signals from layer U_M.

Since the irrelevant features generated by occluding objects are thus eliminated, only local features relevant to the occluded pattern are transmitted to higher stages of the network. This model, like the neocognitron, has some tolerance for the absence of local features, and can recognize a target pattern correctly even if all of the local features of the target pattern do not reach higher stages. Hence the model can recognize occluded patterns correctly.

The cells in the backward paths are arranged in the network making a mirror image of the cells in the forward paths. The output signal of the recognition layer U_{C4} is sent back to lower stages through backward paths. More specifically, there are backward connections from W_{Cl} to W_{Sl}, and then to W_{Cl-1}. At the same time, there are one-to-one excitatory connections from U_{Sl} to W_{Sl}.

As has been mentioned before, only one cell can be active at a time in layer U_{S4}, and hence in U_{C4}. Since connections are made in a one-to-one fashion from U_{C4} to W_{C4}, only one cell is active also in W_{C4}. The active cell sends a backward signal to only one cell in the corresponding cell-plane of W_{S4} that is situated at the same location as the maximum-output cell in the corresponding cell-plane of U_{S4}.

After finishing the learning, by which forward connections have been strengthened, the backward connections leading from a cell of W_{Sl} are made to have the same strength as the forward connections converging to the corresponding cell of U_{Sl} [3]. In other words, the backward connections diverging from a cell in W_{Sl} and the forward connection converging to the corresponding cell of U_{Sl} make a mirror image to each other, but

Restoring Partly Occluded Patterns: A Neural Network Model with Backward Paths

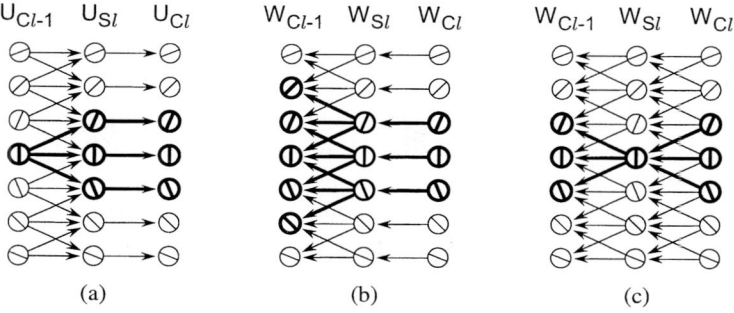

Fig. 3. Deblurring among features by backward connections from W_{Cl} to U_{Sl}.

the directions of signal flow are opposite. These connections from W_{Sl} to W_{Cl-1} work for reconstruction of local features in the backward paths.

In the forward paths, C-cells are inserted to tolerate positional error of local features that are extracted by the presynaptic S-cells. The response of U_{Sl} is spatially blurred by the connections from U_{Sl} to U_{Cl}. The spatial blur is very useful for robust recognition of deformed patterns. The blurring operation is also performed among resembling features. The blurring among features is produced by a low threshold value for S-cells. Figure 3(a) illustrates this situation. To simplify the illustration, only line-extracting cells are drawn in the figure, but, actually, there are cells extracting many other complex features in the network. We assume here that S-cells have already been trained to extract oriented lines. The threshold of the S-cells is set low enough to respond, not only to the stimulus of their own preferred orientation, but also of slightly different orientations. The blurring among features is thus produced by a low threshold value of S-cells. The response of a cell-plane of U_{Sl} is spatially blurred and relayed to the corresponding cell-plane of U_{Cl}. Blurring among features is not taken place between U_{Sl} and U_{Cl}.

Although the blur in space and among features is very useful for robust recognition of deformed patterns, some deblurring operation is required in the backward paths to reconstruct a sharp image of partly occluded patterns. In our model, backward signals from W_{Cl} and the signals from the forward layer U_{Sl} are simply added at W_{Sl} of the backward paths, where the former signals are usually much blurred than the latter signals. If both signals are transmitted to the lowest stage of the network without mutual interaction, a blurred image would appear strongly in W_0, and a clear reconstruction of the pattern could not be expected. It is desired that, in the backward paths of the network, the sharper signals from U_{Sl} predominate over the blurred signals from W_{Cl} in the locations where both signals exist, and the blurred signals are used only in the places where sharper signals are missing. This desired operation is automatically performed in two steps: by the backward connections from W_{Sl} to W_{Cl-1}, and by the backward connections from W_{Cl-1} to W_{Sl-1}. The former connections work mainly for spatial deblurring, and the latter mainly for deblurring among resembling features.

We will discuss here the deblurring among resembling features in more detail. Suppose that the same response as U_{Cl} that is shown in Figure 3(a) has appeared in W_{Cl} by the backward signals from W_{Sl+1}. If the backward signals from W_{Cl} are sent back to W_{Sl} in a simple one-to-one fashion as shown in Fig. 3(b), however, the response of W_{Sl} diverges further in W_{Cl-1}. In this illustration, five cell-planes of different preferred orientations respond.

To prevent such an excessive divergence among features, deblurring among features is taken place between W_{Cl} and W_{Sl}, as shown in Fig. 3(c). Cells of W_{Sl} have the same characteristics as S-cells in the forward paths, and receive inhibitory signals in a shunting manner. The training of their input connections starts after the self-organization of the forward paths has been finished. Suppose a training pattern (a vertical line in this particular example) is presented to the input layer U_0 of the network, and U_{Cl} has responded as shown in Fig. 3(a). This response is directly relayed to W_{Cl}, and a cell of W_{Sl} that becomes the seed learns to respond selectively to this activity pattern of W_{Cl}. In contrast to the learning of the forward connections, however, the seed cell is determined by competition, not among cells of W_{Sl}, but among cells of U_{Sl}: Since there is one-to-one correspondence between cells in the forward and backward cells in the network, if a cell of U_{Sl} wins the competition, the corresponding cell of W_{Sl} is appointed as the seed cell and learns the activity pattern of W_{Cl}, which is equivalent to U_{Cl}. In the particular case illustrated in Fig. 3(a), the seed cell, and hence all cells of the cell-plane, learns to respond selectively to the situation where the three cell-planes of W_{Cl} are active.

Layer W_G in the backward paths correspond to layer U_G in the forward paths. The positive and negative contrast components of a restored pattern are expected to appear in this layer.

Layer U_{S1} in the forward paths receives signals from W_G, as well as from U_G, and extract oriented edges. The sum of these two signals appears in U_{S1}. The connections from W_G to U_{S1} are the same as those from U_G to $U_{S1'}$. The inhibitory signals from the masker layer U_M, however, suppress only the signals from U_G, and not the signals from backward paths W_G.

Multiple positive feedback loops are thus generated in the network by the forward and the backward paths. The response of the network gradually changes while signals circulate in the feedback loops.

Layer W_0 is a virtual layer, which is utilized to monitor the response of the model. To observe how the information of an occluded pattern is extracted and interpolated by the model, we try to reconstruct a pattern in W_0 from the response of layer W_G. The author does not insist, however, such a layer as W_0 actually exists in the real biological brain. It is not plausible that the brain reconstructs a retinal image again in a higher center to perceive it. It would be natural, however, that information sufficient for such reconstruction is to be sent to higher stages, in order the brain to perceive or recognize the pattern. Therefore, it might be possible to consider that the response of W_0 shows the image that the model perceives.

The reconstruction of image in W_0 is done by diffusing the response of W_G. On-center cells of W_G send positive signals to W_0, and off-center cells send negative signals. These signals are diffused to the neighboring cells, but the signal of the opposite polarity works as a barrier for the diffusion.

Fig. 4. The learning patterns used to train the network. It should be noted that the test patterns are of a different font.

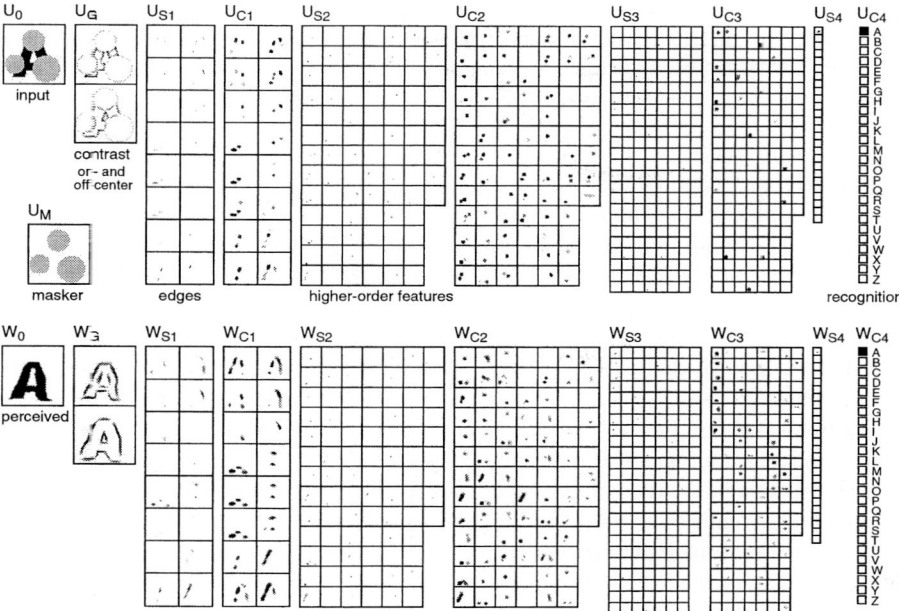

Fig. 5. An example of the response of the cells in the network after 3 times of circulation of signals in the feedback loop.

3 Computer Simulation

The model is simulated on a computer. The network was initially trained to recognize alphabetical characters. Figure 4 shows the learning pattern set used to train the network. To demonstrate that the model can accept deformed patterns that have not been shown during the training phase, alphabetical characters of different fonts are used for the training and for the test. Training patterns are of slanted shape (both thin and thick lines), and upright shape of a larger size with thin lines. To test the behavior of the network that has finished the learning, partly occluded characters of upright shape with thick lines are used.

Figure 5 shows an example of the response of the cells in the network after 3 times of circulation of signals through the feedback loop made by the forward and backward paths. A partly occluded pattern 'A' is presented to the input layer U_0. It should be noted here that pattern 'A' of this font is not included in the learning set. The model has learned the pattern of other fonts. The response of the recognition layer U_{C4} shows that the occluded pattern is recognized correctly as 'A'.

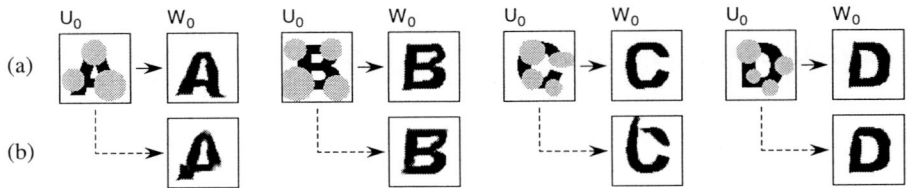

Fig. 6. The responses of W_0, which are restored from partly occluded patterns presented to U_0. (a) The model has already learned the target pattern, but the patterns used for the learning are of other fonts. (b) To emulate a situation where the model has not learned the target patterns yet, the feedback from W_{C4} is manually suppressed.

The original shape of the occluded pattern is restored in layer W_0. The restored image is not identical in shape to the original pattern 'A' before occlusion. It is natural that the model cannot imagine the exact shape in the occluded areas because it has not seen the pattern of this identical shape. It is noteworthy that, despite some deformation, all essential components of pattern 'A' have been correctly restored. The model does not recognize and restore patterns by a simple pattern matching technique. It can accept deformed version of the learned patterns even if they have not been presented in the learning phase.

Figure 6(a) shows how other patterns are restored by this model.

To emulate a situation where the model has not learned patterns 'A', 'B', 'C' and 'D' yet, the response of the recognition layer U_{C4} is manually suppressed. The response of W_0 under this condition is shown in Figure 6(b). It can be seen that the interpolation of missing portion of the input pattern is now made based on the geometrical shape of the unoccluded part of the pattern. In other words, the model has tried to restore the original shape by extrapolating the contours of the unoccluded part of the pattern.

Acknowledgement. This work was partially supported by Grant-in-Aid-for-Scientific-Research #14380169, and Special Coordination Fund for Promoting Science and Technology (Project on Neuroinformatics Research in Vision), both from the Ministry of Education, Culture, Sports, Science and Technology, Japan.

References

1. K. Fukushima: "Recognition of partly occluded patterns: a neural network model", *Biological Cybernetics*, **84**[4], pp. 251–259 (2001).
2. K. Fukushima: "Neocognitron: a hierarchical neural network capable of visual pattern recognition", *Neural Networks*, **1**[2], pp. 119–130 (1988).
3. K. Fukushima: "Neural network model for selective attention in visual pattern recognition and associative recall", *Applied Optics*, **26**[23], pp. 4985–4992 (Dec. 1987).
4. K. Fukushima: "Use of top-down signals for restoring partly occluded patterns", *IJCNN'02*, Honolulu, Hawaii, USA, pp. 17–22 (May 2002).
5. K. Fukushima: "Neocognitron for handwritten digit recognition", *Neurocomputing*, **51**, pp. 161–180 (April 2003).

The InfoMin Criterion: An Information Theoretic Unifying Objective Function for Topographic Mappings

Yoshitatsu Matsuda and Kazunori Yamaguchi

Kazunori Yamaguchi Laboratory,
Department of General Systems Studies,
Graduate School of Arts and Sciences, The University of Tokyo,
3-8-1, Komaba, Meguro-ku, Tokyo, 153-8902, *Japan*.
{matsuda,yamaguch}@graco.c.u-tokyo.ac.jp

Abstract. In this paper, we propose a new objective function for forming topographic mappings, named the "InfoMin" criterion. This criterion is defined as the average of the information transferred through small neighbor areas over a mapping, and its closed form is derived by use of the Edgeworth expansion. If the second-order statistics (namely, normal correlations among neurons) are not zero, the InfoMin criterion is consistent with the C measure (a unifying objective function for topographic mapping proposed by Goodhill and Sejnowski [1]). In addition, the higher-order correlations are dominant in this criterion only if the second-order ones are negligible. So, it can explain many previous models comprehensively, and is applicable to uncorrelated signals such that ZCA or ICA generates as well. Numerical experiments on natural scenes verify that the InfoMin criterion gives a strong unifying framework for topographic mappings based on information theory.

1 Introduction

It is well-known that there are various topographic mappings in the brain system, e.g. the retinotopic map [2], the ocular dominant columns, and the orientation columns [3]. Quite many models have been proposed for explaining the formation of these topographic mappings (e.g. see [4] and [5] as reviews). In order to explain these many models comprehensively, some unifying frameworks have been proposed by defining a general objective function [1][6]. But, the previous frameworks have two defects. First, they are not derived deductively but inductively from many topographic mapping models. The fundamental and comprehensive "principle" under the topographic mapping formation is still unclear. Secondly, they are based on mainly the second-order statistics (namely, the normal correlations among neurons). In spite of that it has been suggested by some models that the higher-order statistics play an important role for forming topographic mapping [7][8], the previous frameworks do not involve such higher-order statistics explicitly.

In this paper, a new objective function for topographic mappings (named "the InfoMin criterion") is proposed by the information-theoretic approach[1]. It has been shown that such an approach is quite effective for explaining the developments of the feature preferences of neurons [9][10][11], and there exist some information theoretic models for topographic mappings also (e.g. [12], [13], and [14]). But, the most of such topographic mapping models are specific and thus do not give a comprehensive framework. In addition, they do not utilize the higher-order statistics except for a few models such as topographic ICA [8]. On the other hand, the InfoMin criterion gives a deductive and unifying framework for topographic mappings and involves the higher-order statistics if the second-order ones are negligible.

This paper is organized as follows. In Section 2, the InfoMin criterion is proposed. First, it is introduced intuitively from the general property of topographic mappings in Section 2.1. Secondly, the information transfer model is given formally in Section 2.2. Then, the mathematical closed form of the InfoMin criterion is obtained in Section 2.3. In Section 3, the relations between the InfoMin criterion and other models (the C measure [1], the ZCA filter preserving spatial relationships [7][11], and topographic ICA [8]) are discussed both analytically and numerically. Some numerical experiments on natural scenes verify that the InfoMin criterion gives a strong unifying framework for topographic mappings. Lastly, this paper is concluded in Section 4.

2 The InfoMin Criterion

2.1 Basic Idea of the InfoMin Criterion

It is the general property of topographic mappings that more correlated neurons are placed nearer, while information theory asserts that the information transferred by correlated neurons is lower than that by uncorrelated ones. So, in topographic mappings, the information transferred by the neurons in a small neighbor area is low. Therefore, we can define an objective function for topographic mappings as "the average of the information transferred through small neighbor areas over a mapping." This objective function is called the "InfoMin" criterion.

2.2 Information Transfer Model

Here, the information transfer model and the InfoMin criterion are described formally.

The information transfer model (Fig. 1) is given as follows:

- The input signal (namely, the values of neurons) $\boldsymbol{S}\ (=(s_i))$ is given according to a stationary probability distribution $P_s(\boldsymbol{S})$.

---

[1] Our previous works [15] have the limitation that input signals should obey a Gaussian distribution.

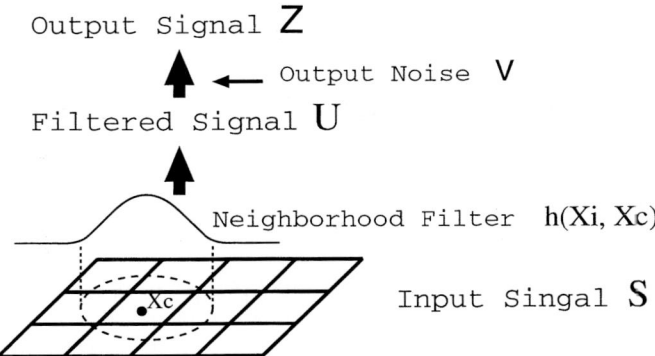

Fig. 1. Information transfer model: An input signal S is arranged in a given low-dimensional array (e.g. a two-dimensional one of 3×4 neurons). The arranged input signal S is filtered through a neighborhood filter h centered at $\boldsymbol{X}_C$. Then, the output signal Z is given as the sum of the filtered signal U and an output noise V.

- The N neurons are arranged in a given low-dimensional array (for example, a two-dimensional 3×4 array of neurons in the cortex). The arrangement corresponds to a mapping. The coordinates of each neuron i in the arrangement are denoted as $\boldsymbol{X}_i = (x_{ik})$.
- The transfer through a small area is regarded as filtering by a neighborhood function $h(\boldsymbol{X}_i, \boldsymbol{X}_C)$, where $\boldsymbol{X}_C = (x_{Ck})$ represents the center of the small neighbor area. The filtered signal $\boldsymbol{U} = (u_i)$ is given as

$$u_i = h(\boldsymbol{X}_i, \boldsymbol{X}_C) s_i. \qquad (1)$$

- An output noise $\boldsymbol{V} = (v_i)$ is added to the filtered signal. $\boldsymbol{V}$ is given according to a probability distribution $P_v(\boldsymbol{V})$ which is independent of $\boldsymbol{S}$.
- The output signal $\boldsymbol{Z} = (z_i)$ is given as

$$\boldsymbol{Z} = \boldsymbol{U} + \boldsymbol{V}. \qquad (2)$$

Now, let $I(\boldsymbol{S}; \boldsymbol{Z})$ be the mutual information between $\boldsymbol{S}$ and $\boldsymbol{Z}$. Then, the InfoMin criterion IM is defined as

$$IM = \int I(\boldsymbol{S}; \boldsymbol{Z}) \, d\boldsymbol{X}_C, \qquad (3)$$

where $I(\boldsymbol{S}; \boldsymbol{Z})$ is averaged over all the small areas placed arbitrarily. The topographic mapping is formed by finding out the arrangement of neurons in the given array which minimizes the IM.

2.3 Closed Form of the InfoMin Criterion

We assume that the noise distribution $P_v(\boldsymbol{V})$ is Gaussian where each v_i is independent and has the same sufficiently large variance Δ^2. Then, the closed

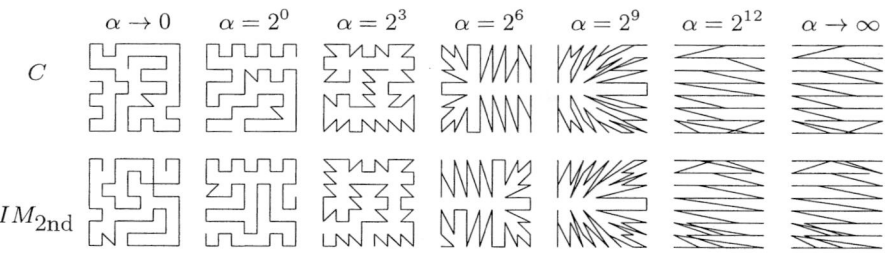

Fig. 2. Comparison between the C measure and $IM_{2\text{nd}}$: The input signal S was given as 50000 samples of image patches consisting of 8×8 pixels. The signal components are arranged in the 1×64 (one-dimensional) array. The arrangements minimizing C or $IM_{2\text{nd}}$ were found out by simulated annealing (SA) [18] for various α. They are represented by joining up the signal components on the 8×8 patch according to the order in the 1×64 array. The SA parameters are as follows. Initial map: random. Move set: pairwise interchanges. Initial temperature: $3 \times$ the mean energy difference over 10,000 moves. Cooling schedule: exponential. Cooling rate: 0.998. Acceptance criterion: 1000 moves at each temperature. Upper bound: 10,000 moves at each temperature. Stopping criterion: zero acceptance at upper bound.

mathematical form of $I(S;Z)$ can be derived by the Edgeworth expansion[2]. By letting $h(X_i, X_C)$ be a radial basis function $g_\alpha(X_i - X_C)$ defined as

$$g_\alpha(X) = \exp\left(\frac{-\sum_k x_k^2}{\alpha}\right) \quad (4)$$

where α is a positive constant, the closed form of IM can be obtained.

We focus our attention on the following two cases in this paper. Note that the constant multipliers and additional terms are neglected here.

1. In the case that the second-order cumulants are not negligible:
   $I(S;Z)$ is given as $-\sum_{i,j}\left(\kappa_u^{ij}\right)^2$, where κ_u^{ij} is the second-order cumulant between u_i and u_j. κ_u^{ij} is given as

   $$\kappa_u^{ij} = \kappa^{ij} h(X_i, X_C) h(X_j, X_C) \kappa^{ij} = \kappa^{ij} g_\alpha(X_i - X_C) g_\alpha(X_j - X_C), \quad (5)$$

   where κ^{ij} is the second-order cumulant between s_i and s_j in the input signal. Thus, the InfoMin criterion on the second-order cumulants, $IM_{2\text{nd}}$, is given as

   $$\begin{aligned}IM_{2\text{nd}} &= -\sum_{i,j}\left(\kappa^{ij}\right)^2 \int \left(g_\alpha(X_i - X_C) g_\alpha(X_j - X_C)\right)^2 dX_C \\ &= -\sum_{i,j}\left(\kappa^{ij}\right)^2 g_\alpha(X_i - X_j).\end{aligned} \quad (6)$$

---

[2] For details of the derivation, see our preprint at
http://www.graco.c.u-tokyo.ac.jp/~matsuda/publications/.

2. In the case that the second-order and the third-order cumulants are negligible:
   $I(S; Z)$ is given as $\sum_{i,j,k,l} \left(\kappa_u^{ijkl}\right)^2 + 6 \sum_{i,j} \left(\kappa_u^{ii}\right)^2 \left(\kappa_u^{jj}\right)^2$ where κ_u^{ijkl} is a fourth cumulant of U. For simplicity, we also assume that the dominant fourth cumulants are κ^{iijj} only. Then, the InfoMin criterion on the fourth-order cumulants, IM_{4th}, is given as

$$IM_{4th} = -\int dX_c \left(\sum_{i,j} \left(\kappa_u^{iijj}\right)^2 - 2 \sum_{i,j} \left(\kappa_u^{ii}\right)^2 \left(\kappa_u^{jj}\right)^2 \right)$$

$$= -\sum_{i,j} \left(\left(\kappa^{iijj}\right)^2 - 2 \left(\kappa^{ii}\right)^2 \left(\kappa^{jj}\right)^2 \right) g_{\frac{\alpha}{2}} (X_i - X_j), \quad (7)$$

where κ^{iijj} is a fourth order cumulant in the input signal S.

The above IM_{2nd} and IM_{4th} are used as an objective function for forming topographic mappings.

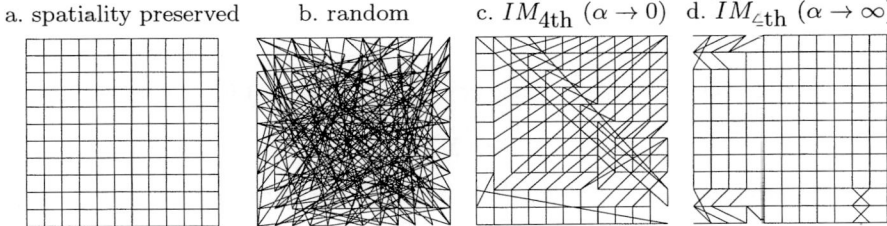

a. spatiality preserved   b. random   c. IM_{4th} ($\alpha \to 0$)   d. IM_{4th} ($\alpha \to \infty$)

Fig. 3. Regeneration of the spatiality preserving (identity) mapping for the ZCA filter: The original signal T was given as 50000 samples of 12×12 image patches. The input signal S is the whitened signal of T through the ZCA filter. The identity mapping (preserving the spatial relationship) is shown for comparison (a). Topographic mappings from the 12×12 image patch to the two-dimensional 12×12 array were formed by minimizing IM_{4th} for $\alpha \to 0$ (c) and $\alpha \to \infty$ (d), where the initial mapping was given randomly (b). The SA parameters were the same as in Fig. 2.

3 Relation to Other Models

3.1 C Measure

Goodhill and Sejnowski proposed the C measure as a unifying objective function for topographic mappings [1]. C is given as follows in the notation of this paper:

$$C = \sum_{i,j} \int (s_i - s_j)^2 P_s dS g_\alpha (X_i - X_j) = \sum_{i,j} \left(\kappa^{ii} + \kappa^{jj} - 2\kappa^{ij} \right) g_\alpha (X_i - X_j). \quad (8)$$

Therefore, IM_{2nd} in Eq. (6) is consistent qualitatively with the C measure if κ^{ii} is a constant and $\kappa^{ij} \geq 0$.

The results of numerical experiments on natural scenes[3] are shown in Fig. 2, which illustrates the mappings from a two-dimensional image signal to a one-dimensional array formed by minimizing C or IM_{2nd} for various α. For $\alpha \to 0$ and $\alpha \to \infty$, g_α is given as

$$g_{\alpha \to 0}(\boldsymbol{X}_i - \boldsymbol{X}_j) = \begin{cases} 1, & i, j \text{ neighboring,} \\ 0 & \text{otherwise,} \end{cases} \quad (9)$$

and

$$g_{\alpha \to \infty}(\boldsymbol{X}_i - \boldsymbol{X}_j) = -\sum_k (x_{ik} - x_{jk})^2 = -|\boldsymbol{X}_i - \boldsymbol{X}_j|^2, \quad (10)$$

respectively in the discrete array structure (the constant multipliers and additional terms are neglected). Fig. 2 verify numerically that the InfoMin criterion is consistent with the C measure, where the resulting mapping became "spikier" for larger α. This consistency shows that the InfoMin criterion gives a unifying framework including many topographic mapping models (e.g. the minimal path length model [17] and the minimal distortion model [13]).

3.2 ZCA Filter

For a signal $\boldsymbol{T}$, the ZCA (zero-phase component analysis) filter is given as

$$\boldsymbol{S} = \boldsymbol{\Sigma}_T^{-\frac{1}{2}} \boldsymbol{T} \quad (11)$$

where $\boldsymbol{S}$ is the filtered signal and $\boldsymbol{\Sigma}_T$ is the covariance matrix of $\boldsymbol{T}$. If $\boldsymbol{T}$ is sampled from natural scenes, it has been known that the filter whitens the given signal with the spatiality relationship preserved [7][11]. In other words, the topographic mapping in the ZCA filter must be the identity mapping (Fig. 3a). In the numerical experiment, after the identity mapping were destroyed randomly (Fig. 3b), new topographic mappings were generated by minimizing IM_{4th} for the two limit cases $\alpha \to 0$ (Fig. 3c) and $\alpha \to \infty$ (Fig. 3d). Note that IM_{2nd} is not available for such a whitened signal. Then, the identity mapping was regenerated approximately with some fracture and distortion. The results verify that the InfoMin criterion also preserves the spatial relationship through the ZCA filter.

3.3 Topographic ICA

Topographic ICA is an ICA (independent component analysis) algorithm with neighborhood interactions [8]. It can find out topographically-ordered independent components (see Fig. 4a). In the comparative experiment, the normal linear ICA was applied first. The calculated independent components were arranged randomly (Fig. 4b), then a topographic mapping was found by minimizing IM_{4th} for $\alpha \to \infty$ (Fig. 4c). The results show that a topographically-ordered

---

[3] The original image data were downloaded at http://www.cis.hut.fi/projects/ica/data/images/.

mapping of independent components can be formed by minimizing IM_{4th} as well as topographic ICA. That is, the InfoMin criterion can simulate topographic ICA.

4 Conclusion

In this paper, we proposed the "InfoMin" criterion in order to give deductively a unifying framework for topographic mappings, and introduced its general closed forms by the Edgeworth expansion. We then derived two specific forms IM_{2nd} (using the second-order statistics) and IM_{4th} (utilizing the higher-order ones) under the typical conditions. The analytical and numerical examinations show that it can comprehensively simulate the C measure, the ZCA filter with the spatiality preserved, and topographic ICA.

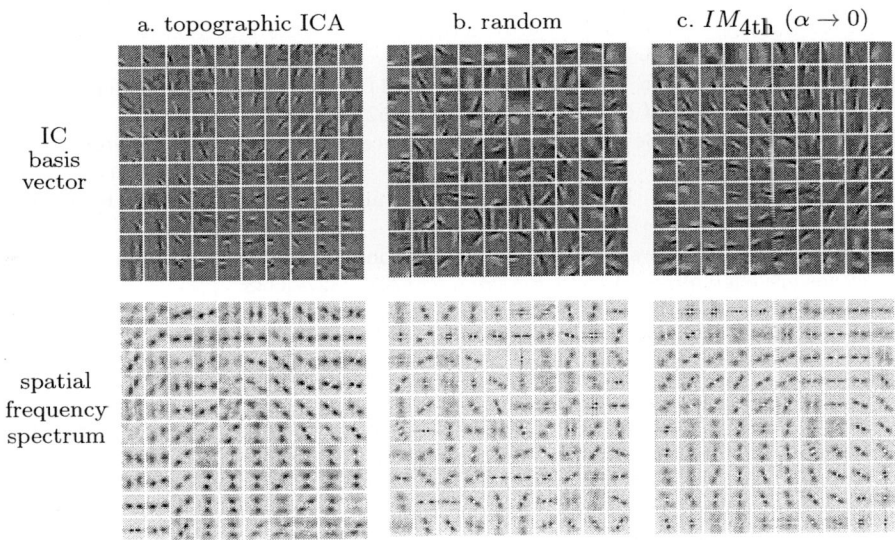

Fig. 4. Comparison of topographic ICA and IM_{4th}: The original signal T is the same as in Fig. 3. (a): The topographic ICA algorithm was applied to T directly for finding 10×10 topographic ICA mapping (with $g(u) = \tanh(u)$, a 3×3 neighborhood ones matrix, and 10000 learning steps). (b): The 100 linear independent components were arranged randomly in the 10×10 array, which was obtained by applying the fast ICA algorithm [19] to T (with $g(u) = u * \exp(-\frac{u^2}{2})$). (c): A topographic mapping was found by minimizing IM_{4th}, where the extracted independent components were used as the input signal S and the SA parameters were the same as in Fig. 2. The upper and lower rows display the IC basis vectors and the corresponding spatial frequency spectrums, respectively.

References

1. Goodhill, G. J. & Sejnowski, T. (1997). A Unifying Objective Function for Topographic Mappings *Neural Computation, 9,* 1291–1303.
2. Tootell, R. B. H., Switkes, E., & Silverman, M. S. (1988). Functional anatomy of macaque striate cortex, II, Retinotopic organization. *The Journal of Neuroscience, 8* (5), 1531–1568.
3. Hubel, D. H., & Wiesel, T. N. (1977). Functional Architecture of macaque monkey visual cortex. *Proceedings of the Royal Society of London B, 198,* 1–59.
4. Swindale, N. V. (1996). The development of topography in the visual cortex: A review of models. *Network: Computation in Neural Systems, 7* (2), 161–247.
5. Erwin, E., Obermayer, K., & Schulten, K. (1995). Models of orientation and ocular dominance columns in the visual cortex: A critical comparison. *Neural Computation, 7,* 425–468.
6. Wiskott, L. & Sejnowski, T. J. (1998). Constrained optimization for neural map formation: A unifying framework for weight growth and normalization. *Neural Computation, 10,* 671–716.
7. Li, Z. & Atick, J. J. (1994). Toward a theory of the striate cortex. *Neural Computation 6* (1), 127–146.
8. Hyvärinen, A., Hoyer, P. O., & Inki, M. (2001). Topographic independent component analysis. *Neural Computation, 13* (7), 1527–1558.
9. Linsker, R. (1988). Self-organization in a Perceptual Network. *Computer, 21* (3), 105–117.
10. Plumbley, M. (1993). Efficient information transfer and anti-Hebbian neural networks. *Neural Networks, 6,* 823–833.
11. Bell, A. J. & Sejnowski, T. J. (1997). The independent components of natural scenes are edge filters. *Vision Research 37* (23), 3327–3338.
12. Linsker, R. (1989). How to generate ordered maps by maximizing the mutual information between input and output signals. *Neural Computation, 1,* 402–411.
13. Luttrell, S. P. (1994). A Bayesian analysis of self-organizing maps. *Neural Computation, 6,* 767–794.
14. Bishop, C. M., Svensen, M., & Williams, C. K. I. (1998). GTM: The generative topographic mapping. *Neural Computation, 10* (1), 215–234.
15. Matsuda, Y., & Yamaguchi, K. (2001). The InfoMin principle: A unifying information-Based criterion for forming topographic Mappings. in *Proceedings of ICONIP,* Shanghai, China, 14–19.
16. Barndorff-Nielsen, O. E. & Cox, D. R. (1989). *Asymptotic techniques for use in statistics.* London; New York: Chapman and Hall.
17. Durbin, R. & Mitchson, G. (1990). A dimension reduction framework for understanding cortical maps. *Nature, 343,* 644–647.
18. Kirkpatrick, S., Gelatt, C. D., & Vecchi, M. P. (1983). Optimization by simulated annealing. *Science, 220,* 671–680.
19. Hyvärinen, A. (1999). Fast and robust fixed-point algorithms for independent component analysis. *IEEE Transactions on Neural Networks, 10,* 626–634.

Short-Term Memory Optical Flow Image

Satoru Morita

Yamaguchi University, 2557 Tokiwadai Ube, Japan

Abstract. Driver takes the attentions for the several objects that include the red road sign, the center line of the road and moving vehicles in the wide region. We introduce the eye movement based on the parallel task model to simulate the eye movement based on the attentions which driver takes for the several objects to the computation model of eye movement. Though viewpoint moves in the wide region to react a moving vehicle in a moment, it is difficult to identify the moving objects in the periphery of the retina, as the resolution is high in the center of the retina, and low in the periphery of it We introduce the eye movement to react the motion in the wide region in a moment by saving the optical flow in the short-term memory to the computation model of eye movement. We call it the short-term memory optical flow image. We successfully simulate the driver's eye movement in an open road to take the attention for the several objects that include the red road sign, the center line of the road and moving vehicles.

1 Introduction

Gibson discussed the optical flow in the field of the vision psychology[1]. We can find many researches related to the optical flow in the computer vision field[2].

Human vision has high resolution at the center of the retina and the low resolution at the periphery of the retina. Human vision is called foveated vision and a CCD device has been developed to generate foveated vision[3]. In this paper, we propose a method to calculate optical flow from foveated vision to simulate human vision.

As soon as moving objects are detected in the periphery of the retina, the viewpoint moves to them reflectively. The vision characteristics related to this motion are important for living creatures. But it is difficult to move the viewpoint over a wide region, as eye movement is controlled in the region of foveated vision[4], On the other hand, the eye movement based on the short-term memory has been reported in the field of recognized psychology. The input information derived from the sensor is saved in the short-term memory[5]. In this paper, we simulate eye movement in the case that the moving object is detected in the periphery of the visual field by introducing the short-term memory to optical flow.

Parallel execution model is important for the modeling of the neural system related to the brain. Brooks discussed the parallel execution model which is called subsumption architecture in the robot field[6]. In this paper, we propose an eye movement based on parallel execution. We simulate the driver's eye movement on an open road, and introduce a computation model of eye movement which employs short-term memories that corresponding to tasks in order to change the region of attention during driving.

In section 2, we explain the short-term memory and optical flow based on foveated vision. In section 3, we explain the control of the viewpoint based on the short-term memory optical flow image. In section 4, we explain eye movement based on certain tasks and demonstrate the efficiency of the computation model by simulating the driver's eye movement.

2 Optical Flow Based on Foveated Vision

The center of the retina is called the fovea. Vision in which resolution is low at the periphery of the retina and high at the center of it is called foveated vision. Because the log-polar mapping model varies its scale in rotation, it is used widely as a image sampling model. Wilson proposed the arrangement of the receptive field according to the mapping model and explained the human sensing facility related to the contrast[7]. The receptive field is located on circles whose center is the center of the retina. In order to realize the types of vision, it is necessary that the resolution diminishes as the radius of the circle grows larger. The eccentricity R_n of the nth circle is defined in the following:

$$R_n = R_0(1 + \frac{2(1-Ov)Cm}{2-(1-Ov)Cm})^n \qquad (1)$$

R_0 is the radius of foveated vision, and C_m is the rate between the eccentricity and the distance from the retina center to the center of the receptive field. Ov is the overlapping rate between the receptive fields in the neighbor. If one receptive field is attached to another receptive field, Ov is zero. If the receptive field reaches to the center of another receptive field, Ov is 0.5. The color in the center of the receptive field used in each pixel of the foveated image. The xy image allocated R and θ in x and y and having RGB value in each pixel is called $R\theta$ image. The radius of foveated vision is $length$, and $R\theta$ image is generated in the region of $R_n < length$. The peripheral information is limited by $length$ when the viewpoint does not move.

The lighting pattern moves as the camera moves. The optical flow is computed by minimizing the following function using the proposition that the motion field is smooth. E is the image intensity.

$$F(u, v, u_x, u_y, v_x, v_y) = e_s + \lambda e_c, \qquad (2)$$

where,

$$e_s = \int\int ((u_x^2 + u_y^2) + (v_x^2 + v_y^2))dxdy$$

$$e_c = \int\int ((E_x u + E_y v + E_t)^2 dxdy$$

$u = \frac{dx}{dt}, v = \frac{dy}{dt}, E_x = \frac{\partial E}{\partial x}, E_y = \frac{\partial E}{\partial y}, E_t = \frac{\partial E}{\partial t}$.

In order to calculate optical flow from the $R\theta$ image, we extend the equation (2) to the following.

$$F(u, v, u_\theta, u_r, v_\theta, v_r) = e_s + \lambda e_c, \quad (3)$$

where, $e_s = \int\int ((u_\theta^2 + u_r^2) + (v_\theta^2 + v_r^2))d\theta dr$
$e_c = \int\int (E_\theta u + E_r v + E_t)^2 d\theta dr$
$u = \frac{d\theta}{dt}, v = \frac{dr}{dt}, E_\theta = \frac{\partial E}{\partial \theta}, E_r = \frac{\partial E}{\partial r}, E_t = \frac{\partial E}{\partial t}$

The equation (3) is solved by the calculus of variations minimizing the following equation.

$$\int\int F(u, v, u_\theta, u_r, v_\theta, v_r)d\theta dr,$$

where,

$$F(u, v, u_\theta, u_r, v_\theta, v_r) =$$
$$(u_\theta^2 + u_r^2) + (v_\theta^2 + v_r^2) + \lambda(E_\theta u + E_r v + E_t)^2 \quad (4)$$

The Euler equation corresponding to the equation is represented in

$$F_u - \frac{\partial}{\partial \theta}F_{u_\theta} - \frac{\partial}{\partial r}F_{u_r} = 0$$

$$F_v - \frac{\partial}{\partial \theta}F_{v_\theta} - \frac{\partial}{\partial r}F_{v_r} = 0 \quad (5)$$

and the following equation is derived from them.

$$\nabla^2 u = \lambda(E_\theta u + E_r v + E_t)E_\theta$$
$$\nabla^2 v = \lambda(E_\theta u + E_r v + E_t)E_r, \quad (6)$$

where,

$$\nabla^2 = \frac{\partial^2}{\partial \theta^2} + \frac{\partial^2}{\partial r^2}$$

The simultaneous differential equation of the elliptical system is solved using the repeating method.

We approximate the computation of optical flow using R_n, θ_m image. Optical flow is calculated by regarding $R_n\theta_m$ image of $n*m$ pixel number as xy image. The first pixel is connected to the last pixel in the θ direction, and optical flows calculated based on the coordinate of the cylindrical shape. As the number of the receptive fields on a radius is $\frac{2*\pi}{C_m(1-O_v)}$, θ_m is $C_m(1-O_v)*m$. u, v vector derived on R_n, θ_m image is translated into the vector in x, y image taking the rotation and size of the pixels into consideration.

$$\begin{bmatrix} x \\ y \end{bmatrix} = S_0 \frac{R_n}{R_0} \begin{bmatrix} cos\theta_m & -sin\theta_m \\ sin\theta_m & cos\theta_m \end{bmatrix} \begin{bmatrix} u \\ v \end{bmatrix} \quad (7)$$

S_0 is the distance between two receptive fields neighboring R_0. The starting point of the optical flow is calculated using the coordinate in $R\theta$ image. It is given by the following equation.

$$x = R_n cos(\theta_m) + c_x$$
$$y = R_n sin(\theta_m) + c_y$$
(8)

c_x, c_y is the coordinate of the retina center.

Image features are extracted from the optical flow. The size of optical flow $I(q)$, the edges defined as $\frac{\partial I(q)}{\partial r} = 0$ or $\frac{\partial I(q)}{\partial \theta} = 0$, and the corners defined as $\frac{\partial I(q)}{\partial r} = 0$ and $\frac{\partial I(q)}{\partial \theta} = 0$ are used. The angle change of optical flow $A(q)$, the edges defined as $\frac{\partial A(q)}{\partial r} = 0$ or $\frac{\partial A(q)}{\partial \theta} = 0$, the corners defined as $\frac{\partial A(q)}{\partial r} = 0$ and $\frac{\partial A(q)}{\partial \theta} = 0$ are used. These features are calculated using $R\theta$ image. We use the features that the size and the angle change of optical flow is more than the constant value to define the next viewpoint.

3 Short-Term Memory Optical Flow Image

Short-term and long-term memory are discussed as the human perceptual model in the psychology field. Input information can be saved in short-term memory for about 20 seconds. After the saved information is managed in these moments, the results are sent to the long-term memory. Though the viewpoint moves quickly, we are not conscious that the image changes suddenly, because we see the image as it is saved in the the short-term memory.

An object is traced in the center of the retina as soon as the object is detected in the retina's periphery. Vision characteristics related to a moving object are important to living creatures, and the optical flow involving in the detection of motion is important in simulating the peripheral vision. We suppose that an moving object is traced in the center of the retina because the object's motion seen previously is saved in the image . So, the motion seen previously is saved in the short-term memory in this paper.

The image generated in short-term memory is the image that you then feel seeing. We recover foveated vision using the previous viewpoint, the movement of the viewpoint, and the input information derived from the receptive field. The system compare the n value of the previous image to the n value of the observing foveated vision for each pixel. If the value of the current foveated image is smaller than the previous one, the image at the pixel is updated and the current time is written in t_i. If it is bigger than the previous one , the image at the pixel is not updated. If the difference between the time t_i and the current time is more than the constant value, the image at the pixel is also deleted from the image at the pixel and 0 is written in t_i. The size of the memory is limited by the constant value related to the time.

The features such as color, gray level, optical flow, edge and corner define the candidate of the next viewpoint. The image in which the color features are saved in the short term is called the short-term memory image, and the image in which the optical flow features are saved is called the short-term memory optical flow image. The next viewpoint is determined by using the features including in the short-term memory feature images.

The next viewpoint is defined using the value n for R_n and the short-term memories corresponding to features and the attention region in the window according to a specific tasks. When the number of the short-term memory feature images is p,

$$f_i = l(\Sigma_{j=0}^{p}(\alpha_j \cdot g(n_i))) \tag{9}$$

is calculated for the ith feature point.

$$ff_i = \frac{f_i}{\Sigma_i f_i} \tag{10}$$

Thus, the next viewpoint is defined by setting the random number by the value ff_i for each i.

Optical flow is a feature frequently used in human peripheral vision, while features such as edge and corner are used in human central vision. It is necessary to change the attention region and the response according to the tasks and features. The response changes according to the feature, the attention region, the weight α_j and the function $g(\cdot)$. For example, if the value n_i is more than 80, $g(\cdot)$ is 1, and if the value n_i is not more than 80, $g(\cdot)$ is 0. When $\alpha_j = 1$ set, edge features are used and the step function is used as $g(\cdot)$, The viewpoint moves to the edge that the many features exist and the resolution is low. The features detected in regard to direction and location are calculated in foveated vision by using the attention region corresponding to the task.

In the experiment, we defined α_j for each task so as to move the viewpoint to red, blue, the moving objects and edges. The short-term memory gives priority to features of the peripheral vision, and assigns a lower priority to features in the central vision. Thus, eye movement in narrow and wide regions can be simulated by employing the short-term memories.

The eye movements of the driver are simulated under conditions that include clear weather and an open road. The time sequence images are obtained at 10 frames per second. The parameters of the foveated image are $R_0 = 7, Cm = 0.3, Ov = 0.3$.

Fig. 1 (a) shows the foveated images observed from the 11th viewpoint to 15th viewpoint. Two images are required to generate the optical flow. Fig. 1 (b) shows optical flows corresponding to five combinations of (a). The small circle shows the center of the viewpoint and the flows around the small circle show optical flow. Fig. 2 (a), and (b) show the short-term memory optical flow image saved 10, and 50 images respectively. Their images are observed at the 20th, and 60th viewpoints. It is used to move the viewpoint. It is found that the large image with high resolution is generated from Fig. 2. The visual field and the resolution required for driving is achieved by using the short-term memory that

50 images are able to be saved, while it is insufficient by using the short-term memory with 10 and 20 images.

4 Driver's Eye Movement Based on Parallel Execution

It is reported that eye movement in an open road differs from the eye movement in a road that contains traffic. We simulate a driver's eye movements in an open road. These eye movements in an open road are classified into these that estimate the road shape and know the situation of some vehicles.

To find the road edges, to find the color such as blue, red and yellow and to find the moving objects are the trigger to execute the events. Determining the situation at the periphery of the vision takes priority over deter ming the road shape. We can estimate the road shape using the short-term memory saved the 50 images if allowed sufficient time to rewrite the memory. In this paper, we use two tasks to know the situations in the right side and in the left side without using tasks to identify the situations at the right and left sides without using a process to determine the situation over a wide region. So we use two short-term memories in which 15 images can be saved without using a short-term memory in which 50 images can be saved. The events are found quickly using two tasks : looking for the mark of the road sign in the left side and paying attention to the moving vehicles in the right side.

A task is divided into two tasks to determine the road shape. One involves moving the viewpoint along the center line of the road from the starting point to the end point and another is to determine the road shape. An edge image observed previously is required to move the viewpoint along the center line of the road while some edge images observed previously are required to determine the road shape. Two short-term memories that corresponds to the two tasks are used. a short-term memory in which the foveated images can be saved in is used to find edges along the center line of the road and we use another short-term memory in which can be saved five foveated images to determine the road shape. The task is simulated by calculating the density of the short-term memory feature image.

We explain the eye movement flow based on some tasks that a task is divided into.

- The generation of events is detected by the computer system.
- As soon as the generated event is detected, a task related to the event is executed using a short-term memory according to the priority of the tasks.
- As soon as the event used due to delete the short-term memory is detected, it is deleted, and the short-term memory is re-set.

The system repeats these processes.

The computer system is realized using the client-server model, and simulates the eye movement based on the certain tasks related to some short-term memory images.

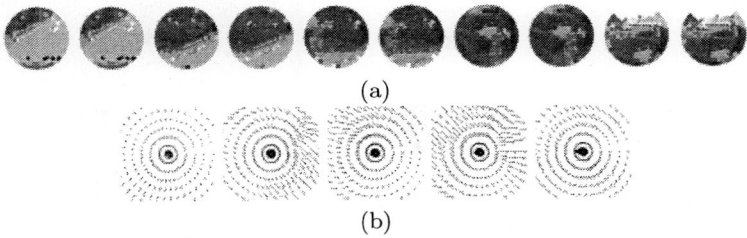

Fig. 1. (a)The foveated images observed from the 11th viewpoint to the 15th viewpoint. Two images are required to generate the optical flow. (b) Optical flows corresponding to five combinations of (a).

Fig. 2. (a) and (b) show short-term memory optical flow image saved 10, and 50 images respectively. Their images are observed at the 20th, and 60th viewpoints. Small circle shows the viewpoint center and the flows around the circle show the optical flow.

We simulate the driver's eye movement in an open road using this model. Time sequence images of ten frames per a second are used in the experiment. $Cm = 0.42, Ov = 0.85$ and $R_0 = 7$ are used as the parameters required to generate the foveated image.

Fig. 3 (a) shows foveated images in which the left image is used for the task observing the red, blue and yellow objects, the middle image is used for the task determining the road shape, the right image is used for the task observing the moving vehicles. Fig. 3 (b) shows the short-term memory feature images related to the optical flow observing the moving vehicles at the 158th viewpoint. Fig. 3(c) and (d) show the integrated short-term memory image and the simulated driver's eye movement. The white blob means the candidate viewpoint. The candidate viewpoint exists in the right in Fig. 3(b). It is found that the resolution and the visual field required in driving are derived from Fig. 3(c). On the other hand, the candidate viewpoint exists in only the neighbor of the center line of the road for the task determining the road shape and exists in the left and right region for the task finding the red and blue sign mark. It is found that the eye movement in Fig. 3(d) is simulated to find the moving object and red, blue and yellow object in the periphery of the visual field while the eye movement is simulated to get edges along the center line of the road in the center of the visual field.

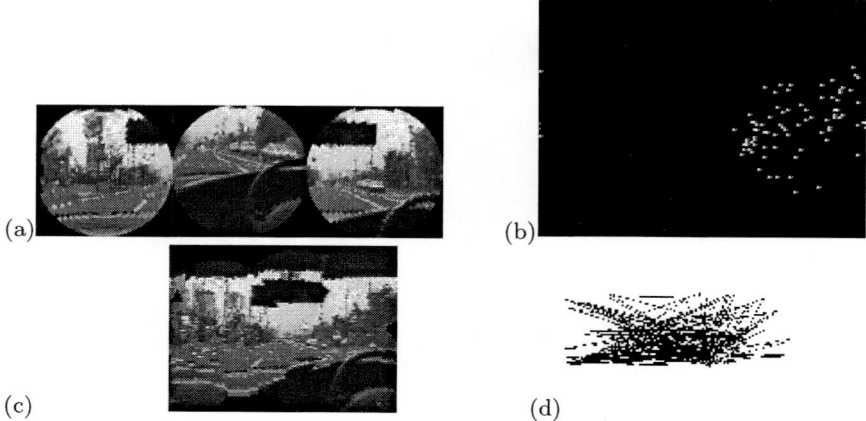

Fig. 3. (a) shows the foveated images for the three tasks related to the driver's eye movement. (b) shows the short-term memory feature images related to the optical flow that observing the moving vehicles at the 158th viewpoint. (c) and (d) show the integrated short-term memory image and the simulated driver's eye movement.

5 Conclusions

We proposed a computation model of eye movement using the short-term memory optical flow image. We successfully simulated the driver's eye movement to take the attention for the several objects that include the red road sign, the center line of the road and moving vehicles.

References

1. E. J. Gibson, J. J. Gibson, O. W. Simith and H. Flock, "Motion Parallax as a Determinant of Perceived Depth," Journal of Experimental Psychology, vol. *, No. 1, pp. 40-51, 1959.
2. B. K. P. Horn and B. G. Schunk, "Determining Optical Flow," Artificial Intelligence, vol. 17, pp. 185-203, 1981.
3. G. Sandini, P. Dario and F. Fantini, "A RETINA LIKE SPACE VARIANT CCD SENSOR," SPIE 1242, pp. 133-140, 1990.
4. H. Yamamoto, Y. Yeshurun and M. D. Levine, "An Active Foveated Vision System: Attentional Mechanisms and Scan Path Covergence Measures," Computer Vision and Image Understanding, Vol. 63, No. 1, pp. 50-65, 1996.
5. R. C. Atkinson and R. M. Shiffrin: "Human memory: A proposed system and its control process," The Psychology of Learning and Motivation, Vol. 2, Academic Press, 1968.
6. R. Brooks, "A Robust Layered Control System for a Mobile Robot," IEEE J. Robotics and Automation, vol. RA-2, pp. 14-23, 1986. pp. 181-194, 1977.
7. S. W. Wilson: "On the retina-cortical mapping," Int. J. Man-Machine Stud. 18, pp. 361-389, 1983.

A Hybrid MLP-PNN Architecture for Fast Image Superresolution

Carlos Miravet[1,2] and Francisco B. Rodríguez[1]

[1] Grupo de Neurocomputación Biológica (GNB), Escuela Politécnica Superior, Universidad Autónoma de Madrid, 28049 Madrid, Spain
{carlos.miravet, francisco.rodriguez}@ii.uam.es
[2] SENER Ingeniería y Sistemas, S. A.,Severo Ochoa 4 (P.T.M.), 28760 Madrid, Spain

Abstract. Image superresolution methods process an input image sequence of a scene to obtain a still image with increased resolution. Classical approaches to this problem involve complex iterative minimization procedures, typically with high computational costs. In this paper is proposed a novel algorithm for superresolution that enables a substantial decrease in computer load. First, a probabilistic neural network architecture is used to perform a scattered-point interpolation of the image sequence data. The network kernel function is optimally determined for this problem by a multi-layer perceptron trained on synthetic data. Network parameters dependence on sequence noise level is quantitatively analyzed. This super-sampled image is spatially filtered to correct finite pixel size effects, to yield the final high-resolution estimate. Results on a real outdoor sequence are presented, showing the quality of the proposed method.

1 Introduction

Image super-resolution methods process an input image sequence of a scene to obtain a still image with increased resolution. From the earliest algorithm proposed by Tsai and Huang [1], superresolution has attracted a growing interest as a purely computational mean of increasing the imaging sensors performance. During last years, a number of approaches have been proposed [2-7]. Of these, methods based on projection onto convex sets (POCS) [4, 5] and, particularly, bayesian MAP methods [6, 7] have gained acceptance due to their robustness and flexibility to incorporate *a priori* constraints. However, both methods approach the solution by iterative procedures highly demanding in terms of computational cost.

In this paper, we propose a neural network based method that learns from examples how to perform image superresolution with significantly lower computational needs. The method is based on a two-step sequential processing scheme that is applied to the input sequence, increasing the image sampling rate and restoring the degradations associated to the low resolution pixel size.

To operate, the algorithm requires the previous knowledge of the geometrical transformations that relate the input sequence frames. To this end, an adaptation of a classical sub-pixel registration procedure [8, 9] has been used.

After registration, a scattered-point interpolation is performed in first place, using the proposed neural architecture. Finally, this densely sampled image is spatially filtered to restore degradations associated to pixel size and any residual artifacts introduced by the interpolation procedure. Filter coefficient generation is described elsewhere due to space constraints. Application of this second processing step yields the final high-resolution image reconstruction.

In next section, we describe in detail the proposed scattered-point sequence interpolation method, and we analyze quantitatively the network parameters dependence on input sequence noise level. Then, we present experimental results on an outdoor sequence and draw some conclusions in last section.

2 Scattered-Point Interpolation

Once the sequence has been registered to sub-pixel accuracy, all pixels of the input sequence could be conceptually projected onto a common reference system, aligned to the reference sequence frame. This results in a distorted (translated, rotated, scaled) superposition of discrete image grids that represent noisy samples of an underlying continuous image, smoothed by the finite pixel size of the acquiring imaging sensor.

In this step of the process, a scattered-point interpolation is performed on the projected image data to increase the image sampling rate to that of the high resolution image. This step will drastically reduce the aliasing artifacts induced by the finite sampling frequency, improving simultaneously the signal-to-noise ratio of the result due to the weighted averaging implicit in the interpolation operation.

The scattered-point interpolation is performed using a probabilistic neural network (PNN), an architecture introduced by Specht [10]. The PNN is a multivariate kernel density estimator, originally with fixed kernel width. This technique is closely related to a non-parametric regression technique, the Nadaraya-Watson estimator [11], and to probability density estimation methods, such as the Parzen windows [12] method.

By means of this interpolation process, the image values at the nodes of a high-resolution grid are estimated. Each node site is handled independently, which makes this process highly amenable to parallel implementation. For each grid site, the nearest pixel in each projected frame of the N-length input sequence is determined, and its pixel value and distance to the target location is stored as an element of an array of size N. This array constitutes the input to our network.

A diagram of the proposed neural architecture is depicted in figure 1. The first network layer is composed of a set of identical units, one per sequence frame. Each unit determines the relative contribution of the correspondent pixel in the input array to the interpolated value provided by the network. This weight is obtained by applying a non-linear kernel function to the pixel distance to the target location. The second network layer contains summation units that add and normalize all contributions to provide the final interpolated image value.

The selection of a kernel shape and width has a significant impact on the quality of the results. Specht proposed several function kernels, including the exponential, to be considered for application. The kernel width of a PNN is commonly obtained by a trial-and-error procedure. A too narrow kernel will typically lead to spiky, noisy estimates of the function to be approximated. On the other hand, a too large kernel width will provide an excessive degree of smoothing, sweeping out the function details.

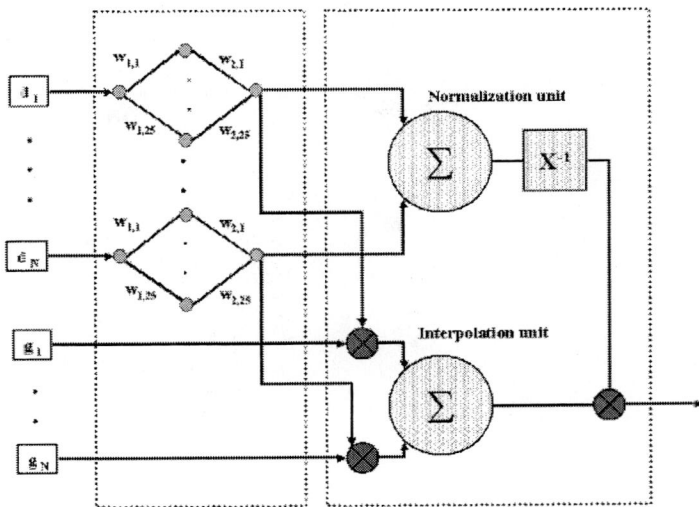

Fig. 1. Hybrid MLP-PNN neural architecture for scattered point image sequence interpolation. The network estimates the image value at a target location as a weighted average of the values $(g_1,\ldots, g_N)$ of pixels closest to that location in each frame of the N-length sequence. First layer MLP networks compute pixel interpolation weights as a function of distance to the target location. Second layer units perform the weighted average operation to obtain the output value

In our system, the kernel function is determined optimally for the image scattered-point interpolation task by a multi-layer perceptron (MLP), constituting the core of PNN first layer units. The MLP weights, identical for all units, are determined by training the full neural architecture on a set of synthetically generated image sequences, where target values are readily available. The details involved in the generation of these sequences are discussed in the section devoted to network training.

For this purpose, we have used a two-layer perceptron with 25 hidden units and hyperbolic tangent activation functions in the first layer, and a single unit with a linear activation function in the output layer. The network has been trained using a conjugate gradient descent [13] method with gradient computed by an adaptation of the backpropagation algorithm [11] to our neural architecture.

Considering the standard sum-of-squares error function, the error for pattern k is given by:

$$E^k = \frac{1}{2}\left(o^k - t^k\right)^2 \qquad (1)$$

where o^k is the network estimate for the pixel location associated to the kth input array, and t^k is the target image value at that location.

Fig. 2. Image set used for synthetic image sequence generation

Using the chain rule, the following expression could be obtained for the derivative of the k pattern error with respect to the output of the sth MLP in our neural architecture:

$$\frac{\partial E^k}{\partial y_s} = \left(o^k - t^k\right) \cdot \frac{\partial o^k}{\partial y_s} = \left(o^k - t^k\right) \cdot \left(\frac{\left(g^k_s \cdot \sum_i y^k_i\right) - \sum_i g^k_i \cdot y^k_i}{\left(\sum_i y^k_i\right)^2} \right) \quad (2)$$

where y^k_s is the output of the sth unit MLP when the network is fed with pattern k, and g^k_s is the value of the sth frame nearest pixel, for input pattern k. Application of the backpropagation algorithm enables the computation of the weight error gradient in terms of this error derivative with respect to the MLP output.

2.1 Network Training

Training data generation. Training of the proposed hybrid MLP-PNN architecture has been conducted using a supervised, learning by examples procedure. In this scheme, low-resolution image data, randomly scattered around a target pixel location, is used as input to the network, which predicts the image value at that location. Comparison with the actual pixel value generates an error term which, accumulated over the complete training set, drives the training procedure.

In our approach, training sequence patterns are generated synthetically from input still images. For this purpose, a training still image set composed of four images of widely different image content was used. This image set is presented in figure 2.

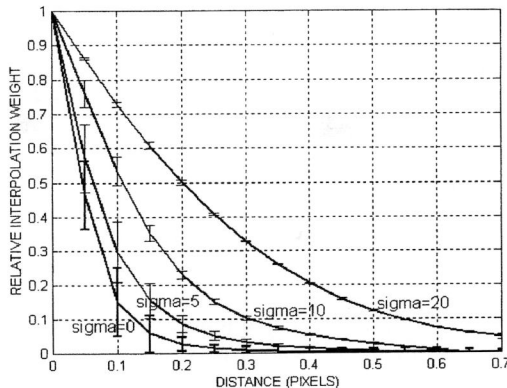

Fig. 3. MLP-derived interpolation kernels for different noise variances

To generate a training pattern from a high-resolution still image, a target location on that image has to be previously selected. This location is generated by a probabilistic procedure, where sites in the vicinity of abrupt changes in gray level are assigned a higher probability. The value of a low-resolution pixel centered at this location is computed by adequate bilinear interpolation and averaging operations. This value constitutes the target output of the network. Network input is composed of a set of low-resolution image data randomly scattered around that target location. Gaussian noise can be added to this input data to train the network for different sequence noise levels. Data sets have been generated for different input noise levels, sequence lengths and low-to-high resolution scale factors.

Training results. The network has been trained on the described synthetic data sets using a conjugate gradient descent method. To avoid local minima, the training procedure was carried out on multiple network realizations with weights randomly initialized, retaining the global minimum. This procedure was validated by comparing the results with those obtained on a subset of cases using a stochastic minimization process based on simulated annealing [14].

In figure 3 are presented the interpolation kernels obtained for training sets with gaussian noise of several standard deviations (0, 5, 10 and 20 gray levels) added to the input low-resolution data. In all cases, the network operates on 25-frame sequences, and provides an output image scaled by a factor of 3 with respect to input sequence frames.

Obtained results show a steady kernel width increase with input data noise level. Intuitively, at low noise levels, preservation of image detail is the primary factor, and kernel widths are adjusted to impose object continuity in the estimated image, avoiding jagged edges typical of sequence nearest-neighbor interpolation. At higher levels, noise becomes a leading factor in the reconstruction error, and kernels widen correspondingly to smooth the results, at the cost of some loss in detail preservation. The training algorithm performs these kernel shape modifications in an autonomous, data-driven manner.

Table 1. Interpolation errors for sequence nearest neighbor and MLP-PNN interpolation schemes

Method	$\sigma=0$	$\sigma=5$	$\sigma=10$	$\sigma=20$
SEQ NN	7.736	9.279	12.635	21.498
MLP-PNN	4.458	5.254	6.143	7.690

In table 1 are presented the obtained interpolation errors for the hybrid MLP-PNN network. Nearest-neighbor sequence interpolation (SEQ NN) has also been included for comparison. In this scheme, the image value at the target location is estimated as the value of the nearest pixel in the projected input sequence.

For zero noise samples, the direct nearest-neighbor scheme provides an interpolation error approximately 70% higher than that of the MLP-PNN network. The difference in the error of both methods increases with the amount of input noise. For input image sequences degraded by additive gaussian noise of 20 gray levels standard deviation, the nearest-neighbor method yields an interpolation error near to 200% higher than that of the corresponding MLP-PNN network.

In a similar way to what has been described so far, preliminary studies were conducted to evaluate interpolation kernel dependence on image content, input sequence length and input/output scale factor. Results, in all cases, reflect a remarkable interpolation kernel independence on these factors, showing the generality of the proposed approach. In a second phase of this study, the effects of other factors, such as misregistration will be analyzed in detail.

3 Experimental Results

The proposed algorithm has been tested with excellent performance on sequences with widely different image content. On figure 4 are presented the results obtained on an outdoor image sequence [15] well suited to test superresolution algorithm performance. The input sequence contains 25 frames showing a car gradually moving away from the viewpoint position. Superresolution results on the car license plate zone are presented for a well-known bayesian method [6], a recently proposed method that obtains superresolution by solving a preconditioned Tikhonov regularization problem [16], and our proposed method. As it appears, the perceptual quality of the results obtained with the bayesian method and the method proposed is similar, and somewhat higher than the quality provided by the Tikhonov regularization method. All three methods provided a very significant increase in quality over direct bilinear interpolation of one sequence frame.

Optimized versions of the bayesian and the proposed method were implemented on a Pentium IV commercial PC platform, and their execution time on the license plate zone of the car sequence was measured. The bayesian method required a processing time of 4.47 s to achieve the reported result. This time is almost 150 times higher than that required by the proposed method (0.03 s). The results corresponding to the preconditioned Tikhonov regularization method were taken directly from those reported by the author, and its execution time was not measured on our platform. However, the reported execution times of this iterative method on similar sequences using a Sparc

20 platform are in the range of 10-100 s, which, even after platform processing power compensation, are more than an order of magnitude higher than those provided by the method proposed.

The very significant decrease obtained in processing time requirements, paves the way to quasi-real time applications of superresolution.

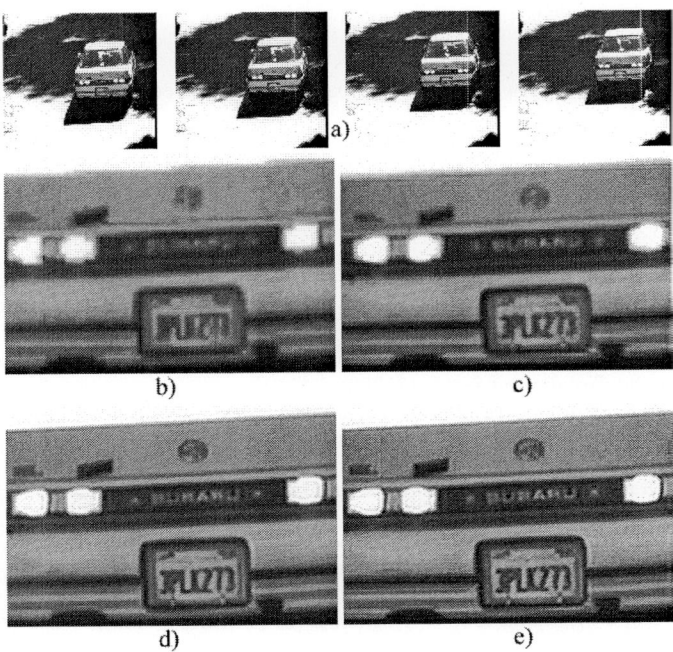

Fig. 4. Superresolution results on the "car" sequence. a) Several input sequence frames; b) bilinear interpolation of the car license plate zone on the central sequence frame; c) results using a preconditioned Tikhonov regularization method (Nguyen *et al*); d) results using a bayesian method (Hardie *et al*); e) results using the hybrid MLP-PNN proposed method. The method proposed provided a measured speed-up factor of about 150 over the execution time of Hardie *et al* method.

4 Conclusions

In this paper is proposed a novel, highly-computationally efficient algorithm for image superresolution. The proposed algorithm is based on the sequential application of scattered-point interpolation and restoration operations on the input sequence data. A hybrid MLP-PNN neural network is used to perform the scattered-point interpolation step, where the MLP is trained on synthetically generated sequences to derive optimum interpolation kernel shapes. The restoration process is performed applying an spatial linear filter optimized for this problem. This filter restores the degradations caused by the input low-resolution image pixel size, and reduces any residual artifacts caused by the interpolation procedure. The filter coefficients have been computed for several input sequence noise levels.

The proposed method have been compared with iterative superresolution methods, providing similar or better quality results with a very significant reduction in computational load, paving the way to quasi-real time applications of superresolution techniques.

Acknowledgments. This work has been partially supported by TIC2001-0572-C02-02 grant.

References

1. R.Y.Tsai and T.S.Huang (Ed.), "Multiframe image restoration and registration", in *Advances in Computer Vision and Image Processing* volume 1, pages 317-339, JAI Press Inc. (1984).
2. S. Borman, R. Stevenson, "Super-resolution from image sequences-a review", *Midwest Symposium on Circuits and Systems* (1998).
3. S.P.Kim, N.K. Bose and H.M. Valenzuela, "Recursive reconstruction of high resolution images from noisy undersampled multiframes". *IEEE Trans. ASSP* 38(6):1013–1027 (1990).
4. D. Granrath and J. Lersch, "Fusion of images on affine sampling grids", *J. Opt. Soc. Am. A*, 15(4), 791–801 (1998).
5. J. Patti, M.I. Sezan and M. A. Tekalp, "Superresolution video reconstruction with arbitrary sampling lattices and non-zero aperture time", *IEEE Trans. Image processing*, vol. 6, pp. 1064–1076 (1997).
6. R. C. Hardie, K. J. Barnard, J. G. Bognar, E. E. Armstrong, and E. A. Watson, "High-resolution image reconstruction from a sequence of rotated and translated frames and its application to an infrared imaging system", *Optical Engineering*, 37(1), 247–260 (1998).
7. R. R. Schultz and R.L. Stevenson. "Extraction of high-resolution frames from video sequences", *IEEE Trans. Image Processing*, vol. 5, n° 6, pp. 996–1011 (1996).
8. B.D. Lucas and T. Kanade, "An iterative image registration technique with an application to stero vision", *International Joint Conference on Artificial Intelligence*, pp. 674–679, Vancouver (1981).
9. M.Irani, S.Peleg, "Improving resolution by image registration", CVGIP: *Graphical Models and Image Processing*. 53, 231–239 (1991).
10. D. Specht, "Probabilistic neural networks", *Neural Networks*, Vol. 3, pp. 109–118 (1990).
11. A.Bishop, *Neural Networks for Pattern Recognition*. Oxford University Press (1995).
12. R. Duda, P. Hart. *Pattern Classification and Scene Analysis*, Wiley-Interscience, New York, (1973).
13. M. Hestenes. *Conjugate Direction Methods in Optimization*, Springer Verlag, New York, (1980).
14. L.Fausset, *Fundamentals of Neural Networks*, Prentice Hall, Englewood Cliffs (1994).
15. http://www.soe.ucsc.edu/~milanfar/MDSP/superres.htm
16. N. Nguyen, P. Milanfar and G. Golub, "A computationally efficient supperresolution image reconstruction algorithm", *IEEE Trans. Image Processing*, vol. 10, n° 4, pp. 573–583 (2001).

Recognition of Gestural Object Reference with Auditory Feedback

Ingo Bax, Holger Bekel, and Gunther Heidemann

Neuroinformatics Group, Faculty of Technology, Bielefeld University,
Postfach 10 01 31, D-33501 Bielefeld, Germany
{ibax,hbekel,gheidema}@techfak.uni-bielefeld.de
http://www.TechFak.Uni-Bielefeld.DE/ags/ni/index_d.html

Abstract. We present a cognitively motivated vision architecture for the evaluation of pointing gestures. The system views a scene of several structured objects and a pointing human hand. A neural classifier gives an estimation of the pointing direction, then the object correspondence is established using a sub-symbolic representation of both the scene and the pointing direction. The system achieves high robustness because the result (the indicated location) does not primarily depend on the accuracy of the pointing direction classification. Instead, the scene is analysed for low level saliency features to restrict the set of all *possible* pointing locations to a subset of highly *likely* locations. This transformation of the "continuous" to a "discrete" pointing problem simultaneously facilitates an auditory feedback whenever the object reference changes, which leads to a significantly improved human-machine interaction.

1 Introduction

Establishing a common *focus of attention* (FOA) is a major task of communication. To influence the spatial FOA humans often use hand gestures. Therefore, pointing direction evaluation is a key topic in the field of human-machine interaction, in particular, gestural reference to objects increasingly attracts interest. However, humans use several modalities at once to establish a common FOA like gesture, speech and gaze direction. Moreover, feedback from the partner is constantly evaluated. In contrast, gesture recognition used in machine vision to direct the FOA is still mostly *stand alone* and *unidirectional*, i.e. without feedback. To compensate for these shortcomings, much effort is spent to increase the *accuracy* of pointing direction recognition. However, we argue that it is not primarily pointing accuracy which leads to good results but interaction with a system. Therefore, a system for gestural object reference recognition should offer three features: (*i*) A basic "understanding" of the scene to limit the set of objects that can be pointed at, (*ii*) feedback to the user to indicate how a gesture was understood, and (*iii*) the possibility to include other modalities like speech.

In this paper, we present a human-machine interaction system that addresses these three points. It allows the user to refer to objects or structures of objects (like buttons of a technical device) by pointing gestures. It relies on the interaction of a neural classifier for pointing directions and a saliency map S generated from context-free attentional mechanisms. The attentional system is related to the approach of Backer et al. [1]; an earlier version was presented in [2,7]. Similarly motivated architectures for FOA were proposed by Itti et al. [9] and Walther et al. [17]. The latter approach is based on the Neocognitron introduced by [3].

The maxima of S are used to select conspicuous image structures. These results are combined with the down-propagated output of the classifier (pointing angle) on a sub-symbolic level using an "attention map" (ATM). The representation of the common FOA as the maximum of the ATM facilitates (*i*) the stabilisation even in the presence of inaccurate or noisy pointing results, (*ii*) an auditory feedback when the indicated point "hops" to a new object and (*iii*) the future integration of spatial anticipations from other modalities.

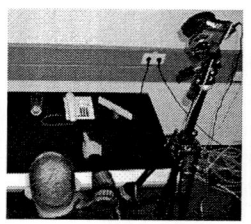
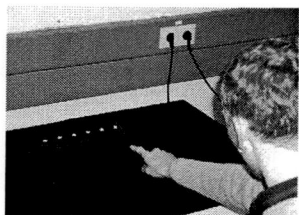

Fig. 1. Left: In a test scenario viewed by a stationary camera a user is pointing to objects on the table. Right: Setting used for system performance evaluation as described in Sect. 3.

2 System Description

The system relies on two data driven processing branches (Fig. 2): From the camera image first three feature maps are calculated (Sect. 2.1) in which different image features stand out (Fig. 5). The saliency map S is calculated as a weighted sum of the feature maps by an adaptive weighting (Sect. 2.2). Maxima of S are considered as "interesting" areas and serve as a possible pointing targets.

In the second branch, a skin colour segmentation module yields candidate regions which might contain a hand. These regions are input to the VPL classifier (Sect. 2.3) which (a) decides if the region is a pointing hand and if so (b) determines the pointing direction. The symbolic output angle is translated back to the sub-symbolic level by calculating a *manipulator map* (Sect. 2.4) which is multiplied to S to obtain the attention map, the maximum of which is the FOA. The *focus shift detection* module (FSD) outputs an auditory feedback to the user, reconsulting intermediate processing results from the ATM module. Next, the single components are described in more detail.

2.1 Generation of Context-Free Feature Maps

We currently use three different methods to generate saliency maps which complement each other: Grey value entropy, local symmetry and edge-corner detection. A *local entropy* map M_1 yields high saliency value for image windows which

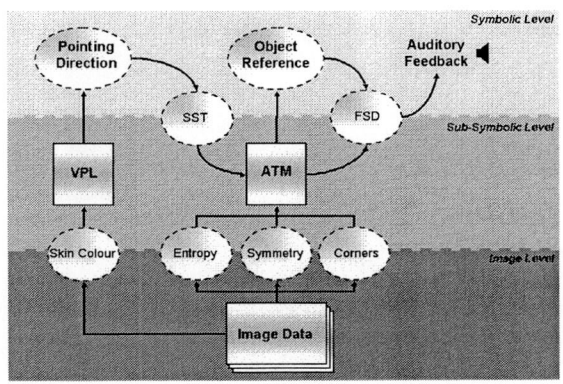

Fig. 2. System architecture. In contrast to approaches which integrate pointing gesture information and object locations on the symbolic level, the pointing angle is down-propagated to the sub-symbolic level using a "symbol-signal-transformer" (SST) and integrated as a spatial weighting of the feature maps.

have a high informational content in the sense of information theory [10]. The window size determines the scale on which structures are evaluated. Here, we use windows large enough to detect large objects (see Fig. 5).

A *symmetry map* M_2 after Reisfeld et al. [13] attracts attention to objects or details which are locally symmetric. The use of symmetry is cognitively motivated e.g. by [12]. The third feature map M_3 concentrates on *edges and corners* as small salient details of objects. Here we use the detector proposed by Harris and Stephens [4], which proved to be superior to other detectors in [15].

2.2 Adaptive Integration Algorithm

From the $N = 3$ feature maps $M_i(x, y)$ the saliency map S is calculated as a weighted sum. S is spatially weighted by the *manipulator map* $L(x, y)$ which codes the pointing direction (Sect. 2.4) to obtain the attention map C (Fig. 3):

$$C(x,y) = S(x,y) \cdot L(x,y) \quad \text{with} \quad S(x,y) = \sum_{i=1}^{N} \theta(w_i \cdot M_i(x,y)), \quad (1)$$

with $\theta(\cdot)$ as a threshold function. The maximum of $C(\cdot, \cdot)$ determines the common FOA of user and machine, which can be used for further processing.

To equalise contributions of the maps M_i, we calculate the contributions $\bar{M}_i$ as a sum over all pixels of each M_i. To reach approximate equalisation of the $\bar{M}_i$, the map weights w_i are adapted by iterating

$$w_i(t+1) = w_i(t) + \epsilon(w_i^s(t) - w_i(t)), \quad 0 < \epsilon \leq 1, \quad (2)$$

with the following target weights w_i^s:

$$w_i^s = \frac{1}{N^2} \cdot \frac{\sum_{k=1}^{N} \bar{M}_k}{\bar{M}_i} \quad \text{with} \quad \bar{M}_i = \frac{\sum_{(x,y)} (M_i(x,y) + \gamma)}{\xi_i}. \quad (3)$$

γ enforces a limit for weight growing. The parameters ξ_i can be used if certain saliency features should a priori be weighted higher. In Sect. 2.4 we make use of this possibility to give entropy higher weight for large-scale selection of objects and low weight when object details are pointed at.

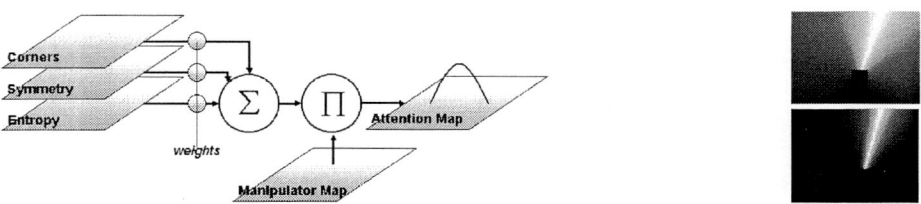

Fig. 3. Left: Processing flow of the ATM-module (central box in Fig. 2). The saliency map S is generated from an (adaptively) weighted superposition of the feature maps. The manipulator map, which allows the coupling of information from other modules like the pointing direction recognition, is multiplicatively overlaid on S. Right: Examples of manipulator maps L ("spotlight of attention"). A wide cone is used as long as the user wants to indicate large objects, a narrow one for precise pointing to details.

2.3 The Neural VPL Classification System

We use the VPL system [5] for visual classification, which was previously applied to several computer vision tasks [6]. "VPL" stands for three processing stages: **V**ector quantisation, **P**CA and **L**LM-network. The VPL classifier combines visual feature extraction and classification by means of a local principal component analysis (PCA) for dimension reduction followed by a classification stage using neural networks, see Fig. 4. Local PCA can be viewed as a nonlinear extension of simple, global PCA [16].

The vector quantisation is carried out on the raw image windows to provide a first data partitioning with N_V reference vectors $\boldsymbol{r}_i \in \mathbb{R}^D, i = 1 \ldots N_V$, using the *Activity Equalisation Algorithm* proposed in [8]. To each reference vector $\boldsymbol{r}_i$ a single layer feed forward network for the successive calculation of the principal components (PCs) as proposed by Sanger [14] is attached. It projects the input $\boldsymbol{x} \in \mathbb{R}^D$ to the $N_P < D$ PCs with the largest eigenvalues: $\boldsymbol{x} \to \boldsymbol{p}_i(\boldsymbol{x}) \in \mathbb{R}^{N_P}, i = 1 \ldots N_V$. In the third stage, to each PCA-net one "expert" neural classifier of the Local Linear Map – type (LLM network) is attached. It performs the final mapping $\boldsymbol{p}_l(\boldsymbol{x}) \to \boldsymbol{y}$. The LLM network is related to the self-organising map [11], see e.g. [5] for details. It can be trained to approximate a nonlinear function by a set of locally valid linear mappings.

The output vector $\boldsymbol{y}$ codes both the decision as to whether the input $\boldsymbol{x}$ is a pointing hand, and, if so, its pointing angle. The three VPL processing stages are trained successively with labelled sample windows of the cropped pointing

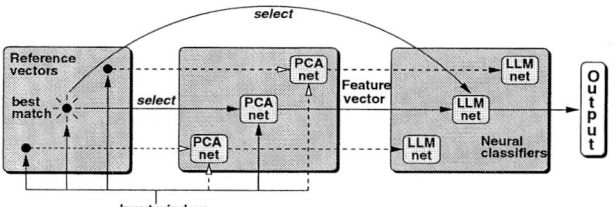

Fig. 4. The VPL classifier performs a local PCA for feature extraction and a subsequent neural classification.

hand plus objects assigned to a rejection class. The rejection class contains other objects which are part of the scenario, e.g. the objects the user points at or parts of the background. In addition, hand postures other than pointing gestures are part of the rejection class, e.g. a fist.

The major advantage of the VPL classifier is its ability to form many highly specific feature detectors (the $N_V \cdot N_P$ local PCs). It could be shown that classification performance and generalisation properties are well-behaved when the main parameters are changed, which are N_V, N_P and the number of nodes in the LLM nets N_L [6].

2.4 Translation from Symbolic to Sub-symbolic Level

Skin colour segmentation and the VPL classifier yield the position of the hand (x_H, y_H) and the pointing direction α, respectively. Both these (symbolic) informations are translated to a manipulator map L and thus back to the sub-symbolic level. The manipulator map shows a "Gaussian cone" of width σ_c which determines the effective angle of beam spread

$$L(x,y) = \frac{1}{\sqrt{2\pi}\sigma_c} \exp\left(-\frac{(\arctan(\frac{y-y_H}{x-x_H}) - \alpha)^2}{\sigma_c^2}\right), \qquad (4)$$

here in the form for the first quadrant for simplicity, see Fig. 3. The cone gives higher weight in the attention map to image regions in the pointing direction and thus "strengthens" salient points in this area.

To facilitate selection of objects on differing scales, σ_c is adjusted online according to the user behaviour. The pointing angles α and hand positions (x_H, y_H) are recorded over the last six frames. If they show large variance, it is assumed that the user has moved the hand on a large scale to select a big object, so also a large σ_c is chosen. In contrast, σ_c is reduced for small variance to establish a "virtual laser pointer" since it is assumed that the user tries to point to detail.

As an additional assistance for coarse / fine selection, the a priori weights ξ_i of (3) are changed such that the large scale entropy map M_1 dominates for large pointing variance whereas the symmetry map M_2 and the corner saliency M_3 are weighted higher for detail selection.

2.5 Auditory Feedback

The FSD module in Fig. 2 detects spatial shifts of the FOA for auditory user feedback. A short "bop" sound is produced when the current FOA shifts to a different maximum $\hat{s}_j$ of the saliency map S. Such an event is detected when

$$\left| \left(\frac{1}{\Delta t} \sum_{i=1}^{\Delta t} \hat{s}^*(t-i) \right) - \hat{s}^*(t) \right| > d, \qquad (5)$$

where $\hat{s}^*(t)$ denotes the maximum of S closest to the FOA (i.e. the maximum of the ATM) in frame t. The parameter Δt has to be adjusted according to the processing frame rate of the system and the threshold d can be estimated by analysing the distance matrix of the maxima $\hat{s}_i$ of the map.

3 Results

Figure 5 shows the results of intermediate processing stages. The user has just slowed down the pointing movement, so the manipulator map shows a cone of medium width in the pointing direction, starting at the approximate position of the hand centre. The parameter ξ_i of the entropy map is decreased while the symmetry map is weighted higher. So the edges of the phone are suppressed while the key pad is highlighted most through the combination of high weighted symmetry map and the manipulator cone.

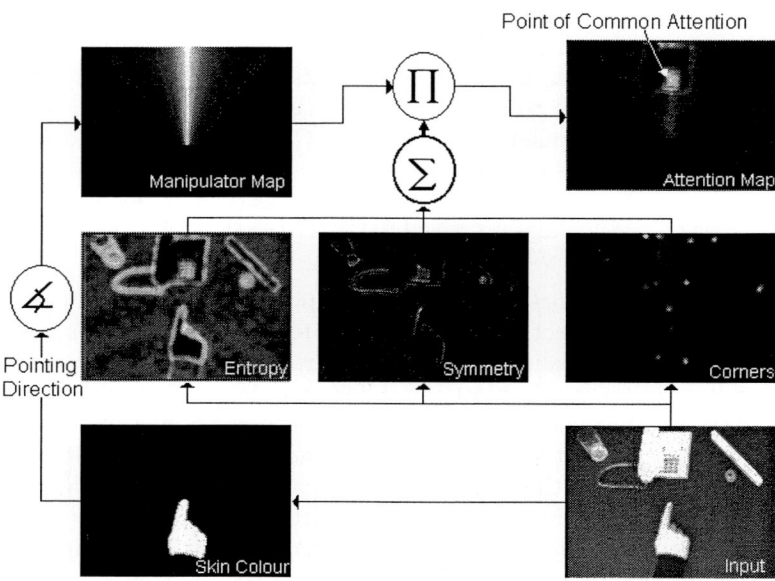

Fig. 5. Processing results for a pointing gesture towards an object. From the input image (bottom right) skin colour is segmented (bottom left); the VPL classifier calculates the angle which is transformed to a manipulator map (top left). The manipulator cone "illuminates" the object; the maxima of the feature maps stand out.

To evaluate the system performance we choose a setup which is based on a "generic" pointing task that can be easily reproduced: A proband points at a row of six white circles on a black table (Fig. 1, right). The distance between the hand and the targets is approximately 40 cm. So the diameter of each circle is of an angular range of 1.7° and the distances between the circle centres vary from an angular resolutions of 4° to 28°. To test performance for pointing to details, circles of a diameter of 0.9° with a distance angle of 2° were used in an additional experiment. A supervisor gives the command to point at one of the circles by reading a randomly generated circle number. We use only the inner four circles to avoid border effects. A match is counted if the system outputs a focus point on the correct circle within three seconds. The experiment was

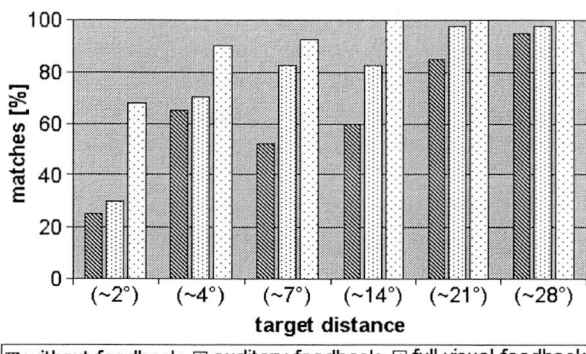

Fig. 6. The chart shows the results of the evaluation experiment. The values are averaged for three probands with 20 items each. On the x-axis the the corresponding angles for a pointing distance of about 40 cm are shown.

repeated under three conditions. As the results in Fig. 6 show, the best match percentages are reached under the *full visual feedback* condition (proband sees system output on a computer screen), whereas the values substantially decrease under the *without feedback* condition at small distances. Under the *auditory feedback* condition (proband hears a "bop" sound, if the focus point shifts from on maximum to another) a better percentage could be reached.

The major result achieved in this test scenario is that system performance can be significantly increased by giving feedback because (*i*) the user is enabled to adjust single pointing gestures to a target and (*ii*) the user can adapt himself or herself to the system behaviour. This way the achievable *effective resolution* can be improved, because it does not solely rely on the accuracy of the pointing gesture recognition anymore. It could be shown that the rather simple means of giving auditory feedback already leads to a better performance.

A limitation is that the hand has to be completely visible, otherwise the VPL classifier gets an unknown input. A "beep" is used as an error signal if the hand is too close to the border. Another restriction is that the saliency operators do not yield maxima on all of the objects or not on the desired locations.

4 Conclusion

We have presented a human-machine interface for visual detection of gestural object reference. It could be shown that using auditory feedback to indicate shifts of the FOA increases performance significantly.

The functionality of the presented system is not limited to the current scenario. Since arbitrary other saliency features like colour or movement can be integrated, the bottom-up focus of attention can be directed to a wide variety of objects. Even more important is the possibility to transform cues from other modules top-down to the sub-symbolic level using further manipulator maps. One of the first steps will be the integration of speech-driven cues to generate spatial large scale anticipations. As precision and user independence are still problems in the field of gesture recognition, a major advantage of the new approach is that it does not require high recognition accuracy. This is achieved by the system's anticipation that only salient image points will be selected.

Acknowledgement. This work was conducted within the scope of the project VAMPIRE (Visual Active Memory Processes and Interactive REtrieval) which is part of the IST programme (IST-2001-34401).

References

1. G. Backer, B. Mertsching, and M. Bollmann. Data- and Model-Driven Gaze Control for an Active-Vision System. *IEEE Trans. PAMI*, 23(12):1415–1429, 2001.
2. M. Fislage, R. Rae, and H. Ritter. Using visual attention to recognize human pointing gestures in assembly tasks. In *7th IEEE Int'l Conf. Comp. Vision*, 1999.
3. K. Fukushima. Neocognitron: A Self-Organizing Neural Network Model for a Mechanism of Pattern Recognition unaffected by Shift in Position. *Biol. Cybern.*, 36:193–202, 1980.
4. C. Harris and M. Stephens. A Combined Corner and Edge Detector. In *Proc. 4th Alvey Vision Conf.*, pages 147–151, 1988.
5. G. Heidemann. *Ein flexibel einsetzbares Objekterkennungssystem auf der Basis neuronaler Netze*. PhD thesis, Univ. Bielefeld, 1998. Infix, DISKI 190.
6. G. Heidemann, D. Lücke, and H. Ritter. A System for Various Visual Classification Tasks Based on Neural Networks. In A. Sanfeliu et al., editor, *Proc. 15th Int'l Conf. on Pattern Recognition ICPR 2000, Barcelona*, volume I, pages 9–12, 2000.
7. G. Heidemann, R. Rae, H. Bekel, I. Bax, and H. Ritter. Integrating Context-Free and Context-Dependent Attentional Mechanisms for Gestural Object Reference. In *Proc. Int'l Conf. Cognitive Vision Systems*, Graz, Austria, 2003.
8. G. Heidemann and H. Ritter. Efficient Vector Quantization Using the WTA-rule with Activity Equalization. *Neural Processing Letters*, 13(1):17–30, 2001.
9. L. Itti, C. Koch, and E. Niebur. A Model of Saliency-Based Visual Attention for Rapid Scene Analysis. *IEEE Trans. PAMI*, 20(11):1254–1259, 1998.
10. T. Kalinke and W. v. Seelen. Entropie als Maß des lokalen Informationsgehalts in Bildern zur Realisierung einer Aufmerksamkeitssteuerung. In B. Jähne et al., editor, *Mustererkennung 1996*. Springer, Heidelberg, 1996.
11. T. Kohonen. Self-organization and associative memory. In *Springer Series in Information Sciences 8*. Springer-Verlag Heidelberg, 1984.
12. P. J. Locher and C. F. Nodine. Symmetry Catches the Eye. In A. Levy-Schoen and J. K. O'Reagan, editors, *Eye Movements: From Physiology to Cognition*, pages 353–361. Elsevier Science Publishers B. V. (North Holland), 1987.
13. D. Reisfeld, H. Wolfson, and Y. Yeshurun. Context-Free Attentional Operators: The Generalized Symmetry Transform. *Int'l J. Comp. Vision*, 14, 1995.
14. T. D. Sanger. Optimal Unsupervised Learning in a Single-Layer Linear Feedforward Neural Network. *Neural Networks*, 2:459–473, 1989.
15. C. Schmid, R. Mohr, and C. Bauckhage. Evaluation of Interest Point Detectors. *Int'l J. of Computer Vision*, 37(2):151–172, 2000.
16. M. E. Tipping and C. M. Bishop. Mixtures of probabilistic principal component analyzers. *Neural Computation*, 11(2):443–482, 1999.
17. D. Walther, L. Itti, M. Riesenhuber, T. Poggio, and C. Koch. Attentional Selection for Object Recognition – a Gentle Way. In *Proc. 2nd Workshop on Biologically Motivated Computer Vision (BMCV'02)*, Tübingen, Germany, 2002.

Multi-chip Implementation of a Biomimetic VLSI Vision Sensor Based on the Adelson-Bergen Algorithm

Erhan Ozalevli and Charles M. Higgins

Department of Electrical and Computer Engineering
The University of Arizona, Tucson, AZ 85721
{erhan,higgins}@neuromorph.ece.arizona.edu

Abstract. Biological motion sensors found in the retinas of species ranging from flies to primates are tuned to specific spatio-temporal frequencies to determine the local motion vectors in their visual field and perform complex motion computations. In this study, we present a novel implementation of a silicon retina based on the Adelson-Bergen spatio-temporal energy model of primate cortical cells. By employing a multi-chip strategy, we successfully implemented the model without much sacrifice of the fill factor of the photoreceptors in the front-end chip. In addition, the characterization results proved that this spatio-temporal frequency tuned silicon retina can detect the direction of motion of a sinusoidal input grating down to 10 percent contrast, and over more than a magnitude in velocity. This multi-chip biomimetic vision sensor will allow complex visual motion computations to be performed in real-time.

1 Introduction

Every organism in nature must struggle to survive within its perceived truth by the help of its senses. What organisms perceive is only a noisy flow of sensation and this does not necessarily represent the perfect truth of their environment, but in fact provides information on their indispensable sensed truth. The biological strategies they have adopted have been proven to be effective and reliable by evolution. In this respect, when building artificial vision systems these biological models can be taken as a reference to deal with real life tasks such as target tracking and object avoidance. These systems employ massively parallel processing in dealing with complex and dynamic visual tasks and by incorporating the same strategy with parallel VLSI design principles in artificial systems, reliable low-power real-time neuromorphic systems can be built.

In this study we present a multi-chip system implementation of an analog VLSI hardware visual motion sensor based on the Adelson-Bergen motion energy model [1]. The Adelson-Bergen spatiotemporal energy model is a biological model and is often used as a model to describe primate cortical complex cells [2],[3]. In addition, it is classified under the correlation-based algorithms which are utilized to explain the optomotor response in flies [4] and direction selectivity in a rabbit's retina [5].

Multi-chip implementations are very suitable especially to achieve 2D optical flow motion computation [8]. These kind of systems integrate analog circuitry with an asynchronous digital interchip communication which is based on the Address-Event Representation (AER) protocol proposed by Mahowald [9] and revised by Boahen [13]. We utilized the same protocol in our implementation of the Adelson-Bergen algorithm to achieve the communication between sender and receiver chips.

A software version of the Adelson-Bergen algorithm was implemented on general-purpose analog neural computer by Etienne-Cummings [6]. Later, Higgins and Korrapati [7] implemented an monolithic analog VLSI sensor based on this algorithm. The main reason why we employed the Adelson-Bergen algorithm in motion computation is that it responds to real-world stimuli better than other algorithms and is therefore more amenable for robotic applications. Here we show that by incorporating the advantages of the model with a modular strategy the computational overload in the front-end chip can be reduced noticeably and the fill factor of the photoreceptors can be kept high. In addition the analog hardware implementation of the model exploits the subthreshold behavior of MOS transistors and therefore consumes little power. Furthermore, it works in real time, adapts to its environment and utilizes a massively parallel processing biological strategy by aligning in parallel arrays in the silicon retina.

2 Algorithm

The Adelson-Bergen algorithm is a spatiotemporal frequency tuned algorithm which obtains its direction selectivity by integrating quadrature filters with a nonlinearity. This algorithm is used in motion computation to extract the Fourier energy in a band of spatiotemporal frequencies regardless of phase of the stimulus. In this study, the Adelson-Bergen algorithm has been implemented (in a modified form; see Figure 1) by making use of Neuromorphic principles [10] and simplified without modifying the basic idea of spatiotemporal energy model.

Firstly, the spatial filtering in the model is trivialized by simply taking photoreceptor outputs separated by a $\Delta\Phi$ spatial distance between adjacent photoreceptors. Secondly, temporal filters in the model are implemented by employing an integrating circuit. Here we demonstrate that the integrating receiver circuitry can be used to attain a phase difference close to 90 degrees. This novel technique of using an integrator instead of a low-pass filter as a temporal filter enables us to exploit the advantages of multi-chip strategy in motion computation and to decrease the computational overload. Finally, the nonlinearity required to realize the algorithm is attained in the implementation by making use of the mathematical properties of rectification.

3 Hardware Architecture

In this section, the hardware architecture of the Adelson-Bergen algorithm is explained in detail. The overall organization of the multi-chip system is illus-

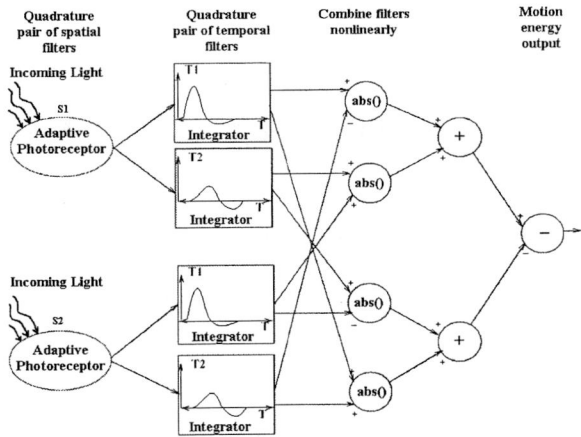

Fig. 1. Modified Adelson-Bergen spatiotemporal energy model

trated in Figure 2. The system consists of two chips, namely sender and receiver chips. These chips communicate by using the AER protocol [13] (Figure 4a) and perform all computations in current mode to minimize the space and maximize the fill-factor of the front-end chip.

In this implementation, the sender chip is employed to sense the intensity changes in the environment with respect to its adapted background and send this information to the receiver chip. It includes an array of pixels that discretize space and incorporates a photoreceptor, transconductance amplifier, rectifier and AER interface circuitry. In order to sense the intensity changes in the environment we used adaptive photoreceptors (Figure 3a) by Liu [11]. This photoreceptor provides a continuous-time signal that has a low gain for static signals and a high gain for transient signals. In addition to the photoreceptor output, an internal feedback voltage in this circuit is utilized in the motion computation to obtain information on the change of the adapted background level of its environment. This feedback voltage represents the running average of the illumination level of the background and the time interval of the averaging operation can be changed by altering the adaptation time. In the next stage, the response of the photoreceptor is compared with its feedback voltage and converted to current by making use of a transconductance amplifier shown in Figure 3b. In this way, we obtain a bandpass characteristic from the photoreceptor and transconductance amplifier pair. This characteristic ensures that very high frequencies are attenuated and offset or in this case the background level, is removed. After that, the output current of the transconductance amplifier is rectified by utilizing a full-wave rectifier (Figure 3c) in order to acquire separate currents for negative and positive intensity changes. Lastly, the communication interface circuitry that sends these intensity changes to the corresponding pixels

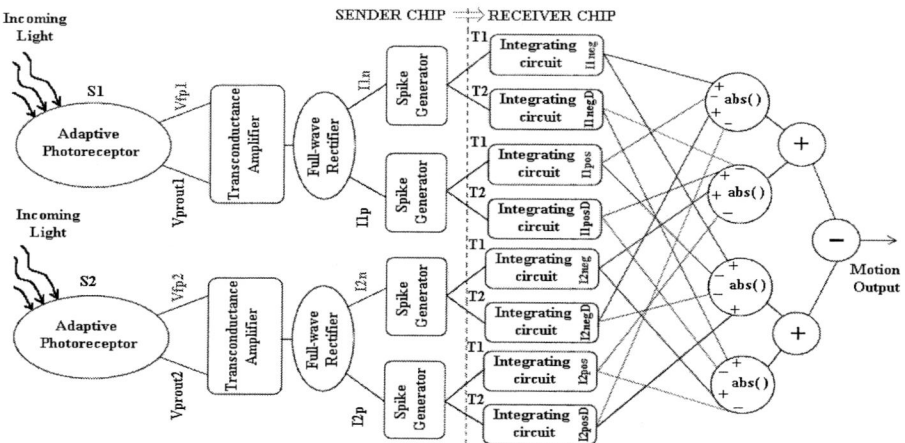

Fig. 2. The multi-chip implementation of the Adelson-Bergen algorithm. V_{prout} and V_{fb} represent the photoreceptor's output and feedback response, respectively. In addition, I_p and I_n refer to positive and negative parts of the rectified signal, and in the receiver part, I_{pos} and I_{neg} represent the integrated versions of these signals. Lastly, I_{posD} and I_{negD} are the signals that are delayed relative to I_{pos} and I_{neg}.

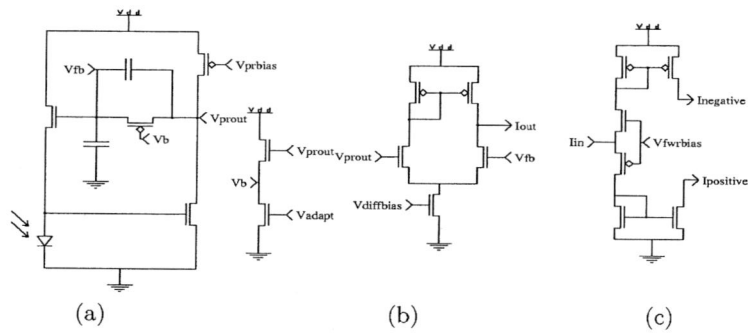

Fig. 3. (a) Adaptive photoreceptor circuit by Shih-Chii Liu. (b) Transconductance amplifier circuit. (c) Full-wave rectifier circuit.

in the receiver chip is implemented. This interface circuitry generates spikes with a frequency proportional to the amplitude level of the intensity change.

The receiver chip is utilized to achieve small field motion computation by making use of the information obtained from the sender chip. It is composed of the AER communication circuitry and corresponding pixels of the sender chip. In this implementation, the integrating circuit is employed not only to integrate the incoming spikes but also to attain necessary delays. The integrating receiver circuit has a particular spike frequency f_0 for which the charging and discharging current are the same on average keeping output voltage at a steady state value.

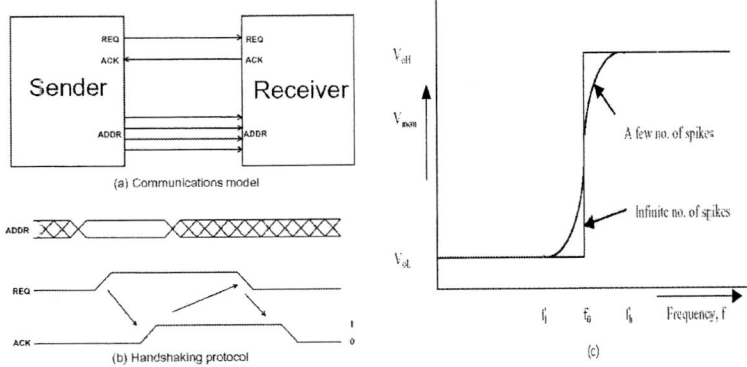

Fig. 4. AER protocol summary. (a) The model for AER transmission: a sender chip communicates with a receiver chip via request, acknowledge and address lines. (b) The handshaking protocol for transmission using the control and address lines: a request with a valid address leads to an acknowledgment, which in turn leads to falling request and falling acknowledge. (c)Vout vs. frequency sketch.

In Figure 4c, the relationship between the voltage output and incoming spike frequency is illustrated. Similar to low-pass characteristics, this circuit can be incorporated to obtain the necessary delay and is therefore amenable to be used as a temporal filter. Accordingly, the positive or negative part of the signal is integrated by two integrating circuits tuned to different temporal frequencies in order to obtain a similar configuration as it was achieved with monolithic implementation [7]. As a result, the integrated positive and negative parts of the signal are summed, subtracted and absolute valued to perform the motion computation illustrated in Figure 2. The formulation of the final output is shown below.

$$I_{out} = |I_{1neg} + I_{2negD} - I_{1pos} - I_{2posD}| + |I_{2neg} + I_{1posD} - I_{1negD} - I_{2pos}|$$
$$- |I_{1neg} + I_{2posD} - I_{1pos} - I_{2negD}| - |I_{2neg} + I_{1negD} - I_{2pos} - I_{1posD}| \quad (1)$$

4 Characterization Results

In this section, characterization results of the multi-chip implementation are presented. The experiments are performed by using computer-generated sinusoidal grating stimuli on an LCD screen. In the experiments, each time one parameter is changed the others are held constant. In order to remove the phase dependence of the sensor and prevent artifacts, output voltages are averaged over 10 temporal periods of stimuli. The output of the sensor is obtained in current mode and converted to voltage by utilizing current sense amplifier with a 3.9 megohm feedback resistor.

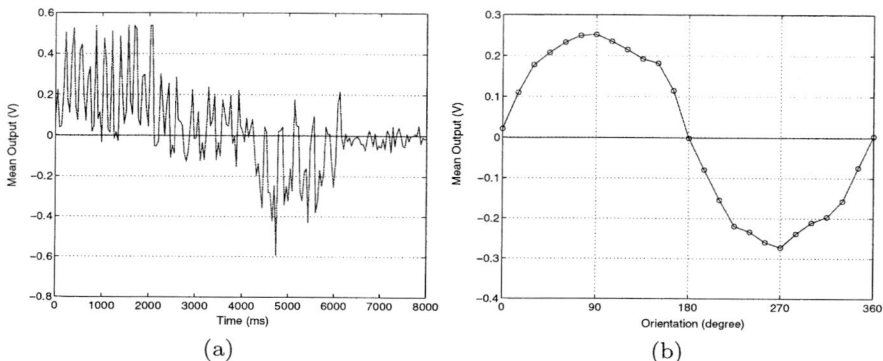

Fig. 5. (a) Output of the motion sensor. In the interval 0-2 seconds, a preferred direction sinusoidal stimulus is presented. Between 2-4 seconds, a sinusoidal stimulus moving orthogonal to the sensor orientation is presented. After that, sensor is exposed to a null direction sinusoidal stimulus. Lastly, no stimulus is presented between 6-8 seconds. (b) Orientation sweep. A sinusoidal stimulus is presented at varying directions relative to the motion sensor, which is optimally oriented for a stimulus at 90 degrees.

The first experiment is performed by using sinusoidal grating stimuli to test the direction selectivity of the sensor for preferred, null, orthogonal motion, and no-motion cases. As can be seen in Figure 5a, the mean response of the sensor quite clearly indicates the direction of the stimulus. In the second experiment, it is proved that the sensor shows sinusoidal dependence to orientation sweep of sinusoidal grating (Figure 5b) as expected from the theoretical results of Adelson-Bergen algorithm. At 90 degrees the motion output gives its positive peak response and at 270 degrees the sensor output reaches its negative maximum. In the last experiment, the sensor is tested to acquire the spatial and temporal frequency characteristics of the sensor. The response of the sensor to a temporal frequency sweep is shown in Figure 6a. The output of the sensor peaks at around 1 Hz and, as is obvious from the temporal frequency response, the sensor responds to a velocity range of more than one order of magnitude. These responses justify the use of integrating circuit as a temporal filter in the motion computation. The response of the sensor to a spatial frequency sweep is illustrated in Figure 6b. The plot of the multi-chip sensor peaks around 0.4 cycles/pixel and the sensor shows a strong spatial aliasing around 0.9 cycles/pixel. Lastly, in Figure 6c, the spatiotemporal response of the sensor is illustrated. This plot shows the mean output of the model in response to sinusoidal gratings varying in both spatial and temporal frequency. The mean output is plotted for spatial frequencies on the X-axis versus temporal frequencies on the Y-axis. It is obvious from the graph that the model responds best to a particular spatiotemporal frequency for which it is tuned and the response decreases at other frequencies.

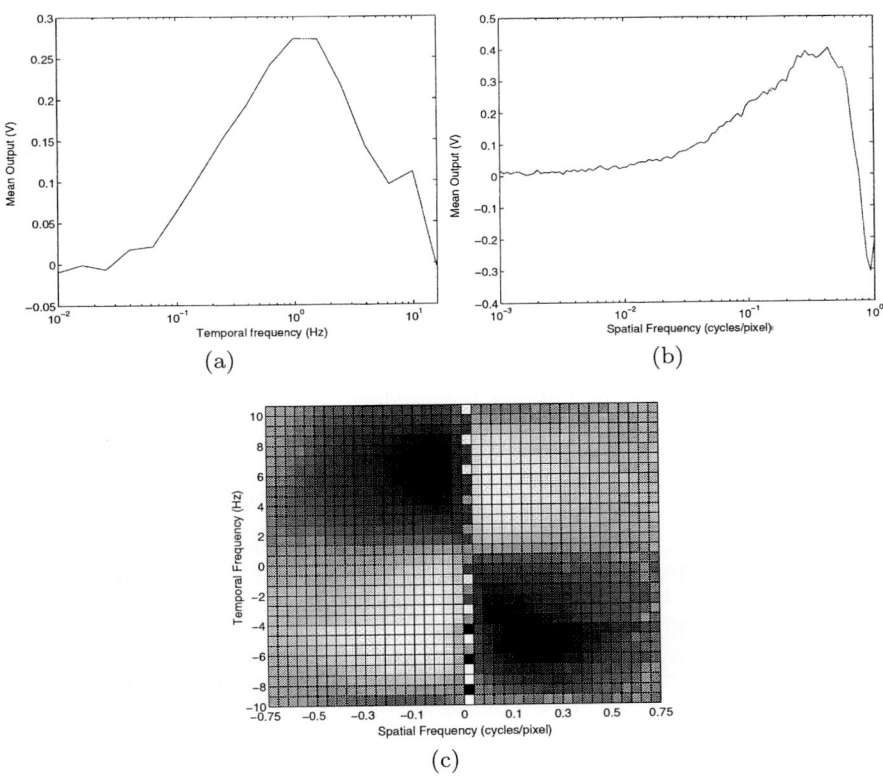

Fig. 6. Spatio-temporal frequency tuning of the sensor. (a) Temporal frequency sweep. (b) Spatial frequency sweep: note the onset of spatial aliasing. (c) Spatio-temporal frequency plot: light colors indicate positive and dark colors indicate negative average response.

5 Discussion

We have described and characterized a novel spatiotemporal frequency tuned multi-chip analog VLSI motion sensor and presented a new technique to realize the temporal filters needed for motion computation. The characterization results clearly elucidate the fact that by using this technique, we can obtain a reliable, low-power and real time multi-chip Neuromorphic motion processing system while retaining many of the advantages of monolithic implementation.

The multi-chip sensor responds to optimal spatial frequencies over a velocity range of more than an order of magnitude. Since the motion sensor is tuned to spatiotemporal frequencies, the main concern is to increase the range of the spatial and temporal frequencies and the contrast level to which it can respond. As seen from the spatiotemporal plot (Figure 6c), the response range of the multi-chip motion sensor is increased in comparison to monolithic implementation by Higgins and Korrapati [7]. The area of this region increased two times compared to the monolithic implementation. Besides, the immunity of the sensor to low contrast levels is improved. These results clearly indicate the improvement in the performance while the motion computation capability of the system is vastly increased compared to any space limited monolithic system. Furthermore, 2D motion computation can be easily achieved with this implementation by using a single sender chip with two two receivers and manipulating the x and y connections of the address lines of the second receiver.

By using a multi-chip system, we obtained 36 pixels in a standard 1.5μm CMOS process and 2mm-by-2mm die size. In a new designed sender chip, positive and negative parts of the rectified signal will be sent through with a novel technique implemented in the AER system. With this implementation, we are expecting to exceed the number of pixels that can currently be realized on a single chip.

References

1. E.H. Adelson and J.R. Bergen: "Spatiotemporal energy models for the perception of motion," J. Opt. Society of America, vol. 2, no. 2 (1985), pp. 284–299
2. S.J. Nowlan and T.J. Sejnowski: "Filter selection model for motion segmentation and velocity integration," J. Opt. Soc. America, vol. 11, no. 12 (1994), pp. 3177–3200
3. D.J. Heeger, E.P. Simoncelli, and J.A. Movshon: "Computational models of cortical visual processing," Proc. Natl. Acad. Sci., vol. 93 (1996), pp. 623–627
4. Hassenstein, B. and W. Reichardt: "Systemtheoretische Analyse der Zeit-, Reihenfolgen- und Vorzeichenauswertung bei der Bewegungsperzeption des Rüsselkäfers Chlorophanus." Z. Naturforsch (1956), 11b: 513–524
5. Barlow, H.B. and W.R. Levick: "The mechanism of directionally selective units in the rabbit's retina." J. Physiology (1965), 178: 447–504
6. R Etienne-Cummings, J. Van der Spiegel, and P. Mueller: "Hardware implementation of a visual-motion pixel using oriented spatiotemporal neural filters," IEEE Transactions on Circuits and Systems-II, vol. 46, no. 9 (1999), pp. 1121–1136
7. Higgins, C.M. and S. Korrapati: "An analog VLSI motion energy sensor based on the Adelson-Bergen algorithm." In Proceedings of the International Symposium on Biologically Inspired Systems, (2000)
8. C. M. Higgins and C. Koch: "A Modular Multi-Chip Neuromorphic Architecture for Real-Time Visual Motion Processing," Analog Integrated Circuits and Signal Processing 24(3) (September, 2000), pp. 195–211
9. M.A. Mahowald: "VLSI analogs of neuronal visual processing: A synthesis of form and function." PhD thesis, Department of Computation and Neural Systems, California Institute of Technology, Pasadena, CA., (1992)
10. C. A. Mead: "Neuromorphic electronic systems," Proceedings of the IEEE, vol. 78 (1990), pp. 1629–1636
11. S-C. Liu: "Silicon retina with adaptive filtering properties," Analog Integrated Circuits and Signal Processing, 18 (2/3) (1999), pp. 1–12
12. Mead, C.A.: "Analog VLSI and Neural Systems." Addison-Wesley, Reading, (1989)
13. K. Boahen: "A throughput-on-demand 2-D address-event transmitter for Neuromorphic chips," in Proc. Of the 20th Conference on Advanced Research in VLSI, Atlanta, GA (1999)

Speech Recognition

Client Dependent GMM-SVM Models for Speaker Verification

Quan Le and Samy Bengio*

IDIAP, P.O. Box 592, CH-1920 Martigny, Switzerland
{quan,bengio}@idiap.ch

Abstract. Generative Gaussian Mixture Models (GMMs) are known to be the dominant approach for modeling speech sequences in text independent speaker verification applications because of their scalability, good performance and their ability in handling variable size sequences. On the other hand, because of their discriminative properties, models like Support Vector Machines (SVMs) usually yield better performance in static classification problems and can construct flexible decision boundaries. In this paper, we try to combine these two complementary models by using Support Vector Machines to postprocess scores obtained by the GMMs. A cross-validation method is also used in the baseline system to increase the number of client scores in the training phase, which enhances the results of the SVM models. Experiments carried out on the XM2VTS and PolyVar databases confirm the interest of this hybrid approach.

1 Introduction

Speaker verification techniques use acoustic signal to determine whether a person is who he claims to be or not. They have many applications, such as access control, transaction authentication or voice mail. A good introduction to the field can be found in [5].

State-of-the-art speaker verification systems are based on a generative model of speech sequences for each client, and another generative model for modeling impostors. Every time a client tries to access the system, the decision is taken using the ratio between the likelihood that the utterance was generated by the client model and the likelihood that the utterance was generated by the impostor model. For text independent speaker verification, where there is no prior knowledge about what the speaker will say, the most successful generative models have been Gaussian Mixture Models (GMMs) [8]. Such a system has several advantages. It provides a framework for handling variable length sequences, can be trained using reliable techniques like the Expectation Maximization algorithm (EM) [4], and is scalable with respect to the number of clients.

However, it is well known that for a classification problem, a better solution should in theory be to use a discriminative framework: in that case instead of

---

* The authors would like to thank the Swiss National Science Foundation for supporting this work through the National Center of Competence in Research (NCCR) on "Interactive Multimodal Information Management (IM2)".

constructing a model independently for each class, one constructs a unique model that decides where the boundaries between classes are.

In this paper we combine these two models using an idea mentioned in [1] in which instead of using the so-called log likelihood ratio criterion (the Bayesian decision) the GMM scores (scores from the world and client models as well as the log likelihood ratio or both) are used as input to train a discriminative model. Depending on the amount of data, we can have one discriminative model for all clients as in [1], or it can be extended to having one model for each speaker.

Based on the fact that in real world tasks it is not easy to collect lots of data from each client, a cross-validation technique is applied in order to increase the number of client scores used to train the discriminative model.

The rest of the paper is organized as follows. Section 2 presents the baseline speaker verification system using GMMs. Section 3 describes the hybrid system, including the combining method and the cross-validation technique to create more client accesses. Experiments on the XM2VTS and PolyVar databases are presented in Section 4. Finally, conclusions are drawn in Section 5.

2 The Baseline Speaker Verification System

The speaker verification problem can be considered as a statistical hypothesis testing problem where we test the hypothesis that the speaker is the true person that he claims to be (in which case, he is called a client) against the hypothesis that he is not (in which case he is called an impostor). Given an utterance $\mathbf{X} = \{\mathbf{x}_1, .., \mathbf{x}_T\}$, we are interested in $P(S_i|\mathbf{X})$ the probability that speaker S_i has pronounced utterance $\mathbf{X}$. Using Bayes theorem, we can write it as follows:

$$P(S_i|\mathbf{X}) = \frac{p(\mathbf{X}|S_i)P(S_i)}{p(\mathbf{X})} \quad (1)$$

where $p(\mathbf{X}|S_i)$ is the likelihood that utterance $\mathbf{X}$ was generated by speaker S_i, $P(S_i)$ is the prior probability of speaker S_i and $p(\mathbf{X})$ is the unconditional likelihood of utterance $\mathbf{X}$.

Let us assume that $P(\overline{S}_i|\mathbf{X})$ is the probability that utterance $\mathbf{X}$ was pronounced by any other speaker. When $P(\overline{S}_i|\mathbf{X})$ is the same for all clients, we replace it by a speaker independent model $P(\Omega|\mathbf{X})$. Using Bayesian criterion, we then derive the decision rule:

$$\text{if } P(S_i|\mathbf{X}) > P(\Omega|\mathbf{X}) \text{ then } \mathbf{X} \text{ was generated by } S_i. \quad (2)$$

Using equation (1), inequality (2) can be rewritten as:

$$\text{Test}(\mathbf{X}) = \frac{p(\mathbf{X}|S_i)}{p(\mathbf{X}|\Omega)} > \frac{P(\Omega)}{P(S_i)} = \delta_i. \quad (3)$$

Since it is more convenient to deal with *log-likelihood ratio statistics* rather than *likelihood ratio statistics*, taking the logarithm of (3) leads us to inequality:

$$\text{test}(\mathbf{X}) = \log p(\mathbf{X}|S_i) - \log p(\mathbf{X}|\Omega) > \log \delta_i = \Delta_i. \quad (4)$$

The distribution of feature vectors $\mathbf{x}_t$ extracted from a speaker's speech is often modeled by a Gaussian mixture density. Using the i.i.d. assumption, the likelihood of a sequence $\mathbf{X} = \{\mathbf{x}_1,..,\mathbf{x}_T\}$ given a GMM can be computed as follows:

$$p(\mathbf{X}|\theta) = \prod_{t=1}^{T} p(\mathbf{x}_t|\theta) = \prod_{t=1}^{T} \sum_{n=1}^{N} w_n \cdot \mathcal{N}(\mathbf{x}_t; \boldsymbol{\mu}_n, \boldsymbol{\Sigma}_n) \tag{5}$$

where the parameter set of the GMM is $\theta = \{w_n, \boldsymbol{\mu}_n, \boldsymbol{\Sigma}_n\}$ with $w_n \in \mathbb{R}, \boldsymbol{\mu}_n \in \mathbb{R}^d, \boldsymbol{\Sigma}_n \in \mathbb{R}^{d^2}$ being respectively the prior probability, the mean vector, and the covariance matrix of the nth Gaussian component and d is the dimension of acoustic vectors:

$$\mathcal{N}(\mathbf{x}; \boldsymbol{\mu}_n, \boldsymbol{\Sigma}_n) = \frac{1}{(2\pi)^{\frac{d}{2}} \sqrt{|\boldsymbol{\Sigma}_n|}} \exp\left(-\frac{1}{2}(\mathbf{x} - \boldsymbol{\mu}_n)^T \boldsymbol{\Sigma}_n^{-1} (\mathbf{x} - \boldsymbol{\mu}_n)\right). \tag{6}$$

In general, diagonal covariance matrices are used to limit the model size.

From a large amount of speech data, maximum likelihood estimates of $P(\mathbf{X}|\Omega)$, the world model, is obtained using the Expectation-Maximization algorithm [4]. Then, based on sequences of training vectors belonging to a particular speaker S_i, the client model $P(\mathbf{X}|S_i)$ is trained via a Bayesian adaptation technique from the world model [6,8].

The system might have two types of errors: *false acceptance* (FA), when the system accepts an impostor, and *false rejection* (FR), when the system rejects a client. In order to be independent on the specific dataset distribution, the performance of the system is often measured in terms of these two different errors as follows:

$$\text{FAR} = \frac{\text{number of FAs}}{\text{number of impostor accesses}}, \tag{7}$$

$$\text{FRR} = \frac{\text{number of FRs}}{\text{number of client accesses}}. \tag{8}$$

Various evaluation measures can be constructed based on FAR and FRR. In this paper, we used the *Half Total Error Rate* (HTER):

$$\text{HTER} = \frac{FAR + FRR}{2}. \tag{9}$$

Moreover, in order to select a decision threshold (Δ_i), the system is often tuned on a validation set to optimize a criterion which could be different. For instance, the *Equal Error Rate* (EER), where FAR is equal to FRR, is often used.

3 Hybrid System

3.1 Support Vector Machines

Support Vector Machines (SVMs) [9,2] are built upon two key ideas: *maximizing the margin* and the *kernel trick*.

In the case where data is linearly separable, the SVM simply looks for the separating hyperplane with the largest margin, with respect to the labeled training set

$$f^{max} = \arg\max_{f} \min_{i} \frac{y_i f(\mathbf{x}_i)}{\|\mathbf{w}\|} \tag{10}$$

$$\text{where } f(\mathbf{x}) = (\mathbf{x} \cdot \mathbf{w}) + b = \sum_{i=1}^{l} \alpha_i y_i (\mathbf{x_i} \cdot \mathbf{x}) + b \tag{11}$$

$$\text{and } \mathbf{w} = \sum_{i=1}^{l} \alpha_i y_i \mathbf{x}_i \tag{12}$$

where l is the number of training examples, $\mathbf{x}, \mathbf{w} \in \mathbb{R}^N$, $b \in \mathbb{R}$, $\alpha_i \in \mathbb{R}$ is the contribution of sample i in the final solution, $y_i \in \{-1, 1\}$ are the label corresponding to the training set $\{\mathbf{x_i}\}$ and $sign\,(f(\mathbf{x}))$ is the classification rule. α_i and b are determined in the training process. This choice follows Vapnik's *Structural Risk Minimization* principle [9].

Since data only appears in the training problem in the form of dot products, we can avoid the need to explicitly represent the acting vectors. This trick can be used for the case where data is not linearly separable. We first map data into a very high dimensional space (also called the feature space) which is more suitable for classification, and then use a linear classifier. The dot product operation in the data space can therefore be replaced by *kernels* such as Radial Basis Functions (RBF) [2]. The training algorithm's complexity will then depend only on the dimension of the input space and the training set size, rather than the dimension of the feature space.

The final output of an SVM is then a linear combination of the training examples projected in the feature space through the use of the kernel:

$$y = \text{sign}\left(\sum_{i=1}^{l} y_i \alpha_i K(\mathbf{x}, \mathbf{x}_i) + b\right) \tag{13}$$

where $(\mathbf{x_i}, y_i)$ are input/class from the training set, $\mathbf{x}$ is the current input, y is the desired class $\in \{-1, +1\}$, and $K(\cdot, \cdot)$ is a kernel function.

3.2 Postprocessing GMM Scores by SVMs

In most speaker verification systems, the decision is taken using inequality (4) in which a universal threshold Δ is chosen to minimize the optimization criterion (HTER or EER for instance). It is equal to choosing a line from a family of parallel lines $\log p(\mathbf{X}|S_i) - \log p(\mathbf{X}|\Omega) = C$ which optimizes the criterion. This choice is the optimal solution when the distribution of data is perfectly estimated, which is usually not the case. Replacing this line by a more general and possibly non-linear function such as SVMs [1] might help to correct the scores from GMMs.

When the kernel chosen is the dot product, the discriminative model is the line which maximizes the *margin* between positive and negative examples. Since the log-likelihood ratio is known to contain important information (inequality (4)) which is not easy to recover when using SVMs with only scores from GMMs, it is put together with two log-likelihood scores from the world and client models as a 3-dimensional input vector for SVMs. "Client dependent" discriminative models were used in our experiments with the meaning that SVMs were trained and tested on the same population of clients to learn somehow their statistics[1]. If there is enough data for each client (enough client accesses), we can use speaker specific SVMs. It will better adapt discriminative models to each particular client[2], and also reduce the training time for the discriminative models since the complexity of the training algorithm for SVMs is quadratic on the number of examples.

One of the problems with SVMs is then the imbalance between the number of client and impostor accesses (with the XM2VTS database there are about 100 times more impostor accesses than client accesses). Here we use an empirical solution to increase the number of client scores based on a cross-validation method.

3.3 Using Cross-Validation to Increase the Number of Client Scores

It is generally not possible to collect a lot of speech data from each client, so it is important to use properly the collected data. In most speaker verification systems, the speech data set of each client is divided into two sets. The first part (called training client data set) is used to build the client model, while the second part is used to compute client scores for training the decision boundary for other clients or for measuring the performance of the system. We propose here to use cross-validation to obtain client scores from the training client data set. Firstly, the speech data set for each client is divided into N disjoint parts of equal size. For each part, a client model is built from the $(N-1)$ other parts, and off-training set scores are computed from the left-out part (Figure 1). This process is repeated for all N parts. The final client model is then trained using all data from the client training data set. When N is big enough the union from the $(N-1)$ data parts will be almost the same as the whole data set. So it is expected that the model obtained from these data will be similar to the final client model, and all off-training set scores computed from all N data parts in this way can be put together for training the decision model. By this way we will have scores from training client data set. These additional client scores can be used for various purposes, here we simply put them with other data for training a more accurate SVM model.

---

[1] For this approach, choosing whether or not to retrain the SVM for a new client is a trade-off between the accuracy and the use of computing resources.

[2] The speaker specific discriminative model approach is scalable with respect to the number of clients. For each new client, one only needs to train a new SVM for him.

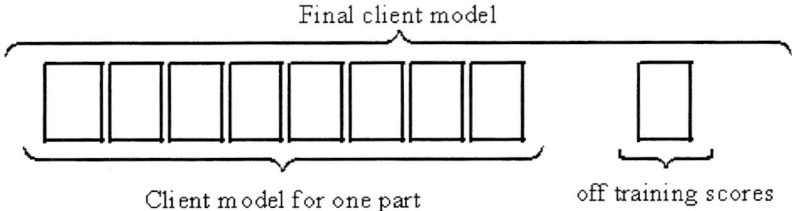

Fig. 1. Illustration of the cross-validation idea on one part of training client data set.

4 Experiments

4.1 The PolyVar Database

Database Description. In the first experiment, we used the *PolyVar* telephone database [3] that contains two sets (called development population and evaluation population) of 19 clients as well as another population of 56 speakers (28 men and 28 women) used for the world model. The database contains different numbers of recording sessions for each speaker, where one recording session contains 17 words. For each client 20 sessions were used, 10 of them (called training client model data set) for adapting the world model to the client model and the other 10 sessions for test only.

Results from Text Independent Experiments. The speech signal was sampled every 10 ms and then parameterized into 16 *Linear Frequency Cepstral Coefficients* (LFCC) coefficients as well as energy, complemented by their first derivatives, for a total 34 coefficients[3].

To determine the number of Gaussians for the world model, we used a simple validation technique, training on 90% of the available training set for the world model and selecting the model with the highest likelihood over the remaining 10%. This led us to a GMM with 256 Gaussians. The client models were adapted from the world model using the training client data set (10 sessions) of each client. For the baseline system a global threshold is estimated based on scores from the test set of the development population and the performance of the system is estimated on the scores of the test set of the evaluation population. In the hybrid system, the cross-validation technique is applied to create scores (called training scores) from the training client data, in which training client data set is divided into 10 parts (according to 10 sessions). All other experiments were done on the system using the cross-validation technique. In the first experiment, an universal decision threshold Δ is estimated on the cross-validation system using

---

[3] For all experiments with the XM2VTS and PolyVar databases, a voice activity detection module was used to discard silence frames.

the HTER criterion (as in the baseline system). Then one universal linear SVM is trained from the training scores (with 17860 impostor accesses and 3230 client accesses) of the evaluation population (for comparing with the baseline system), and the performance is measured on the test data (the evaluation population consisting of 3230 client accesses and 13262 impostor accesses). In the last experiments, we estimated one decision threshold per client, and correspondingly estimated one linear SVM per client (trained by 170 client accesses and 940 impostor accesses).

Table 1 gives the results of these experiments on the test set of the evaluation population. We can see that the universal linear SVM obtains better results than the baseline system, and the speaker specific linear SVMs system yields the best performance.

Table 1. Results from the PolyVar database.

System	HTER(%)
256 Gaussians baseline	5.770
Global threshold on Cross-validation system	5.765
Universal linear SVM on Cross-validation system	5.320
Threshold per client on Cross-validation system	5.710
Linear SVM per client on Cross-validation system	5.146

4.2 Experiments on the XM2VTS Database

Database Description. In a second series of experiments, we used the XM2VTS database [7] and its associated experimental protocol, the Lausanne protocol. The database contains four recording sessions of 295 subjects taken at one month intervals. In each session, one speech shot consisting of two sentences was made. The sentences were the same for all speakers to allow the simulation of impostor accesses by all subjects. Sentences were chosen to compensate for prosodic and co-articulation effects. The database was divided into three sets: training set for building client models, evaluation set for computing the decision threshold and test set for estimating the performance of different verification algorithms.

Results. During the preprocessing step, the speech signal was sampled every 10 ms and then parameterized into LFCC coefficients, keeping 16 coefficients and their first derivative, as well as the energy together with its first derivative, for a total of 34 features.

The world model (GMM with 600 Gaussians, the number of Gaussians was chosen using the same technique as described above) was then trained from the world data set (taken from another speaker verification database because of the limited amount of data in the XM2VTS database) and adapted to client models. In the baseline system using the configuration 2 of the XM2VTS database, two sessions per client (each session has two sentences) were used for training client models, one session for estimating decision threshold, and one for measuring performance of the system. Using the cross-validation idea, we merged the client data from the training set and the evaluation set into one training client model data set consisting 3 sessions. This data set is divided into 6 parts (according to 6 sentences in 3 sessions) and the cross-validation technique is used to create client scores. The resulting client model is better estimated (trained by 3 sessions) and we also have more client scores in the enrollment phase. In the first experiment, to test the cross-validation system we simply compute the decision threshold as in the baseline system and measure the performance. In the second experiment, one linear SVM is trained from the training scores (including 40,000 impostor accesses and 1,200 client accesses), and the performance is then measured on the test data (112,000 impostor accesses and 400 client accesses). Because there are only six utterances for one client in the enrollment phase, we did not have enough data to obtain a separate threshold per client (with or without SVM postprocessing).

Results from Table 2 show that the cross-validation system got better result than the baseline system, and using SVM further improved the result. In fact, to the best of our knowledge, the result obtained here is the best ever reported on that subset.

Table 2. Results from the XM2VTS database.

System	HTER(%)
600 Gaussians baseline	1.155
Global threshold on Cross-validation system	1.060
Universal linear SVM on Cross-validation system	0.92

5 Conclusions

In this paper we proposed the use of a cross-validation technique to increase the number of client scores used to select the decision function for speaker verification systems. These scores are then used to train SVM models for taking the decision, instead of using the classical thresholding method. Results from experiments on the XM2VTS and PolyVar databases show that the hybrid generative-discriminative model is a promising approach.

References

1. S. Bengio and J. Mariéthoz. Learning the decision function for speaker verification. In *IEEE Intl. Conf. on Acoustics, Speech, and Signal Processing ICASSP*, 2001.
2. C. J. C. Burges. A tutorial on support vector machines for pattern recognition. *Data mining and Knowledge Discovery*, 2(2):1–47, 1998.

3. G. Chollet, J.-L. Cochard, A. Constantinescu, C. Jaboulet, and P. Langlais. Swiss french polyphone and polyvar: telephone speech databases to model inter- and intra-speaker variability. IDIAP-RR 1, IDIAP, 1996.
4. A. P. Dempster, N. M. Laird, and D. B. Rubin. Maximum-likelihood from incomplete data via the EM algorithm. *Jrnl. of Royal Statistical Society B*, 39 1–38, 1977.
5. S. Furui. Recent advances in speaker recognition. *Lecture Notes in Computer Science*, 1206:237–252, 1997.
6. J. Mariéthoz and S. Bengio. A comparative study of adaptation methods for speaker verification. In *Intl. Conf. on Spoken Language Processing ICSLP*, 2002.
7. K. Messer, J. Matas, J. Kittler, J. Luettin, and G. Maitre. XM2VTSDB: The extended M2VTS database. In *Second International Conference on Audio and Video-based Biometric Person Authentication AVBPA*, March 1999.
8. D. A. Reynolds, T. F. Quatieri, and R. B. Dunn. Speaker verification using adapted gaussian mixture models. *Digital Signal Processing*, 10:19–41, 2000.
9. V. N. Vapnik. *The Nature of Statistical Learning Theory*. Springer-Verlag, New York, NY, USA, 1995.

Frequency and Wavelet Filtering for Robust Speech Recognition

Murat Deviren and Khalid Daoudi

INRIA-LORIA (Speech Group) B.P. 101 - 54602 Villers les Nancy. France.
www.loria.fr/equipes/parole, {deviren,daoudi}@loria.fr

Abstract. Mel-frequency cepstral coefficients (MFCC) are the most widely used features in current speech recognition systems. However, they have a poor physical interpretation and they do not lie in the frequency domain. Frequency filtering (FF) is a technique that has been recently developed to design frequency-localized speech features that perform similar to MFCC in terms of recognition performances. Motivated by our desire to build time-frequency speech models, we wanted to use the FF technique as front-end. However, when evaluating FF on the Aurora-3 database we found some discrepancies in the highly mismatch case. This led us to put FF in another perspective: the wavelet transform. By doing so, we were able to explain the discrepancies and to achieve significant improvements in recognition in the highly mismatch case.

1 Introduction

State-of-the-art automatic speech recognition (ASR) systems are based on probabilistic modeling of the speech signal using Hidden Markov Models (HMMs). These models lead to the best recognition performances in ideal "lab" conditions or for easy tasks. However, in real world conditions of speech processing (noisy environment, spontaneous speech, non-native speakers...), the performance of HMM-based ASR systems can decrease drastically. One of the major reasons for this discrepancy is the fact that, while speech temporal dynamics are well captured by HMMs, the frequency dynamics (which are phonetically very informative) are weakly modeled in classical HMM-based systems. The primary motivation behind the work presented in this paper is our ongoing effort to build statistical speech models which can capture *both* temporal and frequency dynamics of speech (but this is not the scope of this paper).

To address the problem of modeling frequency dynamics, one needs to work with speech features that are localized in the frequency domain and, preferably, that have a meaningful physical interpretation. The most widely used features in speech recognition systems are Mel-frequency cepstral coefficients (MFCC). These features are calculated by a Mel-scale filtering of the power spectrum followed by discrete cosine transform (DCT) of the logarithmic filter-bank energies. The DCT decorrelates the filter-bank energies at the cost of loosing frequency localization. Therefore, MFCC features have a poor physical interpretation and they lie in an artificial domain which do not allow for the analysis of frequency dynamics of speech. Nevertheless, MFCC-based parameterizations lead to the best recognition performances and it is difficult to compete with them. In general, when a new parameterization is proposed, it may improve performances with respect to MFCC, but only in clean or noisy conditions, rarely in both. Motivated by our desire to build time-frequency speech models, we wanted to investigate whether it was possible to design speech parameterizations which have the advantages of MFCC but not their disadvantages. By looking at the literature addressing the same problem, we were attracted by the frequency filtering (FF) technique developed by Nadeu et al [1,2] because of it's simplicity and the reported results. The principle of this technique is to filter the log filter-bank energies by first or second order linear filters in order to decorrelate them. It has been reported [1,3,2,4] that FF leads to recognition performances similar to or better than MFCC, in clean and artificial noise conditions. However, when we tested FF in real noise conditions (using Aurora 3 database [5]) we found some discrepancies. The scope of this paper is to show that, by looking at the frequency filtering approach [1,2] from a wavelet filtering perspective, it is in fact possible to design speech features that are localized in the frequency domain, and that perform at least as well as MFCC in *all* conditions.

In the next section we briefly recall the main lines of the frequency filtering approach introduced by Nadeu et al [1,2]. In Section 3, we describe our experimental setting to evaluate this technique in real-world conditions. The evaluations are presented in Section 4. In Section 5 we consider frequency filtering from another perspective and associate the selection of a frequency filter to the selection of a wavelet filter. Finally in Section 6, we present experiments using multi-resolution wavelet decompositions of spectral energies.

2 Frequency Filtering

To overcome the limitations imposed by MFCCs, Nadeu et al [1,2] proposed a simple logarithmic filter-bank energy (logFBE) based parameterization which consists of a linear filtering of logFBE features that quasi-decorrelates them. The basic principle of this technique, called *frequency filtering* (FF), is to design a filter that would equalize the variance of the cepstral coefficients. Nadeu et al [1,2] report that a simple first or second order FIR filter can achieve this goal. The transfer functions of these two filters, that we note FF1 and FF2 as in [2, 4], are respectively given by: $H_{FF1}(z) = 1 - z^{-1}$; $H_{FF2}(z) = z - z^{-1}$.

That is, if the logFBE sequence of a given frame is: $S = \{S(1), S(2), ..., S(Q)\}$ then the resulting filtered features are

$$S_{FF1} = \{S(1) - 0, S(2) - S(1), ..., S(Q) - S(Q-1)\},$$
$$S_{FF2} = \{S(2) - 0, S(3) - S(1), ..., 0 - S(Q-1)\}.$$

Here Q denotes the number of filter-banks used in the spectral representation. In the same spirit, Paliwal [3] designed different filters and reported that the one that achieves the best results is (we call it FF3): $H_{FF3}(z) = 1 - z^{-2}$.

$$S_{FF3} = \{S(3) - S(1), ..., 0 - S(Q-1), 0 - S(Q)\}$$

Note that FF3 is just a shifted version of FF2. Besides decorrelating logFBEs, frequency filtering also has the effect of weighting different regions in the cepstrum. This liftering effect is another advantage of this technique as compared to DCT. A discussion on this aspect can be found in [2].

FF-based parameterizations have been evaluated on different databases in clean and artificial noise conditions [1,3,2,4]. They have been shown to give equivalent or better performances as compared to MFCCs. Thus, the FF technique seems to be a serious candidate to address our problem. Here we recall that our primary objective is to have a frequency localized parameterization that perform equivalent (not even better) to MFCC, but in *all* conditions. Frequency filtering yields well localized features because of the small length of the filters used. Thus, what remains is to evaluate this FF technique in real world conditions. If the (good) behavior observed in clean and artificial noise conditions is again observed in real world conditions, then frequency filtering provides a solution to our problem. From this point of view, the Aurora 3 Speechdat-Car database provides a very good experimental setting to evaluate the performances of the FF technique. Indeed, this database was recorded in real noise and therefore includes several degradations that occur in real world conditions. Moreover, this database was designed especially to give the speech recognition community a test bed to evaluate "seriously" alternative parameterizations to MFCC.

3 Experimental Setup

Of course, we started the evaluation using the Aurora-3 Speechdat-car German database because it is the smallest one. The utterances in the database consist of German digit sequences recorded in different driving conditions. The database is divided into 3 subsets according to the mismatch between training and test sets: well match (WM), medium mismatch (MM) and high mismatch (HM). We report results for each of these subsets using different parameterizations.

The baseline parameterization is obtained using the ETSI SQL W1007 standard front-end [5]. This is a cepstral analysis scheme where 13 Mel-frequency cepstral coefficients are extracted from 23 Mel filter-bank energies. The analysis is performed on 25ms Hamming windowed frames with 10ms frame shift. A notch filtering is applied to compensate signal offset. Pre-emphasis filter with $a = 0.97$ is used. The Mel filter-bank has 23 frequency bands in the range from 64 Hz to half of the sampling frequency. The resulting feature vector consists of 12 cepstral coefficients (excluding c0) and logarithmic frame energy. The first and second time derivatives (Δ and $\Delta\Delta$) are also appended as dynamic features in all the experiments presented in this paper.

The recognition is performed using the HTK software. The digits are modeled as whole word HMMs with 16 emitting states per word and left-to-right non-skipping transition topologies. The output density of each state is modeled with a mixture of 3 Gaussians using diagonal covariance matrices. Two silence models are used : 1) 3 state silence HMM to model pauses before and after each utterance, 2) single state short pause HMM for modeling pauses between words.

4 Frequency Filtering in Real Noise Conditions

It was reported in [1,2] that the number of Mel-scale filter-banks has to be carefully chosen because it effects the performances of the FF technique (a discussion is given in [2] and we will come back to this point in Section 6). Thus, in the experiments presented in this section, we evaluate FF-based parameterizations obtained by filtering 12 Mel filter-bank energies as the original authors do in [1,2,4]. We also incorporate the same energy feature as in MFCC parameterization, i.e. log frame energy. Obviously, this also leads to a fair comparison between MFCC and FF given that the features dimension is the same in both parameterizations.

Previous results on FF-based parameterizations report that this technique performs at least as good as MFCCs in clean an artificial noise conditions. The filters that perform the best were found to be FF1, FF2 and FF3 [1,3,2] and that they generally lead to similar recognition scores. We now evaluate the behavior of FF1, FF2 and FF3 in real world conditions. The recognition scores of FF-based parameterizations and the baseline MFCC parameterization are shown in Table 1. We observe that the recognition accuracy of FF1, FF2 and FF3 features are almost equivalent to MFCCs on well matched and medium mismatched conditions. So far, this is consistent with the previous results on FF-based parameterizations [1,3,4]. However, in high mismatched conditions only FF1 still performs similar to MFCCs and there is a significant degradation in the performance of FF2 and FF3 features. One may conclude that under real world noise conditions FF1 is superior to the other two filters. But this would be a rather fast conclusion because a natural question is: what is the inherent reason that causes a huge discrepancy between these similar derivative type filtering techniques? Indeed, all these filters have been designed using the same principle, so what is the reason for this discrimination between FF1 and {FF2, FF3}? In the next section, we argue that a possible explanation can be given by looking at these filters from another perspective: *the wavelet transform*.

Table 1. Word accuracies (%) using 12 Mel-scale filter-banks for FFs and 23 filter-banks for MFCCs. Total number of static features is 13.

	MFCC	FF1	FF2	FF3
WM	90.58	90.80	90.10	89.68
MM	79.06	79.80	79.21	78.62
HM	74.28	73.17	**64.80**	**63.78**

5 Frequency Filtering and Wavelet Transform

Our starting point is to notice that FF1 is nothing but applying the simplest orthogonal wavelet transform: the Haar wavelet transform [6]. Indeed, the transfer function of the high pass filter of the Haar wavelet is: $H_{Haar}(z) = \frac{1}{\sqrt{2}} H_{FF1}(z)$

Thus, given that wavelets are known for their decorrelation properties, a certain decorrelation is achieved when using FF1. Similarly, FF2 and FF3 are nothing but applying the Haar transform to the odd and even sequences of the input sequence (up to a shift factor for FF3). If the odd and even sequences are viewed as approximations of the input sequence, then FF2 and FF3 can be seen as an erroneous way to implement the dyadic Haar decomposition. Indeed, to implement the latter correctly, the approximations should be computed using the low pass filter of the Haar wavelet. Thus, from this point of view, the discrepancy of FF2 and FF3 is probably due to this erroneous implementation. We emphasize here that we are completely ignoring the motivations and the analysis given by the original authors and we are looking at these filters from a different angle. We now proceed to check whether our reasoning makes sense.

Let's assume that the fundamental reason behind the relatively good performances of FF1 is the decorrelation property of the corresponding wavelet (the Haar wavelet). It is well known that decorrelation generally increases with the number of vanishing moments of the analyzing wavelet. Therefore (if our reasoning is correct), if we replace the Haar filter (FF1) with a wavelet with a higher number of vanishing moments, we should get at least similar performances as FF1. We must however be careful on the choice of the degree of the corresponding filter (or equivalently the length of the corresponding FIR). Indeed, choosing a highly regular wavelet would not only lead to boundary artifacts, but also (and more importantly) it would loosen the frequency localization of the resulting features. The wavelet which fulfills the desired requirements is the Daubechies 4-tap filter (Daub4). This wavelet belongs to the same family as the Haar wavelet (actually, the Haar wavelet is Daubechies 2-tap filter), it has 2 vanishing moments while the Haar wavelet has only 1, and the length of it's FIR is 4. The transfer function of the high pass filter of Daub4 is: $H_{Daub4}(z) = 0.129z + 0.224 - 0.836z^{-1} + 0.483z^{-2}$.

The recognition scores obtained with the Daub4 filter are shown in Table 2. If we do not consider the medium mismatch case, our reasoning is verified since we get a similar performance in well match case and a significantly improved performance in high mismatch case.

Table 2. Word accuracies (%) using FF of 12 Mel-scale filter-banks with Haar and Daub4 wavelets. Total number of static features is 13.

	MFCC	Haar (= FF1)	Daub4
WM	90.58	90.80	90.30
MM	79.06	79.80	76.94
HM	74.28	73.17	78.21

However, we have a rather disturbing discrepancy in medium mismatch case because it is inconsistent with how a parameterization should behave. One would expect that the recognition performance degrades as the mismatch between training and test data increases. In our experiments the performance of the recognizer for the high mismatch case is higher than the performance in medium mismatch. After spending a lot of time to understand this behavior, we realized that it is mainly due to the Speechdat-Car-German database. Indeed, a lot of people working on this database finds the same discrepancy as reported by several papers in the special session "Aurora: Speech Recognition in Noise" in ICSLP'2002 (see [7] for instance). Therefore, the scores in MM should not be given a lot of credit. In summary, these experiments suggest that, looking at FF from a wavelet filtering perspective provides an explanation for the discrepancy of FF2 and FF3 and the good behavior of FF1. Moreover, this perspective can lead to significant improvement in the recognition accuracy in the HM case.

At this point we can conclude that, putting the frequency filtering in a wavelet filtering perspective *seems* to provide a solution to our problem. That is, depending on the desired frequency localization of the spectral features, one can choose the appropriate wavelet with the appropriate number of vanishing moments to decorrelate the logFBEs. Of course, more experiments and evaluations need to be done in order to have a precise idea on the behavior of wavelet filters.

6 Multi-resolution Frequency Filtering

In the previous section we proposed a formal perspective to tune the decorrelation and localization properties of frequency filtering. Another aspect that influences the localization property of the resulting parameterization is the resolution of the initial spectral representation. As reported in [2], the choice of number of filter-banks (Q) that is used to compute logFBEs is a critical aspect in frequency filtering. This parameter specifies the resolution of the initial spectral representation. For high Q, logFBEs will include many details that may not carry useful information for discrimination. On the other hand if Q is too small there may not be sufficient resolution in the spectral representation [2]. In [8, 4], Q is tuned to achieve the spectral resolution that yields the best recognition performance. In this section we would like to investigate if it is possible to avoid this tuning. Since we have paraphrased frequency filtering in a wavelet filtering perspective, a way to do so is to apply a multi-resolution wavelet decomposition and evaluate the performance of frequency filtering at multiple resolutions. We note here that multi-resolution wavelet analysis is the usual way wavelets are used in speech parameterization as an alternative to the DCT operation [9,10,11].

The wavelet decomposition of a signal $s_0 = \{S_0[k]\}$ at resolution j ($j > 0$) is recursively obtained by :

$$D_{j+1}[n] = \sum_k h[k - 2n]S_j[k], \ S_{j+1}[n] = \sum_k l[k - 2n]S_j[k]$$

where $h[n]$ and $l[n]$ are the high-pass and low-pass decomposition filters. $d_j = \{D_j[k]\}$ and $s_j = \{S_j[k]\}$ are the detail and scaling coefficients respectively. The properties of the wavelet basis is specified by the decomposition filters $h[n]$ and $l[n]$. The reader is referred to [6] for further details on wavelet analysis. In terms of frequency filtering, d_1 is the decimated frequency filtered sequence where $h[n]$ is the frequency filter.

Table 3. Word accuracies (%) using DWT on 23 Mel-scale filter-banks with Haar wavelet. The size of the feature vector for each case is indicated inside the parenthesis.

	(d_1) (13)	$(d_1 + d_2)$ (19)	$(d_1 + d_2 + d_3)$ (21)	$(d_2 + d_3)$ (10)
WM	83.01	88.14	91.08	89.04
MM	64.42	76.57	78.77	71.89
HM	71.88	77.75	78.82	74.65

In our experiments we use 23 filter-banks as specified by the ETSI SQL W1007 front-end standardization for the Aurora database. This selection specifies an initial resolution that is found to be optimal for this database [5]. Moreover, we would like to start with an initial resolution that is detailed enough to allow a range of resolutions to analyze. We conduct experiments using 3-level ($j = 1, 2, 3$) wavelet decompositions using the Haar and Daub4 wavelets. The results are shown in Tables 3 and 4, respectively. In the first columns we report the results when only d_1 (which denote the finest level detail coefficients) is used as static features. In this case the number of static parameters is 13 (the same as MFCCs). We observe that the recognition performance at the first decomposition level is inferior to MFCC and FF techniques previously reported in Tables 1 and 2. The main reason for this degradation is the initial resolution selection which is optimal for MFCCs but not for frequency filtering. In the second columns we compute the detail coefficients at the second level and construct an appended feature vector to see the contribution of the coefficients at the second level. Although the number of parameters is only slightly increased (13 to 19) there is a considerable improvement in the recognition performance. Going one step further, we append the coefficients at the third decomposition level. This case is reported in the third columns of Table 3 and 4. We observe that the performance is comparable to and even (especially in high mismatch conditions) better than MFCC and fixed resolution FF parameterizations. From these results we can conclude that frequency filtering at different resolutions have complementary discriminative information. With appropriate integration of information from different resolutions we can achieve performance improvements. However we should note that this improvement comes with the cost of increasing the number of parameters, and also with a loss in frequency localization as compared to fixed resolution FF.

Finally in the last columns we discard the first level detail coefficients (d_1), i.e. the highest resolution, and use the combination of lower resolution coefficients ($d_2 + d_3$). By doing so we reduce the number of coefficients to 10 and also eliminate the highest resolution coefficients which may include non-discriminative information as reported in [2]. With the decreased number of parameters, the recognition performance is still remarkable. These results confirm that the highest resolution coefficients are not as discriminative as lower resolutions. We note that a similar approach has been proposed in [9] where a spline wavelet is used for decomposition.

Table 4. Word accuracies (%) using DWT on 23 Mel-scale filter-banks with Daub4 wavelet. The size of the feature vector for each case is indicated inside the parenthesis.

	(d_1) (13)	$(d_1 + d_2)$ (19)	$(d_1 + d_2 + d_3)$ (21)	$(d_2 + d_3)$ (10)
WM	74.19	85.25	89.40	88.56
MM	58.49	71.96	77.23	75.26
HM	62.86	78.26	81.17	76.83

In summary, these experiments suggest that a way to avoid tuning $\mathcal{Q}$ is to use a full wavelet decomposition of logFBEs. Then, if there is a desire to reduce the computational complexity, fine resolution detail coefficients could be removed.

7 Conclusion

In this paper, we addressed the problem of designing frequency-localized speech features that can perform at least as well as MFCC in all conditions. The recently introduced frequency filtering technique has been shown to solve this problem in clean and artificial noise conditions. But when we evaluated it in real-noise conditions using Aurora 3 German database, we found some discrepancies. By looking at frequency filtering from a wavelet filtering perspective, we were able to explain the FF discrepancies and to achieve significant improvements in recognition accuracy in the highly mismatch case. However, at this point we can not draw any decisive conclusions because more experiments need to be done (using the full Aurora 3 database, other databases, sub-word models...). But we can say that the framework of the frequency and wavelet filtering approaches has definitely a huge potential to provide a solution to this problem, and that more investigations should be conducted in this framework.

References

1. Nadeu, C.: On the decorrelation of filter-bank energies in speech recognition. In: Eurospeech. (1995)
2. Nadeu, C., et al: Time and frequency filtering of filter-bank energies for robust HMM speech recognition. Speech Communication **34** (2001) 93–114
3. Paliwal, K.: Decorrelated and liftered filter-bank energies for robust speech recognition. In: Eurospeech. (1999)
4. Marsal, P., et al: Comparison and combination of RASTA-PLP and FF features in hybrid HMM/MLP speech recognition system. In: ICSLP. (2002)
5. Hirsch, H., Pearce, D.: The AURORA experimental framework for the performance evaluation of s.r. systems under noisy conditions. In: ASR2000, Paris, France (2000)

6. Mallat, S.: A wavelet tour of signal processing. Academic Press (1999)
7. Macho, D., et al: Evalutaion of noise-robust DSR front-end on AURORA databases. In: ICSLP. (2002)
8. Nadeu, C.: On the filter-bank parameterization front-end for robust HMM speech recognition. In: Robust Methods for S. R. in Adverse Conditions, Finland (1999)
9. Gowdy, J., Tufekci, Z.: Mel-scaled discrete wavelet coefficients for speech recognition. In: ICASSP. (2000)
10. Sarikaya, R., Pellom, B.L., Hansen, J.H.L.: Wavelet packet transform features with application to speaker identification. In: IEEE Nordic Signal Proc. Symp. (1998)
11. Sarikaya, R., Hansen, J.H.L.: High resolution speech feature extraction parameterization for monophone-based stressed speech recognition. IEEE Signal Processing Letters **7** (2000) 182–185

Robotics and Control

Unsupervised Learning of a Kinematic Arm Model

Heiko Hoffmann and Ralf Möller

Cognitive Robotics, Max Planck Institute for Psychological Research,
Amalienstr. 33, D-80799 Munich, Germany
{hoffmann,moeller}@psy.mpg.de

Abstract. An abstract recurrent neural network trained by an unsupervised method is applied to the kinematic control of a robot arm. The network is a novel extension of the Neural Gas vector quantization method to local principal component analysis. It represents the manifold of the training data by a collection of local linear models. In the kinematic control task, the network learns the relationship between the 6 joint angles of a simulated robot arm, the corresponding 3 end-effector coordinates, and an additional collision variable. After training, the learned approximation of the 10-dimensional manifold of the training data can be used to compute both the forward and inverse kinematics of the arm. The inverse kinematic relationship can be recalled even though it is not a function, but a one-to-many mapping.

1 Introduction

A basic task in controlling a robot arm is to establish a relation between joint angles and end-effector coordinates. A model that determines the end-effector coordinates from the joint angles is called a forward model. On the other hand, the transformation from end-effector coordinates to joint angles is established by an inverse model. While forward models are one-to-one or many-to-one mappings, inverse models can be one-to-many. Feedforward neural networks are function approximators and therefore fail to learn a one-to-many mapping [3].

Steinkühler and Cruse [10] therefore suggested to use a recurrent neural network (RNN) to solve the redundant problem. In a RNN, all variables are combined in a single pattern, and there is no distinction between input and output at training time. Output values are retrieved by completion of a partially defined pattern, the input. Steinkühler and Cruse used a hard-wired RNN with predefined connections and weights. Here, we present an abstract RNN modeling the manifold of stored patterns by unsupervised learning from the training examples.

We apply this network for learning and recall to the kinematic model of a 6 degree-of-freedom robot arm. Each collected training pattern contains 6 joint angles, 3 end-effector coordinates, and the collision state. In the training phase, a local principal component analysis (local PCA) method is used to determine a model of the manifold of the training data. In geometrical terms, it is approximated by a collection of hyper-ellipsoids. It is assumed that the training patterns lie on a lower-dimensional manifold embedded in the pattern space. In the application phase, a pattern completion is performed. The input part of a test pattern defines the offset of a constraint in the pattern space. The output is determined from the intersection of the constraint space and the approximated data manifold. The presented network has better generalization abilities than a Hopfield network [2], which only restores isolated patterns under the condition that they are uncorrelated or orthogonal.

Section 2 describes training and recall in the abstract recurrent neural network. Section 3 explains the application of the model to a kinematic arm model and presents the results, which are discussed in Sec. 4.

2 Unsupervised Learning and Recall in an Abstract RNN

2.1 Training

The training algorithm is an extension of Neural Gas to local PCA. Neural Gas [4] is a robust vector quantization technique with soft competition between the units. It is an online method, where the model is updated after each presented pattern. A network contains N units, with unit index $k = 1, ..., N$. In Neural Gas, each unit contains a center vector c_k. For each presentation of a training pattern x, all centers are ranked from 0 to $N-1$ in ascending order of their distance d_k (Euclidean in Neural Gas) to x. The rank r_k of a center determines its individual weight $\alpha_k = \varepsilon \cdot \exp(-r_k/\varrho)$. The centers are updated with

$$c_k \leftarrow c_k + \alpha_k \cdot (x - c_k) \ . \tag{1}$$

The learning rate ε and the neighborhood range ϱ decrease exponentially during training, so that the algorithm converges and descends from soft to hard competition. The unit centers are initialized by randomly chosen examples from the training set.

We extend the units to hyper-ellipsoids defined by a center c_k, m principal axes w_{ki} with half axis length $\sqrt{\lambda_{ki}}$, and a spherical complement with radius $\sqrt{\lambda_k^*}$ in the $n-m$ minor dimensions. The w_{ki} and λ_{ki} are the estimates of the eigenvectors and eigenvalues of the local covariance matrix of the training data. The distance measure is extended from a Euclidean distance to a normalized Mahalanobis distance plus reconstruction error [1],

$$d_k(x) = y_k^T \Lambda_k^{-1} y_k + \frac{1}{\lambda_k^*}(\xi_k^T \xi_k - y_k^T y_k) + \ln \det \Lambda_k + (n-m)\ln \lambda_k^* \ . \tag{2}$$

$\xi_k = x - c_k$ is the deviation between the input vector x and the center of the unit c_k, and the vector $y_k = W_k^T \xi_k$ contains the coordinates of ξ_k in the system of the first m vectors w_{ki}, which are the columns of W_k. The eigenvalues are comprised in the diagonal matrix Λ_k. The second term in (2) is the reconstruction error divided by λ_k^*. The logarithmic terms take care of the normalization. λ_k^* depends on the estimate of the residual variance σ_k^2 which is updated according to

$$\sigma_k^2 \leftarrow \sigma_k^2 + \alpha_k \cdot (\boldsymbol{\xi}_k^T \boldsymbol{\xi}_k - \mathbf{y}_k^T \mathbf{y}_k - \sigma_k^2) \ . \tag{3}$$

The residual variance is evenly distributed among all $n-m$ minor dimensions by

$$\lambda_k^* = \frac{\sigma_k^2}{n-m} \ . \tag{4}$$

To adjust the principal axes and their lengths, one step of an online PCA method is performed:

$$\mathbf{W}_k, \Lambda_k \leftarrow \mathrm{PCA}\{\mathbf{W}_k, \Lambda_k, \boldsymbol{\xi}_k, \alpha_k\} \ . \tag{5}$$

For simplicity, we omit the index k in the rest of this section. We use a PCA algorithm similar to RRLSA [6]. RRLSA is a sequential network of single-neuron principal component analyzers based on deflation of the input vector [9, 8]. While the $\mathbf{w}_i$ are normalized to unit length, internally the algorithm works with unnormalized $\tilde{\mathbf{w}}_i$,

$$\tilde{\mathbf{w}}_i \leftarrow \tilde{\mathbf{w}}_i + \alpha \cdot (\boldsymbol{\xi}^{(i)} y_i - \tilde{\mathbf{w}}_i), \quad i = 1, \dots, m \ , \tag{6}$$

where a neuron i (with the weight vector $\tilde{\mathbf{w}}_i$) sees the deflated input vector $\boldsymbol{\xi}^{(i)}$,

$$\boldsymbol{\xi}^{(i+1)} = \boldsymbol{\xi}^{(i)} - \mathbf{w}_i y_i \quad \text{with} \quad \boldsymbol{\xi}^{(1)} = \boldsymbol{\xi} \ . \tag{7}$$

After each online step, the eigenvalue and eigenvector estimates are obtained from

$$\lambda_i = \|\tilde{\mathbf{w}}_i\|, \quad \mathbf{w}_i = \frac{\tilde{\mathbf{w}}_i}{\|\tilde{\mathbf{w}}_i\|}, \quad i = 1, \dots, m \ . \tag{8}$$

The eigenvector estimates are initialized with random orthogonal vectors. The eigenvalues λ_i and the variance σ^2 are initialized with the value 1.

Since the orthogonality of $\mathbf{W}$ is not preserved for each step, the algorithm has to be combined with an orthogonalization method, here we used Gram-Schmidt [5]. Orthogonality is essential for the computation of the distance (2).

2.2 Recall

After learning, the manifold of training patterns is represented by a collection of hyper-ellipsoids with centers $\mathbf{c}_k$, direction vectors $\mathbf{w}_{ki}$, lengths $\sqrt{\lambda_{ki}}$ of the principal axes, and the complement λ_k^*. An input to the network (one part of the components of $\mathbf{p} \in \mathbb{R}^n$) defines the offset of a constraint space $\mathbf{x}(\boldsymbol{\eta})$ spanning over all possible output values:

$$\mathbf{x}(\boldsymbol{\eta}) = \mathbf{M}\boldsymbol{\eta} + \mathbf{p} \ . \tag{9}$$

η is a collection of q free parameters (q being the dimension of the network output) in the subspace. $\mathbf{M}$ is a $n \times q$ matrix.

Recall of the complete pattern takes place in two steps. First, for each unit k determine the point $\hat{\mathbf{x}}_k \in \mathbb{R}^n$ on the constraint subspace with smallest distance (2) to $\mathbf{c}_k$. Second, choose the unit k^* resulting in the smallest distance $d_{k^*}(\hat{\mathbf{x}}_{k^*})$. The corresponding $\hat{\mathbf{x}}_{k^*}$ yields the desired output values (see Fig. 1 A).

The distance d_k as a function of the free parameters η can be written as:

$$d_k(\mathbf{x}(\eta)) = (\mathbf{M}\eta + \boldsymbol{\pi}_k)^T (\mathbf{W}_k \Lambda_k^{-1} \mathbf{W}_k^T + \frac{1}{\lambda_k^*}\{\mathbf{I} - \mathbf{W}_k \mathbf{W}_k^T\})(\mathbf{M}\eta + \boldsymbol{\pi}_k) \quad (10)$$
$$+ \ln \det \Lambda_k + (n-m) \ln \lambda_k^* ,$$

with $\boldsymbol{\pi}_k = \mathbf{p} - \mathbf{c}_k$. We derive with respect to η:

$$\frac{\partial d_k}{\partial \eta} = 2\,\mathbf{M}^T \mathbf{D}_k \mathbf{M} \eta + 2\,\mathbf{M}^T \mathbf{D}_k \boldsymbol{\pi}_k \quad (11)$$

with

$$\mathbf{D}_k = \mathbf{W}_k \Lambda_k^{-1} \mathbf{W}_k^T + \frac{1}{\lambda_k^*}\{\mathbf{I} - \mathbf{W}_k \mathbf{W}_k^T\} . \quad (12)$$

Setting the derivative equal to zero yields,

$$\hat{\eta}_k = -(\mathbf{M}^T \mathbf{D}_k \mathbf{M})^{-1} \mathbf{M}^T \mathbf{D}_k (\mathbf{p} - \mathbf{c}_k) . \quad (13)$$

The function d is convex. Therefore, $\hat{\eta}_k$ is closest to the center. Thus, $\hat{\mathbf{x}}_k = \mathbf{M}\hat{\eta}_k + \mathbf{p}$. The presented algorithm always gives a unique output for a given input. This approach has the advantage over a recall mechanism using gradient descent relaxation that it does only recall the global minimum on the constraint. Local minima on a constraint may not relate to the data manifold.

Equation (9) defines a general linear constraint. In the special case of constraint planes parallel to the coordinate axes, arbitrary components can be assigned the role of input and output variables. This is exploited for the application to a kinematic robot arm control task, where the same network is used as an inverse model and as a forward model without relearning, as described in the following.

3 Kinematic Arm Model

A robot arm with 6 rotatory degrees of freedom is simulated. It corresponds to a real robot arm in our lab. Figure 1 B shows the setup of the model. An arm model with the geometry of the arm and its environment can determine a collision between different parts of the arm and between the arm and the environment.

The training set was generated by randomly choosing 50 000 joint angle sets. Angles were chosen from a uniform interval of ±120 degrees centered at a predefined zero position. For each joint angle set, the end-effector position was

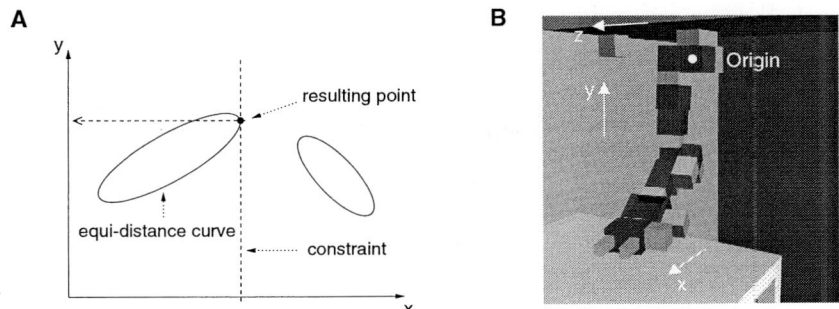

Fig. 1. *A.* Pattern recall. The input x defines the offset of a constraint space from zero. In this space the point closest to a unit center is chosen. Its y-value is the desired output. The ellipses describe the points having same distance d_k to unit k. *B.* Simulated robot arm. Location of the origin and axes of the end-effector coordinate system are shown

determined from the arm model. It was also calculated if the angle set resulted in a collision. Thus, each training pattern is 10-dimensional and contains 6 joint angles, 3 end-effector coordinates, and one collision variable. Only training patterns with an end-effector position inside a workspace of 500 × 500 × 500 mm above the table were included in the training set. Further more, the patterns were chosen such that half of the set were collision trials and half no-collision trials. All values were scaled such that they fit in a 10-dimensional cube with side length 1. Collision was encoded by a binary value 0 or 1. That means the subsets of collision patterns and no-collision patterns had zero variance in the collision variable, which in the training could lead to undefined values of the distance measure. Therefore, random noise was added to all pattern values. This noise was uniformly distributed in the interval [-0.0001,0.0001] and added whenever a pattern was drawn from the pattern set.

Three networks with different number of units ($N = 50, 100, 200$) were trained and tested. All networks were trained using the parameter set $T = 400\,000$ (the number of training steps), $m = 6$, $\varrho(0) = 10$, $\varrho(T) = 0.0001$, $\varepsilon(0) = 0.5$, $\varepsilon(T) = 0.001$. The number of principal eigenvectors m was chosen after inspecting the eigenvalues of a test run without dimension reduction ($m = 10$). Only the first 6 eigenvalues noticeably differed from zero. The training of a network with 200 units took about 33 minutes on an Athlon XP 2200+ with 1 GB RAM. After learning, the number of training patterns were approximately evenly assigned to the N different units of a network. For $N = 200$, the number of assigned patterns to a unit ranged between 32 and 403, with a mean of 250 and a standard deviation of 73. The distribution was nearly Gaussian. Table 1 shows the performance of the network with $N = 200$.

For the inverse direction, the constraint space specified the end-effector coordinates and the collision state, and the network had to find the joint angles.

Table 1. Position and collision errors for an abstract RNN with $N = 200$ units, compared with a multilayer perceptron (MLP). Results are shown for different directions of recall, forward and inverse. The inverse model takes the desired collision state as an additional input variable (third column). Position errors are averaged over all test patterns, and are given with standard deviations. In the inverse case, the collision error is the percentage of trials deviating from the collision input value. In the forward case, it is the erroneous number of collision state predictions

Network	Direction	Input	Position error (mm)	Collision error (%)
RNN	Inverse	No collision	27 ± 15	5.1
RNN	Inverse	Collision	23 ± 13	7.7
RNN	Forward	–	44 ± 27	11.4
MLP	Inverse	No collision	310 ± 111	30.1
MLP	Forward	–	93 ± 48	13.4

Position errors were calculated between the desired end-effector coordinates and the ones obtained by feeding the joint angles produced by the network into the analytical geometric arm model. Collision errors were obtained in a similar way. Desired end-effector coordinates were taken from a $11 \times 11 \times 11$ grid inside the working space.

In the forward direction, the 6 joint angles were constrained, and the network had to find the end-effector coordinates and the collision state. The position error and collision prediction error were computed by directly comparing the network output with the result from the geometrical model. The test pattern set used here was randomly generated in the same way as the training set. It contained 1331 patterns (the same number as for the inverse direction).

Table 2 shows the dependence of the network performance on the number of units. Performance increases with increasing network size. Obviously, the manifold is better approximated the more units are used.

Table 2. Performance of an abstract RNN for different number of units

Direction	Input	Error	$N = 50$	$N = 100$	$N = 200$
Inverse	No collision	Position (mm)	48	38	27
Inverse	No collision	Collision (%)	4.8	4.9	5.1
Inverse	Collision	Position (mm)	47	35	23
Inverse	Collision	Collision (%)	8.2	9.1	7.7
Forward	–	Position (mm)	74	56	44
Forward	–	Collision (%)	16.3	13.7	11.4

The distribution of the position error in the space of test pattern can be seen in Fig. 2. This data is taken from the inverse direction test with no-collision as input. Higher errors can be seen at the border of the workspace (e.g. right bottom corner in both images). The error flow field is not continuous. Different regions are visible.

The abstract RNN results were compared with the performance of a multilayer perceptron (MLP). We used a simple structure with one hidden layer containing 200 neurons (smaller or higher numbers did not improve the performance) and trained 2000 epochs of resilient propagation [7]. Training and test sets were the same as for our network. As can be seen in Tab. 1, the MLP cannot cope with the redundant inverse problem, and performs worse on the forward problem.

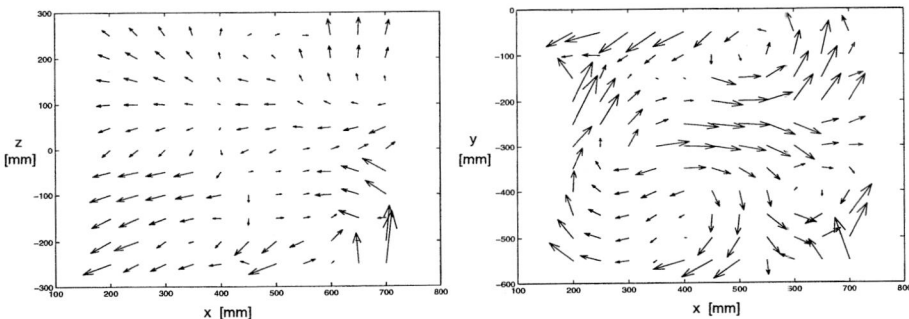

Fig. 2. The position errors of the inverse model with input 'collision' (here $N = 200$). *Left*: horizontal plane (approximately 70 mm above the table). *Right*: vertical plane through the origin ($z = 0$).

4 Discussion

We presented an abstract recurrent neural network model with unsupervised learning. The model is applied to a kinematic arm control task and could learn the direct and the inverse kinematics with one and the same network, coping with the redundancy of the inverse direction. In contrast to Steinkühler and Cruse [10], the network is not restricted to learning geometric relationships, but can include additional variables such as a collision state.

The discrete collision variable splits the training data into two parallel hyperplanes, one including all collision trials and the other all no-collision trials. The distance (2) between the two hyper-planes is much bigger than any other distance between data points inside one hyper-plane. As a result, most of the hyper-ellipsoids stay within one of the hyper-planes (for $N = 200$ all but 9 units had mid-points and eigenvectors within one of the hyper-planes).

The discontinuity of the error (as seen in Fig. 2) results from the change to the next best fitting unit (the closest hyper-ellipsoid). Different regions in the error flow field correspond to different hyper-ellipsoids. As can be seen from (9) and (13), the relation between input and output is locally linear. The local linear models do not necessarily join continuously. So far, no better solution was found to avoid these discontinuities. The vortex like flow fields in Fig. 2 probably result from the error arising from approximating a trigonometric function with a locally linear model.

Recent work focuses on learning a visuo-motor model using a real robot arm. There, the image of an object and the joint angles required to grasp the object are associated.

Acknowledgments. The authors would like to thank Wolfram Schenck for providing an implementation of the MLP network used in this work, Henryk Milewski for implementing the geometric arm model, and Bruno Lara for comments on the manuscript.

References

1. Hinton, G. E., Dayan, P., Revow, M.: Modeling the Manifolds of Images of Handwritten Digits. IEEE Transactions on Neural Networks **8** (1997) 65–74
2. Hopfield, J. J.: Neural Networks and Physical Systems with Emergent Collective Computational Abilities. Proceedings of the National Academy of Sciences, USA **79** (1982) 2554–2558
3. Jordan, M. I., Rumelhart, D. E.: Forward Models: Supervised Learning with a Distal Teacher. Cognitive Science **16** (1992) 307–354
4. Martinetz, T. M., Berkovich, S. G., Schulten, K. J.: "Neural-Gas" Network for Vector Quantization and its Application to Time-Series Prediction. IEEE Transactions on Neural Networks **4** (1993) 558–569
5. Möller, R.: Interlocking of Learning and Orthonormalization in RRLSA. Neurocomputing **49** (2002) 429–433
6. Ouyang, S., Bao, Z., Liao, G.-S.: Robust Recursive Least Squares Learning Algorithm for Principal Component Analysis. IEEE Transactions on Neural Networks **11** (2000) 215–221
7. Riedmiller, M., Braun, H.: A Direct Adaptive Method for Faster Backpropagation Learning: The RPROP Algorithm. Proceedings of the IEEE International Conference on Neural Networks (1993) 586–591
8. Rubner, J., Tavan, P.: A Self-Organizing Network for Principal-Component Analysis. Europhys. Lett. **10** (1989) 693–698
9. Sanger, T. D.: Optimal Unsupervised Learning in a Single-Layer Linear Feedforward Neural Network. Neural Networks **2** (1989) 459–473
10. Steinkühler, U., Cruse, H.: A Holistic Model for an Internal Representation to Control the Movement of a Manipulator with Redundant Degrees of Freedom. Biological Cybernetics **79** (1998) 457–466

A Design of CMAC Based Intelligent PID Controllers

Toru Yamamoto[1], Ryota Kurozumi[1], and Shoichiro Fujisawa[2]

[1] Hiroshima University, Graduate School of Education, 1-1-1 Kagamiyama, Higashi-Hiroshima, Japan
{yama, zumi3}@hiroshima-u.ac.jp
[2] Takamatsu National College of Technology
{fujisawa}@takamatsu-nct.ac.jp

Abstract. PID control schemes have been widely used for most industrial processes which are represented by nonlinear systems. However, it is difficult to find an optimal set of PID gains. On the other hand, Cerebellar Model Articulation Controller (CMAC) has been proposed as one of artificial neural networks. This paper presents a new design scheme of intelligent PID controllers whose PID gains are generated by using CMACs. The newly proposed control scheme is numerically evaluated on a simulation example.

1 Introduction

Owing to the rapid progress of the computer technology in recent years, lots of works about intelligent control schemes have been developed in the field of control engineering. However, PID control algorithms still continue to be widely used for most industrial control systems, particularly in the chemical process industry. This is mainly because PID controllers have simple control structures, and are simple to maintain and tune. Therefore, it is still attractive to design control systems with PID structure. Most tuning schemes of the PID gains that give a great influence on a control performance have been already proposed[ZN1, CHR1,Su1]. However, it is difficult to find a suitable set of PID gains, because most processes are represented by nonlinear systems.

The other side, in recent years, the structure and the mechanism of the human brain are partially clarified by the medical research. Then, various neural networks (NNs) are proposed under the knowledge of the cerebral activity [RM1, Ha1], and they have been already applied about a pattern recognition, a pattern matching problem and learning control. These technology of the NNs enables us to deal by the nonlinear systems, and they have a important role in the field of control[NP1,HSZG1,GR1]. They can be classified into two types. The one is that the control input is generated in the output layer of the NN, and the other is that the control parameters such that the PID gains are adjusted in the output layer of the NN. In this paper, the former is called the direct output type and the latter is called the parameter adjusting type.

By the way, a Cerebellar Model Articulation Controller (CMAC) has been proposed[Al1,Al2] as a kind of NNs, and applied for a process control[YK1] and manipulator control. The CMAC is based on a learning scheme that has the common memory reference structure. In this paper, a new design scheme of intelligent PID controllers whose PID gains are generated by using CMACs is proposed. The proposed control scheme is called as CMAC-PID in this paper. According to the newly proposed scheme, the computational burden can be drastically reduced by the high-generalized ability of the CMAC. Moreover, PID control structure can realize robust tracking for untrained reference signals. The newly proposed scheme is numerically evaluated on a simulation example.

2 CMAC Based Intelligent PID Controller

2.1 Outline of CMAC-PID Controller

First, the controlled object is described as the following formula.

$$y(t) = f(\boldsymbol{u}, \boldsymbol{y}) \tag{1}$$

Now, $\boldsymbol{u}$ and $\boldsymbol{y}$ denote the histrical input and output signals, and defined as

$$\left.\begin{aligned}\boldsymbol{u} &:= [u(t-1), u(t-2), \cdots, u(t-m)] \\ \boldsymbol{y} &:= [y(t-1), y(t-2), \cdots, y(t-n)].\end{aligned}\right\} \tag{2}$$

In this paper, n and m are assumed to be known in advance. Moreover, f is defined as a nonlinear function. Next, the following PID control scheme is considered:

$$\begin{aligned}u(t) = {} & u(t-1) + K_I e(t) - K_P \{y(t) - y(t-1)\} \\ & - K_D \{y(t) - 2y(t-1) + y(t-2)\}.\end{aligned} \tag{3}$$

The control error is defined as the following expression:

$$e(t) := w(t) - y(t). \tag{4}$$

Furthermore, K_P, K_I and K_D are the proportional, integral and differential gains, respectively. (3) is called the velocity-type PID control scheme or the I-PD control scheme. The PID gains included in (3) greatly affect the performance of the closed-loop system. Therefore, it is important to find a suitable set of PID gains, in designing the PID controller. Particularly, for nonlinear systems such as chemical processes, the tuning of PID gains is considerably difficult. Therefore, in this paper, the CMAC-PID control scheme is newly proposed, whose PID gains are tuned by CMACs. Fig. 1 shows the block diagram of the proposed CMAC-PID control system. Furthermore, the detailed figure of 'PID Tuner' included in Fig. 1 is shown Fig. 2. The 'PID Tuner' has three CMACs, and each CMAC is trained so as to generate the optimal gain. Thus, in this paper, consider the following cost function to train the CMACs:

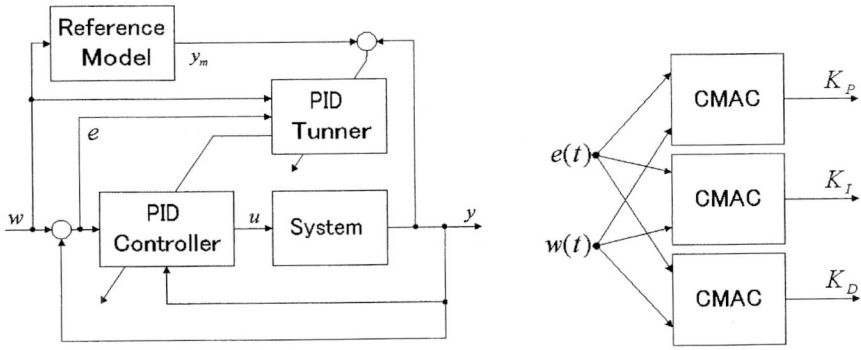

Fig. 1. Schematic figure of the CMAC based PID control system.

Fig. 2. Schematic figure of the PID tuner.

$$J = \frac{1}{2}\varepsilon(t)^2$$
$$\varepsilon(t) = y_m(t) - y(t) ,\qquad(5)$$

where $y_m(t)$ denotes the output of the reference model. To minimize the cost function (5), consider the following gradients:

$$\left.\begin{array}{l}\dfrac{\partial J}{\partial K_P} = \dfrac{\partial J}{\partial \varepsilon(t)}\dfrac{\partial \varepsilon(t)}{\partial y(t)}\dfrac{\partial y(t)}{\partial u(t)}\dfrac{\partial u(t)}{\partial K_P}\\[4pt]\dfrac{\partial J}{\partial K_I} = \dfrac{\partial J}{\partial \varepsilon(t)}\dfrac{\partial \varepsilon(t)}{\partial y(t)}\dfrac{\partial y(t)}{\partial u(t)}\dfrac{\partial u(t)}{\partial K_I}\\[4pt]\dfrac{\partial J}{\partial K_D} = \dfrac{\partial J}{\partial \varepsilon(t)}\dfrac{\partial \varepsilon(t)}{\partial y(t)}\dfrac{\partial y(t)}{\partial u(t)}\dfrac{\partial u(t)}{\partial K_D}.\end{array}\right\}\qquad(6)$$

Furthermore, (6) can be rewritten by

$$\left.\begin{array}{l}\dfrac{\partial J}{\partial K_P} = \{y_m(t) - y(t)\}\{y(t) - y(t-1)\}\dfrac{\partial y(t)}{\partial u(t)}\\[4pt]\dfrac{\partial J}{\partial K_I} = -\{y_m(t) - y(t)\}e(t)\dfrac{\partial y(t)}{\partial u(t)}\\[4pt]\dfrac{\partial J}{\partial K_D} = \{y_m(t) - y(t)\}\{y(t) - 2y(t-1)\\[4pt]\qquad\qquad + y(t-2)\}\dfrac{\partial y(t)}{\partial u(t)}.\end{array}\right\}\qquad(7)$$

These gradients are utilized in training the CMACs. Here, $\partial y(t)/\partial u(t)$ is a system Jacobian, and it is assumed that the sign of the system Jacobian is constant and known.

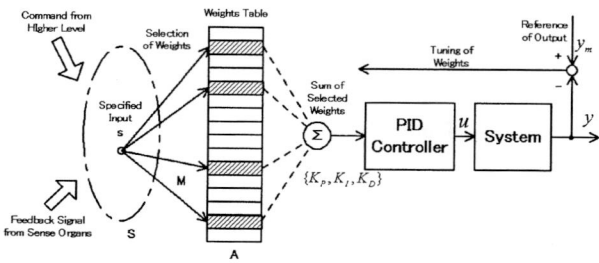

Fig. 3. Conceptual figure of CMAC.

2.2 CMAC

The CMAC is a numerical model which artificially imitates information processing in the cerebellum. The CMAC is trained by referring and updating values of the weight table that has the distributed common memory structure. Fig. 3 shows the conceptual figure of the CMAC. CMAC is defined as the following mapping relationship:

$$S \to M \to A \to \{K_P, K_I, K_D\} \ . \tag{8}$$

The input vector S is first converted into the set of the labels M, and using M, the set of values A is referred. Finally, the total value of A corresponds to PID gains $\{K_P, K_I, K_D\}$.

According to the above mapping relationship, the CMAC refers the weight $\boldsymbol{W}_h(t)$ from K weight tables. The following expression shows the output from the CMAC:

$$\{K_P(t),\ K_I(t),\ K_D(t)\} = \sum_{h=1}^{K} \boldsymbol{W}_h(t) \ . \tag{9}$$

Moreover, the CMAC is trained by updating the weights according to the following rule:

$$\boldsymbol{W}_h^{new}(t) = \boldsymbol{W}_h^{old}(t) - g\frac{\boldsymbol{\delta}(t)}{K} \ , \tag{10}$$

where $h = 1, 2 \cdots, K$, and K is the number of the weight table. Moreover, g is the learning coefficient and $\boldsymbol{\delta}(t)$ is the gradient which is given by (7), namely,

$$\boldsymbol{\delta}(t) = \left\{ \frac{\partial J}{\partial K_P},\ \frac{\partial J}{\partial K_I},\ \frac{\partial J}{\partial K_D} \right\} \ . \tag{11}$$

The volume of memory required in training the CMAC can be reduced by the common memory structure. In contrast, the necessary number of learning iterations can be also reduced significantly, because of the generalizing action.

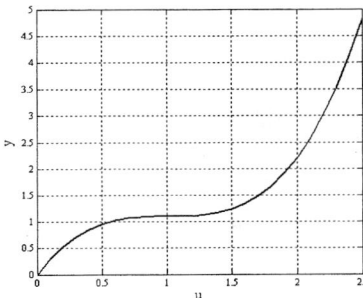

Fig. 4. Steady state properties of the controlled object.

3 Simulations

In this section, the newly proposed control scheme is numerically evaluated on a simulation example. For comparison purpose, the conventional PID controller whose PID gains are fixed, and the conventional CMAC scheme in which the control input is directly generated, were firstly employed.

3.1 Conventional Control Schemes

Consider the following nonlinear system expressed by a Hammerstein model:

$$\left. \begin{array}{l} y(t) = 0.6y(t-1) - 0.1y(t-2) \\ \qquad +1.2x(t-1) - 0.1x(t-2) \\ x(t) = 1.5u(t) - 1.5u^2(t) + 0.5u^3(t) \ . \end{array} \right\} \quad (12)$$

Fig. 4 shows the static properties of the controlled object. It shows that the controlled object has high nonlinearities around $y(t) = 1.1$. First, for comparison purpose, the control result by Chien, Hrones & Reswick (CHR) method[CHR1], which is well-known as a PID parameter tuning method, is shown in Fig. 5. Here, PID gains are calculated as $K_P = 0.04$, $K_I = 0.06$, $K_D = 0.18$. The reference signal $w(t)$ is following:

$$w(t) = \begin{cases} 1 \ (1 \leq t \leq 100) \\ 2 \ (101 \leq t \leq 200) \\ 3 \ (201 \leq t \leq 300) \ . \end{cases} \quad (13)$$

In Fig. 5, the solid line and the dashed line denote the output of the controlled object and the reference signal, respectively. At the second step of Fig. 5, the tracking performance is not enough owing to the nonlinearities. Moreover, for comparison purpose, a simulation result of the conventional CMAC scheme is shown in Fig. 6 in which the control input is directly generated by the CMAC. The parameters included in CMAC are determined as follows:

$$n = 2, \ m = 2, \ K = 4, \ g = 10^{-6} \ , \quad (14)$$

and the following gradient is used:

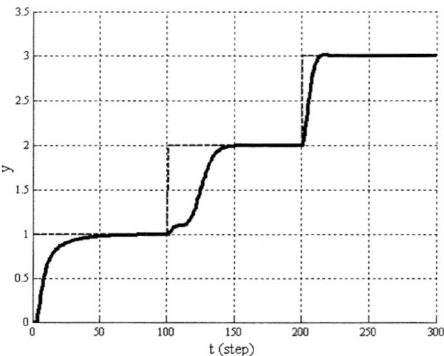

Fig. 5. Control result using the conventional PID control scheme.

$$\delta(t) = \frac{\partial J}{\partial u(t)} = -\{y_m(t) - y(t)\} \ . \tag{15}$$

Here, the reference model is given by

$$y_m(t) = 0.7 y_m(t-1) + 0.3 w(t-1) \ . \tag{16}$$

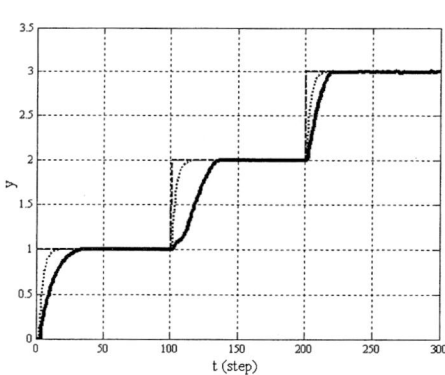

Fig. 6. Control result using the CMAC controller.

The CMAC is trained 2×10^5 trials. In Fig. 6, the solid line and the dotted line denote the outputs of the controlled object and the reference model, respectively.

Next, the newly proposed scheme was employed, and the control result is shown in Fig. 7, and the corresponding PID parameters are shown in Fig. 8. The tracking performance is fairly improved in comparison with the conventional methods.

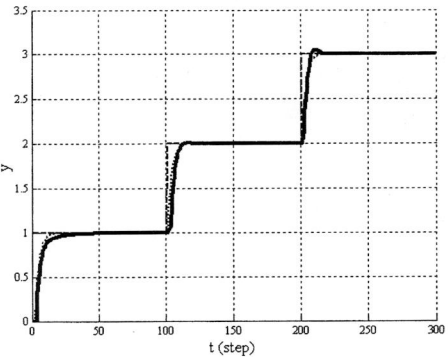

Fig. 7. Control result using the proposed scheme.

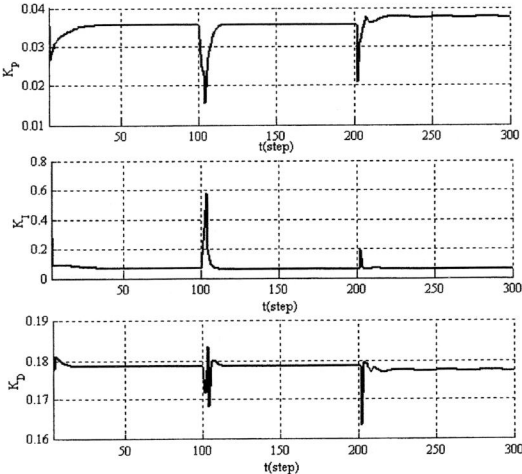

Fig. 8. Obtained PID gains using the proposed scheme.

The proposed scheme uses three CMACs that is shown in Fig. 2, in which each PID gain is adjusted in each CMAC. The parameters included in the CMACs are determined as follows:

$$n = 2, \ m = 2, \ K = 4, \ g = 10^{-4} \ . \tag{17}$$

Moreover, the initial values of the weight tables of the CMACs are set to the PID gains by the CHR method. The CMACs are trained 6×10^3 trials. From these results, it is clear that the newly proposed control scheme works well.

4 Conclusion

In this paper, a CMAC based intelligent PID controller has been newly proposed for nonlinear systems. The proposed method is numerically evaluated on the simulation example, and the features of the proposed method are summarized as follows.

- Owing to the high-generalized ability of the CMAC, the proposed scheme does not need large learning time with comparison to the conventional maltilayed NN.
- The proposed method can use the PID gain adjusted by the conventional PID tuning scheme as the initial values of the CMAC-PID controller. Therefore, the computational burden can be drastically reduced.
- Since the proposed controllers has a PID control structure, the robust tracking can be realized for untrained reference signals.

In order to improve the control performance and the learning cost, the tile cording method must be further developed. This is in our future work.

References

[ZN1] J. G. Ziegler, N. B. Nichols: Optimum settings for Automatic controllers. *Trans. ASME*, vol. 64. no. 8. (1942) 759–768

[CHR1] K. L. Chien, J. A. Hrones, J. B. Reswick: On the automatic control of generalized passive systems. *Trans. ASME* vol. 74. (1972) 175–185

[Su1] Suda: PID control. Asakura Publishing Company (1992)

[RM1] Rumelhart, D, E., J. L. McCelelland, the PDP Research Group: Parallel distributed processing. *MIT Press* Cambridge (1986)

[Ha1] Haykin, S.: Neural networks. *Macmillan College Publishing Company Inc.* New York (1994)

[NP1] Narendra, K. S., K. Parthasarathy: Identification and control of dynamical systems using neural networks. *IEEE Trans. on Neural Networks* NN-1 (1990) 1–27

[HSZG1] Hunt, K. J., D. Sbarbaro, R. Zbikowski, P. J. Gawthrop: Neural networks for control systems. *–A Survey* Automatica vol. 28. (1992) 1083–1112

[GR1] Gupta, M. M., D. H. Rao: Neuro-control systems theory and applications. *IEEE Press* New York (1993)

[Al1] J. S. Albus: A new approach to manipulator control cerebellar model articulation control (CMAC): *Trans. on ASME, J. of Dynamic Systems, Measurement, and Control*, vol. 97. no. 9. (1975) 220–227

[Al2] J. S. Albus: Data storage in the control cerebellar model articulation control (CMAC). *Trans. on ASME, J. of Dynamic Systems, Measurement, and Control*, vol. 97. no. 9. (1975) 228–233

[YK1] T. Yamamoto, M. Kaneda: Intelligent controller using CMACs self-organized structure and its application for a process system. *IEICE Trance. Fundamentals*, vol. E82-A. no. 5. (1999) 856–860

Learning to Control at Multiple Time Scales

Ralf Schoknecht[1] and Martin Riedmiller[2]

[1] Institute of Logic, Complexity and Deduction Systems
University of Karlsruhe, 76128 Karlsruhe, Germany
ralf.schoknecht@ilkd.uni-karlsruhe.de
[2] Lehrstuhl Informatik 1
University of Dortmund, 44227 Dortmund, Germany
martin.riedmiller@udo.edu

Abstract. In reinforcement learning the interaction between the agent and the environment generally takes place on a *fixed* time scale, which means that the control interval is set to a fixed time step. In order to determine a suitable *fixed* time scale one has to trade off accuracy in control against learning complexity. In this paper, we present an alternative approach that enables the agent to learn a control policy by using multiple time scales simultaneously. Instead of preselecting a fixed time scale, there are several time scales available during learning and the agent can select the appropriate time scale depending on the system state. The different time scales are multiples of a finest time scale which is denoted as the primitive time scale. Actions on a coarser time scale consist of several identical actions on the primitive time scale and are called *multi-step actions* (MSAs). The special structure of these actions is efficiently exploited in our recently proposed MSA-Q-learning algorithm. In this paper, we use the MSAs to learn a control policy for a thermostat control problem. Our algorithm yields a fast and highly accurate control policy; in contrast, the standard Q-learning algorithms without MSAs fails to learn any useful control policy for this problem.

1 Introduction

Reinforcement Learning (RL) can be successfully applied to learning discrete time control policies for dynamical systems [5,7]. The control problem is formulated as a dynamic optimisation problem and modelled as a Markov Decision Process (MDP). This MDP corresponds to the following learning situation. An agent (the controller) interacts with the environment (the plant) by selecting an action a (control signal) from the available finite action set $\mathcal{A}$ and receiving feedback about the resulting immediate reward r. As a consequence of the action the environment makes a transition from a state s to a state s'. Accumulated over time the obtained rewards yield an evaluation of every state concerning its long-term desirability. This value function is optimised during learning and by greedy evaluation of the value function an optimal policy can be derived.

In a discrete time control problem as described above the agent can change the action only at fixed predetermined time steps. The temporal difference between two subsequent time steps is called control interval or time scale. In some regions of the state space a fine time scale is needed in order to provide the necessary reactivity when a switch of action is required. Moreover, the finer the time scale is the higher is the stationary accuracy that can be achieved with a finite action set. This means that a given goal state can be achieved with lower tolerance if the action can be changed more frequently. From a learning perspective, however, the agent needs many decisions to reach the goal if the time scale is too fine. This makes the learning problem more complex [1]. Thus in order to determine a suitable fixed time scale one has to trade off reactivity and stationary accuracy against learning complexity. In this paper we present an alternative approach that allows to learn a control policy on multiple time scales simultaneously.

The main idea is to let the agent explicitly select abstract actions that correspond to larger time steps than the primitive time step. Such *multi-step actions* (MSAs) consist of a sequence of the same primitive action that is applied for several consecutive time steps. The MSA is executed as a whole and can be interpreted as acting on a coarser time scale. In many control problems such abstract actions are *building blocks* of optimal paths because between action switches the same primitive action will be applied for several consecutive time steps. Thus, the MSAs allow to make larger steps towards the goal and can therefore reduce the number of decisions to reach the goal. We combine different length MSAs, i.e. different time scales, in *one* action set. This allows to leave the decision about the appropriate time scale to the agent. The special structure of the action set is efficiently exploited in the *MSA-Q-learning* algorithm. In [6] we showed that the MSA framework is suitable for considerably speeding-up reinforcement learning.

The MSA framework uses an action set with a hierarchical structure where temporally abstract actions on coarser time scales are composed of actions on finer time scales with the primitive time scale being at the bottom of the hierarchy. There are other hierarchical concepts of temporal abstraction that have been proposed in recent years to improve the scalability of reinforcement learning in large state spaces with many decisions from the start state to the goal state. The main contributions are the *Option* approach [8], the *Hierarchy of Abstract Machines* (HAM) [3] and the *MAXQ* approach [1]. The two latter are based on the notion that the whole task is decomposed into subtasks each of which corresponds to a subgoal. The subgoals are preselected regions in the state space. A temporally abstract action corresponds to a subgoal. Thus, executing this action leads the agent all the way to the subgoal. In this way, larger steps in the state space are made and the number of decisions to reach the goal is reduced. The option approach is formulated in a very general way so that it is not restricted to subgoal-related abstract actions. However, the main algorithm, *intra-option Q-learning* [8], requires that abstract actions be subgoal-related. Hence, the minimal requirement for the efficient application of existing hierarchical RL algorithms is that a decomposition of the whole problem into suitable subproblems is known. Thus, problems from technical process control, e.g. the thermostat control considered here, cannot profit from these approaches because suitable subgoals are not known in advance or do not exist at all. However, the MSA framework described in this paper is suited for many problems where no decomposition into subproblems is known in advance.

We apply this approach to a thermostat control problem [4]. In this problem a finer control interval is necessary in order to achieve high stationary accuracy when the system state is close to the goal state. However, far away from the goal it is optimal to apply the same action for several consecutive time steps. The solution proposed in [4] is to partition the state space into two regions, namely the neighbourhood of the goal state and the rest of the state space. Then, two controllers are learned separately, a coarse controller using a coarse time scale outside the goal neighbourhood and a fine controller using a fine time scale inside. Upon crossing the region boundary the controller is switched. This approach has the disadvantage that the partitioning must be determined prior to learning. As this will not be possible in general, a heuristic approximative partitioning must be used. In the MSA framework presented here the agent can autonomously select where to use which time scale. Thus, there is the possibility of controlling at different time scales without having an explicit partitioning of the state space. We show that a fast and highly accurate control policy is learned with our approach. In contrast, the standard Q-learning algorithms without MSAs fails to learn any useful control policy for this problem.

2 Reinforcement Learning with Multi-step Actions

As described we consider a discrete time RL problem with a primitive time step τ. Primitive actions last exactly one such primitive time step. In the following, the set of primitive actions is denoted as $\mathcal{A}^{(1)}$. We define the set of all *multi-step actions* (MSAs) of *degree* n as $\mathcal{A}^{(n)} = \{a^n | a \in \mathcal{A}^{(1)}\}$ where a^n denotes the MSA that arises if action a is executed in n consecutive time steps. The next decision is only made after the whole MSA has been executed. In order to retain the possibility of learning optimal policies different time scales are combined in one action set. We denote such combined action sets as $\mathcal{A}^{(n_1,\ldots,n_k)} = \mathcal{A}^{(n_1)} \cup \ldots \cup \mathcal{A}^{(n_k)}$.

Figure 1 shows how the concept of MSAs is implemented in a learning algorithm called MSA-Q-learning. The agent maintains Q-functions for all time scales it is acting on. When executing action $a^{\Delta t}$ of degree Δt in a state s_t the agent goes to state $s_{t+\Delta t}$ and updates the corresponding Q-value. If the trajectory is aborted before the action $a^{\Delta t}$ is fully executed then the corresponding shorter transition of length dt is updated. When executing a MSA on a coarse time scale Δt all MSAs on finer time scales are executed implicitly. MSA-Q-learning uses the training information efficiently by also updating all these lower level actions. The corresponding updates are carried out backward in time. This ensures a faster propagation of the correct values.

input: $\mathcal{T} = (i_1, \ldots, i_n) = (1, 20)$: list of time scales
  $H = 300$: horizon; after H primitive time steps a trajectory is aborted
  $\alpha = 0.1$: learning rate
  $\gamma = 0.99$: discount factor
  $\epsilon = 0.1$: exploration; 10% of all actions are selected randomly
  $num\_trajectories = 50000$: number of training trajectories
  $r_{goal} = 5.0$; $r_{outside} = -0.1$: immediate reward inside/outside goal region
  $R_{violation} = -15.0$: terminal reward for constraint violation
$\mathcal{A}^{\mathcal{T}} = \text{init\_action\_set}(\mathcal{T})$
$Q = \text{init\_Q\_function}(0)$ // zero initialised Q-function
$traj = 0$
while $traj < num\_trajectories$
 $t = 0$
 $s_t = \text{select\_start\_state}()$
 $trajectory\_status = \text{NOT\_FINISHED}$
 while $trajectory\_status == \text{NOT\_FINISHED}$
  if (rand() $> \epsilon$) $a^{\Delta t} = \arg\max_{a' \in \mathcal{A}} Q(s_t, a')$
  else $a^{\Delta t} = \text{select\_random\_action}()$ (a: primitive action, Δt time scale)
  $sum\_r = 0$ // after while loop sum_r contains accumulated reward
  $dt = 0$
  while $(dt < \Delta t) \wedge (trajectory\_status == \text{NOT\_FINISHED})$
   if in_goal_region(s_{t+dt}) $r_{t+dt} = r_{goal}$
   else $r_{t+dt} = r_{outside}$
   $sum\_r = sum\_r + \gamma^{dt} * r_{t+dt}$
   $s_{t+dt+1} = \text{next\_state}(s_{t+dt}, a)$
   if $t + dt + 1 \geq H$
    $trajectory\_status = \text{HORIZON\_REACHED}$
   if constraint_violation(s_{t+dt+1})
    $trajectory\_status = \text{CONSTRAINT\_VIOLATION}$
    $R = R_{violation}$
   $dt = dt + 1$
  if ($trajectory\_status == \text{NOT\_FINISHED}$)
   $R = \max_{a' \in \mathcal{A}} Q(s_{t+dt}, a')$
  if ($trajectory\_status \neq \text{HORIZON\_REACHED}$)
   $Q(s_t, a^{\Delta t}) = (1 - \alpha) Q(s_t, a^{\Delta t}) + \alpha[sum\_r + \gamma^{dt} R]$
  precompute the rewards for all intermediate states and all MSAs
   for $i \in \{t, \ldots, t + dt\}, j \in \{l \in \mathcal{T} | l < \Delta t \wedge i + l \leq t + dt\}$
    $r(s_i, a^j) = \sum_{k=i}^{i+j-1} \gamma^{k-i} r_i$
  for all time scales $\delta t \in \mathcal{T}$ with $\delta t \leq dt$ in descending order (generally $dt == \Delta t$)
   for $i = t + dt - \delta t$ down to $i = t$
    $Q(s_i, a^{\delta t}) = (1 - \alpha) Q(s_i, a^{\delta t}) + \alpha[r(s_i, a^{\delta t}) + \gamma^{\delta t} \max_{a' \in \mathcal{A}} Q(s_{i+\delta t}, a')]$
  $t = t + dt$
 $traj = traj + 1$

Fig. 1. The MSA-Q-learning algorithm. The reading and writing operations for the Q-function are given for a tabular representation. In presence of function approximation these operations must be replaced by the corresponding methods of the function approximator. The input parameters are set to the values used in the thermostat control task.

3 Thermostat Control

In many manufacturing applications it is important to keep a liquid (water, oil, chemical substance) at a certain temperature. Reasons for this may be that a chemical reaction only has the desired outcome, if the temperature is kept within (very) tight bounds. This is the case for example in wafer production processes, but many more industrial applications exist. They considerably vary with respect to the type and the amount of the liquids used, resulting in a broad range of different process characteristics. This variety makes it very difficult and costly to design a controller that shows good control characteristics in every application situation. Reinforcement learning seems to be a promising approach to overcome this problem because the control law can easily be adapted to varying scenarios by learning.

3.1 System Description

The hardware structure shown in Figure 2 is a common apparatus for liquid temperature control with a very broad application range. There is a heating device which is used to directly heat a liquid within a smaller *internal* tank (about 1 litre). This liquid is then pumped through a tube which is going through a larger *external* tank, thereby emitting energy and thus heating the liquid in the external tank (typically 10–60 litres). The temperature of the liquid in the external tank thus can be controlled by first heating the internal liquid. The temperature of the external liquid now depends on many parameters, for example, the type of the internal and the external liquid, the amount of internal liquid that is pumped through the tube per minute, the size of the internal and the external tank, the environment temperature, external disturbances and the type of the tube.

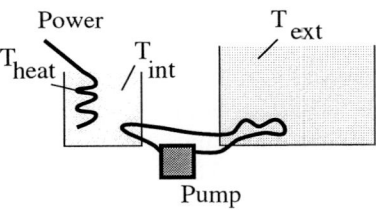

Fig. 2. Typical hardware structure to control the liquid temperature in the external tank (right)

3.2 Control Task

The control task is to keep the liquid temperature in the external tank, T_{ext}, at a certain target temperature T_{ext}^{target}, i.e. $|T_{ext} - T_{ext}^{target}| < \delta$. This part of the state space is called the goal region. The system state is completely described by a three dimensional state vector, that contains the temperature of the internal tank, T_{int}, the temperature of the external tank, T_{ext}, and the temperature measured at the heating device, T_{heat}. The available control action is to apply varying power to the heating device, u_{heat}, which is measured in percent of the maximum heating energy (device depending, e.g. $2000J$). This results in an increase of the temperature of the internal liquid, T_{int}, which finally heats the external liquid. A problem arises from the time delays that might occur due to the overall hardware structure. Depending on the ratio of internal and external liquid, it may require hours to heat the external liquid to a certain temperature. The control task considered in the following, for example, requires approximately one hour to reach its specified target temperature of $T_{ext}^{target} = 40°C$ from the initial temperature of 20°C. However, during all this time, the process must be controlled so exactly, that finally the temperature of the external tank T_{ext} differs from its target value by less than $\delta = 0.1°C$.

3.3 Formulation of the Reinforcement Learning Problem

As the state space is continuous, we use an interpolating grid-based function approximator for the Q-functions with the Kaczmarz update rule [2]. The domain of the function approximator corresponds to the region of the state space that is relevant for the control task. This region is 20°C − 70°C for T_{int} and T_{ext} and 20°C − 90°C for T_{heat}. Leaving this region represents a constraint violation. The general resolution of the grid in the different dimensions varies and gets finer in the vicinity of the stationary state that corresponds to the goal. For T_{int} and T_{heat} the resolution varies between 1°C 10°C, for T_{ext} the resolution varies between 0.05°C and 5°C.

In order to formulate the above control task as a RL problem we need to specify the immediate reward that is obtained in every state. We set the immediate reward to 5.0 inside the goal region and -0.1 outside. Upon a constraint violation the control trajectory is aborted and the agent receives a terminal reward of -15.0. This corresponds to a desired control behaviour that avoids a constraint violation and that reaches the goal region as quickly as possible and permanently stays within this region.

4 Results

We use MSA-Q-learning with the action set $\mathcal{A}^{(1,20)}$. The primitive time step is $\tau = 20s$, i.e. control interactions take place either at 20s or at 400s. During training the controller performance is assessed every 100 training episodes by measuring the discounted reward accumulated over a test episode without exploration. The learning curves depicted in Figure 3(a) are averaged over 30 training runs with 50000 training episodes each. The accumulated discounted reward is plotted against the number of training episodes where each training episode consists of 300 primitive time steps unless it is aborted because the relevant region of the state space is left. With $\mathcal{A}^{(1,20)}$ a good controller is already learned after 25000 training episodes which takes (only!) three minutes on an AMD Athlon™ processor with 1666 Megahertz. We also applied the standard Q-learning algorithm with the primitive action set $\mathcal{A}^{(1)}$ to the thermostat control problem. Figure 3(a) shows that nothing is learned within the first 50000 episodes. But even with 1 Million episodes no useful control policy that reaches the goal region could be learned. Thus, the control task seems to be unsolvable when using only the primitive action set.

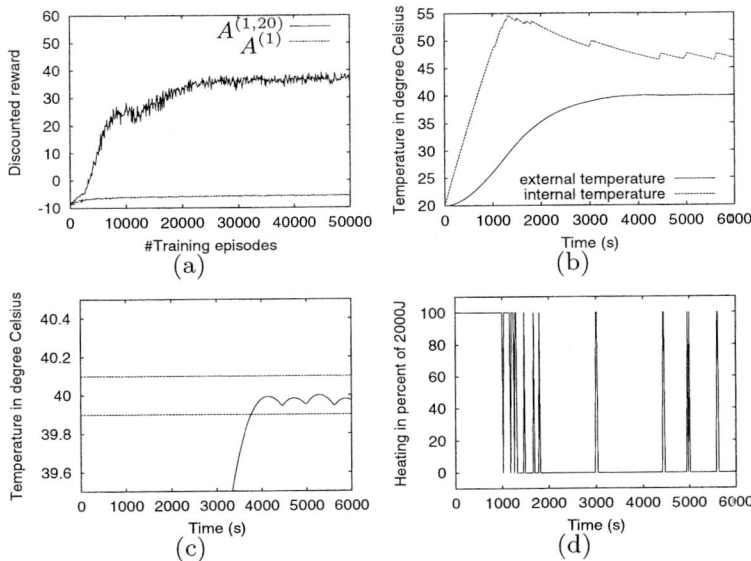

Fig. 3. Thermostat control problem. (a) Learning curve for MSA-Q-learning ($\mathcal{A}^{(1,20)}$, solid) and for standard Q-learning ($\mathcal{A}^{(1)}$, dashed). (b) Control behaviour (T_{ext}, T_{int}) of the learned controller. (c) Enlargement of the control behaviour (T_{ext}) in the goal region. (d) Sequence of heating actions during control.

In Figure 3(b) the control behaviour of the controller learned after 25000 episodes is depicted. The temperature of the external tank T_{ext} (solid) reaches the 40°C level and keeps it. The controller has learned to heat the internal tank (dashed) to about 55°C and to keep a level of about 47°C afterwards in order to achieve the right temperature in the external tank. Figure 3(c) shows an enlargement of the goal region. The control goal is reached after 3780s which is approximately one hour. After reaching the control goal the required high stationary accuracy of 0.1°C is permanently kept. Figure 3(d) shows the learned sequence of heating actions that produces the charts (b) and (c). Until about 1000s the heating is constantly on. Then the controller learned to anticipate the long time delay until the heat of the liquid in the internal tank is transferred to the external tank. Note, that the temperature of the internal tank drops from about 1300s until 3000s while the temperature of the external tank still rises in that period of time. When the system is close to the goal region the controller switches to the pattern of shortly heating the internal tank from time to time in order to avoid that the temperature in the external tank drops too far.

In [4] the same control problem is learned using a controller that switches between a coarse and a fine time scale whenever the absolute value of the difference between the temperature of the external tank and the target temperature crosses the 1°C boundary. This control approach yields a controller that reaches the goal region already after 3500s. But the controller overshoots so considerably that the goal region is left again and is permanently reached not before 6000s. Thus, the

MSA controller with mixed time scales shows a better control behaviour that achieves a considerably higher reward. The reason for the overshooting of the combined controller in [4] lies in the training of the coarse controller. The control objective of the coarse controller is to achieve a tolerance of less than 1°C as fast as possible and to keep that accuracy permanently. However, this specification allows an overshooting of 1°C above the target temperature. Therefore, the heating will be turned on longer in order to achieve the target value faster. When the control is then switched to the fine controller that requires an accuracy of 0.1°C the right time for turning off the heating is already past and an overshooting over the 0.1°C tolerance boundary is inevitable. The same problem would be encountered if the 1°C tolerance region was defined as a subgoal. Therefore, a decomposition with *suitable* subgoals is not obvious for the thermostat control problem. Approaches that are based on a task decomposition are therefore not directly applicable here.

5 Conclusions

We showed that the MSA-Q-learning algorithm learns a successful control policy for a thermostat control problem where standard Q-learning without multi-step actions (MSAs) fails to learn any useful control policy. The success of the MSAs is due to an implicit reduction of the problem size, which enables the agent to reach the goal with less decisions. Moreover, the MSA-Q-learning algorithm efficiently uses training experience from multiple explicitly specified time scales. The concept of MSAs can be especially applied to unstructured domains for which a decomposition in suitable subtasks is not known in advance or does not exist at all. The thermostat control problem, that we addressed here, is a typical representative of such an unstructured domain. We discussed why selecting unsuitable subgoals can lead to a bad control behaviour such as considerable overshooting. In contrast, the MSA approach learns a good control behaviour without overshooting very quickly. Moreover, the learned controller meets the high requirements in stationary accuracy that are indispensable for a practical deployment in the important field of thermostat control.

References

1. T. G. Dietterich. Hierarchical reinforcement learning with the MAXQ value function decomposition. *Journal of Artificial Intelligence Research*, 13:227–303, 2000.
2. S. Pareigis. Adaptive choice of grid and time in reinforcement learning. *NIPS*, volume 10. MIT Press, 1998.
3. R. E. Parr. *Hierarchical Control and Learning for Markov Decision Processes*. PhD thesis, University of California, Berkeley, CA, 1998.
4. M. Riedmiller. High quality thermostat control by reinforcement learning – a case study. In *Proceedings of the Conald Workshop 1998*, CMU, 1998.
5. M. Riedmiller. Concepts and facilities of a neural reinforcement learning control architecture for technical process control. *Journal of Neural Computing and Application*, 8:323–338, 2000.

6. R. Schoknecht and M. Riedmiller. Speeding-up reinforcement learning with multi-step actions. *ICANN*, LNCS 2415, pages 813–818, 2002. Springer.
7. R. S. Sutton. Generalization in reinforcement learning: Successful examples using sparse coarse coding. *NIPS*, volume 8, pages 1038–1044. MIT Press, 1996.
8. R. S. Sutton, D. Precup, and S. Singh. Between mdps and semi-mdps: A framework for temporal abstraction in reinforcement learning. *AI*, 112:181–211, 1999.

The Evolution of Modular Artificial Neural Networks for Legged Robot Control

Sethuraman Muthuraman, Grant Maxwell, and Christopher MacLeod

School of Engineering, The Robert Gordon University,
Schoolhill, Aberdeen AB10 1FR, U.K.
{s.muthuraman-e, g.m.maxwell, chris.macleod}@rgu.ac.uk

Abstract. This paper outlines a system that allows a neural network, which is used to control a robot, to evolve in a structured but open-ended way. The final intention of the research is that, as the network develops, intelligence will eventually emerge. This is accomplished by placing the robot in a developing environment and allowing both this environment and the robot's body form, sensors and actuators to become more complex and sophisticated as time passes. As this development takes place, neural network modules are added to the control system. The result is that the robot's complexity and that of the neural network grows with its environment. Results are presented showing the system in operation on a simulated legged robot.

1 Introduction

Evolutionary Artificial Neural Networks [1,2] have proved useful in several application areas. However, they have failed, as yet, to deliver a convincing route to robotic intelligence, although some large projects have had this as their final aim [3]. Some of the reasons for this failure have been discussed elsewhere [4,5] and are briefly outlined below.

In most implementations of standard evolutionary methods, such as Genetic Algorithms or Evolutionary Strategies, the network is coded directly into the string [1,2]. However, in biology, there is no such thing as direct coding. In fact the human genome does not contain enough information space to directly code even a small part of the brain. Instead, what are coded are proteins, which are mechanically, electrically or chemically active and can self assemble themselves into a larger and more complex whole [5,6].

One of the results of this type of coding and operation is that cells like neurons can form themselves into functional clusters or groups - effectively modules. Genetic mistakes can make new clusters available; these can add functionality to an existing network, so growing its topology [7]. Growth of networks as a method of development is discussed by MacLeod and Maxwell [8]. Gallinari [9] discusses why modular structures like these make effective systems.

For reasons discussed in [5], it would be difficult to model the full biological system practically, within the limits of current technology. This means that we must look to other methods of introducing a modular structure into the evolutionary process.

One possibility is to look at the development process at a cellular rather than a molecular level. Here, organisation in the nervous system proceeds through steps of cell placement, migration, proliferation and connection formation. This results in modules which are available to the network for evolution as discussed in [7]. We have chosen to simulate this by adding modules to the network - a type of Incremental Evolution [8]. Figure 1 shows how the modules are connected to each other and to the sensor and actuators. Connections are added in the evolution space by an Evolutionary Strategy [10].

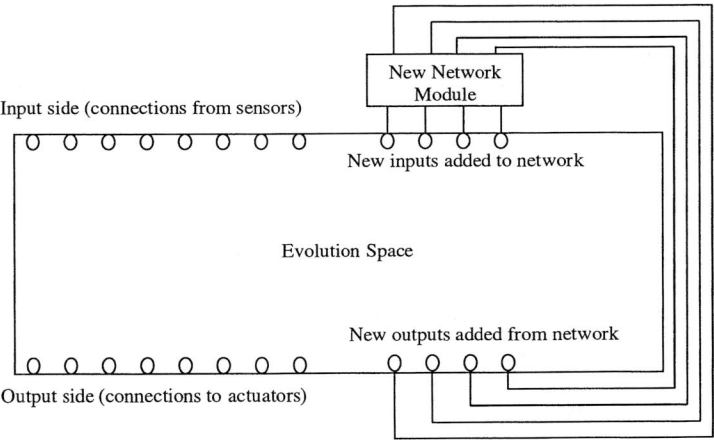

Fig. 1. Module connectivity

2 Evolution of Body Plan and Environment

Perhaps a more important feature of biological evolution concerns the Evolutionary Environment in which the creature finds itself. The first animals had a simple body plan and lived in a simple environment; for example, sponges (Porifera) are fixed to rocks. Later, more complex, animals such as Jellyfishes (Cnidaria) lived in the open ocean. This is a more complex environment, but still simple compared with others; for example, there is no need for obstacle avoidance. A jellyfish, however, can swim and so, as the environment developed, so did the body plan of the animal and the actuators and sensors available to it. We can follow this reasoning through progressively more complex environments and body plans to the level of the human animal.

Likewise, it makes sense for a robot to start developing in a simple environment and to master this before progressing on to more complex situations and for the controlling network to first master simple situations with simple actuators and sensors before "deconstraining" itself and becoming more complex. This is the approach we have adopted here. We start with a simple legged robot and allow the body plan to become more complex (for example, by allowing the legs to develop another degree of freedom).

3 Experiments with Simple Functions

Our initial experiments were concerned with finding out whether it is possible to grow a modular neural network to control a single function, such as a simple leg (as opposed to training one large network to do it). Figure 2 shows the actuator model used, which is a simulation of a physical robot in which each leg has two degrees of freedom (one passive and one active); this is discussed in detail in McMinn [11]. This model has been shown to be accurate, as simulations using it work well with the actual robot.

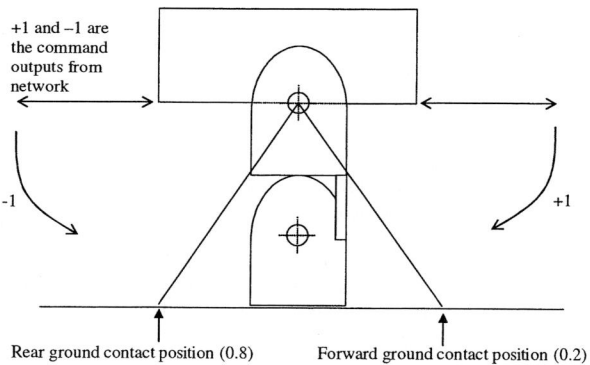

Fig. 2. Actuator model used

Modules, each containing several neurons, are added to the control system one by one. To illustrate this, figure 3 shows the initial network, with just one module; figure 4 shows how a second module is added to the network. (In order to simplify the presentation of these networks, a double-headed arrow is used to indicate a connection in both directions between a pair of neurons.) Each module is trained using the Evolutionary Strategy outlined in McMinn [11], until its fitness did not increase further. These weights were then retained and a further module was added. Only the weights of the new module are trained. This is a form of incremental learning [12]. It is important because the biological brain, with its billions of neurons, could not possibly afford to reconfigure itself each time an evolutionary change took place. New structures must have been built upon older ones (while retaining the older structure's functionality).

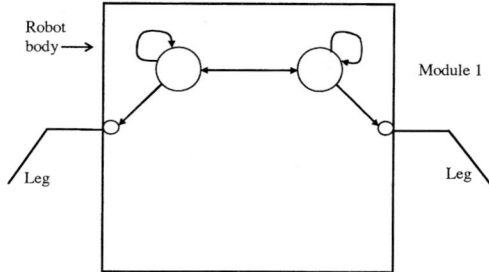

Fig. 3. Initial network

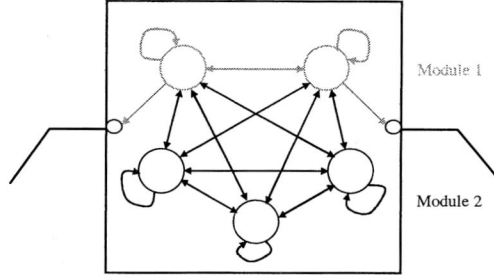

Fig. 4. Network with two modules

It was found that this system attained maximum fitness, but both the neural model and the connection pattern of the new module were critical to the method's success. Simple models, such as those used in other legged robot research [13], did not have enough flexibility to allow the additional modules to evolve satisfactorily. The 'Spike Accumulation and delta-Modulation' model was adopted [14]; the neuron's operation is described as follows:

$$U(k) = \sum_{j=1}^{n} W_j(k) X_j(k) + \alpha V(k-1) \qquad (1)$$

$$Y(k) = G[U(k) - T] \qquad (2)$$

$$V(k) = U(k) - pY(k) \qquad (3)$$

where U(k) is the leaky integration of the input pulses, α (a feedback factor) is a positive constant with a value less than 1, G[z] is the threshold function, T is the firing threshold, Y(k) is the output and p is a constant which controls the internal state of the neuron after a pulse has been generated. This neuron proved flexible enough to evolve the more complex networks (for example, those used to produce the results shown in figure 8).

The reason that the connection pattern is important is that a fully interconnected pattern means that all neurons in the previous module are effected by the new module. While some of these connections cause improvements in fitness, this may be counteracted by other connections which cause a decrease. The simplest way of overcoming this is to use the Evolutionary Algorithm to choose the connections in the network as well as the weights; this was also used to select the values of α, T and p for each neuron.

Figure 5(a) shows the outputs achieved with just one two-neuron module, using a slightly modified version of McMinn's neuron [10]. Figure 5(b) shows the outputs from a network with five modules, each of two neurons. In both cases the outputs were taken from the first neurons in the network. Figure 6 shows the overall improvement in fitness as different modules are added to the network. Finally, the network reaches maximum possible fitness (maximum possible distance travelled). The next stage in the process is the development of the robot's body plan and its environment.

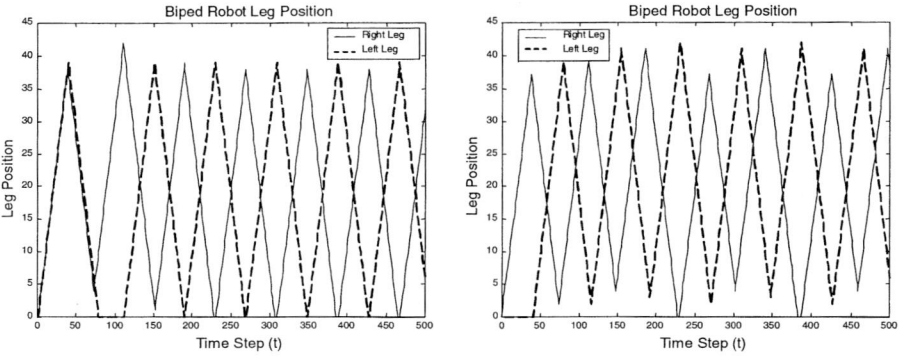

Fig. 5. Outputs from (a) a single module (b) a network of five modules

4 Multiple Functions

In our experimental system, after evolving a control system for single degree of freedom legs, the next stage was to add a second degree of freedom (see figure 7). Having deconstrained the actuator, the network is then grown until maximum fitness is reached. In this case, as before, the previously evolved structures are retained and new network structures are evolved as separate modules. Connections are allowed between any of the new neurons and those of the previous modules. Figure 8(a) shows the leg positions with one module. Figure 8(b) shows the leg positions after the fitness has reached a maximum with four modules in the system. Figure 9 shows how the fitness increases with the addition of new modules. Similar results were obtained for galloping and walking for quadrupeds.

The network structure resulting from the system outlined appears, to the casual observer, to be a fully interconnected network. However, closer inspection

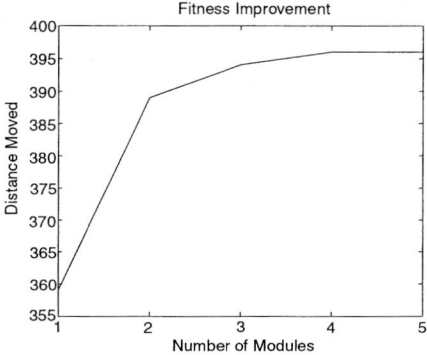

Fig. 6. Increasing fitness with additional modules

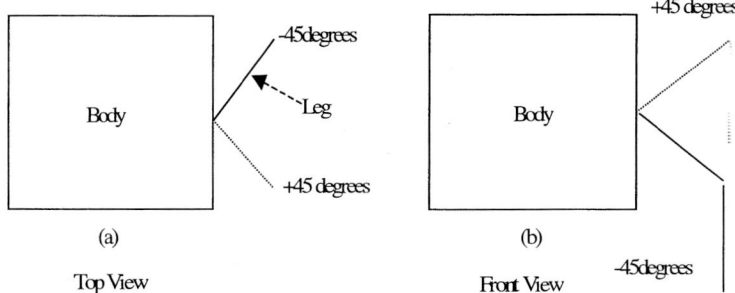

Fig. 7. Start condition of actuator after deconstraint

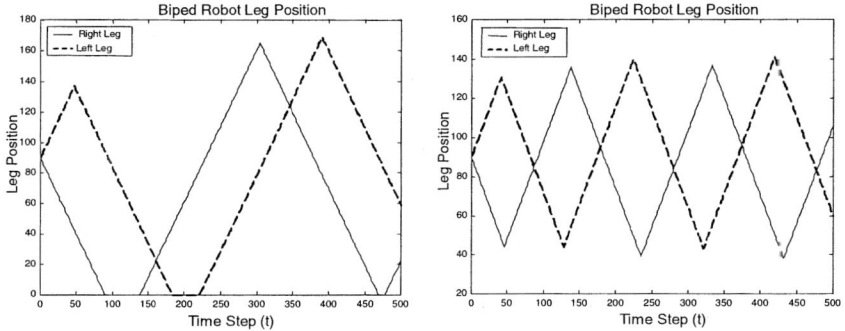

Fig. 8. Leg positions with (a) one module (b) four modules

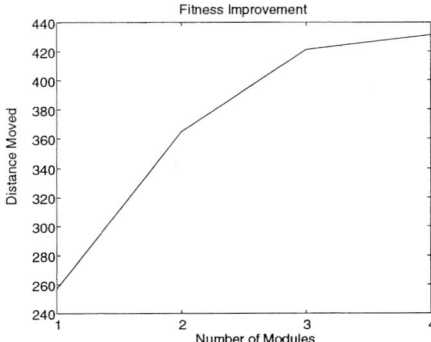

Fig. 9. System fitness

of its functionality shows that different areas of the network are specialised to handle different functions – a structure similar to that present in the biological brain, where localised regions of an apparently interconnected structure perform specific tasks. This is a direct result of the evolutionary process.

5 Conclusions and Future Directions

Our initial results show the applicability of the technique to the evolution of robotic control systems. It has been shown that the method allows a network to build up, from a simple to a complex form and in a potentially open-ended way. The system has been successfully used to create neural control systems, up to the level of those required for quadruped robots. The ultimate aim is to have an algorithm which can grow without constraint until a sophisticated level of intelligence and environmental interaction is attained.

The next experiments will concentrate on incorporating the ideas outlined above into a more advanced robot with a vision system. The network will be able to grow and incorporate both locomotion and vision into the same structure. To do this the neuron model may have to assume a new degree of flexibility in that neural units for pattern recognition are different to those generally used to generate a time dependant output.

Another area that will have to be addressed in larger networks is localising the neural module's connections. At present the networks used are small enough to allow any neuron to be connected to any other. However, in large networks this becomes impractical and smaller connection areas, (for example, only to the previous module layer) may be required.

We also plan to investigate the reuse of successfully evolved modules in "copy and paste" evolution. This would mimic that biological scenario of whole strings of DNA being copied to other areas within the genome and would be useful in evolving repeating structures.

References

1. Schaffer, J. D. et al: Combinations of Genetic Algorithms and Neural Networks: A Survey of the State of the Art. Proceedings of COGANN-92, IEEE Comp Soc Press (1992) 1–37
2. Vonk, E., Jain, L. C., Johnson, R. P.: Automatic Generation of Neural Network Architecture using Evolutionary Computation. World Scientific (1997)
3. de Garis, H.: CAM_BRAIN: The evolutionary engineering of a billion neuron artificial brain by 2001 which grows / evolves at electronic speeds inside a cellular automata machine. Neuroinformatics and Neurocomputers (1995) 62–69
4. MacLeod, C., Maxwell, G.: Evolutionary Electronics. Practical Electronics, August (1999)
5. MacLeod, C., McMinn, D. et al: Evolution by Devolved Action: Towards the Evolution of Systems. In: Appendix B of McMinn, D.: Using Evolutionary Artificial Neural Networks to Design Hierarchical Animat Nervous Systems, PhD Thesis, The Robert Gordon University, Aberdeen, UK (2002)
6. Alberts, B., Bray, D. et al.: The Molecular Biology of the Cell. 3rd ed. Garland Publishing (1994)
7. Fritzsch, B.: Evolution of the Ancestral Vertebrate Brain. In: Arbib, M. A.: The Handbook of Brain Theory and Neural Networks, The MIT press, (1998) 373–376
8. MacLeod, C., Maxwell G. M.: Incremental Evolution in ANNs: Neural Nets which Grow. Artificial Intelligence Review. Kluwer, 16 (2001) 201–224
9. Gallinari, P.: Training of Modular Neural Net Syetems. In: Arbib, M. A. (ed): The Handbook of Brain Theory and Neural Networks, The MIT Press, (1998) 582–585
10. McMinn, D., Maxwell, G., MacLeod, C.: An Evolutionary Artificial Nervous System for Animat Locomotion. EANN 2000: Proceedings of the International Conference on Engineering Applications of Neural Networks, Kingston Upon Thames, UK (2000) 170–176
11. McMinn, D.: Using Evolutionary Artificial Neural Networks to Design Hierarchical Animat Nervous Systems. PhD Thesis, The Robert Gordon University, Aberdeen, UK (2002)
12. Guo-Jian, C.: Incremental Learning of Self-organising Variable Topology Neural Networks. Shaker Verlag, Aachen (2001)
13. McMinn, D., Maxwell, G., MacLeod, C.: Evolutionary Artificial Neural Networks for Quadruped Locomotion. Proceedings of the International Conference on Neural Networks ICANN 2002, Madrid, (2002) 789–794
14. Shigematsu, Y., Ichikawa, M., Matsumoto, G.: Reconstitution studies on brain computing with the neural network engineering. In: Ono, T., McNaughton, B., Molotchnikoff, S. Rolls, E., Nishijo, H. (Eds.): Perception, memory and emotion: frontiers in neuroscience. Elsevier, (1996) 581–599

Dimensionality Reduction through Sensory-Motor Coordination

Rene te Boekhorst[1], Max Lungarella[2]*, and Rolf Pfeifer[3]

[1] Adaptive Systems Research Group, University of Hertfordshire, UK
r.teboekhorst@herts.ac.uk
[2] Neuroscience Research Institute, Tsukuba AIST Central 2, Japan
max.lungarella@aist.go.jp
[3] Artificial Intelligence Laboratory, University of Zurich, Switzerland
pfeifer@ifi.unizh.ch

Abstract. The problem of category learning has been traditionally investigated by employing disembodied categorization models. One of the basic tenets of embodied cognitive science states that categorization can be interpreted as a process of sensory-motor coordination, in which an embodied agent, while interacting with its environment, can structure its own input space for the purpose of learning about categories. Many researchers, including John Dewey and Jean Piaget, have argued that sensory-motor coordination is crucial for perception and for development. In this paper we give a quantitative account of why sensory-motor coordination is important for perception and category learning.

1 Introduction

The categorization and discrimination of sensory stimuli, and the generation of new perceptual categories is one of the most fundamental cognitive abilities [1,2]. Perceptual categorization [1] is of such importance that a natural organism incapable of making perceptual discriminations will not have much of a chance of survival, and an artificial device, such as a robot, lacking this capability, will only be of limited use. Traditionally the problem of categorization has been investigated by adopting a disembodied perspective. Categorization models like ALCOVE (Attention Learning COVEring Map) [3] or SUSTAIN (Supervised and Unsupervised STratified Adaptive Incremental Network) [4] implement categorization as a process of mapping an input vector consisting of "psychologically relevant dimensions" onto a set of output (category) nodes. The problem with these traditional approaches is, roughly speaking, that they do not work in the real world, e.g., when used on real robots, because they neglect the fact that in the real world there are no input vectors that have been preselected by the designer, but continuously changing sensory stimulation. Moreover, these models do not properly take into account that the proximal stimulation originating from objects varies greatly depending on distance and orientation, and on other factors that we do not discuss here.

Recently Clark and Thornton [5] have introduced the concept of *type-2 problems* to denote datasets for which the mapping from input nodes to output nodes cannot

---
* R.t.B and M.L: Work done at the Artificial Intelligence Laboratory in Zurich.

be extracted by means of learning algorithms and statistical procedures used in classic categorization models. In contrast, whenever the aforementioned mapping can be learned from data alone, the data are said to correspond to a *type-1 problem*. According to Clark and Thornton, the main difficulty in category learning is the generation of appropriate (type-1) data. As far as we know, there are two main strategies to achieve this. The first was suggested by Clark and Thornton themselves [5], and relies on an improvement of the internal processing, which could be based on already learned things, for instance. The second approach is derived from the basic tenets of embodied cognitive science and consists of exploiting processes of sensory-motor coordination [2,6]. As suggested more than one century ago by John Dewey [7], categorization can be conceptualized as a process of sensory-motor coordinated interaction – see also [1,2,8]. Sensory-motor coordination involves object-related actions, which can be used to structure the agent's input (sensory) space for the purpose of learning about object categories. The structuring of the sensory space can be thought of as a mapping from a high dimensional input space to a sensory space with a smaller number of dimensions. The important point to note is that the dimensionality reduction does not necessarily have to be the result of internal processing only, but may be the result of an appropriate embodied interaction. From the account given above, we derive two working hypotheses:

- Dimensionality reduction in the sensory space is the result of a sensory-motor coordinated interaction of the system with the surrounding environment. This leads to the emergence of correlations among the input variables (sensors) and between these and the motor outputs.
- The particular temporal pattern of these correlations can be used to characterize the robot-environment interaction, i.e., it can be considered to be a "fingerprint" of this interaction.

More specifically, we expect clearer correlations in the case of a robot that is driven by *sensory-motor dynamics*, rather than in a robot that moves on the basis of a set of fixed and preprogrammed instructions. Here, *sensory-motor dynamics* is defined as the dynamics of a system that is characterized by continuous feedback between sensory input and motor output.

In what follows, we describe how these two hypotheses were experimentally tested in a real robot. In section 2 we give an overview of the experimental setup we employed and of the five experiments we performed. Then in section 3 we describe and motivate the statistical methodology, which we used to analyze the time-series collected during the robot experiments. Finally, in the two last sections, we discuss what we have learned and point to some future work.

2 Real-World Instantiation and Environmental Setup

All experiments described in this paper were carried out with a circular wheeled mobile robot called $Samurai^{TM}$. This mobile device is equipped with a ring of 12 ambient-light (AL) and 12 infrared (IR) sensors, and a standard off-the-shelf color CCD camera for vision (Fig. 1). The two wheels allow for independent translational and rotational

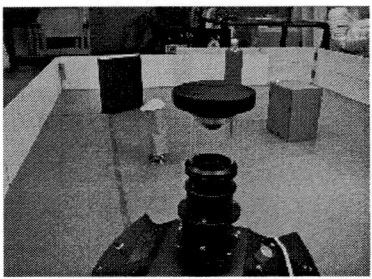

Fig. 1. Environmental setup. Object of different shape can be seen in the background. In a typical experiment the robot started in one corner of the arena, and dependent on its in-built reflexes, it tried to avoid obstacles, circled around them, or just tracked a moving obstacle (the small cylinder in the front). Note that the omnidirectional camera on the robot was not used for the experiments discussed in the paper.

movements. For the purpose of this study the original 128x128 pixel array was compressed into a 100 dimensional vector, whose elements were calculated by taking the spatial average of the pixel intensity [1] over adjacent verticular rectangular image patches. Video frames were recorded at a rate of $7Hz$. In the course of each experimental session, the input data coming from three (exteroceptive) sensory modalities (AL, IR, and vision), and the difference between the left and right motor speed (angular velocity), were transferred to a computer and stored in a time-series file, yielding a 125 dimensional data vector per time step. The following five experiments were carried out in a simple environment (a square arena) consisting either of stationary or moving objects (Fig. 1). Each experiment was replicated 15 times. The resulting time series of each run consist of $N = 100$ time steps.

- *Experiment 1 – Control setup:* The robot moved forward in a straight line with a constant speed. A static red object was placed in its field of view, in the top left corner at the end of the arena. The behavior of the robot displayed no sensory-motor coordination.
- *Experiment 2 – Moving object:* The complexity of the control setup was slightly increased by letting the same object move with a constant speed. As in experiment 1, the behavior was not sensory-motor coordinated.
- *Experiment 3 – Wiggling:* The robot was programmed to move forward in an oscillatory manner. As in experiment 1 and 2, there is no sensory-motor coordination.
- *Experiment 4 – Tracking 1:* Simple sensory-motor coordination was implemented by letting the robot move in such a way that it kept, as long as possible, a static object in the center of its field of view, while moving forward towards the object. This behavior was sensory-motor coordinated.

---

[1] The statistical analysis described in this paper is based on the intensity map of the image, which is obtained by computing the spatial average of the red, green and blue color map.

- *Experiment 5 – Tracking 2:* As in Experiment 4, but now the robot had to keep a moving object in the center of its field of view, while moving towards the object – simple sensory-motor coordination.

The control architectures for the five experiments were designed so as to be as simple as possible for the task at hand, i.e., the output of the control architecture of experiments 1 to 3 consisted of a pre-programmed sequence of motor commands, whereas in the case of experiments 4 and 5, a feedback signal proportional to the error due to a not centered tracked object was used in order to compute the new motor activations.

3 Statistical Analysis

The most straightforward statistical approach would be to correlate the time series of all variables (difference, AL, IR, and preprocessed camera image) of the 125 dimensional data vector with each other. However, by doing so we would run into the Bonferroni problem [9]: 5% of that very large number of correlations would be significant by chance alone (accepting a significance level of $\alpha = 0.05$). Moreover, the result of this operation would be strongly biased due to the preponderance of the image data. Additional difficulties would arise from the fact that the computed correlation coefficients would have to be combined into a single and meaningful number, and due to the variance of the input data, this number would change over time.

In order to avoid incurring into the Bonferroni problem, we reduced – as a first step – the number of variables by performing a principal component analysis (PCA) on each of the three sensory modalities separately. The main idea of Principal Component Analysis (PCA) is to compress the maximum amount of information of a multivariate data set into a limited (usually small) number of principal components (PCs). These principal components are linear combinations of the original variables and in this way the high-dimensional data are projected onto a space of reduced dimensionality. The axes are chosen in order to maximize the variance of the projected data. The usefulness of this method is exemplified by a PCA performed on the camera image data (see Fig. 2). In the case of natural images, a PCA would result in a principal component to which contribute especially those pixel locations whose intensity values correlate strongly in time and thus probably originate from one and the same object. The image reconstructed from the PCA is, however, far from perfect. This is probably due to the fact that the PCs are mere linear combinations of *all* variables considered and, in addition, they do not take into account the sign of their contribution to a given PC. They therefore include also those variables that correlate only weakly or strongly negatively with a given PC. As an alternative, we constructed so-called *average factors* (AF), which are the mean values calculated (for each time step) over only those variables that load significantly high on a PC and are of the same sign. The comparison of a reconstruction based on 5 PCs with one based on 5 AFs is shown in Fig. 2d and 2e. Also for the other experiments we found that the image data could be adequately described by about 5 to 10 AFs. The AL data and the IR readings could be combined into an average of up to 4 AFs.

Next, the correlations between the AFs representing the reduced sensory space and the angular data (from the wheel encoders) were computed and brought together into

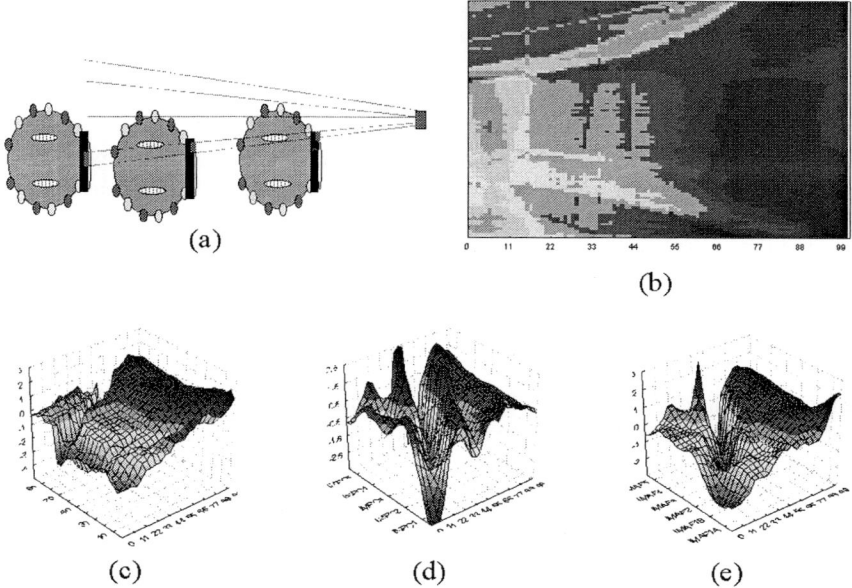

Fig. 2. Use of dimension reduction techniques, exemplified by the image data. (a) How the robot perceives an object when approaching it (experiment 1, no sensory-motor coordination). Moving forward, the image of a static object shifts to the periphery of the visual field. (b) A contour plot of the image data displayed as a time series of the pixel intensities. Vertical axis: pixel locations. Horizontal axis: time steps. The peripheral shift shows up as an upward curving trace. (c) A $3D$ plot of (b) with pixel intensity plotted along the vertical axis. Here the trace is visible as a trough cutting through a landscape with a ridge on the right side. (d) A reconstruction of (c) based on the first 5 PCs, which explain 95% of the variance. (e) The same as (d) but based on *average factors*.

a correlation matrix $\mathbf{R}$. One way of summarizing the information in this matrix is to estimate $1-|\mathbf{R}|$, $|\mathbf{R}|$ being the determinant of the correlation matrix. The measure $1-|\mathbf{R}|$ has been put forward as a general measure of the variance explained by the correlation among more than 2 variables and has actually been proposed to quantify the dynamics of order and organization in developing biological systems [10]. The dynamics of this measure could be captured by calculating it for a window of W subsequent time steps, and by recomputing this quantity after the window has been shifted ahead one step in time. An obvious shortcoming of this technique is that the end of the data sequence is tapered to zero, i.e., the time series is truncated at $N - W - 1$ data points, where N is the length of the data sequence. This represents a clear loss of information, since events occurring in the tapered region are missed.

As an alternative, we computed the correlations for increasingly larger windows of 4,5, to N time steps, but with a decreasing influence of the past, i.e., by giving less weight to data points further back in time. This was achieved by weighting the contribution of the correlation coefficient at time $t = T$ (the current point in time) by a decay function $w_{t,\alpha}$

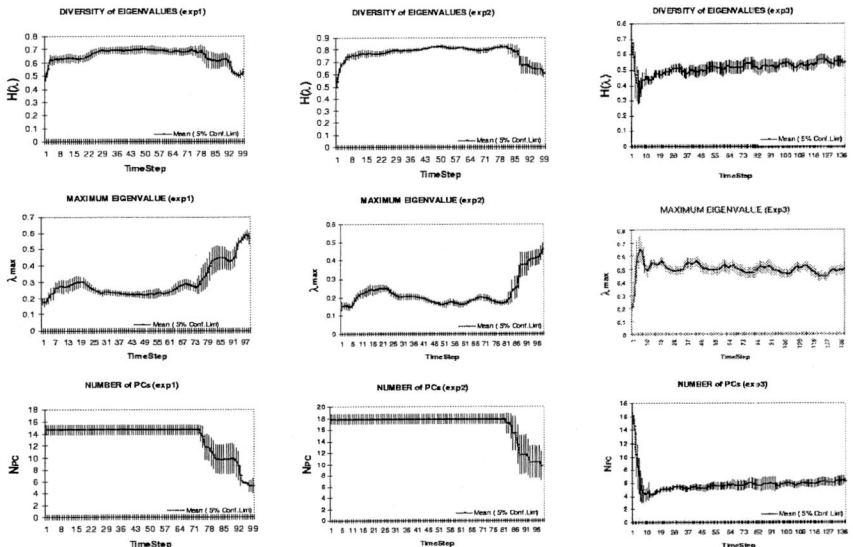

Fig. 3. Results of experiments 1–3 (no sensory-motor coordination). Left: experiment 1. Center: experiment 2. Right: experiment 3. From top to bottom (and for all columns) the vertical axes are $H(\lambda)$, λ_{max}, and N_{pc}. In all graphs the horizontal axis denotes time. The curves are the means from up to 15 experimental runs and the bars are the associated 95% confidence limits around those means. For details refer to text.

(where α is a parameter controlling the steepness of decay) leading to the calculation of the weighted correlation coefficient:

$$r_T^* = \frac{\sum_{t=0}^T w_{t,\alpha} x_t y_t - \sum_{t=0}^T w_{t,\alpha} x_t \sum_{t=0}^T w_{t,\alpha} y_t / N}{\left[\sum_{t=0}^T w_{t,\alpha} x_t^2 - \left(\sum_{t=0}^T w_{t,\alpha} x_t\right)^2 / N\right]\left[\sum_{t=0}^T w_{t,\alpha} y_t^2 - \left(\sum_{t=0}^T w_{t,\alpha} y_t\right)^2 / N\right]}. \quad (1)$$

As a decay function, we chose a half-gaussian function $w_{t,\alpha} = e^{ln(\alpha(t-T))^2} u_{-1}(t)$, where $u_{-1}(t)$ is the *Heaviside-function*, which is 1 for $t > 0$ and 0 for $t \leq 0$. This yields a matrix of weighted correlation coefficients $\mathbf{R}^*(\mathbf{t})$ for each sampled point at time t. Unfortunately, the determinant of a correlation matrix is highly sensitive to outliers. In other words, $1 - |\mathbf{R}^*|$ could not be used as a measure of the dynamics of the correlation among the input and output variables.

Another way of characterizing a weighted correlation matrix, is by the set λ of its eigenvalues, λ_i ($i = 1, 2, \ldots, F$), where F is the number of AFs. The ith eigenvalue equals the proportion of variance accounted for by the ith PC and hence contains information about the correlation structure of the data set. In fact, this boils down to yet another PCA, this time on the averaged factors. We propose 3 indices to capture the statistical properties of the robot's sensory data; they combine the eigenvalues λ_i into a single quantity (and that, like $\mathbf{R}^*$, has to be calculated for each time step t). The first one is the *Shannon Entropy* $H(\lambda) = \sum_{i=1}^{N} p(\lambda_i) \log p(\lambda_i)$ [11]. This index attains its

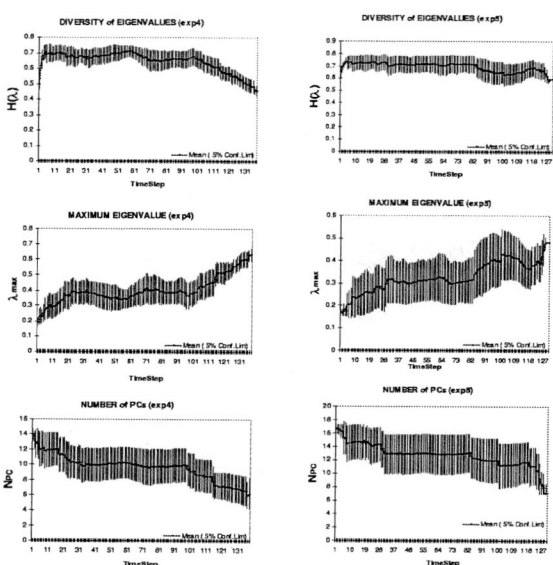

Fig. 4. Results of experiments 4 and 5 (sensory-motor coordination). Left: experiment 4. Right: experiment 5. From top to bottom (and for all columns) the vertical axes are $H(\lambda)$, λ_{max}, and N_{pc}. The horizontal axis denotes time. For details refer to text.

maximum for $p(\lambda_i) = 0.5$ ($i = 1, 2, \ldots, N$), i.e., when the variance is evenly accounted for by all PCs. A high value of $H(\lambda)$ therefore represents a lack of correlational structure among the variables. When $H(\lambda)$ is low, the total variance of the data matrix is concentrated in one or only a few PCs and hence points to strong correlations. Another way to quantify the same effect is the so-called *Berger-Parker Index* (BPI), which measures "dominance" as $D = \lambda_{max}/\sum_{i=1}^{N} \lambda_i$. Since the eigenvalues of a correlation matrix are arranged in decreasing order and sum up to unity, this results in $D = \lambda_{max} = \lambda_1$. The third measure is the number of PCs (eigenvalues) that together explain 95% of the total variance. We will refer to it as N_{pc}.

4 Experiments and Discussion

The outcomes of the statistical analyses described in the previous section are summarized in Fig. 3 and 4. What do these results tell us with respect to the impact of sensory-motor coordination? The most conspicuous difference between architectures with and without sensory-motor coordination appears to be in the variance of the introduced indices. The curves of the experiments with sensory-motor coordination (experiments 4 and 5) display a very large variance (represented by the errorbars). Furthermore in these experiments the curves for H_λ and N_{pc} decrease more or less monotonously (whereas λ_{max} rises), implying a steady increase in correlation among the AFs. The large variance is due to the fact that in some experiments these changes set in much earlier than in others (in some instances the decrease was so late, that they resembled the outcomes of experiments 1 and 2). But this does not imply that in the case of no sensory-motor coordination no reduction of dimensionality occurs. In experiments 1 and 2 there is a reduction. However, it takes place only at the end of the runs. Experiment 3 is odd – see Fig. 3, third column. Although the experiment is not sensory-motor coordinated, the calculated indeces show the strongest reduction in dimensionality of all experiments! Note that after an initial increase, the correlations seem to decrease again (see λ_{max}, for instance). One possible explanation is that the oscillatory movement forces a large part of the sensory input in the same phase, leading to strong correlations in the case when the robot is distant from objects (beginning of the experiment) and to weaker correlations otherwise.

5 Conclusion and Future Work

To summarize, the curves do indeed give a *fingerprint* of the robot-environment interaction (note how the oscillations of the robot are also manifest in the λ_{max} curve of experiment 3) and sensory-motor coordination does lead to a reduction of dimensionality in the sensory input. However, despite this very definite impact on the correlations of the sensory data, the results are not entirely straightforward. Further investigation, in particular more complex sensory-motor setups, is required.

Acknowledgements. This research was supported in part by grant number 11.65310.01 of the Swiss National Science Foundation.

References

1. G.M. Edelman. *Neural Darwinism: The Theory of Neural Group Selection.* Basic Books: New York, USA, 1987.
2. R. Pfeifer and C. Scheier. *Understanding Intelligence.* MIT Press, Cambridge, MA, USA, 1999.
3. J.K. Kruschke. Alcove: An exemplar-based connectionist model of category learning. *Psychological Review*, 99:22–44, 1992.
4. B.C. Love and D.L. Medin. Sustain: A model of human category learning. In *Proc. of the 5th National Conference on Artificial Intelligence (AAAI-98)*, pages 671–676, 1998.
5. A. Clark and T. Thornton. Trading spaces. *Behavioral Brain Sciences*, 20:57–90, 1997.
6. C. Scheier and R. Pfeifer. Information theoretic implications of embodiment for neural network learning. In *Proc. of Int. Conf. on Articial Neural Networks*, 1997.
7. J. Dewey. The reflex arc concept in psychology. *Psychological Review*, 3:357–370, 1981. Original work published in 1896.
8. E. Thelen and L. Smith. *A Dynamic Systems Approach to the Development of Cognition and Action.* MIT Press, Cambridge, MA, USA, 1994.
9. G.W. Snedecor and W.G. Cochran. *Statistical Methods.* Iowa State University Press, Ames, Iowa, USA, 1980.
10. P.R. Banerjee, S. Sibbald and J. Maze. Quantifying the dynamics of order and organization in biological systems. *J. of Theoretical Biology*, 143:91–112, 1990.
11. C.E. Shannon. A mathematical theory of communication. *Bell Syst. Tech. J.*, 27:379–423, 623–653, 1948.

Learning Localisation Based on Landmarks Using Self-Organisation

Kaustubh Chokshi, Stefan Wermter, and Cornelius Weber

Hybrid Intelligent Systems, School of Computing and Technology, University of Sunderland
St. Peter's Campus, Sunderland SR6 0DD, United Kingdom
http://www.his.sunderland.ac.uk/

Abstract. In order to have an autonomous robot, the robot must be able to navigate independently within an environment. Place cells are cells that respond to the environment the animal is in. In this paper we present a model of place cells based on Self Organising Maps. The aim of this paper is to show that localisation can be performed even without having a built in map. The model presented shows that the landmarks are selected without any human interference. After training, a robot can localise itself within a learnt environment.

1 Introduction

Ideally an autonomous robot should have a self-contained system which allows it to adapt and modify its behaviour to all possible situations it might face. The classical method is to pre-define the internal model of the robot relating it to the external world. The problem which arises is that the external world is very complex thus making it often unpredictable [2]. With a pre-defined program the robot can navigate only within a highly controlled environment [8].

There are various ways to address the problem of localisation. The most common approach is to ignore the errors of localisation [7]. This has the advantage of being simple but a major disadvantage is that it cannot be used as a global planning method. To overcome this problem, another technique updates the robot location by bar codes and laser sensors in the environment, thus giving it an explicit location. This method was purely motivated by the "*go until you get there*" philosophy [7]. Another approach was to use topological maps where symbolic information for localisation at certain points for instance gateways was being used [3,12,4]. With gateways as a navigational strategy the robot can change its direction for instance at intersections of hallways. Here the robot is not concerned with how long the hallway is but it knows that at the end of the hallway there is an intersection. Therefore the gateways are critical for localisation, path planning and map making. The main disadvantage here is that it is very hard to have unique gateways. Another technique of localisation is to match raw sensor data to an a priori map [7]. Usually the sensors used are distance sensors such as sonar, infrared, laser etc. The problem here is that the sensor data rarely comes in without noise but it can be used in highly restricted environments. It is used in certain industrial robots who operate in highly controlled environments but they fail to work in dynamic environments. This problem is overcome by generating small local maps and then integrating them with larger maps. The use of small local maps motivates the need of good map building [7].

More sophisticated systems either identify added artificial landmarks or natural landmarks. Landmarks can be defined as *a distinctive object or a place in the environment which help localisation*. In other words landmarks are distinct objects in the habituated environment. In a natural environment the landmarks would be chosen as those objects that have noticeable geometric properties.

In this paper we present a model that learns to form landmarks for helping the robot to navigate. In order to generate an internal representation, we use vision to identify landmarks. This paper focuses on a type of landmark localisation which depends on extracting novel features from the environment in order to localise itself. Landmarks can be defined as distinguishable input patterns. In other words each category of input activates different output neurons. In our approach we have developed Self Organising Maps which classify the input images for localisation.

2 Self Organising Maps Based on Place Codes for Localisation

Self Organising Maps (SOM) [6] networks learn to categorise input patterns and to associate them to different output neurons or a set of output neurons. Each neuron, j, is connected to the input through a synaptic weight vector $\mathbf{w}_j = [w_{j1}....w_{jm}]^T$. At each iteration, the SOM [6] finds a winning neuron $\mathbf{v}$ by minimising the following:

$$v(x) = arg\ min_j \|x(t) - w_j\|, \qquad j = 1, 2, ...n \qquad (1)$$

$\mathbf{x}$ belongs to an *m*-dimensional input space, $\|.\|$ is the Euclidean distance, while the update of the synaptic weight vector follows:

$$w_j(t+1) = w_j(t) + \alpha(t) h_{j,v(x)}(t) [x(t) - w_j(t)], \qquad j = 1, 2, ...n, \qquad (2)$$

This activation and classification are based on features extracted from the environment by the network. Feature detectors are neurons that respond to correlated combinations of their inputs. These are the neurons that give us symbolic representations of the world outside. In our experiments once we get symbolic representations of the features in the environment we use these to localise the robot in the environment.

The removal of redundancy by competition is thought to be a key aspect of how the visual system operates [11]. Competitive networks also reduce the dimensions of the input vector as a set of input patterns, in our case pixels of the input image vector. The representation of a location is done by activation of a neuron.

The sparsification performed by the competitive networks is very useful for preparing signals for presentation to pattern associators and auto associators, since this representation increases the number of patterns that can be associated or stored in such networks [11,13]. Although the algorithm is simple, its convergence and accuracy depend on the selection of the neighbourhood function, the topology of the output space, a scheme for decreasing the learning rate parameter, and the total number of neuronal units [5].

We are making use of a simple scenario for our symbolic representations of the world model. For this experiment the overall goal for the robot is to navigate between two desired locations. When it is navigating between those two locations, it should be able to localise itself. In the environment we provide a random colour coded rectangles on the wall, along with some distinguishable features like cubes and pyramids randomly kept in the environment like in the figure 1(b). During experimentation, the robot was able to make its own symbolic representation of the world model based on unsupervised learning.

Hippocampal pyramidal cells called place cells have been discovered that fire when an animal is at a certain location in its environment [9]. In our model, place cells can provide candidate locations to the path integrator and place cells could localise the robot in a familiar environment. Self-localisation in animals or humans often refers to the internal model of the world outside. As seen in a white water maze experiment [10] even though a rodent was not given any landmarks, it could still reach its goal by forming its own internal representation of landmarks of the world outside. It is seen in humans and animals that they can create their own landmarks, depending on the firing of place cells. These cells change their firing patters in an environment when prominent landmarks are removed from the environment. With this evidence from computational neuroscience it is reasonable to assume that place cells could prove to be an efficient way of localisation using vision.

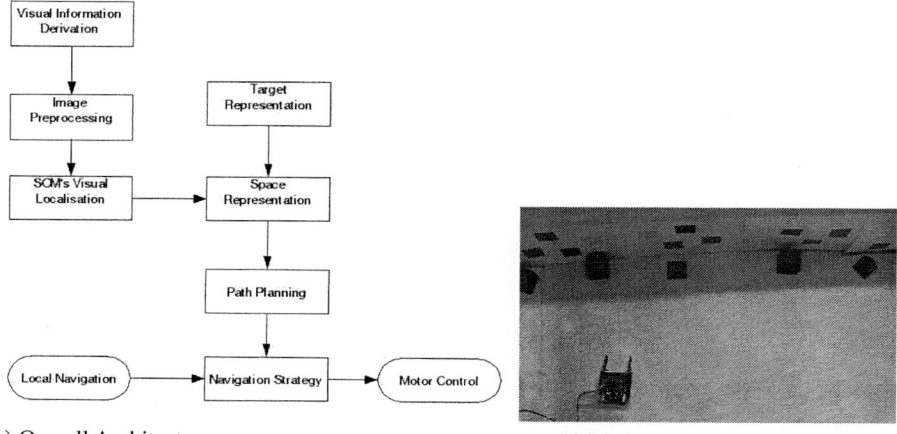

(a) Overall Architecture (b) Birds eye view of Scenario used

Fig. 1. (a) Architecture of Navigation strategy being developed. The focus of this paper is on visual landmark recognition. (b) This figure provides the birds eye view of the overall scenario which is being used for experiments. In this picture, we can see Khepera robot looking at the wall which have colour rectangles and pyramids and cubes kept adjacent to the wall.

2.1 Architecture

In figure 1 (a) visual information derivation is a module which is responsible for getting the images from the robot's camera. The image preprocessing module is responsible for normalising the images for the network. The SOM is responsible for the localisation of the robot in the environment. There are various ways in which the robot can be instructed as to where its target for navigation is. We are currently experimenting as to how to translate the place code output by the SOM's network into a spatial representation. Once we can map both the target representation and the current location of the robot into the same spacial representation, then we can have a simple path-planning module which directs the robot to its goal. The path planning module provides output to the motors. This forms the global navigation strategy. We have implemented the local navigation strategy using reactive behaviour. Both the global navigation strategy and the local navigation strategy meet each other in the navigation strategy module which is mostly responsible for choosing which navigation strategy to choose. Accordingly it chooses the output from either the global navigation strategy or local navigation strategy into motor control commands.

2.2 Visual Data Pre-processing

The images in original format were of 360 x 480 pixels. A total of 75 images were used for learning. Images were in 24 bit colour RGB format. In order to reduce the dimensionality of the images without losing valuable information, we first reduced the dimensions of the colours within the images. We chose blue of the the RGB cube as given in the equation 4, here N represents the whole picture.

$$N = (a_{ijk}) \in \mathbb{A}^{3mn}, \quad i = 1, 2, \ldots, m \quad j = 1, 2, \ldots, n \quad k = 1, 2, 3 \quad (3)$$
$$B = (b_{ij}) \in \mathbb{A}^{mn}, \quad i = 1, 2, \ldots, m \quad j = 1, 2, \ldots, n \quad b_{ij} := a_{ij3} \quad (4)$$

$\mathbb{A}$ is is the set of possible pixel values. The values are between 0 and 255, and can be represented as $\mathbb{A} = \{0, 1, 2, \ldots, 255\}$, $m = 17$, $n = 27$.

The images were reduced to a size of 17 x 27. An example of the reduced image with only one colour pane of the cube can be seen in figures 2 and 3. This image in turn was converted into a single vector to be presented to the network. It was done as explained from equations 5 to 7.

$$A = \begin{pmatrix} a_{11} & \cdots & a_{1n} \\ a_{21} & \cdots & a_{2n} \\ \vdots & \ddots & \vdots \\ a_{m1} & \cdots & a_{mn} \end{pmatrix} \quad A_i = (a_{i1}, \ldots, a_{in}) \quad i = 1, 2, \ldots, m \quad (5)$$

$$V = (v_l) := (A_1, \ldots, A_m) \in \mathbb{A}^{mn} \quad l = 1, 2, \ldots, mn \quad (6)$$

Equation 6 is a concatenation of A_i of A. In other words,

$$v_{(i-1)n+j} := a_{ij} \quad i = 1, 2, \ldots, m \quad j = 1, 2, \ldots, n \quad (7)$$

2.3 Self Organisation of Landmarks

The SOM learns to classify patterns. The network receives an input image of size 17 x 27 and the output is the activation of a cell to indicate the place where the robot is. The aim of the experiment was to study whether the robot can develop an internal representation of the world model at a symbolic level. It was studied by providing the robot with an environment where it can create its own internal representations, rather than giving explicit landmarks to the robot.

Each activation in the output layer of the SOM represents place codes. The results, which are given in figure 2 and 3 show how the SOM has classified different landmarks in different sections of the map, with neighbouring images having the same landmark; there are clusters of sections which are formed. Each cluster on the maps represents a place code, related to its landmark. Each neuron activation gives us a representation in x, y and z co-ordinates of the environment, where x represents the vertical coordinate of the environment, y represents the horizontal coordinate and z represents the head direction of the robot. These three inputs do not participate in the input of the neural network of the SOM's. They are purely deduced by the output of the SOM.

Cluster Formation. The basic property of a SOM network is to form clusters of information relating to each other, in our case landmarks. In the next step we take advantage of these clusters to know which local area the robot is in and to give directions to the robot.

A cluster is a collection of neurons which are next to each other representing the same landmark. Figure 2 shows that when the robot was approaching the desired landmark, there were activations in the neighbouring neurons. This is due to clustering of similar images around the landmark. There are multiple similar images that are being represented by a single neuron, making the cluster a bit smaller and richer in information. On the other hand figure 3 shows the landmarks which were at a distance to the location represented in figure 2. Two landmarks that were given to the robot at a distance would be mapped not only in different clusters but also distant from each other.

By their very definition, landmarks are features in the environment. This was the reason behind a formation of these clusters by SOM's. The landmarks that were chosen by the SOM were quite significant in the image and distinguished features from the rest of the environment and other landmarks.

(a) Input Image   (b) Input Image   (c) Neuron Activation   (d) Input Image   (e) Neuron Activation

Fig. 2. Here image (a) and image (b) have the same neuron activation as seen in (c). These two images were taken at a close distance overlooking the same landmark. Image (d) has a different activation in the neighbourhood as seen in (e), because the images and location were not very different from (a) and (b).

(a) Input Image   (b) Activation

Fig. 3. The input image represented in figure (a) is different from those images in figure 2 and as we can see the activations are also at a distance to each other i.e. the cluster of this image is at a significant distance compared to the cluster of the images represented in figure 2.

Noise handling by the Network. A natural environment is full of noise. For a robust model of navigation the robot must still be able to navigate. At the present stage there are unknown clusters formed when the landmarks are modified or removed from the environment. This is similar to how place cells behave [9,1]. These clusters are also formed if there is noise added to the environment i.e. by adding or replacing objects in the environment.

In figure 4 the first half of the input image was cleared and black colour was presented in the image as seen in the figure. Even with 50% covered the landmark is still visible to the network. This behaviour was also observed with other landmarks and clusters. The network is able to do pattern completion and is trained to have its focus on a particular significant landmark in the environment. We have seen that the network starts to become uncertain once the noise level reaches around 50%.

(a) Image with 50% noise (b) Activation (c) Image with 80% noise (d) Activation

Fig. 4. In image (a) we see that even if there is high amount of noise the activation as seen in (b) is in the neighbourhood of the original activation as seen in figure 2 whereas there is a random, but specific activation with images with 80% of noise added to them

The aim of the experiment was to explore the place code to localise the robot in the area. Therefore it is less important which neuron in the cluster is active, but the neuron in the cluster relating to place code is important for localisation. Therefore our measurement of robustness for a particular place code falls into two categories either right or wrong. In figure 5 we examine the network's response to the noise for a particular place code. We have shown the effectiveness of the networks averaged over all the place codes in the network shown in figure 5.

We have use the same place code as shown in the images in figure 2. In figure 5 we can clearly see that the correct individual neuron is activated even with 40% noise which demonstrates effective noise handling by the network. At the cluster level we can see that the noise handling by the network is even better as it can handle noise upto 60%. Noise resistance could be improved if the responses were averaged over several images.

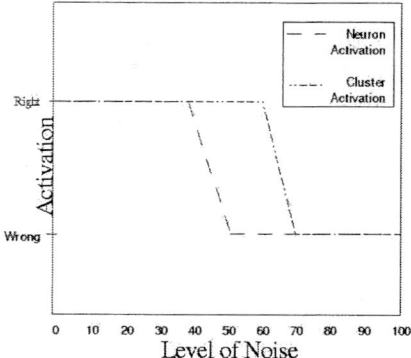

Fig. 5. Here the correctness of the activation of a location shown in figure 2. The x-axis represents the 10% of noise introduced and the y-axis represents the whether the activation was correct or not. The correctness of activations were examined at two levels the first being correctness of a neuron being active and the second being the correctness of a neuron in the right cluster being active.

Unknown clusters caused by high volumes of noise, would not matter a lot in navigation as long as most of the landmarks in the environment are not removed. The property of place cells shows us that an animal or a human can navigate even if there are significant landmarks missing from the environment, since the place cells continue to fire. It is only when a series of landmarks are not found that the animal or a human would get lost, which is similar to the behaviour of our model.

3 Conclusion

In this paper we have described a place cell model based on a SOM for navigation. The model was successful in learning the locations of the landmarks even when tested with distorted images. Visual landmarks were associated with the locations in a controlled environment. This model clusters of neighbouring landmarks next to each other. The landmarks that are away from each other are also relatively away from each in the map. Rather than preprogramming localisation algorithms as internal modules, our SOM's architecture demonstrates that localisation can be learnt in a robust model based on external hints from the environment. The noise handling of the network is also very efficient. This model was developed to learn landmarks in an environment, by having maps divided into cluster of neurons for different parts of the environment. This model is successful in localising the robot in an environment.

Acknowledgements. This research is partially sponsored by a FET-IST grant for MirrorBot project, by the EU to Prof. Wermter, under grant IST-2001-35282. We are grateful to Christo Panchev, Wolfgang Schmidle and Garen Arevian for their support on the paper.

References

1. Angelo Arleo. *Spatial Learning and Navigation in Neuro-Mimetic Systems, Modeling the Rat Hippocampus.* PhD thesis, Swiss Federal Institute of Technology, Lausanne, EPFL, Switzerland, 2000. http://diwww.epfl.ch/mantra/team/arleo/.
2. Angelo Arleo and Wulfram Gerstner. Spatial cognition and neuro-mimetic navigation: A model of hippocampal place cell activity. *Biological Cybernetics, Special Issue on Navigation in Biological and Artificial Systems,* 83:287–299, 2000.
3. Peter Bonasso and Robin Murphy, editors. *Artificial Intelligence and Mobile Robotics: Case Studies of Successful Robot Systems.* The MIT Press / AAAI Press, London, 1998.
4. W. Burgard, A.B. Cremers, D. Fox, D. Hähnel, G. Lakemeyer, D. Schulz, W. Steiner, and S. Thrun. Experiences with an interactive museum tour-guide robot. *Artificial Intelligence,* 114(1-2):3–55, 1999.
5. Michel Haritoppulos, Hujun Yin, and Nigel M. Allinson. Image denoising using self-organising map-based non-linear independent component analysis. *Neural Networks: Special Issue, New Developments in Self Organising Maps,* 15(8-9):1085–1098, October – November 2002.
6. T. Kohonen. *Self-organizing Maps.* Springer Series in Information Sciences. Springer-Verlag, Berlin, Germany, 3rd ed edition, 2001.
7. Robin R. Murphy. *Introduction to AI Robotics.* The MIT Press, London, England, 2000.
8. Ulrich Nehmzow. *Mobile Robotics: A Practical Introduction.* Springer Verlag, London, 2000.
9. A. D. Redish and D. S. Touretzky. Navigating with landmarks: computing goal locations from place codes. 1997.
10. A. David Redish. *Beyond Cognitive Map from Place Cells to Episodic Memory.* The MIT Press, London, 1999.
11. Edmund Rolls and Gustavo Deco. *Computational Neuroscience of Vision.* Oxford University Press, New York, 2002.
12. S. Thrun, M. Beetz, M. Bennewitz, W. Burgard, A.B. Cremers, F. Dellaert, D. Fox, D. Hähnel, C. Rosenberg, N. Roy, J. Schulte, and D. Schulz. Probabilistic algorithms and the interactive museum tour-guide robot minerva. *International Journal of Robotics Research,* 19(11):972–999, 2000.
13. Stefan Wermter, Jim Austin, and David Willshaw, editors. *Emergent Neural Computational Architectures Based on Neuroscience.* Springer, Berlin, 2001

Signal Processing

Spatial Independent Component Analysis of Multitask-Related Activation in fMRI Data

Zhi-ying Long[1], Li Yao[1], Xiao-jie Zhao[1], Liu-qing Pei[1], Gui Xue[2], Qi Dong[2], and Dan-ling Peng[2]

[1] Department of Electronics, Beijing Normal University, Beijing, P.R.China, 100088
[2] Department of Psychology, Beijing Normal University, Beijing, P.R.China, 100088
{yaoli@bnu.edu.cn}

Abstract. Independent component analysis (ICA) is a technique to separate the mixed signal into independent components without priori assumptions about the hemodynamic response to the task. Spatial ICA (SICA) is applied widely in fMRI data because the spatial dimension of fMRI data is larger than their temporal dimension. The general linear model (GLM) is based on a priori knowledge about stimulation paradigm. In our study, a two-task cognitive experiment was designed, and SICA and GLM were applied to analyze these fMRI data. Both methods could easily find some common areas activated by two tasks. However, SICA could also find more accurate areas activated by different single task in specific brain areas than GLM. The results demonstrate that ICA methodology can supply us more information or the intrinsic structure of the data especially when multitask-related components are presented in the data.

Keywords. Independent component analysis; general linear model; multitask-related activation; functional magnetic resonance imaging; data-driven method; hypothesis-driven method.

1 Introduction

Functional magnetic resonance imaging (fMRI) based on blood oxygen level-dependent (BLOD) contrast has become a powerful noninvasive tool providing spatial and temporal information about human brain functions during a wide range of cognitive task (Ogawa et al., 1992) [14]. Because fMRI data are complex mixtures of signals resulting from task-related brain hemodynamic changes as well as from respiration, motion, machine artifacts, and other processes, it is a challenge to effectively separate the task-related changes from the entire fMRI signal. Current analysis techniques of fMRI data based on BOLD can be categorized mainly into two approaches, hypothesis-driven and data-driven methods.

Hypothesis-driven methods, like the General Linear Model (GLM) (Friston, 1996) [7], attempt to fit data to hypotheses specified by the examiner. Typically, the famous software package, SPM99-statistical parametrical mapping (Wellcome Department of

Cognitive Neurology, London, UK, http://www.fil.ion.ucl.ac.uk/spm/), is based on the GLM and has so far dominated the analysis of fMRI data. In the GLM, see equation (1), $\mathbf{Y}$ is an $i \times j$ data matrix with i being the number of time points in the experiment and j being the total number of voxels in all slices. $\mathbf{X}$ is an $i \times k$ "design matrix" containing the time courses of all k factors hypothesized to modulate the BOLD signal. β is a $k \times j$ matrix of k spatial patterns to be estimated. And ε is a matrix of noise or residual errors typically assumed to be independent, zero-mean, and Gaussian distributed.

$$\mathbf{Y} = \mathbf{X}\beta + \varepsilon \tag{1}$$

Here, $\mathbf{X}$ is a given matrix (model), parameters in β can be got by a least-squares estimate.

Data-driven methods, like independent component analysis (ICA), do not rely on priori assumptions of the time courses of activation, but rather attempt to determine the intrinsic structure of the data. ICA was originally developed to solve problems similar to the "cocktail party" problem in which many people are speaking at the same time (Bell and Sejnowski, 1995) [2]. Later ICA was also applied to the analysis of electroencephalograph (EEG) data (Makeig et al., 1997) [10]. In both situations, the independent components in time can usually be separated from mixed signals, and the process is called temporal ICA (TICA). However, because the spatial dimension is much larger than the temporal dimension in fMRI data, spatial ICA (SICA), which can decompose mixed signals into the independent components in space, was applied to fMRI data firstly (McKeown et al., 1998) [11]. ICA can also be expressed by equation (1), but the variables of two ICA models have different meanings. When SICA is concerned, $\mathbf{X}$ is an $i \times k$ matrix containing the time courses of all k independent components and unknown, β is a $k \times j$ matrix, spatial map of all k independent components.

In ICA algorithm, there are some hypotheses: (1) independent components are high-order statistically independent, (2) the mixed signal is combined linearly by independent components, (3) the distribution of independent components is non-Gaussian, sub-Gaussian or super-Gaussian.

Since ICA was firstly applied to fMRI data, some researchers have done a lot of work on it, such as, a direct comparison of SICA and TICA (Calhoun, et al., 2001)[4], a hybrid ICA(Mckeown et al., 2000) [13], a finger-typing task examined with ICA(Chad, et al., 2000)[5] and so on. In fact, ICA has more advantages in cognitive paradigm for which the detailed models of brain activity are not clear. For many hypothesis-driven methods in fMRI, the hemodynamic response model should be accurately estimated. But such response waveforms may vary in different brain areas and even in different tasks. It really brings some difficulties to hypothesis-driven methods. However, data-driven method ICA is less sensitive to the hemodynamic response model. It is easy to detect the activation in single task experiment by ICA algorithm or GLM and the results are almost same. Now Multitask cognitive experiment design is becoming more and more popular, because researchers are more concerned with the difference between tasks. In our study, a two-task cognitive experiment was designed, and SICA was applied to analyze the fMRI data. Compared with the hypothesis-driven method, ICA algorithm could not only separate the component that was highly correlated with two-task related activation but also get the components that was highly correlated with each single task related activation in a specific brain area. So we can obtain more information and know well the intrinsic structure of fMRI data by ICA, although these information still need to be explained more deeply.

2 Experiment and Methods

2.1 Cognitive Task

Material and behavioral performance: 40 pairs of Chinese characters or English words were arranged into 4 blocks. Half of them were semantic related and half were not. The duration for experiment block and baseline block is 30s and 21s respectively. During experimental condition, subjects were asked to judge whether the paired words were semantic related or not. Each pair of stimulus was presented for 2500ms, followed by a blank for 500ms. For the control condition, fixation cross was presented in the same manner as experimental condition. Time course of the English and Chinese word pair was BAABABBA, where A was the English task and B was the Chinese task.

2.2 Data Acquisition

The fMRI data was acquired in a 2.0 T GE/Elscint Prestige whole-body MRI scanner (GE/ Elscint Ltd., Haifa, Israel). Gradient-echo echo-planar imaging was acquired consisting of 20 axial slices(TR=3000 ms, TE=60ms, field of view 375×210mm, matrix size 128×72, 6 mm thickness, no gap, 136 repetitions per time series). A T1-weighted anatomic scan(TR=25ms, TE=6ms, field of view=220×220mm, matrix size 220×220, slice thickness=2mm, no gap) consisting of 80 slices was acquired.

2.3 Data Preprocessing

The data were preprocessed by SPM99. First using the software, the functional images were realigned and a mean image was created, and the anatomic image was co-registered to the functional mean image. Then the data were spatially normalized into a standard space and resliced to 3×3×4mm voxels. Last the data were spatially smoothed with a 9×9×12 full-width at half maximum(FWHM) Gaussian kernel to improve the spatial signal noise ratio(SNR).

2.4 SPM Analysis

An experimental model was designed. The ideal signals were convolved with a canonical hemodynamic response function. The type of response was box-car response. The data were regressed onto the GLM to estimate the parameters that minimized the error square sum. By creating different contrasts, we got three kinds of activations. The first was the overlap activation of two tasks. The second was activated mainly by Chinese task. And the third was activated mainly by English task. One point that should be emphasized is that in the second and third case, the activation included both the overlap and the areas that were more strongly acted by one task than the other.

2.5 ICA Process

Some ICA algorithms have been used so far for SICA of fMRI time-series. In this paper, the fixed-point was applied to our fMRI data (Hyvärinen, 1999)[8].

In fMRI experiment, each of the psychomotor task and artifacts, such as stimulation, subtle head movements, physiological pulsation and so on, may be represented by one or more spatially independent components. Consistently task-related (CTR) components are the most related with the reference function, and transiently task-related (TTR) components appear to be time-locked to the task-block design during part of the trial (McKeown 1998)[11]. Here a reference function is created by convolving the block design of the experiment with a fixed model of the hemodynamic reference function.

After preprocessed and temporal smoothed, the data were simultaneously whitened and reduced in dimension to 60 components (~99.99% of information was retained) by principle components analysis (PCA). All voxels inside the brain were extracted and SICA were performed. The time courses of two-task related components were easily found (See Fig. 1). Applying SICA to some specific brain areas, we got single-task related components and their activated voxels (See Fig. 3 and Fig. 4). To display voxels contributing significantly to a particular component map, the map values were scaled to z-scores, and voxels whose absolute z-scores were greater than some threshold ($|z|>2.5$) could be considered as the activated voxels for that component.

In temporal smoothing, we adopted five-point temporal moving-average to raise the SNR. It was found the CTR component was most highly correlated with the reference function when compared with three or seven-point temporal smooth.

3 Experiment Results

3.1 Detection of Two-Task Related Activation

The results are shown in Fig. 1. When ICA algorithm was used on the whole brain, it was easy to detect the two-task related components, which included CTR and TTR components.

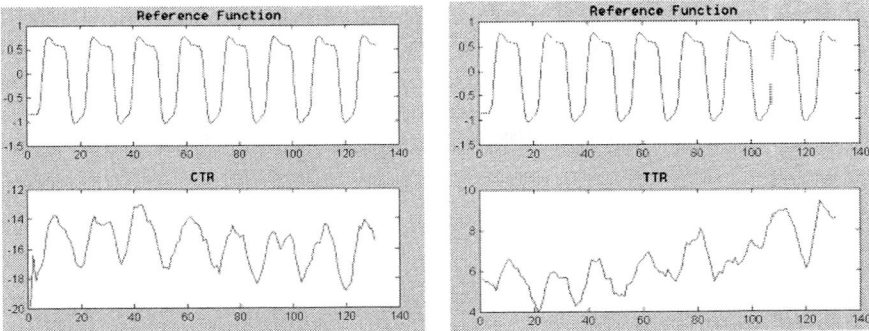

Fig. 1. The left wave is the time course of CTR component. The right one is the TTR component.

The activated areas by two-task related component with two different methods are shown in Fig. 2, from which we can see that two different methods get similar results and both CTR and TTR components contribute to the two-task activation commonly. And ICA results show more activated areas in the right hemisphere than SPM.

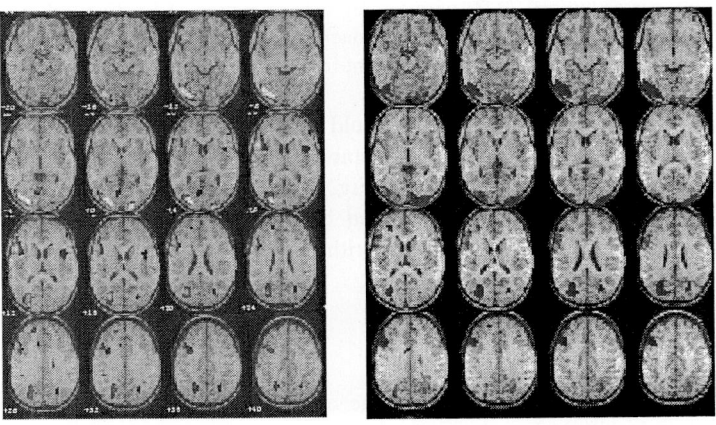

Fig. 2. The overlap areas activated by two tasks from slice 9 to slice 24. The left is the SPM results. The ICA results are shown in the right, in which the red areas are the spatial maps of the CTR components and the blue corresponds to the TTR components.

3.2 Detection of Single Task Activation

The areas, which were dominantly activated by Chinese task, could be easily found by SPM. But some of those areas may also be activated by English task. And it is difficult to detect the activation only by Chinese or by English. We used ICA to decompose the data of those areas into several ICA components, among them single task-related components were found (See Fig.3).

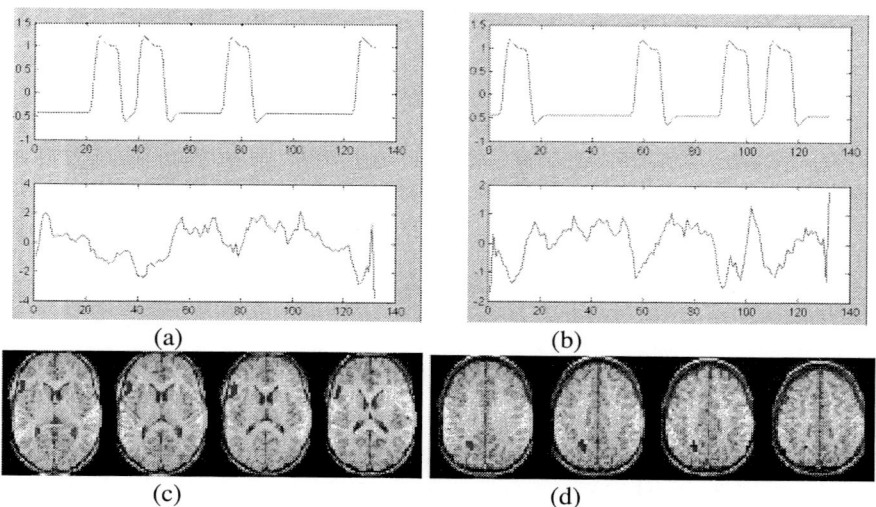

Fig. 3. Results of component time course and its spatial mapping. (a) The ICA component that was highly correlated(r=0.6319) with the reference function of Chinese task. (b) The component that was highly correlated(r=0.7223) with the reference function of English task. (c) Activated voxels (|z|>2.5) of Chinese task-related component from slice 15 to slice 18. (d) Activated voxels(|z|>2.5) of English task-related component from slice 22 to slice 25.

In the same way mentioned above, we could also perform ICA on the areas mainly activated by English task. The spatial mapping of the single task-related components and associated time courses are shown in Fig. 4. Compared with Fig. 3, we can see in the specific areas such as mainly activated by Chinese or English task, the voxels activated only by single task with ICA algorithm are almost same.

4 Discussion

It is obvious that we can easily detect the activation in single task experiment by means of ICA algorithm. For the multitask, the case will become more complex because it is difficult to know the relationship between tasks, especially often in cognitive experiments. Three cases usually appear. 1) All the tasks act on some common areas without significant difference. 2) One task activates some areas more strongly than the others. 3) Some areas are activated by only one task, without the interference of the others. Usually one or more cases may exist in a multitask experiment. We can find the multitask-related independent component in case 1 and single task-related in case 3 by ICA algorithm. In our experiment, when analyzing the whole brain with ICA, it is easy to get the two-task related components, which demonstrates that the two tasks must activate some common areas without significant difference (See Fig 2).

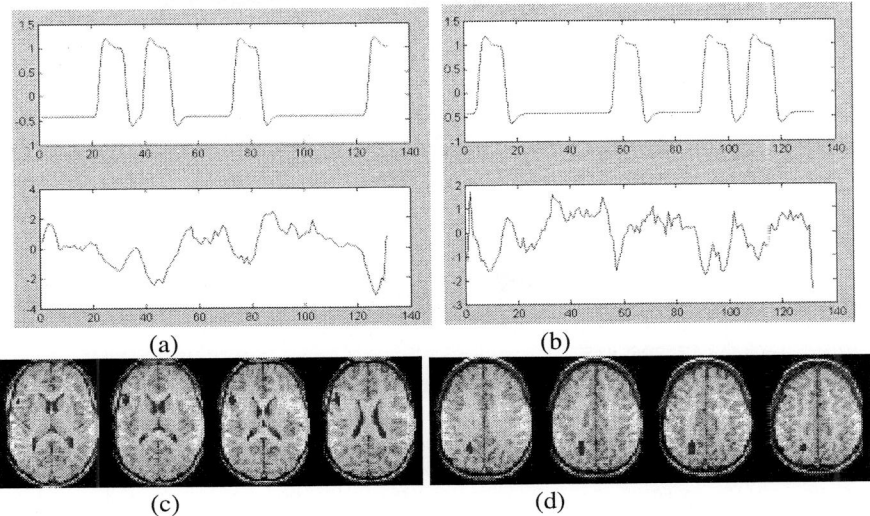

Fig. 4. Results of component time course and its spatial mapping. (a) The ICA component that was highly correlated(r=0.7273) with the reference function of Chinese task. (b) The component that was highly correlated(r=0.6712) with the reference function of English task. (c) Activated voxels (|z|>2.5) of Chinese task-related component from slice 16 to slice 19. (d) Activated voxels(|z|>2.5) of English task-related component from slice 22 to slice 25.

Some differences exist in ICA and SPM. Firstly in SPM, in order to test whether the parameters estimated are best fit for the model, a T-statistic or F-statistic for each voxel is formed. During the T or F test, not the state but the difference between two different states is compared, such as the dynamic and static state or the dynamic states of two different tasks. So ICA can get more accurate activation of single task than SPM in multitask experiment (See Fig. 3 and Fig. 4). Secondly for SPM, only spatial activation is got without any temporal information, while we can acquire both temporal and spatial information in ICA. Therefore we can see that the overlap areas consist of the activation of CTR and TTR components and their corresponding time courses are also known (See Fig. 2 and Fig. 1). Thirdly in ICA algorithm, all independent components must contain some information of data and some of them may be interesting to us while others may not. But sometimes we may also find some unexpected new component with corresponding spatial mapping and it is almost impossible for SPM to do so. In our experiment, the activation mainly by one task was estimated by SPM, but it could also be affected by the other tasks. In order to look for the activation only by any single task, we selected some interesting areas to analyze, which is discussed in 3.2. And we found after reducing the range, the single task-related components appeared and their spatial mappings could also be determined (Fig. 3 and Fig. 4), which were very hard for SPM to detect such accurate areas. Comparing with two-task activation, we could see that the single task activation was too small to find them on the whole brain because they might be submerged by some other noises. Since the ICA model in equation (1) is noiseless, large noise may destroy decomposition of useful components. So when we focused on some special areas, the SNR in these specific areas was higher than in the whole brain and single task-related components appeared.

Therefore it is necessary to temporal smooth the raw data in order to raise the SNR. And how to improve the ICA model's anti-noise ability is also worth studying further.

References

1. Andersen A.H., Gash D.M., Malcolm J.A. (1998) Principal component analysis of the dynamic response measured by fMRI: a generalized linear systems framework. Magn Reson Imaging 17: 795–815.
2. Bell A.J., Sejnowski T.J. (1995) An information-maximization approach to blind separation and blind deconvolution. Neural Computation 7:1129–1159.
3. Biswal B.B, Ulmer J.L. (1999) Blind source separation of multiple signal sources of fMRI data sets using independent component analysis. J. Comput. Assist. Tomogr 23: 265–271,
4. Calhoun V. D., Adali T., Pearlson G.D., and Pekar J.J. (2001) Spatial and temporal independent component analysis of functional MRI data containing a pair of task-related waveforms. Hum. Brain Mapp 13: 43–53.
5. Chad H. M., Victor M. H., Dietmar C., Michelle Q., and M. E. M. (2000) Whole-brain functional MR imaging activation from a finger-typing task examined with independent component analysis. AJNR Am J Neuroradiol 21: 1629–1635.
6. Esposito F., Formisano E., Seifritz E., Goebel R., Morrone R., Tedeschi G.,and Francesco D.S. (2002) Spatial independent component analysis of functional MRI time-series: to what extent do results depend on the algorithm used? Hum. Brain Mapp. 16: 146–157.
7. Friston, K. J. (1996) Statistical parametric mapping and other analyses of functional imaging data. Brain Mapping: The Methods (Toga A.W. and Mazziotta J.C., Eds.) [C]. San Diego: Academic Press, 363–396.
8. Hyvärinen A. (1999) Fast and robust fixed-point algorithms for independent component analysis. IEEE Trans Neural Networks 10: 626–634.
9. Hong Gu, Wolfgang Engelien, Hanhua Feng, David A. Silbersweig, Emily Stern, Yihong Yang. (2001) Mapping transient, randomly occurring neuropsychological events using independent component analysis. NeuroImage 14: 1432–1433.
10. Makeig S., Jung T.P., Bell A.J., Ghahremani D., Sejnowski T.J. (1997) Blind separation of auditory event-related brain responses into independent components. Proc. Natl. Acad. Sci. USA 94: 10979–10984.
11. Mckeown M. J., Makeig S., Brown G.G., Jung T.-P., Kindermann S. S., Bell A. J., and Sejnowski T. J. (1998a) Analysis of fMRI data by separation into independent spatial components. Hum. Brain Mapp. 6: 160–188.
12. Mckewon M. J., Jung T.-P., Makeig S., Brown G., Kindermann S. S., Lee, T.-W., and Sejnowski T. J. (1998b) Spatially independent activity patterns in functional MRI data during the stroop color-naming task. Proc. Natl. Acad. Sci. USA 95: 803–810.
13. Meckeown M. J. (2000) Detection of consistently task-related activations in fMRI data with hybrid independent component analysis. NeuroImage 11: 24–35.
14. Ogawa S., Tank D.W., Menon R., Ellermann J.M., Kim S.G., Merkle H., and Ugurbil K.(1992) Intrinsic signal changes accompanying sensory stimulation: Functional brain mapping with magnetic resonance imaging. Proc. Natl. Acad. Sci. USA 89: 5951–5955.

Closed Loop Stability of FIR-Recurrent Neural Networks

Alex Aussem

LIMOS (UMR CNRS 6158), University Blaise Pascal, Clermont-Ferrand II,
63173 AUBIERE Cedex FRANCE
alex@isima.fr, http://www.isima.fr/aussem

Abstract. In this paper, the problems of stability of a general class of discrete-time delayed recurrent neural networks are re-investigated in light of some recent results. These networks are obtained by modeling synapses as Finite Impulse Response (FIR) filters instead of multiplicative scalars. We first derive a sufficient conditions for the network operating in closed-loop to converge to a fixed point using Lyapunov functional method; the symmetry of the connection matrix is not assumed. We then show how these conditions relate to other conditions ensuring both the existence of the error gradient other arbitrary long trajectories and the asymptotic stability of the fixed points at each time step.

1 Introduction

Recently, a number of new theoretical results on the qualitative analysis of the behavior of some continuous specific delayed-based neurodynamics described by differential equations with delays have attracted much interest (see [5], [6] and references therein). In this paper, we draw from their work to derive some new sufficient conditions for the global asymptotic stability of a general class of so-called (discrete) FIR-recurrent neural networks operating in closed-loop by using Lyapunov functional method and some analysis techniques, which are independent of delays and connectivity. In this discrete delayed-based fixed point recurrent architecture, the classic synaptic scalar multiplication is replaced by a convolution product [2], [11]. Interestingly, we will see that these conditions also enforce, at each iteration, the global asymptotic stability of the unique equilibrium solution, as well as the convergence of the gradient-based procedure as the trajectory length goes to infinity.

2 A Fixed Point FIR-Recurrent Model

For purpose of generality, we consider a fairly broad class of fixed points discrete-time delayed fully recurrent architectures obtained by modeling the recurrent synapses as FIR filters [2], [11], given a coupled set of discrete equations in the form

$$v_k(j) = g(s_k(j)),$$
$$s_k(j) = \sum_{d=0}^{D}\sum_{i=1}^{N} w_{ij}^d v_{k-d}(i), \qquad (1)$$

where N is the number of units, $v_k(j)$ is the activity if the the j-th unit at iteration k, w_{ij}^d is the weight connecting neurons i to j with delay d. D is the order of the FIR filter, in other word D is the maximum synaptic delay. For notational convenience, we won't distinguish between input, hidden, output and bias units in (1); as it stands, the system (1) operates in closed loop fashion. We make the mild assumption that the nonlinear activation function, $g()$ is a nondecreasing continuously differentiable which takes a global maximum $\mu = \max_x(g'(x))$. Consequently, $g()$ is uniformly Lipschitz, i.e. there exists a constant $\mu > 0$ such that $|g(x) - g(y)| \le \mu|x - y|$, for any x,y $\in \mathbb{R}$. Sigmoïd functions are typically included in this formulation.

The resulting FIR-recurrent structure encompasses a large variety of synaptic delay-based forward, locally and globally recurrent neural architecture proposals that have emerged in the literature (see for instance the taxonomy in [8]). It is important to stress that cycles of delay zero are *allowed* in the architecture; therefore fixed point recurrent networks of the type discussed by Almeida [1] and Pineda [10] are also included in this framework, resulting in that the system is not guaranteed to settle down, at each iteration k, to an equilibrium solution. This point will be discussed later. For simplicity, we assume first that an equilibrium points exists at each iteration.

3 Closed Loop Stability

In many applications, long-term iterated prediction (or data synthesis) is usually achieved by feeding the output estimate back to form a closed loop system, once the network is trained. The system is then iterated forward in time to achieve predictions as far into the future as desired according to (1). Although the method is not optimal in the nonlinear case, the iterated predictions usually show better performance than direct prediction [11]. Nonetheless, the iterated dynamics of nonlinear systems can be quite complex, e.g., isolated fixed points, limit cycles, chaos. In this paper, attention is focused on the problem of deriving conditions for the closed loop iterated system to ultimately converge to a fixed point. For the system operating in closed loop to ultimately settle down to a steady state for *any* choice of initial conditions, it should be *globally asymptotically stable* (Khalil, 1996),

Definition 1. *The equilibrium point* $\mathbf{v}^\star$ *of the system (1) operating in closed loop is globally asymptotically stable if* $\lim_{k\to\infty} \mathbf{v}_k = \mathbf{v}^\star$ *for any initial activation vector* $\mathbf{v}_0$.

Networks for which a Lyapunov function can be exhibited, such as the Hopfield model or pure feedforward networks, are guaranteed to be globally asymptotically stable. Unfortunately, little is known when the symmetry of the connection matrix is not assumed anymore.

Assume the existence of $s^\star(j) = g^{-1}(v_k^\star(j)), \forall j$, an equilibrium point of (1). Let $\mathbf{s}^\star$ be the corresponding vector and let $\boldsymbol{\alpha}_k = \mathbf{s}_k - \mathbf{s}_k^\star$. We have

$$\alpha_k(j) = \sum_{d=0}^{D} \sum_{i=1}^{N} w_{ij}^d \left(g(s_{k-d}^\star(i) + \alpha_{k-d}(i)) - g(s_{k-d}^\star(i)) \right). \tag{2}$$

Obviously, $(0, 0, \ldots, 0)^T$ is an equilibrium point of (2). Remind that $\mu = \max_x(g'(x))$ under the mild assumption that the nonlinear activation function, $g()$, is $\mathcal{C}^1$ with bounded derivatives. We may now state the fundamental result of this paper:

Theorem 1. *The closed loop system (1) admits a globally asymptotically stable equilibrium point if the following inequalities are satisfied*

$$\mu \sum_{d=0}^{D} \sum_{i=1}^{N} |w_{ij}^d| < 1, \quad \forall j = 1, \ldots, N. \tag{3}$$

Proof. The existence of a fixed point of the map (2) can be shown by the well known Brouwer's fixed point theorem. The uniqueness of the fixed point will follow from the global asymptotic stability to be established below. The map is continuous on a bounded closed and convex set. $g()$ is a one-to-one mapping; $\mathbf{s}^\star$ is given by $g^{-1}(v_k^\star(j))$. To prove the global asymptotic stability of $\mathbf{s}^\star$ in (1), it is sufficient to prove the global asymptotic stability of the trivial solution of (2). So, we consider the Lyapunov function defined at time $k \geq D$ by

$$V(\boldsymbol{\alpha}_k^D) = \sum_{j=1}^{N} \sum_{d=0}^{D} |\alpha_{k-d}(j)| + \mu \sum_{i=1}^{N} \sum_{j=1}^{N} \sum_{d=0}^{D} \sum_{n=k-d+1}^{k} |w_{ij}^d| |\alpha_n(j)|. \tag{4}$$

where the vector $\boldsymbol{\alpha}_k^D$ of size $(D+1)N$ is the vector $\boldsymbol{\alpha}_{k-D}, \boldsymbol{\alpha}_{k-D+1}, \ldots, \boldsymbol{\alpha}_k$. The system (1) is iterated in a *sequential asynchronous* and we assume without loss of generality that all neurons are updated in sequential order starting from 1 to N. By definition of μ, $g(s+\alpha) - g(s) \leq \mu\alpha$ for all s, α. Let

$$\Delta V_k := V(\boldsymbol{\alpha}_{k+1}^D) - V(\boldsymbol{\alpha}_k^D) \tag{5}$$

Calculating the difference ΔV_k along the solution of Eq. (2), we get

$$\Delta V_k = \sum_{j=1}^{N}(|\alpha_{k+1}(j)| - |\alpha_{k-D}(j)|)$$
$$+ \mu \sum_{i=1}^{N}\sum_{j=1}^{N}\sum_{d=0}^{D}\sum_{n=k-d+1}^{k} |w_{ij}^d|(|\alpha_{n+1}(j)| - |\alpha_n(j)|),$$
$$\leq \sum_{d=0}^{D}\sum_{i=1}^{N}\sum_{j=1}^{N} |w_{ij}^d| |g(s_{k+1-d}^\star(i) + \alpha_{k+1-d}(i)) - g(s_{k+1-d}^\star(i))|$$
$$- \sum_{j=1}^{N} |\alpha_{k-D}(j)| + \mu \sum_{i=1}^{N}\sum_{j=1}^{N}\sum_{d=0}^{D} |w_{ij}^d|(|\alpha_{k+1}(j)| - |\alpha_{k+1-d}(j)|),$$
$$\leq \mu \sum_{d=0}^{D}\sum_{i=1}^{N}\sum_{j=1}^{N} |w_{ij}^d||\alpha_{k+1}(i)| - \sum_{j=1}^{N} |\alpha_{k-D}(j)|. \tag{6}$$

For all integer, K,
$$\sum_{k=D}^{K+D-1} \Delta V_k = V(\boldsymbol{\alpha}_{K+D}^D) - V(\boldsymbol{\alpha}_D^D)$$
$$\leq -\sum_{k=1}^{K}\sum_{j=1}^{N}\left[1 - \mu \sum_{d=0}^{D}\sum_{i=1}^{N} |w_{ij}^d|\right] |\alpha_{k+D}(j)|,$$
$$+ \mu \sum_{k=1}^{D+1}\sum_{d=0}^{D}\sum_{i=1}^{N}\sum_{j=1}^{N} |w_{ij}^d||\alpha_{k+K}(i)|$$
$$- \sum_{k=0}^{D}\sum_{j=1}^{N} |\alpha_k(j)|. \tag{7}$$

It follows from (2) that for all k, $|\alpha_k(j)| < 2\mu \sum_{d=0}^{D}\sum_{i=1}^{N} |w_{ij}^d| < 2$. Let
$$r := \min_{1 \leq j \leq N}\left[1 - \mu \sum_{i=1}^{N}\sum_{d=0}^{D} |w_{ij}^d|\right] > 0. \tag{8}$$

It follows from (7) that
$$\lim_{K \to \infty}\left\{V(\boldsymbol{\alpha}_{K+D}^D) + r\sum_{k=1}^{K}\sum_{j=1}^{N} |\alpha_{k+D}(j)|\right\} < \infty. \tag{9}$$

Therefore
$$\sum_{k=D}^{\infty}\sum_{j=1}^{N} |\alpha_k(j)| < \infty. \tag{10}$$

It follows that

$$\lim_{k\to\infty}\sum_{j=1}^{N}|\alpha_k(j)| = 0. \tag{11}$$

Thus, $\lim_{k\to\infty}\|\alpha_k\| = 0$. The zero solution of (2) is a globally asymptotically stable for any delays, thus the equilibrium point $\mathbf{v}^\star$ of (1) is also globally asymptotically stable. This completes the proof.

□

The idea of the demonstration is inspired by the paper by Cao and Zhou [5] and the paper by Feng and Palmondon [6]. This result can be view as a generalization of the formula given by Mandic and Chambers for the recurrent NARMA Perceptron (page 129, [9]).

4 Discussion

In the previous analysis, we did not assume the symmetry of the connection matrix and it may easily be seen from the demonstration above that the existence and the asymptotic stability of a unique equilibrium point is also guaranteed for certain non Lipschitzian non differential and non strictly monotonously increasing output functions as long as there exists a positive constant μ such that $\mu = \sup_{x\neq 0} g(x)/x$. Consider now Eq. (3); let the $N \times N$ matrix $\mathbf{W}^d$ contains all adaptive weights of delay $d \leq D$, i.e. $\mathbf{W}^d = [\mathbf{w}^d(1), \mathbf{w}^d(2), \ldots, \mathbf{w}^d(N)]$ where $\mathbf{w}^d(j) = [w^d_{1j}, \ldots, w^d_{Nj}]^T$. Clearly, inequality (3) may be written into an equivalent form,

$$\mu \sum_{d=0}^{D} \|\mathbf{W}^d\|_1 < 1, \tag{12}$$

where $\|\ \|_1$ refers to the compatible matrix norm $\|\mathbf{A}\|_1 = \sup_{x\neq 0} \|\mathbf{A}x\|_1/\|x\|_1$. Written in matrix form, it appears that the above condition is also a sufficient condition for the existence/uniqueness/stability of the fixed point at each time step and for the gradient-based training convergence as we will see next. For this reason, the condition (12) has a wide adaptive range and can be applied to the design of stable delayed neural network that are a special cases of FIR-recurrent networks.

Fixed point stability – Condition (12) for the network closed loop convergence apply to all recurrent FIR architecture proposals as well as fixed point recurrent networks, regardless of delay and connectivity. Interestingly, the existence and uniqueness of the network activation vector, at each time step, are also guaranteed since $\mu \sum_{d=0}^{D} \|\mathbf{W}^d\|_1 < 1$ implies a weaker condition $\mu \|\mathbf{W}^0\|_1 < 1$ which is clearly a sufficient condition for the input-output mapping to be contracting (see for instance [7], [9]), hence the result.

Gradient-based training convergence – The introduction of time delays leads to somewhat more complicated training procedure because the current state of a unit may depend on several events having occurred in the neighboring neurons at different times. Classically, the goal is to find a procedure to adjust the weight components w_{ij}^d so that a given fixed initial conditions $\mathbf{v}_0$ and a set of input vectors $\{\mathbf{i}_k\}$ taken from the training set result in a set of fixed points (the existence of which is guranteed by (12)), whose components along the output units have a desired set of values. This is generally accomplished by minimizing some error function $E = \sum_{k=0}^{K} E_k$ which measures the errors between the desired and the actual fixed point values along an epoch starting at iteration 0 up to K. Consider for instance the gradient $\partial E_K/\partial w$ due to error signal at time K. $\partial E_K/\partial w$ may be expressed as a series other K elements. When a gradient-based training algorithm is used, the question we are faced with is whether the sum is diverging or remains bounded as K goes to infinity.

Definition 2. *The gradient based training procedure is said to be convergent, at each intermediate time step, if for all weight w, $\lim_{K\to\infty} \partial E_K/\partial w$ exists.*

To answer this question, consider the matrix $\partial \mathbf{v}_K/\partial \mathbf{v}_{K-n}$ as a function of n. It is shown in [3] that when condition (12) holds, $\exists \rho \in [0,1)$ and $\exists M > 0$ such that

$$\|\frac{\partial \mathbf{v}_K}{\partial \mathbf{v}_{K-nD}}\| < M\rho^n. \tag{13}$$

As $\partial E_K/\partial w$ may be expressed as a series of exponentially decaying terms (see the generalized delta rule in [2] for details), the conditions for the *error gradient back flow convergence* are also fulfilled when condition (12) holds. With this in mind, we may now state the following corollary:

Corollary 1. *If $\mu \sum_{d=0}^{D} \sum_{i=1}^{N} |w_{ij}^d| < 1$, for all $j = 1,\ldots,N$, then the FIR-recurrent network has the following properties:*

- *The network admits a unique equilibrium point globally asymptotically stable, $\mathbf{v}_k^\star$, at each iteration k, The latter may be obtained by the method of successive approximation starting from an arbitrary initial conditions. The convergence is asymptotically linear.*
- *The network operating in closed loop converges to a unique fixed point globally asymptotically stable, $\lim_{k\to\infty} \mathbf{v}_k^\star = \mathbf{v}^\star$, starting from any initial conditions.*
- *The gradient-based training procedure is convergent at each intermediate time step.*

Link to regularization – The inequality (12) reminds us of a specific regularizing term usually added to the cost function to penalize non smooth functions. The links between regularization and Bayesian inference are well established. It can easily be shown that, in the Gaussian case, minimizing the regularized cost is equivalent to maximizing the posterior solution assuming the following prior on the weights:

$$P(w \mid \alpha) \propto \prod_{d=0}^{D} \exp\left(-\alpha \|\mathbf{W}^d\|\right) \qquad (14)$$

where the hyper-parameter, α, parameterizes the distribution. Therefore, formal regularization *enforces* the network closed loop convergence to a fixed point, whatever prior is used (e.g., Gaussian prior, Laplace prior). In addition, formal regularization also *stabilizes* the training procedure by indirectly enforcing the error back flow decay when back propagated reversely in time. This result highlights the links between the analysis of the iterated dynamics stability and the well known *forgetting behavior* [4] of recurrent neural networks owing to the *vanishing gradient* phenomenon.

5 Conclusion

In this paper, the problems of stability of a general class of fixed point FIR-recurrent neural networks were investigated in light of some recent results. A new stability criterion was derived for the network operating in closed-loop using Lyapunov functional method based on the norm of delayed-connection matrixes; symmetry was not assumed. These conditions were shown to be in nice agreement with other related sufficient conditions ensuring the error gradient back flow convergence.

References

1. Almeida, L.B.: Backpropagation in perceptrons with feedback. Neural Computers (1987) 199–208.
2. Aussem, A., Murtagh, F., Sarazin, M.: Dynamical recurrent neural networks - towards environmental time series prediction. International Journal of Neural Systems **6** (1995) 145-170
3. Aussem, A.: Sufficient Conditions for Error Back Flow Convergence in Dynamical Recurrent Neural Networks. Neural Computation **14** (2002) 1907–1927
4. Bengio, Y., Simard, P., Frasconi, P.: Learning long-term dependencies with gradient descent is difficult. IEEE Transactions on Neural Networks **5** (1994) 157–166.
5. Cao, J.D., Zhou, D.M.: Stability Analysis of Delayed Cellular Neural Networks. Neural Networks **11** (1998) 1601–1605
6. Feng, C., Plamondon, R.: On the Stability Analysis of Delayed Neural Networks. Neural Networks **14** (2001) 1181–1188
7. Khalil, H.K.: Nonlinear Systems. Prentice-Hall, Upper Saddle River, NJ, (1996)
8. Kremer, S.C.: Spatiotemporal Connectionist Networks: A Taxonomy and Review. Neural Computation **13** (2001) 249–306
9. Mandic, D.P., Chambers, J.A.: Recurrent Neural Networks for Prediction. Learning Algorithms, Architectures and Stability. John Wiley & Sons, Chichester, England (2001)
10. Pineda, F.J.: Generalization of back-propagation to recurrent neural networks. Physical Review Letters **59** (1987) 2229–2232
11. Wan, E.A.: Finite Impulse Response Neural Networks with Applications in Time Series Prediction. Ph.D. Thesis, Stanford University, CA, (1993)

Selective Noise Cancellation Using Independent Component Analysis

Jun-Il Sohn[1] and Minho Lee[2]

[1]Dept. of Sensor Engineering,
[2]School of Electronic & Electrical Engineering,
1370 Sankyuk-Dong, Puk-Gu, Taegu 702-701, Korea
mholee@knu.ac.kr

Abstract. We propose a new ANC system that selectively cancels only the noise signal in the mixture at a specific local position. The BSS separates the desired sound signal from the unwanted noise signal and is used as a preprocessor of the proposed ANC system. In order to enhance the performance of noise separation, we propose a teacher-forced BSS learning algorithm. The teacher signal is obtained form a loudspeaker of the ANC system. Computer simulation and experimental results show that the proposed ANC system effectively cancels only the noise signals from the mixtures with human voice.

1 Introduction

When the desired signal, such as a speech signal, exists with a noise signal in the same area, conventional Active Noise Control (ANC) system deletes not only the noise signal but also the desired sound signal [1]. A Blind Source Separation (BSS) algorithm can separate the independent source signals from the mixture without any prior information except a number of independent sources [2, 3, 4]. Thus, a more effective ANC system with a selective cancellation function can be achieved by blind source separation [5].

In this paper, we propose a new active noise control system that removes only noise signal around the desired position. Our proposed system employs the BSS algorithm as a preprocessor to separate original signal from mixture. The separated noise signal is fed into ANC system of the proposed system, and the desired signal to be separated by the BSS is used as target signal in ANC. The coefficients of ANC system are updated to reduce the difference between target signal and received signal at the specific microphone that is located at the place to be silent. However, the BSS algorithm will make errors in separating the independent sources, and the adaptive filter for implementing the ANC system also has an error to cancel the separated noise signal. In this case, canceling the noise signal through the output of the loudspeaker also acts as an additional independent source signal. Resultantly, the BSS algorithm may fail to separate the noise signal and desired sound signal through failing to consider the output of ANC system as the effect of the additional independent source. In order to enhance the separation performance of the BSS and whole selective noise control system, we use an additional microphone to consider the loudspeaker in the

ANC system as an additional independent source. Also, we use a priori knowledge of the output of the ANC system in constructing the BSS algorithm. The loudspeaker signal output of the ANC system, that is a priori information, is used for finding the coefficients of demixing matrix. This creates a new learning algorithm for the separation of the mixtures, or so called "teacher forced BSS learning algorithm".

Computer simulation results show that speech signals successfully remain around a microphone by selectively reducing a ship engine noise. The proposed ANC system with an additional microphone and the teacher forced BSS learning algorithm is more effective to cancel only the noise signal than that combined with BSS algorithm without an additional microphone and the teacher forced BSS learning algorithm. The experimental result shows a possibility that the proposed selective noise control system can cancels only the noise signals from mixture.

2 Selective Noise Control System Using Active Noise Control and Blind Source Separation

Fig. 1 shows the proposed selective noise control system with two microphones using a BSS [5]. Let it be assumed that two independent source signals are voice and noise. The mixtures of two independent source signals are received at two microphones through the space. Our aim is to retain only the voice signal around microphone 2 while selectively eliminating the effect of noise.

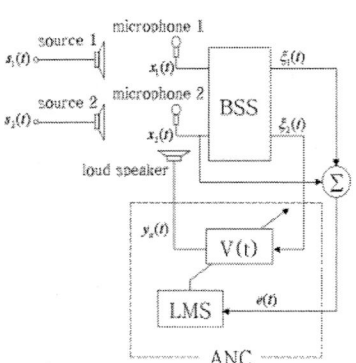

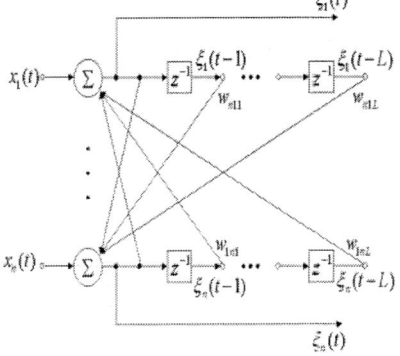

Fig. 1. The selective noise control system network with two microphones

Fig. 2. The dynamic recurrent neural model

In general, the order of the signals separated by the BSS is unknown; however, it is possible to identify the permutation order of the BSS output signals using a simple heuristic and/or statistical method such as a comparison of the kurtosis of the separated signals [5]. Separated noise signals passes through the adaptive filter of the ANC system. Assuming that the microphone 2 and the loud speaker are close by, the received signal $X(t)$ can be expressed as follows:

$$X(t) = H(t) * S(t) + [h'(t) * y_a(t) \quad y_a(t)]^T \tag{1}$$

where $S(t)$ is the independent source signals, $y_a(t)$ is the output of ANC system, $h'(t)$ is the transfer function between the loud speaker and the microphone 1, and the symbol $*$ is convolution operator.

In order to retain only the desired source signal around microphone 2, the error function of the ANC system is defined as Eq. (2).

$$e(t) = \varepsilon^2 = \{\xi_1(t) - x_2(t)\}^2 \tag{2}$$

$$= \{\xi_1(t) - (h_{21}(t) * s_1(t) + h_{22}(t) * s_2(t) + y_a(t))\}^2$$

where $h_{ij}(t)$ denotes the $(i,j)-th$ polynomial element in the mixing matrix $H(t)$. The adaptive filter is trained in an on-line manner to minimize the error function as shown in Eq. (2). Eq. (3) shows the update rule of the filter coefficients.

$$v_k(t+1) = v_k(t) + \mu\varepsilon(t)\xi_2(t-k) \quad \text{where } k = 1, 2, \cdots, L \tag{3}$$

in which $v_k(t)$ means $k-th$ coefficient of the adaptive filter. μ represents the step size, and $\varepsilon(t) = \xi_1(t) - x_2(t)$. In the case where the BSS successfully separates the independent source signals and the ANC system generates the anti-noise signal completely, the received signal at the microphone 2 converges to the desired source signal [5].

In order to consider the convolved mixture characteristics in BSS, a dynamic recurrent neural network for realizing a BSS algorithm was used. Fig. 2 shows the structure of dynamic recurrent neural network. The dynamic ICA learning algorithm can be derived as follows [6]:

$$w_{ijk}(t+1) = w_{ijk}(t) - \eta_t \frac{dL(W(t))}{dw_{ijk}(t)} = w_{ijk}(t) - \eta_t f_i(\xi_i(t))\xi_j(t-k) \tag{4}$$

in which $L(W(t))$ is the loss function for maximum likelihood defined by $L(W(t)) = -\log|\det W(t)| - \sum_{i=1}^{n} \log p_i(\xi_i(t))$ and $\xi_j(t-k)$ represents the delayed output of the network. The $w_{ijk}(t)$ is the synaptic weight between $x_i(t)$ and $\xi_j(t-k)$, and $f_i(\xi_i(k)) = -\frac{d\log(p_i(\xi_i(k)))}{d\xi_i(k)}$. The choice of the non-linear function is important problem because it deeply influences the separation ability of the neural network. Pearlmutter and Parra used linear combinations of parametric basis functions [7]. Taleb and Jutten employed multi-layer perceptron in order to adaptively estimate the 'score function' of the sources [8]. Fiori proposed adaptive-activation-function neurons to adaptively estimate the probability density function of the sources [9], while Welling and Weber proposed a maximum-likelihood approach to blind separation based on the well-known expectation/maximization (EM) algorithm [10]. In recent, the flexible independent component analysis deals with the design method of the nonlinear function for a signal that can be represented the generalized Gaussian probability distribution as follows [11]. By the flexible independent component analysis, the nonlinear function is given as follows:

$$f_i(\xi_i) = |\xi_i|^{\alpha_i - 1} sign(\xi_i) \qquad (5)$$

where α_i is a positive real number.

3 Improvement of the Selective Noise Control System

It is difficult to derive the exact global minimum of the error function shown in Eq. (2), and the BSS algorithm will make errors in separating the independent sources. Additionally, the adaptation process of the adaptive filter cannot completely generate the anti-noise signal. In this case, the separation performance of the BSS algorithm is reduced by the effect of the ANC system loudspeaker and as a result, it is difficult to cancel only the unwanted noise signal among the mixtures. The output signal generated by the incomplete ANC system creates an additional independent signal, which makes the BSS become an overcomplete problem [12]. In order to avoid the overcomplete situation, the proposed system employs an additional microphone to consider the effect of a loudspeaker in the BSS algorithm. By the way, if we regard the output of the ANC as another independent source, then one of the separated signals in the BSS should be the output signal of the ANC. This means that one of the outputs of the BSS is no longer a blind source and we can use the known loudspeaker signal as a target to enhance the separation performance of the dynamic recurrent neural network as shown in Fig. 2.

Fig. 3 shows the proposed selective noise control system with three microphones and a teacher-forced dynamic ICA learning algorithm. In this figure, the line between microphone 3 and the third output node of the BSS allocates the ANC output value to BSS output directly. The $i-th$ output signal, $\xi_i(t)$, of a dynamic recurrent neural network can be represented as:

$$\xi_i(t) = f(x_i(t), \xi_j(t), \xi_j(t-k), W) \qquad (6)$$

where the delay parameter $k = 1, 2, \cdots, L$ and $j \neq i$ and $x_i(t)$ are external input signals for the $i-th$ output node. $\xi_j(t)$ and $\xi_j(t-k)$ are the signals of $j-th$ output node and its delayed values, respectively. W represents the weight vector.

If we know the delayed value of a target signal for $j-th$ output node, the Eq. (6) can be replaced by Eq. (7).

$$\xi_i(t) = f(x_i(t), \xi_j(t), \delta_j(t-k), W) \qquad (7)$$

where $\delta_j(t-k)$ represents the delayed value of the target signal for the $j-th$ output node. Using the exact delay signals of a known output as shown in Eq. (7) enhances the separation performance of the BSS algorithm through avoiding the adverse effect of the dynamic recurrent neural network's inexact output signal during the training phase [13]. The accurate delayed value of the recurrent neural network helps the learning process by reducing the training time and increasing the accuracy, and thus, we can obtain more accurate training result [14]. Two further nodes, whose values were obtained through an unsupervised learning process to minimize mutual information, are still unknown. One of these two outputs is a desired source signal, which is used to derive the error function in Eq. (2) for the adaptation of the filter coefficient with the ANC system. The other is the separated noise signal, which is used as the input of the ANC system.

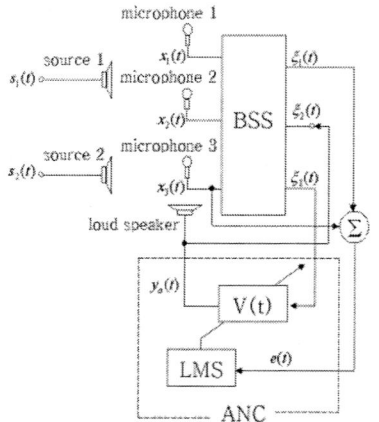

Fig. 3. The selective noise control system with three microphones

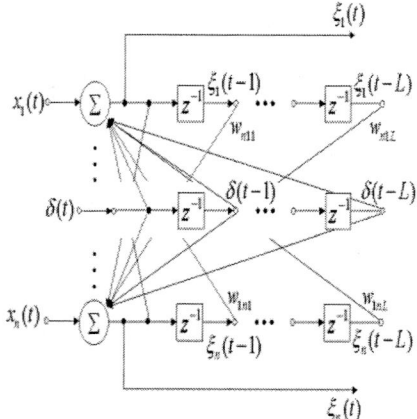

Fig. 4. The dynamic recurrent neural network for teacher forced dynamic ICA learning

Fig. 4 shows the dynamic recurrent neural network with a teacher-forced dynamic ICA learning algorithm for realizing the BSS algorithm where $\delta_i(t)$ is the target value of i-th output node, which is given by $y_a(t)$, and $\delta_i(t-k)$ is its delayed value. The delayed value of $\xi_i(t)$ is presented by $\xi_i(t-k)$. Since the output of the ANC system's loudspeaker can be used, the delayed values of known signal are used as a teacher signal for the delayed neurons of the recurrent neural network. Thus, two kinds of outputs are considered. One is the independent source signal that is separated by BSS algorithm and the other is the loudspeaker signal that is known without learning. In the latter case, the teacher-forced learning algorithm can be applied to a structure possibly similar to the nonlinear filter built on a static neural network [14].

The output of this neural network is given as the following equation:

$$\xi_i(t) = x_i(t) + \sum_{k=0}^{L} \sum_{j \neq i, j \in T \cup Y}^{n} w_{ijk}(t)\xi_j(t-k) \qquad (8)$$

where $\xi_j(t-k) = \begin{cases} \delta_j(t-k) & j \in T \\ y_j(t-k) & j \in Y \end{cases}$. $\delta_j(t-k)$ and $y_j(t-k)$ represent the delayed target value obtained from the loudspeaker output and the delayed output of the network obtained through unsupervised learning, respectively. T and Y denote the teacher domain and output domain, respectively. The delayed values in the teacher node are the weighted sum that determines the values of the other output nodes. Thus, the proposed teacher forced dynamic ICA learning is as follows:

$$w_{ijk}(t+1) = \begin{cases} w_{ijk}(t) - \eta_t f_i(\xi_i(t))\delta_j(t-k), & if \quad j \in T \quad and \quad i \neq j \\ w_{ijk}(t) - \eta_t f_i(\xi_i(t)) y_j(t-k), & if \quad j \in Y \quad and \quad i \neq j \end{cases} \quad (9)$$

In the proposed scheme, the weights connected to the teacher node are unnecessary and thus the output of loudspeaker output can be directly used. The delayed term of the teacher node is also known and used for learning and separating the unknown independent sources.

4 Computer Simulation and Experimental Results

In computer simulation, the speech signal and the sound noise signal induced by a ship engine were used as the two original independent source signals. The received signals $x_i(t)$ in the linear mixtures were generated using the linear mixing matrix, and the received signals in the convolved mixtures were generated by $H(t)$ that has 100th order delay terms and random values in [-1, 1]. The goal is to cancel the effect of noise signal by a ship engine around a specific microphone. We compare the performance of the proposed systems by Signal-to-Noise Ratio (SNR) and Mean Opinion Score (MOS) test. In case of convolved mixture, since the phase of resultant signals may change, we use MOS test instead of using SNR comparison. Table 1 shows the average of SNR in linear mixtures and the result of the MOS in convolved mixtures. From these results, we can know that our proposed systems are effective to remove only the noise signal, and additive microphone and employment of teacher forced BSS learning algorithm remarkably improve the selective cancellation performance of noise signal.

Table 1. The comparison of the SNR and MOS

	Before the proposed system operate	The proposed system with 2 microphones	The proposed system with 3 microphones	The proposed system with 3 microphones and teacher forced dynamic ICA learning
SNR	-7.8162dB	-5.3197dB	-0.7743dB	0.9967dB
MOS	3	3.364	3.546	3.909

In order to show the efficiency of the proposed system in real situation, we implement the proposed system with three microphones and teacher-forced dynamic ICA learning, and applied the proposed system to cancel only the noise signal from mixtures with voice and car engine noise in the office and many kinds of furniture and equipment are filled in the office.

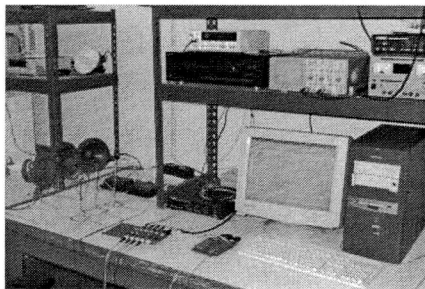

Fig. 5. The picture of the proposed system in the office

Fig. 5 shows the picture of the proposed system in the office. In this system, digital audio tape recorders generate original source signals, voice and noise. After the received signals at each microphone are amplified and filtered by LPF with the cut-off frequency at 500Hz, the computer gets the received signals using a data acquisition board. The algorithm of the proposed system with BSS and ANC system works in the IBM PC that generates an output signal. The generated signal is propagated through the output channel of the data acquisition board, LPF, audio amp and speaker. Fig. 6 (a) shows voice signal in frequency domain, Fig. 6 (b) shows the received mixture with the voice and engine noise of the car at the microphone 3 in frequency domain when the proposed system is not operating and Fig. 6 (c) shows the received mixture at the microphone 3 when the proposed system is operating. In this figure, we can see that the noise around 375Hz is reduced and shape of the received signal at microphone 3 resembles the shape of the original voice signal in the frequency domain. This means that the noise signal is selectively removed and that the voice signal remained around microphone 3 in the office.

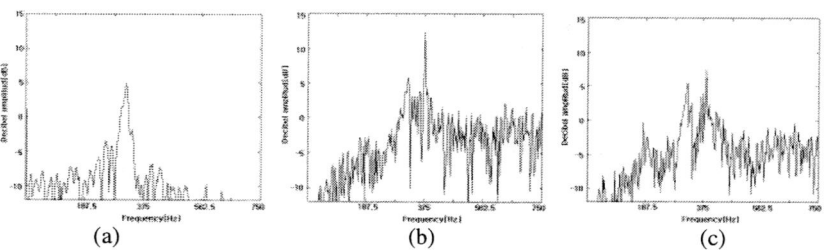

Fig. 6. The result of experiment using voice and engine noise in frequency domain. (a) The voice signal. (b) The received mixture with the voice and engine noise at the microphone 3, when the proposed system is not operating. (c) The received mixture with the voice and engine noise at the microphone 3, when the proposed system is operating

5 Conclusion

We proposed a new selective noise control system using blind source separation. In order to enhance performance of the proposed system, we considered another microphone for the output of ANC and also proposed teacher forced dynamic ICA learning algorithm. Through the computer simulation and experimental results, we could know that our proposed system reduces only the noise signal.

Acknowledgment. This research was funded by the Brain Science & Engineering Research Program of the Ministry of Korea Science and Technology.

References

1. Kuo, S.M., Morgan, D.R.: Active noise control systems; Algorithm and DSP Implementations. John Wiley & Sons (1996) 1–51
2. Yang, H.H., Amari, S.I.: Adaptive on-line learning algorithms for blind separation: Maximum entropy and minimum mutual information. Neural Computation, Vol. 9. (1997)
3. Lee, T.W., Bell, A., Orglmeister, R.: Blind source separation of real world signals. International Conference on Neural Network, Vol. 4. (1997) 129–2134
4. Comon, P. Independent component analysis, A new concept?. Signal Processing, Vol. 36. (1994) 287–314
5. Sohn, J.I., Lee, M. Selective attention system using active noise controller. Neurocomputing, Vol. 31. (2000) 197–204
6. Choi, S., Cichocki, A.: Adaptive blind separation of speech signals: Cocktail party problem. International Conference on Speech Processing (1997) 617–622
7. Pearlmetter, B.A., Parra, L.C.: Maximum likelihood blind source separation: A context-sensitive generalization of ICA, Neural Information Processing System (1996) 613–619
8. Taleb, A., Jutten, C.: Entropy optimization-application to source separation, International Conference on Artificial Neural Networks (1997) 529–534
9. Fiori, S.: Blind signal processing by the adaptive activation function neurons. Neural Networks, Vol. 13. (1996) 597–611
10. Welling, M., Weber, M.: A Constrainsed E.M. Algorithm for independent component analysis. Neural Computation, Vol. 13. (2001)
11. Choi, S., Cichock, A.I., Amari, S.I.: Flexible independent component analysis. The Journal of VLSI Signal Processing, Vol. 26. (2000) 25–38
12. Lee, T.W., Lewicki, M.S., Girolami, M., Sejnowski, T.J.: Blind source separation of more sources than mixtures using overcomplete representations. IEEE Signal Processing Letters, Vol. 4. (1999)
13. Bae U.M., Lee, S.Y.: Combining ICA and top-down attention for robust speech recognition. Neural Information Processing Systems, Vol. 13. (2000)
14. Williams, R.J., Zipser, D.: A learning algorithm for continually running fully recurrent neural network, Neural Computation, Vol. 1. (1989) 270–280

Expert Mixture Methods for Adaptive Channel Equalization

Edward Harrington

Research School of Information Sciences and Engineering
The Australian National University
Canberra, ACT 0200
edward.harrington@anu.edu.au

Abstract. Mixture of expert algorithms are able to achieve a total loss close to the total loss of the best expert over a sequence of examples. We consider the use of mixture of expert algorithms applied to the signal processing problem of channel equalization. We use these mixture of expert algorithms to track the best parameter settings for equalizers in the presence of noise or when the channel characteristics are unknown, maybe non-stationary. The experiments performed demonstrate the use of expert algorithms in tracking the best LMS equalizer step size in the presence of additive noise and in prior selection for the approximate natural gradient (ANG) algorithm.

1 Introduction

At the receiver of a communications system we would like to recover the original symbol transmitted. A number of factors hinder that recovery. The first factor is the Inter-Symbol Interference (ISI) caused by the communications channel [9]. The ISI is reduced by applying a filter at the receiver called an equalizer. Another factor of hindrance is the possible presence of noise. A common problem with adaptive equalization given noise and ISI is the appropriate selection of parameters like step-size (learning rate) or the equalizer length. We can also consider the possibility that the interference is non-stationary, i.e. varies over time. The consequence of such variability is that not one single equalizer maybe suitable over the entire transmission. This makes the mixture of experts algorithms [6,5,3,2] which track the best expert from a pool of experts applicable. In this paper we investigate mixture of experts algorithms in connection with the problem of channel equalization in different scenarios.

2 System Model

The basic signal model consists of a transmitted binary signal $y_t \in \{-1, +1\}$ (t denotes time and we only consider the binary case in this paper; this could be extended to complex or multi-class, suitable for quadrature modulation types).

As shown in Figure 1, y_t is transmitted over a communications channel $\mathbf{c} = (c_0, \ldots, c_{L-1})$, resulting in the signal at the receiver r_t,

$$r_t = \sum_{l=0}^{L-1} y_{t-l} c_l + n_t, \tag{1}$$

where n_t is Additive Gaussian White Noise (AGWN) which is assumed to have zero mean and variance $\sigma_{n_t}^2$. We consider a equalizer of length $d = 2K + 1$. The equalizer produces an estimate $\hat{y}_t$ of the transmitted signal y_t via

$$\hat{y}_t = \sum_{i=1}^{d} w_{t,i} x_{t,i}, \tag{2}$$

where the instances are $\mathbf{x}_t = [r_{t-K}, \ldots, r_t, \ldots, r_{t+K}]'$. Throughout the paper (except section 6.3) we assume that the transmitted labels $y_1, \ldots, y_T$ are known at the receiver. This corresponds to the standard technique of first transmitting a known sequence for tuning the equalizer. Our techniques can also be applied to the more difficult problem of blind equalization where the labels are not known; some preliminary results are given in section 6.3.

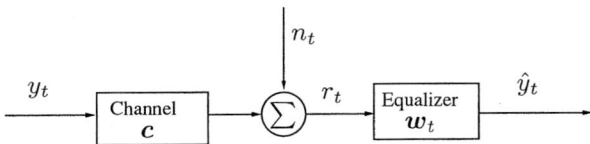

Fig. 1. Communications system discrete time model with channel equalization applied at the receiver.

3 Adaptive Equalizers

Optimal removal of the ISI can be achieved given perfect knowledge of the channel. Having complete knowledge of the channel may not be possible especially when the channel is time varying. This gives rise to the use of adaptive equalizers which attempt to track the changes. In this section we will discuss a number of different adaptive equalizers.

Given the residual $\xi_t = y_t - \hat{y}_t$ consider gradient method updates of the form

$$f(w_{t+1,i}) = f(w_{t,i}) - \eta_t \frac{\partial L(\xi_t)}{\partial w_{t,i}}, \tag{3}$$

where $\mathbf{w}_t$ is the vector used to produce $\hat{y}_t$ as in (2), f is possibly a nonlinear function used to modify the weights, $\eta_t > 0$ is the learning rate, and L is a loss function.

In general (3) can be used with a number of different gradient based equalizers. In this paper we only consider LMS [11] with loss function $L(\xi_t) = \frac{1}{2}\xi_t^2$.

We will now consider a number of different examples of $f(w_{t,i})$. The simplest case is the Stochastic Gradient Descent (SGD) algorithm where $f(w_{t,i}) = w_{t,i}$ and

$$w_{t+1,i} = w_{t,i} - \eta_t \frac{\partial L(\xi_t)}{\partial w_{t,i}}. \qquad (4)$$

Compared to gradient methods like the SGD algorithm the Exponentiated Gradient (EG) algorithm [5] has better convergence when the target weight vector is known to be sparse. The existence of sparse communications channels motivates the inclusion of the EG algorithm in this discussion on adaptive equalizers. The EG update is derived from the general update by substituting $f(w_{t,i}) = \ln(w_{t,i})$ in (3) giving,

$$w_{t+1,i} = w_{t,i} \exp\left(-\eta_t \frac{\partial L(\xi_t)}{\partial w_{t,i}}\right). \qquad (5)$$

Both SGD and EG algorithms can be generalised by replacing the gradient with the natural gradient [1] that takes into account a Riemannian metric in the weight space. For brevity we will not go into more detail concerning the NG algorithm. Rather we are interested in the simpler and easier to implement first order approximation, the Approximate Natural Gradient algorithm (ANG) [8]. Mahony and Williamson introduce a different interpretation of the NG algorithm, that the true weight vector $\boldsymbol{w}^*$ is drawn at random from some prior distribution [1] $\phi(w_{t,i})$. The ANG algorithm is given by,

$$w_{t+1,i} = w_{t,i} - \eta_t \frac{\partial L(\xi_t)}{\partial w_{t,i}} \frac{1}{\phi(w_{t,i})^2}. \qquad (6)$$

In order to develop intuition about (6) consider the EG case of ANG, where the prior $\phi(w_{t,i}) = 1/w_{t,i}$. In this case if the $w_{t,i}$ is small in value then the prior will be high and the opposite is true when $w_{t,i}$ is large. Hence there is a warping of the weight space to suit the fact that the target weight is sparse.

4 Mixture of Experts

We are interested in mixtures of experts, in particular the online algorithms of fixed-share from [3]. First we will discuss the simplest algorithm referred to as the *static expert* algorithm [6,10]. In the static expert case each expert $i = 1, \ldots M$ makes a prediction $\hat{y}_{t,i}$ at trial t (this could be a neural network, decision tree,

---

[1] We consider in this paper the standard parameterization of [7] i.e. $w_{t,i} = \gamma(z_{t,i}) = z_{t,i}$, though in [7] they consider the more general case of the transform $\gamma(z_{t,i})$ where $w_{t,i} \neq z_{t,i}$ hence replacing $w_{t,i}$ with $z_{t,i}$ in (6).

or as in our case equalizers) and is assigned a weight $v_{t,i}$. The overall prediction of the mixture of experts $\hat{y}_t^m$ in the weighted average case is given by,

$$\hat{y}_t^m = \sum_{i=1}^{M} p_{t,i}\hat{y}_{t,i}, \qquad (7)$$

where $p_{t,i} = v_{t,i}/V_t$ and $V_t = \sum_{i=1}^{M} v_{t,i}$. The key to the ability to perform close to the best expert's prediction is in the loss update. The loss update for the static-expert is

$$v_{t+1,i} = v_{t,i} \exp(-\nu L(\xi_{t,i})), \qquad (8)$$

where $\nu > 0$ is the learning rate, and $\xi_{t,i} = y_t - \hat{y}_{t,i}$ is the residual of expert i at trial t. Hence if an expert has large losses then the weight $v_{t,i}$ associate with that expert will become exponentially small.

We define the total loss for the weighted average for the sequence of examples $z = ((x_1, y_1), \ldots, (x_T, y_T))$ as $L_{WA}(z) = \sum_{t=1}^{T} L(\xi_t^m)$ where $\xi_t^m = y_t - \hat{y}_t^m$. Similarly the total loss for expert i over the same sequence z is expressed as $L_{z,i} = \sum_{t=1}^{T} L(\xi_{t,i})$ where $\xi_{t,i} = y_t - \hat{y}_{t,i}$.

The static-expert algorithm for the weighted average has been shown in [4] to have for a large class of loss functions L and range of learning rates ν the loss bound

$$L_{WA}(z) \leq \min_{1 \leq i \leq M}(L_{z,i}) + \frac{1}{\nu} \ln M. \qquad (9)$$

This is a nice bound saying that the worst that the total loss of the weight average $L_{WA}(z)$ will be is the loss of the best expert plus the term $\frac{1}{\nu} \ln M$ which is a constant over the sequence z.

It is worth exploring the worst case bounds on $\frac{1}{\nu}$ specifically the loss function for LMS to understand the expected performance. Given $|\xi_{t,i}| \leq \xi_{\max}$ using the squared loss function $L(\xi_{t,i}) = \frac{1}{2}\xi_{t,i}^2$ then from [6] the bound (9) holds for all ν such that $\frac{1}{\nu} \leq \xi_{\max}^2$.

It is not always the case that one expert will be the best over all T examples. The *fixed-share* algorithm divides a small fraction α of the total weight uniformly over all the experts. This prevents the weight of any expert getting too low. Thus, if an expert that previously performed poorly starts to perform well, its weight can recover faster. The fixed-share algorithm's weight update for $0 \leq \alpha < 1$ is

$$v_{t+1,i} = (1-\alpha)v_{t,i}\exp(-\nu L(\xi_{t,i})) + \alpha/(M-1)(V_t - v_{t,i}\exp(-\nu L(\xi_{t,i}))). \qquad (10)$$

Noting that the fixed-share update is constructed in such a way that the following: $\sum_{i=1}^{M} v_{t+1,i} = \sum_{i=1}^{M} v_{t,i} \exp(-\nu L(\xi_t))$.

For analysing the fixed-share algorithm, we consider for some fixed k all possible partitionings of the trial sequence $t = [1, 2, \ldots, T]$ into $k+1$ segments $[t_0, \ldots, t_1), [t_1, \ldots, t_2), \ldots, [t_k, \ldots, t_{k+1})$. The accumulated loss over segment j for the best expert i is denoted by $L(z_j, i) = \sum_{s=t_{j-1}}^{t_j - 1} L(\xi_{s,i})$ where $\xi_{s,i} =$

$y_s - \hat{y}_{s,i}$. For any partitioning to segments z_j and assignments of experts i_j to each segment, the fixed-share algorithm satisfies

$$L_{WA}(z) \leq \sum_{j=1}^{k+1}(L_{z_j,i_j}) + \frac{\ln M}{\nu} + \frac{(T-k-1)}{\nu}\ln\frac{1}{1-\alpha} + k/\nu\left[\ln\frac{1}{\alpha}+\ln(M-1)\right]. \tag{11}$$

(Assumptions about L and ν are as for (9)). The optimal choice of the fraction of total weight $\alpha^* = k/(T-1)$ can be determined by taking the derivative of the bound (11).

5 Mixture of Equalizer Scenarios

5.1 Choosing the Step-Size η

A well understood property of gradient methods in the presence of noise is their sensitivity to the choice of step size or learning rate η. For constant η, the final MSE (Mean Squared Error) of such gradient methods comprises of $J_{min} + J_\eta$: the first component is the minimum achievable MSE (MMSE) and the second component J_η is the measurement noise, dependent on the value of η. In the case of LMS the measurement MSE is given by $J_\eta \sim \eta d J_{min}$, where d is the equalizer's filter length. In determining the best η there is a trade-off between rate of convergence and the final MSE. The larger we make η the faster the initial convergence, although the final MSE maybe higher. This motivates the first application of mixture of experts, using a mixture of M LMS algorithms with different step sizes.

A large body of research (refer to [9]) has been devoted to finding the most appropriate step size to accelerate the convergence of LMS. The simplest and most common proposed method for fast convergence of LMS is to start with a large step size and decrease it over time. Usually the methods require some adaptive feedback to determine when to decrease η. Two potential problems arise with this approach: difficulty to analyse the MSE above without a constant step size, and the feedback may become unstable if the initial step size chosen is too high. When considering a mixture of LMS algorithms each LMS has a constant step-size. There is no penalty in performance if one step size is too high, and thus becomes unstable, the fixed-share algorithm will make its weight small and still perform close to the best LMS algorithm.

5.2 Choice of Prior ϕ in ANG Algorithm

One problem for the ANG of equation (6) is the selection of a suitable prior $\phi(w_{t,i})$. If the channel is not sparse, then we might want to try a $\phi(w_{t,i}) = 1$. We propose that we can use a mixture of ANG algorithms with different parameter settings using the fixed-share algorithm. One method proposed in [7] was to run different ANG algorithms with different parameter settings taking the one with best average MSE of a number of Monte-Carlo trials. This is not always practical scheme because it is not online and assumes that the parameters are constant over the entire signal transmission. Alternatively the fixed-share algorithm tracks the best prior in a truely online manner.

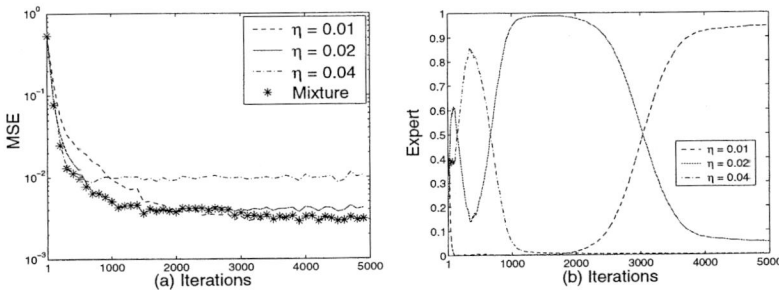

Fig. 2. Experimental results selecting the step size η with the lowest MSE, (a) MSE for each individual LMS algorithm and their resulting mixed prediction $\hat{y}^m$, (b) weight given to each LMS prediction versus iterations.

6 Experiments

All the results were produced over 500 Monte-Carlo trials using the fixed-share algorithm.

6.1 Choosing the Step-Size

The first experiment tests the idea of choosing the most appropriate step-size with a mixture of LMS algorithms in the presence of additive noise. The channel from [9, pages 631] $c_A = (0.04, -0.05, 0.07, -0.21, 0.72, 0.36, 0, 0.21, 0.03, 0.07)$ was used. We tried the step sizes, $\eta = 0.01, 0.02, 0.04$, for three different independently run LMS algorithms. Each LMS algorithm had a weight vector or equalizer of length $d = 31$.

The training data was generated from a binary sequence filtered by c_A and adding zero mean Gaussian noise with variance, $\sigma_n^2 = 10^{-3}$. The results shown in Figure 2(a) illustrate the effectiveness in selecting the value of η which has the lower MSE. We found that the higher we made ν the faster the selection of η corresponding to the lower MSE. The value of $\nu = 10$ was used to suit the fact that the loss is small in this application. It was observed that the value of α over the range 0.01 to 0.001 had little effect on the result of Figure 2(b).

6.2 ANG Prior Selection

We consider the specific case of ANG with the inverse power law prior $\phi(w_{t,i}) = (1/(w_{t,i}^\beta + \zeta))$ with $\zeta = 0.1, 0.3$ and $\beta = 0.125, 0.5$. A sparse channel was created

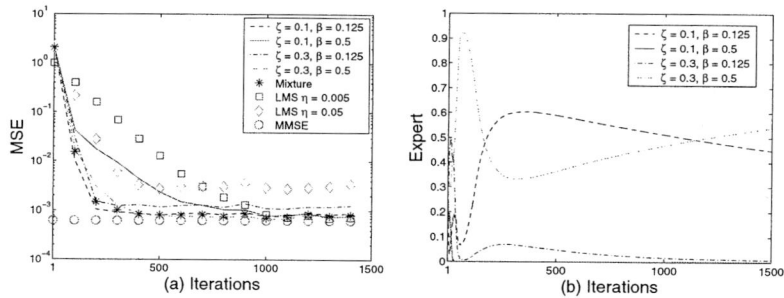

Fig. 3. Experimental results for ANG mixture with inverse power law priors ($1/(w_{t,i}^{\beta} + \zeta)$), (a) MSE comparison to LMS, (b) expert weights using squared loss.

with length of $L = 15$, with value zero except at positions $[1, 5, 10]$ which had the values $[0.1, 1, -0.1]$ respectively. The model included additive Gaussian noise with variance of 0.025^2 which has the corresponding theoretical minimum of the MMSE (see Figure 3) of 6.25×10^{-4}. From the results in Figure 3 (a) we see that the mixture has a faster convergence compared to LMS with $\eta = 0.005$ given both converge to the MMSE. LMS was also plotted with the same $\eta = 0.05$ as used by the ANG mixture, though it converged to a higher MSE. Figures 3(a) and (b) also demonstrates how the fixed-share algorithm selects the appropriate prior at particular iterations with $\alpha = 0.001$ and $\nu = 10$.

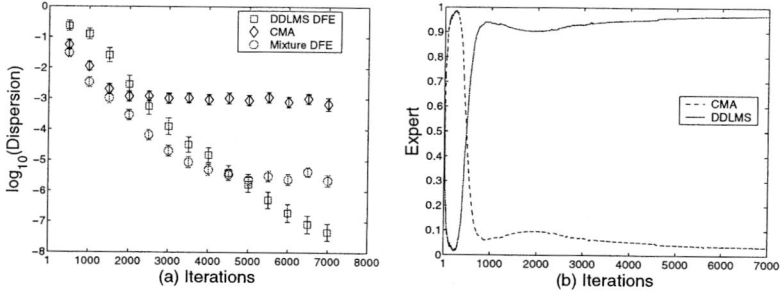

Fig. 4. Experimental results for Mixture DFE, (a) log natural of the dispersion comparing three equalizers, CMA, DDLMS DFE and Mixture DFE, (b) weighting for each expert, CMA and DDLMS DFE.

6.3 Blind DFE

Preliminary results look promising for the problem of providing a stability to the switch between CMA (blind equalizer) and Decision Feedback Equalization (DFE) in decision directed mode. We do not cover the theory of DFE's here, for brevity (see [9]). We set $\nu = 10.0$, and the $\eta = 0.01$ for both CMA and DDLMS against channel c_A. The length of the forward filter of the DFE, feedback filter of the DFE and CMA was 31. We used CMA Dispersion loss function. Figure 4 demonstrated that the mixture outperformed the DDLMS DFE and successfully switched from CMA to DDLMS DFE to make decisions. Note the DDLMS DFE after 5000 iterations outperforms the mixed DFE, this appears to be due CMA still contributing to the final decision in the mixture. Figure 4(a) also displays the 95% confidence interval, noting that the DDLMS DFE interval is the largest.

7 Conclusions

We proposed and applied the online algorithms for tracking the best expert to adaptive equalization. The advantage is that the methods we propose are truly online hence able to handle non-stationary conditions. One area for further research maybe using mixture of expert algorithms in determining the best equalizer length.

Acknowledgments. We would like to thank Jyrki Kivinen, Gunnar Rätsch and Bob Williamson for their help regarding this work. Edward is an employee of the Defence Science and Technology Organisation, Australia.

References

1. S. Amari, (1998) Natural gradient works efficiently in learning. *Neural Computation*, **10(2)**:251–276.
2. R.B. Gramacy, M.K. Warmuth, S.A. Brandt and I. Ari, (2002) Adaptive Caching by Refetching. *Advances in Neural Information Processing Systems 15*, to appear.
3. M. Herbster and M.K. Warmuth, (1998) Tracking the best expert. *Journal of Machine Learning*, **32(2)**:151–178.
4. J. Kivinen and M.K. Warmuth, (1999) Averaging expert predictions. In P. Fischer and H.U. Simon, editors, *Proc. 4th European Conference on Computational Learning Theory*, pp 153–167, Springer LNAI 1572, Berlin.
5. J. Kivinen and M.K. Warmuth, (1997) Additive versus exponentiated gradient updates for linear prediction. In *Journal of Information and Computation*, **132(1)**:1–64.
6. N. Littlestone and M.K. Warmuth, (1994) The weighted majority algorithm. In *Journal of Information and Computation*, **108(2)**:212–261.
7. R.K. Martin, W.A. Sethares, R.C. Williamson and C.R. Johnson, (2002) Exploiting Sparsity in Adaptive Filters. *IEEE Transactions on Signal Processing*, **50(8)**:1883–1894.
8. R.E. Mahony and R.C. Williamson, (2001) Prior knowledge and preferential structures in gradient descent learning algorithms. *Journal of Machine Learning Research*, **1**:311–355.
9. J.G. Proakis, (2001) *Digital Communications, 4th Edition.* McGraw-Hill.
10. V. Vovk, (1998) A game of prediction with expert advice. In *Journal of Computer and System Sciences*, **56**:153–173.
11. B. Widrow and M.E. Hoff, (1960) Adaptive switching circuits. *1960 IRE WESCON Convention Record*, pt. 4, pp. 96–104.

A Relaxation Algorithm Influenced by Self-Organizing Maps

Michiharu Maeda

Kurume National College of Technology
1-1-1 Komorino, Kurume, Japan
maedami@kurume-nct.ac.jp

Abstract. A relaxation algorithm influenced by self-organizing maps for image restoration is presented in this study. Self-organizing maps have been hitherto studied for the ordering process and the convergence phase of weight vectors. As another approach of self-organizing maps, a novel algorithm of image restoration is proposed. The present algorithm creates a map containing one unit for each pixel. Utilizing pixel values as input, the image inference is carried out by self-organizing maps. Then, an updating function with a threshold is introduced, so as not to respond to a noisy input sensitively. Therefore, the inference of original image proceeds appropriately since any pixel is influenced by surrounding pixels corresponding to the neighboring setting. In the restoration process, the effect of the initial threshold and the initial neighborhood on accuracy is examined. Experimental results are presented in order to show that the present method is effective in quality.

1 Introduction

Self-organizing neural networks realize the network utilizing the mechanism of the lateral inhibition among neurons with the local topological ordering. In addition, the neighboring neurons would always respond for neighboring inputs [1,2]. In short, the outputs respond locally for the localized inputs clearly. Therefore, huge amounts of information are locally represented and their expressions form a configuration with topological ordering. As an application of self-organizing neural networks, for example, there are the combinatorial optimization problem, pattern recognition, vector quantization, and clustering [3]. Thus, though a number of self-organizing models exist, they differ with respect to the field of application. On self-organizing maps, the ordering and the convergence of weight vectors are mainly argued [4]. The former is a problem on the formation of topology preserving map, and outputs are constructed in proportion to input characteristics [5]–[7]. For instance, there is the traveling salesman problem as an application of feature maps, which is possible to obtain good results by adopting the elastic-ring method with many elements compared to inputs [8],[9]. The latter is a problem on the approximation of pattern vectors, and the method expresses enormous input-information to a little output. Especially, it is an important problem for the convergence of weight vectors, and it is mainly argued when self-organizing neural networks are applied to vector quantization [10]–[15]. In the meantime, the inference of original image is carried out, by using the model of Markov random field formulated statistically, from the concept that any pixel is affected in circumference pixels [16,17].

In this study, a novel algorithm according to relaxation process influenced by self-organizing maps for image restoration is presented. The present method forms a map in which one element corresponds for each pixel. Image restoration is carried out by self-organizing maps using pixel values as input. To begin with, it is introduced a renewal function with a threshold in proportion to the difference between input and inferred values. According to the function, it does not respond to an input including the noise oversensitively. Furthermore, as any pixel is influenced by circumference pixels corresponding to the neighboring setting, the inference of original image is appropriately promoted. In the restoration process, the effect of the initial threshold and the initial neighborhood on accuracy is examined. Experimental results are presented in order to show that the present method is effective in quality.

2 Self-Organizing Maps

For self-organizing maps, there exists Kohonen's algorithm which is known as a plain and useful learning. In this algorithm, the updating of weights is modified to involve neighboring relations in the output array. In the vector space R^n, the input $\boldsymbol{x}$ which is generated on the probability density function $p(\boldsymbol{x})$ is defined. Thus $\boldsymbol{x}$ has the components from x_1 to x_n. The output unit y_i is generally arranged in an array of one- or two-dimensional maps, and is completely connected to the inputs by way of w_{ij}.

Let $\boldsymbol{x}(t)$ be an input vector at step t and let $\boldsymbol{w}_i(0)$ be weight vectors at initial values in R^n space. For input vector $\boldsymbol{x}(t)$, we calculate the distance between $\boldsymbol{x}(t)$ and the weight vector $\boldsymbol{w}_i(t)$, and select the weight vector as a winner c minimizing the distance. The process is written as follows:

$$c = \arg\min_i \{\|\boldsymbol{x} - \boldsymbol{w}_i\|\}, \tag{1}$$

where $\arg(\cdot)$ gives the index c of the winner.

With the use of the winner c, the weight vector $\boldsymbol{w}_i(t)$ is updated as follows:

$$\Delta \boldsymbol{w}_i = \begin{cases} \alpha(t)\,(\boldsymbol{x} - \boldsymbol{w}_i) & (i \in N_c(t)), \\ 0 & (\text{otherwise}), \end{cases} \tag{2}$$

where $\alpha(t)$ is the learning rate and is a decreasing function of time ($0 < \alpha(t) < 1$). $N_c(t)$ has a set of indexes of topological neighborhoods for the winner c at step t.

3 Image Restoration

A large number of weights are used in comparison with inputs when self-organizing maps are adapted to the traveling salesman problem, and good solutions based on the position of weights after learning have been approximately

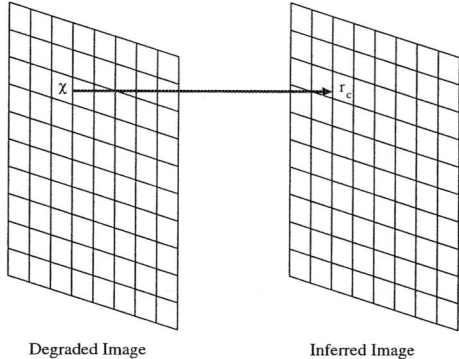

Degraded Image   Inferred Image

Fig. 1. Correspondence between degraded image and inferred image.

obtained. Furthermore, when self-organizing maps are applied to vector quantization, a few weights compared to inputs are utilized for the purpose of representing huge amounts of information as a small number of units, and many discussions have been made.

In this study, a relaxation algorithm influenced by self-organizing maps is proposed with the same number both of inputs and weights in order to infer the original image from a degraded image provided beforehand. Here, an input χ as the degraded image and a weight r_i as the inferred image are defined. A map forms that one element reacts for each pixel, and the image inference is executed by self-organizing maps using the pixel values as the input.

To begin with, r_i is randomly distributed near the central value of gray scale as an initial value. Next, a degraded image with $l \times m$ size is given. χ is arbitrarily selected among them, and let r_c be an inferred image corresponding to χ. As shown in Fig.1, both of the positions χ and r_c agree under the image. Therefore, the inferred image r_i is updated as follows:

$$\Delta r_i = \begin{cases} \alpha(t)\Theta\left(\chi - r_i\right) & (i \in N_c(t)), \\ 0 & (\text{otherwise}), \end{cases} \quad (3)$$

where $\Theta(a)$ is a function in which the value changes with a threshold $\theta(t)$ presented as follows:

$$\Theta(a) = \begin{cases} a & (|a| \leq \theta(t)), \\ 0 & (\text{otherwise}). \end{cases} \quad (4)$$

In case of learning according to self-organizing maps, the weights tend to react sensitively for the noisy inputs. Therefore, in order to avoid the tendency, Eq.(3) is adopted, instead of Eq.(2).

Using these functions, the weights are updated until the termination condition is satisfied. The image restoration is appropriately promoted as given in the next section.

Figure 2 shows an example of the arrangement of topological neighborhood. The circle signifies the weight and the line which connects the circles denotes the

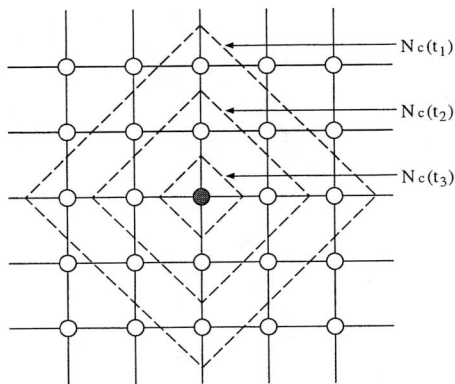

Fig. 2. Distribution of topological neighborhoods.

topological neighborhood. In this figure, the black circle expresses the weight of the winner c. As the set of the topological neighborhoods changes $N_c(t_1)$, $N_c(t_2)$, and $N_c(t_3)$ when the time varies t_1, t_2, and t_3, it is shown that the number of set decreases with time.

The image restoration (IR) algorithm is presented as follows.

[*IR algorithm*]

Step 1 Initialization:
Give initial weights $\{r_1(0), r_2(0), \cdots, r_{lm}(0)\}$ and maximum iteration T_{max}. $t \leftarrow 0$.

Step 2 Self-organization:
(**2.1**) Choose an input χ at random among $\{\chi_1, \chi_2, \cdots, \chi_{lm}\}$.
(**2.2**) Select r_c corresponding to the input χ.
(**2.3**) Update r_c and its neighborhoods according to Eq.(3).
(**2.4**) $t \leftarrow t + 1$.

Step 3 Condition:
If $t = T_{max}$, then terminate, otherwise go to Step 2.

In this study, a peak signal to noise (PSN) ratio P is used as the quality measure for the image restoration. PSN ratio P is presented as follows:

$$P = 10 \log_{10}(\sigma/E) \text{ [dB]} \tag{5}$$

where σ and E are the square of gray-scale length (i.e., $\sigma = (Q-1)^2$) and the mean square error between the original image and the restored image, respectively.

4 Numerical Experiments

In the numerical experiments, the image inference is performed to restore the degraded image with the size $l \times m = 512 \times 512$ and the gray-scale $Q = 256$.

(a) Degraded image i (b) Restored image i

Fig. 3. Degraded image i with 512 × 512 size and 256 gray-scale, and example of restored image i.

The degraded image contains the uniform noise of 25% in comparison with the original image, as shown in Fig. 3 (a). That is to say, the noise is included 25% pixels which are randomly chosen among the 512 × 512 pixels, and the chosen pixels are given 0 to 255 value at random. The initial weights are distributed near the central value of the gray scale Q. The parameters are chosen as follows: $l = 512$, $m = 512$, $T_{max} = 100 \cdot lm$, $N(t) = N_0 - \lfloor N_0 t/T_{max} \rfloor$, and $\theta(t) = \theta_0 - \lfloor \theta_0 t/T_{max} \rfloor$.

For the present algorithm of image restoration, Fig. 3 (b) shows an example of image restoration with the initial neighborhood $N_0 = 3$ and the initial threshold $\theta_0 = 118$. According to the technique given in this study, the degraded image is restorable.

Figure 4 shows the effect of the initial threshold θ_0 (i.e., I in this figure) on accuracy in PSN ratio P for each of initial neighborhood $N_0 = 1, 2, \cdots, 5$. In this case, P yields the maximum when $N_0 = 3$ and $I = 118$. Figure 3 (b) was restored by these values.

As an example of the complicated image, Fig. 5 (a) shows the degraded image. As well as the above-mentioned image, the degraded image contains the uniform noise of 25% compared to the original image. The condition of the computation is equal to that of the earlier description. According to the present algorithm, an example of image restoration with the initial neighborhood $N_0 = 2$ and the initial threshold $\theta_0 = 113$ is shown in Fig. 5 (b). It is proven that the degraded image can be also restored in this case.

Figure 6 presents the effect of the initial threshold θ_0 (i.e., I in this figure) on accuracy in PSN ratio P for each of initial neighborhood N_0. P yields the maximum when $N_0 = 2$ and $I = 113$. Using these values, an example of results for image restoration is given in Fig. 5 (b).

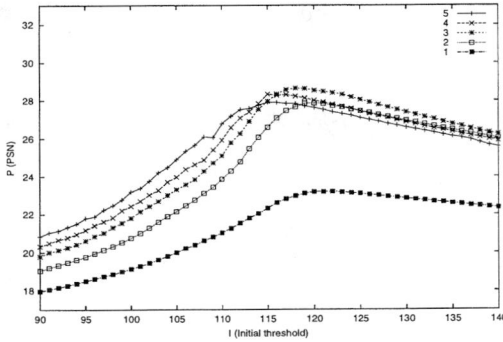

Fig. 4. PSN ratio and initial threshold for image i.

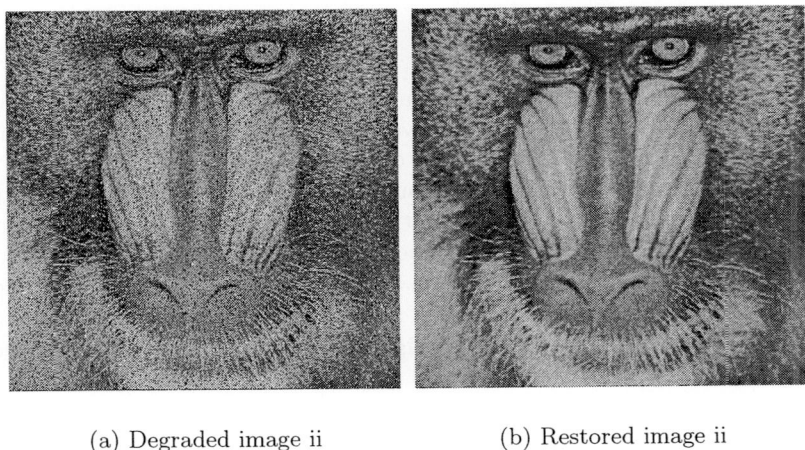

(a) Degraded image ii (b) Restored image ii

Fig. 5. Degraded image ii with 512 × 512 size and 256 gray-scale, and example of restored image ii.

Table 1 summarizes PSN ratio for results of the present method and the median filter. Here, the size of the median filter mask is 3 × 3. It is proven that the present method excels the median filter for both of images i and ii. The reason is that, weights do not oversensitively react a noisy input as introducing the updating function with the threshold in proportion to the difference between the input value and the inferred image, and the inference of original image appropriately proceeds since any pixel is influenced by surrounding pixels corresponding to the neighboring setting.

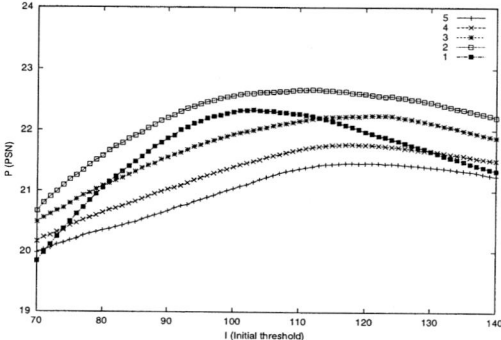

Fig. 6. PSN ratio and initial threshold for image ii.

5 Conclusions

In this study, a relaxation algorithm influenced by self-organizing maps for image restoration has been presented and its validity has been shown through numerical experiments. The present method created a map containing one unit for each pixel. Utilizing pixel values as input, the image inference was carried out by self-organizing maps. Then, an updating function with a threshold according to the difference between the input value and the inferred pixel was introduced, so as not to respond to a noisy input sensitively. Therefore, the inference of original image proceeded appropriately since any pixel was influenced by surrounding pixels corresponding to the neighboring setting. Finally, more effective techniques of the present algorithm will be studied for the future works.

Table 1. PSN ratio for results of the present method and the median filter.

	Present method	Median filter
Image i	28.7 dB	27.4 dB
Image ii	22.7 dB	19.5 dB

References

1. Grossberg, S.: Adaptive pattern classification and universal recoding: I. Parallel development and coding of neural feature detectors. Biol. Cybern. **23** (1976) 121–134
2. Willshaw, D.J., Malsburg, C.: How patterned neural connections can be set up by self-organization. Proc. R. Soc. Lond. B. **194** (1976) 431–445
3. Hertz, J., Krogh, A., Palmer, R.G.: Introduction to the theory of neural computation. Addison-Wesley (1991)

4. Kohonen, T.: Self-organizing maps. Springer-Verlag Berlin (1995)
5. Bauer, H.-U., Pawelzik, K.R.: Quantifying the neighborhood preservation of self-organizing feature maps. IEEE Trans. Neural Networks **3** (1992) 570–579
6. Martinetz, T., Schulten, K.: Topology representing networks. Neural Networks **7** (1994) 507–522
7. Villmann, T., Herrmann, M., Martinetz, T.M.: Topology preservation in self-organizing feature maps: Exact definition and measurement. IEEE Trans. Neural Networks **8** (1997) 256–266
8. Durbin, R., Willshaw, D.: An analogue approach to the traveling salesman problem using an elastic net method. Nature **326** (1987) 689–691
9. Angéniol, B., Vaubois, G. de La C., Le Texier, J.-Y.: Self-organizing feature maps and the traveling salesman problem. Neural Networks **1** (1988) 289–293
10. Ritter, H., Schulten, K.: On the stationary state of Kohonen's self-organizing sensory mapping. Biol. Cybern. **54** (1986) 99–106
11. Ritter, H., Schulten, K.: Convergence properties of Kohonen's topology conserving maps, Fluctuations, stability, and dimension selection. Biol. Cybern. **60** (1988) 59–71
12. Tanaka, T., Saito, M.: Quantitative properties of Kohonen's self-organizing maps as adaptive vector quantizers. IEICE Trans. **J75-D-II** (1992) 1085–1092
13. Martinetz, T.M., Berkovich, S.G., Schulten, K.J.: "Neural-gas" network for vector quantization and its application to time-series prediction. IEEE Trans. Neural Networks **4** (1993) 558–569
14. Maeda, M., Miyajima, H., Murashima, S.: An adaptive learning and self-deleting neural network for vector quantization. IEICE Trans. Fundamentals **E79-A** (1996) 886–1893
15. Maeda, M., Miyajima, H.: Competitive learning methods with refractory and creative approaches. IEICE Trans. Fundamentals **E82-A** (1999) 1825–1833
16. Geman S., Geman D.: Stochastic relaxation, Gibbs distributions, and the Bayesian restoration of images. IEEE Trans. Pattern Anal. Mach. Intel. **6** (1984) 721–741
17. Maeda, M., Ohta, M., Miyajima, H.: An algorithm of statistical mechanics for image restoration. Proc. IEICE Int. Symp. Nonlinear Theory and Its Applications **1** (2001) 107–110

A Gradient Network for Vector Quantization and Its Image Compression Applications

Hatice Doğan and Cüneyt Güzeliş

Dokuz Eylül University, Engineering Faculty
Electrical-Electronics Dept., Kaynaklar Buca
İzmir-Türkiye
`hatice.dogan@eee.deu.edu.tr`
`cuneyt.guzelis@eee.deu.edu.tr`

Abstract. The ultimate goal of vector quantization (VQ) is to encode the signal into representative code vectors such that it can be represented digitally in a compact way. This task can be formulated as an optimization problem, namely the minimization of the total distance between the signal and the code vectors. In this paper, we formulate VQ as a constrained binary integer programming problem by eliminating the code vectors, where the constraints that partition the signal space are linear. We propose a two dimensional Gradient Network to solve this problem. The performance of this solution method is tested on image compression applications and the results are compared with the ones obtained by the well-known k-means algorithm.

1 Introduction

Vector quantization is a powerful technique widely used in signal processing especially for compression. The objective of VQ is to efficiently encode the signal into a digital representation that compactly represents the original signal while preserving the essential information contained in the original signal [1]. Design of a vector quantizer is a multidimensional optimization problem in which total quantization error is minimized. The optimal vector quantizer must satisfy two necessary conditions: (i) Nearest neighbor condition: for a given codebook each data vector is mapped to the closest code vector in according to an appropriate distance measure (ii) Centroid condition: for a given partition each code vector must be the center of its region.

Many clustering methods have been proposed on the design of an optimal vector quantizer [2]. Among these k-means clustering or Generalized Lloyd Algorithm is the well-known technique, which is based on the application of the (i) and (ii) successively. Indeed this can be classified as a relaxation type gradient-based iterative procedure. In the literature, the clustering problem that is crucial for VQ, formulated as a 0-1 quadratic programming problem, where the binary variables represent the probability that a data point is assigned to a certain cluster. Hopfield network had been used and were shown to outperform conventional iterative techniques when the clusters are well defined [3]. In these methods, k-means clustering algorithm is mimicked [4], [5].

The new formulation for posing the clustering in an optimization framework is firstly introduced in [6]. Where the clustering of finite number of samples is formulated as a linearly constrained binary integer programming problem. Contrary to [4], [5], two necessary rules for an optimum vector quantizer are combined in [6] as a unique rule by substituting (ii) into (i). [6] then proposes a two dimensional Gradient Neural Network to solve the obtained optimization problem.

In this paper, a new Gradient Network with a completely different dynamics is proposed for the same purpose. To increase the convergence speed of the network and to escape from the local minima, new terms namely noise and acceleration terms are incorporated to the dynamics of the network. The newly developed dynamics is superior to the one in [6] in terms of providing successful image compression application reported in the paper.

This paper is organized as follows: VQ is reviewed in Section 2, our formulation is introduced in Section 3, the new Gradient Network is presented in Section 4, the results in image compression are given in Section 5 and conclusions are given in the Section 6.

2   Vector Quantization (VQ)

A vector quantizer Q is a mapping of n-dimensional space $\mathbf{R}^n$ into a finite subset C of $\mathbf{R}^n$. Design of a vector quantizer is accomplished by generating a codebook from the training data using the total quantization error. The k- means clustering algorithm is usually used for this purpose. Given a finite set of observations of data vector $\mathbf{x}_j$, $j=1,...,L$ where $\mathbf{x}_j \in \mathbf{R}^n$ and given k cluster centers, the optimal partitioning of the data samples is achieved by the following optimization:

$$\min \quad \sum_{i=1}^{k} \sum_{j=1}^{L} m_{ij} \left\| \mathbf{x}_j - \mathbf{c}_i \right\|^2$$

$$subject\ to\ (s.t.) \quad m_{ij} \in S = \left\{ m_{ij} \middle| \sum_{i=1}^{k} m_{ij} = 1,\ m_{ij} \in \{0,1\} \right\} \tag{1}$$

where m_{ij} indicates the membership of data vector $\mathbf{x}_j$ to i'th cluster i.e. $m_{ij}=1$ if $x_j \in C_i$ and 0 otherwise, $\mathbf{c}_i$ denotes the center of the cluster C_i. Constraints provide that no data vector can be assigned to more than one cluster.

3   VQ as a Binary Integer Optimization Problem

We formulate the clustering problem as the minimization of the distance between the data vectors and the centers of the clusters. Our cost function is the total quantization error, which we want to minimize it, is shown in (2):

$$\min \quad \sum_{j=1}^{L}\left\|\mathbf{x}_j - \sum_{i=1}^{k} m_{ij}\mathbf{c}_i\right\|_2^2 \qquad (2)$$

$$\text{s.t.} \quad m_{ij} \in S$$

If (1) and (2) are compared, it can be seen that they are equal on the constraint set. But if the constraints are satisfied in the steady state of an associated dynamics, they have different gradients and contrary to (1) the error is calculated once for every data vector in (2), this reduces the computation time.

(2) can be written in matrix form as follows:

$$\min_{\mathbf{C},\mathbf{M}} \quad \|\mathbf{X} - \mathbf{CM}\|_F^2 \qquad (3)$$

$$\text{s.t.} \quad m_{ij} \in S$$

Where $\mathbf{X}$ is the data matrix, $\mathbf{C}$ is the centers matrix and $\mathbf{M}$ is the indicator matrix that indicates which objects belongs to which cluster. It is well-known that $\mathbf{C}^* = \mathbf{XM}^+$ is the solution of this problem. $\mathbf{M}^+$ denotes the Moore-Penrose pseudo inverse of $\mathbf{M}$. Substituting of the $\mathbf{C}^*$ in (3) and using the properties $\mathbf{M}^+\mathbf{MM}^+ = \mathbf{M}^+$ and $\|\mathbf{A}\|_F^2 = tr\{\mathbf{AA}^T\}$ we obtain:

$$\min_{\mathbf{M}} \quad -\sum_{i=1}^{k} \frac{1}{\sum_{j=1}^{L} m_{ij}} \|\mathbf{Xm}_i^T\|_2^2 \qquad (4)$$

$$\text{s.t.} \quad m_{ij} \in S$$

The function that is minimized for this problem will be constructed using a penalty function approach. That is, the energy function will consist of the objective function and penalty functions to enforce the constraints. The first term is the average distortion; second term provides that no data vector can be assigned to more than one cluster in the final partition and the third term guaranties $m_{ij} \in \{0,1\}$. The cost function that is expressed as a binary integer optimization problem is given below:

$$E(\mathbf{m}) = -\sum_{i=1}^{k}\sum_{r=1}^{L}\sum_{j=1}^{L}\frac{1}{\sum_{s=1}^{L} m_{is}} \mathbf{x}_j^T \mathbf{x}_r m_{ij} m_{ir} + B\sum_{j=1}^{L}\left(\sum_{i=1}^{k} m_{ij} - 1\right)^2 + C\sum_{j=1}^{L}\sum_{i=1}^{k} m_{ij}(1 - m_{ij}) \qquad (5)$$

where B and C are positive penalty coefficients. This cost function can be minimized with a dynamics, for instance with a dynamical neural networks.

4 Gradient Network

Hopfield neural network approach has been widely used for solving optimization problems. The energy of the Hopfield network does not increase with time and its minima are stable steady states of the network. The energy function has typically many minima that represent valid solutions to the problem, deeper minima corresponds to good solutions and the deepest minima to the best solution. The dynamics of the two dimensional Hopfield network is described by (5)-(7) and the energy function of it, is shown in (8).

$$V_{ij} = g(u_{ij}) = \frac{1}{2}\left(1 + \tanh\frac{u_{ij}}{\lambda_0}\right) = \frac{1}{1 + e^{-2u_{ij}/\lambda_0}} \tag{6}$$

$$\frac{du_{ij}}{dt} = \sum_r \sum_h T_{ij,rh} V_{rh} - I_{ij} \tag{7}$$

$$E = -\sum_i \sum_j \sum_r \sum_h T_{ij,rh} V_{ij} V_{rh} + \sum_i \sum_j I_{ij} V_{ij} \tag{8}$$

V_{ij} is the binary state of the neuron (ij) and $T_{ij;rh}$ is the interconnection weight between the neuron (ij) and the neuron (rh) and $g(\cdot)$ is the transfer function of the neurons that relates the input u_{ij} to the output V_{ij}. λ_0 determines the steepness of the transfer function. The simulation of this network by computer implies a numerical integration of (7). The discrete dynamics is described by:

$$\frac{\Delta u_{ij}}{\Delta t} = \sum_r \sum_h T_{ij,rh} V_{rh} - I_{ij} \tag{9}$$

The input potential to neuron (ij) at step k+1 is defined with respect to potential at step k as follows [7]:

$$u_{ij}(k+1) = u_{ij}(k) + \Delta t \left(\sum_r \sum_h T_{ij,rh} V_{rh} - I_{ij} \right) \tag{10}$$

To find a solution, the network is started at a randomly selected state. It evolves until it reaches a minimum of the function E and stops there forever.

Gradient Network, which is designed to minimize the cost function, is a natural extension of the original formulation of Hopfield and Tank. It consists of kxL neurons, which are mutually interconnected. The columns of the network represent the data vectors that are to be classified and the rows of the network represent the given classes and m_{ij}'s are the outputs of the neurons. As a new feature distinguishing the proposed network from the one in [6], a noise term **N** and a positive function $\eta(t)$ are incorporated to the dynamics of the network in order to escape from the local minima and to increase the convergence speed, respectively.

During the optimization process the additive noise should approach zero in time so that the network itself will become deterministic prior to reaching the final solution [8]. Adding a noise term to the cost, the energy function will be described as:

$$E_{new} = E + c(t) \sum_{i=1}^{k} \sum_{j=1}^{L} n_{ij} m_{ij}. \tag{11}$$

Where E_{new} is termed the perturbed form of the energy function, n_{ij} is an element of **N** which is an independent white noise source and $c(t)$ is the parameter controlling the magnitude of noise that must be selected in such a way that it approaches zero as time t tends to *"infinity"*. Our choice is:

$$c(t) = ke^{-\alpha t}. \tag{12}$$

Where $n_{ij} \in [0,1]$, $k = 10^{10}$ and $\alpha = 0,9$.

Searching for optimal values of B and C coefficients at (5) is time consuming and laborious. In order to alleviate the calculation of them, we can adopt the winner-take-all rule to the outputs of the neurons that are in the same column. By this way we can automatically satisfy both of the two constraints. Gradient Network is shown in the Fig. 1. The interconnection weight between neurons is:

$$T_{ij;ir} = \frac{1}{\sum_{j=1}^{L} m_{ij}} \mathbf{x}_j^T \mathbf{x}_r. \tag{13}$$

Note that $T_{ij;ir}$'s here are dependent on the neuron outputs m_{ij}'s, differing the proposed nonlinearly weighted model from the original Hopfield network as well as from the network proposed in [6], whose parameters were defined independent of these terms. The dynamics of the Gradient Network is given in (14)-(16). $\eta(t)$ is a scalar positive function of time that determines the displacement to be taken in the direction of the vector $d = -\nabla E(m_{ij})$.

$$\frac{dU_{ij}}{dt} = -\eta(t)\left[\frac{\partial E}{\partial m_{ij}} + c(t)n_{ij}\right]$$
$$= \eta(t)\left[2\frac{\mathbf{m}_i\mathbf{y}_j}{me} - \frac{\mathbf{m}_i\mathbf{Y}\mathbf{m}_i^T}{me^2}\right] - \eta(t)c(t)n_{ij} \tag{14}$$

$$U_{ij}(t+1) = U_{ij}(t) + \frac{dU_{ij}(t)}{dt} \tag{15}$$

$$m_{ij}(t+1) = \begin{cases} 1 & if\ i = \max\{U_{1,j}(t),...,U_{k,j}(t)\} \\ 0 & otherwise. \end{cases} \tag{16}$$

Where $\mathbf{m}_i$ and $\mathbf{m}_j$ stands for the rows and the columns of the **M** respectively, $\mathbf{Y}=\mathbf{X}^T\mathbf{X}$, $\mathbf{y}_j$ stands for the columns of the **Y** and $me=\mathbf{m}_i.\mathbf{e}$ where $\mathbf{e}=[1...1]^T$, $\mathbf{e} \in \mathbf{R}^n$.

It is possible to find a convenient $\eta(t)$ in order to ensure the network reach a local minima after a specified period of time, say T_s [8]. The displacement $\eta(t)$ is selected by experimentally. In our experimental study we found the function $\eta(t)=t^{90}(T_s-t)^{90}$.

Once all the parameters have been chosen, a typical simulation of the Gradient Network proceeds as follows:

1. Initialize the input and the output of neurons in a random way
2. Iteratively calculate the dynamics.
3. Go back to step 2 until the network converges.

Randomly choosing the initial input and output values of the neurons provides good approximation to global minimum as observed in the simulations of the considered Gradient Network.

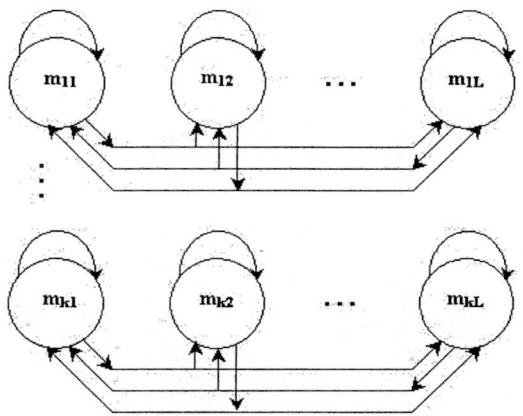

Fig. 1. The structure of the proposed Gradient Network.

5 Results in Image Compression

To compress an image the whole image is divided into L blocks (a block represents a training vector, which occupies lxl components) and mapped onto the two dimensional Gradient Network which consists of a grid of kxL neurons.

The performance of the k-means clustering and the proposed Gradient Network algorithm were compared for real images. The codebook design is the primary problem in image compression based on VQ. The data vectors were extracted from 128x128 images, which were divided into 4x4 blocks to generate nonoverlapping 16 dimensional vectors respectively. The codebook size was chosen as 128. The peak signal to noise ratio (PSNR), which is defined for an NxN image as follows, was evaluated in the reconstructed images:

$$PSNR = 10\log_{10} \frac{255 \times 255}{\frac{1}{N}\sum_{x=1}^{N}\sum_{y=1}^{N}(f_{xy} - \hat{f}_{xy})^2} \qquad (17)$$

where f_{xy} and $\hat{f}_{xy}$ are the pixel gray levels from the original and the reconstructed images and 255 is the peak gray level.

Algorithms were tested with 20 different initial conditions. Fig. 2 shows the original and reconstructed images obtained by using the Gradient Network and k-means clustering. The average PSNR results of algorithms are given in Table 1.

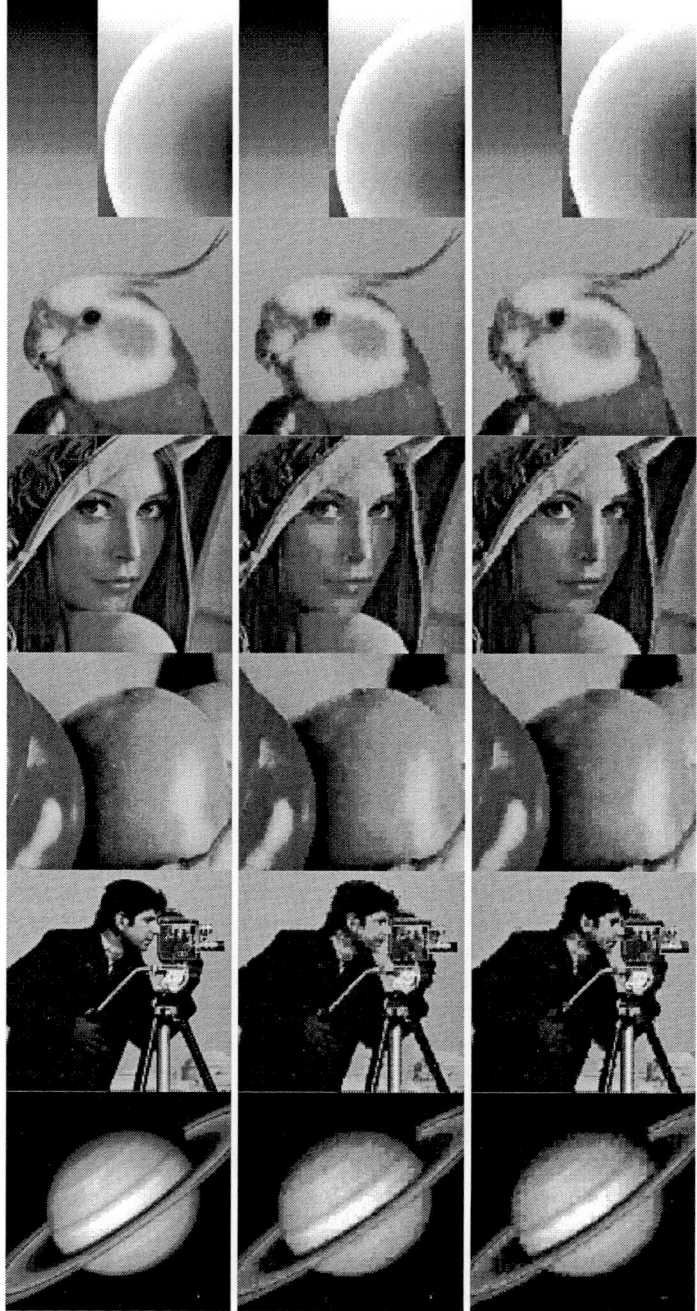

Fig. 2. Column 1: Original images. Columns 2-3: Reconstructed images obtained by using the Gradient Network and k-means clustering respectively. Compression ratio: 8:1

Table 1. Average PSNRs of reconstructed images

Images	Proposed Gradient Network	K-means
Circle-bar	39.843	36.888
Bird	33.082	32.638
Lena	27.856	27.525
Peppers	31.728	31.425
Cameraman	25.790	24.732
Saturn	31.576	30.517

6 Conclusions

A two dimensional Gradient Network has been introduced for vector quantization in image compression. Though the proposed model, like all gradient related methods, can not ensure the global minimum, its performance is better than the k-means clustering algorithm, as approved by the experimental results. It has two major advantages: in our energy function, optimization is done according to the one variable which indicates the membership of the data vector so instead of iteratively updating the codebook as in k-means clustering, the codebook is updated just once after the last iteration and because of it works in parallel, computation time can be reduced by way of parallel processing.

References

1. Ahalt S.C., Fowler J.E.: Vector Quantization using Artificial Neural Network Models. Proceedings of The Int. Workshop on Adaptive Methods and Emergent Techniques for Signal Processing and Communications. (1993) 42–61
2. Gray R.M., Neuhoff D.L.: Quantization. IEEE Transactions on Information Theory, Vol. 44, No. 6. (1998) 2325–2383
3. Smith K.A.: Neural Networks for Combinatorial Optimization A Review of More Than A Decade Research. Informs Journal on Computing, Vol.11, No. 1. (1999)
4. Kamgar-Parsi B., Gualtieri J.A, Devaney J. E., Kamgar-Parsi B.: Clustering with Neural Networks. Biological Cybernetics 6, (1990) 201–208
5. Kamgar-Parsi B., Kamgar-Parsi B.: On Problem Solving with Hopfield Neural Networks. Biological Cybernetics 62, (1990) 415–523
6. Doğan H.,Güzeliş C.: VQ As an Integer Optimization Problem and Gradient Artificial Neural Network Solution (In Turkish). Proceeding of SIU2002, (2002) 266–271
7. Joya G., Atencia M.A., Sandoval F.: Hopfield Neural Networks for Optimization Study of The Different Dynamics. Neurocomputing Vol. 43, (2002) 219–237
8. Sammouda R., Noboru N., Nishitani H.: A Comparison of Hopfield Neural Network and Boltzmann Machine in Segmenting MR Images of the Brain. IEEE Transactions on Nuclear Science, Vol. 43, No. 6 (1996) 3361–3369

Multi-scale Switching Linear Dynamical Systems

Onno Zoeter* and Tom Heskes

SNN, University of Nijmegen
Geert Grooteplein 21, 6525 EZ, Nijmegen, The Netherlands
{orzoeter, tom}@snn.kun.nl

Abstract. Switching linear dynamic systems can monitor systems that operate in different regimes. In this article we introduce a class of multi-scale switching linear dynamical systems that are particularly suited if such regimes form a hierarchy. The setup consists of a specific switching linear dynamical system for every level of coarseness. Jeffrey's rule of conditioning is used to coordinate the models at the different levels.
When the models are appropriately constrained, inference at finer levels can be performed independently for every subtree. This makes it possible to determine the required degree of detail on-line. The refinements of very improbable regimes need not be explored.
The computational complexity of exact inference in both the standard and the multi-class switching linear dynamical system is exponential in the number of observations. We describe an appropriate approximate inference algorithm based on expectation propagation and relate it to a variant of the Bethe free energy.

1 Introduction

In a *linear dynamical system* (LDS) a hidden state variable $\mathbf{x}_t$ is assumed to evolve with Markovian, linear Gaussian dynamics, of which only noisy measurements $\mathbf{z}_t$ are available. In a *switching linear dynamical system* (SLDS) this model is extended with discrete switch states s_t that denote the *regime* the system is in. Within every regime the state $\mathbf{x}_t$ evolves with different dynamics and also the observation model $p(\mathbf{z}_t|\mathbf{x}_t, s_t)$ might be different. The regime itself also follows a first-order Markov process. The model equations read

$$p(\mathbf{x}_t|\mathbf{x}_{t-1}, s_t = j, \boldsymbol{\theta}) = \mathcal{N}(\mathbf{x}_t; A_j \mathbf{x}_{t-1}, Q_j) \quad p(\mathbf{z}_t|\mathbf{x}_t, s_t = j, \boldsymbol{\theta}) = \mathcal{N}(\mathbf{z}_t; C_j \mathbf{x}_t, R_j)$$

$$p(s_t = j|s_{t-1} = i, \boldsymbol{\theta}) = \Pi_{i \to j} ,$$

with $\mathcal{N}(.;.,.)$ the Gaussian probability density function, and $\boldsymbol{\theta}$ the parameters in the model. The prior $p(s_1|\boldsymbol{\theta})$ is taken multinomial and $p(\mathbf{x}_1|s_1, \boldsymbol{\theta})$ Gaussian.

In this article we are concerned with models where the regimes s_t have natural refinements in sub-regimes as defined below. We will restrict ourselfs to models with two levels: a fine grained and a coarse grained level. Extensions to multiple levels are straightforward. At the coarse grained level, we refer to the discrete

---
* O. Zoeter is supported by the Dutch Competence Centre Paper and Board

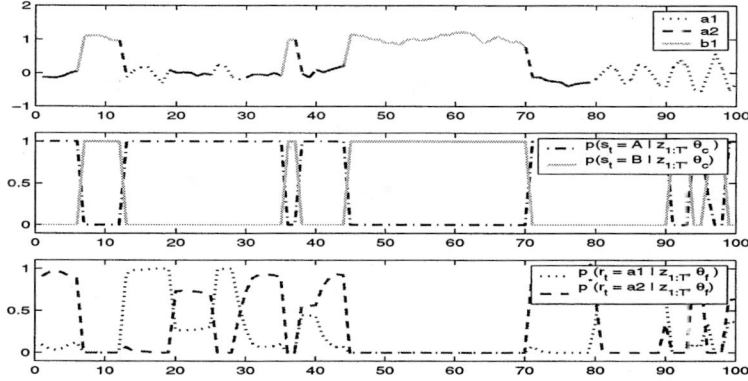

Fig. 1. A simple example: $M_c = \{A, B\}$, $\text{ch}(A) = \{a_1, a_2\}$, and $\text{ch}(B) = \{b_1\}$. Synthetic data was generated from $\boldsymbol{\theta}_f$ (top; colors indicate regimes as they were generated). First, posteriors for coarse regimes are inferred (middle). Then, with these results fixed, refinements of A and B are inferred independently (bottom; only results for submodel A are shown).

state as s_t, and to the continuous state as $\mathbf{x}_t$. We denote the set of regimes that s_t can take on with M_c. At the fine level we use r_t, $\mathbf{y}_t$ and M_f. The hierarchy, or grouping, we have in mind is a parent-child relationship $\text{ch}(.)$: for every $j \in M_f$ there is exactly one $m \in M_c$ for which $j \in \text{ch}(m)$ holds.

In the multi-scale setup of this article there are two different models: one for the coarse and one for the fine level. First the state and regime are inferred in the coarse model. Then, given the posterior probabilities for the coarse parent regimes, a refinement is inferred in the second model. Jeffrey's rule of conditioning is used to ensure that the posterior weights of the children add up to that of the parent. A simple example with synthetic data is presented in Fig. 1 (Matlab code with the full model description is available at www.snn.kun.nl/~orzoeter/multiscale.html). The two model setup is discussed in Sect. 2. In Sect. 3 restrictions for the fine level model are introduced so that refinements of the coarse regimes can be inferred independently. This way, in an on-line application, only probable regimes need to be explored in greater detail. In Sect. 4 we show how a deterministic approximation overcomes the computational complexity implied by the SLDS.

2 The Fine Level Model

The model for the first level is a basic SLDS. For the fine level model we want to ensure that the posterior probabilities of being in a child of m sum to the posterior probability of being in m in the coarse model:

$$\sum_{r_1 \in \text{ch}(s_1)} \cdots \sum_{r_T \in \text{ch}(s_T)} p(r_{1:T}|\mathbf{z}_{1:T}, \boldsymbol{\theta}_f) = p(s_{1:T}|\mathbf{z}_{1:T}, \boldsymbol{\theta}_c) \ .$$

To enforce these constraints we introduce extra random variables $\tilde{s}_{1:T}$ that have a link satisfying

$$p(r_t = j | r_{t-1} = i, \tilde{s}_t = m, \boldsymbol{\theta}_f) = 0 , \quad \text{if } j \neq \text{ch}(m) , \tag{1}$$

i.e. the link rules out the combination of a parent m with a "cousin" j. The motivation behind the introduction of $\tilde{s}_t$ is that we can now put constraints on the *sum* over possible values of r_t: $\sum_{j \in \text{ch}(m)} p(r_t = j | \mathbf{z}_{1:T}, \boldsymbol{\theta}_f)$, instead of only on individual values. If $p(s_{1:T} | \mathbf{z}_{1:T}, \boldsymbol{\theta}_c)$ is crisp, making the fine model agree with the coarse can be done by treating $\tilde{s}_{1:T}$ as observations ("hard clamping").

If, however, $p(s_{1:T} | \mathbf{z}_{1:T}, \boldsymbol{\theta}_c)$ is not crisp, for example if it is the result of inference at the coarse level, we have to ensure that the marginal over $\tilde{s}_{1:T}$ is kept fixed to $p^*(\tilde{s}_{1:T} = \text{path}_i) \equiv p(s_{1:T} = \text{path}_i | \mathbf{z}_{1:T}, \boldsymbol{\theta}_c)$ ("soft clamping"). This is done by Jeffrey's rule of conditioning:

$$p^*(\tilde{s}_{1:T}, r_{1:T}, \mathbf{y}_{1:T} | \mathbf{z}_{1:T}, \boldsymbol{\theta}_f) \equiv p(r_{1:T}, \mathbf{z}_{1:T} | \tilde{s}_{1:T}, \mathbf{z}_{1:T}, \boldsymbol{\theta}_f) p^*(\tilde{s}_{1:T}) , \tag{2}$$

We denote probabilities that have the constraints on $\tilde{s}_{1:T}$ enforced with $p^*(.)$.

3 Independent Submodels

The fine level model described in Sect. 2 ensures consistency with the already inferred coarse model. It is however necessary to treat the refinements of all coarse regimes together in one large model for the second level. In this section we will alleviate this requirement by making appropriate choices for the state and regime transition probabilities such that the sub-models become independent.

The idea is that the model is restricted such that whenever there is a switch in coarse regimes ($\tilde{s}_{t-1} \neq \tilde{s}_t$) the discrete and continuous latent states at the fine level uncouple (see Fig. 2). I.e. when $\tilde{s}_{t-1} \neq \tilde{s}_t$, $\{r_t, \mathbf{y}_t\}$ does not depend on $\{r_{t-1}, \mathbf{y}_{t-1}\}$. For the continous state this is accomplished by introducing a "reset" after a switch in $\tilde{s}$: the new state is drawn from a Gaussian prior:

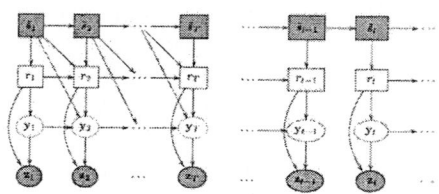

Fig. 2. Graphical structure corresponding to the fine level model. Left: when $\tilde{s}_{t-1} \neq \tilde{s}_t$, right: when $\tilde{s}_{t-1} \neq \tilde{s}_t$.

$$p(\mathbf{y}_t | \mathbf{y}_{t-1}, r_t = j, \tilde{s}_{t-1} = l, \tilde{s}_t = m, \boldsymbol{\theta}_f) = \begin{cases} \mathcal{N}(\mathbf{y}_t; A_j \mathbf{y}_{t-1}, Q_j) & : l = m \\ \mathcal{N}(\mathbf{y}_t; \boldsymbol{\nu}_j, \Sigma_j) & : l \neq m . \end{cases}$$

The regime transition probability is constrained similarly:

$$p(r_t = j | r_{t-1} = i, \tilde{s}_{t-1} = l, \tilde{s}_t = m, \boldsymbol{\theta}_f) = \begin{cases} 0 : j \notin \text{ch}(m) & (3-a) \\ \Pi_{i \to j | m} : l = m, j \in \text{ch}(m) & (3-b) \\ \pi_{j | m} : l \neq m, j \in \text{ch}(m) . & (3-c) \end{cases}$$

Case (3-a) encodes the already discussed constraint that every child has only one parent (1). Case (3-b) describes the probability of jumping between regimes within one subtree ("brothers"). These probabilities are fully modeled. Case (3-c) states that if a jump at the coarse level occurs, the fine level regime is drawn from a prior. Note that, to make notation not too complex, we have left out a possible dependence of $\mathbf{y}_t$ on r_{t-1}, and a dependence of r_t on $\tilde{s}_{t-1}$. Crucial for the sub-models to become independent is only the conditional independence depicted in Fig. 2 for the case $\tilde{s}_{t-1} \neq \tilde{s}_t$.

The conditional independencies in the model allow us to write

$$p(r_{1:T}, \mathbf{y}_{1:T} | \mathbf{z}_{1:T}, \tilde{s}_{1:T}, \boldsymbol{\theta}_\mathrm{f}) \propto \prod_{\substack{t=2 \\ \tilde{s}_{t-1}=\tilde{s}_t}}^{T} p(\mathbf{z}_t, \mathbf{y}_t, r_t | \mathbf{y}_{t-1}, r_{t-1}, \tilde{s}_t, \boldsymbol{\theta}_\mathrm{f}) \prod_{\substack{t=1 \\ \tilde{s}_{t-1} \neq \tilde{s}_t}}^{T} p(\mathbf{z}_t, \mathbf{y}_t, r_t | \tilde{s}_t, \boldsymbol{\theta}_\mathrm{f})$$

$$= \prod_{m \in M_\mathrm{c}} \left\{ \prod_{\substack{t=2 \\ \tilde{s}_{t-1}=\tilde{s}_t=m}}^{T} p(\mathbf{z}_t, \mathbf{y}_t, r_t^{(m)} | \mathbf{y}_{t-1}, r_{t-1}^{(m)}, \tilde{s}_t = m, \boldsymbol{\theta}^{(m)}) \times \right.$$

$$\left. \prod_{\substack{t=1 \\ \tilde{s}_{t-1} \neq \tilde{s}_t = m}}^{T} p(\mathbf{z}_t, \mathbf{y}_t, r_t^{(m)} | \tilde{s}_t = m, \boldsymbol{\theta}^{(m)}) \right\}, \qquad (4)$$

where $\boldsymbol{\theta}^{(m)}$ are the disjoint parameter sets that together form $\boldsymbol{\theta}_\mathrm{f}$, and $r_t^{(m)}$ are variables ranging over ch(m). The boundary $t = 1$ can be taken into account by setting $\tilde{s}_0 \neq m$ for all m.

The marginal $p^*(\tilde{s}_{1:T})$ is fixed, so by (4) the posterior $p^*(\tilde{s}_{1:T}, r_{1:T}, \mathbf{y}_{1:T} | \mathbf{z}_{1:T}, \boldsymbol{\theta}_\mathrm{f})$ in (2) factors into independent subtree terms. Therefore these terms, and hence filtered or smoothed one-slice posteriors, can be computed independently.

4 Approximate Inference

4.1 The Coarse Level Model

The computational complexity of exact inference in an SLDS is exponential in the number of observations. One way to see this is to look at the posterior

$$p(\mathbf{x}_t | \mathbf{z}_{1:T}) = \sum_{s_{1:T}} p(\mathbf{x}_t | s_{1:T}, \mathbf{z}_{1:T}) p(s_{1:T} | \mathbf{z}_{1:T}) ,$$

where for notational convenience we drop the dependence on $\boldsymbol{\theta}_\mathrm{c}$. Every regime history $s_{1:T}$ gives rise to a different Gaussian $p(\mathbf{x}_t | s_{1:T}, \mathbf{z}_{1:T})$. Since $s_{1:T}$ is not observed, we have to take every possible history into account and integrate these out. So the exact posterior is a mixture with $|M_\mathrm{c}|^T$ components. In this section we therefore describe a greedy approximate inference strategy for the SLDS. An adaptation for the fine level SLDS from Sect. 2 is presented in Sect. 4.2.

The approximation is a particular form of *expectation propagation* [4]. We present it here in the spirit of the sum-product algorithm [3]. For ease of notation and interpretability we treat $\mathbf{u}_t = \{s_t, \mathbf{x}_t\}$ together as one *conditionally*

Gaussian distributed random variable. Slightly abusing notation, we will use the sum sign for the combined operation of summing out s_t and integrating out $\mathbf{x}_t$. The posterior distribution can be written as a product of *local potentials*, ψ_t:

$$p(\mathbf{u}_{1:T}|\mathbf{z}_{1:T}) \propto \prod_{t=1}^{T} \psi_t(\mathbf{u}_{t-1}, \mathbf{u}_t), \text{ with } \psi_t(\mathbf{u}_{t-1}, \mathbf{u}_t) \equiv p(\mathbf{z}_t|\mathbf{u}_t)p(\mathbf{u}_t|\mathbf{u}_{t-1}),$$

and $\psi_1(\mathbf{u}_0, \mathbf{u}_1) \equiv p(\mathbf{z}_1|\mathbf{u}_1)$. We are interested in one and two-slice marginals of the joint posterior. To avoid having to construct the entire posterior, these marginals are computed by local operations where *messages* are sent between nodes in a graph. We distinguish *variable nodes* that are associated with $\mathbf{u}_t$'s and *function nodes* that are associated with ψ_t's. The message from ψ_t forward to $\mathbf{u}_t$ is called $\alpha_t(\mathbf{u}_t)$ and the message from ψ_t back to $\mathbf{u}_{t-1}$ is referred to as $\beta_{t-1}(\mathbf{u}_{t-1})$. In a chain, variable nodes simply pass on the messages they receive. The message passing scheme is depicted in Fig. 3.

We denote the approximation of $p(\mathbf{u}_t|\mathbf{y}_{1:T})$ by $q_t(\mathbf{u}_t)$. It is computed by multiplying all incoming messages from neighboring function nodes: $q_t(\mathbf{u}_t) \propto \alpha_t(\mathbf{u}_t)\beta_t(\mathbf{u}_t)$. Associated with every function node is an approximate two-slice belief that we denote by

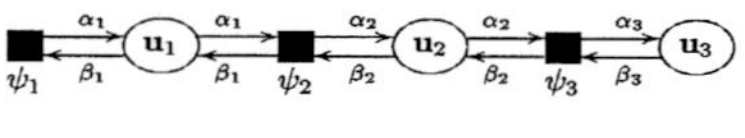

Fig. 3. Message propagation.

$p(\mathbf{u}_{t-1}, \mathbf{u}_t|\mathbf{y}_{1:T}) \approx \hat{p}_t(\mathbf{u}_{t-1}, \mathbf{u}_t)$. Throughout the procedure we will ensure, using greedy approximations, that both $\hat{p}_t$ and q_t are conditionally Gaussian (CG) distributed. New messages from function node ψ_t to variable node $\mathbf{u}_{t'}$, where t' can be $t-1$ or t are computed as follows.

1. Construct a two-slice belief by multiplying the potential corresponding to the local function node ψ_t with *all* messages from neighboring variable nodes to ψ_t, yielding

$$\hat{p}_t(\mathbf{u}_{t-1}, \mathbf{u}_t) \propto \alpha_{t-1}(\mathbf{u}_{t-1})\psi_t(\mathbf{u}_{t-1}, \mathbf{u}_t)\beta_t(\mathbf{u}_t).$$

2. The one-slice marginal $\hat{p}_t(\mathbf{u}_{t'}) = \sum_{\mathbf{u}_{t''}} \hat{p}_t(\mathbf{u}_{t''}, \mathbf{u}_t)$, with $t'' = \{t-1, t\}\setminus t'$, is not CG, but more complex: for every value of $s_{t'}$, $\mathbf{x}_{t'}$ follows a *mixture* of Gaussians. Find $q_{t'}(\mathbf{u}_{t'})$ that approximates $\hat{p}_t(\mathbf{u}_{t'})$ best in Kullback-Leibler (KL) sense:

$$q_{t'}(\mathbf{u}_{t'}) = \operatorname*{argmin}_{q \in \text{CG}} \sum_{\mathbf{u}_{t'}} \hat{p}_t(\mathbf{u}_{t'}) \log \frac{\hat{p}_t(\mathbf{u}_{t'})}{q_{t'}(\mathbf{u}_{t'})}.$$

It can be shown that $q_{t'}$ follows by "collapsing" the mixture

$$q_{t'}(\mathbf{u}_{t'}) \propto \text{Collapse}\left(\sum_{\mathbf{u}_{t''}} \hat{p}_t(\mathbf{u}_{t''}, \mathbf{u}_t)\right).$$

Where $\text{Collapse}(p_{ij}\mathcal{N}(\mathbf{x}; \boldsymbol{\mu}_{ij}, \Sigma_{ij})) \equiv p_j\mathcal{N}(\mathbf{x}; \boldsymbol{\mu}_j, \Sigma_j)$, with $p_j = \sum_i p_{ij}$, $\boldsymbol{\mu}_j = \sum_i p_{i|j}\boldsymbol{\mu}_{ij}$, $\Sigma_j = \sum_i p_{i|j}(\Sigma_{ij} + (\boldsymbol{\mu}_{ij} - \boldsymbol{\mu}_j)(\boldsymbol{\mu}_{ij} - \boldsymbol{\mu}_j)^T)$, and $p_{i|j} = p_{ij}/p_j$.

3. Infer the new message by division. All messages not sent from ψ_t remain fixed, in particular β_t and α_{t-1}, so new messages are computed as

$$\alpha_t(\mathbf{u}_t) = \frac{q_t(\mathbf{u}_t)}{\beta_t(\mathbf{u}_t)}, \quad \beta_{t-1}(\mathbf{u}_{t-1}) = \frac{q_{t-1}(\mathbf{u}_{t-1})}{\alpha_{t-1}(\mathbf{u}_{t-1})}.$$

For filtering the messages are initialized with $\mathbf{1}$, and steps 1. to 3. are performed for $t = 1 : T$ sequentially. For the best smoothed posterior the above steps are iterated (e.g. using forward-backward passes) until convergence.

Fixed points of steps 1. to 3. correspond to stationary points of a "Bethe free energy"

$$\mathcal{F}_{\mathrm{EP}}(\hat{p}, q) = \sum_t \sum_{\mathbf{u}_{t-1,t}} \hat{p}_t(\mathbf{u}_{t-1,t}) \log \frac{\hat{p}_t(\mathbf{u}_{t-1,t})}{\psi_t(\mathbf{u}_{t-1,t})} - \sum_t \sum_{\mathbf{u}_t} q_t(\mathbf{u}_t) \log q_t(\mathbf{u}_t), \quad (5)$$

subject to the constraints that all $\hat{p}_t$'s and q_t's sum to 1, and "weak" consistency constraints:

$$\mathrm{Collapse}\Big(\sum_{\mathbf{u}_{t-1}} \hat{p}_t(\mathbf{u}_{t-1}, \mathbf{u}_t)\Big) = q_t(\mathbf{u}_t) = \mathrm{Collapse}\Big(\sum_{\mathbf{u}_{t+1}} \hat{p}_{t+1}(\mathbf{u}_t, \mathbf{u}_{t+1})\Big).$$

This relationship is analogous to the one between the Bethe free energy and loopy belief propagation [6]. The only difference is that the strong consistency constraints are replaced by the weak ones: i.e. here overlapping beliefs only have to agree on their *expectations*. The proof of this claim is similar to the one in [6] and follows by constructing the Lagrangian and setting its derivatives to 0. In the resulting stationary conditions the Lagrange multipliers added for the weak consistency constraints have a one-to-one correspondence with messages α_t and β_t: the multipliers form the canonical parameters of the messages. Given this relationship the mapping between fixed points of the message passing scheme and staticnary of points of $\mathcal{F}_{\mathrm{EP}}$ follows easily.

Iterating above steps can be seen as a procedure that greedily tries to find one and two-slice marginals that approximate the exact beliefs as good as possible and are pairwise consistent *after a collapse*. The details of the approximation are beyond the scope of this text. We refer the interested reader to [2].

4.2 The Fine Level Model

At the fine level we treat the marginal $p^*(\tilde{s}_{1:T}) \equiv p(s_{1:T}|\mathbf{z}_{1:T}, \boldsymbol{\theta}_c)$, as fixed and use Jeffrey's rule of conditioning and the extra $\tilde{s}_t$ nodes to ensure that the fine level model is consistent with the coarse level model. In the approximate inference procedure described in the previous section $p(s_{1:T}|\mathbf{z}_{1:T}, \boldsymbol{\theta}_c)$ is approximated by overlapping two-slice marginals. We use these to enforce consistency: $p(\tilde{s}_{t-1}, \tilde{s}_t|\mathbf{z}_{1:T}, \boldsymbol{\theta}_f) = \hat{p}_t(s_{t-1}, s_t)$. So, effectively, distant interactions are disregarded.

We will first describe an approximation scheme for the general fine level model and deal with independent sub-models later. The approximation is based on a free energy identical to (5) but now with definition $\mathbf{u}_t \equiv \{\tilde{s}_t, r_t, \mathbf{y}_t\}$ and the constraints that all $\hat{p}_t$'s and q_t's sum to one replaced by

$$\sum_{r_{t-1,t}, \mathbf{y}_{t-1,t}} \hat{p}_t(\mathbf{u}_{t-1}, \mathbf{u}_t) = p^*(\tilde{s}_{t-1}, \tilde{s}_t)$$

(since $\sum_{\tilde{s}_{t-1,t}} p^*(\tilde{s}_{t-1}, \tilde{s}_t) = 1$ proper normalization is automatically enforced). In the way new messages are computed only the first step needs to be changed:

1′. Construct a two-slice belief that has the correct marginal over $\tilde{s}_{t-1,t}$:

$$\hat{p}_t(\mathbf{u}_{t-1}, \mathbf{u}_t) \propto \frac{\alpha_{t-1}(\mathbf{u}_{t-1})\psi_t(\mathbf{u}_{t-1}, \mathbf{u}_t)\beta_t(\mathbf{u}_t)}{\sum_{\substack{r_{t-1,t}\\ \mathbf{y}_{t-1,t}}} \alpha_{t-1}(\mathbf{u}_{t-1})\psi_t(\mathbf{u}_{t-1}, \mathbf{u}_t)\beta_t(\mathbf{u}_t)} p^*(\tilde{s}_{t-1,t}) \,.$$

Fixed points of this new message passing scheme correspond to stationary points of $\mathcal{F}_{\mathrm{EP}}$ with the changed normalization constraints. The proof is analogous to the proof for the standard case presented in Sect. 4.1. (see also [5] for a related algorithm). The intuition behind the free energy is similar: the adapted message passing scheme tries to find one and two-slice marginals that approximate the exact beliefs as good as possible, are pairwise consistent after a collapse, *and* are consistent with the soft-assignments to regimes in the coarse level model.

Having established a way to infer posteriors for a general fine level model, we now adapt the above message passing scheme such that independent sub-models as described in Sect. 3 can be handled independently.

One possible way to adapt the scheme is to work with discrete variables $r^{(m+)}$ that range over $\mathrm{ch}(m) \cup \bar{m}$, where $\bar{m}$ is a special state that encodes "not in subtree m". This would however imply some inefficiency, since when we are refining regime m we are not interested in a continuous state associated with $\bar{m}$, nor in the mode $\hat{p}_t(\bar{m}, \bar{m})$. Instead, the inference algorithm for sub-model m only computes the required parts of the two-slice joint $\hat{p}_t$. In the remainder define $\mathbf{u}_t \equiv \{r_t^{(m)}, \mathbf{y}_t\}$ and

$$\psi_t^{(mm)}(\mathbf{u}_{t-1,t}) \equiv p(\mathbf{z}_t, \mathbf{u}_t | \mathbf{u}_{t-1}, \tilde{s}_{t-1} = \tilde{s}_t = m, \boldsymbol{\theta}^{(m)})$$
$$\psi_t^{(\bar{m}m)}(\mathbf{u}_t) \equiv p(\mathbf{z}_t, \mathbf{u}_t | \tilde{s}_{t-1} \neq \tilde{s}_t = m, \boldsymbol{\theta}^{(m)}) \,,$$

with $\psi_1^{(mm)}(\mathbf{u}_{0,1}) \equiv 0$ and $\psi_1^{(\bar{m}m)}(\mathbf{u}_0) \equiv p(\mathbf{z}_1, \mathbf{u}_1 | \tilde{s}_1, \boldsymbol{\theta}^{(m)})$.

To infer the refinements of the coarse regime m we use the message passing scheme of the general fine level, but with steps 1. and 2. adapted as follows.

1″. Construct the required parts of the two-slice marginal as

$$\hat{p}_t^{(mm)}(\mathbf{u}_{t-1,t}) = p^*(\tilde{s}_{t-1} = \tilde{s}_t = m)\left(Z_t^{(mm)}\right)^{-1}\alpha_{t-1}(\mathbf{u}_{t-1})\psi_t^{(mm)}(\mathbf{u}_{t-1,t})\beta_t(\mathbf{u}_t)$$

$$\hat{p}_t^{(\bar{m}m)}(\mathbf{u}_t) = p^*(\tilde{s}_{t-1} \neq \tilde{s}_t = m)\left(Z_t^{(\bar{m}m)}\right)^{-1}\psi_t^{(\bar{m}m)}(\mathbf{u}_t)\beta_t(\mathbf{u}_t)$$

$$\hat{p}_t^{(m\bar{m})}(\mathbf{u}_{t-1}) = p^*(\tilde{s}_{t-1} = m \neq \tilde{s}_t)\left(Z_t^{(m\bar{m})}\right)^{-1}\alpha_{t-1}(\mathbf{u}_{t-1}) \,,$$

with $Z_t^{(mm)}$, $Z_t^{(\bar{m}m)}$, and $Z_t^{(m\bar{m})}$ the proper normalization constants of the r.h.s. *before* weighting with p^*.

2″. In a forward pass compute $q_t(\mathbf{u}_t) = \text{Collapse}\left(\hat{p}_t^{(mm)}(\mathbf{u}_t) + \hat{p}_t^{(\bar{r}m)}(\mathbf{u}_t)\right)$. In a backward pass compute $q_{t-1}(\mathbf{u}_{t-1}) = \text{Collapse}\left(\hat{p}_t^{(mm)}(\mathbf{u}_{t-1}) + \hat{p}_t^{im\bar{m}}(\mathbf{u}_{t-1})\right)$.

The exposition has been restricted to two levels, but we can extend the approach to any number of scales. The approximations of $p^*(r_{t-1} = r_t = j|\mathbf{z}_{1:T})$, $p^*(r_{t-1} = j \neq r_t|\mathbf{z}_{1:T})$, and $p^*(r_{t-1} \neq j = r_t|\mathbf{z}_{1:T})$ form the constraints for the refinements of regime j and can be computed from the $\hat{p}_t$'s.

5 Discussion

We have introduced a class of switching linear dynamical system models that allows iterative refinement of regimes. If properly restricted, the models at levels of finer detail can be inferred independently. One of the advantages of this is that relatively complex models can be tracked at reasonable computational costs since only those regimes that have reasonable probability need to be refined. For instance to refine coarse regime A in Fig. 1, $t = 45 : 70$ can be disregarded.

The hierarchy and independence between sub-models allows recursive maximum likelihood fitting of parameters using an EM algorithm. In [7] this approach is used to interactively fit a hierarchical SLDS. An appealing line of future research is to use the multi-scale setup as a basis for greedy model learning.

The notion of multiple scales in statistical models is not new. There are many uses of multi-scale models in various disciplines. Our method shares with [1] the "top-down" construction of the hierarchy and the use of Jeffrey's rule to synchronize models at different scales. To our knowledge the work presented here is the first to enforce constraints in hybrid models for which exact inference is intractable. The approximate inference method from Sect. 4.2 is very general. Extensions to trees, or even structures containing cycles, are possible. It therefore paves the way for interesting combinations of previously proposed multi-scale models.

References

1. M. Ferreira, M. West, H. Lee, and D. Higdon. A class of multi-scale time series models. Unpublished.
2. T. Heskes and O. Zoeter. Expectation propagation for approximate inference in dynamic Bayesian networks. In *UAI-2002*, pages 216–223, 2002.
3. F. Kschischang, B. Frey, and H. Loeliger. Factor graphs and the sum-product algorithm. *IEEE Transactions on Information Theory*, 47(2):498–519, 2001.
4. T. Minka. Expectation propagation for approximate Bayesian inference. In *Proceedings of UAI-2001*, pages 362–369, 2001.
5. Y. Teh and M. Welling. The unified propagation and scaling algorithm. In *Advances in Neural Information Processing Systems 14*, page (in press). MIT Press, 2002.
6. J. Yedidia, W. Freeman, and Y. Weiss. Generalized belief propagation. In *NIPS 13*, pages 689–695, 2001.
7. O. Zoeter and T. Heskes. Hierarchical visualization of time-series data using switching linear dynamical systems. Submitted.

Time-Series Prediction

Model Selection with Cross-Validations and Bootstraps – Application to Time Series Prediction with RBFN Models

Amaury Lendasse[1], Vincent Wertz[1], and Michel Verleysen[2]

Université catholique de Louvain
[1] CESAME, av. G. Lemaître 3, B-1348 Louvain-la-Neuve, Belgium
{lendasse, wertz}@auto.ucl.ac.be,
[2] DICE, pl. du Levant 3, B-1348 Louvain-la-Neuve, Belgium
verleysen@dice.ucl.ac.be

Abstract. This paper compares several model selection methods, based on experimental estimates of their generalization errors. Experiments in the context of nonlinear time series prediction by Radial-Basis Function Networks show the superiority of the bootstrap methodology over classical cross-validations and leave-one-out.

1 Introduction

Nonlinear modeling has raised a considerable research effort since decades, including in the field of artificial neural networks. Nonlinear modeling includes the necessity to *compare* models (for example of different complexities) in order to select the "best" model among several ones. For this purpose, it is necessary to obtain a good approximation of the generalization error (or "expected loss") of each model (the generalization error being the average error that the model would make on an infinite-size and unknown test set). In this paper, the terms "model selection" will be used when several models must be compared based on estimations of their generalization errors, in order to select one of them.

Nowadays there exist some well-known and widely used methods able to fulfill this task. Among them we can cite:

- the hold-out (HO) which consist in removing data from the learning set and keeping them for validation; HO is also called "validation" [1], or "external validation" for example in chemometrics, etc.
- the Monte-Carlo cross-validation (or simply "cross-validation", CV), where several HO validation sets are randomly and sequentially drawn;
- the k-fold cross-validation, where the initial set is randomly split into k roughly equal parts, each one being used successively as a validation set;
- Leave-One-Out (LOO) is a k-fold cross-validation where the size of the validation set is 1;
- the bootstrap [2, 3], which consists in drawing sets *with replacement* from the original sample and using these sets to estimate the generalization errors (boostrap 632 and 632+ are improved versions of the original bootstrap):

All these methods of estimating generalization errors have been shown to be asymptotically roughly equivalent (see for example [4]), with some exceptions and limitations:
- LOO is less biased [5, 2] but its variance is unacceptable [6];
- cross-validation is consistent (i.e. converges to the generalization error when the size of the sample increases) if the size of the validation set grows infinitely faster than the size of the learning set (which is counter-intuitive!) [7];
- cross-validation is almost unbiased [2];
- bootstrap is downward biased but has a very low variance [2];
- most recent bootstrap methods (632 and 632+) are almost unbiased and also have a low variance [2].

Given this list of possible model selection methods and criteria, the purpose of this paper is to compare experimentally these methods in the context of (1) highly nonlinear regression (making complex model structures unavoidable) and (2) a small number of data points or input-output pairs (which is often the case in real-world applications in medium- or high-dimensional spaces).

An important argument in favor of simple, reliable model selection methods is the following. In the context of nonlinear regression or model identification, the learning time (or computational complexity) may be far from negligible. In some cases, for example when one tries a single model structure and has a large validation set at disposal, this might not be a concern. However, in most situations, first one has to try many different model structures (for example of different complexities, different number of neurons in the hidden layers of multi-layer perceptrons, etc.); and secondly the use of resampling methods (CV, LOO, bootstrap,...) is necessary because of the small size of the original sample at disposal. This might multiply the learning time by several hundreds or thousands, making computation time a real concern, even on up-to-date powerful machines.

Therefore, this paper will consider the various model selection methods in the context of nonlinear regression with relatively small sample, from the point of view of performances and computational complexity.

This will be illustrated on a standard time series prediction benchmark, the Santa Fe A series [8]. This particular example has been chosen for illustration because [8] (1) the ideal regressor is known, avoiding the supplementary problem of choosing its size, (2) if the rules of the Santa Fe competition are followed, we have a small set of data (1000), (3) the relation to learn is highly nonlinear, and (4) making the hypothesis of a stationary process, we have a very large test set at disposal (8000 data), used to obtain a very good approximation of the generalization error (independently from the model selection method) for comparison purposes. According to our previous experience [9], we chose to approximate this series by a Radial-Basis Function network with 100 Gaussian kernels, the learning being achieved by the method presented in [10].

2 Model Selection Methods

This section presents the different methods enumerated in the introduction. The initial data used for the learning phase are the N pairs (x_i, y_i) with x_i representing the d-

dimensional input vectors and y_i the scalar outputs. Theses pairs form the learning dataset X. Each of the methods below computes an approximation of the generalization error obtained with a model g. The generalization error is defined by:

$$E_{gen}(g) = \lim_{N \to \infty} \sum_{i=1}^{N} \frac{(g(x_i) - y_i)^2}{N}, \quad (1)$$

with (x_i, y_i) the elements of an infinite test dataset and $g(x_i)$ the approximation of y_i obtained with the model g. The selected model will be the model minimizing this estimate of the generalization error.

2.1 Monte-Carlo Cross-Validation

The consecutive steps of the Monte-Carlo cross-validation method are:
1. One randomly draws without replacement some elements of the dataset X; these elements form a new learning dataset X_{learn}. The remaining elements of X form the validation set X_{val}. Usually, two third of the elements of X are used in X_{learn} and one third in X_{val} [1]; this rule will be used in the following.
2. The training of the model g is done using X_{learn} and the error $E_k(g)$ is calculated according to:

$$E_k(g) = \frac{\sum_{i=1}^{N/3} \left(g(x_i^{val}) - y_i^{val} \right)^2}{N/3}, \quad (2)$$

with (x_i^{val}, y_i^{val}) the elements of X_{val} and $g(x_i^{val})$ the approximation of y_i^{val} by model g.
3. Steps 1 and 2 are repeated K times, with K as large as possible. The error $E_k(g)$ is computed for each repetition k. The average error is defined by:

$$\hat{E}_{gen}(g) = \frac{\sum_{k=1}^{K} E_k(g)}{K}. \quad (3)$$

A particular case of the Monte-Carlo cross-validation method is the Hold-Out method, where the number K of repetitions is equal to 1.

2.2 k-fold Cross-Validation

The k-fold cross-validation method is a variant of the Monte-Carlo cross-validation method. The consecutive steps of this method are:
1. One divides the elements of the dataset X into K sets of roughly equal size. The elements of *the kth* set form the validation set X_{val}. The other sets form a new learning dataset X_{learn}.
2. The training of the model g is done using X_{learn} and the error $E_k(g)$ is calculated according to:

$$E_k(g) = \frac{\sum_{i=1}^{N/K}\left(g(x_i^{val}) - y_i^{val}\right)^2}{N/K}, \qquad (4)$$

with (x_i^{val}, y_i^{val}) the elements of X_{val} and $g(x_i^{val})$ the approximation of y_i^{val} by model g.

3. Steps 1 and 2 are repeated for k varying from 1 to K. The average error is computed according to (3).

A particular case of the k-fold cross-validation method is the Leave-One-Out, where K is equal to N.

2.3 Bootstrap

The consecutive steps of the bootstrap method, developed by Efron [2], are:

1. In the dataset X, one draws randomly N samples with replacement. These new samples form a new learning set X_{learn} with the same size as the original one. The validation set X_{val} is the original learning set X. This process is called re-sampling.
2. The training of the model g is done using X_{learn} and the errors $E_k^{val}(g)$ and $E_k^{learn}(g)$ obtained with this model are calculated according to the following equations:

$$E_k^{learn}(g) = \frac{\sum_{i=1}^{N}\left(g(x_i^{learn}) - y_i^{learn}\right)^2}{N}, \qquad (5)$$

with $(x_i^{learn}, y_i^{learn})$ the elements of X_{learn} and $g(x_i^{learn})$ the approximation of y_i^{learn} obtained by model g;

$$E_k^{val}(g) = \frac{\sum_{i=1}^{N}\left(g(x_i^{val}) - y_i^{val}\right)^2}{N}, \qquad (6)$$

with (x_i^{val}, y_i^{val}) the elements of X_{val} and $g(x_i^{val})$ the approximation of y_i^{val} by model g.

3. The optimism $D_k(g)$, a measure of performance degradation (for the same model) between a learning and a validation set, is computed according to:

$$D_k(g) = E_k^{val}(g) - E_k^{learn}(g). \qquad (7)$$

4. Steps 1,2 and 3 are repeated K times, with K as large as possible. The average optimism $\hat{D}(g)$ is computed by:

$$\hat{D}(g) = \frac{\sum_{k=1}^{K} D_k(g)}{K}. \qquad (8)$$

5. Once this average optimism is computed, a new training of the model g is done using the initial dataset X; the learning error $E_m^I(g)$ is calculated according to:

$$E_m^I(g) = \frac{\sum_{i=1}^{N}\left(g(x_i)-y_i\right)^2}{N},\qquad(9)$$

with (x_i, y_i) the elements of X and $g(x_i)$ the approximation of y_i obtained using the model g.

6. Step 5 is repeated repeated M times, with M as large as possible. For each repetition m the learning error $E_m^I(g)$ is computed. The apparent error $\hat{E}^I(g)$ is defined as the average of errors $E_m^I(g)$ over the M repetitions. In the case of a linear model g, this repetition is not necessary; learning of a linear model gives a unique set of parameters, making all learning errors $E_m^I(g)$ equal. With nonlinear models, this repetition performs a (Monte-Carlo) estimate of the most probable apparent error obtained after training of g.

7. Now we have an estimate of the apparent error and of the optimism, their sum gives an estimate of the generalization error:

$$\hat{E}_{gen}(g) = \hat{E}^I(g) + \hat{D}(g).\qquad(10)$$

A particular case of bootstrap method is the bootstrap 632 [3]. In this method, $\hat{E}_{gen}(g)$ is calculated according to:

$$\hat{E}_{gen}(g) = .368\hat{E}^I(g) + .632\hat{D}^{632}(g),\qquad(11)$$

with $\hat{D}^{632}(g)$ an optimism estimated only on the data that are not selected during the re-sampling (see [3] for details).

3 Radial-Basis Function Networks and Time Series Prediction

The nonlinear models that have been chosen in this paper are the RBFN [11]. These approximators have the well-known property of universal approximation. Other approximators as Multi-Layers Perceptrons could have been chosen. However, the goal of this paper is not to compare different families of approximators: RBFN have been chosen for the simplicity of their training phase. Indeed, a possible learning algorithm for RBFN [10] consists in a three-folded strategy (separated computation of kernel centers, widths and weights). As a consequence, the weights are simply calculated as the solution of a linear system.

The problem of time series prediction is a common problem in many different fields as finance, electricity production, hydrology, etc. A set of successive points (the time series) is known; the goal is to predict the next unknown value. To perform this task, a model is needed, that associates some previous values of the time series to the next one. This model has the following form:

$$y(t) = g(y(t-1), y(t-2), ..., y(t-n)), \quad (12)$$

where n is the lag order [1]. Model g can be linear or nonlinear. In this paper, the class of models we have chosen is a set of RBFN with different numbers C of Gaussian kernels but with a given size for the regressor. The problem of model selection is then to choose one of the models in the set, i.e.: how many Gaussian kernels must be used?

4 Experimental Results

We illustrate the methods described in the previous section on a standard benchmark in time-series prediction. The Santa Fe A time series [8] has been chosen mainly for the large number of data available for the training stage (1000) as well as for the test stage (8000). These two numbers correspond to the rules of the Santa Fe competition, as detailed in [8]. According to [8], we also choose $n = 6$.

We trained 7 RBFNs on the Santa Fe learning dataset, for C = 20, 40, 60, 80, 100, 120 and 140 respectively. This number of models is kept small to avoid a too large computational time; indeed the goal is not to find the best among an infinite set of models but to compare the performances of the different model selection methods.

Having a huge (8000 samples) test set makes it possible to have a very good approximation of the true generalization error:

$$E_{gen}(g) = \lim_{N \to \infty} \sum_{i=1}^{N} \frac{(g(x_i) - y_i)^2}{N} \approx \sum_{i=1}^{8000} \frac{(g(x_i) - y_i)^2}{N}. \quad (13)$$

In practice, for similar reasons as those argued in favour of a Monte-Carlo evaluation (step 6) of the apparent error $\hat{E}^I(g)$ in the bootstrap (use of nonlinear models), a Monte-Carlo method (with $M = 100$ repetitions) is used to evaluate $E_{gen}(g)$ for each model. Then, according to Fig. 1 (a), the best RBFN model has a number C of Gaussian kernels equal to 100.

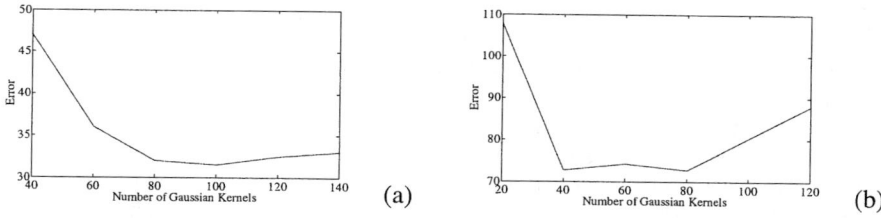

Fig. 1. (a) Estimation of the true generalization error; (b) Estimation of the generalization error by a Monte-Carlo cross-validation method.

Fig. 1 (b) shows the estimation of the generalization error by a Monte-Carlo cross-validation method. The optimal number of Gaussian kernel is 80 (another number of kernels that could be chosen -according to the parsimony principle- is 40, corresponding to a local minimum).

Figure 2 (a) shows the estimation of the generalization error by a Leave-One-Out method. The optimal number of Gaussian kernels is 80.

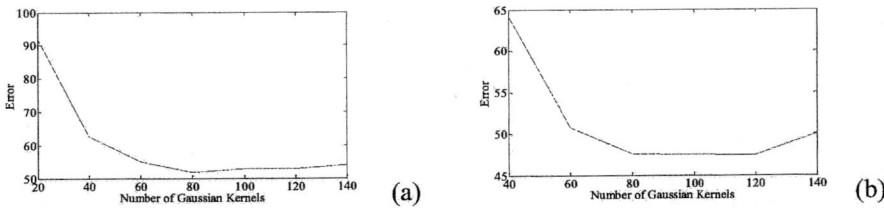

Fig. 2. (a) Estimation of the generalization error by Leave-One-Out; (b) Estimation of the generalization error by the classical bootstrap.

Fig. 2 (b) shows the estimation of the generalization error by the classical bootstrap. The optimal number of Gaussian kernels is between 80 and 120. In this case, again according to the parsimony principle, it is advised to choose $C = 80$.

Figure 3 shows the estimation of the generalization error by the bootstrap 632. The optimal number of Gaussian kernels is 100.

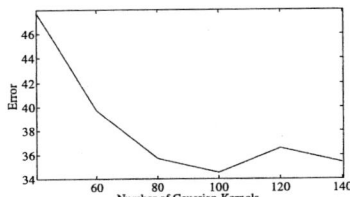

Fig. 3. Estimation of the generalization error by the bootstrap 632.

5 Conclusion

A number of similar experiments have been conducted, with the purpose of comparing model selection methods based on empirical estimations of the generalization error: Monte-Carlo cross-validation, Leave-One-Out, bootstrap, bootstrap 632. They all lead to similar conclusions: bootstrap methods, and in particular the bootstrap 632, give the best estimations of the generalization error.

Although theoretical results (briefly summarized in the introduction) show that all these methods are roughly asymptotically equivalent, this is no more the case in real applications, with limited number of data.

Concerning the computation time, the number of repetitions in the cross-validation and bootstraps may be tuned, which is not the case with the Leave-One-Out. This allows, in our 1000 learning data experiments, to strongly reduce the computational costs associated with cross-validation and Bootstraps.

However, in accordance with theoretical results, cross-validation has a much higher variance than bootstraps. Using the same number of repetitions in cross-validation and bootstraps highlights the advantages of the bootstraps.

Such results have also been published in different contexts, namely classification [5]. This paper extends these results to regression, and time series prediction in particular.

Acknowledgements. Michel Verleysen is Senior research associate at the Belgian National Fund for Scientific Research (FNRS). The work of A. Lendasse and V. Wertz is supported by the Interuniversity Attraction Poles (IAP), initiated by the Belgian Federal State, Ministry of Sciences, Technologies and Culture. The scientific responsibility rests with the authors.

References

1. Ljung, L.: System Identification - Theory for the user, 2nd ed, Prentice Hall, 1999.
2. Efron, B., Tibshirani, R. J. An introduction to the bootstrap, Chapman & Hall, 1993.
3. Efron, B, Tibshirani, R.: Improvements on cross-validation: The .632+ bootstrap method. J. Amer. Statist. Assoc. (1997) 92:548–560.
4. Stone, M.: An asymptotic equivalence of choice of model by cross-validation and Akaike's criterion, J. Royal. Statist. Soc., B39, 44–7, 1977.
5. Kohavi, R.: A study of Cross-Validation and Bootstrap for Accuracy Estimation and Model Selection, Proc. of the 14th Int. Joint Conf. on A.I., Vol. 2, Canada, 1995.
6. Efron, B.: Estimating the error rate of a prediction rule: improvements on cross-validation. Journal of American Statistical Association, (1983) **78**(382):316–331.
7. Shao, J., Tu, D.: The Jackknife and Bootstrap, Springer Series in Statistics, Springer-Verlag, New York (1995).
8. Weigend, A. S., Gershenfeld, N. A.: Times Series Prediction: Forecasting the future and Understanding the Past, Addison-Wesley Publishing Company (1994).
9. Simon, G., Lendasse, A., Wertz, V., Verleysen, M.: Fast approximation of the bootstrap for model selection, submitted to ESANN03, Bruges (Belgium), April 2003.
10. Benoudjit, N., Archambeau, C., Lendasse, A., Lee, J., Verleysen, M.: Width optimization of the Gaussian kernels in Radial Basis Function Networks, ESANN 2002, European Symposium on Artificial Neural Networks, Bruges (2002) 425–432.
11. Moody, J., Darken, C.: Learning with localised receptive fields, Proceedings of the 1988 Connectionist Models Summer School, San Mateo, CA (1989).

A Hybrid Neural Architecture and Its Application to Temperature Prediction

Srimanta Pal[1], Jyotirmay Das[1], and Kausik Majumdar[2]

[1] Electronics and Communication Sciences Unit
Indian Statistical Institute, 203 B T Road, Calcutta 700 108
[2] Electronics and Telecommunication Engineering
Jadavpur University, Calcutta – 700 032
{srimanta, jdas}@isical.ac.in

Abstract. We first investigate the effectiveness of multilayer perceptron networks for prediction of atmospheric temperature. To capture the seasonality of atmospheric data we then propose a hybrid network, SOFM-MLP, that combines a self-organizing feature map (SOFM) and multilayer perceptron networks (MLPs). The architecture is quite general in nature and can be applied in other application areas. We also demonstrate that use of appropriate features can not only reduce the number of features but also can improve the prediction accuracies.

1 Introduction

The measurement and prediction of lower atmospheric parameters are necessary for different applications such as avionics, pollution dispersal, communication and so on. Weather forecasting requires estimation of temperature, rainfall, humidity, wind speed, wind direction, atmospheric pressure etc. well in advance. Often it is very difficult to get an accurate prediction result because of many other factors like topography of a place, surrounding structures and environmental pollution etc. The problem becomes more difficult due to continuous change of the dynamics of lower atmosphere.

Here we focus on prediction of temperature based on past measurements of various atmospheric parameters. Our data set consists of the following information obtained for a day from the meteorology department: (1) mean sea level *pressure* at 1730 Hrs. and 0630 Hrs., (2) *vapor pressure* at 1730 Hrs. and 0630 Hrs., (3) *relative humidity* at 1730 Hrs. and 0630 Hrs., (4) *maximum temperature* at 1730 Hrs., (5) *minimum temperature* at 0630 Hrs., and (6) *rainfall*. We have daily observation on these variables for the period 1989-95. Also we have the normal maximum and minimum temperatures over 365 days of a year.

Here first we study the effectiveness of multilayer perceptron network (MLP) [1] for prediction of the maximum and the minimum temperatures. Next we propose a hybrid network which uses both self-organizing feature map and MLP to realize a much better prediction system. Then we demonstrate that use of appropriate features such as temperature gradient can not only reduce the number of features but also can improve the prediction accuracies.

2 Organizing the Data

For day t, we have observations on 9 variables, let us denote that by $\mathbf{x}_t \in R^9$. Now let us assume that the maximum (Mt) and the minimum (mt) temperatures for day t (Mt_t, mt_t) is defined by the atmospheric conditions of past K days. Thus we will attempt to predict (Mt_t, mt_t) using $X_t = (\mathbf{x}_{t-1}, \mathbf{x}_{t-2}, \cdots, \mathbf{x}_{t-K}) \in R^{9K}$. If $K = 2$, then we will use $(\mathbf{x}_{t-1}, \mathbf{x}_{t-2}) \in R^{18}$ to predict (Mt_t, mt_t).

Let N be the total number of days for which observations are available. To train the network we generate input-output pairs (X, Y). Here we will have $N - K$ pairs. $X = \{X_N, X_{N-1}, \cdots, X_{N-K}\}$ and $Y = \{Y_N, Y_{N-1}, \cdots, Y_{N-K}\}$ where $Y_j = (Mt_j, mt_j)$.

After obtaining (X, Y) we partition X (and also Y) randomly as X_{tr} (Y_{tr}) and X_{te} (Y_{te}) such that $X_{tr} \bigcup X_{te} = X$, $X_{tr} \bigcap X_{te} = \phi$. X_{tr} is then used for training the system and X_{te} is used to test the system. So our network will have $9K$ input nodes and 2 output nodes. In our data set $N = 2555$, $|X_{tr}| = 2285$ and $|X_{te}| = 270$.

3 Results with MLP

The MLP network consists of several layers of neurons of which the first one is the input layer and the last one is the output layer, remaining layers are called hidden layers. There are complete connections between the nodes in successive layers but there is no connection within a layer. Every node, except the input layer nodes, computes the weighted sum of its inputs and apply a sigmoidal function to compute its output, which is then transmitted to the nodes of the next layer [1]. The objective of the MLP learning is to set the connection weights such that the error between the network output and the target output is minimized. The network weights may be updated by several methods of which the backpropagation technique is the most popular one. In this work we use the backpropagation learning. It is known that under a fairly general assumption a multilayer perceptron with only one hidden layer is sufficient to compute a uniform approximation of a given training set [1]. Hence in this study we restrict ourselves to a three-layer network i.e., one hidden layer.

We have made several runs of the MLP net with different number of hidden nodes (h) and fixed number of input (18) & output (2) nodes. Table 1 reports some typical performance on the test data for $h = 10, 15, 20$ and 25 nodes. The table shows the cumulative percentage of prediction within different ranges. For example, the 3rd row of the 'max' column with $h = 10$ shows that on the test data the network could make prediction with $\leq \pm 2°C$ error in 80.68% cases. It is interesting to note that the networks with $h = 10, 15$ and 20 perform reasonably well but the performance degrades with increase in the number of hidden nodes beyond 20. With $\pm 2°C$ error the best result that the networks could achieve is little more than 80%. This is reasonable but not quite satisfactory.

One of the possible reasons for this can be the presence of seasonality. So we now

Table 1. Cumulative Percentage Frequency Table (Test sample)

Range	% Frequency of Temperature							
°C	$h=10$		$h=15$		$h=20$		$h=25$	
	max	min	max	min	max	min	max	min
$\leq +1.0$	52.40	40.75	50.48	40.41	51.37	45.21	34.38	40.68
$\leq +1.5$	69.59	58.90	66.44	58.36	66.71	64.04	49.45	59.04
$\leq +2.0$	80.68	76.16	79.04	74.59	80.34	78.84	62.74	76.85
$\leq +2.5$	87.60	87.12	87.40	86.85	87.19	88.90	72.19	87.53
$\leq +5.0$	98.77	99.79	98.42	99.86	98.77	99.86	95.68	99.79

propose a hybrid network which can account for seasonality of data. Our basic philosophy would be as follows. We like to group the vectors in (X) into a set of homogeneous subgroups. Then for each subgroup we will train a separate feedforward network. For prediction, first we have to chose the appropriate trained MLP and then apply the test input to that net to get the prediction. The partitioning of the training data as well as the selection of the desired trained MLP will be done using a self-organizing feature map (SOFM). So before describing the prediction network, we first briefly describe the SOFM.

4 SOFM Network

SOFM [2] has the interesting property of achieving a distribution of the weight vectors that approximates the distribution of the input data. This property of the SOFM can be exploited to generate prototypes which in turn can partition the data into homogeneous groups. We want to use this property.

The self-organizing feature map is an algorithmic transformation A_{SOFM}^D : $R^p \rightarrow V(R^q)$ that is often advocated for visualization of metric-topological relationships and distributional density properties of feature vectors (signals) $X = \{\mathbf{x}_1, \cdots, \mathbf{x}_N\}$ in R^p. SOFM is implemented through a neural-like network architecture as shown in Figure 1. The visual display produced by A_{SOFM}^D helps to form hypotheses about topological structure present in X. Here we concentrate on $(m \times n)$ displays in R^2, in principle X can be transformed onto a display lattice in R^q for any q.

The feature mapping algorithm starts with (usually) a random initialization of the weight vectors $\mathbf{v}_{ij}$ (Fig.1). For notational clarity we suppress the double subscripts. Now let $\mathbf{x} \in R^p$ enter the network and let t denote the current iteration number. Find $\mathbf{v}_{r,t-1}$, that best matches $\mathbf{x}$ in the sense of minimum Euclidean distance in R^p. This vector has a (logical) "image" which is the cell in O_2 with subscript r. Next a topological (spatial) neighborhood $N_r(t)$ centered at r is defined in O_2, and its display cell neighbors are located. A 3×3 window, $N(r)$, centered at r corresponds to updating nine prototypes in R^p. Finally, $\mathbf{v}_{r,t-1}$ and the other weight vectors associated with cells in the spatial neighborhood $N_t(r)$ are updated using the rule $\mathbf{v}_{i,t} = \mathbf{v}_{i,t-1} + h_{ri}(t)(\mathbf{x} - \mathbf{v}_{i,t-1})$. Here r is

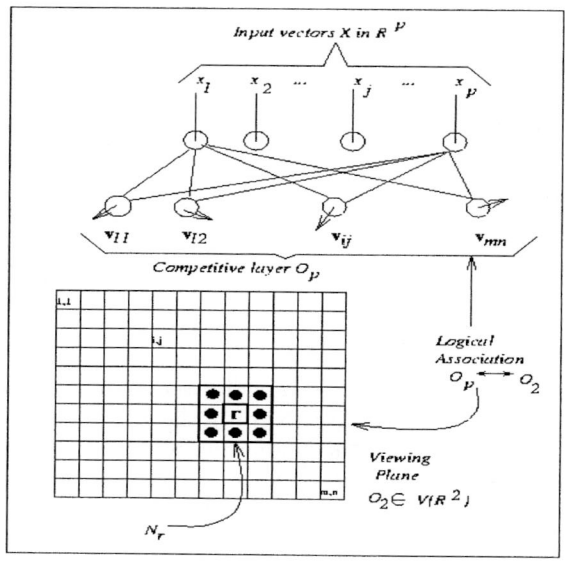

Fig. 1. The SOFM architecture

the index of the "winner" prototype $r = \underbrace{arg\ min}_{i}\{\|\mathbf{x} - \mathbf{v}_{i,t-1}\|\}$ and $\| * \|$ is the Euclidean norm on R^p. The function $h_{ri}(t)$ which expresses the strength of interaction between cells r and i in O_2 usually decreases with t, and for a fixed t it decreases as the distance (in O_2) from cell r to cell i increases. $h_{ri}(t)$ is usually expressed as the product of a learning parameter α_t and a lateral feedback function $g_t(dist(r,i))$. A common choice for g_t is $g_t(dist(r,i)) = e^{-dist^2(r,i)/\sigma_t^2}$. α_t and σ_t both decrease with time t. The topological neighborhood $N_t(r)$ also decreases with time. This scheme, when repeated long enough, usually preserves spatial order in the sense that weight vectors which are metrically close in R^p generally have, at termination of the learning procedure, visually close images in the viewing plane.

5 SOFM-MLP Hybrid Network

The architecture of the proposed hybrid network is shown in Fig. 2. It has eight layers. The first layer with p nodes scales the data – it is the scaling interface between user and the system at the input side. The second and third layers constitute the SOFM layer. The output of the scaling layer is fed as input to the SOFM layer. In Fig. 2 layer 2 (input) with p nodes and layer 3 (output) with k nodes together is called the SOFM layer. The fourth layer has kp nodes. This kp nodes constitute the input layer of a set of k MLP networks. Without loss of generality, we assume that each of the k MLP networks has only one hidden layer, although it could be more than one and different for different MLP nets. Let the nodes in layer four be numbered as N_i, $i = 1, 2, \cdots, kp$. Nodes N_1 to N_p will be the input nodes of the first MLP (M_1); similarly, nodes $N_{(k-1)p+1}$ to N_{np} will be the input nodes of MLP, M_k. As mentioned earlier, $p = 9K$. The jth input node of MLP M_i gets two inputs from the previous layers : the jth normalized input (say x_j) and the output of the ith node of the SOFM output node (say o_i). Each node of layer 4 computes the product of the two inputs it receives, i.e., the jth input node of M_i computes $x_j.o_i$ as output and passes it on the first hidden layer of the MLP net, M_i. Since only one output of the SOFM layer will be one and rest of the outputs will be zero, only one of the MLP nets, which is connected to the winner node, will get the normalized input unattenuated. So only one of the MLP will be activated and other will produce zero output. Each MLP, M_i will

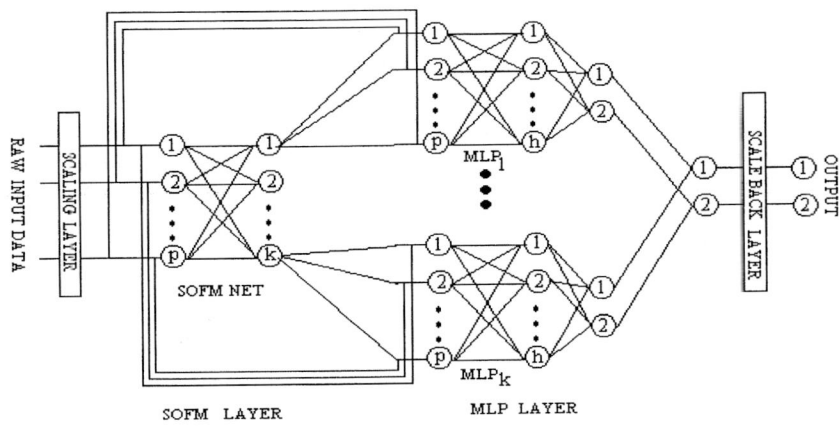

Fig. 2. A hybrid neural net for temperature forecasting.

have two output nodes. Let us denote these nodes by O_{ij}^6 where i corresponds to the ith MLP, M_i and $j = 1, 2$, where 1 corresponds to the minimum temperature and 2 corresponds to the maximum temperature. In Fig. 2 layers 4 - 6 together constitute the MLP layer. The outputs of this MLP-layer are then aggregated in layer 7 which has just two nodes one for the minimum temperature and the other for the maximum temperature. Let us denote these two nodes by m and M. Now nodes O_{i1}^6, $\forall\ i = 1, 2, \cdots, k$ are connected to node m and O_{i2}^6, $\forall\ i = 1, 2, \cdots, k$ are connected to node M. All connection weights between layer 6 and 7 are set to unity, and nodes m and M compute the weighted sum of all inputs as the output which are then passed to the scaling layer.

At this point, readers might wonder why are we using a self-organizing map, why not a clustering algorithm. The prototypes generated by SOFM not only preserves topology but also density. We want to exploit this density preservation property. If there is a dense cluster in the input space then SOFM will place more prototypes there; consequently, we will have more competitive MLPs for dense regions. Hence finer details of the process can be modeled better and this will result in an enhancement of overall performance. None of clustering algorithms has this density matching property.

5.1 Implementation and Results of the SOFM-MLP Hybrid Net

In the training process, first $\mathbf{X}_{tr}$ is normalized by the input normalization (i.e., scaling) layer. Then with the normalized $\mathbf{X}_{tr}$ the SOFM net is trained. Once the SOFM training is over, then $\mathbf{X}_{tr}$ is partitioned into k subsets, $\mathbf{X}_{tr}^{(l)}$, $l = 1, 2, \cdots, k$ as follows:
$$\mathbf{X}_{tr}^{(l)} = \{\mathbf{x}_t \in R^p \mid ||\mathbf{x}_l - \mathbf{v}_l|| = \min_j ||\mathbf{x}_l - \mathbf{v}_j||\}.$$
Thus, $\mathbf{X}_{tr}^{(l)}$ is the set of input vectors for which the lth prototype, $\mathbf{v}_l$ of the SOFM becomes the winner. Let $\mathbf{Y}_{tr}^{(l)}$ be the set of output vectors associated with vectors in $\mathbf{X}_{tr}^{(l)}$. Now we train k multilayer perceptron nets $M_1, M_2, \cdots, M_k$, where M_l is trained with $(\mathbf{X}_{tr}^{(l)}, \mathbf{Y}_{tr}^{(l)})$. Note that, each of M_l, $l = 1, 2, \cdots, k$ will have the same number of nodes in the input layer, i.e., $p = 9K$ and the same number of nodes in the output layer, i.e., 2 nodes. But the number of nodes in the hidden layer could be different for different M_l. This training is done off-line and during training, we do not consider the output of the SOFM. Once the training of both SOFM and k MLP's are over, now we are in a position to use the hybrid net for prediction of temperatures.

A test input vector $\mathbf{x}_t \in R^{9K}$ is applied to the first layer. The first layer normalizes it and the normalized input then goes to the SOFM layer. $\mathbf{x}_t$ makes the output of only one of k SOFM output node, say of lth node, high (1) and sets the rest $(k-1)$ outputs as zero. The normalized $\mathbf{x}_t$ and output of the ith SOFM node are now fed to the ith MLP M_i, $i = 1, 2, \cdots, k$. Consequently, only the lth MLP will be active and rest of the MLP will be inactive. The integrated output from the MLP layer will be nothing but the output of the lth MLP, which will then be scaled back to the original scale by the output scaling layer – and these become our prediction for the maximum and the minimum temperature of day $t+1$.

Tables 2 and 3 compare the performance of direct use of MLP and the proposed SOFM-MLP hybrid network. Table 2 shows the performance on the test data for direct MLP with architectures $h = 15$ and $h = 20$ while Table 3 depicts the performance on the test data when each of the $(k = 8)$ MLPs uses $h = 15$ and $h = 20$ in the hidden layer. For the SOFM layer we have used 8 nodes thereby the training data were partitioned into 8 homogeneous subgroups. For this data the choice of 8 was made based on a few experiments. In this case, use of more than 8 nodes results in some clusters with very few data points. Each MLP is trained 5 times with different random initialization and Table 3 represents the average prediction accuracy over these runs. Comparing Table 3 with Table 2 we find that within $\pm 1°C$ error, the SOFM-MLP shows an improvement between 2.5% to 7.5% over the direct use of MLP. This improvement is reduced to about

2.5% to 6.5% within $\pm 2°C$ error. If we consider the maximum deviation and the average deviation we get a consistently better result for SOFM-MLP.

Table 2. Whole data of Last 3 days (Direct MLP)

Range °C	% Frequency of Temperature			
	$h=15$		$h=20$	
	max	min	max	min
$\leq +1.0$	54.72	57.18	53.16	55.79
$\leq +1.5$	71.47	73.46	71.33	72.10
$\leq +2.0$	83.82	85.25	81.26	83.51
$\leq +3.0$	91.72	92.71	91.53	92.12
Maximum Deviation	6.313	5.813	6.268	5.722
Average Deviation	1.137	1.108	1.142	1.122

Table 3. Whole data of Last 3 days (SOFM-MLP)

Range °C	% Frequency of Temperature			
	$h=15$		$h=20$	
	max	min	max	min
$\leq +1.0$	61.29	59.82	60.74	58.89
$\leq +1.5$	76.73	75.12	76.14	74.86
$\leq +2.0$	88.07	87.47	87.82	86.10
$\leq +3.0$	94.73	93.21	93.12	93.28
Maximum Deviation	5.806	5.813	5.617	5.626
Average Deviation	1.063	1.082	1.071	1.094

6 Performance Evaluation with New Features

So far we have used entire information available for the past three days to predict the temperatures for the next day. As a result the number of input features become 27 making the learning task a difficult one.

For any learning task the use of appropriate features is a key factor determining the success of the learning process. In this case also if we can use some derived features that are better suited for the task at hand we are expected to get better prediction. With a view to achieving this we have used local gradients of the temperature sequences as features. The local gradient is computed as follows. Suppose t_1, t_2, t_3, t_4 are the maximum temperatures recorded for the last 4 days. So the temperature gradient or changes of temperature are $t_1 - t_2$, $t_2 - t_3$, $t_3 - t_4$. Similarly, there are 3 components for minimum temperatures. Here we use 15 features containing 9 features giving the atmospheric conditions of today and 6 temperature gradients as discussed above. The advantage with this scheme is that (1) it reduces the number of input features and (2) it gives an idea to the MLP network about the changes in the maximum and minimum temperatures. This can make the learning task simpler. Our results in the next section indeed reveal this.

Tables 4 and 5 show the performance of the MLP and SOFM-MLP on the test data with new features discussed above. These Tables shows that with smaller architecture (small number of input units) the performance of an ordinary MLP is consistently better for all cases with deviations less or equal to $\pm 1.5°C$. For deviations less or equal to $\pm 2°C$ the performance of MLP network with gradients as features is also consistently better than the corresponding MLP using 27 features. Now we find that for deviation less or equal to $\pm 2°C$ SOFM-MLP with gradient as the features exhibits consistently better performance than the corresponding SOFM-MLP using all 27 features. This is clearly a significant improvement because with the new features we are using a much smaller network.

Table 4. Temperature Gradient (Direct MLP)

Range °C	% Frequency of Temperature			
	$h=10$		$h=15$	
	max	min	max	min
$\leq \pm 1.0$	59.83	61.11	57.20	60.30
$\leq \pm 1.5$	75.85	76.84	75.21	76.43
$\leq \pm 2.0$	87.67	88.32	86.08	87.99
$\leq \pm 2.5$	91.37	92.73	91.89	92.23
$\leq \pm 3.0$	93.61	94.81	93.40	93.86
Maximum Deviation	5.762	5.415	5.900	6.028
Average Deviation	1.083	1.059	1.098	1.075

Table 5. Temperature Gradient (SOFM-MLP)

Range °C	% Frequency of Temperature			
	$h=10$		$h=15$	
	max	min	max	min
$\leq \pm 1.0$	64.89	62.64	64.17	62.29
$\leq \pm 1.5$	80.16	77.82	79.54	77.56
$\leq \pm 2.0$	89.26	87.13	88.76	87.29
$\leq \pm 2.5$	93.86	91.77	93.61	91.85
$\leq \pm 3.0$	95.70	95.83	95.28	94.73
Maximum Deviation	4.928	5.102	5.027	4.892
Average Deviation	0.951	1.021	0.979	1.031

7 Conclusion and Discussion

We summarize our achievements and observations below:
(*i*) The proposed hybrid SOFM-MLP network consistently performs better than the conventional MLP network. (*ii*) Use of gradient as features instead of the raw observations can reduce the required size of the network and make the training task simpler yet achieving better performance. (*iii*) Feature selection is an important factor for better prediction of atmospheric parameters. In this regard we can use a feature selection MLP [3] and this is likely to reduce the network size and improve the results.

Acknowledgements. The authors are grateful to the help rendered by Prof. N. R. Pal for his valuable suggestions and comments in the preparation of the manuscript. They are also thankful to the Director General, India Meteorological Department (IMD) for providing the data.

References

1. Haykin S., *Neural Networks A comprehensive Foundation*. Macmillan College Publishing Co., New York, 1994.
2. T. Kohonen, "The self-organizing map," *Proc. IEEE*, **78**(9), pp. 1464–1480, 1990.
3. N. R. Pal and K. Chintalapudi, *A connecionist system for feature selection*, Neural, parallel and scientific computation, **5**(3), pp. 359–381, 1997.

Risk Management Application of the Recurrent Mixture Density Network Models[*]

Tatiana Miazhynskaia[1], Georg Dorffner[2], and Engelbert J. Dockner[3]

[1] Austrian Research Institute for Artificial Intelligence,
Schottengasse 3, A-1010 Vienna, Austria, phone:+431.5336112-15
tatiana@oefai.at
[2] Austrian Research Institute for Artificial Intelligence and
Department of Medical Cybernetics and Artificial Intelligence,
University of Vienna, Freyung 6/2, A-1010 Vienna, Austria,
georg@ai.univie.ac.at
[3] Department of Business Studies, University of Vienna,
Brünner Strasse 72, A - 1210 Vienna, Austria,
Engelbert.Dockner@univie.ac.at

Abstract. We consider the generalization of the classical GARCH model in two directions: the first is to allow for non-linear dependencies in the conditional mean and in the conditional variance and the second concerns specification of the conditional density. As a tool for non-linear regression we use neural network-based modeling, so called recurrent mixture density networks, describing conditional mean and variance by multi-layer perceptrons. All of the models are compared for their out-of-sample predictive ability in terms of Value-at-Risk forecast evaluation. The empirical analysis is based on return series of stock indices from different financial markets. The results indicate that for all markets the improvement in the forecast by non-linear models over linear ones is negligible, while non-gaussian models significantly dominate the gaussian models with respect to most evaluation tests.

1 Introduction

Modeling and forecasting volatility of financial time series have been a popular research topic for the last several years. One reason for this development is that in today's new global financial architecture more emphasis is placed on measuring and managing financial market risks. The most famous model widely used in practice is GARCH which captures several "stylized facts" of asset return series (heteroskedasticity, volatility clustering, excess kurtosis). But the latest studies have found that there exist additional empirical regularities that can

---

[*] This work was funded by the Austrian Science Fund under grant SFB#010: "Adaptive Information Systems and Modeling in Economics and Management Science". The Austrian Research Institute for Artificial Intelligence is supported by the Austrian Federal Ministry of Education, Science and Culture.

not be described by classical GARCH model, such as leverage effect, fat tails of conditional distribution and so on.

We consider the generalization of the classical GARCH model in two directions: the first is to allow for non-linear dependencies in the conditional mean and in the conditional variance and the second concerns specification of the conditional density. As a tool for non-linear regression we use neural network-based modeling, so called recurrent mixture density networks ([1],[2]), describing conditional mean and variance by multi-layer perceptrons. Concerning distributions, we compare three different density specifications: models with normal distribution (heteroskedastic, but neither skewed nor leptokurtic); models with a Student's t-distribution (heteroskedastic, not skewed but leptokurtic); two component mixtures of gaussians (heteroskedastic, skewed and leptokurtic in a time-dependent manner).

For empirical analysis we used return series of the Dow Jones Industrial Average (USA), FTSE 100 (Great Britain) and NIKKEI 225 (Japan) over a period of more than 12 years. We got dynamical Value-at-Risk (VaR) predictions by each our model and evaluated the quality and accuracy of the VaR models with a number of statistical tests: the Basle Committee's traffic light test; exceptions testing and conditional coverage test. Moreover, we checked for the efficiency of the VaR measure, providing a quantitative basis for the incorporation of VaR prediction in regulatory capital requirements (calculation of the lost interest yield connected with the dynamically computed model-based capital reserves). In such a way, we continue the work in [2] and [3] in the direction of risk management application.

2 Description of Models

As a benchmark we use classical GARCH(1,1) model (see [4]) with conditional normal distribution and AR(1) process for mean equation for financial data returns r_t, i.e.

$$r_t = \mu_t + e_t, \quad e_t \sim \mathbf{N}(0, \sigma_t^2),$$
$$\mu_t = a_1 r_{t-1} + a_0,$$
$$\sigma_t^2 = \alpha_0 + \alpha_1 e_{t-1}^2 + \beta_1 \sigma_{t-1}^2.$$

One possible extension of this GARCH model is to substitute the conditional normal distribution by a Student's-t distribution with ν degrees of freedom in order to allow for excess kurtosis in the conditional distribution.

The second direction of the extension of the classical GARCH model is to allow for non-linear dependencies in the conditional mean and in the conditional variance. As a tool for non-linear regression we used neural network-based modeling, so called recurrent mixture density networks, describing conditional mean and variance by multi-layer perceptrons (MLP) (see [1] and [3] for detailed discussion).

In the simplest case an MLP with one input unit, one layer of hidden units and one output unit realizes the mapping

$$\tilde{f}(x_t) = g\left(\sum_{j=1}^{H} v_j h(w_j x_t + c_j) + s x_t + b\right), \quad (1)$$

where H denotes the number of hidden units, w_j and v_j the weights of the first and second layer, s the shortcut weight, and c_j and b the bias weights of the first and second layer. In general, the activation function h of the hidden units is chosen to be bounded, non-linear, and increasing as, e.g., the hyperbolic tangent. The activation function of the output unit may be unrestricted, e.g. $g(x) = x$. In general, MLP can approximate any smooth, non-linear function with arbitrary accuracy as the number of hidden units tends to infinity (see [5]). In such a way, MLP can be interpreted as a non-linear autoregressive model of first order and can be applied to predict the parameters of conditional density of the return series.

Recurrent mixture density network models RMDN(n) approximate the conditional distributions of returns by a mixture of n Gaussians:

$$\rho(r_t|I_{t-1}) = \sum_{i=1}^{n} \pi_{i,t} k(\mu_{i,t}, \sigma_{i,t}^2), \quad (2)$$

where $k(\mu_{i,t}, \sigma_{i,t}^2)$ is the gaussian density and the parameters $\pi_{i,t}$, $\mu_{i,t}$, and $\sigma_{i,t}^2$ of the n gaussian components are estimated by three MLPs. The MLPs estimating the priors and the centers are standard MLPs (1) with r_{t-1} as input. The MLP estimating the variances is recurrent and has the form

$$\sigma_{i,t}^2 = g\left(\sum_{j=1}^{H} v_{ij} h\left(w_{j0} e_{t-1}^2 + \sum_{k=1}^{n} w_{jk} \sigma_{k,t-1}^2 + c_j\right)\right.$$
$$\left. + s_{i0} e_{t-1}^2 + \sum_{k=1}^{n} s_{ik} \sigma_{k,t-1}^2 + b_i\right).$$

The activation function of the n output units is chosen as $g(x) = |x|$ to ensure non-negative network outputs.

The most appealing feature of RMDN models is time-dependence of the higher-order moments(skewness and kurtosis) and it is in contrast to the properties of GARCH and GARCH-t models.

We note that an RMDN model with one Gaussian component ($n = 1$) can be interpreted as a non-linear extension of a GARCH model.

There are two other models that must be introduced in order to analyze the influence of linear and non-linear functions and density specification on the performance of return series models ([3]). The first is non-linear GARCH-t models in the framework of RMDN models, replacing the weighted sum of normal densities in (2) by the density of the t-distribution. These models will be called

RMDN(n)-t models in the following. Secondly, one must study the performance of mixture models for the case that only linear functions are allowed. More precisely, in all three MLPs estimating the parameters of the mixture model the activation function h of the hidden units are supposed to be linear. These linear mixture models are referred to as LRMDN(n) models in the following.

3 Data Sets

In our numerical experiments we used three data sets related to different financial markets:

1. daily closing values of the American stock index Dow Jones Industrial Average (DJIA);
2. daily closing values of the FTSE 100 traded at the London Stock Exchange;
3. daily closing values of the Japan index NIKKEI 225.

The taken time interval for all data sets was 13 years from 1985 to 1997. All data were transformed into continuously compounded returns r_t (in percent) in the standard way by the natural logarithm of the ratio of consecutive daily closing levels. In order to take care of stationarity issues and increase the reliability of the empirical analysis, all time series were divided into overlapping segments of a fixed length of 700 trading days, where the first 500 returns of each segment form a training set, the next 100 points form a validation set and the remaining 100 returns are used for testing. The training sets are used to optimize the parameters of each model. The validation sets are used for an "early stopping" strategy to avoid overfitting for the neural networks models and independent test sets are reserved for out-of-sample model performance evaluation. The test sets are not overlapping.

4 Error Measure and Estimation Procedure

We fitted GARCH(1,1), RMDN(1), GARCH(1,1)-t, RMDN(1)-t, LRMDN(2) and RMDN(2) models to each of the training sets separately. The number of hidden units of the MLPs in the RMDN-models was chosen to be $H = 3$. The parameters of all models were optimized with respect to the average negative loglikelihood of the sample (loss function). The optimization routine was a scaled conjugate gradient algorithm. We performed optimization of RMDN models with several parameter initializations in an attempt to approach a global optimum. For the models with t-distribution, the degrees-of-freedom parameter was additionally optimized by a one-dimensional search routine.

5 Risk Management Application

A primary tool for financial risk assessment is the Value-at-Risk (VaR) methodology, where VaR is a measure of the maximum potential change in value of a portfolio with a given probability over a pre-set horizon. As soon as the probability distribution of the return is specified, VaR can be calculated using $(100\text{-}p)\%$ percentile r_p^* of this distribution as VaR = today's price $\cdot (\exp(r_p^*) - 1)$. For more information on VaR see, for instance, [6] and [7].

We proceeded in the following way:
The parameters of each model were fixed within every segment and we computed a forecast of tomorrow's return distribution as well as VaR estimates given the past data for every point in the test part of this segment. As usual in bank policy, we chose $p = 1\%$ and considered the 99% level on one-day VaR measures of the investment in the portfolio of stocks, corresponding to DJIA, FTSE 100 or NIKKEI 225 stock indices. In such a way, we got VaR estimate series for the whole data samples. Comparing the realization of the indices with VaR estimates, we determined the indicator variable θ_t as the outcome of a binomial event: either one-day actual loss L_t on trading activity is less than VaR_t estimates (a success), or the loss on the activity exceeds the potential loss estimates (a failure), i.e.

$$\theta_t = \begin{cases} 1, & if\ L_t\ <\ \text{VaR}_t, \\ 0, & \text{otherwise.} \end{cases} \qquad (3)$$

We assess now the quality and accuracy of VaR predictions and of the models underlying them in a number of ways, considering our three stock index series. Such testing is often referred to as "backtesting" (see, e.g. [6]).

5.1 Test 1: Basle Traffic Light

This is the backtesting framework developed by the Basle Committee on Banking Supervision ([8]). Any bank must hold regulatory capital against their market risk exposure. These capital charges are based on VaR estimates generated by the banks' own VaR models and a multiplication factor defined by supervising authorities according to the traffic light concept of the Basle Committee on Banking Supervision. According to this concept, internal banks' models are classified into three zones. This classification into green, yellow or red zones depends on how often the actual losses exceed the daily 99% VaR predictions over a period of n trading days. Based on such classification, the necessary capital reserves are assigned. Green zone means that the multiplication factor of 3 is applied to the VaR value, yellow results in a higher (add-on) factor between 3 and 4, whereas red normally means rejection of the model.

Our backtesting period covers the whole sample period with $n = 2300$ that exceed the 250 days that are typically used in practice.

The results of the hypothetical classification are listed in Table 1.

All the models for FTSE 100 data are in acceptable zones. For other markets the models with t-distribution together with mixture density networks yield the most reliable setup. Among the non-gaussian models, the linear mixture density network performs best. The gaussian models are mostly rejected. This test also indicates the bad performance of the RMDN(2) model on DJIA data set.

Table 1. Classification according to the Basle rules. The column "failures" give the number of failures in the whole sample for the corresponding index

Model	DJIA		FTSE 100		NIKKEI 225	
	failures	zone	failures	zone	failures	zone
GARCH(1,1)	45	red	32	yellow	39	yellow
RMDN(1)	48	red	26	green	43	red
GARCH(1,1)-t	30	green	29	green	35	yellow
RMDN(1)-t	39	yellow	25	green	32	yellow
LRMDN(2)	30	green	27	green	27	green
RMDN(2)	44	red	30	green	34	yellow

5.2 Test 2: Proportion of Failures

Kupiec (1995) presents a more sophisticated approach to the analysis of exceptions based on the observation that a comparison between daily profit or loss outcomes and the corresponding VaR measures gives rise to a binomial experiment. The outcomes of the binomial events θ_t (3) are distributed as a series of draws from an independent Bernoulli distribution and the verification test is based on the proportion of failures (PF) in the sample. For more details, see [9].

Table 2 summarizes the performance of our models with respect to the proportion of failures test. The column denoted by "failures" give the number of failures in the whole sample for the corresponding index. The next column shows whether the null hypothesis H0: $p^* = 0.01$ can be rejected at the 5% significance level. The results from the table are consistent with the previous test.

Table 2. PF test. The largest number of failures that could be observed in the samples without rejecting the null H0 at the 5% confidence level is 32 for sample size 2300 points

Model	DJIA		FTSE 100		NIKKEI 225	
	failures	H0: $p^* = 0.01$	failures	H0: $p^* = 0.01$	failures	H0: $p^* = 0.01$
GARCH(1,1)	45	rejected	32	not rejected	39	rejected
RMDN(1)	48	rejected	26	not rejected	43	rejected
GARCH(1,1)-t	30	not rejected	29	not rejected	35	rejected
RMDN(1)-t	39	rejected	25	not rejected	32	not rejected
LRMDN(2)	30	not rejected	27	not rejected	27	not rejected
RMDN(2)	44	rejected	30	not rejected	34	rejected

5.3 Test 3: Lost Interest Yield

The common downside of the tests above is that all of them only count the number of excesses, so that a model which has many very small excesses will be rejected while a model with few very high excesses will be accepted. Moreover, financial institutions prefer VaR models that are not only able to pass in backtesting but that provide small VaR predictions, while overestimated VaR implies banks have excessive risk capital. Therefore, to check the efficiency of the VaR measure we developed a new test, providing a quantitative basis for the incorporation of VaR prediction in regulatory capital requirements.

Any financial institution must hold regulatory capital to cover their potential market risk exposure. We used dynamically computed daily VaR estimates generated by our VaR models and assumed for simplicity that capital reserves equal to the VaR estimates will be held for 1 day. When actual portfolio loss L_t does not exceed the predicted loss for this day, we considered the required capital lost for investment for 1 day and computed the continuously compounded lost interest yield as $\text{VaR}_t \cdot (e^{i/250 \cdot 1} - 1)$ with some interest rate i. In the case of excessive losses (portfolio loss L_t is greater than VaR_t) banks will have additional capital charges as a penalty, so that the lost interest yield $= \text{VaR}_t \cdot (e^{i/250 \cdot 1} - 1) +$ Penalty, where, e.g., Penalty $= 1.2 \cdot (L_t - VaR_t) \cdot e^{i/250 \cdot 1}$ to cover higher transaction costs of capital transference.

According to this strategy, we calculated lost yield summing over all test points and then scaled them to remove the dependency on the portfolio size. These relative lost interest yields for all our data sample are depicted in Fig 1.

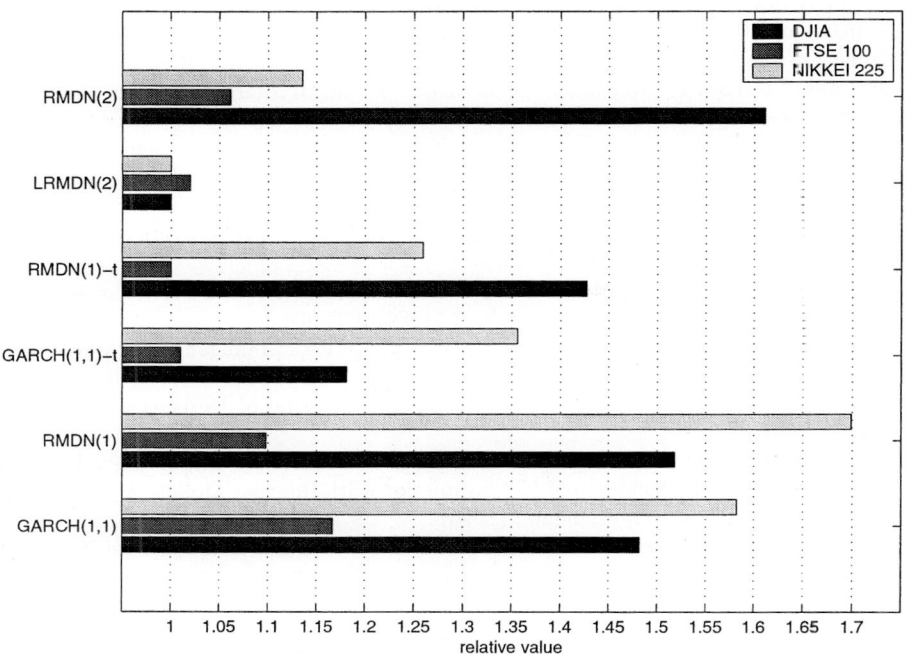

Fig. 1. Lost Interest Yield

For all the markets the best model is the linear mixture density network. In general, this test clearly rejects linear and non-linear gaussian models and favours the mixture density models over the models with t-distributions.

6 Discussion and Conclusions

We analyzed the impact of non-linearity and of non-gaussian distributions versus the classical GARCH model. The statistical tests clearly favour non-gaussian models over gaussians ones. But within non-gaussian models themselves there is some difference across the markets and while both the models with t-distribution and mixture density networks are capable to capture fat tails elements in the conditional distribution, only mixture density networks allow for time-varying skewness and kurtosis which are common in financial markets. Further, we found no significant differences in performance between linear and non-linear models for all data series except DJIA, where the tests support only linear GARCH-t and linear mixture density network. With respect to the efficiency test, for all the markets the best model is the linear mixture density network.

References

1. Bishop, C.: Mixture density networks. Technical report, Neural Computing Research Group Report: NCRG/94/004, Aston University, Birmingham (1994)
2. Schittenkopf, C., Dorffner, G., Dockner, E.J.: Volatility prediction with mixture density networks. In Niklasson, L., Bodén, M., Ziemke, T., eds.: ICANN 98 – Proceedings of the 8th International Conference on Artificial Neural Networks, Springer (1998) 929–934
3. Schittenkopf, C., Dorffner, G., Dockner, E.J.: Forecasting time-dependent conditional densities: a seminonparametric neural network approach. Journal of Forecasting **19** (2000) 355–374
4. Bollerslev, T.: A generalized autoregressive conditional heteroskedasticity. Journal of Econometrics **31** (1986) 307–327
5. Hornik, K., Stinchcombe, M., White, H.: Multilayer feedforward networks are universal approximators. Neural Networks **2** (1989) 359–366
6. Dowd, K.: Beyond Value at Risk: the New Science of Risk Management. John Wiley & Sons, England (1998)
7. Duffie, D., Pan, J.: An overview of value at risk. Journal of Derivatives **4** (1997) 7–49
8. Basle Committe on Banking Supervision Basle, Switzerland: Supervisory Framework for the Use of 'Backtesting' in Conjunction with Internal Models Approach to Market Risk Capital Requirements. (1996)
9. Kupiec, H.: Techniques for verifying the accuracy of risk management models. Journal of Derivatives **3** (1995) 73–84

Hierarchical Mixtures of Autoregressive Models for Time-Series Modeling

Carmen Vidal and Alberto Suárez

Computer Science Department
Escuela Politécnica Superior
Universidad Autónoma de Madrid
Ciudad Universitaria de Cantoblanco, Madrid 28049, Spain
alberto.suarez@ii.uam.es

Abstract. A hierarchical mixture of autoregressive (AR) models is proposed for the analysis of nonlinear time-series. The model is a decision tree with soft sigmoidal splits at the inner nodes and linear autoregressive models at the leaves. The global prediction of the mixture is a weighted average of the partial predictions from each of the AR models. The weights in this average are computed by the application of the hierarchy of soft splits at the inner nodes of the tree on the input, which consists in the vector of the delayed values of the time series. The weights can be interpreted as *a priori* probabilities that an example is generated by the AR model at that leaf. As an illustration of the flexibility and robustness of the models generated by these mixtures, an application to the analysis of a financial time-series is presented.

1 Introduction

The idea of combining the results of simple models to carry out the analysis of complex patterns lies at the heart of many successful automatic learning paradigms. In this work, we propose to use a collection of simple (linear) autoregressive models articulated in a hierarchical mixture in order to model stochastic time series with some degree of non-linearity. The combined model can be thought of as a hierarchical mixture of competing experts [1], or alternatively as a decision tree with soft splits and linear models at the leaves [2,3]. The final prediction, which involves the whole tree structure, is obtained by a convex combination of the individual expert predictions at the leaves. This modeling strategy is different from that of connectionist models (for instance, a multilayer perceptron with AR models at the leaves), where units collaborate to yield a prediction.

Mixtures of experts have been employed in many pattern recognition and control tasks [4,1,5]. Mixture density networks [6] and non-hierarchical mixtures [7,8,9] have also been used for time series analysis. In this paper we show how hierarchical mixtures of autoregressive (AR) models can be used in time-series analysis to extract relevant information about the full time-dependent conditional probability distributions. In certain applications of time-series analysis one is interested in models that predict more than just the conditional mean. Hierarchical mixtures of AR models can be used to produce robust estimates of, for instance, the tails of the distributions of expected financial returns, which are very important in financial risk analysis.

2 Hierarchical Mixtures of Autoregressive Models

Consider the time series

$$\{X_0, X_1, X_2, \ldots, X_T\}, \qquad (1)$$

which is assumed to be stationary. The building blocks of the mixtures studied in this work are linear autoregressive models of the form

$$X_t = \boldsymbol{\phi}^\dagger \cdot \tilde{\mathbf{X}}_{(t-1)}^{(t-m)} = \phi_0 + \phi_1 X_{t-1} + \phi_2 X_{t-2} + \ldots + \phi_m X_{t-m} + u_t, \qquad (2)$$

with the definitions $\boldsymbol{\phi}^\dagger = (\phi_0\,\phi_1\,\phi_2\,\ldots\phi_m)$, for the vector of coefficients of the autoregressive models, and

$$\left(\mathbf{X}_{(t-1)}^{(t-m)}\right)^\dagger = (X_{t-1}\,X_{t-2}\,\ldots X_{t-m}), \quad \left(\tilde{\mathbf{X}}_{(t-1)}^{(t-m)}\right)^\dagger = \left(1\,\left(\mathbf{X}_{(t-1)}^{(t-m)}\right)^\dagger\right) \quad (3)$$

for the vector of delayed values of the time series (plus a *bias* term if a tilde appears in the notation). The last term in (2) is assumed to be zero-mean white noise with a probability distribution $P(u_t)$.

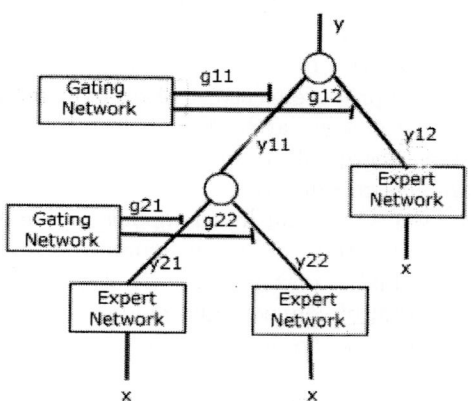

Fig. 1. Architecture for a mixture of 3 experts with hierarchy

The architecture of the hierarchical mixture is a decision tree, T, with soft splits at the inner nodes and autoregressive models, such as the ones given by

(2), at the leaves or terminal nodes (see Fig. 1 for a decision tree with two levels and three experts at the leaves). The global tree prediction consists in a convex combination of the partial predictions of the experts in each of the leaves

$$\hat{X}_t = \sum_{l \in \tilde{T}} g_l \hat{X}_t^{(l)}; \quad \hat{X}_t^{(l)} = \phi_l^\dagger \cdot \tilde{\mathbf{X}}_{(t-1)}^{(t-m)}, \tag{4}$$

where $\{t_l\}_{l \in \tilde{T}}$ is the set of leaf nodes of the tree.

The weights in the average are found by applying the hierarchy of soft splits at the inner nodes of the decision tree. Consider the split at the inner node t_i. Assuming that the instance characterized by the delay vector $\mathbf{X}_{(t-1)}^{(t-m)}$ has been assigned to node t_i with a weight $g_i(\mathbf{X}_{(t-1)}^{(t-m)})$, the weights for the child nodes are

$$g_{iL}(\mathbf{X}_{(t-1)}^{(t-m)}) = g_i\left(\mathbf{X}_{(t-1)}^{(t-m)}\right) \frac{1}{1 + \exp\left\{\boldsymbol{\theta}_i^\dagger \cdot \mathbf{X}_{(t-1)}^{(t-m)} - a_i\right\}}$$

$$g_{iR}(\mathbf{X}_{(t-1)}^{(t-m)};) = g_i\left(\mathbf{X}_{(t-1)}^{(t-m)}\right)\left(1 - g_{iL}(\mathbf{X}_{(t-1)}^{(t-m)};)\right). \tag{5}$$

where g_{iL} (g_{iR}) stands for the weight of the left (right) child nodes of t_i. The space of instances is partitioned by a soft sigmoidal splits centered at the oblique hyperplane $\boldsymbol{\theta}_i^\dagger \cdot \mathbf{X}_{(t-1)}^{(t-m)} - a_i$. If the weight in the root node, t_0, is initialized to one ($g_0 = 1$), Equation (5) guarantees that

$$\sum_{l \in \tilde{T}} g_l\left(\mathbf{X}_{(t-1)}^{(t-m)}\right) = 1, \tag{6}$$

which makes a probabilistic interpretation for the weights possible: The value $g_l(\mathbf{X}_{(t-1)}^{(t-m)})$ is the *a priori* probability that point X_t in the time-series is generated by the model l, given that $\mathbf{X}_{(t-1)}^{(t-m)}$ has been observed.

The parameters of the model are $\left\{\boldsymbol{\theta}_i, a_i; \ t_i \in T - \tilde{T}\right\}$ i.e., the $(m-1)$ parameters that characterize the soft splits at each of the inner nodes, $\left\{\boldsymbol{\phi}_l; \ t_l \in \tilde{T}\right\}$, the $(m+1)$ parameters of the AR model at each of the leaf nodes, and the parameters that characterize the distribution of innovations. For each Autoregressive model there is a different stochastic source for the innovations. We then make the assumption that the innovations in model l are Gaussian white noise with zero mean and variance σ_l^2. Provided that a sufficient number of models are used, any non-Gaussian process can be mimicked by the mixture.

According to the probabilistic interpretation of the hierarchical mixture, the model parameters are fixed by optimization of the likelihood function

$$\mathcal{L} = \prod_{t=m}^{T} \sum_{l \in \tilde{T}} g_l\left(\mathbf{X}_{(t-1)}^{(t-m)}\right) P(X_t - \phi_l^\dagger \cdot \tilde{\mathbf{X}}_{(t-1)}^{(t-m)}; 0, \sigma_l), \tag{7}$$

where $P(x; \mu, \sigma)$ is the probability density function for a normal distribution of mean μ and variance σ^2. The likelihood function depends on the parameters of the splits through the quantities g_l, which are calculated by iteration of Eq. (5) from the root node t_0 to the terminal node t_l. Despite the fact that hierarchical mixtures are parameter-rich models, we expect them to exhibit good generalization properties, at least for the types of data we investigate. This resilience to overfitting has also been documented in other compound models [5].

3 Application to Financial Time Series

Financial time series, such as the evolution of the price of a given asset in the stock market, the exchange rate between a pair of currencies, or the market value of a portfolio, present some special features that need to be taken into account when being analyzed. While prices of financial products do not seem to be drawn from a stationary probability distribution, the daily returns obtained by log-differencing the original series can be modeled by a stationary process. Unfortunately, the series of returns obtained by this procedure seem to be rather unpredictable. This last observation can be readily understood if markets are efficient; financial products traded in an efficient market incorporate in the actual market price all available information (including all rational expectations of the *future* evolution of the prices). If this hypothesis is correct, the availability of a reliable trend predictor for the prices leads to the emergence market pressures (offer/demand) that tend to annul the detected trends: Assume that the market believes a given asset is undervalued (an upward trend is detected); such a belief is translated into an increase in the number buying orders by agents expecting to profit from this upward trend. The increase in demand pushes the price of the asset upwards. Asset prices will continue to rise until the identified future trend is annulled. A symmetric argument can be used for overvalued assets, whose price will drop up to the level marked by the expectations of the market.

This simple argument rules out the possibility of learning a reliable predictor from the time-series of log-returns in an efficient market. There are however other tasks, besides prediction, that are of interest: In financial risk analysis [10] one is interested in estimating the frequency of large variations in the price of a financial product. It is therefore extremely important that the models developed to analyze the time-series of returns remain accurate at the tails of the distribution, so that they are useful tools in financial risk analysis. It is well known in the econometrics literature that linear AR models with Gaussian noise, although well-suited to the study of small fluctuations in series of financial returns, fail to capture the tails of the distribution, which is highly leptokurtic (the so-called *heavy tails*). More realistic models that incorporate heteroskedasticity (ARCH, GARCH) are also unable to fully account for these heavy tails. There exists several possible ways to extend the "classical" AR models in order to account for this observation. One possibility is assume a more complex form for the noise distribution (e.g., hyperbolic distributions [11], mixtures of Gaussians [12], extreme value distributions [13]), etc. Another choice is to use combinations of autoregressive models [14,15,8,9]. We propose to use hierarchical mixtures of autoregressive models to account for the leptokurtosis of financial time series.

These hierarchical mixtures generate expected distributions of financial returns that can account better than simple linear models for the observed frequency of large (tail) events. In this work the usefulness of these hierarchical models is illustrated through the analysis of the time series of returns of the IBEX35 index (Spanish stock market). The data used are the daily returns of the index corresponding to 1912 trading days between 1993 and 2001 (see Fig. 2).

3.1 Analysis of the IBEX35 Time Series

In this section we fit mixtures of up to 3 AR(1) experts to model the conditional probability distribution of the IBEX35 returns. Longer delays than a single day have been also tested, but were discarded because they do no lead to a significant improvement in the quality of the fits. This is in agreement with the absence of linear correlations among the residuals of an AR(1) fit.

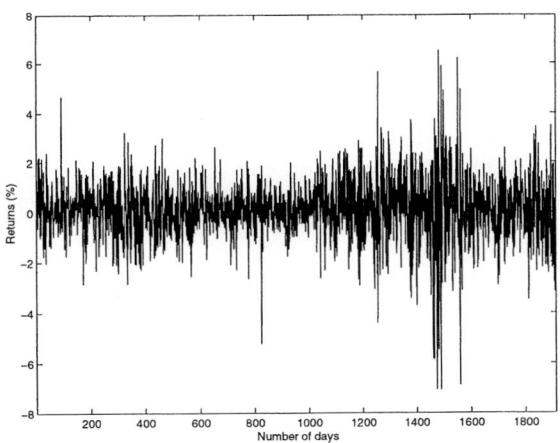

Fig. 2. Series of daily returns for the IBEX35

When articulating the prediction of 3 AR models, two architectures are possible: a non-hierarchical mixture with all experts at the same level (see Ref. [9]) or a hierarchical mixtures with two levels (see Fig. 1). Results of both architectures are reported for comparison.

In the experiments, the data are partitioned into a training set of the first 1000 values of the series (approximately 4 years of data) and then tested on the remaining 912. In order to make a comparison across different models, the actual values of the time-series are transformed by a Rosenblatt transformation [16]: the inverse of the standard normal cumulative distribution function is applied on the cumulative distribution function predicted by the mixture for the actual time-series value. If the model were correct, the transformed values would correspond to a random Gaussian variable of mean zero and unit variance. Deviations from normality signal the failure of the models to estimate the conditional

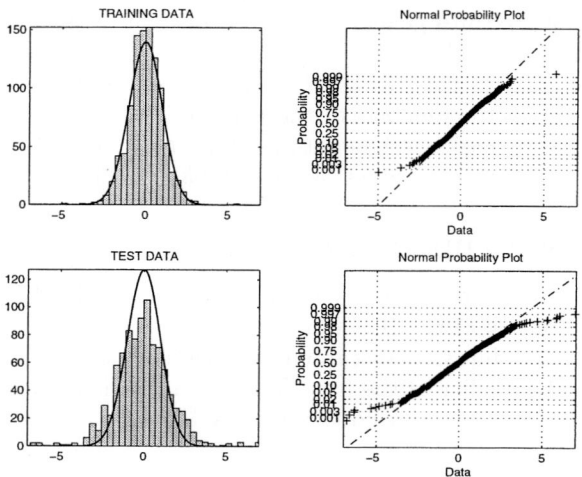

Fig. 3. Residuals for an AR(1) fit to the IBEX35 data.

probability distribution of the returns. Figs. 3-5 present, on the left-hand side, a comparison between the histogram of transformed values and the theoretical al normal $N(0,1)$ distribution, and, on the right-hand side, a quantile-quantile plot of the theoretical percentiles and the empirical percentiles.

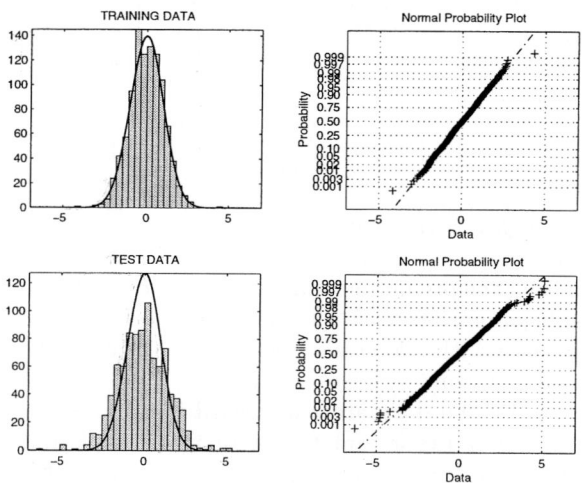

Fig. 4. Transformed values for a Mixture of 3 AR(1) fit to the IBEX35 data (no hierarchy).

The inadequacy of a linear Gaussian AR(1) model is apparent even in the training data (see Fig. 3). The tails of the empirical distribution have clearly more

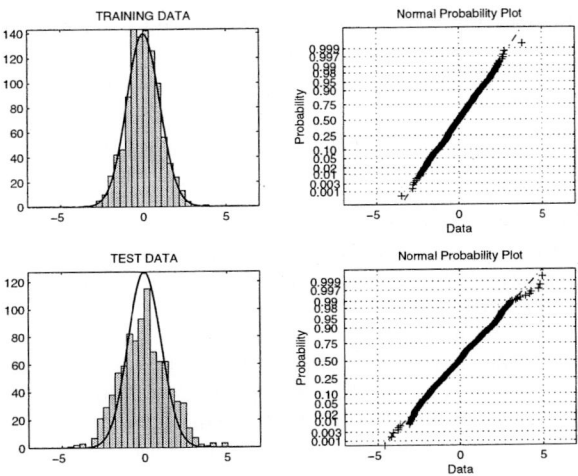

Fig. 5. Transformed values for a Mixture of 3 AR(1) fit to the IBEX35 data (with hierarchy).

weight than what a simple AR(1) predicts. Non-hierarchical mixtures of 3 AR(1) experts fit data quite well for the training set (Fig. 4), with the possible exception of points at the tails, which might be outliers or fluctuations due to sampling errors. The fit to the test data is reasonable, although the models systematically underpredict the frequency of events near the mode of the distribution and in the tails. The hierarchical mixture of 3 AR(1) models (Fig. 5) performs reasonably well (even at the tails, which is the interesting region in risk analysis) for the both the training and test sets.

4   Summary and Conclusions

A hierarchical mixture of models combines the prediction of different experts placed at the leaves of a decision tree. The weights of the prediction of each expert in the combination is determined by the sigmoidal splits in the decision tree. The models can be applied to financial time series using linear autoregressive models as experts. Financial time series are notoriously difficult to predict: Arguments of market efficiency hint at the practical futility of point prediction tasks for prices of financial products. For this reason, the present research has focused on modeling some features of financial time series that are not annulled by market pressures upon detection. In particular, the hierarchical mixtures of AR models introduced seem to be able to capture some statistical features of financial time series that are relevant for the analysis of financial risk. These models are robust, and apparently their performance is not deteriorated by overfitting to the data used in training them.

Acknowledgments. This work has been supported by CICyT grant TIC2001-0572-C02-02.

References

1. M. I. Jordan and R. A. Jacobs. Hierarchical mixtures of experts and the EM algorithm. *Neural Computation*, 6:181–214, 1994.
2. A. Suárez and J. F. Lutsko. Globally optimal fuzzy decision trees for classification and regression. *IEEE Trans. on Pattern Analysis and Machine Intelligence*, 21(12):1297–1311, 1999.
3. V. Medina–Chico, A. Suárez, and J. F. Lutsko. Backpropagation in decision trees for regression. In Luc De Raedt and Peter Flach, editors, *Lecture Notes in Artificial Intelligence: Proceedings of the 12th European Conference on Machine Learning*, volume 2167, pages 348–359, Berlin, 2001. Springer.
4. M. I. Jordan and R. A. Jacobs. Adaptive mixtures of local experts. *Neural Computation*, 3:79–87, 1991.
5. R. Jacobs and M. Tanner. Mixtures of X. In A. J. C. Sharkey, editor, *Combining Artificial Neural Nets*, pages 267–296, London, 1999. Springer.
6. C. Schittenkopf and G. Dorffner. Risk-neutral density extraction from option prices: Improved pricing with mixture density networks. *IEEE Transactions on Neural Networks*, 12(4):716–725, 2001.
7. A. S. Weigend, M. Mangeas, and A. N. Srivastava. Nonlinear gated experts for time series: Discovering regimes and avoiding overfitting. *International Journal of Neural Systems*, 6(4):373–399, 1995.
8. C. S. Wong and W. K. Li. On a mixture autoregressive model. *Journal of the Royal Statistical Society B*, 62:95–115, 2000.
9. A. Suárez. Mixtures of autorregressive models for financial risk analysis. In J. R. Dorronsoro, editor, *Lecture Notes in Computer Science: Artificial Neural Networks-ICANN 2002*, volume 2167, pages 1186–1191, Berlin, 2002. Springer.
10. P. Jorion. *Value at Risk: The new Benchmark for Controlling Market Risk*. McGraw-Hill, New York, 1997.
11. E. Eberlein and U. Keller. Hyperbolic distributions in finance. *Bernoulli*, 1:281–299, 1995.
12. J. Hull and A. White. Value at risk when daily changes in market variables are not normally distributed. *Journal of Derivatives*, 5(3):9–19, 1998.
13. P. Embrechts, C. Kluplelberg, and T. Mikosch. *Modelling Extremal Events for Insurance and Finance*. Springer-Verlag, Berlin, 1997.
14. H. Tong. *Non-linear Time Series. A Dynamical System Approach*. Oxford University Press, New York, 1996.
15. G. González-Rivera. Smooth transition GARCH models. *Studies in Nonlinear Dynamics and Econometrics*, 3:61–78, 1998.
16. M. Rosenblatt. Remarks on a multivariate transformation. *Annals of Mathematica Statistics*, 23(3):470–472, 1952.

Intelligent and Hybrid Systems

A Simple Constructing Approach to Build P2P Global Computing Overlay Network

Dou Wen, Jia Yan, Liu Zhong, and Zou Peng

Group 613, Dept. of Computer Science, Changsha Institute of Technology,
410073, Hunan, China
{douwen,phillipliu}@vip.sina.com

Abstract. We describe a peer-to-peer self-organizing overlay network for our global computing system. The preliminary simulation results show that the network has some small-world characteristics such as higher clustering coefficient and short path length, which leads to an efficient heuristic task scheduling algorithm on which any volunteer peer with limited knowledge about the global network can dispatch its excrescent computation tasks to powerful nodes globally, in a way contrary to the current global computing system in which a global broker is responsible for the task scheduling. We argue that our approach is a starting point to eliminate the broker component which makes current global systems unscalable.

1 Introduction

This paper describes a peer-to-peer self-organizing overlay network on which we build a java based general-purpose global computing system, Paradropper. The goal of Paradropper project is to implement a unified computing network on which anyone can submit (contribute) his/her computing jobs (resources) in a unified overlay network via unified user-friendly GUI. The most desirable feature of our system is its peer-to-peer architecture. Current global computing systems such as Javelin++[1] and Bayanihan[2] are essentially center-based. The centralized architecture leads to some problems in scalability and accessibility. Firstly, in systems such as Javelin++ and Bayanihan, there is a broker component which is responsible for registering, task dispatching, job submitting, load balancing and synchronizing. When there are many computing jobs managed by the broker, it becomes a bottleneck of the whole computing network and a potential single point of failure. Though the two projects both prompt a broker network [1] (in Bayanihan, a similar concept is called server pool) approach to avoid this situation, we argue that the maintaining cost of the broker network cannot be neglected. Secondly, in most other general-purpose global computing systems (including above two systems), there must be one or more well-known sites to host the brokers, non-professional clients and volunteers need firstly to know these brokers address for submitting their computing jobs or registering their computers. This in a sense will frustrate those volunteers who do not want to know any troublesome details of how to contribute their computational resources. So how to eliminate the broker component (or weaken its functions?) is a key issue of the system scalability and accessibility.

The peer-to-peer overlay network has been widely used in file-sharing and data-sharing applications, many researches [3, 4, 5] has proved that a well-designed peer-to-peer topology would make the applications built on it more scalable and assessable. In this paper, we investigate the possibility of using a pure peer-to-peer network to construct computing network. Our preliminary work show that, by constructing a small-world network with clustering characteristic, any volunteer peer with limited knowledge about global network can dispatch its computation tasks to the more powerful nodes globally, without the help of a global broker component. In another word, our work lightens the broker's overload by unleashing its scheduling and registering responsibility. In addition, and any peer can join the computing network just by starting the (Paradropper) program without any knowledge about broker (like the situation in some pure decentralized file-sharing application). Our ongoing work is dealing with eliminating other responsibility of the broker component, such as heartbeat detecting, termination detecting, load balancing, and synchronizing, etc. The final goal of our project is to eliminate the whole broker component completely.

The paper is organized as follows: in section 2 we discuss the construction of Paradropper network. In section 3 we prompt a heuristic task scheduling algorithm. In section 4 a conclusion is given.

2 The Construction of Paradropper Network

Many researches have shown that peer-to-peer networks have some self-organizing network characteristics, which contribute to peer's easily and effectively searching for data. These characteristics include (1) high clustering coefficient, (2) short path length and (3) power-law distribution of node degree, etc. All these characteristics help peers relying on limited local knowledge to make routing decisions rather than depending on global knowledge. After Milgram[6] prompted the famous 6-degrees of separation notion by a social experiment, Watts et al. [7] started by looking at graphs and the metrics for graphs common in social networks. Two key ideas they focused on were clustering and path length. The first concept is a formal way to state how "cliquish" a graph is, i.e., how tightly the links of a node in the graph are connected to each other. For convenience, we give the formal graph theory definitions about these concepts:

Definition 1. The connectivity of a vertex v, k_v, is the number of attached edges.

Definition 2. Let d(i, j) be the length of the shortest path between the vertices i and j, then the characteristic path length, L, is d(i, j) averaged over all C_n^2 pairs of vertices.

Definition 3. The neighborhood of a vertex v, $\Gamma_v = \{i : d(i,v) = 1\}$ so $(v \notin \Gamma_v)$

Definition 4 The local clustering coefficient, C_v, is: $C_v = \dfrac{|E(\Gamma_v)|}{C_{k_v}^2}$, where $|E(\bullet)|$ gives a sub graph's total number of edges.

Definition 5. The clustering coefficient, C, is C_v averaged over all vertices.

Watts et al. have discovered that almost all the self-organizing networks have two basic characteristics :(1) higher clustering coefficient than the random network (2) short path length, and the latter lead to the famous small-world phenomenon in social network and many self-organizing networks. Unfortunately, Watts's network constructing approaches are based on regular network (rewired lattice), and not suitable for dynamic network constructing and maintaining. There are other researches [8] also prompt some approaches which are more suitable for dynamic network constructing, but these approaches seem to be dedicated to constructing only low diameter network without more concerning about clustering characteristic which is important in our system. In this paper, we prompt a very simple construction approach, and the simulation show that our approach is very suitable for constructing small-world network with clustering characteristic.

2.1 The Construction of Paradropper Computing Network

We use the following approach to construct Paradropper network:

At bootstrapping stage, every new volunteer computer interacts with an entry point cache, which randomly selects an in-network volunteer (we call it network entry point) as response to the new participator.
(1) The new volunteer then send a message to the entry point, if the entry point's neighbor number is beyond the upper bound Z, it will accept the new node as its new neighbor, otherwise, refuse it. In the later situation, the new node will ask the cache again for a new entry point.
(2) If the entry point accepts the new node, it will send notify messages to part of his old neighbors. Let the number is K.
(3) These K neighbors who received the notify message will also try to build a neighbor relationship with the new node.

In social terms, when you have a new friend, you would likely introduce him (her) to part of your old friends. We argue that it is the main reason why in social network the probability of our friends know each other is very high. The clustering characteristic emerges when we introduce new friends to our old friends. The rewiring behavior described by Watts can also be explained by our model: some nodes have friends in several clusters. These nodes play the re-wiring roles just like those nodes selected randomly in Watts's lattice network.

Practically, a volunteer computer can only have limited neighbors. Suppose when an entry point accepts a new node as a new neighbor, it will introduce the new node to maximum K number of his old neighbors. In Paradropper, we let the upper bound of a volunteer can have neighbors is 2K, i.e., Z=2K. Sometimes, not all the K neighbors notified will accept the new node as a new neighbor because of the upper bound Z. Let us suppose every in-network volunteer computer knows how many neighbors his neighbors have. The notify message will first send to neighbors whose neighbor number is below the upper bound Z. The reason why we take Z as 2K is empirically: we find when $1<K<Z-1$(If $K = Z-1$, the network will become a complete graph and stop to grow as the nodes number in network reach Z), the constructed network appears almost the same properties with slightly decreasing in clustering coefficient when $K \to Z-1$ and slightly increasing in path length when $K \to 1$. More details about K and Z are discussed in our technical report [9].The Fig. 1 illustrate the construction of 5 nodes network.

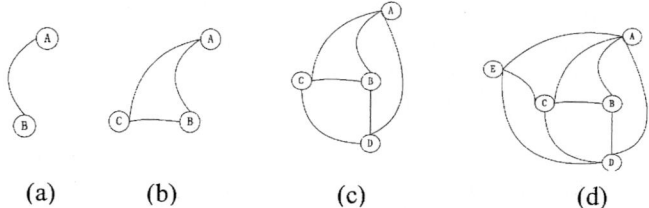

Fig. 1. A Simple illustration of Paradropper Network Construction. (a) add a new volunteer B.(b) add a new volunteer C from entry point A, A introduce it to B.(c) add a new volunteer D from entry point B, B introduce it to A, C.(d) add a new volunteer E from entry point C, C introduce it to A, D.

2.2 Paradropper Network Simulation

We use simulation approach to investigate the properties of Paradropper network, i.e. clustering coefficient and path length. A simulator was build with java. We use undirected graph to represent Paradropper network and vertex to represent volunteer computer. A failure simulation thread make some links disable (every 500ms) randomly, and another recovery thread periodically check if there is node with no neighbor (every 1000ms), if so, give it an entry point randomly and make it re-connect to the network again. We have tried scale of 100,400, 600, 1000 nodes, with K = 2, 4, 8, 10, 20. The results are shown in Fig. 2, 3. The simulation result show that our construction approach leads to a self-organizing overlay network, with the clustering coefficient is very high and the path length decrease sharply with limited K. For example, when scale is 100, K=4, the clustering coefficient $C \approx 0.65$, and when the scale became 1000, C just has some slight change($C \approx 0.67$).

The path length decrease sharply with the increasing of upper bound Z, while the clustering coefficient seems get little affected. In fact, the C gets slightly increased when the nodes have a higher upper bound Z. This phenomenon can be explained easily: when Z becomes larger, the whole network gets more tightly. In an extreme situation, when Z=N-1(N is the scale of the network) and K=Z, the whole network will become a complete graph gradually with C=1 and the path length L=1. The failure simulation results are omitted here in the case of limited space. Actually, with the interaction between the failure thread and recovery thread, the clustering coefficient waves at a slight scope, and the network partitioned occasionally but could be repaired at last. The explanation is intuitive: when a node lost some of its neighbors, the local clustering efficient C_v will decrease and the global clustering coefficient C trends to decrease with a lot of nodes lost their neighbors. But as we discussed in section 2.1, when a node finds itself lost all its neighbors, it will asks the entry point cache to give it a new entry point to re-join to the network, so its C_v will increase and the global C will recovery with the work of the recovery thread. The path length is in the same situation, when a node lost some of its neighbors, it means that node lost some possible shortest path to some other nodes. In an extreme situation, this will make the whole graph "partition". But the recovery algorithm will merge these partitions as long as there is enough running time.

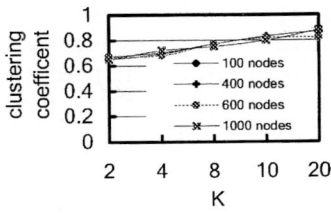
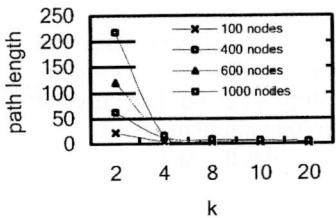

Fig. 2. Simulation result of clustering coefficient.

Fig. 3. Simulation result of path length.

3 Scheduling Algorithm

Here scheduling means routing tasks to volunteer peer efficiently, i.e., with a high probability, tasks are more likely to be routed to the powerful peers in Paradropper network. In a random network, deciding to whom to send the task is sightless. Because Paradropper network is close to a self-organizing network with high clustering coefficient and short path length, we could implement a very simple but efficient heuristic scheduling algorithm.

As we discuss above, every Paradropper peer has limited neighbors. In each routing step, the idlest neighbor is selected as the target. In every peer, there is a variable *Workload* recording the current workload of the peer. Whenever the peer accepts a task, its Workload increase by 1, and whenever the peer finishes a task, its Workload decreases by 1. Here we use the number of tasks the peer accepted to represent the workload of a peer. It's a coarse granularity workload representation, but we thought it is enough to explain our scheduling algorithm here.

A new volunteer has the workload 0. When the workload of a peer gets changed (accept a task or finish a task), the peer will notify all its neighbor using a notify message. In the case of limited space, here we omit the formal representation.

A *time-to-live* value is used to limit the hops of a task message. Because Paradropper network has a short path length, in most case, a peer could reach any peer in limited hops (in our system, we set the *ttl* to 11). An intuitionistic procedure is shown in Fig. 4(a).

Can a random network do the same thing? No. For example, a random network can not deal with the following case shown in Fig. 4(b). In Fig. 4(b), the solid line means there is an edge between two nodes, dash line means there is a possible edge(exist with probability) between two nodes. When node A accepts a task, according to our scheduling algorithm, there is a chance for A to schedule the task to E directly, if the edge between A and E exist. If the edge A-E do not exist, the task will be send to node C. There is also a chance for C to schedule the task to E directly, if the edge between C and E exist. If not, the task will be send to node D while the node E has the lowest workload. In a random network the probability of an edge existing between A and E is very low, so does the edge between C and E. Therefore there is a high probability that the task will be routed to D at last. In Paradropper network, because the average clustering coefficient is very high, which means the probability of B's neighbors knowing each other (have edge between them) is very high. Suppose the clustering coefficient is P, then the probability of A and E have a neighbor relationship is P, and the probability of which E and C have a relationship is also P. Consider our simulation results, the average clustering coefficient is 0.8, then the probability that the task will be scheduled to E is $P + (1-P) \times P = 0.96$. So the task is likely to be sent to E with a high probability.

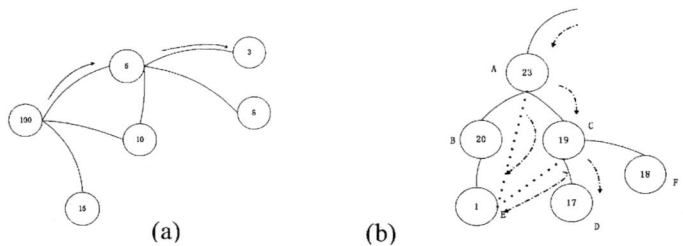

Fig. 4. Task scheduling in Paradropper network. (a) task scheduling in Paradropper network, the task will be routed to the neighbor with the lowest workload. (b) in a random network, node A will likely schedule task to node D while in a high clustering network, node A will likely schedule task to D.

A simulation is done to show a large scale scheduling result. In our simulation, we setup a 1000 nodes network (K=10), every node has a *superfactor*. When a node accepts a task, it increases its workload by its *superfactor*. More powerful node has the smaller *superfactor*. The distribution of the nodes is square of the superfactor. For example, the number of nodes with superfactor 10 is 100.(which is close to a Zipf distribution). A thread every t1 (1-200) ms randomly submit a random number of tasks, and hold t2 (1-2000) ms to mimic the executing procedure. After t2 ms, the workloads of these nodes decrease by their superfactor. After enough time, we randomly select 4 sampling point to check the accepted tasks of different kinds of nodes, the result is shown in Fig. 5. As the result indicated, those powerful nodes (with lower superfactor) have got more tasks than those weaker nodes. It implies that our scheduling algorithm can not only be used to dispatch tasks, but also can be used to balance loading of the whole computing network. When a node get overload, it can re-send its excrescent computation tasks to the network. With high probability, the re-sent tasks will be accepted by those powerful nodes (nodes with low workload). Someone may argue that even if in a random network we could do the same thing. As we discuss above, because of the poor clustering characteristic, scheduling in a random network will miss many nodes which are more suitable for those tasks. For a more accurate discussion, we prompt the concept of *scheduling efficiency* to evaluate and compare the scheduling capability between our network and random network. From Fig. 6 we can conclude that the scheduling efficiency with our network is far superior to random network.

Suppose that there is a super node in the Paradropper network, its initialized workload and superfactor are always 0, and the initialized workload and superfactor of other nodes are value large then 1. We randomly submit N tasks to the network and count the number of tasks accepted by the super node, let the number is W. We define $E=W/N$ as the *scheduling efficiency*. In scales of 100, 600 and 1000 nodes, we get the scheduling efficiency E which is shown in Fig. 6.

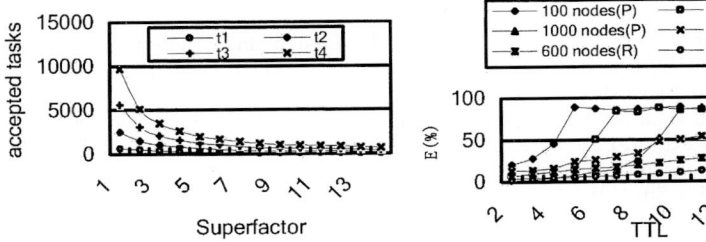

Fig. 5. Accepted tasks using our scheduling algorithm, 1000 nodes, K=10.

Fig. 6. Scheduling efficiency E in our simulation network and random network. (P: Paradropper, R: random network).

As we see in Fig. 6, the E can reach very high level in Paradropper network with limited TTL, compared to the low level in random network. Fig. 5, 6 shows that, even if without any global knowledge of the computing network, the topology of Paradropper network and our heuristic scheduling algorithm make it possible for any volunteer to route tasks anywhere and anytime to the most powerful nodes in the network with high probability. This means that we need not a global broker to schedule the tasks dispatching or node registering in our computing network expressly.

4 Conclusion

In this paper, we prompt a simple and practical approach to build our peer-to-peer global computing network, the simulation results show that, our approach lead to a network with higher clustering coefficient and short path length, which has been used to implement our heuristic scheduling algorithm. Our experimental results also suggest that the global broker components existing in current global computing systems could be eliminated (at least be weakened) from our peer-to-peer computing network in order to make system more scalable and accessible. Our current work proves that at least the scheduling and registering responsibility of broker component could be unleashed.

References

1. M. O. Neary, S. P. Brydon, P. Kmiec, S. Rollins, P. Capello, "Javelin++: Scalability Issues in Global Computing," Proceedings of the ACM Java Grande 1999 Conference, June 12–14, 1999, San Francisco, California.
2. Luis F. G. Sarmenta, "Volunteer Computing", Ph.D. Thesis, MIT Department of Electrical Engineering and Computer Science, March 2001.
3. H. Zhang , A. Goel, R. Govindan. "Using the Small World Model to Improve Freenet Performance. Proceedings, IEEE Infocom., 2002
4. A. Montresor, "Anthill: a Framework for the Design and Analysis of Peer-to-Peer Systems", 4th European Research Seminar on Advances in Distributed Systems (ERSADS '01), Bertinoro, Italy (May 2001).
5. A. Montresor, Hein Meling, Ozalp Babaoglu, "Towards Self-Organizing, Self-Repairing and Resilient Peer-to-Peer Systems", Proceedings of the 1st International Workshop on Future Directions in Distributed Computing, Bertinoro, Forlì, Italy, June 2002.
6. S. Milgram: The Small World Problem, Psychology Today 1(1), 60–67 (1967)
7. D. J. Watts and S. H. Strogatz. Collective dynamics of 'small-world' networks, Nature 393, 440--442 (1998). Networks, Nature 393, 440–442 , 1998.
8. G. Pandurangan, P. Raghavan, E. Upfal, Building Low-Diameter P2P Networks, Proceedings of the 42nd Annual IEEE Symposium on the Foundations of Computer Science (FOCS), 2001
9. http://paradropper.nudt.edu.cn

Option Pricing with the Product Constrained Hybrid Neural Network

Paul Lajbcygier

School of Business Systems, Monash University, Clayton,
Australia
`Paul.Lajbcygier@infotech.monash.edu.au`

Abstract. It is well known that conventional option pricing models have systematic, statistically and economically significant errors or residuals. In this work an artificial neural network (ANN), which estimates the residuals from the most accurate conventional option pricing model, so as to improve option pricing accuracy, is constrained in such a way so that pricing must be rational at the option-pricing boundaries. These constraints lead to statistically and economically significant out-performance relative to both the most accurate conventional and non-constrained ANN option pricing models.

1 Introduction

Biases in the Black-Scholes model ([1]) model have been documented in many different global markets and have grown since the October 1987 stock-market crash ([2]).

There have been numerous extensions, but despite these numerous and extensive efforts modern option-pricing models still exhibit systematic, significant and persistent bias ([3, 4]).

As an alternative to the program of generalizing the underlying assumptions of the Black-Scholes option pricing model, researchers have begun to use statistical regression techniques to provide more accurate option pricing. A growing literature has shown that statistically based regression techniques, such as artificial neural networks (ANNs), are able to improve option pricing ([8-11]).

The rest of the paper considers a novel ANN for option pricing. Firstly, a review of the relevant literature is provided, then a detailed discussion of a new type of ANN option pricing model (OPM) is considered-the product constrained hybrid (PCH) OPM, is made, the option pricing data is considered next, finally the results and the conclusions are presented.

2 Literature Review

The 'hybrid' approach, which estimates the residuals from conventional OPMs, has been shown to provide more accurate option pricing than so-called pure (P) approaches that attempt to model the entire option-pricing surface.

The reasons for the good performance of the hybrid approach are that:

- The conventional model is quite accurate and therefore represents a good 'building block' for statistically based models (such as ANNs) that can augment their performance.
- Accurate option pricing can still be achieved for illiquid options such as deep-in-the-money or very long maturity options which have very few transactions and which pose a problem for 'data-hungry' statistically based 'pure' option-pricing approaches.
- The sharp at-the-money discontinuity that occurs naturally for short maturity options presents a problem for pure approaches.
- The pure approaches are not particularly robust to changes in volatility.

A number of hybrid option pricing papers have been completed. The first was by Gulekin et al ([5]), who estimated the residuals with linear regression for Chicago Board Options Exchange (CBOE) call options for 1975-1976. They found statistically significant out-performance using their approach. Eales et al. ([6]) estimated biases using simulation and linear regression. Shashtri et al. ([7]) estimated the residuals using linear regression. None of these studies was sophisticated nor detailed, however the hybrid approach provided accurate option pricing in each.

A hybrid approach is used in [8], where the conventional parametric model is augmented by an ANN. ANNs have the ability to model interaction and non-linearity between variables and therefore are well-suited to modeling option residuals. It has been found that the use of a hybrid-ANN approach "achieves the same pricing accuracy as the more complex pure network." Furthermore, it has been found that "this is particularly promising as the network part in the combined model is extremely simple. Therefore, the computational burden is reduced and the interpretation of the model facilitated." The hybrid ANN approach is verified and extended by Hanke ([9, 10]). Due to this success of ANNs in hybrid OPMs, hybrid-ANN models are the focus of this work.

3 The Product Constrained Hybrid Option Pricing Model

The aim of this section is to introduce the product-constrained-hybrid neural network. Since this approach uses the conventional option pricing models (OPMs) as a building block, the conventional model is introduced first.

The modified Black model equation is as follows:

$$f_{MB}(\bar{x}) = FN(d_1) - XN(d_2) \tag{1}$$

where $d_1 = (\ln(F/X) + (\sigma^2/2)(T-t))/\sigma\sqrt{T-t}$, $d_2 = d_1 - \sigma\sqrt{T-t}$.

In each of these equations, F refers to the value of the underlying future, X to the exercise price, r to the risk-free interest rate over the lifetime of the option, σ represents the volatility of the underlying, T represents the expiry time, t the time now, T-t the time to expiry and, N() is the standard cumulative normal distribution.

The choice of implied standard deviation (i.e. volatility, σ) is crucial to the accuracy of an option pricing model. It can be shown that the optimal weighted implied standard deviation (ISD) is the vega weighted DERISD. DERISD uses a weighting scheme based on vega, where:

$$\text{VEGA} = \Lambda_{imp,i} = F\sqrt{T-t}\, N'(d_1') \tag{2}$$

where N'() is the standard normal distribution.

$$\text{DERISD} = \left(\sum_{i=1}^{K} \sigma_{imp,i}^2 \Lambda_{imp,i}^2\right)^{1/2} \Big/ \left(\sum_{i=1}^{K} \Lambda_{imp,i}^2\right)^{1/2} \tag{3}$$

In general, hybrid models which use the MB OPM as a building-block can be expressed as:

$$\hat{f}_{Hybrid}(\bar{x}) = f_{MB}(\bar{x}) - \hat{f}(\bar{x}) \tag{4}$$

where $\hat{f}(\bar{x})$ represents a non-parametric regression such as an ANN.

The novel aspect of this work utilizes intrinsic option boundary pricing conditions to constrain the non-parametric regression $\hat{f}(\bar{x})$, so that rational pricing is achieved at these boundaries.

There are two types of constraints utilized: maturity and model constraints. Maturity constraints use the fact that, when an option reaches maturity, the pay-off is certain and the standard MB OPM gives the correct solution.

That is, if F/X>1, as $t \to T, d_1 \to \infty, d_2 \to \infty$, for the MB OPM $N(d_1) \to 1, N(d_2) \to 1$ and therefore, $f_{MB}(\bar{x}) \to F - X$. On the other hand, if F/X<1, as $t \to T, d_1 \to -\infty, d_2 \to -\infty$, for the MB OPM $N(d_1) \to 0, N(d_2) \to 0$ and therefore, $f_{MB}(\bar{x}) \to 0$.

Even though we considered the MB OPM to find this value, this expiry pay-off is OPM-independent: when *F/X>1*, F-X is the pay-off that the call option holder will receive regardless of the model used to price the option prior to maturity; when

$F/X<1$, it must be zero. Any conventional OPM, including the MB OPM, will provide this correct value. Therefore, any non-zero value of the non-parametric regression $\hat{f}(\vec{x})$ will yield incorrect option pricing. Consequently, a new constrained hybrid (CH) OPM is proposed so that:

$$\hat{f}(\vec{x}) = 0, t = T \tag{5}$$

Two other constraints, referred to as model constraints, are also considered. A model constraint is used to keep the resulting hybrid model consistent with some of the extremes of the underlying modified Black model.

The first model constraint follows from this argument: as $\sigma \to 0, d_1 \to \infty, d_2 \to \infty$, for the MB OPM $N(d_1) \to 1, N(d_2) \to 1$ and therefore, $f_{MB}(\vec{x}) \to F - X$.

This result implies that the MB OPM value will not change when the underlying exhibits zero volatility (that is, the underlying is assumed not to move in the future). The following constraint on the hybrid non-parametric regression must be enforced to utilize this model constraint:

$$\hat{f}(\vec{x}) = 0, \sigma = 0 \tag{6}$$

The second model constraint occurs when F/X=0 as $F/X \to 0, d_1 \to -\infty, d_2 \to -\infty$, in the MB OPM $N(d_1) \to 0, N(d_2) \to 0$ and therefore, $f_{MB}(\vec{x}) \to 0$.

In other words, for a zero moneyness option, the pay-off is zero. The hybrid constraint must be:

$$\hat{f}(\vec{x}) = 0, F/X = 0 \tag{7}$$

These arguments engender 3 new models. Each of these models use multiplicative scaling that ensures the constrained ANN will output zero when each input will be zero. The first model, the hybrid OPM (H), does not use any constraints. The second model, the constrained hybrid (CH) OPM uses only the maturity constraint. Finally, the PCH (product constrained hybrid) OPM utilizes each of these constraints. The details of the innovative neural network are described in detail in [11].

In principle, benefit comes from this more complex constrained approach because strong boundary condition non-linearity, which occurs in regions with sparse amounts of data, is modeled exactly. Of course, no transactions occur exactly at the option pricing boundaries. Instead, the constraints utilized in the PCH OPM serve to change the regression surface so that the performance is improved in the locale of the option pricing boundaries, where the actual transactions occur.

4 Data Considerations

The data used to estimate the PCH ANN architecture model is considered in this section. The data set comprises all call options transacted on the SFE on the All Ordinaries (AO) Share Price Index (SPI) futures from January 1993 to December 1995. The data is time-stamped to the second and has volume, premium and strike price associated with it.

The data were divided into half-yearly periods (i.e. 931, 932, 941, 942, 951, 952). To test the consistency of the estimated OPM, a model on each half-year data set was estimated and then tested out- of-sample on the next half-year data set (e.g. estimate on 931 and test on 932). If a model performs better than the optimal conventional model, out-of-sample, for every period we can be very confident that the model is reliable (and that its strong performance was not due to a spurious fit). Each model's performance is reported (below) for the next, out-of-sample, half-year period.

Many subtle details associated with the collection and transformation of data have been omitted in this section. A more thorough and detailed explanation can be found in [11].

5 Results

Fig. 1 shows the fit of each of the hybrid ANNs considered in this work for the 1st half of 1994 (i.e. 941) period. The hybrid neuroshell (HN) and hybrid (H) OPMs are similar in construction: they are not constrained in any way. However, the HN OPM was estimated using proprietary software (whereas the H OPM was constructed by the author and uses multiplicative scaling); furthermore, the number of hidden units was chosen using early stopping (rather than cross-validation as for the H OPM); the HN OPM utilized standard scaling (rather than the multiplicative scaling of the H OPM); and the HN OPM DERISD input variable was scaled (the H OPM DERISD variable was not scaled).

By studying each ANN in turn in Fig. 1, it is possible to see the effect of each the constraints in turn on the pricing surface. The H surface (which has no constraints) is extremely large (top, left-hand panel). The CH surface (top, right-hand panel) is constrained to be zero at T-t=0 and, therefore, the entire surface has been molded to meet that constraint (compare with the H surface). Finally, the PCH surface (bottom, left-hand panel) is constrained to be zero at T-t=0 and DERISD=0, the extra DERISD constraint serves to make the regression surface symmetrical around zero (i.e. f(x)=0). Note that f(x) is not zero when T-t=0 for the H and HN models and therefore they are in error.

Having examined the effect of the constraints on each of the model, next we consider how each model performed for each half-year. A number of error measures were compared over each period to determine which OPM provided the most accurate option pricing for each period.

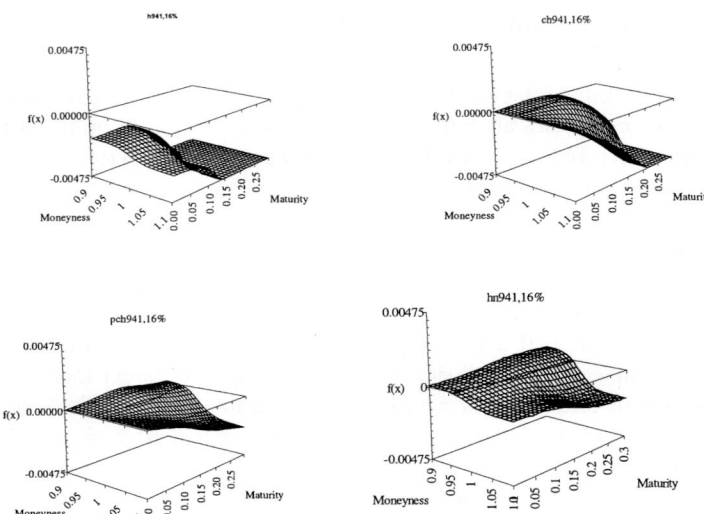

Fig. 1. It is possible to see the effect of the constraints on the pricing surface for the 941 period. The H surface is extremely large. The CH surface is constrained to be zero at T-t=0 and therefore the entire surface has changed. Finally the PCH surface is constrained to be zero at T -t=0 and DERISD=0 and therefore it is centered

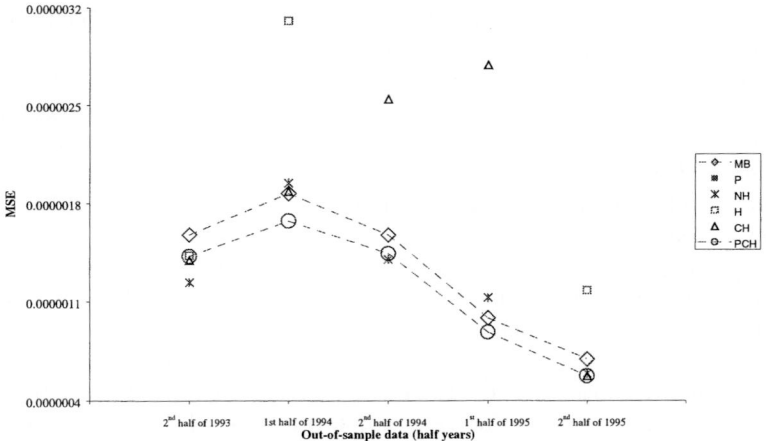

Fig. 2. The MSE for each technique considered for each half-yearly out-of-sample data set. The left-most column represents the performance of the techniques estimated on data from the first half of 1993 (i.e. 931) and tested on the second half of the 1993 year (i.e. 932). The modified Black model (MB), the optimal conventional model, is joined by dashed lines. The product-constrained hybrid model (PCH), the only model which consistently out-performs the MB, also shown. The H and P performance is so poor, it is "off-the-scale". P is the pure ANN OPM (i.e. not hybrid)

Fig. 2 shows the performance of each model, using mean-squared error (MSE), for each half-year. The PCH OPM (i.e. circles) dashed line does not cross the MB OPM (i.e. diamonds) dashed line, indicating that the PCH model has a lower MSE for each out-of-sample data set. It should be noted that the PCH model does not have the lowest MSE for each out-of-sample data set. However, it has the consistently lowest MSE of any model.

A comparison of PCH with HN (its nearest rival) at the option boundary conditions provides a very satisfying result (see [11]). The MSE of the shortest maturity (i.e. 0 to 0.05 years) interval for PCH is statistically significantly smaller than the shortest maturity for HN, in four of five periods. The MSE of the lowest DERISD (i.e. 0 to 12.5%) options is statistically smaller for PCH in three of five periods. In other words, the PCH constraints provide more accurate option pricing than the best ANN hybrid OPM -the HN OPM, in the locale of the boundary conditions, as hoped.

To conclude, the comparison between OPMs over different periods has clearly indicated that the PCH (unlike the HN OPM) consistently and significantly outperformed the optimal conventional model, the MB OPM, in each period. The PCH OPM is an incremental improvement upon its nearest rival the HN OPM.

References

1. F. Black and M. Scholes, The pricing of options and corporate liabilities, *Journal of Political Economy* (1973), 81, 637–654.
2. M. Rubinstein, Implied binomial trees, *The Journal of Finance* (1994), 49, 771–818.
3. G. Bakshi, C. Cao and Z. Chen, Empirical performance of alternative option pricing models, *The Journal of Finance* (1997), LII, 2003–2049.
4. G. Bakshi, C. Cao and Z. Chen, Pricing and hedging long-term options, *Journal of Econometrics*. (1998).
5. N. Gultekin, R. Rogalski and S. Tinic, Option Pricing Model Estimates, Some Empirical Results, *Financial Management* (1982), Spring 1982, 58–69.
6. J. Eales and R. J. Hauser, Analyzing biases in valuation models of options on futures, *The Journal of Futures Markets* (1990),10,211–228.
7. K. Shastri and K. Tandon, An empirical test of a valuation model for American options on futures contracts, *Journal of Financial and Quantitative Analysis*. (1986), 21, 377–392.
8. U. Anders, O. Korn and C. Schmitt, Improving the pricing of options -A neural network approach, Centre for European Economic Research, Mannheim (1996).
9. M. Hanke, Option Pricing using Neural Networks vs. Black-Scholes: An Empirical Comparison of the Pricing Accuracy of two Fundamentally Different Option Pricing Methods, *Journal of Computational Intelligence in Finance* (1999), 7, 26–34.
10. M. Hanke, Neural Network Approximation of Option Pricing Formulas for Analytically Intractable Option Pricing Models, *Journal of Computational Intelligence in Finance* (1997), 5, 20–27.
11. P. Lajbcygier, Improving option pricing with the product-constrained-hybrid neural network and booting, PhD, Monash University, Melbourne (2000).

Self-Organizing Operator Maps in Complex System Analysis

Pasi Lehtimäki, Kimmo Raivio, and Olli Simula

Helsinki University of Technology,
Laboratory of Computer and Information Science,
P.O. Box 5400, FIN-02015 HUT, Finland

Abstract. The growth in amount of data available today has encouraged the development of effective data analysis methods to support human decision-making. Neuro-fuzzy computation is a soft computing hybridisation combining the learning capabilities of the neural networks with the linguistic representation of data provided by the fuzzy models. In this paper, a framework to build temporally local neuro-fuzzy systems for the analysis of nonstationary process data using self-organizing operator maps is described.

1 Introduction

During the last decades, the developments in the computer technology have enabled the efficient processing and storage of large data sets. As a result, new computation paradigms to obtain human comprehensible descriptions of such data items have emerged. Soft computing techniques like neural networks, fuzzy logic and genetic algorithms provide an acceptable solution for various data modelling tasks due to their tolerance against imprecision and uncertainty, while being computationally robust and efficient. The benefits of different soft computing techniques are combined in various hybrid systems. For example, in neuro-fuzzy systems the learning capability of neural networks is combined to the interpretable rule-based representation of data provided by the fuzzy systems [14].

However, most of the neural network models and fuzzy systems are designed for stationary environments in which the data has time-independent statistics. In many applications, the data is generated by a complex system that is allowed to change its configuration and parameters during the operation, resulting in a nonstationary process with time-dependent statistics [8,15]. In this paper, a framework to design neuro-fuzzy systems for nonstationary process analysis using self-organizing operator maps is described.

Next in this paper, motivation and theory for the operator maps are presented. Then, the most typical choices for the map operators and an approach to control their complexity are presented. Finally, an operator map with multiple local neuro-fuzzy models as the map operators is applied in the analysis of the third generation (3G) cellular network performance.

2 Operator Maps

The Self-Organizing Map (SOM) has been widely used in various data analysis problems due to its simplicity and ability to provide a highly visual representation of data. The SOM produces a nonlinear projection from the measurement space into a low-dimensional grid suitable for data visualisation [9].

The basic SOM is usually applied in problems in which it is of interest to visualise the spatial properties of the data. For time-series data containing an additional temporal dimension, it is usually of interest to also know *when* or under what circumstances certain spatial properties occur. This information is usually represented in terms of a sequence of past observations and predictive modelling is used to estimate the possible dependence between the current and past observations.

However, most of the predictive modelling methods assume that the available time-series data is stationary, that is, the system responses to the same input are time-independent and thus all similar in the whole data set. In many real-world applications the systems tend to produce different responses to the same input at different parts of the process. In order to analyse the behavior of such systems, the data can be assumed to be piecewise stationary, that is, the data is generated through switching between finite number of different generating models, resulting in so-called switching time-series [8].

One of the most flexible extensions of the SOM suitable for the analysis of switching time-series is the operator map [9]. In operator maps, the map units or operators are generalized to be parametric models that are able to describe the interesting behavioral patterns in different parts of the data. The most common choices for the operators are:

- probabilistic models [5];
- linear time-series models [11,6,15];
- adaptive nonlinear time-series models [12].

Next, a general procedure to train operator maps consisting of various linear and nonlinear local time-series models is presented.

2.1 Training of Operator Maps

The training of operator maps requires the definition for the similarity between the observations and the behavior represented by the operators of the map. For predictive time-series models describing the behavioral patterns in the data, a suitable similarity measure is the mean-square prediction error (MSE) produced by the operator m given the system input $x(n)$ and the true output $y(n)$. In such a situation, the error function to be iteratively minimized by the operator map becomes [9]:

$$E(t) = \frac{1}{2N} \sum_{m \in L} \sum_{n=1}^{N} h_{c(n),m}(t,n)[y(n) - \hat{y}^{(m)}(t,n)]^2, \qquad (1)$$

where L is the lattice of map units, $h_{c(n),m}(t,n)$ is the value of the neighborhood function between map unit m and best-matching operator $c(n)$ for nth sample at epoch t. Since multiple consecutive observations are needed when estimating a temporally local model from data, a single operator is assigned as the winner map unit for a sequence of consecutive data samples in computation of $c(n)$.

The map training consists of updating the parameters of the operator m by minimizing the error measure $E(t)$ with a gradient descent algorithm

$$\theta_m(t+1) = \theta_m(t) - \alpha(t)\frac{\partial E(t)}{\partial \theta_m(t)}. \tag{2}$$

After training, each operator is specialized into a certain kind of dependence between the system input $x(n)$ and output $y(n)$ that may hold valid only for a short period of time. When the environment changes its configuration, the current operator predicting the process no longer explains the observations and thus must be replaced by a new operator suitable for the new environment. Thus, a nonstationary process is represented by a sequence of stationary process segments each modelled by a separate operator. Next, choices for operator parameterisations suitable for different situations are presented. Detailed update rules for the parameters of the presented operator types are given in [12].

Adaptive filter: In many situations, it is sufficient that the operators are represented by linear predictive models. In this case, the output of the operator m is defined by [3]:

$$y^{(m)}(n) = \sum_{i=1}^{M} w_i^{(m)} x_i(n), \tag{3}$$

where M is the dimension of the input space, $w_i^{(m)}$ is the ith weight of the mth adaptive filter corresponding to the ith input variable $x_i(n)$. The advantages of this map unit parameterisation are the easy interpretation of the model parameters as correlation between variables and the efficient optimization of the parameters. Since the model is linear in parameters, a solution corresponding to the global minima can be obtained.

Multilayer perceptron (MLP): In order to model any temporally local nonlinear dependence between the past and current observations, the parameterisation of the map units can be generalized according to the MLP. In such a case, the output of the ith neuron in layer l of a single operator m is [3]:

$$y^{(m,l)}(n) = \varphi\left(\sum_{j=0}^{M_{l-1}} w_{ij}^{(m,l)} y_j^{(m,l-1)}(n)\right), \tag{4}$$

where $y_j^{(m,l-1)}(n)$ is the jth input component for the neurons at layer l, $w_{ij}^{(l)}$ is the jth synaptic weight of the neuron i at layer l, M_{l-1} is the number of inputs for layer l and φ is a nonlinear activation function. The main disadvantage of the MLP operators is the lack of interpretation for the estimated mapping.

Adaptive neuro-fuzzy inference system (ANFIS): In the analysis of spatio-temporal data, a human-comprehensible description about the process is needed. An adaptive model suitable for this purpose is the ANFIS model based on the zero-order Sugeno fuzzy inference system [7]. In ANFIS, the dependence between the model input and output can be represented by a set of human-friendly fuzzy rules of the form: if x_1 is A and x_2 is B then y is r, where A and B are linguistic labels and r is a crisp consequent part parameter of the fuzzy rule. The output of an operator m in this case is:

$$y^{(m)}(n) = \frac{\sum_k \prod_{\forall i,j \in R_k^m} \mu_{ij}^{(m)}(x_i(n)) r_k^{(m)}}{\sum_l \prod_{\forall i,j \in R_l^m} \mu_{ij}^{(m)}(x_i(n))}, \quad (5)$$

where $\mu_{ij}^{(m)}(x_i(n))$ is the value of the jth premise part membership function for the ith input component, $r_k^{(m)}$ is the crisp consequent part parameter of kth rule of the map unit m and R_k^m is the set of premise part membership functions that belong to the kth rule of the operator m.

2.2 Model Selection Using Regularization

In order to obtain a good generalisation capability for the map units, a suitable complexity for the operators must be selected. This can be done by minimizing the risk functional $R(\theta) = R_{emp} + \lambda \phi[f(x,\theta)]$ where R_{emp} is the empirical risk or the training error produced by the operator map and $\phi[f(x,\theta)]$ is a user-selected penalty functional used to penalize the operators from unnecessary complexity. The goal in model selection is then to find the value for the regularization parameter λ that provides the best generalisation for the map with new data.

The penalty term $\lambda\phi[f(x,\theta)]$ can also be defined implicitly in the choice of approximating functions, when the form of the approximating functions corresponds to the penalty term $\phi[f(x,\theta)]$ and the number of approximating functions corresponds to the regularization parameter λ [1].

Different methods or types of operators can be compared using double resampling [2]. At first, the data set is divided into learning, validation and prediction sets and then, all methods using different forms of approximating functions are used to solve the problem with different number of approximating functions using the training set. The best number of approximating functions for each method is selected according to the modelling error computed on the basis of the validation set. Finally, the best models of each method are compared using the modelling error computed with the prediction set.

3 Analysis of 3G Cellular Network Performance

The 3G cellular networks provide a wide set of new services for the mobile network users. In order to obtain an efficient usage of the available radio network resources, modern methods are required in the analysis of cellular network performance. The behavior of 3G cellular networks has previously been analysed in [13,16,10] using self-organizing feature maps.

3.1 Cellular Network

The data used in this work is generated using wideband code division multiple access (WCDMA) radio network simulator [4]. The network consists of base stations (mobile cell) in the area of Helsinki, each measuring a wide set of state variables and quality variables at high sampling rate. The state variables include, for example, the number of users (nUsr) in the cell and the downlink average transmission power (dlTxp) and the quality variables include the downlink frame error rate (dlFER).

3.2 Results of Macro-Cellular Network Scenario

In this experiment, the performance of the downlink direction traffic of a macro-cellular network scenario consisting of 31 base stations with sector antennas and one base station with omnidirectional antenna was analysed. For this purpose, the number of users and the downlink average transmission power were selected as the input variables and the downlink frame error rate as the output variable for the performance model. In order to model temporal dependencies, a single delayed sample for both input variables was used. Since the data set consisted of 18 000 data samples from each 32 mobile cells, the amount of data was reduced by averaging over 5 samples due to the high computational effort needed in map training.

Several operator maps consisting of 16 local operators in a rectangular lattice of size $[4 \times 4]$ were trained using the adaptive filter, 2-layer MLP and ANFIS operators. For a comparison, the same data set was modelled by the corresponding single global models, that is, the maps of size $[1 \times 1]$. The map training consisted of rough training of 2500 epochs with large learning rate and neighborhood radius, followed by fine tuning of 2500 epochs with small learning rate and neighborhood radius. The bubble neighborhood function $h_{c(n),m}(t) = \mu[\sigma(t) - d(r_c, r_m)]$ was used, where $\sigma(t)$ is the decreasing neighborhood radius and μ is the unit step function. The length of the subprocess over which the mean-square error was computed in winner map unit search was 400 samples.

In Table 1, the results of the model selection are summarized. According to the validation errors, the best single MLP model included 3 hidden layer neurons and the best MLP map included 10 hidden layer neurons in each operator. The best single ANFIS model consisted of 4 fuzzy rules and the best ANFIS map consisted of 3 fuzzy rules in each map operator. The best method according to the prediction errors is the ANFIS operator map with 3 fuzzy rules. In general, the operator maps with multiple local models are able to model the data more accurately than a single global model. Also, the nonlinear ANFIS and MLP operators perform better than the linear adaptive filters.

3.3 Analysis of Cellular Network Performance Using ANFIS Map

When analysing the network performance, it is of interest to know when the cells generate high values of the frame error rate, especially when the number

Table 1. Comparisons of different operator maps. The best complexity for the map operators is selected according to the validation error computed from the separate validation data set. λ describes the value of the regularization parameter: for MLP it is the number of hidden neurons in a single map unit and for ANFIS it is the number of rules in a single ANFIS operator. For linear adaptive filters, there is no parameter to adjust the model complexity. The best models of each operator parameterisation are compared using a separate prediction data set.

Operator type	Map size	λ	Learning error (MSE)	Validation error (MSE)	Prediction error (MSE)
linear	1×1	–	4.262	3.174	2.600
linear	4×4	–	1.660	1.306	1.043
MLP	1×1	3 neurons	1.996	1.504	1.424
MLP	1×1	5 neurons	2.053	1.568	–
MLP	1×1	10 neurons	2.059	1.557	–
MLP	4×4	3 neurons	1.078	0.810	–
MLP	4×4	5 neurons	1.076	0.806	–
MLP	4×4	10 neurons	1.038	0.784	0.669
ANFIS	1×1	2 rules	2.031	1.534	–
ANFIS	1×1	3 rules	2.213	1.724	–
ANFIS	1×1	4 rules	1.652	1.219	1.239
ANFIS	4×4	2 rules	1.026	0.806	–
ANFIS	4×4	3 rules	0.975	0.756	0.639
ANFIS	4×4	4 rules	0.955	0.773	–

of network users is low. In operator maps of multiple local ANFIS operators, this information is provided by the fuzzy rules of the operators with the highest values for the consequent part parameters $r_i^{(m)}$.

In Figure 1(a), such rules of each operator in the best ANFIS map are shown. These rules can be used to track the input variable conditions resulting in high values of system output. For example, the map units {7, 11} tend to produce high dlFER values when the number of users in the cell drops from high to low and the transmission power drops from high to medium, in contrast with the map unit {6} in which the similar drop in the number of users and an increase in transmission power from medium to high produces the bad quality. The map unit {12} seems to generate bad performance when there is a rapid growth in number of users with transmission power being constantly medium.

The visualisation of the rules of the ANFIS operators as shown in Figure 1(a) can be used to examine the spectrum of the data generating models in a piecewise stationary process. However, the trained operator map can be used to analyse also the long-term behavior of mobile cells using the so-called *trajectories*. A trajectory is a sequence of best-matching map units computed from a sequence of consecutive process segments. Thus, it can be used to analyse how the segments of the piecewise stationary process change in time, thus forming a single nonstationary process. In Figures 1(b)–(d), the trajectories of mobile cells 2, 10 and 31 on the best map of ANFIS operators are shown. According to the figure, the

1 if nUsr(n) is very high nUsr(n−1) is very high dfTxp(n) is very med dfTxp(n−1) is very med then dfFer is 0.70	5 if nUsr(n) is very med nUsr(n−1) is very high dfTxp(n) is very high dfTxp(n−1) is very med then dfFer is 0.72	9 if nUsr(n) is very high nUsr(n−1) is very high dfTxp(n) is very high dfTxp(n−1) is very med then dfFer is 0.74	13 if nUsr(n) is very high nUsr(n−1) is very high dfTxp(n) is very high dfTxp(n−1) is very med then dfFer is 0.73
2 if nUsr(n) is very med nUsr(n−1) is very high dfTxp(n) is very med dfTxp(n−1) is very med then dfFer is 0.70	6 if nUsr(n) is very low nUsr(n−1) is very high dfTxp(n) is very high dfTxp(n−1) is very med then dfFer is 0.76	10 if nUsr(n) is very high nUsr(n−1) is very^2 high dfTxp(n) is very high dfTxp(n−1) is very med then dfFer is 0.72	14 if nUsr(n) is very med nUsr(n−1) is very high dfTxp(n) is very^2 low dfTxp(n−1) is very high then dfFer is 0.73
3 if nUsr(n) is very high nUsr(n−1) is very^2 high dfTxp(n) is very med dfTxp(n−1) is very med then dfFer is 0.72	7 if nUsr(n) is very low nUsr(n−1) is very High dfTxp(n) is very med dfTxp(n−1) is very High then dfFer is 0.70	11 if nUsr(n) is very low nUsr(n−1) is very high dfTxp(n) is very med dfTxp(n−1) is very High then dfFer is 0.74	15 if nUsr(n) is very high nUsr(n−1) is very med dfTxp(n) is very high dfTxp(n−1) is very low then dfFer is 0.77
4 if nUsr(n) is very med nUsr(n−1) is very med dfTxp(n) is very med dfTxp(n−1) is very^2 high then dfFer is 0.72	8 if nUsr(n) is very med nUsr(n−1) is very high dfTxp(n) is very high dfTxp(n−1) is very med then dfFer is 0.71	12 if nUsr(n) is very high nUsr(n−1) is very low dfTxp(n) is very high dfTxp(n−1) is very med then dfFer is 0.72	16 if nUsr(n) is very med nUsr(n−1) is very high dfTxp(n) is very med dfTxp(n−1) is very med then dfFer is 0.73

(a)   Cell 2 (b)   Cell 10 (c)   Cell 31 (d)

Fig. 1. (a) Rule plane 3 of the best ANFIS operator map. The centers of the Gaussian premise part membership functions are described by the user-selected label set {LOW, Low, low, med, high, High, HIGH}. The shape of the membership functions are described by $\mu_{very^n A}(x) = \mu_A(x)^{n+1}$. The trajectories of the mobile cells (b) 2, (c), 10 and (d) 31 of the mobile network on the map of ANFIS models.

cells 10 and 31 visit the map units representing undesirable behavior. The cell 2 represents normal operation.

4 Discussion

In this paper, a SOM-based method for unsupervised segmentation and segment description of nonstationary process data using a set of local neuro-fuzzy operators was described. The benefits of the method include the support for visual analysis in terms of the linguistic representations of the topologically ordered neuro-fuzzy operators and a measure for the accuracy of the obtained map in terms of the prediction errors. Also, it is possible to include a priori information about modelled system by importing fixed fuzzy rules to the operators.

The drawbacks of the method include the high computational requirements resulting from the regularization framework used in model selection. Also, each operator was assigned the same average complexity instead of optimizing the complexity of the operators separately. In addition, the nonlinear parameter optimization used in MLP and ANFIS maps was based on the back-propagation algorithm only guaranteeing local minima. It is also known, that the ANFIS model suffers from the curse of dimensionality, making it difficult for the system to solve high-dimensional modelling problems.

References

1. Vladimir Cherkassky and Filip Mulier. *Learning from data: concepts, theory and methods*. John-Wiley & Sons, Inc., 1998.
2. J. H. Friedman. An overview of predictive learning and function approximation. In *From Statistics to Neural Networks, Proc. NATO/ASI Workshop*. Springer Verlag, 1994.
3. Simon Haykin. *Neural Networks: a comprehensive foundation*, 2nd edition. Prentice-Hall, Inc., 1999.
4. Seppo Hämäläinen, Harri Holma, and Kari Sipilä. Advanced WCDMA radio network simulator. In *Personal, Indoor and Mobile Radio Communications*, volume 2. pages 951–955, Osaka, Japan, September 12–15 1999.
5. Jaakko Hollmen, Volker Tresp, and Olli Simula. A self-organizing map algorithm for clustering probabilistic models. In *Ninth International Conference on Artificial Neural Networks*, volume 2, pages 946–951, September 1999.
6. Heikki Hyötyniemi, Ari S. Nissinen, and Heikki N. Koivo. Evolution based self-organization of structures in linear time-series modeling. In *3rd Nordic Workshop on Genetic Algorithms*, pages 135–152, Helsinki, Finland, August 1997.
7. Jyh-Shing Roger Jang. ANFIS: Adaptive-network-based fuzzy inference system. *IEEE Transactions on Systems, Man, and Cybernetics*, 23(3), May/June 1993.
8. Athanasios Kehagias and Vassilios Petridis. Predictive modular neural networks for unsupervised segmentation of switching time series: The data allocation problem. *IEEE Trans. Neural Networks*, 13(6):1432–1449, 2002.
9. Teuvo Kohonen. *Self-Organizing Maps, 3rd edition*. Springer, 2001.
10. Jaana Laiho, Kimmo Raivio, Pasi Lehtimäki, Kimmo Hätönen, and Olli Simula. Advanced analysis methods for 3G cellular networks. Technical Report A 65, Helsinki University of Technology, 2002.
11. Jouko Lampinen and Erkki Oja. Self-organizing maps for spatial and temporal ar models. In *Scand. Conf. on Image Analysis (SCIA)*, pages 120–127, Helsinki, Finland, 1989.
12. Pasi Lehtimäki. *Self-Organizing Operator Maps in Complex System Analysis*. Master's Thesis, Helsinki University of Technology, 2002.
13. Pasi Lehtimäki, Kimmo Raivio, and Olli Simula. Mobile radio access network monitoring using self-organizing map. In *Proceedings of the 10th European Symposium on Artificial Neural Networks*, 2002.
14. Sushmita Mitra and Yoichi Hayashi. Neuro-fuzzy rule generation: survey in soft computing framework. *IEEE Trans. Neural Networks*, 11(3):748–768, 2000.
15. Ari Nissinen. *Neural and evolutionary computing in modeling of complex systems*. PhD thesis, Control Engineering Laboratory, Helsinki University of Technology, 1999.
16. Kimmo Raivio, Olli Simula, and Jaana Laiho. Neural analysis of mobile radio access network. In *IEEE International Conference on Data Mining*, pages 457–464, November 29 – December 2 2001.

Optimization of a Microwave Amplifier Using Neural Performance Data Sheets with Genetic Algorithms

Filiz Güneş[1] and Yavuz Cengiz[2]

[1] Yıldız Technical University, Electronics and Communication Engineering Department, Yıldız – Beşiktaş, İstanbul – Turkey, gunes@yildiz.edu.tr
[2] Süleyman Demirel University, Electronics and Communication Department, Isparta -Turkey , ycengiz@mmf.sdu.edu.tr

Abstract. In this work, the neural performance data sheets of the transistor are employed to determine the feasible design target space in the optimization of a microwave amplifier. In order to obtain these data sheets the ANN model of the active device is utilized to approximate the small-signal [S] and noise [N] parameter functions in the operation domain. Inputting of these characterization parameters into the performance characterization of the device results in the triplet of gain G_T, noise F, and input VSWR V_i and its source (Z_S) and load (Z_L) termination functions in the operation domain, from which the neural performance data sheets can be obtained. The genetic algorithms with the binary (BGA) and decimal (CPGA) numbers are utilized in the multi-objective optimization process for the global minimum of the objective function which is expressed as a function only gain of a matching circuit, in the negative exponential form to ensure the rapid convergence . Here optimization of a microwave amplifier with the Π - type matching circuits is given as a worked example and its resulted performance ingredients are compared with the design targets.

1 Introduction

Optimization is one of the fundamental processes frequently encountered in the engineering problems and is highly nonlinear in terms of the descriptive parameters of the system. An optimization process generally contains two fundamental problems:
(i) The first is to form a feasible Design Space which is defined in terms of the design variables and targets; (ii) The second is that the global minimum of the error (objective) function governing the optimization must be obtained with respect to the design variables within the feasible design space.
For optimization of a microwave amplifier, design variables are generally the matching circuit parameters whose lower and upper limits are very often determined by the technology to be utilized in the realization stage of the design. Nevertheless, design targets are still one of the main problems of the amplifier optimization. Generally, the optimization is focused on the transducer power gain (G_T) over a frequency band of operation without controlling the other performance criteria such as the noise (F), the input standing wave ratio (V_i). Certainly, within the optimization process one can

easily embed the desired performance goals without knowing the physical limits and / or compromise relations among F, V_i and G_T appropriately. Unfortunately this process often fails to attain the desired goals. However, the Neural Performance Data Sheets (NPDS) of the transistor overcomes all the above-mentioned handicaps and embeds the compatible (F, V_i, G_T) triplets with their source (Z_s) and load (Z_L) terminations together over a predetermined frequency band of operation. However, a work has recently been completed [1] that gives gain-bandwidth limitations of a microwave transistor whose fundamentals will be focused in the next section. So optimization of a microwave amplifier is a multi – objective design problem with a mix of equality and inequality constraints.

Mathematical nonlinear programming algorithms have emerged as the method of the choice for applications in engineering optimizations problems. The more efficient of this class of methods are generally gradient based, and required at last the first–order derivates of both objective and constrained functions with respect to the design variables. With this "slope-tracking" ability, gradient–based can easily identify a relative optimum closest to the initial guess of the optimum design. There is no guarantee of locating global optimum if the design space is known to be nonconvex. These methods are also inadequate in problems where design space is discontinuous, as the derivatives of both the objective function and constraints may become singular across the boundary of discontinuity.

In engineering design problems, the mix of continuous, discrete and integer design variables has been approached by treating all variables as continuous, and then rounding specific variable either up or down to the nearest integer or discrete variable. This simple rounding procedure often fails completely, resulting in either a suboptimal design, or in some cases, even generating an infeasible design.

Genetic algorithms belong to a category of stochastic search techniques which can work an almost all kinds of design spaces and without any restriction on types of design variables. These algorithms have their philosophical bases in Darwin's Theory of survival of the fittest. Design alternatives representing a population in a given generation are allowed to reproduce and cross among themselves with bias allocated most fit members of the population. The mechanics of genetic search is to move from a population of designs to another population of designs; these is in contrast to the point to point search available in traditional mathematical programming networks; therefore is highly applicable to the problem search in a nonconvex / disjoint design space with mix of continuous, discrete and integer design variable and offers a better possibility of locating a global optimum. Properties of the genetic algorithm used in the optimization will be given in the optimization section.

2 Neural Performance Data Sheets for a Microwave Transistor

2.1 Neural Performance Data Block Diagram

Neural performance data sheets for a microwave transistor can be obtained from the neural block diagramme given in the Fig.1. According to this block diagramme, this work can be described in three main stages.

In the first stage the signal and noise behaviours of the small–signal transistor are modeled by a Multiple Bias and Configuration, Signal–Noise neural network .So the scattering (S) and noise (N) parameters can result from the output of this neural network as the functions of the Configuration Type (CT), the bias condition (V_{DS}, I_{DS}) and the operation frequency (f). This part of the work can be considered as the function approximations of the eight scattering and four noise parameters [2,3].

The second stage consists of determining of the compatible performance (F_{req}, V_{ireq}, G_{Treq}) triplets and their associated source (Z_{sreq}) and load (Z_{Lreq}) terminations. In this part of the work the performance characterization theory of the transistor is employed, which is given in [4] and [5] using respectively, the impedance [z] and scattering [S] parameter approaches. The input of the second block is the (S) and (N) parameters resulting from the Signal–Noise neural network and the free variables of $F_{req} \geq F_{min}$, $V_{ireq} \geq 1$ and $G_{T\,min} \leq G_{T\,req} \leq G_{T\,max}$.

The second block results in the following triplets and termination data in the operation domain of the device :

$$(F_{req}, V_{ireq}, G_{Tmax}) \Leftrightarrow Z_{Smax} = R_{Smax} + jX_{Smax}; Z_{Lmax} = R_{Lmax} + jX_{Lmax}$$

$$(F_{req}, V_{ireq}, G_{Tmin}) \Leftrightarrow Z_{Smin} = R_{Smin} + jX_{Smin}; Z_{Lmin} = R_{Lmin} + jX_{Lmin}$$

$$(F_{req}, V_{ireq}, G_{Treq}) \Leftrightarrow Z_{Sreq} = R_{Sreq} + jX_{Sreq}; Z_{Lreq} = R_{Lreq} + jX_{Lreq}$$

The third stage of the work is to obtain the neural performance data sheets using the interrelations among the performance measure components F, V_i, G_T and the operation parameters CT, V_{DS}, I_{DS}, f of the transistor. These can give all the necessary information to design a microwave amplifier with optimum performance because the F, V_i, G_T ingredients can be determined only by the active devices in the amplifiers with the lossless and reciprocal matching circuits.

Two approaches can be followed in the utilization of the (F, V_i, G_T) triplet and the Z_s, Z_L functions in the design of the microwave amplifiers circuits :

1. Only the (F, V_i, G_T) triplet function can be employed to provide the design targets over the predetermined bandwidth to the optimization process of the parameters of the front- and back-end matching networks that was recently applied and completed by Aliyev [6].
2. In the second approach only the Z_s, Z_L termination functions can be employed in the design of the front- and back-end matching networks, respectively, to obtain corresponding performance (F, V_i, G_T) triplet over the predetermined bandwidth. This approach is used in this work by combining the genetic algorithm for the data processing in the optimization, which will be given in the

optimization section. Next, a worked example will be given to obtain neural design characteristics for the transistor NE329S01 which is used as the active device of the amplifier circuit.

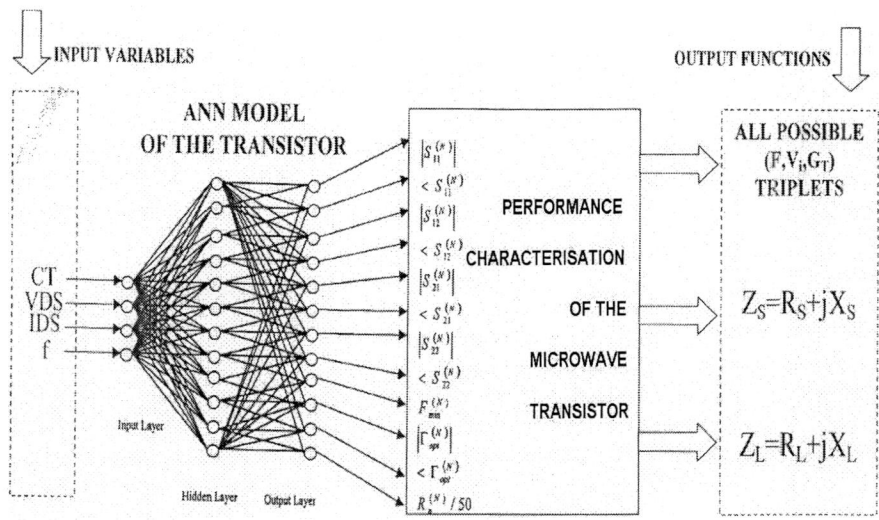

Fig. 1. A Neural Block Diagram of the Performance Data Sheets

2.2 Worked Example and Design Targets

The characteristics in the Figs. 2 and 3 give respectively, variations of the triplet of (F = 0.46 dB, $V_i = 1$, G_{Tmax} (f)) and the source (Z_s) and load (Z_L) terminations for the triplet of (F = 0.46 dB, $V_i = 1$, $G_T = 12$ dB) of the low noise, high quality transistor NE329S01 biased at $V_{CE} = 2$ V, $I_C = 10$ mA with the operation bandwidth 2 – 18 GHz. As seen from the Figs. 3a and 3b, Z_s (ω) and Z_L (ω) functions form a design target subspace that provides an operation with the triplet of F = 0.46 dB, $V_i = 1$ and $G_T = 12$ dB over the band of 2 – 11 GHz which cannot go further because of incapability of the transistor.

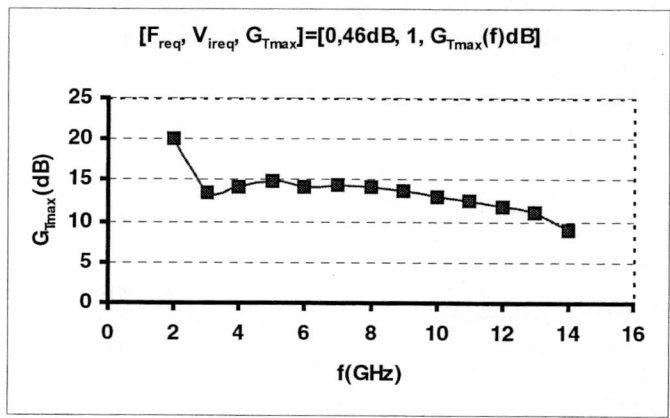

Name of the Transistor: NE 329S01
Bias Condition:
$V_{CE} = 2$ V; $I_C = 10$ mA
Operation Bandwidth: 2–18 GHz

Fig. 2. [0,46dB, 1, G_{Tmax}(f)] Triplet for the Transistor Ne329s01

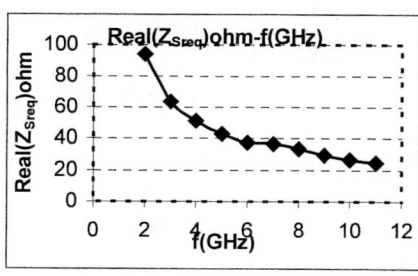
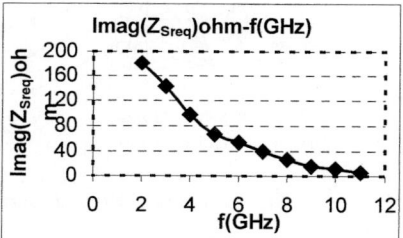

(a) Source Termination

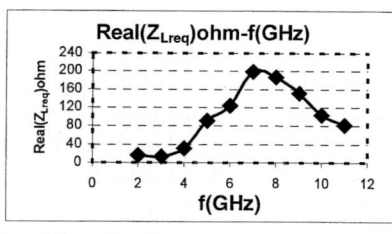
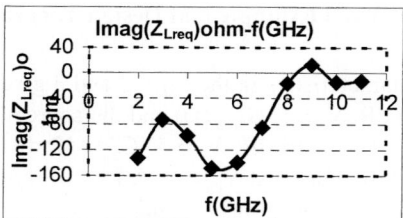

(b) Load Termination

Fig. 3. Termination Functions of the (0,46db, 1, 12db) Triplets for the Transistor Ne329s01

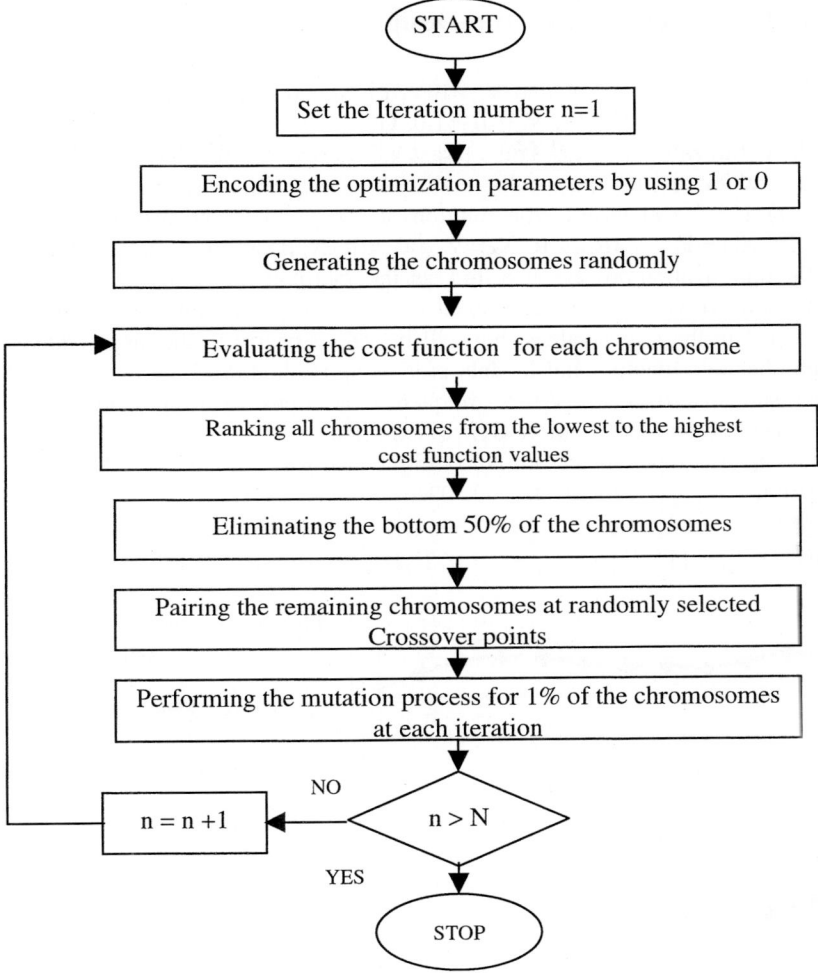

Fig. 4. The flow diagram of the genetic algorithm

3 Optimization Algorithm: Genetic

In optimization of the matching circuits in front and back-ends of the active device, the genetic algorithms with binary (BGA) and decimal (CPGA) coded numbers are used, whose main flow diagram is given in the Fig. 4. Parameters constituting a chromosome are represented by floating-point number in CPGA. CPGA has the advantage of the accurate representation of the continuous parameters also requires less storage and computing time than BGA since it does not need conversion between binary and decimal numbers.

4 Computed Performances and Design Variables

NE329S01 is biased at I_c = 5mA and V_{CE}=10V, for which the termination functions $Z_s(\omega_i)$, $Z_L(\omega_i)$ for $F_{req}(\omega_i)$=0,46dB, $V_{ireq}(\omega_i)$=1,0, $G_{Treq}(\omega_i)$) =12dB, i= 2,...11 are supplied into the optimization process as the target values over the operation bandwidth. These target values are the physically realizable $Z_s(\omega_i)=R_s(\omega_i)+jX_s\omega_i)$; $Z_L(\omega_i)$ = $R_L(\omega)+jX_L(\omega_i)$, i = 2,...11 termination solutions to the simultaneous nonlinear equations of $F(R_s, X_s) = F_{req}$, $V_i(R_s,X_s,R_L,X_L)=V_{ireq}$, $G_T=(R_s,X_s,R_L,X_L)=G_{Treq}$ for the transistor. Since the optimization process also find out the approximately solution set to the same equations in terms of the predetermined variables, so the resulted values will no longer be equal to the target values, but will be values nearly to the target values, ruled by the objective function and its data processing method. So Figure 5a, 5b and 5c give the resulted $G_T(\omega)$,$F(\omega)$, $V_i(\omega)$ - frequency variations. Realized bandwidth of the amplifier is between 2 GHz and 11 GHz as expected.

∏-type matching circuit parameters for NE329S01 transistor are found as follows:
ℓ_1 = 14.608cm, ℓ_2= 13.970cm, ℓ_3 = 0.503cm, Z_{o1} = 85.185Ω, Z_{o2} = 51.995 Ω
Z_{o3} =167.1842 ; ℓ_4 = 14.291 cm, ℓ_5 = 13.678 cm, ℓ_6 = 14.197 cm,
Z_{o4} =199.988 Ω ,Z_{o5} = 114.411 Ω,, Z_{o6} =193.972 Ω (Results of the CPGA)

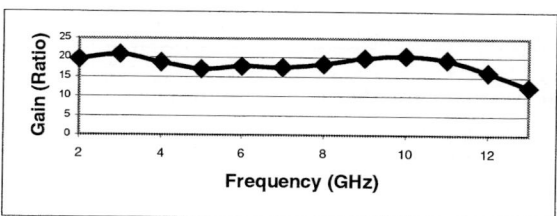

Fig. 5a. G_T (ratio) Variation of the Microwave Amplifier

G_{Treq}(ratio)=15.85
V_{ireq}(ratio)=1.0
F_{req}(ratio)=1.11

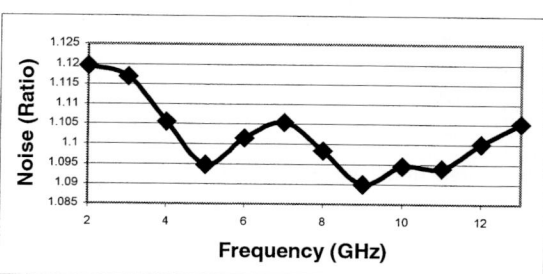

Fig. 5b. Noise (ratio) Variation of the Microwave Amplifier

G_{Treq}(ratio)=15.85
V_{ireq}(ratio)=1.0
F_{req}(ratio)=1.11

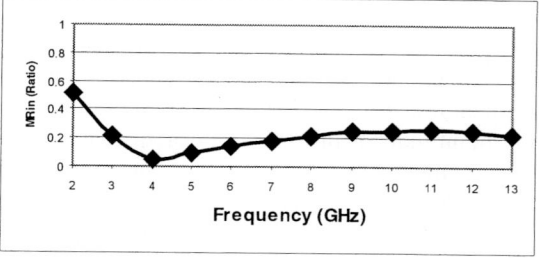

Fig. 5c. Input Reflection Coefficient Variation of the Microwave Amplifier of 5a and 5b.

5   Conclusions

Quality of the microwave amplifier performance can be determined by the flat gain level (G_T) as well as the percent of the maximum power delivered into the input port, which is characterized by the module square of the input reflection coefficient (V_i), over the operation bandwidth. Noise figure (F) is also important performance ingredient depending on the position of the amplifier in system order. In order to have feasible(F, V_i, G_T) triplets for the design, the potential characteristics of the transistor are obtained from the Neural Performance Data Sheets which are expected to be replaced for the Manufacturers Data Sheets. So the feasible performances of Gain, Input VSWR and Noise Figure can be taken into account simultaneously over the predetermined operation bandwidth in a Multi-Objective Error Function. The global minimum of this Error function are found by BGA and CPGA techniques. The resulted Design Space can be utilized efficiently in the realization by the MMIC (Monolithic Microwave Integrated Circuit) technology.

References

1 Güneş, F., Tepe, C.: Gain-Bandwidth Limitations for a Microwave Transistor". Int. J RF Microwave CAE, Vol.12, No:6, (2002), 483–495 .
2 Güneş, F., Gürgen, F., Torpi H.: Signal-Noise Neural Network Model for Active Microwave Device, IEE Proc. Circuit Devices and Systems Vol. 143 No :1, (1996): 1–8
3 Güneş, F., Torpi, H., Gürgen F.:A Multidimensional Signal-Noise Neural Model for Microwave Transistors, IEE Proc. Circuit Devices and Systems Vol. 145 No:2, (1998) 111–117.
4 Güneş, F., Güneş M., Fidan, M.: Performance Characterization of a Microwave Transistor, IEE Proc. Circuits Devices System, Vol. 141, No:5, (1994) 337–344
5 Güneş, F., Çetiner, B.A.:Smith: Chart Formulation of Performance Characterization for a Microwave Transistor, IEE Proc. Circuits Devices Syst. Vol. 145, No:6, (1998)1–10.
6 Aliyev, Ilgar: Design of the Microwave Amplifier using the Performance (F,V_i ,G_T) Triplets, MSc Thesis submitted to the Science Research Institute of Yıldız Technical University, Istanbul, Turkey (2001)

Adaptive Stochastic Classifier for Noisy pH-ISFET Measurements

Tong Boon Tang, Hsin Chen, and Alan F. Murray

School of Engineering and Electronics,
The University of Edinburgh,
Edinburgh EH9 3JL, UK
{tbt, hc, afm}@ee.ed.ac.uk

Abstract. Sensor drift is an inevitable measurement problem and is particularly significant in the long term. The common practice is to have an auto-calibration facility (including standard buffers or accurate integrated actuators) mounted on the monitoring system. However, this approach may not be feasible when the monitoring system is miniaturized to the size of a capsule. In this paper, we develop an adaptive stochastic classifier using analogue neural computation to produce constantly-reliable classification for noisy pH-ISFET measurements. This classifier operates at the signal-level fusion and auto-calibrates its parameters to compensate the sensor drift, with simple learning rules. The ability of the classifier to operate with a drift of 85 % of the pH-ISFET's full dynamic range is demonstrated. This sensor fusion highlights the potential of neural computation in miniaturized multisensor analytical microsystems such as Lab-in-a-Pill (LIAP) for long-term measurements.

1 Introduction

Driven by current Lab-on-a-Chip and System-on-Chip (SoC) technological trends, it is now possible to shrink a complex multisensor microsystem into the size of a capsule [1]. However, it is then inherently more difficult to extract useful information from what is now far noisier sensor data. Our primary interest is in a simple data-fusion algorithm that is robust to noise, hardware-amenable and thus able to underpin an intelligent sensor fusion system (ISFS). Since sensor drift is an unavoidable problem especially in the long term, an ISFS should be **autonomous adaptive** and possibly capable to **classify** noisy sensory data into categories.

Our prototype capsule [1] contains standard PN-junction silicon diode temperature sensor [2] and ion-sensitive field effect transistor (ISFET) pH sensor [3]. The ISFET suffers from four different types of sensor drift. The type of drift, which we confront most, is due to the instability of the reference electrode. One approach to eliminate the drift is to use two different pH-sensitive layers (e.g. Ta_2O_5 and oxynitride/Si_3N_4) in differential mode. However, this design suffers from crosstalk between the transistors when some protons (by-product of enzyme reaction) diffuse to the ion-insensitive transistor and cause a false signal. This, combined with our interest in miniaturization of the multisensor microsystem [1], means that we choose to use a single ISFET for each pH measurement.

In this study, we choose to employ neural computation, in particular Continuous Restricted Boltzmann Machine (CRBM) [4], to calibrate the ISFET's drift. The CRBM has been shown to be a stochastic generative model that can model continuous data with a simple training algorithm. The following sections present our investigation on the potential of CRBM in our application - performing reliable classification of noisy data that suffers from sensor drift.

2   Neural Computation

This section briefs the CRBM model, while detailed description should be referred to [4]. The CRBM has one visible and one hidden layer with inter-layer connection defined by a weight matrix $\{\mathbf{W}\}$. A stochastic neuron j has the following form:

$$s_j = \varphi_j \left(\sum_i w_{ij} s_i + \sigma \cdot N_j(0,1) \right), \quad (1)$$

with $\quad \varphi_j(x_j) = \theta_L + (\theta_H - \theta_L) \cdot \dfrac{1}{1 + \exp(-a_j x_j)} \quad (2)$

where s_i refers to input from neuron i, and $N_j(0,1)$ represents a unit Gaussian noise with zero mean. The noise component $\sigma \cdot N_j(0,1)$ allows the CRBM to perform probabilistic *analogue* neural computation without quantization and hence avoid unnecessary loss of information which a binary RBM suffers from [5,6,7]. To enhance efficient learning, the noise scaling factor σ in visible layer is set to a constant value close to the input data's standard deviation, while σ in hidden layer is set to 0.4 in order to avoid overfitting problem [8]. Parameter a_j is the noise-control factor which controls the slope of the sigmoid function, such that a neuron j behaves deterministically (small a_j), or continuous-stochastically (moderate a_j), or binary-stochastically (large a_j). θ_H and θ_L are then simply two constants defining the sigmoid function's asymptotes.

Both $\{a_j\}$ and $\{w_{ij}\}$ can be trained by "Minimizing Contrastive Divergence" (MCD) learning [5]. The simplified MCD learning rule [8] requires only addition and multiplication, and is therefore hardware-amenable.

3   Sensor Model

This section introduces the mathematical models of the temperature and the pH sensors.

3.1   Temperature Sensor

The signal conditioning circuit is illustrated in Fig. 1a. The output voltage V_{out} is linearly proportional to the environmental temperature T. In our application [1], the sensor should operate within a dynamic range of 0 - 70 °C with a sensitivity of 31.5 mV/°C. Results from fabricated integrated sensors [1] show that the temperature sensor can be represented by:

$$V_{out}(t) = 31.5 \times T + 1030 + \tau_{temp}(t) + a_{temp} N_{temp}(t) \quad (3)$$

at time t. The terms $\tau_{temp}(t)$, a_{temp} and $N_{temp}(t)$ refer to non-linear sensor drift function, noise magnitude and random Gaussian noise function (due to background noise of the sensing environment). Units for $V_{out}(t)$ and T are mV and °C respectively.

3.2 pH Sensor

The signal conditioning circuit is depicted in Fig. 1b. This sensor provides a dynamic range of pH 1 - 10. Experiment [1] reveals that the ISFET has a sensitivity of 23.5 mV/pH with 16 µA of excitation current. Thus, a first-order model for the output voltage V_{out} of a particular ISFET (with an unique V_T) at time t will be:

$$V_{out}(t) = 18 \times T - 23.5 \times pH + V_T + \tau_{pH}(t) + a_C N_C(t) \qquad (4)$$

The term $\tau_{pH}(t)$ refers to non-linear pH sensor drift function while a_C and $N_C(t)$ refer to the composition noise magnitude and random Gaussian noise function for both temperature and pH sensing variances. Units for $V_{out}(t)$ and T are mV and °C respectively.

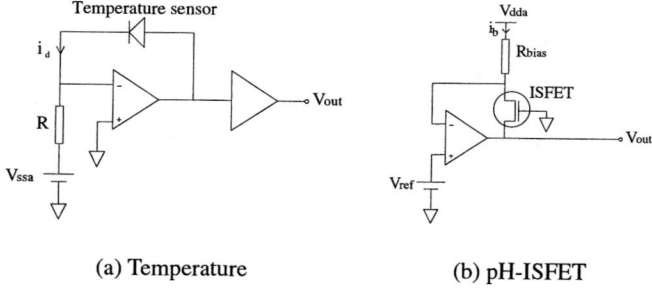

Fig. 1. Signal conditioning circuits for the sensors

4 Experiments and Discussion

In this study, we investigate the CRBM's ability to model the measurement signals from one temperature sensor and ten pH-ISFET sensors. The 11-dimensional measurement data are generated according to (3) and (4), with a_{temp} and a_c being set to 0.013 and 0.053 which correspond to their experimentally-recorded levels (20 mV and 80 mV) [1]. With $\theta_H = 1$ and $\theta_L = -1$, all generated data are also renormalized into ± 1.

Fig. 2a shows the training data consisting of two sets of measurements. The sensors are exposed to a pH 4 liquid in the first set (cluster A), while to a pH 10 liquid in the second set (cluster B). Since both sets of measurement have the same ambient temperature of 37 °C, the mean values of the temperature sensor (first visible unit in Fig.2a) in both sets are the same. As the characteristics of the sensors are defined by the fabrication process, the only variation between the ten ISFETs is the threshold voltage. Therefore, the two data clusters have similar distributions (Fig. 2a).

A CRBM model (implemented in Matlab) with five hidden unit, including the bias unit, is trained to model the two clusters of data. The noise-scaling constant σ is set to 0.05 for visible units, in accordance with a_{temp} and a_c, and to 0.4 for the hidden units. To test CRBM's ability to classify noisy sensory data, both weights $\{w_{ij}\}$ and noise-control factors $\{a_j\}$ are updated in the first 30,000 epochs. The results of CRBM functioning as a classifier after 30,000 epochs' training are discussed in Sec.4.1. Sec.4.2 then examines the trained CRBM's ability to trace any subsequent shift in training data after 30,000 epochs, by turning ON the learning of some particular parameters. Finally, Sec.4.3 further complicates the task by removing one cluster in the training data, and demonstrates that the CRBM remains able to trace the shift and classify noisy data.

4.1 CRBM as a Classifier

After the initial 30,000 training epochs, the bias unit H0 in the hidden layer encodes the underlaying shape (i.e. mean) of the training data distribution, as depicted in Fig. 2b. This is due to its state (permanently '+1') which allows it to learn faster (with a larger weight change $\Delta\hat{\omega}_{i0}$) than the other hidden units that have near-zero initial states. On the other hand, the hidden unit H1 has a set of large values ($\sim$ -0.6) of receptive field for visible units V2-11 (Fig. 2c) and a large noise control factor a_h (2.6956) relative to other hidden units' as shown in Fig. 3a. These point to the mechanism whereby a CRBM models two such clusters of data. The large values imply that the activity/state of the hidden unit H1 is very sensitive to the particular elements in the input data vector. Consequently, it is possible to classify the unknown input data into cluster A or B by simply observing the activity of the hidden unit with large a_h, in this case H1. Furthermore, we realize that the activity of the hidden unit can be a measure of confidence for this high-level abstraction of information. As indicated in Fig. 3b, a clear separation (lowest upper boundary - highest lower boundary = 0.65) of H1's response to two different clusters shows that a 100 % accuracy on classification is easily achieved.

4.2 Tracing Sensor Drift

After the initial 30,000 training epochs, sensor drift is introduced to the first pH sensor (second visible unit V2). For simplicity, we set $\tau_{temp}(t) = 0$ and $\tau_{pH}(t) = 5$ mV per 5000 epochs. If all weights ω_{ij} remain updated simultaneously as in Sec. 4.1, all ω_{ij} will "compete" to respond to any shift in the mean of the data distribution, due to their stochastic nature. Since the experiment in Sec. 4.1 indicates that the receptive field of the bias unit H0 in the hidden layer describes the mean of the training data distribution, we thus propose that only H0's receptive field be updated with the latest distribution after the initial 30,000 epochs.

After 230,000 epochs, the reconstruction data distribution, as depicted in Fig. 4b, has a notable shift of 0.2 units approximately in the V2 axis from the reconstructed data at epoch 30,000 (Fig. 4a). This shift coincides with the controlled shift of 0.2 unit in the training data. Further evidence is shown in Fig. 4c where the receptive field of the

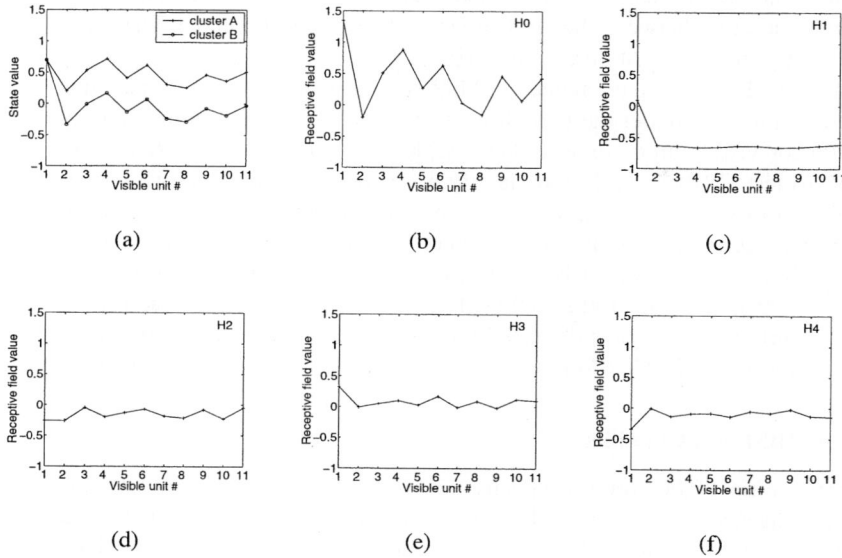

Fig. 2. (a) The mean values for the two clusters training data in the initial 30,000 epochs. (b) - (f) The receptive field values for all the hidden units H0-4 respectively after its initial training period 30,000 epochs

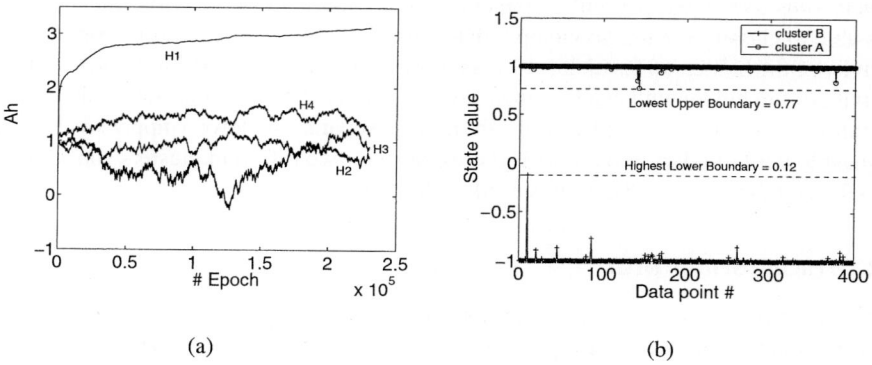

Fig. 3. (a) The noise control factor for hidden units over the entire experimental period. (b) The activities for the hidden unit H1 for a set of 400 training data points for both clusters A and B after its initial training period 30,000 epochs

bias unit in the hidden layer for visible unit V2 has been adjusted by 0.4752 unit to "trace" the change in the input data whilst the other w_{ij} remain almost unchanged. This result consolidates the argument that a learning CRBM, under a useful and constrained configuration, can adapt to environmental changes such as sensor drift whilst present an unchanging (autonomously re-calibrated) representation of drifting data to subsequent layers of processing - at least in this relatively simple real example.

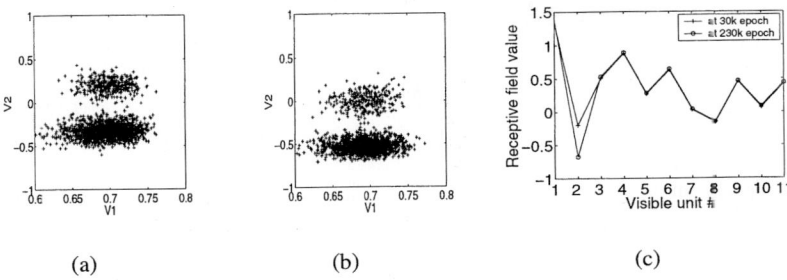

Fig. 4. (a) Reconstruction data distribution for the first two visible units after 30,000 epochs. (b) Reconstruction data distribution for the first two visible units after 230,000 epochs (c) Receptive fields for the bias unit H0 in the hidden layer at 30,000 and 230,000 epochs

4.3 Single Cluster Updating

When a microsystem is monitoring on its surrounding environmental parameters, often there is only a single class of data available over a long period of time. This may cause a serious problem for a **learning** system such as above because of catastrophic interference. When new data distribution (a single cluster) is presented, the system tends to adopt a new set of parameters to re-generate the new distribution, and consequently lose its ability to classify.

To investigate the CRBM's ability to learn an incomplete training data without losing classifying ability, cluster B in training data is removed after epoch 30,000, and the same drift as in Sec. 4.2 is introduced to the remaining training cluster A. As predicted, despite the effort of inhibiting the learning for all (except bias unit) weights, the CRBM parameters are adjusted to re-generate only one cluster of data. We found that this is due to a strong "compensation" from the noise-control factor a_j. We therefore repeated the experiment with learning in a_j switched OFF after the initial 30,000 epochs.

Fig. 5a shows promisingly that the CRBM is still able to re-generate two clusters at epoch 230,000 despite the current training data has only single drifting cluster of data for updating its parameters. Besides, a notable shift in the V2-axis is learnt. Further evidence is given in Fig. 5b whereby the receptive field of bias unit H0 in hidden layer has a large change (0.4651) for V2 and very small adjustment (less than 0.0199) for the rest. This is encouraging and reinforces the potential of this form neural computation in dealing with noisy and drifting integrated-sensor data. One example of its possible application will be a location indicator for a capsule that monitors the gastrointestinal (GI) tract [9].

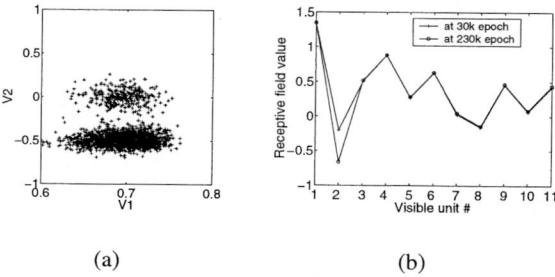

Fig. 5. Experiment on using a single cluster to update a CRBM's parameters. (a) Reconstruction data for the first two visible units after 230,000 epochs. (b) Receptive fields for the bias unit H0 in the hidden layer at 30,000 and 230,000 epochs

5 Conclusion

The stochastic neural algorithm CRBM shows its ability to learn the 11-dimensional probabilistic distribution of the analogue sensor data with merely 5 hidden units. Additionally, we have demonstrated its ability to classify noisy data with reasonable confidence. With proper configuration, this classifier is further capable to counteract at least simple sensor drift to improve its reliability, by "auto-calibrating" key parameters instead of re-learning a new set of receptive fields for every newly-drifted data distribution. Finally, we demonstrated that a CRBM is able to adapt to sensor drift despite the training data is incomplete. Therefore, we anticipate that neural computation such as CRBM can find a niche in the increasingly complicated distributed multisensor systems as a form of intelligent sensor fusion.

Acknowledgment. This work is supported by the Scottish Higher Education Funding Council (RDG 130). The authors would like to thank Dr. Erik A. Johannessen for helpful discussion on chemical sensors and signal conditioning circuits.

References

1. Tang, T.B., et al: Towards a Miniature Wireless Integrated Multisensor Microsystem for Industrial and Biomedical Applications. IEEE Sensors Journal: Special Issue on Integrated Multisensor Systems and Signal Processing **2(6)** (December 2002) 628–635
2. Rashid, M.H.: Microelectronics Circuit Analysis and Design. Boston: PWS Publishing Company (1999)
3. Bergveld, P.: Development, operation, and application of the ion-sensitive field effect transistor as a tool for electrophysiology. IEEE Trans. on Biomedical Eng. **19** (1972) 342–351
4. Chen, H., Murray, A.F.: A Continuous Restricted Boltzmann Machine with a Hardware-Amenable Learning Algorithm. Proc. of the International Conference on Artificial Neural Networks (2002) 358–363
5. Hinton, G.E.: Training Products of Experts by Minimizing Contrastive Divergence. Neural Computation **14(8)** (2002) 1771–1800

6. Smolensky, P.: Information processing in dynamic systems: Foundations of harmony theory. Parallel Distributed Processing: Explorations in the Microstructure of Cognition **1** (1986) 195–281
7. Murray, A.F.: Novelty detection using products of simple experts – a potential architecture for embedded systems. Neural Networks **14** (2001) 1257–1264
8. Chen, H., Murray, A.F.: A Continuous Restricted Boltzmann Machine with an Implementable Training Algorithm. IEE Proc. of Vision, Image, Signal Processing, in press (2003)
9. Lei, W., et al: Integrated micro-instrumentation for dynamic monitoring of the gastro-intestinal tract. Proc. of the 2nd Annual International IEEE EMB Special Topic Conference on Microtechnologies in Medicine and Biology (2002) 219–222

Comparing Support Vector Machines, Recurrent Networks, and Finite State Transducers for Classifying Spoken Utterances*

Sheila Garfield and Stefan Wermter

University of Sunderland, School of Computing and Technology,
Centre for Hybrid Intelligent Systems, Sunderland, SR6 0DD, United Kingdom
{stefan.wermter,sheila.garfield}@sunderland.ac.uk
http://www.his.sunderland.ac.uk/

Abstract. This paper describes new experiments for the classification of recorded operator assistance telephone utterances. The experimental work focused on three techniques: support vector machines (SVM), simple recurrent networks (SRN) and finite-state transducers (FST) using a large, unique telecommunication corpus of spontaneous spoken language. A comparison is made of the performance of these classification techniques which indicates that a simple recurrent network performed best for learning classification of spontaneous spoken language in a robust manner which should lead to their use in helpdesk call routing.

1 Introduction

Spontaneous spoken language is disfluent [1] and as a result errors in recognition of speech input can arise due to background noise, speaking style, disfluencies, out-of-vocabulary words, parsing coverage or understanding gaps [2]. Spontaneous speech also includes filled pauses and partial words. Spoken dialogue systems must be able to deal with these as well as other discourse phenomena such as anaphora and ellipsis, and ungrammatical queries [2,3].

A general research question arises whether certain symbolic, statistical or neural network methods can be used effectively to classify faulty telephone utterances. In order to address this question we have chosen symbolic finite state transducers, statistical support vector machines and simple recurrent neural networks. So far there has been little work on comparing and evaluating such techniques on substantial real world corpora although we believe that such a study is crucial to suggest more effective techniques and architectures for the future.

In this paper we describe an approach to the classification of recorded operator assistance telephone utterances. We describe experiments in a real-world scenario utilising a large, unique corpus with 4 000 utterances of spontaneous spoken

---

* This research has been partially supported under grant ML846657 to Professor S. Wermter. The authors thank Mark Farrell and David Attwater of BTexact Technologies for their helpful discussions.

language. The paper is structured as follows: Section 2 provides an overview of the corpus used; Sections 3 and 4 outline the experimental work using SVMs and FSTs and Section 5 is an evaluation and comparison of these techniques with the SRN; and finally Section 6 draws together conclusions.

2 Description of the Helpdesk Corpus

Our task is to learn to classify real incoming telephone utterances into a set of service level classes. For this task a corpus from transcriptions of recorded operator assistance telephone calls was used [4]. Examination of the utterances reveals that the callers use a wide range of language to express their problem, enquiry or to request assistance [5].

1. *"could I book a wake up call please"*
2. *"could you check for conversation please"*
3. *"I'm in on my own and I've just got a phone call and I picked it up and it was just gone and it happened yesterday as well at the same time"*

2.1 Call Transcription

A corpus based on transcriptions of the first utterances of callers to the operator service is the focus of the investigation. A number of service levels or call classes, primary move types and request types [4] were identified after analysis of the utterances. As shown by the example in Table 1, the *call class* is the classification of the utterance and is associated with the service that the caller requires. The *primary move* is a subset of the first utterance, it is like a dialogue act and gives an indication of which dialogue act is likely to follow the current utterance. The *request* type identifies whether the request is explicit or not [6].

Table 1. Example call from the corpus

Call	Call Class	Primary Move Type	Request Type
yeah could I book a wake up call please	alarm call	action	explicit

Four separate call sets of 1 000 utterances each were used in this study. The call sets are split so that 80% of utterances are used for training and 20% of utterances used for testing. The average length of an utterance in the training set is 16.05 words and in the test set the average length of an utterance is 15.52 words. An illustrative example of the breakdown of utterances is given in Table 2, however for illustration not all call classes are shown. The part of the utterance identified as the primary move was used for both the training and test sets.

Table 2. Breakdown of utterances in training and test sets from call set 1. Note: For illustration purposes not all classes are shown

1 000 utterances
Total of 712 utterances in Training set
Total of 205 utterances in Test set
Total of 83 utterances not used since they did not contain a primary move

Classes:	class 1	class 2	class 3	class 4	class 5	class 6	class 7	class 8	class 9	class n
in train set:	261	11	41	3	85	32	6	16	28	...
in test set:	59	3	21	1	29	11	2	4	7	...

2.2 Semantic Vector Representation

The experiments use a semantic vector representation of the words in a lexicon [7]. These vectors represent the frequency of a particular word occurring in a call class and are independent of the number of examples observed in each class. The number of calls in a class can vary substantially. Therefore we *normalise* the frequency of a word w in class c_i according to the number of calls in c_i (2). A *value* $v(w, c_i)$ is computed for each element of the semantic vector as the *normalised* frequency of occurrences of word w in semantic class c_i, divided by the *normalised* frequency of occurrences of word w in all classes. That is:

$$Normalised\ frequency\ of\ w\ in\ c_i = \frac{Frequency\ of\ w\ in\ c_i}{Number\ of\ calls\ in\ c_i} \qquad (1)$$

where:

$$v(w, c_i) = \frac{Normalised\ frequency\ of\ w\ in\ c_i}{\sum_j Normalised\ frequency\ for\ w\ in\ c_j},\ j \in \{1, \cdots n\}\ . \qquad (2)$$

3 Support Vector Machines

A support vector machine is a binary classifier which divides the problem space into two regions via a *dividing line* or *hyperplane*. This hyperplane separates positive examples from negative examples with a maximum margin [8,9,10] between it and the nearest data point of each class. SVMs can deal with non-linearly separable classes and can handle noisy data. SVMs can learn or generalise from labelled training data and consequently can be automatically constructed.

Classifiers were constructed [11] with different kernel functions: polynomial, RBF and sigmoid [9,12]. For each of these kernel functions we performed two series of experiments. In the first series the value of tuning parameter C, the error penalty, was chosen randomly; in the second series this parameter was selected automatically. Several values for C were determined empirically; the aim was to select a value that reduced the test error to a minimum while at the same time constructing a classifier that was able to perform successfully on individual classes. Other parameters were kept constant, that is, the classifiers were constructed using the same values except the error penalty C.

The input sequences generated are composed of feature-value pairs, for example, 1:0.106232, where the 'feature', in this case '1', is the position of the word in the utterance and the 'value', '0.106232', is the frequency of occurrence of that word for the particular class under investigation, (see also Section 2.2).

A classifier was constructed [11] for each class in a *one-versus-all* approach, that is, the training and test sets used positive examples for the particular class in question and negative examples of all the other classes. The classifier in each case was trained and then tested on the utterance sequences generated from four call sets used in [13]. Table 3 shows the overall F-score performance (combined recall and precision [14]) of each of the trained classifiers on the four call sets. We will later analyse and compare this performance in Section 5.

Table 3. Training and test set. F-score results of SVM on 4 000 utterances

	Training Set			Test Set		
	RBF	Sigmoid	Polynomial	RBF	Sigmoid	Polynomial
Call set 1	89.31	75.70	77.00	56.71	57.82	64.36
Call set 2	89.89	81.06	81.77	58.46	60.51	63.82
Call set 3	88.92	79.78	78.50	57.88	59.58	66.66
Call set 4	91.23	84.09	83.92	57.57	60.51	65.26

4 Finite-State Machines

A finite-state machine is a formal machine that consists of states, transitions, one start state, any number of final states and an alphabet [15,16]. While their representation and their output is both easily understood and interpreted the foundation of a finite-state machine is the regular expression and these must be manually pre-specified to encode an utterance classification.

In order to create the regular expressions, the utterances in the call set are symbolically tagged to enable identification of possible patterns or strings and substrings in the utterances. This means that each word in the utterance is tagged with a symbolic representation of the class associated with that word based on the highest frequency of occurrence as shown by the example utterance *"how do I cancel it or can't I"* in Table 4. Thus in the lexicon, the word "how" is most frequently associated with the "class 4" class based on the frequency of occurrence. These symbolic tags represent the sequence for a specific utterance. The higher frequency of class 4 would indicate that this utterance is classified as class 4.

The same 4 000 utterances were used as in the previous experiment and transducers were constructed for each class. Transducers were constructed for

Table 4. Example sequence

how	do	I	cancel	it	or	can't	I
class 4	class 4	class 8	class 4	class 1	class 4	class 4	class 8

each class using regular expressions which were hand-crafted. The tagged training sets were used as reference sets whilst creating the regular expressions based on sequences of classes identified in the symbolic representation of the utterances. Once the transducers were constructed each was tested against the data sets for the other classes. The transducer produces an output for each sequence in the input file. A successful output is the semantic label of the class for which the transducer has been constructed while an unsuccessful output is '0'.

The overall F-score performance of the transducers on each of the four call sets is shown in Table 5.

Table 5. Training and test set. F-score results of FST on 4 000 utterances

	Training Set	Test Set
Call set 1	38.75	40.59
Call set 2	36.31	35.91
Call set 3	41.43	37.21
Call set 4	34.58	33.59

5 Evaluation and Comparison with Simple Recurrent Network

The overall test recall and precision rates for each of the SVM classifiers and the FST are shown in Figure 1 for each of the four call sets.

In an initial comparison of the three techniques SRN, SVM and FST the average recall and precision performance on the test set across three classes for each technique is shown in Figure 2. The SRN network and its performance has been described in more detail in [13] which is why we concentrated here on the description of SVM and FST in this paper. The performance of the SRN, SVM and the FST on individual call classes for recall and precision on the unseen test data for call set 1 is shown in Figure 3.

From the results on the test set, shown in Figure 3, the performance is varied across each technique and it is evident that no one technique performs well on every class and, in some cases, both the SRN and the SVM produce exactly the same recall result, for example, class 3 recall percentage. Generally, the performance of the SRN is better than that of the SVM and the FST. One possible reason why the performance of the SRN is better than that of the other

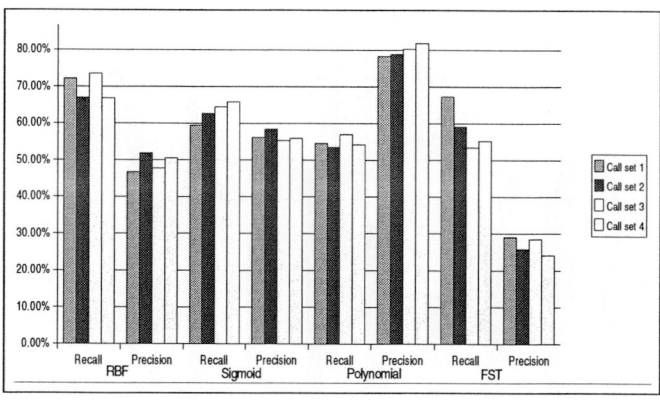

Fig. 1. Test results of SVM and FST

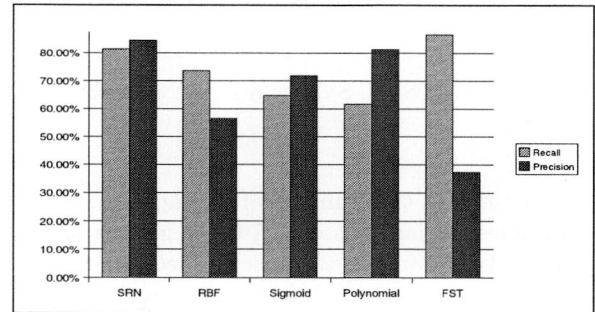

Fig. 2. Test set. Comparison of average performance on three classes for the SRN, SVM and FST

techniques is that the SRN is able to make use of sequential memory in the form of its context layer. That is, the information stored in the context layer does assist the network in assigning the correct class to an utterance.

However, in the case of class 3 the precision rate for both the SVM and the FST is below 50%. This is a possible indication that the method of representation of the semantic content of the utterances in this particular class is inadequate and does not allow either technique to consistently classify the utterances.

On the other hand the recall performance of the FST on this class is significantly better than that of the SVM. It can be concluded that the means by which the semantic content is presented to the FST generally enables this technique to perform more effectively with regard to recall than the SVM but in most cases not as well with regard to precision performance. It is evident that the hand-crafted regular expressions do not capture a fine enough level of granularity in the semantics of this type of utterance for the FST to accurately classify the utterances consistently when precision performance is considered.

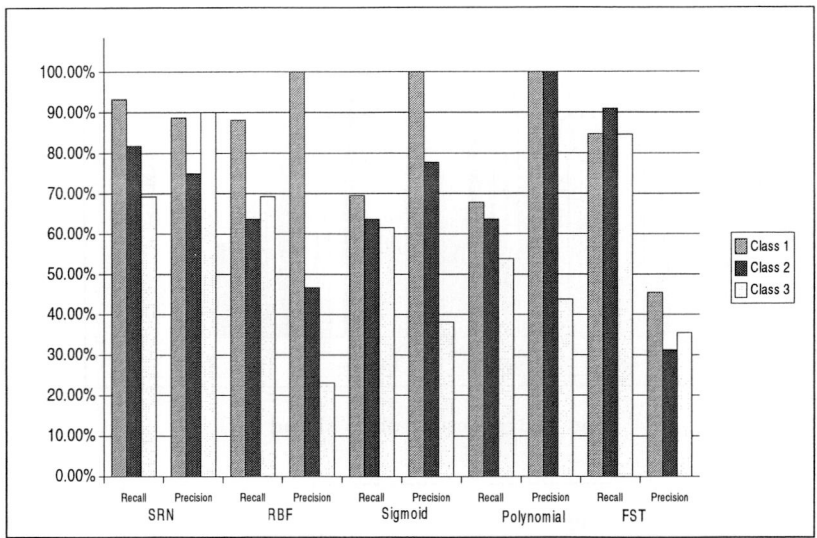

Fig. 3. Test set. Comparison of SRN, SVM and FST. Note: For illustration purposes three classes are shown

One factor to consider is the number of examples in each of the classes. The number of examples in class 1 is over 5 times greater than that of class 3. Consequently, if one or two examples are misclassified or not classified in a small number of examples the impact on the result is much greater and produces a greater difference to the result but the same is not true for a larger set of examples.

SVMs are a promising method for learning classification from examples. Classifiers can be automatically constructed and, depending on the task, achieve a smooth trade-off between recall and precision [17]. Finite-state machines can handle strings of any length and this is of particular significance in this task because the length of the caller's utterance is variable. However, the SRN overall outperformed both the SVM and FST and provided better overall results due to its context layer.

6 Conclusion

The SRN network was compared to the other approaches identified and the main result from this work is that the performance of the simple recurrent network is better when factors such as noise in the utterance and the number of classes are taken into consideration. However, a combination of techniques might yield even improved performance. The SVM allows a trade-off between recall and precision and as a result for classes that are problematic to the SRN the SVM might be a better alternative. Whilst the FST does not allow a trade-off between recall and precision again it could be used for those classes with very few and problematic examples because it can achieve almost perfect performance, that is 100%, on both recall and precision for very few examples. The drawback to this approach is that it requires hand-crafted regular expressions which are time-consuming to construct. One additional factor that must be considered is the number of examples available for training and testing as this does influence performance. Based on this detailed study of 4 000 utterances we conclude that an SRN-based architecture combined with SVM models is the most promising candidate to improve classification performance even further.

References

[1] Abney, S.: Statistical Methods and Linguistics. In: Klavans, J. and P. (eds): The Balancing Act. MIT Press, Cambridge, MA (1996)
[2] Glass, J.R.: Challenges for Spoken Dialogue Systems. Proceedings of IEEE ASRU Workshop. Keystone, CO (1999)
[3] Clark, H.: Speaking in Time. Speech Communication 36 (2002) 5-13
[4] Durston, P.J. and Kuo, J.J.K. et al.: OASIS Natural Language Call Steering Trial. Proceedings of Eurospeech, Vol2 (2001) 1323-1326
[5] Edgington, M., Attwater, D. and Durston, P.: OASIS – A Framework for Spoken Language Call Steering. Proceedings of Eurospeech '99 (1999)
[6] Attwater, D.: OASIS First Utterance Version 2.10 Release Note, 100CS:QUAL:REL:005 Version. (2000)
[7] Wermter, S., Panchev, C., Arevian, G.: Hybrid Neural Plausibility Networks for News Agents. Proceedings of the National Conference on Artificial Intelligence. Orlando, USA (1999) 93-98
[8] Chapelle, O. and Vapnik, V.: Model Selection for Support Vector Machines. In: Solla, S., Leen, T. and Muller, K-R. (eds): Advances in Neural Information Processing Systems 12. MIT Press, Cambridge, MA (2000)
[9] Opper, M. and Urbanczik, R.: Universal Learning Curves of Support Vector Machines. Physical Review Letters 86,19 (2001) 4410-4413
[10] Feng, J. and Williams, P.: The Generalization Error of the Symmetric and Scaled Support Vector Machines. IEEE Transactions on Neural Networks 12, 5 (2001)
[11] Joachims, T.: Making Large-Scale SVM Learning Practical. In: Schölkopf, B., Burges, C. and Smola, A. (eds): Advances in Kernel Methods: Support Vector Learning. MIT Press, Cambridge, MA (1999)
[12] Moghaddam, B. and Yang, M-H.: Sex with Support Vector Machines. In: Leen, T.K., Dietterich, T.G. and Tresp, V. (eds): Advances in Neural Information Processing Systems 13. MIT Press, Cambridge, MA (2001) 960-966
[13] Garfield, S. and Wermter, S.: Recurrent Neural Learning for Helpdesk Call Routing. Proceedings of the International Conference on Artificial Neural Networks (2002) 296-301
[14] Van Rijsbergen, C.J.: Information Retrieval. 2nd edition. Butterworths, London. (1979)
[15] Roche, E. and Schabes, Y.: Finite-state Language Processing. MIT, London (1997)
[16] Jurafsky, D. and Martin, J.H.: Speech and Language Processing. Prentice Hall, New Jersey (2000)
[17] Dumais, S.: Using SVMs for text categorization. IEEE Intelligent Systems (1998) 21-23

Selecting and Ranking Time Series Models Using the NOEMON Approach

Ricardo B.C. Prudêncio and Teresa B. Ludermir

Center of Informatics – Federal University of Pernambuco
P. O. Box 7851. Cidade Universitária, Recife – PE, Brazil. 50.732-970
{rbcp,tbl}@cin.ufpe.br

Abstract. In this work, we proposed to use the NOEMON approach to rank and select time series models. Given a time series, the NOEMON approach provides a ranking of the candidate models to forecast that series, by combining the outputs of different learners. The best ranked models are then returned as the selected ones. In order to evaluate the proposed solution, we implemented a prototype that used MLP neural networks as the learners. Our experiments using this prototype revealed encouraging results.

1 Introduction

Time series forecasting has been widely used to support planning and decision-making processes [1]. Several models have been developed to forecast time series, such as the Exponential Smoothing and the Box-Jenkins models, among others [1]. Given a set of candidate models to choose, a forecaster may either select *one* best model for all series, or he/she may select the best model for each time series. The former is called an *aggregate* selection rule and the latter an *individual* selection rule [2].

Although aggregate rules are simple to implement, empirical research has shown that there is no single model that performs better than the others in all series [3]. This fact motivated several authors to develop individual rules, commonly associating characteristics of the series to the best model. An approach that formalizes this knowledge in a reusable way is to use expert systems [3]. However, the process of acquiring knowledge from experts may be very expensive and time-consuming [4]. In this scenario, an interesting alternative is the use of Machine Learning (ML) techniques [5].

The ML algorithms were already used to model selection in different works [6][7][8][9]. In general, these works used a learner as a classifier that suggests just one model among the set of candidate ones. We believe that to provide a ranking of models is a more informative solution for model selection. In our work, we proposed to use the NOEMON approach [10] to select and rank time series models. This approach generates a ranking by combining the outputs of different learners. In our work, we implemented a prototype using MLP (Multi-Layer Perceptron) neural networks [11] as the learners, and performed experiments using a large set of time series. Our results revealed that the models suggested by our prototype were in average more accurate than the models suggested by different aggregate selection rules.

In section 2, we present the use of ML algorithms to model selection. Section 3 brings a brief explanation about the NOEMON approach and its application to model selection. In section 4, we present the description of the implemented prototype. Section 5 presents the experiments and results obtained by this prototype. Finally, we have the conclusion and future work in section 6.

2 Machine Learning to Model Selection

As we have previously said, a way to select time series models is using expert systems. The knowledge used in these systems is extracted from forecasting experts and it is expressed in the form of rules. In this context, we highlight the Rule-Based Forecasting system [3], which implemented an expert system with 99 rules, associating time series features (such as level discontinuities, basic trend...) to the available models. Although these systems can express knowledge in a practical and reusable way, the process of knowledge acquisition depends on human experts, which are often scarce and expensive [4]. In this scenario, ML techniques are an interesting alternative to acquire knowledge [5]. These techniques can be used to automatically learn from data, leading to potential improvement of performance, easy adaptability to new types of data, and a reduced need for experts [4].

The use of ML algorithms to model selection was originally proposed by [6], and adopted in other different works. In [6], the author used decision trees to select among six available models. As training examples, he used a set of 67 time series described by six features: level of detail (quarterly or yearly), the number of turning points, autocorrelation coefficients, trend, coefficient of determination, and error of the linear regression model. In [7], a neural network system was used to select among several exponential smoothing models, using the autocorrelations. In [8], the authors used a neural network to select a group of models and another neural network to select a single model of the group. In [9], the authors used a decision tree algorithm to select between the simple exponential smoothing model and a neural network model.

In general, these works treat the model selection as a classification problem where the class attribute represents the best candidate model to forecast the series, and then, they use a ML algorithm as the classifier. In this context, each training example consists of a time series described by a set of *time series features*, associated to the class attribute. The value of this attribute is commonly defined by experimenting all candidate models, and by choosing the one that obtained the best forecasting results for the series. A set of such examples is given as input of the ML algorithm, responsible for discovering knowledge associating the features to the candidate models.

3 NOEMON Approach to Model Selection

Previous works used ML techniques to suggest either one single model or a small group of models among the set of candidate ones. We believe that a more informative and flexible solution for model selection is to provide a ranking of the candidate models. First, if enough resources are available, more than one model may be used to forecasting a time series. Second, if the user has some preference for a specific subset of candidate models, he/she can select the model that get the best rank among the models of interest. In our work, we proposed the use of the NOEMON approach [10] to select and rank time series models. This approach has been recently used to select algorithms for classification problems and the results has been very promising [10]. In our work, we adapted the NOEMON approach to the model selection problem.

The NOEMON generates a ranking of models for each time series given as input, and suggests to the user the models that get the top position in the ranking. To generate a ranking of n models, the NOEMON uses (n 2) classifiers (learners), each one associated to a specific pair of models. For constructing the classifier associated to a pair (X, Y), the NOEMON adopts the following procedure. First, it defines a set of learning examples where each example corresponds to a time series described by a set of features and associated to a class attribute (either 'X' or 'Y'). The class attribute is assigned according to the model (X or Y) which obtained the best forecasting results for that series. At following, the NOEMON applies a ML algorithm, which will be responsible for associating new time series either to the class 'X' or to the class 'Y'.

Given a new time series as input, NOEMON collects the outputs of the (n 2) classifiers for the series. At following, NOEMON defines a score for each candidate model by counting how many times the model appears among the (n 2) collected outputs. The ranking is then generated by sorting the scores associated to the models. As an example, suppose that we have 3 available models (X, Y and Z). The NOEMON construct (3 2) = 3 classifiers C_1, C_2 and C_3, associated to the pairs (X, Y), (X, Z) and (Y, Z), respectively. Now, suppose that the outputs of the three classifiers for a new time series be 'Y', 'X' and 'Y', respectively. In this case, the scores associated to the models X, Y and Z are 1, 2 and 0, respectively. By sorting these values, the NOEMON generates the ranking [Y, X, Z] and consequently suggests the model Y as the best one for the input series. In fact, the model Y is supposed to be better than X according to the classifier C_1, and better than Z according to the classifier C_3.

4 The Implemented Prototype

In order to verify the viability of our proposal, we implemented and tested a prototype. In our prototype, the NOEMON approach was used to rank and select the following models: *Random Walk (RW)*, *Holt's Linear Exponential Smoothing (HL)* and *Auto-Regressive model (AR)*. We choose these models based on criteria suggested in [8]. First, the models should be well established in the literature and commonly used in practice. The models should also require a minimal degree of user intervention and they should represent different forecasting procedures.

For these models, the NOEMON creates 3 different classification problems, each one associated to the pairs of models: (RW, HL), (RW, AR) and (HL, AR). For each problem, the NOEMON uses a ML algorithm as classifier. At following, we described the most important points in the construction of these classifiers.

4.1 Time Series Features

We followed some criteria to define the time series features. First, we tried to choose features that can be reliably identified, avoiding any subjective analysis, such as visual inspection of plots. According to [12], judgmental identification is time consuming, requires expertise, and has a low degree of reliability. Second, we tried to use features that had already been used by other authors. Finally, we tried to use a manageable number of features. Based on these criteria, we defined the following features:
1. *Length of the time series (LEN)*: number of observations of the series.
2. *Basic Trend (BT)*: slope of the linear regression model. Large values of this feature suggest the existence of a global trend in the series.
3. *Ratio of Turning Points (TP)*: percentage of turning points in the series (100* number of turning points divided by the length of the series). A point X is a turning point of a series if $X_{t-1} < X_t > X_{t+1}$, or $X_{t-1} > X_t < X_{t+1}$. This feature attempts to measure the degree of oscillation in a series.
4. *First Coefficient of Autocorrelation (AC1)*: Large values of this feature suggest that the value of the series at a point influences the value at the next point.
5. *Type of the time series (TYPE)*: categorical variable that indicates the source of the data. It is represented by 6 categories: 'micro', 'macro', 'industry', 'finances', 'demographic' and 'others'.

4.2 Definition of the Training Examples

For each pair of models (X, Y), the NOEMON stores a set of training examples where each example has two parts: (1) the *features* describing a time series (see Section 4.1); and (2) the *class* attribute, which has one of the values 'X' or 'Y'. In order to assign the class attribute, we observed the forecasting performance of the models on a sample which was not used to estimate them. We used the first T observations of the series to estimate the models and the last H observations to test the models. We compared the Mean Absolute Error (MAE) obtained by each model on these h points, and assigned to the class attribute the model which obtained lower MAE.

4.3 Definition of the ML Technique

In our implementation of NOEMON, we decided to use MLP (Multi-Layer Perceptron) neural networks [11] as the classifiers. A reason for this choice is the good performance of neural networks when compared to other ML algorithms in several problems [13]. Another advantage of the MLP model is the reduced amount of time needed to generate an output to a given input pattern. This feature is crucial to NOEMON since it has to collect the outputs of (n 2) classifiers ($O(n^2)$) in order to generate a ranking. In the original implementation of NOEMON [10], the authors used the KNN algorithm, which requires less computation during training, but more computation to return an output [5]. Using an eager algorithm, such as the MLP neural network, the prototype can efficiently answer the new queries of the user.

In our prototype, we used a MLP with one hidden layer. The input layer represents the time series features (see Section 4.1). The first four features were normalized and the categorical feature 'TYPE' was represented by 5 binary attributes, each one associated to one of the categories 'micro', 'macro', 'industry', 'finances', and 'demographic'. In the case of the category 'others', all 5 input received the value 0. The output layer represents the class of the input pattern, i.e. the model associated to the time series.

5 Experiments and Results

We describe here the experiments that evaluated the performance of our prototype. In our experiments, we used the 645 yearly time series of the M3-Competition [14]. Although, these series only represent certain economic and demographic domains, they represent a convenient sample for expository purposes [2]. The series of the M3-Competition has been commonly used as a benchmarking sample to evaluate model selection strategies [2][3][8].

For each series, we estimated the three candidate models using the first observations and we used the last $H = 6$ observations to evaluate the performance of the models. This number was defined following the definitions of the M3-Competition [14]. In table 1, we present the class distributions for each classification problem.

Table 1. Class distributions.

	(RW, HL)	(RW, AR)	(HL, AR)
RW	281	344	–
HL	364	–	379
AR	–	301	266

The set of 645 examples was equally divided into training, validation and test sets, each one composed of 215 examples. The number of hidden nodes was defined by a trial-and-error procedure. We trained networks using 2, 4 and 6 hidden nodes (five times for each configuration), and then saved the trained network which obtained the lowest Sum of Squared Errors (SSE) in the validation set. The training process was performed by the standard Backpropagation algorithm [11], using 0.002 as the value of the learning rate.

5.1 Classification Performance

Here, we present the classification performance obtained by the MLPs in the previously defined classification problems. The MLPs were compared to the *default classifier*, which always associates a new example to the most frequent class (for example the class 'HL' in the problem (RW, HL)). Table 2 shows the classification test error obtained by the MLPs, the default test error and the gain obtained by using the MLPs. As we can see, for each pair of models, we obtained a gain in the classification error when the MLPs were used. These results showed us that the networks were able to learn relationships associating the time series features to the forecast models. We observed that the best test result (around 18%) was obtained in the problem (RW, AR), where the classes are more equally distributed.

Table 2. Classification performance of the MLPs

	(RW, HL)	(RW, AR)	(HL, AR)
% Test Error Default	89/215 (41.40%)	106/215 (49.30%)	86/215 (40.00%)
% Test Error NN	78/215 (36.28%)	66/215 (30.70%)	72/215 (33.49%)
Obtained Gain	5.12%	18.6%	6.51%

5.2 Quality of the Suggested Rankings

The quality of a suggested ranking for a series was evaluated by measuring the similarity to the ideal ranking, which represents the correct ordering of the models according to the MAE error. In our work, we used the Spearman's rank correlation coefficient [15] to measure the similarity between a suggested and the ideal rankings. Given a series i, we calculate the squared difference between the suggested and the ideal ranks for each model j (D^2_{ij}). Then we calculate the sum of these squared differences for all models. Finally, the Spearman coefficient is defined by the equation:

$$SRC_i = 1 - (6. \sum_j D^2_{ij})/(n^3 - n) \qquad (1)$$

where n is the number of models. The larger is the value of SRC_i, the greater is the similarity between the suggested and the ideal rankings for the series i.

In order to evaluate the rankings generated for series in the test set, we calculated the average of the Spearman's correlation for all these series.

$$SRC = (1/215) \sum_{i \in \text{test set}} SRC_i \qquad (2)$$

The NOEMON approach was compared to an aggregate ranking method, where the same ranking is suggested for all series. This ranking was defined by observing the number of series in which each candidate model obtained the best performance (see table 1). In our case, the aggregate ranking was [HL, RW, AR]. In table 3, we show the average Spearman coefficient for the rankings generated by NOEMON and for the aggregate ranking. As we can see, the rankings generated by the NOEMON method were in average more correlated to the ideal ranking.

Table 3. Average Spearman coefficient of the NOEMON and aggregate methods

Method	SRC
Aggregate	0.15
NOEMON	0.38

5.3 Forecasting Performance

We evaluated here the NOEMON approach as an individual selection rule. As we have previously said, the NOEMON selects the models that get the top position in the ranking. When more than one model is selected for a given series, the final forecasting is the simple average of the forecasts generated by the selected models. In our experiments, we compared the NOEMON method with three aggregate selection rules. The first one is merely to use RW as the forecast model for all series, the second is to use HL and the third is to use the AR model.

In order to compare the quality of the selection rules for all series in the test set, we considered the *Percentage Better (PB)* measure [2]. This measure associated to a selection method i is defined as follows:

$$PB_i = 100 * (1/m) \sum_{j \in \text{test set}} \sum_{t=T+1}^{T+6} \delta_{ijt} \quad (3)$$

where,

$$\delta_{ijt} = 1 \quad \text{se } |e_{Rjt}| < |e_{ijt}|$$
$$0 \quad \text{otherwise.}$$

In the above definition, R represents a reference rule which serves as a basis for comparison. The e_{ijt} is the one-step-ahead error obtained by the method i in the series j at time t, and m is the number of times in which $|e_{Rjt}| \neq |e_{ijt}|$. Hence, PB_i indicates in percentage terms, the number of times the error obtained by the reference method R was lower than the error obtained using the rule i, for all series and all points of test. Values greater than 50 for PB_i, indicates that the models selected by the rule i are in average, more accurate than the models suggested by the reference rule R.

In table 4, we show the PB estimates of the NOEMON method for the 215 series of test, using the three aggregate rules as the reference methods. As we can see, for all aggregate rules the PB measure was lower than 50%. Although the PB measure was not significantly low for the rule HL, it was nevertheless lower than 50%. These results indicate that the individual rule provided by the NOEMON method was in general more accurate than the aggregate rules.

Table 4. Comparative forecasting performance measured by PB

Aggregate Method	PB
RW	36.0
HL	47.9
AR	37.3

6 Conclusion

In this work, we proposed the use of the NOEMON approach to rank and select time series models. In order to evaluate the proposed solution, we implemented a prototype to select between three widespread models. In our prototype, we used MLP neural networks as the classifiers of NOEMON. In our experiments, the trained MLPs obtained a good classification performance for all the classification problems created by the prototype. We also observed that the rankings generated by NOEMON were well correlated to the ideal rankings, and the forecasting accuracy of the selected models was improved when the NOEMON approach was used. As future work we intend to improve the performance of this prototype by augmenting the set of time series features and by performing feature selection for each pair of models.

References

1. Montgomery, D. C., Johnson, L. A. and Gardiner, J. S.: Forecasting & Time Series Analysis. McGraw Hill, New York (1990)
2. Shah, C.: Model Selection in Univariate Time Series Forecasting Using Discriminant Analysis. International Journal of Forecasting, 13 (1997) 489–500
3. Collopy, F. and Armstrong, J.S.: Rule-based Forecasting: Development and Validation of an Expert Systems Approach to Combining Time Series Extrapolations. Management Science, 38(10) (1992) 1394–1414
4. Arinze, B., Kim, S-L. and Anandarajan M.: Combining and Selecting Forecasting Models Using Rule Based Induction. Computers & Operations Research, 24(5) (1997) 423–433
5. Mitchel, T.: Machine Learning, MacGraw Hill, New York (1997)
6. Arinze, B.: Selecting Appropriate Forecasting Models Using Rule Induction. Omega-International Journal of Management Science, 22(6) (1994) 647–658
7. Chu C-H, Widjaja D: Neural Network System for Forecasting Method Selection. Decision Support Systems, 12(1) (1994) 13–24
8. Venkatachalan, A. R. and Sohl, J. E.: An Intelligent Model Selection and Forecasting System. Journal of Forecasting, 18 (1999) 167–180
9. Prudêncio, R. B. C. and Ludermir, T. B.: Selection of Models for Time Series Prediction via Meta-Learning. Proceedings of the 2th International Conference on Hybrid Intelligent Systems (HIS' 02), Santiago, Chile, IOS Press (2002) 74–83
10. Kalousis A. and Theoharis, T.: NOEMON: Design, Implementation and Performance Results of an Intelligent Assistant for Classifier Selection. Intelligent Data Analysis, 3(5) (1999) 319–337
11. Rumelhart, D. E., Hinton, G. E., Williams, R. J.: Learning Representations by Backpropagation Errors. Nature, 323 (1986) 533–536
12. Adya M., Collopy. F., Armstrong, J.S. and Kennedy, M.: Automatic Identification of Time Series Features for Rule-Based Forecasting. Int. Jour. of Forecasting, 17(2) (2001) 143–157
13. Shavlik, J. W., Mooney, R.J. and Towell, G.G.: Symbolic and Neural Learning Algorithms: An Experimental Comparison. Machine Learning, 6(2) (1991) 111–143
14. Makridakis S., Hibon M.: The M3-Competition: Results, Conclusions and Implications. International Journal of Forecasting, 16(4) (2000) 451–476
15. Soares, C. and Brazdil, P.: Zoomed Ranking: Selection of Classification Algorithms Based on Relevant Performance Information. Principles of Data Mining and Knowledge Discovery: 4th European Conference (PKDD-2000), Springer-Verlag, (2000) 126–135

Optimization of the Deflection Basin by Genetic Algorithm and Neural Network Approach

Serdal Terzi[1], Mehmet Saltan[2], and Tulay Yildirim[3]

[1] Technical Education Faculty, Suleyman Demirel University, Isparta 32260, Turkey
sterzi@tef.sdu.edu.tr
[2] Faculty of Engineering-Architecture, Suleyman Demirel University, Isparta 32260, Turkey
msaltan@mmf.sdu.edu.tr
[3] Faculty of Electric-Electronics Eng., Yildiz Technical University, Istanbul 34349, Turkey
tulay@yildiz.edu.tr

Abstract. This paper introduces a new concept of integrating artificial neural networks (ANN) and genetic algorithms (GA) in modeling the deflection basins measured on the flexible pavements. Backcalculating pavement layer moduli are well-accepted procedures for the evaluation of the structural capacity of pavements. The ultimate aim of the backcalculation process from Nondestructive Testing (NDT) results is to estimate the pavement material properties. Using backcalculation analysis, in-situ material properties can be backcalculated from the measured field data through appropriate analysis techniques. In order to backcalculate reliable moduli, deflection basin must be realistically modeled. In this work, ANN was used to model the deflection basin characteristics and GA as an optimization tool. Experimental deflection data groups from NDT are used to show the capability of the ANN and GA approach in modeling the deflection bowl. This approach can be easily and realistically performed to solve the optimization problems which do not have a formulation or function about the solution.

1 Introduction

Nondestructive Testing (NDT) and backcalculating pavement layer moduli are well-accepted procedures for the evaluation of the structural capacity of pavements [1]. NDT enables the use of a mechanistic approach for pavement design and rehabilitation because in-situ material properties can be backcalculated from the measured field data through appropriate analysis techniques [2]. In order to backcalculate reliable moduli, it is essential to accomplish several deflection tests at different locations along the highway sections having the same layer thicknesses [1]. However, this is not enough to backcalculate pavement layer moduli. If and only if deflection basin is realistically modeled, elastic pavement layer moduli obtained from backcalculation results will reflect actual behavior. In deflection methods, commercially available devices are the Dynaflect, Road Rater and Falling Weight Deflectometer (FWD). The most common property found by NDT is the elastic modulus of each pavement layer.

In recent years, one of the most important and promising research field has been "Heuristics from Nature", an area utilizing some analogies with natural or social systems and using them to derive non-deterministic heuristic methods and to obtain very good results. Artificial Neural Networks (ANN) and Genetic Algorithms (GA) are among the heuristic methods [3].

The use of ANN is proliferating with high rate in simulation. On the other hand, GAs belong to a class of probabilistic search methods that strike excellent balance between exploration and exploitation of the search space. They are different from random algorithms, as they combine elements of directed and stochastic search methods. They have been successfully applied to optimization problems, transportation problems, etc. [4].

The GA and ANN are especially appropriate to tackle the deflection basin modeling problems. Their advantages can be made completely use of, i.e. the ability of ANN to learn complex nonlinear relationships, and that of GA to find the optimum solutions.

2 Backcalculation of Pavement Layer Moduli

Highway and transportation agencies have an increased responsibility for maintenance, rehabilitation on management of highways, particularly with regard to asphaltic concrete pavements. Efficient and economical methods are required to determine the structural properties of existing pavements realistically from non-destructive test data. This kind of evaluation is one of the most efficient and economical methods and has been increasingly used in the pavement engineering community. Pavement structural properties may be generally stated in terms of resilient modulus which is a key element in mechanistic pavement analysis and evaluation procedures.

Backcalculation generally refers to an iterative procedure whereby the layer properties of the pavement model are adjusted until the computed deflections under a given load agree with the corresponding measured values. NDT and backcalculating pavement layer moduli are well-accepted procedures for the evaluating of the structural capacity of pavements. NDT is meant to produce numerous deflection bowls. The ultimate aim of the backcalculation process from NDT results is to estimate the pavement material properties. The backcalculation procedure is to find the set of parameters corresponding to the best fit of the measured deflection bowls. Even if the deflections are measured accurately, backcalculation process does not give accurate results unless the backcalculation procedure is realistic.

FWD delivers a load to a pavement surface; then deflections are measured at several points of observation around the load. If layer elastic moduli are found so that the analytic deflections nearly coincide with measured deflections, the set of elastic moduli may be considered to represent average elastic moduli of real pavement structure. So far, Least Squares Method (LSM) was used for modeling both computed and measured deflection basin in backcalculation procedures. However, it can be said that LSM does not accurately model the deflection bowl. If the deflection basin is modeled as realistic as possible, then pavement layer moduli values obtained from backcalculation will give more realistic results. More precision is needed from the backcalculation procedures, and more realistic models will reduce the size of systematic errors. This will make it possible to predict the remaining life of a pavement realistically in the field immediately after it has been tested. For this reason, in this work, deflection basin was modeled using ANN and GA technique as a realistic approach.

3 FWD Testing Device

In order to simulate the truck loading on the pavement, a circular plate is dropped on the pavement from a certain height. The height is adjusted according to the desired load level. Underneath the circular plate a rubber pad is mounted to prevent the shock loading. Seven geophones are generally mounted on the trailer (the number of geophones can change). When the vertical load is applied on the pavement, the geophones collects the data in a byte form. Using the calibration factors, the bytes can be converted to the real deflections.

The FWD is a trailer mounted device which applies a load to the pavement surface through a circular plate. FWD testing has been established world-wide as one of the most effective tools for measuring deflections for pavement evaluation purposes [5]. Benkelman beam and Dynaflect which are other mostly used devices in the developing countries only give the information about underneath the circular plate whereas the FWD gives the information about other six points which are away from the circular plate. Hence, the effect of the wheel loading can also be seen in other points when FWD is used.

There are many types of FWDs which can apply the same loading. The frequencies of loading change between 0.025 and 0.030 sec; the applied loads vary between 6.7-156 kN. The loads are generally applied in a sinusoidal form [6], [7], [8]. The loading time of 0.030 sec represents the wheel loading moving at a speed of 30 km/h and $\pm$ 0.023 mm deviations can be seen from the FWD measurements [9]. A crew can be carried out 200-300 FWD measurements in a day.

4 Integration of GA and ANN

4.1 The Optimization Plan

Fig 1. gives a short draft of the optimization plan. Firstly, the identification of the system input variables and their constraints are defined. The system input variables consist of control variables and uncontrolled variables. The control variables are the targets (layer thickness, elastic moduli, etc.) that the system is to respond for achieving a fitness function, such as minimized layer thickness, maximized elastic moduli, etc. Uncontrolled variables are those measurable quantities (deflection values, etc.) that may not be controlled by the system, but instead may affect the system performance. The constraints of the input variables define the boundaries of the search space. They should be set based on real life operating experience and knowledge about the system and component features/characteristics.

The development of the GA population of the input variables is the next step for use in the probabilistic-based optimum search. This is followed by the prediction of the system outputs based on an ANN model of the system. For the layer thickness and/or the elastic moduli, the fitness function usually addresses deflection values. While the fitness requirements are being updated from time to time, a new generation of the population will be produced and gone through the same evaluation process. This process continues until the maximum number of generations has been reached. The final population of the generation groups is designed as the "winner" and rewarded as the final generation of lowest layer thickness or highest elastic moduli (final fitness) [8].

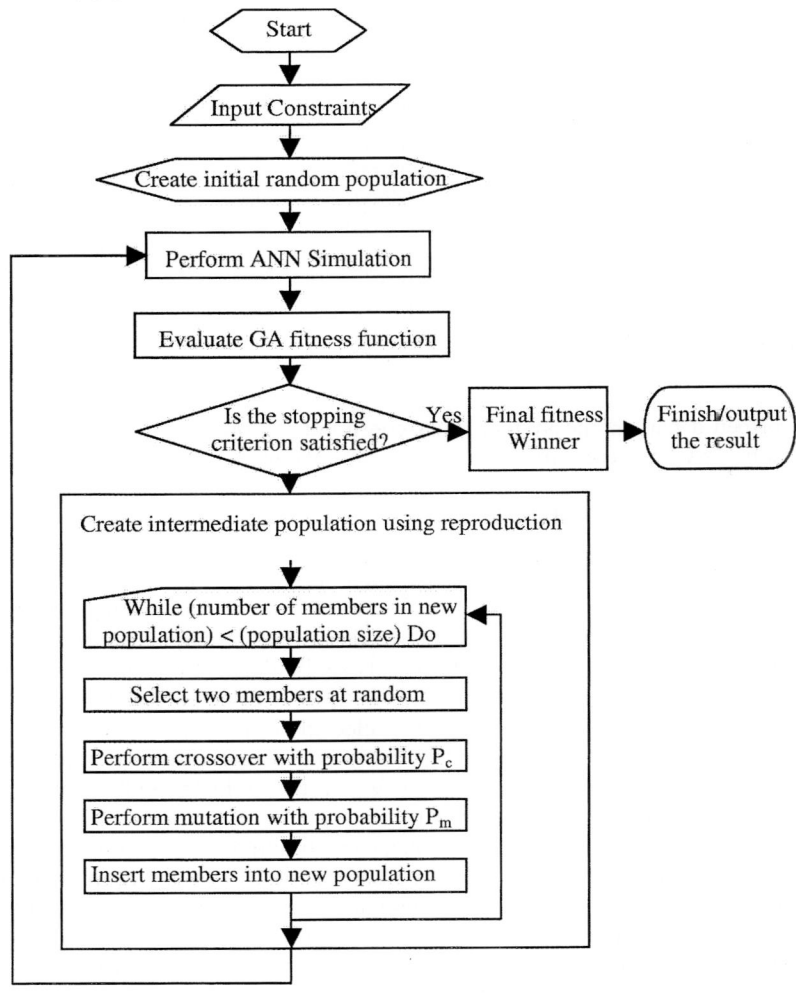

Fig. 1. Optimization process based on GA and ANN [9]

5 A Case Study

A deflection measurement system with deflection values, layer thickness and elastic moduli was studied. In the system model, there were seven inputs representing the seven deflection points. The outputs were two variables representing layer thickness and elastic moduli.

The operation of deflection basins have to be limited to certain ranges of operating parameters. These boundaries are showed in Table 1. Relationship between deflection basins are:

$$x_1 > x_2 > x_3 > x_4 > x_5 > x_6 > x_7 \tag{1}$$

where x are deflection basin points.

Table 1. Relationship between deflection basins

Deflection Basin Point	Minimum	Maximum
1	0.07000	0.11500
2	0.05000	0.06500
3	0.03000	0.04000
4	0.02000	0.02400
5	0.01575	0.01650
6	0.01195	0.01275
7	0.00990	0.01047

These formed a part of the system input constraints in the optimum search. In real applications, however, there may be different limit values.

5.1 ANN System Representation

The ANN modeling consists of two steps: First step is to train the network; second step is to test the network with data, which were not used in training step [10]. During the training stage the network uses the inductive-learning principle to learn from a set of examples called the training set [11]. In this study, data set includes 114 samples. For training set, 95 samples (approximately 80 %) were selected and the test set were formed by 19 samples (approximately 20 %) selected as randomly on data set.

Logarithmic sigmoid transfer function was used as the activation function for hidden layers and output layers. The values of the training and test data were normalized to within the range from 0 to 1.

Levenberg-Marquardt Back-propagation training was repeatedly applied until the evaluation standard was reached. The configuration 7-4-2 appeared to be most optimal topology [12]. The configuration is shown in Fig 2. The decrease in mean square error (MSE) which shows the performance with epoch during the training process is shown in Fig 2. The regression curves which are symbolized as R^2 of individual output variables are shown in Fig 3.

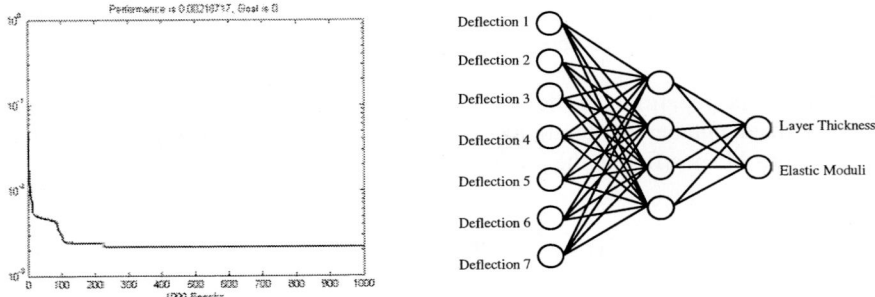

Fig. 2. ANN model of the deflection basins and training results based on 7-4-2 configuration

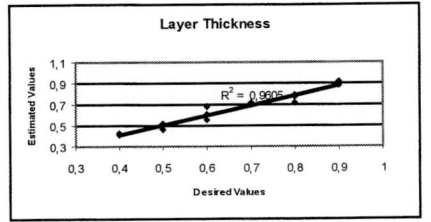 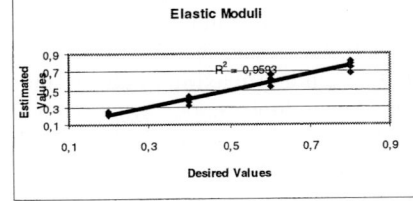

Fig. 3. The regression curves of individual output variables

5.2 Searching by Genetic Algorithm

The flow chart in Fig 1. drafts the key features of the GA evolution program in use. The program can be summarized in four main steps:

1. Step 1: To initialize a population. The size of populations was 10, which is a trade-off between an efficient searching process and avoidance of pre-mature convergence. The initial population was chosen randomly within the assigned input constraints. Binary codes were used to code the non-binary parameters. The number of bits in the binary string was set to 16 for each of the seven input variables, hence came up with 20 bit chromosomes. This is adequate judging from required precision in defining the numerical values of each input variable.
2. Step 2 To evaluate each chromosome by applying the ANN model and the cost function to the decoded sequences of the variables. The results were obtained for entire population. They were compared to give the ranked fitness values.
3. Step 3: To use the three genetic operators to alter the composition of the offspring in the next generation. These included the following.
    3.1. *Selection operator:* Based on the ranked fitness values, a selection of a new population was made with respect to the probability distribution, i.e. the Roulette-Wheel method.
    3.2. *Crossover operator:* Recombination to the individuals in the new population was applied. The single-point crossover index was randomly selected.
    3.3. *Mutation operator:* Performed on a bit-by-bit basis. The probability of mutate was taken of four times on each loop.

The above values of P_c, perform crossover with probability, and P_m, perform mutation with probability, were determined by working experience with the problem in hand.

4. Step 4. Cyclic repetition of the above steps 2 and 3. The algorithm was stopped after a fixed number of iterations. This depended on the maximum number of generations M specified in the program. In our case, M=200.

6 Results of Optimization

Two optimal control cases were studied for a layer thickness and an elastic moduli.
   Case 1: Minimization of layer thickness
   Case 2: Maximization of elastic moduli
   Separate solutions were performed for each case using steps mentioned above. It was found at the end of the solutions that minimum layer thickness value was 4.08 cm and maximum elastic modulus value was 4532 MPa. Deflection basins giving lower limit, upper limit and minimum layer thickness and maximum elastic moduli values are shown in Fig. 4. While minimum layer thicknesses are near to upper limits, maximum elastic moduli values are close to lower limits. The reason of this can be explained that genetic algorithms runs with random working principle.

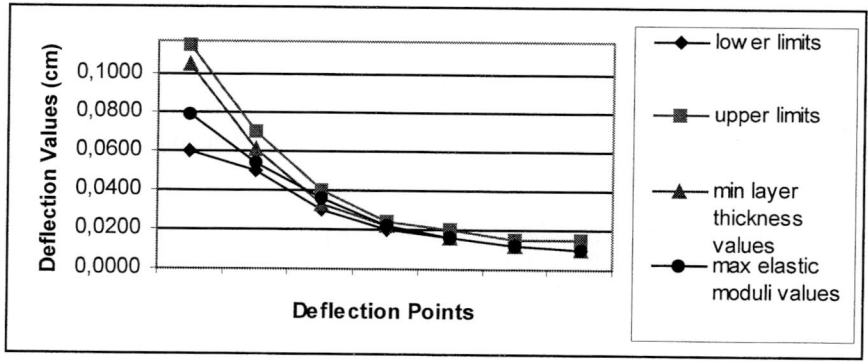

Fig 4. Optimum deflection values and limits

7 Conclusions

Modeling the deflection basin is very important in backcalculating flexible pavement layer moduli. In this work, a model for the deflection basins measured on the flexible pavements has been presented. The ANN and GA approach was applied to model deflection basin. Both ANN and GA are especially appropriate for investigating the complex deflection basin form in evaluating the structural capacity of the flexible pavements, taking the ability of ANN to learn complex nonlinear pavement behavior, and that of GA to search for optimum solution. A concept of integrating these two techniques has been introduced through an example on deflection basins measured on the surface of a flexible pavement.

This new methodology can help the highway agency for estimating deflection basin in backcalculation process of flexible pavement layer moduli.

Some models formed in solution of a number of problems are based on assumptions and cannot reflect the reality. Solutions of the optimization problems which do not have a formulation or function about the solution can be easily and realistically performed using approach presented here.

References

1. Uzan, J., Lytton, R.L., Germann, F.P.: General procedure for backcalculating layer moduli. Nondestructive testing of pavements and backcalculation of moduli, ASTM STP 1026, USA (1989) 217–228
2. Kang, Y.W.: Multi-frequency backcalculation of pavement-layer moduli, Journal of Transportation Engineering, ASCE, Vol.124.no.1, USA (1998) 73–81
3. Colorni, A., Dorigo, F., Maffioli, F., Maniezzo, V., Righini, G., Trubian, M.: Heuristics from nature for hard combinatorial optimization problems. Int. Trans. In Oper. Res., 3, 1, pag. 1–21
4. Chow, T. T., Zhang, G. Q., Lin, Z. L. and Song, C. L.: Global optimization of absorption chiller system by genetic algorithm and neural network, Energy and Buildings, Volume 34, USA (2002) 103–109
5. Saltan, M.: Modeling deflection basin using neuro-fuzzy in backcalculating flexible pavement layer moduli, Pakistan Journal of Information and Technology Vol.1 No.2, Pakistan (2002) 180–187
6. Stolle, D.F.E.: Modelling of dynamic response of pavements to impact loading. Computers and Geotechnics, Vol.11 n.1 (1991) 83–94
7. Stolle, D.F.E., Jung, F.W.: Estimate of average subgrade moduli using the FWD. Canadian Geotechnical Conference, Canada (1991) 5111–5118
8. Hossain, M., Zaniewski, J., Rajan, S.: Estimation of pavement layer moduli using nonlinear optimization technique. Journal of Transportation Engineering, ASCE, Vol.120, no.3, USA (1994) 376–393
9. Shaat, A.A., Kamal, M.A.: The effective use of Deflectograph testing in quantifying pavement strength and seasonal variations. PTRC Summer Annual Meeting, USA (1991)
10. Kaseko, M.S., Lo, Z-P. and Ritchie, S.G.: Comparison of traditional and neural classifiers for pavement-crack detection. Journal of Transportation Engineering, Volume 120, No 4, USA (1994) 552–569
11. Lingras, P.: Classifying highways: hierarchical grouping versus kohonen neural networks. Journal of Transportation Engineering, Volume 121, No 4, USA (1995) 364–368
12. Demuth, H., Beale, M.: Neural Network Toolbox, User Guide, Version 4. The MathWorks, Inc. (2001)

Inversion of a Neural Network via Interval Arithmetic for Rule Extraction

Carlos Hernández-Espinosa, Mercedes Fernández-Redondo, and
Mamen Ortiz-Gómez

Universidad Jaume I, Campus de Riu Sec, D. de Ingeniería y Ciencia de los Computadores,
12071 Castellón, Spain. espinosa@icc.uji.es

Abstract. In this paper we propose a new algorithm for rule extraction from a trained Multilayer Feedforward network. The algorithm is based on an interval arithmetic network inversion for particular target outputs. The types of rules extracted are N-dimensional intervals in the input space. We have performed experiments with four databases and the results are very interesting. One rule extracted by the algorithm can cover 86% of the neural network output and in other cases 64 rules cover 100% of the neural network output.

1 Introduction

Neural networks have been applied to a great number of applications and one of the most widely used neural network paradigms is Multilayer Feedforward. However, in same applications it is not only sufficient a correct classification of an input, it is also necessary an explanation of the classification [1]. One example is the medical diagnosis field, in this case, we need to provide a correct classification of the symptoms (the disease) and an explanation of the classification for the doctor. The intelligent systems in this field are conceived as an aid for the doctor and not as a substitution of the doctor. Therefore, they should provide an explanation capability.

A fundamental problem of neural networks is that the information they encode can not be easily understood by humans, for example, it is difficult to give an explanation on how they solve a particular problem.

One of the methods to solve this problem is rule extraction from a trained neural network. With this method, we tray to convert the information contained in a neural network in a set of rules that can be understood by a person.

There are many algorithm for rule extraction [2–8]. They differ in the type of rules extracted and many other characteristics. However, they lack from a common problem, the computational cost of the extraction of rules increases exponentially with the number of parameters in the neural network (weights or neurons). So, it is usually of crucial importance the application of pruning algorithms to reduce the size of the network previously to the application of the rule extraction method.

In this paper, we propose a new algorithm for rule extraction from a trained Multilayer Feedforward network based on interval arithmetic. The algorithm is based in a network inversion for a particular target using the interval arithmetic properties. The type of rules extracted are N-dimensional intervals in the input space.

This new algorithm has the problem of an exponential computational cost increase with the number of inputs in the network, but other parameters like the number of weights or hidden units does not affect significantly the computational cost.

2 Theory

This section is divided in four subsection. The first one reviews the basic properties of interval arithmetic. The second explains how to calculate the output of a neural network for an interval input. Subsection three describes the interval arithmetic inversion algorithm, and finally in the fourth we explain the rule extraction algorithm.

2.1 Interval Arithmetic Basis

First, we will review the basic operations of interval arithmetic used in this paper. They are sum of intervals, multiplication of an interval by a number and the exponential [9].

The sum of two intervals is an interval whose upper limit is the sum of the upper limits of the intervals and whose lower limit is the sum of the lower limits of the intervals. See equation 1.

$$A + B = [a^L, a^U] + [b^L, b^U] = [a^L + b^L, a^U + b^U] . \qquad (1)$$

Where the superscripts L and U denote the lower and upper limits of the interval.

The second property is the product of a real number by an interval. In this case the final interval depends on the sign of the real number. See equation 2.

$$m \cdot A = m \cdot [a^L, a^U] = \begin{cases} [m \cdot a^L, m \cdot a^U] & \text{if } m \geq 0 \\ [m \cdot a^U, m \cdot a^L] & \text{if } m < 0 \end{cases} . \qquad (2)$$

Another interesting property is the exponential function of an interval. It is interesting because it is often used in the transfer function of a neural network.

Since the exponential function is monotonically increasing the result is an interval whose lower limit is the exponential of the lower limit and whose upper limit is the exponential of the upper limit. See equation 3.

$$\exp(A) = \exp([a^L, a^U]) = [\exp(a^L), \exp(a^U)] . \qquad (3)$$

2.2 Interval Output of Multilayer Feedforward for an Input Interval

With these three basic properties, we can calculate the output of the usual Multilayer Feedforward for an input interval, i.e., in the case we use intervals as the inputs of the neural network.

In this situation the output of the neural network becomes an N-dimensional interval where N is the number of output units.

Also, all the intermediate values of the neural network, like the output of the hidden units, becomes intervals.

The interval outputs of the hidden units can be calculated with equation 4.

$$H_{P,j} = [H_{P,j}^L, H_{P,j}^U] = f(Net_{P,j}) = f([net_{P,j}^L, net_{P,j}^U]) = [f(net_{P,j}^L), f(net_{P,j}^U)] \quad (4)$$

$$\text{where } Net_{P,j} = \sum_{i=1}^{Ninputs} w_{j,i} \cdot I_{P,i} + \theta_j \quad Net_{P,i} = [net_{P,j}^L, net_{P,j}^U]$$

$$\text{where } net_{P,j}^L = \sum_{i=1, w_{j,i} \geq 0}^{Ninputs} w_{j,i} \cdot I_{P,i}^L + \sum_{i=1, w_{j,i} < 0}^{Ninputs} w_{j,i} \cdot I_{P,i}^U + \theta_j$$

$$net_{P,j}^U = \sum_{i=1, w_{j,i} \geq 0}^{Ninputs} w_{j,i} \cdot I_{P,i}^U + \sum_{i=1, w_{j,i} < 0}^{Ninputs} w_{j,i} \cdot I_{P,i}^L + \theta_j$$

Where f is the standard sigmoid function, $I_{P,j} = [I_{P,j}^L, I_{P,j}^U]$ the input interval and $H_{P,j} = [H_{P,j}^L, H_{P,j}^U]$ the output intervals of the hidden units.

In equation 4, we have to distinguish between positive and negative weights because of the same distinction in the property of multiplication of a real number by an interval.

Analogously for the interval outputs of the neural network we have the equation 5.

$$O_{p,k} = [O_{P,k}^L, O_{P,k}^U] = f(Net_{P,k}) = f([net_{P,k}^L, net_{P,k}^U]) \quad (5)$$

$$\text{where } net_{P,k}^L = \sum_{j=1, w_{k,j} \geq 0}^{Nhidden} w_{k,j} \cdot H_{P,j}^L + \sum_{j=1, w_{k,j} < 0}^{Nhidden} w_{k,j} \cdot H_{P,j}^U + \xi_k$$

$$\text{and } net_{P,k}^U = \sum_{j=1, w_{k,j} \geq 0}^{Nhidden} w_{k,j} \cdot H_{P,j}^U + \sum_{j=1, w_{k,j} < 0}^{Nhidden} w_{k,j} \cdot H_{P,j}^L + \xi_k$$

Where f is the standard sigmoidal function and $O_{P,k} = [O_{P,k}^L, O_{P,k}^U]$ is the interval output of the neural network.

With these equations we can calculate the transformation of an interval in the inputs into an interval at the outputs across the neural network structure.

2.3 Network Interval Arithmetic Inversion

The aim of a neural network inversion algorithm is to fix a particular output of the network and obtain an input or set of inputs whose output is the previously fixed output.

In the case of interval arithmetic inversion the objective is the same, but in this case the fixed output is an interval and obviously the obtained input will be an interval.

The algorithm for interval arithmetic inversion is basically the same algorithm of neural network inversion [10], but in this case, the target will be an interval vector and the error function will be the one of equation 6.

$$E_p = \frac{1}{4} \cdot \sum_{k=1}^{Noutput} \left\{ \left(t_{p,k}^U - o_{p,k}^U\right) + \left(t_{p,k}^L - o_{p,k}^L\right) \right\}. \tag{6}$$

After we fix an interval output, the inversion is accomplished by selecting and initial interval vector as the initial input $\{[i_1^L(0), i_1^U(0)], [i_2^L(0), i_2^U(0)], \ldots, [i_N^L(0), i_N^U(0)]\}$ and applying an iterative gradient descent algorithm similar to Backpropagation that will minimize the error value by changing the initial input. The equations are basically in 7.

The process is iterative, we calculate the interval output of the neural network for the initial interval input. After that, we apply equations 7 and we obtain a new input interval. With this new input interval we can calculate again the output interval and iterate in this way the process.

$$i_{P,k}^L(n) = i_{P,k}^L(-1) - \eta \frac{\partial Error}{\partial i_{P,k}^L} \quad ; \quad i_{P,k}^U(n) = i_{P,k}^U(n-1) - \eta \frac{\partial Error}{\partial i_{P,k}^U} \tag{7}$$

The values of the partial derivates of equation 7 are in equation 8 and 9:

$$\frac{\partial Error}{\partial i_{P,k}^L} = -\frac{1}{2} \left\{ \sum_{k=1}^{Noutput} \left(t_{P,k}^L - o_{P,k}^L\right) o_{P,k}^L (1-o_{P,k}^L) \cdot \left\{ \sum_{i}^{w_{k,i} \geq 0, w_{i,l} \geq 0} w_{k,i} \cdot H_{P,i}^L \cdot (1-H_{P,i}^L) \cdot w_{i,l} + \sum_{i}^{w_{k,i}<0, w_{i,l}<0} w_{k,i} \cdot H_{P,i}^U \cdot (1-H_{P,i}^U) \cdot w_{i,l} \right\} + \sum_{k=1}^{Noutput} (t_{P,k}^U - o_{P,k}^U) \cdot o_{P,k}^U \cdot (1-o_{P,k}^U) \cdot \left\{ \sum_{i}^{w_{k,i} \geq 0, w_{i,l}<0} w_{k,i} \cdot H_{P,i}^U \cdot (1-H_{P,i}^U) \cdot w_{i,l} + \sum_{i}^{w_{k,i}<0, w_{i,l} \geq 0} w_{k,i} \cdot H_{P,i}^L \cdot (1-H_{P,i}^L) \cdot w_{i,l} \right\} \right\}. \tag{8}$$

$$\frac{\partial Error}{\partial i_{P,k}^U} = -\frac{1}{2} \left\{ \sum_{k=1}^{Noutput} \left(t_{P,k}^L - o_{P,k}^L\right) o_{P,k}^L (1-o_{P,k}^L) \cdot \left\{ \sum_{i}^{w_{k,i} \geq 0, w_{i,l}<0} w_{k,i} \cdot H_{P,i}^L \cdot (1-H_{P,i}^L) \cdot w_{i,l} + \sum_{i}^{w_{z,i}<0, w_{i,l} \geq 0} w_{k,i} \cdot H_{P,i}^U \cdot (1-H_{P,i}^U) \cdot w_{i,l} \right\} + \sum_{k=1}^{Noutput} (t_{P,k}^U - o_{P,k}^U) \cdot o_{P,k}^U \cdot (1-o_{P,k}^U) \cdot \left\{ \sum_{i}^{w_{k,i} \geq 0, w_{i,l} \geq 0} w_{k,i} \cdot H_{P,i}^U \cdot (1-H_{P,i}^U) \cdot w_{i,l} + \sum_{i}^{w_{k,i}<0, w_{i,l}<0} w_{k,i} \cdot H_{P,i}^L \cdot (1-H_{P,i}^L) \cdot w_{i,l} \right\} \right\}. \tag{9}$$

2.4 Rule Extraction Algorithm

The type of rules we want to obtain are N-dimensional intervals in the input space like the following:

If $x_1 \subset [a^L_1, a^U_1]$, $x_2 \subset [a^L_2, a^U_2]$, ..., $x_N \subset [a^L_N, a^U_N]$ then $\{x_1, x_2, ..., x_N\} \in$ Class K.

If the input is contained in the N-dimensional interval $[a^L_i, a^U_i]$ the output is a particular class (class K in the example).

We should obtain the limits of the intervals a_i, b_i. They limit a N-dimensional interval in the input space and the whole N-dimensional interval has to be included in a classification class. An interval neural network inversion is used to get the intervals.

In order to obtain a rule, first, we will select a target value of the following type for one classification class (for example, class number 2): $\{[0,0.5]_{Class1}, [0.5,1.0]_{Class2}, [0,0.5]_{Class3}, ..., [0,0.5]_{ClassN}\}$. An output vector inside the above interval suppose a correct classification inside the class number 2 because neuron number 2 is activated and the rest neurons are not.

Second, we will apply the inversion algorithm for the target. We expect that the initial input interval will evolve to give an interval whose output is inside the target interval selected, in this case, the final input interval will correspond to a valid rule.

We have performed simulations with three types of initial intervals in several two dimensional examples. And the conclusion is that if the initial interval is a point correctly classified by the target interval, during the inversion, the point will expand to an interval, the final output limits of the interval input will generally touch the borders of the classification class and the final results will normally correspond to a valid rule. We can see several examples in Fig. 1.

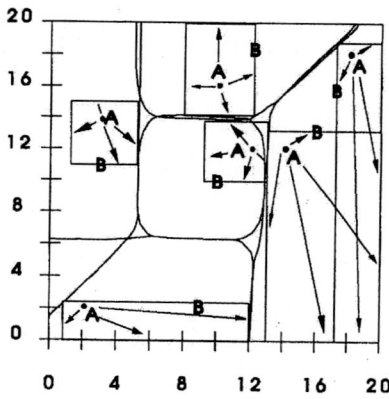

Fig. 1. Example of point expansion by interval arithmetic inversion. A is the initial point, B is the final interval

It is obvious that we can exploit this behavior of this type of initial intervals in order to propose an algorithm which can convert the information contained in the neural network into rules. The algorithm can be resumed as follows:

a) Select an initial point and calculate the output of the neural network for this input.
b) Select a target of the type described above, this target should agree with the classification class of the output of the neural network for the initial point.
c) Apply the inversion algorithm and extract a rule.

d) Select a new point which is not included in the rules we have obtained before, and calculate the output of the neural network for this new point.
e) Select a target which agrees with the output of the neural network for this new point.
f) Apply the inversion algorithm and extract a new rule.
g) If we have not cover the whole input space go to step d).

In order to test whether we have covered the input space and select a new initial point we can scan the input space with equally spaced points and test if the points are included in the rules. The space between the points will also influence the final accuracy of the set of rules.

The problem of this scanning method is that its yields a computational complexity increase with the increase of the number of inputs and it can not be used with a high number of inputs. The methods of input or feature selection will play an important role to apply this algorithm [11].

There are other specific characteristics of this method. A rule will always have an output interval inside the target described above, so there will not be incorrect classification of points by the rule. Also another consequence is that there will not be overlapping among rules of different classes. And finally, the set of rules will not usually cover the total space of the neural network input, for example, the output {0.1, 0.8, 0.7} is not in the initial target intervals because two output units are activated and if an input has this output it will not be covered. We can say that the points where the classification of the neural network is not clear are not covered by the rules.

3 Experimental Results

We have tested the neural network rule extraction algorithm with four database from the UCI repository of machine learning databases. The databases are Balance Scale (BALANCE),), Liver Disorders (BUPA) and two of the Monk's Problems (MONK1 and MONK 2). We have selected this databases because the input dimensionality is at most six (http://www.ics.uci.edu/~mlearn/MLRepository.html).

We have applied the rule extraction algorithm to ten networks for each database which were trained with different random initialization of weights and different partition of data among training, cross-validation and test.

In a rule extraction algorithm of this type we think that the two most important criterion for the results are the fidelity of the rules and the number of rules extracted. By fidelity of rules, we should understand how the results reproduced the behavior of the neural network.

In table 1 we have the results for the four databases.

The second column (Prec. Space) is the distance in the input space between the points generated to construct the rules. A lower number means a higher number of points and therefore a higher number of rules.

We have randomly generate 10.000 point inside the input space with the condition that only one output unit is activated. The third column (Percentage) is the mean percentage of point covered by the rules and the fourth column (Not Cover) the mean percentage of points which were not cover for the ten networks of each database.

Columns five and six are two mean percentages, in this case we have generated randomly 10.000 points without restriction inside the input space. The fifth column (Total Percentage) is the mean percentage of points cover by the rules and the sixth column (Total Not Cover) is the mean percentage of points not covered by the rules.

The seventh column (Number of Rules, Nrule) is the mean number of rules generated by the algorithm for the ten networks of each database. Column number eight is the minimum number of rules generated for a network and column number nine is the percentage of covering of this minimum number of rules.

Table 1. Results of the rule extraction algorithm

Database	Prec. Space	Percentage	Not Cover	Total Percentage	Total Not Cover	Number of Rules (Nrule).	Nrule minimum	Percentage Nrule minimum
BALANCE	0.2	74.15	25.84	65.57	34.42	331.3	323	74.96
BALANCE	0.13	83.14	16.86	73.75	26.25	745.9	671	82.04
BUPA	0.2	92.59	7.41	92.59	7.41	6357.1	64	100
BUPA	0.13	85.11	14.89	85.11	14.89	19289.5	1	89.27
MONK1	0.2	81.10	18.90	81.10	18.90	8899.5	5036	82.44
MONK1	0.13	81.31	18.69	81.31	18.69	47211.4	35842	82.56
MONK2	0.2	93.21	6.79	93.21	6.79	7288	64	100
MONK2	0.13	83.16	16.84	82.69	17.31	12943.1	1	87.57

We can see that, in general, the number of rules increases with the precision of the scanning space as it was expected. We can see very interesting results in the minimum number of rules, for example for the databases BUPA and MONK2 sixty four rules are enough to completely cover the input space. Also, in BUPA and MONK2 one rule cover more that 85% of the input space.

As we commented before, the rules will only cover the input space where only one output unit is activated and the rest are not. We can evaluate the maximum percentage of points not covered by subtracting the columns "Percentage" and "Total Percentage", they are 8.58% for the database BALANCE, 0.% for BUPA, 0% for MONK1 and 0.47% for MONK2. As we can see this effect is not so important in the experimental results.

The results of mean percentage of covering are in general good. But if we want to increase the percentage of covering we can generate random points outside the covering of the rules and extract new rules from this points. In a rule the initial point is usually covered by the rule (see Fig. 1), therefore the new rule will usually cover part of the input space not cover by the rest of the rules (the initial point is not contained in any rule).

We have applied this technique with the database BALANCE which got the lower percentage of covering and the results are in Table 2, using 5000 new points.

As we can see the mean percentage of covering by the rules (column three) increases from 74.15 to 95.15, so this is a good technique to increase the performance of our rule system.

Table 2. Results of the rule extraction algorithm

Database	Number of Points	Percentage	Not Cover	Total Percentage	Total Not Cover	Number of Rules (Nrule).	Nrule minimum	Percentage Nrule minimum
BALANCE	5.000	95.19	4.81	85.45	14.54	2963	2706	95.87

4 Conclusions

We have presented a new algorithm for rule extraction from a trained Multilayer Feedforward neural network. The algorithm is based on an interval arithmetic network inversion for particular interval target outputs. The type of rules extracted are N-dimensional intervals in the input space. The experimental results are encouraging, one rule extracted by the algorithm can cover 86% of the input space of the neural network, and in other cases 64 rules cover 100% of the neural network.

Acknowledgments. This research was supported by a Spanish CICYT project number TIC2000-1056.

References

1. A. Maren, C. Harston y R. Pap, Handbook of Neural Computing Applications, Academic Press Inc., 1990.
2. Lu, H., Setiono, R., Liu, H., "Effective Data Mining Using Neural Networks", IEEE Trans. on Knowledge and Data Engineering, vol. 8, no. 6, pp.957–961, 1996.
3. Thrun, S., "Extracting Rules from Artificial Neural Networks with Distributed Representations", Advances in Neural Information Processing Systems 7, pp. 505–512, 1995.
4. Gupta, A., Lam, S.M., "Generalized Analytic Rule Extraction for Feedforward Neural Networks", IEEE Trans. on Knowledge and Data Engineering, vol. 11, no. 6, pp. 985–991, 1999.
5. Narazaki, H., Shigaki, I., Watanabe, T., "A Method for Extracting Approximate Rules from Neural Network", Proc. of the IEEE Int. Conf. on Fuzzy Systems, vol. 4, pp. 1865–1870, 1995.
6. Palade, V., Neagu, D.C., Puscasu, G., "Rule extraction from neural networks by interval propagation", Fourth Int. Conf. on Knowledge-Based Intelligent Engineering Systems and Alllied Technologies, pp. 217–220, 2000.
7. Greczy, P., Usui, S., "Rule extraction from trained artificial neural networks", Behaviormetrika, vol. 26, no. 1, pp. 89–106, 1999.
8. Taha, I.A., Ghosh, J., "Symbolic interpretation of artificial neural networks", IEEE Trans. on Knowledge and Data Engineering, vol. 11, no. 3, pp. 448–463, 1999.
9. Alefeld, G., Herzberger, J., Introduction to Interval Computations, Academic Press, New York, 1983.
10. Linden, A. and Kinderman, J., "Inversion of Multilayer Nets", in Proc. of the Int. Conf. on Neural Networks, Washington D.C., vol. 2, pp. 425–30, 1989.
11. Fernandez, M., Hernandez, C., "Analysis of Input Selection Methods for Multilayer Feedforward", Journal Neural Network World, vol. 10, no. 3, pp. 389–406, 2000.

Implementation of Visual Attention System Using Bottom-up Saliency Map Model

Sang-Jae Park[1], Sang-Woo Ban[2], Jang-Kyoo Shin[2], and Minho Lee[2]

[1]Dept. of Sensor Engineering, [2]School of Electronic and Electrical Engineering,
Kyungpook National University
1370 Sankyuk-Dong, Puk-Gu, Taegu 702-701, Korea
mholee@knu.ac.kr

Abstract. We propose a new active vision system that mimics human-like bottom-up visual attention using saliency map model based on independent component analysis. We consider the feature bases reflecting the biological features and psychological effect to construct the saliency map model, and the independent component analysis is used for integration of the feature bases to implement human-like visual attention system. Using the CCD camera, a DSP board, and DC motors with PID controllers, we implement an active vision system that can automatically select a visual attention area.

1 Introduction

Considering the human-like selective attention function, top-down or task dependent processing can affect how to determine the saliency map as well as bottom-up or task independent processing [1]. In a top-down manner, the human visual system determines salient locations through perceptive processing such as understanding and recognition. It is well known that perception is one of the most complex cerebral activities. Recently, Vidhya and Itti proposed a goal oriented attention guidance model that guides attention according to a topographic attention guidance map [2]. Walther et. al. proposed an attentional selection for object recognition by combining the spatial attention with object recognition [3]. However, these are all based on the feature bases similar with those of the bottom-up visual attention and use a simple feedback path for inhibition. These models do not reflect the human-like top-down mechanism sufficiently. On the other hand, with bottom-up processing, the human visual system determines salient locations obtained from features that are based on the basic information of an input image such as intensity, color, and orientation. [1]. Bottom-up processing is a function of primitive selective attention in the human vision system since humans selectively attend to a salient area according to various stimuli in the input scene.

Previously, Itti and Koch introduced more brain-like model to generate the saliency map. Based on Treisman's results [4], they used three types of bases such as intensity, orientation, and color information to construct a saliency map in a natural scene [1]. Koike and Saiki proposed that a stochastic WTA enables the saliency-based search model to cause the variation of the relative saliency to change search efficiency, due to stochastic shifts of attention [5]. In a hierarchical selectivity mechanism, Sun and Fisher integrated visual salience from bottom-up groupings and the top-down attentional setting [6]. Ramström and Christensen calculated saliency with respect to a given task using a multi-scale pyramid and multiple cues. Their saliency computations were based on game theory concepts, specifically a coalitional game [7]. However, the weight values of these feature maps for constructing the saliency map are still determined artificially.

On the other hand, Barlow suggested that human visual cortical feature detectors might be the end result of a redundancy reduction process [8], in which the activation of each feature detector is supposed to be as statistically independent from the other as possible. We suppose that the saliency map is one of the results of redundancy reduction of the human brain [9]. The scan path that is a sequence of salient locations may be the result of the roles of our brain for information maximization. In the Sejnowski's result using the ICA, the edge filter is derived from the redundancy reduction of a natural scene [10]. Buchsbaum and Gottschalk found opponent coding to be most efficient way to encode human photoreceptor signals [11]. Wachtler and Lee used ICA for hyperspectral color image and obtained their color opponent basis from analysis of trichromatic image patches [12]. It is well known that the human retina has preprocessing features such as cone opponent coding and edge detection [13], and that extracted information is delivered to the visual cortex through the lateral geniculate nucleus (LGN). Symmetrical information is also an important feature of determining the salient object, which is related to the function of LGN.

In this paper, we propose a new saliency map that considers the preprocessing mechanism of cells in the retina and LGN with an on-set and off-surround mechanism prior to the redundancy reduction in the visual cortex. The proposed saliency map also considers intensity information to reflect human psychological factor in Treisman's result [4]. Our saliency map was developed by integration of the feature maps and is finally constructed by applying the ICA that offers the greatest redundancy reduction. In addition, since the successive salient regions are highly dependent on the size and the shape of mask that needs to avoid the duplicate consideration of the salient region, we suggest a way to determine suitable mask size and shape by considering symmetrical information of the selected salient region.

2 Saliency Map Model Based on Color Information

2.1 Architecture of Saliency Map Model

The photoreceptor transforms an optical signal into an electrical signal. The transformed signals for the static image are divided into two processing for color opponent coding and edge detection if we do not consider motion information. The extracted visual information and psychological factor such as intensity are transmitted to the visual cortex through the LGN. Fig. 1 shows a proposed saliency map model. The extracted visual information is transmitted to the visual cortex through the LGN in which symmetrical information can be extracted by edge information. That extracted information is used as a preprocessor in the model for the visual cortex to find a saliency region.

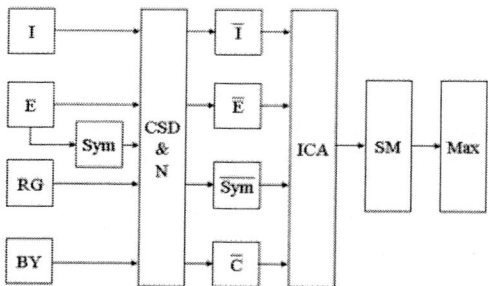

E : edge feature map, Sym : symmetry feature map, RG : red-green opponent coding feature map, BY : blue-yellow opponent coding feature map, CSD & N : center-surround difference and normalization, ICA : independent component analysis, SM : saliency map , Max : max operator

Fig. 1. The architecture of the proposed saliency map model

In the course of preprocessing, we used a Gaussian pyramid with different scales from 0 to n level, in which each level is made by subsampling of 2^n, thus constructing five feature maps [9]. Consequently, five feature maps are obtained by the following equations.

$$I(c, s) = |I(c) \ominus I(s)| \quad (1)$$

$$E(c, s) = |E(c) \ominus E(s)| \quad (2)$$

$$Sym(c,s) = |Sym(c) \ominus Sym(s)| \quad (3)$$

$$RG(c,s) = ||R(c) - G(c)| \ominus |G(s) - R(s)|| \quad (4)$$

$$BY(c,s) = ||B(c) - Y(c)| \ominus |Y(s) - B(s)|| \quad (5)$$

where " $\ominus$ " represents interpolation to the finer scale and point-by-point subtraction. Totally, 30 feature maps are computed because the five feature maps individually have 6 different scales [1]. Feature maps are combined into four "conspicuity maps," as shown in Eq. (6) where $\bar{I}$, $\bar{E}$, $\overline{Sym}$ and $\bar{C}$ stand for intensity, edge, symmetry, and color opponency, respectively. These are obtained through across-scale addition "$\oplus$".

$$\bar{I} = \bigoplus_{c=2}^{4} \bigoplus_{s=c+3}^{c+4} N(I(c,s)), \quad \bar{E} = \bigoplus_{c=2}^{4} \bigoplus_{s=c+3}^{c+4} N(E(c,s)),$$

$$\overline{Sym} = \bigoplus_{c=2}^{4} \bigoplus_{s=c+3}^{c+4} N(S(c,s)), \quad \bar{C} = \bigoplus_{c=2}^{4} \bigoplus_{s=c+3}^{c+4} N(RG(c,s) + BY(c,s)) \quad (6)$$

Compared with Itti and Koch's model, we use different bases such as intensity, edge, symmetry, and color opponent coding feature maps instead of using intensity, orientation, and color feature maps. The proposed model reflects human psychological phenomenon and more biologically realistic visual pathways by considering of the roles of retina cells and the LGN. In this paper, we use unsupervised learning to determine the relative importance of different bases used to generate a suitable salient region.

After the convolution between channel of the feature maps and the filters obtained by ICA learning, the saliency map is computed by summation of all feature maps for every location [9].

2.2 Inhibition-of-Return with Adaptive Mask

The saliency map model generates the most salient location in the scene. In our brain, there is an inhibition-of-return (IOR) function for which the currently attended location is prevented from being attended again [14]. If we do not have the IOR function, attention would endlessly be attracted towards the most salient stimulus. In order to pay attention and to scan our visual environment thoroughly, we need to consider the IOR function in the saliency map model by employing a suitable mask for the most salient region.

Since successive salient locations depend highly on the size and shape of the mask used to implement the IOR function, we must develop a suitable masking method. If an object in a natural scene is selected as the most salient location, the symmetrical property of the object may be used as a guideline to determine the suitable size and shape of the mask because an object has symmetrical property, in general. Thus, if the value representing the degree of symmetry, which is obtained by NTGST, is larger than a threshold value, we use the noise-tolerant generalized symmetry transformation (NTGST) and dilation function of the morphology algorithm to decide the region of IOR [15]. If a selected salient location does not include an object, it may not have symmetry information. As a result, the value representing the degree of symmetry is small. In this case, we mask the region that has high pixel value above a specified threshold in the saliency map. After masking this region, we find the next salient point that excludes the previous salient object [16].

3 Implementation of Active Vision System Based on Saliency Map Model

Fig. 2 (a) shows the architecture of the implemented active vision system that can imitate human visual selective attention. Fig. 2 (b) shows a photograph of the implemented active vision system with 5 degrees of freedom, and Fig. 2 (c) is the implemented motor driving circuit and DSP board.

We use a CCD type camera as an image sensor, and an image data is transferred to the IBM PC at a speed of 30 frames per second. The saliency map model which is implemented in IBM PC generates a target point and transfers it to the DSP board using RS232C serial communication in each sampling instant. The PID controller with suitable control gains generates a proper control signal that is used to bring the selected salient area into the focus of CCD camera. A DSP board using TMS320C32 is used to implement the PID controller, and it activates a driver circuit for the DC motor. The DC motor is driven by power supplied to the motor driver. The motor driver uses LMD18200. A PWM generator and a counter circuit are designed by using a field programmable gate array (FPGA), EPM7128SLC84-15 of Altera Co.

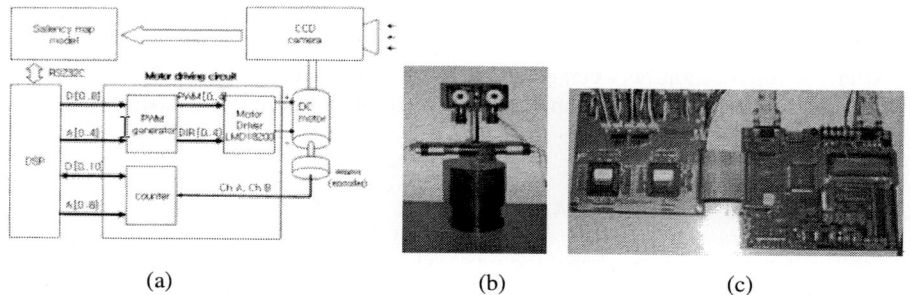

Fig. 2. The implemented active vision system; (a) Architecture of the proposed active vision system, (b) A picture of the implemented system, (c) A picture of the implemented motor driving circuit(left) and DSP board(right)

The encoder is used as a position sensor of the CCD camera that is connected to the DC motor.

4 Computer Simulation and Experimental Results

4.1 Computer Simulation Results of the Proposed Saliency Map Model

Fig. 3 (a) shows the computer simulation results of the proposed saliency map model. The preprocessed feature maps ($\overline{I}$, $\overline{E}$, $\overline{Sym}$, $\overline{C}$) from color natural image are convolved by the ICA filters to construct a saliency map ($\overline{SM}$). Fig. 3 (b) shows the successive eye scan paths of a complex natural image in a street1 scene, and the arrows represent the successive salient regions. At first, we compute the most salient region. Then an appropriate focus area centered by the most salient location is masked off, and the next salient location in the input image is calculated using the salient map model. This means that a previously selected salient location is not considered duplicate.

4.2 Computer Simulation Result of the Proposed Saliency Map Model with Adaptive Mask

After we compute the most salient region from an input image, an appropriate focus area centered by the most salient location is masked off, and the next salient location in the input image is calculated using the salient map model. If the selected salient region contains an object, then the masked region is dilated from a center point of a salient region to a region with symmetry information. Thus, we can find the shape and size of an object in input image. If the selected salient region does not have an object, that is the value representing the degree of symmetry calculated by NTGST is lower than a threshold, we mask the region that has the higher pixel value rather than a threshold value. In order to show the simulation results in a case in which the selected salient region does not include an object, we consider the street2 image without

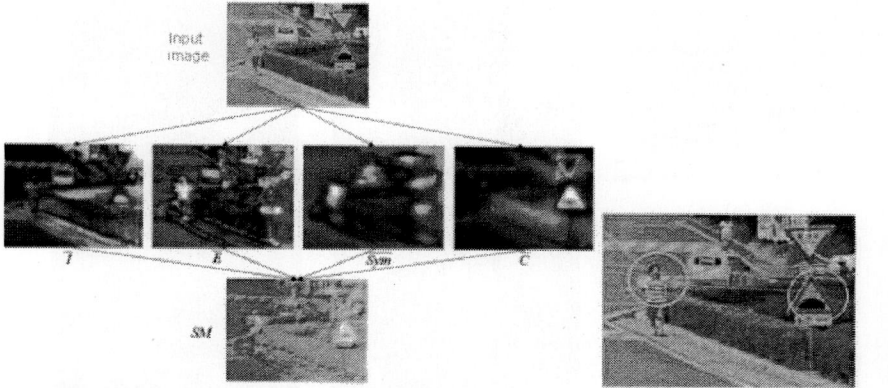

(a) Generated four feature maps and saliency map   (b) Successive salient regions

Fig. 3. Computer simulation result of proposed saliency map model of a natural image

consideration of intensity and symmetry feature basis, because the salient regions in our simulation examples include an object in most cases if all of the four feature maps are considered. Fig. 4 (a) and (b) are the street2 input image, saliency map of input image, respectively. Fig. 4 (c) is a symmetry map for the street2 image. We can determine the mask size and shape of the first and the second salient regions by using symmetrical information, but the third salient location does not have symmetry as shown in Fig. 4 (c). In this case, we use pixel values above a specified threshold value in the saliency map for the mask, as shown in Fig. 4 (f).

4.3 Experimental Results of Active Vision System with the Proposed Saliency Map Model

Fig. 5 shows the result of an active vision system with a saliency map model using a CCD camera, DC motors, and a DSP board. Fig. 5 (a) is the first input scene from the CCD camera, and Fig. 5 (b) is the saliency map of the first input scene. Fig. 5 (c) is the second input scene after the CCD camera moves to the salient location shown in Fig. 5 (b). Fig. 5 (d) is the saliency map of the second input scene shown in Fig. 5 (c).

5 Conclusions

We proposed a new active vision system that mimics human-like bottom-up visual attention. The proposed system used a saliency map model based on four preprocessed feature maps. The feature maps were used as input signals of a neural network to realize ICA filters which imitate the function of the visual cortex to reduce redundancy. In order to consider the IOR function, we also considered a suitable masking method using symmetrical property if the salient region has an object. Based

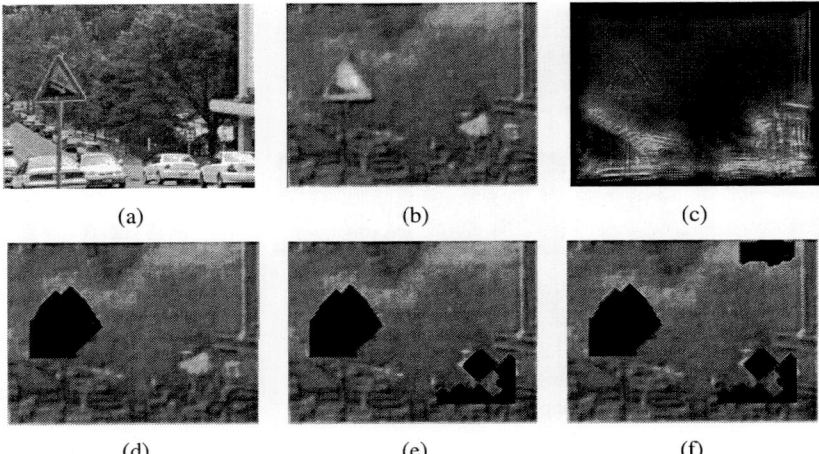

Fig. 4. Adaptive masking of the street2 image; (a) Street2 input image, (b) Saliency map, (c) Symmetry map for street2 image without using intensity and symmetry feature maps, (d) The first salient location with the mask based on symmetry information, (e) The second salient location with the mask based on symmetry information, (f) The third salient location with the mask based on the pixel value in the saliency map

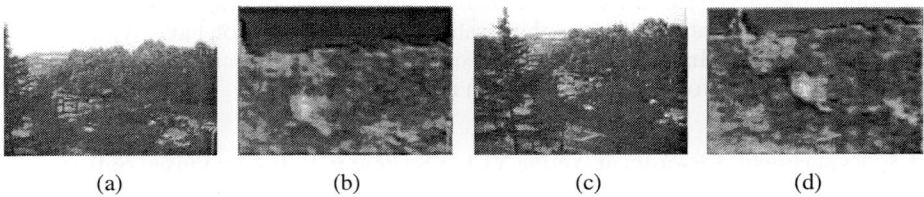

Fig. 5. Active vision system with the proposed saliency map model; (a) The first input image of CCD camera, (b) The saliency map of (a), (c) The second input image of CCD camera,(d) The saliency map of (c)

on the saliency map, we implemented a human-like visual selective attention system. Computer simulation and experimental results showed that the proposed method gives a reasonable salient region. Further research is necessary to consider a new method for symmetry feature maps because the NTGST demands a large calculation time. Additionally, the integration of the proposed saliency map model and eye movement model such as saccade and smooth pursuit is currently under investigation.

Acknowledgement. This work was supported by grant No.R05-2003-000-11399-0 from the Basic Research Program of the Korea Science & Engineering Foundation.

References

1. Itti, L., Koch, C., Niebur, E.: A model of saliency-based visual attention for rapid scene analysis, IEEE Trans. Patt. Anal. Mach. Intell. Vol. 20. no. 11. (1998) 1254–1259
2. Navalpakkam, V., Itti, L.: A Goal Oriented Attention Guidance Model, BMCV 2002. LNCS 2525. (2002) 453–461
3. Walther, D., Itti, L., Riesenhuber, M., Poggio, T., Koch, C.: Attentional Selection for Object Recognition – A Gentle Way, , BMCV 2002. LNCS 2525. (2002) 472–479
4. Treisman, A.M., Gelde, G.: A feature-integration theory of attention, Cognitive Psychology, Vol. 12. no. 1. (1980) 97–136
5. Koike, T. Saiki, J.: Stochastic Guided Search Model for Search Asymmetries in Visual Search Tasks, BMCV 2002. LNCS 2525. (2002) 408–417
6. Sun, Y., Fisher, R.: Hierarchical Selectivity for Object-Based Visual Attention, BMCV 2002. LNCS 2525. (2002) 427–438
7. Ramström, O., Christensen, H.I.: Visual Attention Using Game Theory," BMCV 2002. LNCS 2525. (2002) 462–471
8. Barlow, H.B., Tolhust, D. J.: Why do you have edge detectors? Optical society of America Technical Digest, Vol. 23. (1992) 172
9. Park, S.J., Shin, J.K., Lee, M.: Biologically Inspired Saliency Map Model for Bottom-up Visual Attention, BMCV 2002. LNCS 2525. (2002) 418–426
10. Bell, A.J., Sejnowski, T.J.: The independent components of natural scenes are edge filters, Vision Research, Vol. 37. (1997) 3327–3338
11. Buchsbaum, G., Gottschalk, A.: Trichromacy, opponent colours coding and optimum colour information transmission in the retina, Proc. R. Soc. London Ser. B. Vol. 220. (1983) 89–113
12. Wachtler, T., Lee, T.W., Sejnowski, T.J.: Thromatic structure of natural scenes, J. Opt. Soc. Am. A. Vol. 18. No. 1. (2001)
13. Derrington, A.M., Lennie, K.J.: Chromatic mechanisms in lateral geniculate nucleus of macaque, J. Physio. Lond. Vol. 357. (1984) 241–265
14. Itti, L., Koch, C.: Computational Modeling of Visual Attention, Nature Reviews Neuroscience, Vol. 2. No. 3. (2001) 194–203
15. Park, C.J., Oh, W.G., Cho, S.H., Choi, H.M.: An efficient context-free attention operator for BLU inspection of LCD, IASTED SIP. (2000) 251–256
16. Park, S.J., An, K.H., Lee, M.: Saliency map model with adaptive masking based on independent component analysis, Neurocomputing. Vol. 49. (2002) 417–422

A Self-Growing Probabilistic Decision-Based Neural Network for Anchor/Speaker Identification*

Y.H. Chen[1], C.L. Tseng[1], Hsin-Chia Fu[1], and H.T. Pao[2]

[1] Department of Computer Science and Information Engineering,
{yhchen,cltseng,hcfu}@csie.nctu.edu.tw,
[2] Department of Management Science,
National Chiao-Tung University,
300 Hsinchu, Taiwan ROC
htpao@cc.nctu.edu.tw

Abstract. In this paper, we propose a new clustering algorithm for a mixture Gaussian based neural network, called Self-growing Probabilistic decision-based neural networks (SPDNN). The proposed Self-growing cluster learning (SGCL) algorithm is able to find the natural number of prototypes based on a self-growing validity measure, Bayesian Information Criterion (BIC). The learning process starts with a single prototype randomly initialized in the feature space and grows adaptively during the learning process until most appropriate number of prototypes are found. We have conduct numerical and real world experiments to demostrate the effectiveness of the SGCL algorithm. In the results of using SGCL to trainin the SPDNN for anchor/speaker identification, we have observed noticeable improvement among various model-based or vector quantization-based classification schemes.

1 Introduction

The last two decades have seen a growing number of researcher and practitioner apply neural networks (NNs) to a variety of applications associated with pattern classification and function approximation. In these applications, data clustering techniques have been applied to discover and to extract hidden structure in a data set. In general, clustering is an unsupervised learning process [1,4]. A variety of competitive learning schemes have been developed. Different algorithms in this paradigm such as winner-take-all (WTA)[3], LBG (or generalized Lloyd) [7] and k-Means [8] have been well recognized. In general, selecting the appropriate number of prototypes is a difficult task in the competitive learning, as we do not usually know the number of clusters in the input data a priori. It is therefore desirable to develop an algorithm that has no dependency on the initial prototype locations and is able to adaptively generate prototypes to fit the data patterns.

---
* This research was supported in part by the National Science Council under Grant NSC 90-2213-E009-047.

In this paper, we propose a new learning algorithm for the Self-growing Probabilistic decision-based neural networks (SPDNN) to better estimate density functions corresponding to different pattern classes. We also developed a new Self-growing cluster learning (SGCL) algorithm, that is able to find the natural number of components based on a self-growing validity measure, Bayesian Information Criterion (BIC). The learning process starts with a single component randomly initialized in the feature space and grows adaptively until most appropriate number of components are found. In our experiments on anchor/speaker identification, we observed noticeable improvement among various model-based or vector quantization-based classification schemes.

The remainder of this paper is organized as follows. In Section 2, we describe in detail the architecture of SPDNN and the SGCL Algorithm. Section 3 presents the experimental results on clustering analysis and anchor/speaker identification. Finally, Section 4 gives the summary and concluding remarks.

2 Self-Growing Probabilistic Decision-Based Neural Network

As shown in Figure 1, Self-growing Probabilistic Decision-based Neural Network (SPDNN)[2] is a multi-variate Gaussian neural network [6]. The training scheme of SPDNN is based on the so-called *LUGS* (Locally Unsupervised Globally Supervised) learning. Detail description of the SPDNN model will be given in the following sections.

2.1 Discriminant Functions of SPDNN

Given a set of iid patterns $\mathbf{X}^+ = \{x(t); \ t = 1, 2, \cdots, N\}$, we assume that the likelihood function $p(\mathbf{x}(t) \mid \omega_i)$ for class ω_i is a mixture of Gaussian distributions. Define $p(x(t) \mid \omega_i, \Theta_{r_i})$ as one of the Gaussian distributions which comprise $p(x(t) \mid \omega_i)$, where Θ_{r_i} represents the parameter set $\{\mu_{r_i}, \Sigma_{r_i}\}$ for a cluster r_i in a subnet i:

$$p(\mathbf{x}(t) \mid \omega_i) = \sum_{r_i=1}^{R_i} P(\Theta_{r_i} \mid \omega_i) p(\mathbf{x}(t) \mid \omega_i, \Theta_{r_i}),$$

where $P(\Theta_{r_i} \mid \omega_i)$ denotes the prior probability of the cluster r_i. By definition, $\sum_{r_i=1}^{R_i} P(\Theta_{r_i} \mid \omega_i) = 1$, where R_i is the number of clusters in ω_i. The discriminate function of the multi-class SPDNN models the log-likelihood function

$$\varphi(\mathbf{x}(t), \mathbf{w}_i) = \log p(\mathbf{x}(t) \mid \omega_i) = \log \left[\sum_{r_i=1}^{R_i} P(\Theta_{r_i} \mid \omega_i) p(\mathbf{x}(t) \mid \omega_i, \Theta_{r_i}) \right], \quad (1)$$

where $\mathbf{w}_i = \{\mu_{r_i}, \Sigma_{r_i}, P(\Theta_{r_i} \mid \omega_i), T_i\}$. T_i is the output threshold of a subnet i. In most general formulations, the basis function of a cluster should be able to approximate the Gaussian distribution with a full rank covariance matrix,

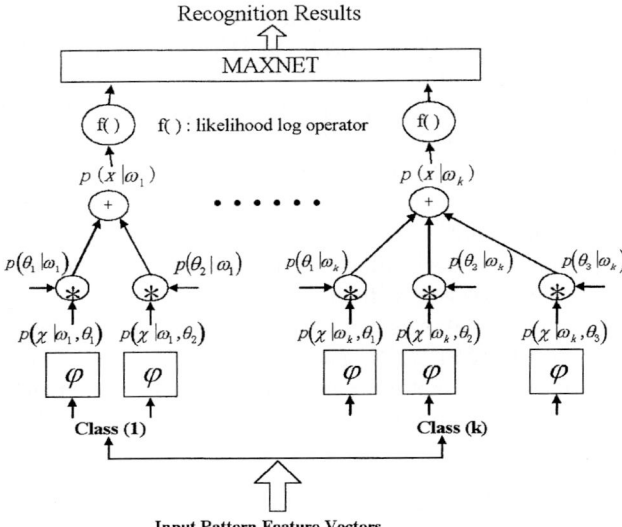

Fig. 1. The schematic diagram of a *k-class* SPDNN.

i.e., $\varphi(\mathbf{x}, \omega_i) = -\frac{1}{2}\mathbf{x}^T \Sigma_{r_i}^{-1} \mathbf{x}$, where Σ_{r_i} is the covariance matrix. However, for applications which deal with high-dimension data but a finite number of training patterns, the training performance and storage space requirements discourage such matrix modeling. A natural simplifying assumption is to assume uncorrelated features of unequal importance. That is, suppose that $p(\mathbf{x}(t) \mid \omega_i, \Theta_{r_i})$ is a D-dimensional Gaussian distribution with uncorrelated features:

$$p(\mathbf{x}(t) \mid \omega_i, \Theta_{r_i}) = \frac{1}{(2\pi)^{\frac{D}{2}} |\Sigma_{r_i}|^{\frac{1}{2}}} \cdot \exp\left[-\frac{1}{2} \sum_{d=1}^{D} \frac{(x_d(t) - \mu_{r_i d})^2}{\sigma_{r_i d}^2}\right], \qquad (2)$$

where $\mathbf{x}(t) = [\mathbf{x}_1(t), \mathbf{x}_2(t), \cdots, \mathbf{x}_D(t)]^T$ is the input, $\mu_{r_i} = [\mu_{r_i 1}, \mu_{r_i 2}, \cdots, \mu_{r_i D}]^T$ is the mean vector, and diagonal matrix $\Sigma_{r_i} = diag[\sigma_{r_i 1}^2, \sigma_{r_i 2}^2, \cdots, \sigma_{r_i D}^2]$ is the covariance matrix. As shown in Figure 1, an SPDNN contains K subnets which are used to represent a K-category classification problem. Inside each subnet, an elliptic basis function (EBF) serves as the basis function for each cluster r_i:

$$\varphi(\mathbf{x}(t), \omega_i, \Theta_{r_i}) = -\frac{1}{2} \sum_{d=1}^{D} \alpha_{r_i d}(x_d(t) - \mu_{r_i d})^2 + \theta_{r_i} \qquad (3)$$

where $\theta_{r_i} = -\frac{D}{2}\ln 2\pi + \frac{1}{2}\sum_{d=1}^{D} \ln \alpha_{r_i d}$. After passing an exponential activation function, $\exp\{\varphi(\mathbf{x}(t), \omega_i, \Theta_{r_i})\}$ can be viewed as a Gaussian distribution, as described in (2), except for a minor notational change: $\frac{1}{\alpha_{r_i d}} = \sigma_{r_i d}^2$.

2.2 Learning Rules for SPDNN

Recall that the training scheme for SPDNN follows the LUGS principle. The locally unsupervised (LU) phase for the SPDNN learns proper number and location of clusters in a class of input patterns. The network learning enters the GS phase after the LU training is converged. As for the globally supervised (GS) learning, the decision-based learning rule is adopted.

Unsupervised Training for LU learning. We have developed a new Self-growing cluster Learning (SGCL) algorithm that is able to find appropriate number and location of clusters based on a self-growing validity measure, Bayesian Information Criterion (BIC) [5].

Bayesian Information Criterion (BIC). Given a set of patterns $\mathbf{X}^+ = \{\mathbf{x}(t); t = 1, 2, \cdots, N\}$ and a set of candidate models $\mathcal{M} = \{M_i \mid i = 1, \ldots, L\}$, each model associated with a parameter set $\mathbf{w}_i$. Suppose two candidate models M_1 and M_2 are used to model a data set $\mathbf{X}^+$, the BIC difference ΔBIC_{21} [5] can be defined as :

$$\Delta BIC_{21} = BIC(M_2, \mathbf{X}^+) - BIC(M_1, \mathbf{X}^+).$$

Raftery et al.,[9] suggested that there is strong evidence for favoring M_2 against M_1, when the value of BIC difference is between 6~10, and if ΔBIC_{21} is larger than 10, M_2 is decisively better than M_1.

BIC-based Self-growing Cluster Learning. There are two aspects with respect to self-growing rules:

I1: *Which cluster should be split?*
I2: *How many clusters are enough?*

Among several clusters over a class of data set, a cluster with highest value of ΔBIC_{21} will be selected as a candidate for splitting, and the splitting process terminates when none of ΔBIC_{21} is favoring for splitting. Detail computing processes are depicted in the following SGCL algorithm.

Self-Growing Cluster Learning (SGCL) algorithm

1. Starts with one cluster, and initialize its center μ_i and covariance Σ_i by the sample mean and variance of data set $\mathbf{X}^+$;
2. Temporarily split each cluster and estimate their mean and variance of the two temporal clusters by the EM clustering algorithm;
3. Compute $\Delta BIC_{21} = BIC(M_2, \mathbf{X}^+) - BIC(M_1, \mathbf{X}^+)$, where BIC_2 and BIC_1 are the Bayesian Information Criterion of the new (2) and the old (1) clusters respectively;
4. If ΔBIC_{21} is larger than a predetermined threshold, the situation favors splitting, and then a global EM based clustering on data set $\mathbf{X}^+$ is performed, otherwise NEXT;
5. If there are clusters which has not been tested for splitting, select a cluster and go to step 2, otherwise terminate the splitting process.

Global supervised learning. During the **supervised learning** phase, training data are used to fine tune the decision boundaries of each class. At the beginning of each supervised learning phase, use the still-being-trained SPDNN to classify all the training patterns $\mathbf{X}_i^+ = \{\mathbf{x}_i(1), \mathbf{x}_i(2), \cdots, \mathbf{x}_i(M_i)\}$ for $i = 1, \cdots, L$. $\mathbf{x}_i(m)$ is put into class ω_i if $\varphi(\mathbf{x}_i(m), \mathbf{w}_i) > \varphi(\mathbf{x}_i(m), \mathbf{w}_k), \forall k \neq i$. According to the classification results, the training patterns for each class i can be divided into three subsets:

- $D_1^i = \{\mathbf{x}_i(m); \mathbf{x}_i(m) \in \omega_i, \mathbf{x}_i(m) \text{ is correctly classified into } \omega_i \}$;
- $D_2^i = \{\mathbf{x}_i(m); \mathbf{x}_i(m) \in \omega_i, \mathbf{x}_i(m) \text{ is misclassified into another class } \omega_j \}$;
- $D_3^i = \{\mathbf{x}_i(m); \mathbf{x}_i(m) \notin \omega_i, \mathbf{x}_i(m) \text{ is misclassified into class } \omega_i \}$.

The following reinforced and antireinforced learning rules [6] are applied to the corresponding misclassified subnets.

$$\text{Reinforced Learning}: \mathbf{w}_i^{(m+1)} = \mathbf{w}_i^{(m)} + \eta \nabla \varphi(\mathbf{x}_i(m), \mathbf{w}_i) \quad (4)$$

$$\text{Antireinforced Learning}: \mathbf{w}_j^{(m+1)} = \mathbf{w}_j^{(m)} - \eta \nabla \varphi(\mathbf{x}_i(m), \mathbf{w}_j), \quad (5)$$

where η is a user defined learning rate ($0 < \eta \leq 1$).

3 Experimental Results

In this section, experimental results are presented in two parts. The first part uses an synthetic data set and the second part explores the ability of SPDNN for anchor/speaker identification. In each part we perform EM based learning scheme with six different initialization methods for the training of an SPDNN. These six different initialization methods are briefly explained in the followings. (1) Regular EM method: Using EM learning method with initial *Gaussian mean* values determined by randomly selected seeds from training data. (2) Model K-means method: Using EM learning method with initial *Gaussian mean* values determined by K-means clustering. (3) Model single-Link method: Using EM learning method with initial *Gaussian mean* values determined by single-link hierarchical clustering. (4) Model average-Link method: Using EM learning method with initial *Gaussian mean* values determined by average-link hierarchical clustering. (5) Model complete-Link method: Using EM learning method with initial *Gaussian mean* values determined by complete-link hierarchical clustering. (6) Self-growing method: Using EM learning method with initial *Gaussian mean* values determined by the proposed BIC-based self-growing method. *Experiment 1: Synthetic data set drawn from a distribution of six mixture Gaussian clusters*

The synthetic data set contains 600 data points, which are evenly divided into six Gaussian clusters. Figure 2 depicts the self-growing and *EM* learning processes from one up to six clusters. The number of mixture Gaussian clusters is limited to an upper bound of 10. As shown in Figure 3, the learning curve of the proposed method rises to its peak value when the number of cluster reaches 6, which is the predefined number of clusters in the data set.

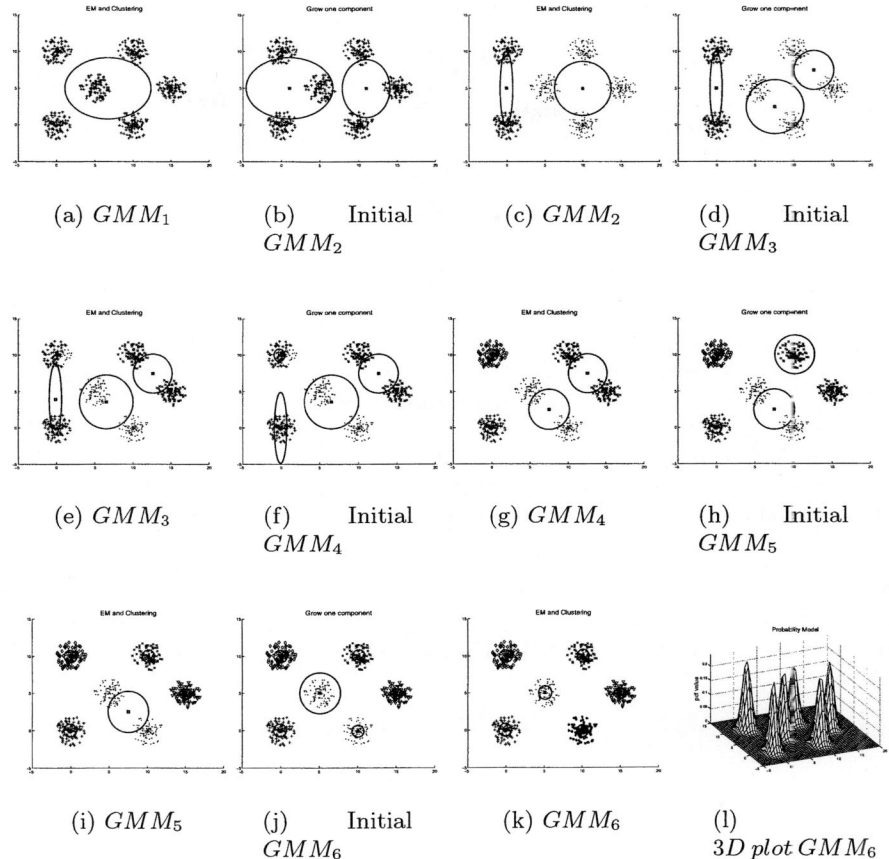

Fig. 2. The learning process of self-growing with synthetic data.

Experiment 2: Anchor/speaker identification

The anchor/speaker identification experiments were conducted in the following manner. Speech data were collected from 19 female and 3 male anchor/speakers, of the evening TV news broadcasting programs in Taiwan. For each speaker, there are 180 TV news briefing of approximately 25 minutes sampling over 6 months. The speech data are partitioned into 5 second segments, which corresponds to 420 features vectors (mfcc). Each speaker was modeled by a SPDNN trained by three different amount of speech data (30, 60 and 90 seconds). Testing were done using the rest of speech data. Each segment of 5 second speech data was treated as a separate test utterance.

There is no theoretical way to estimate the number of mixture components *a prior*. For speaker modeling, the objective is to choose the minimum of compo-

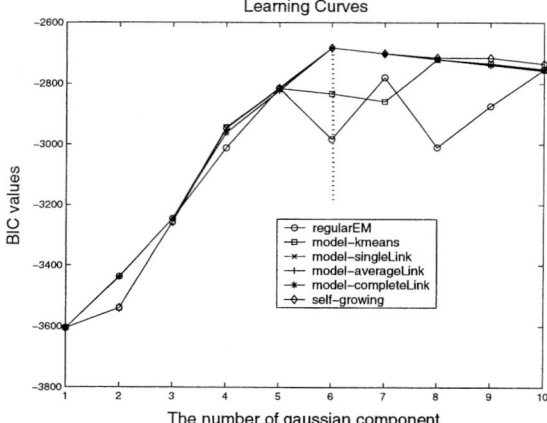

Fig. 3. The BIC learning curves of the six different methods on the synthetic data. The learning curve of the Self-growing method peaks at GMM_6. It seems that the proposed SMGL method suggests a nature number of clusters for the synthetic data set.

nents necessary to adequately model a speaker for good speaker identification. Figure 4 shows, the learning curve of (BIC values) versus the number of Gaussian components used in building a SPDNN speaker model.

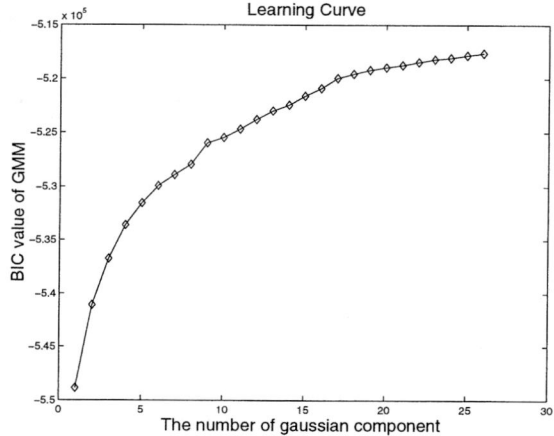

Fig. 4. The learning curve of the SPDNN anchor/speaker identification system. The BIC values indicate a quick increase from 1 to 8 mixture components, and leveling off above 16 components.

Several observations were made from these results. First, the quick increase in the BIC values from 1 to 8 mixture components, and leveling off above 16 components. Thus, the next set of experiments were performed by using

1. different amount (30, 60, and 90 seconds) of training speech data
2. different dimension of mfcc (mel-frequency features).

As shown in Table 1, by using different amount of training data and *mfcc* feature dimension, the number of mixture components corresponding to peak BIC values, ranges from 12 to 30. The performance evaluation was then computed as the percent of correctly identified segment overall test utterance segments.

$$\% \text{ correct identification} = \frac{\# \text{ correctly identification segments}}{\text{Total } \# \text{ of segments}} \times 100\%$$

The complete identification rates are also shown in Table 1. In the lower part of Table 1, the identification rates were tested from an SPDNN with fixed (32) components. It seems that the identification performance from self-growing SPDNN is slightly better than the fixed component model.

Table 1. Self-growing number of clusters and speaker identification performance for different amount of training speech data and dimension of *mfcc* feature vectors. In the body of the table, the first number is the mean value of the number of clusters, the second number after '/' is the variance and the number in parentheses indicates the percentage (%) of identification performance.

Amount of Training speech	Dimension of mfcc			
	12	16	20	24
	Identification performance by Self-growing SPDNN			
30s	12.32/1.45(89.51)	13.32/2.03(92.00)	14.84/2.54(94.24)	15.8/2.12(94.81)
60s	17.31/2.16(90.28)	19/1.19(95.08)	20.84/2.41(96.81)	23.05/2.80(96.95)
90s	20.32/2.67(93.44)	23.79/2.55(96.46)	25.94/2.97(97.78)	30.21/3.6(97.90)
	Identification performance by fixed component SPDNN			
90s	32(92.57)	32(95.60)	32(97.39)	32(97.71)

4 Concluding Remarks

In this paper, we have presented a BIC based learning scheme for the training of SPDNN. This learning scheme tries to tackle a long standing critical problem in clustering, the difficulty in determining the number of clusters. During the learning process, according to the split validity criterion (BIC), one prototype is chosen to split into two prototypes. This splitting process terminates when the BIC values of each cluster reaches their highest points. We have conducted experiments on TV news anchor/speaker identification to demonstrate the proposed learning scheme. The experimental results show that the learning scheme is indeed a powerful, effective, and flexible technique in classifying clusters.

References

1. C. Dacaestecker, "Competitive clustering," in *Proc. IEEE Int. Neural Networks Conf.*, vol. 2, 1988, p. 833.

2. H. C. Fu, H.Y. Chang, Y.Y. Xu, and H.T. Pao, "User Adaptive Handwriting Recognition by Self-growing Probabilistic Decision-based Neural Networks," in *IEEE Transaction on Neural Networks*, Vol. 11, No.6, Nov. 2000.
3. J. Hertz, A. Krogh, and R. G. Palmer, *Introduction to the Theory of Neural Computation*. New York: Addison-Wesley, 1991.
4. J. M. Jolion, P. Meer, and S. Bataouche, "Robust clustering with applications in computer vision," in *IEEE Trans. Pattern Anal. Machine Intell.*, vol. 13, pp. 791–802, Aug. 1991.
5. R.E. Kass, "Bayes Factors, in *Journal of the American Statistical Association*," **90**, pp.773–795, 1995.
6. Shang-Hung Lin, S.Y. Kung, and L.J. Lin, "Face Recognition/Detection by Probabilistic Decision-based Neural Networks," in *IEEE Transactions on Neural Networks*, Vol. 8, No. 1, pp. 114–132, 1997.
7. S. P. Lloyd, "Least squares quantization in PCM," in *IEEE Trans. Inform. Theory*, vol. 28, pp. 129–137, 1982.
8. J. MacQueen, "Some methods for classification and analysis of multivariate observations," in *Proc. 5th Berkeley Symp. Math. Statist. Probability.* Berkeley, CA: Univ. California Press, 1967, pp. 281–297.
9. A. E. Raftery, *Bayesian Model Selection in Social Research.* University of Washington Demography Center Working paper no 94–12, September 1994.

Unsupervised Clustering Methods for Medical Data: An Application to Thyroid Gland Data

Songül Albayrak

Computer Engineering Department, Yildiz Technical University
Istanbul, Turkiye
sbayrak@yildiz.edu.tr

Abstract. The purpose of this paper is to examine the unsupervised clustering methods on medical data. Neural networks and statistical methods can be used to develop an accurate automatic diagnostic system. Self-Organizing Feature map as a Neural Network model and K-means as a statistical model are tested to predict a well defined class. To test the diagnostic system, thyroid gland data is used for the application. As a result of clustering algorithms, patients are classified normal, hyperthyroid function and hypothyroid function.

1 Introduction

The amount of data is rapidly growing at the result of scientific measurements and experiments. In the area of medicine, devices used to obtain data by experimental measurement have been developing and the traditional manual data analysis has become inefficient and methods for efficient computer-based analysis are indispensable. Neural network, statistical methods and machine learning algorithms are currently being tested on many medical prediction problem to achieve accurate automatic diagnosis [7].

In literature, breast cancer, heart disease, hepatitis, liver disorders, lymphography, Pima Indians diabetes have been investigated and usually statistical methods, such as decision trees, Bayes classifier and standard linear discrimination etc., have been used. Furthermore, Baxt used backpropagation to identify myocardial infarction on a coronary artery disease database, Rosenberg et al. found performance of a radial basis function network to be comparable with that of human experts and superior to various backpropagation methods and for breast cancer detection, researchers have successfully applied backpropagation, ART and fractal analysis[7].

In this work, unsupervised clustering methods were performed to cluster the patients into three clusters by using thyroid gland data obtained by Dr. Coomans[1]. To measure the thyroid gland functions, five different tests were applied to patients and the test results were used by other researchers for the classification purpose. In a very recent work, L. Ozyilmaz and T. Yildirim are investigated the supervised classification methods to develop a medical diagnostic system on this data [2]. In the work presented here, self-organizing feature map and K-means algorithms are used as an unsupervised clustering method to cluster the patients. As a result of clustering algorithms, patients status are classified normal, hyperthyroid function and hypothyroid function.

In this paper, some information about clustering algorithms, K-means and Self-Organizing Feature Map algorithm, used in this application and the thyroid gland data are also given.

2 K-means Clustering

The ability to determine characteristic prototypes or cluster centers in a given set of data plays a central role in the design of pattern classifiers based on the minimum distance concept. K-means algorithm is based on the minimization of the squared distances from all points in a cluster domain to the cluster center. This procedure consists of the following steps [3].

Step1: Choose K initial cluster centers $z_1(1)$, $z_2(1)$, $z_K(1)$. These are arbitrary and are usually selected as the first K samples of the given sample set.

Step 2: At the t th iterative step distribute the samples {x} among the K cluster domains, using the relation,

$$x \in S_j(t) \quad \text{if} \quad \|x - z_j(t)\| < \|x - z_i(t)\| \tag{1}$$

for all i=1,2,...,K, i≠j , where $S_j(t)$ denotes the set of samples whose cluster center is $z_j(t)$.

Step 3: From the results of Step 2, compute the new cluster centers $z_j(t+1)$, j=1,2,...,K, such that the sum of the squared distance from all points in $S_j(t)$ to the new cluster center is minimized. In other words, the new cluster center $z_j(t+1)$ is computed so that the performance index is minimized. The $z_j(t+1)$ which minimizes this performance index is simply the sample mean of $S_j(t)$. Therefore, the new cluster center is given by

$$z_j(t+1) = \frac{1}{N_j} \sum_{x \in S_j(t)} x \quad j=1,2,...,K \tag{2}$$

where N_j is the number of samples in $S_j(t)$. The name "K-means" is obviously derived from the manner in which cluster centers are sequentially updated.

Step 4: If $z_j(t+1)=z_j(t)$ for j=1,2, . . . ,K, the algorithm has converged and the procedure is terminated. Otherwise go to Step 2.

3 Self-Organizing Feature Map (SOFM) Algorithm

Self-Organizing Mapping is a kind of neural network which is based on competitive learning. The output neurons of the network compete among themselves to be activated, with the result that only one output neuron or one neuron per group wins the competition. The output neurons that win the competition are called winner-take-all neurons. One way of inducing winner-take-all competition among the output neurons is to use lateral inhibitory connections between them [4,5,6].

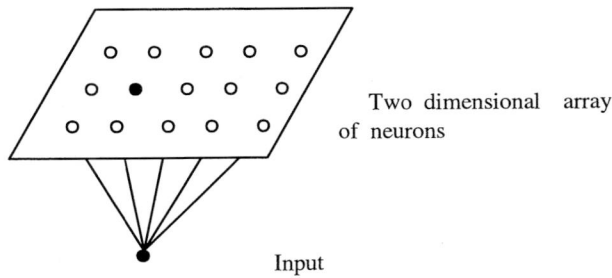

Fig. 1. Two-dimensional lattice of neurons that are fully connected to the inputs.

In a self-organizing feature map, the neurons are placed at the nodes of a lattice that is usually one or two dimensional. The neurons become selectively tuned to various input patterns in the course of a competitive learning process. The location of the neurons (i.e. winning neuron) so tuned tend to become ordered with respect to each other in such a way that a meaningful coordinate system for different input feature is created over the lattice.

There are three basic step involved in the application of the algorithm after initialization. These three steps are **sampling, similarity matching** and **updating steps** and are repeated until the map formation is completed. The algorithm is summarized as follows:

1. Initialization: Choose random values for the initial weight vector $w_j(0)$. The only restriction here is that the $w_j(0)$ must be different for $j=1,2,...,N$, where N is the number of neurons in the lattice. It may be desirable to keep the magnitude of the weights small.

2. Sampling: Draw a sample x from the input distribution with a certain probability; the vector x represents the sensory signal.

3. Similarity Matching: In the formulation of adaptive algorithm, it is convenient to normalize the weight vectors w_j to constant Euclidean norm (length). In such a situation, **the best-matching criterion** described here is equivalent to the **minimum Euclidean distance between vectors**. If we use the mapping i(x) to identify the neuron that best matches (winning) the input vector x, we may determine i(x) by applying the following condition;

$$i(x) = \arg\min_{j} \|x(t) - w_j(t)\| \quad j = 1,2,...,N \qquad (3)$$

t represents the iteration count.

4. Updating: Adjust the synaptic weight vectors of all neurons, using the update formula

$$w_j(t+1) = \begin{cases} w_j(t) + \eta(t)[x(t) - w_j(t)] & j \in A_{i(x)}(t) \\ w_j(t) & \text{otherwise} \end{cases} \qquad (4)$$

where $\eta(t)$ is the learning-rate parameter, and $A_{i(x)}(t)$ is the neighborhood function centered around the winning neuron i(x); both $\eta(t)$ and $A_{i(x)}(t)$ are varied dynamically during learning for best results.

5. Continuation: Continue with step 2 until noticeable changes in the feature map are observed.

3.1 Selection of Parameters

The learning process involved in the computation of a feature map is stochastic in nature, which means that the accuracy of the map depends on the number of iterations of the SOFM algorithm. Moreover, the success of map formation is critically dependent on how the main parameters of the algorithm, namely, the learning rate parameter η and the neighborhood function A_i are selected. Unfortunately, there is no theoretical basis for the selection of these parameters. They are usually determined by a process of trial and error [5].

The learning-rate parameter: $\eta(t)$ is used to update synaptic weight vector $w_j(t)$ should be time varying. In particular, during the first 1000 iterations or so, $\eta(t)$ should begin with a value close to unity; thereafter should be decreased gradually by staying above 0.1. The exact form of variation of $\eta(t)$ with t is not critical; it can be linear, exponential, or inversely proportional to t. It is during this initial phase of the algorithm that the topological ordering of the weight vectors $w_j(t)$ takes place. This phase of the learning process is called the ordering phase. The remaining iterations of the algorithm are needed principally for the fine tuning of the computational map; this second phase of the learning process is called the convergence phase at a small value for a fairly long period of time, which is typically thousands of iterations[5].

Neighborhood Function: For topological ordering of the weight vectors $w_j(t)$ to take place, careful consideration has to be given to the neighborhood function $A_i(t)$. Generally, the function $A_i(t)$ is taken to include neighbors in a square region around the winning neuron, as illustrated in Fig.2. For example, a "radius" of one includes the winning neuron plus the eight neighbors. However, the function may take other forms, such as hexagonal or even a continuous Gaussian shape. In any case, the neighborhood function $A_i(t)$ usually begins such that it includes all neurons in the network and then gradually shrinks with time[5].

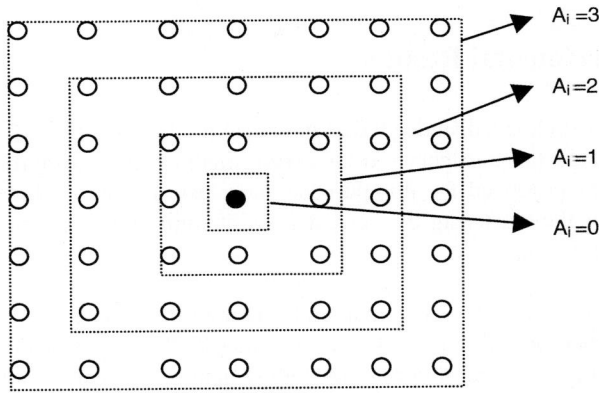

Fig. 2. Square topological neighborhood Ai, of varying size, around "winning" neuron i, identified as a black circle.

4 The Functions and Properties of the Thyroid Gland

The thyroid gland is the biggest gland in the neck. It is situated in the front neck bellow the skin and muscle layers. The thyroid gland takes the shape of a butterfly with the two wings being represented by the left and right thyroid lobed which wrap around the trachea. The sole function of the thyroid is to make thyroid hormone. This hormone has an effect on nearly all tissues of the body where it increases cellular activity. The function of the thyroid therefore is to regulate the body's metabolism [9].

The thyroid gland is prone to several very distinct problems, some of which are extremely common. Production of too little thyroid hormone causes hypo-thyroidism or production of too much thyroid hormone causes hyper-thyroidism.

In this work, thyroid database [10] are investigated to cluster by unsupervised methods. This data set contains 3 classes and 215 samples. These classes are assigned to the values that correspond to the hyper-, hypo- and normal function of the thyroid gland. The followings give the 5 tests which are applied to patients to measure the thyroid functions. 5 dimensional feature vector is obtained as $x=[x_1,x_2,x_3,x_4,x_5]$ from the applied tests

1-T3-resin uptake test (A percentage)
2-Total Serum thyroxin as measured by the isotopic displacement method.
3-Total Serum triiodothyronine as measured by radioimmuno assay
4-Basal thyroid-stimulating hormone (TSH) as measured by radioimmuno assay
5-Maximal absolute difference of TSH value after injection of 200 micro grams of thyrotropin-releasing hormone as compared to the basal value.

5 Experimental Results

K-means which is a distance based statistical method and SOFM algorithms were used for analyzing the unsupervised clustering methods on the thyroid gland data. Pascal codes were produced for this purpose and clustering was achieved over 215 thyroid data. After the clustering the correct classification rate was obtained as 78.1% for K-means algorithm.

Two different structure, 1-D map and 2-D map, have been used for SOFM. 1-D map has 20 lattice of nodes and 2-D map includes 7x7 lattice of nodes. SOFM method has the same $\eta(t)=1/\sqrt{t}$ learning rate for both structure. Correct classification rate obtained with 2-D SOFM was 96.3% while it was 93.0% for 1-D SOFM. Overall results were given in table 1. As can be seen from the results, SOFM gives the better results than K-means clustering.

Table 1. Performance comparison on the Thyroid gland data

Classifiers	Correct Classified sample	Correct Classification rate
K-means	168	78.1 %
1-D SOM (20 nodes)	200	93.0 %
2-D SOM (7x7 nodes)	207	96.3 %

6 Conclusion

In this work, unsupervised clustering methods have been used for the purpose of medical diagnosis. Thyroid gland data was used as an application. SOFM which is the unsupervised neural network structure gives the better results than statistical based K-means clustering methods for this specific problem. In the application, size of lattice, learning rate and neighborhood function in the SOFM are the most important factors on the performance of clustering process. If the size of lattice is increased, the performance of the clustering process increases while the speed of the system decreases. However, to speed up the SOFM algorithm, due to its suitable structure, parallel programming can be used. This work has demonstrated the motivation for research in medical diagnosis using unsupervised clustering methods.

References

1. Coomans, D., Broeckaert, I., Jonckheer, M., Massart D.L.: Comparison of Multivariate Discrimination Techniques for Clinical Data - Application to the Thyroid Functional State. Methods of Information in Medicine, Vol.22, (1983) 93–101
2. Ozyilmaz L., Yildirim T., Diagnosis of Thyroid Disease using Artificial Neural Network Methods, Proceedings of the 9'th International Conference on Neural Information Processing (. ICONIP'02) (2002)
3. Tou, J.T., Gonzalez R.C., Pattern Recognition Principles, Addison-Wesley Publishing Company (1974)
4. R.J. Schalkoff, Pattern Recognition: Statistical, Structural and Neural Approaches, John Wiley & Sons, Inc. (1992)
5. Haykin S., Neural Networks: A Comprehensive Foundation, Macmillan College Publishing Company, New York (1994)
6. N.K. Bose, P.Liang, Neural Network Fundamentals with Graphs, Algorithms and Applications, Mc Graw Hill (1996)
7. Carpenter A.G., Markuzon N., ARTMAP-IC and medical diagnosis: Instance counting and inconsistent cases, Elsevier Neural Networks 11, 323–336, (1998)
8. Deng D., Kasabov N., On-line Pattern Analysis by Evolving Self-Organizing Maps, (2000)
9. www.endocrineweb.com/thyroid.html, 2002
10. www.ics.uci.edu/pub/ml-repos/machine-learning-database/, 2001

Protein Sequence Classification Using Probabilistic Motifs and Neural Networks

Konstantinos Blekas, Dimitrios I. Fotiadis, and Aristidis Likas

Department of Computer Science, University of Ioannina, 45110 Ioannina, Greece
and Biomedical Research Institute, FORTH – Hellas, 45110 Ioannina, Greece
{kblekas,fotiadis,arly}@cs.uoi.gr

Abstract. The basic issue concerning the construction of neural network systems for protein classification is the sequence encoding scheme that must be used in order to feed the network. To deal with this problem we propose a method that maps a protein sequence into a numerical feature space using the matching local scores of the sequence to groups of conserved patterns (called *motifs*). We consider two alternative schemes for discovering a group of D motifs within a set of K-class sequences. We also evaluate the impact of the background features (2-grams) to the performance of the neural system. Experimental results on real datasets indicate that the proposed method is superior to other known protein classification approaches.

1 Introduction

Consider a finite set of characters $\Sigma = \{\alpha_1, \ldots, \alpha_\Omega\}$, where $\Omega = |\Sigma|$. Any sequence $S = a_1 a_2 \ldots a_L$, such that $L \geq 1$ and $a_i \in \Sigma$, is called a *sequence* over the alphabet Σ. In the case of proteins, the alphabet Ω is the set of 20 aminoacids. Protein sequence classification constitutes an important problem in biological sciences. It deals with the assignment of sequences to known categories based on homology detection properties (sequence similarity). We use the term *family* or class to denote any collection of sequences that are presumed to share common characteristics.

Various approaches have been developed for solving this problem. Most of them are based on appropriately modeling protein families, either directly or indirectly. Direct modeling techniques use a training a set of sequences to build a model that characterizes each family of interest. Hidden Markov models (HMMs) are a widely used probabilistic method for protein families [1] that provides a probabilistic measurement (score) of how well an unknown sequence fits to a family. The classification is then made by selecting the class label of the most likely model [1]. Indirect techniques use an *encoding* stage to extract useful sequence features. In this way, sequences of variable length are transformed into fixed-length input vectors that are subsequently used for training discriminative models, such as neural networks [2].

In biological sequences, *motifs* or patterns can be considered as islands of aminoacids conserved in the same order of a given family [3]. Since they enclose significant homologous attributes, they can be seen as local features characterizing the sequences. The *background* information also constitutes another source of information for sequence data. A common way to determine background features, also termed as *global* features, is to use the *2-gram* encoding scheme that counts the occurrences of two consecutive characters in sequences [2]. In the case of protein sequences (generated from the alphabet of the 20 aminoacids), there are 400 possible such 2-gram features.

Several neural network schemes have been applied that follow alternative encoding schemes and training methods [4],[2]. These approaches are characterized by the enormous size of the extracted input vectors, the imbalance between global and local features (more emphasis on global features) and the need for large training sets (since the number of network inputs is very large). For example in [4],[2] only one feature was responsible for carrying local information, while all the others were 2-gram features. Another class of discriminative model used for classifying sequences is the Motif Alignment and Search Tool (MAST) [5]. The MAST algorithm estimates the significance of the match of a query sequence to a family model as the product of the p-values of each motif match score. This measure (E-value) can then be used to select the family of the unknown sequence.

In this paper, we focus on building efficient neural classifiers for discriminating multiple protein families by using appropriate local features extracted from efficient probabilistic motif models. As motifs constitute family diagnostic signatures, our aim is to formulate a neural network scheme that exploits motif-based (local) features. It can be considered as a combination of an unsupervised and a supervised learning technique. In the first stage, we identify probabilistic motifs in a training set of multi-class sequences. We assume two alternative ways, depending on whether or not taking into account the class labels. For this purpose we use the MEME algorithm [6] that follows iteratively a two-component mixture model approach. The discovered motifs are then used to convert each sequence to a numerical feature vector that subsequently can be applied to a typical feedforward neural network. Using a Bayesian regularization training technique [7],[8], the neural network parameters are adjusted and therefore a classifier is obtained suitable for predicting the family of an unlabeled sequence. The next section describes the proposed method, while experimental results obtained using real sets of protein sequences are presented in Section 3. Finally, in Section 4 we present our conclusions.

2 The Proposed Method

Consider the problem of classifying a set of N protein sequences $\mathbf{S} = \{S_i, i = 1, \ldots, N\}$ into K classes. The set $\mathbf{S}$ is a union of positive example datasets $\mathcal{S}_k$ from K different classes, i.e. $\mathbf{S} = \{\ \mathcal{S}_1 \cup \ldots \cup \mathcal{S}_K\ \}$, and can be seen as a subset of the complete set of all possible sequences over the aminoacid alphabet Σ ($\mathbf{S} \subseteq \Sigma^*$). The proposed protein classification scheme consists of three main stages. A supervised technique is first applied for discovering probabilistic motifs in a set of

K protein families. This follows a feature vector generator that converts protein sequences into feature vectors. Finally, a neural network is used for assigning a protein family to each input vector.

2.1 Discovering Probabilistic Motifs in Sequences

A motif M_j of length W_j can be probabilistically modeled using a position weight matrix (PWM_j) that follows a multinomial character distribution. Each column (l) of the matrix corresponds to a position l in the motif sequence ($l = 1, \ldots, W_j$). The column elements provide the probability $p_{\alpha_\xi, l}$ of each character α_ξ of the alphabet $\Sigma = \{\alpha_\xi, \xi = 1, \ldots, \Omega\}$ to appear in the position l, where $\Omega = 20$ for proteins. Let $s_p = a_{p,1} \ldots a_{p,W_j}$ denote a segment of length W_j beginning at position p and ending at position $p + W_j - 1$ of a sequence S of length L. Totally, there are $L - W_j + 1$ such subsequences. Then, we can define the probability that s_p matches the motif M_j, or has been generated by the model PWM_j corresponding to that motif, using the following equation:

$$P(s_p|M_j) = \prod_{l=1}^{W_j} p_{a_{p,l}, l} \,. \tag{1}$$

Several approaches have been proposed for discovering probabilistic motifs in a set of unaligned biological sequences [3], such as the CONSENSUS, Gibbs sampler and MEME methods. Among these, the MEME algorithm [6] applies a two-component mixture model to discover one motif of length W_j. The first component of the model describes the motif (PWM_j), while the other models the background information, formulated by a probabilistic vector ρ of size Ω. Multiple motifs can be found by sequentially fitting another two-component model to the set of sequences that remain after removing the subsequences that correspond to the occurrences of the already identified motifs[1]. MEME uses the Expectation Maximization (EM) algorithm to maximize the log-likelihood function of the model [6], i.e. to estimate the elements of the corresponding position weight matrix. Furthermore, MEME provides with a strategy for locating efficient initial parameter values in order to prevent the EM algorithm from getting stuck in local optima [6]. The D motif models PWM_j ($j = 1, \ldots, D$) discovered by MEME can be of either fixed or variable length W_j. In our experimental studies both types of motifs will be examined.

In order to discover a group of motifs from a training set containing sequences of K classes, two alternative approaches can be followed. The first approach is to apply the MEME algorithm K times, one for each protein family, respectively. Then, the union of the discovered groups of motifs D_k ($k = 1, \ldots, K$) can form the final group of D motifs. These will be termed as *class-dependent* motifs. An alternative approach is to apply the motif discovery algorithm only once to the total training set $\mathbf{S}$, ignoring class labels. In this way, we do not allow the

---

[1] The model assumes that there are zero or more non-overlapping motifs in each sequence.

algorithm to directly create K protein family profiles, but rather to discover D *class-independent* motifs. During experiments both motif discovery strategies will be considered and evaluated.

Following the probabilistic framework of PWM_j for modeling motifs, we can sequentially compute the corresponding position-specific score matrix ($PSSM_j$) in order to score a sequence. The $PSSM_j$ is a log-odds matrix calculating the logarithmic ratio $r_{\alpha_\xi,l}$ of the probabilities $p_{\alpha_\xi,l}$ suggested by the PWM_j and the corresponding general relative frequencies ρ_{α_ξ} of aminoacids α_ξ in the family. Given a motif model M_j, the score value $f(s_p|M_j)$ of a subsequence s_p can be defined as:

$$f(s_p|M_j) = \sum_{l=1}^{W_j} \log(\frac{p_{a_{p,l},l}}{\rho_{a_{p,l}}}) = \sum_{l=1}^{W_j} r_{a_{p,l},l} \ . \qquad (2)$$

At the sequence level, the score value of a sequence S against a motif M_j can be determined as the maximum value among all scores of the possible subsequences of S, i.e. $f(S|M_j) = \max_{1 \leq p \leq L-W_j+1} f(s_p|M_j)$. Thus, if we assume that we have discovered a group of D motifs, we can translate each sequence S_i into a D-dimensional feature vector $\mathbf{x}_i$ by calculating the score values $x_{ij} = f(S_i|M_j)$ ($j = 1, \ldots, D$).

2.2 Construction of the Neural Classifier

The last stage in our methodology is to implement and train a feed-forward neural network that will be able to map the input vectors $\mathbf{x}_i$ into the K protein classes of interest. To construct the neural classifier we use the training set $\mathbf{X} = \{\mathbf{x}_i, \mathbf{t}_i\}$, $i = 1, \ldots, N$. The target vector $\mathbf{t}_i$ is a binary vector of size K indicating the class label of input $\mathbf{x}_i$, i.e. $t_{ik} = 1$ if the corresponding sequence S_i belongs to the class k, and 0 otherwise. In an manner analogous, the output of the classifier is represented by a K-dimensional vector $\mathbf{y}_i$. Based on this scheme, the predicted class $h(\mathbf{x}_i)$ of an unlabeled feature vector $\mathbf{x}_i$ is given by the index of the output node with the largest value y_{ik}, i.e. $h(\mathbf{x}_i) = c: \ y_{ic} = \max_{1 \leq k \leq K} y_{ik}$. Setting a threshold value θ ($\in [0,1]$), we can restrict the classifiers' decision only to those input vectors whose maximum output value surpasses this threshold. In this case we can write:

$$h(\mathbf{x}_i, \theta) = c: \ y_{ic} = \max_{1 \leq k \leq K} y_{ik} \ \wedge \ y_{ic} \geq \theta \ . \qquad (3)$$

Parameter θ can be used to specify the sensitivity of the classifier.

In order to train the neural network we use the Gauss-Newton Bayesian Regularization (GNBR) learning algorithm [8]. The GNBR algorithm applies an iterative procedure for Bayesian regularization of the network parameters and implements a Gauss-Newton approximation to the Hessian matrix $\mathbf{H}$ of the regularized objective function [7],[9]:

$$F(\mathbf{w}) = \beta E_X(\mathbf{w}) + \alpha E_W(\mathbf{w}) = \frac{\beta}{2} \sum_{i=1}^{N} \{\mathbf{y}_i - \mathbf{t}_i\}^2 + \frac{\alpha}{2} \sum_{j=1}^{N_W} w_j^2 \ , \qquad (4)$$

where **w** corresponds to the vector of the network weights and the N_W represent the number of network parameters. The E_X and E_W indicate the sum of the squared errors and the sum of the squares of the network weights, respectively.

At each step, the objective function $F(\mathbf{w})$ is minimized using the Levenberg-Marquardt algorithm to provide a solution $\mathbf{w}_{MP}$. Then, optimal values for parameters α and β at the minimum point $\mathbf{w}_{MP}$ can be computed as follows [7],[9]:

$$\hat{\alpha} = \frac{\gamma}{2E_W(\mathbf{w}_{MP})} \text{ and } \hat{\beta} = \frac{N - \gamma}{2E_X(\mathbf{w}_{MP})}, \quad (5)$$

The quantity γ represents the effective number of network parameters **w** and can be defined as $\gamma = N_W - 2\hat{\alpha}\text{Tr}\hat{\mathbf{H}}^{-1}$. The GNBR algorithm exploits the approximation of the Hessian provided by the minimization method [8]. In cases where the number of effective parameters is equal to the actual ones ($\gamma \approx N_W$), more hidden units must be added to the network. It must be noted that in our experiments, the best results for the GNBR algorithm were obtained by scaling the network inputs in the range $[-1, 1]$.

3 Experimental Results

Several experiments have been conducted to evaluate the proposed method. In all K-class classification problems, each protein family $\mathcal{S}_k$ ($k = 1, \ldots, K$) was randomly partitioned into training and test sequences, with the training set being only a small percentage (5 - 10%) of the family dataset. Experiments have been carried out using the MEME algorithm to discover either groups of $D_k = 5$ *class-dependent* motifs for each family, or a group of $D = 5 \times K$ *class-independent* motifs using the total training dataset (ignoring the class labels). In this way two datasets are created containing D-dimensional feature vectors, denoted by $\mathbf{X}_s$ for the class-dependent case and $\mathbf{X}_g$ for the class-independent case, respectively. To evaluate classification performance, ROC (Receiver Operating Characteristic) analysis was used. More specifically, we used the ROC_{50} curve which is a plot of the sensitivity as a function of false positives for various decision threshold values θ until 50 false positives are found.

We have selected the two real (public) datasets in our experimental study. The first dataset (nearly 2000 sequences) consists of $K = 6$ families depicted from the PROSITE database, which is a large collection of protein families. The second one (nearly 1800 sequences) contais $K = 7$ subfamilies from the G-protein coupled receptors (GPCR) superfamily. The difficulty of recognizing GPCR subfamilies arises from the fact that their classification has been made based on chemical properties rather than sequence homology.

In the first series of experiments we assessed the impact of using 2-grams (background features). To do this, we constructed a new feature space consisting of only global features. In particular, we defined the feature g_{iq} as the relative frequency of each 2-gram q ($q = 1, \ldots, \Omega^2$) in a sequence S_i. Furthermore, we ignore *redundant* 2-grams and consider only the n_g features g_{iq} that occur frequently (at least half of the N training sequences). Therefore, the new created dataset, called **G**, would contain n_g global features of the input sequences. In summary, we have created five different sets of features: $\mathbf{X}_s, \mathbf{X}_g, \mathbf{X}_s \cup \mathbf{G}, \mathbf{X}_g \cup \mathbf{G}$ and **G** for each problem and we measured their discriminative ability. The neural network architecture had one hidden layer of either 10 for the cases $\mathbf{X}_s$ and $\mathbf{X}_g$, or 20 nodes for the other three datasets.

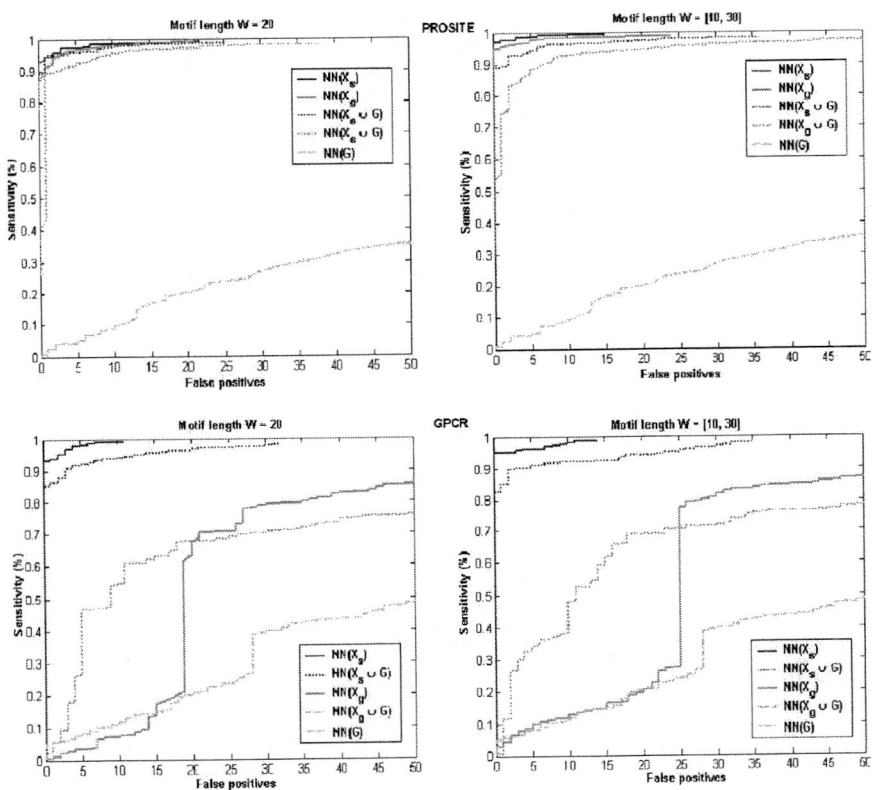

Fig. 1. ROC_{50} curves illustrating the performance of the neural classifier on the two datasets using the five different feature vectors.

Figure 1 displays the ROC_{50} curves obtained after training the five neural classifiers. For each problem two different graphs are presented concerning motifs of fixed length ($W = 20$) and of variable length ($W \in [10, 30]$). As it is obvious, motif-based features itself constitute an excellent source of information that lead to the construction of efficient classifiers. In all cases, the neural networks trained by mixed (local and global) features (e.g. $\text{NN}(\mathbf{X}_s \cup \mathbf{G})$) exhibit lower classification accuracy compared to the corresponding classifier trained with only motif-based features (e.g. $\text{NN}(\mathbf{X}_s)$). Furthermore, the 2-gram features alone (case $\text{NN}(\mathbf{G})$) do not seem to contain significant discriminant information. The best classification results were obtained with the network NN($\mathbf{X}_s$). This indicates that the class-dependent motifs achieve better allocation among the K families and thus more efficient modeling, in comparison with the class-independent case.

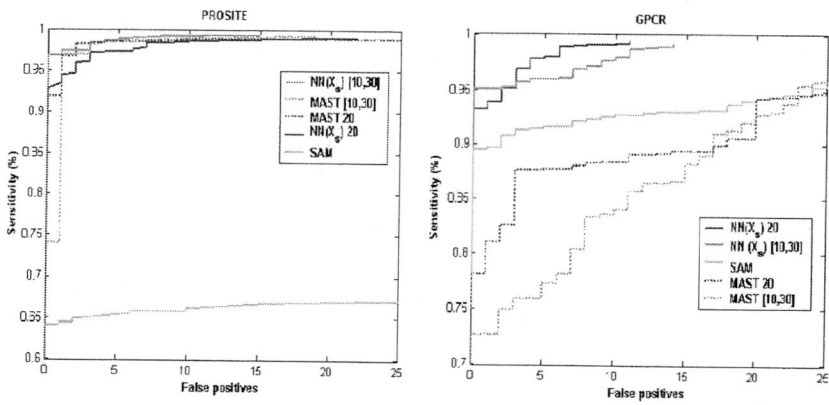

Fig. 2. ROC$_{25}$ curves for the three methods (neural (NN), MAST and SAM) on the two datasets.

During the second series of experiments we have compared the best neural classifier (NN($\mathbf{X}_s$)) with two other protein classification methods, namely the MAST homology detection algorithm [5] and the SAM method based on HMMs [1]. As it has already been discussed, both methods create (indirectly or directly) a probabilistic model-profile for each family and they classify each test sequence into the class with the best score value (minimum E-value). Figure 2 provides comparative results for the two datasets. Five ROC curves are presented until 25 false positives were found (ROC$_{25}$). The performance of the neural classifier and MAST was given by two curves concerning motifs of fixed ($W = 20$) and variable length ($W = [10, 30]$), respectively. In the case of MAST and SAM methods, ROC curves were obtained by setting several E-value thresholds. When the lowest estimated E-value was greater than the threshold then the test sequence was considered unclassified.

The superior classification of the proposed neural approach is obvious from the plotted curves in all problems, offering greater sensitivity rates with perfect specificity (zero false positives). The classification improvement is more clear in the GPCR dataset. A sensitivity rate of 99.30% was measured with only 11 false positives, while the corresponding results for MAST and SAM are (95.76%, 25) and (95.38%, 25), respectively. A last observation is that, although the MAST approach uses the same groups of motifs, our method seems to offer a more efficient scheme for combining the motif match scores, in comparison with their p-values as suggested by MAST.

4 Conclusions

In this paper we have presented a neural network approach for the classification of protein sequences. The proposed methodology is motivated by the principle that in biological sequence analysis motifs can provide major diagnostic features. Based on the MEME algorithm, we discover probabilistic motifs in a set of K-class sequences. Two alternative ways have been suggested depending on whether or not the class labels are taken into account. Then, numerical feature vectors are generated by computing the matching score of the sequences to each motif. At the second stage, the extracted feature vectors are used as inputs to a feed-forward neural network trained using a Bayesian Regularization algorithm that provides the class label of a sequence. Experimental results clearly illustrate the superiority of our neural approach in comparison with other probabilistic methods. In addition, we have shown that background features do not provide a useful source of information for the classification task, since they do not lead to performance improvement. Future work is focused on studying alternative methods both in the classification and the motif discovery stage.

References

1. Hughey R. and Krogh A. Hidden Markov models for sequence analysis: Extension and analysis of the basic method. *CABIOS*, 12(2):95–107, 1996.
2. Wang J.T.L., Ma Q., Shasha D., and Wu C.H. New techniques for extracting features from protein sequences. *IBM: Systems Journal*, 40(2):426–441, 2001.
3. Bréjova B., DiMarco C., Vinař T., Hidalgo S.R., Holguin G., and Patten C. Finding patterns in biological sequences. Project Report for CS798g, University of Waterloo, 2000.
4. Ma Q. and Wang J.T.L. Application of Bayesian neural networks to protein sequence classification. In *ACM SIGKDD Int. Conf. on Knowledge Discovery and Data Mining*, pages 305–309, Boston, MA, USA, Aug 2000.
5. Bailey T.L. and Gribskov M. Combining evidence using p-values: application to sequence homology searches. *Bioinformatics*, 14:48–54, 1998.
6. Bailey T.L. and Elkan C. Fitting a mixture model by expectation maximization to discover motifs in biopolymers. In *Second International Conference on Intelligent Systems for Molecular Biology*, pages 28–36, Menlo Park, California, 1994. AAAI Press.
7. MacKay D.J.C. Bayesian interpolation. *Neural Computation*, 4:415–447, 1992.
8. Foresse F.D. and Hagan M.T. Gauss-Newton approximation to Bayesian regularization. In *Proceedings of the 1997 International Joint Conference on Neural Network*, pages 1930–1935, 1997.
9. Bishop C.M. *Neural Networks for Pattern Recognition*. Oxford Univ. Press Inc., New York, 1995.

On a Dynamic Wavelet Network and Its Modeling Application

Yasar Becerikli[1,*], Yusuf Oysal[2], and Ahmet Ferit Konar[3]

[1]Kocaeli University, Computer Engineering Depart., Izmit Turkey
becer@kou.edu.tr
[2]Anadolu University, Computer Eng. Depart., Eskisehir Turkey
yoysal@anadolu.edu.tr
[3]Dogus University, Computer Eng. Depart., Istanbul, Turkey
fkonar@dogus.edu.tr

Abstract. This study presents a nonlinear dynamical system modeling with dynamic wavelet networks (DWNs). Wavelet is widely used in processing of signals and data. It has been also shown that wavelet can be effectively used in nonlinear system modeling. For this, dynamic wavelet networks (DWNs) structure based on Hoppfield networks has been developed. DWN has a lag dynamic, non orthogonal mother wavelets as activation function and interconnection weights. Network weights are adjusted based on supervised training. With fast training algorithms (quasi-Newton methods), wavelet networks are trained. In this paper, Mexican Hat wavelet. First, a phase-portraits based example is given. For this, it has been shown that DWN has chaos properties. The last, a dynamical system with discrete-event is modeled using DWN. There is a localization property at discrete-event instant for time-frequency in this example.

1 Introduction

Wavelet theory is widely used in signal and image processing and function approximation [1]-[4]. There are many studies about modeling and control with artificial neural networks (ANNs) [4]-[9]. In the standard ANN, nonlinearity obtains with all activation functions. These type networks are known universal approximator and some problems force. Recently, new solution approaches have been developed both of ANN and wavelet techniques [3][4][10][11]. Many methods necessitate the past of input-output data for controlling and estimation of unknown systems. As an alternative method, wavelet networks can be used for modeling of nonlinear dynamic systems [10]-[12]. In this study, as the DNN and DFN [13]-[16] based on Hopfield networks, DWN mathematical model has been developed.

In 2th section, wavelet and DWN structure present. It has been shown in an example that DWN has some properties in nonlinear systems in 3th section. In section 4, the gradient calculation and sensitivity analysis have been explained for training of DWN. In the last section, a simulation example presents using a continuous dynamic system with discrete-event.

---

* Corresponding author

2   Dynamic Wavelet Networks Model Structure

DWN has unconstraint interconnection parameters, dynamic units and wavelet activation functions. Fig. 1 shows diagram of a DWN with three-neurons. Wavelet neuron input over a lag dynamic transports to output via wavelet activation function (see Fig. 4)

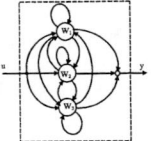

Fig. 1. DWN schematic diagram with three-neuron

Wavelets are usually explained as basis functions which are compact (closed and bounded), orthogonal (or orthonormal) and have time-frequency localization properties. But, to provide all of those properties is very difficult. Basis functions are called "activation function" in ANN literature and can be with global or local feature in time. The local basis functions are only active near the center, the value tends to zero far from the center, but global basis functions don't. The most important disadvantage of orthonormal compact basis functions doesn't able to obtain in the closed analytical form. The local basis functions are only active for certain inputs. In addition, the generalization errors decrease [17]. The most important local function is Gaussian and general Gaussian;

$$\phi(x) = \exp(-\tfrac{x^2}{2}), x \in R \ , \ \phi(\tfrac{x-\mu}{\sigma}) = \exp(-\tfrac{1}{2}\left(\tfrac{x-\mu}{\sigma}\right)^2), x \in R \qquad (1), (2)$$

where $\phi \in L^2(R)$, μ is center or translation, σ is standard deviation or dilation. The localization of Gaussian function in time is shown in Fig. 2(a). But, Gaussian function is not local in frequency Fig. 2(b).

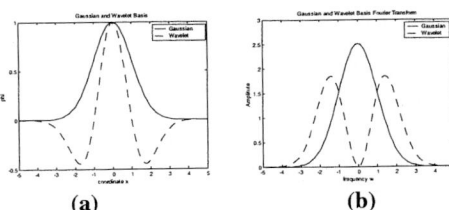

Fig. 2. (a) Gaussian (solid) and wavelet (dashed) basis functions (b) The Fourier transform of Gaussian (solid) and wavelet (dashed) basis functions

If a function is described in a bounded interval and has very small value outside, then that function is local in time. The local function in time can be shifted by changing its center. If the frequency spectrum of the local function in time is described in a bounded frequency interval and has very small value outside and also can be shifted by changing its dilation, then that function is local in frequency.

Gaussian based ANN doesn't have localization capability in frequency. As shown in Fig. 2 (b), Gaussian function is not local in frequency. Therefore, it is very difficult to use it [18]. It is very effective way to use wavelet functions with time-frequency localization properties [19]. The time and frequency envelope of the Mexican Hat function (second derivative of Gaussian) is shown in Fig. 3. First derivative of the Gaussian function can be used [20][21]. Mexican Hat basis function can be easily write on the analytical form and can be found its Fourier transform [10],

$$\phi(x_i) = (1 - x_i^2)\exp(-\tfrac{x_i^2}{2}), x \in R \; , \; \phi(\omega) = \sqrt{2\pi}\omega^2 \exp(-\tfrac{\omega^2}{2}), \omega \in R \qquad (3),(4)$$

where ω is a real frequency. The equation (3) can be generalized as follows;

$$\phi_i(\tfrac{x_i - \mu_i}{\sigma_i}) = (1 - (\tfrac{x_i - \mu_i}{\sigma_i})^2)\exp(-\tfrac{1}{2}(\tfrac{x_i - \mu_i}{\sigma_i})^2) \qquad (5)$$

Wavelet functions have efficient time-frequency localization properties [20]. As in Fig. 3, if the dilation parameter is changed, the support region width of the wavelet function changes, but the number of cycles doesn't change. When the dilation parameter decreases, the peak point of the spectrum shifts to higher frequency. Equation (3) has been used as a mother wavelet [10]. N dimensional mother wavelet can be given in the separable structure with product rule as follows [3][11][19]-[21];

$$\Phi_i(x) = \prod_{j=1}^{N} \phi_j(\tfrac{x_j - \mu_{ij}}{\sigma_{ij}}) \qquad (6)$$

where $x_j \in R^N$ is input and N is input number. A function y=f(x) can be represented with wavelets obtaining from the mother wavelet, [19]-[21] below;

$$y_i = h_i(x) = \sum_{j=1}^{N_w} c_{ij}\Phi_j(x) + a_{i0} + \sum_{k=1}^{N} a_{ik}x_k \qquad (7)$$

where c_{ij} is coefficients of mother wavelets, N_w is the number of wavelets, a_{i0} is a mean or bias term and a_{ik} is the linear term coefficients of this approach.

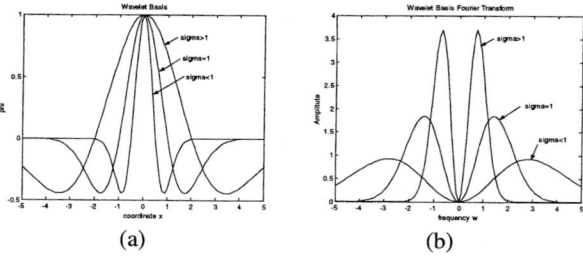

Fig. 3. Illustration of the dilation parameter effect (a) Mexican Hat wavelet function (b) Its Fourier transforms

Wavelet function in this structure will be used in DWA given Fig. 1.The structure used in [13]-[16] has been adapted to this network. Wavelets in equations (6) and (7) will be used as activation function in the network. Each activation function has a single input/single output (SISO) and can be re-expressed as follows;

$$\Phi_i(x_i) = \phi_i(\tfrac{x_i-\mu_{ij}}{\sigma_{ij}}) \;,\; y_i = h_i(x_i) = \sum_{j=1}^{N_w} c_{ij}\phi_i(\tfrac{x_i-\mu_{ij}}{\sigma_i}) + a_{i0} + a_{i1}x_i \qquad (8),(9)$$

$$\phi_i(\tfrac{x_i-\mu_{ij}}{\sigma_{ij}}) = (1-(\tfrac{x_i-\mu_{ij}}{\sigma_{ij}})^2)\exp(-\tfrac{1}{2}(\tfrac{x_i-\mu_{ij}}{\sigma_{ij}})^2) \qquad (10)$$

The mathematical expression of DWN can be written as in DNN/DFN [13]-[16].

By a DWN, we mean a network with unconstrained connectivity and with dynamic elements (lag dynamics) in its wavelet processing units. The processing unit is called the wavelon, representing a single dynamic wavelet neuron. Fig. 4 shows a general computational model of DWN. Each wavelon has a dynamic unit. Mathematical computational model equations are summarized as follows;

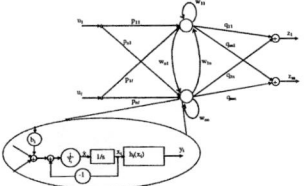

Fig. 4. General mathematical computational model diagram of DWN

$$z_i = \sum_{j=1}^{n} q_{ij} y_j \;,\; i=1.....M \quad,\quad y_j = h_j(x_j),\; j=1.......n \qquad (11),(12)$$

$$T_i \dot{x}_i = -x_i + \sum_{j=1}^{n} w_{ij} y_j + \sum_{j=1}^{L} p_{ij} u_j + b_i \;,\; x_i(0) = x_{i0} \qquad (13)$$

All parameters, initial conditions and input trajectories are given, the outputs of DWN can be calculated using numerical methods (5th order Runga Kutta-Butcher).

3 Illustrative Example for DWN

DWN can model any nonlinear physical dynamic systems. DWN has some behaviors (limit cycle, oscillator, and chaos etc.) that properties only belong to nonlinear systems. In this application, the number of mother wavelet is taken $N_w=3$.

DWN diagram with two-input/two-output and two-wavelon is shown in Fig. 5.

DWN as a Chaotic System
As an application, chaotic Lorenz [22] system has been used. Three-wavelon DWN can be trained and some parameters have been found by training belows

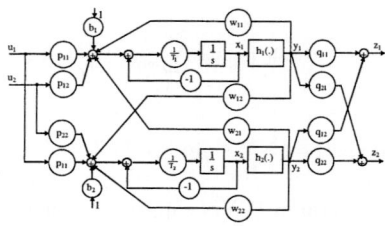

Fig. 5. State diagram of DWN with two-wavelon/two-input/two-output

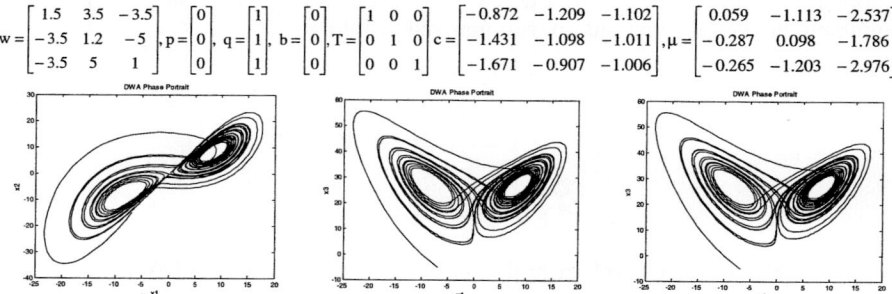

Fig. 6. The state-space trajectories of DWN as a chaotic system

DWN has behaved as a chaotic system ($x_i(0)$, i=1,2,3) as shown in Fig. 6
The DWN successfully captures behaviors of a nonlinear physical dynamic system

4 Parameter Optimization Based on Adjoint Sensitivity Analysis for DWN Training

The DWN training is to encapsulate a given set of trajectories by adjusting network parameters. This is done by minimizing the cost functional (error functional). The gradient-based algorithms have been used for this problem. The cost gradients w.r.t. network parameters are required for the algorithm. Our focus is to use adjoint sensitivity analysis for calculating the cost gradients w.r.t. all DWN parameters.

A performance index (PI) or cost is selected in the simple quadratic form;

$$J = \tfrac{1}{2}\int_0^{t_f}[z(t)-z^d(t)]^T[z(t)-z^d(t)]dt \tag{14}$$

where $e(t)=z(t)-z^d(t)$ is error function. $z(t)$ is DWN model response (output), $z^d(t)$ is desired (target) system response. The cost sensitivities w.r.t. various parameters;

$$\frac{\partial J}{\partial p_{ij}}, \frac{\partial J}{\partial w_{ij}}, \frac{\partial J}{\partial q_{ij}}, \frac{\partial J}{\partial T_i}, \frac{\partial J}{\partial b_i}, \frac{\partial J}{\partial c_{ij}}, \frac{\partial J}{\partial \mu_{ij}}, \frac{\partial J}{\partial \sigma_{ij}}, \frac{\partial J}{\partial a_{ij}} \tag{15}$$

The output weight gradients can be easily obtained by differentiating (11) and (14)

$$\frac{\partial J}{\partial q_{ij}} = \int_0^{t_f} [z_i(t) - z_i^d(t)] \frac{\partial z_i}{\partial q_{ij}} dt = \int_0^{t_f} e_i(t) y_j dt \qquad (16)$$

One approach to solving constrained dynamic optimization problem is based on the use of calculus of variations which is called "adjoint" method for sensitivity computation [5]-[8][13]-[16][23]. Differential equation number to be solved only depend on wavelon number, doesn't depend on DWN parameters. A new dynamical system defined with adjoint state variables λ_i is obtained;

$$-\dot{\lambda}_i = -\frac{1}{T_i}\lambda_i + \frac{1}{T_i}\sum_j w_{ij} y_j' \lambda_j + e_i(t)\sum_j q_{ij} y_j' \quad , \quad \lambda_i(t_f) = 0 \qquad (17)$$

$$y_i' = \frac{\partial h_i(x_i)}{\partial x_i} = -\sum_{j=1}^{N_w} c_{ij}\left(3\phi_i + 2(\frac{x_i - \mu_i}{\sigma_{ij}})^2\right)(\frac{x_i - \mu_i}{\sigma_{ij}^2}) + a_{i1} \qquad (18)$$

There are **n** quadratures for computing the sensitivities. The integration of the differential equations must be performed backwards in time, from t_f to 0. Let **p** be a vector containing all network parameters. Then, the cost gradients w.r.t. parameters are given by the following quadratures;

$$\frac{\partial J}{\partial p} = \int_0^{t_f} (\frac{\partial f}{\partial p})^T \lambda dt \qquad (19)$$

Gradients can be easily derived. The detailed results can be found in the literature [13]-[16]. We assume that at each iteration, gradients of the PI w.r.t. all DWN parameters is computed. Updating rule of parameters is below;

$$p^{k+1} = p^k + \tau^k d^k, \quad d^k = -H^k g_p^k, \quad g = \frac{\partial J}{\partial p} \qquad (20)$$

where d is the search direction, τ is the optimal step size along the search direction, g is the cost gradient with respect to parameter and $H \cong (\nabla_p J)^{-1}$ is the inverse of the approximate Hessian matrix. Broyden-Fletcher-Golfarb-Shanno (BFGS) gradient method has been used for updating of network weights [14][15][24].

5 Simulation Example

As an application, a nonlinear piecewise-continuous scalar function (discrete-event system) [11] has been considered in the dynamic structure (passing through **1/s**) by adding a control function and this function is wanted to model with DWN. For this, **f(x)** function is buried to $\dot{x} = f(x,u), x(t_0) = x_0, 0 \le t \le t_f$ expression as below;

$$\dot{x} = f(x,u) = \begin{cases} -2.186x - 12.864 + u, & -10 \le x < -2 \\ 4.246x + u, & -2 \le x < 0 \\ 10.\exp(-0.05x - 0.5) * \sin((0.03x + 0.7)x) + u, & 0 \le x < 10 \end{cases} \quad (21)$$

Modeling structure is shown in Fig. 7 (a). The used unit step gain functions $k_i(x)$ (i=1,2,3) are given in Fig. 7 (b). This process has been trained by DWN with a wavelon at time interval $t \in [0,10]$. The control function to be applied to the system input was selected for enough shaking the system as shown in Fig. 8 (a). The initial condition was taken x_0=-0.4. At the beginning of the training some modeling parameters were set to p_{ij}=1 and T_i=1, but the others were started randomly. After the training, process and DWN output are as in (a). The right-hand side of equation (13) for u(t)=0 (that is $\hat{f}(x)$, static side of DWN) has been successfully fitted to the real function f(x) given by right-hand side of equation (21) for u(t)=0 (see Fig. 8 (b)). As can be seen that, the joint point at x=-2 was successfully modeled with DWN.

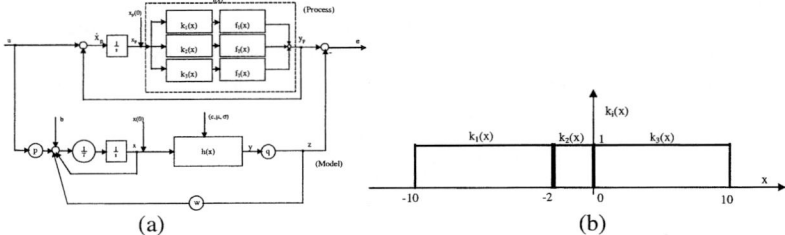

Fig. 7. (a) Modeling diagram of discrete-event system (b) The unit step gain functions

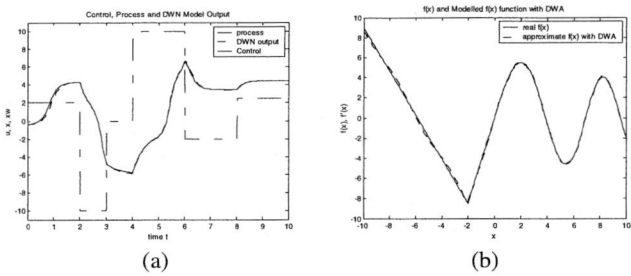

Fig. 8. The modeled process with DWN (a) Control input (dashed-dotted line), DWN output (dashed line) and process output (solid line) (b) DWN approximation $\hat{f}(x)$ (dashed line) and real function f(x) (solid line)

6 Conclusions and Future Works

In this work, we presented an intelligent method to be used in modeling, control and the other applications. Any nonlinear physical dynamic system can be captured by DWN. Simulation results show that the dynamic network structure can grow more accurate by wavelet approximators.

All of the results presented here were obtained with the help of a trained DWN which generated the model response policy close to the target process. In the illustrative examples, the dynamic networks used have some nonlinear dynamic system behaviors such as chaotic, etc.

In the simulation presented here, we used a nonlinear system with discrete-event system. The network was successfully used for modeling the target process. Therefore, DWN has produced satisfactory results. The exact Hessian based optimization algorithm for application to DWN is valuable approximation to speed up training time. In addition, the local and orthogonal wavelet usage in these areas can increase the training speed for DWN.

References

[1] Erdol, N. and Başbuğ, F., "Wavelet Transform Based Adaptive Filters: Analysis and New Results", IEEE Tran. on Signal Processing, vol 44(9), pp. 2163–2169, 1996
[2] S. G. Mallat, "Multifrequency Channel Decompositions of Images and Wavelet Models", IEEE Trans. on ASSP, Vol.37, No.12, pp. 2091–2109, December, 1987
[3] J. Zhang, G. G. Walter and at all, "Wavelet Neural Networks for Function Learning", IEEE Trans. on Signal Processing, Vol.43, No.6, pp.1485–1497, June, 1995
[4] Q. Zhang, "Using Wavelet network in Nonparametric Estimation", IEEE Trans. on Neural Networks, Vol.8, No.2, March, 1997
[5] T. Samad, and A. Mathur, "System Identification with neural Networks.' Technical Report CSDD-89-I4920-2, Honeywell SSDC, 3660 Technology Drive, Minneapolis, MN 55418, 1988.
[6] T. Samad, and A. Mathur, "Parameter estimation for process control with neural networks." International Journal of Approximate Reasoning, 1992.
[7] A.F. Konar, and T. Samad, "Hybrid Neural Network/ Algorithmic System Identification." Technical Report SSDC-91-I4051-1, Honeywell SSDC, 3660 Technology Drive, Minneapolis, MN 55418, 1991.
[8] M. Gherrity, "A learning algorithm for analog, fully recurrent neural networks." Proc. Int. Joint Conf. on Neural Networks, Vol. 1, pp. 643–644, 1989.
[9] K.S. Narendra, and K. Parthasarathy, "Identification and Control of Dynamical Systems using Neural Networks." IEEE Trans. on Neural Networks, Vol.1, No.1, March, 1990.
[10] Y. Tan, X. Dang, F. Liang, and C.Y. Su, "Dynamic Wavelet Neural Network for Nonlinear Dynamic System Identification", Proc. of the 2000 IEEE, Int. Conf. on Control Applications, Alaska, USA, September, 2000.
[11] Q. Zhang and A. Benveniste, "Wavelet Networks", IEEE Trans. on Neural Networks, Vol.3, No.6, November, 1992
[12] D. Wang, J.A. Romagnoli and A.A Safavi, "Wavelet Based Adaptive M-Estimator for Nonlinear System Identification", AIChE Journal, Vol.6, No.8, August, 2000
[13] A.F. Konar, and T.Samad, "Dynamic Neural Networks." Technical report SSDC-92-I 4142-2, Honeywell Technology Center, 3660 Technology Drive, Minneapolis, MN 55418, 1992
[14] Y. Becerikli, " Neuro-Optimal Control", Ph.D Thesis, Sakarya University, Sakarya, Turkey, July 1998
[15] Y. Oysal, "Feuro Modeling and Optimal Fuzzy Control", Ph.D Thesis, Sakarya University, Sakarya, Turkey, January 2002
[16] A.F. Konar, Y. Oysal, Y. Becerikli and T. Samad, "Dynamic Fuzzy Network for Real-Time Applications", TAINN'99, Boğaziçi Üniversitesi, İstanbul , Haz. 1999

[17] J. Leonard, and M. Kramer, "Radial Basis Function Networks for Classifying Process Faults", IEEE Control Systems, Vol.31, 1991
[18] R. Sanner and J-J. E. Slotine, "Gaussian Networks for direct Adaptive Control", IEEE Trans. on Neural Networks, Vol.13, No.6, pp. 837–863, 1992.
[19] M. Cannon and J-J. E. Slotine, "Space Frequency Localized basis Function Networks for Nonlinear System Estimation and Control", Neurocomputing, Vol.9, No.3, pp.293–342, 1995
[20] S. Mallat, "A Theory for Multiresulation Signal Decomposition: the Wavelet Representation", IEEE Trans. On Pattern Analysis and Machine Intelligence, Vol.11, No.7, pp.674–693,1989
[21] Y. Oussar, I. Rivals, et al, "Training Wavelet Networks for Nonlinear Dynamic Input-Output Modeling", Neurocomputing, Vol.20, pp.173–188,1998.
[22] H.K. Khalil,: "Nonlinear Systems", Prentice-Hall, Inc., 1996.
[23] A.F:, Konar, Y. Becerikli, and T. Samad: "Trajectory Tracking with Dynamic Neural Networks", IEEE, Int. Sym. On Intelligent Control (ISIC'97), İstanbul 1997.
[24] P.E. Gill, W. Murray, and M.H. Wright, "Practical Optimization", Academic Press Ltd., 1993.

Neural Network Hardware

Low Power Digital Neuron for SOM Implementations

Roberta Cambio and David C. Hendry

School of Engineering and Physical Sciences, University of Aberdeen,
Kings College, Aberdeen, Scotland, AB24 3UE
{r.cambio,d.c.hendry}@eng.abdn.ac.uk

Abstract. As applications of the Self-Organising Map emerge in portable devices, power dissipation becomes a crucial design issue. The digital implementation of the SOM which is introduced in this paper meets low power requirements by means of increasing silicon area while reducing the number of clock cycles required to process each element of an input vector. Designs of a single neuron requiring two clock cycles, one clock cycle, and $\frac{1}{2}$ clock cycle per element of the input vector are presented. The designs offer a reduction in power of a factor of 3 for an increase in silicon area of some 33%. The contribution of each routine composing training and classification to total power is also illustrated.

1 Background

The Self Organising Map (SOM) [1] algorithm has been used in a variety of applications ranging from process and machine monitoring to robot-arm control and telecommunications. If the dimensionality of the problem is not very high and computing is not required in real time, a workstation running a SOM software can satisfy the requirements. However, this approach can not be effective when real-time or high-performance is required, hence the need for custom hardware which accelerates the execution of the SOM algorithm arises. In this context a number of designs have been proposed, for a review of which see [3]. The chips described in [5], [6] and [2] are examples of a trend towards general processing elements, closely resembling RISC or VLIW processors with reduced arithmetic capabilities [3]. In fact the three designs show a Single Instruction stream Multiple Data stream (SIMD) architecture in which each neuron corresponds to one processor element in the SIMD array. Each processor element is a simple RISC processor with a small instruction set.

As portable applications, such as mobile phone handsets, have become an interesting market for the SOM, most of the design efforts must be focused on power dissipation. Some researchers [2] integrated an array of 256 processors onto a single die using a $0.65 \mu m$ process. This device uses a 50MHz clock, giving a total measured power dissipation of 3W with a 5V supply when operating at its maximum classification rate. With current VLSI processes of $0.13 \mu m$ and below, at least 1024 processors, and possibly 4096 processors, may be placed on a single die. Clock frequencies of at least 200MHz are known to be feasible. With such increasing processor count, and increasing clock frequency, power dissipation is as much an issue in such a design as silicon area.

This paper presents a design approach for a single neuron which gives a useful reduction in the dissipated power of the SOM circuitry for such applications.

2 Method

In the SOM algorithm, or the closely related LVQ (Learning Vector Quantisation) algorithm, each neuron stores a *reference vector*, represented here as $m_i = (\mu_{i1}, \mu_{i2}, \ldots, \mu_{in}) \in \Re^n$ where μ_{ij} are scalar values, i is the neuron index, and j the index of a reference vector element. Each neuron undergoes a *classification* step composed of two routines, which will be called respectively *Calc_distance* and *Find_active* throughout the paper in order to ease their reference. During *Calc_distance* an input vector $x = (\xi_1, \xi_2, \ldots, \xi_n) \in \Re^n$ is communicated to all neurons. The distance d_i from each reference vector m_i to the input vector x is then calculated. Usually the Euclidean distance is chosen, which requires n multiplications and a square root. Since multipliers require large chip area in digital designs, the Manhattan distance is preferred to the Euclidean distance, hence defining the distance d_i as:

$$d_i = \sum_{j=1}^{n} |\xi_j - \mu_{ij}|$$

In this way the necessary chip area is minimized and the number of processing elements which could fit onto a single chip is maximized.

Following the calculation of the d_i *Find_active* finds the minimum such distance, and the neuron with that minimum distance becomes the *active* neuron. If the network is to undergo *training* then the *neighbourhood* of the active neuron is identified during a routine which will be called *Neighbourhood*. Neurons in the neighbourhood will be moved closer to the current training input vector by modifying their reference vectors during a successive routine which will be referred to as *Update*.

In this paper we consider the power requirements of an initial training (continuous iterations of a classification step and a training step) of a single neuron followed by a classification phase (repeated execution of a classification step). It is clear that power requirements for a training step (that is, during the exection of *Neighbourhood* and *Update*) are substantially less than those required for classification since only a small subset of the total number of neurons will operate during a training step. It is assumed that all neurons outwith the neighbourhood are placed in a low-power mode, by for example gating the clock signal to such neurons. Training schemes for the SOM begin with 25% or more of the available neurons within the neighbourhood, but this figure typically drops so that the neighbourhood includes only the active neuron and its nearest neighbours, approximately 1% of the available neurons for a 256 processor array [1]. As such the distance calculation requires the bulk of the supplied power, and therefore is the first target for power reduction.

The approach taken is to construct designs of varying performance levels with a view to saving power by requiring fewer clock cycles for the execution of the distance calculation. In both [7] and [8] such a strategy was reported as reducing power for CISC processors, RISC processors and DSP processors. In this strategy datapaths of varying complexity implement *Calc_distance*. A simpler datapath (such as the 2 clocks design below) offers reduced area but requires additional clock cycles. A more complex datapath (such as the $\frac{1}{2}$ clock design) requires greater area but completes the calculation in fewer clocks. Both designs require instruction decoding, instruction delivery and delivery of the input vector.

Table 1. Two clock cycles per element pipeline

Opcode	\multicolumn{5}{c}{Clock Cycle}
	1	2	3	4	5
DST $j+1$	IX	DE	$d_i = d_i + \|\Delta d_i\|$ fetch $\mu_{i,j+1}$		
SUB		IX		DE	$\Delta d_i = \xi_j - \mu_{i,j}$	
DST $j+2$			IX	DE	$d_i = d_i + \|\Delta d_i\|$ fetch $\mu_{i,j+2}$

Table 2. One clock cycle per element pipeline

Opcode	\multicolumn{4}{c}{Clock Cycle}
	1	2	3	4
DS1 $j+1$	IX	DE	fetch $\mu_{i,j+1}$; $\Delta d^+ = \xi_j - \mu_{i,j}$; $d_i = d_i + \|\Delta d^-\|$	
DS1 $j+2$		IX	DE	fetch $\mu_{i,j+2}$; $\Delta d^+ = \xi_{j+1} - \mu_{i,j+1}$; $d_i = d_i + \|\Delta d^-\|$

Three designs, requiring respectively 2, 1, or $\frac{1}{2}$ clock cycles per element of the input vector have been compared for their power dissipation. Since each processor is an element of an SIMD array, no instruction fetch is required. Instructions and where required data are supplied to the processor by an external *array controller* which is not considered here. One clock cycle is required to propagate the instruction and data to all processors within the array, denoted by IX in the tables 1, 2 and 3 below. Each instruction is then decoded, again requiring a single clock cycle, denoted by DE below.

2 clocks. The neurons in this design use a two-stage pipeline consisting of an instruction decode phase and an instruction execute phase. Two instructions

Table 3. $\frac{1}{2}$ clock cycle per element pipeline

Opcode	1	2	Clock Cycle 3	4
DS2 $j+2$	IX	DE	fetch $\mu_{i,j+2}, \mu_{i,j+3}$ $\Delta d_1^+ = \xi_j - \mu_{ij}$ $\Delta d_2^+ = \xi_{j+1} - \mu_{i,j+1}$ $\Delta d^+ = |\Delta d_1^-| + |\Delta d_2^-|$ $d_i = d_i + \Delta d^-$	
DS2 $j+4$		IX	DE	fetch $\mu_{i,j+4}, \mu_{i,j+5}$ $\Delta d_1^+ = \xi_{j+2} - \mu_{i,j+2}$ $\Delta d_2^+ = \xi_{j+3} - \mu_{i,j+3}$ $\Delta d^+ = |\Delta d_1^-| + |\Delta d_2^-|$ $d_i = d_i + \Delta d^-$

are required to calculate the distance between a single element of the input vector ξ_j and the corresponding element $\mu_{i,j}$ of the reference vector. The SUB instruction computes $\Delta d_i = \xi_j - \mu_{i,j}$ with ξ_j being supplied by a global bus to all processors. The DST instruction then adds this distance increment to the accumulated distance, $d_i = d_i + |\Delta d_i|$ and fetches $\mu_{i,j+1}$ from local memory. A single ALU is required. This is illustrated in the pipeline diagram of table 1.

1 clock. Again a two stage pipeline is used for instruction decode and execute. A single instruction computes $\Delta d_i = \xi_{j+1} - \mu_{ij+1}$ for the $j+1$th element, $d_i = d_i + |\Delta d_i|$ for the jth element and fetches μ_{ij+2} from memory in a single clock. Thus, excepting additional clock cycles at the start and end of the iteration over j needed to prime and flush the calculation, a single clock cycle is needed for each element of the input vector.

Two ALUs and additional intermediate registers are required. Table 2 shows the operation of the pipeline. In this table the superscript - denotes the value of a register at the start of the clock cycle, while a superscript of + denotes the value to be assigned to a register at the end of a clock cycle.

$\frac{1}{2}$ clock. In this design two elements of the input vector are processed per clock. Additional ALUs and registers are required. Two input vector elements are now assumed to be supplied via a wider input bus to an individual processor. Both elements are processed in parallel and their contribution to the total distance summed.

A single instruction initiates the fetch from memory of the reference vector elements for the next cycle, calculates two distance increments (Δd_1 and Δd_2), sums the absolute values of distance increments from the previous cycle and accumulates the total distance as shown in table 3.

It is worthwhile to mention that the additional hardware required by the 1 clock model and the $\frac{1}{2}$ clock model to implement *Calc_distance* helps to improve *Update* as well. In fact, while the 2 clocks model requires six clock cycles to update each reference vector element, 1 clock takes only two clock cycles for each element and $\frac{1}{2}$ clock further reduces this time to one clock cycle.

As far as the implementation of *Find_active* is concerned, the two clock model initially used a downcounting method. According to this method, each neuron decrements its distance by one until one neuron reaches zero. This method is clearly slow and may require many clock cycles, especially at the beginning of training when the reference vectors are not yet tuned. Moreover, it involves all neurons with an evident impact on power dissipation. Hence this method was substituted by a technique which uses a comparator tree external to the neural array. This comparator receives distances sent by all neurons and identifies the smallest among them. Consequently *Find_active* is reduced to output the distance followed by the identification number in case the current neuron is the winning neuron. All the three models described in this paper use such an implementation of *Find_active*.

3 Results

The designs above provide varying levels of performance and power dissipation. Power dissipation has therefore been computed for two cases: 1) with all three designs clocked at the same frequency (50MHz) and 2) with clock speeds of 200MHz, 100 MHz and 50MHz for the 2 clocks, 1 clock and $\frac{1}{2}$ clock designs respectively. The latter case is the most relevant comparison since the same data throughput is maintained (ignoring additional clock cycles to prime and flush the pipelines). Power figures for the two cases are shown in table 4. In both cases a single neuron was trained and then used for classification purposes.

Where differing clock frequencies are used two effects come into play. The first is simply the increased transition activity due to the faster clock. The second is that for the higher clock speeds, designs must be synthesised at that higher clock speed to meet the faster timing constraints. This further adds to the dissipated power due to the additional gates and resulting logic transitions. The 2 clock model illustrates this point: when synthesised for operation at 50Mhz the design requires 4.7mW, but at 200MHz the design requires not 4 x 4.7mW = 18.8mW, but 21.00mW as table 4 shows.

For all the three models a Register Transfer Level description was synthesized to a netlist with Synopsys Design Compiler. The target library was a $0.18\mu m$ standard cell library characterized for dynamic power estimation. Wire-load models appropriate to the size of each circuit were used to estimate capacitative loads. The netlists were then simulated with Synopsys VSS and no layout parasitics were back annotated since the design process was not extended downto the layout level. Result of a simulation was a file specifying the switching activity of the nets in the circuit. Finally, this file was read by Synopsys Power Compiler to estimate power. The power figures given include dynamic power only; this is a sum of the dynamic power dissipated inside each library cell and the dynamic power dissipated by toggling nets. Power due to leakage current is omitted. Area figures are in units of a single 2-input NAND gate and assume a placement utilisation of 80%.

Table 4. Power Dissipation and Area

Design	Same Clock Rate (50MHz)		Same Classification Rate	
	Power (mW)	Area	Power (mW)	Area
2 Clock	4.7	5255	21.00 (200MHz)	5737
1 Clock	5.25	5864	10.83 (100MHz)	6188
$\frac{1}{2}$ Clock	5.86	7594	5.86 (50MHz)	7594

Table 5. Power by major sub-component

Subcomponent	Design		
	$\frac{1}{2}$ clock (50MHz)	1 clock (100MHz)	2 clocks (200MHz)
Total Power	5.86mW	10.83mW	21.00mW
Memories	2.23mW (38%)	4.55mW (42%)	9.03mW (43%)
Clock Drivers	0.82mW (14%)	1.52mW (14%)	2.73mW (13%)
ALUs, Decode	0.41mW (7%)	0.76mW (7%)	2.52mW (12%)
Other (buses, muxes, registers, connect)	2.40mW (41%)	4.01mW (37%)	6.72mW (32%)

Table 6. Power Dissipated by each Routine

Routine	$\frac{1}{2}$ clock (50MHz)	1 clock (100MHz)	2 clocks (200MHz)
Total Power	5.86mW	10.83mW	21.00mW
Calc_distance	3.15mW (54%)	6.62mW (61%)	14.00mW (67%)
Find_active	2.04mW (35%)	2.70mW (25%)	2.89mW (14%)
Neighbourhood	0.15mW (3%)	0.19mW (2%)	0.37mW (2%)
Update	0.51mW (9%)	1.29mW (12%)	3.01mW (14%)

As may be seen from the third column of table 4, use of the $\frac{1}{2}$ clock per input element design gives a threefold reduction in dynamic power at the cost of a one third increase in area compared to the 2 clocks design.

Table 5 gives the percentage of the total power (for equivalent data rates) to major identifiable units within each design. A major component of the power in each is that due to the memories (both for the reference vectors and local storage). All designs here use synchronous RAM synthesised to standard cell flip-flops (this gives the minimum area for the size of memories used).

The power requirements of the additional ALUs and registers in the $\frac{1}{2}$ clock per element design are not significant, being much less than the additional power required in the 2 clocks per element design due to the higher clock frequency and subsequent increased switching activity.

Table 6 shows power dissipation of each routine for the three models working at the same data throughput. Calc_distance is clearly the routine with the highest impact on total power since it is executed during both the initial training and the following classification phase. As expected, its percentage over total power decreases as the number of clock cycles per element of the input vector decreases. In particular, use of the $\frac{1}{2}$ clock design per input gives a fourfold reduction in

Calc_distance's power. On the other hand, the contribution of Update is in the order of 10% of total power and diminishes with the reduction in the number of clock cycles. In fact Update recalculates the distance between the input vector and the reference vector and modifies the latter. Hence, when a classification step is followed by a training step, the power Update dissipates can be clearly as big as the power Calc_distance dissipates. However, if a training phase is followed by a classification phase, Update is limited to the first and its effect on total power results low. In more detail the $\frac{1}{2}$ clock design causes a sixfold reduction in the power dissipated by Update. Similarly the contribution due to Neighbourhood is quite modest. As far as Find_active is concerned, it evidently does not affect power significantly when the four routines are executed in a row since the minimum is calculated by a comparator tree and a single neuron simply sends its distance and, in case of victory, its identification number. When a neuron goes through training and classification, instead, Find_active's contribution to total power becomes higher because of the frequency of its execution.

4 Conclusions

In this paper a digital implementation of the SOM is presented. Special emphasis is placed on the power dissipation of a single neuron. It is demonstrated that power can be considerably decreased through a strategy of increasing area to provide additional parallelism within a neuron, so enabling a reduction in the number of clock cycles requested to calculate the distance between an input vector and a neuron's reference vector. It is estimated that the reduction in power is approximately 1/3, for a 33% increase in area. It is also shown that the Calc_distance routine counts for more than 50% of the power dissipated by a training phase followed by a classification phase, justifying our attention to that routine. The $\frac{1}{2}$ clock design guarantees a successful fourfold reduction in the fraction of power due to Calc_distance and, as a result of the hardware modifications requested by Calc_distance, a sixfold reduction in the fraction of power due to Update.

References

1. T. Kohonen "Self-Organizing Maps" 3rd ed. Springer 2001, *Springer Series in Information Sciences 30*
2. N. Lightowler, A.R. Allen, H. Grant, D.C. Hendry, C.T. Spracklen "The Modular Map" *Neural Networks* IJCNN'99 Vol. 2, pp 851–856
3. P. Ienne, T. Cornu, G. Kuhn "Special-Purpose Digital Hardware for Neural Networks: An Architectural Survey" Journal of VLSI Signal Processing Systems Vol 13 1996 pp. 5–25.
4. R. Tawel, N. Aranki, G.V. Puskorius, K.A. Marco, L.A. Feldkamp, J.V. James, G. Jesion, T.M. Feldkamp "Custom VLSI ASIC for automotive applications with recurrent networks" Neural Networks Proceedings, 1998, IEEE World Congress on Computational Intelligence. The 1998 IEEE International Joint Conference on, Vol 1, 1998, pp. 598–602.

5. S. Rüping, M. Porrmann and U. Rückert *SOM Accelerator System* Neurocomputing 21 (1998) pp. 31–50
6. M. S. Melton, T. Phan, D. S. Reeves and D. E. Van den Bout *The TInMANN VLSI Chip* IEEE Transactions on Neural Networks, Vol. 3, No. 3, May 1992, pp. 375–383
7. K. Roy and S. C. Prasad *Low-power CMOS VLSI circuit design* John Wiley and Sons, Inc. 2000
8. V. Tiwari, S. Malik, A. Wolfe, M.T.-C. Lee *Instruction Level Power Analysis and Optimisation of Software* Journal of VLSI Signal Processing, 1996

Direction Selective Two-Dimensional Analog Circuits Using Biomedical Vision Model

Masashi Kawaguchi[1], Kazuyuki Kondo[1], Takashi Jimbo[2], and Masayoshi Umeno[3]

[1] Department of Electrical Engineering, Suzuka National College of Technology,
Shiroko, Suzuka, Mie 510-0294 Japan
{masashi, kondo}@elec.suzuka-ct.ac.jp,
http://www.suzuka-ct.ac.jp/elec/
[2] Department of Environmental Technology and Urban Planning Graduate School of Engineering, Nagoya Institute of Technology, Gokiso-cho, Showa-ku, Nagoya, 466-8555 Japan
jimbo@elcom.nitech.ac.jp
[3] Department of Electronic Engineering, Chubu University,
1200 Matsumoto-cho, Kasugai, Aichi 487-8501 Japan
umeno@solan.chubu.ac.jp

Abstract. We propose herein a motion detection artificial vision model which uses analog electronic circuits. The proposed model is comprised of four layers. The first layer is a differentiation circuit of the large CR coefficient, and the second layer is a differentiation circuit of the small CR coefficient. Thus, the speed of the movement object is detected. The third layer is a difference circuit for detecting the movement direction, and the fourth layer is a multiple circuit for detecting pure motion output. We first designed a one-dimensional model, which we later enhanced to obtain a two-dimensional model. The model was shown to be capable of detecting a movement object in the image. Moreover, the proposed model can be used to detect two or more objects, which is advantageous for detection in an environment in which several objects are moving in multiple directions simultaneously.

1 Introduction

We propose herein a motion detection artificial vision model using analog electronic circuits. A neuro chip and an artificial retina chip are developed to comprise the neural network model and simulate the biomedical vision system. At present, basic image processing, such as edge detection and reverse display of an image has been achieved. [1][2] We measured the shape of the output waves produced by the input movement signal using an electronic circuit simulator (SPICE).
The retina consists of the inside retina and outside retina. The inside retina sends the nerve impulses to the brain, whereas the outside retina receives optical input from the visual cell. As a result, the outside retina emphasizes spatial changes in optical strength. Recently, the network between the amacrine cell, the bipolar cell and the

ganglion cell has been clarified theoretically, which has led to active research concerning the neuro device, which models the structure and function of the retina.

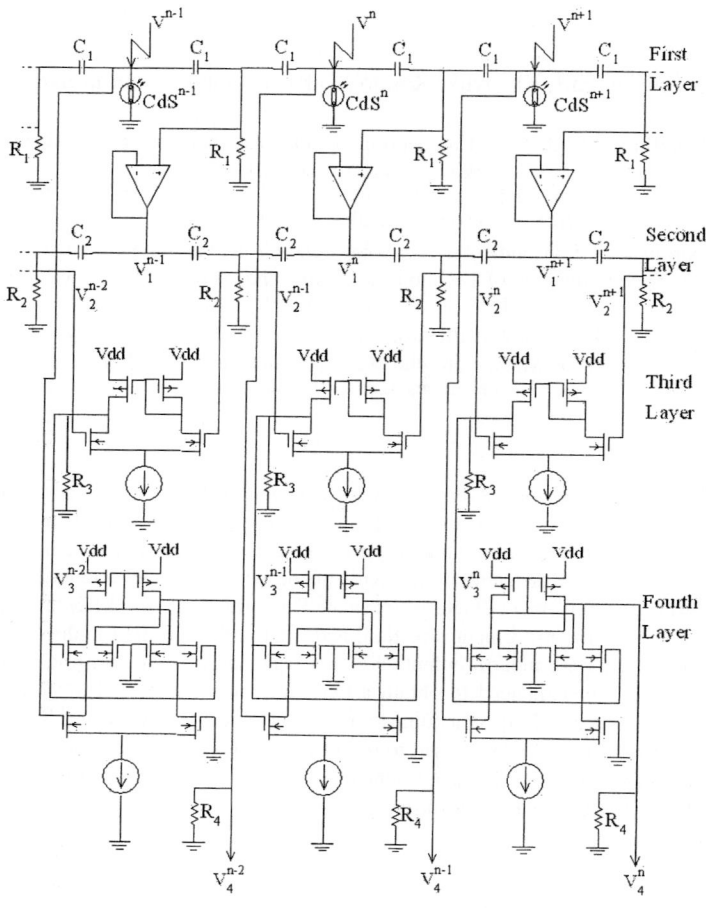

Fig. 1. One-Dimensional Four-Layered Direction Selective Motion Detection Model

Easy image processing, reversing, edge detection, and feature detection, have been achieved by technologies such as the neuro chip and the analog VLSI circuit. Some motion detection models are proposed in the recent research.
One paper describes the application of an analog VLSI vision sensor to active binocular tracking.[3] Another model is presented the implementation of a visual motion detection algorithm on an analog network. The algorithm is on Markov random field(MRF)modeling. Robust motion detection is achieved by using a spatiotemporal neighborhood for modeling pixel interactions. Not only are the moving edges detected, but also the inner part of moving regions.[4] The other model is an analog MOS circuit inspired by an inner retina. The analog circuit produces signals of motion of edges

which are output in an outer retinal neural network. Edge signals are formed into half-wave rectified impulses in 2 types of amacrine cells, and fed back to the wide field amacrine cell in order to modulate width of impulses.[5]

In the present study, we propose a motion detection model in which the speed is detected by differentiation circuits. The surface layer is composed of the connections of capacitors. In the inner layer, the movement direction is detected by difference circuits. When the object moves from left to right, a positive output signal is generated, and when the object moves from right to left, a negative output signal is generated. We show this model is able to detect the speed and direction of a movement object by the simple circuits. Despite the large object size, this model can detect the motion. The connection of this model is between adjacent elements, making hardware implementation easy.

2 One-Dimensional Model

We first composed a one-dimensional model, the structure of which is shown in Fig. 1.

2.1 First Layer Differentiation Circuits (First Layer)

The current is given by equation (1), where the input voltage is denoted by V^n and the capacitance is denoted by C_1. The current into a capacitor is the derivative with respect to time of the voltage across the capacitor, multiplied by the capacitance. The output voltage V_1^n is given by equation (2).

$$I = C_1 \frac{dV^n}{dt} \tag{1}$$

$$V_1^n = IR_1 = C_1 R_1 \frac{dV^n}{dt} \tag{2}$$

Equation (2) is multiplied the resistance R_1, calculating the voltage potential. Buffer circuits are realized by operational amplifiers between the first layer and the second layer. In the first layer, there are also the CdS Photoconductive Cells. Using CdS cells, this model is not affected by object luminance. When the object is high luminance, the resistances of CdS cells are low. Some currents flows to ground through the CdS. Therefore, despite the high luminance, the input Voltage V_1^n is not affected.

2.2 Second Layer Differentiation Circuits (Second Layer)

The second Layer is also composed of differentiation circuits; however, the CR coefficient is small compared that of the first layer differentiation circuits. The output of

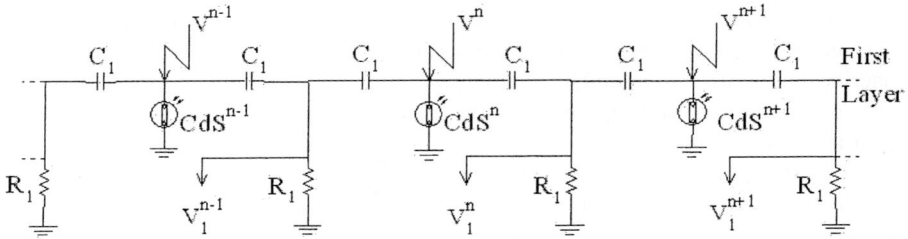

Fig. 2. First Layer Differentiation Circuits

first layer, V_1^n, is differentiated again, and the output of the second layer is assumed to be V_2^n, calculating the voltage potential. Using two layer differentiation circuits, this model can detect the motion despite the large object size.

$$I = C_2 \frac{dV_1^n}{dt} \tag{3}$$

$$V_2^n = IR_2 = C_2 R_2 \frac{dV_1^n}{dt} \tag{4}$$

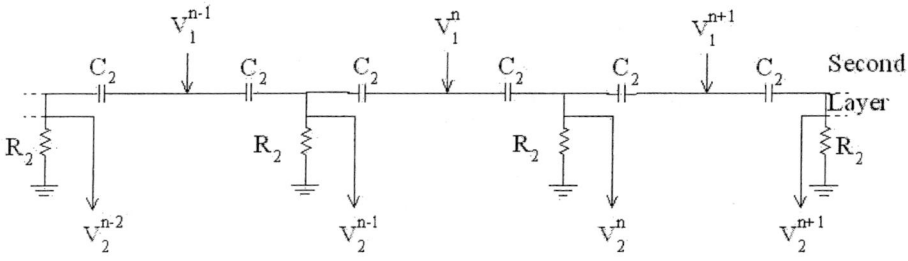

Fig. 3. Second Layer Differentiation Circuits

2.3 Difference Circuits (Third Layer)

The third layer consists of difference circuits realized by MOSFET. In Figure 4, the bottom I_b is a current source. The manner in which I_b is divided between Q_1 and Q_2 is a sensitive function of the difference between V_2^{n+1} and V_2^n, and is the essence of the operation of the stage. We assume the MOSFET device is in the sub-threshold region, the I-V characteristics follows the exponential characteristics, then the drain current ID in the sub-threshold region is exponential in the gate voltage V_g and source voltage V_s. V is electric potential of current source I_b. I_0 and κ are coefficients.

$$V_3^n = (I_1 - I_2)R_3 = I_b R_3 \tanh \frac{\kappa(V_2^{n+1} - V_2^n)}{2} \tag{5}$$

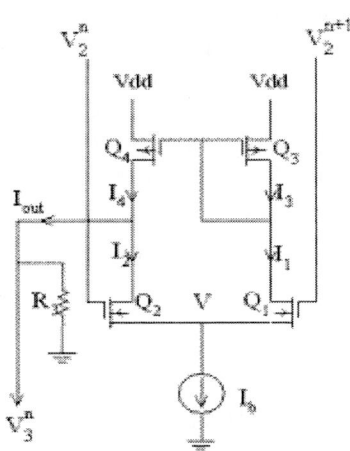

Fig. 4. Difference circuits(Third layer)

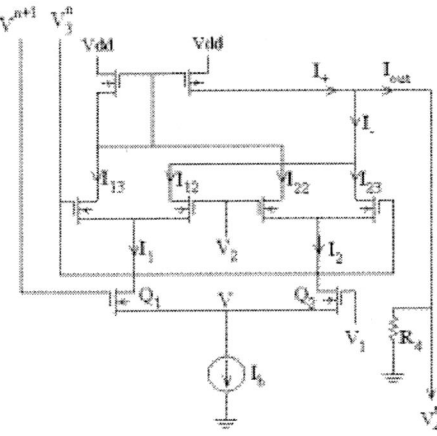

Fig. 5. Gilbert multiple circuits(fourth layer)

2.4 Gilbert Multiple Circuits (Fourth Layer)

The fourth layer is comprised of Gilbert multiple circuits. We show it in Figure 5. We assume the MOSFET device is in the sub-threshold region, the I-V characteristics follows the exponential characteristics, then the drain current I_D in the sub-threshold region is exponential in the gate voltage V_g and source voltage V_s. The result for the two drain currents of the differential pair were derived in Equation (6).
I_4^n is the output current of the fourth layer, R_4 is the earth resistance, and V_4^n is the final output. I_4^n corresponds to I_{out} in Figure 5. Using multiple circuits, this model can detects the pure output of movement. We set the parameter of circuits as follows. In the first layer, C_1=0.1μF, R_1=1kΩ. We used the μA741 as a buffer circuits. In the second layer, C_2=0.1μF, R_2=100kΩ. At the difference circuits, we used the VP1310 and VN1310 as MOSFET.[6][7]

$$V_4^n = I_4^n R_4 = I_\partial R_4 \tanh \frac{\kappa V_3^n}{2} \tanh \frac{\kappa V^{n+1}}{2} \tag{6}$$

3 The Two-Dimensional Model

We enhanced the one-dimensional model to obtain a two-dimensional model. The first layer (surface layer) is an array of capacitors, similar to a lattice, which has a simple structure and allows easy differentiation.

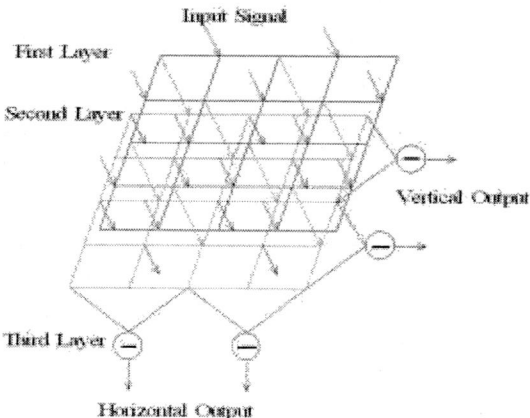

Fig. 6. Structure of the two-dimensional model

The second layer is also an array of capacitors similar to a lattice. The third layer consists of a subtraction circuit realized via a MOSFET.[8][9] The structure of the two-dimensional model is shown in Fig. 6. In Fig. 7 and Fig. 8 are final outputs of two-dimensional model. These output are for two objects moving simultaneously: one object is moving from left to right and the other object is moving from bottom to top.

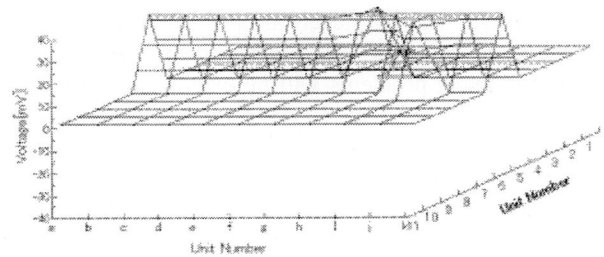

Fig. 7. Horizontal output for two objects moving simultaneously

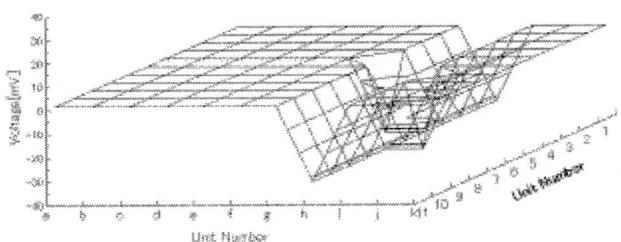

Fig. 8. Vertical output for two objects moving simultaneously

These results indicate that the two-dimensional model is able to detect the speed and the direction of the movement object in both one and two dimensions. Moreover, the output of the vertical direction can be deleted by adding a threshold circuit to each output terminal. As a result, element detection of the pure direction of the movement can be performed

4 Conclusion

We designed the motion detection analogue electric circuit using a biomedical vision system. We constructed one-dimensional model and two-dimensional model. The capacitor in the surface layer was arranged in a similar manner to the lattice in the two-dimension model. As a result, a simple circuit and an equivalent output result were obtained. The realization of an integration device will enable the number of elements to be reduced. The proposed model is robust with respect to fault tolerance. Moreover, the connection of this model is between adjacent elements, making hardware implementation easy.

The proposed model is applicable to movement sensors, measurement of road traffic volume, speed measurement, and counting the number of pedestrians in an area. Using the analog circuit not only simplifies the structure, but also provides excellent fault tolerance, as compared to digital circuits. Using the proposed model, moving objects can be detected even if two or more objects are present. This is advantageous for detection in environments in which several objects are moving in multiple directions simultaneously. The following problems will be examined in a future study. In two-dimensional model, we constructed 10*10 scale model. The enhancement for large-scale model is the future problem. And the detecting range of the moving object speed is about 10 terminals per seconds. Wide range speed detection is also future study. To solve this problem, very well matching transistors are needed. Finally, this model attempts to aid in the clarification of the biomedical vision system, particularly the mechanism of motion recognition. From a technological viewpoint, the proposed model facilitates clarification of the mechanism of the biomedical vision system, which should enable design and simulation by an analog electric circuit for detecting the movement and speed of objects.

References

1. Mead, C.: Analog VLSI and Neural Systems, Addison Wesley Publishing Company, Inc., (1989)
2. Chong, C. P., Salama, C. A. T., Smith. K. C.: Image-Motion Detection Using Analog VLSI, IEEE Journal of Solid-State Circuits Vol.27, No.1(1992) 93–96
3. Lu, Z., Shi, B. E.: Subpixel Resolution Binocular Visual Tracking Using Analog VLSI Vision Sensors, IEEE Transactions on Circuits and Systems-II: Analog and Digital Signal Processing, Vol.47, No.12 (2000)1468–1475
4. Luthon, F., Dragomirescu, D.: A Cellular Analog Network for MRF-Based Video Motion Detection, IEEE Transactions on Circuits and Systems-I: Fundamental Theory and Applications, Vol.46, No.2 (1999)281–293
5. Yamada, H., Miyashita, T., Ohtani, M., Yonezu, H.: An Analog MOS Circuit Inspired by an Inner Retina for Producing Signals of Moving Edges, Technical Report of IEICE, NC99-112 (2000) 149–155
6. Kawaguchi, M., Jimbo, T., Umeno, M.: Motion Detection Artificial Vision Model by the Two-Dimensional Analog Electronic Circuits, in Proc. ICONIP2000, Taejon, KOREA, (2000) FBP29
7. Kawaguchi, M., Shao, C., Jimbo, T., Umeno, M.: Motion Detecting Two-Dimensional Three-Layers Analog Electronic Circuits Using Biomedical Vision Model, Neural Information Processing, Fudan University Press, in Proc. ICONIP2001, Shanghai, CHINA (2001) 1225–1230
8. Kawaguchi, M., Jimbo, T., Umeno, M.: Motion Detection Two-Dimensional MOS Analog Electronic Circuits Using Biomedical Vision Model, in Proc.SCI2001, Orlando, USA, Vol.6, (2001)309–314
9. Kawaguchi, M., Jimbo, T., Umeno, M.: Motion Detecting Artificial Retina Model by Two-Dimensional Multi-Layered Analog Electronic Circuits, IEICE Transactions, E86-A-2(2003)387–395

Review of Capacitive Threshold Gate Implementations

V. Beiu[1], M.J. Avedillo[2] and J.M. Quintana[2]

[1]School of Electrical Engineer and Computer Science.
Washington State University. Pullman, WA 99164-2752, USA
vbeiu@eecs.wsu.edu

[2]Instituto de Microelectrónica de Sevilla, Centro Nacional de Microelectrónica,
Edificio CICA, Avda. Reina Mercedes s/n, 41012-Sevilla, SPAIN
{avedillo, josem}@imse.cnm.es

Abstract. This is an in-depth survey paper on capacitive hardware implementations of threshold logic gates. The different VLSI solutions include the switched capacitor and the floating gate and their variations. It will be shown how the distinct original proposals from both categories have evolved to become quite similar. The problems with this kind of implementations are pointed out, and their applications are discussed.

1 Introduction

In the last decade the tremendous impetuous of VLSI technology has made neurocomputer design a really lively research topic. Research on hardware implementations of neurons has recently been very active. This has included extensive investigation on implementations of threshold logic gates (TLGs), one of the well-known neuron models. TLGs compute the weighted sum of their n inputs, $x_1, x_2, \ldots, x_n$, and compare it to the threshold θ. They produce an output 1 iff the weighted sum is equal or greater than the threshold. They are defined by $n+1$ real numbers: threshold θ and weights w_1, w_2, $\ldots$, w_n, where weight w_i is associated with input variable x_i.

In addition of being useful as a neuron model, there are many theoretical results showing that TLGs are more powerful/efficient than classical Boolean gates. These have been another motivation to investigate VLSI implementations of such gates.

The number of proposed TLGs implementations reported in the literature starting from the mid 50's is in the order of hundreds. Three different categories have been identified [1]: pure CMOS solutions, capacitive solutions, and conductance solutions. This paper focuses only on capacitive implementations.

The concept underlying capacitive TLGs is the use of an array of capacitors to implement the required weighted sum of inputs introduced as early as mid 60's [2]. Distinct circuits structures have been proposed which differ in the way the value of the threshold is set, and in the circuit techniques used to carry out the comparison involved in determining the output value. Capacitive threshold-logic gates have been classified into two major groups: Capacitive Threshold Logic (**CTL**), and Neuron MOS (ν**MOS**), also known as multi input floating gate transistor (MIFG or MFMOS). Although their current developments have become increasingly similar the paper describes them separately, starting from the two different original approaches in order to show the convergent evolution. For this reason, sometimes the reader might disagree with a particular solution being included in a given category. The paper is organized as follows: Sections 2 and 3 describe νMOS-based and CTL-based solutions respectively. Finally, Section 4 summarizes the evolution, problems and suitable applications of the capacitive TLGs.

2 Neuron-MOS Based Solutions

Neuron-MOS (νMOS) TLGs are based on the νMOS transistor [3], [4]. This transistor has a buried floating polysilicon gate and a number of input polysilicon gates capacitively coupled to the floating gate. The voltage of the floating gate becomes a weighted sum of the voltages on the input gates, and controls the current in the transistor channel.

The most simple νMOS-based TLG is the complementary inverter using both *p*- an *n*-type νMOS devices [2] [5] [6] [7]. A schematic of this TG is shown in Fig. 1. It consists of a floating gate, which is common to both the PMOS and the NMOS transistors, and a number of input gates ($V_1, V_2, ..., V_n$), corresponding to the threshold gate inputs plus an extra input (indicated by V_C in Figure 1) for logic threshold adjustment, as will be explained later. Without using the extra control input, and assuming the charge in the floating gate is zero, the voltage in the floating gate is given by $V_F = (\sum C_i V_i)/C_{tot}$, $1 \leq i \leq n$, where C_i is the coupling capacitance between the *i*-th input and the floating gate, and C_{tot} is the total capacitance, including the parasitic capacitances at the floating gate C_c, $C_{tot} = \sum C_i + C_c$, $1 \leq i \leq n$. As V_F becomes higher than the inverter threshold voltage, V_{TH}, the output switches to logic 0.

In the case of the simple, **static νMOS**, the gate's threshold is adjusted via the threshold programming voltage V_C. It is obvious that this νMOS TLG is very simple and very compact. However, there are a number of well-known problems. Degradation in the long-term stability is anticipated due to the use of a floating gate. Sensitivity to parasitic charges in the floating gate and to process variations could limit its effective fan-in, unless adequate control is provided. In particular, ultraviolet light (UV) erasure is required for initialisation/reprogramming. This gate also has large DC power consumption. Different schemes have been proposed to alleviate at least part of these problems.

The problem of large power dissipation in the simple static νMOS TGL was solved by the **deep-threshold νMOS TLG** [8]. The gate is composed of a deep-threshold νMOS inverter and a two-staged buffer as depicted in Figure 1b. Deep-threshold inverters have transistors (NMOS and PMOS) with a threshold voltage large enough so that there is not DC pass current at whatever multiple logic levels the potential of the common floating gate is. This gate dissipates significantly less power than conventional static νMOS TGL (a reduction by a factor 1/30 has been reported for a case study consisting of a number detector). There is a penalty in speed. However the power reduction

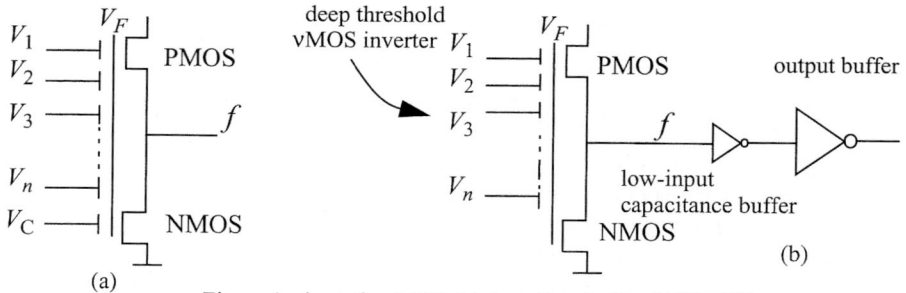

Figure 1: a) static νMOS; b) deep-threshold νMOS TGL

compensates the increase in delay. Thus, this gate exhibits better power-delay products. For the above case study the PDP figure of merit are 1/3.5 and 1/6 of those using standard CMOS technology and a conventional νMOS implementation respectively.

In the **clock-controlled νMOS** TLG [9] [10], shown in Figure 2, a clock-driven switch is attached to the floating gate to initialize the floating-gate charge (reset phase). This switch short-circuits the floating gate and the inverter output, thus biasing the inverter at the most sensitive point of the inverting characteristics. At the same time the logical threshold of the gate is correlated with the physical threshold of the inverter. That means that, in each reset phase, the floating-gate charge is refreshed, avoiding the problems of parasitic capacitances and long-term stability. The inverter threshold is also automatically readjusted, reducing the sensitivity to process and ambient parameters variations, and increasing the fan-in of the gates. The gate is not very fast: a neuron with 32 synapses of 5-bit accuracy in 0.8 μm CMOS exhibit delays in the range 3–17 ns [11]. These dynamic versions of the νMOS have relatively high static power and might require multiple clock phases. Although this type of gates was introduced as νMOS, it is quite similar to he CTL gate in figure 4.

The static power consumption of the basic νMOS TLG can be eliminated, and its speed increased, by a current comparison between a νMOS transistor and a reference device, using a positive feedback circuit [9]. The symmetry of the layout is important in this solutions. Figure 3 depicts the circuit schematics of TLGs operating on this basis. Fig. 3a shows a configuration called **sense-amplifier** νMOS TLG [10]. Other variations are described in [12] [13] and [14]. Although these circuits do not have an offset cancellation mechanism, fluctuation in device parameters can be compensated by the differential configuration. Speed improvements by a factor of 5 and power savings for this gate over the static νMOS are reported. Finally, Fig. 3b shows the configuration called charge recycling threshold logic (**CRTL**) gate [15]. In fact, the CRTL gate achieves the lowest power consumption when compared with clocked νMOS [10], and other TLG implementations [14], [16]. CRTL have been tested for process variations at 45 corners, and seem to be robust. A 4-bit carry look ahead adder using CRTL gates was implemented in a 0.25 μm double poly CMOS process [17]. It can be operated at a frequency in excess of 400MHz. At 100MHz with V_{DD} = 2 V, dissipates 0.5 mW, *i.e.*,

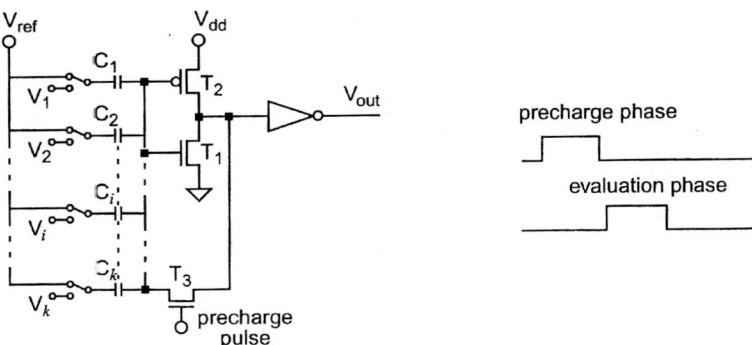

Figure 2: clock-controlled νMOS TGL

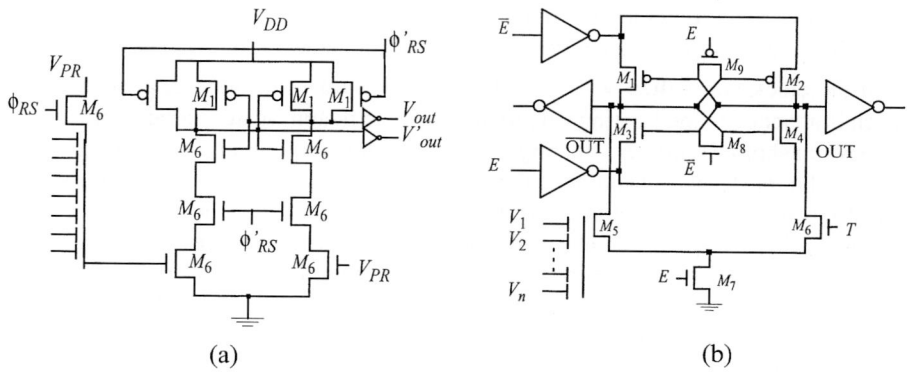

Figure 3: a) sense-amplifier vMOS TGL, b) CRTL

15-20% lower power dissipation than other capacitive TLGs Very recently, a novel self-timed threshold logic (STTL) has been proposed [18]. The solution is low power (as being differential), and eliminates the clock at the expense of a double rail signalling and the additional "enable generate" block. It is too early to say if the power reduction due to the elimination of the clock and its distribution is off-balanced by the "enable generate" block required by each gate. Obviously, low power solutions have to be used in designing this block. The only results reported so far is a (7,3) counter in a 0.25μm double poly CMOS, which has a delay of 1.4ns and dissipates 870 μW@2V when driven by a 300MHz enable signal.

3 CTL Based Solutions

Originally introduced in 1987 [19], the main idea of capacitive solutions was to use switched capacitors, switches and inverters, and to take advantage of the inherent saturation of the inverters to implement the neuron non-linearity without additional elements. This first approach required a somehow complex three-phase clock. The principle of capacitive synapse was presented also in [20] with the same three-phase clock. It has quickly evolved into a simpler two-phase clock solution [21], known as the capacitive threshold logic (**CTL**) gate. Its conceptual circuit schematic is shown in Fig. 4 for an n-input gate. It consists in a row of capacitors C_i, $i = 1, 2, ..., n$, with capacitances proportional to the corresponding input weight, $C_i = w_i \times C_u$, and a chain of inverters which functions as a comparator to generate the output. This TLG operates with two nonoverlapping clock phases Φ_R and Φ_E. During the reset phase, Φ_R is high and the row voltage V_R is reset to the first inverter threshold voltage while the capacitor bottom plates are precharged to a reference voltage V_{ref}. Evaluation begins when Φ_E is at a logic 1, setting gate inputs to the capacitor bottom plates. As a result, the change of voltage in the capacitor top plates is given by $\Delta V_R = (\sum C_i(V_i - V_{ref}))/C_{tot}$, $1 \leq i \leq n$, where C_{tot} is the row total capacitance including parasitics. Choosing adequate definitions for V_{ref} and C_i as functions of the input weight and threshold values,

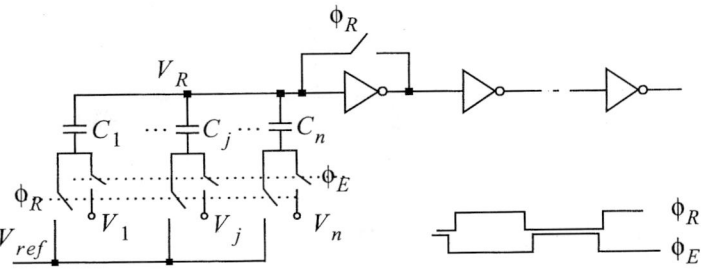

Figure 4: Capacitive Threshold Logic (CTL)

the above relationship can be expressed as $\Delta V_R = (\sum(w_i x_i - \theta) C_i V_{DD})/C_{tot}$, $1 \leq i \leq n$. Together with the comparison function of the chain of inverters give the TG operation: $V_o = V_{DD}$ if $\sum w_i x_i \geq \theta$, $1 \leq i \leq n$, and $V_o = 0$ if $\sum w_i x_i < \theta$, $1 \leq i \leq n$. Computation of a large number of input vector between two consecutive reset phases is possible.

Experimental results from different CTL gates fabricated in a standard-CMOS technology [21], [22], have shown the proper functionality of this type of TLG and its large fan-in capability (fan-in < 128-256). This later feature is due to the auto-offset cancellation technique widely used in chopper-type CMOS comparators. Originally, CTL gates needed a double-poly process. In [22] the MOS capacitor is used with a small penalty on the fan-in (fan-in < 64). The main drawbacks of CTL gates are: their large delays, their large area (the estimated area of the unit capacitor is equivalent to several minimum sized inverters), their DC power consumption, and the threshold value programming mechanism. Developments after the CTL have been proposed which overcome some of its limitation. We briefly summarize some of them here.

The fact that the threshold value is set by an analogue reference voltage complicates its integration. This problem is solved by the improved CTL gate [22] which operates exclusively with binary input logic levels. Another solution for this problem is the Capacitor Programmable CTL gate (**CP-CTL**), [23] which does not rely on the presence of additional external voltages. Fig. 5 depicts its circuit schematic. The CTL gate is augmented with a number of capacitors. The programming of the gate is now achieved by setting V_{ref}, V_{eval1}, V_{eval2}, and V_{reset} to readily available voltage levels. Different combinations of GND, V_{DD} and $V_{DD}/2$ (programming methods) can be used.

Finally, another variation called Balanced-CTL (**B-CTL**) [24] is shown in Fig. 6. The requirement for a highly precise reference voltage is eliminated by implementing functions with thresholds equal to 0. This is not a restriction on the class of functions that can be implemented, since any threshold logic function (TLF) can be converted into an equivalent TLF with threshold equal to zero by inverting certain inputs, and changing the sign of their associated weights. The basic structure is formed by two banks of capacitors (Bank A and Bank B in Fig. 6). Both banks are connected to a differential amplifier that determines which bank has a larger number of inputs at logic one. That bank has a higher voltage level on its common line. This gate implements threshold functions with thresholds equal to zero if the inputs having positive weights are con-

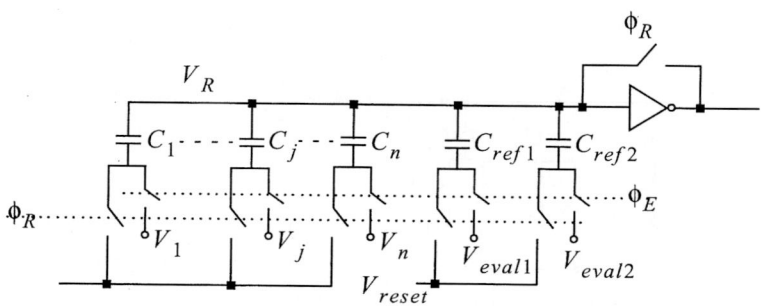

Figure 5: Capacitive Programmable CTL (CP_CTL)

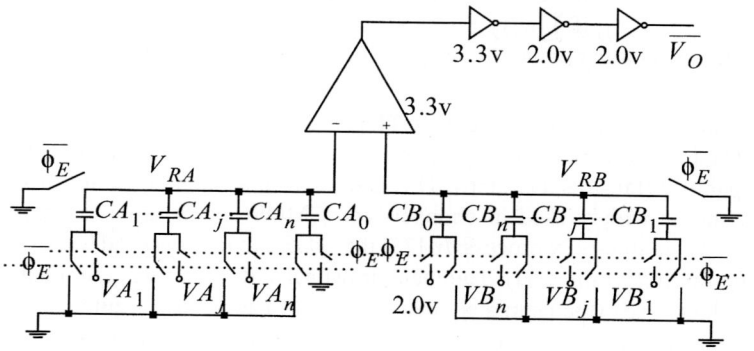

Figure 6: Balanced CTL (B-CTL)

nected to one bank and the inputs having negative weights are connected to the other one. One additional half capacitor unbalanced the voltage level at the amplifier inputs in case both banks have an identical number of high-level inputs. B-CTL gates operate from one clock that switches the gate between two states: reset and evaluate. Their main characteristics are high fan-in and low power consumption.

4 Analysis

Although originally CTL and vMOS approaches were different: static versus clocked and different mechanisms for setting the threshold value, their current developments have become increasingly similar. Advanced representative solutions from both categories are differential and allow straightforward implementation of both positive and negative weights. In addition they exhibit low power dissipation. Recently [17], the capacitor sharing technique has been introduced which allows significant area reduction in those networks of TLGs where two or more gates share inputs with same associated weights.

Capacitive implementations are multivalued in nature. Each distinct weighted sum of inputs is represented by and analog voltage. This translates in reduced noise margins and sensitivity to process variations which could limit the effective fan in. In [25] a very thorough analysis with respect to parameter variations, namely capacitances and the sensing amplifiers of vMOS TLGs using a dynamic comparator latch for sensing is carried out. The dominant mismatch originates from the input offset voltage variations of the sensing circuits. Measured results show that the most critical components are the comparators circuits. Improved noise margins can be traded off for increased layout areas and increased power consumption (due to increased capacitances). They conclude that this is a problem that will be exacerbated in future CMOS technologies, since lower supply voltages and increased device mismatch will have a diminishing effect on the threshold window, sensing margins, signal to noise ration, and reliability. In addition, it is claimed that a careful comparison with the area consumption of a standard CMOS logic circuit is absolutely necessary. However, [25] explicitly mentions that there are applications where capacitive devices can be employed advantageously, like threshold logic circuits with low logic depth implemented in fault tolerant architectures requiring high functional densities (e. g. data processing architectures in image sensors). In fact, a commercial finger print sensor array for image processing based on this kind of implementations exits [26].

References

1 V. Beiu, J.M. Quintana and M.J. Avedillo: "VLSI Implementations of Threshold Logic: A Survey" accepted for publication at *IEEE Trans. on Neural Networks* special number on Hardware Implementations.
2 J.R. Burns, N.J. Trenton and R.A. Powlus, "Threshold circuit utilizing field effect transistors", U.S: Patent 3 260 863, Jul. 12, 1966.
3 T. Shibata, and T. Ohmi, "A functional MOS transistor featuring gate-level weighted sum and threshold operations," *IEEE J. Solid-State Circuits*, vol. SC-39, pp. 1444–1455, June 1992.
4 T. Shibata, "Intelligent VLSI Systems Based on a Psychological Brain Model", Proceedings IEEE International Symposium on intelligent Signal Processing and Systems, pp. 323-332, November 2000.
5 T. Shibata, and T. Ohmi, "Neuron MOS binary-logic integrated circuits—Part I: Design fundamentals and soft-hardware-logic circuit implementation," *IEEE Trans. Electron Devices*, vol. ED-40, pp. 570–576, Mar. 1993.
6 T. Shibata, and T. Ohmi, "Neuron MOS binary-logic integrated circuits—Part II: Simplifying techniques of circuit configuration and their practical applications," *IEEE Trans. Electron Devices*, vol. ED-40, pp. 974–979, May 1993.
7 E. Rodríguez-Villegas, G. Huertas, M.J. Avedillo, J.M. Quintana, and A. Rueda, "A practical floating-gate Muller-C element using vMOS threshold gates," *IEEE Trans. Circuits Syst. II*, vol. CAS2-48, pp. 102–106, Jan. 2001.
8 H.Y. Kwon, K. Kotani, T. Shibata and T. Ohmi: "Low Power Neuron-MOS Technology for High-Functionality Logic Gate Synthesis", *IEICE Trans. Electron.*, Vol. E80-C, No. 7, pp. 924-929, Jul. 1997.
9 K. Kotani, T. Shibata, M. Imai, and T. Ohmi, "Clocked-neuron-MOS logic circuits employing auto-threshold-adjustment," *Proc. ISSCC'95*, San Francisco (USA), 1995, pp. 320–321, 388

10. K. Kotani, T. Shibata, M. Imai, and T. Ohmi, "Clocked-controlled neuron-MOS logic gates," *IEEE Trans. Circuits Syst. II*, vol. CAS2-45, pp. 518–522, Apr. 1998.
11. R. Lashevsky, K. Takaara and M. Souma, "Neuron MOSFET as a way to design a hreshold gates with the threshold and input weigths alterable in real time", *Proc APCCAS'98*, Chiangmai (Thailand), 1998, pp. 263-266.
12. W. Weber, S. Prange, R. Thewes, and E. Wohlrab, "A neuron MOS transistor-based multiplier cell," in *IEDM Technical Digest*, 1995, pp. 21.5.1–21.5.4.
13. W. Weber, S.J. Prange, R. Thewes, E. Wohlrab, and A. Luck, "On the application of Neuron MOS transistor principle for modern VLSI design," *IEEE Trans. Electron Devices*, vol. ED-43, pp. 1700–1708, Oct. 1996.
14. H.Y. Huang, and T.N. Wang, "CMOS capacitor coupling logic (C^3L) logic circuits," *Proc. Asia Pacific* pp. 33-36 *AP-ASIC*, Cheju (Korea), 2000, pp. 33–36.
15. P. Celinski, J.F. López, S. Al-Sarawi, and D. Abbott, "Low power, high speed, charge recycling CMOS threshold logic gate," *Electron. Lett.*, vol. 37, no. 17, pp. 1067–1069, Aug. 2001.
16. M.J. Avellido, J.M. Quintana, A. Rueda, and E. Jiménez, "A low-power CMOS threshold-gate," *Electron. Lett.*, vol. 31, pp. 2157–2159, Dec. 1995.
17. P. Celinski. S. Al-Sarawi, D. Abbot, J.F. Lopez, "Low depth carry lookahead adder addition using charge recycling threshold logic," *Proc. ISCAS 2002*, pp. 469-472, Scottsdale (USA).
18. P. Celinski, J.F. López, S. Al-Sarawi and D. Abbott, "Compact parallel (m, n) Counters based on Self-Timed Threshold Logic", *Electronics Letters*, Vol. 38, No. 13, pp. 633-635, Jun 2002.
19. Y.P. Tsividis, and D. Anastassiou, "Switched-capacitor neural networks," *Electron. Lett.*, vol. 23, pp. 958– 959, mo. 1987.
20. U. Çilingiroglu, "A purely capacitive synaptic matrix for fixed-weight neural networks," *IEEE Trans. Circuits Syst. II*, vol. CAS2-38, pp. 210–217, Apr. 1991.
21. H. Özdemir, A. Kepkep, B. Pamir, Y. Leblebici, and U. Çilingiroglu, "A capacitive threshold-logic gate," *IEEE J. Solid-State Circuits*, vol. SC-31, pp. 1141–1150, Aug. 1996.
22. Y. Leblebici, F.K. Gürkaynak, and D. Mlynek, "A compact 31-input programmable majority gate based on capacitive threshold logic," *Proc. International Symposium on Circuits and Systems ISCAS'98*, Monterey (USA), vol. 2, 1998, pp. 105–108.
23. A. Stokman, S. Cotofană, and S. Vassiliadis, "A versatile threshold logic gate," *Proc. Annual Semiconductor Conference CAS'98*, Sinaia, (Romania), 1998, pp. 163–166.
24. J. López García, J. Fernández Ramos, and A. Gago Bohórquez, "A balanced capacitive threshold logic gate," *Proc. Design of Circuits and Integrated Systems* (DCIS'2000), Montpellier (France), 2000.
25. A. Luck, S. Jung, R. Brederlow, R. Thewes, K, Goser, and W. Weber, "On the design robustness of threshold logic gates using multi-input floating gate MOS transistors," *IEEE Trans. Electron Devices*, vol. ED-47, pp. 1231–1240, Jun. 2000.
26. S. Jung, R. Thewes, T. Scheiter, K.F. Goser, and W. Weber, "A low-power and high performance CMOS fingerprint sensing and encoding architecture", *IEEE Journal of Solid State Circuits*, Vol. 34, no. 7, pp. 978-984, Jul. 1999.

Constructive Threshold Logic Addition
A Synopsis of the Last Decade

Valeriu Beiu

Washington State University, School of EE & CS
102 Spokane Str., PO Box 642752, Pullman, WA 99164-2752, USA
vbeiu@eecs.wsu.edu

Abstract. This paper presents a comprehensive review of the constructive results obtained over the last tvelwe years for the addition of two binary numbers using threshold logic gates. Such solutions are intended for very practical VLSI implementations. A comparison of nine different solutions is included.

Keywords. Threshold logic, addition, circuit/VLSI complexity.

1 Introduction

In this paper we shall consider feedforward artificial *neural networks* (NNs) of perceptrons for computing addition. NNs are made of 'neurons' composed of a cell body and many outgrowths: the *axon* (the 'output' of the neuron), and the *dendrites*. Formally, a *network* is a graph having several input nodes, and some (at least one) output nodes. If a synaptic *weight* is associated with each edge, and each node computes the weighted sum of its inputs to which a nonlinear activation function is then applied $f_i(X_i)$ $= f_i(x_{i,1}, ..., x_{i,\Delta}) = \sigma_i(\sum_{j=1}^{\Delta} w_j x_{i,j} + \theta_i)$, the network is a NN, with the synaptic *weights* $w_j \in \mathbb{R}$, $\theta_i \in \mathbb{R}$ known as the *threshold*, $\Delta \in \mathbb{N}$ being the *fan-in*, and σ_i an activation function. If the underlying graph is *acyclic*, the NN does not have feedback connections, and can be layered. This is the well-known multilayer feedforward NN. If the activation function σ_i is the sign, the node is a threshold logic gate (TLG), and the NN is a threshold logic circuit (TLC). Two cost functions have been used to characterize NNs: *depth*, i.e., the number of edges on the longest input-to-output path, or number of layers, and *size*, i.e., the number of nodes.

In the last decade the impetus of VLSI technology has made neurocomputer design a really lively topic. Hundreds of designs have been build, while several are available as commercial products [3, 12]. For VLSI implementations the *area* of the connections counts, and the *area* of one neuron can be related to its associated *weights*. That is why several authors have taken into account cost functions which can be linked to VLSI implementations by the assumptions one makes on how the *area* scales with the *weights* and the *thresholds* [2, 4]. It is worth emphasizing that it is quite desirable to limit the range of parameter values, because: the maximum value of the *fan-in* [22], and the

---

This material is based on research partly sponsored by the Air Force Research Laboratory under agreement number F29601-02-2-0299. The U.S. Government is authorized to reproduce and distribute reprints for Governmental purposes notwithstanding any copyright notation thereon. The views and conclusions contained herein are those of the author and should not be interpreted as necessarily representing the official policies or endorsements, either expressed or implied, of the Air Force Research Laboratory or the U.S. Government.

maximal ratio between the largest and the smallest *weight*, cannot grow over a certain (technological) limit [15].

This paper will detail many constructive results obtained over the last twelve years for the addition of two binary numbers using TLGs. The main problem concerns the reduction of the *size* in small (constant) *depth*, while also reducing the *weights*, and possibly the *fan-ins*. If the results are constructive, they are interesting both for CMOS implementations [25, 6, 7], and for (future) quantum implementations where TLGs are a perfect fit [21]. Still, TLGs (or their variations) have rarely been used in practice. The two earliest examples are *Mark I Perceptron*, built by Rosenblatt (1958), and Widrow's *memistor* (1960). These were followed by:

- the floating point co-processor MIPS R2010 in 1988 [26] (the implementation of the gates was originally discovered by Lerch in 1973 [31]);
- the SUN Sparc V9 in 1995 [32, 33];
- the Itanium 2 microprocessor in 2002 [40].

Currently, the devices which could get central stage positions in the (near) future are: single electron tunneling (SET) devices and resonant tunneling devices (RTDs). SET technology combines large integration and ultra low power dissipation. RTDs are already operating at room temperature, and appear to hold the most promise as a short/medium term solution. They have already been used for implementing TLGs [44]. These are the reasons why a clear understanding of the known *depth–size* and *weights–fan-ins* tradeoffs for addition could prove useful for VLSI designers.

2 Addition Revisited

The addition of two n-bit binary numbers, an augend $X = x_{n-1}x_{n-2} \ldots x_1x_0$ and an addend $Y = y_{n-1}y_{n-2} \ldots y_1y_0$, is defined as the unsigned sum of the addend added to the augend $S = s_n s_{n-1} \ldots s_1 s_0$. A well established method for this computation is [14, 28, 34, 45, 57]: $c_i = (x_i \wedge y_i) \vee (x_i \wedge c_{i-1}) \vee (y_i \wedge c_{i-1})$, $c_{-1} = 0$, $s_i = x_i \oplus y_i \oplus c_{i-1}$ for $i = 0, 1, \ldots, n-1$, and $s_n = c_n$. The sum bits s_i can also be computed as $s_i = (x_i \wedge y_i \wedge c_{i-1}) \vee [\overline{c_i} \wedge (x_i \vee y_i \vee c_{i-1})]$, which is implementable by one TLG (the equation was presented in [13], and later rediscovered in [47]). The c_i are known as the "carry" bits, and addition reduces to computing the carries [30, 45, 57], e.g., based on an associative operator "o" defined as $(g, p) \text{ o } (g', p') = [g \vee (p \wedge g'), p \wedge p']$ and $(G_i, P_i) = (g_i, p_i) \text{ o } (G_{i-1}, P_{i-1})$, for $2 \leq i \leq n$.

2.1 Boolean Logic

Many of the known adders have been built using Boolean bounded *fan-in* logic gates. It has also been proven that a *depth*-2 circuit of AND-OR logic gates for addition must have exponential *size* [55]. Some authors have formulated the problem of minimizing the latency in carry-skip and block carry-lookahead adders [19, 23, 49] as multidimensional dynamic programming [17, 58]. Others have investigated implementations based on spanning trees [36]. Still, most of the effort has been devoted to practical implementations [27, 36, 38, 46, 58]. Some very interesting results using *fan-ins* larger than two have also been reported. Such extensions of solutions like the ones introduced in [14, 29] have been presented by Ong and Atkins [43], and later by Ngai and Irwin [42], while similar extensions for a hybrid prefix algorithm were detailed in [23]. Han et al. [23] thorough analysis has led to the conclusion that for all the operand length $n \leq 1024$, *the optimal fan-in for the hybrid prefix algorithm is either* 3 *or* 4. They also mentioned that increasing the *fan-in* affects the time performance of the circuitry in three different ways: (*i*) the *depth* decreases from O (log$n$) to O (log$n$/logΔ); (*ii*) the processing *delay* of each element increases due to the need to implement more complex logic; (*iii*) the *delay* is also increased due to the larger *fan-out* capacitance. Obviously, TLGs are ideal candidates for implementing the complex logic gates, as potentially maintaining, or even reducing, the *delay* of the processing elements for large *fan-in*s.

2.2 Threshold Logic

From the very beginning, there have been two different ways of approaching TLC: theoretical and practical. The theoretical approach falls under the well-established computational circuit theory. Results from computational TLC theory could be useful for VLSI implementations. Such results are of interest to hardware designers, as long as they are *constructive*. The particular case of Boolean functions (BFs) has been intensively studied [37, 45, 48]. The first lower bound on the *size* of a TLC for 'almost all' *n*-ary BFs ($f : \mathbb{B}^n \to \mathbb{B}$, where $\mathbb{B} = \{0, 1\}$) was given by Nechiporuk [41]: $size \geq 2\,(2^n/n)^{1/2}$. A very tight upper bound for the same case was proven in $depth = 4$ [35]: $size \leq 2\,(2^n/n)^{1/2} \times \{1 + \Omega\,[(2^n/n)^{1/2}]\}$. A similar existence lower bound of $\Omega\,(2^{n/3})$ for arbitrary BFs was detailed in [50, 55].

Beside *size* and *depth*, other aspects of interest to VLSI designers are those related to technological limitations like *fan-in* and range of *weights*. The precision of the *weights* is linked to very practical noise margins, and/or power dissipation problems [12]. That is why theoretical research has also focused on *weights*, or more precisely on the capabilities of TLG with restricted *weights*. It has been proven that any TLG could be implemented with integer *weights*, and also that the number of bits per *weight* is $O\,(\Delta \log \Delta)$ [39]. The bound is tight as Håstad has presented a function having *weights* up to $2^{(\Delta \log \Delta)/2 - \Delta}$, *i.e.*, requiring $\Omega\,(\Delta \log \Delta)$ bits per *weight* [24].

Particular classes of functions allow for simpler implementations, *i.e.*, small(er) *weights* and *fan-ins*, shallow *depth* and polynomial *size*. That is why arithmetic operations (addition, multiplication, division) have been among potential candidates. Addition has been considered as a challenging function [1, 51]. Obviously, beside minimum *depth* or minimum *size*, those solutions having small(er) *fan-ins* and small(er) *weights* were of interest [11, 18, 52, 54, 57] (the *area* of a VLSI implementation depends on the sum of the *weights*). An existence *depth*-2 solution of polynomial *size* is well known [53]. It was followed in 1991 [1] by the first constructive *depth*-2 majority gate circuit (*i.e.*, TLGs with *weights* of −1, or +1) of *size* $O\,(n^4)$.

Two other constructions for addition based on AND-OR logic gates have been detailed in 1991 [55]. Because AND and OR gates can be simulated by TLGs, they have been considered as unbounded *fan-in* TLGs:
- a *depth*-3 TLC of *size* $O\,(n^2)$, or more precisely $n^2/2 + 7n/2 - 1$ (*Theorem* 7);
- a *depth*-7 TLC of *size* $O\,(n \log n)$ was constructed in four steps (*Lemma* 4).

Going for a lower *depth* (in this case from 7 to 3) increases the *size* complexity from

O (nlog$n$) to O (n^2). From their own lower bound results [54], the authors concluded that "*a substantial reduction in size is not possible without increasing the depth beyond 3.*" As we shall see, it did not take too long to constructively prove better.

In 1993-1994, a first improvement reduced the *depth*-7 construction from [55] to *depth*-5, while still having the same O (nlog$n$) *size* complexity [9, 10, 11]. The solution is based on a class of linearly separable functions $I\!F_\Delta$ of Δ input variables computing the carries: $f_\Delta = f_\Delta (g_{\Delta/2-1}, p_{\Delta/2-1}, \ldots, g_0, p_0) = \vee_{j=0}^{\Delta/2-1} [g_j \wedge (\wedge_{k=j+1}^{\Delta/2-1} p_k)]$, where by convention $\wedge_{i=a}^{a-1} p_i = 1$. The input variables are pair-dependent, *i.e.*, in each of the $\Delta/2$ pairs of two input variables: $(g_{\Delta/2-1}, p_{\Delta/2-1}), \ldots, (g_0, p_0)$ one variable is "dominant" (*i.e.*, when a dominant variable is 1, the other variable forming the pair will also be 1). Because the BFs from *Step* 3 and *Step* 4 of *Lemma* 4 from [55] are $I\!F_\Delta$ functions, the *depth*-7 construction can be shrunk to *depth*-5 by replacing the AND-OR gates from the intermediate layers with TLGs implementing f_Δ functions.

By mid 1994, a linear *size* solution of 7n was obtained in *depth*-4 [2, 11]. This was a substantial reduction in *size* from O (nlog$n$) to O (n), but not yet in *depth*-3. The solution was in fact a class of constructive solutions based on $I\!F_\Delta$. By varying the *fan-in*, the solutions span *depths* from 4 to 3 + log$n$, while the *sizes* vary from 7n to 2$n$log$n$ + 5n. Several variations are possible depending on the way the sum bits s_i are implemented: (*i*) classical AND-OR solutions, or (*ii*) using the last layer from [55]. A better alternative is to use the equation $s_i = (x_i \wedge y_i \wedge c_{i-1}) \vee [\overline{c_i} \wedge (x_i \vee y_i \vee c_{i-1})]$ (known since 1969 [13]). Now, the *depth* is reduced by one and the *size* by 2n (with respect to the case when the last layer would be implemented by a classical AND-OR solution). *This is the first depth-3 solution having linear size* 5n (a substantial reduction over [55]). This solution has exponential *weights*. Decreasing the *fan-in* from 2n to 4, the *depth* increases from 3 to 2 + log$n$, and the *size* from 5n to 3n + 2$n$log$n$, while the *weights* decrease from 2^n to 4. This class of adders has been used to prove inclusions amongst many circuit complexity classes, including three NN complexity classes [8].

In 1995-1996, three other *depth*-3 solutions have been presented [16, 56]. Another linear *size* solution [1] of 6n + 2$\lceil n/\sqrt{n} \rceil$ was achieved in *depth*-3 [56]. This solution exhibits a larger *size* than the previous solution, but the *weights*, while still exponential, are smaller $2^{\lceil \sqrt{n} \rceil}$. A solution having polynomially *weights* O (n^k) was also detailed in [56]. It has O (n^2/$k$log$n$) *size* in *depth*-3, for any $1 \leq k \leq n/\log n$. By varying k, the *sizes* cover the interval from $2n^2$/log$n$ + 8n to 10n, but for those solutions approaching 10n, the *weights* are (again) exponential $n^{n/(c\log n)} = 2^{n/c}$.

Finally, in 1999, three other solutions have been detailed.
- Yeh et al. [59] (see also [60]) present a *depth* (log$n$ + 2) / logΔ + 1.44log$k$ majority gate circuit having *size* O [2$n$log(k+1)/Δ] for any positive integer k.

---

[1] In this paper $\lceil x \rceil$ is the ceiling of x, and $\lfloor x \rfloor$ is the floor of x; all the logarithms are taken to base 2 (except explicitly mentioned otherwise).

Constructive Threshold Logic Addition   749

Table 1. Constructive TLCs for addition (chronological order).

Author(s) Year Ref.	Delay/depth (#layers)	Size (#gates)	Max *weight*	Max *fan-in*	Remarks
Siu & Bruck 1990 [53]	2	n^c	—	—	Existence.
Alon & Bruck 1991 [1]	2	$O(n^4)$	$\{-1, 0, +1\}$	n^4	Constructive TLC.
Siu et al. 1991 [55]	3	$(n^2 + 7n - 2)/2$	$\{-1, 0, +1\}$	$2n$	Constructive (AND-OR).
	7	$O(n\log n)$	$\{-1, 0, +1\}$	$2n$	
Beiu et al. 1994 [10, 11]	5	$O(n\log n)$	2^n	$2n$	Constructive TLC.
Beiu 1994 [2, 11]	$3 + \left\lceil \frac{\log n}{\log \Delta - 1} \right\rceil$	$5n + 2n \left\lceil \frac{\log n}{\log \Delta - 1} \right\rceil$	$2^{\Delta/2}$	Δ	Constructive class of TLCs based on carry lookahead [14, 23, 29]. See also Beiu & Taylor 1996 [8].
	4	$7n$	2^n	$2n$	
	d	$2dn - n$	$2^{\sqrt[d-3]{n}}$	$2^{\sqrt[d-3]{n}}$	
	$3 + \frac{\log n}{\log(\log w_{max})}$	$5n + \frac{2n \log n}{\log(\log w_{max})}$	w_{max}	$2 \log w_{max}$	
Beiu et al. 1994 [10, 11] using Betts 1969 [13]	$2 + \left\lceil \frac{\log n}{\log \Delta - 1} \right\rceil$	$3n + 2n \left\lceil \frac{\log n}{\log \Delta - 1} \right\rceil$	$2^{\Delta/2}$	Δ	Constructive class of TLCs obtained by implementing the last layer from [2, 10, 11] using the equation presented in [13].
	3	$5n$	2^n	$2n$	
	4	$7n$	$2^{\sqrt{n}}$	$2\sqrt{n}$	
	d	$2dn - n$	$2^{\sqrt[d-2]{n}}$	$2^{\sqrt[d-2]{n}}$	
	$2 + \frac{\log n}{\log(\log w_{max})}$	$3n + \frac{2n \log n}{\log(\log w_{max})}$	w_{max}	$2 \log w_{max}$	
Vassiliadis et al. 1996 [56]	3	$6n + 2\lceil n/\lceil\sqrt{n}\rceil \rceil$	$2^{\lceil \sqrt{n}\rceil}$	$2\lceil n/\lceil\sqrt{n}\rceil\rceil + 3$	Constructive.
	3	$2n \left(\frac{n}{m \log n} - 1 \right) + 13n$	$O(n^k)$	max $\{2m\log n, 4\lceil n/(m\log n) + 2\rceil\}$	Constructive $1 \leq k \leq n/\log n$.
Yeh et al. 1999 [59]	$\frac{\log n + 2}{\log \Delta} + 1.44 \log k$	$O\left[\frac{2n\log(k+1)}{\Delta} \right]$	$\{-1, 0, +1\}$	Δ	Constructive class of TLCs.
Beiu 1999 [5]	$1 + \left\lceil \frac{\log n}{\log \Delta - 1} \right\rceil$	$\frac{n\Delta}{2} + 2n \left\lceil \frac{\log n}{\log \Delta - 1} \right\rceil$	$2^{0.7\Delta}$	Δ	Constructive class of TLCs using a modified first and second layer for reducing the depth by 1 (see also [7]).
	2	$n^2 + 2n$	$2^{1.4n}$	$2n$	
	3	$n\sqrt{n} + 4n$	$2^{1.4\sqrt{n}}$	$2\sqrt{n}$	
	4	$n\sqrt[3]{n} + 6n$	$2^{1.4\sqrt[3]{n}}$	$2\sqrt[3]{n}$	
	d	$n\sqrt[d-1]{n} + 2n(d-1)$	$2^{1.4\sqrt[d-1]{n}}$	$2^{\sqrt[d-1]{n}}$	
	$1 + \frac{\log n}{\log(\log w_{max}^{0.7})}$	$\frac{2n\log n}{\log(\log w_{max}^{0.7})} + O(n)$	w_{max}	$1.4 \log w_{max}$	
Ramos & Bohórquez 1999 [47]	2	$2n$	2^n	$2n + 1$	Constructive class of TLCs based on using Betts' equation [13] together with a modification of the classic carry lookahead method.
	3	$4n - 2\lceil n/\sqrt{n}\rceil$	$2^{\lceil n/\sqrt{n}\rceil}$	$2\lceil n/\sqrt{n}\rceil + 1$	
	4	$6n - 2\lceil n/\sqrt[3]{n}\rceil$	$2^{\lceil\sqrt[3]{n}\rceil}$	$2\lceil\sqrt[3]{n}\rceil + 1$	
	d	$2(d-1)n - 2(d-3)\sqrt[d-1]{n^{d-2}}$	$2^{\sqrt[d-1]{n^{d-2}}}$	$2^{\sqrt[d-1]{n^{d-2}}} + 1$	
	$1 + \frac{\log n}{\log(\log w_{max})}$	$\frac{2n \log n}{\log(\log w_{max})} + O(n)$	w_{max}	$2\log w_{max} + 1$	

- Beiu [5] improves on [2, 10, 11] by lowering the *depth* to 2 in $n^2 + 2n$ *size*, with exponential *weights*. A new *depth*-3 solution having *size* $n\sqrt{n} + 4n$ and *weights* $2^{1.4\sqrt{n}}$ is also presented. This new class of solution is based on modified f_Δ functions, which have no restrictions on the input variables. The *weights* of these functions are the Fibonacci numbers extended to to negative values using Binet's formula $\text{Fib}_{-m} = (-1)^{m+1} \text{Fib}_m$, hence the *weights* are bounded by $2^{0.7\Delta}$.
- Ramos and Bohórquez [47] solution has its roots in [56] and [13]. They rediscovered the equation for s_i from [13], obtaining a *depth*-2 linear *size* $2n$ solution with exponentially bounded *weights* 2^n, and a *depth*-3 solution of *size* $4n$ having *weights* bounded by $2^{\sqrt{n}}$ (these result directly from [56] using [13]). The novelty comes from improving the *depth*-3 solution by reducing the *size* to $4n - 2\lceil n/\sqrt{n}\rceil$, and by extending this last solution to arbitrary limited *weights*.

For an easier comparison, all these solutions are presented in a compact form in chronological order in *Table 1*.

3 Conclusions

The paper has presented several classes of TLCs for computing the addition of two binary numbers. They show many interesting *depth-size* tradeoffs, which can be directly translated into allowed ranges of *weights* and *fan-ins*, strongly influencing the overall *area*, *delay* and *power consumption* of VLSI implementations. The improvements reported have been as follows:
- in *depth*-2, the *size* has been reduced from $O(n^4)$ with constant *weights* [1], to $O(n^2)$ with exponential *weights* [5], and finally to $O(n)$ with exponential *weights* [47];
- in *depth*-3, the *size* has been reduced from $O(n^2)$ with constant *weights* [55], to $O(n)$ with exponential *weights* [2, 10, 11], while two other $O(n)$ solutions with exponential *weights* have been reported later: [56] and [47];
- in *depth*-4, the *size* has been reported $O(n)$ with exponential *weights* [2, 11], while another $O(n)$ solution was reported in [47];
- in *depth-d*, a $2nd - n$ *size* solution was reported in [2, 10, 11], and was improved to $2n(d-1) - 2(d-3)\sqrt[d-1]{n^{d-2}}$ in [47].

Finally, interesting questions remain: Could one improve by allowing super-polynomial *weights*? What could be obtained with sub-linear *weights*? What could be obtained in sub-logarithmic *depth*?

References

1. N. Alon, J. Bruck: Explicit construction of depth-2 majority circuits for comparison and addition. Res. Rep. RJ 8300 (75661), IBM Almaden Res. Center (1991) [Also in: Proc. ISIT'93, 433 (1993); SIAM J. Disc. Math., 7(1), 1-8 (1994); US Patent 5357528 (10/18/1994)]

2. V. Beiu: Neural Networks Using Threshold Gates: A Complexity Analysis of Their Area- and Time-Efficient VLSI Implementations, PhD dissertation, Katholieke Univ. Leuven, Belgium (1994)
3. V. Beiu: Digital integrated circuit implementations, Chapter E1.4 in [20] (1996)
4. V. Beiu: On the circuit and VLSI complexity of threshold gate COMPARISON. Neurocomputing, 19(1-3), 77-98 (1998)
5. V. Beiu: Neural addition and Fibonacci numbers. Proc. IWANN'99, LNCS 1607, Vol. 2, 198-207 (1999)
6. V. Beiu: Adder and multiplier circuits employing logic gates having discrete, weighted inputs and methods of performing combinatorial operations therewith. US Patent 6205458 (03/20/2001)
7. V. Beiu: Adder having reduced number of internal layers and method of operation thereof. US Patent 6438572 (08/20/2002)
8. V. Beiu, J.G. Taylor: On the circuit complexity of sigmoid feedforward neural networks. Neural Networks, 9(7), 1155-1171 (1996)
9. V. Beiu, J.A. Peperstraete, J. Vandewalle, R. Lauwereins: Comparison and threshold gate decomposition. Proc. MicroNeuro'93, 83-90 (1993)
10. V. Beiu, J.A. Peperstraete, J. Vandewalle, R. Lauwereins: Area-time performances of some neural computation. Proc. SPRANN'94, 664-668 (1994)
11. V. Beiu, J.A. Peperstraete, J. Vandewalle, R. Lauwereins: Addition using constrained threshold gates. Proc. ConTI'94, 166-177 (1994)
12. V. Beiu, J.M. Quintana, M.J. Avedillo: VLSI implementation of threshold logic: A comprehensive survey. IEEE Trans. Neural Networks (Special Issue on Hardware Implementations), 14(5), in press (2003)
13. R. Betts: Majority logic binary adder. US Patent 3440413 (04/22/1969)
14. R.P. Brent, H.T. Kung: A regular layout for parallel adders. IEEE Trans. Comput., 31(3), 260-264 (1982)
15. J. Bruck, J.W. Goodmann: On the power of neural networks for solving hard problems. J. Complexity, 6(2), 129-135 (1990)
16. S.A. Cannas: Arithmetic perceptrons. Neural Computation, 7(1), 173-181 (1995)
17. P.K. Chang, M.D.F Schlag, C.D. Thomborson, V.G. Oklobdzija: Delay optimization of carry-skip adders and block carry-lookahead adders using multidimensional programming. IEEE Trans. Comput., 41(8), 920-930 (1992)
18. S. Cotofana, S. Vassiliadis: Low weight and fan-in neural networks for basic arithmetic operations. Proc. IMACS'97, Vol. 4, 227-232 (1997)
19. R.W. Doran: Variants of an improved carry look-ahead adder. IEEE Trans. Comput., 37(9), 1110-1113 (1988)
20. E. Fiesler, R. Beale (eds.): Handbook of Neural Computation. New York: Inst. of Physics (1996)
21. K.F. Goser, C. Pacha, A. Kanstein, and M.L. Rossmann: Aspects of system and circuits for nanoelectronics. Proc. IEEE, 85(4), 558-573 (1997)
22. D. Hammerstrom: The connectivity analysis of simple associations –or– How many connections do you need. In D.Z. Anderson (ed.): Neural Inform. Proc. Sys., New York: Inst. of Physics, 338-347 (1988)
23. T. Han, D.A. Carlson, S.P Levitan: VLSI design of high-speed, low-area addition circuitry. Proc. ICCD'87, 418-422 (1987)
24. J. Håstad: On the size of weights for threshold gates. SIAM J. Discr. Math., 7(3), 484-492 (1994)
25. H. Jeong: Neural network implementation of a binary adder. US Patent 5016211 (05/14/1991)
26. M.G. Johnson: A symmetric CMOS NOR gate for high-speed applications. IEEE J. Solid-State Circuits, 23(10), 1233-1236 (1988)
27. T.P. Kelliher, R.M. Owens, M.J. Irwin, T.-T. Hwang: ELM a fast addition algorithm discovered by a program. IEEE Trans. Comput., 41(9), 1181-1184 (1992)
28. V.M. Khrapchenko: Asymptotic estimation of addition time of a parallel adder. Problemy Kibernetiki, 19, 107-125 (1967). English transl., Syst. Th. Res., 19, 105-122 (1970)
29. P.M. Kogge, H.S. Stone: A parallel algorithm for the efficient solution of a general class of recurrence equations. IEEE Trans. Comput., 22(8), 783-791 (1973)
30. R.E. Ladner, M.J. Fischer: Parallel prefix computations. J. ACM, 27(4), 831-838 (1980)

31. J.B. Lerch: Threshold gate circuits employing field-effect transistors. US Patent 3715603 (02/06/1973)
32. L.A. Lev et al.: A 64-b microprocessor with multimedia support. IEEE J. Solid-State Circuits, 30(11), 1227-1238 (1995)
33. L.A. Lev: Fast static cascode logic gate. US Patent 5438283 (08/01/1995)
34. H. Ling: High speed binary adder. IBM J. Res. Develop., 25(2-3), 156-166 (1981)
35. O.B. Lupanov: On circuits of threshold elements. Dokl. Akad. Nauk SSSR, 202, 1288-1291 (1971). English transl., Sov. Phys. Dokl., 17(2), 91-93 (1972)
36. T. Lynch, E.E. Swartzlander Jr.: A spanning tree carry lookahead adder. IEEE Trans. Comput., 41(8), 931-939 (1992)
37. R.C. Minnik: Linear-input logic, IRE Trans. Electron. Comput., 10(1), 6-16 (1961)
38. R.K. Montoye: Area-time efficient addition in charge based technology. Proc. DAC'81, 862-872 (1981)
39. S. Muroga: Threshold Logic and Its Applications. New York: Wiley (1971)
40. S.D. Naffziger, G. Colon-Bonet, T. Fischer, R. Reidlinger, T.J. Sullivan, T. Grutkowski: The implementation of the Itanium 2 microprocessor. IEEE J. Solid-State Circuits, 37(11), 1448-1460 (2002)
41. E.I. Nechiporuk: The synthesis of networks from threshold elements. Problemy Kibernetiki, 11(1), 49-62 (1964). English transl., Automation Express, 7(1), 27-32 and 35-39 (1964)
42. T.F. Ngai, M.J. Irwin: Regular area-efficient carry-lookahead adders. Proc. ARITH 7, 9-15 (1985)
43. S. Ong, D.E. Atkins: A comparison of ALU structures for VLSI technology. Proc. ARITH 6, 10-16 (1983)
44. C. Pacha, U. Auer, C. Burwick, P. Glösekötter, A. Brennemann, W. Prost, F.-J. Tegude, K.F. Goser: Threshold logic circuit design for parallel adders using resonant tunneling devices. IEEE Trans. VLSI Syst., 8(10), 558-572 (2000)
45. I. Parberry: Circuit Complexity and Neural Networks. Cambridge, MA: MIT Press (1994)
46. N.T. Quach, M.J. Flynn: High-speed addition in CMOS. IEEE Trans. Comput., 41(12), 1612-1615 (1992)
47. J.F. Ramos, A.G. Bohórquez: Two operand binary adders with threshold logic. IEEE Trans. Comput., 48(12), 1324-1337 (1999)
48. N.P. Red'kin: Synthesis of threshold circuits for certain classes of Boolean functions. Kibernetika, 5(1), 6-9 (1970). English transl., Cybernetics, 6(1), 540-544 (1973)
49. T. Rhyne: Limitations on carry lookahead networks. IEEE Trans. Comput., 33(4), 373-374 (1984)
50. V.P. Roychowdhury, A. Orlitsky, K.-Y. Siu: Lower bounds on threshold and related circuits via communication complexity. IEEE Trans. Info. Th., 40(2), 467-474 (1994)
51. K.-Y. Siu, J. Bruck: Neural computations of arithmetic functions. Proc. IEEE, 78(10), 1669-1675 (1990)
52. K.-Y. Siu, J. Bruck: On the power of threshold circuits with small weights. SIAM J. Discr. Math., 4(3), 423-435 (1991)
53. K.-Y. Siu, J. Bruck: Neural computing with small weights. In J.E. Moody, S.J. Hanson, R.P. Lippmann (eds.): Advs. Neural Inform. Proc. Sys. 4, San Mateo: Morgan Kaufmann, 944-949 (1992)
54. K.-Y. Siu, V. Roychowdhury, T. Kailath: Computing with almost optimal size threshold circuits. Tech. Rep., Info. Sys. Lab., Stanford University (1990) [Also in: Proc. ISIT'91, 370 (1991); in S.J. Hanson, J.D. Cowan and C.L. Giles (eds.): Advs. Neural Inform. Proc. Sys. 5, San Mateo: Morgan Kaufmann, 19-26 (1993)]
55. K.-Y. Siu, V.P. Roychowdhury, T. Kailath: Depth-size tradeoffs for neural computations. IEEE Trans. Comput., 40(12), 1402-1412 (1991)
56. S. Vassiliadis, S. Cotofana, K. Berteles: 2-1 addition and related arithmetic operations with threshold logic. IEEE Trans. Comput., 45(9), 1062-1067 (1996)
57. I. Wegener: The Complexity of Boolean Functions. Stuttgart: Wiley–Teubner (1987)
58. B.W.Y. Wei, C.D. Thompson: Area-time optimal adder design. IEEE Trans. Comput., 39(5), 666-675 (1990)
59. C.-H. Yeh, E.A. Varvarigos, B. Parhami, H. Lee: Optimal-depth threshold circuits for multiplication and related problems. Proc. Asilomar'99, Vol. 2, 1331-1335 (1999)
60. C.-H. Yeh, E.A. Varvarigos, B. Parhami: Optimal-depth circuits for prefix computation and addition. Proc. Asilomar'2000, Vol. 2, 1349-1353 (2000)

CrossNets: Neuromorphic Networks for Nanoelectronic Implementation

Özgür Türel and Konstantin Likharev

Stony Brook University, Stony Brook, NY 11794-3800, U.S.A.
Ozgur.Turel@sunysb.edu, klikharev@notes.cc.sunysb.edu

Abstract. Hybrid "CMOL" integrated circuits, incorporating advanced CMOS devices for neural cell bodies, nanowires as axons and dendrites, and single-molecule latching switches as synapses, may be used for the hardware implementation of extremely dense (~10^7 cells and ~10^{12} synapses per cm^2) neuromorphic networks, operating up to 10^6 times faster than their biological prototypes. We are exploring several "CrossNet" architectures that accommodate the limitations imposed by CMOL hardware and should allow effective training of the networks without a direct external access to individual synapses. CrossNet training in the Hopfield mode have been confirmed on a software model of the network.

1 Introduction

The recent demonstration of first single-molecule transistors [1-4] gives every hope for the development, within the next decade or so, of "CMOL" integrated circuits [5] with density beyond 10^{12} functions per cm^2. Such a circuit (Fig. 1) would combine a level of advanced (e.g., 45-nm-node [6]) CMOS fabricated by the usual lithographic patterning, a few layers of parallel nanowire arrays formed, e.g., by nanoimprinting [7], and a level of molecular devices that would self-assemble on the wires from solution. CMOL circuits allow to combine advantages of their nanoscale components (e.g., reliability of CMOS circuits and miniscule footprint of molecular devices) and circumvent their drawbacks (e.g., low voltage gain of molecular devices).

Earlier we suggested [8] a simple 2-terminal device (latching switch) that allows single-molecule implementation and might be the basis of BiWAS (binary-weight, analog-signal) synapses in several network architectures sustaining the ultimate areal density of the synapses. The further study has indicated [9], however, that in order to allow effective training, 3-terminal devices, enabling Hebbian plasticity, may be necessary. The goal of this work is to demonstrate that dense "CrossNet" structures using the 3-terminal single-electron devices, may really allow effective training, at least in the Hopfield mode, without tutor's access to individual synaptic weights.

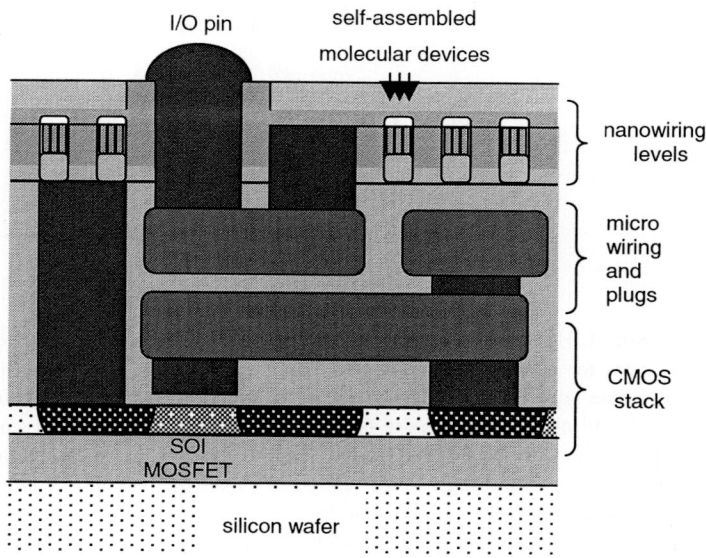

Fig. 1. The concept of CMOL (hybrid CMOS/nanowire/molecular) circuit [5]

2 Hebbian Synapse

Figure 2a shows schematics of our 3-terminal latching switch. It is essentially a combination of two well known components [5]: a single-electron transistor connecting two nanowires (modeling an axon and a dendrite, respectively), and a single-electron trap. The device and physics of the device operation are essentially the same as for the 2-terminal switch [8, 9], besides that now the signal applied to the trapping island comes equally from two sources: an axon coming from the source cell j and an axon leaving the target neural cell j'. This is why the net voltage $V = V_j + V_{j'} = (V_0/2) \times (\pm x_j \pm x_{j'})$ depends on activity $x_j(t)$ of both cells. (We accept such normalization that $|x_j|_{max} = 1$). Due to the random character of single-electron tunneling, V only determines the rates of electron injection into the trap ($\Gamma_\uparrow$), opening the transistor; and its ejection from the trap ($\Gamma_\downarrow$), closing the transistor. The rates, in turn determines the dynamics of probability p to have the transistor open:

$$dp/dt = \Gamma_\uparrow(1 - p) - \Gamma_\downarrow p. \tag{1}$$

The theory of single-electron tunneling shows that, in a good approximation, the rates may be presented as

$$\Gamma_{\uparrow\downarrow} = \Gamma_0 \exp\{\pm(V - S)/T\}, \tag{2}$$

where Γ_0, S, and T are constants depending on physical parameters of the synapse. (The last parameter is the effective temperature expressed in voltage units.) Despite the random character of the switching, the strong nonlinearity of Eq. (2) allows to limit the degree of device fuzziness. In fact, solving Eqs. (1), (2) for the case when signals are applied for sufficiently long time, we get

$$p = \tfrac{1}{2}[1 + \tanh(V - S)/T], \qquad (3)$$

so that if $V_0 - S, S \gg T$ and $|x_j| \approx 1$, we get $p \approx 1$ for $\pm\mathrm{sgn}(x_j)\pm\mathrm{sgn}(x_{j'}) = 2$, and $p \approx 0$ for any other combination of signal signs. Let us connect in parallel 4 switches with all possible sign combinations, sending each output current to cell j' with the same polarity as that of the feedback axonic voltage $V_{j'}$. Then we get a composite synapse with an almost deterministic weight that satisfies the "clipped Hebb rule" [13] $w_{jj'} \propto \mathrm{sgn}(x_j x_{j'})$.

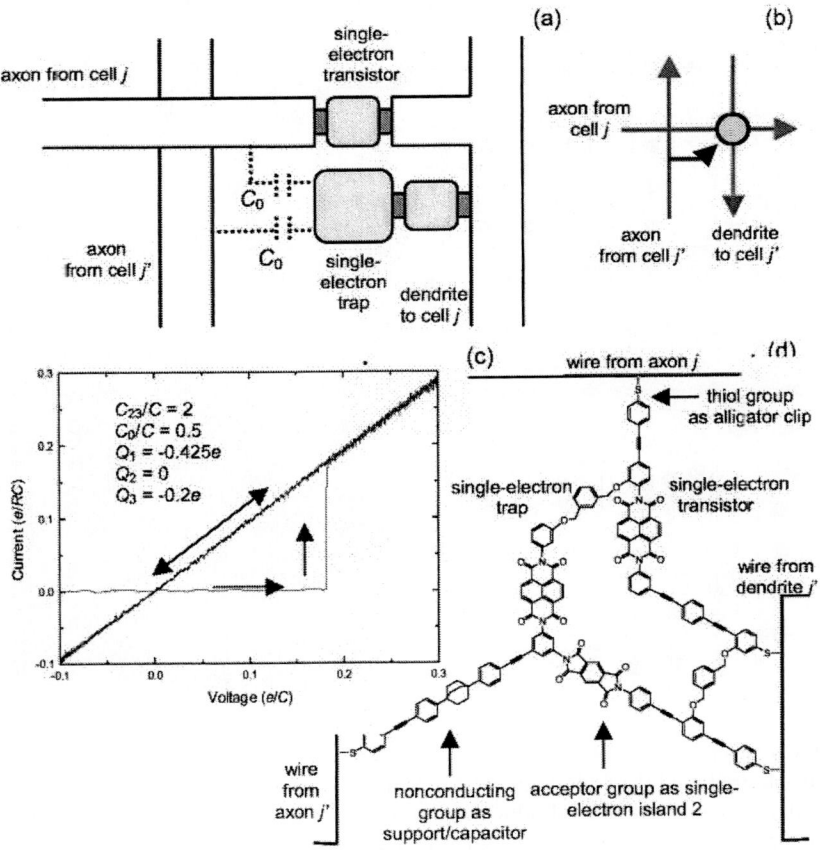

Fig. 2. Three-terminal single-electron latching switch: (a) schematics [9], (b) circuit notation used in Fig. 3, (c) result of simulation [8], and (d) possible molecular implementation [10]. C and R are the capacitance and resistance of each tunnel junction (shown dark-gray in panel a); Q_i are the background charges [5] of the single-electron islands (light gray)

3 CrossNets

We have suggested a family [9] of Distributed Crossbar Networks ("CrossNets") in which neural cell bodies (implemented within the fire rate model, see gray cells in Fig. 3) are inserted sparsely into large, uniform 2D arrays of synapses clustered into identical "plaquettes" (green cells). Each pair of sufficiently close cells are connected in two directions, via two composite (4-switch) Hebbian synapses each way. Various Cross-Nets differ only by the gray cell insertion rule. In particular, in InBar (Fig. 3) the cells sit on a square lattice inclined relative to that of synaptic plaquettes. The incline enables each cell to be connected with $4M = 4/\tan^2\alpha$ other cells.

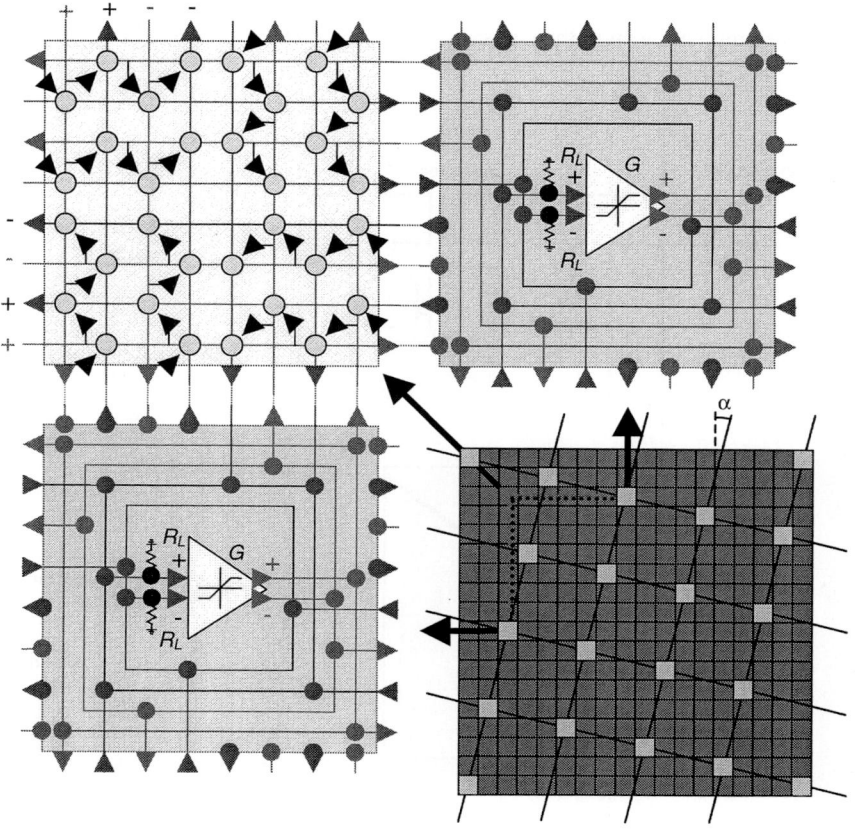

Fig. 3. CrossNet: synaptic plaquettes (green cells) and somas (gray cells) and their connection with axonic (red) and dendritic (blue) wires. Solid points on the somatic cell borders denote open-circuit terminations of the dendritic and axonic wires; due to these terminations the neural cells in the same row or column of the InBar do not interact. The bottom right panel shows the most explored CrossNet architecture, the Inclined Crossbar ("InBar"). In that panel, dashed red and blue lines show the particular connections show in the rest of the figure, while this violet lines indicate the square lattice formed by the somatic cells in InBar. These lines may be used for input/output of signals from individual cell (but not an individual synapse)

4 Hopfield Training

CrossNet training algorithms should take into account the following peculiarities of these networks:
 - in CMOL-implemented networks, no external access to an individual synapse is possible (though individual somas may be accessed);
 - CrossNets, by their very structure, are deeply recurrent.

These peculiarities do not allow the straightforward use of most known techniques of neural network training [11, 12], and new techniques should be developed.

We have started with the development of techniques of training InBar to operate as a Hopfield network. In the first, most straightforward method each pair $\{j, j'\}$ of cells is taught in turns. (Due to the network locality, cell pairs separated by large Manhattan distances, $r > M$, may be trained simultaneously.) For this, one of the cells of the pair is fed with external signal $(V_0/P) \times \sum_p \xi_j^p \xi_{j'}^p$, where ξ_j^p is the j-th pixel of the p-th image of the training set of P images, while the second cell is fed with positive signal V_0, with $V_0 \gg T$. In this way, each of two synapses connecting the cell pair is exposed to training only once and, as described in Sec. 2 above, the probabilities of connection of its synapses are well saturated to provide virtually deterministic weights

$$w_{jj'} \approx \mathrm{sgn} \sum_p \xi_j^p \xi_{j'}^p. \tag{4}$$

Such synaptic weights are known to work very well for fully connected Hopfield networks [11, 13]. Our numerical experiments have confirmed its efficiency for such localized networks as CrossNets. As an example, Fig. 4 shows the result of the restoration of one of three black-and-white images, being spoiled initially by flipping 40% of randomly selected pixels. In this case, the final restoration is perfect.

However, as the number of taught images P is increased, we see that the number of errors grow. For a "global" (fully connected) Hopfield network of N cells, the rule (4) is well known [13] to provide capacity $P_{max} \approx 0.1N$, i.e. just ~30% below that for the continuous Hebb rule $w_{jj'} \propto \sum_p \xi_j^p \xi_{j'}^p$. In CrossNets, the synaptic connections only extend to $4M \ll N$ cells. To our knowledge, no analytical theory had been developed for this case, but from what we knew about randomly diluted Hopfield networks (see, e.g., Ref. 14), we expected P_{max} to be proportional to M. Our analytical estimate [15] has confirmed this expectation, giving $P_{max} \approx [4/\pi f^2(m)]M$, where m is the average fraction of wrong bits in the restored image, and the function $f(m)$ is defined by equation: $m = \{1-\mathrm{erf}[f(m)]\}/2$. For $m = 1\%$, this formula gives $P_{max} \approx 0.5M$, compatible with our numerical results.

In our second training method, the InBar matrix is considered to be partitioned to pixel panels with P cells each. Then each couple of cells from different pixels is fed sequentially by external signals according to the following rule: $V_{j,\pi} = V_0 \xi_\pi^p$, $V_{j+p,\pi'} = V_0 \xi_{\pi'}^p$, where j is the cell number in the pixel, while π is the pixel number. In this way, each 4-group of synapses is again exposed to training only once and probabilities of connection of its synapses are saturated to provide almost deterministic weights $w_{j,\pi,\ j+p,\pi'} \approx \xi_\pi^j \xi_{\pi'}^{j+p}$. The advantage of this method is that it does not require the external tutor system to provide multiplication of the taught signals. Our analysis and numerical experiments have shown, however, that although this method also works, it provides a lower network capacity: $P_{max} \approx [2/f(m)]M^{1/2}$.

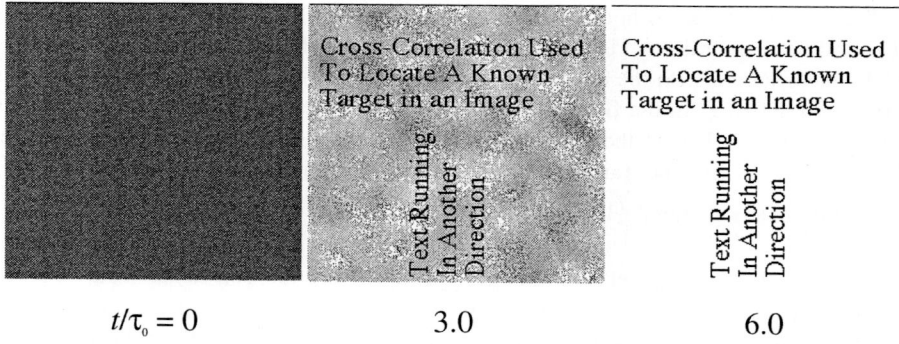

Fig. 4. The process of recall of one of three trained black-and-white images by an InBar-type CrossNet with 256×256 neural cells and connectivity $M = 64$. The initial image (left panel) was obtained from the trained image (identical to the one shown in the right panel) by flipping 40% of pixels. $\tau_0 = MR_L C_0$ is the effective time constant of intercell interaction, C_0 is the dendrite wire capacitance per one plaquette.

5 Runtime Training Prospects

The applied value of Hopfield networks is rather limited [11, 12]. Much more important would be the continuous ("runtime") training of CrossNets as image classifiers. Our plans for such training are based on the following important feature of these networks.

Due to the signal sign symmetry of CrossNets (Fig. 3), if the latching switches are connected randomly, with probability $p = 1/2$, the average synaptic weight vanishes: $\langle w_{jj'} \rangle = 0$. This means that in the absence of synaptic adaptation, the increase of the effective somatic gain $g \equiv GR_L/R$ (where G is the linear voltage gain of the somatic cell amplifier, and R_L is its load resistor – see Fig. 3), cannot lead to a global latch-up of all the cells in one of two possible saturated states. Simulations show that, similarly to the non-Hebbian case [8, 9], an increase of g above a certain threshold value $g_t \approx 1/\sqrt{M}$ leads to ac self-excitation of the network. Near the threshold this excitation has a form of almost sinusoidal oscillations with a period of a few τ_0, but at $g \gg g_t$ the activity is almost completely chaotic.

In order to train a CrossNet in runtime, we propose to set the initial shift S [see Eq. (2)] to zero. Then, according to Eq. (3), at $V = 0$ the synapse connection probability p settles to 0.5, and at sufficient gain $g > g_t$ the system goes to chaos. (If the somatic amplifiers are saturated at $V_s \lesssim T/\ln(1/\Gamma_0\tau)$, this activity as such does not generate noticeable synaptic adaptation.) Now we insert external input signals to a subset of I ($N/M \sim I \ll N$) cells, and monitor activity of even smaller number of cells, $O \ll I$, as output signals. Most cells, not belonging to either input or output subsets, serve as a huge hidden "layer" (though this term is hardly applicable to our, deeply recurrent, networks).

As soon as the input/output combination is favorable, the external tutor increases parameter S (either globally or quasi-globally, in the vicinity of each output cell producing desirable output), so that the synaptic connection probability changes in accordance with the signal combination in this particular instant. Thus the chaotic activity should serve for driving the system through the phase space of possible signal states, enabling the tutor to pin down the favorable combinations. We hope that this method will be able to overcome the typical limitations of the firing rate models with chaotic bursts serving for cell synchronization, similarly to spikes in biological neural systems and their integrate-and-fire models [11, 12]. The verification of this idea is our first priority for the near future.

6 Conclusions

Due to potentially low cost of chemically-directed self-assembly of single-molecule devices, CrossNets based on the CMOL technology may become the first artificial neuromorphic networks with the areal density comparable to that of the cerebral cortex, $\sim 10^7$ neurons per cm^2, operating at much higher speed at acceptable power consumption P. (Specifically, the estimated constant τ_0 of intercell interaction is close to 20 ns, i.e. approximately 6 orders of magnitude smaller than the cortex, for the relatively high power $P = 100$ W/cm^2. The power may be reduced with the proportional system slowdown: $P\tau_0 \approx$ const.)

If created and trained to perform high-quality image classification and feature detection, these networks may create a viable market for CMOL circuits. In this case, large-scale ($\sim 30\times30$ cm^2) CMOL circuits comparable in integration scale with the human cerebral cortex ($\sim 10^{10}$ cells at $\sim 10^{14}$ synapses) may become available.(In order to allow relatively rare but fast communications between its distant parts, such systems should have hierarchical organization including, as a minimum, flat CrossNet blocks connected by high-speed lines.)

Equipped with broadband sensor/actuator interfaces, such hierarchical systems may be capable, after a period of initial supervised training, of further self-training in the process of interaction with environment (read self-evolution), with the speed several orders of magnitude higher than that of their biological prototypes. Needless to say, the development of such self-evolving systems would have a major impact on all information technologies and the society as a whole.

Acknowledgments. Fruitful discussions with P. Adams, J. Barhen, V. Protopopescu, and T. J. Sejnowski are gratefully acknowledged. I. Muckra has provided great help with network simulations. A. Mayr has kindly allowed the use of Fig. 2d before publication of Ref. 10. The work was supported in part by ARDA via ONR, DOE (both directly and via ORNL), and NSF. Most numerical calculations have been carried out on *Njal* computer cluster that was acquired with a grant from DoD's DURIP program via AFOSR.

References

1. Park, H. et al.: Nanomechanical Oscillations in a Single C_{60} Transistor. Nature **407** (2000) 57–60
2. Zhitenev, N. B., Meng, H., Bao, Z.: Conductance of Small Molecular Junctions. Phys. Rev. Lett. **88** (2002) 226801 1–4
3. Park J. et al: Coulomb Blockade and the Kondo Effect in Single-Atom Transistors. Nature **417** (2002) 722-725
4. Liang, W. J. et al.: Kondo Resonance in a Single-Molecule Transistor. Nature **417** (2002) 725–729
5. Likharev, K.: Electronics Below 10 nm. To be published in: Korkin, A. (ed.): Nano and Giga Challenges in Microelectronics. Elsevier, Amsterdam (2003). Preprint available on the Web at http://rsfq1.physics.sunysb.edu/~likharev/nano/NanoGiga036603.pdf
6. International Technology Roadmap for Semiconductors, 2001 Edition, 2002 Update. Available on the Web at http://public.itrs.net/Files/2001ITRS/Home.html
7. Zankovych, S. et al: Nanoimprint Lithography: Challenges and Prospects. Nanotechnology **12** (2001) 91–95
8. Fölling, S., Türel, Ö., Likharev, K. K.: Single-Electron Latching Switches as Nanoscale Synapses. In: Proc. of the 2001 Int. Joint Conf. on Neural Networks. Int. Neural Network Society, Mount Royal, NJ (2001) 216–221
9. Türel, Ö., Likharev, K. K.: CrossNets: Possible Neuromorphic Networks Based on Nanoscale Components. Int. J. of Circuit Theory and Appl. **31** (2003) 37–54
10. Likharev, K., Mayr, A., Muckra, I., Türel, Ö: CrossNets: High-Performance Neuromorphic Architectures for CMOL Circuits. Report at the 6th Conf. on Molecular-Scale Electronics (Key West, FL, December 2002), to be published by the New York Acad. Sci. (2003)
11. Hertz J., Krogh A., Palmer R. G.: Introduction to the Theory of Neural Computation. Perseus, Cambridge, MA (1991)
12. Dayan, P., Abbott, L. F.: Theoretical Neuroscience. MIT Press, Cambridge, MA (2001)
13. van Hemmen, J. L., Kühn, R.: Nonlinear Neural Networks. Phys. Rev. Lett. **57** (1986) 913–916
14. Derrida, B., Gardner, E., Zippelius, A.: An Exactly Soluble Asymmetric Neural Network Model. Europhys. Lett. **4** (1987) 167–173
15. Türel, Ö., Muckra, I. Likharev, K. K.: Possible Nanoelectronic Implementation of Neuromorphic Networks, Accepted for presentation at the Int. Joint Conf. on Neural Networks (Portland, OR, July 2003), preprint available on the Web at http://rsfq1.physics.sunysb.edu/~likharev/nano/IJCNN03.pdf

Cognitive Science

The Acquisition of New Categories through Grounded Symbols: An Extended Connectionist Model

Alberto Greco[1], Thomas Riga[1], and Angelo Cangelosi[2]

[1] Psychology Division, Department of Anthropological Sciences, University of Genoa,
vico S. Antonio 7, Genoa, Italy
greco@disa.unige.it   thomasriga@yahoo.com
[2] Centre for Neural and Adaptive Systems, School of Computing, University of Plymouth,
Drake Circus, PL4 8AA Plymouth, UK
acangelosi@plymouth.ac.uk

Abstract. Solutions to the symbol grounding problem, in psychologically plausible cognitive models, have been based on hybrid connectionist/symbolic architectures, on robotic approaches and on connectionist only systems. This paper presents new simulations on the use of neural network architectures for the grounding of symbols on categories. In particular, the connectivity patterns between layers of the networks will be manipulated to scale up the performance of current connectionist models for the acquisition of higher-order categories via grounding transfer.

1 The Grounding of Symbols in Categories

Cognitive models dealing with linguistic and symbol-manipulation tasks can use symbols that are either grounded or ungrounded (i.e. self-referential). Grounded symbols are those inherently significant to the cognitive system, such as an agent, and not mediated by the interpretation of an external user. Self-referential symbolic systems are those that use symbols that have no grounding in any other module of the cognitive agent. It has been claimed [5] that the cognitive relevance and psychological plausibility of a self-referential symbolic system is diminished as a result of the symbol grounding problem. To solve the problem, Harnad [5] suggested that symbols should be intrinsically linked to the agent's ability of acquiring categories from everyday experience it has of its environment. In particular, it is necessary that some basic symbols are directly grounded on sensorimotor categories. Subsequently, new (grounded) categories can be formed through the combination of previously grounded basic symbols.

Hybrid symbolic-connectionist models were originally proposed as ideal candidates for solving the symbol grounding problem [6]. More recently, alternative approaches have been introduced. Robotics approaches to symbol grounding focus on social learning and interaction between agents (including robots, internet agents and humans) to ground shared symbol communication systems. This has been implemented, for example, in experiments on robotic language games [9]. Fully connectionist models have also been proposed to deal with the symbol grounding problem [1,7,8]. For example, in [1] the ability of neural networks to acquire a small set of basic categories through direct sensorimotor grounding was tested. The same networks were subsequently trained to acquire new higher-order categories solely through combination of the name of basic categories (symbolic theft). These networks were able to transfer the grounding from sensorimotor categories to higher-order categories learnt via symbol combination. Such an approach has also been used in evolutionary simulations of language origins [2].

Research on the connectionist implementation of grounded symbolic cognitive agents is still in progress. In particular, effort has focused on the design of modular connectionist architectures and its contribution in dealing with the nature/nurture debate (e.g. [3]). This paper presents new simulations based on the manipulation of the connectivity pattern of multi-layer perceptrons for the grounding of symbols on categories. In addition, it will deal with some problems of current connectionist architectures, such as the scaling up of categories and symbols.

2 Simulation One

In the first model, Cangelosi, Greco and Harnad's [1] model (CGH, thereafter) will be expanded to deal with larger category sets, and to look at different aspects of the transfer of grounding. In previous studies [10], the same fully-connected architecture from CGH was used with larger category sets. These included extra entry-level categories (e.g. 3 basic categories, each constituted by 2 exemplars), larger entry-level categories (2 basic categories, each constituted by 3 exemplars), and more high-order levels of categories (27 basic order categories which form 9 high-order categories, which then form 3 higher-order categories). Fully connected multi-layer perceptrons failed to transfer the grounding in any of the three levels of extension of the model. This indicated a significant shortcoming of the proposed neural network model [1] for the symbol grounding. This paper presents a series of new simulations in which some of these limitations have been overcome by manipulating the pattern of connections between groups of units.

The goal of the first simulation is to use a fully connectionist architecture to scale up the performance of CGH with more categories (4x4 basic and 4 higher-order categories).

2.1 The Stimulus Set

The total stimulus set consisted of 396 images, 216 for the training and 180 for the generalization test (cf. prototypical stimuli in Fig. 1). These images were derived from the animal picture set of the second experiment of CGH [1]. Each stimulus consists of a 50x50 pixel image. A single image can represent an isolated shape, a texture or an animal obtained by combining a specific shape and texture. Four different animal shapes (e.g. a horse shape), four textures (e.g. a striped pattern) and four animals (zebra = horse shape + stripes pattern) were used. The four shapes and the four textures constitute the (basic) entry-level categories. These are learned through direct sensorimotor grounding in categorization and naming learning stages. The four animals constitute the higher-order categories and are learned through symbolic theft. These are also used for the grounding transfer test only.

The training stimulus set was augmented by placing each image of the 8 entry-level categories into 27 different positions on the retina. This resulted in 215 training images. The testing set was also augmented by placing the 4 animals in 45 different positions in the retina image (9 spatial translation of the shapes x 4 translation of the texture position).

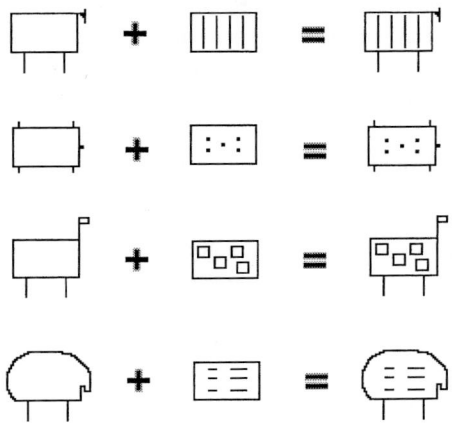

Fig. 1. Prototype of categories used in simulation 1. (Left) The shapes and textures of the Entry-Level categories. (Right) Higher-Level categories.

2.2 The Neural Network and Training Procedure

The architecture of the network has been significantly changed with respect to that of CGH. In GCH, a standard multi-layer perceptron with one hidden layer was used. Here, the networks also have one hidden layer, but the connections to and from hidden units are modularly organized. The network contains 61 input units, 49 for the retina and 12 for the category names (Fig. 2). The same type and number of units are used in the output layer. The 49 (7x7) retina input units consists of gaussian receptive field units. These process the 50x50 pixels of the original image, each using a square receptive field of 11x11 pixel [1,4]. Retina units are divided into two groups, the periphery and the center. The 6 hidden units are also divided into two groups of 3 units each, one specialized for shapes and one for textures. The periphery input units send connections only to the 3 shape hidden units. The retina central units send connections only to the texture hidden units. This is due to the fact that the units in the periphery of the retina encode the part of the image representing the various animal shapes. The central units encode the texture in the center of images. Twelve localist symbolic input and output units encode the category names (4 entry-level shapes, 4 entry-level textures, 4 higher-level animals).

The networks were trained using the error backpropagation algorithm. Training was similar to that of CGH and consisted of three stages: prototype sorting, entry-level learning and higher-level naming and imitation (Fig. 3a). During the prototype sorting stage (i.e. entry-level categorization), networks learn the basic categories (4 animal shape and 4 textures) by receiving input exclusively from the retina images and responding with a retina representation of the prototype of the category (e.g. a fixed, centered shape of a horse). The entry-level learning stage consists of two network activation cycles, the naming and imitation cycles. In the naming cycle, the network sees the retina image and responds in output with the prototypical retinal image and the localist unit encoding the category name. In the imitation, only the symbolic units are used in both the input and the output layers. During the first two stages, learning occurs through direct trial and error experience supervised by corrective feedback ('sensorimotor toil'). Therefore, names acquired this way can be considered as symbols grounded in retinal input. In the higher-level stage the networks acquired new names defined solely on the basis of symbolic strings containing combinations of previously grounded names ('symbolic theft').

The final stage consisted of the grounding transfer test. New retina images exhibiting combinations of previously learned shapes and textures (e.g. images of zebras obtained by combining a horse shape and the striped pattern) were presented to the networks. The test aims to establish whether the networks, which have never seen these images before, are able to correctly categorize and name images with entry- and higher-level symbols.

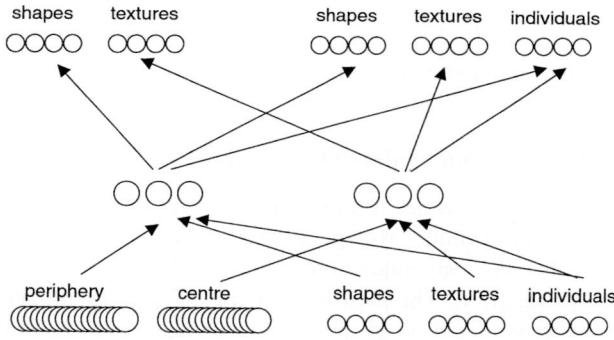

Fig. 2. Neural network architecture for simulation 1

2.3 Results

The simulation consisted of the training of 10 networks with different initial random weights. The momentum was 0.9 for all stages. The learning rate was 0.2 for the first stage and 0.5 for stages two and three. The stimuli were always presented in random order. All networks completed the three training tasks successfully. After training, all networks learnt the various entry- and higher-level categories. The percentage of images correctly categorized in all training stages is 100%. The percentage of correct responses (i.e. production of the correct output name) was computed by using the unit with highest activation to select the name of the input image.

The results on the grounding transfer test were also very positive. The percentage of higher-order animal images correctly categorized and named was 80.4%. This clearly shows that grounding is "transferred" from directly grounded names to higher-order ones (grounding transfer). Moreover, the networks were able to give the correct sensorimotor response when they received the name of a higher-level category in input (inverse grounding transfer).

This model dealt well with a scaled up stimulus set of 4x4 basic categories and 4 higher-order categories. However, the separation of input and output retina units into peripheral and central units was somewhat artificial. This separation was essential to achieve successful grounding transfer results. It is likely that this was due to the design of stimuli with no overlap in the retina for the position of the animal shapes and the texture pattern. In the next model, this problem will be dealt with by using a stimulus set with complete overlap of entry-level category features.

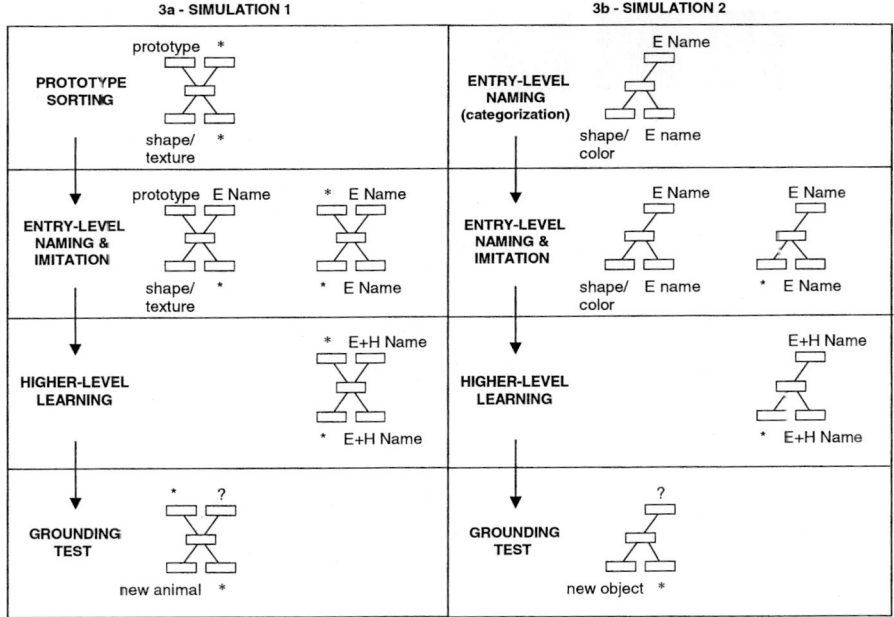

Fig. 3. Training and test stages for simulation one (3a) and two (3b). EL = Entry-Level, HL=Higher-level categories.

3 Simulation Two

This simulation will use a new neural network architecture and a new set of categorization stimuli. The objective is to avoid the artificial division of retina units into peripheral and central units. This division did not have any plausible justification, but was simply introduced to facilitate the network in the classification of the specific set of animal picture stimuli. Only the modular organization of hidden-to-output connections will be preserved.

3.1 The Stimulus Set

The stimuli consisted of 81 abstract images, 54 for training purposes and 27 reserved for testing. Each image, constituted by a 5x5 pixel drawing, was obtained by combining 3 different shapes (square, cross, dots) with 3 different colors (red, green, blue) in 9 different positions (Fig. 4). Every pixel of the image is presented to the network with three input units, coding the primary color components (red, green, blue: RGB).

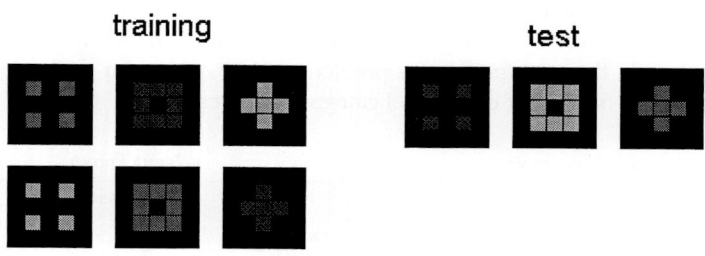

Fig. 4. Sample training and testing stimuli for simulation 2

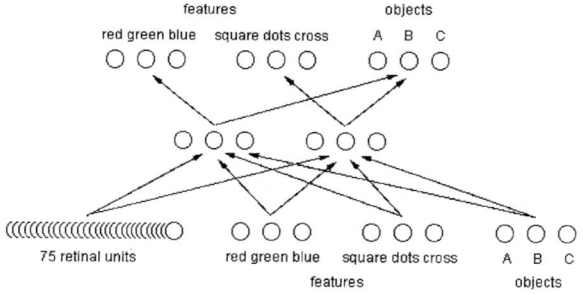

Fig. 5. The neural network architecture of simulation 2

The names of categories are encoded with localist symbolic input and output units. These may contain the names of the categories of different visual features (e.g. blue, square), the name of the object as a whole, or a full description of the objects (e.g. blue + square = object A).

This new stimulus set is intended to be more flexible than the one used in Simulation one. Specifically, in this simulation the distinction between the periphery and the center of the retina image becomes irrelevant since the color and shape completely overlap.

3.2 The Neural Network and Training Procedure

A three-layer, feedforward neural network was used (Fig. 5). The input layer consisted of a retina with 75 units and a symbolic input group containing nine units. The retina had three units for each of the 25 pixels, measuring its RGB component. The symbolic input group consisted of nine units receiving names for the colors, shapes and objects perceived. The hidden layer had six units, organized into two separated groups of three units each. The output layer was structured in the same way as the symbolic input group, with nine units representing the symbolic output.

The input layer was fully connected to the hidden layer. The symbolic output units representing the names for the objects were fully connected to all hidden units. The output units indicating shapes were only connected to the first three hidden units, whilst those indicating colors had connections solely to the last three hidden units. This modular connectivity forces the functional division of the hidden layer into a group dedicated to categorizing shapes and a group to classify colors. Note that the retina units are not artificially divided into two groups as in simulation one.

The error backpropagation algorithm was used to train the network. Training was organized in three stages: Entry-Level naming, Entry-Level imitation and naming, and Higher-Level learning (Fig. 3b). In the Entry-Level naming stage the neural nets are initially trained to categorize (through naming) the color and shape of objects perceived on the retina. The retinal stimuli and names for colors and shapes are presented simultaneously in input. The networks learn to respond to the symbolic and retinal stimuli indicating the corresponding names for the color and shape in output. In the Entry-level imitation and naming stage an extra imitation learning cycle is executed in addition to the repetition of the naming cycles. Imitation consists on the use of only the symbolic units in both the input and the output layers. During these first two stages the networks learn through direct trial and error experience supervised by corrective feedback. Visual stimuli are categorized and linked to arbitrary grounded names.

In the third training phase (Higher-Level learning), networks acquire new higher-order categories through symbolic descriptions only. New categories are built by combining grounded names. Each description contains the name of a shape, a color and the name of a object that is new to the network. The grounding test is performed at the end of training.

3.3 Results

The training procedure was replicated with 30 networks having different initial random seeds. The momentum was 0.9 for all stages. The learning rate was 0.2 for the first stage and 0.5 for stages two and three. The stimuli were presented in random order during Entry-Level (EL) categorization and in sequential order afterwards.

All 30 networks completed the three training tasks successfully. The networks categorized the colors and shapes of the training stimuli correctly, with a success rate of 100%. The percentage of correct responses (i.e. production of the correct output name for the shape/color/object input) was computed using a winner-takes-it-all approach in which the unit with highest activation determines the name of the input image.

After the networks had completed the final stage, 27 retinal stimuli depicting new objects were presented to the networks for the first time, in order to check if grounding had been "transferred" from directly grounded names to higher-order categories. The rate of correct test responses for the 30 nets was 85%. Even when the networks had never seen the test images before, they were able to categorize most of them correctly.

4 Conclusion

In this paper we have presented two simulations that model autonomous cognitive systems, immune to the symbol grounding problem: the connections between symbols and their meanings are direct and intrinsic to the system, without need for mediation by an external interpreter.

Our results reinforce the approach to symbol grounding based on fully connectionist models. The same network processes both the sensorimotor grounding and the generation of new categories through symbolic learning. The modular organization of the hidden units suggests that it is important that sensorimotor grounding be separated for different classification features. In fact, when a fully distributed network was used [10], the grounding transfer was difficult to achieve.

In order to improve the psychological plausibility and scalability of connectionist approaches to the symbol grounding, various extensions of the models presented here are being studied. For example, alternative learning algorithms like Kohonen's self organizing map and Hebbian learning are being tested for the basic categorization stage.

Acknowledgements. Cangelosi's contribution to the research was supported by the EPSRC (GR/N01118).

References

1. Cangelosi A, Greco A, Harnad S (2000). From robotic toil to symbolic theft: Grounding transfer from entry-level to higher-level Categories. *Connection Science*, 12: 143–162
2. Cangelosi A, Harnad S (2000). The adaptive advantage of symbolic theft over sensorimotor toil: Grounding language in perceptual categories. *Evolution of Communication*, 4: 117–142
3. Elman JL, Bates EA, Johnson MH, Karmiloff-Smith A, Parisi D, and Plunkett K (1996). *Rethinking Innateness: A Connectionist Perspective on Development.* Cambridge: MIT
4. Jacobs RA, Kosslyn SM (1994). Encoding shape and spatial relations: The role of receptive field size in coordinating complementary representations. *Cognitive Science*, 18: 361–386.
5. Harnad S (1990). The symbol grounding problem. *Physica D*, 42: 335–346
6. Harnad S (1993). Grounding symbols in the analog world with neural nets. *Think*, 2: 12-78
7. Harnad S, Hanson SJ, Lubin J (1995). Learned categorical perception in neural nets: Implications for symbol grounding. In Honavar V, Uhr L (Eds) *Symbol Processors and Connectionist Network Models in Artificial Intelligence and Cognitive Modeling: Steps toward principled integration.* Academic Press (p. 191–206)
8. Plunkett K, Sinha C, Moller MF, Strandsry O (1992). Symbol grounding or the emergence of symbols? Vocabulary growth in children and a connectionist net. *Connection Science*, 4(3-4): 293–312
9. Steels L (2002). Grounding symbols through evolutionary language games. In Cangelosi A, Parisi D (Eds) *Simulating the Evolution of Language*, (p. 211–226), London: Springer
10. Stuart EJ, Cangelosi A (1999). Unpublished data. University of Plymouth

A Neural Model of Binding and Capacity in Visual Working Memory

Gwendid T. van der Voort van der Kleij[1], Marc de Kamps[2], and Frank van der Velde[1]

[1] Cognitive Psychology Unit, University of Leiden Wassenaarseweg 52,
2333 AK Leiden, The Netherlands
{gvdvoort, vdvelde}@fsw.leidenuniv.nl
[2] Robotics and Embedded Systems, Department of Informatics,
Technische Universität München, Boltzmannstr. 3,
D-85748 Garching bei München, Germany
kamps@in.tum.de

Abstract. The number of objects that can be maintained in visual working memory without interference is limited. We present simulations of a model of visual working memory in ventral prefrontal cortex that has this constraint as well. One layer in ventral PFC constitutes a 'blackboard' representation of all objects in memory. These representations are used to bind the features (shape, color, location) of the objects. If there are too many objects, their representations will interfere in the blackboard and therefore the quality of these representations will degrade. Consequently, it becomes harder to bind the features for any object maintained in memory, which reduces the capacity of working memory.

1 Introduction

Recent investigations [1] have shown that humans have the ability to maintain a number of visual objects in visual working memory. A remarkable characteristic of this finding is that the number of objects that can be maintained in working memory without interference (i.e., loss of information) is limited (to about four), but the number of object features (e.g., shape, color, location, motion, etc.) is unlimited for each of the objects. A model of visual working memory in prefrontal cortex (PFC) has been presented that can explain this characteristic [2]. Basically, this model is characterized by a 'blackboard' that can link different 'processors' to one another. The processors in this case are networks for feature identification (shape, color, location). One layer in ventral PFC functions as the blackboard, containing representations that consist of conjunctions of (partial) 'identity' (shape, color) information and location information. This blackboard serves to bind the information processed in each of the specialized feature networks. Objects in working memory are stored in the blackboard. When too many objects are put in working memory, their representations in the blackboard interfere. Consequently, an object's representation in the blackboard muddles and the capacity of the blackboard to bind the features of an object degrades.

After getting deeper into this model of visual working memory, we present simulations that confirm our expectations that the model is limited in the number of visual objects that it can maintain without interference.

2 Blackboard Architecture of Visual Working Memory in PFC

Our model of visual working memory in PFC is based on a neural blackboard architecture that is used in a simulation of object-based attention in the visual cortex [3]. We assume that the neural blackboard architecture is located in the ventral prefrontal cortex (V-PFC) [2]. This is in line with human neuroimaging studies and recent monkey studies [4]. Activation in V-PFC is sustained (reverberating) activation, characteristic of working memory activation in the cortex.

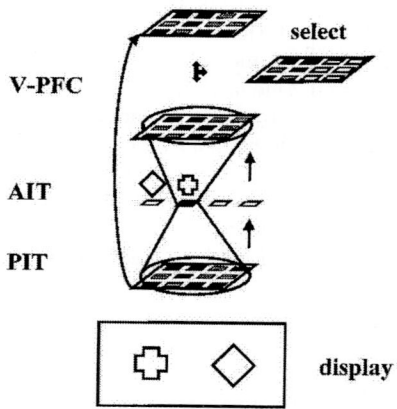

Fig. 1. A blackboard architecture in prefrontal cortex (PFC). PIT = posterior inferotemporal cortex; AIT = anterior infero-temporal cortex; V-PFC = ventral prefrontal cortex.

In the model (figure 1), the ventral prefrontal cortex (V-PFC) has a layered structure with representations similar to the representations in the visual (temporal) cortex. First, the posterior infero-temporal cortex (PIT) connects to one of the layers in V-PFC (for the purpose of illustration: the top layer in figure 1). As in PIT itself, the representations in this layer of V-PFC consist of conjunctions of location and (partial) identity (object-feature) representations (shape, color). In turn, another layer of V-PFC (the bottom layer in figure 1) is connected to the higher-level areas in the visual cortex, in which location and (location-invariant) object identity information are processed and represented (in figure 1 illustrated for the anterior infero-temporal cortex (AIT), where the shape of an object is processed and represented). These connections are similar to the connections of the feedback network of the visual cortex in [3]. They have a 'fan-out' structure, which means that they connect to all possible representations that are selective for an activated feature (on every possible position). As a result, the representations in the bottom layer of V-PFC consist of distributed identity representations. The bottom and top layer of V-PFC interact in a manner similar to the interaction between the feedforward and feedback networks of the visual cortex in [3], using similar microcircuits. This interaction results in the selective activation of a third layer in V-PFC (the 'select' layer in figure 1). In particular, in the select layer there is activation on locations in which there is a substantial match in activation between the top and bottom layer of V-PFC.

Figure 1 illustrates the selection process in the V-PFC model. In figure 1, two objects are processed in the visual cortex, and their PIT representations also activate the representations in the top layer of V-PFC. The activation of one of the objects (the cross) is selected (attended) in AIT (e.g., due to a competition between both figures in AIT). This identity activation of the cross in AIT activates the bottom layer of V-PFC. As a result, the interaction between the top and bottom layer activate the representations in the select layer that are selective for the features (e.g., shape, color, position) of the cross. The activation in the select layer can be used to activate the other features of the cross [3,5].

2.1 Feature Binding in Working Memory

The nature of the representations in V-PFC and the connections with the higher-level areas in the visual cortex produces the behavioral effects described before. The blackboard architecture of V-PFC results in a binding of the feature representations of the objects maintained in memory. Therefore, the features of an object can be retrieved (selected) in working memory as long as the representations of the objects stored in V-PFC do not interfere. However, when too many objects are present in a display, their representations in V-PFC will interfere, which results in loss of information. As more objects are present in a display, the amount of interference increases, and it can be expected that the quality of the representation of an object in V-PFC becomes less. As a consequence, it becomes harder to correctly bind the feature representations of the object that are maintained in memory. V-PFC might end up binding wrong feature representations for an object that is attended to. We carried out simulations to see whether our model of the visual working memory shows this behavior.

3 Simulations

For the simulations we used the same neural network model of (the ventral pathway in) the visual cortex that is used in the simulation of object-based attention in the visual cortex [3]. It basically consists of a feedforward network that includes the areas V1, V2, V4, PIT and AIT, and of a feedback network that carries information about the identity of the object to the lower areas in the visual cortex (V1 - PIT). The model shares the basic architecture and characteristics (i.e., the nature of the representations) of the visual cortex. For the purpose of our simulations, we trained 5 feedforward neural networks to identify 9 different objects on 9 possible positions (using backpropagation). After a feedforward neural network had successfully learnt this task, its corresponding feedback network was trained as well (using Hebbian learning) [3]. This resulted in having 5 instances of the visual cortex model, with each instance having slightly different connection weights between its layers.

The layers of the visual working memory were subsequently simulated as follows. The activation in the top layer of V-PFC is simulated as a copy of the activation in PIT after a display is processed feedforwardly through the visual cortex [3]. This is done because the representations in this layer of V-PFC are similar to the representations in PIT. For reasons of simplicity, the bottom layer of V-PFC, which is connected to many higher-level areas in the visual cortex, is simulated being connected to just one of these areas, AIT. The connections from AIT to this layer are similar to the connections between AIT and PIT in the feedback network of the visual cortex [3]. These connections are therefore copied from a trained feedback network and the representation in this layer equals the representation in PIT in the feedback neural network.

During the simulations, displays consisting of N (different) objects, with N ranging from 2 to 9, are presented to V1. For each N, 180 random displays are presented to each instance of the model. Objects in a display are placed on separate, non-overlapping, positions. Let us see what happens in our model after presentation of a single display (i.e., one trial). First, the visual cortex processes the display. The feedforward neural network gradually transforms the retinotopic information in the primary visual cortex into identity-based information. The representations of the objects in PIT also activate the representations in the top layer of V-PFC, that receives its information from PIT. This layer of V-PFC stores the objects in the display. Now suppose that one of the represented objects is attended to (selected). The attended object activates its shape representation in AIT, and consequently, all representations in the bottom layer of V-PFC that are selective for the shape of the object. The question now arises whether it is possible to bind the shape of the attended object with its other features (e.g., its location), despite the fact that $N-1$ other objects are also present in the display. If the representation of the attended object in the top layer of V-PFC is still intact (i.e., is not severely affected by the representations of other objects), the interaction between the top and bottom layer can activate the representation in the select layer that is selective for the attended object. This implies that this representation should be activated in the select layer on a position that corresponds to the location of the attended object in the display. But, in the case that the N representations of the objects in the top layer interfere too much, and make each other's representations 'fuzzy', the interaction between the top and bottom layer cannot uniquely activate the representation that is selective for the attended object anymore. Instead, it might wrongly activate a representation that (originally) is selective for another object. Feature binding of the selected object then fails. The chance of this happening will likely rise as the number of objects represented in the top layer of V-PFC increases.

For example, if a cross and a diamond are presented in a display (figure 1), the cross on the left and the diamond on the right, then this display will be represented in the top layer of V-PFC. Selecting the cross in AIT subsequently activates the distributed representations of the shape of the cross at any possible position in the bottom layer of V-PFC. By means of the interaction between the top and the bottom layer, the representation of the cross on the left position in the select layer will be activated. But, in the case that the representation of the cross and the representation of the diamond in the top layer are interfering too much, the selection of the cross in AIT could result in the incorrect activation of a representation on the right in the select layer. Let us see how our model of visual working memory behaved.

4 Results

In our model of visual working memory, the representation in the encode layer embodies the match between the representation in the top and the bottom layer of V-PFC.

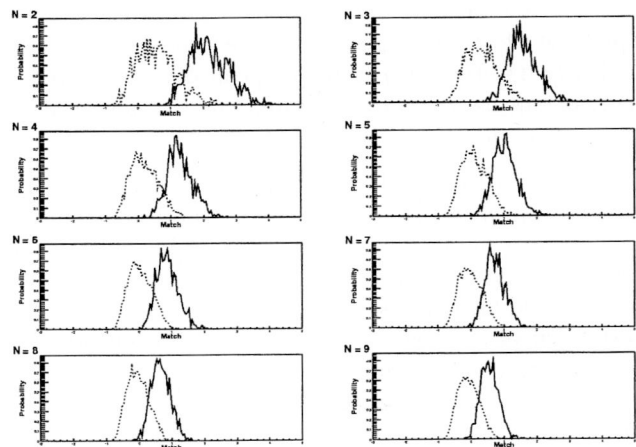

Fig. 2. Probability distribution of match (i.e., standardized positive covariance per position) for positions of attended objects (solid line) and for positions of unattended objects (dashed line) in the top layer in V-PFC. Y-axis: probability. X-axis: match, from negative (left) to positive (right).

The artificial neurons can have activation values in the range -1 to 1. Positive and negative activation can be regarded as activity of separate populations of neurons [6]. Thus, negative activation in the bottom layer and negative activation in the top layer is also a match. Therefore, we simulated the interaction between the top and the bottom layer of V-PFC by computing the covariance between them. Note that these covariance values offer two kinds of information; the match (positive covariance) and the mismatch (negative covariance). After every presentation of a display with N objects, the positive covariance for every possible position of an object in the blackboard (top) layer was summed and subsequently standardized by the average positive covariance per position during that trial. The same was done for the negative covariance. We will further refer to this standardized positive and negative covariance as the match and mismatch respectively.

It may be clear that within every trial, one position in the top (and select) layer corresponds to the position of the attended object in the display, and $N-1$ positions in these layers correspond to positions of objects in the display that are unattended. The rest of the positions in the top and select layer $(9-N)$ correspond to locations in the display where no object was presented.

Figure 2 shows the probability distribution over several amounts of match for positions in the top layer of attended objects and unattended objects separately. For each number of objects in working memory, data of all 5 instances of the neural network model are averaged over all relevant trials. Note that for successful binding to occur, the match should be high on the position of the attended object and low on positions of unattended objects (as the mismatch should be respectively low and high). Only then the position of the attended object can be clearly distinguished from the positions of unattended objects in terms of match. As can be seen in the figure, this is the case if the number of objects held in working memory is low.

Figure 3 shows the probability distribution over several amounts of mismatch for positions in the top layer of attended objects and unattended objects separately. Again, for each number of objects in working memory, data of all 5 instances of the neural network model are averaged over all relevant trials. Note that for successful binding to occur, the mismatch should be low on the position of the attended object and high on positions of unattended objects (as the match should be respectively high and low). Only then the position of the attended object can be clearly distinguished from the positions of unattended objects in terms of mismatch. Again, as can be seen in the figure, this is the case if the number of objects held in working memory is low.

However, figures 2 and 3 show that the probability distribution of match and mismatch for the positions of attended objects and for the positions of unattended objects start to overlap more and more as the number of objects in working memory increases. This means that the position of the attended object cannot be reliably selected on the basis of positive covariance. As the load on the visual working memory gets higher, positions of unattended objects will more frequently be selected instead. In other words, the binding process starts to break down.

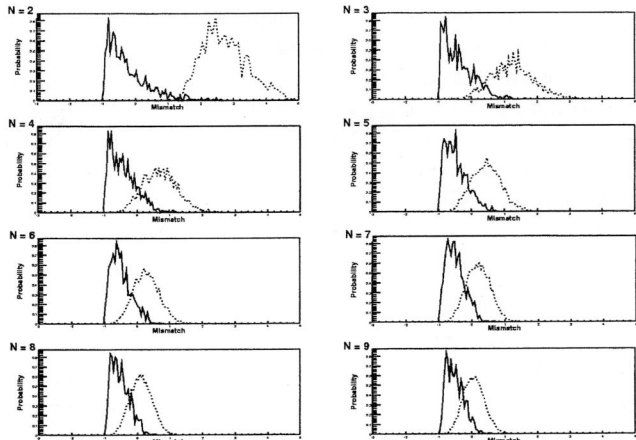

Fig. 3. Probability distribution of mismatch (i.e., standardized negative covariance per position) for positions of attended objects (solid line) and for positions of unattended objects (dashed line) in the top layer in V-PFC. Y-axis: probability. X-axis: mismatch, from negative (left) to positive (right).

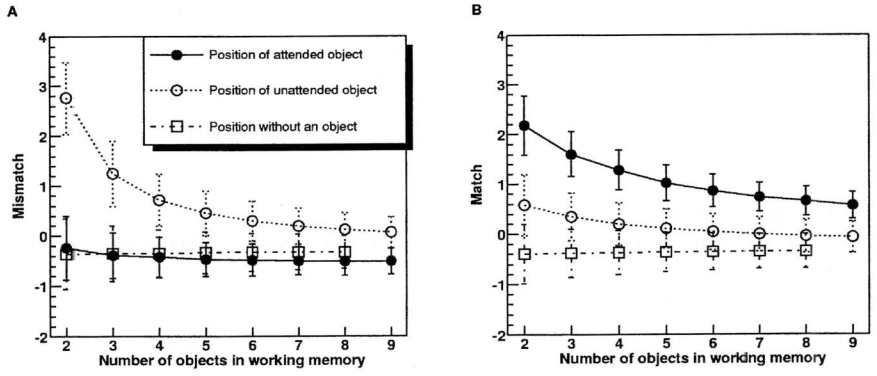

Fig. 4. (A) Mismatch (mean and rms) on positions of attended objects (solid line), on positions of unattended objects (dot-dot line) and on positions without an object (dash-dot line) in the top layer in V-PFC. (B) Idem, but then for match (i.e., standardized positive covariance per position).

The mean amount of match for positions of attended objects, positions of unattended objects and positions with no object is presented in figure 4B together with its root mean square (rms). Picking the position of the attended object instead of a position of an unattended or empty position on the basis of match information clearly becomes very hard as the number of objects in working memory increases. Does mismatch information enable us to point out the right position of an attended object when the number of objects stored in memory increase? The answer is given in figure 4A, and appears to be negative. The distinction between attended and unattended objects gets lost here as well. Filling up the working memory makes the level of mismatch that can be detected in the top layer on the position of the attended object more and more similar to the level of mismatch on other positions. Thus, based on mismatch information, binding begins to fail as well.

5 Discussion

The simulations point out that the model of visual working memory that we presented is limited in the number of objects that it can maintain in memory without interference (i.e., loss of information). Our model cannot successfully bind the feature(s) of the attended object anymore as it gets loaded with more objects. This is in accordance with findings about visual working memory [1]. However, when exactly the limit in visual working memory is reached will depend on other factors as well, like the level of alertness and the contrast of the objects with the background. We predict that this limit is also partly dependent on the distance between objects in a display. Objects that are close to each other activate more common neurons in the top layer of V-PFC than objects that are far from each other. More overlap between representations of objects in the top layer of V-PFC leads to more interference and thus enhances the chance of binding the wrong features for an attended object.

References

1. Vogel, E.K., Woodman, G.F., Luck, S.J.: Storage of features, conjunctions, and objects in visual working memory, Journal of Exp. Psychol.: HPP **27** (2001) 92–114
2. Van der Velde, F., de Kamps, M.: A model of visual working memory in PFC, Neurocomputing (2003) (in press)
3. Van der Velde, F., de Kamps, M.: From knowing what to knowing where: Modeling object-based attention with feedback disinhibition of activation, J. Cognitive Neurosci. **13** (4) (2001) 479–491
4. Duncan, J.: An adaptive coding model of neural function in prefrontal cortex, Nature Rev. Neurosci. **2** (11) (2001) 820–829
5. De Kamps, M., van der Velde, F.: Using a recurrent network to bind form, color and position into a unified percept. Neurocomputing **38-40** (2001) 523–528
6. De Kamps M., van der Velde, F.: From artificial neural networks to spiking neuron populations and back again. Neural Networks **14** (2001) 941–953

Neural Network: Input Anticipation May Lead to Advanced Adaptation Properties

Andrei Kursin

Information Systems Department
Kharkiv Polytechnic Institute
21 Frunze str., Kharkiv, 61002, Ukraine.
kursin@kharkov.ua

Abstract. Network architecture is proposed, which is built according to principle of input anticipation. The network constantly anticipates the incoming input, compares the anticipation with the real input data and modifies its internal structure to ensure better anticipation in the future. It is argued that such network may exhibit advanced adaptation properties.

1 Introduction

Maturana and Varela [1] derive cognitive properties of living organisms from their ability for structural coupling with the environment. In structural coupling an organism changes its structure to successfully operate in given environment, namely to preserve its integrity or autopoiesis – the process of constant self-reproduction. Following Nature, it would be reasonable to apply the same design in order to achieve cognitive properties in an artificial system. Artificial systems usually don't require autopoiesis, so we need to select appropriate homeostatic factor(s) for the system to maintain and rules for system structure modification to ensure this maintenance. In this paper I advance a hypothesis that, thinking of an artificial neural network, the homeostasis required may consist in coherent activity of network elements. On a higher level it gives rise to the principle of input anticipation. A network working according to this principle constantly anticipates its input, compares the anticipations with the real input data and modifies its structure for better anticipation in the future, i.e. for better structural coupling with the environment. This hypothesis is based on the data from physiology and cognitive psychology concerning anticipatory character of animal neural system activity.

I argue that input anticipating network can exhibit advanced adaptive and learning properties, which make them promising candidates for using in autonomous adaptive agents. Relatively slow progress with traditional neural network models in this field – especially in adaptation to complex environments – justifies search for novel network architectures. The only homeostatic adaptive architecture I know has been proposed by Yemelianov-Yaroslavsky [2]. He based network processing and adaptation on the principle of optimization under limited energy resources. I think that coherence/anticipation principle provides more direct and simple solution for the adaptation problems addressed in [2]. Besides, anticipation offers more elegant solution for adaptation to the environment that unfolds in time.

2 Anticipation in Physiology and Cognitive Psychology

Predictive character of animal nervous system activity is stressed in a number of works in physiology and cognitive psychology. Anokhin [3, 4] proved that nervous system – along with initiation of certain action – creates an image of the expected result – a result acceptor. Later the actual result of the action – as it is perceived by the receptors – is compared with the preformed image and the comparison result influence the following action being taken. Thoroughly justified with experiments on the most basic reflexes like respiratory instinct, this theory let us to assume that prediction or anticipation is one of the basic functions of animal neural system

Anticipatory character of perception was revealed by Naisser [5]. He argues that perception is guided by a perceptive cycle that consists in continuous generation of perceptive schemata. The schemata direct the process of perception, anticipate and select the data coming from receptors, while being at the same time subject to change and even replacement in case of their incoherence with the incoming data.

Vitiaev [6] argues that internal representation of goal, which is necessary for any goal-directed activity, is also a kind of prediction formed by a nervous system. Comparison of activity results with the internal image of goal allows judging whether the goal is reached and directs the decision search activity.

3 Anticipatory Neural Network Architecture

Before delving into details of the network architecture I want to sketch out a general picture of its expected functioning. Let's imagine a neural network whose input is exposed to certain systematically organized environment. The network acts e.g. like a pattern recognizer, recognizing the environment objects affecting its input. Since the environment is systematic, the network input sequences would also possess certain systematic character. It would be reasonable not to do each recognition step from scratch but to use information gathered on previous steps or (putting it in another way) to generate certain expectations regarding the subsequent input(s) after a successful recognition step. To enable the network self-learning we should endow it with the ability to compare the real input with the predicted one and modify itself according to the result of the comparison. For this reason we need the network to be able to detect and maintain coherence of activity of its elements because in internal network terms any disparity between a prediction and the real input can manifest itself in nothing else like incoherence in neuronal activity. Actually the network should be able to do three things: 1) to recognize objects; 2) to spread activation among recognition steps and 3) to maintain coherent activity of its elements – and they can lead to rather interesting self-adaptation properties. Let's see how these three things can be implemented.

The most promising for introducing the anticipation principle are – in my view – the neural network architectures based on neural assemblies [7, 8, 9]. Despite of the differences among them, such architectures exhibit essential similarities in network structure and general dynamics. Making certain generalization from these architectures I assume the following.

- The neural network consists of an *input layer* being affected by the environment and an *internal layer*, which is a pool of neural assemblies. The network may also include an output layer or be connected with similar network modules in a kind of super-network [7] but these possibilities aren't considered here.
- The network is scarcely connected; i.e. a neuron connects only to relatively small part of other neurons in the network (no more than square root of total number of neurons [7]).
- The input layer neurons form only output connection to the inner layer, have no input connections and no connections among themselves.
- Neural assemblies of the internal layer are distinguished by denser connectivity of their neurons. They are innate and the weights of intra-assembly connections are assumed non-modifiable.
- The assemblies are overlapping; i.e. one neuron belongs to several assemblies [7, 10]. Assemblies (namely, neurons belonging to different assemblies) are connected with modifiable associative links.
- Each assembly is a potential internal representation of certain idea [7] or, strictly speaking, certain class of environment effects on the input layer. Such potential is actualized in learning process by strengthening connections from certain input layer neurons to certain assembly.
- The number of assemblies in the network is assumed sufficient for the task the network is designed for. So that there is always a reserve of "sleeping" neurons and assemblies intended for possible learning.

The network also contains a *control center* ("reinforcement/inhibition system" [8, 9]) that modulates the activity of the assemblies by means of influencing the neuron activation thresholds. The control center synchronizes the network processing distinguishing several phases in it [7, 11]. Usually two phases minimum are distinguished: search phase and selection phase. Search phase starts with perceiving current environment effect on the input layer. Through the inter-neuron connections the input layer excitation is projected onto the inner layer and activates neurons of certain assemblies. The control center modulates the activation for the projection to be rather wide, ensuring sufficient space for subsequent selection. Then after certain time period the selection phase begins. Increasing neuron activation thresholds, control center narrows the set of active assemblies to one, which is the most active. If the operation succeeds, that assembly is assumed to be the sought-for inner representation for the current environmental affect. The neural assembly, on which the input layer excitation projection is finally focused, experiences an outburst of activity called *firing*. Excitation from the firing assembly is spread through associative links to other assemblies in the network.

There are various approaches to interpreting and using this post-selection excitation. In [7] the effect of such excitation is simply cleared off so none of the results of current activity would contaminate the next recognition step. In [8, 9] it is acknowledged that such excitation is useful for forming context for the future steps. The anticipation principle being proposed consists in treating such excitation not as simply a context but as *a form of expectation or a predictive image for the subsequent input*. The prediction formed inside the network is useful because it facilitates the network reaction on the subsequent step. The inter-network predictive chains are learned by strengthening appropriate associative links between the assemblies. Note that the anticipatory function doesn't mean that the network predicts what exactly will be on its input layer. It rather gets more inclined to receive certain input than other.

4 Three-Stage Neuron Model

The anticipation function is not very useful if the network cannot compare the preformed anticipatory image with the real input data and modify own internal structure (via changing associative link weights) to ensure better predictions. The comparison function can be based on three-stage neuron activation model proposed in [2]. This model distinguishes three stages of neuron activation: *inactive* (or low active), *semi-active* and *highly active*. Typically a neuron cycles among the states in the above-mentioned order. But it can also return to inactive state from semi-active one if it doesn't get enough input activation to reach highly active level. The state transitions have certain semantics: highly active – inactive transition is considered positive, semi-active – inactive transition is negative. 3-stage neuron should "want" that as much as possible of its semi-activations would end in highly active states. This thesis has two consequences. First, assemblies of such neurons act as mutual aid groups [2], in which the neurons, due to their dense connectivity, help each other to reach high activation level. Second, such activation model suggests a specific rule for modification of input connection weights. Namely, a neuron strengthens the active input links on experiencing positive state transition and weakens them on negative one. The strengthening and weakening occurs proportionally to the amount of work done by a link in the nearest history.

The 3-stage activation model gets the following meaning on the network level. Semi-active neurons constitute a prediction image. The neurons can get sufficient activation to reach highly active level only under coherent activity: either in the inner layer or between input and inner layers, i.e. when prediction formed agrees with the input data. A 3-stage neuron acts not only as a generator and selective amplifier of activity but also as a detector of activity coherence. It is the root of coherent activity maintenance function, upon which the anticipation function of the network is built.

It should be expected that an anticipation formed would always be rather wider than its part that would actually hold up. Consequently, the criterion of successful processing of the network would be maintenance of certain ratio between the number of neurons reaching high activation level and the number of going out semi-active neurons. When the number of fired neurons is below the necessary level, it means that the inner state of the network doesn't match the state of the input layer, the prediction fails, the inner representation for current input is not found, and the network enters *critical state*. Seeking its way out of the critical state the network should modify its structure to generate better predictions. A kind of unsupervised learning should take place. I think that an anticipatory neural network can demonstrate advanced learning properties.

5 Learning

Critical state in such network means that none of the inner layer assemblies gets enough input activation to reach high activity level. Input activation for an assembly consists of activation transferred from the previous step and activation received from the input layer on current step. The fact that they don't sufficiently converge on any assembly represents actually the incoherence between the anticipatory image and the real input.

What are the possible ways out of that situation? Wickelgren [7] for example recruits one of the sleeping assemblies to represent the novel input data. The recruitment is achieved with special mechanism called *chunking*. The recruited assembly is the one having most physical connections to the currently active input image.

For an anticipatory neural network such technique cannot be useful. A freshly recruited assembly has no sufficiently strong associative output links to form anticipation for the next step. So after coming out of critical state on the current step the network highly probably enters it again on the next one. The appropriate technique for such network model, I think, is in mutual help among neural assemblies. Let's consider this technique in detail.

In critical situation none of the assemblies gets strong activation but there should be a set of partially excited assemblies whose neurons are presumably in semi-active state. The following can be assumed.
1. A portion of the set of partially excited assemblies consists of already engaged assemblies which don't have enough physical connection to the currently active neurons in the input layer to get sufficient input activation (remind that the network is scarcely connected).
2. Entering critical state awakens "sleeping" assemblies, which constitute the other portion of partially excited assemblies. Among them there certainly are those ones that have enough physical connections to the current input image. But input connections of freshly awaken neurons are week and such assemblies cannot receive sufficient excitation from the input as well.
3. The current input nevertheless would be often substantially similar to those learned by "old" assemblies. So substantial overlap between them and the freshly awaken assemblies should be expected.

I think that resolving critical situation is possible through joint firing of one of the semi-active old assemblies and one of the awakened. This can be obtained with modulation of global network parameters: lowering activation thresholds and increasing the number of neurons that can simultaneously reach highly active state. This process is influenced by possible overlap between "old" and "fresh" assemblies and existence of – though possibly weak – associative links between them. In this act of joint firing the "fresh" assembly helps the "old" one to fire, i.e. that the neurons of the "old" assembly follow the positive state transition curve, while the "old" assembly with its strong associative links helps the "fresh" one to form appropriate prediction.

If resolving critical situation is followed by a successful anticipation, it is necessary to memorize useful changes in the network structure. Inter-neuron connections are modified by the neurons (see above) accordingly to the dynamics of their state transitions. Though it would be unwise to leave learning decision on such low level. For effective learning the control center modulates the influence that the neurons have on their input connections, so that such influence be minimal in routine mode (when anticipations mainly hold up) and maximal on successful solving a critical situation favoring learning useful changes in network structure. In case of repetition of the same input data the "old" and the "fresh" assemblies continue joint firing for certain period while the links of the "fresh" assembly grow strong enough that it would be able to take a lead and fire alone.

I call such critical situation solving technique and learning that occurs hereat as "metaphorization" because the process highly resembles using metaphor in human thinking – in the most general sense of the word – like a way to understand something with the help of an inner image of another thing [12]. It can become a very promising kind of learning due to the fact that here a newly learned model inherits appropriate properties of old template model with its associative links. This can serve a basis of rapid learning in complex intellectual systems.

Note that due to the overlap among the assemblies, "metaphorization" process can solve recognition failures of different complexity – from noisy input data (in this case the "fresh" assembly minimally deviates from the "old" one) to the situations when the inter-assembly overlap is minimal, which looks more line metaphor using in the above mentioned sense.

6 Model of an Adaptive System

Thus organizing network processing according to the anticipatory principle let us make rather plausible assumptions concerning the existence of advanced leaning and adaptation properties in such network. I think that being rather simple, this principle nevertheless allows building highly scalable powerful solutions. In conclusion, I want to outline architecture of an autonomous self-adapting system based on such a network.

Let's assume that the neural network input layer is exposed to certain environment. Assume for simplicity that on each step only one object in the environment affects the network's input layer. The network finds a neural assembly inside itself that matches this input. We can consider this assembly an inner representation or model of the external object. Through its associative links, the found model forms anticipations as to the subsequent object. The network reads the next input and the cycle repeats. Actually the neural network predicts only elementary events on its input layer but for complex systematically organized environment such anticipation is impossible without reflecting the environment structure in the structure of the network. Through "metaphorization" in its simple forms neural assemblies undergo the process of generalization tending to represent not unique objects but classes of similar objects. Associative links among neural assemblies, representing, essentially, possible temporal sequences, indirectly reflect cause-effect relations in the environment. Trajectories of migration from one object model to another in the inner space of the network can serve as inner models of possible situations in the environment. To enable existence of hierarchies of generalizing models we can introduce additional layers of neurons with longer reaction time.

7 Conclusion

The neural network model described here is yet hypothetical. The future task is to build working model of it and experimentally test the hypotheses. The aim of this paper was to draw attention to the anticipation principle. Neurophysiological data serve as either a source of inspiration in designing artificial neural network models or means to validate them. There are a lot of skepticism stressing the enormous simplification of artificial neural networks comparing to natural ones, which is explained either by development of relatively young research field or still rather restricted computational resources available for experiments. A reasonable strategy in such situation, I think, is to follow the most general principles of natural neural network functioning. Anticipation principle is one of them, thoroughly grounded on experimental physiological data. I intended to show how fruitful might be introduction of the principle into artificial neural network calculations.

References

1. Maturana, H.R., Varela, F.J.: Autopoiesis and Cognition: The Realization of the Living. Reidel, Dordrecht (1980)
2. Yemelianov-Yaroslavsky, L.B., Intellectual quasi-biological system. Inductive automaton. Nauka, Moscow (1990) (in Russian). English version at http://www.aha.ru/~pvad/concept.htm.
3. Anokhin, P.K.: The Functional System Theory as a Basis for Development of Physiological Cybernetics. In: Kuzin, A.M. et al. (eds.): Biological Aspects of Cybernetics. USSR Academy of Sciences Publishing House, Moscow (1962) 74–91 (in Russian)
4. Anokhin, P.K.: Functional System. In: Annual of the Great Medical Encyclopedia, Vol. 1. (1968) 1300–1322 (in Russian)
5. Neisser, U.: Cognition and Reality. Principles and Implications of Cognitive Psychology. W.H. Freeman and Company, San Francisco (1976)
6. Vitiayev, E.E.: Goal-making as Brain Working Principle. In: Models of Cognitive Processes, Proc. of Institute for Mathematics, Siberian Department, Russia Academy of Sciences, Novosibirsk (1997) 9–52 (in Russian).
7. Wickelgren, W.A.: Webs, Cell Assemblies, and Chunking in Neural Nets. In: Canadian Journal of Experimental psychology. Vol. 53. 1 (1999) 118–131
8. Amosov, N.M. et. al.: Automata and Intelligent Behavior. Naukova Dumka, Kiev (1973) (in Russian)
9. Amosov, N.M., Goltzev, A.D., Kussul E.M.: Functional Organization of Brain Processes and Their Concern with Neural Network Structures, Kibernetika 5 (1988) 113–119 (in Russian)
10. Palm, G.: Neural Assemblies. Studies of Brain Function. Vol VII. Springer, Berlin Heidelberg New York (1982).
11. Braitenberg, V.: Cell assemblies in the cerebral cortex. In: Heim, R. and Palm, G. (eds.): Theoretical Approaches to Complex Systems – Lecture Notes in Biomathematics, Vol. 21. Springer Verlag, Berlin (1978) 171–188.
12. Lakoff, G., Johnson, M.: Metaphors We Live By. University of Chicago Press, Chigaco (1980).

Acceleration of Game Learning with Prediction-Based Reinforcement Learning – Toward the Emergence of Planning Behavior –

Yu Ohigashi[1], Takashi Omori[1], Koji Morikawa[2], and Natsuki Oka[2]

[1] Graduate School of Engineering, Hokkaido University,
Kita 13 jyou Nishi 8 chome, Kita, Sapporo, Hokkaido, 060-8628, Japan
{y_ohigashi,omori}@complex.eng.hokudai.ac.jp
[2] Humanware Technology Research Laboratory,
Matsushita Electric Industrial Co., Ltd.,
3-4, Hikaridai, Seika, Soraku, Kyoto, 619-0237, Japan
oka@mrit.mei.co.jp, morikawa@crl.mei.co.jp

Abstract. When humans solve a problem, it is unlikely that they use only the current state of the problem to decide upon an action. It is difficult to explain the human action decision strategy by means of the state to action model, which is the major method used in conventional reinforcement learning (RL). On the contrary, humans appear to predict a future state through the use of past experience and decide upon an action based on that predicted state. In this paper, we propose a prediction-based RL model (PRLmodel). In the PRL model, a state prediction module and an action memory module are added to an actor-critic type RL, and the system predicts and evaluates a future state from a current one based on an expected value table. Then, the system chooses a point of action decision in order to perform the appropriate action. To evaluate the proposed model, we perform a computer simulation using a simple ping pong game. We also discuss the possibility that the PRL model may represent an evolutionary change in conventional RL as well as a step toward modeling of hmuan planning behavior, because state prediction and its evaluation are the basic elements of planning in symbolic AI.

1 Introduction

When we compare the behavior in simple game play of a human and a learning agent that uses Reinforcement Learning (RL), we find that their behavior is not the same even though both players play the game well. Why do their actions differs even when they play the same game? Let's look at the case of the action acquisition by RL. An RL agent acquires optimum action strategies by updating a state value and an action probability distribution based on a reward from the environment through iterative trial and error. That is, RL is a state to action learning model that learns the optimum action for the perceived current state.

In contrast, in addition to the perceived current state, humans can use past experience to predict how an environment will change next and decide upon an

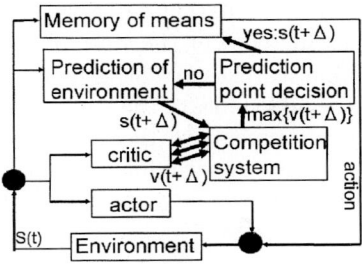

Fig. 1. PRL model

action based on the predicted state. Therefore, in this study, we assume that the human learning strategy is the one based on a state to prediction to action model and that this determines an action by using the current state and the predicted state.

In this paper, we propose prediction-based RL model (PRL model), which is able to select and perform the appropriate action based on the predicted state. The prediction is made by using an extension of RL, namely, a prediction module is added to a conventional actor-critic RL model. To evaluate the effectiveness of the prediction, we run a computer simulation and compare the performance of PRL with that of RL.

2 Prediction-Based Reinforcement Learning Model

2.1 The PRL Model

The PRL model is an extension of an actor-critic RL model to which two modules of "Prediction of Environment(PE)" and "Memory of Means(MM)", have been added(Fig. 1). The PE module carries out a prediction about an object that the agent cannot control in an environment. The MM module memorizes the optimum action for the predicted state and the current state combination in order to change the current state to a target state.

The basic idea of this model is that an agent chooses the optimum action based on the current state and the predicted state, and that the state prediction is acquired through the use of a memory of past experiences. When the agent decides upon an action, it has to resolve two problems.

One is which timing, or prediction point, to adopt for the action decision. The other is how to choose the optimum action from the predicted state and the current state. For each of the problems, a processing flow is described below.

– Timing

1. The agent predicts the state $state(t+1)$ from the state $state(t)$ using the PE module. The prediction is limited to a part of the state. For example,

in the ping pong game simulation described later, a ball position of the next time step is predicted, but the state of agent action is not.

2. A competition system searches for corresponding states in the critic value table and refers expected values of the states. As the prediction is limited to a part of the environment, to the object, and does not include the agent action, multiple states with different agent states correpond to the predicted state. The competition system select the state with maximum value out of the found states.

3. The prediction point decision module receives the selected state value along a time course and decides which predicted state should be adopted for deciding upon the current action. To do this, first, the module compares the value of the selected prediction state in the last prediction step and that of the current prediction step. If the former value is small, the module does not adopt the current prediction state and returns to step 1. Conversely, if the former value is large, the module adopts the last prediction state and uses it to decide upon the current action. As a result, the prediction point with the highest value is selected.

The point here is that the agent chooses the timing of the predicted state by referring to the critic value table which has been built from past experiences. This extended system thus makes use of basic RL knowledge in a different way.

− Action decision
The action decision module chooses the optimum action from the adopted prediction state and the current state. The agent regards the adopted prediction state as the target state. The MM module stores a set of action memoryies for an agent to approach the target state from the current state. Lastly, the MM module outputs the optimum current action that the agent should take. The method by which the MM module acquires memory content is an issue which will be addressed in future research. Here, we assume that the MM module is built by observing several next states that occur as a result of performing actions in the current state. We also assume that some memory content is given in advance.

When the agent decides upon and performs the current action, the agent gets a reward from the environment. The actor and critic modules of our model also learn based on this reward in the same way as in the actor-critic RL model. However, the learning equation in our model differs from that of RL as follows.

$$TDerror = reward + \alpha V(S_{t+\Delta}) - V(S_t) \quad (1)$$

This means that the time step for TD learning is adjusted to the length Δ of prediction steps. This modification results in acceleration of RL learning because an expected value of Δ steps apart state propagates in a single time trial.

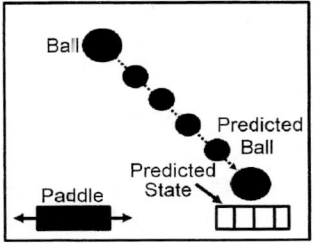
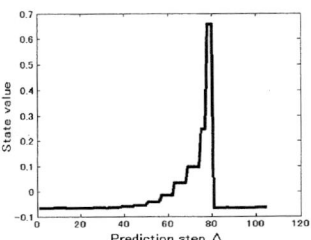

Fig. 2. Ping pong game   **Fig. 3.** State value

2.2 Application to a Simple Ping Pong Game

The PRL model is applied to a simple ping pong game in which an agent operates a paddle with the actions left, right, or stay and hits back a ball to acquires a reward. The process of the PRL model used in the game is as follows.

1. The agent perceives the current state from a display of the game. The variables that represent the state consist of the ball position (B_x, B_y), the direction θ of the ball movement, and the position P_x. Thus, the state space of the game is four dimensional.
2. The PE module predicts the ball state of the next step from the current ball state.
3. The competition system module receives the predicted ball state, and searches the critic value table entries corresponding to multiple paddle states. The module compares those state value and selects the state with the maximum value.
4. The prediction point decision module judges whether the agent should use the selected predicted state for the action decision or not. The agent repeats the processing from step 2 through step 4 until a predicted state is adopted. If the prediction of the environment can predict the next ball state correctly, the agent can predict the ball trajectory (plotted by a broken line in Fig. 2). The transition of the selected state value along the trajectory is shown in Fig. 3. Then, if the learning of the critic value table is sufficient, the predicted state value that should be adopted by the prediction point decision module is the local maximal value shown in Fig. 3. The adopted point corresponds to the place where the ball is hit by the paddle.
5. The MM module outputs the optimum action that the agent should take for the current paddle state and the paddle state of the adopted predicted state.

If the learning of the critic nearly converges, the PRL model can predict the critical position for hitting the ball and select the action that moves the paddle to the correct position.

2.3 Addition of Predcition and Mean Memory Pairs

In this study, we used a simple ping pong game as the sample task and added the ball position prediction module and a memory of paddle action means. However, we believe that if we prepared a PE module and an MM module for a different object or a different game scene, our model would be able to cope with various problems beyond those of a simple ping pong game. The change proposed here from an RL to a PRL model through the addition of PE and MM modules is important in the sense that this change is an evolutional stage in learning.

3 Computer Simulation

3.1 Environment

In this study, we run a computer simulation of the ping pong game(Fig. 2). From the game panel, the player sees a paddle and a ball in two-dimensional space. The x/y-coordinates of the space are defined within the range $[0, 1]$. The direction of the ball movement is represented by an angle between $-\pi$ and π, a zero designating the down direction. The paddle can perform one of three actions: staying, moving left, or moving right at each time step. These are the only actions that the player can take. The ball complies with the physical law of moving straight with a constant speed and rebounding off the wall. The goal of this game is for the agent to hit back the ball by operating the paddle. By hitting the ball, the agent gets a positive reward. A negative reward is given when the agent misses the ball by using an incorrect paddle operation. A small negative reward is also given for each left or right movement of the paddle in order to discourage unnecessary movement. We define an episode of game play as starting from when the ball begins to move up until the paddle hits back or misses the ball. We call an episode an epoch. The state of the game scene is discretized by dividing each of the x/y-coodirnates into ten equal parts and the direction of the ball movement into twelve equal parts. Thus, the state space of the game is the ball x-coordinate (10) * the ball y-coordinate (10) * the direction of the ball movement (12) * the paddle x-coordinate (10) = 10 * 10 * 12 * 10 = 12,000 states in total. This is a typical box states of conventional RL.

3.2 Setup of the PRL Model

The PE moduel calculates the ball position of the next step using a neural network. The neural network is trained by a backpropagation rule with real ball trajectory data of the game. The maximum number of prediction steps is limited to 100. If no predicted state is adopted until the maximum number of steps is reached, the agent performs a soft max action selection rule that is commonly used as an action selection rule of conventional actor-critic based RL. The MM module is implemented by reference to a table from which the agent can find the optimum action from the current paddle state and the target paddle state. In this study, we assume that the PE module and the MM module have

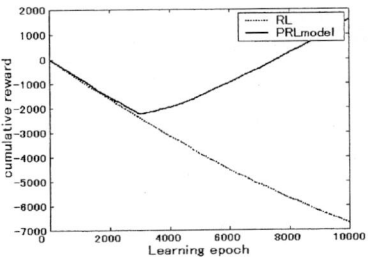

Fig. 4. Cumulative reward

already been learned because it should not be difficult for an agent to learn those two functions if the appropriate parameters for the input and output of the modules are selected in advance and they acquire past experiences in the initial RL learning phase (see section 3.3).

3.3 Task

A learning agent have learned ping pong game play for 10000 epochs by using both the actor-critic RL model and the proposed PRL model. We evaluated these two models by monitoring their respective cumulative reward and probability of ball hitting. After a 100 epochs learning period, we performed a 100-epochs evaluation task in which the agent does not learn the evaluation of their ability in the current state. For the evaluation of RL learning method, we used both the soft max action selection rule and the greedy method. The initial ball position of the task was random. For evaluation of PRLmodel learning, the model learned using the actor-critic method for the initial 3000 epochs in order to bootstrap the critic table, and then the PRL model was applied by using the learned critic table. The learning parameter of the TD learning for both models was $\alpha = 0.1$. The action selection probability of both models was initialized to $\frac{1}{3}$. The initial value of the critic table was set to zero. The parameters for the ping pong game were: the paddle speed = 0.1, paddle width = 0.2, ball radius = 0.02, and ball speed = 0.1. The reward settings for the simulation were: ball hitting = +1.0, ball missing = -1.0, and paddle moving left or right = -0.01.

3.4 Result

Figure 4 shows the transition of cumulative reward for both the actor-critic model and the PRL model. There was no difference in their performance during the first 3000 epochs because the PRL model was not working during initial learning. After the PRL model became active, the performance of the PRL model was better than that of the actor-critic method because of its use of the PE and MM structure. The reasons for this result are that the probability of

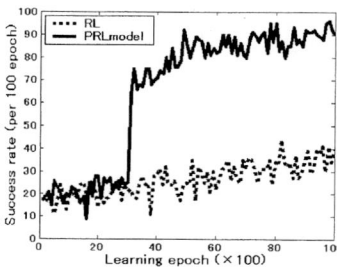
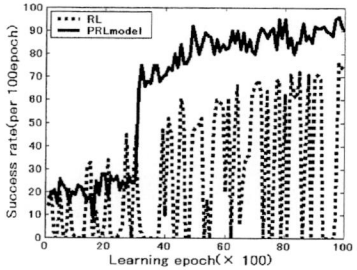

Fig. 5. Test performance (RL:soft max)   **Fig. 6.** Test performance (RL:greedy)

ball hitting by using the PRL model became high even in unlearned states and the ratio of unnecessary actions decreased because the optimum action choice was selected based on the accuracy of the ball hitting position prediction.

Figure 5 shows the result of the test run after each set of 100 learning epochs. The action selection rule of the actor-critic method was the soft max rule. After the initial bootstrap epochs, it is clear that the performance of the PRL model greatly surpassed that of the actor-critic method. The major factor in this high performance is that the PRL model decides upon its optimum action by using the state along the predicted ball trajectory. Moreover, even under an insufficient learning condition, it could by using RL find some learned states by RL near the ball hitting position.

Figure 6 shows the performance of actor-critic RL in which the action selection rule was changed to the greedy method in the test run. The performance of RL shown in Fig. 6 is better than that in Fig. 5. However, as shown in Fig. 6, the performance rapidly deteriorates when RL encounters an unlearned state. The performance of the PRL model exceeds that of the actor-critic method in performance, precision and stability.

In the literature, $TD(\lambda)$ method, that uses experience of a few step befor, for the learning, is proposed. But the performance of $TD(\lambda)$ did not exceed RL so much in this task.

4 Discussion and Conclusion

We proposed a prediciton-based reinforcement learning model (PRL model) which is able to determine the optimum action based on the predicted state by adding PE and MM modules to a traditional actor-critic model. In the computer simulation, we showed that the advantage of this method of prediction lies in the agent being able to select the optimum action for a state which it has not yet learned by using the learned state along the predicted trajectry. A side effect of the use of this pediction method is that the use of the PRL model leads to an acceleration in learning because the propagation of TD is accelerated by the steps Δ of the adopted prediction. The combination of the state prediction and the evaluation of the predicted state are the basic elements for planning in the symbolic AI field. However, this concept of planning is not limited to the in symbolic system. Even in real world RL problems, it should be possible to model planning using similar functional modules. Using the PRL model the behavior of the agent in the ping pong game looks like human behavior, in that the agent waits for the ball to come and does not move the paddle unnecessarily. However, we have not yet evaluated the agent's behavior sufficiently. In the simulation, the modules of the PRL model are given with already sufficiently learned states. The learning of those modules in the initial RL phase will be an important factor in the complete emergence of PRL from RL.

The importance of the PRL model presented here is that it is a first step, a slight extension of conventional RL. We believe that a planning behavior model can emerge from the PRL model through the addition of further modules, like working memory. We hope the trial presented in this paper will be a first step toward the successful computational modeling of the human planning process.

References

1. Sutton, R.S., Learning to predict by the method of temporal differences, Machine Learning, 3, pp. 9–44, 1988.
2. Sutton, R.S. and Barto, A.G., Reinforcement Learning: An Introduction, MIT Press, Cambridge, MA, 1998.
3. Yasuharu Koike and Kenji Doya, A Driver Model Based on Reinforcement Learning with Multiple-Step State Estimation, IEICE Transactions, Vol. J84-D-II, No. 2, pp. 370–379.
4. Kazuyuki Samejima, Ken'ichi Katagiri, Kenji Doya and Mituo Kawato, Multiple Model-based Reinforcement Learning of Nonlinear Control, IEICE Transactions, Vol. J83-DII, No. 9, pp. 2092–2106.
5. Christian Balkenius and Jan Moren, Dynamics of a Classical Conditioning Model, ICANN 98, Perspectives in Neural Computing, Springer-Verlag, 1999.
6. Watkins, C.J.C.H.(1989). Learning from Delayed Rewards. Ph.D. thesis, Cambridge University.
7. Rummery, G.A., and Niranjan, M. (1994). On-line Q-learning using connectionist systems. Technical Report CUED/F-INFENG/TR 166. Engineering Department, Cambridge University.

Computational Neuroscience

The Interaction of Recurrent Axon Collateral Networks in the Basal Ganglia

Mark D. Humphries, Tony J. Prescott, and Kevin N. Gurney

Department of Psychology, University of Sheffield, Sheffield, S10 2TP, UK,
{m.d.humphries, a.j.prescott, k.gurney}@shef.ac.uk,
http://www.shef.ac.uk/~abrg

Abstract. We have proposed that the basal ganglia act as the central switching mechanism for the action selection system of the vertebrate brain. Simulation of our functional model of basal ganglia demonstrated that their output was consistent with this action selection hypothesis. Here we extend this model by incorporating anatomically-inspired local inhibitory axon collateral networks into two basal ganglia nuclei (globus pallidus and substantia nigra pars reticulata). Through simulation it is demonstrated that the basal ganglia's ability to function as a selection mechanism is impaired by the individual addition of the collateral networks but slightly improved when they co-exist. Therefore, we predict the existence of local axon collaterals in the entopeduncular nucleus because of its functional equivalence with the substantia nigra pars reticulata. We conclude that the action selection hypothesis is supported by the continued functioning of the basal ganglia model as a switching mechanism following appropriate anatomically-inspired additions.

1 Introduction

Whenever an animal has two or more actions that it could potentially execute, we may say that these actions are in competition for selection. Though this competition is not necessarily resolved in favour of a single action, it is essential that any actions selected are appropriate to the current circumstances and are mutually compatible. There is, then, a selection problem: how is the competition between actions resolved, while respecting the constraints of appropriateness and compatibility?

We have argued that in any system in which distributed functional modules compete for expression (in this case, groups of neurons), the competition is best resolved by a central switching mechanism rather than direct communication between the modules [1]. This was based on the smaller number of connections needed for, and the ease of adding new modules to, a central switching mechanism. The latter is an important consideration if we are to explain how evolutionary processes created such a system. To function correctly, a central switching mechanism requires input from all functional modules, and its output must contact systems which can express the selected competitor(s).

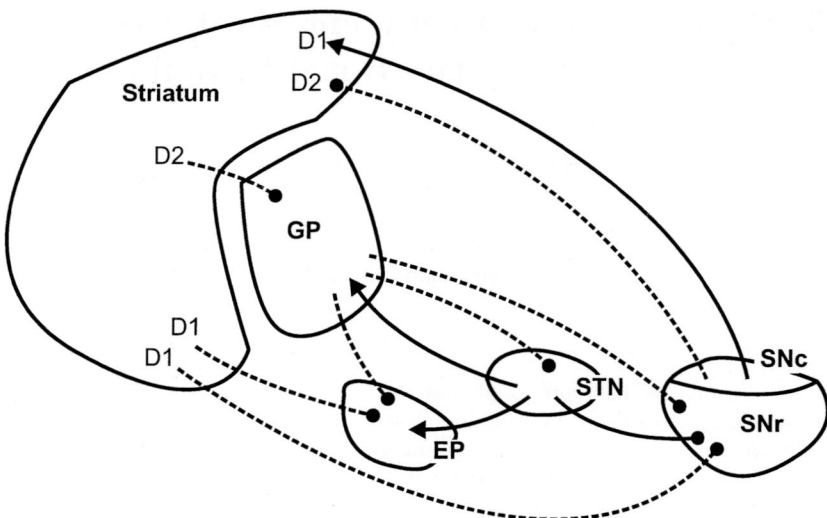

Fig. 1. The connectivity, relative position, and relative size of the nuclei that comprise the rat basal ganglia. Excitatory pathway: solid line; inhibitory pathway: broken line. GP: globus pallidus. STN: subthalamic nucleus. SNc: substantia nigra pars compacta. SNr: substantia nigra pars reticulata. EP: entopeduncular nucleus.

With this in mind we identified the basal ganglia, shown in Figure 1, as a candidate central switching mechanism for action selection in the vertebrate brain [2]. The extensive afferent input from thalamus and all of cortex to the striatum (or caudate-putamen), the major input nucleus of the basal ganglia, we interpret as sufficient to cover all possible functional modules representing actions. Similarly, the efferent connections to thalamic and brainstem motor structures from the basal ganglia output nuclei (substantia nigra pars reticulata and the entopeduncular nucleus) could allow for the expression of the selected action(s).

Based on this anatomy, we proposed a new functional architecture of the basal ganglia, illustrated in Figure 2. Each action is assumed to be represented in a separate processing channel as there are multiple anatomical channels running in parallel throughout the basal ganglia [3]. Each action has associated with it a level of urgency or *salience* which is derived in the striatum from its widespread inputs and expressed in the firing rate of its output. The converging multi-modal information provided by these inputs from brain regions associated with sensory and motor processing, memory, emotion, and proprioceptive (body-state) information means that the salience level of an action is potentially a direct measurement of its appropriateness to the current circumstances of the animal.

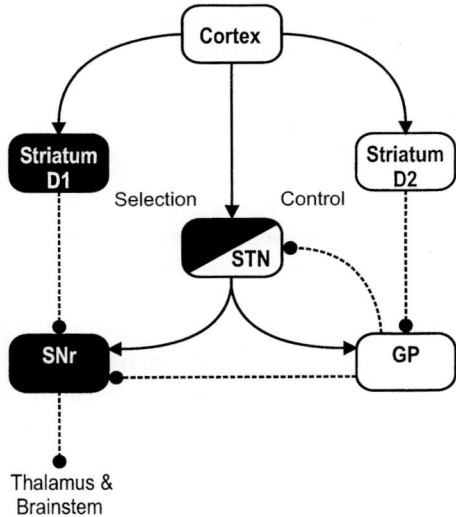

Fig. 2. The proposed new functional anatomy of the basal ganglia, from [4]. The subthalamic nucleus (STN) is half-shaded as it plays a role in both selection and control pathways. Solid line: excitatory. Dashed line: inhibitory.

We made the further assumption that local inhibitory axon collateral networks in the striatum resolve competitions between sets of incompatible actions. This was based on two factors. First, the massive convergence of striatal neurons on their afferent targets suggests that multiple channels in striatum converge on single channels in globus pallidus (GP), substantia nigra pars reticulata (SNr), and the entopeduncular nucleus. Second, the extent of local axon collateralisation suggests that the striatum is delineated into many separate processing domains, each domain being a relatively self-contained lateral inhibition network [5].

The selection of a particular action occurs as follows. A large salience in a striatal channel results in the corresponding channel in the SNr or entopeduncular nucleus being inhibited. Thus the tonic inhibition that the channel's neurons exert over their target neurons in thalamus and/or brainstem is removed. This, in turn, allows the target neurons to respond to any consequent excitatory input. As this process only involves the striatum (specifically the D1-receptor neurons) and the output nuclei, this pathway is termed the *selection* pathway.

In simulation our model of basal ganglia functional architecture (the *intrinsic* model) gave results consistent with the selection of salient actions, and switching to a higher salience action from a currently selected action [6].

In this paper we augment the intrinsic model through the addition of further anatomically constrained pathways. In particular we explore the possibility that the local competition in striatum is complemented by axon collateral network competitions within GP and SNr. The existence of functional inhibitory local axon collaterals within both these nuclei has been established [7,8] but they have, to our knowledge, not yet been incorporated into functional or computational models of the basal ganglia.

2 Method

In each nucleus a channel is represented by a single leaky-integrator neuron. The equations describing the activation a_i and output y_i of the ith striatal D1 and D2 and subthalamic nucleus channels are as given in [6]. All inter-nucleus connections were channel-specific except those from the subthalamic nucleus which provided diffuse projections to the GP and SNr [9].

The new model incorporates local axon collaterals in each of GP and SNr. The collaterals form a complete set of reciprocal inhibitory connections between channels in both nuclei. While the anatomical data does not support global collateral networks, we assume that the channels in our model represent a local sub-set of all possible channels in each nucleus. We now describe the new equations for GP and SNr which incorporate the collateral input.

A GP channel receives input from the corresponding striatal D2 population channel y_i^g, input Y^+ from all the subthalamic nucleus channels, and input from local axon collaterals Y_p (the sum of the output of every other GP channel). Let the weights of the striatum D2 to GP connection be w_{gp}, the subthalamic nucleus to GP connection be w_{sp}, and the collateral connection be w_{pp}. Then the activation at equilibrium $\tilde{a}_i^p$ of the ith GP channel is given by

$$\tilde{a}_i^p = w_{sp}Y^+ - w_{gp}y_i^g - w_{pp}Y_p. \quad (1)$$

If ϵ_p is the output threshold term, then the output y_i^p of the ith GP channel is

$$y_i^p = [\tilde{a}_i^p - \epsilon_p]H(\tilde{a}_i^p - \epsilon_p) \quad (2)$$

where $H()$ is the Heaviside step function. Thus, we can now define the local collateral input Y_p to the ith GP channel as the sum of all other GP channel outputs $Y_p = \sum_{j \neq i}^n y_j^p$, where n is the number of channels in GP, and y_j^p is the output of the jth GP channel.

A SNr channel receives input from four sources: the corresponding striatal D1 population channel y_i^e, GP channel y_i^p, diffuse subthalamic nucleus input Y^+, and local axon collateral input Y_b. The strength of the synaptic connections from striatum D2, GP, subthalamic nucleus, and other local channels are w_{eb}, w_{pb}, w_{sb}, and w_{bb}, respectively. The equilibrium activation $\tilde{a}_i^b$ of the ith SNr channel is thus given by

$$\tilde{a}_i^b = w_{sb}Y^+ - w_{pb}y_i^p - w_{eb}y_i^e - w_{bb}Y_b. \quad (3)$$

Letting ϵ_b be the output threshold term, the output y_i^b of a SNr channel is

$$y_i^b = [\tilde{a}_i^b - \epsilon_b]H(\tilde{a}_i^b - \epsilon_b). \quad (4)$$

Thus, the local collateral input Y_b to the ith SNr channel can now be defined as $Y_b = \sum_{j \neq i}^n y_j^b$, where n is the number of channels in SNr, and y_j^b is the output of the jth SNr channel.

3 Simulation Results

Three models with six channels were simulated: one with the GP collateral network (GP-only), one with the SNr collateral network (SNr-only), and one with both (Combined). The collateral connection weights were set equal (to facilitate comparison) and low (modelling the small number of synapses) so that $w_{pp} = w_{bo} = 0.2$. The SNr output threshold ϵ_b was adjusted for each model so that its tonic output was ~ 0.15, identical to that of the previous (intrinsic) model. Thus, for the SNr-only model $\epsilon_b = -0.35$, for the GP-only model $\epsilon_b = -0.02$, and for the Combined model $\epsilon_b = -0.17$. All other parameter values were set as in the original intrinsic model [6].

Salience values were directly input to striatum. Each model was simulated 121 times, covering the salience input pairs c_1 and c_2 from 0 to 1 in steps of 0.1. The input to channel 1 began at time $t = 1$; the input to channel 2 began at $t = 2$. No other channels received input. This gave two time intervals in which SNr output on any channel could change: $I_1 = [1 \leq t \leq 2]$ and $I_2 = [t > 2]$.

Selection of channel i occurred when $y_i^b \leq \theta_s$, where θ_s is the selection threshold (set at 0.05 here). Using this definition, and given the onset times of the salience input, the outcome of a simulation could be characterised by one of four states:

- First, *no selection*, where $y_1^b, y_2^b > \theta_s$ for all t. Neither active channel becomes selected during the simulation.
- Second, *single channel selection*, where $y_1^b \leq \theta_s$ in I_1 and $y_2^b > \theta_s$ in I_2; or $y_1^b > \theta_s$ for all t and $y_2^b \leq \theta_s$ in I_2. A single channel is selected at some point in the duration of the simulation: either channel 1 becomes selected in the first interval or channel 2 becomes selected in the second interval.
- Third, *simultaneous channel selection*, where $y_1^b, y_2^b \leq \theta_s$ in I_2. Concurrent channel selection occurs in the second interval (channel 1 must be selected in the first interval to remain selected in the second interval; but note that selection in the first interval does not mean automatic selection in the second interval).
- Fourth, *channel switching*, where $y_1^b \leq \theta_s$ in I_1 and $y_1^b > \theta_s$ in I_2 and $y_2^b \leq \theta_s$ in I_2. A clean switch between channels: channel 1 is selected in the first interval, then becomes de-selected as channel 2 becomes selected in the second interval.

Figure 3 shows the resulting output states for each of the models across the complete range of inputs. The bottom right plot shows the output states for the original intrinsic model (that is, the model without the added collateral networks) - it illustrates what a successful central switching mechanism should achieve: switching between channel selections over a range of salience pairs, and the successful selection of a single channel for most other pairs. Note that simultaneous selection only occurred following closely-matched high-level inputs. Thus, alternation of behaviours, ambivalent behaviour, or compromise behaviour may result, which are all consistent with such an output and known to occur when two or more highly salient actions are in conflict for expression [10].

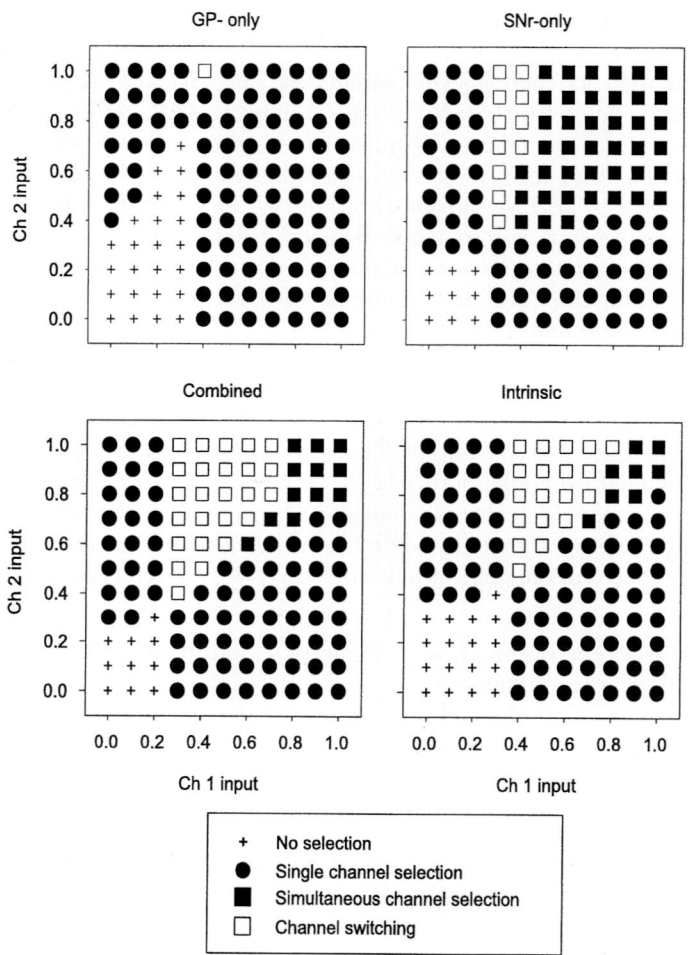

Fig. 3. Output states for the 121 simulations that were run in each of the three models. The bottom right plot shows the equivalent results from the original intrinsic model for comparison purposes.

By contrast, the GP-only and SNr-only models demonstrated that the basal ganglia could fail as a switching mechanism with inappropriate additional pathways. The GP-only model was mostly capable of single-channel selection, otherwise no selection occurred. Conversely, the SNr-only model showed selection of both channels in roughly half of the simulations. However, this was predominantly simultaneous channel selection, which indicated failure of the switching mechanism because it often occurred following a widely separated or low-level salience input pair. Thus, the addition of local inhibitory axon collateral networks to either GP or SNr caused the break-down of the basal ganglia's demonstrable central-switching function (note that both models retained some central-switching function if the connection strengths of other pathways were altered beyond neurophysiologically realistic values).

The striking result is that the addition of collateral networks to both nuclei resulted in a similar output state pattern to the intrinsic model, but with two improvements in terms of the basal ganglia's ability to act a central switching mechanism. First, there was more channel switching; second, there was selection of lower-level salience inputs. We also noted that switching from one selected channel to another occurred consistently faster for the Combined model than for the intrinsic model (for every salience input pair which resulted in *channel switching* for both models). On average, the time taken for a completed switch (the time between $t = 2$ and the first time-point at which both $y_1^t > \theta_s$ and $y_2^b \leq \theta_s$) for the Combined model was $t = 0.049$ less than for the intrinsic model.

The robustness of the Combined model's behaviour following variation of the collateral weights was also tested. We found that the Combined model only functioned correctly (that is, had a similar output pattern to that of the intrinsic model) if the collateral weights were equal and low. For example, if both weights were raised, but kept equal, then the output reverted to that of the SNr-only model. Thus, the Combined model's results support our assumption of low collateral weights, provided that the collaterals do form lateral, inhibitory networks between channels.

4 Discussion

By decomposing the addition of the GP and SNr local axon collateral networks to the intrinsic model into three stages, we have been able to demonstrate three important results. First, it is possible for the basal ganglia model to fail as a central switching mechanism following the addition of inappropriate anatomically-constrained connections which demonstrates that our action selection hypothesis is testable. Second, we have shown that the two collateral networks must co-exist for selection and switching to function correctly and thus have demonstrated the possible existence of complimentary pathways/networks within the basal ganglia. Third, due to the increased number of switchable salience pairs and speed of switching, we suggest that the functional role of the co-existing collateral networks is the general improvement of the basal ganglia's ability to switch between competing actions.

In most of our modelling work we have assumed that the entopeduncular nucleus and SNr are functionally interchangeable because of their neurons' identical afferent inputs, electrical properties, and tonic inhibitory outputs. Here we explicitly modelled the SNr because the evidence for local axon collaterals in the entopeduncular nucleus (or its primate homologue, the internal segment of the globus pallidus) is sparse [11]. However, given that SNr and the entopeduncular nucleus are similar in many functional aspects and, as we have demonstrated, that SNr and GP axon collaterals must co-exist for the basal ganglia to act as a switching mechanism, we predict the existence of functional axon collaterals in the entopeduncular nucleus (or equivalent structure).

Despite this caveat, the success of the basal ganglia model in demonstrating the functions of a switching mechanism following the addition of new, anatomically-constrained, connections reinforces the case for our hypothesis that the basal ganglia is a central switching mechanism in the action selection system of the vertebrate brain.

References

1. Prescott, T.J., Redgrave, P., Gurney, K.: Layered control architectures in robots and vertebrates. Adapt. Behav. **7** (1999) 99–127.
2. Redgrave, P., Prescott, T.J., Gurney, K.: The basal ganglia: A vertebrate solution to the selection problem? Neuroscience **89** (1999) 1009–1023.
3. Alexander, G.E., Crutcher, M.D.: Functional architecture of basal ganglia circuits: neural substrates of parallel processing. Trends Neurosci. **13** (1990) 266–272.
4. Gurney, K., Prescott, T.J., Redgrave, P.: A computational model of action selection in the basal ganglia I: A new functional anatomy. Bio. Cyber. **85** (2001) 401–410.
5. Oorschot, D.E.: Total number of neurons in the neostriatal, pallidal, subthalamic, and substantia nigral nuclei of the rat basal ganglia: a stereological study using the Cavalieri and optical disector methods. J. Comp. Neurol. **366** (1996) 580–599.
6. Gurney, K., Prescott, T.J., Redgrave, P.: A computational model of action selection in the basal ganglia II: Analysis and simulation of behaviour. Bio. Cyber. **85** (2001) 411–423.
7. Deniau, J.M., Kitai, S.T., Donoghue, J.P., Grofova, I.: Neuronal interactions in the substantia nigra pars reticulata through axon collaterals of the projection neurons. An electrophysiological and morphological study. Exp. Brain Res. **47** (1982) 105–113.
8. Stanford, I.M., Cooper, A.J.: Presynaptic μ and δ opioid receptor modulation of $GABA_A$ IPSCs in the rat globus pallidus in vitro. J. Neurosci. **19** (1999) 4796–4803
9. Hazrati, L.N., Parent, A.: Differential patterns of arborization of striatal and subthalamic fibers in the two pallidal segments in primates. Brain Res. **598** (1992) 311–315.
10. Hinde, R.A.: Animal Behaviour. (1966). London: McGraw-Hill.
11. Moriizumi, T., Nakamura, Y., Okoyama, S., Kitao, Y.: Synaptic organization of the cat entopeduncular nucleus with special reference to the relationship between the afferents to entopedunculothalamic projection neurons: an electron microscope study by a combined degeneration and horseradish peroxidase tracing. Neuroscience **20** (1987) 797–816.

Optimal Coding for Naturally Occurring Whisker Deflections

Verena Vanessa Hafner[1], Miriam Fend[1], Max Lungarella[1]*,
Rolf Pfeifer[1], Peter König[2], and Konrad Paul Körding[2]**

[1] Artificial Intelligence Laboratory, Dept. of Inf. Tech., University of Zurich
{vhafner,fend,lunga,pfeifer}@ifi.unizh.ch
[2] Institute of Neuroinformatics, University of Zurich / ETH Zurich
Winterthurerstr. 190, 8057 Zurich, Switzerland
{peterk,koerding}@ini.phys.ethz.ch

Abstract. It is largely unknown how the properties of the somatosensory system relate to the properties of naturally occurring whisker deflections. Here, we analyse representations of simulated neurons that have optimally sparse activity in response to recorded reflections of a rat whisker from surfaces of everyday objects. These representations predict a number of interesting properties of neurons in the somatosensory system that have not been measured yet.

1 Introduction

For about a century it has been known that the vibrissae or whiskers provide an important source of information to rats and other rodents [1]. In particular, rats can distinguish surface properties purely on the basis of cues from their whiskers [2][3]. Rats can furthermore use their whiskers to discriminate objects [4]. As the rat explores its environment, its whiskers are moved over various shapes and surfaces. The whisker deflections caused by these stimulations define the input to the rat's somatosensory system. Although a large number of studies analyses the electrophysiology in this system [5][6][7], the relevant features of its input have remained unknown.

It is evidently difficult to analyse complex natural stimuli. Fortunately, many studies have addressed the properties of natural stimuli in the visual [8][9] and the auditory domain [10][11]. Simulated neurons with optimally sparse activity reproduce much of the properties of neurons in the early visual and auditory areas. Optimally sparse [12] in this context means that the neurons often have an activity close to zero and then sometimes have very high activity. Drawing upon this inspiration, we analyse the somatosensory system with similar methods.

In this paper, we examine the statistics of natural stimuli to the somatosensory system. To do so, we built an artificial whisker system, with a real rat whisker attached to a capacitor microphone. This is in contrast to previous

---

* Current working address: Neuroscience Research Institute (AIST), Tsukuba, Japan
** Current working address: Institute of Neurology, UCL, London, UK

robotics studies, that used simple whisking devices measuring distances or contact only [13][14][15], but do not capture the rich information picked up by natural whiskers.

We analyse if the neurons in the vibrissal system can also be understood in terms of leading to sparse activity in response to these natural inputs. The data coming from our artificial whisker system is analysed in the spectro-temporal domain. Simulated neurons optimally coding for these data are analysed and generate predictions about neurons in the somatosensory system.

2 The Artificial Whisker System

2.1 Hardware

The desired artificial whisker should be functionally comparable to a natural rat whisker and therefore be sensitive to small amplitude deflections and fast oscillations. We attached a rat whisker to the diaphragm of a capacitor microphone using cyanoacrylic super-glue. The change in voltage resulting from whisker deflections is preamplified and digitally recorded. This technique allows us to measure fast oscillations of the whisker even if the amplitude is very low. A schematic drawing of the device is shown in figure 1 left.

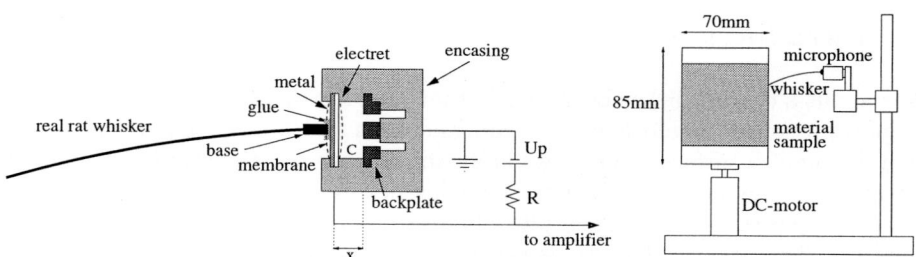

Fig. 1. Left: Basic schematic of the artificial whisker with a capacitor microphone being its main component. The deflection of the membrane is measured by the change of capacitance. The related change of voltage is fed into a preamplifier circuit. Right: Experimental device used to perform some of the experiments described and analysed in this paper.

2.2 Data Obtained

We consider two distinct datasets. Sandpaper data set: we recorded the deflections of whiskers that touched a cylinder rotating with constant speed covered with sandpaper (see figure 1 right). We used a set of natural rat whiskers of different length (37mm-51mm) and distance (20mm-45mm) to the cylinder. Natural object data set: we recorded deflections from a single whisker being manually swept over nine objects and surfaces (fur, leaves, etc.). Data are sampled at 4096Hz. Typical recordings from the two data sets can be seen in figure 2.

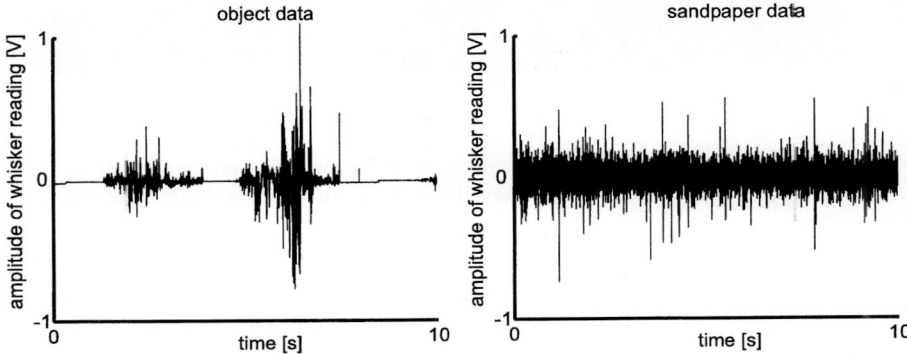

Fig. 2. Data received directly from the artificial whisker system while moving the whisker over an object (natural object data set, left) or while rotating a cylinder covered with sandpaper along the whisker (sandpaper data set, right).

3 Processing Methods

3.1 Representation of the Data

Time varying data are conveniently analysed in spectrogram space, the space spanned by frequency and time. This representation is particularly useful for the whisker system since rats are able to discriminate surfaces of different spatial frequencies [3]. We thus transform the input signals into spectrograms using methods adapted to the analysis of temporally changing signals which are also used for auditory processing. They are available as a matlab package ("NSL Tools" [16]). The resolution on the tonotopic axis is 64 points, covering a frequency range from 4.7Hz to 185.5Hz. In figure 3, three typical samples of such transformed whisker data (recorded with the natural object data set) can be seen. These spectrograms show that whisker deflections lead to a largely conserved frequency-time response. We cut the spectrogram data in windows of 250ms each, overlapping by 10ms. The temporal resolution of these windows is 25 points.

3.2 Spectrotemporal Receptive Fields

For the learning studies, the spectrograms are first compressed by a principal component analysis (PCA) using the first $n_{PCA} = 100$ principal components

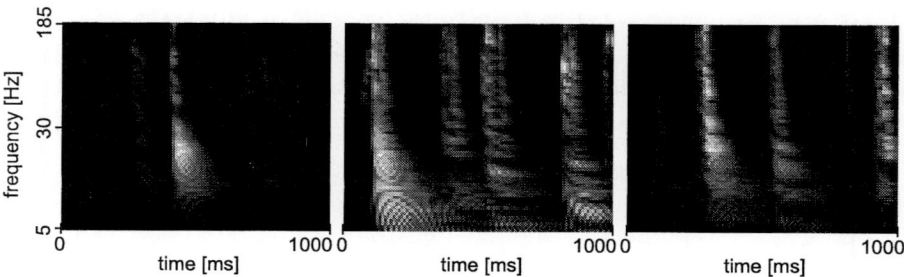

Fig. 3. Sample spectrogram of whisker data recorded with the natural object data set. The frequency axis logarithmically ranges from 4.7Hz to 185.5Hz while time runs from 0 to 1000ms.

(out of $25 \times 64 = 1600$). These components capture more than 96 per cent of the variance. We subsequently assemble a set of 2025 samples of natural object data spectrograms, and a second set of 1050 samples of sandpaper data spectrograms. A set of 32 simulated neurons is trained to optimally code for each of these data. The activity of the neurons is defined as

$$A_i(t) = I(t) W_i(t),$$

where A_i is the activity, W_i is the weight vector of the neuron i. $I(t)$ is the input vector of length n_{PCA} shared by all neurons. The weights connecting each neuron to the spectrogram data, are optimised by scaled gradient descent to minimise the following loss function:

$$\Psi_{total} = \Psi_{cauchy} + \Psi_{std} + \Psi_{decorr} \text{ , with:}$$

- Cauchy: $\Psi_{cauchy} = \frac{1}{n} \sum_i < \ln(1 + A_i(t)^2) >_t$,
  with $< \cdot >_t$ being the average over time t

- Standard deviation: $\Psi_{std} = \frac{1}{n} \sum_i (\sigma_{A_i} - 1)^2$

- Decorrelation: $\Psi_{decorr} = \frac{4 \sum_{i,j} C_{ij}^2}{(n-2)(n-1)}$,
  with $C = cov(A)$ being the $n \times n$ covariance matrix of A

While the Ψ_{cauchy} measures the sparseness of the responses, the two other loss functions ensure the standard criterion used in Independent Component Analysis (ICA) and sparse coding studies that the output variances should be unitary and the output covariances should be vanishing.

4 Results

Simulated neurons are optimised to sparsely encode naturally occurring whisker deflections. Figure 4 shows the general properties of the resulting spectrotemporal receptive fields. Most of the analysed neurons are localised in time, and some are also localised in frequency (figure 4, plots A, F, H, I, and J).

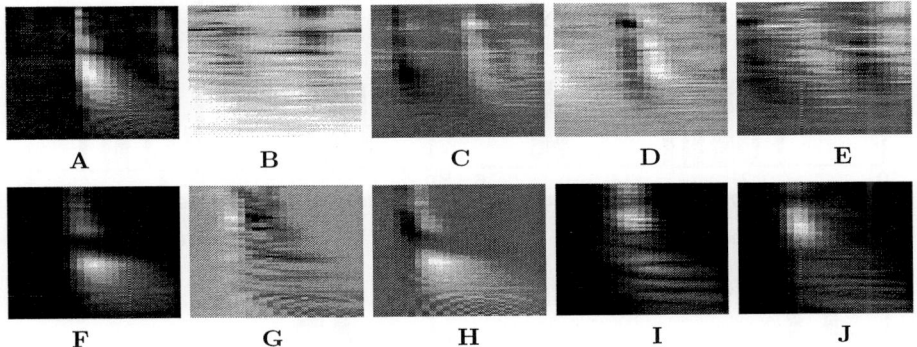

Fig. 4. Five samples each (top row: sandpaper data set, bottom row: objects data set) of typical colour-coded spectrotemporal receptive fields out of 32 neurons. y-axis: frequency (4.7Hz to 185.5Hz), x-axis: time (0 to 250ms).

To further quantify this property, we introduce two measures of localisedness (figure 5). For the analysis, we calculate the average energy over time, and the frequency for each receptive field. We also measure the width of the maximum peak at half the peak value for time localisation, and the octaves $log(f_l/f_h)$ for frequency localisation. More than 87 per cent of the receptive fields from the object data set have a localisation measure in time of less than 100ms. The receptive fields from the sandpaper data set have a localisation measure in time of less than 100ms in only 68 per cent. The percentage of neurons with a tuning width of less than 3 octaves, and thus selective to frequency, is 43 per cent in the object data set and 46 per cent in the sandpaper data set

This is in analogy to sparse simulated neurons in the visual system that obtain localised receptive fields in space and orientation [8]. In addition to this, they are often tuned to changes or even modulations of the energy of the input over time.

This property might be useful for tactile texture recognition. There is some influence of the choice of the stimulus set. The sandpaper data show a stronger degree of modulation selectivity while the natural textures data show a stronger specificity to frequency. To which degree these properties depend on specific properties of the datasets remains an issue for further research.

5 Discussion

Our simulations investigate the optimal coding of naturally occurring whisker deflections. We proceed with the discussion of the properties of the whisker

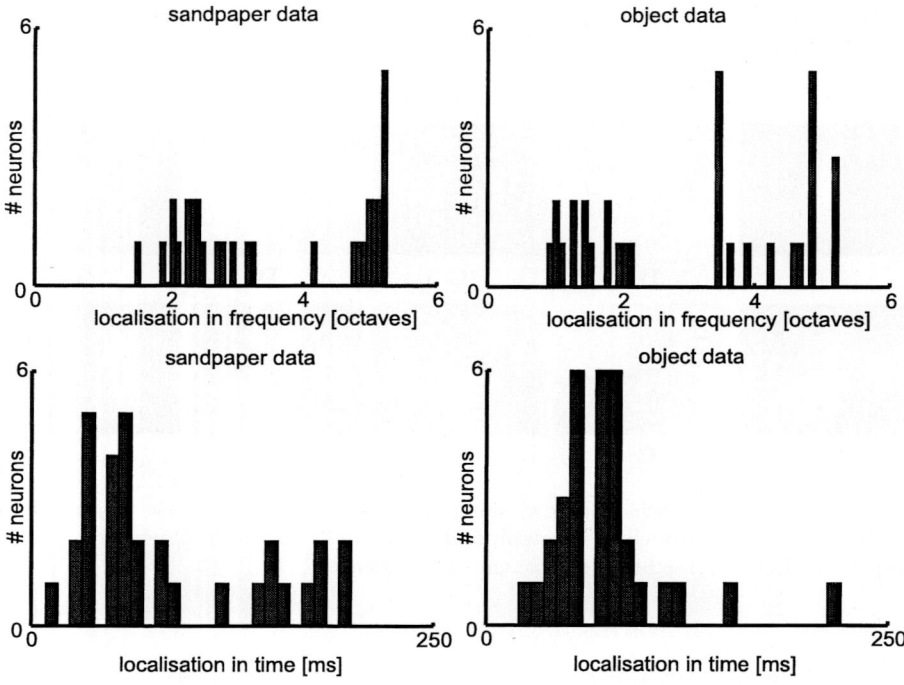

Fig. 5. Histograms showing the localisedness of the spatiotemporal receptive fields for frequency in octaves (top row) and for time in ms (bottom row) for both data sets.

representation in the rodent brain, and based on our results we make predictions of the properties of neurons that have not been measured yet in physiological experiments.

5.1 Choice of the Representation

It is not clear which stimulus features allow rats to perform discrimination tasks involving high spatial frequencies and neither are there physiological studies that analyse the time frequency properties of neurons in the somatosensory system. Since the waveforms of high frequency signals are not a good indicator of their properties (in speech for example, we can scramble the phase spectrum without changing the perceived sounds) a different representation is necessary. Auditory and somatosensory systems share similar temporal stimulus properties (data not shown). Drawing upon this inspiration, we thus represent the whisker data as spectrograms the same way auditory data are typically represented. By training the simulated neurons to have sparse activities on these inputs, we extract salient features from the obtained natural stimuli.

5.2 Physiological Studies

Biological studies have focused mainly on low-frequency stimulation of one or more whiskers and have studied neuronal parameters such as latency of thalamic response [17], cortical response [18][19], and ON or OFF response magnitude [20][21]. The stimulations used for most biological studies consist of air puffs or ramp-hold deflections, either in single trials or with frequencies around the natural whisking frequency of 8Hz. There are no published studies that investigate in the response pattern of neurons in the somatosensory system to stimuli of frequencies between 20 and 200Hz. There is however some preliminary evidence that neurons show complex behaviour in this range (R.S. Petersen, M.E. Diamond, personal communications). The lack of experimental data is particularly surprising since it is known that rats can discriminate surfaces and textures with high spatial frequency, translating into high frequency of whisker stimulations [3].

5.3 Predictions

Our study investigates how such frequencies of obvious behavioural relevance can optimally be encoded by neural representations. Simulated neurons optimally coding for natural stimuli can be viewed as predictions of the, yet unmeasured, neural properties at higher stimulation frequencies.

This study predicts that some neurons in the somatosensory system should not code for the frequency of the whiskers stimulation but rather code for modulation frequencies. Such cells might actually be better detectors for surface texture properties than cells that are just localised in spectrum. Most of them should have temporally localised responses and show some selectivity to stimulation frequency. These predictions can be tested in experimental studies probing the somatosensory system with spectrotemporal patterns.

Acknowledgements. This research has been supported by the IST-2000-28127 European project (AMOUSE), by grant #20-068198.02 of the Swiss National Science Foundation (VVH), and by the Collegium Helveticum for the dialogue of the sciences (KPK). The natural rat whiskers were kindly provided by Mathew Diamond at SISSA, Cognitive Neuroscience sector, Trieste, Italy.

References

1. S. B. Vincent. The function of the vibrissae in the behavior of the white rat. *Behavior Monographs*, 1(5):1–81, 1912.
2. E. Guic-Robles, C. Valdivesco, and G. Guajardo. Rats can learn a roughness discrimination using only their vibrissal system. *Behavioral Brain Research*, 31:285–289, 1989.
3. G. E. Carvell and J. Simons. Biometric analyses of vibrissal tactile discrimination in the rat. *Journal of Neuroscience*, 10(8):2638–2648, 1990.

4. M. Brecht, B. Preilowski, and M. M. Merzenich. Functional architecture of the mystacial vibrissae. *Behavioral Brain Ressearch*, 84(1-2):81–97, 1997.
5. E. Ahissar and A. Arieli. Figuring space by time. *Neuron*, 32:185–201, October 2001.
6. K. D. Miller, D. J. Pinto, and D. J. Simons. Processing in layer 4 of the neocortical circuit: new insights from visual and somatosensory cortex. *Current opinion in neurobiology*, 11:488–497, 2001.
7. C. I. Moore, S. B. Nelson, and M. Sur. Dynamics of neuronal processing in rat somatosensory cortex. *Trends in Neurosciences*, 22(11):513–520, 1999.
8. B. A. Olshausen and D. J. Field. Emergence of simple-cell receptive field properties by learning a sparse code for natural images. *Nature*, 381(6583):607–609, 1996.
9. J. H. van Hateren and D. L. Ruderman. Independent component analysis of natural image sequences yields spatio-temporal filters similar to simple cells in primary visual cortex. *Procedings of the Royal Society London B*, 265:2315–2320, 1998.
10. M. S. Lewicki. Efficient coding of natural sounds. *Nature Neuroscience*, 5(4):356–63, 2002. 1097-6256 Journal Article.
11. K. P. Körding, P. König, and D. J. Klein. Learning of sparse auditory receptive fields. In *Proceedings of the International Joint Conference on Neural Networks (IJCNN)*, 2002.
12. H. B. Barlow. Single units and sensation: a neuron doctrine for perceptual psychology? *Perception*, 1:371–394, 1972.
13. D. Jung and A. Zelinsky. Whisker-based mobile robot navigation. *Proceedings of the IEEE/RSJ International Conference on Intelligent Robots and Systems (IROS)*, 2:497–504, 1996.
14. R. A. Russell. Using tactile whiskers to measure surface contours. In *Proceedings IEEE International Conference on Robotics and Automation*, pages 1295–1300, 1992.
15. M. Kaneko, K. Kanayama, and T. Tsuji. Active antenna for contact sensing. *IEEE Transactions on Robotics and Automation*, 14(2):278–291, 1998.
16. NSL Tools. http://www.isr.umd.edu/CAAR/pubs.html, Neural Systems Laboratory, University of Maryland, College Park, 1998.
17. R. Sosnik, S. Haidarliu, and E. Ahissar. Temporal frequency of whisker movement. I. Representations in brain stem and thalamus. *Journal of Neurophysiology*, 86:339–353, 2001.
18. E. Ahissar, R. Sosnik, K. Bagdasarian, and S. Haidarliu. Temporal frequency of whisker movement. II. Laminar organization of cortical representation. *Journal of Neurophysiology*, 86:354–367, 2001.
19. E. Ahissar, R. Sosnik, and S. Haidarliu. Transformation from temporal to rate coding in a somatosensory thalamocortical pathway. *Nature*, 406:302–305, 2000.
20. H. T. Kyriazi, G. E. Carvell, and D. J. Simons. Off response transformations in the whisker/barrel system. *Journal of Neurophysiology*, 72(1):392–401, 1994.
21. J. A. Hartings, S. Temereanca, and D. J. Simons. High responsiveness and direction sensitivity of neurons in the rat thalamic reticular nucleus to vibrissa deflections. *Journal of Neurophysiology*, 83:2791–2801, 2000.

Object Localisation Using Laterally Connected "What" and "Where" Associator Networks

Cornelius Weber and Stefan Wermter

Hybrid Intelligent Systems Group, School of Computing and Technology, University of Sunderland, Sunderland SR6 0DD, United Kingdom www.his.sunderland.ac.uk
{Cornelius.Weber, Stefan.Wermter}@Sunderland.ac.uk

Abstract. We describe an associator neural network to localise a recognised object within the visual field. The idea extends the use of lateral connections within a single cortical area to their use between different areas. Previously, intra-area lateral connections have been implemented within V1 to endow the simple cells with biologically realistic orientation tuning curves as well as to generate complex cell properties. In this paper we extend the lateral connections to also span an area laterally connected to the simulated V1. Their training was done by the following procedure: every image on the input contained an artificially generated orange fruit at a particular location. This location was reflected – in a supervised manner – as a Gaussian on the area laterally connected to V1. Thus, the lateral weights are trained to associate the V1 representation of the image to the location of the orange. After training, we present an image with an orange of which we do not know its location. By the means of pattern completion a Gaussian hill of activation emerges on the correct location of the laterally connected area. Tests display a good performance with real oranges under diverse lighting and backgrounds. A further extension to include multi-modal input is discussed.

1 Introduction

Once that an object of interest appears in the visual field, it is necessary to localise its position within the visual field before moving the centre of sight toward it and, eventually, to activate a grasping movement prototype [9]. We develop a biologically inspired solution using a recurrent associator network which we want to apply in a bio-mimetic mirror neuron-based robot, MirrorBot.

Our approach extends the framework of intrinsic lateral (horizontal) connections in the cortex toward object recognition and localisation. Horizontal connections within one cortical area have a strong influence on cortical cell response properties. In the visual area V1, for example, they may be responsible for surround effects and for the non-linear response properties of simple and complex cells [11]. This view is supported by connectionist neuron learning paradigms in which lateral connections statistically de-correlate [10] or find correlation structure [1] within the activities of cells in an area. Both paradigms are in accordance with the notion that the lateral connections form an attractor network. The activation patterns which form its attractors correlate nearby cell's activations but de-correlate distant cell's activations. The attractor activation pattern can recover noisy input with maximum likelihood [2]. Such a theoretically derived learning paradigm has successfully explained orientation tuning curves of V1 simple cells as well as complex cell's response properties [13].

Here we apply the learning rule for lateral connections within a cortical area to connections between different, but laterally organised cortical areas. This is justified by the fact that lateral connections between areas – as opposed to hierarchical connections – originate and terminate in the same cortical layers [3]. A different learning rule is applied to the hierarchical connections which form the input to one of our two simulated laterally connected areas (see Fig. 1). This is a rule which leads to feature extraction and can be any rule from the sparse coding / ICA repository. Here we use a sparse coding Helmholtz machine for the bottom-up connections, as previously described [13].

The two laterally connected areas of our model specialise on object recognition and localisation. As such they shall be regarded as exemplary areas within the lateral "what" and the dorsal "where" pathway of the visual system. In the actual implementation, however, in a model where every connection is trained and which uses natural images as input, there are no high-level cortical areas. Instead, our "what" area receives direct visual input, reminiscent of V1 while our "where" area receives directly the representation of a location. Such a representation may actually reside in the superior colliculus [5].

The problem of object localisation is intermixed with recognition: several structures in different locations within the image may match to the object of interest and the best matching location has to be found. For this purpose, saliency maps can be produced [8] or the data may be generated from Bayesian priors [12]. These approaches, however, are missing a neural description. An approach involving shifter neurons [7] takes into consideration the derivative of an object with respect to a shift within the image. It can handle small shifts of complex objects but involves high dimensional neurons which each have an $N \times N$ matrix to the N input neurons. Our approach uses standard neurons with order N connections and handles relatively large shifts. However, tests have been done only with a very simple object, and an extension to general objects is discussed.

2   Theory and Methods

The architecture is depicted in Fig. 1 and consists of a "what" pathway on the left, and a "where" pathway on the right. The "what" pathway consists of an input area and a hidden area. The input area consists of three sub-layers to receive the red, green and blue components of colour images. Its size of 24×16 pixels which is minimal to demonstrate object localisation reflects the computational demand of training. The hidden area of the "what" pathway consists of two layers which we may loosely identify with the simple (lower layer) and complex (upper layer) cells of V1. The lower layer receives bottom-up connections W^{bu} from the input. In the following we will assume that these have already been trained such that the lower layer cells resemble the simple cells of V1 [13]. Since

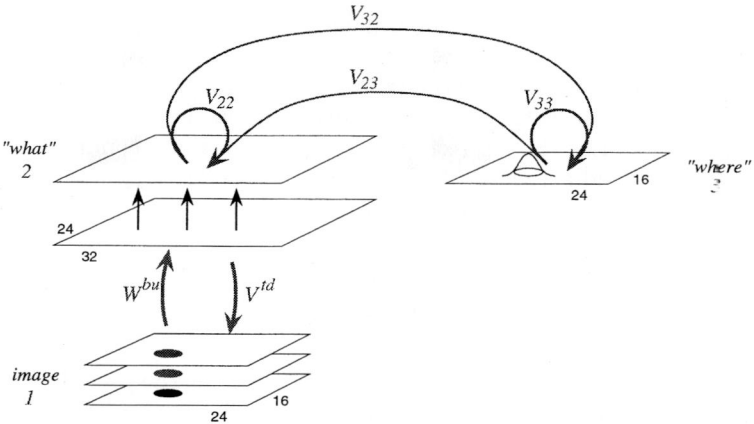

Fig. 1. Model architecture. Left, the pathway of the lower visual system, the retina which receives the image and V1, which we refer to as the "what" area. Feature extracting, hierarchically organised weights are W^{bu}, V^{td} (green). On the right side, the "where" area displays the location of the object of interest. Lateral association weights are V_{22}, V_{33}, V_{23} and V_{32} (red). The small numbers denote simulated area sizes.

colour images are used, a few cells have learnt to encode colour, while the majority has become black-and-white edge detectors. The depicted top-down weights V^{td} were only used to train W^{bu}, but are not used further on. The upper layer of the V1 cells receives a copy of the output of the lower layer cells. After it receives this initial input, it functions as an attractor network which solely updates its activations based on its previous activations. Each cell receives its input from all other neurons via recurrent weights V_{22}. In addition, input arrives from the laterally connected area of the "where" pathway via weights V_{23}.

The "where" pathway on the right of Fig. 1 consists of just one area. Its size of 24 × 16 neurons matches the size of the image input area of the "what" path, because an interesting object within the image should have a representation as an activation at the corresponding location on the "where" area. The "where" neurons are fully connected via recurrent weights V_{33} and in addition receive input from the highest "what" layer via V_{32}. In the following, we will refer to all connections V_{22}, V_{33}, V_{23} and V_{32} collectively as V^{lat}, because they always receive the same treatment, during training as well as during activation update.

Activation Dynamics and Learning rule: The activation update of the "where" and highest level "what" neurons is governed by the following equation:

$$u_i(t+1) = f(\sum_l v_{il}^{lat} u_l(t)) \qquad (1)$$

Activation u_i of neuron i develops through discrete time t using the input via lateral weights v_{il}^{lat} from the other l ("what" and "where") neurons. The lateral weights are not forced to be symmetric, i.e. $v_{il}^{lat} \neq v_{li}^{lat}$ in general.

The lateral weights are trained from the bottom-up input. Their purpose is to memorise the incoming activities $u_i(t=0)$ as activation patterns which they maintain. Since they will not be capable of holding every pattern, they will rather classify these into discrete attractors. In the original top-down generative model [13] these patterns were recalled in a separate mode of operation ("sleep phase") in order to generate statistically correct input data.

Learning maximises the log-likelihood to generate the incoming data distribution by the internal activations $u_i(t)$ if Eq. 1 is applied repeatedly:

$$\Delta v_{il}^{lat} \approx \sum_t (u_i(t=0) - u_i(t)) u_l(t-1). \qquad (2)$$

Transfer Function and Parameters: The transfer function of our continuous rate-coding neurons is:

$$f(h_i) = \frac{e^{\beta h_i}}{e^{\beta h_i} + n} \approx p_i(1) \qquad (3)$$

The function ranges from 0 to 1 and can be interpreted as the probability $p_i(1)$ of a binary stochastic neuron i to be in active state 1. Parameters $\beta = 2$ scales the slope of the function and n is the degeneracy of the 0-state. Large $n = 8$ reduces the probability of the 1-state and accounts for a sparse representation of the patterns which are learned. The introduction of this sparse coding scheme was found to be more robust than the alternative use of variable thresholds. The weights V^{lat} were initialized randomly, self-connections were constrained to $v_{ii}^{lat} = 0$.

Training Procedure: First, the weight matrices W^{bu} and V^{td} were trained on small patches randomly cut out from 14 natural images, as in [13], but with a 3-fold enlarged input to separate the red, green and blue components of each image patch. 200000 training steps had been done. Lateral weights V^{lat} were then trained in another 200000 training steps with W^{bu} and V^{td} fixed. Herefore, within each data point (an image patch), an artificially generated orange fruit was placed to a randomly chosen position. An orange consisted of a disc of 5 pixels in diameter which had a color randomly chosen from a range of orange fruit photos. The mean of the pixel values was subtracted and the values normalised to variance 1. The "where" area received a Gaussian hill of activity on the location which corresponds to the one in the input where the orange is presented. The standard deviation of the Gaussian hill was $\sigma = 1.5$ pixels, the height was 1.

The representation of the image with an orange obtained through W^{bu} on the lower V1 cells was copied to the upper V1 cells. This together with the Gaussian hill on the "where" area was used as initial activation $u_i(t = 0)$ to start the relaxation procedure described in Eq. 1. It is also used as target training value. Relaxtions were done for $0 \leq t < 4$ time steps.

3 Results

Anatomy: Fig. 2 a) shows a sample of weights W^{bu} of our lower V1 cells. Many have developed localized, Gabor function shaped, non color selective receptive fields to the input. A few neurons have developed broader, color selective receptive fields. Similar results have been obtained [4].

Fig. 2 b)-e) shows samples of the lateral connections V^{lat}. Inner-area connections are usually center-excitatory and surround inhibitory in the space of their

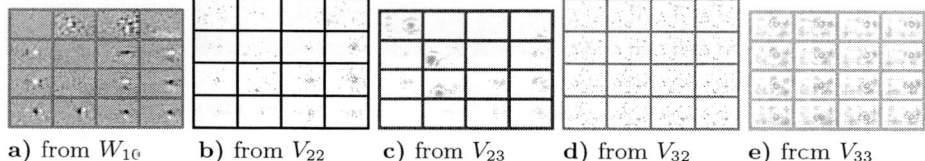

a) from W_{10} b) from V_{22} c) from V_{23} d) from V_{32} e) from V_{33}

Fig. 2. a) The receptive fields (rows of W^{bu}) of 16 adjacent lower V1 ("simple") cells. Bright are positive, dark negative connection strengths to the red, green and blue visual input. Receptive fields of color selective neurons appear colored, because the three color components differ. b)-e) Samples of lateral weights V^{lat}. Positive connections are green, negative are red. b) Within-area lateral connections among the upper V1 ("complex") cells. c) Lateral cross-area connections from the "where" area to upper V1 to the same 16 neurons (same indices) as depicted in a) and b). Connections V_{22} and V_{23} together form the total input to an upper V1 cell. d) Cross-area lateral connections from upper V1 to the "where" area. e) Within-area lateral connections on the "where" area to the same 16 neurons as depicted in d). Connections V_{33} and V_{32} together form the total input to a "where"-area cell. Within-area connections are in general center-excitatory and surround-inhibitory and they are small in the long range. Connections V_{33} establish a Gaussian-shaped hill of activations. Cross-area connections V_{32} influence the position of the activation hill. Self-connections in V_{22} and V_{33} are set to zero.

functional features [13]. Cross-area connections are sparse and less topographic. Strong connections are between the "where" cells and color selective "what" cells, because for orange fruits, color is a salient identification feature.

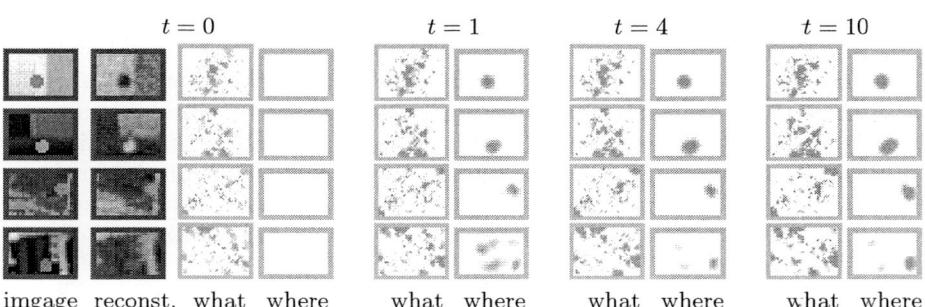

$t=0$ $\qquad$ $t=1$ $\qquad$ $t=4$ $\qquad$ $t=10$

imgage reconst. what where $\quad$ what where $\quad$ what where $\quad$ what where

Fig. 3. Each row shows the network response to a color image which contains an artificially generated orange fruit. From left to right: the image, the reconstruction of the image using feedback weights V^{td}, the representation on the "what" area, the initial zero activities on the "where" area at time $t=0$. Then the activations on the "what" and "where" areas at time $t=1$, then on both at time $t=4$ which is the relaxation time used for training, and then after a longer relaxation of $t=10$ time steps.

The estimated position of the orange on the "where" area is correct in the upper 3 rows. In the difficult example below, at time $t=1$ activity on the "where" area is distributed across many locations and later focuses on a wrong location.

image

what

where

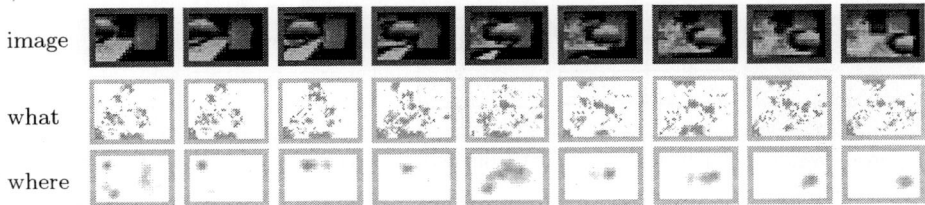

Fig. 4. Localisation on real images taken from the robot camera. The lower two rows show the response on the "what" and the "where" area at iteration time $t = 4$ to the image in the upper row.

Physiology: Figs. 3 and 4 show the relaxation of the network activities after initialization with sample stimuli. In all cases, the "where" area neuron's activations were initialised to zero at time $t = 0$. The relaxation procedure therefore completes a pattern which spans both, the "what" and the "where" area, but which is incomplete at time $t = 0$, as can be seen in Fig. 3.

The activation on the "where" area may resemble a Gaussian already at time $t = 1$, even though at this time, no effective input from the lateral weights V_{33} has arrived. A clearer Gaussian hill of activity evolves at later steps, but since no new information is coming in, the competition may draw a wrong location as a winner, if the representation is very fuzzy initially (Fig. 3, lowest row). Since the attractor shares the "what" and the "where" area, the Gaussian on the "where" area may remain distorted for quite a while.

All weights in the model have been trained on the basis of real images and are therefore irregular. Localisation quality may vary at slightly different object locations within the image. The 5th frame in Fig. 4, for example, leads to an unclean "where" representation. If information from the 4th frame would be taken into account, this may be cleand up. However, for simplicity and consistency with the training procedure, the algorithm processes only one frame at a time.

Fig. 5 shows how the network creates images, if there is no information but the location of the orange fruit. The projection of the corresponding internal representation onto the input creates images with predominantly blue background and a large patch of orange/red color near the location of the imaginated orange.

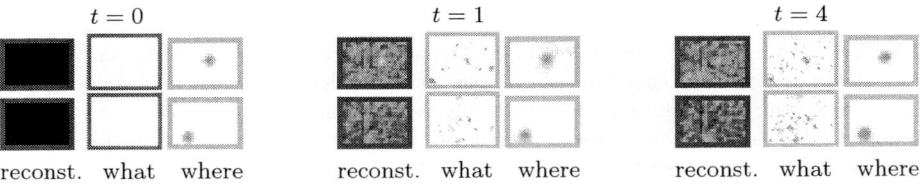

Fig. 5. Each row shows the network response purely from a Gaussian hill of activation on the "where" area. At time $t = 0$ the "what" area does not contain any activations and the reconstructed image is empty. Later, the areas maintain stable activations.

4 Discussion and Future Work

The current model has been trained on one object type, orange fruits. The cross-area lateral connections V_{32} originate predominantly at color selective V1 neurons, taking advantage of a feature specific to our chosen kind of object. For general object localisation, the cross-area lateral connections V_{32} need to be unspecific to object features. Then the object to localise would have to show up on V1 as a region of increased activation (attention). Fig. 6 shows two conceptual architectures which could achieve this. In both cases a third area, e.g. a language area, connects to V1. If it currently represents a specific object (as an orange in the figure) then it shall give an activation bias to those neurons on V1 which represent that object. Then, the lateral connections V_{32} transfer the biased representation to the "where" area, where intra-area connections V_{33} confine the activations to a Gaussian hill on the corresponding position. Note that direct connections between the language area and the "where" area would not make any sense, because an object does not have a preferred position *a priori*. Training would automatically lead to near-zero connections.

The question remains whether the language area should be connected laterally to the V1 area as in Fig. 6 **a)** or hierarchically as in Fig. 6 **b)**. The weight structure is the same, but their usage and training differs. In the lateral version a full representation on all three upper areas has to be present during training. In the hierarchical version the orange/apple features on the now highest level may be extracted by unsupervised training. The latter version is more appealing, because we expect a more abstract object representation to be hierarchically higher than a representation which still contains information on the object location.

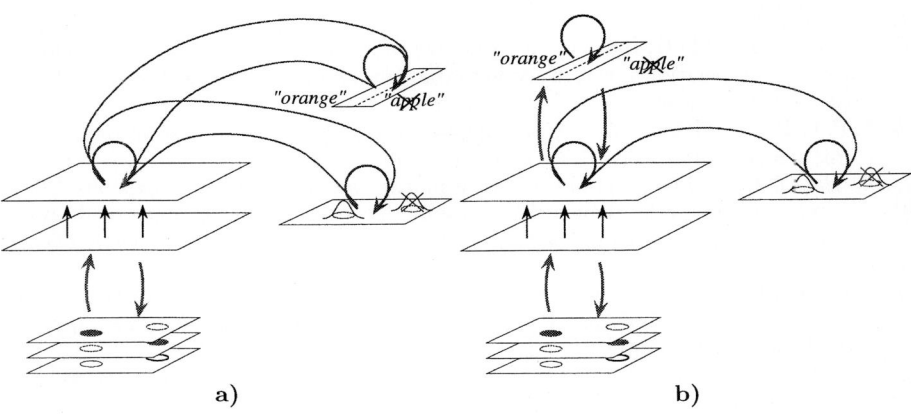

Fig. 6. The model with **a)** a laterally and **b)** a vertically (hierarchically) connected language area. If two trained fruit, like a red orange and a green apple, appear in the visual input, below, then at both corresponding locations in the "where" area a Gaussian may emerge, both competing. Input from another area, like the word "orange" from a language area may then strengthen the corresponding representation on "V1".

Both paradigms, however, are not necessarily contradicting: in the visual system, hierarchical and lateral connection patterns coexist if the vertical hierarchical level difference is small [3]. Two hierarchically arranged areas (with asymmetric connectivity [3]) may therefore use their mutual lateral connections (which are symmetric) for a "top-down" reconstruction. In addition, recent evidence suggests that object representations are distributed across different areas [6], potentially on different hierarchical levels. A model for a data driven arrangement of areas in parallel or hierarchically has been presented [14].

Acknowledgments. This work is part of MirrorBot, a project supported by the EU in the FET-IST programme under grant IST-2001-35282, coordinated by Prof. Wermter.

References

1. P. Dayan. Recurrent sampling models for the Helmholtz machine. *Neur. Comp.*, 11:653–77, 2000.
2. S. Deneve, P.E. Latham, and A. Pouget. Reading population codes: a neural implementation of ideal observers. *Nature Neurosci.*, 2(8):740–5, 1999.
3. D.J. Felleman and D.C. Van Essen. Distributed hierarchical processing in the primate cerebral cortex. *Cerebral Cortex*, 1:1–47, 1991.
4. P.O. Hoyer and A. Hyvärinen. Independent component analysis applied to feature extraction from colour and stereo images. *Network: Comput. Neural Syst.*, 11(3):191–210, 2000.
5. A.K. Moschovakis, G.G. Gregoriou, and H.E. Savaki. Functional imaging of the primate superior colliculus during saccades to visual targets. *Nature Neurosci.*, 4(10):1026–31, 2001.
6. F Pulvermüller. A brain perspective on language mechanisms: from discrete neuronal ensembles to serial order. *Progress in Neurobiology*, 67:85–111, 2002.
7. R.P.N. Rao and D.H. Ballard. Development of localized oriented receptive fields by learning a translation-invariant code for natural images. *Network: Comput. Neural Syst.*, 9:219–37, 1998.
8. R.P.N. Rao, G.J. Zelinsky, M.M. Mayhoe, and D.H. Ballard. Eye movements in iconic visual search. *Vis. Res.*, 42(11):1447–63, 2002.
9. G. Rizzolatti and G. Luppino. Cortical motor system. *Neuron*, 31:889–901, 2001.
10. J. Sirosh and R. Miikkulainen. Topographic receptive fields and patterned lateral interaction in a self-organizing model of the primary visual cortex. *Neur. Comp.*, 9:577–94, 1997.
11. J. Sirosh, R. Miikkulainen, and Y. Choe, editors. *Lateral Interactions in the Cortex: Structure and Function*. Hypertext Book, www.cs.utexas.edu/users/nn/web-pubs/htmlbook96, 1996.
12. J. Sullivan, A. Blake, M. Isard, and J. MacCormick. Bayesian object localisation in images. *Int. J. Computer Vision*, 44(2):111–35, 2001.
13. C. Weber. Self-organization of orientation maps, lateral connections, and dynamic receptive fields in the primary visual cortex. In G. Dorffner, H. Bischof, and K. Hornik, editors, *Proceedings ICANN*, pages 1147–52, 2001.
14. C. Weber and K. Obermayer. *Emergent Neural Computational Architectures*, chapter Emergence of modularity within one sheet of neurons: a model comparison, pages 53–76. Springer-Verlag Berlin Heidelberg, 2001.

Influence of Membrane Warp on Pulse Propagation Time

Akira Hirose and Toshihiko Hamano

Department of Frontier Informatics, The University of Tokyo
7-3-1 Hongo, Bunkyo-ku, Tokyo 113-8656, Japan
http://www.eis.t.u-tokyo.ac.jp/

Abstract. We derive general expressions of pulse propagation time on warped membrane to analyze the cell shape influence on signal processing. In particular, we consider round (Purkinje-like) and cone (pyramidal) cell shapes to compare the theoretical results with computational ones obtained by the two-dimensional membrane potential computation. We also take into account the channel type varieties (Squid, CA3). It is found that membrane-expanding parts have large effects on the propagation time and velocity.

1 Introduction

Recent developments in physiological measuring equipment including optical recording systems and arrayed microelectrodes accelerate investigations based on high resolution and multi-channel measurements. In the near future we can capture precise spatiotemporal dynamics of potential and other entities on the cell membrane. For example, we will be able to elucidate the reason why variously shaped neurons we have in the brain and how the cells process signals differently depending on their shapes. For such pursuit, it is also desired to develop theories to analyze the microscopic or mesoscopic membrane signal dynamics.

The Hodgkin-Huxley equations are the most fundamental membrane potential representation [1]. They give temporal change of potential assuming a cell as a point, i.e., 0 dimensionally. Following them, some 1-dimensional theories were proposed such as the cable theory and the compartmental models [2],[3]. The authors group analyzed the spatiotemporal dynamics of potential, current and generated magnetic fields of CA3 pyramidal cells [4],[5]. We also developed the 2-dimensional membrane potential equations by combining nonlinear channel equations and diffusion equations to investigate numerically, for example, the influence of membrane curvature on the potential propagation parameters [6].

Generally speaking, the cell shape influence is expected small when the membrane potential dynamics is almost linear (e.g., for EPSP). This is because the potential charges all the membrane area homogeneously and widely. Therefore, the dynamics should be affected simply by the total membrane area size.

However, when the potential gets larger and the dynamics becomes nonlinear, the potential grows into a localized pulse with a shorter rise / falling time. Then the spatiotemporal dynamics of the pulse is considered gradually affected by the

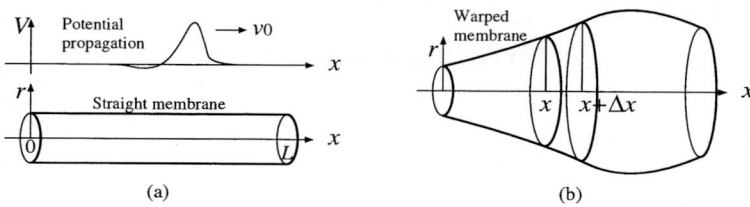

Fig. 1. (a) Straight membrane and (b) warped one.

membrane shape. Recent observations reported that an action potential rising at axon hillock runs backward to soma and dendrites, and that the backward propagation has a large effect on the bursting characteristic [4]. In this way, the influence of the membrane shape on the pulse propagation becomes important more and more for understanding the signal processing dynamics of neurons.

In this paper, we derive general expressions of pulse propagation time on warped membrane to analyze the cell shape influence. In particular, we consider Purkinje-like and pyramidal cell shapes to compare the theoretical results with computational ones obtained by using the two-dimensional membrane potential computation. In the numerical analysis, we take into account the channel type varieties (Squid giant axon's, CA3). It is found that membrane-expanding parts have large effects on the propagation time and velocity.

2 Theory

General analysis. Figure 1 shows straight and warped membrane. They can be parts of soma, dendrite or axon. If the membrane is straight as shown in Fig.1(a) where the radius is constantly r, the pulse (action potential or burst pulse) propagates with a constant velocity v_0. The time required for propagation of distance L is $T_0 = L/v_0$. When the ionic channel densities are not too small, the pulse waveform is preserved by the nonlinear operation of channel conductance.

In this paper, we consider the case where the membrane has a arbitrarily varying line-symmetric shape (variable radius r) as shown in Fig.1(b). When a pulse runs on the membrane where r increases, the diffusive propagation have to charge up a larger capacitance. Hence the propagation velocity will be smaller. We consider the propagation time taking into this effect.

Suppose the frustum in Fig.2(a) is a fraction of the r-varying membrane. We take x axis along the symmetric line while a curvilinear coordinate l on the membrane in direction of the propagation. When the charge of the capacitance at l (linear density c) diffuses forward onto $l + \Delta l$, the membrane capacitance changes to $c + \Delta c$, resulting in a voltage drop (if c increases). Thereby the pulse requires an additional time to propagate by charging up again the capacitance. Accordingly the traveling time increases. The voltage drop (or rise) is expressed as

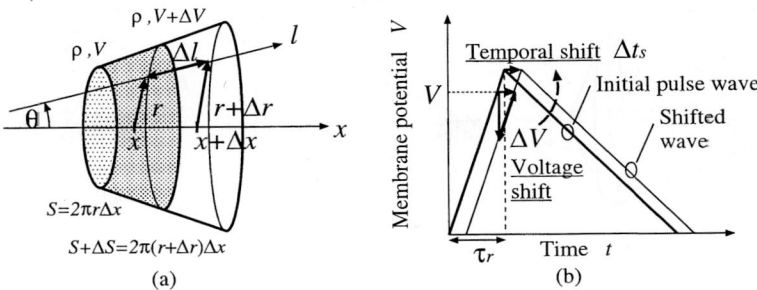

Fig. 2. (a) Membrane area variation and (b) related potential variation and pulse waveform shift in the time domain.

$$\Delta V = -\frac{\rho}{c + \Delta c} - V = \left(1 - \frac{\Delta c}{c}\right)\frac{\rho}{c} - V = -\frac{\Delta c}{c}V \quad (1)$$

For simplicity, we consider a triangular pulse waveform shown in Fig.2(b) with a rise time of τ_r. For a small voltage drop ΔV, the pulse needs an additional charging time of Δt_s. Because we find almost invariant waveform in observations, we can estimate that the shift occurs homogeneously in cooperation with neighbors in time and space domain. We then obtain a small time shift Δt_s for the whole the pulse wave as

$$\Delta t_s = (-\Delta V/V)\tau_r = (\Delta c/c)\tau_r \quad (2)$$

Here we assume that the membrane is homogeneous with a membrane thickness of d and a permittivity of ε. The capacitance (linear density) is $c = \varepsilon 2\pi r/d$. Then we can rewrite (2) in terms of the local radius $r(l)$ as

$$\Delta t_s = \tau_r \left(\varepsilon 2\pi \Delta r/d\right)\big/(\varepsilon 2\pi r/d) = \tau_r (\Delta r/r) \quad (3)$$

Accordingly we can express the local velocity along the membrane $v(l)$ by using the standard velocity on a straight membrane $v_0 \equiv \Delta l/\Delta t_0$ as

$$v(l) = \frac{\Delta l}{\Delta t_0 + \Delta t_s} = v_0 \left(1 + \frac{1}{\Delta t_0}\frac{1}{r}\frac{dr}{dl}\Delta l \tau_r\right)^{-1} = v_0 \left(1 + v_0 \tau_r \frac{1}{r}\frac{dr}{dl}\right)^{-1} \quad (4)$$

Because typical values of the variables are $v_0 = 1[\text{m/s}]$, $\tau_r = 1[\text{ms}]$ and $r = 10$–$100[\mu\text{m}]$, we find that the term $v_0\tau_r/r$ can be considerably large, and that we cannot apply small variation approximation to the denominator. The velocity along x axis can be expressed as

$$v(x) = v_0 \cos\theta \left(1 + v_0 \tau_r \cos\theta \frac{1}{r}\frac{dr}{dx}\right)^{-1} \quad (5)$$

where θ stands for the angle formed by the membrane and x axis, and $\cos\theta = 1/\sqrt{(dr/dx)^2 + 1}$.

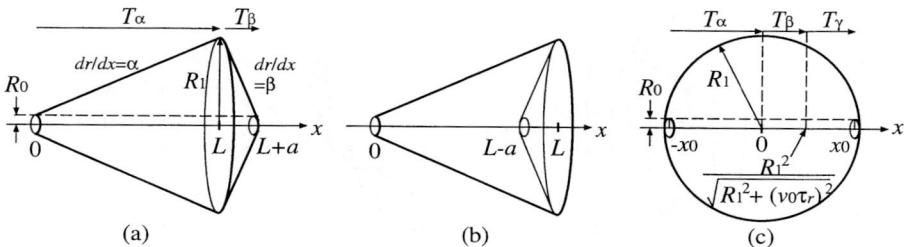

Fig. 3. (a) A modified Pyramidal cell, (b) Pyramidal cell and (c)Purkinje-like cell.

The result yields a propagation time T from x_1 to x_2 as

$$T = \int_{x_1}^{x_2} \frac{dx}{v(x)} = \int_{x_1}^{x_2} \left(\frac{\sqrt{(dr/dx)^2 + 1}}{v_0} + \tau_r \frac{1}{r} \frac{dr}{dx} \right) dx \qquad (6)$$

Example 1: Pyramidal Cell (Figs.3(a),(b)). First we apply the above results to a conically shaped cell illustrated in 3(a). We consider a case where a single pulse is evoked by an external stimulus at $x = 0$. The slope is a constant $dr/dx = \alpha$ in the range of $0 < x < L$ while $dr/dx = \beta$ in $L < x < L + a$. The propagation time of the pulse in each region is then obtained as

$$T_\alpha = \sqrt{\alpha^2 + 1}\,(L/v_0) + \tau_r \ln(R_1/R_0) \qquad (7)$$
$$T_\beta = \sqrt{\beta^2 + 1}\,(a/v_0) - \tau_r \ln(R_1/R_0) \qquad (8)$$

The summation is the total propagation time T_{total}. Because $T_\beta \geq 0$ in principle, when the ratio R_1/R_0 is large, we can estimate $T_{\text{total}} \approx T_\alpha$. That is, by substituting $\alpha = dr/dx = (R_1 - R_0)/L$, we obtain

$$T_{\text{total}} = \sqrt{(R_1 - R_0)^2 + L^2}/v_0 + \tau_r \ln(R_1/R_0) \qquad (9)$$

The first term is almost proportional to R_1 and attributed to geodesic increase, while the second is logarithmic and caused by the additional charging up. If L is chosen constant, the propagation time T_{total} grows in accordance with the increase of R_1 by the summation of these terms.

This result is also applicable to the pyramidal cell shown in 3(b). Furthermore, when we assume a pulse generation at axon hillock $L \pm a$ with synaptic excitations, we can analyze the dynamics in the same way.

Example 2: Purkinje cell (Fig.3(c)). Secondly, we consider a round (Purkinje-like) cell shape shown in Fig.3(c). Since $dr/dx = -x/\sqrt{R_1^2 - x^2}$, we obtain $1/\cos\theta = R_1\sqrt{R_1^2 - x^2}$. The propagation time in expanding region (α region: left-hand side hemisphere of 3(c)) and that in the shrinking one (β region: the

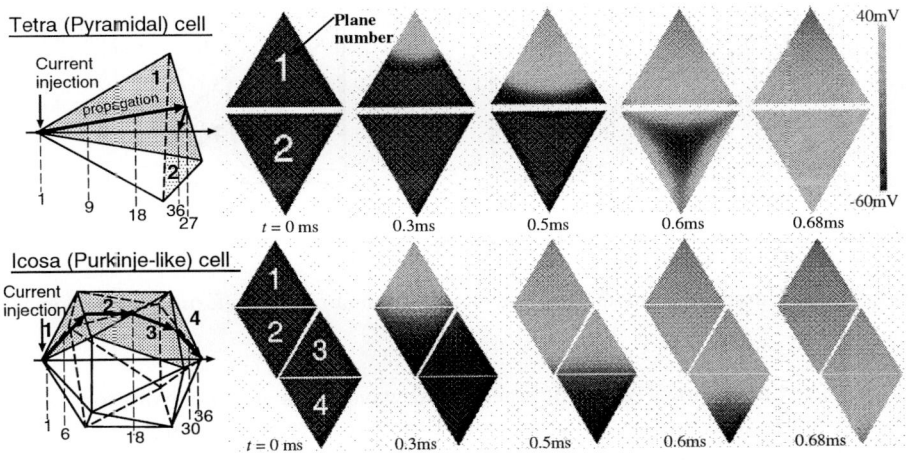

Fig. 4. Pyramidal and Purkinje-like cell shapes for numerical analysis. Pulse propagation appearances are also presented two-dimensionally as temporal evolutions.

integrant in (6) is positive and γ region: the integrant is formally negative) are obtained as

$$T_{\alpha \text{ or } \beta} = \frac{R_1}{v_0}\arcsin\frac{x_0}{R_1} \pm \tau_r \ln\left(\frac{R_1}{\sqrt{R_1^2 - x_0^2}}\right) \quad (+ \text{ for } \alpha, - \text{ for } \beta) \quad (10)$$

and $T_\gamma \approx 0$. In general $x_0 \approx R_1$ and if we assume $T_\beta \approx 0$, then the total propagation time T_{total} is estimated as

$$T_{\text{total}} \approx T_\alpha \approx \pi R_1/(2v_0) + \tau_r \ln(R_1/R_0) \quad (11)$$

Again the time is the sum of R_1 proportional and logarithmic terms.

3 Numerical Analysis and Comparisons

In this paper, we compare the above theoretical result with numerical analysis based on 2-dimensional membrane potential equations [6]. We consider two types of ionic channel models: *Model Squid* is the Squid giant axon channel set [1] and *Model CA3* is the hippocampal CA3 channel set [7].

Figure 4 illustrates the cell shapes under consideration with coordinates for location identification. The tetrahedron is modeled after pyramidal cell, whereas the icosahedron is after Purkinje. Their total surface areas are chosen identical. (For a realistic comparison of pyramidal and Purkinje cells, their sizes are also near to actual ones. But in this paper, we concentrate on the membrane warp effects on the propagation.) Each surface plane is constructed by small triangles. Details are reported elsewhere. We put location indexing number 1 – 36 at equi-interval.

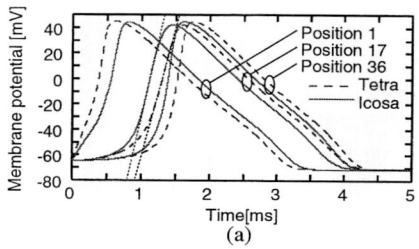 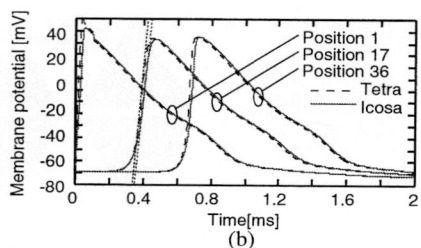

Fig. 5. Computed (a)squid and (b)CA3 channels membrane waveforms in time domain.

Figure 4 also shows rough 2-dimensional waveforms as time evolution. These approximated shapes are different from those in the theory mainly in the fact that the surface is composed of planes instead of conical surface. We can see the wave front is shown as arc. This difference brings some disagreement in the computational results below.

Figure 5 shows computed waveforms at Position 1, 17 and 36 for (a)*Model Squid* and (b)*Model CA3* in time domain. In both cases, the waveforms are found stable. Table 1 shows the numerical calculation conditions and parameters. The rise time τ_r is extracted from the Icosahedron waveform at Position 17 where the membrane has little expansion or shrinkage. Figure 6 presents waveforms in space domain at several time points.

As shown in Table 1, we injected $1[A/m^2] \times$ (area of 5μm sides triangle) current for $500[\mu s]$ (*Squid*) or $100[\mu s]$ (*CA3*). In the case of tetrahedron, the 1/3 current is injected at the top three triangle elements, while for icosahedron, 1/5 at the top five. Since R_0 is important only as the initial charge determiner in the theory, we estimate the initial charge Q. The linear density at the pulse rise is approximately $\rho = Q/\Delta l = Q\Delta\tau_r/v_0$ independent of the cell shape. In the comparison below, the wave is estimated to run $8[\mu m]$(*Squid*) or $1[\mu m]$(*CA3*).

Figure 7 presents the computation results obtained by using the 2-dimensional membrane potential equations: (a1)local velocity, (a2)local traveling time (inverse of local velocity) as functions of position and (a3)pulse peak location as function of time for *Model Squid*, while (b1)-(b3) show those for *Model CA3*. In any cases, the required traveling time becomes very large at the area-expanding positions, i.e., injection points in this case.

Table 1. Chosen or estimated (extracted) parameters.

		Tetra	Icosa		Pulse rise time τ_r [ms]	Squid	CA3
(Input radius	R_0	2.4	4.0[μm])				
Input current (chosen)	I	1.0	1.0[A/m2]	Icosa		0.35	0.1
Equiv. max cell radius	R_1	404	301[μm]	Tetra		0.48	0.1

4 Discussion

The theoretical curves are also presented in Figs.7(a3) and (b3) for $v_0 = 1$[m/s]. They are in good agreement qualitatively at least. That is, in (a)*Model Squid*, the total traveling time is shorter for icosahedron because it goes into a non-expanding region earlier than that for tetrahedron. On the other hand, in (b)*Model CA3*, the velocities are large for both since τ_r is small, resulting in more linear curves. Comparing them with the theoretical result in (9) or (11), we understand that these characteristics arise from (1)membrane shape (warp, i.e., expansion or shrinkage) as well as (2)pulse rise time τ_r determined by channel types and densities.

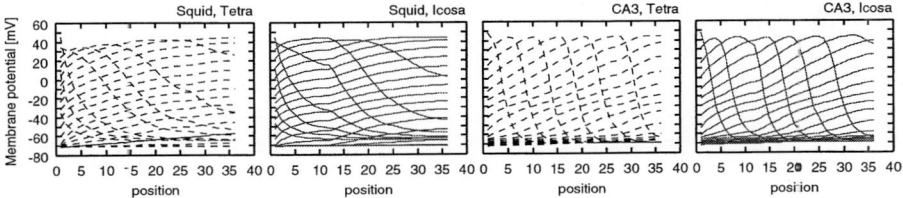

Fig. 6. Computed squid and CA3 channels membrane waveforms in spatial domain with 0.2ms (Squid) or 0.1ms (CA3) sampling intervals.

The slight discrepancy is attributed to the following points. First, in Fig.7(a) *Model Squid*, the tetra case, the expansion ratio $(r + \Delta r)/r$ decreases monotonically (Plane 1 = Position 1 – 27), yielding increase of the local velocity. If the shape is completely a cone as considered in theory, the ratio could be averaged and the velocity would be constant. The velocity is exceedingly increased at 27 because of the expansion end. But next the velocity gets down since the wave front has to be reformed (from expanding fan form to shrinking one) to go around the fold into Plane 2. These effects are not taken into consideration in the theory. After the fold, the velocity increases drastically as estimated in the theory.

Next we examine the results for icosahedron in Fig.7(a). We find a velocity increase even in the early stage (1 – 10) affected by the end of the membrane expansion. Afterward the pulse slows down to charge up the corners, which is the same behavior as that for tetrahedron. Later the behavior is also the same.

In Fig.7(b) for *Model CA3*, the linear parts of theory and computation are very near to each other. At the last part corresponding to shrinkage, the computation yields a longer propagation time probably because the long pulse length weaken the time shortening effect. Totally the computed curves are in good agreement with those for theory.

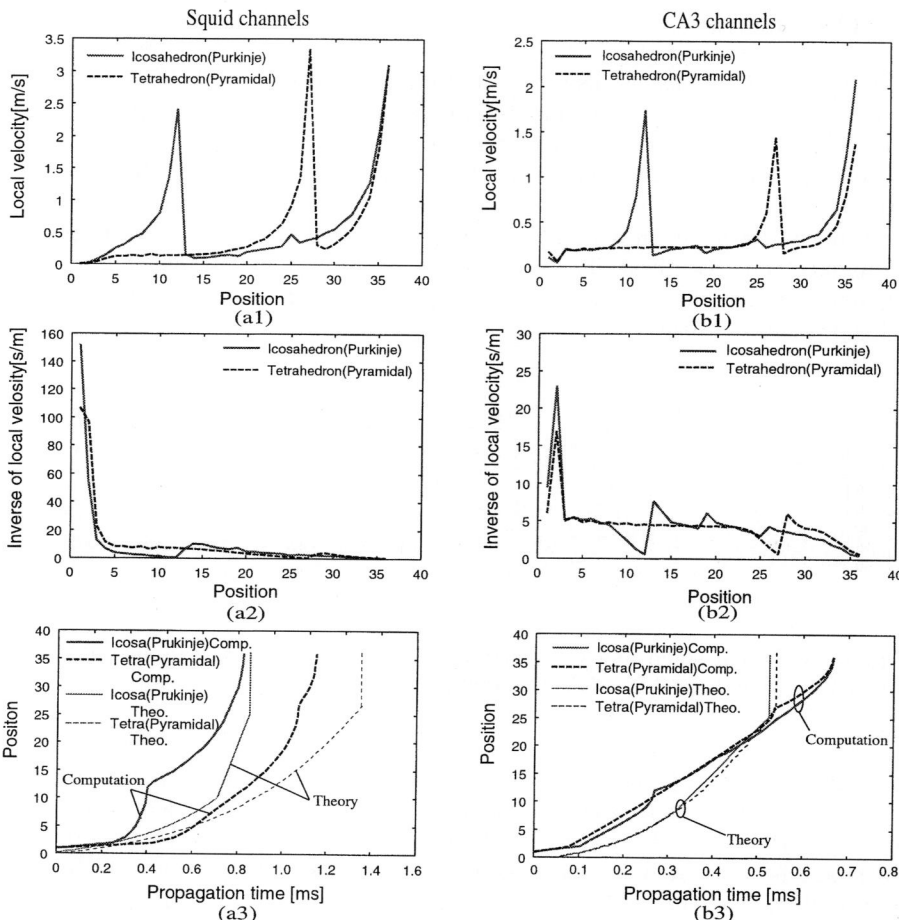

Fig. 7. Computed squid channel curves of (a1) local velocity, (a2) local consumed time and (a3) pulse-peak position (with theoretical ones) as functions of propagation time. Hippocampal CA3 channel curves (b1)-(b3). Propagation time is defined as (Time in Figs.4 & 5) − (Time required for pulse generation after current injection).

5 Conclusion

We have derived the general expressions of the pulse propagation time on warped membrane. As examples, we have considered tetrahedron and icosahedron cell shapes to compare the theoretical results with computational ones based on the two-dimensional membrane potential computation. It has been found that the membrane-expanding parts have a large effect on the propagation time.

References

1. Hodgkin, A.L., Huxley, A.F., "A quantitative description of membrane current and its application to conduction and excitation in nerve," J. Physiol., **117** (1952) 500–544
2. Rall, W., "Theoretical significance of dendritic trees for neural input-output relations," Neural Theory and Modeling, ed., Reiss, R.F., Stanford University Press (1964)
3. Rall, W., "Core conductor theory and cable properties of neurons," In Handbook of Physiology, Sec. 1, The Nervous System, **1**, Behtesda, M.D.: Am. Physiol. Soc. (1977) 39–97
4. Sakatani, S., Hirose, A., "A quantitative evaluation of the magnetic field generated by a CA3 pyramidal cell at EPSP and action potential stages," IEEE Trans. on Biomedical Engineering, **49** (2002) 310–319
5. Murakami, S., Zhang, T., Hirose, A., Okada, Y.C., "Physiological origins of evoked magnetic fields and extracellular field potentials produced by guinea-pig CA3 hippocampal slices," J. Pysiol., **544.1** (2002) 237–251
6. Hirose, A., Murakami, S., "Spatiotemporal equations expressing microscopic two-dimensional membrane potential dynamics," Neurocomputing, **43** (2002) 185–196
7. Traub, R.D., Wong, R.K.S., Miles, R., Michelson, H., "A model of a CA3 hippocampal pyramidal neuron incorporating voltage-clamp data on intrinsic conductances," J. Neurophysiol., **66** (1991) 635–650

Detailed Learning in Narrow Fields – Towards a Neural Network Model of Autism

Andrew P. Papliński[1] and Lennart Gustafsson[2]

[1] Computer Science and Software Engineering,
Monash University, Victoria 3800, Australia
`app@csse.monash.edu.au`
[2] Computer Science and Electrical Engineering,
Luleå University of Technology, S-971 87 Luleå, Sweden
`Lennart.Gustafsson@sm.luth.se`

Abstract. Autism is a developmental disorder in which attention shifting is known to be restricted. Using an artificial neural network model of learning we show how detailed learning in narrow fields develops when attention shifting between different sources of stimuli is restricted by familiarity preference. Our model is based on modified Self-Organizing Maps (SOM) supported by the attention shift mechanism. The novelty seeking and the attention shifting restricted by familiarity preference learning modes are investigated for stimuli of low and high dimensionality which requires different techniques to visualise feature maps. To make learning more biologically plausible we project the stimuli onto a unity hyper-sphere. The distance between a stimulus and a weight vector can now be simply measured by the post-synaptic activities. The modified "dot-product" learning law that keeps evolving weights on the surface of the hyper-sphere has been employed.

1 Introduction: Autism, Restricted Attention Shifting

Autism is a developmental disorder with diagnostic criteria (DSM-IV, 1994 [1]) grouped in three categories: impairments in social interaction, impairments in verbal and nonverbal communication, and restricted repetitive and stereotyped patterns of behavior, interests, and activities. The subcategory of the last category: "encompassing preoccupation with one or more stereotyped and restricted patterns of interest that is abnormal either in intensity or focus" is of particular interest in this paper. It is generally agreed that attention shifting is not normal in autism but the underlying cause is a matter of debate with two main hypotheses, a general attention shifting impairment [2], and attention shifting restricted by familiarity preference or novelty avoidance [3,4,5,6]. A brief review of these hypotheses can be found in [7].

In this paper an artificial neural network model of learning is used to show how detailed learning in narrow fields develops when attention shifting between different sources of stimuli is restricted by familiarity preference. This is a continuation of our earlier work on modelling autism presented in [7,8] where we examined the use of Kohonen Self-Organizing Maps subjected to two-dimensional data. We found that attention shifting restricted by familiarity preference causes the feature map to learn the data from the source with the least variability in its data whereas normal learning, i.e. learning with attention shifts to that source which presents new data, resulted in maps which adapt to the data from both sources. Learning under general attention shifting impairment resulted in maps that were very similar to the maps obtained from normal learning.

2 Artificial Neural Networks and Learning in Autism

Our model of autistic learning is based on Kohonen Self-Organizing Maps (SOMs) [9] with some modifications and addition of the attention shift mechanism. It is well known that a Self-Organizing Map is a competitive neural network in which m neurons, each with p synapses are organized in an l-dimensional lattice (grid) representing the **feature space**. Such a neural network performs mapping of a p-dimensional **input space** into the l-dimensional feature space. In Figure 1 we present an example of a self-organizing map consisting of $m = 12$

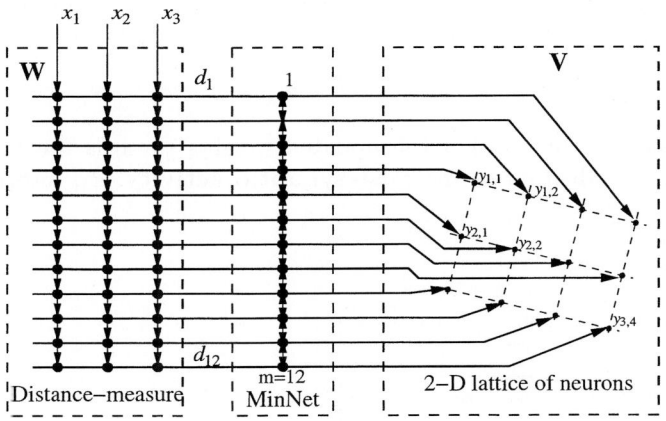

Fig. 1. A 2-D SOM with $p = 3$; $m = [3\ 4]$; $l = 2$

neurons in which the **input space** is 3-dimensional ($p = 3$) and the **feature space** is 2-dimensional ($l = 2$). The first section of the network is a distance-measure layer consisting of $m = 12$ dendrites each containing $p = 3$ synapses excited by p-dimensional stimuli **x** and characterised by the p-dimensional weight vector $\mathbf{w}_i, i = 1, \ldots, m$. The distance-measure layer calculates the distances d_i between each input vector **x** and every weight vector $\mathbf{w}_i$. This distance vector, $\mathbf{d} = [d_1, \ldots, d_m)]$ is passed to the competition layer, the MinNet in Figure 1, which calculates the minimal distance $d_k = \min d_i$ in order to establish the position of the winning neuron k. The competition is implemented through the lateral inhibitive and local self-excitatory connections between neurons in the competitive layer. In addition, every neuron is located at $l = 2$-D lattice and its position is specified by an l–dimensional vector $\mathbf{v}_i$. The synaptic weight vectors, $\mathbf{w}_i$, and the vectors of topological positions of neurons, $\mathbf{v}_i$, are grouped into the $m \times p$ weight matrix W and $m \times l$ position matrix V.

In order to make the distance calculations simpler and more biologically plausible we project our $(p-1)$–dimensional stimuli $\hat{\mathbf{x}}(n)$ onto a unity p–dimensional sphere.

$$\mathbf{d} = W \cdot \mathbf{x} = \cos \boldsymbol{\alpha}, \quad d_j \in [-1, +1] \tag{1}$$

equal to the cosine of the angles between the stimulus and the weight vectors.

For the normalised stimuli, in order to keep the weight vectors on the surface of the unity sphere we used the "dot-product" learning law [9]. For the jth neuron we can write:

$$\hat{\mathbf{w}}_j = \mathbf{w}_j + \eta \cdot \Lambda_j \cdot (\mathbf{x}^T - \mathbf{w}_j), \quad \mathbf{w}_j(n) = \frac{\hat{\mathbf{w}}_j}{||\hat{\mathbf{w}}_j||} \tag{2}$$

where $\mathbf{x}$ is the current stimulus, $\mathbf{w}_j, \mathbf{w}_j(n)$ are the current and the next weight vectors for the jth neuron, respectively, Λ_j is the value of the neighbourhood function, and η is the learning gain. Normalization as in eqn (2) is computationally relatively complex, but for small learning gain $\eta < 1$ it can be shown that the weight update can be expressed in the following elegant form:

$$\mathbf{w}_j(n) = \mathbf{w}_j + \eta \cdot \Lambda_j \cdot (\mathbf{x}^T - \mathbf{w}_j \cdot d_j), \quad d_j = \mathbf{w}_j \cdot \mathbf{x} \tag{3}$$

The modification that pushes the updated weights towards the unity sphere is based on introduction of the **post-synaptic activity**, d_j, into the update equation.

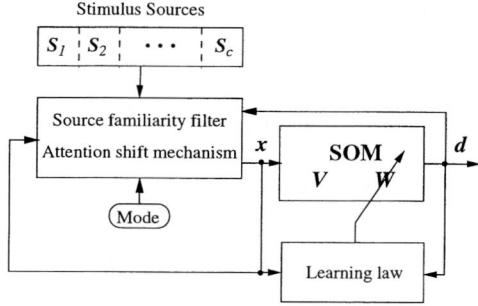

Fig. 2. A block-diagram of the model of autistic learning

The block-diagram of the model of autistic learning which includes source familiarity filter and attention shift mechanism is presented in Figure 2. The central part is the SOM neural network as presented in Figure 1, together with the learning section implementing the learning law, or map formation algorithm, given in eqn (3). At each learning step a stimulus is randomly generated from one of the sources, $S_1, \ldots S_c$. The attention shifting mechanism determines if that stimulus is presented to the map for learning.

In the normal, or **novelty seeking** learning mode, attention is shifted to another source if the new stimulus originates from that source.

In the **attention shifting restricted by familiarity preference** learning mode attention is shifted to another source if that source presents the next new stimulus, but conditionally, depending on the map's familiarity with that source. The map familiarity to a particular source is measured by the time averaged value of the distance between map nodes and the stimuli. When both sources are unfamiliar to the map, i.e. in the beginning stage of self-organization, attention is shifted to an alternate source if that source presented the next stimulus as in the novelty seeking mode. As the map develops some familiarity with the sources, i.e. the node weights begin to resemble the data, attention is shifted with a higher probability to the source which is most familiar to the map. If the map becomes familiar to two or more sources (the average difference between node weights and the data from the sources becomes smaller than a predetermined small value) then attention is unconditionally shifted.

3 Modelling Autistic Learning with Low-Dimensional Stimuli

In the first set of simulations we use three sources generating four classes of two-dimensional stimuli, each class consisting of just two exemplars. Therefore we have in total twenty four two-dimensional stimuli. For the sake of conceptualization we can imagine that the the sources produce **three dialects** of a very limited protolanguage, each with **four protophonemes** (classes) pronounced in **two** slightly different ways. The neural network which is used to model the stimuli consists of sixteen neurons (or nodes) organized in a 4×4 two-dimensional lattice, or grid.

Thanks to the low-dimensionality of stimuli (and weights) it is possible to visualise the **feature map** in the input space. Such a feature map is a plot of synaptic **weights** in the **input space** in which weights of the neighbouring neurons are joined by lines and illustrates the mapping from two-dimensional input space to two-dimensional feature space as shown in Figure 3a. The stimuli originating from a particular source are marked with '+', 'o' and '*', respectively, and are arranged in four pairs (classes). The neuronal nodes are marked with '*' and joined by the straight lines. The map shows the way in which the neuronal 4×4 lattice approximates the input data (stimuli).

The map of Figure 3a has been developed in the novelty seeking mode, that is, in normal learning. Normal learning results in a map where most neurons are "shared" between two stimuli and thereby all stimuli have a good representation in the map. There are also a few "dead" neurons in the map, neurons that are far from all stimuli; this is a very common thing to occur.

There are two parameters visible on the map, namely the attention shift index, and the map "goodness" index. The **attention shift** index is the num-

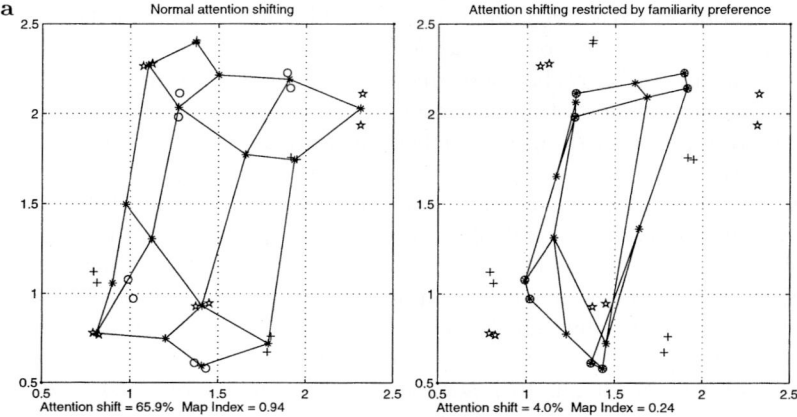

Fig. 3. A 4 × 4 feature map in the 2-D input space developed in the: **a.** novelty seeking, and **b.** attention shifting restricted by familiarity preference learning modes

ber of attention shifts normalised with the total number of stimuli used during learning. With three sources and equal probability of generating a stimulus from each source the attention shift index is clearly equal to 2/3. The **map "goodness" index** is formed from the sum of distances between the class means and weights located in the proximity of the means. This sum of distances will be the largest for the initial value of weights and will be reduced during training. The "goodness index" has been normalized so that a value of 1 represents a map with nodes located at the centres of all data subclasses.

After all these introductions we are ready to consider **detailed learning in a narrow field** characteristic to autistic learning. The feature map presented in Figure 3b is the result of learning when the attention shifting is restricted by familiarity preference. In this mode of learning the attention shifting has ceased (attention shift index is 4%) and as a result only the source with the **lowest variability** (spread), in this case marked by 'o', is learned. The representational capacity of the map now makes it possible to assign one neuron to each of the eight stimuli, i.e. detailed learning in a narrow field, characteristic to autistic learning, has occurred.

4 Modelling Autistic Learning with High-Dimensionality Stimuli

In the second set of simulations the width of the afferent connections, that is, the dimensionality of the stimuli and weight vectors is much higher ($p = 18$). As previously, the neural network which is used to model the stimuli consists of sixteen neurons organized in a 4 × 4 two-dimensional grid. With such a high dimensionality the feature map cannot now be visualised in the input space. However the dimensionality of the **feature space**, that is, the neuronal grid is still low ($l = 2$) and the feature maps can be illustrated in this space by attaching to each neuron stimuli located in the proximity of the relevant weight vector.

The higher-dimensional stimuli are here chosen to be animals and a number of their characteristics, mostly visual. One source contains animals of widely different kinds: mammals, birds, a reptile and fish. The other source contains only cats. There are animals which stand out and there are other animals that are very similar to each other, in some cases separated only by coloration. The animals are listed below:

Source A: Przewalski's horse, Grevy's zebra, Canis lupus (wolf), Dingo, White (mute) swan, Black swan, Atlantic salmon, Rainbow trout, Polar bear, Kodiak bear, White rhinocerous, Hippopotamus, Grey Western kangaroo, Swamp wallaby, Anaconda, Grey whale

Source B: even colored domestic cat, striped domestic cat, black panther, leopard, ocelot, jaguar, lion tiger.

For investigating the generalization properties acquired by the map during learning we also have four **test animals:** black domestic cat, Siamese cat, snow leopard and Eurasian lynx. The animals have been characterized by weight, food, locomotion (fins, wings, two legs, four legs), feet (hooves, claws or other), coloration (black, white, even colored, spotted, striped), facial feature (elongated or short nose), aquatic preference and social structure. Each animal is described by eighteen numbers. We project the animal characterization on a 19-dimensional unity sphere as described in Sect. 2.

In order to assess the categorization characteristics of the maps it is necessary to establish the "likeness" among these animals. In Table 1 pairs of greatest likeness are presented and a measure of their angular distance on the hypersphere. The first animal is chosen and then the animal that most resembles it is calculated. It is clear from Table 1 that the anaconda and the whale stand out

Table 1. Angular distances in the pairs of the closest animals

Source A		
Horse	Zebra	28
Zebra	Horse	28
Wolf	Dingo	55
Dingo	Wolf	55
WSwan	Bswan	38
BSwan	WSwan	38
Salmon	Trout	36
Trout	Salmon	36
PBear	KBear	50
KBear	Pbear	50
Rhino	Hippo	42
Hippo	Rhino	42
Kangaroo	Wallaby	44
Wallaby	Kangaroo	44
Anaconda	PBear	103
Whale	Hippo	406

Source B		
CatEcld	catSiam	9
catstrp	catSiam	9
panther	leopard	12
leopard	panther	12
ocelot	lynxEur	41
jaguar	tiger	40
lion	tiger	45
tiger	jaguar	40
Test cats		
catBlck	catSiam	9
catSiam	catEcld	9
snowLprd	leopard	13
lynxEur	ocelot	41

and that the domestic cats are very similar to each other. There are also many pairs like horse — zebra and a group of three similar big cats, jaguar, lion and tiger. A good map of only sixteen nodes would thus assign one node each for the whale and the anaconda, let the domestic cats share one node, let the three big cats share one node and let a number of pairs of animals share one node per pair. In a map formed by attending to Source B only, a good map would assign one node to each of the cats.

The feature map resulting from the normal, novelty seeking learning is shown in Figure 4a. The map consists of the 4×4 neuronal grid. Each animal is shown

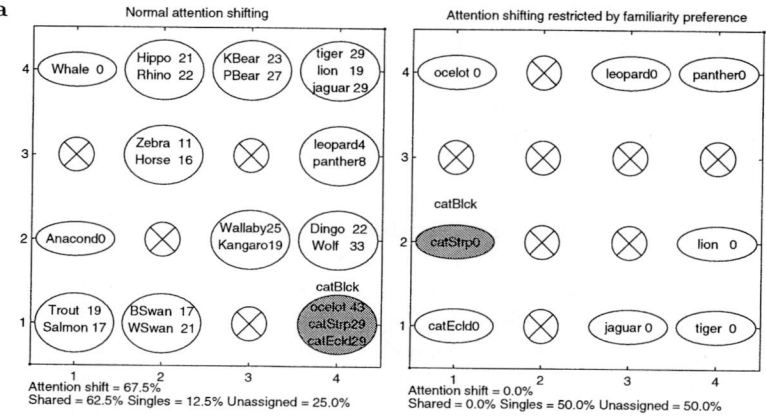

Fig. 4. The feature maps developed in the **a.** novelty seeking, and **b.** attention shifting restricted by familiarity preference learning modes. The shaded ovals represent the network response to a test animal

at the node with the best match of weights. The angular distance between the animal vector and the node weight vector is shown after the animal name. In the map the number of animals for which a given node is the closest varies from three to zero ("dead neurons"). As expected the whale is represented by its own node with distance 0, i.e. a perfect match between the animal and the best matching node has been achieved. As also anticipated the three big cats share one node almost in the middle between them. Other animals are likewise represented as anticipated. Four nodes are dead (unassigned).

The feature map resulting from learning in the attention shifting restricted by familiarity preference mode is shown in Figure 4b. This map, which developed when the attention shifting has ceased, reveals the characteristics of detailed learning in a narrow field, that is, only the stimuli source with the lowest variability, i.e. the cats, is learned. Every cat is represented by its best matching node and all these best matches are perfect because the number of neurons considerably exceeds the number of cats. Several of the nodes marked as "unassigned" have weight vectors which are close to the cats which have been allocated to neighboring (closest match) neurons.

Testing for Generalization: A good map should have acquired some generalization capability, i.e. when presented with a stimulus it has not learned, it should be represented by a node with weights that are similar if such a node exists. We presented the maps from Figures 4a and 4b with the "Black Cat" stimulus which has not been used in learning. In both cases the node closest to this test stimulus is the one allocated to the striped cat, possibly shared with other similar cats. These nodes are shaded in Figure 4.

5 Conclusion

Self-organization of feature maps presented with stimuli from more than one source will result in very different maps depending on the rules for attention shifting between the sources. In learning under novelty seeking the resulting map will represent all sources and group stimuli in an "economic" way — similar stimuli will share the same node. In learning under familiarity preference — a characteristic well-known in autism — the resulting map will represent only the map with the lowest variability and will use its representational capacity so that stimuli with very minor differences, such as the coloration of domestic cats, each have their own nodes. The learning which is modelled by such self-organization corresponds to detailed learning in narrow fields, a characteristic well-known in autism.

Acknowledgements. This work is a result of a cooperation between Luleå University of Technology, Luleå, Sweden and Monash University, Clayton, Australia. We wish to express our appreciation to the Swedish STINT grant scheme and the Monash School of Computer Science and Software Engineering for supporting this cooperation.

References

1. Diagnostic and statistical manual of mental disorders. 4th ed. American Psychiatric Association (1994) Available from: http://www.psychologynet.org.
2. Courchesne, E., Townsend, J., Akshoomoff, N., Saitoh, O., Yeung-Courchesne, R., Lincoln, A., James, H., Haas, R., Schreibman, L., Lau, L.: Impairment in shifting attention in autistic and cerebellar patients. Beh. Neuroscience **108** (1994a) 848–865
3. Kootz, J., Marinelli, B., Cohen, D.: Modulation of response to environmental stimulation in autistic children. Jour. Autism Dev. Dis. **12** (1982) 185–193
4. Dawson, G., Meltzoff, A., Osterling, J., Rinaldi, J., Brown, E.: Children with autism fail to orient to naturally occurring social stimuli. Jour. Autism Dev. Dis. **28** (1998) 479–485
5. Pascualvaca, D., Fantie, B., Papageorgiou, M., Mirsky, A.: Attentional capacities in children with autism: Is there a general deficit in shifting focus? Jour. Autism Dev. Dis. **28** (1998) 467–478

6. Minshew, N., Luna, B., Sweeney, J.: Oculomotor evidence for neocortical systems but not cerebellar dysfunction in autism. Neurology (1999) 917–922
7. Gustafsson, L., Papliński, A.P.: Self-organization of an artificial neural network subjected to attention shift impairments and novelty avoidance: Implications for the development of autism. Jour. Autism Dev. Dis. (2002) to be published.
8. Papliński, A.P., Gustafsson, L.: An attempt in modelling autism using self-organizing maps. In: Proc. 9th Int. Conf. Neural Inf. Proc., Singapore (2002) 301–304
9. Kohonen, T.: Self-Organising Maps. 3rd edn. Springer-Verlag, Berlin (2001)

Online Processing of Multiple Inputs in a Sparsely-Connected Recurrent Neural Network

Julien Mayor and Wulfram Gerstner

Laboratory of Computational Neuroscience
EPFL, CH-1005 Lausanne, Switzerland
julien.mayor@epfl.ch

Abstract. The storage and short-term memory capacities of recurrent neural networks of spiking neurons are investigated. We demonstrate that it is possible to process online many superimposed streams of input. This is despite the fact that the stored information is spread throughout the network. We show that simple output structures are powerful enough to extract the diffuse information from the network. The dimensional blow up, which is crucial in kernel methods, is efficiently achieved by the dynamics of the network itself.

1 Introduction

Information processing in recurrent neural networks has become a fashionable subject and is known as Liquid State Machines (LSM, [1,2]) or echo state networks [3]. They are good candidates to model ultra-short-term memories. The idea underlying those models is that the instantaneous state of the network provides a rich reservoir of non-linear spatio-temporal transformations of the inputs. Information about past input can then be read out with simple, efficient and adaptive readouts. In general learning only acts on the readout structures, the network itself remaining fixed. A set of non-linear transformations of the input is achieved through the use of a sparsely-connected neural network of integrate-and-fire neurons. Tuning the network to an asynchronous irregular firing state allows us to have the needed rich dynamics. In this paper we establish a link between liquid state machines on the one side and the theory of sparsely-connected networks [4] on the other side.

2 The Model

The system we study is a sparsely-connected network of leaky integrate-and-fire (IF) neurons. Such networks are known to have a complex dynamics ([4,5]). Our network is made up of 200 IF neurons, 80% of which are excitatory and 20% inhibitory. Both excitatory and inhibitory neurons are modelled with a membrane time constant of 20ms. They are weakly (connection probability = 0.2) and randomly connected through simple static synapses. We carefully chose the synaptic strengths, $\omega_I = 5\omega_E$, and an external drive consisting of 32 external poisson spike trains with a mean rate of 6.3 Hz, such that the network without additional external input is in an asynchronous and irregular firing regime based on the phase diagram described in [4] (coordinates: $g = 5$ and $\nu_{ext} = 2\nu_{thr}$, specifically we take $\omega_E = 1mV$, $\theta = 5mV$ and $V_{reset} = 0mV$, but other combinations of parameters would give the same results). With a weaker or a stronger input, the system reaches a phase of synchronous irregular firing (respectively slow or fast). The absence of synchrony at the working point of the liquid state machine is important in order to avoid limit cycles (periodic patterns of activity) and therefore indistinguishable moments that share the same phase within these cycles.

We assess the information processing capacity of the network with a procedure analogous to [1] and [3]. We inject simultaneously N independent inputs to N disjoint groups of randomly chosen neurons (see figure 1 left), every neuron receives exactly one input e.g. for $N = 4$ inputs we have 4 groups of 50 neurons in our network of 200 neurons. The inputs are derived from a bounded random walk so that they all share the same underlying statistics. Their auto-correlation profiles can easily be measured, an analysis of which will be done in section 3.3. N readout structures, 'seeing' all neurons of the network are trained to retrieve the amplitude of their corresponding signal a given time T in the past (see figure 1 right). The outputs of the readout structures are simple linear combination of all the membrane potentials i.e.

$$Output(t) = \sum_k w_k u_k(t).$$

Only the weights w_k of the readout structures are tunable, the network itself remaining fixed. We minimise the error :

$$E = [Output(t) - Input(t - T)]^2$$

by an optimal regression on the training set. This $Input(t - T)$ plays the role of a target value for optimisation. After a training period, the weights of the readout structures are frozen and N new input signals are introduced in the network. Outputs of the readout structures are then compared with their corresponding targets.

3 Results and Discussion

In the following section we will discuss the results we obtained by the procedure described above. For all the simulations, the training time is 50000 time steps and performances are obtained on an independant test set of 5000 time steps. Firstly we will show that it is possible to process online many superimposed streams of input. In the second subsection we will show that this is possible despite the fact that information has diffused within the network. In the third subsection we investigate the role of the input statistics and see that the output structures use all the available information in order to minimise the distance

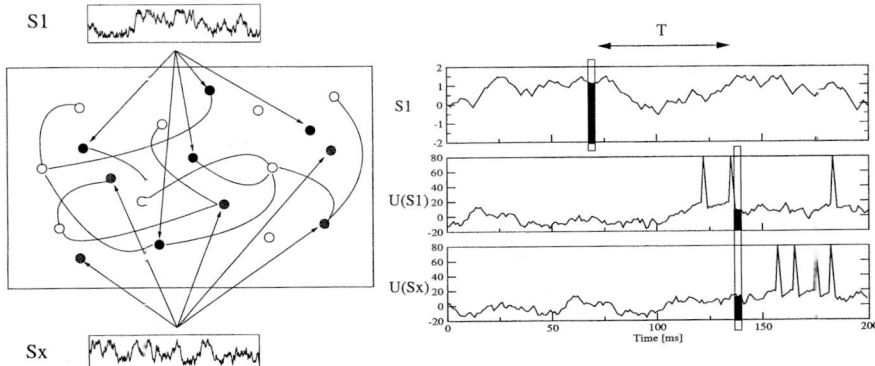

Fig. 1. Left: The different signals are introduced to randomly chosen interconnected neurons. Every neuron receives exactly one input from the exterior. Only two input signals are shown in the figure. Right: Based on the momentary state of all membrane potentials (those receiving directly the signal S1 *and* those receiving any other signal Sx), a readout structure is trained to guess the amplitude of its corresponding input a time T before (referred as delay thereafter).

of its output to the target. Finally it will be shown that simple linear readouts are powerful enough to extract information and perform as good kernel-based methods: in other words, the recurrent neural network provides the necessary dimensional blow up.

3.1 Multiple Inputs

Following the procedure described in the previous section, we inject simultaneously eight independent signals with an autocorrelation time of 95 ms. In figure 2 (left), only four out of the eight input-output pairs are shown. In order to allow a qualitative visual assessment of the performance, inputs are shifted back in time so that they can be directly compared with the output. The time delay shown here is 10ms. In figure 2 (right), the cross-correlations between the output of the readout structures and their corresponding targets are shown as a function of the delay. A significant amount of information is still present up to about 150ms. Although the eight signals excite the network simultaneously, the high dimensionality of the system allows the readout structures to extract any individual signal.

3.2 Information Diffusion

A control has yet to be done. Although the network is generated randomly, coupling might be stronger within a given subset of neurons compared to neurons outside the subset. Information might then stay localized in that part of the network, where it was injected. To rule out this possibility, a closer look at the

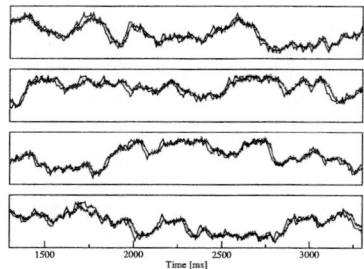 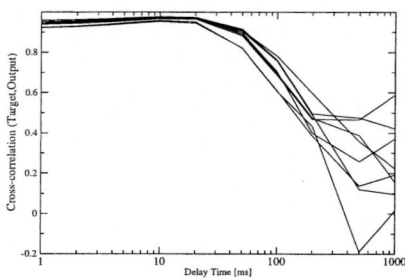

Fig. 2. Left: A sample of four target(black)-output(grey) pairs. Trained delay: 10ms. Right: Cross-correlation curves for the eight target-output pairs.

weights of the readouts was taken. This time we injected simultaneously four different signals. For three different delays and four different readout structures, the sixteen weights with the largest value have been identified. Neurons of the network have been grouped into four groups according to the label of the input they receive. The number of 'large' weights has then been determined in each of the zones. The results are shown as grey-level plots: the horizontal axis is the label of the zones and the vertical axis is the label of the readout structures, the grey-level being the count of large weights that belong to a given readout structure (y-axis) and that 'read' neurons that belong to a given zone (x-axis). The clearer the zone is, the more weights lie in that zone. A diagonal light ridge implies that information is located where it was injected, whereas a rather homogeneous coloration indicates that information is spread out over the network. In figure 3, three different plots are shown. They correspond to delays of 2ms, 20ms and 50ms. Although cross-correlation plots of the figure 2 (right) indicate that information is still extractable up to more than 100ms, the plots corresponding to the 20ms and 50ms delay do not show any significant diagonal trace, compared to the one clearly present for the 2ms delay. The information therefore diffuses in the network without being predominantly stuck locally.

3.3 Auto-correlation versus Cross-Correlations

A step towards a deeper analysis of the characteristics of the network is to have a look at the full cross-correlation curves instead of only sampling the values for the trained delay as done in figure 2 (right). In what follows, only one single input with a short auto-correlation profile excites the network. In figure 4, the thick curves correspond to the cross-correlations between the input and the outputs of readouts trained for different delays. If we have to guess the trained delay by only looking at the input and the output of the network, we might be tempted to say it corresponds to the location of the peak of the cross-correlation curve. This would in fact yield an incorrect answer. A quick examination shows us that

Fig. 3. Greyscale plots giving insight to where the information is (see text). Light areas indicate regions where a given readout structure extracts most of the information. Diagonal clear squares signify information stays where it has been injected (as seen on the left for a delay of 2ms) whereas rather uniform colour distribution means information is spread out among different network regions (as seen for the 20ms (middle) and 50ms (right) delays.

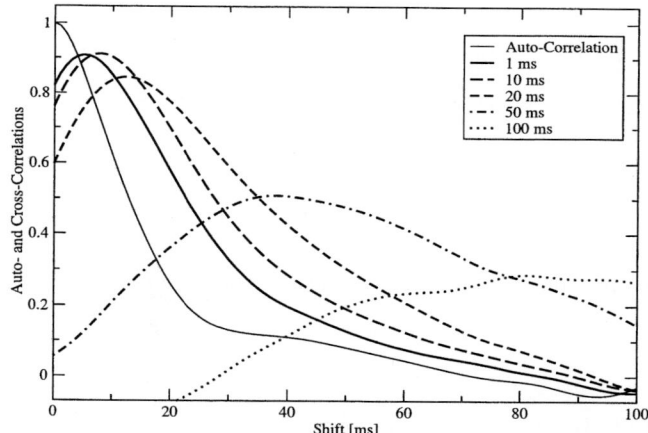

Fig. 4. Auto-correlation curve (thin line starting at the point(0,1)) of the input signal and cross-correlation curves target-output. Note that the cross-correlation curves peak at a shift value that is not the trained delay (eg for the dot-dashed curve; the trained delay is 50ms but the curve peaks around 37ms). For a given shift though, the highest curve has the correct corresponding delay (eg for a 50ms shift, the highest curve is the one trained for a 50ms delay). These curves are in this perspective optimal.

the curves do not peak around values that correspond to the trained delays. Yet another important observation is that for a given shift, the highest curve for this shift correspond to the readout trained for a delay equal to that shift. Although it is in apparent contradiction, the explanation is rather simple. Because the weights are chosen such that they minimise the error $L2$ between the output and the target, they use all the available information. On the one hand they will set their guess by looking in the past, but on the other hand they will also use the fact that the auto-correlation of the target has a certain width. Reading the present and saying this was the past is not completely incorrect, because of this auto-correlation. Minimising the error $L2$ is equivalent to finding the optimal balance between extracting degraded past information and online reading of the present input (correlated with the input some time T ago). Performances are then strongly dependent on the underlying statistics of the target.

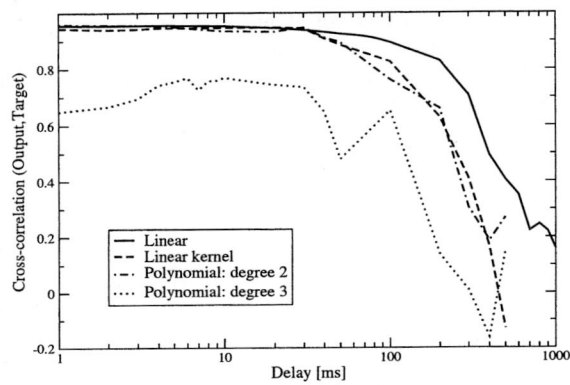

Fig. 5. Comparison between optimal linear output and kernel-based methods.

3.4 Optimal Readouts: Linear versus SVM

In the previous sections, outputs of the readout structures have often been named 'optimal'. Such outputs are not biologically plausible in the sense that they can access the membrane sub-threshold potential instead of only receiving information through action potentials. These structures are intended to provide an upper bound on the information processing capacity of such a network. To justify the use of simple linear outputs we now show that they can extract as much information as possible for a given number of learning examples. A comparison of the performances of such simple readouts to kernel-based methods have been carried out with always the same training set size (50000 time steps). Support vector machines ([6] and therein) are known to be among the most powerful classification tools. Therefore we used SVM (with hierarchical polynomial kernels) in regression [7] as readout structures of our network. None of the kernels succeeded in doing better than the optimal linear output (see figure 5). The linear kernel and the polynomial (degree two) kernel performed almost as well as the linear regression whereas kernels of higher dimensions (polynomial of degree three, Gaussian) showed strong effects of over-fitting. Simple output structures (yet optimal in the linear sense) are powerful enough to extract information from the network for a limited (although big) training set. The dimensional blow up which is crucial in the kernel methods is already efficiently achieved by the rich dynamics of the network.

3.5 Conclusion

We have seen that a sparsely-connected recurrent neural network tuned to be in an asynchronous irregular firing regime has enough degrees of freedom for simple output structures to extract simultaneously informations coming from independent sources, even though patterns are superimposed. We also have seen that statistics of the targets play an important role in the performances of the network. In order to minimise the distance to the target, an optimal trade-off is made between extracting old corrupted information and retrieving not-so-old information correlated in time to the desired target.

References

1. Maass, W., Natschläger, T. and Markram, H.: Real-time computing without stable states: A new framework for neural computation based on perturbations. Neural. Comp. **14(11)** (2002) 2531–2560
2. Maass, W., Natschläger, T. and Markram, H.: Computational models for generic cortical microcircuits. In J. Feng, editor, Computational Neuroscience: A Comprehensive Approach. CRC-Press, 2002. to appear
3. Jäger, H.: Short term memory in echo state networks. GMD Report 152, German National Research Center for information technology, 2002.
4. Brunel, N.: Dynamics of sparsely connected networks of excitatory and inhibitory spiking neurons. J. Comp. Neuro. **8** (2000) 183–208
5. Brunel, N. and Hakim, V.: Fast global oscillations in networks of integrate-and-fire neurons with low firing rates. Neural. Comp. **11** (1999) 1621–1671
6. Schölkopf, B. and Smola, A.: Learning with Kernels. (MIT Press, Cambridge, MA,2002)
7. Collobert, R. and Bengio, S.: SVMTorch: Support Vector Machines for Large-Scale Regression Problems. J. of Machine Learning Res. (2001)

The Spike Response Model: A Framework to Predict Neuronal Spike Trains

Renaud Jolivet[1], Timothy J. Lewis[2], and Wulfram Gerstner[1]

[1] Laboratory of Computational Neuroscience,
Swiss Federal Institute of Technology Lausanne, 1015 Lausanne, Switzerland,
{renaud.jolivet, wulfram.gerstner}@epfl.ch,
http://diwww.epfl.ch/mantra
[2] Center for Neural Science and Courant Institute of Mathematical Sciences,
New York University, New York, NY 10003, USA,
tim.lewis@nyu.edu,
http://www.cns.nyu.edu/~tlewis

Abstract. We propose a simple method to map a generic threshold model, namely the Spike Response Model, to artificial data of neuronal activity using a minimal amount of a priori information. Here, data are generated by a detailed mathematical model of neuronal activity. The model neuron is driven with *in-vivo*-like current injected, and we test to which extent it is possible to predict the spike train of the detailed neuron model from that of the Spike Response Model. In particular, we look at the number of spikes correctly predicted within a biologically relevant time window. We find that the Spike Response Model achieves prediction of up to 80% of the spikes with correct timing ($\pm$2ms). Other characteristics of activity, such as mean rate and coefficient of variation of spike trains, are predicted in the correct range as well.

1 Introduction

The successful mathematical description of action potentials by Hodgkin and Huxley has led to a whole series of papers that try to describe in detail the dynamics of various ionic currents. However, precise description of neuronal activity involves an extensive number of variables, which often prevents a clear understanding of the underlying dynamics. Hence, a simplified description is desirable and has been subject to numerous works. The most popular simplified models include the Integrate-and-Fire (IF) model, the FitzHugh-Nagumo model and the Morris-Lecar model (for a review, see [1]).

In this paper, we make use of the Spike Response Model (SRM), a generic threshold model of the IF type. Similar to earlier work [2], we map the SRM to a detailed mathematical model of neuronal activity. But, in contrast of what has been done in [2], we go beyond the classic Hodgkin-Huxley neuron model of the squid axon and use instead a model of a cortical interneuron. Moreover, we use a different mapping technique that could also be applied to real neurons. We show that such a simple technique allows reliable prediction of the spike train of a fast-spiking interneuron. Prediction of up to 80% of spikes with correct timing is achieved. The model also quantitatively reproduces the subthreshold behavior of the membrane voltage (see Fig. 1) as well as other characteristics of neuronal activity including mean rate and coefficient of variation (C_V).

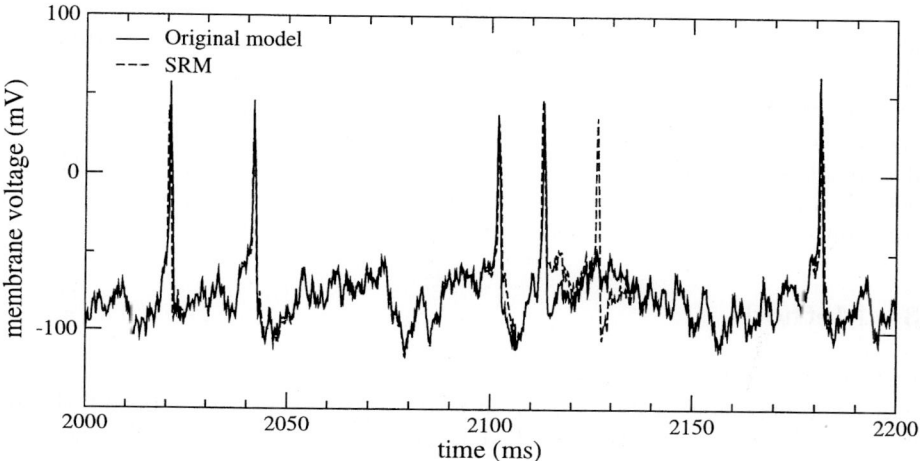

Fig. 1. The prediction of the SRM (dotted line) is compared to the target data (solid line). The model achieves very good prediction of the subthreshold behavior of the membrane voltage. The timing of all the spikes is predicted correctly, except that one extra spike is added at around 2125ms.

2 Model

In this section, we describe the SRM in detail. The state of a neuron is characterized by a single variable u, the membrane voltage of the cell. Let us suppose that the neuron has fired its last spike at time $\hat{t}$. At each time $t > \hat{t}$, the state of the cell is written:

$$u(t) = \eta(t - \hat{t}) + \int_{-\infty}^{+\infty} \kappa(t - \hat{t}, s) I(t - s) ds, \qquad (1)$$

The last term accounts for the effect of an external current $I(t)$. The integration process is characterized by the kernel κ (additional external current). The kernel η includes the form of the spike itself as well as the after-hyperpolarization potential (AHP), if needed. As always, we have a threshold condition to account for spike generation:

$$\text{if } u(t) \geq \theta \text{ and } \dot{u}(t) > 0, \text{ then } \hat{t} = t. \qquad (2)$$

Note that spiking occurs only if the membrane voltage crosses the threshold from below. The threshold itself can be taken either as constant or as time-dependent. We choose:

$$\theta(t-\hat{t}) = \begin{cases} +\infty & \text{if } t-\hat{t} \leq \gamma_{ref} \\ \theta_0 + \theta_1 \exp(-(t-\hat{t})/\tau_\theta) & \text{else} \end{cases}, \quad (3)$$

where γ_{ref} is a fixed absolute refractory period. θ_0, θ_1 and τ_θ are parameters that will be chosen to yield the best fit to a test dataset (target spike train).

The SRM is more general than the classic leaky IF model. In particular, the choice of the kernel κ is not restricted. Moreover, κ is time-dependent since it depends on the time elapsed since the last spike $t-\hat{t}$. Finally, the AHP is described in a more realistic manner than in the leaky IF model where the time constant of the AHP is equal to the membrane time constant.

3 Methods

In this section, we begin by generating a test dataset using a conductance-based neuron model stimulated by *in-vivo*-like time-dependent current. Then, we explain the mapping of the SRM to the data, and finally, define how we quantify the predictive power of the model.

3.1 Generation of the Test Dataset

The test dataset is generated with a Hodgkin-Huxley-like model. The model was originally designed for fast-spiking interneurons [3] and was slightly modified for the present study. Note that an analytical reduction from this detailed model to the SRM is possible [1]. The model is integrated with a time step of 10^{-2}ms. The driving current is a random Gaussian noise with constant mean μ_I and standard deviation σ_I. During integration, the value of the current is changed every 20 time steps ($= 0.2$ms). The sampling frequency of our dataset is 5kHz. This highly variable temporal input is thought to approximate well *in-vivo* conditions [4]. For each spike train, we record the membrane voltage and the driving current. Both are needed later on.

3.2 Mapping of the Model

To realize the mapping of the SRM to the conductance-based neuron model, we proceed in two steps. First, we extract the two kernels characterizing the model (κ and η) and second, we choose a specific threshold (θ) and optimize it in terms of quality of predictions.

Let's start with the kernels. For the sake of simplicity, we assume that the mean driving current is zero but the method can easily be generalized. We start by extraction of the kernel η. It is well known that the shape of spikes is highly stereotyped and presents only little variability. We therefore select one spike train from the dataset generated with the detailed model and align all spikes. The mean shape of the spikes yields η. Detection and alignment of spikes is realized using a threshold condition on the first derivative of the membrane voltage.

Once we are done with η, we extract the kernel κ. Let us limit ourselves to the interval between two consecutive spikes at times t_j and t_{j+1}. Therefore, we can rewrite equation (1) as follows:

$$u(t) - \eta(t - \hat{t}_j) = \int_{-\infty}^{+\infty} \kappa(t - \hat{t}_j, s) I(t-s) ds. \qquad (4)$$

The right-hand side of equation (4) is the convolution product between the driving current and a family of kernels κ parameterized by the variable $t - \hat{t}_j$. It is then possible to find an approximation of the optimal kernel for each timing by the Wiener-Hopf optimal filtering technique [5]. Let us consider each non-zero term of κ as a free parameter and try to minimize the squared distance between data $d(t) = u(t) - \eta(t - \hat{t}_j)$ and prediction $p(t) = \sum_s \kappa(t - \hat{t}_j, s) I(t-s)$ in a time window centered on $t - \hat{t}_j$. Then, the optimal filter for that window is the solution of the following linear system:

$$\begin{pmatrix} C(I,I)_0 & \cdots & C(I,I)_{M+N} \\ \cdots & \cdots & \cdots \\ C(I,I)_{-(M+N)} & \cdots & C(I,I)_0 \end{pmatrix} \begin{pmatrix} \kappa_{-N} \\ \cdots \\ \kappa_{+M} \end{pmatrix} = \begin{pmatrix} C(d,I)_{-N} \\ \cdots \\ C(d,I)_{+M} \end{pmatrix}. \qquad (5)$$

$C(f,g)_i$ is the numerical cross-correlation of vector f with vector g at lag i. M (respectively N) is the maximum positive lag (respectively negative lag) for which κ is non-zero. It is obvious that this filter should be causal and therefore, $N = 0$. Finally, we fit the resulting vector κ with a suitable function (usually an exponential decay). The Wiener-Hopf method requires a window as large as the support of κ. The result is that the dependency on $t - \hat{t}$ cannot be reproduced exactly. However, it is not a crucial point for correct prediction of the timing of the spikes but only for correct prediction of the membrane voltage just after emission of a spike, and only for time lags between 0 and about 30ms (for our dataset). The kernels are plotted in Fig. 2.

The final step is to choose and optimize the threshold. The absolute refractory period γ_{ref} is set to 2ms. All the other parameters: θ_0, θ_1 and τ_θ (see equation (3)) are fitted in order to optimize the coincidence factor Γ using the *downhill simplex method* (see subsection 3.3 for definition of this quantity).

For some technical reasons, we use three spike trains of 10s each to do the mapping of the SRM to the detailed model. However, it is possible to do it with only one spike train.

3.3 Evaluation of Predictions

Once we are done with the mapping, we simulate the conductance-based model and the SRM with the same driving currents. These driving currents are new

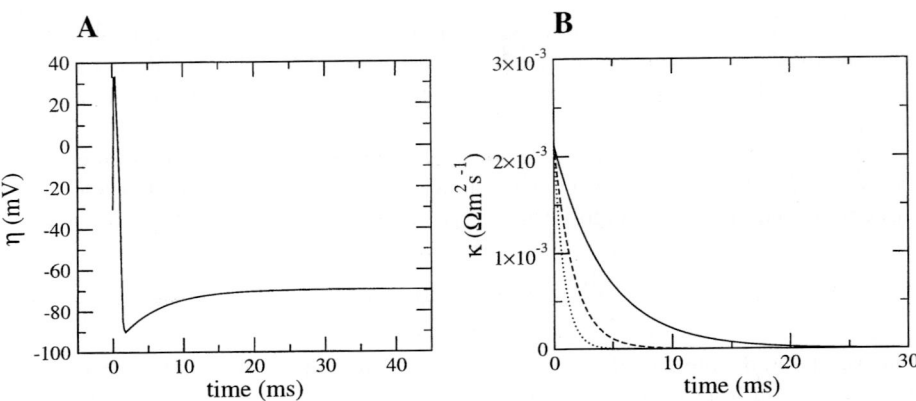

Fig. 2. Kernels extracted by the method described in text. **A.** Kernel η. **B.** Kernel κ at different timings: $t - \hat{t} = 0$ms (dotted line), $t - \hat{t} = 10$ms (dash-dotted line) and $t - \hat{t} = 100$ms (solid line).

and have not been used during optimization. Then, we count the number of spikes in coincidence between both trains within a small time window $\pm\Delta$. As a measure of the quality of the prediction, we use the coincidence factor Γ [2]:

$$\Gamma = \frac{N_{coinc} - \langle N_{coinc}\rangle}{\frac{1}{2}(N_{SRM} + N_{data})}\frac{1}{\mathcal{N}}, \quad (6)$$

where N_{coinc} is the number of coincident spikes, $\langle N_{coinc}\rangle$ is the mean number of spikes that would be predicted correctly by a homogeneous Poisson neuron firing at the same rate as the SRM (it can be calculated exactly), N_{SRM} (respectively N_{data}) is the number of spikes elicited by the SRM (respectively by the conductance-based model) and $\mathcal{N}$ is a normalization factor ensuring that $\max(\Gamma) = 1$. Γ equals 1 if the spike train is predicted exactly and 0 if the prediction is not better than a Poisson neuron (Γ can be lower than 0). The denominator of the first term ensures that the mean frequency of both spike trains is roughly the same.

4 Results

In this section, we show the predictions obtained from the SRM and quantitatively compare the results to the test dataset (target spike trains) generated using the conductance-based model for fast-spiking interneurons. Unless specified, we used a dynamic threshold with $\theta_0 = -49.1$mV, $\theta_1 = 14.9$mV and $\tau_\theta = 20.9$ms.

We test the predictive power of the SRM by comparing the responses of the conductance-based model neuron and the SRM to Gaussian noise current with constant mean μ_I and standard deviation σ_I. Fig. 3 shows the effects of changing

The Spike Response Model: A Framework to Predict Neuronal Spike Trains 851

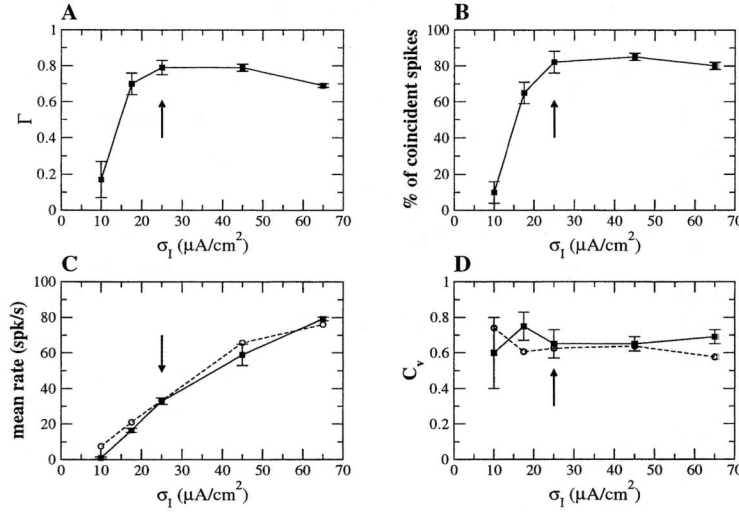

Fig. 3. The neuron is driven with zero mean Gaussian current. Panels A-D show results of the SRM (solid line with squares). In addition, panels C and D show the target values for mean rate and C_V (dotted line with circles). The arrows denote the point for which parameters of the threshold have been optimized (same in the four panels). Mean of five trials is plotted with two standard deviations for each point. **A.** Coincidence factor Γ. **B.** Percentage of coincident spikes. **C.** Mean rate compared to target. **D.** C_V of the interspike interval distribution compared to target.

variance with fixed mean, and Fig. 6 shows effects of changing mean with fixed variance. In both cases, $\Delta = 2$ms and tested spike trains are 10s long.

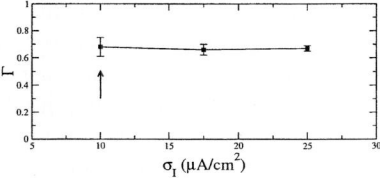 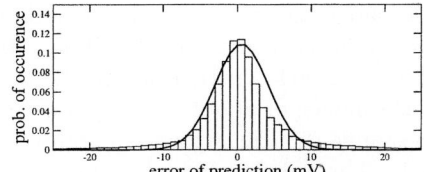

Fig. 4. SRM mapped to data at low rates (here, between $7 - 35$spk/s). Γ is plotted versus the current's standard deviation σ_I ($\mu_I = 0$). The arrow denotes the point for which parameters of the threshold were optimized. The corresponding rates are, from left to right, 7.6, 21.0 and 33.3spk/s. Here, parameters of the threshold are: $\theta_0 = -52.5$mV, $\theta_1 = 37.5$mV and $\tau_\theta = 5.2$ms.

Fig. 5. Normalized histogram of the error of prediction of the membrane voltage. For each time step of one spike train, we report the predicted voltage minus the target voltage. The solid line is a fitted Gaussian distribution centered on mean $\mu = 0.6$mV and with standard deviation $\sigma = 3.7$mV. Effects at the tails are due to missed and added spikes.

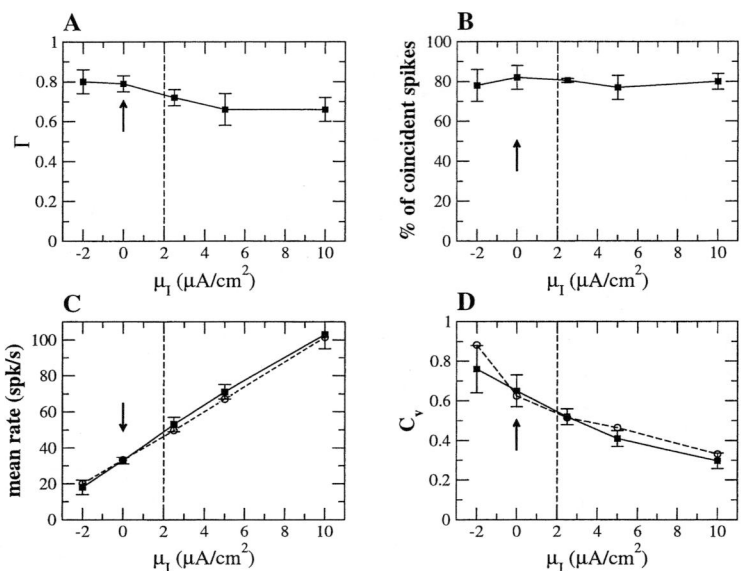

Fig. 6. The neuron is driven with varying mean Gaussian current. The current's standard deviation is held constant at $25\mu A/cm^2$. Panels A-D show results of the SRM (solid line with squares). In addition, panels C and D show the target values for mean rate and C_V (dotted line with circles). Mean of five trials is plotted with two standard deviations for each point. The vertical dotted line is the limit of the subthreshold constant current. The threshold's parameters are the same as in Fig. 3. **A.** Coincidence factor Γ. **B.** Percentage of coincident spikes. **C.** Mean rate compared to target. **D.** C_V of the interspike interval distribution compared to target.

The SRM produces very good predictions of the target spike trains over a broad range of means and standard deviations of the injected current. The model tuned using data at about 30Hz is still good for spike trains at 80Hz (Fig. 3, panel A). If optimized for low rates, the SRM can also achieve good performance of about $\Gamma = 0.7$ for $\sigma_I = 10\mu A/cm^2$ (Fig. 4). Predictions hold in the range 0-35Hz, which is roughly the range of interest for cortical pyramidal cells. The subthreshold behavior of the membrane voltage is also very nicely reproduced (see Fig. 1 and 5). Other standard quantities like the mean rate or the C_V of the interspike interval (ISI) distribution are predicted in the correct range, particularly the mean rate. This indicates that spikes that are missed or added do not modify crucially the pattern of the spike train (Fig. 3, 5 and 6).

The SRM is very robust against some modifications. Predictive power is still very good ($\Gamma > 0.7$) when using a shorter time window for coincidence detection ($\Delta = 1$ms) and using a constant threshold instead of a time-dependent threshold reduces only slightly the range of validity of the model. On the other hand, trying to simplify one of the kernel (η or κ) reduces significantly the quality of predictions (data not shown).

5 Conclusion

Prediction of the activity of neurons was attempted in the past. Keat, Reinagel, Reid and Meister show that it is possible to predict the activity of neurons of the early visual system [6]. However, these neurons produce very stereotyped spike trains with short periods of intense activity followed by long periods of silence. More recently, Rauch, La Camera, Lüscher, Senn and Fusi observed that an IF model can reproduce the mean rate of neocortical pyramidal cells with the same kind of *in-vivo*-like input current [7].

Here, we go one step further and propose a simple and general method to map a threshold model to data of neuronal activity. Once the mapping is realized, the model allows very reliable prediction of many aspects of neuronal activity, such as timing of the spikes, membrane voltage, mean rate and C_V of the ISI distribution. A posteriori, we may interpret the kernel κ as the response kernel of an IF model with time-dependent time-"constant" [1]. The main advantage of this purely numerical approach (compared to an analytical or semi-analytical approach) is that it could, in principle, be extended to experimental data. Therefore, not only do these results provide a basis for theoretical network studies on threshold models, they also offer an approach toward studying the integration of inputs in real neurons.

References

[1] Gerstner, W. and Kistler W., Spiking neurons models: single neurons, populations, plasticity, Cambridge University Press, Cambridge (2002)
[2] Kistler, W., Gerstner, W. and Van Hemmen, L., Reduction of Hodgkin-Huxley equations to a single-variable threshold model, *Neural Comp.* **9**: 1015–1045 (1997)
[3] Erisir, A., Lau, D., Rudy, B. and Leonard, C., Function of specific K^+ channels in sustained high-frequency firing of fast-spiking neocortical interneurons, *J. Neurophysiol* **82**: 2476–2489 (1999)
[4] Destexhe, A. and Paré, D., Impact of network activity on the integrative properties of neocortical pyramidal neurons in vivo, *J. Neurophysiol.* **81**: 1531–1547 (1999)
[5] Wiener, N., Nonlinear problems in random theory, MIT Press, Cambridge (1958)
[6] Keat, J., Reinagel, P., Reid, C. and Meister M., Predicting every spike: a model for the responses of visual neurons, *Neuron* **30**: 803–817 (2001)
[7] Rauch, A., La Camera, G., Lüscher, H.-R., Senn, W. and Fusi, S., *unpublished observations* (2002)

Roles of Motion and Form in Biological Motion Recognition

Antonino Casile and Martin Giese

Laboratory for Action Representation and Learning
University Clinic, Tübingen
{casile,martin.giese@tuebingen.mpg.de}

Abstract. Animals and humans recognize biological movements and actions with high robustness and accuracy. It still remains to be clarified how different neural mechanisms processing form and motion information contribute to this recognition process. We investigate this question using simple learning-based neurophysiologically inspired mechanisms for biological motion recognition. In quantitative simulations we show the following results: (1) Point light stimuli with strongly degraded local motion information can be recognized with a neural model for the (dorsal) motion pathway. (2) The recognition of degraded biological motion stimuli is dependent on previous experience with point light stimuli. (3) Opponent motion features seem to be critical for the recognition of these stimuli.

1 Introduction

Biological movements, like locomotion of humans and animals, are perceived visually with amazing sensitivity and robustness. This was demonstrated in a seminal experiment by Johansson [5]. He demonstrated that complex movements can be recognized from strongly impoverished stimuli that consisted of a small number of moving dots (cf. section 2). Though the form information conveyed by these "point light stimuli" is highly impoverished, subjects perceived the moving dots as human beings and could correctly recognize the executed actions. This has been interpreted as evidence that biological motion recognition is primarily based on the analysis of motion information [6]. Physiological evidence suggests that form and motion information are processed in two separate visual pathways that depart from the primary visual cortex. Form information is processed predominantly in a ventral pathway that includes areas V2, V4 and IT in monkeys. Motion information is processed predominantly in a dorsal pathway that includes areas as MT and MST. This implies that, according to the classical view, biological motion stimuli are mainly processed in the dorsal pathway.

This view has been recently challenged on the basis of results from patients who, in spite of lesions in the dorsal pathway, still could recognize biological motion stimuli [9]. Additional evidence that seems to contradict an involvement of the dorsal pathway has been obtained in experiments using point light displays with strongly degraded local motion information [1].

In this paper we use a learning-based neural network model for the recognition of biological movements. The model includes two separate processing streams for the analysis of form and motion information and allows to test the computational relevance of the two pathways. The model is consistent with neurophysiological data and reproduces a variety of experimental results on biological motion recognition [2]. We show that recognition of previously learned patterns can be accomplished with either pathway alone and depends on the previous learning history. However, generalization between regular (full-body) biological motion stimuli and point light stimuli could be accomplished only in the motion pathway of the model. For this generalization opponent motion features seem to be highly important.

2 Stimuli

In psychophysical experiments different types of stimuli have been used to study biological movement recognition (cf. figure 1). Subjects can easily recognize the direction and type of locomotion (e.g. walking vs. running) from movies of regular (full-body) walkers, and even from static pictures of such walkers (figure 1 (*a*)).

When movies of point light walkers (cf. figure 1 (*b*)) are shown to **naive** subjects, who have never seen such stimuli before they can recognize easily the type and direction of locomotion. If, however, individual frames from such movies are presented as static pictures naive subjects can not recognize the locomotion pattern, and often even do not detect the presence of a human body. This fact was interpreted as evidence for the hypothesis that point light stimuli are recognized using predominantly the dorsal pathway. Of course, after some training, observers can learn to categorize correctly individual static dot configurations. Subjects that have received such previous training will be called **expert** subjects in the following.

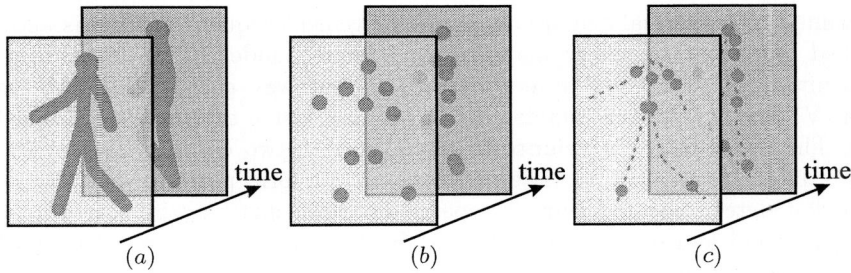

Fig. 1. Stimuli used in our simulations. (*a*) Regular (full-body) walker; (*b*) Point light walker; (*c*) Sequential position stimulus (SPS).

Recently a novel point light stimulus with strongly degraded local motion information has been proposed by Beintema and Lappe [1]. The dots[1] of their **sequential position stimulus (SPS)** are positioned randomly on the limbs of

---

[1] Depending on the experiment, 1 to 8 points were shown.

the walker, i.e. not necessarily on the major joints. They were randomly reassigned to a new limb every p frames ($p = 1...4$). Figure 1 (c) shows an SPS that consists of 8 dots. (The bones of the skeleton are sketched only for illustrative purposes; they are not shown in the real stimulus.) Despite the fact that the local motion information of the SPS is strongly perturbed, subjects could judge the direction of walking with high accuracy. From this it has been concluded that perception of the SPS must be based on the reconstruction of the form of the walker exploiting predominantly mechanisms in the ventral pathway [1], possibly by fitting a kinematic model of the skeleton.

3 Model Description

In this section we give a brief overview of our model. A complete description of the details exceeds the scope of this paper and can be found in [2].

The form and the motion pathway of the model consist of a hierarchy of neural units that are selective for motion and form features with different levels of complexity. The complexity of the extracted features and the position and scale invariance of the detectors increase along the hierarchy. The parameters of the neural detectors are chosen so that they match available neurophysiological results. The highest levels of the hierarchy contain neurons that represent biological motion patterns in terms of learned snapshots (in the form pathway) and characteristic optic flow patterns (in the motion pathway). These neurons are trained with examples of biological motion sequences.

3.1 Form Pathway

The form pathway analyzes biological motion by extracting the form information contained in individual "snapshots" from movement sequences. This is accomplished by recognizing body shapes using a neural model for stationary object recognition (cf. [8]). The first level of the form pathway, corresponding to brain areas V1 and V2, models simple cells in primary visual cortex using Gabor filters. This stage extracts **oriented contours** with two different spatial scales and 8 different orientations. The next level of the form pathway contains neurons that detect oriented **bars** irrespective of their exact positions within the receptive field and of their spatial scale. Such behavior has been observed for complex cells in primary visual cortex (e.g. area V2) and for neurons in area V4. The model achieves position and scale invariance by pooling the responses of the Gabor filters with same preferred orientation, but different spatial positions and scale using a maximum operation [8]. The next-higher level of the form pathway contains neurons that are selective for snapshots from movement sequences. The feed-forward inputs of these **snapshot neurons** are modeled by radial basis function units: $G(u) = exp(-[u - u_0]C[u - u_0])$, where u is the response vector of the complex cells in the previous layer. The centers u_0 and covariance matrix C of the basis functions are learned by training with example movement sequences[2] (see [2]).

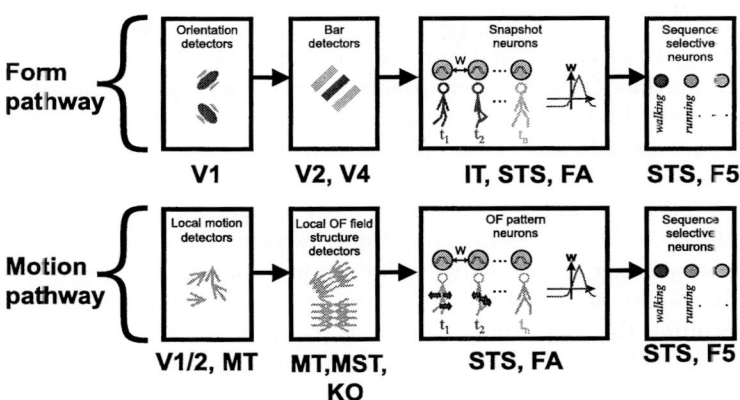

Fig. 2. Overview of the model. See section 3 for details.

3.2 Motion Pathway

The motion pathway recognizes biological movements by analyzing optic flow information. The first level of this pathway consists of **local motion detectors** that compute a motion energy signal that is derived from local optic flow vectors. These neurons model speed- and direction-selective cells in areas V1/2 and MT. The model contains detectors for 4 different motion directions and two speed regimes.

The second level of the motion pathway models neurons which are selective for opponent motion. Such neurons may be located in areas MT, MST and KO. The activities of the opponent motion detectors are obtained by combining the responses of two adjacent subfields with opposite direction selectivity in a multiplicative manner. The response of each subfield is obtained by summation of the responses of local motion detectors with same direction preference. Position invariance is obtained by pooling the responses of opponent motion detectors with different positions using a maximum operation. An inclusion of additional detectors for translational motion at this hierarchy level did not improve the recognition performance for the tested stimuli.

The next-higher level of the motion pathway consists of **optic flow pattern detectors** which are analogous to the snapshot neurons in the form pathway. These neurons are selective for complex global optic flow patterns that arise during individual instances of biological movements. The existence of this type of neurons is a prediction of the model. Their feed-forward input is modeled by

---

[2] Each training movement sequence was represented by 21 snapshot neurons.

radial basis function units that receive their inputs from the opponent motion detectors. They are trained like the snapshot neurons in the form pathway.

3.3 Sequence Selectivity

The analysis of individual snapshots is not sufficient to account for biological motion recognition. Only if the snapshots are presented in the correct temporal order a percept of biological motion arises, implying that biological motion recognition is sequence-selective. One possible neural mechanism of sequence selectivity is based on asymmetric lateral connections between the snapshot neurons in the form pathway and the optic flow pattern detectors in the motion pathway [7]: By these lateral connections the presently active neuron preactivates the neurons encoding future body configurations, and inhibits neurons encoding other body configurations. The activity $H_k^l(t)$ of the snapshot (or OF pattern) neuron encoding the k-th frame belonging to the l-th training sequence obeys the dynamics: $\tau \dot{H}_k^l(t) = -H_k^l(t) + \sum_m w(k-m) f(H_m^l(t)) + G_k^l(t)$; where τ is a time constant, $w(m)$ is an asymmetric interaction kernel, $f(\cdot)$ is a monotonic nonlinear threshold function, and $G_k^l(t)$ is the feed-forward input of the neuron according to section 3.1. It is shown elsewhere [7,3] that for appropriate choice of the interaction kernel (see insets in fig 2) substantial activity arises only if the stimulus frames are presented in the right temporal order.

The highest level of both pathways consists of **sequence selective neurons** which sum the output activities of all the snapshot neurons (or OF pattern detectors) and smooth them over time. The activity $P^l(t)$ of the sequence-selective neuron encoding the response to the l-th stored pattern obeys the dynamics: $\tau_s \dot{P}^l(t) = -P^l(t) + \sum_k H_k^l(t)$, where τ_s is a time constant and $H_k^l(t)$ is the activity of the snapshot neuron or the OF pattern detector encoding the k-th snapshot of the l-th training sequence. Sequence selective neurons might be found in the Superior Temporal Sulcus (STS) and maybe area F5 in monkeys.

4 Simulation Results

In this section we present data showing the generalization properties of the model (figure 3) and the recognition performances for strongly impoverished stimuli (figure 4). All simulations reported here were obtained with a model containing only opponent motion detectors on the second level of the motion pathway. We also tested a model that contained additional translation detectors modeling translation-selective neurons, e.g. in area MT. These detectors did not improve the recognition performance. This implies that opponent motion seems to be the critical feature for the recognition of the tested point light stimuli.

4.1 Generalization: Regular vs. Point Light Stimuli

In a first set of simulations we tried to reproduce Johansson's main result [5]: Naive subjects who have seen only regular walkers can easily recognize point light walkers. Both pathways of the model were trained with regular walker stimuli, and were tested either with regular walkers or point light stimuli walking in the same or in opposite direction.

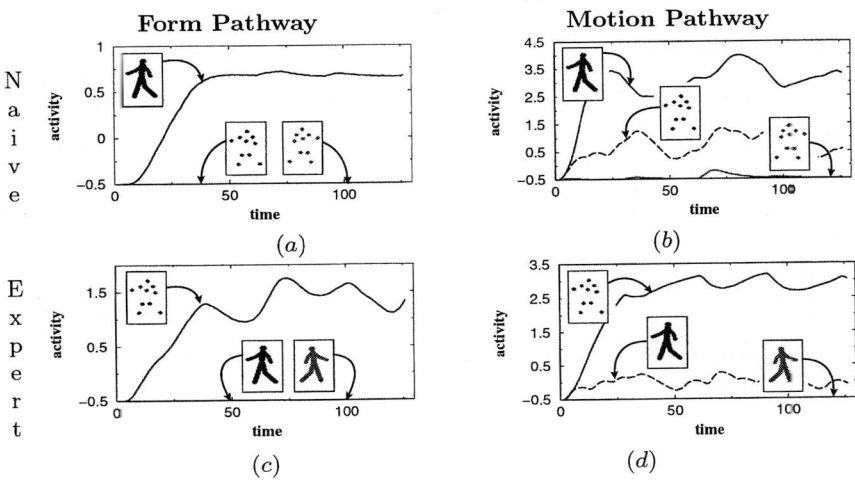

Fig. 3. Generalization to different types of stimuli then previously learned. For each figure the inset in the upper left corner shows the pattern presented during the training. The other insets show patterns presented during testing. Solid lines indicate the response of the sequence selective neurons for the training patterns. The dashed curves show the responses for the other stimulus type, walking in two different directions. Upper (lower) panels indicate the responses for a simulated naive (expert) subject.

Figures 3 (a) and (b) show that regular stimuli elicit activity in both pathways. On the contrary, only the motion pathway is activated when point light stimuli are presented. Moreover, this activity is highly selective for the direction of walking. This result implies that generalization from regular to point light stimuli is possible in the motion pathway of the model, but not in the form pathway.

It is an interesting to test whether a similar generalization occurs when the model is trained with point light walkers and tested with regular walker stimuli. Both pathways of the model were trained with a point light walker and tested with point light walkers or regular stimuli walking in opposite directions. As shown in figures 3 (c) and (d) generalization occurs in the motion pathway, but not in the form pathway. Again the activity in the motion pathway is selective for the walking direction.

These results indicate that generalization to novel types of stimuli can be achieved in the motion pathway much better than in the form pathway – at least for our model.

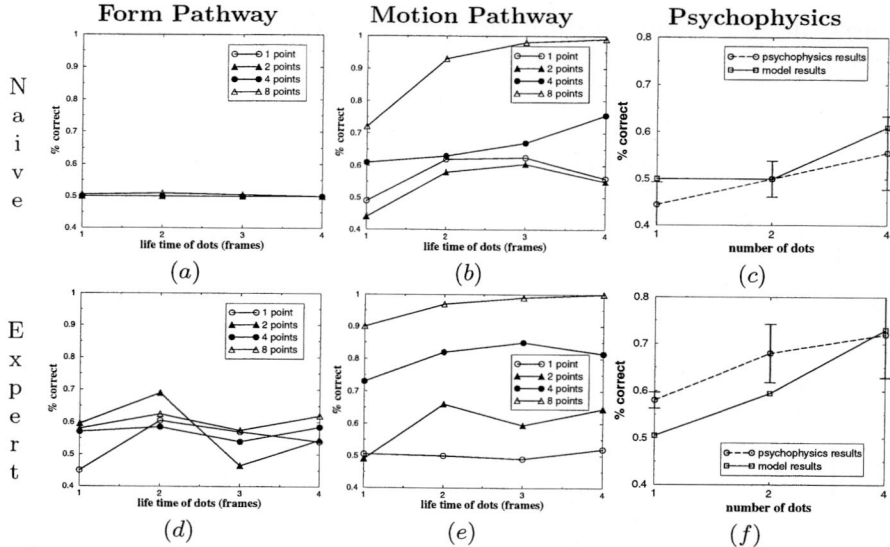

Fig. 4. Percentages of correct direction discrimination of an using either the form pathway (left column) or the motion pathway (central column). The rightmost column shows psychophysics results obtained with 3 naive (upper row) or 5 expert (lower row) subjects and recognition percentages predicted by the model. Error bars are ±1SE.

4.2 Recognition of the Sequential Position Stimulus (SPS)

In a second series of experiments we tested the capability of the model to recognize stimuli with strongly impoverished motion information (cf. Figure 1 (c)). In particular we tested the hypothesis that only form information can be used for recognizing the sequential position stimulus (SPS) [1]. We used SPS containing either 1, 2, 4 and 8 points with lifetimes 'q ranging from 1 to 4 frames. The parameters of the stimulus were closely matched with the experiments in [1].

Two different sequence selective neurons were trained with point light stimuli walking to the right or the left side. The simulated response of the subject was defined by the sequence selective neuron that was, on average, more active. The solid lines in Figure 4 show the average percentages of correct discriminations between stimuli walking leftwards and rightwards over 100 presentations obtained with the model.

Significant differences were found between the simulated naive and expert subjects. For naive subjects recognition rate was always at chance level (50%) when only form information was exploited (panel (a)). A recognition rate above chance level (up to almost 100%) was obtained with the motion pathway (panel (b)). Only expert subjects achieved a recognition rate above chance level (about 60%) using form information (panel(d)). Also for these simulated subjects the best performance was obtained with the motion pathway (panel(e)). Even for stimuli containing just 2 dots recognition was better than chance for lifetimes larger than one frame.

A first important implication of these simulations is that high recognition performances for these impoverished stimuli can be achieved with the motion pathway alone. This disproves that the form pathway is necessary for the recognition of SPS.

A major prediction from these simulations is that a considerable difference for the recognition of SPS should exist between naive and expert observers. We tested this prediction psychophysically. We exactly replicated the experiment from [1] using completely naive subjects, and subjects that had previous experience with point light walkers, but not with the SPS. Panels (c) and (f) show the comparison between our psychophysical results and the predictions from the model for SPS with one frame life time. Consistent with the prediction expert subjects show a higher performance than naive subjects[3]. The deviations between model and data for stimuli with 1 and 2 dots in panel(f) might be caused by special recognition strategies of the expert observers[4].

5 Discussion

In this paper we have used a neurophysiologically inspired model to test how form and motion (optic flow) information contribute to the recognition of biological motion stimuli. From our theoretical analysis we conclude that for the recognition of regular walker stimuli either pathway alone is computationally sufficient. Generalization to novel types of biological motion stimuli (regular vs. point light) was possible only in motion pathway of our model. The recognition of point light stimuli (even with strongly degraded motion information) did not require the form pathway. The recognition of point light stimuli required detectors for opponent motion features, whereas detectors for translational motion were not necessary. This is consistent with fMRI results showing selective activity in the opponent motion sensitive area KO during observation of biological motion (e.g. [10]). It is also consistent with data on patients with lesions in the dorsal pathway that could recognize biological motion when the lesion spared area KO [3].

The proposed model is constrained by neurophysiological results, and by the fact that it reproduces many other experimental results on biological motion recognition [2]. However, we cannot exclude that the form pathway could be changed in a way that improves its performance.

---

[3] We were not able to replicate the high recognition rates reported in [1]. This difference might be due to the fact that our subjects did not have previous experience with SPS.

[4] For example, we observed that the tilt of the spatial region that is covered by the dots over many frames allows a reliable prediction of walking direction. This strategy is not related to biological motion perception, and therefore is not predictable by our model.

We conclude that biological movement recognition under normal conditions is likely based on a fusion of cues, rather than on motion or form information alone. This seems to be particularly the case for stimuli that have been learned previously. Our theoretical study predicts a dominance of motion information for more demanding tasks, like recognition of point light and sequential position stimuli. This conclusion is consistent with results from fMRI experiments and data from neurological patients [9,4].

References

1. J. A. Beintema and M. Lappe. Perception og biological motion without local image motion. *Proceedings of the National Academy of Sciences*, 99(8):5661–5663, April 2002.
2. Martin Giese and Tomaso Poggio. Neural mechanisms for the recognition of biological motion. *Nature Reviews Neuroscience*, 4(3):179–192, March 2003.
3. Martin A. Giese and Lucia M. Vaina. Pathways in the analysis of biological motion: computational model and fmri results. In *Proceedings of the 24th European Conference on Visual Perception (ECVP)*, August 2001.
4. Emily D. Grossman and Randolph Blake. Brain areas active during visual perception of biological motion. *Neuron*, 35:1167–1175, September 2002.
5. Gunnar Johansson. Visual perception of biological motion and a model for its analysis. *Perception and Psychophysics*, 14:201–211, 1973.
6. George Mather, Kirstyn Radford, and Sophie West. Low-level visual processing of biological motion. *Proc. R. Soc. Lon. B: Biological Sciences*, 249(1325):149–155, August 1992.
7. Paul Mineiro and David Zipser. Analysis of direction selectivity arising from recurrent cortical interactions. *Neural Networks*, 10:353–371, 1998.
8. Maximilian Riesenhuber and Tomaso Poggio. Hierarchical models of object recognition in cortex. *Nature Neuroscience*, 2(11):1019–1025, November 1999.
9. Lucia M. Vaina, Marjorie Lemay, Don C. Bienfang, Albert Y. Choi, and Ken Nakayama. Intact "biological motion" and "structure from motion" perception in a patient with impaired motion mechanisms: a case study. *Visual Neuroscience*, 5(4):353–369, October 1990.
10. Lucia M. Vaina, Jeffrey Solomon, Sanjida Chowdhury, Pawan Sinha, and John W. Belliveau. Functional neuroanatomy of biological motion perception in humans. *Proceedings of the National Academy of Sciences*, 98(20):11656–11661, September 2001.

Special Sessions

Semantic and Context Aware Intelligent Systems

Improving the Performance of Resource Allocation Networks through Hierarchical Clustering of High-Dimensional Data*

Nicolas Tsapatsoulis[1], Manolis Wallace[1], and Stathis Kasderidis[2]

[1] School of Electrical and Computer Engineering
National Technical University of Athens
9, Iroon Polytechniou Str., 157 73 Zographou, Athens, Greece
{ntsap,wallace}@image.ntua.gr
http://image.ntua.gr/
[2] Department of Mathematics, King's College London, Strand, WC2R2LS, UK
stathis@mth.kcl.ac.uk
http://www.kcl.ac.uk/

Abstract. Adaptivity to non-stationary contexts is a very important property for intelligent systems in general, as well as to a variety of applications of knowledge based systems in era of "ambient intelligence". In this paper we present a modified Resource Allocating Network architecture that allows for online adaptation and knowledge modelling through its adaptive structure. As in any neural network system proper parameter initialization reduces training time and effort. However, in RAN architectures, proper parameter initialization also leads to compact modelling (less hidden nodes) of the process under examination, and consequently to better generalization. In the cases of high-dimensional data parameter initialization is both difficult and time consuming. In the proposed scheme a high – dimensional, unsupervised clustering method is used to properly initialize the RAN architecture. Clusters correspond to the initial nodes of RAN, while output layer weights are also extracted from the clustering procedure. The efficiency of the proposed method has been tested on several classes of publicly available data (iris, ionosphere, etc.).

1 Introduction

When functioning in an environment with non-stationary contexts both online training and adaptation are critical. Online adaptation during normal operation is a very complex problem because target outputs are not available. The problem is handled either by using reinforcement learning or semi-supervised techniques [1].

Resource Allocating Network (RAN) architectures [2], were found to be suitable for online modelling of non-stationary processes. In this sequential learning

---

* This work has been partially funded by the ORESTEIA IST-2000-26091/TBD project

method the network initially contains no hidden nodes. On incoming training examples, based on two criteria, either the RAN is grown, or the existing network parameters are adjusted using a least mean square gradient descent. The first criterion is based on the prediction error while the second is the novelty criterion. In the cases where hidden neurons are modelled via RBFs ,the novelty criterion states that the distance between the observation and the winning RBF neuron should be greater than a threshold. If both criteria are satisfied, then the data is memorized and a new hidden node is added to the network.

Starting from no hidden nodes is highly inefficient, since outliers in the training data may create unnecessary nodes and, therefore, increase both learning effort and convergence time and deteriorate generalization performance. Unsupervised clustering of the training data provides the means of a successful initialization of RAN architectures that initially contain RBF-type hidden nodes. Clusters can be represented through their mean vector and, either an overall spread (vector spread) or a vector of spreads, corresponding to the spread of elements in each input dimension. Clearly, such kind of parameters can be directly transferred to RBF nodes. It will be shown in subsection 2.4 that the weights connecting the hidden neurons and the output nodes of the neural network can be also easily initialized based on the clustering results.

The number of clusters that are created by an hierarchical clustering procedure does not depend solely on the data; it is also affected by the stopping criterion. In the case of RAN architectures, creating as few clusters as possible is an advantage, while in pruning techniques starting from a relatively high number of hidden nodes is not much a problem. However, in both cases, selecting the stopping criterion of data clustering is not so critical, since structured learning follows.

2 The Modified Resource Allocation Network

The RAN architecture that we adopt consists of three layers: The input layer, containing n nodes, through which an input vector $\underline{x} \in \mathcal{R}^n$ is fed to the hidden nodes, a hidden layer containing $q(t)$ RBF-type hidden nodes (at iteration t), and an output layer, containing p sigmoid nodes [3].

2.1 Learning

Learning is incorporated into the network using the gradient descent method. A squared error criterion is used as a training performance parameter. The squared error $e(t)$ at iteration t is computed in the standard way:

$$e(t) = \frac{1}{2}\sum_{k=1}^{p}(d_k(t) - y_k(t))^2$$

where $d_k(t)$ is the desired output and $y_k(t)$ is the output at node k given by:

$$y_k = \frac{1-e^{2z_k}}{1+e^{2z_k}}, \quad z_k = \underline{w}_k^T \cdot \underline{\phi}$$

where $\underline{w}_k = [w_{k1}\ w_{k2} \ldots w_{kq(t)}]^T$, $k = \in \mathcal{N}_p$, are the weights connecting the RBF neurons with the output nodes and $\underline{\phi}$ is the output of the hidden layer.

Each hidden node represents a single RBF and computes a kernel function of $\underline{x}$ according to the following equation:

$$\phi_j(\underline{x}) = exp\{-\frac{1}{2}\sum_{i=1}^{n}(\frac{x_i - \mu_{ji}}{\sigma_{ji}})^2\}$$

where $\mu_j = [\mu_{j1}, \mu_{j2} \ldots \mu_{jn}]$ and $\sigma_j = [\sigma_{j1}, \sigma_{j2} \ldots \sigma_{jn}]$ are the center and the spreads of the j-th hidden node, respectively. The output of the hidden layer is given by $\underline{\phi} = [\phi_1, \phi_2 \ldots \phi_n]$

The three parameters of the network (μ_j, σ_j, $j \in \mathcal{N}_{q(t)}$ and w_k, $k \in \mathcal{N}_p$) are modified on the basis of update equations taking the following forms:

$$w_{kj}(t+1) = w_{kj}(t) - \eta(t) \cdot a_j \frac{\vartheta e(t)}{\vartheta w_{kj}(t)} \quad (1)$$

$$\mu_{ji}(t+1) = \mu_{ji}(t) - \eta(t) \cdot a_j \frac{\vartheta e(t)}{\vartheta \mu_{ji}(t)} \quad (2)$$

$$\sigma_{ji}(t+1) = \sigma_{ji}(t) - \eta(t) \cdot a_j \frac{\vartheta e(t)}{\vartheta \sigma_{ji}(t)} \quad (3)$$

$\eta(t)$ is the online computed, decreasing with time, learning rate.

Parameter a_j in equations 1,2,3 is related with the j-th hidden node and accounts for soft competitive learning. In particular, a_j indicates the similarity between the j-th hidden node and the input pattern $\underline{x}(t)$, computed using the following equation:

$$a_j = 1 - \frac{\|\underline{x}(t) - \underline{\mu}_j\| - \|\underline{x}(t) - \underline{\mu}_{nearest}\|}{\|\underline{x}(t) - \underline{\mu}_{farthest}\| - \|\underline{x}(t) - \underline{\mu}_{nearest}\|}$$

where $\underline{\mu}_{farthest}$ and $\underline{\mu}_{nearest}$ are centers of the farthest and nearest hidden nodes from $\underline{x}(t)$ respectively, and $\|\cdot\|$ denotes the Euclidean distance.

2.2 Creating a Hidden Node

Training data are supplied to the network in the form of pairs $(\underline{x}(t), \underline{d}(t))$ of input and target vectors. If a new input $\underline{x}(t)$ does not significantly activate any hidden node and the prediction error is significantly large, a new node is created according to the following relations: $q(t) = q(t-1) + 1$, $N_{q(t)} = 1$, $\underline{\mu}_{q(t)} = \underline{x}(t)$, $\sigma_{q(t)} = k \cdot \|\underline{x}(t) - \underline{\mu}_{nearest}\|$ and $w_{kq(t)} = d_k(t) - y_k(t)$, $k \in \mathcal{N}_p$, where k is a constant (overlap factor).

2.3 Updating the Network

If the new input $x(t)$ activates at least one of the hidden nodes, or the prediction error is small, the network parameters are updated based on equations 1,2,3 and 4, 5, 6:

$$\frac{\vartheta e(t)}{\vartheta w_{kj}(t)} = \phi_j(\underline{x}(t))\{d_k(t) - y_k(t)\}\{1 - (y_k(t))^2\} \quad (4)$$

$$\frac{\vartheta e(t)}{\vartheta \mu_{ji}(t)} = \phi_j(\underline{x}(t))\frac{\{x_i(t) - \mu_{ji}(t)\}}{\sigma_{ji}^2(t)}\sum_{k=1}^{p}(w_{kj}(t)\{d_k(t) - y_k(t)\}\{1 - (y_k(t))^2\}) \quad (5)$$

$$\frac{\vartheta e(t)}{\vartheta \sigma_{ji}(t)} = \phi_j(\underline{x}(t))\frac{\{x_i(t) - \mu_{ji}(t)\}}{\sigma_{ji}^3(t)}\sum_{k=1}^{p}(w_{kj}(t)\{d_k(t) - y_k(t)\}\{1 - (y_k(t))^2\}) \quad (6)$$

2.4 Initialization of the Network Parameters

The network is initialized by setting the values of $\underline{\mu}_j$, $\underline{\sigma}_j$, $j \in \mathcal{N}_{q(t)}$ and $\underline{w}_k$, $k \in \mathcal{N}_p$, according to the results of the hierarchical clustering algorithm. In particular, the centers $\underline{\mu}_j$ of the hidden RBF neurons are obtained directly from the centers of the created clusters, while the spreads are set according to the following equation:

$$\sigma_{ji} = \sqrt{\frac{1}{N_j}\sum_{k=1}^{N_j}(\nu_{ji}^k - m_j)^2}$$

where ν_{ji} is the i-th element of the k-th vector of the j-th cluster, $\underline{m}_j$ is the center of the cluster and N_j is the number of vectors of the cluster. Weights $\underline{w}_k$ are determined by considering the way elements of detected clusters are mapped to output classes. Specifically, if $per\%$ of the elements of cluster j belong to class k, then the corresponding hidden node is linked to the class's output node with a weight of $w_{kj} = \frac{per}{100}$.

3 Hierarchical Clustering of High-Dimensional Data

When the count of clusters that exist in a data set is not known beforehand, partitioning methods are inapplicable; an hierarchical clustering algorithm needs to be applied [4]. Their general structure is as follows:

1. Turn each input element into a singleton, i.e. into a cluster of a single element.
2. For each pair of clusters c_1, c_2 calculate a compatibility indicator $CI(c_1, c_2)$. The CI is also referred to as cluster similarity, or dissimilarity, measure.
3. Merge the pair of clusters that have the best CI. Depending on whether this is a similarity or a dissimilarity measure, the best indicator could be the maximum or the minimum operator, respectively.
4. Continue at step 2, until the termination criterion is satisfied. The termination criterion most commonly used is the definition of a threshold for the value of the best compatibility indicator.

This process creates a dendrogram of partitionings on the data.

The core of this generic algorithm is the definition of a unique compatibility indicator among any pair of clusters. When the input space has more than one dimensions, an aggregating distance function, such as Euclidean distance, is typically used as the CI. This, of course, is not always meaningful. Cases exist, in which the "context" can change the similarity or dissimilarity measure to be used. In such cases, a selection of distance function among elements needs to be performed, prior to calculating a CI among clusters.

Real elements are usually grouped together semantically, based on their similarity in a single or a few features. When the total number of features is high, small distances in a small subset of them barely affect the overall distance, when an aggregation of distances in all features is used. Thus, only when the correct subset of features is considered, can elements be compared correctly. In this paper we tackle feature selection based on the following principle: while we expect elements of a given set to have random distances from one another according to most features, we expect them to have small distances according to the features that relate them. We rely on this difference in distribution of distance values in order to identify the *context*, i.e. the features that most probably relate a set of elements.

More formally, let c_1 and c_2 be two clusters of elements. Let also r_i, $i \in \mathcal{N}_F$ be the metric that compares the i-th feature, and F the count of features (the dimension of the input space). A distance (dissimilarity) measure between the two clusters, when considering the i-th feature, is given by

$$f_i(c_1, c_2) = \sqrt[\kappa]{\frac{\sum_{a \in c_1, b \in c_2}[r_i(a_i, b_i)]^\kappa}{|c_1||c_2|}}$$

where e_i is the i-th feature of element e, $|c|$ is the cardinality of cluster c and $\kappa \in R$ is a constant.

The context is a selection of features to consider when calculating an overall distance value. We can define it as a vector $\underline{x}$ of $\mathcal{R}_F^+$, with $\sum_{i=1}^{F} x_i = 1$. Then the overall distance between c_1 and c_2 is calculated as

$$d(c_1, c_2) = \sum_{i=1}^{F}[x_i(c_1, c_2)]^\lambda f_i(c_1, c_2)$$

where $\lambda \in R$ is a constant and x_i is the degree to which f_i is included in the context.

The features that relate c_1 and c_2 are "most probably" the ones that produce the smallest distances f_i. Therefore, the "correct" context can be calculated as the context that produces the best (smallest) overall distance.

When $\lambda = 1$ the optimization is trivial: the feature that produces the smallest distance is the only one selected. The degree to which it is selected is 1. If more than one features produce the best distance, then they are equally selected, as there is no information as to which should be favored.

Table 1. Classification rates and numbers of hidden nodes

	No training	Random	Bayesian	Pre-clustering
Number of rules	3	6	5	3
Classification rate	87.33%	96%	97.3	98%

When $\lambda \neq 1$ and $f_i(c_1, c_2) \neq 0 \forall i \in \mathcal{N}_F$, then it is easy to prove that the best context is given by:

$$x_1(c_1, c_2) = \frac{1}{\sum_{i=1}^{F}[\frac{f_1(c_1,c_2)}{f_i(c_1,c_2)}]^{\frac{1}{\lambda-1}}} \quad \text{and} \quad x_i(c_1, c_2) = x_1 [\frac{f_i(c_1,c_2)}{f_1(c_1,c_2)}]^{\frac{1}{\lambda-1}}$$

where $i \in \mathcal{N}_F$. Proof is omitted for the sake of space.

When $\lambda \neq 1$ and $\exists i \in \mathcal{N}_F : f_i(c_1, c_2) = 0$, then the features for which $f_i(c_1, c_2) = 0$ are the ones the are (equally) selected.

As λ increases, pairs of clusters that are related by fewer features, and thus have greater values in their contexts, are obviously assigned greater distances. It order for distances to be used as compatibility indicators it is, of course, imperative that they are transformed as to become directly comparable to each other, even when different contexts are used for different pairs of clusters. Therefore, the following compatibility indicator is used:

$$CI(c_1, c_2) = \frac{d(c_1, c_2)}{x_\lambda(c_1, c_2)} \quad \text{where} \quad x_\lambda(c_1, c_2) = \sum_{i=1}^{F}[x_i(c_1, c_2)]^\lambda$$

As far as the termination criterion is concerned, a threshold on the growth rate of value of CI is used. In other words, when the best CI starts increasing rapidly, we conclude that all valid clusters have already been detected and are starting to be merged with each other. Therefore, the algorithm terminates.

The average values of features of a detected cluster c_j form the centroid $m_j = [m_{j1}, m_{j1} \ldots m_{jF}]$, i.e. a "virtual" element that is located in the center of the cluster. In this equation, m_{ji} is given by $m_{ji} = \frac{\sum_{a \in c_j} a_i}{|c_j|}$

4 Experimental Results

In order to demonstrate the efficiency of the proposed scheme, we have applied it to several well known data sets. The iris data set contains 150 elements, characterized by 4 features, that belong to three classes; two of these classes are not linearly separable from each other. This is a relatively easy data set, as the number of clusters in the data is equal to the number of classes. For testing purposes, a part of the set was used as training data.

Four different experiments were carried out for the iris data set:

- The network was initialized as described in subsection 2.4, based on the results of the clustering, and was not trained.

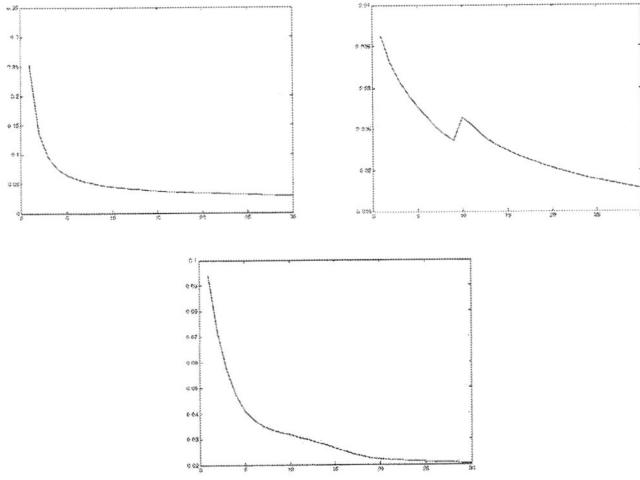

Fig. 1. MSE as a function of epochs: (a)random initialization (b) bayesian initialization (c) with pre-clustering

- The network was initialized with three random hidden nodes
- A bayesian approach was used. Specifically, the three existing classes were used as clusters, and the network was initialized as described in subsection 2.4.
- The network was initialized as described in subsection 2.4, based on the results of the clustering.

As can be seen in Figure 1, where the MSE is presented as a function of the number of epochs, random initialization has an upper bound of performance, which is probably caused by a local minimum that the network has to overcome. Properly initialized approaches, on the other hand, progress much better. The bayesian approach seems to be better, as far as MSE during the first epochs is concerned, but only the network that was initialized using the high – dimensional pre-clustering continues to improve drastically. After a few epochs (about 20), the proposed scheme has an MSE that is considerably lower that those of different approaches.

Moreover, Table 1 presents the classification rate and the number of hidden nodes in the final network. The first remark we can make is that the network that was not trained performed much worse than others, indicating that training is necessary for this data set. As far as the classification rate and the number of rules are concerned, our method converges to a network of just three rules, no more than the classes of the problem, while not loosing in performance when compared to networks with larger numbers of hidden nodes. In addition to the experiments presented herein, our method outperforms others in the literature as well (7 rules, 96.7% [5]) (17 rules, 95.3% [6]) (9 rules, 95.3% [7]) (7 rules, 96% [8]).

Similar results are observer for other data sets as well. Especially for the ionosphere data set, which is clearly a high dimensional data set (it is characterized by 34 features), simpler initialization approaches, such as the bayesian approach, have proven to be totally ineffective.

5 Conclusions

In this paper, we combine an hierarchical clustering algorithm with a modified Resource Allocation Network in order to properly initialize the network parameters and especially the RBF nodes of the hidden layer. RANs are dynamically formed architectures and, thus, provide the means to model non-stationary phenomena. On the other hand, proper initialization serves two purposes: (a) Reduces the learning effort, (b) keeps the number of hidden nodes low and increases generalization performance; this is highly desirable since in RBF networks one may consider the hidden nodes to be "rules" and therefore use the RAN architecture for knowledge extraction from numerical data [9]. The latter is very important since there are several domains in which no estimation about the number of rules that are required to solve a particular problem is available. Moreover, "rules" can be created to model a changing context, given the dynamic nature of RANs.

The classification performance of the proposed network turns out to be excellent. When initiated with three hidden nodes, based on the results of the high – dimensional clustering, outperforms the majority of the soft-computing schemes that were tested on the iris classification problem. It performs similarly in other data sets as well, especially as the dimensionality of the input space increases.

References

1. Vapnik, V.: Statistical Learning Theory. John Willey and sons (1998)
2. Platt, J.: A resource-allocating network for function interpolation. Neural Computing **3**, (1991) 213–225
3. Lee, K., Street, W. N.: Intelligent Image Analysis using adaptive resource allocating networks. Procs of IEEE International Workshop on NN for Signal Processing (2001)
4. Theodoridis, S., Koutroumbas, K.: Pattern Recognition, Academic Press (1998)
5. Nauk, D., Kruse, R.: A neuro-fuzzy method to learn fuzzy classification rules from data. Fuzzy sets and Systems **8** (1997) 277–288
6. Kasabov, N., Woodford, B.: Rule insertion and rule extraction from evolving fuzzy neural networks: Algorithms and applications for building adaptive, intelligent, expert systems. Procs of FUZZ-IEEE'99, (1999) 1406–1411
7. Kasabov, N.: Learning fuzzy rules and approximate reasoning in fuzzy neural networks and hybrid systems. Fuzzy Sets and Systems **82**, (1996) 135–149
8. Halgamuge, S., Glesner, M.: Neural Networks in designing fuzzy systems for real world applications. Fuzzy Sets and Systems **65**, (1994) 1–12
9. Mitra, S., DE, R.K., Pal, S.K.: knowledge-based fuzzy MLP for classification and rule generation. IEEE Trans. Neural Networks **8**,(1997) 1338–1350

Learning Rule Representations from Boolean Data[*]

B. Apolloni[1], A. Brega[1], D. Malchiodi[1], G. Palmas[2], and A.M. Zanaboni[1]

[1] Dipartimento di Scienze dell'Informazione, Università degli Studi di Milano
Via Comelico 39/41, 20135 Milano, Italy
{apolloni,malchiodi,zanaboni}@dsi.unimi.it, andrea@laren.dsi.unimi.it
[2] ST Microelectronics s.r.l., Agrate Brianza (Milano)
giorgio.palmas@st.com

Abstract. We discuss a Probably Approximate Correct (PAC) learning paradigm for Boolean formulas, which we call PAC meditation, where the class of formulas to be learnt is not known in advance. We split the building of the hypothesis in various levels of increasing description complexity according to additional inductive biases received at run time. In order to give semantic value to the learnt formulas, the key operational aspect represented is the understandability of formulas, which requires their simplification at any level of description. We deepen this aspect in light of two alternative simplification methods, which we compare through a case study.

1 Introduction

PAC learning [1] is a very efficient approach for selecting a function within a class of Boolean functions (call them concepts) on the basis of a set of examples of how this function computes. In this paper we will consider an extension of this approach to the case that the class of concepts is not known at the beginning of the learning procedure. Rather we receive requisites of the class a little at a time in subsequent steps of the learning process. Thus at runtime we must be sure of both correctly updating current knowledge on the basis of new requisites and suitably reinterpreting examples in the light of this knowledge, so that the approximation of the hypothesis on the final concept and its readability are not compromised. We learn Boolean formulas through a multi-level procedure that we call *PAC-meditation*:

- at the ground level we have two sets of positive (label 1) and negative (label 0) examples. From subsets of examples with a same label we compute partial consistent hypotheses. Namely each hypothesis is consistent with (i.e. computes the correct labels of) a part of the positive examples and all negative examples, or *vice versa*. The union of the former constitutes an *inner border*

---

[*] Work partially funded by E.C. contract No. IST-2000-26091, "ORESTEIA: mOdular hybRid artEfactS wiTh adaptivE functIonAlity".

and the intersection of the latter an *outer border*. The two nested regions delimit a gap where we look for consistent hypotheses. In Fig. 1 the gap is represented by the dashed area.
– at further abstraction levels the partial consistent hypotheses of the preceding level play the role of labelled examples, where the sampled data are substituted by formulas and the positive and negative labels are substituted by a flag which denotes whether these formulas belong to the inner or outer border. We construct a new pair of borders running the same procedure on the so represented examples (these borders are contoured by bold lines in Fig. 1), with the double benefit of both reducing the gap between the border and increasing their understrandability through the introduction of new symbols.

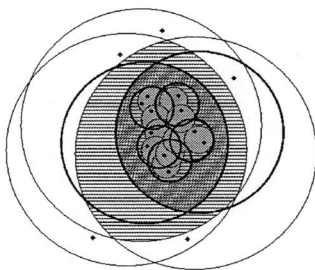

Fig. 1. Inner and outer borders, in the sample space, of a concept at two abstraction levels. Inner borders are delimited by the union of formulas bounded by positive examples (gray circles with thin contour at ground level), outer borders by the intersection of formulas bounded by negative examples (white circles with thin contour at ground level). Bold lines describe higher level formulas. Bullets: positive examples; diamonds: negative examples.

The idea of fitting the formula within minimum and maximum hypotheses is well known in the literature, and acquainted from various perspectives [2] [3]. The formula simplification is performed according to an optimality criterion. We propose one entropic method and an altrernative one based on fuzzy relaxation; numerical case studies show that the latter one proves faster achieving almost the same accuracy as the former. The paper is organized as follows. In section 2 we describe the learning procedure, in section 3 its performance is discussed, and the last section is devoted to concluding remarks.

2 The Inference Process

Let us denote by $X_n \equiv \{0,1\}^n$ the space of boolean vectors $\mathbf{x}$ of size n that can be assigned to the set of propositional variables from $V_n = \{v_1, \ldots, v_n\}$, and by g^* the target of our learning procedure. The block diagram of the inference process is shown in Fig. 2. Given a set of positive and negative examples the procedure core consists of the iterated activation of an *abstraction module* made up of two steps: i) a *Symbols' jump*, where we introduce new symbols to describe (Boolean) properties on the points by the search for an inner and an outer border; and ii) a *Reduction* step, which is devoted to broadening or narrowing these hypotheses with: i) the constraint of not violating consistency; and ii) the aim of narrowing the gap between borders through a simplified version of them. At each abstraction level we may restart the two steps after assuming the minimal hypotheses as positive *meta*points at the previous level, maximal hypotheses as negative metapoints, and searching for new *meta*symbols to describe properties on these points. To avoid tautologies, the new abstraction level must be enriched by pieces of symbolic knowledge that are now available about the properties we want to discover and that translate into additional constraints in rebuilding the borders. Once we are satisfied with the achieved abstraction level (or simply do not plan attaining new formal knowledge), the *Level test* in Fig. 2 addresses us to the *Synthesis step*. Here we collapse the two borders into a single definite formula lying between them which we assume as representative of the properties on the random population we observed.

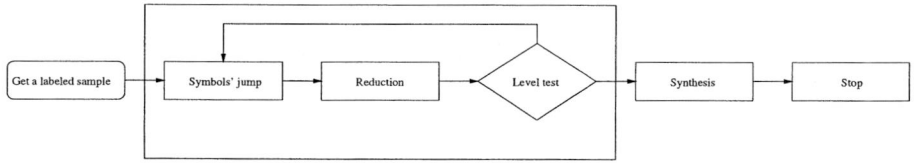

Fig. 2. Block diagram of PAC-meditation.

2.1 Symbol's Jump

Ground level. Starting from $\mathbf{X}_n$, we construct the atomic components of 0-level borders, which we call *canonical monomials* and *clauses*. They are respectively product and sum of propositional variables from V_n. Denoting set(g) the set of literals used by the formula g, we describe the canonical formulas as follows.

Definition 1. *i) given $\mathbf{X}_n$ and a set E^+ of positive examples, a monotone monomial* m *with arguments in V_n is a* canonical monomial *if there exists $\mathbf{x} \in E^+$ such that for each $i \in \{1, \ldots, n\}$, $v_i \in$ set(m) if $x_i = 1$, and $v_i \notin$ set(m) otherwise. ii) given $\mathbf{X}_n$ and a set E^- of negative examples, a monotone clause* c *with arguments in V_n is a* canonical clause *if there exists $\mathbf{x} \in E^-$ such that for each $i \in \{1, \ldots, n\}$, $v_i \in$ set(c) if $x_i = 0$ and $v_i \notin$ set(c) otherwise.*

These formulas do not constrain the final expression of the target g^* of the learning procedure (that we asume to be a monotone formula). Infact, any

Boolean formula on the binary hypercube can be represented either through the union of monomials (DNF) or through the intersection of clauses (CNF). They just represent a set of points that necessarily must belong to g^* given a positive example, or cannot belong to it given a negative one.

First abstraction level. The jump to the first abstraction level is done as follows. Applying the distributive property to the union of two monomials

$$v_i v_j v_k \vee v_l v_m v_n v_r = (v_i \vee v_l v_m) \wedge (v_i \vee v_n v_r) \wedge (v_j v_k \vee v_l v_m) \wedge (v_j v_k \vee v_n v_r) \tag{1}$$

we obtain a new monomial where literals are constituted by clauses and, in turn, literals in the clauses are substituted by monomials. We generalize the operation, keeping groups of at most k_2 monomials and splitting them in such a way that at most k_1 metaclauses arise. As a consequence each metaclause is the union of k_2 monomials. Bounds on k's stand for requisites of conciseness on the formula description, i.e. for a compression of our knowledge that constitutes the true *inductive bias* [4] of our procedure. We do the same with metaclauses.

Climbing abstraction levels. Denoting $\cup^t = \cap^{t-1} = \cap$ if t is odd and $\neq 0$, $\cup$ otherwise, for $t \geq 0$, at the Lth abstraction level we obtain formulas belonging to the families of meta_L_monomials $\mathbf{G}_{n;k_0,k_1,\ldots,k_{\nu-1}}$ and meta_L_clauses $\mathcal{G}_{n;k_0,k_1,\ldots,k_{\nu-1}}$ whose elements g can be written respectively as follows, for $\nu = 2L$, $k'_i \leq k_i$ for each $i < \nu$, $k'_\nu \in \mathbb{N}$ and suitable q

$$g = \begin{cases} \bigcup_{j_0=1}^{k'_0}{}^1 \bigcup_{j_1=1}^{k'_1}{}^2 \cdots \bigcup_{j_\nu=1}^{k'_\nu}{}^{\nu+1} v_{q(j_0,j_1,\ldots,j_\nu)} & \text{for the former and} \\ \bigcup_{j_0=1}^{k'_0}{}^0 \bigcup_{j_1=1}^{k'_1}{}^1 \cdots \bigcup_{j_\nu=1}^{k'_\nu}{}^\nu v_{q(j_0,j_1,\ldots,j_\nu)} & \text{for the latter} \end{cases} \tag{2}$$

In short, we pass from one level to the next adding a pair of operations of the "∩∪" kind for metamonomials and "∪∩" for metaclauses.

2.2 Reduction Step

At a given abstraction level, the *Symbol's Jump* block leaves us with a pair of borders within which any function is a candidate hypothesis for the goal concept g^*. We adopted the general strategy of obtaining the new pair through incremental changes in the original ones that do not induce a trespassing of the inner border beside the outer one, and *vice versa*. Selection of the best simplifications is managed in terms of an optimization task. Two possible approaches (mutual information maximization and fuzzy relaxation) are described in the following.

Mutual information maximization (Fitness Maximization, FM). Given the set of (meta)monomials constituting the inner border, let us focus on monomial a and on any other of the remaining monomials that we denote by b_i. Thus $\mathsf{a} \cup_i \mathsf{b}_i$ is the inner border that contains all n^+ positive points. Let us denote by

A the event: a point belongs to $\mathbf{a}$, and B the event: a point belongs to $\mathbf{b}_i$, for a given i. We mean by H_A the entropy associated to the first partition and by $\mathrm{H}_{A/B}$ the conditional entropy associated to the first partition conditioned to the second one.

The mutual information [5] $\mathrm{I}_{A,B} = \mathrm{H}_A - \mathrm{H}_{A/B}$ can be estimated as in [6]: We numerically discovered [6] that in learning formulas it is suitable to go in the direction of maximizing the mutual information, which is a direction opposite to what is usually suggested (see for instance [7]). In line with [8], the rationale for our strategy lies in the fact that formulas with high mutual information discover a strong structure within data, a structure that we may expect to be preserved in the new unseen data.

Fuzzy relaxation (FR). As an alternative, we may decide to broaden the contours of the inner and outer borders balancing a desirable shortening of the formula f with the undesirable loss of its description power [9]. We account for this trade-off by minimizing a cost function $O(f, \boldsymbol{\lambda})$ that takes into account the formula length and the radious of its fuzzy border, as follows.

Definition 2. *Given a monomial m, for an ordered sequence $\mathbf{d} = (d_1, \ldots, d_\ell)$ of length ℓ of literals from $\mathrm{set}(m)$, let us denote by $\mathbf{d}^k$ its prefix of length k. Let $m_{\mathbf{d}^0} = m$, and $m_{\mathbf{d}^k}$ denote the monomial obtained by flipping from 1 to 0 the crisp membership value of literal d_k in $m_{\mathbf{d}^{k-1}}$. Let us denote $\sigma(\mathbf{d}^k)$ the cardinality of the E subset belonging to $m_{\mathbf{d}^k}$-m. We define the (fuzzy) membership function $\mu_{m_\mathbf{d}}(d_k)$ of a literal d_k in respect to $m_\mathbf{d}$ as follows*

$$\mu_{m_\mathbf{d}}(d_k) = 1 - \frac{\sigma(\mathbf{d}^k)}{\sigma(\mathbf{d})} \qquad (3)$$

An anlogous definition can be given for clauses. In a local interpretation of the membership function we can consider $\mu_{m_\mathbf{d}}(d_k)$ as a probability estimate of finding points that belong to the fuzzy frontier outside the enlargement induced by d_k, and we can define the radius of the frontier as the mean value of the distances of points belonging to each enlargement slice from the crisp monomial m as follows.

Definition 3. *Given a monomial m_i and an ordered sequence $\mathbf{d}_i = (d_1, \ldots, d_\ell)$ of length ℓ of literals from $\mathrm{set}(m_i)$, we call $m_\mathbf{d} - m_i$ the fuzzy frontier of m_i, and*

$$\rho_i = \sum_{k=1}^{\ell} \mu_{m_\mathbf{d}}(d_k) \qquad (4)$$

its radius.

The cost function we want to minimize with respect to the formula f is:

$$O(f, \boldsymbol{\lambda}) = \lambda_1 \sum_{i=1}^{m} L_i + \lambda_2 \sum_{i=1}^{m} \rho_i + \lambda_3 \nu_0 \qquad (5)$$

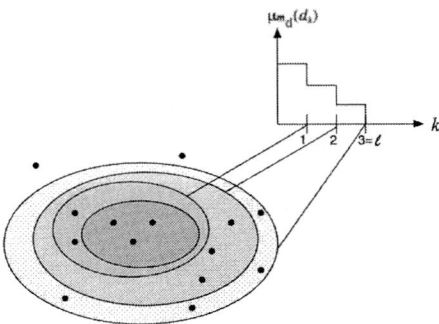

Fig. 3. The fuzzy border of a monomial. Dark region → m; lessening gray regions → progressive enlargements after removal of d_1, d_2, and d_3 from set(m); $\mu_{m_d}(d_k)$ as in Definition 2.

where: $\boldsymbol{\lambda} = (\lambda_1, \lambda_2, \lambda_3)$; f is an inner or outer border; $\sum_i L_i$ is the length of the formula, being L_i the number of literals in the ith atomic formula; ν_0 is the percentage of positive examples left out of the support of f (a short way for accounting the dummy monomial cost).

3 Numerical Results

We discuss effectiveness of our procedure on an artificial instance consisting in recovering formulas in the polynomial hierarchy. The experiments are aimed at learning DNFs on 12 propositional variables drawn randomly in order to have a number of terms ranging between 2 and 7. We considered 100 such formulas. For each of them we generate two kinds of training sets containing 100 examples equally partitioned in positive and negative ones. In the unbiased training set assignments of values 0 or 1 to all the propositional variables are made with same probability 0.5. In the biased training set, instead, value 1 is assigned with probability 0.7 to 4 randomly selected propositional variables, and with probability 0.5 for the others. The test set is constituted by the whole set of 4096 different 12 long Boolean vectors labeled according to the DNF to be recovered. Table 1 reports comparative performances of: a) *PACmed*itation using *FM*, b) *PACmed*itation using *FR*, c) C4.5 [10], the well spread concept learning algorithm, where a decision tree in terms of IF-THEN-ELSE rules is drawn directly by iterated partitioning of the sampled data on the basis of mutually exclusive tests on their range. Performances are evaluated in terms of: i) residual indeterminacy, measured by the number of test set points falling in the gap between inner and outer borders (column *Gap*); ii) compression rate between original and rediscovered formulas (column ρ); and iii) test set classification accuracy.

Concerning accuracy, in methods *FM* and *FR* if we consider correctly classified the points falling in the gap, we get a lower bound to the error percentage (column FFN); if we consider them incorrectly classified, we get an upper bound

Table 1. Comparing the performances of *PACmed*itation, in the *FM* and *FR* release, and C4.5. μ and σ are mean and standard deviation over 100 trials. *Gap* between inner and outer border is measured in number of points falling inside it; ρ is the ratio between the found and original rule lengths; FP, FFP, FN, FFN are percentages of False Positives, Fuzzy False Positives, False Negatives, and Fuzzy False Negatives, respectively. Level 0 and Level 1 are the abstraction levels of PAC meditation; C4.5 results are conventionally reported in the Level 1

			Level 0					Level 1					
			Gap	ρ	FP	FFP	FN	FFN	Gap	ρ	FP	FFP	FN	FFN
FM PACmed	unbias.	μ	23.42	1.22	6.25	5.53	2.61	2.55	11.77	0.63	6.25	5.89	2.58	2.55
		σ	38.34	0.49	4.5	4.11	2.95	2.93	23.86	0.23	4.5	4.4	2.95	2.93
	biased	μ	29.67	1.3	6.85	5.99	3.57	3.35	13.21	0.67	6.85	6.45	3.49	3.35
		σ	37.6	0.6	4.76	4.46	3.47	3.49	21.59	0.28	4.76	4.61	3.54	3.49
FR PACmed	unbias.	μ	149.09	0.93	10.23	5.59	2.53	1.73	124.9	0.78	10.23	6.29	2.17	1.73
		σ	114.1	0.32	6.13	4.87	2.16	2.44	103.9	0.36	6.13	5.05	2.61	2.44
	biased	μ	131.1	0.94	9.9	5.89	2.69	1.73	112.4	0.8	9.9	6.48	2.52	1.73
		σ	109.7	0.35	6.46	5.03	2.9	2.11	104.3	0.31	6.46	5.19	2.7	2.11
C4.5	unbias	μ							1.13		8.45		5.58	
		σ							0.48		6.95		4.72	
	biased	μ							1.2		7.25		6.09	
		σ							0.51		6.51		4.93	

in the (column FN). The same happens with the negative points, for which FFP and FP percentages are defined analogously.

Concerning compression rate, the better behavior of the disjunctive representation is due to the fact that the original formula is a disjunctive form too.

The jump to abstraction level 1 improves all parameters with the sole exception of some accuracy indices. Actually we have a slight increase of the FFP percentages, since the inner border still expands, while FP and FFN remain unchanged such as the outer border.

A slight degradation of all performance indices is registered when we pass from unbiased to biased samples.

The greatest reason for employing *FR*, however, lies in the computing time. Its average in all these trials is 3.6 seconds (with almost 0 variance) on a Pentium IV as a reference architecture, which is one order less than the time (around 72 seconds) taken for *FM*. With these running times we may compete with the C4.5 algorithm ([7]). Table 1 shows that the description lengths of formulas obtained by C4.5 are meanly from 1.3 to 1.9 times greater than those provided by *FR*, with almost equal accuracy, obtained in an average time of 0.03 seconds running a program written in a language compiled into bytecode (while C4.5 is written in a language compiled into machine language).

The fact that standard deviations are almost equal to the means denotes the presence of some rare hard instances causing very high values of the indices, balancing a higher concentration of all the other cases which follow within at most 1 standard deviation from the mean.

4 Conclusions

Confining an unknown function f between one tight and one weak hypothesis is a usual way for the human brain to infer properties about the function and then take operational decisions. It is a functional extension of the confidence interval notion, thus based on statistics on the observed examples. In absence of any indication about f we commit to the example the sole role of watching for inconsistencies. Deciding to bind f through monotone formulas awards the watching points the connotation of delimiters of wide regions in the Boolean hypercube. We transfer to these regions the role of examples of f and make them more and more complex through the addition of some syntactical constraints. This is the main idea of our meditation process. By definition, under the monotonicity assumption, no negative point can be found inside the inner border and no positive point outside the outer one. Then to render the formulas understandable we accept the compromise of reducing the sharpness of the borders. The primary idea is to modify their shape maintaining a robust common structure. This gives rise to an algorithm for learning concepts that proves quite accurate when a monotone formula really underlies the data. Although it does not find the best fitting of the data, the structure it finds underlying them pays in terms of robustness versus the randomness of the training set.

References

1. Valiant L.: A Theory of the Learnable. Communications of the ACM, Vol. 27 (1984) 1134–1142
2. Mitchell, T. M.: Machine Learning. McGraw-Hill Series in Computer Science.The McGraw-Hill Companies, Inc., New York (1997).
3. Selman, B., Kautz, H.: Knowledge compilation and theory approximation. In: Journal of the ACM, Vol. 43. (1996) 193–224
4. Michalski,R. S.: A theory and methodology of inductive learning. In: Machine Learning: An Artificial Intelligence Approach. J. G. Carbonell and T. M. Mitchell (eds.) Tioga, Palo Alto (1983) 83–134
5. Cover, T., Thomas, J.: Elements of information theory, Wiley, New York (1991).
6. Apolloni, B. and Malchiodi, D. and Orovas, C. and Palmas, G.: From synapses to rules. In: Cognitive Systems Research, Vol. 3/2 (2002) 167–201
7. Qunilan, J. R.: C4.5: programs for machine learning. Morgan Kaufmann Publishers. San Mateo, California (1993)
8. Orovas, C. and Austin, J.: A Cellular Neural Associative Array for Symbolic Vision. In: Wermter, S. and Sun, R. (eds.): Hybrid Neural Systems. Springer-Verlag, Berlin Heidelberg New York (2000) 372–386
9. Vapnik V.: The Nature of Statistical Learning Theory. Springer-Verlag, Berlin Heidelberg New York(1995)
10. Ross Quinlan Home Page. http://www.cse.unsw.edu.au/~quinlan/

Weighted Self-Organizing Maps: Incorporating User Feedback

Andreas Nürnberger[1] and Marcin Detyniecki[2][*]

[1] University of California at Berkeley, EECS, Computer Science Division
Berkeley, CA 94720, USA
anuernb@eecs.berkeley.edu
[2] CNRS, Laboratoire d'Informatique de Paris 6, University of Paris 6,
8, rue du Capitaine Scott, 75015 Paris, France
Marcin.Detyniecki@lip6.fr

Abstract. One interesting way of accessing collections of multimedia objects is by methods of visualization and clustering. Growing self-organizing maps provide such a solution, which adapts automatically to the underlying database. Unfortunately, the result of the clustering greatly depends on the definition of the describing features and the used similarity measure. In this paper, we present a general approach to improve the obtained clustering by incorporating user feedback (in the form of drag-and-drop) into the underlying topology of the self-organizing map.

1 Introduction

Today large archives of text, images, audio and/or video sequences are available. In order to access a specific object a great number of indexing methods have been developed. Almost all of these methods are based on a numerical data space, i.e. an index is computed, which is a numerical feature vector that describes the objects. For instance, text documents are frequently indexed by selected key terms and then each term is represented by a number in a dictionary vector. Another examples are images that can be described by color histograms, which are also represented as numerical vectors.

Unfortunately, the existing methods are not aware of either the context or the user preferences. In prior work we implemented a document retrieval system based on growing self-organizing maps [7, 8]. These maps are built based on the provided database taking into account not only neighboring documents, but also introducing new words to the index, if they are considered as relevant. All this, depending completely on the learning context (i.e. the database used for training). Thus, the system automatically enables a user to visualize, search and navigate in arbitrary document collections that can be represented by numerical vectors.

In this article we go one step further. We present an extension of our system that makes it aware of user-feedback in order to adapt the classification of documents. In the following we give a brief introduction to self-organizing systems and the used

---

[*] Both authors contributed equally to this work.

document retrieval system. Then, we outline two complementary learning methods based on user-feedback and a generalized version of these methods. These algorithms were implemented in an interactive image retrieval system.

2 Self-Organizing Systems

Self-organizing maps [3] are a special architecture of neural networks that clusters high-dimensional data vectors according to a similarity measure. The clusters are arranged in a low-dimensional topology that preserves the neighborhood relations in the high dimensional data. Thus, not only objects that are assigned to one cluster are similar to each other (as in every cluster analysis), but also objects of nearby clusters are expected to be more similar than objects of distant clusters. Usually, two-dimensional grids of squares or hexagons are used. Although other topologies are possible, two-dimensional maps have the advantage of an intuitive visualization and thus good exploration possibilities.

Several applications have been proposed for the usage of the maps for the classification and exploration of collections of text documents, images or speech data. Our approach for document retrieval [4] combines conventional keyword search methods with several SOM-based views on the document collection to allow interactive exploration.

In this paper we will focus on different extensions of the basic algorithm in order to allow the integration of user-feedback. Other previous extensions of our model include the implementation of growing self-organizing maps, which eliminates the necessity to define the map size manually, leading to more appropriate mappings of the objects [7, 8]. In [10] we discussed how the system could be applied to collections of objects other than text documents.

2.1 Using the Maps

The SOM algorithm can be applied to arbitrary document collections, as far as a vector description of the considered objects is given. However, it is essential that the vector consists of object features that represent the characteristics of the objects appropriately and that the used vector-similarity translates a real similarity for the objects. More on the construction of the maps, for instance on the training algorithm, can be found in [2]. Here we focus just on the extension.

A trained map represents a clustering of the object collection. A browsable list of objects can be assigned to every grid cell. A screenshot of our implementation for text document retrieval is shown in Fig. 1.

The user can interact with the map by querying by keyword or by example. In both cases the answer to the query will be a particular coloring of the map. For instance, this coloring can translate the similarity of the query to each cell[1]. The user can simply navigate taking into account that the map was built so that similar documents are close to each other.

---

[1] Further details on coloring methods can be found in, e.g., [1, 6].

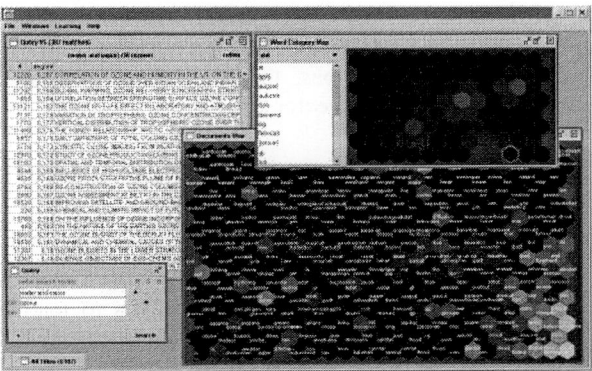

Fig. 1. A text document retrieval system based on the proposed approach [4].

3 Incorporating User Feedback

To allow the user to give feedback information, the tool was extended such that a user can drag one or several objects from one node of the map to another, which in his opinion is more appropriate for the considered objects. Furthermore, the user can mark objects that should remain at a specific node, thus preventing the algorithm from moving them together with the moved object during re-computing the document allocations on the map.
In the following, we describe two user-feedback models that have been designed to solve specific clustering problems [11]. These two approaches modify the underlying similarity measure by increasing or decreasing the importance of individual features.

3.1 Learning a Global Feature Weighting

For the implementation of a global feature weighting scheme, we replaced the Euclidean similarity function used for the computation of the winner nodes by a weighted similarity measure. Therefore, the distance of a given feature vector to the feature vectors of the prototypes is computed by

$$e_s = \left(\sum_i w^i \cdot (x_s^i - y_k^i)^2 \right)^{\frac{1}{2}} \quad (1)$$

where w is a weight vector, y_k the feature vector of an document k and x_s the prototypical feature vector assigned to a node s.
We update the global-weight vector w based on the differences of the feature vectors of the moved document and the vectors of the origin node and of the target node. The goal is to increase the weights of similar features between the document and target node and to decrease the weights of similar features between the document and its

current node. And symmetrically decrease and increase the weights of dissimilar features.

Let y_i be the feature vector of an document i, s be the source and t the target node, x_s and x_t be the corresponding prototypes, then w is computed as described in the following. First we compute an error vector e for each object based on the distance to the prototypes

$$e_{ji}^k = |d_{ji}^k|, \forall k \text{ , where } d_{ji} = \frac{y_i - x_j}{\|y_i - x_j\|} \quad (2)$$

If we want to ensure that an object is moved from the source node to the target node using feature weights, we have to assign higher weights to features that are more similar to the target than to the source node. Thus for each object we compute the difference of the distance vectors

$$f_i = e_{si} - e_{ti} \quad (3)$$

The global weight vector is finally computed iteratively. For the initial weight vector we choose $w^{(0)} = w_1$, where w_1 is a vector where all elements are equal one. Then we compute a new global weight vector $w^{(t+1)}$ by doing a by element multiplication:

$$w^{k(t+1)} = w^{k(t)} \cdot w_i, \forall k \text{ with } w_i = (w_1 + \eta \cdot f_i), \quad (4)$$

where η is a learning rate. The global weight is modified until – if possible – all moved objects are finally mapped to the target node. A pseudocode description of this approach is given in Fig. 2.

Obviously, this weighting approach also affects the assignments of all other documents. The idea is to interactively find a feature weighting scheme that improves the overall classification performance of the map. Without a feature weighting approach the map considers all features equally important.

The global weights can also be used to identify features that the user considers important or less important. If, for example, text documents are used where the features represents terms, then we might get some information about the keywords that the user seems to consider important for the classification of the documents.

3.2 Learning a Local Weighting Scheme

The global weighting scheme emphasizes on general characteristics, which support a good overall grouping of the data collection. Unfortunately, this may lead to large groups of cells with quite similar documents. In this case some features – which are of less importance on a global scope – might be useful for distinguishing between local characteristics. Thus, modifying locally the weights assigned to these features might improve the assignment of the documents to more specific *local* classes.

The proposed learning method used is quite similar to the method described above. However, instead of modifying the global weight w, we modify local weights assigned to the source and the target nodes (noted here w_s and w_t).

As before we first compute an error vector e for each document based on the distance to the prototypes, as defined in equation (2).

```
Compute the weight vectors w_i;
If the global weight vector w is undefined, create
        a vector and initialize all elements to one;
cnt = 0;
Repeat until all documents are moved or cnt > max
        cnt++;
        For all documents i to be moved do
                Compute the winning node n for i;
                if  N≠ t_i  (target for i) then
                     w^k := w^k · w_i^k, ∀k ;
                     normalize w ;
                end if;
        end for;
end repeat;
```

Fig. 2. Pseudocode description of the computation of a global weight.

Then we set all elements of the weight vectors w_s and w_t to one and compute local document weights w_{si} and w_{ti} by adding (subtracting) the error terms from the neutral weighting scheme w_1. Then we compute the local weights iteratively similar to the global weighting approach:

$$w_s^{k(t+1)} = w_s^{k(t)} \cdot w_{si}, \forall k, \text{ with } w_{si} = w_1 + \eta \cdot e_{si} \tag{5}$$

and

$$w_t^{k(t+1)} = w_t^{k(t)} \cdot w_{ti}, \forall k, \text{ with } w_{ti} = w_1 - \eta \cdot e_{ti} \tag{6}$$

where η is a learning rate. The weights assigned to the target and source node are finally normalized such that the sum over all elements equals the number of features in the vector, i.e.

$$\sum_k w_s^k = \sum_k w_t^k = \sum_k 1 \tag{7}$$

In this way the weights assigned to features that achieved a higher (lower) error are decreased (increased) for the target node and vice versa for the source node.

3.3 A Generalized Learning Model

With the local approach we just modified weighting vectors of the source and target nodes. However, as adjacent map nodes should ideally contain similar documents, one could demand that the weights should not change abruptly between nodes. Thus, it is a natural extension of this approach to modify the weight vectors of the neighboring map units accordingly with a similar mechanism as in the learning of the map. Depending on the radius r of the neighborhood function, the result would lie between the local approach (r = 0) and the global approach (r = ∞). In the following, we present such an extension.

As for the local approach we have a weighting vector per node. Then – as before – we start by computing an error vector e for each object based on the distance to the prototypes, as defined in equation (2).

Based on the error vectors e weight vectors of each node n are computed iteratively. For the initial weight vector $w_n^{k(0)}$ we choose vectors where all elements are equal to one. We then compute a new local weight vector for each node by an elementwise multiplication:

$$w_n^{k(t+1)} = w_n^{k(t)} \cdot w_{ni}, \forall k, \text{ with } w_{ni} = w_1 + \eta \cdot \left(g_{sn}^r \cdot e_{si} - g_{tn}^r \cdot e_{ti} \right) \qquad (8)$$

where η is a learning rate and where g_{sn}^r and g_{tn}^r are weighting values calculated using a neighborhood function.

Because two similar prototypes can be projected in distant cells of the map, the neighborhood function should be based on the actual topology of the map. Here we propose to use a linear decreasing function for g_{sn}^r, which equals one for the source node and equals zero at the hull defined by the radius r. The same holds for the target node and g_{tn}^r (see also Fig. 3). Notice that more refined functions can be used as for instance Gaussian-like functions.

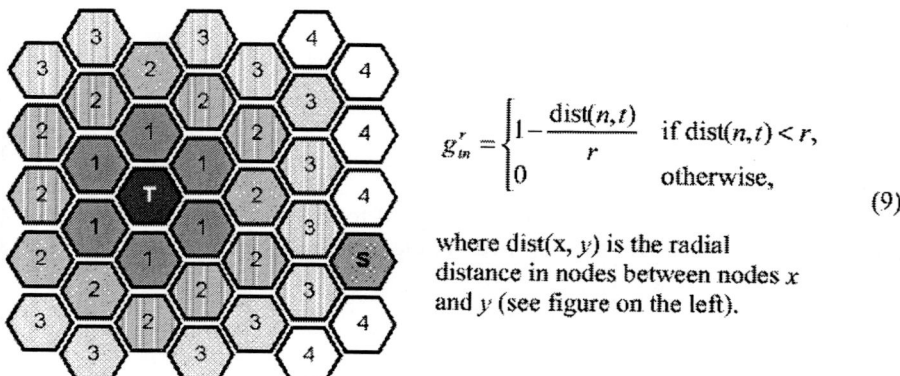

$$g_{tn}^r = \begin{cases} 1 - \dfrac{\text{dist}(n,t)}{r} & \text{if dist}(n,t) < r, \\ 0 & \text{otherwise,} \end{cases} \qquad (9)$$

where dist(x, y) is the radial distance in nodes between nodes x and y (see figure on the left).

Fig. 3. Neighborhood function centered on target node (decreasing to zero for r)

As above, all weights vectors are modified until – if possible – all moved objects are finally mapped to the target node. A pseudocode description of this approach is given in the Fig. 4.

This weighting approach affects the assignments of documents of neighboring cells. The influence of the modification is controlled by the neighborhood function. The idea is that a local modification has a more global repercussion on the map. In this way we can interactively find a feature weighting scheme that improves the classification performance of the map.

```
For each node n compute the weight vectors w_ni
If any of the weight vectors w_n is undefined, then
        created them and initialized all elements to one;
cnt = 0;
Repeat until all documents are moved or cnt > max
     cnt++;
     For all documents i to be moved do
          Compute the winning node N for i;
          if   N≠ t_i (target for i) then
               for all nodes n of the map
```
$$w_n^k := w_n^k \cdot w_{ni}^k, \forall k \; ;$$
```
               end for;
               normalize w_n ;
          end if;
     end for;
end repeat;
```

Fig. 4. Pseudocode description of the computation for the generalized weight scheme.

We note here that the general approach has by construction the local and global approach as limiting models. In fact, depending on the radius r of the neighborhood function, we obtain the local approach for $r \to 0$ and the global approach for $r \to \infty$.

4 Application: An Image Retrieval System

The discussed learning methods were implemented in a java based interactive tool for image retrieval. As sample data set we used subsets of a picture database provided from the California Department of Water Resources. The database contains more than 17,000 color images of scenery, of buildings, animals, people, etc. They are available from the web server of the *Digital Library Project*, University of California, Berkeley (http://elib.cs.berkeley.edu/). Using this platform we verified that the proposed methods are able to capture normal user preferences. A more important study, taking into account a panel of users, should be done in order to make more precise conclusions. More information about the retrieval system and its methods and capabilities can be found in, e.g., [6] and [11].

5 Conclusions

Self-organizing maps provide valuable means for visualization and exploration of any object collection that can be described by numerical vectors. The combination with traditional search and coloring methods allows the design of interactive and user-friendly object retrieval tools. The presented approaches incorporate user-feedback allowing refining the map that was initially trained in an unsupervised manner. In fact, the initial cluster greatly depends on the definition of describing features and the similarity measures. We gather information about the desired similarity measure and then modify the importance of certain features using weights. In other words, we modify the underlying similarity measure and thus considering user specific grouping criteria.

Acknowledgements. The work presented in this article was partially supported by BTexact Technologies, Adastral Park, Martlesham, UK and the European Network of Excellence on Intelligent Technologies for Smart Adaptive Systems (EUNITE). We like to thank the California Department of Water Resources and the Digital Library Project, UC Berkeley, for providing the photos.

References

[1] T. Honkela, S. Kaski, K. Lagus, and T. Kohonen, *Newsgroup Exploration with the WEBSOM Method and Browsing Interface, Technical Report*, Helsinki University of Technology, Neural Networks Research Center, Espoo, Finland, 1996.
[2] T. Kohonen, *Self-Organization and Associative Memory*, Springer-Verlag, Berlin, 1984.
[3] T. Kohonen, Self-Organized Formation of Topologically Correct Feature Maps, *Biological Cybernetics*, 43, pp. 59–69, 1982.
[4] A. Klose, A. Nürnberger, R. Kruse, G. K. Hartmann, and M. Richards, Interactive Text Retrieval Based on Document Similarities, *Physics and Chemistry of the Earth, Part A: Solid Earth and Geodesy*, 25(8), pp. 649-654, Elsevier Science, Amsterdam, 2000.
[5] A. Narasimhalu, *Special issue on content-based retrieval, ACM Multimedia Systems*, 3(1), 1995.
[6] A. Nürnberger and M. Detyniecki, Visualizing Changes in Data Collections Using Growing Self-Organizing Maps, *Proceedings of the International Joint Conference on Neural Networks - IJCNN'2002*, Honolulu, Hawaii, pp. 1912–1917, May, 2002.
[7] A. Nürnberger, Interactive Text Retrieval Supported by Growing Self-Organizing Maps, In: T. Ojala (edt.), *Proc. of the International Workshop on Information Retrieval (IR'2001)*, pp. 61–70, Infotech, Oulu, Finland, 2001.
[8] A. Nürnberger and M. Detyniecki, Content Based Analysis of Email Databases Using Self-Organizing Maps, *Proceedings of the European Symposium on Intelligent Technologies, Hybrid Systems and their implementation on Smart Adaptive Systems – EUNITE'2001*, Tenerife, Spain, pp. 134–142, December, 2001.
[9] A. Nürnberger and M. Detyniecki, User Adaptive Methods for Interactive Analysis of Document Databases, *Proceedings of the European Symposium on Intelligent Technologies, Hybrid Systems and their implementation on Smart Adaptive Systems - EUNITE'2002*, Algarve, Portugal, September, 2002.
[10] A. Nürnberger, and A. Klose, Interactive Retrieval of Multimedia Objects based on Self-Organising Maps, In: *Proc. of the Int. Conf. of the European Society for Fuzzy Logic and Technology (EUSFLAT 2001)*, pp. 377-380, De Montfort University, Leicester, UK, 2001.
[11] A. Nürnberger and A. Klose, Improving Clustering and Visualization of Multimedia Data Using Interactive User Feedback, In: *Proc. of the 9th International Conference on Information Processing and Management of Uncertainty in Knowledge-Based Systems - IPMU 2002*, pp. 993–999, 2002.

Classification and Tracking of Hypermedia Navigation Patterns

Patrick Gallinari, Sylvain Bidel, Laurent Lemoine, Frédéric Piat, and Thierry Artières

LIP6, Université Paris 6, 8 rue du capitaine Scott, 75015, Paris, France
fname.name@lip6.fr

Abstract. We consider the classification and tracking of user navigation patterns for closed world hypermedia. We first propose a series of features characterizing different aspects of the navigation behavior. We then develop Hidden Markov models and a variant of these models called Multi-stream Hidden Markov models to track on line the behavior of a user. We also provide experimental results for the recognition of pre-defined user behaviors, using a home made basis.

1 Introduction

The development and the complexity increase of hypermedia systems accessible by many different users (e.g. through internet) has created a need for developing help tools for the user. Basic mechanisms relying on navigation history or dedicated search engines are already of common use but are insufficient. To go further it is necessary to develop user centric help strategies then to characterize the user in order to define help actions, to infer the relevant action for a user in a given situation [2]. The user modeling field has explored such issues for many years now, some aspects of the problem are already pretty well covered by existing solutions, while many other are still largely open. One reason for that is that the domain is rapidly evolving and adapts continuously to the technology. Another one is that most aspects of human behavior, like measuring satisfaction, inferring user goal, etc, are intrinsically complex and/or subjective, and this difficulty carries to the development of user modeling tools.

We focus here on the characterization of user groups or categories with respect to user navigation in a rich hypermedia system, from the observation of low level traces like clics, scrolls, page access, etc. The goal is to follow individual user navigation and to track its behavior during a session so that an adequate help could be provided to him on line. There have been some studies for defining generic navigation behaviors in hypermedia e.g. [4]. Most agree on 5 or 6 typical behaviors and even if they propose different classifications, they globally offer a coherent vision of typical user behaviors. In our work we use a behavior taxonomy in the different steps of the system development: data gathering, action sequences classification, behavior tracking, behavior interpretation.

We first propose an original set of features for characterizing the different aspects of user navigation from traces in rich hypermedia systems. The sequence of user actions captured by a server is then encoded in a sequence of feature vectors or frames, each frame representing navigation actions for a short duration. For identifying navigation behaviors, we then make use of Hidden Markov Models (HMMs). We also introduce the Multi-Stream HMM (MS-HMM) Model that allows taking into account simultaneously different partially asynchronous feature sets characterizing the user behavior at different time scales. We use these models for user behavior categorization and tracking. Up to now, sequence models – either Markovian models [10] or dynamic Bayesian Networks [8] have mainly been used for predicting user actions or for inferring goals in environments which are described using existing domain specific knowledge.

We first discuss in section 2 the navigation behaviors we want to recognize, the database used in our experiments and the features we propose for characterizing user sequences. In section 3, we introduce sequence models that operate on these feature and present experimental results in section 4.

2 Typical Navigation and Feature Extraction

2.1 Navigation Typology

Although most researchers who proposed typologies of navigation behaviors and search strategies in closed hypermedia systems distinguish broad user strategies (e.g. browsing and searching), there is no general agreement for the generic categorization of more specific behaviors. We adopt here the taxonomy proposed by Canter and al [4] which we found convenient for the type of application we deal with, and adapt it to our problem, we thus distinguish four *elementary behaviors*:
- Scanning: seeking an overview of a theme by requesting an important proportion of its pages but without spending much time on them.
- Exploring: reading thoroughly the pages viewed.
- Searching: seeking a particular document or information.
- Wandering: navigating in an unstructured way without particular goal.

2.2 Navigation Database

For the tests, we used the application « The XXth century encyclopedia », initially a cultural CD-ROM[1] reconfigured as an Internet site. This is a typical "cultural" hypermedia system, it contains about 2k articles (i.e. pages with text, pictures, videos etc...), a full-text search engine and tables of contents where the user can navigate on a 2-level theme hierarchy. Each theme is associated a set of key words. Each article is associated a theme, navigation links towards other articles, and reading times corre-

---

[1] Distributed by Montparnasse Multimédia company.

sponding to the durations required to fully read each of its paragraphs. All the above have been set by the conceivers of the site.

In order to evaluate our methods, we have generated data in a controlled fashion, by asking 26 users to fill out questionnaires by navigating through the encyclopedia. The questions were chosen in order to induce a given navigation behavior from the above typology. For instance, a question asks the user to extract important dates from a particular theme. This leads the user to view several pages of this theme without having to read them thoroughly, it is a "Scanning" behavior. For the "Exploring" behavior, the user was asked to fully read a few articles (pages) etc. The sequences of user actions recorded by the navigator are labelled by the typical behavior expectedly induced. These labels will be used for the evaluation. We gathered 104 data sessions, 26 for each of the 4 *elementary behaviors*. Navigation data are sequences of dated events (page access, click, scroll, query on the search engine...) that are collected all along the user session.

2.3 Navigation Features

Traces are then processed to compute sequences of feature vectors. We computed a frame for every page viewed. Overall, this yields over 400 frames, each representing a period of about one minute in average. We investigated various features and in the end, we are left with 9 features that take advantage of the richness of the information associated to articles (reading time, etc..). These 9 features are divided into three subsets according to the type of information they carry:

- The "reading" subset reflects the extent and the quality of the reading behavior and contains 4 features. We use here the reference reading time for each paragraph, to compute reading rates for the first quarter of the document and for the rest of the document (applies when accessed via scrolling). The time spent on the page(s) and the activity (number of clicks/scroll events) complete this set of features.
- The "resources" subset informs the system about the kind of resources used. They may be articles (the real content of the hypermedia, the leave pages in the tree of themes hierarchy), tables of content (either of 3 levels, containing links to access the themes, sub-themes or articles), or the search engine page. We use the percentage of time spent on these three kinds of resources.
- The "navigation" subset characterizes the navigation focus, whether the user is focused on one theme or spread onto several. We define the distance between two articles as being the distance between their sub-themes in the tree. We then compute the length of the path followed, and the standard deviation of the distances between the pages visited and the focus sub-theme (with the most time spent on).

3 Behavior Models

After the feature extraction step, the navigation information in a user session is represented as a sequence of frames (a frame is a vector of 9 features), each frame corresponds to timely information about the user actions. Let $o_1^T = (o_1, ..., o_T)$ denote a sequence of T frames, o_t being the tth frame in the sequence. We want to identify different types of user behavior, for that we propose a model for the production of frame sequences. This model B will then allow to compute sequence likelihood $P(o_1^T/B)$. We investigated for that two Markovian systems and, as a reference system for the supervised case only, a Multi-Layer Perceptron (MLP).

The MLP is trained (using Back Propagation algorithm) to discriminate between the frames corresponding to different behaviors. It takes a frame as input and outputs a vector of behavior scores, the maximal score corresponds to the recognized behavior. When trained for discrimination, a MLP is known to approximate posterior probabilities $P(B/o_t)$. Then one can use this MLP to classify sequences of frames since, using Bayes Theorem and assuming uniform behaviors priors:

$$\arg\max_B P(o_1^T / B) = \arg\max_B \prod_t P(B/o_t) \qquad (1)$$

Besides, we developed two Markovian systems. The first is based on standard HMMs which have shown strong abilities for various signal modelling and classification tasks. We used one HMM per behavior, with an ergodic topology (any transition allowed) and diagonal covariance Gaussian densities. The underlying hypothesis for HMMs is that the process being modeled is locally stationary and a transition in the Markov model corresponds to a skip from one of its stationary state to another one. A consequence is that all features in the frames are assumed locally stationary and synchronous processes. This assumption does not correspond to the features used here which do not change synchronously. Hence, we propose to use a variant of HMMs called Multi-Stream HMM (MS-HMM) [9], it allows combining multiple partially synchronous information streams or modalities [6, 7]. More precisely in our case, a behavior model is a combination of three HMMs operating on different information stream corresponding to *Reading*, *Ressources* and *Navigation* frame sequences (see §2). The three streams are asynchronous i.e. transitions in the three stream-HMMs may occur at different times, except in some particular states named recombination states that are designed by hand. We choose the entering and leaving states of each stream model as recombination states, i.e. each behavior model is fully asynchronous. This means that, given an entering time and a leaving time in a stream behavior model, one can compute very simply the probability of the corresponding sub-sequence of frames. For example, the probability of a sub-sequence of frames from time b to time e is computed with:

$$P(o_b^e / B) = P(rd_b^e / B_{rd}) P(rs_b^e / B_{rd}) P(n_b^e / B_n) \qquad (2)$$

where B is a behavior MS-HMM model composed of three HMM model B_{rd}, B_{rs}, B_n, working respectively on sequences of frames rd_b^e, rs_b^e, n_b^e which are frames of *reading*, *resources* and *navigation* features. Recombination states will be useful for segmentation tasks as will be seen in §3.3.

3.1 Supervised and Unsupervised Learning

For our experiments, we investigated supervised and unsupervised learning. Supervised experiments aim at investigating the ability to correctly classify and track *elementary behaviours*. Unsupervised experiments aim at investigating the ability to automatically discover typical user behavior from a collection of unlabelled data (user traces), then to classify and track these behaviors.

For supervised learning, we used the labelling of our database into the four elementary behaviors as described in §2. We learned four models, one for each behavior, using a classical learning scheme where each behavior model is trained to maximize the likelihood of associated training sessions.

For unsupervised learning, we consider a mixture of N probabilistic (Markovian only) behavior models. The probability of a frames sequence is given by a mixture of models:

$$P(o_1^T) = \sum_{i=1..N} P(B_i) \cdot P(o_1^T / B_i) \tag{3}$$

where $(B_i)_{i=1..N}$ are N Behavior models, $P(B_i)$ is the prior probability for the ith behavior model B_i and $P(o_1^T / B_i)$ is the likelihood of o_1^T computed by B_i (HMM or MS-HMM). Learning consists in maximizing the likelihood of all training sessions given this mixture model. Since we do not know which behavior a training session belongs to, we use an EM procedure where missing data are posterior probabilities of behavior $P(B_i / o_1^T)$. Here is the sketch of the algorithm, it is close to the one in [3]:

0. Initialise the parameters of all behavior models $(B_i)_{i=1..N}$ and of priors.
1. Iterate until convergence
    i. Estimate missing data using current models.

$$P(B_i / o_1^T) = \frac{P(o_1^T / B_i) P(B_i)}{\sum_{j=1}^{N} P(o_1^T / B_j) P(B_j)} \tag{4}$$

    ii. Re-estimate behavior models with all training sessions. A session o_1^T participates to the re-estimation of model B_i with a weight corresponding to $P(B_i / o_1^T)$.

    iii. Re-estimate behavior models priors:

$$P(B_i) = \frac{1}{\#Training\ sessions} \sum_{o_1^T \in TrainigData} P(B_i / o_1^T) \tag{5}$$

3.2 Behavior Categorization

When sessions correspond to a single *elementary behavior* as it is the case for the recorded sessions (§2), it is useful to categorize whole sessions into one of the 4 *ele-*

mentary behaviors. This amounts to classify sequences using HMMs or MS-HMMs: a session is classified according to the model maximizing the sequence likelihood.

3.3 Behavior Segmentation

When sessions correspond to multiple successive behaviors, we will try to detect the sequence of navigation behaviors of a user along a session. A global Markov model is then built by concatenating the leaving state of each behavior model to the entering state of each behavior model. Then, considering a test session, a dynamic programming algorithm finds the optimal state path for the session, from which we get the sequence of computed behaviors. This is a classical step for standard HMMs, we explain below how it works for MS-HMMs.

To segment a session into elementary behaviors, one builds three large HMMs λ_{rd}, λ_{rs}, λ_n by concatenating all HMMs corresponding respectively to reading features, resources features and navigation features. The global MS-HMM model denoted λ is built from these three asynchronous models, by imposing synchronization points at each leaving state, i.e. the three models are forced to leave a behavior model at the same time in each stream. The likelihood of a session is given by:

$$P(o_1^T / \lambda) = \sum_{S_{rd}, S_{rs}, S_n} P(rd_1^T / S_{rd}, \lambda_{rd}) P(rs_1^T / S_{rs}, \lambda_{rs}) P(n_1^T / S_n, \lambda_n) P(S_{rd}, S_{rs}, S_n / \lambda) \quad (6)$$

where S_{rd}, S_{rs}, S_n are the paths in $\lambda_{rd}, \lambda_{rs}, \lambda_n$. The synchronization consists in setting $P(S_{rd}, S_{rs}, S_n / \lambda)$ to 0 if the constraint is not verified. Otherwise, $P(S_{rd}, S_{rs}, S_n / \lambda)$ is set equal to $P(S_{rd} / \lambda_{rd}) \cdot P(S_{rs} / \lambda_{rs}) \cdot P(S_n / \lambda_n)$.

4 Experiments

We describe now two series of experiments. In a first series we want to categorize whole user sessions. Remember that sessions were built with one typical behavior in mind, so that each session should correspond to one class. In a real situation, this corresponds to the case where a user is supposed to have the same behavior for an entire session. In a second series of experiments, we want to track the behavior of the user and detect its behavior changes. This amounts to segment user sessions into reference behaviors. This is a more realistic situation for most hypermedia users. For our experiments, we concatenated all the elementary user sessions in the database using a random ordering, producing large sessions where the user changes behavior. All the evaluations have been performed using a 26-fold cross-validation.

It must be noticed that, even in a closed and controlled environment like the one we are dealing with, user behavior classification is difficult and has intrinsic limitations. Even with a clear goal in mind, a user goes back and forth between different strategies during a session, which makes difficult an accurate classification. The elementary behaviors we are using are only rough abstract representations of the potential user behavior.

Since we built the database using predefined scenario, we know the label of each elementary session. It is thus possible to perform supervised learning for both classification and segmentation. We performed supervised learning with both HMMs and MS-HMMs. Although this could make sense for user behavior classification in some controlled environments, it is usually more realistic to consider the problem as an unsupervised learning problem where sessions are unlabeled, and the goal is to identify typical user behaviors from scratch. We thus performed experiments with unsupervised learning with HMMs and MS-HMMs. The interpretation of the discovered behaviors is complex and the evaluation of unsupervised methods is an open problem. We thus provide below performances of unsupervised methods with regard to the known labels of elementary sessions. Although this is not really satisfying, this provides interesting hints for measuring the ability of these methods to detect user behaviors. Note that performances obtained using supervised methods provide an upper bound of the performances that could be obtained for session classification and segmentation.

4.1 Session Categorization

Here whole sessions have to be classified according to an underlying behavior. We used two evaluation criterions, the standard *correct classification* (*CC*) percentage, and a *weighted accuracy* (*WA*) criterion where confusions between classes have different weights. The idea behind *WA* is that confusions between behaviors do not all have the same importance since user help actions for some classes may be very similar. In our *WA*, confusions between *Scanning* and *Exploring* and between *Searching* and *Wandering* are set equal to ½ while all other confusions are set equal to 1.

For supervised learning, we trained 4 models, one for each typical behavior. A standard HMM model working on whole frames, has 7 states. A MS-HMM model consists of 3 HMMs, one per feature subset, with 3 states. The number of states in the models have been fixed using cross validation.

For behavior clustering (unsupervised learning), we first determined an "optimal" number of clusters using the F-statistic, which is a cluster homogeneity measure. We found an optimal number of 6 clusters. We then learned a mixture of 6 models. Training sessions were then clustered according to the model with greatest likelihood. After training, each cluster has been labeled into one of the 4 classes according to the majority of labels it contains. *CC* and *WA* criteria may then be computed.

Table 1 sums up our results. Both *CC* and *WA* are reasonably high for supervised models: elementary behaviors can be recognized rather accurately from low-level navigation data. As may be seen, Markovian models perform similarly to MLP although these models do not capture the same kind of information, this shows that the dynamic information is partially handled using Markovian models. Although *CC* and *WA* are noticeably lower for unsupervised training, it can be seen that a reasonable proportion of the sessions is correctly classified. This shows that unsupervised classification on user traces allows capturing valuable information on the user behavior. This also shows the difficulty of this task. Going further in the evaluation of unsupervised systems would necessitate a manual analysis of the clusters, this is beyond the scope of this paper.

Table 1. Behavior classification accuracy and weighted accuracy for 3 supervised systems (HMMs, MS-HMMs, MLP) and 2 unsupervised systems (HMMs and MS-HMMs).

Training mode	System	HMM	MS-HMM	MLP
Supervised	Correct classification	79	76	74
Supervised	Weighted accuracy	85	84	83
Unsupervised	Correct classification	69	65	NA
Unsupervised	Weighted accuracy	78	76	NA

4.2 Session Segmentation

Here, a system has to detect the user behavior changes in a long session, and to recognize these behaviors. A segmentation system receives as input a sequence of frames and outputs a sequence of labels, one for each frame. In our controlled experimental setting, this computed sequence has to be close to the actual label sequence. Different measures have been proposed for comparing discrete sequences, we use here the *edit distance* between computed and desired label sequences [1]. This is a classical measure which computes *insertions*, *deletions* and *substitutions* between the two strings. The *correct recognition* percentage is then 1 minus substitution and deletion percentages. Note that this does not take into account the duration of each detected behavior. We made this choice considering that it was not important to detect the exact time where the user changes his exploration strategy, but rather to detect the change of strategy within a reasonable delay. The Edit distance reflects this idea up to a certain extent.

Both for supervised and unsupervised settings, models are first trained on elementary sessions as for classification. Each model is then associated to one of the 4 predefined classes. Models are then used to segment a large session where elementary sessions have been concatenated. The computed sequence is compared to the desired sequence via the Edit distance. Table 2 shows the experimental results.

Again performances of supervised models are satisfying and only show a small drop compared to the simpler task of classification. MS-HMMs are still 4% higher than simple HMMs. As for categorization, Markovian models perform similarly to MLP. On the other hand, performances of unsupervised systems are 40 % below the supervised upper bound. The lower classification ability carries over segmentation. Also, it must be noticed once again that unsupervised systems are evaluated using supervised labels so that a mismatch between discovered and labelled behaviours lead to poor results and may not reflect the eventual relevance of unsupervised systems.

Table 2. Edit-distance rates between correct and predicted behavior sequences, with substitution cost =1 and deletion cost = insertion cost = 2, for 2 supervised systems and 2 unsupervised systems (standard HMMs and MS-HMMs in both cases + MLP for supervised mode only).

Training mode	Edit-distance	% Correct	% Susbt.	% Del	% Ins
Supervised	HMM	78	14	9	12
Supervised	MS-HMM	75	16	10	10
Supervised	MLP	73	16	11	13
Unsupervised	HMM	35	55	10	14
Unsupervised	MS-HMM	39	50	11	13

5 Conclusion

We proposed a series of new features for categorizing user navigation patterns in rich hypermedia systems. We then developed two sequence models for the classification and tracking of user behavior. Experiments were performed on a representative hypermedia system using a controlled navigation database. Results show that whole session classification performs pretty well even in an unsupervised setting, on the other hand, behavior tracking is more difficult when there is no a priori knowledge of what a typical session is. More work is then needed to limit the drop in performance between classification and segmentation. Still, these are encouraging results for the automatically assisted development of hypermedia user-centric help systems.

Acknowledgement. This project is realized as part of the RNTL project Gicsweb funded by the French Ministry of Industry.

References

1. Atallah, M.J. (ed.), Algorithms and Theory of Computation Handbook, CRC Press LLC, 99.
2. Brusilovsky P., Adaptive Hypermédia, *User Modeling and User-Adapted Interaction*, 2001.
3. Cadez I., Gaffney S., Smyth P., A general probabilistic framework for clustering individuals and objects, *In Proceedings of the Sixth ACM International Conference on Knowledge Discovery and Data Mining*, 2000.
4. Canter D., Rivers R., Storrs G., Characterizing User Navigation through Complex Data Structure, *Behavior and Information Technology*, vol. 4, 1985.
5. Catledge L., Pitkow J., Characterizing Browsing Strategies in the World Wide Web, *Computer Networks and ISDN Systems*, 1995, vol.27, No.6.
6. Dupont S. and Luettin., Using the Multi-Stream Approach for Continuous Audio-Visual Speech Recognition: Experiments on the M2VTS Database, *Int. Conf. on Spoken Language Processing*, 1998.
7. Gauthier N., Artières T., Dorizzi B., Gallinari P., Strategies for combining on-line and off-line informations in a on-line handwriting recognition system, *Int. Conf. Document Analysis and Recognition*, 2001.

8. Horvitz E., Breese J., Heckerman D., Hovel D., Rommelse K., The Lumière Project: Bayesian user modeling for inferring the goals and needs of software users, *UAI 98*.
9. Varga A., Moore R., Hidden Markov Model decomposition of speech and noise, *International Conference on Acoustics, Speech and Signal Processing*, 1990.
10. Zukerman I., Albrecht D., Nicholson A., Predicting users' requests on the WWW, *User Modeling*, 1999.

Self-Aware Networks and Quality of Service*

Erol Gelenbe and Arturo Núñez

School of Electrical Engineering & Computer Science
University of Central Florida
Orlando, FL 32816
{erol,artnpp}@cs.ucf.edu

Abstract. We show how "self-awareness", through on-line self-monitoring and measurement, coupled with intelligent adaptive behaviour in response to observed data, can be used to offer quality of service to network users. We first describe the general principles which govern our design, and briefly describe the experimental packet network system we have built in which users are allowed to specify their QoS objectives. The network uses on-line adaptive traffic routing to try to meet the users' QoS requests. Cognitive or smart packets are used for self-observation, and reinforcement learning with neural networks is implemented at network nodes to seek new paths and deduce improved paths from existing routes. First we show how the network is able to discover routes, beginning with an "empty state" and starting from a random search. Secondly we show how our network can intelligently direct traffic through the Internet to optimize web traffic for a user by offering the best quality of service through different Internet Service Providers.

1 Introduction

At the periphery of the Internet novel networked systems are emerging to offer user oriented flexible services, using the Internet and LANs to reach different parts of the same systems, and to access other networks, users and services. Examples include Enterprise Networks, Home Networks (Domotics), Networks for Military Units and for Emergency Services. The example of home networks is significant in that a family may be interconnected as a unit with PDAs for the parents and children, health monitoring devices for the grand-parents, video cameras connected to the network in the infants' bedroom, connections to smart home appliances, the home education server, the entertainment center, the security system, etc.. As an example, the home network will simultaneously use different wired and wireless communication modalities including WLAN, 3G, wired Ethernet and will tunnel packets through IP in the Internet. Such systems must allow for diverse Quality of Service (QoS) requirements, and they raise interesting issues of intelligence and adaptation to user needs and to the

---

* The research was supported by U.S. Army Simulation and Training Command via NAWC under Contract No. N61339-02-C0117, and NSF under Grants No. EIA0086251 and EIA0203446.

networking environment, including routing, self healing, security and robustness. We investigate these issues via "Self Aware Networks" (SAN) (SAN) which leverage and extending our recent research on "Cognitive Packet Networks (CPN)" [13,15,17]. We have designed and implemented an initial version of a SAN which offers a facility for conducting communications based on user-defined QoS. The SAN *Accepts Direction*, by inputing Goals prescribed by users. It exploits *Self-Observation* with the help of *smart packets (SPs)* so as to be aware of its state including connectivity of fixed or mobile nodes, power levels at mobile nodes, topology, paths and path QoS. It performs *Self-Improvement*, and *Learns from the experience of smart packets* using neural networks and genetic algorithms to determine routing schemes with better QoS. It will *Deduce* hitherto unknown routes by combining or modifying paths which have been previously learned so as to improve QoS and robustness. In a recent paper [15] we showed how a SAN can react to sudden node failures, and to sudden changes in network traffic, in order to re-establish connections which satisfy the user's QoS goal. In this paper we provide experimental results illustrating the use of self-awareness for setting up new network connections autonomously and intelligently through the network using SPs, and controlling traffic flow intelligently, beyond the SAN itself and into the Internet, so as to offer a user the best QoS available via different Internet Service Providers (ISP). QoS is an important issue in network design [9], and a comprehensive survey of the subject would require us to cite many hundreds of papers; thus the work we list here only offers an incomplete view of the subject, though these references do point to other useful sources. There is a large literature on *estimating certain specific quality of service parameters* (e.g. loss or delay) for *given traffic characteristics*[6,7]. Numerous papers deal with the analysis of packet network protocols such as TCP/IP [8,21] from a QoS perspective. Others have examined control techniques which may offer QoS guarantees to different types of traffic [14], while exact solution techniques for queueing models that are motivated by communication systems are still under active investigation [21,23]. The mixed wired and wireless network topologies that are becoming common, including fixed and ad-hoc connections, create the need to rationally exploit dynamically variable routing as a function of network conditions. Applications that use such networks have QoS requirements related to packet delay, loss or jitter, as well as other QoS requirements that reflect the need for greater reliability and low power utilization. Routing policies designed to achieve better QoS have been considered by several authors [10,18,19,20]. QoS based routing algorithms raise research issues related to network probing and on-line measurement, algorithm scalability to large networks, path discovery and set-up times, and computational and traffic overheads. Our approach to SAN in *wired networks and wireless ad-hoc environments* exploits intelligence and adaptivity to offer improved QoS to network users [13,16,17] who will increasingly have elaborate QoS Goals.

1.1 The SAN System Design

The SAN concept makes use of four types of packets: smart packets (SP) for discovery, source routed dumb packets (DP) to carry payload, source routed probe packets (P) to test paths, acknowledgments (ACK) to bring back information that has been discovered by SPs and Ps. Conventional IP packets tunnel through SAN to seamlessly operate mixed IP and SAN networks. SPs are be generated by a user (1) requesting that a path having some QoS value be created to some SAN node, or (2) requesting to discover parts of network state, including location of certain fixed or mobile nodes, power levels at nodes, topology, paths and their QoS. SPs *exploit the experience of other packets* using random neural network (RNN) based Reinforcement Learning [13]. RL will be carried out using a Goal which is specified by the user who generated a request for a connection. The decisional weights of a RNN will be increased or decreased based on the observed success or failure of subsequent SPs to achieve the Goal. Thus RL will tend to prefer better routing schemes, more reliable access paths to data objects, and better QoS. (2) Secondly, the system can **deduce** new paths to users, nodes and data objects by combining previously discovered paths, and using the estimated or measured QoS values of new paths select the best new paths. This is similar conceptually to a genetic algorithm which generates new entities by combination or mutation of existing entities, and then selects the best among them using a fitness function. These new paths will then be tested by forwarding Ps so that the actual QoS or success can be evaluated.

When a SP or P arrives to its destination, an ACK is generated and heads back to the source of the request. It updates *mailboxes* (MBs) in the SAN nodes it visits with information which has been discovered, and provides the source node with the successful path to the node. All packets have a life-time constraint based on the number of nodes visited, to avoid overburdening the system with unsuccessful requests. Currently we have experimented with this "limited number of hops H" constraint using both the numbers of $H = 30$ and $H = 200$. These numbers may appear to be arbitrary, but they correspond to a small multiple m of the diameter d of the network, while the diameter itself will be a good estimate of the size of the network. Thus $d = 10$ we may be dealing with a network of size k^d where k is the typical degree of a node, and H may be selected to be $H = md$, or $H = mlog_k S$ where S is the size of the network in number of nodes.

Our current SAN software is integrated into the Linux kernel 2.2.x, providing a single application program interface (API) for the programmer to access SAN. Our SAN routing algorithms run seamlessly on ad-hoc wireless and wired connections [16], without specific dependence on the nature (wired or wireless) of the links, using QoS awareness to optimize behavior across different connection technologies and wireless protocols. To deal with the non-permanent nature of connections, nodes periodically poll their neighbors, and ACKs, DPs and P packets will be able to revert dynamically to smart behavior if the source route they carry is discovered to be disconnected.

2 Cold Start Connection Set-Up Time Measurements

One of the major requirements of a SAN is that it should be able to start itself with no initial information, by first randomly searching, and then progressively improving its behaviour through experience. Since the major function of a network is to transfer packets from some source S to some destination D, it is vital that the SAN be able to establish a path from S to D even when there is no prior information available in the network. The experiments we will describe in this section address precisely this issue. The network topology we have used in these experiments is shown at the top of Figure 3, with the source and destinations nodes marked at the left and right ends of the diagram. The network contains 24 nodes, and each node is connected to 4 neighbours. Because of the possibility of repeatedly visiting the same node on a path, the network contains an unlimited number of paths from S to D. However, the fact that SPs are destroyed after they visit 30 nodes, does limit this number though it still leaves a huge number of possible paths. In this set of experiments, the network is always started with empty mailboxes, i.e. with no prior information about which output link is to be used from a node, and with neural network weights set at identical values, so that the neural network descison algorithm at nodes initially will produce a random choice. Each point shown on the curves of Figure 3 is a result of 100 repetitions of the experiment under identical starting conditions. Let us first comment on the left-hand top-most curve. An abscissa value of 10 indicates that the number of SPs used was 10, and – assuming that the experiment resulted in an ACK packet coming back to the source – the ordinate gives the average time (over the 100 experiments) that it elapse between the instant that the first SP was sent out, and the first ACK comes back. Note that the first ACK will be coming back from the correct destination node, and that will bring back a valid forward path that can be used by the subsequent useful traffic. We notice that the average set-up time decreases significantly when we go from a few SPs to about 10, and after that, the average set-up time does not improve appreciably. Its value somewhere between 10 and 20 milliseconds actually corresponds to the round-trip transit time through the hops. This does not mean that it suffices to have a small number of SPs at the beginning, simply because this average set-up time is only measured for *successful* SPs; unsuccessful ones are just destroyed after 30 hops.

Thus the top-most curve on the right-hand-side of Figure 3 is needed to obtain a more complete understanding of what is happening. Again for an x-axis value of over 10 packets, we see that the probability of successfully setting up a path is 1, while with a very small number of packets this figure drops down to about 0.65. These probabilities must of course be understood as the empirically observed fraction of the 100 tests which result in a successful connection. The conclusion from these two sets of data is that to be safe, starting with an empty system, a fairly small number of SPs, in the range of 20 to 100, will provide almost guaranteed set-up of the connection, and the minimum average set-up time. The third curve that we show as a result of these experiments provides some insight into the dynamics of the path set-up. Inserting SPs into the network is not instantaneous, and they are fed into the network sequentially by the source. The rate at which they are fed in is determined by the processing time per packet at the source, and also by the link speeds. Since the link speed is $100 Mb/s$ and because SPs are only some $200 Bytes$ long at most, we think that the limiting factor here is the source node's processing time. Since, on the other hand, the previous curves show that connections are almost always established with as few as 10 SPs, and because the average round-trip connection establishment time is quite short, we would expect to see that the connection is generally established before all the SPs are sent out by the source. This is exactly what we observe on this third curve. The x axis shows the number of SPs sent into the network, while the y axis shows the average number sent in (over the 100 experiments) before the first ACK is received. For small numbers of SPs, until the value 10 or so, the relationship is linear. However as the number of SPs being inserted into the network increases, we see that after (on the average) 13 packets or so have been sent out, the connection is already established (i.e. the first ACK has returned to the source). This again indicates that a fairly small number of SPs suffice to establish a connection.

Of course, the experimental results we describe depend on the size of the network and on its topology. In future work we hope to provide a theoretical justification of these results. However our experimental results are important in that they provide experimental support for the ability of the SAN concept to operate autonomously.

2.1 Dynamic QoS Control over the Internet

The Internet, which uses the Internet Protocol (IP) with standard routers and routing tables, with connections mostly using the TCP/IP protocol for flow and error control, is a *de facto* standard for computer communications. Thus any new system we may suggest will have to inter-operate seamlessly with this existing world-wide system. Thus, the purpose of the work presented in this section is two-fold:

- We will demonstrate experimentally the seamless operation of a SAN together with the Internet, and
- We will show how a SAN can be used to *control QoS in the Internet* according to requests formulate by a user.

In order to provide this practical demonstration, we set up the experimental environment described at the top of Figure 2.1. The Workstation (W) shown at the bottom of the figure is used to generate requests to the web server (WS) shown at the left-hand side of the figure. The WS responds to these requests by generating standard Internet IP packets which enter into the CPN SAN set-up at the top of the figure, so that the WS creates connections back to W which tunnel through the SAN. These packets then are dynamically directed back into the Internet via two distinct Internet Service Providers (ISP) ports A30 and A40 shown at the right-hand-side of the figure. From there they merge into the

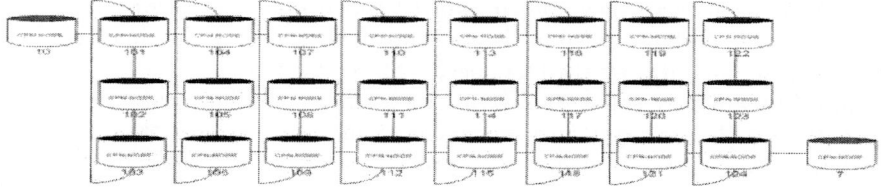

Fig. 1. SAN Network Topology for Cold Start Experiments

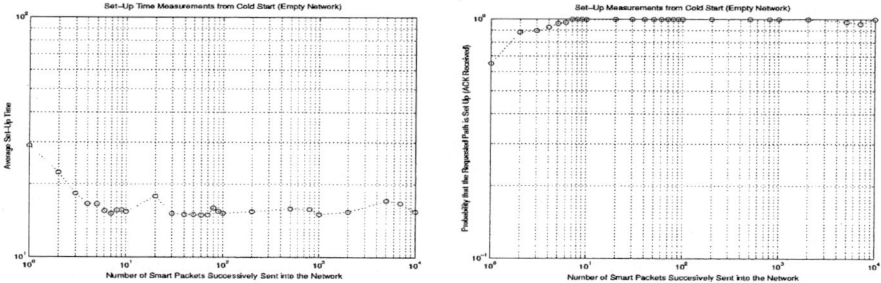

Fig. 2. Average Network Set-Up Time (Left) and Probability of Successful Connection (Right) from Cold Start, as a Function of the Initial Number of Smart Packets

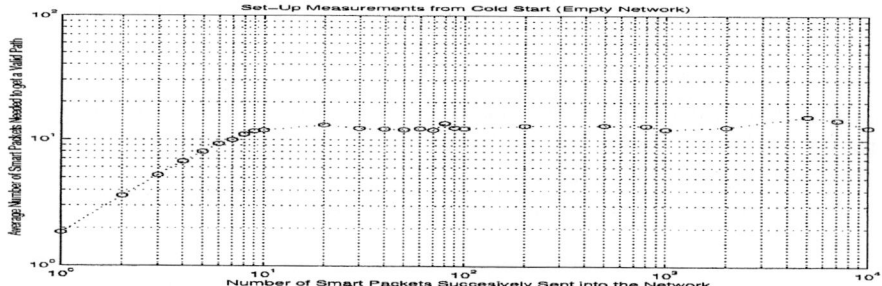

Fig. 3.

Internet, and return to the W as shown on the figure. Thus the experimental setup demonstrates that we are able to seamlessly transmit IP packets into a SAN, and that the SAN can forward them back into the Internet again seamlessly. In the experiments we have run using this set-up, user QoS requested by the W as it makes requests to the WS has been selected to be to minimize delay. Thus we have artificially introduced different delay values at $\overline{A430}$ and $\overline{A40}$ so that the *difference in delay between the two* can be varied. The second top-most set of curves show the fraction of traffic taking A30 (L) and A40 (R) as this delay is varied, and demonstrates that the SAN is indeed dynamically directing traffic quite sharply in response to the user's QoS goal. Figure 6 shows that when the delay through either port is identical, the instantaneous traffic is very similar.

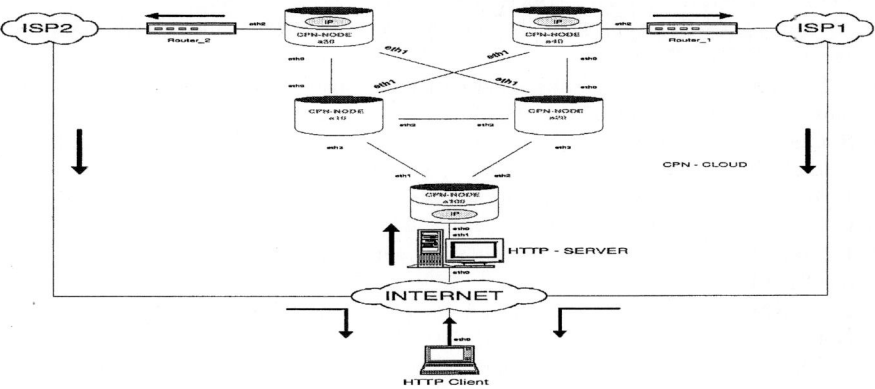

Fig. 4. Experimental Set-Up for Dynamic QoS Control

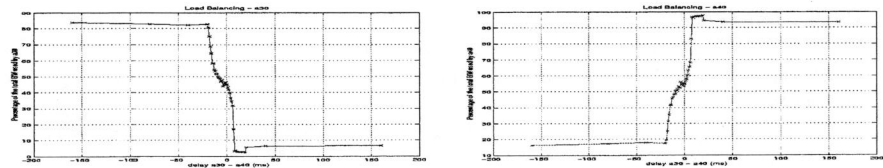

Fig. 5. Percentage of traffic flow through ports A30 (L) and A40 (R) function of difference in delay

References

1. R. Viswanathan, K.S. Narendra "Comparison of expedient and optimal reinforcement schemes for learning systems", *J. Cybernetics*, Vol. 2, pp 21–37, 1972.
2. K.S. Narendra, P. Mars, "The use of learning algorithms in telephone traffic routing – a methodology", *Automatica*, Vol. 19, pp. 495–502, 1983.
3. R.S. Sutton "Learning to predict the methods of temporal difference", *Machine Learning*, Vol. 3, pp. 9–44, 1988.
4. E. Gelenbe. Learning in the recurrent random neural network. *Neural Comp.* 5(1), 154–164, 1993.
5. R. E. Kahn, R. Wilensky "A framework for digital object services", *c.nri.1lib/tn95-01*.

6. E. Gelenbe, X. Mang, Y. Feng "Diffusion cell loss estimates for ATM with multiclass bursty traffic", *Computer Systems–Science and Engineering* 11 (6), 325–334, 1996.
7. V. Srinivasan, A. Ghanwani, E. Gelenbe "Block cell loss reduction in ATM systems", *Computer Comms.*, 19, 1077–1091, 1996.
8. M. May, J.-C. Bolot, C. Diot, A. Jean-Marie "On Internet QoS performance evaluation" INRIA Rept., 1997.
9. D.D. Clark, W. Fang "Adding service discrimination to the Internet", *IEEE/ACM Trans. Net.* 6 (4), 362–373, 1998.
10. S. Chen, and K. Nahrstedt, "Distributed Quality-of-Service routing in ad-hoc networks", IEEE J. Sel. Areas in Comm., 17 (8) 1–19, 1999.
11. U. Halici, "Reinforcement learning with internal expectation for the random neural network" *Eur. J. Opns. Res.*, 126 (2) 2, 288–307, 2000.
12. E. Gelenbe, E. Şeref, Z. Xu. Simulation with learning agents. *Proc. IEEE*, Vol. 89 (2), 148–157, 2001.
13. E. Gelenbe, R. Lent, Z. Xu "Measurement and performance of Cognitive Packet Networks", *J. Comp. Nets.*, 37, 691–701, 2001.
14. J.C.S. Lui, X.Q. Wang "Providing QoS guarantee for individual video stream via stochastic admission control", in K. Goto et al., *Performance and QoS of Next Generation Networking*, Springer, London, 263–279, 2001.
15. E. Gelenbe, R. Lent, Z. Xu "Networking with Cognitive Packets", *Proc. ICANN.*, Madrid, August 2002.
16. E. Gelenbe, R. Lent "Mobile Ad-Hoc Cognitive Packet Networks", *IEEE ASWN*, Paris, July 2–4, 2002.
17. E. Gelenbe et al. "Cognitive packet networks: QoS and performance", Keynote Paper, *IEEE MASCOTS Conference*, San Antonio, TX, Oct. 14–16, 2002.
18. F. Hao, E.W. Zegura, M.H. Ammar "QoS routing for anycast communications: motivation and an architecture for Diffserv networks", *IEEE Comm.* 46 (2), 48–56, 2002.
19. Y.-D. Lin, N.-B. Hsu, R.-H. Hwang "QoS routing granularity in MPLS networks", *IEEE Comm.* 46 (2), 58–65, 2002.
20. M. Kodialam, T.V. Lakshman "Restorable quality of service routing", *IEEE Comm.* 46 (2), 72–81, 2002.
21. A. Chaintreau, F. Baccelli, Ch. Diot "Impact of TCP-like congestion control on the throughput of multicast groups", *IEEE/ACM Trans. on Net.* 10 (4), 2002.
22. E. Gelenbe, K. Hussain "Learning in the multiple class random neural network", *IEEE Trans. on Neural Networks* 13 (6), 1257–1267, 2002.
23. E. Gelenbe, J.M. Fourneau "G-Networks with resets", *Perf. Eval.* 49, 179–191, 2002.

Drawing Attention to the Dangerous

Stathis Kasderidis[1], John G. Taylor[1], Nicolas Tsapatsoulis[2] and Dario Malchiodi[3]

[1] Department of Mathematics, King's College London, Strand, WC2R2LS, UK
stathis@mth.kcl.ac.uk - john.g.taylor@kcl.ac.uk
[2] School of Electrical and Computer Engineering,
National Technical University of Athens,
9, Iroon Polytechniou Str., 15773 Athens, Greece
ntsap@image.ntua.gr
[3] Department of Computer Science, University of Milan,
Via Comelico 39/41, 20135 Milan, Italy
malchiodi@dsi.unimi.it

Abstract. In this paper we present an architecture of attention-based control for artificial agents. The agent is responsible for monitoring adaptively the user in order to detect context switches in his state. Assuming a successful detection appropriate action will be taken. Simulation results based on a simple scenario show that Attention is an appropriate mechanism for implementing context switch detector systems.

1 Introduction

Attention is a very important attribute possessed by many animals. It becomes increasingly under voluntary control and less reflexive as the evolutionary tree is ascended. In this paper we consider the application of this facility to artificial agents. We consider how attention can be introduced into such agents, specifically those involved in the guidance of humans in tasks involving 'wearables'. Seen as a natural part of the *'Disappearing Computer'* project [1], it is necessary to solve the task of fusing what might be a considerable amount of data about the human wearer, leading to possibly crucial decisions as to his/her welfare.
J.G.Taylor has elsewhere [2],[3],[4] introduced attention in engineering control terms; this uses both inverse and forward models [5] in order to optimise information processing used in decision-making. We implement a control architecture, which includes the simplest components: state maps and attention control generator. A simplified scenario is used in simulations to show the case of User Monitoring by the response of the attention system, in particular by adaptively changing the sensor resolution, as well as taking into account the user profile.

2 The User Monitoring Problem

In many circumstances intelligent artefacts would have to monitor their users and decide on behalf of them for their welfare. To facilitate intelligent decision-making the artefacts should be able to adapt their monitoring strategy according to the context of the user. Due to (mainly) power and communication limitations sensors could not be continually polled in their highest sampling rate. This leads to the problem of limited information for effective decision-making. The controlling artefacts then have to adaptively monitor their users by increasing or decreasing the sampling rates of the various sensors involved. This is the User Monitoring Problem. It is an optimization problem in the sense that one has to balance energy and communication overhead against higher resolution information about the user and his environment. A possible strategy for achieving such a balance is attention control.

There are two principle ways in which a state transition could take place. It is either a slow, gradual process (*'adiabatic'*) or a *'sudden'* jump to the new state. According to this we propose a solution to the User Monitoring problem, which consists of two elements. On one hand one uses attention control to capture the fast changes while classifier systems could capture the departure from one context to the other in the slow timescale.

We present now a health monitoring scenario that would make more concrete the User Monitoring Problem. Here we have a user with heart problems, that needs to regularly monitor his heart condition. There is a Heart Rate (HR) sensor attached to the user while a second artefact (his PDA) polls the sensor, controls its sampling rate and informs the user. For simplicity we assume that all the available information is the Heart Rate signal (instead of the ECG). The device acts as the user interface and is able to call the health monitoring service provider in case of an emergency. The software agent resides in the PDA device. A number of events can take place, which induce a change in the state of the user. We use the variable of *Alert Level* to distinguish the user states. The resting state has the *Normal* classification. Additionally two more states are considered. An *Attention Seeking* and a *Dangerous* one. The goal of the agent is to detect successfully the states and take appropriate actions. If an event of interest takes place (either a Heart Attack, or another major stress) we assume that the following cycle of events takes place:

(1) *Rest state* 1 - Initial Steady State, (2) $Pre - cursor\ state$ - indicating the onset of a Heart Attack, (3) $Onset\ of\ Heart\ Attack$ - say with duration of 1 min, (4) *Rest state* 2 - Final Steady State.

The first Rest State is the current equilibrium state where the system uses a default *monitoring level* for the user. We use as default rate 1 sample/min. The second state is a pre-cursor signal which in many phenomena is present and for this reason useful to be exploited for expectation of system change. We make the assumption here that indeed this signal exists in order to simplify the presentation. The existence of a pre-cursor could be exploited by using appropriate rules for the sampling rate setting of the sensor. In a typical setting the sampling rate would be increased on expectation of the main event. In our case the sampling rate is increased to 10 samples/min. The onset of a Heart Attack is manifested by the increase in the mean level of the Heart Rate. At the end of the event the rate returns to another resting state eventually (Rest State 2). During the main event the sampling rate increases to 1 sample/second.

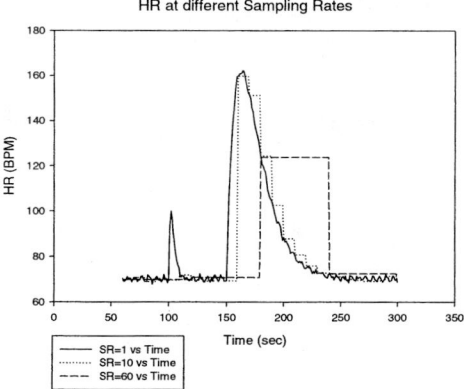

Fig. 1. Heart Rate signal in three different sampling rates: $\frac{1}{60}$ Hz, $\frac{1}{10}$ Hz and 1 Hz.

A typical time course of the Heart Rate series is shown in Figure 1. There we plot the series with the three sampling rates present in our scenario. It is clear that only by using the highest sampling rate ($SR=1$) one can accurately follow the sequence of events. In the figure (and for the rest of the paper) we use the values of 60 (1 sample/60 secs), 10 (1 sample/10 secs) and 1 (1 sample/sec) to indicate the lowest, medium and highest rate.

3 Architecture

The architecture we use is based on that extracted from the human brain, and is shown in Figure 2. Attention is, in the human brain, involved in two forms of control: sensory and motor response [6]. We have made that division explicit, since there is both the need for sensory feedback, to lower level, i.e. to input sensors so as to change sampling rate, as well as in control of motor response for guidance to higher-level systems.

Let us explain now in detail the process that takes place in Figure 2. The user generates a Heart Rate time series, which is sampled at an appropriate rate by the sensor. The output from the sensor is the current instantaneous value of the Heart Rate signal measured in BPM, $HR(t)$. Obviously if one increases the sampling rate he will observe more of the micro-structure of the series (see Figure 1). This raw sensor data is then forwarded to the user's PDA. This has a number of modules that take part in the processing. The first module collects the data and builds an appropriate state representation for the time series; it is called State Vector. The next module in the sequence is the State Classifier system. It uses as input the State Vector and outputs a classification for the Alert Level (State Classification Vector). The classifier system is implemented by some appropriate method [7], [8]. In this way known knowledge can be used for classification purposes.

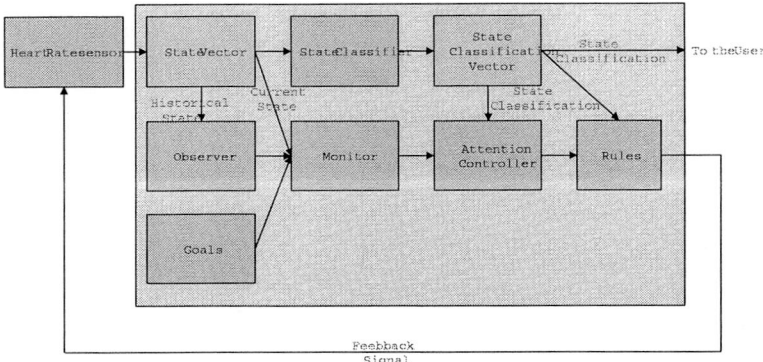

Fig. 2. Proposed Attention Architecture for an agent.

The State Vector we use has a 'Takens' embedding representation [9]. The vector is used in the Observer module as well. This module includes a model for predicting the current state, i.e. $HR(t)$, given a history up to some lag time T. In other words the Observer implements the following mapping:

$$HR(t) = f(HR(t-1), ..., HR(t-T)) \qquad (1)$$

This is achieved by using, for example, an appropriate trained neural network. We also assume that the history of the series up to some lag time T is stored in a *Historical State* vector. However, for simplicity this is not present in Figure 2. At the next step the Observer prediction and the actual state (coming from the State Vector) are compared in the Monitor module. There, a measure of similarity (or closeness), E, is calculated and this is compared against a given threshold. The threshold is a user specific value and it is given by the *User Profile*. In our case the Monitor module calculates the $\|\cdot\|_1$ metric. Other possibilities exist. If the error measure calculated is higher than the threshold value this indicates the existence of an event of interest that needs attending to. The above concept is represented by an Attention Index (AI) given by:

$$AI = 1 - Pr(E > \delta) \qquad (2)$$

where E is the Monitor error measure and δ is the aforementioned threshold. Pr is the probability that the error is larger than the threshold. We assume that a suitable error distribution has been selected. This definition implies that the more 'improbable' is an event the higher is the index that it creates. This is consistent with the fact that unexpected changes in the user state imply in turn a rather large error deviation between the prediction and the current state. As a result higher priority should be given to such events. The Attention Index created together with the State Classification Vector are then forwarded to the Attention Controller. The threshold value δ is provided as a piece of information coming from another module. This is the Goals module. Its main function is to indicate to the system the type of goals we try to achieve as well as help in the creation and processing of new goals. The various properties of the User profile (such as thresholds) are generally fuzzy concepts. For simplicity we assume here that they are crisp numbers. We will not expand further at this point because in our simple scenario the Goals module is not involved any further.

The Attention Controller receives the Attention Index from the Monitor module for further processing. It implements conceptually two distinct functions:

(a) It has a *priority policy* for inducing an order in the space of Attention Events,
(b) It has a *dispatch policy* for deciding which jobs will be dispatched in the next processing stage.

The above structure is a general template for building appropriate Attention Controllers. An example of a priority policy is a competition mechanism. In this paper we adopt a very simple solution: the priority queue model. The ordering in this queue is already defined by the value of the Attention Index. The motivation of definition given in eq. 2 should be now clear: The highest priority event should make use of the system resources for its own processing. This principle is borrowed from the human attention system and it provides effective guidance for control purposes, as we will see in the next section.

Finally, the implementation of actions that are necessary to achieve the desired system behavior, after an Attention Event is dispatched, is left in the Rules module. There, a set of rules, guides the system actions. In our case it is the change of the monitoring level according to the given recognized state. The appropriate rules are as follows (CAL=Current Alert Level, PAL=Previous Alert Level):

If *PAL=Normal* and *CAL =Attention-Seeking* increase rate.
If *PAL=Attention-Seeking* and *CAL =Dangerous* increase rate.
If *PAL=Attention-Seeking* and *CAL =Normal* decrease rate.
If *PAL=Dangerous* and *CAL =Attention-Seeking* decrease rate.

The above rules enable the Rules module to set the appropriate sampling rate in the sensor by means of a feedback signal.

The above description does not include a crucial element of the Architecture, that of learning. There are a number of circumstances where the system will fail. In these cases a reinforcement error learning process takes place using the Error measure calculated in the Monitor for this purpose. Moreover, there is the case of the external user feedback to the system for adaptation purposes. This second process is one of the mechanisms that are provided in the Architecture for the modification of the User Profile set. This set provides actually the various specific thresholds and the model parameters that implement the various models present in the architecture. The first adaptation mechanism present is the off-line training of the models in a supervised way. When errors occur the system stores the data for which the performance was not satisfactory. Supervised training is conducted then for a new determination of the User Profile.

4 Simulation and Results

Using the above architecture we implement the scenario of Section 2 in a simulation. The following assumptions are made:

1. A User Profile exists that guides the system for Heart Attack detection, i.e. the thresholds for the specific user are given. We distinguish three cases: (i) *Normal* [60-80], (ii) *AttentionSeeking* [80-100], (iii) *Dangerous* [>100].
2. One time series alone is used; that of the Heart Rate. No data fusion is necessary due to other sources.
3. A User model (State Classifier) has been implemented using an appropriate technique [7],[8] that distinguishes the classes of events described above.
4. We use a synthetic Heart Rate signal.
5. The Heart Attack pattern is described by an appropriate functional form, e.g. $f(x) = a_1 x e^{-a_2 x}$. The parameters are sampled from Normal distributions for the various events. We assume knowledge of the mean and variances of these distributions for training a neural network prediction model for the Observer.
6. A number of threshold values are used. Results in Figure 3 are generated by using the value of δ.

We train a back-propagation 3-5-1 fully connected model to learn the 'profiles' of a heart attack. The two-parameter family of the pulses mentioned above represents the Heart Attacks profiles. A standard pre-cursor signal is present having a similar form with the main event signal but with less amplitude. The simulation is run for a period of 300 seconds. Two events take place. One pre-cursor event at 100 secs and the main event (Heart Attack) at 150 secs. Typical results are presented in Figure 3. We use only the simplistic rules, mentioned in the previous section, for controlling the sampling rate. Obviously more complete strategies can be used.

The first diagram shows the Heart Rate signal and the prediction of the Observer's model. The solid line represents the HR signal sampled with a variable sampling rate according to the rules applied at the given moment. This is what the user would see. The dotted line represents the prediction of the Observer model. Compare the perceived signal from the part of the user at variable rate with the same signal at the highest sampling rate at Figure 1. The second diagram shows the sensor sampling rate with time. The third diagram indicates the system activity. This has two components. The solid line represents the state classification. The dotted line is the activity of the Attention Controller. The Alert Level is shown as 0 for Normal, 1 for Attention Seeking and 2 for Dangerous. The creation of an attention event is indicated by the value of 3.

The simulation starts with the highest sampling rate of 1 Hz (1 sample/sec). Due to no other activity, no rule is fired so this sampling rate remains unchanged. However, the default monitoring policy is at 1 sample/min. The former rate was chosen so as to show in the first part, 0-100 secs, the close agreement between the prediction of the Observer with the HR series. At 100 sec the pre-cursor signal arrives. A few seconds later the deviation of the Observer prediction and the actual HR series is larger than the threshold. An attention event is created.

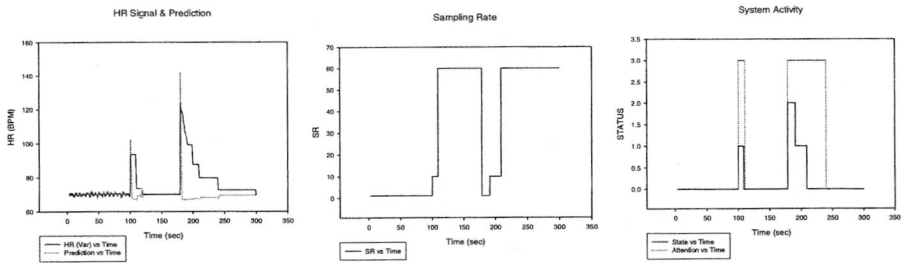

Fig. 3. Simulation results: (a) HR signal, (b) Sampling Rate and (c) System Activity.

This in turn fires the rule that sets the new sampling rate. The new rate is 0.1 Hz. At the same time the HR signal rises from the Normal Alert Level to the Attention Seeking one. This is shown in the System Activity diagram. Eventually the pre-cursor signal levels off and the Observer prediction follows again the HR series time course. At this point the firing of attention events stops. At the same time the rule for setting the sampling rate to the default level, $\frac{1}{60}$ Hz, is activated. This is represented in the Sampling Rate diagram as the value 60.

A period of inactivity exists until the main event arrives at 150 secs. Again the Observer's prediction differs from the HR series, so an attention event is fired. This changes both the sampling rate and the Alert Level classification. The sampling rate goes to 1Hz and the Alert Level takes the value of Dangerous. As the event progresses in time, the Alert Level drops to Attention-Seeking. As a consequence the sampling rate drops to 0.1Hz (10 in Sampling Rate diagram). Eventually the HR signal levels off and the sampling rate returns to the default level of $\frac{1}{60}$ Hz, while no other attention activity is generated.

Some comments are now in due. The first one is related to activation of the rules. The rules are used after an attention event is created. However, there are two ways in which such an event can come to existence. The first one is the deviation of the Observer's prediction from the actual signal. This is intended to capture sudden changes in the signal and indicate fast transitions from one equilibrium state to another. The second way in which attention is caught is by comparing the previous time step's (or steps') State Classification with the current one. An alteration indicates a (typically) slow transition process. These two ways implement the necessary schemes that detect user context switches. See also discussion in Section 2. The second point concerns the prediction ability of the Observer model. One conceptually estimates this model in a stationary regime and then uses it to discover deviations from the actual state. There are two possibilities for such deviations to occur: (a) the model is correct in its prediction and indeed the actual state is different from what was expected, or (b) the model prediction is simply wrong and nothing out of the ordinary has happened. The first is distinguished from the second by using the classification history trace of the State Classifier. If the history indicates that we do have a change in the state we probably deal with the former case. Otherwise the Observer has failed and needs further estimation. This incremental improvement can be implemented as either a supervised learning scheme (off-line) or as a reinforcement scheme (on-line) using the Monitor Error level.

5 Conclusion and Discussion

The attention-based control scheme described in Section 3 is part of the ORESTEIA Architecture for attention-based agents [10]. There, an agent is composed by a number of artefacts partitioned in four levels. At the first level the sensors and actuators exist. In the second one pre-processing facilities are provided. The third level involves local decision makers and the fourth one has global decision makers. Attention control is used in both the third and fourth level

The data fusion problem due to a number of sensors is, currently, under development. The problem here lies in the creation of a proper state representation that captures effectively the environment and user states. In some cases, sensors of different modalities contribute correlated but distinct information about the occurrence of an external event. All the sensor measurements are different aspects of the same stimulus applied either on the environment or directly on the user. Building such a representation is a context capturing problem.

Additionally, learning needs to be present so as the system would be able to adapt better to its environment. Adaptation is achieved by improving the classification power of the State Classifiers and the prediction ability of the Observer model. The latter can be used in order to predict further into the future so as to enable the system to have a more proactive behavior than it currently has.

References

1. Disappearing Computer Project. http://www.disappearingcomputer.org
2. Taylor J. G.: Attentional movement: the control basis for Consciousness. Soc. Neuroscience Abstracts **26**, item 893.3, (2000), 2231.
3. Taylor J. G.: Attention as a neural control system. Proc. Int. Joint Conf. Neural Networks (IJCNN'01), (2001), 262-276.
4. Taylor J. G.: Paying attention to Consciousness. Trends in Cognitive Sciences **6**, (2002), 206-210.
5. Miall R. and Walpert D. M.: Forward models for physiological motor control. Neural Networks **9**, (1996), 1265-1279.
6. Rushworth M. F. S. et al.: The left parietal cortex and motor attention. Neuropsychologia **33**, (1997), 1261-1273.
7. Tsapatsoulis N., Wallace M., and Kasderidis S.: Improving the Performance of Resource Allocation Networks through Hierarchical Clustering of High Dimensional Data. Int. Conf. of Art. Neural Networks (ICANN'03).
8. Apolloni B. et al.: Learning rule representations from boolean data. Int. Conf. of Art. Neural Networks (ICANN'03).
9. Abarbanel H.: Analysis of Observed Chaotic Data. Springer Verlag (1996).
10. FET DC ORESTEIA Project. http://www.image.ntua.gr/oresteia.

ASK – Acquisition of Semantic Knowledge

Trevor P. Martin[1]

Artificial Intelligence Group, Dept of Engineering Mathematics,
University of Bristol, Bristol, BS8 1TR, UK
Trevor.Martin@bris.ac.uk

Abstract. Any computerised information storage system contains assumptions about the form and content of stored information, and the nature of queries. Most obviously, retrieving data from a relational database assumes knowledge of tables and attribute domains. In semi-structured and unstructured data, assumptions may be less explicit but are still present. For example, using a TF-IDF index assumes that the user is aware of the „correct" keywords to be used in queries. One way around this is to implement an ontology, i.e. a „concept dictionary" indicating sets of query terms which are equivalent and containing a hierarchy of concepts e.g. plant is a supertype of tree, which in turn is a supertype of oak. Such a hierarchy can be used to generalise or specialise queries. Manually creating an ontology is a very labour-intensive process In this paper we describe a system which automatically acquires a concept dictionary. The concept dictionary should be regarded as a property of the whole system, i.e. the data and the querying mechanism, not just the data. It makes term similarity explicit and can form the basis for personalisation, by automatically translating a user's terms into those understood by the system.

1 Introduction

Large quantities of data are stored in computer-based systems. Frequently, data is collected and then under-utilised - in itself, the data is useless unless it can be queried, retrieved and explored in order to realise its value. Intelligent information management involves sophisticated mechanisms for searching, extracting and presenting information, meta-data techniques in which a rich array of 'data about the data' is stored, the ability to configure data to different users with different needs and the ability to make inferences from data when appropriate.

A key feature of intelligent information is the use of an ontology, which can relate different concepts in terms of similarity as well as in a hierarchical fashion. In this paper, we suggests a way of generating the ontological information that is implicit in a system, and describe a prototype implementation to demonstrate the validity of the concept. Current information access techniques and ways of assessing system performance are briefly considered. The remainder of the paper outlines a prototype software package which can be used to semi-automatically generate an ontology.

---

[1] This work was supported by BT under the Short Term Fellowship Scheme

2 Data Storage and Access

The form of the data to be stored allows us to identify a spectrum - at one extreme is the relational database which requires complete and well-known data, with a rigidly specified schema and a formal, highly structured querying mechanism. In return for this rigidity and adherence to structure, guarantees can be made about the semantics, integrity and consistency of the data. Data extraction, conversion, transformation, and integration are all well-understood database problems, with clear theoretical underpinnings (see for example [13, 17]). As soon as data moves away from the confines of this completely known and specified format, problems begin to arise. For example, null values are necessary when data is unknown or irregular, leading to well-known problems of interpretation. If a query does not return an expected solution, the system is incorrect and possibly inconsistent.

At the other end of the spectrum, we have completely unstructured data consisting of free text and multimedia components. The process of extracting and searching for data within these „documents" has given rise to the field of information retrieval - see [1] or [18]. Unstructured data is largely free of formal semantics and generally requires human interpretation to make sense of the data.

Falling in the middle of this spectrum, overlapping with both extremes, we have semi-structured data such as classified directories, product catalogues, help systems, and much of the world wide web. In semi-structured data there are compulsory components, for example a business name and telephone number in a classified directory, and there are optional, less-structured components such as a description of products and services offered. Again, access is typically by means of matching a query to a description of the documents. We note that identifying the „right" and „wrong" answers to a query can be subject to interpretation. Documents are generally described as „relevant" (or not) to a query. This is clearly a matter of degree in some cases, and all we can say about a „wrong" answer is that it makes the system less inaccurate, rather than logically inconsistent as a database would be.

In the most common information retrieval model, each document is described by a set of keywords or index terms, each of which is given a weight in the interval [0, 1], calculated according to how well the term distinguishes a document from others in the collection – see for example [16]. Probably the most common method of calculating weights is TF-IDF. A query may be expressed in natural language, some restricted form of natural language, or as a set of keywords. In all cases, it is reduced to an n-dimensional vector over the set keywords extracted from the documents, and the degree of match between the query and a document is given by the cosine of the angle between the two vectors. Many variations of this model have been proposed, including probabilistic retrieval, fuzzification of the vector model, neural nets, Bayesian nets, etc - see chapter 2 of [1] for a more complete discussion of classical information retrieval methods, and some recent extensions.

Performance is normally measured by *precision* - the proportion of retrieved documents that are relevant and *recall* - the proportion of relevant documents that are retrieved.

Many intranet search engines and document retrieval systems use the vector representation with the TF-IDF technique or some variation of it.

2.1 Uncertainty in Data and Queries

Although the modelling of uncertainty has been an active topic within the uncertainty research communities (particularly fuzzy - see [3, 4, 6, 7, 9, 15]), it has not been addressed as such an important topic by the database and information retrieval communities. In the latter case, uncertainty is present by virtue of the fact that the data is free text, and queries are expressed using natural language terms. Most algorithms which return ranked lists of solutions obtained by matching query terms with document contents implicitly handle uncertainty.

In the former case, the avoidance of methods to handle uncertainty is perhaps due to the view that the relational model is formulated in terms of crisp and well-specified values and that better definition is required in data or queries, rather than explicit methods to handle uncertainty. Fuzzy researchers consider attribute uncertainty in either queries or data (or both) i.e. situations where
  (i) a stored attribute value is not known precisely (John's height is *about 180cm*)
  (ii) a query attribute value is not known precisely (find people with *high* salaries)
  (iii) a tuple may satisfy a relation to some degree (John is a *fairly fluent* speaker of Spanish)

2.2 Clustering and Query Expansion

Additional refinement of a search engine can be achieved by clustering documents in some way. Given a successful retrieval, a set of 'similar' documents can be presented on demand. The most obvious (and time consuming) approach to clustering is manual classification of documents. For example, Yahoo uses a hierarchical labelling to assign each web page to a particular category. Documents can be retrieved by navigation through the category hierarchy as well as by keyword search.

Documents can be clustered automatically using the keyword vectors extended by synonyms, stemmed variations of the keywords and terms which are frequently close to the keyword in the text. These term sets also enable *query expansion* in which query terms can be replaced in order to improve the set of documents retrieved. By incorporating an ontology, retrieval performance can be enhanced; however, it is easy for such a system to overgeneralise and retrieve completely unrelated documents [10].

3 Query Expansion and Ontologies

It would appear to be impossible currently to implement a „universal" AI based ontology containing human-level knowledge. Lenat's Cyc system [11] started with the aim of constructing a knowledge base of „common sense", which could be embedded into other knowledge-based systems. It now contains over one million rules and is therefore likely to overgeneralise without an expert user. The *EDR Electronic Dictionary* [8] is a machine-tractable dictionary that catalogues lexical knowledge of Japanese and English and has a unified thesaurus-like concept classification. WordNet is a lexical database „inspired by current psycholinguistic theories of human lexical memory" [14] and intended to act as a cross between a

dictionary and a thesaurus. The database contains nouns, verbs, adjectives and adverbs plus examples of their usage. Of particular relevance are
- synonym sets, showing words which are interchangeable in some contexts,
- hypernym/hyponym sets showing hierarchical relations between nouns (e.g. oak - tree - plant)
- meronyms/holonym sets, relating (bicycle has-part wheel, rim part-of wheel)

Any of these systems could be used as the basis for the ASK knowledge extraction process (see also [12] for comparison). WordNet was chosen because of its availability and prior use within the related systems.

Recognising that universal thesauri and ontologies are too general to be of use for query expansion in a relatively limited domain, we therefore try to extract only the subset of ontological information relevant to the query mechanism and data. It is essential to recognise that the ontology is derived with respect to the complete system, and is not simply a property of the stored data. Because of interactions between the actual data stored and the mechanism used to access the data, it is not possible to treat the data as a stand-alone body of knowledge which can give rise to an ontology on its own. The implicit or explicit assumptions within the query mechanism also affect the ontology – e.g. if the query mechanism is a TF-IDF scheme, then the significance of different keywords will vary according to the set of documents to be indexed.

To illustrate this idea of acquiring a concept hierarchy, let us take two queries $Q1$ and $Q2$, with their corresponding answer sets $S1$ and $S2$. Assume that

$Q1$ = „find a garage in Bristol"

and

$Q2$ = „find car repair in Bristol"

and that the system returns a set of answers to the second query, S2, which is a subset of S1. We can deduce that „car repair" is a more restricted category than „garage". Such generalisation or specialisation of the queries can come from a human expert or from an automatic system such as WordNet [14] - see also next section. For example, WordNet gives *hotel* as a synonym for the noun *inn*. If this is a valid equivalence for the query system, we would expect a query searching for *hotels* in a particular location to give approximately the same set of answers as a query searching for *inns*.

This mechanism can also be used to detect retrieval errors within the system. For example, the terms *car hire* and *car rental* are synonymous in English so that queries

$Q1$ = „car hire in Bristol"

and

$Q2$ = „car rental in Bristol"

should lead to the same set of answers. If a system returns different sets, it indicates that modification is needed to make these synonymous queries behave identically.

Formally we let $Q(x)$ denote a query predicate that returns *true* or *false* according to whether an entry x is relevant to that query. Then the set of solutions

$SQ = \{ x \mid Q(x) \}$

is the set of all entries x that satisfy (are relevant to) the query Q. We can then say that for two queries, Q and P:

Q generalises P if $SP \subseteq SQ$
Q specialises P if $SQ \subseteq SP$
Q is equivalent to P if $SQ = SP$

ASK – Acquisition of Semantic Knowledge

Note that these are *conjunctive* sets, i.e. SQ represents the set of all entries which are relevant to the query Q. We represent this information as a relation to avoid confusion:

$Relevant \subseteq Query \times Entry$

For example, consider the following subset

id	Query	Answer Entry
1	car hire in Bristol	Eurodollar rent a car
2	car hire in Bristol	Autorent (UK)
3	car rental in Bristol	Eurodollar rent a car
4	car rental in Bristol	Autorent (UK)

The process of answering a query is equivalent to computing tuples in this relation. Knowledge about the relations between different queries (generalisation, specialisation, equivalence) provides a means of checking that the query answering process computes the correct tuples. Thus

$Relevant(Q, E) \leftarrow Relevant(P, E)$ when Q generalises P
$Relevant(P, E) \leftarrow Relevant(Q, E)$ when Q specialises P
$Relevant(Q, E) \leftrightarrow Relevant(P, E)$ when Q is equivalent to P

We could use these rules to compress a cache database - given that the two queries in the table above are equivalent, we need only store rows 1 and 2 to answer either query. More importantly, if we extract the relationship between two queries from the content, we can generate the set of answers without executing the query.

Allowing partial relevance converts this crisp relation to a fuzzy relation, and we must expand the definitions of generalisation, specialisation and equivalence to cater for partial inclusion and approximate equality. We define the degree to which a query P generalises a query Q using the mass assignment framework [2]. The support for the rule

$Relevant(P, E) \leftarrow Relevant(Q, E)$

is calculated from the conditional probability

$$\Pr(P \mid Q) = \frac{|\{x : Relevant(P, x) \land Relevant(Q, x)\}|}{|\{x : Relevant(Q, x)\}|}$$

where the calculation is performed over the mass assignment elements in the supported relation (see [5] for details).

This can be used to check that the query system is retrieving the correct answers. By feeding in a query and then a generalised, specialised or equivalent query; it can also be used to deduce that these relations (generalisation, specialisation, equivalence) hold to some degree between queries by comparing sets of answers.

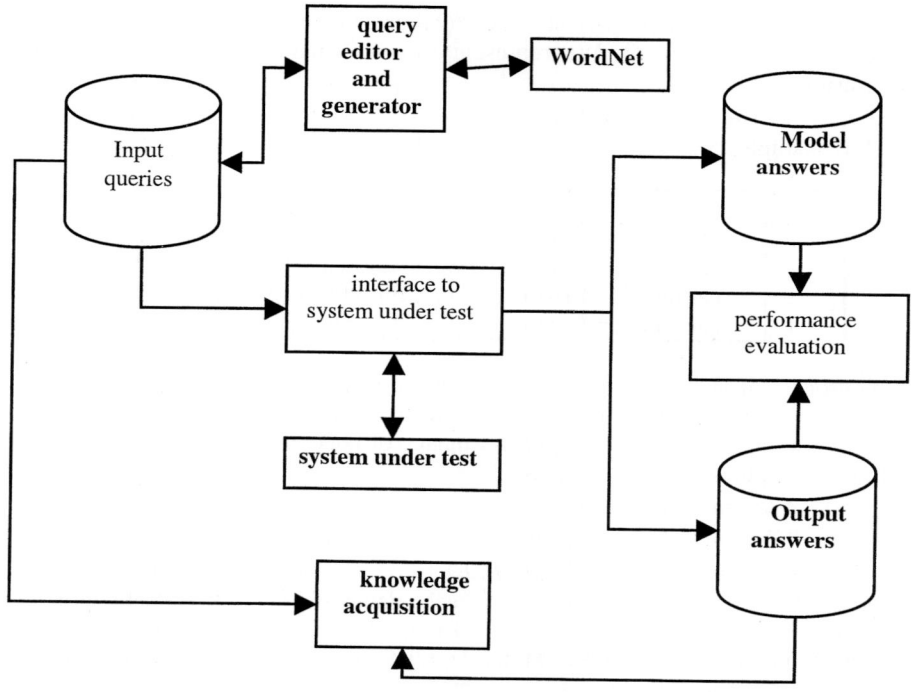

Fig. 1. Architecture of ASK software

3.1 Architecture and Implementation

The prototype software has been implemented in Java and tested on the YPA system [10] which is an interface to semi-structured databases. There are two modes of operation - one is to run a set of queries and compare the answers produced to a set of model answers, giving a performance measure (recall and precision). The second mode of operation is to derive the concept hierarchy implied by a set of queries and answers. The two modes are not exclusive, but we focus on the second mode here.

The queries and corresponding system answers are stored in a database Queries are assumed to be expressible as ASCII text although this does not rule out the possibility of testing a menu- or form-based system. Queries are stored with an explicit tree structure, showing the source of a particular query. Answers are also assumed to be expressed as ASCII text (this could include markup such as HTML). The system under examination is expected to return an ordered list of answer entries, with associated rankings. A method for checking the equality of answer entries is needed, so that sets of answers to different queries can be compared. By default, the answer entries are compared character by character; within the YPA, each answer entry has an identifier, which simplifies identification of equivalent answer entries. Rankings in the YPA are in the range [0, 100] and are treated as the probability that an answer entry is relevant to the query.

Model answers have been derived by a combination of manual methods (searching through the raw data) and examination of the system's answers. A more sophisticated version of the ASK software would build up model answers by allowing the user to accept or reject the system's answers with a user-defined ranking.

A small amount of code is necessary to interface the ASK code with the system under test. The interface runs as a separate thread and communicates with the test system by means of an output stream, to send queries to the test system, and a (tokenised) input stream to obtain answers from the test system. Each query and answer must be identified uniquely, so that this process can be asynchronous and answers can be returned in any order.

A query editor enables a user to create new queries or to derive queries from existing queries. A new query is derived from an existing query by replacing one term (noun or noun phrase) Compared to the starting query, the new query may be *generalised*, *specialised* or *similar*, and the expectation is that the corresponding answer set will be approximately a superset, subset or equal to the answer set of the original query. Each derived query indicates how it is related to its parent (similar, specialisation, generalisation). The degree to which this relation holds true (as indicated by the answers to the queries) is used to derive new knowledge.

This knowledge is stored in a tree structure, reflecting the query hierarchy. It can be exported in any desired format that is derivable from its text-based representation. Exporting the knowledge would be further enhanced by a mechanism to import knowledge from the system designer, so that user-specified domain knowledge could be incorporated, validated and treated on the same basis as acquired knowledge.

4 Results

A database of 40 queries has been used to test the software on YPA version 0.8. Although relatively small, this is sufficient to show the validity of the approach. The average recall is 20% and the average precision is 23%, judged by the model answers (NB many of the queries were hand chosen because they did not elicit accurate responses from the YPA system, leading to these poor figures). With the derived knowledge, an average precision of 91% and recall of 82% was found.

In view of the fact that some of the YPA answers sets are empty, the knowledge derivation step was run on the model answers. Clearly this is a slightly artificial test, in that the model answers and the derived queries were produced manually and hence there is a degree of circularity possible in this test. Further work is needed with a larger set of queries and an improved query system.

5 Summary

A prototype software package has been implemented to test the performance of systems storing semi-structured data, and to extract ontological knowledge from such systems in the form of a concept hierarchy. Such extracted knowledge is a property of the query system (including the data) and could be used to improve the performance of the system or to aid personalisation by translating a user's preferred terms into the system's terms. The methods have been tested on the YPA query system and found to improve performance considerably. Further testing is required for conclusive results, particularly by investigating large databases and the „export" of knowledge.

References

1. Baeza-Yates, R. and B. Ribeiro-Neto, *Modern Information Retrieval*. 1999, Harlow, UK: Addison Wesley.
2. Baldwin, J.F., *The Management of Fuzzy and Probabilistic Uncertainties for Knowledge Based Systems*, in *Encyclopedia of AI*, S.A. Shapiro, Editor. 1992, John Wiley. p. 528–537.
3. Baldwin, J.F., *Mass Assignments and Fuzzy Sets for Fuzzy Databases*, in *Advances in the Shafer Dempster Theory of Evidence*, M. Fedrizzi, J. Kacprzyk, and R.R. Yager, Editors. 1992, John Wiley.
4. Baldwin, J.F. and T.P. Martin. *Management of Uncertainty in Databases Models using Fril*. in *EUFIT-95*. 1995. Aachen, Germany.
5. Baldwin, J.F. and T.P. Martin. *Towards Inductive Support Logic Programming*. in *IFSA-NAFIPS 2001*. 2001. Vancouver: IEEE Press.
6. Bosc, P. and B. Bouchon-Meunier, *Databases and Fuzziness – Introduction*. International Journal of Intelligent Systems, 1994. **9**(5): p. 419.
7. Dubois, D., H. Prade, and R.R. Yager. *Information Engineering and Fuzzy Logic*. in *FUZZ-IEEE 96*. 1996. New Orleans: IEEE Press.
8. EDR, *Japan Electronic Dictionary Research*, http://www.iijnet.or.jp/edr/. 1995, Japan Electronic Dictionary Research Institute.
9. Kacprzyk, J., B.P. Buckles, and F.E. Petry, *Fuzzy Information and Database Systems*. Fuzzy Sets and Systems, 1990. **38**(2): p. 133.
10. Kruschwitz, U., et al., *Extracting Semi-structured Data - Lessons Learnt*, in *Lecture Notes in Computer Science 1835*. 2000. p. 406–417.
11. Lenat, D.B., *CYC: A Large-Scale Investment in Knowledge Infrastructure*. Communications- Acm, 1995. **38**(11): p. 32.
12. Lenat, D.B., G.A. Miller, and T. Yokoi, *CYC, WordNet, and EDR: Critiques and Responses*. Communications- Acm, 1995. **38**(11): p. 45.
13. Maier, D., *The Theory of Relational Databases*. 1983: Pitman.
14. Miller, G.A., *WordNet: A Lexical Database for English*. Communications- Acm, 1995. **38**(11): p. 39.
15. Miyamoto, S. and M. Umano, *Fuzzy Databases and Information Retrieval*. International Journal Of Intelligent Systems, 1996. **11**(9): p. 611.
16. Salton, G. and M.J. McGill, *Introduction to Modern Information Retrieval*. 1983, New York: McGraw Hill.
17. Ullman, J.D., *Principles of Database and Knowledge-Base Systems Parts 1 and 2*. 1988: Computer Science Press.
18. van Rijsbergen, C.J., *Information Retrieval*. 2nd ed. 1979, London, UK: Butterworths.

An Adaptable Gaussian Neuro-Fuzzy Classifier[*]

Minas Pertselakis, Dimitrios Frossyniotis, and Andreas Stafylopatis

National Technical University of Athens
School of Electrical and Computer Engineering
9, Iroon Polytechneiou Str., Zografou, 157 80, Athens, Greece
`{mper, dfros}@cslab.ntua.gr, andreas@cs.ntua.gr`

Abstract. The concept of semantic and context aware intelligent systems provides a vision for the Information Society where the emphasis lays on computing applications that can sense context from the people and the environment and wrap that knowledge into adaptable behavior. In this framework the proper and automatic classification of data gathered by sensors is of major importance. Our approach describes a model that operates as a self-evaluating classifier using on-line re-clustering, addressing adequately the basic issues of modern demands. The novelty of the model lies in a flexible and efficient initialization technique that first partitions the data space utilizing Gaussian distributions and then merges clusters so as to produce an effective partitioning.

1 Introduction

The area of context-aware computing is aimed at the adaptation of the behavior of an application as a function of its current environment [1]. This environment can be characterized as a physical location, a semantic data space or a user profile. A context-aware application can sense the environment and interpret the events that occur within it, reacting accordingly. In heterogeneous environments where semantic integration is often required, the information to be accessed is heterogeneous and attribute correspondences could be fuzzy. In this framework, applications and algorithms should be able to automatically analyze vast amounts of data, extract or exchange knowledge and make decisions in a given context.

Fuzzy neural models have the ability to operate and adapt in both numeric as well as linguistic environments. In addition, they can handle fuzzy attributes and can be adaptive through learning from data. Therefore, in a context-aware computing environment, an adaptive neuro-fuzzy model should be self-evaluating and able to facilitate fast learning through data-driven knowledge embedded in its architecture. More specifically, in order to embed data-driven or expert knowledge in a neuro-fuzzy model, the usual way is to apply a clustering or partitioning method. In the clustering approach the centers of fuzzy rules are initialized as cluster vectors

---

[*] Work partially funded by E.C. contract No.IST-2000-26091,\"ORESTEIA:Modular hybrid artefacts with adaptive functionality".

extracted from the input data set [2]. A learning algorithm is utilized then to fine tune the rules based on the available training data. Partitioning methods divide the input-output cross space into finer regions. Each partition is supposed to represent an *if-then* rule [3]. Both approaches present low adaptability: The number of rules that describe the physical phenomenon under examination is estimated heuristically and does not change during the learning phase.

Our approach includes a context-aware intelligent classifier model that provides self-awareness by reconfiguring its "weak" fuzzy rules when necessary. The proposed system is trained using a novel initialization procedure. This procedure combines both a partitioning method and a clustering algorithm capable of extracting fuzzy rules from a well-fined partitioned dataset in a non-heuristic way.

2 The Integrated Classifier Model

The proposed model consists of three components: the trained classifier module, the Observer and the Catalyst (Fig. 1). The trained classifier could be any of the classifiers proposed in the literature [4]. We chose to use the Subsethood-Product Fuzzy Neural Inference System (SuPFuNIS, [5]), since it utilizes Gaussian distributions and performs very well as a classifier. The Observer is an incorporated mechanism that is constantly aware about the output status Y, tracks down the history of the input data X and is responsible for Catalyst's activation. This activation takes place when we have a reasonable number of input patterns that produce inaccurate or too fuzzy outputs. The Observer, locates this area of effect in the input-output cross space, by re-clustering the inputs that produced the low confident output and only them, based on the multi-clustering fusion algorithm, presented in the following section. From the resulting clusters, we pick the one with most data points (the most serious problem).

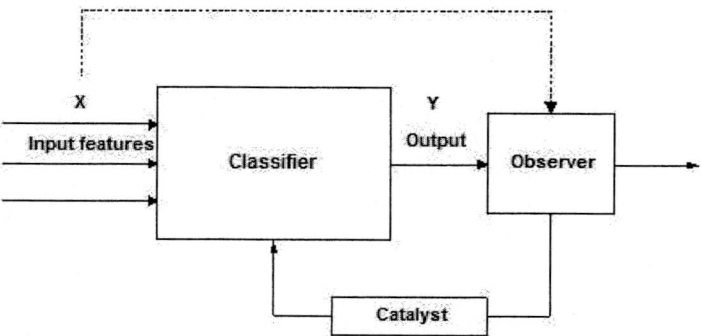

Fig. 1. The classifier model

Given the output result and the input data, we discern the following cases, which are realized by the catalyst:

1) **Null.** The new cluster is not powerful enough to create a new rule (i.e. not sufficient number of data or low density). Nothing happens to the system, though it can be affected from this, later on.
2) **Amputation.** The newly formed cluster belongs to an existent cluster, as a part of it. In that case the new cluster represents a new rule that classifies inputs mainly to the secondary class, which the older cluster was pointing to. The old rule (cluster) enhances the power of its major indicated class, reducing at the same time, the power of the others.
3) **Birth.** The newly formed cluster is independent. The observer checks to see if this new cluster is too remote (i.e. distant to the common data space) and if it is, it requests a general retraining or update. Otherwise, a new rule is added, with a heavier weight towards the output's major class, and a lighter towards the other classes.

Since this model could be implemented in context-aware systems, such as health monitoring devices, or car status interfaces (see [10]), the computational error should be kept minimal and the model should be adaptive. The above model adequately addresses each of these aspects. A short description of the classifier module used is following.

2.1 The Classifier Module

Based on the SuPFuNIS model we implemented a subsethood product fuzzy neural classifier with the following characteristics:

(a) SuPFuNIS uses a tunable input fuzzifier that is responsible for fuzzification of numeric data. Numeric inputs are fuzzified using a feature-specific Gaussian spread.
(b) All information that propagates from the input layer is fuzzy. The model uses a composition mechanism employing a fuzzy mutual subsethood measure to define the activation that propagates to a rule node along a fuzzy connection.
(c) It aggregates activities at a rule node using a *fuzzy inner product*: a product of mutual subsethoods, which is different from the most common approach to use a fuzzy *min* conjunction operator.

Learning. Learning is incorporated into SuPFuNIS using the gradient descent method. The free parameters of the system, meaning both the centers w_{ij}^c (v_{jk}^c) and spreads w_{ij}^σ (v_{jk}^σ) of antecedent (consequent) connections and the spreads x_i^σ of the input features, are modified on the basis of update equations. Evaluation of partial derivatives required in weight update equations, as well as the analytic computations of the mutual subsethood, the net activation product and the defuzzified output, can be found in [5].

SuPFuNIS initialization method. In the SuPFuNIS model, the number of clusters determines the number of rules and the clustering is done in the input-output cross space. Thus, the centroids and boundaries of clusters can be applied as the values of the centers and spreads of fuzzy weights that fan in and out of a rule node. The employed clustering technique is the fuzzy c-means (FCM) algorithm [6] in conjunction with the Xie-Beni validity index [7] to cluster the given dataset and choose the best cluster, respectively.

3 Knowledge Extraction from Numeric Data

One of the methods to extract initial knowledge from the training data set is to cluster the data using a clustering technique. Cluster-based initialization has been known to improve the rate of learning as well as the performance of the system.

It is evident, though, that different clustering algorithms and even multiple replications of the same algorithm produce different partitioning results, due to random or parameterized initialization. For instance, SuPFuNIS employs the FCM algorithm, as described above, to partition the data set because it is simple and fast. Nevertheless, its performance depends on the initial cluster centers and, in addition, the user predefines the number of clusters. Therefore, it is necessary to run FCM several times, each time with a different number of clusters, to discover the right figure that results in the best performance of the classification system (Fig. 2).

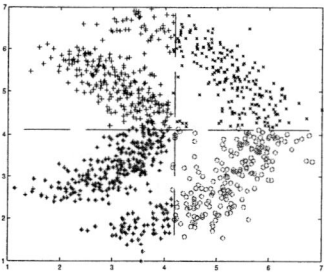 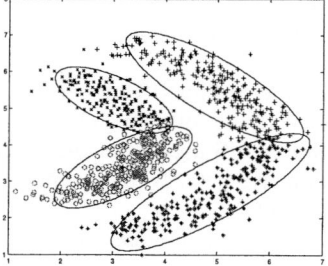

Fig. 2. Partitioning artificial data using FCM with Xie-Beni index for 4 clusters (predefined)

Fig. 3. Partitioning same data using Multi-Clustering Gaussian Fusion resulting in 4 clusters

To overcome these rigid restrictions we developed a multi-clustering fusion algorithm. A variant of this algorithm has been firstly introduced in [8], while, in this paper, we present a different configuration of the method, including adoption of Gaussian distributions as well as a new approach for specifying merging criteria for ellipsoid clusters (Fig. 3). According to this technique, the data are assumed to have been generated by several parameterized Gaussian distributions, so the data points are assigned to different clusters based on their posterior probabilities. In this direction, we believe that finding the optimal number of ellipsoid clusters in the data set can improve the robustness of the classification system. The proposed partitioning approach consists of two main phases: the partitioning and the fusion procedure.

3.1 Partitioning Procedure

In the Partitioning procedure, a basic clustering algorithm is applied for a number of iterations, Iter, so as to accomplish a distinct partitioning of N data points to a predefined number C of clusters. In our implementation, we incorporate the proposed methodology in the context of k-means as the basic clustering algorithm. The basic clustering algorithm partitions the data set in a different way for each iteration, creating a problem of deciding which cluster of one run corresponds to which in another run. This algorithm tackles this problem using the similarity between the clusters produced during successive runs. By determining the percentage of points of a cluster in the t-th run belonging to clusters of the $t-1$-th run, each cluster of the new run is assigned to one of the previous run, resulting in a cluster renumbering process.

After renumbering, if pattern $\vec{x}$ is assigned to cluster q, then a positive vote is given to cluster q and a negative one to all other clusters. This process defines a voting scheme, during which a voting table VT (of dimension $N \times C$) is updated, so that $VT(i,j)$ denotes the membership degree of pattern $\vec{x}_i$ to cluster j, where $i=1,...,N$, and $j=1,...,C$. Using the VT table and the relation between the data points of one cluster with all the remaining clusters, a table NRT (of dimension $C \times C$) can be produced, so that $NRT(i,j)$ represents the neighbourhood relation between clusters i and j.

For each cluster, a different Gaussian distribution (ellipsoid) is assigned and the specification of the Gaussian parameters is based on the expectation-minimization algorithm (EM, [9]). Thus, based on regular EM steps, fine-tuning of the parameters is carried out until convergence.

3.2 Fusion Procedure

After the parameters for each Gaussian distribution are specified, the Fusion procedure takes place and finds the optimal number of ellipsoids in the data set according to some predefined criteria. From the decomposition of the covariance matrix K_j of the j-th ellipsoid, we compute the angle $\phi_{kij} \in \left(-\frac{\pi}{2}, \frac{\pi}{2}\right)$ between the k major axis' eigenvector and the i-th dimension for each ellipsoid.

Given also the neighbourhood relation (table NRT) among ellipsoids, the fusion procedure commences with the predefined number C of ellipsoids and merges the ones that fulfill the following conditions:
1. Both ellipsoids are neighbour to each other,
2. The two angle vectors $(\varphi_{1i}, \varphi_{2i})$, where $i=1...(d-1)$, between the two ellipsoids satisfy one from the rules below for every i (d is the problem dimensionality):

A) φ_{1i} and φ_{2i} have the same sign, and $abs\ (\varphi_{1i}-\varphi_{2i}) < 70°$, or (2)

B) φ_{1i} and φ_{2i} have different sign, and (3)
$(180° - [abs\ (\varphi_{1i}) + abs\ (\varphi_{2i})] < 20°$ or $[abs\ (\varphi_{1i}) + abs\ (\varphi_{2i})] < 20°)$

The next step is to merge these ellipsoids into one and to reconfigure the voting table accordingly, by adding the votes of the second ellipsoid to the first one. The fusion procedure is running iteratively until the algorithm fails to find any pair of ellipsoids to merge.

4 Experimental Results

This section presents a comparative experimental evaluation of the proposed approach using different initialization techniques. Results concern the effectiveness of the classification module rather than the integrated classifier model as described in Section 2. A systematic assessment of the latter based on an involved experimental setup is ongoing [10]. In the following, the case of random initialization will be referred to as *Random-SuPFuNIS,* whereas the classifier resulting from using the FCM partitioning method combined with the Xie-Beni index will be referred to as *FCM-SuPFuNIS*. Similarly, using the proposed multi-clustering gaussian fusion algorithm for partitioning and for initializing the classifier will be referred to as *Multi-Fusion-SuPFuNIS*.

Two benchmark data sets were used to demonstrate the performance of the *Multi-Fusion-SuPFuNIS*: the Clouds and Pima Indians data sets. The Clouds artificial data from the ELENA project, ftp://ftp.dice.ucl.ac.be/pub/neural-nets/ELENA/databases, are two-dimensional produced by three different Gaussian distributions. There are 5000 samples in the data set belonging to three clusters, which are relatively highly overlapped (see Fig.4). The Pima Indians set contains 8-dimensional data and can be obtained from the UCI data set repository ftp://ftp.ics.edu/pub/machine-learning-databases. It is based on personal data from 768 Pima Indians obtained by the National Institute of Diabetes and Digestive and Kidney Diseases. For each data set and for each number of rules, five experiments were performed with random splits of the data into training and test sets of fixed size, from which *mean* classification accuracy was calculated. More specifically, for the Clouds we used 2500 for training and 2500 for testing, while for the Pima Indians we used 500 for training and 268 for testing respectively. The results of our experiments are shown in Tables 1 and 2. Both number of clusters (rules) produced by each partitioning method and test accuracy of the respective classifier system are shown. Note that, for the *Random-SuPFuNIS* and for the *FCM-SuPFuNIS*, we give several results according to the number of rules, contrary to the *Multi-Fusion-SuPFuNIS* where the number of rules is computed in advance. For all the experimental cases considered we used twenty training epochs for the classifier.

Table 1. Experimental results for the Clouds data set

Number of Rules	3	5	8	10	15	20
Random-SuPFuNIS	78.58%	79.07%	72.3%	79.62%	85.96%	87.44%
FCM-SuPFuNIS	75.72%	88.40%	88.30%	88.90%	88.10%	88.70%
Multi-Fusion-SuPFuNIS	Number of Rules produced = 5　Generalization accuracy　　= 89.36%					

Table 2. Experimental results for the Pima Indians data set

Figures 5 and 6 show the application of the proposed approach to Clouds data at

Number of Rules	3	5
Random-SuPFuNIS	75.8%	76.63%
FCM-SuPFuNIS	76.2%	76.13%
Multi-Fusion-SuPFuNIS	Number of Rules produced = 4	
	Generalization accuracy = 79.48%	

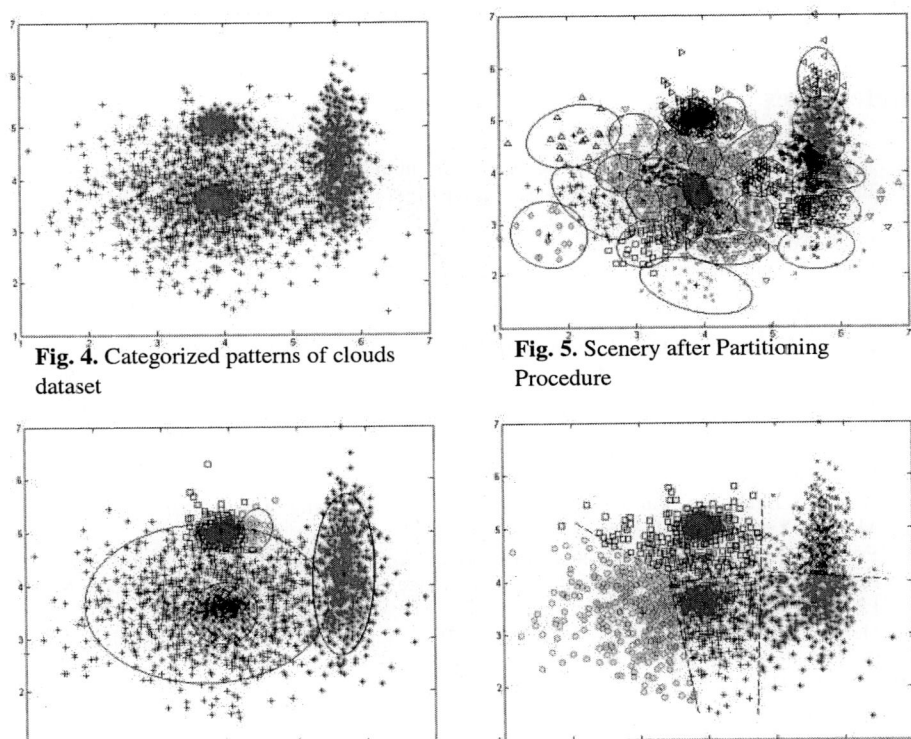

Fig. 4. Categorized patterns of clouds dataset

Fig. 5. Scenery after Partitioning Procedure

Fig. 6. Scenery after Fusion Process resulting in five clusters

Fig. 7. Best Partitioning result of FCM – Xie-Beni index for the same number of clusters

the end of each procedure, respectively, whereas Fig. 7 presents the best partitioning obtained by FCM – Xie-Beni combination. It is clear that the multi-clustering gaussian fusion method yields a much more accurate partitioning result with respect to the actual dataset structure.

5 Conclusions

In this paper we propose a classifier model that employs a novel multi-clustering initialization procedure. The major strengths of this intelligent model are its economy of parameters, fast learning and the ability to learn and adequately perform even in heterogeneous environments, where significant changes of the sensed data characteristics can be manifested. Ongoing and future work includes experimental evaluation of the integrated model using real-data test sets in non-stationary environments.

References

1. Abowd, G.: Software engineering issues for ubiquitous computing. Proceedings of the International Conference on Software Engineering, pp. 5–84, (1999).
2. Nauck, D., Kruse, R.: A neuro-fuzzy method to learn fuzzy classification rules from data. Fuzzy Sets and Systems, Vol.89, pp. 277–288, (1997).
3. Lin, Y., Cunningham, G. A. III, Coggeshall, S. V.: Using fuzzy partition to create fuzzy systems from input–output data and set the initial weights in a fuzzy neural network. IEEE Trans. Fuzzy Systems, Vol. 5, pp. 614–621, (1997).
4. Kovacs, T.: Learning Classifier Systems Resources. CSRP-00-19, (2000) [http://citeseer.nj.nec.com/article/kovacs02learning.html]
5. Paul, S., Kumar, S.: Subsethood-Product Fuzzy Neural Inference System (SuPFuNIS). IEEE Trans. On Neural Networks, Vol. 13, No. 3, pp. 578–599, (2002).
6. Bezdek, J.C.: Pattern Recognition with Fuzzy Objective Function Algorithms. Plenum Press, New York, (1981).
7. Xie, X., Beni, G.: Validity measure for fuzzy clustering. IEEE Trans. Pattern Anal. Machine Learning, Vol. 3, pp. 841–846, (1991).
8. Frossyniotis, D., Pertselakis, M., Stafylopatis, A.: A Multi-Clustering Fusion Algorithm. Proceedings of the Second Hellenic Conference on Artificial Intelligence (SETN2002), LNAI 2308, pages 225–236, Springer-Verlag, Thessaloniki, (2002).
9. Dempster, A.P., Laird, N.M., Rubin, D.B.: Maximum likelihood from incomplete data via the EM algorithm. Roy. Statist. Soc. B, 39: 1–38, (1977).
10. Modular Hybrid Artefacts with Adaptive Functionality (ORESTEIA), IST Project, 2001-2003. [http://www.image.ntua.gr/oresteia/index.html]

Knowledge Refinement Using Fuzzy Compositional Neural Networks

Vassilis Tzouvaras, Giorgos Stamou, and Stefanos Kollias

Image, Video and Multimedia Laboratory
Institute for Computer and Communication Systems
Department of electrical and Computer Engineering
National Technical university of Athens, Greece
tzouvaras@image.ntua.gr
{gstam,stefanos}@softlab.ntua.gr

Abstract. Fuzzy relations as representational tools and fuzzy compositional operators as reasoning components, are user in this paper in order to represent knowledge expressed in semantic rules. Furthermore, neural representation and resolution of composite fuzzy relation equations provides knowledge refinement and adaptation to a specific context. A two-layer fuzzy compositional neural network is proposed in this work, with a learning algorithm changing the weights and minimize the error of the small context changes.

1 Introduction

Machine learning systems, fuzzy rule based systems and hybrid neurofuzzy systems are widely used for the representation and adaptation of semantic descriptions [5],[3],[1], [8]. Built-in a priori knowledge permits robustness, while learning allows for addition, removal and updating of the semantic description in order to adapt to environmental changes. Artificial neural networks are well suited for the adaptive analysis of subsymbolic information, composed of the descriptions generated for the segments. On the other hand, knowledge-based fuzzy logic techniques are capable of including and refining rules that form the basis for symbolic outputs. Hybrid connectionist-symbolic models constitute a promising approach towards developing more robust and versatile intelligent systems. The main focus of such models is the representation of symbolic descriptions of knowledge, in terms of rules in subsymbolic, numeric descriptions used by neural networks for learning and adaptation. The issue of learning includes both representation and automatic acquisition of knowledge. Recent research focuses on the real challenge of integrating learning methods with complex representations [7]. A generic hybrid architecture will be examined in this paper for this purpose. The proposed architecture uses a subsymbolic representation of the semantic knowledge in the form of fuzzy compositional neural networks.

2 Two-Layered Fuzzy Compositional Neural Networks

Let $y = [y_1, y_2, ..., y_m]$ denote a fuzzy set defined on the set of output predicates, the truth of which will be examined. Actually, each y_i represents the degree in which the i-th output fuzzy predicate is satisfied. The input of the proposed system is a fuzzy set $x = [x_1, x_2, ..., x_n]$ defined on the set of the input predicates, with each x_i representing the degree in which the i-th input predicate is detected. The proposed system represents the association $f: X \to Y$ which is the knowledge of the system, in a neurofuzzy structure. After the evaluation of the input predicates, some output predicates represented in the knowledge of the system can be recognized with the aid of fuzzy systems' reasoning [3]. One of the widely used ways of constructing fuzzy inference systems is the method of approximate reasoning which can be implemented on the basis of compositional rule of inference [3]. The need for results with theoretical soundness lead to the representation of fuzzy inference systems on the basis of generalized sup-t-norm compositions [8],[2]. A t-norm (triangular norm) is a function $t: [0,1] \times [0,1] \to [0,1]$ satisfying for any $a, b, d \in [0,1]$ the next four conditions:

1. $t(a,1) = a$ and $t(a,0) = 0$
2. $b \leq d$ implies $t(a,b) \leq t(a,d)$
3. $t(a,b) = t(b,a)$
4. $t(a, t(b,d)) = t(t(a,b), d)$

Moreover, it is called *Archimedean* iff

1. t is a continuous function
2. $t(a,a) < a$, $\forall a \in (0,1)$ (idempotent)

The class of t-norms has been studied by many researchers [11], [15], [26]. Using the definition of t-norms, two additional operators $\hat{\omega}_t, \breve{\omega}_t : [0,1] \times [0,1] \to [0,1]$ are defined by the following relations:

$$\hat{\omega}_t(a,b) = \begin{cases} 1 & a < b \\ a \hat{\otimes}^t b & a \geq b \end{cases}, \quad \breve{\omega}_t(a,b) = \begin{cases} 0 & a < b \\ a \breve{\otimes}^t b & a \geq b \end{cases}$$

where $a \hat{\otimes}^t b = \sup\{x \in [0,1] : t(a,x) = b\}$, $a \breve{\otimes}^t b = \inf\{x \in [0,1] : t(a,x) = b\}$.

With the aid of the above operators, compositions of fuzzy relations can be defined. These compositions are used in order to construct fuzzy relational equations and represent the rule-based symbolic knowledge with the aid of fuzzy inference [7].

Let X, Z, Y be three discrete crisp sets with cardinalities n, l and m respectively, and $A(X,Z)$, $B(Z,Y)$ be two binary fuzzy relations. The definitions of sup-t and inf-$\hat{\omega}_t$ compositions are given by

$$(A \circ^t B)(i,j) = \sup_{k \in N_l} t\{A(i,k), B(k,j)\}, i \in N_n, j \in N_m$$

$$(A \circ^{\hat{\omega}_t} B)(i,j) = \inf_{k \in N_l} \hat{\omega}_t\{A(i,k), B(k,j)\}, i \in N_n, j \in N_m$$

Let us now proceed to a more detailed description of the proposed neurofuzzy architecture (Figure 1). It consists of two layers of *compositional* neurons which are extensions of the conventional neurons [7]. While the operation of the conventional neuron is described by the equation:

$$y = \alpha\left(\sum_{i=1}^{n} w_i x_i + \vartheta\right),$$

where α is non-linearity, ϑ is threshold and w_i are the weights, the operation of the sup-t compositional neuron is described by the equation:

$$y = a\left\{\sup_{j \in N_n}(t\; x_i, w_i)\right\},$$

where t is a fuzzy intersection operator (a t-norm) and α is the following activation function $a'(z) = \begin{cases} 0 & x \in (-\infty, 0) \\ x & x \in [0,1] \\ 1 & x \in (0, +\infty) \end{cases}$.

A second type of compositional neuron is constructed using the $\hat{\omega}_t$ operation. The neuron equation is given by:

$$y = a'\left\{\inf_{j \in N_n} \hat{\omega}_t(x_i, w_i)\right\}$$

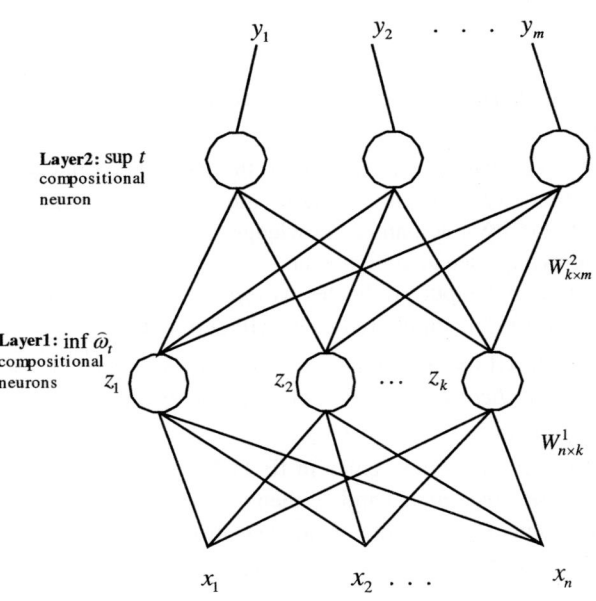

Fig. 1. The fuzzy compositional neural network

The proposed architecture is a two-layer neural network of compositional neurons. The first layer consists of the $\inf - \hat{\omega}_t$ neurons and the second layer consists of the sup-t neurons. The system takes as input, the input predicates and gives to the output the recognized output predicates. The first layer computes the antecedents of the fuzzy rules, while the second implements the fuzzy reasoning using the modus ponens schema.

The rules describing the events are generally of the form "if *input predicate (1)* and ... and *input predicate (n)* then *output predicate (i)*". Each rule consists of an antecedent (the *if* part of the rule) and a consequence (the *then* part of the rule). The set of the rules of the system is given in symbolic form by the expert and is used in order to initialize the neurofuzzy network (giving its initial structure and weights). During the learning process the number of neurons in the hidden layer and the weights of the two layers may change with the aid of a learning with the objective of the error minimization. The learning algorithm that supports the above network is applied in each layer independently. During the learning process, the weight matrices are adapted in order to approximate the solution of the fuzzy relational equation describing the association of the input with the output. Using a traditional minimization algorithm (for example the steepest descent), we cannot take advantage of the specific character of the problem. The algorithm that we use is based on a more sophisticated *credit assignment* that "blames" the neurons of the network using the knowledge about the topographic structure of the solution of the fuzzy relation equation [7]. After the learning process, the network keeps its transparent structure and the new knowledge represented in it can be extracted in the form of fuzzy IF-THEN rules.

3 Knowledge Representation and Refinement

In the process of knowledge representation, the IF-THEN rules are inserted into the proposed neurofuzzy system. This refers to automatically transforming the structured knowledge provided by a semantic knowledge database (encyclopaedia) in order to perform the followings (see also Figure 1).

(a) Define the required input predicates as *input predicate(1)*, *input predicate(2)*,..., *input predicate(n)*. The input predicates will define the set $X = \{x_1, x_2, ..., x_n\}$.

(b) Define the required output predicates as *output predicate(1)*, *output predicate(2)*, ..., *output predicate(n)*. The output predicates will define the set $Y = \{y_1, y_2, ..., y_m\}$.

(c) Insert the a priori knowledge given in IF-THEN rules of the form "if *input predicate(1)* and *input predicate(2)* and ... then *output predicate(5)*" into the neurofuzzy structural elements (the weights of the neurofuzzy system). The number of different antecedents (IF parts of the rules) defines the set $Z = \{z_1, z_2, ..., z_l\}$. The predicates could be associated with confidence levels in order to produce the antecedents; this means that the antecedents could have the form (*input predicate(1)*, *input predicate(2)*, 0.7, 0.9), with the 0.7 and 0.9 values corresponding to confidence levels. The above degrees are used in order to define the weights $\mathbf{W}^1_{ij}, i \in N_n, j \in N_l$ of the first layer. Furthermore, the consequences could also be associated with confidence levels, i.e. "if *input predicate(1)* and *input predicate(2)* and ... then *output predicate(5) with confidence 0.7*". These values are used in order to define the weights $W_{ij}^2, i \in N_l, j \in N_m$ of the second layer.

The knowledge refinement provided by the proposed neurofuzzy system will be now described. Let $X = \{x_1, x_2, ..., x_n\}$ and $Y = \{y_1, y_2, ..., y_m\}$ be the input and output, respectively, predicate sets and let also $R = \{r_1, r_2, ..., r_p\}$ be the set of rules describing the knowledge of the system. The set of antecedents of the rules is denoted by $Z = \{z_1, z_2, ..., z_l\}$ (see the structure of the neurofuzzy system given in Figure 1). Suppose now that a set of input-output data $D = \{(A_i, B_i), i \in N_q\}$, where $A_i \in F(X)$ and $B_i \in F(Y)$ ($F(*)$ is the set of fuzzy sets defined on $*$), is given sequentially and randomly to the system (some of them are allowed to reiterate before the first appearance of some others). The data sequence is described as $(A^{(q)}, B^{(q)})$, $q \in N$, where $(A^{(i)}, B^{(i)}) \in D$. The problem that arise is the finding of the new weight matrices $W_{ij}^1, i \in N_n, j \in N_l$ and $W_{ij}^2, i \in N_l, j \in N_m$ for which the following error is minimised:

$$\varepsilon = \sum_{i \in N_q} \|B_i - y^i\|$$

where $y^i, i \in N_q$ is the output of the network when the input A_i is given. The process of the minimisation of the above error is based on the resolution of the following fuzzy relational equations:

$$W^1 \circ^{\bar{\omega}_t} A = Z$$
$$Z \circ^t W^2 = B,$$

where t is a continuous t-norm and Z is the set of antecedents fired when the input A is given to the network.

Roughly speaking, the above equations describes a generalised two-layered *fuzzy associative memory* (FAM) with the property of the *perfect recall* and the property of *generalization*. One-layered fuzzy associative memories have been originally proposed by Kosko [4] and have played an important role in fuzzy systems theory. The model proposed by Kosko does not support the total recall property. Moreover, for this case Kosko claims that this is not a desirable characteristic, although in the case of the single input-single output memory it is mentioned as the most useful property of FAMs. For the resolution of the above problem the adaptation process changes the weight matrices W^1 and W^2 in order to approximate a solution of the above fuzzy relational equations. During its operation the proposed network can generalize in a way that is inspired from the theory of fuzzy systems and the *generalized modus ponens*. Let us here describe the adaptation of the weights of the second layer (the adaptation of the first layer is similar). The proposed algorithm converges independently for each neuron. For simplicity and without loss of generality, let us consider only the single neuron case. The response of the neuron $f^{(k)}$ at time k is given by

$$f^{(k)} = \sup_{i \in N_l} t(z_i^{(k)}, w_i^{(k)}),$$

where $w_i^{(k)}$ are the weights of the neuron and $z_i^{(k)}$ the input, at time k. The desired output at time k is $B_i^{(k)}$. The algorithm has as following:
- Initialize the weights as $w_i^{(0)}$, $i \in N_l$.
- Process the input $\mathbf{z}^{(k)}$ and the desired output $B^{(k)}$, compute the response of the network $f^{(k)}$ and update the weight accordingly (on-line variant of learning):

$$w_i^{(k+1)} = w_i^{(k)} + \Delta w_i^{(k)}$$

$$\Delta w_i^{(k)} = \eta l_s$$

$$l_s = \begin{cases} \eta_1\left(\breve{\omega}_t\left(z_i^{(k)}, B^{(k)}\right) - w_i^{(k)}\right), & \text{if } w_i^{(k)} < \breve{\omega}_t\left(z_i^{(k)}, B^{(k)}\right) \\ \eta_2\left(w_i^{(k)} - \hat{\omega}_t\left(z_i^{(k)}, b^{(k)}\right)\right), & \text{if } w_i^{(k)} > \hat{\omega}_t\left(z_i^{(k)}, B^{(k)}\right) \end{cases},$$

where η, η_1, η_2 are the learning rates. The adaptation is activated only if $\left|\varepsilon\left(B^{(k)}, y^{(k)}\right)\right| > \varepsilon_c$, where ε_c is an error constant.

If the t-norm is Archimedean, then the learning signal is computed as:

$$l_s = \left(\hat{\omega}_t\left(z_i^{(k)}, b^{(k)}\right) - w_i^{(k)}\right), \text{ if } z_i^{(k)} \geq b^{(k)} \text{ and } z_i^{(k)} \neq 0, \text{ else } l_s = 0.$$

With the aid of the above learning process (and similar for the first layer, since the operator $\hat{\omega}_t$ is also used in order to solve the fuzzy relational equation of the first layer [3]), the network approximates the solutions of the fuzzy relational equations given above and thus minimize the error.

4 Simulation Results

In this section we present some simulation results illustrating the operation of the proposed system. We demonstrate the performance of the proposed network before and after the adaptation procedure. The system has 10 input predicates, $X = \{x_1, x_2, ..., x_{10}\}$, 8 antecedents, $Z = \{z_1, z_2, ..., z_8\}$, and 3 output predicates, $Y = \{y_1, y_2, y_3\}$. The rules of the network, $R = \{R_1, R_2, ..., R_{10}\}$, which describe the knowledge of the system, are shown in the Table 1. The four data that are used to adapt the weights of the network are:

([.9 .6 .7 .7 0 0 0 0 0 0], [.8 0 0])
([0 0 0 .6 .5 .9 0 0 0 0], [0 0 .7])
([.7 .9 0 0 0 0 0 0 0 .8], [.7 0 0])
([0 0 0 .5 0 0 .9 0 0 .7], [0 .8 0])

The weights of the two layers are initialized using the rules shown in Table 1. The antecedent part is used for $\mathbf{W}^1$, and the output (consequence) is used for $\mathbf{W}^2$. The two matrices are shown below.

$$W^1 = \begin{bmatrix} 1 & 1 & 1 & 1 & 0 & 0 & 0 & 0 & 0 \\ 1 & 0 & 1 & 1 & 0 & 0 & 0 & 1 & 0 & 0 \\ 0 & 1 & 1 & 1 & 0 & 0 & 0 & 0 & 1 & 0 \\ 0 & 0 & 0 & 0 & 1 & 1 & 1 & 0 & 0 & 0 \\ 0 & 0 & 0 & 1 & 0 & 0 & 1 & 0 & 0 & 1 \\ 0 & 0 & 1 & 0 & 1 & 0 & 0 & 1 & 1 & 0 \\ 1 & 1 & 0 & 0 & 0 & 0 & 0 & 0 & 0 & 1 \\ 0 & 0 & 0 & 1 & 1 & 1 & 0 & 0 & 0 & 0 \end{bmatrix}, \quad W^2 = \begin{bmatrix} 0 & 0 & 1 \\ 0 & 1 & 0 \\ 0 & 1 & 0 \\ 0 & 0 & 1 \\ 0 & 1 & 0 \\ 1 & 0 & 0 \\ 1 & 0 & 0 \\ 0 & 0 & 1 \end{bmatrix}$$

Table 1. The set of rules of the system

R	Antecedent	Output
1	$x_1 + x_2 + x_3 + x_4$	y_1
2	$x_1 + x_3 + x_4 + x_8$	y_2
3	$x_2 + x_3 + x_4 + x_9$	y_2
4	$x_5 + x_6 + x_7$	y_3
5	$x_4 + x_7 + x_{10}$	y_2
6	$x_3 + x_5 + x_8 + x_9$	y_1
7	$x_1 + x_2 + x_{10}$	y_1
8	$x_4 + x_6 + x_7$	y_3

We have used the Yager t-norm [3] with parameter value p=2, and learning rate $\eta = 1$. The neurons are adapted independently, and after 10 iterations the weights of the two layers are given by:

$$W^1 = \begin{bmatrix} .8 & .75 & .65 & 1 & 0 & 0 & 0 & 0 & 0 & 0 \\ 1 & 0 & 1 & 1 & 0 & 0 & 0 & .7 & 0 & 0 \\ 0 & .65 & 1 & 1 & 0 & 0 & 0 & 0 & 1 & 0 \\ 0 & 0 & 0 & 0 & .76 & 1 & 1 & 0 & 0 & 0 \\ 0 & 0 & 0 & .5 & 0 & 0 & 1 & 0 & 0 & 1 \\ 0 & 0 & 1 & 0 & 1 & 0 & 0 & .7 & 1 & 0 \\ 1 & .8 & 0 & 0 & 0 & 0 & 0 & 0 & 0 & 1 \\ 0 & 0 & 0 & .67 & 1 & .9 & 0 & 0 & 0 & 0 \end{bmatrix}, \quad W^2 = \begin{bmatrix} 0 & 0 & .9 \\ 0 & 1 & 0 \\ 0 & .75 & 0 \\ 0 & 0 & 1 \\ 0 & 1 & 0 \\ .8 & 0 & 0 \\ 1 & 0 & 0 \\ 0 & 0 & 1 \end{bmatrix}$$

We observe that the adaptation procedure has refined the knowledge of the system. The error of the system, as shown in Figure 2 became zero. In Figure 2 the error performance is illustrated, using learning rates, 0.5 and 1.

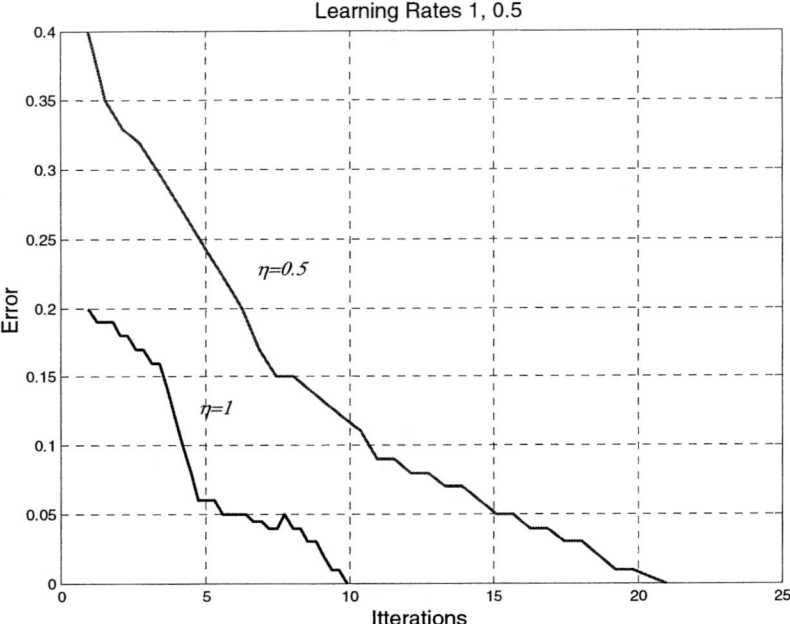

Fig. 2. The error of the neural network during the adaptation process

References

1. Hirota, K. and W. Pedrycz (1996), Solving fuzzy relational equations through logical filtering, *Fuzzy Sets and Systems* 81, pp. 355–363.
2. Jenei, S., (1998) "On Archimedean triangular norms." Fuzzy Sets and Systems, 99, pp. 179–186.
3. G. Klir and Bo Yuan, Fuzzy Sets and Fuzzy Logic: Theory and Applications, New Jersey, Prentice Hall, 1995.
4. Kosko, B., *Neural networks and fuzzy systems: a dynamical approach to machine intelligence*, Prentice Hall, Englewood Cliffs (1992).
5. C.-T. Lin, C.S. Lee, *Neural fuzzy Systems: A neuro-fuzzy synergism to intelligent systems*, Prentice-Hall, Englewood Cliffs, NJ, 1995.
6. G.B. Stamou, S. G. Tzafestas, "Resolution of composite fuzzy relational equations based on Archimedean triangular norms", Fuzzy Sets and Systems, 120, pp. 395–407, 2001.
7. G.B. Stamou, S. G. Tzafestas, "Neural fuzzy relational systems with a new learning algorithm", *Mathematics and computers in simulation,* pp. 301–304, 2000.
8. G. B. Stamou and S. G. Tzafestas, Fuzzy Relation Equations and Fuzzy Inference Systems: an Inside Approach, IEEE Trans. on Systems, Man and Cybernetics, Vol. 99, Num. 6, (1999), 694–702.

Complex-Valued Neural Networks: Theories and Applications

Phase Singular Points Reduction by a Layered Complex-Valued Neural Network in Combination with Constructive Fourier Synthesis

Motoi Minami and Akira Hirose

Department of Electronic Engineering, Graduate School of Engineering,
The University of Tokyo
7-3-1 Hongo, Bunkyo-ku, Tokyo 113-8656, Japan
minami@eis.t.u-tokyo.ac.jp, ahirose@ee.t.u-tokyo.ac.jp
http://www.eis.t.u-tokyo.ac.jp/

Abstract. We propose a novel layered complex-valued neural network to reduce singular points (SP's) in phase images to obtain digital elevation maps (DEM's) through phase unwrapping. First we prepare a SP-free distorted image for a wrapped image data by constructive Fourier synthesis. We patch fractions of the SP-free image at the SP locations of the raw image and, then, feed it to estimation layer of the network as the initial image. The estimation layer interacts with raw-image layer with a complex-valued neurodynamics to yield a better estimation in which the SP number is reduced. The proposal reduces the calculation cost of unwrapping process and also increases the accuracy of the output DEM.

1 Introduction

Digital elevation maps (DEM's) are constructed by unwrapping the wrapped phase images obtained by interferometric radar systems such as Interferometric Synthetic Aperture Radars (InSAR's). The phase data in general include interference noise generated by diffraction and refraction of electromagnetic wave [1]-[3]. Therefore, although the phase image should be conservative, expressing geographical height, it contains many (highly densely) rotational components (phase singular points: SP's). This noise cannot be eliminated by conventional filtering [4].

Researches have been vigorously conducted to overcome the noise and obtain a high-quality DEM with a realistic calculation cost [5]. For example, the branch-cut method is a generally applicable means of phase unwrapping (PU). However, as the SP number increases, the calculation cost also increases in geometric progression while the resultant DEM is degraded. Therefore it is significantly important to reduce the SP numbers and, at the same time, maintain the phase data quality.

The authors group proposed the complex-valued Markov random field (CMRF) model to describe statistically the InSAR images [6]. We presented a SP reduction method by estimating noise-free phase data based on the CMRF model, and demonstrated a high-quality and low-calculation-cost PU process. We have also proposed a layered complex-valued neural network that realizes an adaptive geographical surface-usage clustering by incorporating the phase information with reflectance [7].

In this paper, we propose a novel SP reduction method by using a modification of the clustering layered complex-valued neural network. First we construct a SP-free but distorted wrapped phase image by a constructive Fourier synthesis. We patch fractions of the CFS image at positions of SP's in the raw phase image. Then we feed the patched data to the complex-valued network where an estimation layer and a raw-image layer interact with each other to yield an improved estimation image. By iteration of the elemental process, we reduce the SP number and obtain a better phase image information. We demonstrate the effectiveness of our proposal by applying it to an actual observation data.

2 Construction and Neurodynamics

Figure 1(a) shows an example of interferometric radar image of Mt. Fuji in Japan. The phase of radar electromagnetic (reflected) wave delays in accordance with the distance to the object. The phase expresses the distance and, in the case of airplane or satellite observation, the geographical height. One can imagine the mountain shape by seeing the phase image. However, this task is a very sever one for a computer because the data contains a dense rotations or SP's, although the image should be a conservative field. Figure 1(b) indicates the SP locations. Because of the SP's, we cannot determine the geographical height. The PU is a process that solves this problem, unwrap the 2π-wrapped phase and obtain an estimated DEM.

Suppose we carry out the PU process with our brain. An elementalistic expression is as follows. We look the whole phase image first. If we find an inconsistent point, i.e., SP, we interpret the inconsistency is caused by noise, and correct the data so that the image becomes totally conservative to obtain a DEM. We intend to realize the human action by using a complex-valued layered neural network.

Figure 2 shows the construction of a three-layer complex-valued neural network (128×128 neurons, corresponding to pixels). The upper is the raw-image layer (RI layer) which the raw phase image with SP's is directly fed to. The second is the estimation layer (E layer) which is the working area where we obtian a estimation result. The neurons have local connections and perform a nonlinear local averaging. The third is the singular-point-free layer (SP-free) that holds a singular-point free image (described below). The fourth is the SP detection layer (SPD layer) whose two outputs modulate the RI–E and SP-free–E connections.

The SP-free but distorted image is constructed as follows. First we apply the discrete Fourier transform (DFT) to the raw phase image to obtain a two-dimensional discrete spectrum. Then we arrange the spectrum lines in decreasing order of magnitude. We choose largest n lines to reconstruct a real spatial image

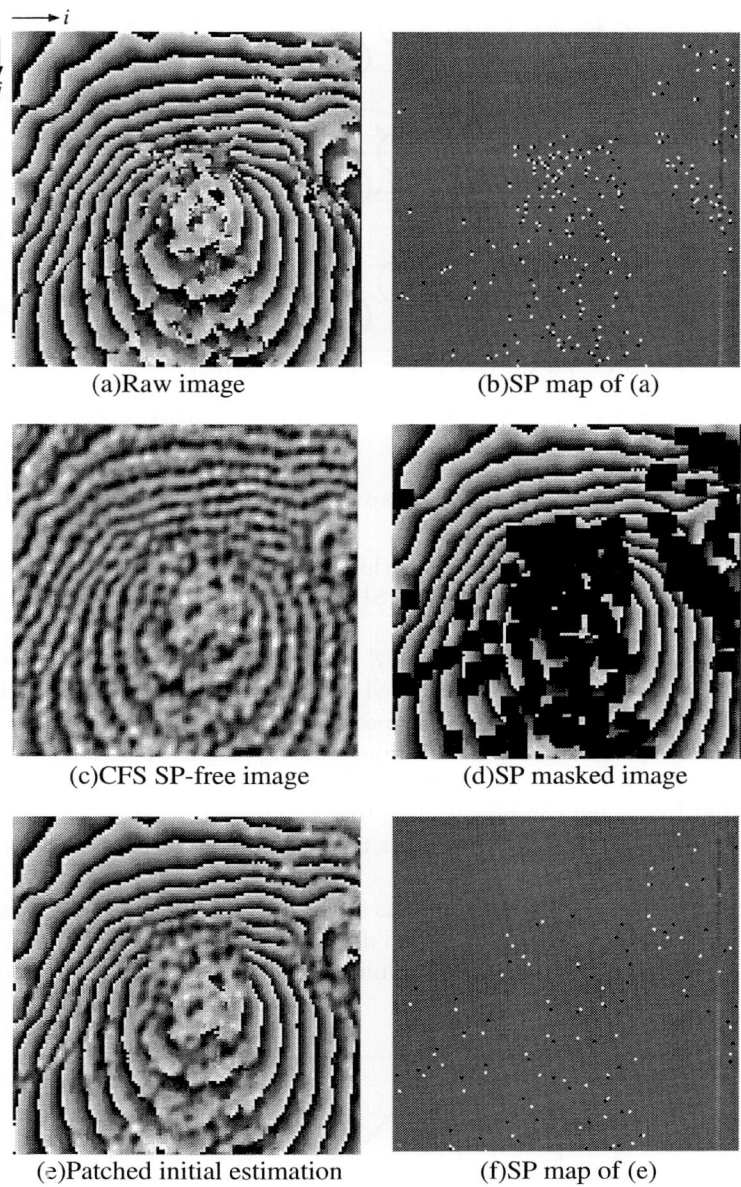

Fig. 1. (a) Input raw phase data, (b) SP map of (a) (white: positive SP, black: negative SP, total #SP=324), (c) constructively Fourier synthesized SP-free image, (d) SP masks (black squares), (e) patched image as an initial estimation and (f) SP map of (e) (#SP=120).

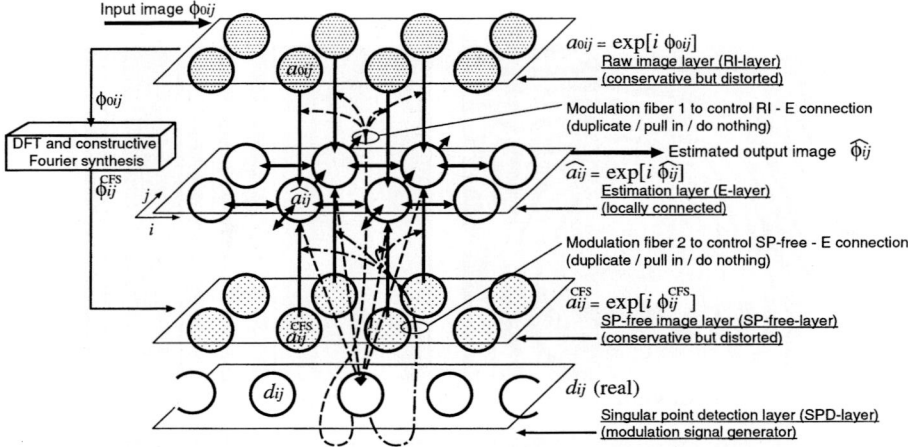

Fig. 2. Construction of the complex-valued neural network for estimation.

by the inverse DFT (IDFT). We call this process the constructive Fourier synthesis (CFS). Figure 1(a) presents the SP number variation versus the threshold number n.

When we construct an image by CFS with only the large-magnitude elements (small n), the SP number in the obtained image is zero. If n is beyond a threshold n_{th}, the SP number increases, makes a peak, and decreases down to a certain floor level. In this paper, we use the CFS image at n_{th} as the SP-free one (Fig.1(c)). Though it gives a rough shape of contour, it also contains large distortion (less high spatial-frequency components) so that the image is rather sinusoidal than saw-tooth like. Therefore, it is difficult to tell in which direction the gray scale slope goes down or up.

We determine the neurodynamics as follows. First we feed a raw phase image obtained by InSAR to the RI-layer and duplicate it onto E-layer. The SPD-layer detects SP's in the E-layer and determines the mask positions (Fig.1(d)). The

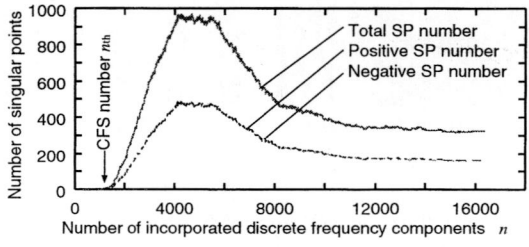

Fig. 3. Number of singular points versus number of incorporated discrete frequency spectrum components.

8×8 pixels' data around an SP in E-layer are exchanged with those in SP-free layer (Fig.1(e)). In this operation, we patch them spatially gradually not to generate extra SP's, but we cannot get rid of SP's left (Fig.1(f)). Moreover, the patched parts are distorted. The network realizes adaptively a relaxation of distortion, a local and nonlinear smoothing as well as approximation of the raw input image at the same time obeying the following dynamics.

We define raw image pixel values at (i,j) as ϕ_{0ij}, estimated phase image $\hat{\phi}_{ij}$, SP-free image obtained by CFS ϕ_{ij}^{CFS}. In the neural network, the variables are corresponding complex-valued numbers: $a_{0ij} = \exp[j\phi_{0ij}]$ (where $j \equiv \sqrt{-1}$) (RI-layer), $\hat{a}_{ij} = \exp[j\hat{\phi}_{ij}]$ (E-layer), $a_{ij}^{\text{CFS}} = \exp[j\phi_{ij}^{\text{CFS}}]$ (SP-free-layer), respectively. We also define energy E as a function of estimation $\hat{a} \equiv \hat{a}_{ij}$ as

$$E(\hat{a}) = \frac{1}{2}\sum_{i,j}\left[\sum_{\text{n.n.}}|\hat{a}_{ij} - \hat{a}_{\text{n.n.}}|^2 + \lambda(\arg[\hat{a}_{ij}] - \arg[a_{0ij}])^2\right] \quad (1)$$

where $\sum_{\text{n.n.}}$ stands for nearest neighbor (four pixels) summation, and λ determines the magnitude of effectiveness of the raw image to the estimation.

By employing the complex numbers as mentioned above, instead of phase itself, we can introduce the periodic structure of phase in a natural way. The summation can also be meaningful because the metric of the information space is constructed purposively. That is, the representation is consistent with the fact that the phase image is a result of reflection, diffraction and interference of electromagnetic wave, that has amplitude as well as phase, instead of sole phase.

We determine the neurodynamics for the estimation phase image $\Delta \hat{a}_{ij}$ that reduces the energy E in (1) as

$$\Delta(\arg[\hat{a}_{ij}]) = -K\frac{\partial E}{\partial \arg[\hat{a}_{ij}]} = -K\left[\sum_{\text{n.n.}}\sin[\hat{a}_{ij} - \hat{a}_{\text{n.n.}}] + \lambda(\arg[\hat{a}_{ij}] - \arg[a_{0ij}])\right] \quad (2)$$

where K denotes the speed of adaptation.

Figure 4 is a schematic diagram of the total processing to obtain a DEM from a raw image. A SP-free image is prepared for a raw image. SP's are detected and the initial image is patched. The above neural process is then iterated for a sufficient reduction of SP's. Finally an unwrapping process (the branch-cut method in this paper) is applied to the SP-reduced estimation phase image to get an phase unwrapped image as a DEM.

3 Results and Discussion

Figure 1(e) is the patched initial image to which the SP reduction complex-valued neurodynamics is applied. A typical parameter set is $K = 0.1$ and $\lambda = 0.2$. A unit SP reduction process consists of 50 times repetitions of neural relaxation for each pixel (2), and this unit is iterated.

Figure 5 shows the SP reduction versus iteration number. The initial SP number 324 is reduced to a floor level of 173. On the other hand, Fig.6(a) shows

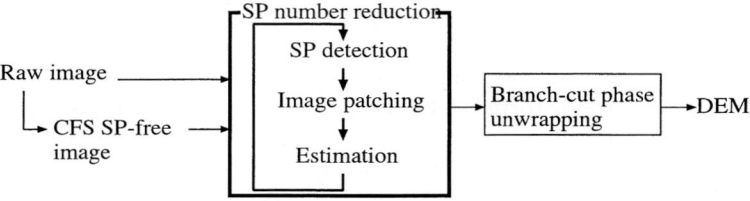

Fig. 4. Schematic diagram of total processing.

the estimated phase image with reduced SP's, while Fig.6(b) is a corresponding SP map. In fact, the SP floor value is larger than that of the initial patched image. However, most of the details in Fig.6(a) are expressed much better than in the patched initial image Fig.1(e).

We can also find in Fig.6(b) that very closely located SP pairs in Fig.1(b) have been removed, while SP pairs with distance remain almost as it was. In our previous work, we found that the close pairs are attributed to noise and should be eliminated, whereas the distant pairs usually meaningful as geographical information and should be reflected in the resulting DEM (See [6]). In this sense also, we can say that our neurodynamics works ideally.

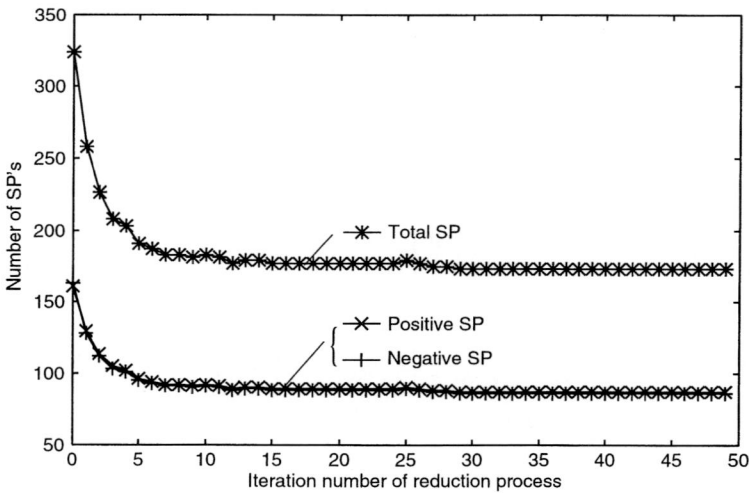

Fig. 5. Reduction of SP numbers versus process iteration number.

Figure 7 compares the resulting DEM's. Figure 7(a) is obtained directly for the raw image without SP reduction, while Fig.7(b) is for the SP reduced estimation image processed by the complex-valued neural network. In Fig.7(a),

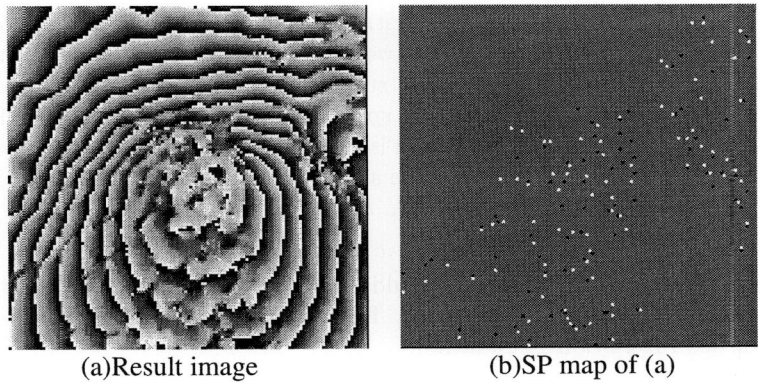

Fig. 6. (a) SP reduced image and (b) SP map of (a) (#SP=173).

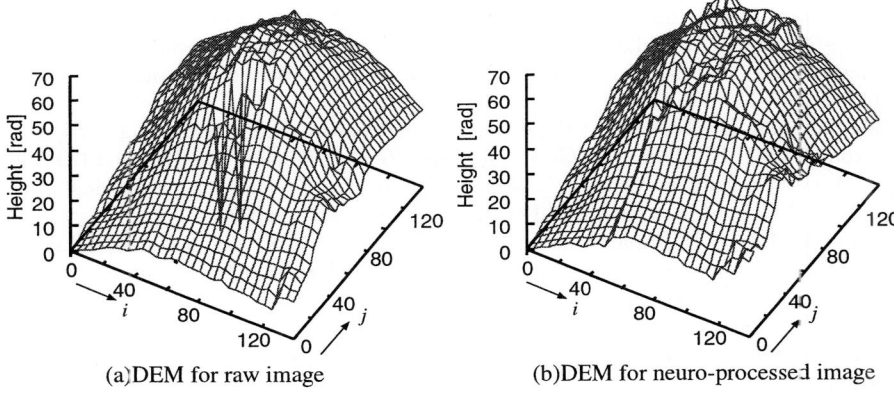

Fig. 7. (a) Unwrapped DEM obtained directly from the raw image and (b) that from neurally preprocessed estimation image.

we can find a deep hole area where the unwrapping process failed. However, in Fig.7(b), the area is removed and all the region is unwrapped successfully. As to the calculation cost, the branch-cut phase unwrapping problem is classified to NP-hard (linear Steiner tree problem) [6]. This is a big problem in a large image in particular. The calculation cost is also found reduced to a great extent.

4 Conclusion

We have proposed a novel complex-valued neural method to reduce the singular point number in the phase image to improve the DEM quality and reduce the calculation cost of the phase unwrapping process. We have applied the method to an actual InSAR image and demonstrated the effectiveness of our proposal. By employing the complex numbers, we can introduce the periodic structure of phase in a natural way. The neural summation can also become meaningful because the metric of the information space is constructed purposively for this application. That is, the representation is consistent with the fact that the phase image is a result of reflection, diffraction and interference of electromagnetic wave that has the complex-valued entity, i.e., amplitude as well as phase.

Acknowledgment. The authors would like to thank Dr. Masanobu Shimada at NASDA for supplying InSAR data. This work was partly supported by the Casio Science Promotion Foundation.

References

1. R.M. Goldstein, H.A. Zebker, C.L. Werner, "Satellite radar interferometry: two-dimensional phase unwrapping," Radio Science, **23** (1988) 713–720
2. Jong-Sen Lee, A.R. Miller, K.W. Hoppel, "Statistics of phase difference and product magnitude of multi-look processed Gaussian signals," Waves in Random Media, **4** (1994) 307–319
3. M. Shimada, H. Hirosawa, "Slope corrections to normalized RCS using SAR interferometry," IEEE Trans. on Geoscience and Remote Sensing, **38** (2000) 1479–1484
4. R.M. Goldstein, C.L. Werner, "Radar interferogram filtering for geophysical applications," Geophysical Research Letters, **25** (1998) 4035–4038
5. Jong-Sen Lee, K.P. Papathanassiou, T.L. Ainsworth, M.R. Grunes, A. Reigber, "A new technique for phase noise filtering of SAR interferometric phase images," IEEE Trans. on Geoscience and Remote Sensing, **36** (1998) 1456–1465
6. A.B. Suksmono, A. Hirose, "Adaptive noise resuction of InSAR image based on complex-MRF model and its application to phase unwrapping problem," IEEE Trans. on Geoscience and Remote Sensing, **40** (2002) 699–709
7. A. Hirose, M. Minami, "Complex-valued region-based-coupling image clustering neural networks for interferometric radar image processing," IEICE Trans. on Electron., **E84-C** (2001) 1932–1938

Quantum Adiabatic Evolution Algorithm for a Quantum Neural Network

Mitsunaga Kinjo[1], Shigeo Sato[1,2], and Koji Nakajima[2]

[1] PRESTO, Japan Science and Technology Co., Kawaguchi, 332-0012, Japan
[2] Research Institute of Electrical Communication, Tohoku University, Sendai, 980-8577, Japan

Abstract. In this paper, a new quantum algorithm for solving the combinatorial optimization problems is discussed. It is based on the quantum adiabatic evolution algorithm. We propose a new method for synthesizing a Hamiltonian inspired by a Hopfield network in order to improve calculation cost. The quantum system given by a new Hamiltonian has neuron-like interactions and shows quantum behavior. We present simulation results of the new algorithm for the 4-queen problem.

1 Introduction

Recent development of nano-device fabrication technology is remarkable. An advantage of such nano-technology is to utilize quantum dynamics. Quantum dynamics has powerful possibility as shown in literatures [1,2] related to quantum computing or quantum information. One can expect such performance enhancement is also possible on a neural network. Unfortunately, a quantum neural network has not been studied well. As a first step, we discuss the possibility of performance enhancement of a neural network taking quantum dynamics into consideration. In the following sections, we introduce a quantum computation algorithm proposed by Farhi et al. and study neuron-like interactions embedded in the Hamiltonian. The calculation cost of our algorithm is $O(N^2)$ as compared with the cost $O(2^N)$ of the conventional algorithm. Finally, we discuss the applications and the relation between neural and quantum computing.

2 Quantum Adiabatic Evolution Algorithm

The quantum computation algorithm utilizing the adiabatic Hamiltonian evolution is proposed by Farhi et al. [3,4], in order to solve instances of the satisfiability problem. They demonstrate that the quantum adiabatic evolution algorithm works effectively for several NP-complete problems [5,6]. The adiabatic Hamiltonian evolution is given by the following equation,

$$H(t) = \left(1 - \frac{t}{T}\right) H_I + \frac{t}{T} H_F, \tag{1}$$

where H_I and H_F are the initial and the final Hamiltonians, respectively. All possible candidates are set in the initial state, since the eigenvector of H_I corresponds to the lowest energy is given by the superposition of all states. And H_F is chosen so that its ground state satisfies the required condition for the solution related to a target problem. T is a parameter which controls the rate of the Hamiltonian evolution. The quantum system evolves to the desired final ground state adiabatically, where T should be sufficiently large compared to the time constant of the quantum system. However, it is not guaranteed that this algorithm operates correctly when there exists any degeneracy in energy levels or any energy level crossing during the evolution [7]. By utilizing adiabatic evolution algorithm, a combinatorial optimization problem can be solved. We confirm that this algorithm works well for the 4-queen problem [8], where we suppose that each qubit corresponds to each neuron of a Hopfield Network [9]. The state vector $|\psi\rangle$ of the whole system is given by the product of all qubit states. In order to clarify the relationship between a qubit and a neuron, we give a number for each state as follows,

$$|x_{16}\rangle \cdots |x_2\rangle |x_1\rangle \equiv |x_{16} \cdots x_2 x_1\rangle \equiv |n\rangle, \tag{2}$$

where each qubit $|x_i\rangle$ takes $|0\rangle$ or $|1\rangle$ exclusively. The final Hamiltonian H_F is obtained by the cost function used in the Hopfield network. H_F has ϵ_n which corresponds to the cost for the state $|n\rangle$ as a diagonal element like the following equation,

$$H_F = \begin{pmatrix} \epsilon_0 & & & 0 \\ & \epsilon_1 & & \\ & & \ddots & \\ 0 & & & \epsilon_{2^{16}-1} \end{pmatrix} = \sum_{n=0}^{2^{16}-1} \epsilon_n |n\rangle\langle n|. \tag{3}$$

And the initial Hamiltonian H_I must satisfy that its ground state is expressed by a linear combination of all states. Thus the H_I is given as follows,

$$\begin{aligned} H_I &= \left(\sigma_x^{(0)} + \sigma_x^{(1)} + \cdots + \sigma_x^{(2^{16}-1)}\right) \\ &= (\sigma_x \otimes I \otimes \cdots \otimes I + I \otimes \sigma_x \otimes \cdots \otimes I \\ &\quad + \cdots + I \otimes I \otimes \cdots \otimes \sigma_x), \end{aligned} \tag{4}$$

where σ_x and I denote the x-component of the Pauli spin matrix and the 2×2 identity matrix, respectively. The time evolution of the system is obtained according to the following Schrödinger equation,

$$|\psi(t+1)\rangle = U(1)|\psi(t)\rangle = e^{-\frac{iH(t)}{\hbar}}|\psi(t)\rangle. \tag{5}$$

Here, the operator $U(1)$ is given by Padé approximation[12]. Note that there are two variables for time, one is for $|\psi(t)\rangle$ and the other is for $H(t)$. Updating of $|\psi(t)\rangle$ is done 10000 times for each change of Hamiltonian $H(t)$. The fatal disadvantage of this algorithm is that the calculation cost of 2^N, where N is the number of neurons, is necessary in order to obtain the above mentioned

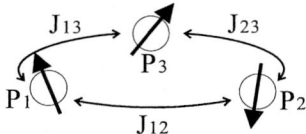

Fig. 1. Illustration of 3 spins and their interactions

Hamiltonian H_F, and there is no difference compared with a heuristic search. Therefore, the key of application is how we choose more effective H_F with less calculation cost.

3 Quantum Neural Computing Employing Adiabatic Hamiltonian Evolution

A full-connection neural network has N^2 synapses. The synaptic weights w_{ij}s for a combinatorial optimization problem are given by comparing the cost function and the energy E of a Hopfield network. It has been known well that E decreases with time. However, since the state change is driven by local feature of the energy surface, the network would often be trapped at local minima. It may be possible to avoid such local minima if the quantum dynamics with the adiabatic evolution algorithm can be introduced to the neural network. In this section, we show a new H_F comprising non-diagonal elements in consideration with an analogy to an artificial neural network. Then we evaluate the new adiabatic evolution method by numerical simulations.

3.1 Hamiltonian Synthesis Based on Interaction between Neurons

Let us consider spin qubits [10,11] in the following sections for convenience. Note that the following discussion can be applied to any quantum computer by a proper mathematical treatment. Suppose we have electron or nuclear spins as shown in Fig. 1 and regard them as neurons. The states up and down along to z-direction correspond to $|0\rangle$ and $|1\rangle$, respectively. In this case, their interactions correspond to synaptic couplings. The Hamiltonian of a quantum system comprising two spin-$\frac{1}{2}$ particles is given by,

$$H = J(\boldsymbol{\sigma}_1 \cdot \boldsymbol{\sigma}_2) = J \begin{pmatrix} 1 & 0 & 0 & 0 \\ 0 & -1 & 2 & 0 \\ 0 & 2 & -1 & 0 \\ 0 & 0 & 0 & 1 \end{pmatrix}, \quad (6)$$

where J represents the exchange interaction of two spins, $\boldsymbol{\sigma}_i$ is the Pauli spin matrix. The Hamiltonian of this system has an eigenvector $|01\rangle - |10\rangle$ as the ground state if $J > 0$. Therefore, we can measure the states $|10\rangle$ or $|01\rangle$ if

Table 1. Relation between a qubit and a neuron

Hamiltonian	Ground States	Measured States	Interaction	Synaptic Weight
$\begin{pmatrix} E & 0 & 0 & 0 \\ 0 & E & A & 0 \\ 0 & A & E & 0 \\ 0 & 0 & 0 & E \end{pmatrix}$	$\|01\rangle - \|10\rangle$	$\|01\rangle, \|10\rangle$	inhibitory	$w < 0$
$\begin{pmatrix} E & 0 & 0 & A \\ 0 & E & 0 & 0 \\ 0 & 0 & E & 0 \\ A & 0 & 0 & E \end{pmatrix}$	$\|00\rangle - \|11\rangle$	$\|00\rangle, \|11\rangle$	excitatory	$w > 0$

the system is in the ground state. This result is similar to the behavior of the 2-neuron network having inhibitory interaction. Such relation between a qubit and a neuron is shown in Table 1, where we use the rather simplified Hamiltonian. $E(\geq 0)$ and A denote the magnitude of diagonal and non-diagonal elements, respectively.

Here we define the final Hamiltonian for a N-qubit system as given by the following equation,

$$H_F \equiv E \cdot H_D + \frac{A}{2} \sum_{ij, i \neq j}^{N} H_{ij}, \qquad (7)$$

where H_D is the $2^N \times 2^N$ identity matrix, H_{ij} denotes interaction between qubits as follows,

$$H_{ij} = I \otimes \cdots \otimes I \otimes u_i \otimes I \otimes \cdots \otimes I \otimes u_j \otimes I \otimes \cdots \otimes I \\ + I \otimes \cdots \otimes I \otimes l_i \otimes I \otimes \cdots \otimes I \otimes l_j \otimes I \otimes \cdots \otimes I, \qquad (8)$$

where u_i, u_j, l_i, and l_j change depending on the sign of the synaptic weight $w_{ij}(= w_{ji})$ as,

$$w_{ij} > 0 : u_i = \lambda_{UT}, u_j = \lambda_{UT}, l_i = \lambda_{LT}, \text{ and } l_j = \lambda_{LT},$$
$$w_{ij} < 0 : u_i = \lambda_{UT}, u_j = \lambda_{LT}, l_i = \lambda_{LT}, \text{ and } l_j = \lambda_{UT},$$

$$\lambda_{UT} \equiv \begin{pmatrix} 0 & 1 \\ 0 & 0 \end{pmatrix}, \text{ and } \lambda_{LT} \equiv \begin{pmatrix} 0 & 0 \\ 1 & 0 \end{pmatrix}. \qquad (9)$$

For example, suppose the symmetric synaptic weights given as follows,

$$W = \begin{pmatrix} 0 & -1 & 1 \\ -1 & 0 & -1 \\ 1 & -1 & 0 \end{pmatrix}. \qquad (10)$$

Then H_F is given by Eq.(7) as,

$$H_F = E \cdot H_D + A(H_{21}^{\text{inhibitory}} + H_{31}^{\text{excitatory}} + H_{32}^{\text{inhibitory}})$$

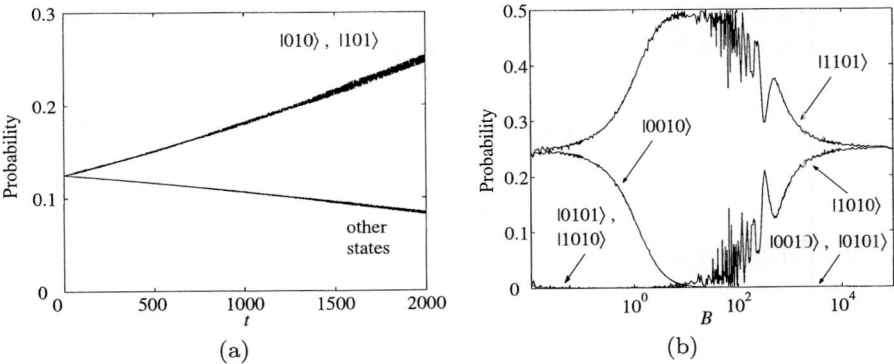

Fig. 2. (a)State evolution with H_F synthesized from the 3-neuron interactions in Eq.(10). (b)Probability changes as a function of B after adding a bias qubit to the network

$$\begin{aligned}
&= E \cdot H_D + A(I \otimes \lambda_{UT} \otimes \lambda_{LT} + I \otimes \lambda_{LT} \otimes \lambda_{UT}) \\
&\quad + A(\lambda_{UT} \otimes I \otimes \lambda_{UT} + \lambda_{LT} \otimes I \otimes \lambda_{LT}) \\
&\quad + A(\lambda_{UT} \otimes \lambda_{LT} \otimes I + \lambda_{UT} \otimes \lambda_{LT} \otimes I) \\
&= \begin{pmatrix}
E & 0 & 0 & 0 & 0 & A & 0 & 0 \\
0 & E & A & 0 & 0 & 0 & 0 & 0 \\
0 & A & E & 0 & A & 0 & 0 & A \\
0 & 0 & 0 & E & 0 & A & 0 & 0 \\
0 & 0 & A & 0 & E & 0 & 0 & 0 \\
A & 0 & 0 & A & 0 & E & A & 0 \\
0 & 0 & 0 & 0 & 0 & A & E & 0 \\
0 & 0 & A & 0 & 0 & 0 & 0 & E
\end{pmatrix}.
\end{aligned} \tag{11}$$

Here we consider the simplest case $E = 0$, because it does not play any role in this study. Note that we do not consider the case where the interactions change for each qubit. We focus on only the sign of interactions and suppose the magnitudes of interactions are same. The simulation results shown in Fig. 2-(a) indicate that the degenerated states $|010\rangle$ and $|101\rangle$ are observed with the equal probability 0.25. This is because the eigenvector of H_F is given by the linear combination of the solution states and other non-solution states. Though the probability is not so high, but it has been confirmed that the new method has possibility for application.

3.2 How to Introduce a Bias Neuron to the Quantum System

It is important to consider a quantum bias neuron, since a neural network often needs certain bias. Here we add one bias qubit as the MSB. Generally, the bias neuron always outputs 1. Therefore, the bias qubit must be $|1\rangle$. It can be realized by applying z-direction magnetic field B only to the bias qubit. Thus the new adiabatic Hamiltonian evolution is given by the following equation,

$$H(t) = \left(1 - \frac{t}{T}\right) H_I + \frac{t}{T} H_F + H_{\sigma_z}, \tag{12}$$

where

$$H_{\sigma_z} = (\sigma_z B) \otimes I \otimes \cdots \otimes I \tag{13}$$

and H_I and H_F should be calculated by the same procedure in consideration of the additional bias qubit.

For example, suppose the synaptic weights are given as follows,

$$W = \begin{pmatrix} 0 & -1 & 1 & 1 \\ -1 & 0 & -1 & -1 \\ 1 & -1 & 0 & 1 \\ 1 & -1 & 1 & 0 \end{pmatrix}, \tag{14}$$

where the 4-th neuron operates as a bias neuron. Usually the synaptic weights to the bias neuron (w_{4j}) should be zero. However, we suppose the matrix in Eq.(14), since a symmetrical weight matrix is required for synthesizing H_F. By applying enough large B, such effect caused by unnecessary connections is neglected. The probability of $|1101\rangle$ and $|1010\rangle$ after the adiabatic evolution are shown as a function of B in Fig.2-(b). The state $|0101\rangle$ is almost zero independent of B. When B is zero, we can observe both $|0010\rangle$ and $|1101\rangle$ with the same probability 0.25. When B is smaller than 10, $|1101\rangle$ is larger than $|0010\rangle$ and the difference between these two states increases with increasing B gradually. The difference has a peak when B is in the region from 10 to 100. When B is larger than 100, the difference becomes small, and finally these states come to have the same probability 0.25. This behavior is unique characteristic of a quantum system and has never been seen on an ordinary neural network since its state should be fixed to '1101' independent of the magnitude of such bias. Therefore, B must be chosen appropriately so that the system operates correctly. The simulation results of the adiabatic evolution shown in Fig.3 indicate that the state $|1101\rangle$ is observed with the probability 0.5. It can be seen that asymmetric behavior can be obtained by introducing a bias qubit.

3.3 Application of the New Proposed Algorithm to the 4-queen Problem

We have simulated this new algorithm for the 4-queen problem, which is one of the combinatorial optimization problems. By the same way discussed in above sections, H_F is given automatically. Please note that we use the synaptic weights proposed in [13] and parameters $A = -1$, $B = 200$ are chosen. The simulation results are shown in Fig. 4. In actual numerical simulations, 8 qubits are fixed and only 9 qubits can change as follows,

$$|x_b\; 0x_8x_70\; x_600x_5\; x_400x_3\; 0x_2x_10\,\rangle, \tag{15}$$

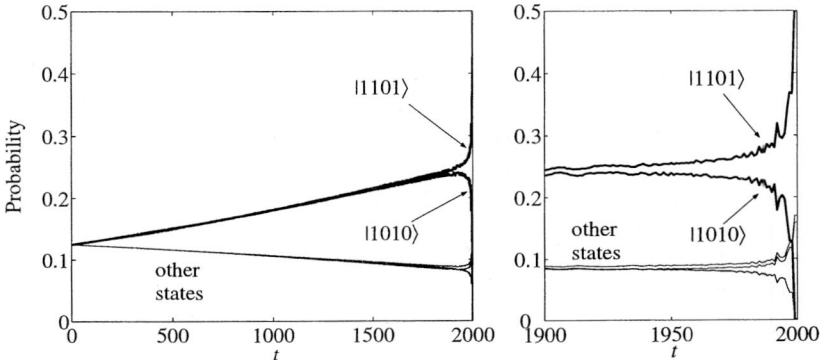

Fig. 3. State evolution with H_F synthesized by adding one bias neuron to the 3-neuron network

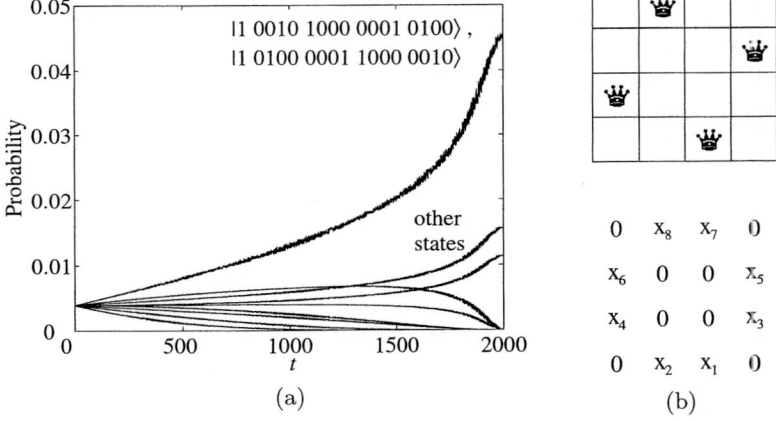

Fig. 4. (a)State evolution with H_F given by the proposed algorithm for the 4-queen problem. (b)An example of the successful configuration of queens and qubit representation

where the most significant qubit x_b is added as a bias qubit. This is due to the restriction of the limited memory size of the PC. The optimal states $|1\ 0010\ 1000\ 0001\ 0100\rangle$ and $|1\ 0100\ 0001\ 1000\ 0010\rangle$ have the same largest probability 4.5%. The probability of the solution states is still small. However, these results indicate that the probability of the optimal states is always larger than non-optimal states. Therefore, further improvement will be achieved if we can incorporate WTA-like mechanism to our system.

4 Conclusion

In order to introduce quantum dynamics to a neural network, the relation between the adiabatic evolution algorithm and a Hopfield network is discussed. We have proposed a new method for generating the final Hamiltonian derived from synaptic weights and external bias. Neuron-like operation has been confirmed by simulations. Even though the obtained results for the probability of optimal states are not sufficient, the first approach for realizing a quantum neural network has been demonstrated. Further improvement will be achieved by introducing dissipative or decoherence effect such as WTA.

References

1. Shor, P.W.: Polynomial-time algorithm for prime factorization and discrete logarithms on a quantum computer. SIAM J. Comput. **26**, (1997) 1484.
2. Grover, L.K.: A fast quantum mechanical algorithm for database search. in Proceedings of the Twenty-Eighth Annual ACM Symposium on the Theory of Computing, Philadelphia, PA, May, (1996) 212–219.
3. Farhi, E., Goldstone, J., Gutmann, S., Lapan, J., Lundgren, A., Preda, D.: A quantum adiabatic evolution algorithm applied to random instances of an NP-complete problem. Science **292**, (2001) 472.
4. Farhi, E., Goldstone, J., Gutmann, S., Sipser, M.: Quantum computation by adiabatic evolution. quant-ph/0001106.
5. Farhi, E., Goldstone, J., Gutmann, S.: A numerical study of the performance of a quantum adiabatic evolution algorithm for satisfiability. quant-ph/0007071.
6. Farhi, E., Goldstone, J., Gutmann, S., Lapan, J., Lundgren, A., Preda, D.: A quantum adiabatic evolution algorithm applied to random instances of an NP-complete problem. quant-ph/0104129.
7. Messiah,A.: Quantum Mechanics. Dover, New York, (1999) p. 739.
8. Kinjo, M., Sato, S., Nakajima, K.: Advantage and disadvantage of the quantum adiabatic evolution algorithm for combinatorial optimization problems. Abstracts of the 10th JST International Symposium (ISQC), Tokyo, Japan, March, (2002), P-2.
9. Tank, D.W., Hopfield, J.J.: Simple 'neural' optimization networks: An A/D converter, signal decision circ uit, and a linear programming circuit. IEEE Trans. Circuits Syst. **35**, (1988) 1273.
10. Loss, D., DiVincenzo, D.P.: Quantum computation with quantum dots. Phys. Rev. A, **57**, (1997), 120–126.
11. Kane, B.E.: A silicon-based nuclear spin quantum computer. Nature, **393**, (1998) 133–137.
12. Golub, G.H., van Loan, C.F.: Matrix Computations, 3rd Ed. Johns Hopkins University, Baltimore, MD, (1996) 572.
13. Tagliarini, G.A., Page, E.W.: Solving constraint satisfaction problems with neural networks. Proceedings of the IEEE International Conference on Neural Networks, **3**, (1987) 741–747.

Adaptive Beamforming by Using Complex-Valued Multi Layer Perceptron

Andriyan Bayu Suksmono[1] and Akira Hirose[2]

[1]Dept. of Electrical Engineering, Institut Teknologi Bandung
Jl. Ganesha No. 10, Bandung (40132), Indonesia
suksmono@radar.ee.itb.ac.id
[2]Grad. School of Frontier Sciences, University of Tokyo
7-3-1 Hongo, Bunkyo-ku, Tokyo 113-8656, Japan
ahirose@ee.t.u-tokyo.ac.jp

Abstract. We propose a complex-valued multilayer perceptron (CVMLP) neural network for adaptive beamforming. The complex-valued backpropagation algorithm (CVBPA) has been used to train the network. Experiments for a narrowband signal with multiple beam pointings and multiple nulls steering has been conducted. By using a 7-2-1 CVMLP topology and linear activation function, it is demonstrated that the beamforming by using CVMLP outperforms beamforming using complex-valued least mean square (CLMS) algorithm in terms of faster learning convergence and better interferences suppressions.

1 Introduction

Adaptive beamforming (ABF) is a technique to adaptively construct beampatterns of an array of sensors (antenna), so that the beams can be pointed to directions of desired signals and the nulls can be steered to unwanted interferences directions. The ABF technique has been used in many engineering applications such as radar, sonar, seismics, medics, wireless communications, etc. Introduction of ABF concepts and its applications can be found in many literatures [1]-[6].

Many ABF techniques have been developed [6]. In practical case, the correlation matrix for signal and noise that is necessary in optimum beamforming are not available. Therefore, researchers develop the dynamic adaptive method that capable to shape the beampattern based on derived information from the array output, array signals etc. The proposed method in this paper is a variant of the dynamic adaptive method.

One of the first dynamic adaptive methods is the LMS-based ABF proposed by Widrow et.al. [7] for ABF of antenna systems. In the LMS method, the steering mechanism is performed by adapting the weights of the array by minimizing a squared-error of the signals.

Artificial neural network (ANN) is an interconnected multiprocessor system that can be used for adaptive signal processing applications with many advantages. In [8], a multilayer-ANN based ABF system has been used to remove aberrations of echoes arrival time in medical ultrasound imaging system.

Recent progress shows that the ANNs that posses complex-valued weights have more advantages in some applications, especially for those that involved complex-valued information to be manipulated [9], [10]. The data in a delay-and-sum beamforming system is naturally represented as complex numbers. Therefore, we propose a complex-valued multilayer perceptron (CVMLP) to be incorporated in the ABF system.

The proposed CVMLP-ABF system uses complex-valued backpropagation algorithm (CVBPA) [11]-[14] for learning. As the real valued BPA has been developed based on the LMS, the CVBPA has been based on the complex-valued LMS (CLMS) algorithm [15]. We employ a 7-2-1 CVMLP architecture for ABF with a linear activation function. In experiments with narrow band signals with multiple beam pointing and multiple null steering, we shows the advantages of using CVMLP-ABF over CLMS-ABF.

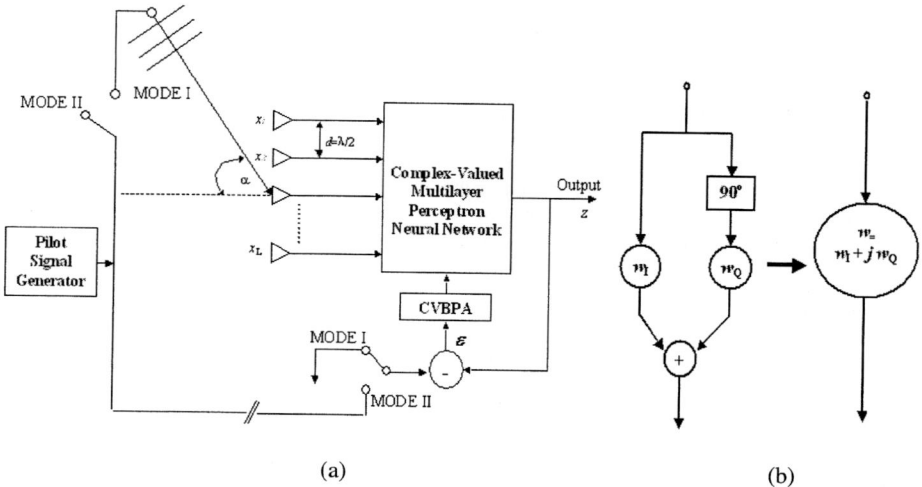

Fig. 1. (a) CVNN-based beamformer and (b) Complex representation of weighting factor

2 Adaptive Beamforming by Using Complex-Valued Multi Layer Perceptrons

2.1 System Construction

Figure 1 (a) shows the block diagram of the proposed CVMLP-ABF system, which adopts Widrow's two-mode adaptation [7]. At present time, we use a uniform linear array (ULA) that consist of 7 (seven) sensors equispaced by $d=\lambda/2$ distances, where λ is the wavelength of the signals. As it is commonly used in the array processing, the output of the sensors will enter a three-port device (Fig. 1(b)) that gives a two output signals called the inphase (I) and quadrature (Q) components. These signals are compactly represented by complex-valued signals. Then the signal in each channel is weighted by a complex-valued weight **w**.

In the CVMLP-ABF system, the weights are arranged in a multilayer interconnected multiprocessor system. In the experiment, we use 7 (seven) neuron units in the input layer, 1 (one) hidden layer that has 2 (two) neuron units, and 1 (one) neuron in the output layer. Each of the neuron posses complex-value. Figure 2. shows a topology of an (L-M-N) multilayer perceptron neural network.

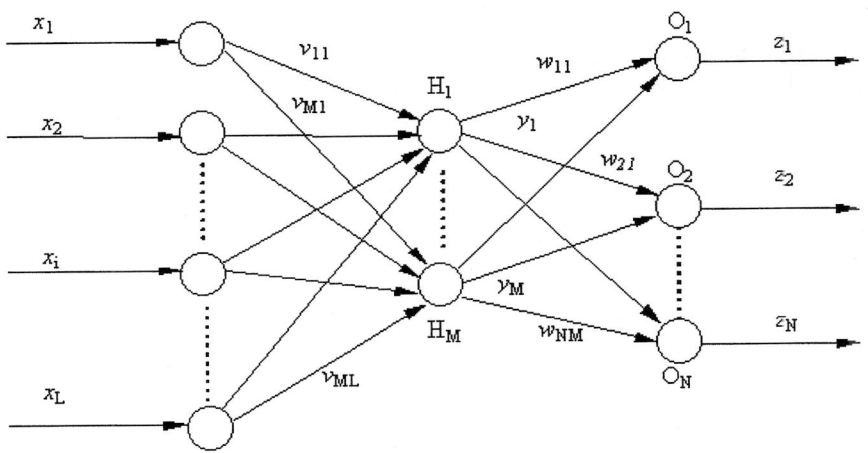

Fig. 2. Topology of the L-M-N multi layer perceptron neural network

In the figure, $x_1...x_L$ denote the network input, $v_{11}...v_{ML}$ denote the weight of the hidden layer, $w_{11}...w_{NM}$ denote the weight in output layer, $y_1...y_N$ are the output of the hidden layer and $z_1...z_N$ are the network output.

2.2 Neurodynamics

During the learning process, the CVMLP weights are updated by using CVBPA as follows:

Output Units:

$$w_{kj}^{new} = w_{kj}^{old} + \Delta w_{kj} \tag{1}$$

$$\Delta w_{kj} = \eta(t_k - z_k)\overline{f}'(O_k)\overline{y}_j \tag{2}$$

Hidden Units:

$$v_{ji}^{new} = v_{ji}^{old} + \Delta v_{ji} \tag{3}$$

$$\Delta v_{ji} = \eta \overline{x}_i \overline{f'}(H_j) \sum_k \delta_k w_{kj} \tag{4}$$

$$\delta_k = (t_k - z_k) \tag{5}$$

where η is the learning speed, t_k is the target signal, f' is the derivative of the activation function, and the bar above variables (or functions) indicates complex conjugate operation.

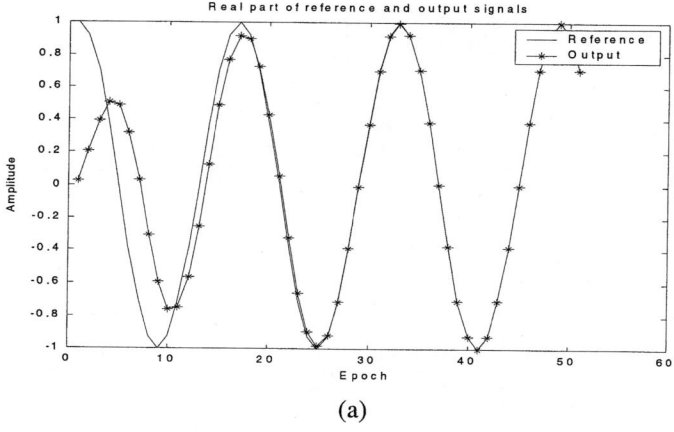

(a)

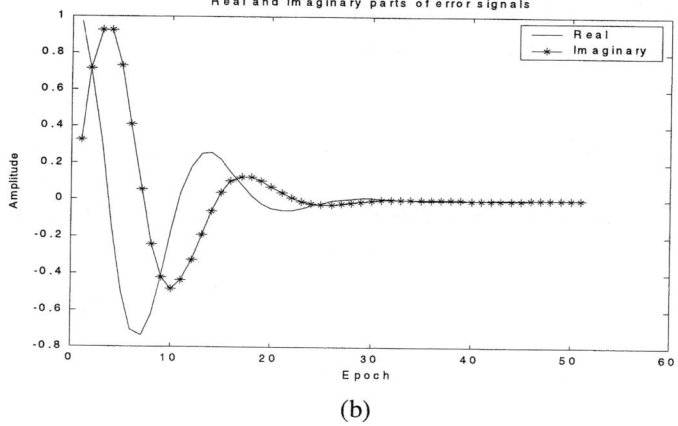

(b)

Fig. 3. (a) Comparison between the output signal and the reference signal and (b) real and imaginary part of the error signal. The CVMLP network is learning to point a beam at $+20°$ direction

During the adaptation process by the CVBPA rules, the output signal become similar to the reference signal, and the error between them are reduced. Figure 3 shows (a) comparison between the real part of output signal and the reference, and (b) display the real-and imaginary-part of the error signal during the learning to point a beam at +20° direction. We observe that the output signal gradually adapts the reference signal and the error signal decreasing to zero for both real and imaginary parts.

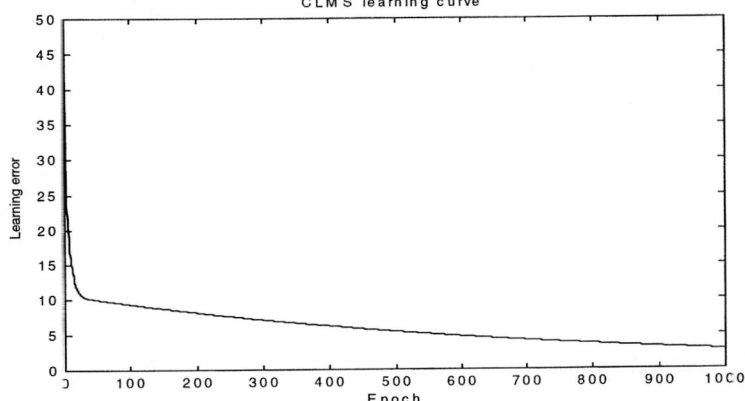

Fig. 4. Error learning curve for CLMS training

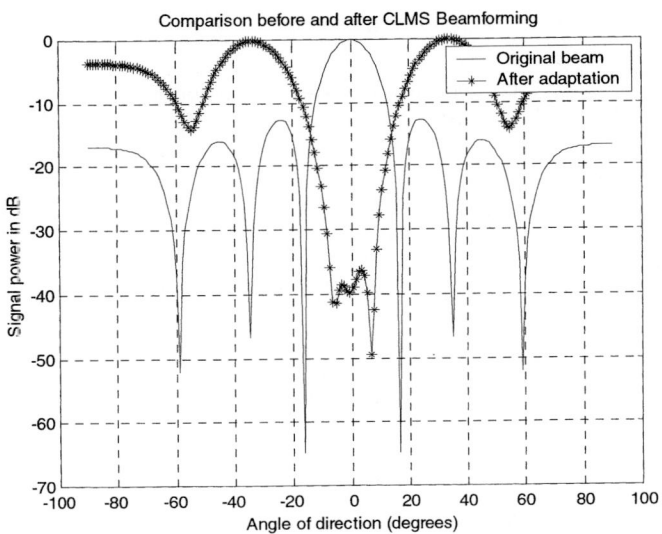

Fig. 5. Comparison of beampattern before- and after-adaptation using CLMS algorithm

3 Experiments with Multiple Beams and Multiple Interferences

In the experiment, we use harmonics sequences (Fig.3.(a)) to train the network. The array is trained to look at desired signals that come from −14° and +14°, and to suppress interferences from -7°, 0° and +7° directions. During the training process, a zero sequence has been used as a reference to null the interference, and (complex) sinusoid has been used as a reference to steer the beam. The length of the training signal sequence is 50 samples. The training is performed sequentially, with one cycle corresponding with training for each angle, and is performed iteratively for each cycle. We iterate the cycle 1000 times.

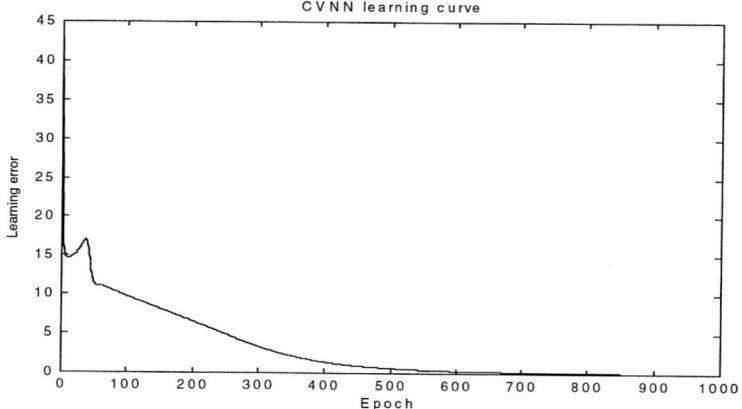

Fig. 6. Error learning curve for CVMLP training

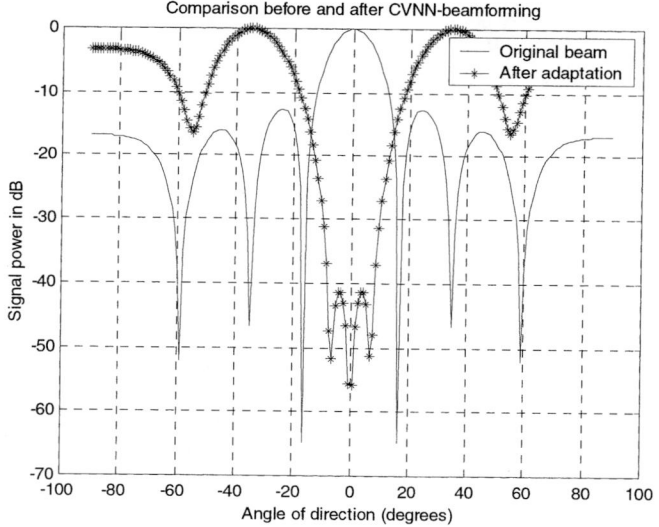

Fig. 7. Comparison of beampattern before- and after-adaptation using CVMLP algorithm

In first the experiment, we use CLMS algorithm to update the weight. Initially, all of the weights are set to 1+j. Figure 4 shows the plot of total error curve, and Fig. 5 is a comparison of the beampattern before-and after-adaptation. We observe in the learning curve that the error has been decreased gradually. The gain to intended beam directions {-15°, +15°} have been increased, and the gain to intended nulls {-7°, 0°, +7°} have been decreased.

In the second experiments, we employ a 7-2-1 CVMLP for beamforming. As to the CLMS case, we initially set the weights to 1+j and perform the adaptation by CVBPA. The error curve for CVMLP adaptation is depicted in Fig. 6 and the resulting beam is depicted in Fig. 7.

Measurements of the differences of the beam patterns before-and after-adaptation for both of the CLMS and CVMLP have been made. The results are listed in Table.1. In the table, the positive sign in the gain means that there has been amplification (the desired response for beam pointing) and negative sign means there has been attenuation (the desired response for null steering).

According to the error curves, we observe that the CVMLP has a faster convergence speed than the CLMS does. The CLMS error curve is monotonically decreasing, while in the CVMLP, for some instance at 10th –80th iteration, the curve is momentarily increasing and then it is monotonically decreasing. At the 600th iteration, the error curve for CVMLP approaching zero, while the CLMS is still high.

Table 1. Performance comparison of CLMS and CVMLP beamforming

No	Steering	GAIN (dB)	
		CLMS	CVMLP
1	Beam-1: -15°	+3.5	+1.2
2	Null-1: -7°	-38.9	-49.4
3	Null-2: -0°	-39.0	-55.8
4	Null-3: +7°	-39.3	-44.8
5	Beam-2: +15°	+11.7	+9.5

A closer observation shows amplification for beam pointings and attenuations for interferences suppressions (nulls steering) as listed in Table I. The beam pointing amplifications for CLMS are slightly better than CVMLP does, i.e. 2.3 dB at –15° and 2.2 dB at+15°. On the other hand, all of the nulls are lower in CVMLP than in CLMS, i.e. 10.5 dB, 16.8, and 5.5 dB at –7°, 0° and +7°, respectively.

The results above indicate that the changing in the information topology by inserting a hidden layer to construct CVMLP, instead of a single layer in the CLMS, improves the learning ability of the adaptive system. This learning ability has been shown in the improvement of interferences suppression and the learning speed of the CVMLP.

4 Conclusions and Further Directions

We have presented an adaptive beamforming by using CVMLP. A 7-2-1 CVMLP network topology and linear activation function has been used. By using CBPA algorithm in the learning process, the proposed CVMLP-based adaptive beamformer has successfully steered 2 (two) beams and 3 (three) nulls as desired. The comparison with CLMS based beamformer has been made. It has been shown in the experiments that the CVMLP outperforms CLMS in terms of faster learning ability and better interference suppression. In the near future, the usage of non-linear activation function and the application possibilities of the CVMLP-ABF will be explored.

References

1. H. Krim and M. Viberg: Two Decades of Array Signal Processing: The Parametric Approach. IEEE Signal Processing Magazine (July 1996) 87–94.
2. B.D Van Veen and K.M Buckley: Beamforming: A Versatile Approach to Spatial Filtering. IEEE ASSP Magazine (April 1998) 4–24.
3. D.H. Johnson and D.E. Dudgeon: Array Signal Processing-Concepts and Techniques. Prentice Hall (1993).
4. B. Widrow and S.D. Stearns: Adaptive Signal Processing. Prentice Hall (1985).
5. J.E. Hudson: Adaptive Array Principles. IEE EM Waves Series 11 (1991).
6. L.C. Godara: Application of Antenna Arrays to Mobile Communications, Part II: Beamforming and Direction-of-Arrival Considerations. Proceedings of the IEEE (August 1997) 1195–1245.
7. B. Widrow, P.E. Mantey, L.J. Griffiths, and B.B. Goode: Adaptive Antenna Systems. Proc. of the IEEE, 55 (1967) 2143–2159.
8. M. Nikoonahad and D.C. Liu: Medical Ultrasound Imaging Using Neural Networks. Electronics Letter, Vol. 26, No. 8 (April 1990) 545–546.
9. A. Hirose: Coherent Neural Networks and Their Applications to Control and Signal Processing: in Soft Computing in Systems and Control Technology, ed. S.G. Tzafestas, World Scientific Pub. Co. (May 1999) 397–422.
10. A.B. Suksmono and A. Hirose: Interferometric SAR Image Restoration Using Monte-Carlo Metropolis Algorithm. IEEE Trans. on Signal Processing, Vol. 50, No. 2 (Feb. 2002) 290–298.
11. H.L Leung and S. Haykin: The Complex Backpropagation Algorithm. IEEE. Trans. on Signal Processing, Vol. 39, No. .9 (Sept. 1991) 2101–2104.
12. N. Benvenuto and F. Piazza: On the Complex Backpropagation Algorithm. IEEE. Trans. on Signal Processing, Vol. 40 No. 4 (April 1992) 967–969.
13. G.M. Georgiou and C. Koutsougeras: Complex Domain Backpropagation. IEEE Trans. on Circuits and Systems II, Vol. 39, No. 5 (May 1992) 330–334.
14. A. Hirose: Continuous Complex-valued Backpropagation Learning. Electronics Letters, Vol. 28, No. 20 (Sept. 1992) 1854–1855.
15. B. Widrow, J. McCool, and M. Ball: The Complex LMS algorithm. Proc. of the IEEE (April 1975) 719–720.

A Complex-Valued Spiking Machine

Gilles Vaucher

Supélec – Electronics, Signal Processing and Neural Networks team
Avenue de la Boulaie, BP 81127, 35511 Cesson-Sévigné Cedex, France
Gilles.Vaucher@supelec.fr

Abstract. The technique presented in this article comes from the formalization of some passive electric properties of the dendritic trees in biological neurons using a complex-valued spatio-temporal coding. The introduction of this coding in the complex-valued neural networks makes it possible to give an algebraic formalization to the spiking neural networks. Our finality in term of applications is the processing of spatio-temporal patterns in the field of human-computer interactions. This technique was thus evaluated by simulation on handwritten character recognition and, audio and visual speech recognition problems. To improve the performances of it we present in this paper a design methodology which helps building multinetwork spiking machines. The implementation of a pen oriented interface made for an industrialist illustrates the method.

1 Induction Process Leading to the STAN[1]

Our approach takes its roots in the works undertaken by neurobiologists to model the passive electric properties of the dendritic trees, in particular Rall's work [15]. This approach is based on a certain modeling of the PSPs[2] and of their composition. On the basis of the formalization made by Agmon-Snir [15], which characterizes one $PSP(t)$ by its moments of order k ($m_k = \int_{-\infty}^{+\infty} t^k \mathrm{PSP}(t) dt$), we keep only the first two moments each one of them being respectively associated to a strength $s = m_0$ and a date $d = m_1 = m_0$ (see figure 1.a). By binding s to the module of a complex number z and d to its phase, it then becomes possible to make the sum, supposed linear, of two PSPs correspond to the sum of two complex numbers (see figure 1.b).

The date d not being bounded whereas the measurement of the phase of an ordinary complex number is, two ways were studied to bind the phase to time: (1) the use of a nonlinear function (the tangent function); (2) the abandonment of the ordinary complex numbers to the profit of the hyperbolic or parabolic ones in which the measurement of the phase is not bounded what makes it possible to link phase and time linearly. For more clearness, only the first solution is retained in the following of this paper; for more details about the second, see [17–19].

---

[1] Spatio-Temporal Artificial Neuron
[2] Post-Synaptic Potentials

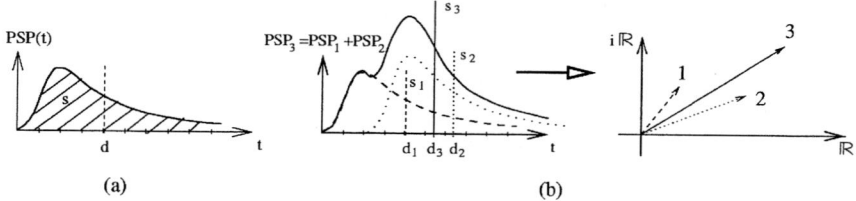

Fig. 1. (a) Characterization of a PSP limited to the 1st order, by its strength s and its mean date d. (b) Summation of two PSPs and corresponding representation in complex

In the complex-valued ST[3] algebra presented here, the product operation is used as in the Mc Culloch & Pitts neuron to model the contribution to the neuron potential of an input stimulus according to the characteristics of the corresponding synapse. In the product $x_j \overline{w_j} = \eta_{x_j} \eta_{w_j} e^{i(\varphi_{x_j} - \varphi_{w_j})}$, the weight w_j of the synapse j plays in our approach a double part: (1) it weights the input x_j via its module η_{w_j} and (2) it delays x_j via its phase φ_{w_j}. The sum of such products $\sum_j x_j \overline{w_j}$ then code in a simplified way the PSP which results from the ST summation of several PSPs.

However, so that the ST code of a resulting PSP takes account of the modifications (attenuation, delay) supported by each PSP during its transmission in the tree, it is advisable to supplement the algebra with a propagation operator $\mathcal{P}$. The *potential* is then written: $\sum_j \mathcal{P}_j(x_j \overline{w_j})$. This *potential* then formalizes, within the framework of our modeling, the PSP at soma level which results from the composition of the PSPs induced by the asynchronous synaptic impulses received in various localizations of the dendritic tree. Brought back to a function of time t, the expression of $\mathcal{P}$ retained for the ordinary complex numbers is:

$$z_{t+\Delta t} = \mathcal{P}_{\Delta t}(z_t) = \mathcal{P}_{\Delta t}(\eta_t e^{i\varphi t}) = \eta_t e^{-\mu_S \Delta t} e^{i \arctan(\mu_T \Delta t + \tan \varphi_t)} \quad (1)$$

z being a complex of module η and phase φ, and (μ_S, μ_T) a couple of positive constants. It is important to note that the $\mathcal{P}$ operator, defined by (1), models the neuron dynamic which is, thus formalized, autonomous (i.e. $\mathcal{P}_{\Delta t_1} \circ \mathcal{P}_{\Delta t_2} = \mathcal{P}_{\Delta t_1 + \Delta t_2}$).

The complex-valued ST algebra thus defined (more details in [17]) makes it possible to enrich the traditional Mc Culloch & Pitts neuron model by the capacity to process vectored sequences of spikes. This extended neuron model, named STAN, may then be directly integrated in complex-valued neural networks to build networks and learn weights.

---

[3] Spatio-Temporal

2 Deduction Process Leading to the STANNs[4]

The STANNs result from the enrichment of traditional ANN architectures, by using the previously defined ST coding of the data and of the parameters. In practice, this ST coding which has two degrees of freedom translates a received numerical event (spike), defined by an amplitude and a date, in a complex number while making correspond one to one: (1) the amplitude of the event and the module η of the complex number and (2) the date of the event and the phase φ of the complex number. And, the complex representation z of the events evolves in the course of time t by applying the $\mathcal{P}$ operator (cf (1) and figure 2). The two constants μ_S and μ_T of the $\mathcal{P}$ operator are both fixed at $1 = TW$[5], TW[6] being the duration of a sort of slipping temporal window, duration which is characteristic of the short-term memorisation process formalized by $\mathcal{P}$[7].

The ST coding is used to build each component of the input vectors X of the neurons. It also intervenes in the coding of the weight vectors W to code, with complex numbers, vectored sequences of spikes of reference. Two classes of networks were developed. In the first, a network is a set of neurons which communicate their data in an algebraic form and in a synchronous way, as in the traditional ANNs. In the second, the neurons are autonomous and exchange spikes in an asynchronous way as in the traditional spiking neurons. The models of this second class differ however from traditional spiking neurons by the formalization which is made of them, the algebraic approach replacing here the analytical techniques based on differential equations usually used for these models [5].

The first class is composed of a ST-MLP [14] which is an adaptation of the complex valued multi-layer perceptron [4, 6], a ST-RBF [11] with kernels equipped with an hermitian distance and a ST-SOM1 [12] which extends the use of the self-organizing maps of Kohonen to hermitian spaces.

The second class contains for its part a ST-WTA [17, 19] which is an ST adaptation of the *Winner Takes All* model, a ST-Kmeans [3] which is just a transposition of the Kmeans algorithm to our ST coding, a ST-RCE [3] which is an adaptation to hermitian spaces of the Reilly-Cooper-Elbaum algorithm and finally a ST-SOM2 [2] which differs from the ST-SOM1 by the addition of spheres of influence making it possible during the exploitation for each unit at any time to decide by itself if it must or not produce a spike on the output.

Table 1 gathers the whole set of the STANN models currently developed by classifying them according to the type of the implemented training and the mode of communication used during the exploitation.

---

[4] Spatio-Temporal Artificial Neural Networks
[5] More details about this choice in [2].
[6] Temporal Window
[7] While fixing μ_T at zero, the coding then corresponds to the one used in the traditional leaky integrate & fire model (with a single degree of freedom).

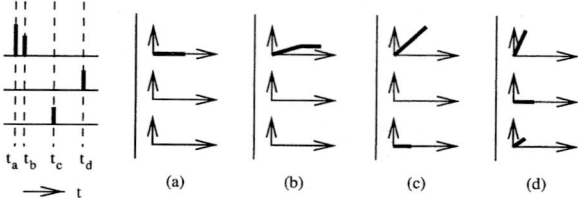

Fig. 2. Vectored sequence of spikes, ST coded component by component: (a) The 1st received spike is initially coded by a complex number whose module is equal to the amplitude of the spike and whose phase is null (the date of the spike being referred at the present time). (b) When the 2nd spike arises, it is summed to the previous complex number transformed by $\mathcal{P}$, the $\mathcal{P}$-transform taking account of the time run out between the two spikes. (c-d) Successive coding of the 3rd and 4th spikes received on the other inputs, from which finally the ST representation of the whole vectored sequence of spikes ensues.

Table 1. The different types of STANN models

Training	During exploitation	Algebraic and synchronous communication	Asynchronous spike exchanges
Unsupervised		ST-SOM1	ST-Kmeans ST-SOM2
		ST-RBF	ST-WTA
Supervised		ST-MLP	ST-RCE

3 SM[8] Design

As regards human-computer interactions, considering a traditional user-software interface of command-responses type, the introduction of a SM into a uni or multi-modal recognition module at the perception level is done by splitting up the interface into three blocks. The first ensures the acquisition of the signals (stylus movement, audio or video signal), their pre-processing and their conversion in spikes. The second one is made of the SM whose task is to translate the numerical events (spikes) produced by the first block into symbolic events (letters, words, commands) sent to the third block. Finally this third block is the more traditional part of the interface; its behaviour may be described using a finite-state automata.

3.1 Spike Production

The first step of the process after signal acquisition is traditional. It consists of a transformation of the raw signals towards a *good* representation space in which the data present properties of invariance and robustness to noise. In practice, depending on the modality processed, traditional transforms from the literature are used: (1) for handwriting, differential data coding and Freeman decomposition,

---
[8] Spiking Machine made of STANNs.

(2) for visual speech, Hough transform, rotation & projection in the colour-space, principal component analysis and independent component analysis and (3) for audio speech, cepstrum decomposition.

After this first step the signal is translated to vectored flows of spikes either at the acquisition frequency of the raw signals or when local triggers are detected. To facilitate the recognition task, some new components are added on which a spike means the identification of a local trigger. For example: pen ups for handwriting, mouth closing for visual speech and silence periods for audio speech[9].

3.2 Synthesis of the SM

Whereas the techniques of spike generation used in the first block are specific to the considered modality[10], the following method proposed to build the SM wants to be generic.

It consists in building a feed-forward architecture made of several STANNs in cascade. A little like a RBF network, we build the first layers (hidden layers) with STANNs composed of neurons having a radial output function and trained with an unsupervised algorithm, and we finish the architecture (output layer) with a STANN trained with a supervised algorithm.

The use in series of several hidden layers making characteristic extraction is justified in certain applications by the need of analyzing the vectored sequences of spikes as sequence of sub-sequences and that in an iterative way; these layers operating on the vectored sequences of spikes within temporal windows of an increasing duration, in some way like the hidden layers of a *time delay neural network* do. Thus this process is similar to that which consists in analyzing a sentence by cutting it out in words (drawn from a dictionary), those words being themselves broken up into letters (drawn from an alphabet).

Each hidden layer ensures then a double transformation: the first one (S → V transform) which translates the vectored sequences of spikes, received by the layer, into an hermitian vector by using the ST coding[11]. During the course of time, this hermitian vector follows under the effect of the $\mathcal{P}$ operator a trajectory which is continuous except at the time of the reception of the spikes.

The second transformation (V → S transform) *a contrario* converts a trajectory in the hermitian space into a vectored sequence of spikes. In fact, during the training, the various trajectories are sampled to produce a set of points in the hermitian space on which the layer carries out a vector quantization. By associating to each neuron a hyper-sphere of influence of radius r[12], one observes

---

[9] More details about this first block in [2, 3, 8, 9, 11, 13, 14, 16].

[10] Researches for a generic technique are however done and some promising results in audio and video were obtained [7, 8].

[11] To make the explanation of the method simpler, it is supposed here that the connectivity between close layers is complete. In addition, by using a unique TW per layer, the hermitian vector is thus identical for all the neurons of a layer.

[12] r is computed from the dimensions of the corresponding Voronoï block.

at the output of the layer a vectored sequence of spikes at the frequence of the layer activation, as illustrated on figure 3.a.

The analysis of the sequences as a composition of sub-sequences is thus made by applying the two transformations alternatively (figure 3.b).

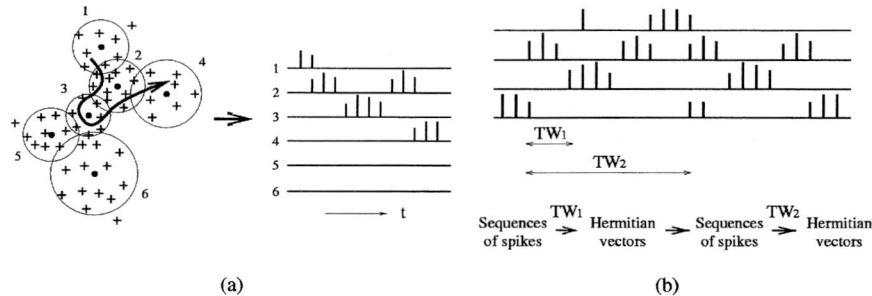

Fig. 3. (a) The V → S transform; case of a layer made of six neurons. (b) Analysis of sequences as a composition of sub-sequences

4 Applications

4.1 Simulated Applications

The STANNs were used in several works for on-line handwritten character recognition [14] as well as for unimodal (visual [3], audio [9]) and bimodal (audio-visual [16]) speech recognition. These works initially limited to simulations made it possible to study the performances of the STANNs.

Thus, a first study [11, 13] in on-line handwritten character recognition (the 26 small letters of the English alphabet) made with a multi-writer database (14 writers) developed by the IRISA[13] led, during the test phase, to a quality of recognition good but inhomogeneous (between 62% and 100% of recognition, according to the letters in question). The confusion observed between certain letters, like h and k or m and n, corresponds in fact to that made by a human expert, and it can only be solved by adding contextual information.

A second study [2, 3] in visual speech recognition of isolate digits (10 digits pronounced in French) in single-speaker conditions made it possible to obtain a good recognition rate of 78% on the test base. Among the video-only results reported by others at the time of the study, there was none in similar conditions which was more than 60% correct. So, our results were quite encouraging, even if no real benchmarking was followed. In [8], these results were thereafter improved on the same database with the same architecture, only by changing the preprocessing, and 90% of good recognitions were then obtained.

---

[13] Institut de Recherche en Informatique et Systèmes Aléatoires, Rennes (35), France.

A third study [9] in audio speech recognition of isolate digits (digits 1 to 4 pronounced in English) made on the multi-speaker database (12 speakers) Tulips1 [10] gave, in multi-speaker mode, 94% of good recognitions and, in unknown-speaker mode, 82%. This work having been primarily centered on the study of a spike generation technique adapted to the audio signal, the neural architecture been thus simplified, these results remain to be improved; traditional techniques give currently better results.

Lastly, to evaluate, there still on the methodological plan, the multimodal performances of the models, a last study [16] in audio-visual recognition of digits (digits 0 to 9 pronounced in French), made on the first 10 people of the European M2VTS[14] database, showed an improvement from 10 to 19% of the rate of a bi-modal recognition compared to an audio unimodal recognition, this improvement being more significant on the presence of noise on the sound signal[15].

4.2 Industrial Application

During these various studies, the implementation was gradually refined to lead to the design methodology presented section 3. This method was recently evaluated within the framework of an industrial experimentation in partnership with France Telecom R&D. It was entrusted to a group of three students in computer science of Supélec, nonspecialists in human-computer interactions, with an aim of validating the potentialities of the method as regards user-software development [1].

The study consisted in developing a pen-oriented interface for acquiring forms with mobile terminals, the capture being done by using the Graffiti$^{(R)}$ alphabet. The letters, digits, punctuation and extended character set having been structured into four group of symbols, four SMs were synthesized.

As in [14, 20], the generation of spikes is made by projecting each stylus movement (differential coding) on the four orientations: right, up, left, down (simplified Freeman decomposition) (figure 4). Each SM is made up of: (1) one ST-SOM which splits up the character lines into primitives (thus producing an alphabet of characteristic elementary lines)[16] and (2) one ST-RCE which ensures the classification of the characters analysed as sequences of primitives (Global TW).

Six writers produced 150 examples of each symbol. During the simulations, the examples of five writers were used for the training whereas those of the last one were used for the tests. These tests led to 85% of good recognition, 2% of errors and 13% of ambiguities. These last correspond to examples located at the intersection of several coding cells associated to different classes in the ST-RCE. In such cases, it is then possible to produce a *beep* at the user interface level to signal the recognition problem. At last, in exploitation, the system was

---

[14] Multi-Modal Verification for Teleservices and Security applications
[15] The rate of good recognition passes from 76 to 86% when the sound is not disturbed and from 49 to 68% when a white noise with a signal to noise ratio of 10dB is added.
[16] The *length* of the characteristic lines depends on the value of the TW of the layer.

tested by two users out of the project. One, confirmed, obtained a rate of good recognition of 90% and the other, beginner in the use of Graffti$^{(R)}$ and in the use of the interface, saw its rate of good recognition falling to 70% at the beginning.

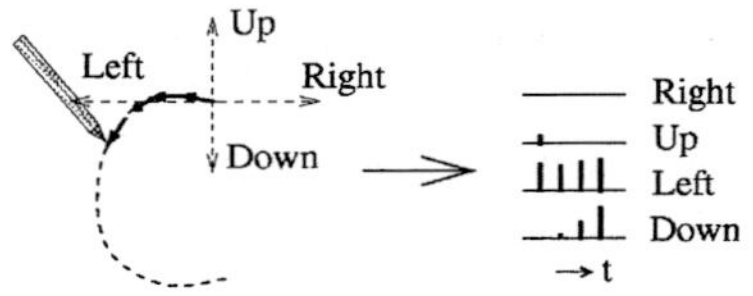

Fig. 4. Conversion of a handwritten letter into a vectored sequence of spikes

5 Conclusion and Discussion

Finally, the STAN spiking neuron model corresponds at the same time to an enrichment of the Mc Culloch & Pitts model by the addition of a second degree of freedom on the processed data and to an extension to the 1st order (according to Agmon-Snir) of the traditional integrate & fire neuron. The intermediate situation occupied by the STAN makes thus possible the processing of vectored sequences of spikes while using the important capital of algorithms developed for the ANNs, in particular those conceived for complex-valued neural networks. The family of models that results from this, tested in the field of the human-computer interactions, gives promising results.

Moreover, the proposed design methodology has the aim to facilitate the synthesis of spiking neural networks in the field of human-software interfaces development, their role being to translate the spatio-temporal patterns produced by the user into data and commands sent to a software application.

In addition to the potentialities of genericity and multi-modal fusion offered by the event-driven kernel of a SM, the industrial study evoked above showed that the synthesized systems built with such an approach are not much greedy in memory and computing power needs. This technique thus appears promising to develop embedded applications intended for mobile use on low power terminals having only a small power supply. This point was validated by an implementation in a Java$^{(TM)}$ *applet* of a pen-oriented interface in which the handwritten character recognition task is done at each displacement of the stylus[17]. This is made possible thanks (1) to the mechanism of short-term memorizing present in each neuron and (2) to the event-driven nature of the implementation in which only a limited number of connections are considered at each slice of time.

The industrial study made it also possible to validate the method, since the nonspecialists in handwritten character recognition who implemented it devoted only one and half human×months to the recognition part of the application to obtain altogether acceptable results; the more so as a significant part of this time was devoted to the construction of the database.

---

[17] Recognition in 10ms with a Pentium I, 233MHz.

However, the design methodology of a SM has still some difficult steps which require a certain know-how: the choice of the number of hidden layers, the choice of the number of neurons in these layers and the choice of the TW associated with each layer. We thus work currently on the automation of these choices. Lastly, insofar as the hidden Markov models are tools largely used for this type of application, a relative positioning of the two approaches remains to be carried out.

Acknowledgements. We make a point of thanking J.-F. Dreyfus and E. Roché which were the first ones to contribute to the study of the integration of the ST coding in ANNs. Our thanks are also addressed to N. Mozayyani, A.R. Baig, D. Mercier and to R. Séguier for their work on the preprocessing of the signals leading to the spike generation. In addition we wish to underline the contribution of N. Mozayyani and A.R. Baig to the progressive working-out of the design method. Lastly, we will greet the work of quality carried out by A. Ardouin, N. Brouard, C. Moreau and R. Plouvier, with the indirect support of J. Champseix, X. Cochi, E. Edouard, F-M. Grattepain and G. Viclin, during the realization of the industrial application presented at the end of this paper; it is the opportunity to thank France Telecom R&D and in particular S. Rouchy for this collaboration.

References

1. A. Ardouin and N. Brouard and C. Moreau and R. Plouvier and S. Rouchy and G. Vaucher. Un exemple d'interface orienté stylo à base de STANN. In *Journées Neurosciences et Sciences de l'Ingénieur*, Sept 2002.
2. A.R. Baig. *Une approche méthodologique de l'utilisation des STAN appliquée à la reconnaissance visuelle de la parole*. PhD thesis, Univ. Rennes 1 – Supélec, avril 2000.
3. A.R. Baig and R. Séguier and G. Vaucher. A Spatio-Temporal Neural Network applied to Visual Speech Recognition. In *Int. Conf. on ANN*, pp. 797–802, Sept. 1999.
4. G.M. Georgiou and C. Koutsougeras. Complex domain backpropagation. *IEEE trans. on circuits and systems – II: Analog and digital signal processing*, 39(5):330–4, May 1992.
5. W. Gerstner and W. Kistler. *Spiking Neuron Models*. Cambridge Univ. Press, 2002.
6. A. Hirose. Continuous complex-valued back-propagation learning. *Electronics Letters*, 20(20):1854–5, Sept 1992.
7. D. Mercier. *Hétéro-association de signaux audio-vidéo par réseaux de neurones*. PhD thesis, Univ. Rennes 1 – Supélec, 2003.
8. D. Mercier and R. Séguier. Un prétraitement simplifié pour les STANN – Illustration en lecture labiale. In *Journées Neurosciences et Sciences de l'Ingénieur*. Sept 2000.
9. D. Mercier and R. Séguier. Spiking neurons (STANNs) in Speech Recognition. In *3rd WSEAS Int. Conf. on Neural Networks and Applications*, Feb 2002.
10. J.R. Movellan. Visual Speech Recognition with Stochastic Networks. vol. 7, pp. 851–8. MIT Press, Cambridge. 1995. In *Advances in Neural Information Processing Systems*. G. Tesauro, D.S. Touretzky and T. Leen (eds).

11. N. Mozayyani. *Introduction d'un codage spatio-temporel dans les architectures classiques de réseaux de neurones artificiels.* PhD thesis, Univ. Rennes 1 – Supélec, Juil. 1998.
12. N. Mozayyani and V. Alanou and J.-F. Dreyfus and G. Vaucher. A spatio-temporal data-coding applied to Kohonen maps. In *Int. Conf. on ANN*, vol. 2, pp. 75–79. EC2 et Compagnie, Oct. 1995.
13. N. Mozayyani and A.R. Baig and G. Vaucher. A Fully-Neural Solution for on-Line Handwritten Character Recognition. *IEEE Int. Joint Conf. on Neural Networks*, pp. 160–4, May 1998, Alaska.
14. N. Mozayyani and G. Vaucher. A spatio-temporal perceptron for on-line handwritten character recognition. In Springer, editor, *Int. Conf. ANN*, pp. 325–30, Oct 1997.
15. W. Rall and H. Agmon-Snir. Cable Theory for Dendritic Neurons, in *Methods in Neuronal Modeling*, chap. 2, pp. 27–92. MIT Press, 1998. C. Koch and I. Segev (eds).
16. R. Séguier and D. Mercier. Audio-Visual Speech Recognition, One Pass Learning with Spiking Neurons. In *Int. Conf. on ANN*, Aug 2002.
17. G. Vaucher. *A la recherche d'une algébre neuronale spatio-temporelle.* PhD thesis, Univ. Rennes 1 – Supélec, Déc 1996.
18. G. Vaucher. An algebra for recognition of spatio-temporal forms. In D facto publications, editor, *European Symp. on ANN*, pp. 231-6, April 1997.
19. G. Vaucher. An algebraic interpretation of PSP composition. BioSystems, 48 (1–3):241–6, Sept–Dec 1998.
20. G. Vaucher and A.R. Baig and R. Séguier. A Set of Neural Tools for Human-Computer Interactions: Application to the Handwritten Character Recognition, and Visual Speech Recognitions Problems. *Neural Computing & Applications*, 9:297–305, dec 2000.

The Behavior of the Network Consisting of Two Complex-Valued Nagumo-Sato Neurons

Iku Nemoto

Tokyo Denki University School of Information Environment
Inzai, Chiba, 270-1382, Japan
nemoto@sie.dendai.ac.jp

Abstract. We previously proposed a complex-version of the Nagumo-Sato model of a single neuron and studied its behavior. Here we investigate the behavior of the network consisting of two such neurons. This is a preliminary report focusing on the fixed points of the dynamics of symmetric circuits, meaning that the two neurons have the same parameter values, and on some experimental results showing interesting orbits. When the network is asymmetric, the analysis becomes quite difficult due to the large number of parameters.

1 Introduction

Several researchers have proposed the use of complex values in neural networks and studied their behaviors (Kono and Nemoto, 1991, Birx and Pipenberg,1993, Hirose, 1992, Hirose and Onishi, 1999, Nemoto and Kubono, 1996, Nitta and Furuya, 1991, Noest, 1988, Nemoto and Saito, 2002). The use of complex values in neural networks seems to be a natural consequence considering that the impulse trains in the biological neural networks contain important information in the temporal relationship between them; synchrony of impulse trains occurring in two sites in the brain has been discussed in relation to association of features in visual recognition and also to mice's perception of their spatial location. Complex numbers are capable of approximately representing the amplitudes (alternatively, the frequencies) and the phases of impulse trains by their real and imaginary parts, respectively. This is of course in analogy to the use of complex numbers in treating electric circuits.

We previously proposed a complex-valued version of the Nagumo-Sato model (N-S model) of a single neuron (Nemoto and Saito, 2002). The original model had been studied extensively by Hata, 1982, who had proven rigorously that it produces 'discontinuous chaos' under certain conditions. The discontinuous chaos occurs on a measure-0 set in the parameter space and thus cannot be observed experimentally. Aihara, Takabe and Toyoda, 1990, introduced the logistic output function in the place of the original step (threshold) function in the N-S model, which made the chaotic behavior intrinsically involved in the original model explicitly observable. Our complex version used complex values for all the parameter values but preserved the discontinuity of the threshold function, which introduced another kind of (experimentally observable) chaos not derived from the discontinuity of the threshold function but from the expanding factor in the mapping. The existence of chaos was not theoretically proved but experimentally shown by positive Lyapunov exponents and high sensitivity to the initial conditions.

In this report, we study the behavior of the network having two complex-valued neurons connected to each other. In particular, we study the fixed points of its dynamics including their stability and compare them with those in the single neuron model. We then show some examples of chaotic behavior in this network.

2 The Model

We present a general model first and then narrow it down to a more specific one for the present study. Let $\mathbf{R}$ and $\mathbf{C}$ be the fields of real and complex numbers, respectively. Let $\eta_i(n) \in \mathbf{C}$ and $\xi_i(n) \in \mathbf{C}$ be the membrane potential and the output of the i-th neuron at time n, respectively. The dynamics of the network is described by

$$\eta_i(n) = A_i - \frac{1}{\alpha_i} \sum_{l=0}^{n} \beta_i^l \xi_i(n-l) + \sum_{j=1}^{N} w_{ij} \sum_{l=0}^{n} \gamma_i^l \xi_j(n-l) \quad (1)$$

$$\xi_i(n+1) = \Theta(\eta_i(n)) = \begin{cases} 0 & (|\eta_i(n)| < 1) \\ \dfrac{\eta_i(n)}{|\eta_i(n)|} & (|\eta_i(n)| \geq 1) \end{cases} \quad i = 1, 2, ..., N \quad (2)$$

where $\beta_i, \gamma_i, c_i \in \mathbf{C}$, $\alpha_i > 0$ and $w_{ij} \in \mathbf{R}$. Equation (1) without the third term would be exactly the same as the complex-valued N-S model (Nemoto & Saito, 2002). The coefficient w_{ij} represents the influence of the j-th output on the i-th neuron and γ_i the temporal change of the degree of the reception of the influence by the i-th neuron. We may take w_{ij} to be complex numbers but it would be easier to see the effects of connecting the neurons with real w_{ij} at least for a first step.

Now we make the change of variables as follows to convert the above system into a dynamical system of the form $\mathbf{x}(n+1) = \mathbf{f}(\mathbf{x}(n))$. Let

$$\begin{aligned} \zeta_i(n) &= 1 + \alpha_i \beta_i A_i - \sum_{l=0}^{n-1} \beta_i^l \xi_i(n-l) \\ \delta_i(n) &= \sum_{j=1}^{N} w_{ij} \sum_{l=0}^{n} \gamma_i^l \xi_j(n-l) \\ z_i(n) &= \zeta_i(n) + \alpha_i \delta_i(n) \end{aligned} \quad (3)$$

Then, we get the dynamical system:

$$\zeta_i(n) - 1 = \begin{cases} \beta_i(\zeta_i(n-1) - c_i), & |z_i(n-1) - c_i| < \alpha_i \\ \beta_i(\zeta_i(n-1) - c_i) - \dfrac{z_i(n-1) - c_i}{|z_i(n-1) - c_i|}, & |z_i(n-1) - c_i| \geq \alpha_i \end{cases} \quad (4)$$

$$\delta_i(n) = \gamma_i \delta_i(n-1) + \sum_{j=1}^{N} w_{ij} \Theta_j \qquad (5)$$

$$\Theta_j = \begin{cases} 0, & |z_i(n-1) - c_i| < \alpha_i \\ \dfrac{z_i(n-1) - c_i}{|z_i(n-1) - c_i|}, & |z_i(n-1) - c_i| \geq \alpha_i \end{cases}$$

$$z_i(n) = \zeta_i(n) + \alpha_i \delta_i(n) \qquad (6)$$

Like in the one unit model we may consider $z_i(n)$ to represent the state of the network, although $z_i(n)$ alone is not sufficient to determine $z_i(n+1)$. When $|z_i(n) - c_i| \geq \alpha_i$, the i-th neuron is considered to fire with the phase of the impulse train being $\arg(z_i(n) - 1)$, and if $|z_i(n) - c_i| < \alpha_i$, it is in the resting state.

The model we study here consists of 2 neurons and satisfies:

$$N = 2, \beta_i = \beta, \gamma_i = \gamma, c_i = c, \alpha_i = \alpha, i = 1, 2 \qquad (7)$$

3 Fixed Points

For investigation of the fixed points and their stability, we further simplify the dynamics by putting $w_{12} = w_{21} = w_c$, $w_{11} = w_{22} = w_a$. We assume that the dynamics starts with both neurons in the same initial condition, and then the orbits of the both neurons will be identical. Therefore in this case,

$$\zeta_1(n) = \zeta_2(n), \ \delta_1(n) = \delta_2(n), \ z_1(n) = z_2(n), \quad n = 1, 2, \mathrm{K} \qquad (8)$$

First we consider the fixed points within the *critical circle* $C_\alpha = \{z \mid |z - c| < \alpha\}$. From $\delta_i(n) = \gamma \delta_i(n-1)$, we get $\gamma_i(n) = 0$ and then it is trivial to see that the common inner fixed point for both neurons is $z_i^* = (1 - \beta c)/(1 - \beta)$ which is exactly the same as in the one unit model. We say that the dynamics of the symmetric circuit is *symmetric* when the initial condition is identical for the two neurons. To study the stability of the fixed point, we use the orthogonal representation: $\zeta_k = \zeta_k^R + i\zeta_k^I$, $\delta_k = \delta_k^R + i\delta_k^I$, $k = 1, 2$ and study the map $\mathbf{f}$ defined by

$$(\zeta_k^R(n+1), \zeta_k^I(n+1), \delta_k^R(n+1), \delta_k^I(n+1)) = \mathbf{f}(\zeta_k^R(n), \zeta_k^I(n), \delta_k^R(n), \delta_k^I(n)) \qquad (9)$$

Within the critical circle the two neurons are completely independent of each other and still follow the same orbit as mentioned above. Therefore, we only have to consider

$$\nabla \mathbf{f} = \begin{pmatrix} \beta^R & -\beta^I & 0 & 0 \\ \beta^I & \beta^R & 0 & 0 \\ 0 & 0 & \gamma^R & -\gamma^I \\ 0 & 0 & \gamma^I & \gamma^R \end{pmatrix} \qquad (10)$$

where $\beta^R, \beta^I, \delta^R, \delta^I$ are the real and imaginary parts of the respective constants. It is easily seen that $|\nabla f| = |\beta|^2 |\gamma|^2$ and thus the inner fixed points are always stable for the natural assumption: $|\beta| < 1, |\gamma| < 1$.

To obtain the outer fixed point ($|z^* - c| \geq \alpha$), we have to solve

$$\zeta^* - 1 = \beta(\zeta^* - c) - \frac{z^* - c}{|z^* - c|} \tag{11}$$

$$\delta^* = \gamma\delta^* + (w_a + w_c)\frac{z^* - c}{|z^* - c|} \tag{12}$$

$$z^* = \zeta^* + \alpha\delta^* \tag{13}$$

Solving (9) for ζ^* and (10) for δ^*, substituting the result into (11) and putting $z^* = c + re^{i\theta}$, we get

$$e^{i\theta} = \frac{(1-c)(1-\gamma)}{\gamma(1-\gamma)(1-\beta) - \alpha(w_c + w_a)(1-\beta) + (1-\gamma)} \tag{14}$$

Taking the absolute value (=1) of the both sides, we get the quadratic equation for r:

$$r^2 |\gamma'|^2 |\beta'|^2 - 2r(W_\alpha |\beta'|^2 \operatorname{Re}[\gamma'] - |\gamma'|^2 \operatorname{Re}\beta') + |\gamma' - W_\alpha \beta'|^2 - |\gamma'|^2 |1-c|^2 = 0 \tag{15}$$

where $\gamma' = 1-\gamma$, $\beta' = 1-\beta$, $W_\alpha = \alpha(w_a + w_c)$. The solution r, if positive, is substituted into (12) to obtain θ. Outer fixed points should be considered to have 8 variables: $\zeta_k^R, \zeta_k^I, \delta_k^R, \delta_k^I : k = 1, 2$ because the two neurons influence each other through w_{ij}. Therefore, in this case, ∇f is an 8×8 matrix. However, ∇f is decomposed into 4 sub-matrices, each 4×4 in dimension, as:

$$\nabla f = \begin{pmatrix} A_{11} & B_{12} \\ B_{21} & A_{22} \end{pmatrix} \tag{16}$$

Here

$$A_{ii} = \begin{pmatrix} \beta^R - \frac{1}{r_i} + \frac{Z_{iR}^2}{r_i^3} & -\beta^I + \frac{Z_{iR}Z_{iI}}{r_i^3} & \alpha\left(-\frac{1}{r_i} + \frac{Z_{iR}^2}{r_i^3}\right) & \frac{\alpha Z_{iR}Z_{iI}}{r_i^3} \\ \beta^I + \frac{Z_{iR}Z_{iI}}{r_i^3} & \beta^R - \frac{1}{r_i} + \frac{Z_{iI}^2}{r_i^3} & \frac{\alpha Z_{iR}Z_{iI}}{r_i^3} & \alpha\left(-\frac{1}{r_i} + \frac{Z_{iI}^2}{r_i^3}\right) \\ \frac{w_{ii}}{r_i}\left(1 - \frac{Z_{iR}^2}{r_i^2}\right) & -\frac{w_{ii}Z_{iR}Z_{iI}}{r_i^3} & \gamma^R + \frac{\alpha w_{ii}}{r_i}\left(1 - \frac{Z_{iR}^2}{r_i^2}\right) & -\gamma^I - \frac{\alpha w_{ii}Z_{iR}Z_{iI}}{r_i^3} \\ -\frac{w_{ii}Z_{iR}Z_{iI}}{r_i^3} & \frac{w_{ii}}{r_i}\left(1 - \frac{Z_{iI}^2}{r_i^2}\right) & -\gamma^I - \frac{\alpha w_{ii}Z_{iR}Z_{iI}}{r_i^3} & \gamma^R + \frac{\alpha w_{ii}}{r_i}\left(1 - \frac{Z_{iI}^2}{r_i^2}\right) \end{pmatrix} \tag{17}$$

where $Z_{iR} = \operatorname{Re}[z_i - c_i]$, $Z_{iI} = \operatorname{Im}[z_i - c_i]$ and

$$B_{ii} = \begin{pmatrix} 0 & 0 & 0 & 0 \\ 0 & 0 & 0 & 0 \\ \frac{w_{ij}}{r_j}\left\{1-\frac{Z_{jR}^2}{r_j^2}\right\} & -\frac{w_{ij}Z_{jR}Z_{jI}}{r_j^3} & \gamma^R + \frac{\alpha w_{ij}}{r_j}\left\{1-\frac{Z_{jR}^2}{r_j^2}\right\} & -\gamma^I - \frac{\alpha w_{ij}Z_{jR}Z_{jI}}{r_j^3} \\ -\frac{w_{ij}Z_{jR}Z_{jI}}{r_j^3} & \frac{w_{ij}}{r_j}\left\{1-\frac{Z_{jI}^2}{r_j^2}\right\} & \gamma^I - \frac{\alpha w_{ij}Z_{jR}Z_{jI}}{r_j^3} & \gamma^R + \frac{\alpha w_{ij}}{r_j}\left\{1-\frac{Z_{jI}^2}{r_j^2}\right\} \end{pmatrix} \quad (18)$$

At the fixed point of the symmetric circuit with symmetric dynamics, $A_{11} = A_{22} = A$ and $B_{12} = B_{21} = B$ and then

$$\nabla f \bigg|_{z^*} = \begin{pmatrix} A & B \\ B & A \end{pmatrix} \quad (19)$$

The eigenvalues λ of this matrix are easily seen to be the solutions of the equation:

$$|A + B - \lambda E| \, |A - B - \lambda E| = 0 \quad (20)$$

that is, they are the eigenvalues of $A + B$ and $A - B$.

Fig. 1 (a) shows the trace of the fixed points when $\theta = \arg(\beta)$ changes from 0 to 2π. The other parameter values are: $\alpha = 0.3, c = -0.5, |\beta| = 0.6, \gamma = 0.9 e^{i\pi/9}$, $w_{11} = w_{22} = w_{12} = w_{21} = 1$. Three orbits with $\theta = -\pi/45, 0, 2/9\pi$, each consisting of 1800 points from the 200-th iterate to 2000-th iterate are shown. The initial point is $\zeta_i(0) = 1$. The small circle around c is the critical circle and the larger one is centered around 1 with radius 1. (b) shows the absolute values of the eigenvalues as

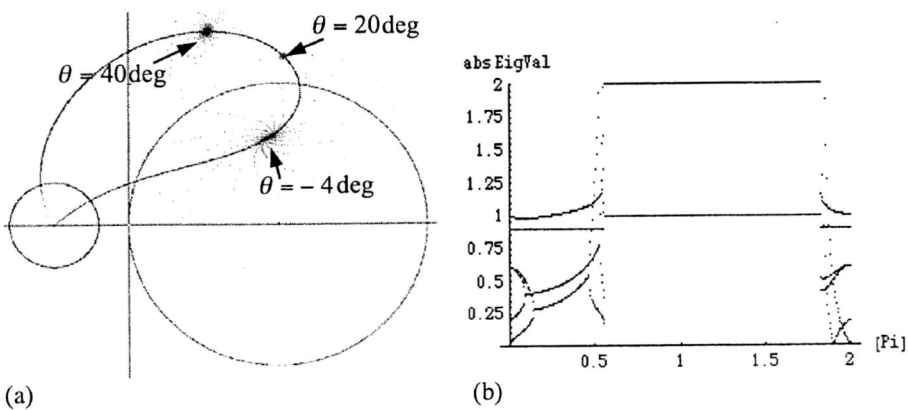

Fig. 1. Fixed points in the symmetric dynamics of the symmetric circuit of two complex-valued neurons. (a) The trace of the fixed points as θ changes from 0 to 2π. Three orbits are also shown. (b) The absolute values of the eigenvalues plotted against θ.

$\theta = \arg(\beta)$ changes. It is seen that the fixed points are unstable for a wide range of θ for this example. Fig. 2(a) shows the traces of fixed points calculated similarly for the same parameter values except for the connecting coefficients. Note that for the symmetric dynamics of the symmetric circuit, w_{ij} plays their part only in the form $W = \sum_{i,j=1}^{2} w_{ij}$. The traces in Fig. 2(a) are for $W = 0, 1, 2, 3, 4$. $W = 0$ naturally corresponds to the single-neuron case. The traces of fixed points in Fig. 2(b) are for $W = 2$ and for various values of $\varphi = \arg\gamma$ the rest of the parameter values being the same, with some orbits converging to the curves. It can be seen that near $\varphi = 0$, the fixed points are extremely sensitive to the value of φ. The stability of the fixed points on the curves is not to be seen here but the eigenvalues can be calculated similarly to Fig. 1(b).

We saw similar characteristics of orbits when $\theta = \arg\beta$ changes on one trace of fixed points as in Fig. 1 and 2 to those seen in the one-neuron circuit; with θ increasing, fixed point becomes unstable at some point, breaking up into period-2 periodic points and as θ increases further, we encounter quasi-periodic closed curves.

4. Some Examples of Orbits

So far it has been quite difficult to rigorously obtain other characteristics such as period-2 periodic points and their stability. We here show some of the orbits we found interesting. Fig. 3(a) shows the transition from fixed points to closed-curve-like orbits which are probably pseudo periodic as $\theta = \arg\beta$ increases. (b) shows an example where an infinitesimal difference in the initial conditions of the two units makes a large difference in the result. The circuit is symmetric but the initial condi-

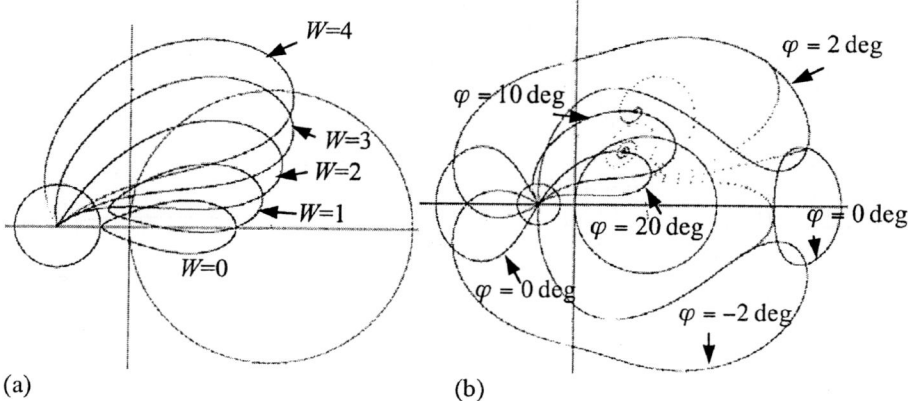

(a) (b)

Fig. 2. Traces of fixed points like the ones in Fig. 1. In (a), curves for several values of $W = \sum w_{ij}$ are shown for $\alpha = 0.3, c = -0.5, |\beta| = 0.6, \gamma = 0.9\exp\{i\pi/9\}$, and in (b), $\varphi = \arg\gamma$ is taken as the parameter.

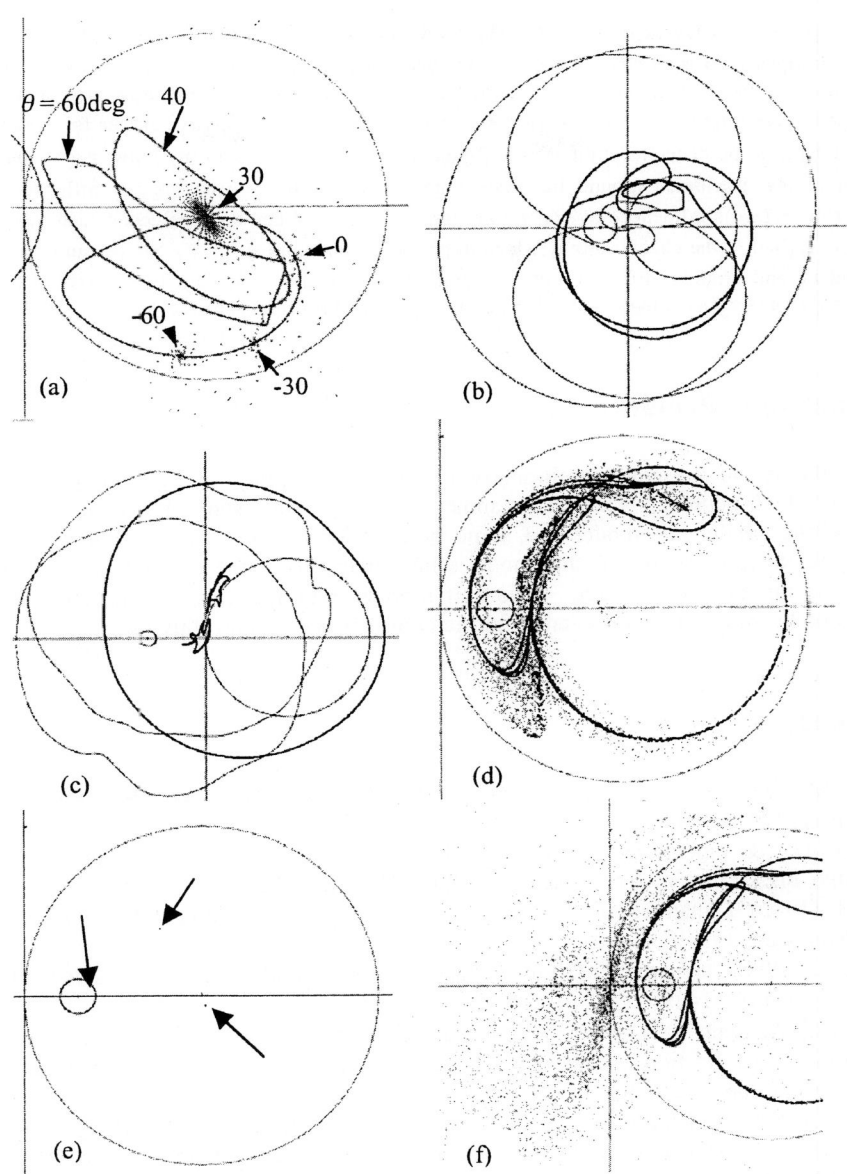

Fig. 3. Some example orbits. The parameter values are (a): $\alpha = 0.6, c = -0.5, |\beta| = 0.5, \gamma = 0.695 e^{i3\pi/2}, w_{ij} = 1, i = 1,2$; (b): $\alpha = 0.3, c = -0.5, \beta = 0.6 e^{i4\pi/3}, \gamma = 0.7 e^{i\pi/9}, w_{ij} = 1, i,j = 1,2$; (c): $\alpha = 0.1, c = -0.7, \beta = 0.6 e^{i2\pi/3}, \gamma = 0.8 e^{i\pi/9}, w_{11} = w_{12} = 1, w_{22} = w_{21} = 0$; (d): $\alpha = 0.1, c = 0.3, \beta = 0.98 e^{i\pi/6}, \gamma = 0.8 e^{i2\pi/3}, w_{11} = w_{22} = w_{21} = 0, w_{12} = 0.3$; (e): the same as (d) except for $w_{12} = w_{21} = 0.3$; (f): different initial conditions are assumed for the 2 units.

tion is: $\zeta_1(0)=1, \zeta_2(0)=\exp\{10^{-14} i\pi\}$. The thick curve shows the orbits $z_1(n), z_2(n)$; they look superimposed on each other but they never become equal as the thin curves shows which represents the orbit of $z_1(n) - z_2(n)$. (c) shows 2 small closed curves representing $z_1(n)$ and a large one representing $z_2(n)$. The 2-turn curve shows $z_1(n) - z_2(n)$. The two curves for $z_1(n)$ are considered to be generated from period-2 points. The thick points in (d) show $z_2(n)$ and the thin points distributed around the thick points show $z_1(n)$. $z_2(n)$ is not influenced by $z_1(n)$ but $z_1(n)$ is influenced by $z_2(n)$ through $w_{12} = 0.3$. When they influence each other by $w_{12} = w_{21} = 0.3$, the chaotic orbits reduce to period-3 points in (e). In (f), the two units are independent and slightly different initial conditions are assumed for the two units. The difference $z_1(n) - z_2(n)$ shown by the thin points imply that the orbit is chaotic.

5. Concluding Remarks

In this report we presented preliminary results of the study of the circuit of 2 complex-valued neurons. They show some interesting orbits some of which reflect those of the single unit model and some quite different from them. We should investigate those behaviors of this model which may reflect the neurophysiological aspects of the biological brain. Two-unit models, unit meaning an ensemble of neurons in this case, would be suitable for many instances of neural activities.

References

Aihara, M., Takabe, T., & Toyoda, M. (1990). Chaotic neural networks. *Physics Letters A, 144*, 333-340.
Birx, D. D., & Pipenberg, S.J. (1993). A complex mapping network for phase sensitive classification, *Transactions of IEEE, NN-4*, 127-135.
Hata, M. (1982). Dynamics of Cainiello's equation. *Journal of Mathematics of Kyoto University, 22*, 155-173.
Hirose, A. (1992). Dynamics of fully complex-valued neural networks. *Electronics Letters, 28*, 1492-1429.
Hirose, A., & Onishi, H. (1999). Proposal of relative-minimization learning for behavior stabilization of complex-valued recurrent neural networks, *Neurocomputing, 24*, 163-171.
Kono, T., & Nemoto I. (1991). Complex-valued neural networks. *Technical Report of the Inststitute of Electronics, Information and Communication Engineers, NC90-69*, 7-12. in Japanese.
Nemoto, I. & Saito, K. (2002). A complex-valued version of Nagumo-Sato model of a single neuron and its behavior. *Neural Networks, 15*, 833-853.
Nitta, T., & Furuya, T. (1991). A complex back-propagation learning. *Transactions of Information Processing Society of Japan, 34*, 29-38.
Noest, A.J. (1988). Phasor neural networks. In D.Z. Anderson (Es.), *Neural Information processing systems (pp. 584-591)*. New York: American Institute of Physics.

On Activation Functions for Complex-Valued Neural Networks
– Existence of Energy Functions –

Yasuaki Kuroe, Mitsuo Yoshida, and Takehiro Mori

Department of Electronics and Information Science
Kyoto Institute of Technology
Matsugasaki, Sakyo-ku, Kyoto 606-8585, Japan
kuroe@dj.kit.ac.jp

Abstract. Recently models of neural networks that can directly deal with complex numbers, complex-valued neural networks, have been proposed and several studies on their abilities of information processing have been done. One of the important factors to characterize behavior of a complex-valued neural network is its activation function which is a nonlinear complex function. This paper discusses the properties of activation functions from the standpoint of existence of an energy function for complex-valued neural networks. Two classes of complex functions which are widely used as activation functions in the models of complex-valued neural networks are considered. We investigate the properties of activation functions which assure existence of energy functions and discuss about how to find out complex functions which satisfy the properties.

1 Introduction

In recent years, there have been increasing research interests of artificial neural networks and many efforts have been made on applications of neural networks to various fields. As applications of the neural networks spread more widely, developing neural network models which can directly deal with complex numbers is desired in various fields. Several models of complex-valued neural networks have been proposed and their abilities of information processing have been investigated.

One of the important factors to characterize behavior of a complex-valued neural network is its activation function which is a nonlinear complex function. In the real-valued neural networks, the activation is usually chosen to be a smooth and bounded function such as a sigmoidal function. In the complex region, however, there are several possibilities in choosing an activation function because of a variety of complex functions. In [8] the properties that a suitable activation should possess are discussed for complex-valued backpropagation of complex-valued feedforward neural networks.

It is well known that one of the pioneering works that triggered the research interests of neural networks in the last two decades is the proposal of models for neural networks by Hopfield [1,2]. He introduced the idea of an energy function to formulate a way of understanding the computation performed by fully connected neural networks and showed that a combinatorial optimization problem can be solved by the neural networks. In the real-valued neural networks energy functions have been applied to various problems such as qualitative analysis of neural networks, synthesis of associative memories, optimization problems etc. ever since.

In this paper we consider a class of fully connected complex-valued neural networks which are a complex-valued extension of the Hopfield-type neural networks. We discuss the properties of activation functions from the standpoint of existence of an energy function for the complex-valued neural networks. The problems are to investigate existence conditions of an energy function and how to find out complex functions which satisfy the conditions. We have already obtained an existence condition of an energy function for the complex-valued neural networks [3]. In this paper we consider two classes of complex functions which are widely used as activation functions in the models of complex-valued neural networks proposed so far. Based on the existence condition we investigate the properties of the complex functions which assure the existence of an energy function and discuss about how to find them.

In the following, the imaginary unit is denoted by i ($i^2 = -1$). The set of complex (real) numbers is denoted by $\boldsymbol{C}$ ($\boldsymbol{R}$). The n-dimensional complex (real) space is denoted by $\boldsymbol{C}^n$ ($\boldsymbol{R}^n$) and the set of $n \times m$ complex (real) matrices is denoted by $\boldsymbol{C}^{n \times m}$ ($\boldsymbol{R}^{n \times m}$). For $A \in \boldsymbol{C}^{n \times m}$ ($\boldsymbol{a} \in \boldsymbol{C}^n$), its real and imaginary parts are denoted by A^R ($\boldsymbol{a}^R$) and A^I ($\boldsymbol{a}^I$), respectively. A^t ($\boldsymbol{a}^t$) denotes the transpose of A ($\boldsymbol{a}$) and A^* ($\boldsymbol{a}^*$) denotes the conjugate transpose of A ($\boldsymbol{a}$).

2 Model of Complex-Valued Neural Networks

Consider a class of complex-valued neural networks described by differential equations of the form:

$$\begin{cases} \tau_j \dfrac{du_j}{dt} = -u_j + \sum_{k=1}^{n} w_{jk} x_k + \theta_j \\ x_j = f(u_j) \end{cases} \quad j = 1, 2, \cdots, n \qquad (1)$$

where n is the number of neurons comprising the neural network, $x_j \in \boldsymbol{C}$, $u_j \in \boldsymbol{C}$ and $\theta_j \in \boldsymbol{C}$ are the output, the membrane potential and the threshold value of the jth neuron, respectively, $\tau_j \in \boldsymbol{R}$ is the time constant ($\tau_j > 0$), and $w_{jk} \in \boldsymbol{C}$ is the connection weight from the kth neuron to the jth neuron, and $f(\cdot)$ is an activation function which is a nonlinear complex function ($f : \boldsymbol{C} \to \boldsymbol{C}$).

Note that the neural network described by (1) is a direct complex-valued extension of the real-valued neural network of Hopfield type. In the real-valued neural networks, the function $f(\cdot)$ is usually chosen to be a smooth (continuously differentiable) and bounded function such as a sigmoidal function. In the complex region, however, we should recall the Liouville's theorem, which says that 'if $f(z)$

is analytic (differentiable) at all $z \in \mathbf{C}$ and bounded, then $f(z)$ is a constant function'. Since a suitable $f(z)$ should be bounded, it follows from the theorem that if we choose an analytic function for $f(z)$, it is constant over the entire $\mathbf{C}$, which is clearly not suitable, as is discussed in [8]. In this paper, in place of analytic function we choose a function which satisfies the followings as an activation function. Let us express $f(u)$ by separating into its real and imaginary parts as:

$$f(u) = f^R(u^R, u^I) + i f^I(u^R, u^I) \qquad (2)$$

where $f^R : R^2 \to R$ and $f^I : R^2 \to R$. We assume the followings for the activation function $f(\cdot)$.

Assumption 1 *(i) $f^R(u^R, u^I)$ and $f^I(u^R, u^I)$ are continuously differentiable with respect to u^R and u^I, and*
(ii) there exists some $M > 0$ such that $|f(\cdot)| \le M$.

In order to write (1) in an abbreviated form, we define vectors $\boldsymbol{u} \in \boldsymbol{C}^n$, $\boldsymbol{x} \in \boldsymbol{C}^n$, $\boldsymbol{\theta} \in \boldsymbol{C}^n$ and $\boldsymbol{f} : \boldsymbol{C}^n \to \boldsymbol{C}^n$ by $\boldsymbol{u} := (u_1, u_2, \cdots, u_n)^t$, $\boldsymbol{x} := (x_1, x_2, \cdots, x_n)^t$, $\boldsymbol{\theta} := (\theta_1, \theta_2, \cdots, \theta_n)^t$ and $\boldsymbol{f}(\boldsymbol{u}) := (f(u_1), f(u_2), \cdots, f(u_n))^t$, respectively, and matrices $T \in \boldsymbol{R}^{n \times n}$ and $W \in \boldsymbol{C}^{n \times n}$ by $T = \mathrm{diag}(\tau_1, \tau_2, \cdots, \tau_n)$ and $W = \{w_{jk}\}$. With this notation, the model of complex-valued neural networks (1) is rewritten as

$$\begin{cases} T \dfrac{d\boldsymbol{u}}{dt} = -\boldsymbol{u} + W\boldsymbol{x} + \boldsymbol{\theta} \\ \boldsymbol{x} = \boldsymbol{f}(\boldsymbol{u}) \end{cases} \qquad (3)$$

3 Existence Condition of Energy Function

We now give an existence condition of an energy function for the network (3), which will be the basis of the discussions on the activation functions in this paper. An energy function for the network (3) is defined by the analogy to that for real-valued Hopfield neural networks as follows [3].

Definition 1. *$E(\boldsymbol{x})$ is an energy function of the complex valued network (3) if $E(\boldsymbol{x})$ is a mapping $E : \boldsymbol{C}^n \to \boldsymbol{R}$ and the derivative of E along the trajectories (3), denoted by $\left.\dfrac{dE(\boldsymbol{x})}{dt}\right|_{(3)}$, satisfies $\left.\dfrac{dE(\boldsymbol{x})}{dt}\right|_{(3)} \le 0$. Furthermore $\left.\dfrac{dE(\boldsymbol{x})}{dt}\right|_{(3)} = 0$ if and only if $\dfrac{d\boldsymbol{x}}{dt} = 0$.*

It can be shown that, if all the equilibrium points of the network (3) are isolated and (3) has an energy function, then no nontrivial periodic solutions exist and each solution of (3) converges to an equilibrium point as $t \to \infty$ [3].

A sufficient condition for the existence of an energy function is obtained as follows [3].

Definition 2. *A complex function $f : C \to C$ satisfying Assumption 1 is said to belong to $\mathcal{F}^\mathcal{E}$ ($f(\cdot) \in \mathcal{F}^\mathcal{E}$), if f satisfies the following three conditions.*

$$\text{(i)} \ \frac{\partial f^R}{\partial u^R} \ne 0, \quad \text{(ii)} \ \frac{\partial f^R}{\partial u^I} = \frac{\partial f^I}{\partial u^R}, \quad \text{(iii)} \ \frac{\partial f^R}{\partial u^R} \frac{\partial f^I}{\partial u^I} - \frac{\partial f^R}{\partial u^I} \frac{\partial f^I}{\partial u^R} > 0 \qquad (4)$$

for all $u \in C$.

Theorem 1. *The complex-valued neural network (3) has an energy function if the connection weight matrix W is a Hermitian matrix, $W^* = W$, and the activation function $f(\cdot) \in \mathcal{F}^\mathcal{E}$.*

This theorem can be proved by defining an energy function as

$$E(\boldsymbol{x}) := -\frac{1}{2}(\boldsymbol{x}^* W \boldsymbol{x} + \boldsymbol{\theta}^* \boldsymbol{x} + \boldsymbol{x}^* \boldsymbol{\theta}) + \sum_{j=1}^{n} G(x_j^R, x_j^I) \qquad (5)$$

where

$$G(x^R, x^I) := \int_0^{x^R} g^R(x, 0) dx + \int_0^{x^I} g^I(x^R, y) dy \qquad (6)$$

and $g = f^{-1}$; $g(x) = g^R(x^R, x^I) + i\, g^I(x^R, x^I)$ [3].

4 Existence Conditions on Activation Functions

In the complex region there are several possibilities in choosing an activation function because of a variety of complex functions. In this section we investigate what kinds of complex functions satisfy the existence condition of an energy function and discuss how to find them. We consider the following two classes of complex functions $f(\cdot)$ which are used in most of the models of complex-valued neural networks proposed so far. Let us express u in the polar representation as $u = re^{i\theta}$.

- Type A: $\qquad f(u) = f^R(u^R) + i\, f^I(u^I) \qquad (7)$
- Type B: $\qquad f(u) = \psi(r) e^{j\phi(\theta)} \qquad (8)$

In type A, $f^R(\cdot)$ and $f^I(\cdot)$ are nonlinear real functions, $f^R : R \to R$ and $f^I : R \to R$. In Type B, $\psi(\cdot)$ and $\phi(\cdot)$ are nonlinear real functions, $\psi : R_{0+} \to R_{0+}$, $\phi : R \to R$, where $R_{+o} = \{x \mid x \geq 0\ x \in R\}$. Note that in Type A the real and imaginary parts of an input go through nonlinear functions separately, and in Type B the magnitude and the phase of an input go through nonlinear functions separately. Most of the activation functions yet proposed for the models of complex-valued neural networks belong to either of Type A or B.

For the activation functions of Type A, the following theorem is obtained immediately from Theorem 1.

Theorem 2. *Consider the activation function f of Type A: $f(u) = f^R(u^R) + i f^I(u^I)$. Suppose that f^R and f^I are continuously differentiable with respect to u^R and u^I, respectively, and are bounded. $f \in \mathcal{F}^\mathcal{E}$ if and only if*

$$\text{(i)}\ \frac{\partial f^R}{\partial u^R} > 0,\ \frac{\partial f^I}{\partial u^I} > 0\ \ \text{or}\ \ \text{(ii)}\ \frac{\partial f^R}{\partial u^R} < 0,\ \frac{\partial f^I}{\partial u^I} < 0 \qquad (9)$$

for all $u \in \boldsymbol{C}$.

In the above theorem, there are two cases, (i) and (ii), in which an activation function satisfies the existence conditions (4) of energy functions (belongs to $\mathcal{F}^\mathcal{E}$). However, it is sufficient to consider only one of them because they are equivalent in the following sense. Suppose that the activation function satisfies the case (ii). Letting $h := -f$, $\hat{x} := -x$ and $\hat{W} := -W$, the model of the complex-valued neural network (3) can be rewritten as

$$\begin{cases} T\dfrac{d\boldsymbol{u}}{dt} = -\boldsymbol{u} + \hat{W}\hat{\boldsymbol{x}} + \boldsymbol{\theta} \\ \hat{\boldsymbol{x}} = h(\boldsymbol{u}) \end{cases} \tag{10}$$

Clearly, $\hat{W}$ is a Hermitian matrix and $h \in \mathcal{F}^\mathcal{E}$, which arrives at the case (i).

The following theorem can be obtained for the activation functions of Type B.

Theorem 3. *Consider the activation function f of Type B: $f(u) = \psi(r)e^{i\phi(\theta)}$ where $u = re^{i\theta}$. Suppose that ψ is continuously differentiable with respect to r for $r \geq 0$ and bounded, and $\phi(\theta)$ is continuously differentiable with respect to θ. $f \in \mathcal{F}^\mathcal{E}$ if and only if*

$$\dfrac{d\psi(r)}{dr} > 0 \text{ for all } r \geq 0, \quad \lim_{r \to 0} \dfrac{\psi(r)}{r} > 0 \quad \text{and} \tag{11}$$

$$\phi(\theta) = \theta + n\pi \tag{12}$$

where n is an integer.

The proof of this theorem will be given in Appendix. It is seen from the theorem that the activation of Type B must take the form:

$$f(u) = \psi(r)e^{i\theta} \quad \text{or} \quad f(u) = -\psi(r)e^{i\theta}$$

for belonging to $\mathcal{F}^\mathcal{E}$ because $\phi(\theta) = \theta + n\pi$. Note also that the latter form is reduced to the former one by rewriting the model of the complex-valued neural network (3) as (10).

5 Discussions

It is known that, in the case that the neural network (3) is real-valued, that is, $\boldsymbol{u}$, $\boldsymbol{x}$, $\boldsymbol{\theta}$, W and T are all real numbers and $f(\cdot)$ is a real nonlinear function ($f : \boldsymbol{R} \to \boldsymbol{R}$) in (3), an existence condition of energy function on the activation function is that $f(\cdot)$ is continuously differentiable, bounded and monotonically increasing (the condition on the connection weight matrix is $W^t = W$). It is seen from Theorem 2 that, for the case that the activation function is of Type A in the complex-valued neural network (3), the existence condition is a direct extension of that of the real-valued Hopfield type neural networks. On the other hand, for the case that the activation function is of Type B, only the condition on its magnitude function is similar to that of the real-valued networks (Theorem 3).

Note that, the activation function of Type B satisfying the existence condition (belonging to $\mathcal{F}^\mathcal{E}$) does not vary the phase of an input signal.

There have been several activation functions proposed for complex-valued neural networks. Typical examples are as follows.

$$f(u) = \frac{1}{1+e^{-u^R}} + i\frac{1}{1+e^{-u^I}} \quad \text{[5], [9]} \tag{13}$$

$$f(u) = \tanh(u^R) + i\tanh(u^I) \quad \text{[10],[11]} \tag{14}$$

$$f(u) = \frac{u}{|u|} \quad \text{[6], [7]} \tag{15}$$

$$f(u) = \tanh(|u|)\exp(i\arg u) \quad \text{[12]} \tag{16}$$

$$f(u) = \frac{u}{c + \frac{1}{\gamma}|u|} \quad (c, \gamma : \text{real positive constants}) \quad \text{[8] ,[13]} \tag{17}$$

$$f(u) = \frac{1}{1+e^{-u}} \quad \text{[4]} \tag{18}$$

The functions (13) and (14) are of Type A and satisfy the conditions of Theorem 2. The functions (15), (16) and (17) are of Type B. Among them (16) and (17) satisfy Theorem 3, but (15) does not because it is not defined at $u = 0$. The function (18) is neither of Type A nor Type B and does not belong to $\mathcal{F}^\mathcal{E}$, but is analytic. It is concluded, therefore, that the complex-valued neural network with the activation function (13), (14), (16) or (17) and a Hermitian weight matrix W has an energy function (5).

In [8] G. M. Georgiou et al. discuss about properties that a suitable activation should possess for complex-valued backpropagation of complex-valued feedforward neural networks. Their suggested properties are:

1. $f(\cdot)$ is nonlinear and bounded,
2. $f(\cdot)$ is not entirely analytic and the partial derivatives $\frac{\partial f^R}{\partial u^R}, \frac{\partial f^R}{\partial u^I}, \frac{\partial f^I}{\partial u^R}$ and $\frac{\partial f^I}{\partial u^R}$ exist and are bounded, and
3. $\frac{\partial f^R}{\partial u^R}\frac{\partial f^I}{\partial u^I} - \frac{\partial f^R}{\partial u^I}\frac{\partial f^I}{\partial u^R} \neq 0$ for all $u \in \mathbf{C}$.

They propose the function (17) as an activation function which satisfies these properties and give its hardware implementation. They show that if the property 3 is violated, no learning takes place in complex domain backpropagation. Note that, in addition to the property 3, the positive definite and symmetry conditions ((ii) and (iii) of Definition 2) are required for existence of an energy function.

By utilizing Theorems 2 and 3 other functions which satisfy the existence conditions can be easily found out because there are a large choice of the real functions $f^R(u^R)$, $f^I(u^I)$ in Type A and $\psi(r)$ in Type B which are continuously differentiable and monotonically increasing. It seems to be challenging to find out complex functions belonging to $\mathcal{F}^\mathcal{E}$ which are neither of Type A nor Type B, but are of the general form (2) or

$$f(u) = \psi(r,\theta)e^{j\phi(r,\theta)} \tag{19}$$

This problem remains for future study. Note also that the discussions here are based on the condition $f(\cdot) \in \mathcal{F}^{\mathcal{E}}$ which is a sufficient condition for existence of an energy function. To derive another existence condition is also a subject for future study.

6 Conclusion

In this paper we investigated existence conditions of energy functions for complex-valued Hopfield-type neural networks. Emphasized were the properties of the activation functions which assure the existence of an energy function for the networks. Two classes of activation functions which are used in most of the models of complex-valued neural networks were considered. We investigated properties of activation functions which assure existence of energy functions and discussed about how to find out complex functions which satisfy the properties.

References

1. J. J. Hopfield, "Neurons with graded response have collective computational properties like those of two-state neurons", *Proc. Natl. Acad. of Sci. U.S.A.*, Vol.81, pp. 3088–3092, 1984.
2. J. J. Hopfield and D. W. Tank, ""Neural" Computation of Decisions in Optimization Problems", *Biol. Cybern.*, Vol. 81, pp. 141–152, 1985.
3. Y. Kuroe, N. Hashimoto and T. Mori, "On Energy Function for Complex-valued Neural Networks and Its Application", *CD-ROM Proc. of 9th International Conference on Neural Information Processing (ICONIP'02)* Nov., 2002.
4. H. Leung and S. Haykin, "The Complex Backpropagation Algorithm", *IEEE Transactions on Signal Processing*, Vol.39, pp. 2101-2104, 1991.
5. D. L. Birx, S. J. Pipenberg, "Chaotic Oscillators and Complex Mapping Feed Forward Networks (CMFFNS) for Signal Detection in Noisy Environments", *Proc. IEEE IJCNN'92*, Vol. II, pp. 881–888, 1992.
6. A.J.Noest, "Phaser Neural Network," *Neural Information Processing Systems*, pp. 584–591, D.Z.Anderson,ed., AIP, New York, 1988.
7. A. J. Noest, "Associative Memory in Sparse Phasor Neural Networks", *Europhysics Letters*, Vol. 6, No. 6, pp. 469–474, 1988.
8. G. M. Georgiou and C. Koutsougeras, "Complex Domain Backpropagation", *IEEE Transactions on Circuits and Systems-II*, Vol. 39, No. 5, pp. 330–334, 1992.
9. N. Benvenuto and F. Piazza, "On the Complex Backpropagation Algorithm" *IEEE Transactions on Signal Processing*, Vol.40, pp. 967–969, 1992.
10. G. Kechriotis and E. S. Manolakos, "Training Fully Recurrent Neural Networks with Complex Weights", *IEEE Transactions on Circuits and Systems-II*, Vol.41, No.3, pp. 235–238, 1994.
11. M. Kinouchi and M. Hagiwara, "Learning Temporal Sequences by Complex Neurons with Local Feedback", *Proc. IEEE ICNN '95*, Vol. VI, pp. 3165–3169, 1995.
12. A. Hirose, "Applications of Complex-Valued Neural Networks to Coherent Optical Computing Using Phase-Sensitive Detection Scheme", *Information Sciences - Applications*, Vol. 2, No. 2, pp. 103–117, 1994.
13. N.Hashimoto, Y. Kuroe and T.Mori, "Theoretical Study of Qualitative Behaviors of Self-Correlation Type Associative Memory on Complex-valued Neural Networks," *Trans. of IEICE*, Vol.J83-A, No.6, pp.750-760, June 2000 (in Japanese).

A Outline of Proof of Theorem 3

Suppose that the activation function f is of Type B. From (8), $\frac{\partial f^R}{\partial u^R}$, $\frac{\partial f^R}{\partial u^I}$, $\frac{\partial f^I}{\partial u^R}$ and $\frac{\partial f^I}{\partial u^I}$ are obtained in the polar representation as follows.

$$\begin{cases} \dfrac{\partial f^R}{\partial u^R} = \dfrac{\partial \psi}{\partial r} \cdot \cos\phi(\theta) \cdot \cos\theta + \dfrac{\psi(r)}{r} \cdot \dfrac{\partial \phi}{\partial \theta} \cdot \sin\phi(\theta) \cdot \sin\theta \\[6pt] \dfrac{\partial f^R}{\partial u^I} = \dfrac{\partial \psi}{\partial r} \cdot \cos\phi(\theta) \cdot \sin\theta - \dfrac{\psi(r)}{r} \cdot \dfrac{\partial \phi}{\partial \theta} \cdot \sin\phi(\theta) \cdot \cos\theta \\[6pt] \dfrac{\partial f^I}{\partial u^R} = \dfrac{\partial \psi}{\partial r} \cdot \sin\phi(\theta) \cdot \cos\theta - \dfrac{\psi(r)}{r} \cdot \dfrac{\partial \phi}{\partial \theta} \cdot \cos\phi(\theta) \cdot \sin\theta \\[6pt] \dfrac{\partial f^I}{\partial u^I} = \dfrac{\partial \psi}{\partial r} \cdot \sin\phi(\theta) \cdot \sin\theta + \dfrac{\psi(r)}{r} \cdot \dfrac{\partial \phi}{\partial \theta} \cdot \cos\phi(\theta) \cdot \cos\theta \end{cases} \quad (20)$$

By using the above relations, the conditions (ii) and (iii) in Definition 2 are rewritten as the following conditions, (21) and (22), respectively.

$$\frac{\partial f^R}{\partial u^I} - \frac{\partial f^I}{\partial u^R} = \left(\frac{\partial \psi}{\partial r} + \frac{\psi(r)}{r} \frac{\partial \phi}{\partial \theta} \right) \sin(\phi(\theta) - \theta) = 0 \quad (21)$$

$$\frac{\partial f^R}{\partial u^R} \frac{\partial f^I}{\partial u^I} - \frac{\partial f^R}{\partial u^I} \frac{\partial f^I}{\partial u^R} = \frac{\psi(r)}{r} \cdot \frac{\partial \psi}{\partial r} \cdot \frac{\partial \phi}{\partial \theta} > 0 \quad (22)$$

It can be seen that the conditions (21) and (22) are equivalent to the following conditions.

$$\frac{d\psi(r)}{dr} > 0 \text{ for all } r \geq 0, \quad \lim_{r \to 0} \frac{\psi(r)}{r} > 0 \quad (23)$$

$$\phi(\theta) = \theta + n\pi \quad (24)$$

Thus the condition (ii) and (iii) in Definition 2 are equivalent to the conditions (11) and (12) in Theorem 3. By using (12), $\frac{\partial f^R}{\partial u^R}$ is calculated as follows.

$$\frac{\partial f^R}{\partial u^R} = \frac{\partial \psi}{\partial r} \cos^2\theta \cos(n\pi) + \frac{\psi(r)}{r} \sin^2\theta \cos(n\pi)$$

$$= \begin{cases} \dfrac{\partial \psi}{\partial r} \cos^2\theta + \dfrac{\psi(r)}{r} \cdot \sin^2\theta & (\text{n: even}) \\[6pt] -\dfrac{\partial \psi}{\partial r} \cos^2\theta - \dfrac{\psi(r)}{r} \sin^2\theta & (\text{n: odd}) \end{cases} \quad (25)$$

From (11) and (25), we can obtain the condition (i) in Definition 2; $\frac{\partial f^R}{\partial u^R} \neq 0$. This completes the proof.

The Computational Power of Complex-Valued Neuron

Tohru Nitta

National Institute of Advanced Industrial Science and Technology (AIST),
Tsukuba Central 2, 1-1-1 Umezono, Tsukuba-shi, Ibaraki, 305-8568 Japan.
tohru-nitta@aist.go.jp

Abstract. There exist some problems that cannot be solved with conventional usual 2-layered real-valued neural networks (i.e., a single real-valued neuron) such as the XOR problem and the detection of symmetry. In this paper, it will be proved that such problems can be solved by a 2-layered complex-valued neural network (i.e., a single complex-valued neuron) with the orthogonal decision boundaries. Furthermore, it will be shown that the fading equalization problem can be successfully solved by the 2-layered complex-valued neural network with the highest generalization ability.

1 Introduction

It is expected that complex-valued neural networks (for example, [2,3]) whose parameters (weights and threshold values) are all complex numbers, will have applications in fields dealing with complex numbers such as telecommunications, speech recognition and image processing with the Fourier transformation.

This paper clarifies the computational power of complex-valued neuron [5]. The main results may be summarized as follows. The XOR problem and the detection of symmetry problem which cannot be solved with 2-layered real-valued neural networks, can be solved by 2-layered complex-valued neural networks with the orthogonal decision boundaries, which reveals a potent computational power of complex-valued neural nets. Furthermore, the fading equalization problem can be successfully solved by the 2-layered complex-valued neural network with the highest generalization ability.

2 The Complex-Valued Neuron

This section describes the complex-valued neuron used in the analysis. First, we will consider the following complex-valued neuron. The input signals, weights, thresholds and output signals are all complex numbers. The net input U_n to a complex-valued neuron n is defined as:

$$U_n = \sum_m W_{nm} X_m + V_n, \qquad (1)$$

where W_{nm} is the (complex-valued) weight connecting complex-valued neurons n and m, X_m is the (complex-valued) input signal from complex-valued neuron m, and V_n is the (complex-valued) threshold value of neuron n. To obtain the (complex-valued) output signal, convert the net input U_n into its real and imaginary parts as follows: $U_n = x + iy = z$, where i denotes $\sqrt{-1}$. The (complex-valued) output signal is defined to be

$$1_C(z) = 1_R(x) + i1_R(y), \quad z = x + iy \qquad (2)$$

where 1_R is a real-valued step function defined on $\boldsymbol{R}$, that is, $1_R(u) = 1$ (if $u \geq 0$), $1_R(u) = 0$ (otherwise) for any $u \in \boldsymbol{R}$ ($\boldsymbol{R}$ denotes the set of real numbers).

Decision boundary is a boundary by which the pattern classifier classifies patterns, and generally consists of hypersurfaces. We analyzed the decision boundary of a single complex-valued neuron and discovered that the decision boundary for the real part of an output of a complex-valued neuron and that for the imaginary part intersect orthogonally [4].

3 The Computational Power of Complex-Valued Neuron

In this section, we will show the computational power of a single complex-valued neuron described above, based on the properties on the decision boundary discovered in [4].

Minsky and Papert [1] clarified the limitations of 2-layered real-valued neural networks (i.e., no hidden layers): in a large number of interesting cases, the 2-layered real-valued neural network is incapable of solving the problems. A classic example of this case is the exclusive-or (XOR) problem which has a long history in the study of neural networks, and many other difficult problems involve the XOR as subproblem. Another example is the detection of symmetry problem. Rumelhart, Hinton, & Williams [6] showed that the *3-layered* real-valued neural network (i.e., with one hidden layer) can solve such problems including the XOR problem and the detection of symmetry problem and the interesting internal representations can be constructed in the weight-space.

As described above, the XOR problem and the detection of symmetry problem cannot be solved with the 2-layered real-valued neural network. Then, first, contrary to expectation, it will be proved that such problems can be solved by the *2-layered* complex-valued neural network (i.e., no hidden layers) with the orthogonal decision boundaries, which reveals a potent computational power of complex-valued neural nets. In addition, it will be shown as an application of the above computational power that the fading equalization problem can be successfully solved by the 2-layered complex-valued neural network with the highest generalization ability. Rumelhart, Hinton and Williams [6] showed that increasing the number of layers made the computational power of neural networks high. In this section, we will show that extending the dimensionality of neural networks to complex numbers originates the similar effect on neural networks. This may be a new directionality for enhancing the ability of neural networks.

3.1 The XOR Problem

In this section, it is proved that the XOR problem can be solved by *2-layered* complex-valued neural network (i.e., no hidden layers) with the orthogonal decision boundaries.

The input-output mapping in the XOR problem is shown in Table 1.

Table 1. The XOR problem

Input		Output
x_1	x_2	y
0	0	0
0	1	1
1	0	1
1	1	0

In order to solve the XOR problem with complex-valued neural networks, the input-output mapping is encoded as shown in Table 2 where the outputs 1 and i are interpreted to be 0, 0 and $1+i$ are interpreted to be 1 of the original XOR problem (Table 1), respectively.

Table 2. An encoded XOR problem for complex-valued neural networks

Input	Output
$z = x + iy$	$Z = X + iY$
$-1-i$	1
$-1+i$	0
$1-i$	$1+i$
$1+i$	i

We use a 1-1 complex-valued neural network (i.e., no hidden layers) with a weight $w = u + iv \in \mathbf{C}$ between the input neuron and the output neuron where $\mathbf{C}$ denotes the set of complex numbers (we assume that it has no threshold parameters). The activation function is defined to be

$$1_C(z) = 1_R(x) + i1_R(y), \quad z = x + iy \qquad (3)$$

where 1_R is a real-valued step function defined on $\mathbf{R}$, that is, $1_R(u) = 1$ (if $u \geq 0$), $1_R(u) = 0$ (otherwise) for any $u \in \mathbf{R}$. The decision boundary of the 1-1 complex-valued neural network described above consists of the following two straight lines which intersect orthogonally:

$$[u \quad -v] \begin{bmatrix} x \\ y \end{bmatrix} = 0, \qquad (4)$$

$$[v \quad u] \begin{bmatrix} x \\ y \end{bmatrix} = 0 \qquad (5)$$

for any input signal $z = x+iy \in C$ where u and v are the real and imaginary parts of the weight parameter $w = u + iv$, respectively. The expressions (4) and (5) are the decision boundaries for the real and imaginary parts of the 1-1 complex-valued neural network, respectively. Letting $u = 0$ and $v = 1$ (i.e., $w = i$), we have the decision boundary shown in Fig. 1, which divides the input space (the decision region) into four equal sections, and has the highest generalization ability for the XOR problem. On the other hand, the decision boundary of the 3-layered real-valued neural network for the XOR problem does not always have the highest generalization ability. In addition, the required number of learnable parameters is only 2 (i.e., only $w = u + iv$), whereas at least 9 parameters are needed for the 3-layered real-valued neural network to solve the XOR problem [6], where a complex-valued parameter $z = x + iy$ (where $i = \sqrt{-1}$) is counted as two because it consists of a real part x and an imaginary part y.

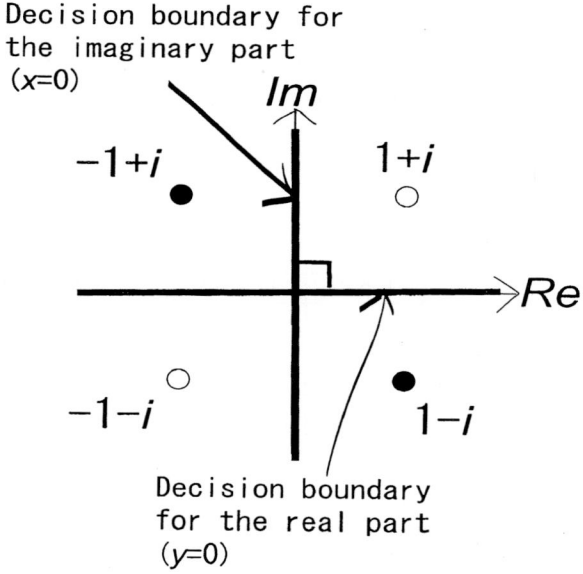

Fig. 1. The decision boundary in the input space of the 1-1 complex-valued neural network that solves the XOR problem. *The black circle* means that the output in the XOR problem is 1, and *the white one* 0

3.2 The Detection of Symmetry

Another interesting task that cannot be done by 2-layered real-valued neural networks is the detection of symmetry problem [1]. In this section, a solution to this problem using *2-layered* complex-valued neural network (i.e., no hidden layers) with the orthogonal decision boundaries is given.

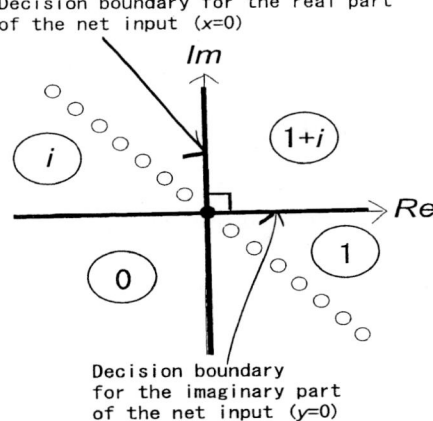

Fig. 2. The decision boundary in the net-input space of the 6-1 complex-valued neural network that solves the detection of symmetry problem. Note that the plane is not the *input* space but the *net-input* space because the dimension of the input space is 6 and the input space cannot be written in a 2-dimensional plane. *The black circle* means a net-input for a symmetric input, and *the white one* asymmetric. There is only *one* black circle at the origin. *The four circled complex numbers* mean the output values of the 6-1 complex-valued neural network in their regions, respectively

The problem is to detect whether the binary activity levels of a one-dimensional array of input neurons are symmetrical about the centre point. For example, the input-output mapping in the case of 3 inputs is shown in Table 3. We used patterns of various lengths (from 2 to 6) and could solve all the cases with 2-layered complex-valued neural networks. Only a solution to the case with 6 inputs is presented here because the other cases can be done by the similar way.

Table 3. The detection of symmetry problem with 3 inputs. Output 1 means that the corresponding input is symmetric, and 0 asymmetric

Input			Output
x_1	x_2	x_3	y
0	0	0	1
0	0	1	0
0	1	0	1
1	0	0	0
0	1	1	0
1	0	1	1
1	1	0	0
1	1	1	1

We use a 6-1 complex-valued neural network (i.e., no hidden layers) with weights $w_k = u_k + iv_k \in \boldsymbol{C}$ between an input neuron k and the output neuron ($1 \leq k \leq 6$) (we assume that it has no threshold parameters). In order to solve the problem with the complex-valued neural network, the input-output mapping is encoded as follows: an input $x_k \in \boldsymbol{R}$ is encoded as an input $x_k + iy_k \in \boldsymbol{C}$ to the input neuron k where $y_k = 0$ ($1 \leq k \leq 6$), the output $1 \in \boldsymbol{R}$ is encoded as $1+i \in \boldsymbol{C}$, and the output $0 \in \boldsymbol{R}$ is encoded as 1 or $i \in \boldsymbol{C}$ which is determined according to inputs (for example, the output corresponding to the input $^t[0\ 0\ 0\ 0\ 1\ 0]$ is i). The activation function is the same as in expression (3).

The decision boundary of the 6-1 complex-valued neural network described above consists of the following two straight lines which intersect orthogonally:

$$[u_1 \cdots u_6 \ -v_1 \cdots -v_6] \begin{bmatrix} x_1 \\ \vdots \\ x_6 \\ y_1 \\ \vdots \\ y_6 \end{bmatrix} = 0, \quad (6)$$

$$[v_1 \cdots v_6 \ u_1 \cdots u_6] \begin{bmatrix} x_1 \\ \vdots \\ x_6 \\ y_1 \\ \vdots \\ y_6 \end{bmatrix} = 0 \quad (7)$$

for any input signal $z_k = x_k + iy_k \in \boldsymbol{C}$ where u_k and v_k are the real and imaginary parts of the weight parameter $w_k = u_k + iv_k$, respectively ($1 \leq k \leq 6$). The expressions (6) and (7) are the decision boundaries for the real and imaginary parts of the 6-1 complex-valued neural network, respectively. Letting $^t[u_1 \cdots u_6] = {}^t[-1\ 2\ -4\ 4\ -2\ 1]$ and $^t[v_1 \cdots v_6] = {}^t[1\ -2\ 4\ -4\ 2\ -1]$ (i.e., $w_1 = -1 + i, w_2 = 2 - 2i, w_3 = -4 + 4i, w_4 = 4 - 4i, w_5 = -2 + 2i$ and $w_6 = 1 - i$), we have the orthogonal decision boundaries shown in Fig. 2 which successfully detect the symmetry of the $2^6 (= 64)$ input patterns.

In addition, the required number of learnable parameters is 12 (i.e., 6 complex-valued weights), whereas at least 17 parameters are needed for the 3-layered real-valued neural network to solve the detection of symmetry [6] where a complex-valued parameter $z = x + iy$ (where $i = \sqrt{-1}$) is counted as two as in Section 3.1.

3.3 The Fading Equalization Technology

In this section, it is shown that 2-layered complex-valued neural networks with orthogonal decision boundaries can be successfully applied to the fading equalization technology.

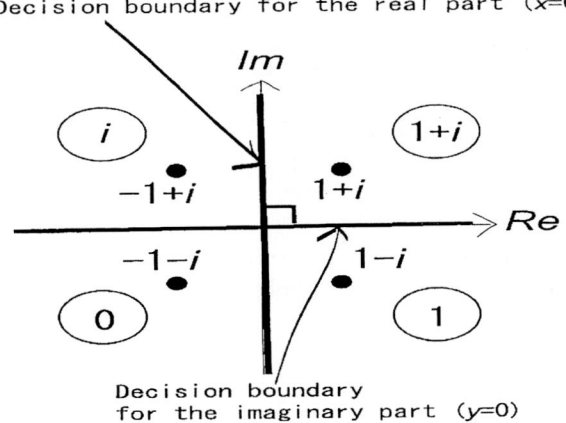

Fig. 3. The decision boundary in the input space of the 1-1 complex-valued neural network that solves the fading equalization problem. *The black circle* means an input in the fading equalization problem. *The four circled complex numbers* mean the output values of the 1-1 complex-valued neural network in their regions, respectively

Channel equalization in a digital communication system can be viewed as a pattern classification problem. The digital communication system receives a transmitted signal sequence with additive noise, and tries to estimate the true transmitted sequence. A transmitted signal can take one of the following four possible complex values: $-1-i, -1+i, 1-i$ and $1+i$ ($i = \sqrt{-1}$). Thus the received signal will take value around $-1-i, -1+i, 1-i$ and $1+i$, for example, $-0.9 - 1.2i$, $1.1 + 0.84i$ or something because some noises are added to them. We need to estimate the true complex values from such complex values with noises. Thus, the method with an excellent generalization ability is needed for the estimate. The input-output mapping in the problem is shown in Table 4.

Table 4. The input-output mapping in the fading equalization problem

Input	Output
$-1-i$	$-1-i$
$-1+i$	$-1+i$
$1-i$	$1-i$
$1+i$	$1+i$

We use the same 1-1 complex-valued neural network as in Section 3.1. In order to solve the problem with the complex-valued neural network, the input-output mapping in Table 4 is encoded as shown in Table 5. Letting $u = 1$ and $v = 0$ (i.e., $w = 1$), we have the orthogonal decision boundary shown in Fig. 3, which has the highest generalization ability for the fading equalization problem,

Table 5. An encoded fading equalization problem for complex-valued neural networks

Input	Output
$-1-i$	0
$-1+i$	i
$1-i$	1
$1+i$	$1+i$

and can estimate true signals without errors. In addition, the required number of learnable parameters is only 2 (i.e., only $w = u + iv$).

4 Conclusions

Rumelhart, Hinton and Williams [6] showed that increasing the number of layers made the computational power of neural networks high. The results of this paper suggest that extending the dimensionality of neural networks to complex numbers originates the similar effect on neural networks. This may be a new directionality for enhancing the ability of neural networks.

References

1. Minsky, M. L., Papert, S. A.: Perceptrons. MIT Press, Cambridge (1969)
2. Nitta, T., Furuya, T.: A Complex Back-propagation Learning. Transactions of Information Processing Society of Japan, 32(10), (1991) 1319–1329 (in Japanese)
3. Nitta, T.: An Extension of the Back-propagation Algorithm to Complex Numbers. Neural Networks, 10(8), (1997) 1392–1415
4. Nitta, T.: An Analysis on Fundamental Structure of Complex-valued Neuron. Neural Processing Letters, 12(3), (2000) 239–246
5. Nitta, T.: Submitted to a journal (2003)
6. Rumelhart, D. E., Hinton, G. E., Williams, R. J.: Parallel Distributed Processing (Vol. 1). MIT Press (1986)

Computational Intelligence and Applications

Recommendation Models for User Accesses to Web Pages

Ş. Gündüz and M.T. Özsu

[1] Department of Computer Science, Istanbul Technical University
Istanbul, Turkey, 34390
gunduz@cs.itu.edu.tr
[2] School of Computer Science, University of Waterloo
Waterloo, Ontario, Canada N2L 3G1
tozsu@db.uwaterloo.ca

Abstract. Predicting the next request of a user as she visits Web pages has gained importance as Web-based activity increases. There are a number of different approaches to prediction. Markov models and their variations, collaborative filtering models, or models based on pattern recognition techniques such as sequence mining, association rule mining, clustering user sessions or user, have been found well suited for this problem. In this paper we review these techniques and also highlight two new models that we have proposed. They consider the user access patterns to the pages as well as the time spent on these pages. We report experimental studies that show that the proposed methods can achieve a better accuracy than the other approaches.

1 Introduction

Web mining is defined as the use of data mining techniques to automatically discover and extract information from Web documents and services [8]. With the rapid growth of the World Wide Web, the study of modelling and predicting a user's access on a Web site has become more important. It has been used to improve the Web performance through caching and prefetching, to recommend related pages, improve search engines and personalize browsing in a Web site. Given a user's (who may, for example, be a customer in an e-commerce site) current actions, the goal is to determine which Web pages (items) will be accessed (bought) in the near future.

In general, Web mining is a common term for three knowledge discovery domains that are concerned with mining different parts of the Web: Web Content Mining, Web Structure Mining, and Web Usage Mining [25]. While Web content and structure mining utilize real or primary data on the Web, Web usage mining works on the secondary data such as Web server access logs, proxy server logs, browser logs, user profiles, registration data, user sessions or transactions [1],

---

[1] The term *server session* is defined as the click stream of page views for a single visit of a user to a Web site [25]. In this paper we will use this term interchangeably with "user session" and "user transaction".

cookies, user queries, and bookmark data. Web usage mining refers to the application of data mining techniques to discover usage patterns from these secondary data, in order to understand and better serve the needs of Web-based applications. The usage data collected at different sources will represent the navigation patterns of different segments of the overall Web traffic, ranging from single-user, single-site browsing behavior to multi-user, multi-site access patterns. The information provided by the data sources can all be used to construct/identify several data abstractions, such as users, server sessions, episodes, click stream, and page views [12].

In this paper, we survey the research in the area of recommendation systems. Recommender systems collect ratings from web users explicitly or implicitly. Most of the models based on implicitly gathered information are based on data mining methods, which attempt to discover patterns from a variety of data sources. Web usage mining is one of these methods for building recommender systems. In this paper, we attempt to put the research done in a way from the web usage mining point of view.

The rest of the paper is organized as follows. Section 2 briefly reviews the work related to Web mining and recommendation systems. Section 3 presents the proposed models. Finally, in Section 4 we conclude and discuss future work.

2 Recommendation Systems for Internet

It is often necessary to make choices without sufficient personal experience of the alternatives. In everyday life, we rely on recommendations from other people either by word of mouth, recommendation letters, movie and book reviews printed in newspapers, or general surveys. Recommender systems assist and augment this natural social process. Since World Wide Web serves as a huge, widely distributed, global information service center for every kind of information such as news, advertisements, consumer information, financial management, education, government, e-commerce, health services, and many other information services, it becomes more important to find the useful information from these huge amount of data. Recommender systems on Internet help people make decisions in these complex information space where enormous volume of information is available to them. This section describes some approaches used in recommender systems.

2.1 Recommender Systems Based on Collaborative Filtering

One of the most successful and widely used technologies for building recommendation systems is collaborative filtering (CF). The term collaborative filtering is introduced first by Tapestry [9]. Collaborative filtering systems collect visitor opinions on a set of objects, using ratings provided by the users or implicitly computed, to form peer groups and then learns from the peer groups to predict a particular user's interest in an item. It is often based on matching, in real-time, the current user's profile against similar records (nearest neighbors) obtained by the system over time from other users. The ratings collected by the system may be both implicit and explicit.

Explicit voting refers to a user consciously expressing his or her preference for a title, usually on a discrete numerical scale. Some example of systems that use this approach include SIFT [27], Tapestry [9] and the system in [16]. The GroupLens project [11] is purely collaborative filtering approach that automated prediction by collecting explicit user ratings and employing statistical techniques. The lack of explicit user ratings as well as the sparse nature and the large volume of data poses limitations to standard collaborative filtering. As a result it becomes hard to scale collaborative filtering techniques to a large number of items, while maintaining reasonable prediction performance and accuracy. A number of optimization strategies have been proposed and employed to remedy this shortcoming. These strategies include similarity indexing and dimensionality reduction to reduce real-time search costs.

Since purely collaborative approaches are subject to certain limitations mentioned above, content-based approaches are used to address some of these limitations. These systems work by comparing text descriptions or other representations associated with an item. A hybrid approach to recommendations combines aspects of both content-based and collaborative filtering. Balabonovic and Shoham [2] developed a system that helped users to discover new and interesting sites that are of users' interest. The hybrid approach used in this model retains the advantages both a content based and collaborative approach while overcoming disadvantages of each.

The system in [3] aims at offering on-line innovative services to support the trade fair business process and a great number of exhibitors organized in a Web-based virtual fair. The WebWatcher [10] is an assistant agent that helps the user by using visual representations of links that guide the user to reach a particular target page or goal. It learns by creating and maintaining a log file for each user and from the user feedback it improves its guidance.

Implicit rating used for collaborative filtering can be divided into three categories: rating based on examination, when a user examines an item; rating based on retention, when a user saves an item; and rating based on reference, when a user links all or part of an item into an other item. PHOAKS [26] represents people by their mention of uniform resource locators(URL) in Usenet messages. An URL in a Usenet messages is considered an implicit rating. The process of recommendation in PHOAKS entails mining URLs, filtering irrelevant links via a number of heuristics and computing a weight for each. Finally the output is relevant URL's and associated weights. Siteseer [20] is another collaborative system that uses implicit ratings. Its recommendation function is based on bookmark folder representation of people. Bookmark are an implicit declaration of interest of Web users. The output of the recommendation function is set of bookmarks.

2.2 Automated Recommender Systems

Recently, a number of approaches have been developed dealing with specific aspects of Web usage mining for the purpose of automatically discovering user profiles. For example, Perkowitz and Etzioni [19] proposed the idea of optimizing the structure of Web sites based co-occurrence patterns of pages within usage data for the site.

Another recommendation system is called Letizia [13], which learns the areas that are of interest to a user by recording the users' browsing behavior. It performs some tasks at idle times (when a user is not reading a document and is not browsing). These tasks include looking for more documents that are related to the user's interest or might be relevant to future requests.

Schechter et al [22] have developed techniques for using path profiles of users to predict future HTTP requests, which can be used for network and proxy caching. Spiliopoulou et al [24], Cooley et al [5], and Mobasher [15] have applied data mining techniques to extract usage patterns from Web logs, for the purpose of deriving marketing intelligence. Shahabi et al [23], and Nasraoui et al [18] have proposed clustering of user sessions to predict future user behavior. Yan et al [28] use Web server logs to discover clusters of users having similar access patterns. The system proposed in [28] consists of an offline module that will perform cluster analysis and an online module which is responsible for dynamic link generation of Web pages. There have been attempts to use association rules [17], sequential patterns [1], and Markov models [7,21] in recommender systems.

2.3 Methodology for Automated Recommender Systems

The overall process of automated recommendation can be divided into three components [25]. Since the data source is Web server log data for Web usage mining, the first step is to clean the data and prepare for mining the usage patterns. The second step is to extract usage patterns, and the third step is to build a predictive model based on the extracted usage patterns. Fundamental methods of data cleaning and preparation have been well studied [25]. The prediction step is the real-time processing of the model, which considers the active user session and makes recommendations. Once the mining tasks are accomplished, the discovered patterns are used by the online component of the model to provide dynamic recommendations to users based on their current navigational activity. The Web server keeps track of the active user session as the user browser makes HTTP requests. This can be accomplished by a variety of methods such as URL rewriting, or by temporarily caching the Web server access logs. The produced recommendation set is then added to the last requested page as a set of links before the page is sent to the client browser.

3 Web Usage Based Recommendation Models

An important feature of the user's navigation path is the time that a user spends on different pages [23]. The time spent on a page is a good measure of the user's interest in that page, providing an implicit rating for it. If a user is interested in the content of a page, he or she will likely spend more time there compared to the other pages in his or her session. In this paper, we present two new models that use the time spent on visiting pages and study the impact of time, that a user spent on each page during her single visit to a web site. The first model (User Interest Model) uses only the visiting time and visiting frequencies of pages without considering the access order of page requests in user sessions. The resulting model has lower run-time computation and memory requirements, while providing predictions that are at least as precise as previous proposals. The second model (Click-stream tree model) uses both the sequences of visiting pages and the time spent on that pages. As far as we know, existing tools for mining two different information types like the order of visited Web pages and the time spent on those pages, are hard to find. Therefore, we concentrate in this study on a model that well reflects the structural information of a user session and handles two-dimensional information.

For the first step of the models, we use cleaning and filtering methods in order to identify unique users and user sessions. The cleaning step is the same for both of the proposed models. Since the cleaning procedure is beyond the scope of this paper, the details of this procedure are not given here. In this research, we use server logs from the NASA Kennedy Space Center server collected over the months of July and August 1995 [14]. Approximately 30% of these cleaned transactions are randomly selected as the test set, and the remaining part as the training set. This section describes the proposed models.

3.1 User Interest Model

The User Interest Model clusters the transactions in the training set according to the similar amount of time in similar pages. We employ a model based clustering algorithm and partition user sessions according to the similar amount of time that is spent on similar pages within a session. The model parameters are learned with EM algorithm [6] under the assumption that the data come from a mixture of Poisson distributions. To confirm our assumption, that the data in each dimension have been generated by a Poisson distribution, the histogram of the occurrence of each of the ten possible values at each dimension has been plotted. The histograms verify our assumption. For the last step, the transactions in the test set are assigned to one of the clusters that has the highest probability given the visiting time of current transaction's active page. The recommendation engine then predicts three pages that have the highest recommendation score in the active cluster. A hit is declared if any one of the three recommended pages is the next request of the user. The hit-ratio which is the number of hits divided by the total number of recommendations made by the system is 43% for the NASA data set.

3.2 Click-Stream Tree Model

The user sessions produced in the first step are clustered based on a similarity metric. Since user sessions are ordered URL requests, we can refer to them as sequences of Web pages. The similarity between sessions is then calculated using a dynamic programming approach such that only the identical matching of page sequences and the time spent on that pages has a similarity value of 1. Using these pair-wise similarity values, a graph is constructed whose vertices are user sessions and edges are the calculated similarity values. In this study an efficient and fast graph partitioning algorithm called Cluto is used for graph partitioning [4]. We generate a click-stream-tree for each cluster. First a *root* node, which is labelled as "null", is generated for the click-stream-tree. When inserting a session in the tree, the first page of the session is stored as a child of the root node if the root node does not have a child with the same page and time information. If it has a child node with the same page and time information, the count of the corresponding node is incremented by one. The second page in the path is stored in a node that is a child of the first page's node. This may continue until the last page in the session. We start the algorithm with an empty tree of Web pages, which contains only the root node. The tree of a cluster is then constructed by inserting all the sessions in that cluster as mentioned above. The recommendation engine is the real time component of the model that selects the best path for predicting the next request of the active user session. When a request is received from an active user, a recommendation set consisting of three different pages that the user has not yet visited, is produced using the best matching user session[2]. For the first two requests of an active user session all clusters are explored to find the one that best matches the active user session. For the remaining requests, the best matching user session is found by exploring the top-N clusters that have the highest N similarity values computed using the first two requests of the active user session. The rest of the recommendations for the same active user session are made by using the top-N clusters. The resulting click-stream trees are then used for recommendation. Table 1 show the results of that model.

Table 1. Results in % of the NASA data set. Visiting time is normalized between 1 and 2.

No.Of Clusters	Top-N					
	1		2		3	
	H-R	CS-R	H-R	CS-R	H-R	CS-R
5	57.41	96.47	59.22	98.80	59.79	99.65
10	54.68	91.10	56.15	93.15	57.18	94.53
15	52.61	88.15	54.65	91.15	55.95	92.43
20	50.79	84.45	52.47	86.37	53.51	87.85
25	49.59	81.47	52.17	85.28	53.11	86.50
30	48.75	80.06	51.29	84.92	52.15	85.77

4 Conclusion and Future Work

In summary, in this survey we provide a snapshot of recommendation methods by presenting the most representative techniques of collaborative filtering and

---

[2] The user session that has the highest similarity to the active user session is defined as the best session.

data mining. We have also considered the problem of modelling the behavior of a Web user during a single visit to the Web site. We proposed two models. The first model uses only the time information of the visiting pages whereas the second one uses both the time information and the access order of page requests. Our experimental results indicate that the techniques discussed here are promising, each with its own unique characteristics, and bear further investigation and development.

The field of recommender systems is still young and much work lays ahead. Given the huge amount of information available on the Internet and increasingly important role that the Web plays in today's society, data mining services on the Internet will become one of the most important and flourishing subfields in data mining. With the increasingly use of data mining tools on Internet, an important issue to face is privacy protection and information security. Evaluation of recommender systems is still a challenge. In the feature, there may be a development of new measures that go beyond those used for recommender systems to deal with more complex systems and that not only consider quantitative but sociological and economical factors as well.

Since recommender systems are becoming widely used by Web sites, a careful evaluation of their performance gets more important. However, for data mining part of recommender systems the question of how well found patterns match the user's concept of useful recommendation is often neglected.

References

1. R. Agrawal and R. Srikant. Mining sequential patterns. In *Proceedings of the International Conference on Data Engineering (ICDE)*, March 1995. Taipei, Taiwan.
2. M. Balabonovic and Y. Shoham. Learning information retrieval agents: Experiments with automated web browsing. *On-line Working Notes of The AAAI Spring Symposium Series on Information Gathering from Distributed, Heterogenous Environment*, 1995.
3. P. Buono, M. F. Costabile, S. Guida, A. Piccinno, and G. Tesoro. Integrating user data and collaborative filtering in a web recommendation system. In *Proceedings of the Eight International Conference on User Modeling*, 2001. Sonthofen, Germany.
4. Cluto. http://www-users.cs.umn.edu/ karypis/cluto/index.html.
5. R. Cooley, B. Mobasher, and J. Srivastava. Data preparation for mining world wide web browsing patterns. *Journal of Knowledge and Information Systems*, 1(1), 1999.
6. A. P. Dempster, N.M. Laird, and D.B. Rubin. Maximum likelihood from incomplete data via the em algorithm. *Journal of Royal Statistical Society*, 39(1):1–38, 1977.
7. M. Deshpande and G. Karypis. Selective markov models for predicting web-page accesses. In *Proceedings of the First SIAM International Conference on Data Mining (SDM'2001)*, 2001.
8. O. Etzioni. The world wide web: Quagmire or gold mine. *Communications of the ACM*, 39(11):65–68, 1996.
9. D. Goldberg, D. Nichols, B. Oki, and D. Terry. Using collaborative filtering to weave an information tapestry. *Communications of the ACM*, 35(12) 61–70, 1992.

10. T. Joachims, D. Freitag, and T. Mitchell. Webwatcher: A tour guide for the world wide web. *The 15th International Conference on Artificial Intelligence*, 1997. Nagoya, Japan.
11. J. A. Konstan, B. N. Miller, D. Maltz, J. L. Herlocker, L. R. Gordon, and J. Riedl. Grouplens: Applying collaborative filtering to usenet news. *Communications of the ACM*, 40(3):77–87, 1997.
12. R. Kosala and H. Blockeel. Web mining research: A survey. *ACM SIGKDD Explorations*, 2(1):1–15, 2000.
13. H. Lieberman. Letizia: An agent that assists web browsing. In *Proceedings Of the 1995 International Joint Conference on Artificial Intelligence*, 1995. Montreal, Canada.
14. NASA Kennedy Space Center Log. http://ita.ee.lbl.gov/html/contrib/NASA-HTTP.html.
15. B. Mobasher, H. Dai, T. Luo, and M. Nakagawa. Discovery of aggregate usage profiles for web personalization. In *Proceedings of the Web Mining for E-Commerce Workshop (WebKDD'2000)*, 2000.
16. J. Mostafa, S. Mukhopadhyay, W. Lam, and M.Palakal. A multilevel approach to intelligent information filtering: Model, system and evaluation. *ACM Transactions on Information Systems*, 15(4):368–399, 1997.
17. A. Nanopoulos, D. Katsaros, and Y. Manolopoulos. Effective prediction of web-user accesses: a data mining approach. In *Proceedings of WEBKDD workshop*, 2001. San Francisco, CA, USA.
18. O. Nasraoui, R. Krishnapuram, and A. Joshi. Mining web access logs using a fuzzy relational clustering algorithm based on a robust estimator. In *Proceedings of Eight International World Wide Web Conference*, 1999. Toronto, Canada.
19. M. Perkowitz and O Etzioni. Adaptive web sites. *Communications of the ACM*, 43(8):152–158, 2000.
20. J. Rucker and M. J. Polano. Siteseer: Personalized navigation for the web. *Communications of the ACM*, 40(3):73–25, March 1997.
21. R. R. Sarukkai. Link prediction and path analysis using markov chains. In *Proceedings of the Ninth International World Wide Web Conference*, 2000. Amsterdam.
22. S. Schechter, M. Krishnan, and M. D. Smith. Using path profiles to predict http requests. In *Proceedings of 7th International World Wide Web Conference*, November 1998. Brisbane, Australia.
23. C. Shahabi, A. Zarkesh, J. Adibi, and V. Shah. Knowledge discovery from users web-page navigation. In *Proceeding of the IEEE RIDE97 Workshop*, pages 20–29, April 1997. Birmingham, England.
24. M. Spiliopoulou and L. C. Faulstich. Wum: A web utilization miner. In *In Proceedings of EDBT Workshop WebDB98*, 1999. Valencia, Spain.
25. J. Srivastava, R. Cooley, M. Deshpande, and P. N. Tan. Web usage mining: Discovery and application of usage patterns from web data. *ACM SIGKDD Explorations*, 1(2):12–23, 2000.
26. L. Terveen, W. Hill, B. Amento, D. McDonald, and J. Creter. Phoaks: A system for sharing recommendations. *Communications of the ACM*, 40(3):59–62, March 1997.
27. T.W Yan and H.Garcia Molina. The sift information dissemnination system. *ACM Transactions on Database Systems*, 24(4):529–565, 1999.
28. Y. Yan, M. Jacobsen, Garcïa-Molina H, and U. Dayal. From user access patterns to dynamic hypertext linking. In *Proceedings of the Fifth International World Wide Web Conference*, 1996. Paris, France.

A Spectral–Spatial Classification Algorithm for Multispectral Remote Sensing Data

Hakan Karakahya[1], Bingül Yazgan[2], and Okan K. Ersoy[3]

[1] Istanbul Technical University, Informatics Institute
Advanced Technologies in Engineering
Satellite Communication and Remote Sensing Program, 34469 Maslak
Istanbul-Türkiye
karakahya@be.itu.edu.tr
[2] Istanbul Technical University, Faculty of Electrical and Electronic Engineering
Electronics and Communication Dept., 34469 Maslak
Istanbul-Türkiye
yazgan@ehb.itu.edu.tr
[3] Purdue University, School of Electrical and Computer Engineering
West Lafayette, Indiana, USA
ersoy@purdue.edu

Abstract. This paper aims at achieving improved land cover classification performance over conventional per-pixel classifiers as well as spectral-spatial classifiers such as ECHO (Extraction and Classification of Homogeneous Objects) algorithm. The proposed algorithm is a two-stage process, which makes use of the contextual information from neighboring pixels. First, a spatial filter is used to achieve more homogeneous regions. Secondly, maximum likelihood pixel classifier is employed to classify the land covers. The experimental results indicate that improved classification accuracy and smoother (more acceptable) thematic maps are achieved than what is obtained with the other methods considered.

1 Introduction

Conventionally, a pixel-based approach is often used to classify a remote sensing image, which means that each pixel is classified individually on the basis of its spectral measurements alone. The spectral characteristics of each pixel are compared with the spectral characteristics of areas with known land cover. The pixel is then assigned to the land cover class, which has statistically the most similar spectral characteristics. Per-pixel approaches like the Maximum Likelihood (ML), Fisher Linear Likelihood and Minimum Distance to Mean (MD) classifiers have been used widely in many remote sensing applications. The classification of remotely sensed images based on the information provided by individual pixels can be improved further by including contextual information in terms of a pixel's relation with its neighboring pixels.

The well-known ECHO algorithm, developed by Kettig & Landgrebe, is such a classifier, which exploits the relation of a pixel with its neighboring pixels [1,2,3]. ECHO is based on a single-pass object-seeking region-growing segmentation algorithm. The goal of the segmentation process is to locate the homogeneous objects in the scene. Since each homogeneous object represents a statistical sample, a sample classifier (ML Sample Classier) is used to classify the objects. In this way, the classification of each pixel in the sample is a result of the spectral properties of its neighbors as well as its own.

A similar approach is used in the SSC (Spectral and Spatial Classifier) method. The SSC method uses the same segmentation algorithm to locate the homogeneous objects. It assumes that neighboring pixel information does not contribute significantly to an improved classification of the homogeneous image parts. Therefore, for each homogeneous region, the average spectral signature is computed and assigned to every pixel of that region. These homogeneous regions are then classified using a Minimum Distance to Mean algorithm [4].

In this paper, a new spectral-spatial classification approach is proposed and tested, which takes the spatial as well as the spectral information into account, aiming at improving the classification performance. The proposed algorithm is a two-stage process. First, a spatial filter is used to achieve more homogeneous regions. Secondly, the maximum likelihood pixel classifier is employed to classify the land covers. The experimental results indicate that superior results are achieved as compared to both conventional per-pixel classifiers and the ECHO algorithm in terms of the classification accuracy and acceptability of the thematic maps.

The paper is organized as follows: the spatial filtering stage is introduced in Section 2. The maximum likelihood classifier is reviewed in Section 3. The experimental results are given in Section 4, and the conclusions are discussed in Section 5.

2 Spatial Filtering Stage

In the first stage, spatial filtering is used to make use of spatial information and to achieve more homogeneous regions. In contrast to the algorithms like ECHO and SSC, the proposed algorithm does not utilize an image segmentation algorithm. Instead the algorithm tests each pixel to determine if it is a part of a homogeneous region, and if positive, the value of the pixel is converted to the mean value of the region made up of a rectangular window centered by the tested pixel. A spatial filter is used for this purpose.

The spatial filter is a simple mean filter, which uses standard deviation as a homogeneity criterion. It starts with a window of size, say, 5x5, centered by the tested pixel. The homogeneity test is achieved by testing if the standard deviation is below a threshold, say, 2. If the test is positive, the mean value of the pixels in the window is assigned to the center pixel. If the test fails, the window size is reduced, say, to 3x3. The same homogeneity test is applied in this window. If the homogeneity test is positive, the mean value of the pixels in the window is assigned to the center pixel. If the test fails, 3 minimum and 3 maximum valued pixels are excluded from the window, and the mean value of the remaining pixels is assigned to the center pixel. The new multispectral pixels are obtained by applying this procedure to all the bands of the multispectral remote sensing data. An example of how the spatial filtering results in more homogeneous regions is shown in Figure 1. The outliers in the homogeneous regions are also smoothed out.

Spatial filtering results in more homogenous regions, and thus the end result is somewhat similar to what is obtained with image segmentation. The variance in homogeneous regions is reduced since the pixel values in a homogeneous region approach the mean value of that region. This also results in improved spectral separability, as discussed in Section 4.

(a)

72	70	72	70	71	67	65	68	67	66
73	72	73	71	72	68	68	69	65	68
73	74	68	71	72	68	66	66	67	64
72	73	71	73	71	67	68	66	70	67
73	71	70	73	72	67	64	67	68	68
mean=71.72 variance=1.79					mean=66.96 variance=2.12				

(b)

72	71.8	71.6	70.6	69.67	67.67	67.22	66.92	66.68	66.64
71.92	71.76	71.56	71.11	70	68	67.22	66.92	66.68	66.84
72	71.92	71.72	71.33	71	68	67.33	66.96	66.3	67.04
72.08	72.08	71.88	71.22	71.33	67.67	66.56	67	66.92	67.24
72	72.04	71.84	71.67	71.67	67.33	66.33	67	66.92	67.44
mean=71.51 variance=0.4					mean=67.09 variance=0.18				

Fig. 1. The effect of the spatial filter. (a) two regions representing two different land covers including one pixel outliers, (b) regions after spatial filtering.

3 Maximum Likelihood Pixel Classifier

The ML classifier is one of the most popular pixel-based classification methods in remote sensing, in which a pixel with the maximum likelihood is classified into the corresponding land cover. The ML decision rule simply states that, given an unknown feature vector $\underline{X}$, we select a class W_i such that

$$p(\underline{X}|W_i) = \max_j p(\underline{X}|W_j) \tag{1}$$

Given that $p(\underline{X}|W_i)$ is estimated by fitting a multivariate normal probability density function to the mean and covariance of the training vectors of class i, the ML discriminant function can be written as:

$$g_i(\underline{X}) = \ln(p(W_i)) - 0.5\ln|\Sigma_i| - 0.5(\underline{X} - \underline{\mu_i})^T \Sigma_i^{-1}(\underline{X} - \underline{\mu_i}) \tag{2}$$

ML classifier is popular because of its robustness and simplicity. However, care must be taken in using it because there will be some errors in the results if the size of sample data is not sufficiently large to estimate the mean vectors and covariance matrices of the land covers, and/or the distributions of the population does not follow the Gaussian distribution, and/or the classes have much overlap in their distribution resulting in poor separability.

4 Experiments

The performance of the proposed algorithm is evaluated using the Flightline C1 (FLC1) data set [5]. FLC1 is a historically significant data set, covering the southern part of Tippecanoe County, Indiana. It follows a county road from the Grandville Bridge over the Wabash River just south of South River Road (West Lafayette) to near State Highway 25. Though collected with an airborne scanner in June 1966, this data remains contemporary. Key attributes that make it valuable, especially for illustrative purposes, are that it has more than a few spectral bands (12 bands), contains a significant number of vegetative species or ground cover classes, including many regions (e.g., fields) containing a large numbers of contiguous pixels from a given class (thus facilitating quantitative results evaluation).

The data set consists of 949 scan lines with 220 pixels per scan line, or 208,780 pixels. The scanner used had an instantaneous field of view (IFOV) of 3 milliradians and was flown at an altitude of 2600 ft above terrain. Each pixel was digitized to 8-bit precision. In the experiments reported, the total number of training samples is 11414, the total number of test samples is 70635, and the number of classes is 9.

Table 1. Training and test field performances.

First 3 Features			First 6 Features			12 Features		
Classifier	Accuracies		Classifier	Accuracies		Classifier	Accuracies	
	Training	Test		Training	Test		Training	Test
Proposed	92.1	76.69	Proposed	98.08	92.52	Proposed	99.78	96.39
ECHO	89.4	76.6	ECHO	97.6	89.6	ECHO	99.5	94.4
ML	69.5	54.5	ML	87.6	79.8	ML	99	93.3
MD	56.4	42.3	MD	62.8	44.8	MD	86.4	72.8
Fisher	68.6	51.6	Fisher	84.3	68.4	Fisher	96	85.7

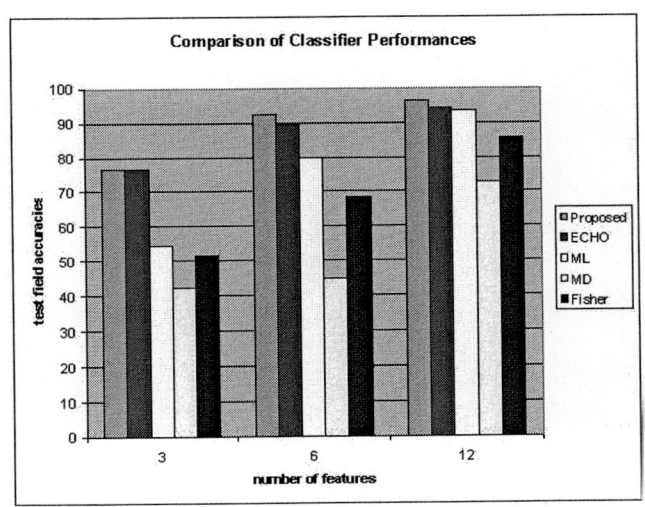

Fig. 2. Comparison of test field performances of the classifiers.

The proposed algorithm is performed and its performance is compared to the conventional per-pixel classifiers, namely, Maximum Likelihood, Minimum Distance to Mean, the Fisher Linear Likelihood and the spectral-spatial classifier ECHO methods, for 3 cases: using first 3 features, first 6 features and all the features available (12 bands). The training and test field performances are summarized in Table 1. Figure 2 shows a graphical comparison of the test field performances. Figure 3 shows the thematic maps generated by the proposed algorithm, ECHO and the ML methods using all the features.

Fig. 3. Thematic maps. (a) Original image; (b) thematic map generated by the proposed algorithm; (c) thematic map generated by ECHO; (d) thematic map generated by ML; (e) color coding map for classification results.

5 Conclusions

A two-stage spectral-spatial classification approach for remote sensing data is proposed. It integrates contextual information with spectral information by spatial filtering, yet it is still a per-pixel classifier. According to the experimental results, the performance of the proposed algorithm -feature extraction using a spatial filter followed by a ML pixel classifier- outperformed the conventional per-pixel classifiers and gave consistently better results than ECHO for all cases considered. Moreover, it produced more acceptable thematic maps.

We carried out the classification by the simple ML classifier. If more powerful classifiers are used, classification accuracy may be further improved. Future work will involve search for more effective spatial filter and homogeneity criterion.

References

1. Kettig R.L., Landgrebe D.A.: Computer Classification of Remotely Sensed Multispectral Image Data by Extraction and Classification of Homogeneous Objects. Ph.D. Thesis No. 27208, School of Electrical Engineering, Purdue University, West Lafayatte, IN (1975)
2. Kettig R.L., Landgrebe D.A.: Classification of Multispectral Image Data by Extraction and Classification of Homogeneous Objects. IEEE Transactions on Geoscience Electronics, Vol. GE-14, No. 1 (1976) 19–26
3. Landgrebe D.A.: The Development of A Spectral-Spatial Classifier for Earth Observational Data. Pattern Recognition, Vol. 12 (1980) 165–175
4. De Jong S.M., Hornstra T., Maas H.G.: An Integrated Spatial and Spectral Approach to the Classification of Mediterranean Land Cover Types: the SSC Method. Journal of Applied Geosciences, Vol. 3(2) (2001) 176–183
5. Ghassemian H., Landgrebe D.A.: On-Line Object Feature Extraction for Multispectral Scene Representation. TR-EE 88-34, Purdue University, West Lafayatte, IN (1988)

Neural Network Based Material Identification and Part Thickness Estimation from Two Radiographic Images

Ibrahim N. Tansel[1], Reen Nripjeet Singh[1], Peng Chen[1], and
Claudia V Kropas-Hughes[2]

[1] Mechanical Engineering Department, Florida International University
10555 West Flagler Street, (EAS-3473), Miami, FL 33174
[2] Air Force Research Laboratory, AFRL/MLLP, Bldg. 655, R166
2230 Tenth Street, Wright-Patterson AFB, Ohio, 45433-7746

Abstract. Radiographic inspection provides extensive information about the characteristics and conditions of parts even if they are hidden behind the walls. A dual energy method is originally proposed to estimate the thickness of parts from two radiographic images by using analytical expressions. Use of neural networks is proposed when the material properties have nonlinear characteristics. Aluminum and brass test pieces were identified and their thickness was estimated from two images obtained at different energy levels.

Keywords: Neural network, dual energy, radiography

1 Introduction

Radiographic images have been successfully used in Nondestructive Testing (NDT) to evaluate the geometry and condition of the parts. Digitization of the images by scanning the film or direct capture of the data by using panels or other means allows estimation of the thickness of a part. When two parts overlap, it is possible to estimate their thickness by using simple analytical expressions and data from two radiographic images obtained at two different energy levels as long as the characteristics of the materials can be represented with linear expressions. In actual test cases, radiographic images are not obtained at ideal conditions. The difference of the intensity of the X-ray cannot be detected at the thick and thin sections of the parts because of the non-liner characteristics of the components of the system. Also, registration of multiple images is very time consuming. Use of neural networks is proposed to identify the material and to estimate the part thickness in this paper. In this study, experimental data was primarily collected to identify single material and its thickness when only two materials are considered.

Dual-Energy method has been successfully used to identify different materials and chemical composition [1-4]. The intensity of the penetrated X-ray from a material can be represented by using linear expressions as long as the part thickness is within certain range depending on the selected X-ray beam intensity [4]. However, beam hardening, film characteristics, and digitization process creates extremely non-linear regions when the penetration is very low and very high.

Some of the Artificial Neural Networks (ANN) are capable to learn the nonlinear input and output relationships [5]. Training of the Back-propagation (BP) type ANN [6] takes much longer than most of the other similar methods such as Abductory Induction Mechanism (AIM) and user involvement is required to determine the key parameters of the network. However, reliability of the BP algorithm is found better than the other approaches when limited number of training cases is available [7]. Also, very compact networks are created for mapping applications.

ANNs have been frequently used for classification of radiographic images. Classification accuracy of ANNs has been compared with the decision trees [8] and ANNs were found more accurate. Other researchers have successfully used the ANNs for evaluation of radiographic images to classify agricultural products [9] and tissue characteristics [10-11].

In this paper, the theoretical background of the dual energy method, use of ANNs for identification and thickness estimation, preparation of the experimental data, and performance of the developed package are presented in the following sections.

2 Theoretical Background

BP is one of the basic and most frequently used neural networks and extensive literature is available on the topic [6].

Transmissions of the X-rays through the materials are mainly influenced with photoelectric absorption and Compton scattering [1-4]. Wojcik et al. [4] estimated the thickness of the materials when two of them were overlapped by using the following equations:

$$L1 = k1\ T\ (E1) + k2\ T\ (E2) + k3\ T\ (E1) + k4\ T\ (E2) + k5\ T\ (E1)\ T\ (E2) \quad (1)$$

$$L2 = k6\ T\ (E1) + k7\ T\ (E2) + k8\ T\ (E1) + k9\ T\ (E2) + k10\ T\ (E1)\ T\ (E2) \quad (2)$$

Where L1, and L2 are the thickness of materials and k1 to k10 are constants. Constants are estimated from the experimental results by using the nonlinear least square method. If I0 (E) is the original X-ray beam intensity, T (E) = ln (I0 (E)/I (E)). T (E1) and T (E2) correspond to the T (E) values obtained at two different energy levels.

3 Proposed Procedure for Part Thickness Estimation by Using Artificial Neural Networks and Developed Program

Two BP type ANNs were used to estimate the thickness of two materials. Each neural network had two inputs and one output. Single ANN with two inputs and two outputs could also be used; however, the authors believe that the accuracy of the ANNs would be slightly compromised. The inputs are the values of two pixels that correspond to the same point at two different images. Images are obtained at two different energy levels. The proposed neural network system is outlined in the Fig. 1.

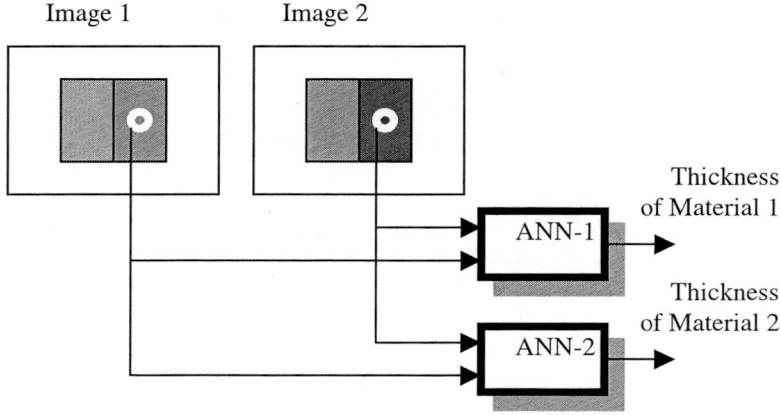

Fig. 1. The proposed ANN system for estimation of the thickness of materials.

Training data for the ANNs was prepared from the radiographic images. Ideally, the data for dual energy method is collected by using step wedges. Three to ten step wedge is prepared by using each material [4]. A Radiographic image is taken by putting them on top of each other. Wedges are arranged to make $90°$ angle. This arrangement allows gathering information for a large number of possible combination of the materials.

The proposed procedure is capable to identify the thickness of two overlapping materials in ideal test conditions; however, in this study materials and their thickness were selected to simulate the actual inspections. The densities of the test materials were very different and a 0.6 mm brass step wedge was used to observe the nonlinear gray level thickness relationship. Under these difficult conditions, main objective of our tests was to identify the material and its thickness when one of two considered material is selected in the image. The experimental data was collected by using 5 to 6 step wedges when they were located side by side. Only a few combinations of the overlaps were tested by putting test pieces with constant thickness on top of each other. The gray level of the images were estimated from the test images by using the following equation:

$$G'(L_1, L_2) = G(L_{1t}) - L_2 ((G(L_{1tb}, L_{2tb}) - G(L_{1tb})) / L_{2tb}) (R(L_{1t}, L_{1tb})) \qquad (3)$$

Where G' (L_1, L_2) are the estimated gray level of the image when the material 1 has L1, and material 2 has L2 thickness. G (L_{1t}) is the experimentally obtained gray level of the image when the thickness of the step wedge (material 1) is L_{1t}. $G(L_{1tb}, L_{2tb})$ is the gray level of the image when two blocks are put on each other with the thickness of L_{1tb} (material 1) and L_{2tb} (material 2). $G(L_{1tb})$ corresponds to the gray level when the block of material 1 with L_{1tb} thickness is exposed to X-ray. This equation is written by assuming that material 1 is a very dense material (brass) compared to material 2 (aluminum). In this case, the relationship between the gray level and part thickness can be kept pretty linear if the maximum thickness of material 2 is selected reasonable. A nonlinear relationship is observed between the thickness of the material 1 and the gray level. $R(L_{1t}, L_{1tb})$ represents this characteristic. A constant was used for each L1t value to represent this function. The constant was selected bigger than 1 when L1t < L1tb and smaller than 1 when $L_{1t} > L_{1tb}$.

The prepared program read the image file, stored the information of each pixel, and displayed the image by using the API function Calls- LoadImage, SetBitmap and BitBlt respectively. Two images were displayed in separate picture boxes. Information for each image was stored in separate arrays. User selects the identical point in both images by using the mouse. The gray level of the corresponding point was given to the neural network as two inputs. Each ANN estimated the thickness of one of the material. The user interface of the program is presented in Fig.2.

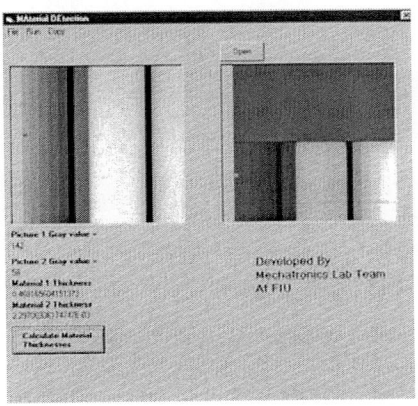

Fig. 2. User interface of the developed program.

4 Experimental Procedure

The arrangement of the step wedges and test blocks are presented in Fig.3. The aluminum step wedge and test block are on the left. The larger test block and the step wedge at the right are made of brass. To obtain the radiographic images ARACOR Tomoscope was used in the preview mode. This system had a Fein Focus 225 KeV X-ray source, and fiber optic scintillators with four CCD image sensors. The digital radiographic images were obtained at 45 KeV and 140KeV settings and are presented in Fig.4.

5 Results and Discussion

Two training files for two neural networks were prepared by using the Eq. 3 and the data obtained from the digital images presented in Fig.4. The calculated semi-experimental gray levels for different material combinations are presented with 3-D graphs in Fig. 5. Two BP type ANNs in Fig.1 were trained by using these semi-experimental values. ANNs used one hidden layer with 5 nodes.

Fig. 3. Aluminum (on the left) and brass (on the right) step wedges and test blocks.

Fig. 4. Radiographic images of the blocks at 45 KeV (top) and 225 KeV (bottom).

The thickness of the material at different points was estimated by using the developed program in Fig. 2 and the results are presented in Fig.6. Even though, one of the materials (brass) had a very nonlinear characteristics (at the test conditions), and gray level of the image of the blocks slightly varied at constant thickness, the program identified the materials very accurately. The thickness estimation of the ANNs for aluminum was excellent. The results for the brass were acceptable at the test conditions.

6 Conclusion

Use of Artificial Neural Networks (ANN) was proposed to estimate the thickness of overlapping materials at actual inspections. Two images of the step wedges and test pieces were obtained at two different energy levels. Very linear relationship was observed between the thickness of aluminum and gray level when a step wedge with

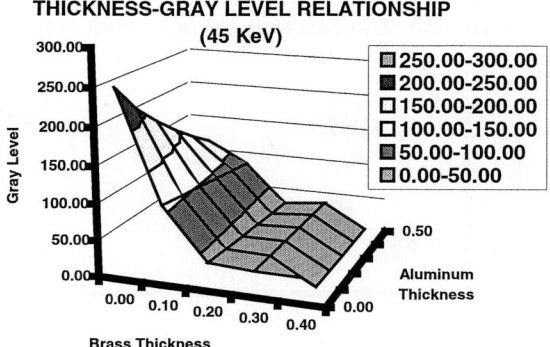

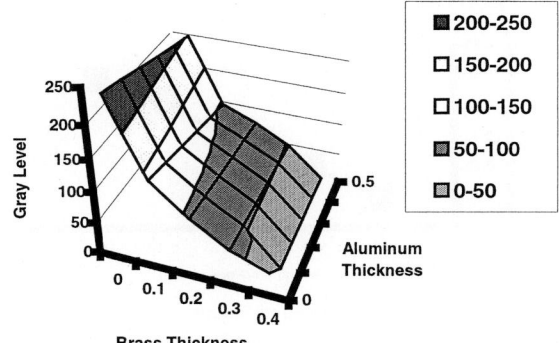

Fig. 5. Material thickness versus gray level when aluminum and brass materials overlap.

0.5-inch thickness was exposed to 45 KeV. A similar characteristic of the brass was very nonlinear when a 0.6-inch thick brass step wedge was exposed to 225 KeV. The information related to brass and aluminum thickness was completely useless at the images obtained at the 45KeV and 225KeV respectively. ANNs were trained by using the data obtained from these images and an analytical expression.

The performance of the proposed procedure and the developed program were tested by using the different points of the same images. ANNs estimated the thickness of the Aluminum very accurately in the tests. The nonlinear characteristics of brass and varying gray levels at constant thickness reduced the accuracy of the estimations. When the materials overlapped, the program detected it; however, the accuracy of the thickness estimations was limited.

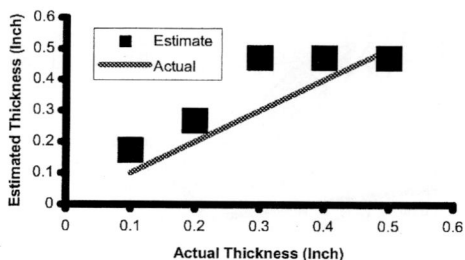

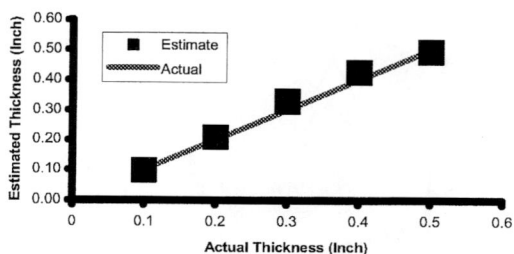

Fig. 6. The estimation accuracy of proposed procedure. Thickness estimations were very good for aluminum (top). Same estimations for brass were reasonable if the nonlinear characteristic of brass at the test conditions is considered.

Acknowledgement. Mr. Ed Porter and Mr. Dan Daniels of Wright Patterson AFB prepared the digital radiographic images. Authors appreciate contributions of both engineers to the study.

References

1. Berodias, G., Peix, M.G.: Nondestructive Measurement of Density and Effective Atomic Number by Photon Scattering, Materials Evaluation, Vol. 46, Aug. 1988, pp. 1209–1213.
2. Engler, P., Friedman, W.D.: Review of Dual-Energy Computed Tomography Techniques, Materials Evaluation, Vol.48, May 1990, pp. 623–629.
3. Robert-Coutant, C., Moulin, V., Sauze, R., Rizo, P., Casagrande, J.M: Estimation of the Matrix Attenuation in Heterogeneous Radioactive Waste Drums Using Dual-Energy Computed Tomography, Nuclear Instruments and Methods in Physics Research A Vol. 422, 1999, pp.949–956.
4. Wojcik, R., Majewski, S., Parker, F.R., Winfree, W.P.: Single shot dual energy reverse geometry X-radiography, Nuclear Science Symposium. IEEE Meeting: November 2, 1996, pp. 811–815.

5. Principe, J.C., Euliano, N.R., Lefebvre W. C.: Neural and Adaptive Systems: Fundamentals through Simulations, John Wiley & Sons, New York, 2000.
6. Rumelhart, D.E., Hilton, G., Williams, R.J.: Learning Internal Representations by Error Propagation, Parallel Distributed Processing:Explorations in the Micro-structure of Cognition, Vol.1, Ed. E. Rumelhart, J.L. McClelland, MIT Press, 1986, pp. 319–362.
7. Tansel, I.N., Bao, W.Y., Tansel, B., Jordahl, C.M.: Modeling, Contamination with Trainable Networks, Fuzzy Logic and Evol. Programming, Intelligent Engineering Systems Through Artificial Neural Networks, Vol.5, Ed. CH. Dagli, M. Aksoy, C.L. Philip Chen, B.R. Fernandez, J. Ghosh, ASME Press, 1995, pp.823–828.
8. Perner, P, Zscherpel, U. Jacobsen, C.: A comparison between neural networks and decision trees based on data from industrial radiographic testing, Pattern Recognition Letters, Vol. 23, 2001, pp. 47–54.
9. Casasent, David, Chen, Xue-Wen: New training strategies for RBF neural networks for X-ray agricultural product inspection," Pattern Recognition, Vol. 36, No. 2, 2003, pp. 535–547.
10. Bocchi, L., Coppini, G., De Dominicis, R., Valli, G.: Tissue characterization from X-ray images, Medical Engineering & Physics, Vol. 19, No. 4, 1997, pp. 336–342
11. Kim, J. K., Park, J. M., Song, K. S., Park, H. W.: Texture analysis and artificial neural network for detection of clustered microcalcifications on mammograms, Neural Networks for Signal Processing – Proceedings of the IEEE Workshop, 1997, pp. 199–206.

Selection of Optimal Cutting Conditions by Using the Genetically Optimized Neural Network System (GONNS)

W.Y. Bao, Peng Chen, I.N. Tansel, N. S. Reen, S.Y. Yang, and D. Rincon

Mechanical Engineering Department
Florida International University
Center for Engineering and Applied Sciences
Miami, FL 33174

Abstract. The Genetically Optimized Neural Network System (GONNS) is proposed to select the optimal cutting conditions in micro-end-milling operations. Two Backpropagation (BP) type Artificial Neural Networks (ANN) represented the characteristics of feed and thrust direction cutting forces. Genetic algorithm found the optimal cutting conditions by evaluating the cutting force estimations of two ANNs. The GONNS is a very convenient computational tool for optimization problems when systems have complex relationship and some experimental data is available.

1 Introduction

Human operators can select optimal operating conditions after they learn the characteristics of a system through trial and error. It is beneficial to have a computer program that is capable of learning the complex characteristics of the system from experimental data and selecting the optimal conditions. In micro-end-milling operations tool life is very short and unpredictable compared to the conventional metal cutting process. Many manufacturers change these tiny tools according to a very conservative schedule to avoid tool breakage during the machining operation. The main concern of many manufacturers is to keep the feed direction cutting force within a certain range to obtain an acceptable tool life without breaking the tool during the middle of the machining operation. In this paper, an optimization procedure is proposed to emulate the expert's decision-making process by using Genetically Optimized Neural Network System (GONNS).

GONNS [1-3] was mainly developed to select the optimal material and operating conditions in composite material manufacturing. It uses multiple Backpropagation (BP) type Artificial Neural Networks (ANN) [4-7] to represent the characteristics of a system. A Genetic algorithm [8-11] optimizes this complex system by adjusting the values of the inputs of the ANNs [4] by following an efficient procedure that mimics nature. There could be one or more genetic algorithms in the system depending on the problem.

In the following section, the theoretical background of the components of GONNS and their architecture will be introduced and performance of the system will be evaluated on the experimental data.

2 Theoretical Background

BP [4-7] is one of the basic and most frequently used ANNs. A user determines the number of inputs, outputs, hidden layers, and nodes at the hidden layers. In most applications, each node is connected to all the nodes of the next layer. The hidden and output layer nodes multiply the incoming values by weight and process the result with a transfer function. Sigmoid is the most commonly used transfer function. Linear, Gaussian, and various hyperbolic functions are also used depending on the need. The network starts to process the incoming training signals with arbitrary parameters. The error is calculated by comparing the output of the network with the provided data of the training file. All the nodal weights are adjusted by back-propagating the errors through the network. All the weights of the network should be adjusted at each training iteration. This process is repeated many times until the network's output errors are reduced to a minimum. The speed and stability of the network is controlled by the learning rate and the momentum selected by the user respectively.

Genetic algorithms use the biological evolution principles including natural selection, and survival of the fittest [8-11]. The user determines the number of the binary digits to be assigned for each parameter and their boundaries. Additional bits can be assigned for switches. All the parameters and the switches are represented with a chromosome. The algorithm tries to find the best 0 and 1 combination of this string either to minimize or to maximize the objective function. Penalty functions might be used to force some of the parameters to stay in a selected range. The user generally selects the population size, the number of children for each set of parents, and the probability of mutation. The chromosomes are generated randomly for the first generation. Generally genetic algorithms follow a five-step optimization procedure. These steps are the following: selection of the mating parents, selection of the hereditary chromosome from parents, gene crossover, gene mutation, and creation of next generation.

The cutting forces of micro-end-milling operations can be estimated by using analytical expressions [12]. In this study, GONNS were used instead of the analytical expressions. The ANNs are capable to represent the characteristics of many systems as long as quality of the available data is acceptable.

3 Proposed Optimization System Based on the GONNS

The proposed GONNS is presented in Figure 1. Two BP type ANNs and one genetic algorithm based optimizer were used. ANNs estimate the maximum feed and thrust direction-cutting forces after the training process. The inputs of both the ANNs are the depth of cut, feed rate and radius. A genetic algorithm tries to keep one of the forces in a given range while trying to minimize the other one. Most of the time, the feed direction cutting force is higher than the thrust direction cutting force and its maximum value in each rotation is correlated with the tool life. In this study, the tool diameter was fixed. The range of the feed direction cutting force was given to obtain the desired tool life. The program tried to find the optimal depth of cut and feed rate to minimize the thrust direction cutting force. It is possible to set the program to fix any one or two of the input parameters. Similarly, a range could be given for the thrust direction cutting force and minimization of the feed direction cutting force can be requested.

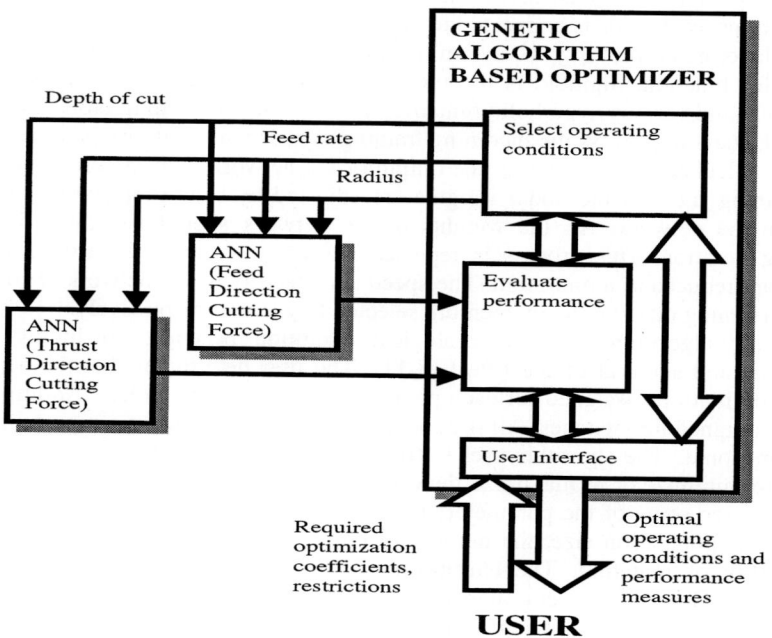

Fig. 1. The architecture of the proposed GONNS.

4 Experimental Setup and Data Collection

The experimental set-up is presented in Figure 2. A work piece was installed on a Kistler 9257B 3-component piezoelectric dynamometer to monitor the feed and thrust direction-cutting forces. Nicolet 310 and Integra model 10 digital oscilloscopes were used to monitor and save the cutting force data. Experiments were performed on Fadal 3 CNC milling machines.

5 Results and Discussion

In the experiments, two-flute end mills with 0.020", and 0.0625" diameter were used to machine the POCO-3 graphite workpiece. Spindle speed was 15,000 rpm and 50% overlapping climb milling operations were performed with both tools. The maximum cutting forces were found at 16 different cutting conditions and presented in the Table 1 and 2.

Selection of Optimal Cutting Conditions

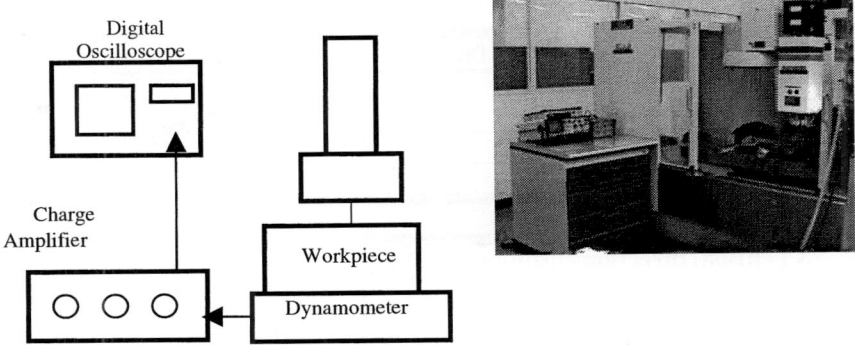

Fig. 2. The diagram and the picture of the experimental setup.

Table 1. Observed maximum cutting forces with the 0.020" diameter end-mill.

X (Thrust) direction cutting force (N)	Feed rate (ipm)		
Depth of cut (inch)	20	70	120
0.05	3.75	6.75	---
0.03	4.85	6.5	---
0.01	4.5	5.425	5.15

Y (Feed) direction cutting force (N)	Feed rate (ipm)		
Depth of cut (inch)	20	70	120
0.05	8.25	16.5	---
0.03	7.5	13.25	---
0.01	5	8.75	10

BP type ANNs were trained by using the values in Table 1 and 2. The feed direction cutting force is correlated with productivity and tool life. Productivity increases when the tool moves faster, removes more material and has a larger diameter. On the other hand, tool life decreases with increasing feed direction cutting force if the cross-sectional area is kept constant (Fig.3). In this study tool diameter was fixed since that parameter is mostly selected according to the part geometry. To keep the productivity high, the maximum possible feed direction cutting force with acceptable tool life should be selected. To keep the resultant cutting force minimum, a range was given for the feed direction cutting force and minimization of the thrust direction cutting force was requested. Population size, child number, cross-probability, mutation-probability, creep-probability was selected as 6, 1, 0.2, 0.1, and

Table 2. Observed maximum cutting forces with the 0.0625" diameter end-mill.

X (Thrust) direction cutting force (N)	Feed rate (ipm)		
Depth of cut (inch)	30	65	100
0.15	6.8	14.9	28.6
0.1	6.8	12.7	19.9
0.062	6.2	7.9	20.1

X (Thrust) direction cutting force (N)	Feed rate (ipm)		
Depth of cut (inch)	30	65	100
0.15	23.5	30	70
0.1	16.25	24.5	42.5
0.062	14.5	20	37.5

0.05 respectively during the optimization process. The selected fixed parameters and the estimated optimal values are presented in Table 3. Four neurons were used at the hidden layers of the ANNs. Pentium II processor at 266MHz clock speed was used for the optimization. Optimum values were found in less than 500 iterations. The program completed 2000 iterations in less than one minute in all the studied cases. Most of the optimization results were very similar for both ANNs.

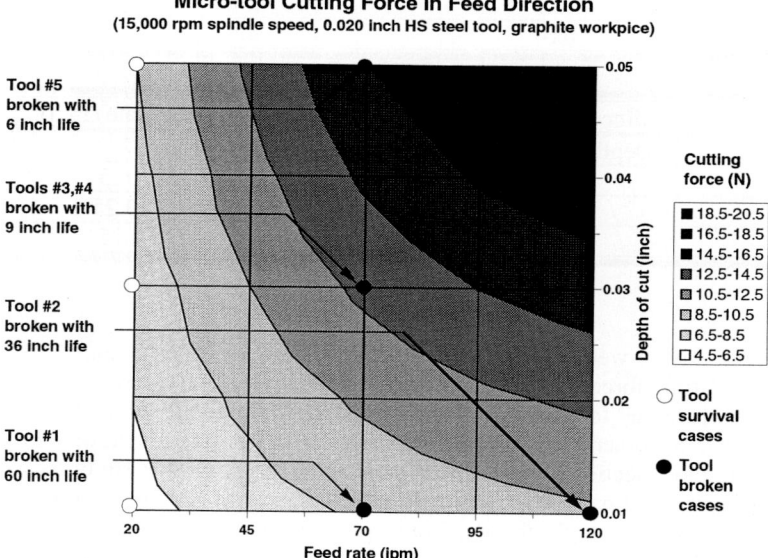

Fig. 3. Some of the training cases, tool life and typical cutting force estimations with a trained ANN.

Table 3. The results of the optimization when 4 nodes were used at the hidden layer. The range of the depth of cut and the feed rate were 0.01"-0.15" and 20ipm-120ipm respectively.

Given values to the optimization program		Results of the optimization			
		Optimized output values of the ANNs		Estimated input values to work at the optimal conditions	
Fixed Radius (inch)	Feed force Range (N)	Optimal Feed force (N)	Optimal Thrust Force (N)	Depth of cut (inch)	Feed rate (inch per minute)
0.03	22-28	28.00	12.974	0.071	83.867
0.04	34-40	40.00	18.97	0.081	95.781
0.05	45-50	45.00	21.538	0.084	101.881

6 Conclusion

GONNS was proposed to select the optimal cutting conditions in micro-end-milling operations. Two ANNs represented the cutting forces while the genetic algorithm found the optimal operating conditions to minimize one of the cutting forces while keeping the other in the given range. The proposed method can also be used in conventional machining operations. In that case additional ANNs could be used to represent the relationship between the cutting conditions and the manufacturing cost, wear, lubrication efficiency, quality index, and many other parameters. Optimization can be performed either to minimize one of the parameters, such as cost, while keeping the others such as cutting forces, quality index, and others in an acceptable range. In most of the micro-end-milling operations in aerospace, biomedical, and mold making applications, current market conditions do not require highly efficient mass production and similar data is not generally available.

Using ANNs represented the characteristics of two cutting forces in the horizontal plane. The proposed approach is very convenient to establish the model from the experimental data. Analytical approach requires fewer experiments to find the coefficients and estimate the cutting forces in many different cutting conditions. However, operator should be trained better, and unexpected discrepancies might be experienced between the estimation of the model and the experimental data in actual cutting conditions.

The general-purpose optimization program allows the user to consider large number of clusters. Each cluster can be assigned to a different type of manufacturing operation such as machining, casting and using composites. Up to six ANNs can be used in each cluster to represent the relationship between the inputs and outputs. The proposed approach is capable to optimize all the clusters at the same time and to select the best one. The optimal manufacturing method and operating conditions would be obtained with this procedure. GONNS can be easily implemented to many applications, from initial design of complex systems to the preparation of diets for patients.

References

1. I.Tansel, S. Y.Yang, C. Shu, W.Y. Bao, N. Mahendrakar: Introduction to Genetically Optimized Neural Network Systems (GONNS), Smart Engineering Systems: Neural Networks, Fuzzy Logic, Evolutionary Programming, Data Mining, and Rough Sets, edited by Drs. Dagli, Akay, Buczak, Ersoy, and Fernandez, ASME Press, New York, 1999, pp.331–336.
2. S.Y. Yang, I.N. Tansel, C.V Kropas-Hughes: Selection of Optimal Material and Operating Conditions in Composite Manufacturing – I – Computational Tool, Int. Jour. of Mach. Tools and Manufacturing, Vol.43, No.2, 2003, pp.169–173.
3. S.Y. Yang, V. Girivasan, N. R. Singh, I.N. Tansel, C.V Kropas-Hughes: Selection of Optimal Material and Operating Conditions in Composite Manufacturing – II – Complexity, Representation of Characteristics and Decision Making, Int. Jour. of Mach. Tools and Manufacturing, Vol.43, No.2, 2003, pp.175–184.
4. D.E. Rumelhart, G. Hilton, R.J. Williams: Learning Internal Representations by Error Propagation, Parallel Distributed Processing:Explorations in the Microstructure of Cognition, Vol.1, Ed. E. Rumelhart, J.L. McClelland, MIT Press, 1986
5. J.E. Dayhoff: Neural Network Architectures: An Introduction, Van Nostrand Reinhold, 1990
6. R. Hecht-Nielsen: Neurocomputing, Addison-Wesley Publishing Company, Inc., 1990
7. DARPA: Neural Network Study, AFCEA International Press, Fairfax, VA, Vol. 23/1, 1988.
8. D.E. Goldberg: Genetic Algorithms in Search, Optimization and Machine Learning, Addison-Wesley, Reading, MA, 1989
9. D.L. Carroll: Chemical Laser Modeling with Genetic Algorithms, AIAA Jour. Vol.34, No.2, 1996, pp.338–346.
10. G. Winter, P. Cuesta, J. Periaux, M. Galan: Genetic Algorithm in Engineering and Computer Science, John Wiley & Sons, 1996.
11. Scott Robert Ladd: Genetic Algorithms in C++, M&T Books, 1996.
12. W.Y. Bao, I.N. Tansel: Modeling Micro-End-Milling Operations –II: Tool Run-out, Int. Jour. of Mach. Tools and Manufacturing, Vol.40, No.15, 2000, pp.2175–2192.

Building RBF Neural Network Topology through Potential Functions

Natacha Gueorguieva[1] and Iren Valova[2]

[1]Computer Science, City University of New York, Staten Island, NY 10314
`natachag@postbox.csi.cuny.edu`
[2]Computer and Information Sciences, University of Massachusetts Dartmouth, N. Dartmouth, MA 02747
`ivalova@umassd.edu`

Abstract. In this paper we propose a strategy to shape adaptive radial basis functions through potential functions. DYPOF (DYnamic POtential Functions) neural network (NN) is designed based on radial basis functions (RBF) NN with a two-stage training procedure. Static (fixed number of RBF) and dynamic (ability to add or delete one or more RBF) versions of our learning algorithm are introduced. We investigate the change of cluster shape with the dimension of the input data, the choice of univariate potential function, and the construction of multivariate potential functions. Several data sets are considered to demonstrate the classification performance on the training and testing exemplars as well as compare DYPOF with other neural networks.

1 Introduction

The goal of object classification is the extraction of a compact set of features from a high-dimension image space to a significantly lower feature space that corresponds to a smaller number of hidden neurons comparing to these of input layer. Thus the neural network encodes inputs in a smaller dimension by retaining most of the important information.

Multilayered networks (MLNs), coupled with the backpropagation (BP) algorithm are successfully applied to solve various problems in pattern classification and clustering. The following two major criticisms are commonly raised against the BP algorithm: 1) It is computationally intensive because of its slow convergence speed; 2) there is no guarantee that the absolute minima can be achieved. The convergence can be improved by different proposed techniques as controlling the learning rate in the course of the training [1][3] by introducing input normalization before presenting them to the network [4], enhancement of conjugate gradient search [5], etc. On the other hand, RBF neural networks have recently attracted extensive interests in the research community because of the following characteristics: a) they are universal approximators [1][5][6]; b) high learning speed due to locally tuned neurons [7]; c) they have a very compact topology [2].

The Radial Basis Function Neural Networks (RBFNs) correspond to a particular class of function approximators, which can be trained using a set of training patterns. The learning strategy used in RBFNs consists of approximating an unknown function with a linear combination of non-linear functions called basis functions. The latter have radial symmetry with respect to a center. The universal approximation capabilities of RBFNs presented and proved in [5] [8] [9] guarantee the existence of an approximator that with a high, but finite number of units, can achieve an approximation with every degree of precision. The result however does not suggest any direct method for constructing it meaning that it is not always possible to find the best approximation within a specified class of approximators even when the analytical expression of the function is given.

The architecture underlying RBF networks has been defined independently from their mathematical representation and presented several times under different names. Initially presented in the neural network framework [7] RBFNs were reintroduced as a particular case of regularization networks [6]. Independently, the fuzzy logic community developed the fuzzy controllers [10] whose effectiveness relies on the same approximation principles. Closely related to the fuzzy approach, it was proposed to use the RBFN for mapping and refining propositional knowledge [11]. With a very different approach in the mainstream of applied statistics [12], the problem of regression and classification, and more generally density estimation, were faced by means of kernel estimators that were strongly related to RBFN.

2 Formalism of Potential Functions

RBFNs with potential functions (PFs) perform a mapping based on a set of generated potential fields over the domain of input space by a number of potential function entities (PFEs) [13]. If we denote by $U(x, x_j)$ the potential function, which is connected to the learning pattern $x_j \in \aleph, j = 1, 2,..., M$, the appearance of training patterns corresponds to the generation of potential functions $U(x, x_1), U(x, x_2),..., U(x, x_M)$ defined over the space $\aleph$, which could be used in construction of the cluster separation functions [13]. Without loss of generality we may consider the case of two distinguished clusters K_1 and K_2. Thus the potential functions generated by the learning patterns $x_1, x_2,..., x_m \in \aleph$ included in subclusters K_1^* and K_2^* can be represented in the form

$$U'(x) = \sum_{x_v \in K_1^*} U(x, x_v); \qquad U''(x) = \sum_{x_\rho \in K_2^*} U(x, x_\rho), \text{ where } m = v + \rho \qquad (1)$$

Thus there exists at least one separation function $f(x) = U'(x) - U''(x)$, which will be positive for the samples belonging to one of the clusters (for example K_1) and respectively negative for K_2.

Let denote by $U_n(x)$ the accumulative potential build after n iterations. The following four cases are possible on the $(n+1)$ step of training:

$$x_{n+1} \in K_1, \quad U_n(x_{n+1}) > 0, \qquad (2)$$
$$x_{n+1} \in K_2, \quad U_n(x_{n+1}) < 0,$$
$$x_{n+1} \in K_1, \quad U_n(x_{n+1}) < 0,$$
$$x_{n+1} \in K_2, \quad U_n(x_{n+1}) > 0.$$

In general, we assume that the accumulative potential $U_n(x)$ built on the n-th training step can be written in the following form:

$$U_n(x) = \sum_{x_k^- \in K_1} U(x, x_k) - \sum_{x_q^- \in K_2} U(x, x_k) \qquad (3)$$

where $x_k^- \in K_1$ and $x_q^- \in K_2$.

Method of potential functions assumes that there exists a separation function $f(x)$ defined in the space $\aleph$, which can be represented by the expansion

$$f(x) = \sum_{i=1}^{N} w_i \varphi_i(x) \qquad (4)$$

For the potential function we will use a function of two variables of the form

$$U(x, x^*) = \sum_{i=1}^{\infty} \lambda_i^2 \varphi_i(x) \, \varphi_i(x^*) = \sum_{i=1}^{\infty} \psi_i(x) \psi_i(x^*) \qquad (5)$$

where $\varphi_i(x)$ $(i=1,2,...)$ is a linearly independent system of orthonormal functions; λ_i are real numbers different from zero for $i = 1,2,...N$ satisfying the condition

$$\sum_{i=1}^{\infty} \lambda_i^2 < \infty .$$

The relation between the potential function $U(x, x_n)$ and approximating function $f^*(x)$ is given by the next equation, which determines the iterative updates of the estimations $f_r(x)$.

$$f_{n+1}(x) = q_n f_n(x) + r_n U(x, x_{n+1}) \qquad (6)$$

where q_n, and r_n are numeric sequences which depend on one or on all of the following factors: number of iteration n, the value of the current estimation f_n for the next input x_{n+1} ($f_n(x_{n+1})$) and from the value of approximating function f^* for x_{n+1} - $f^*(x_{n+1})$ if it is available. For our considerations we set $q_n \equiv 1$ and choose the following form for r_n:

$$r_n \equiv \gamma_n \left\{ F(f_n(x_{n+1}), f^*(x_{n+1})) + \mu_{n+1} \right\} \qquad (7)$$

where $F(f_n, f^*)$ is a function of two variables; μ_n is a noise which appears during the measurement of $f^*(x)$ and γ_n is a non-negative numeric sequence satisfying the following conditions: $\sum_{n=1}^{\infty} \gamma_n = \infty$; $\gamma_n = const$; $\lim_{n \to \infty} \gamma_n = 0$; $\sum_{n=1}^{\infty} \gamma_n = \infty$; $\sum_{n=1}^{\infty} \gamma_n^2 = \infty$;

The weight update received from (4) takes the following form:

$$w_{n+1}^i = q_n w_n^i + r_n \lambda_i^2 \varphi_i(x_{n+1}) \qquad (8)$$

Let $\psi_i(x) = \lambda_i \varphi_i(x)$ and $\tilde{w}_n^i = w_n^i / \lambda_i$. Then

$$f_n(x) = \sum_i w_n^i \varphi_i(x) = \sum_i \tilde{w}_n^i \psi_i(x) \qquad (9)$$

Thus (8) takes the form:

$$\tilde{w}_{n+1}^i = q_n \tilde{w}_n^i + r_n \psi_i(x_{n+1}) \qquad (10)$$

where $\sum_{i=1}^{\infty} \lambda_i^2 < 0$ and $\lambda_i \neq 0$.

The weight update under the above assumption determined by (8) and (10) could be obtained by

$$w_{n+1}^k = w_n^k + \gamma_{n+1} sign[f^*(x_{n+1}) - \sum_{n=1}^{N} w_n^k \varphi^k(x_{n+1})] \varphi^k(x_{n+1}) \qquad (11)$$

3 Topology Determination, Initialization, and Training of DYPOF

Considering RBF models, the neural networks are regarded as a mapping from feature hyperspace to clusters. We set the number of inputs to be equal to that of features (i.e. dimension of the input space), and the number of outputs to be equal to that of clusters. Initially, the number of neurons in hidden layer 1 is set to 25, and the number of hidden units in hidden layer 2 equals 8.

The following is a brief description of the learning algorithm.

Learning Phase:
Step L1. Invoke one cycle learning procedure at the i-th learning cycle where one learning cycle implies the presentation of all patterns of the training set to the neural network. The one cycle learning procedure includes the following stages:

Stage 1: Select a training pattern $x_t \in K_q$, $1 \leq q \leq N$ from the learning set and calculate $U_k^{(i)}(x_{k+1})$, where i is the number of training cycle.

Stage 2. Update $\text{PFE}^{(K_q)}$ with $U(x, x_t)$ and set the cumulative potential $U_1^{(K_q)}(x) = U(x, x_t)$. Update the output cluster separated function for cluster K_q in the following way: $f_1^{(K_q)}(x) = U_1^{(K_q)}$.

Stage 3. Select the next training pattern $x_v \in K^p, 0 < p \le l$, where l is the total number of clusters.

Step L2. Calculate the network performance at the end of i-th learning cycle:

$$P^{(i)} = \left(\sum_p E_p(i) \right)^{1/2} = E_p(i) = \frac{\left| S_i^{(x^*)} \right|}{|S|}, \text{ where } S_i^{(x^*)} \text{ is a subset of } S$$

($S_i^{(x^*)} \subset S$) which includes all patterns x^* which require weight adjustment; $|S|$ and $\left| S_i^{(x^*)} \right|$ are the cardinalities of the training and the reduced training sets. The condition for algorithm convergence is $\left| S_i^{(x^*)} \right| = 0$.

Step L3. If $i = l$ increment it by 1 return to Stage 4 of step L2. Otherwise goto to the next step L5.

Step L4.

$$\text{If } \left| S_i^{(x^*)} \right| = 0, \text{ the algorithm has converged;}$$

$$\text{else} \begin{cases} \text{if } i \le i^{max} \text{ goto Step L6;} \\ \text{otherwise go to Dynamic Learning Phase.} \end{cases}$$

Step L5. Calculate the DYPOF performance improvement $\varepsilon_{i-1,i}$ between the i-1-th and i-th learning cycles $\varepsilon_{i-1,i} = P^{(i-1)} - P^{(i)}$. Then follow the condition

$$\begin{cases} \text{if } \varepsilon > 0 \text{ and } \varepsilon_{i-1,i} < \varepsilon, \text{increment } i \text{ by one and goto Stage 4 of step L2;} \\ \text{else goto Dynamic Learning Phase.} \end{cases}$$

Dynamic Learning Phase:

Step D1. Add a new unit to the hidden layer 1 (new one dimensional activation function).

Step D2. If the cardinality of the set $|\Psi(x)| = |\phi_1(x), \phi_2(x), ..., \phi_n(x)| < k_{max}$ then update the units of hidden layer 2 and goto **Step L1**; otherwise continue to the next step.

Step D3. Add a new unit to the hidden layer 2 (new multivariate potential function) and goto **Step L1**. Repeat this step until there are no further changes in cumulative potentials requiring the weight update for all inputs of the training set.

4 Experiments and Discussion

The simulations involve sets of two-dimensional artificial patterns created by Hermite and Legendre polynomials used as one-dimensional activation potential functions. The 2d space was chosen for better visualization, although multiple dimension patterns were also tested. The different implementations showed very similar results and performances for the learning set of patterns being used. Therefore instead on concentrating on a distinction between different polynomial systems as nonlinearities we will show the classification outcomes of two learning sets. The lines through the pattern sets represent decision boundaries that are derived by DYPOF neural network. The optimal topology of DYPOF network is determined during the training. The DYPOF classification results were compared to the results obtained by using the MLP of the comparable complexity. The MLP has performed significantly poorer then the DYPOF network on experimental data set with noise.

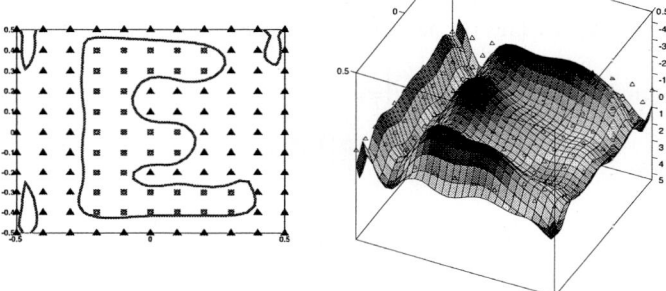

Fig. 1. 2D and 3D decision boundaries for TS1 (number of neurons in hidden layer 1 is set to 45, in hidden layer 2 – 8)

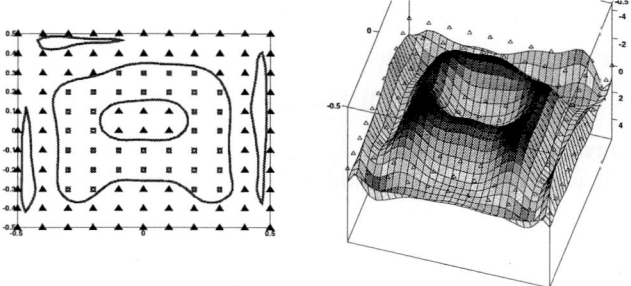

Fig. 2. 2D and 3D decision boundaries for TS2 (number of neurons on hidden layer 1 equals 85, in hidden layer 2 – 12)

Figures 1a and 2a present the decision boundaries for two training sets (TS), labeled TS1 and TS2. These boundaries are based on cumulative potentials generated by Hermite polynomials. Both training sets consist of 121 patterns, 36 of which belong to cluster $K^{(1)}$ and 81 – to cluster $K^{(2)}$ for TS1. Cluster $K^{(1)}$ is assigned to 37 samples of TS2 and respectively the number of samples belonging to $K^{(2)}$ for the same training set is 84. Figure 1 presents the simulation results after increasing of number of neurons of hidden layer 1 to 45 during the dynamic learning phase. The two clusters of TS1 and TS2 are not well separated during the learning phase (sixteen incorrect classifications for TS1 and seventeen for TS2. Figure 1 demonstrates the simulation results in 2D and 3D after increasing the number of hidden neurons of the first layer from 25 during the learning phase to 45 during the dynamic learning phase and number of neurons of the second hidden layer remains 8 during the training. Figure 2 shows the decision boundaries in 2D and 3D after structural changes of hidden layer 1 and hidden layer 2 due to invocation of dynamic learning phase. The NN was forced to make structural changes in the second hidden layer after the number of hidden neurons of the first layer reached 45 and continue with the increase of neurons of layer 1 to 85 after the layer 2 hits the maximum allowed number of 12. Figure 3 illustrates the smooth clustering maps of both training sets created by DYPOF.

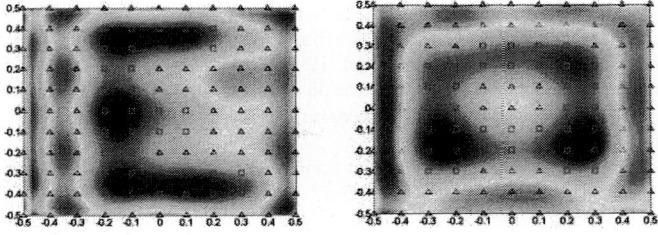

Fig. 3. Cluster maps of TS1 and TS2 as created by DYPOF

It was found that DYPOF achieves very good performance in terms of error rates of classification and learning efficiency. The synthesized potential fields allow smooth approximation of the training data, and thus continuous associations. We have observed that incrementing i^{max} and $i^{max}_{d_1}$ by one do not improve considerably the classification properties and causes NN fluctuations and slow convergence.

Based on the simulations, we conjecture that a better performance would be achieved by designing a preprocessing phase aimed to connect the initial parameters with the existing geometrical properties of the cluster domain (average distance of samples, standard deviation etc.).

5 Conclusions

The proposed approach for RBF NN topology development through potential functions has demonstrated automatic capacity correction of functions that separate the cluster and automatic NN topology selection in the sense that both the optimal number and locations of the basis functions are automatically obtained during training. We observed that extracting of a small number of supporting patterns from the training data that are relevant to the classification further improves the convergence rate of DYPOF. Uniqueness of the solution is achieved during the learning phase and is then modified during the dynamic learning phase in a clusters dependent way. The efficiency and performance characteristics achieved by DYPOF match or are better than these of sophisticated classifiers based on MLP and traditional RBF tested on the same artificial training data. The comparison of results shows that the decision boundaries created by DYPOF are much closer to one of the two clusters. This is a result of the non-linear transform from the pattern space to the potential function space, which performs a position dependent scaling of distance.

References

[1]   J.Park, J.Wsandberg, Universal Approximation Using Radial Basis Functions Network, *Neural Comput.*, vol. 3, pp. 246–257, 1991.
[2]   S.Lee, RKil, A Gaussian Potential Function Network With Hierarchically Self-Organizing Learning, *Neural Networks*, vol. 4, pp. 207–224, 1991.
[3]   A.Bors, I.Pitas, Median Radial Basis Function Neural Network, *IEEE Trans. Neural Networks*, vol. 7, pp. 1351–1364, Sept. 1996.
[4]   H.Leung, V.Zue, Phonetic Classification Using Multi-Layer Perceptrons, in *IEEE Int. Conf. Acoust., Speech, Signal Processing*, vol. 1, Albuquerque, NM, April 1990, pp. 525–528.
[5]   J.Park, I.Sandberg, Approximation and Radial-Basis-Function Networks. *Neural Computation*, 5(3), pp. 305–316, 1993.
[6]   F.Girosi, T.Poggio, Networks And The Best Approximation Property, *Biol. Cybern.*, vol. 63, pp. 169–176, 1990.
[7]   J.Moody, C.Darken, Fast Learning In Network Of Locally-Tuned Processing Units, *Neural Comput.*, vol. 1, pp. 281–294, 1989.
[8]   K.Hornik, M.Stinchcombe, H.White, Multilayer Feed_Forward Networks Are Universal Approximators. *Neural Networks*, 2:359–366, 1989.
[9]   T.Chen, H.Chen, Approximation Capability To Functions Of Several Variables Nonlinear Functionals And Operators By Radial Basis Function Neural Networks. IEEE Transactions on Neural Networks, 6(4):904–910, 1995.
[10] H.Berenji, Fuzzy Logic Controllers. In Yager R., Zadeh L., (Eds), An Introduction to Fuzzy Logic Applications in Intelligent Systems. Kluver Academic Publishers, 1992.
[11] V.Tresp, J.Hollatz, and Ahmad S., Representing probabilistic rules with networks of gaussian basis functions. *Machine Learning*, 27:173–200, 1997.
[12] D.Scott, Multivariate Density Estimation. Wiley, 1992.
[13] N.Gueorguieva, I.Valova, J.Tovar, Dynamic-Node Neural Network Architecture Learning: A Potential Function Approach. *Proceedings of the Artificial Neural Networks in Engineering Conference (ANNIE'02)*, St. Louis, Missouri, pp. 39–44, 2002.

Use of Magnetomyographic (MMG) Signals to Calculate the Dependency Properties of the Active Sensors in Myometrial Activity Monitoring

C. Bayrak[1], Z. Chen[1], J. Norton[2], H. Preissl[2], C. Lowery[2], H. Eswaran[2], and J. D. Wilson[3]

[1] Computer Science Department, University of Arkansas at Little Rock, Little Rock, AR 72204
{cxbayrak | zchen | jdwilson}@ualr.edu
[2] Department of Obstetrics and Gynecology, University of Arkansas for Medical Sciences, Little Rock, AR 72203
{NortonJonathanD | htpreissl | lowerycurtisl | eswaranh}@uams.edu
[3] GIT, University of Arkansas at Little Rock, Little Rock, AR 72204

Abstract. The uterus is able to accomplish the remarkable task of maintaining an environment which suppresses uterine burst activity during the development of the fetus but keeps tone and initiates and coordinates the individual firing of myometrial cells. These cells produce organized contractions, causing the expulsion of the fetus from the mother's body. Past studies suggest that the uterus passes through a preparatory process before entering labor. This can happen preterm, leading to increased risk for the fetus. In order to understand the dynamical properties of the uterus, we have developed a preliminary analysis tool [1] that makes it possible to identify where and how the contraction starts and ends, and how it progresses, in terms of intensity, length, and path. Using these properties, we are hoping to differentiate false labor from true labor using the intercellular activities. The **my**ometrial **a**ctivity **m**odeling (MyAM) will help to determine the regions of localized activation, propagation velocity and direction, and the spread of activity as a function of distance. Through a better understanding of the electrophysiological basis of uterine contractions, better interventions (e.g., drug) can be undertaken which may be effective for suppression of preterm labor or induction of labor at term. Current methodologies lack sensitivity and specificity for prediction of labor, so it is difficult to plan appropriate interventions [2][3]. The MyAM will provide more detailed and precise information regarding the initiation and propagation of electromyographic activity in the human uterus.

1 Introduction

For an understanding of uterine contractility, it is necessary to incorporate current knowledge of anatomy and electrophysiology of the uterus in any analysis and modeling tool. The uterine wall is comprised of the endometrium, myometrium, and serosa. The myometrium consists of smooth muscle fibers that are arranged in overlapping tissue-like bands; the exact arrangement is a highly debated topic. Like cardiac cells [4], uterine myometrial cells can generate either their own impulses – pacemaker cells – or can be excited by the action potentials propagated from other neighboring cells – pacefollower cells. Unlike cardiac cells, however, each myometrial cell can alternately act as a pacemaker or a pacefollower. There is no evidence of the existence of a fixed anatomic pacemaker area on the uterine muscle [5]. The spontaneous oscillations in the membrane potential of the autonomously active pacemaker cells lead to the generation of an action potential burst when the threshold of firing is reached. The electrical activity arising from these pacemaker cells excites neighboring cells, because they are coupled by electronic synapses called gap junctions. It is assumed that the action potential burst can originate from any uterine cell, thus the pacemaker cell can shift from one contraction to another [6]. Garfield et al. and others have shown the gap junctions are sparse throughout pregnancy but increase during delivery in various species [6]. The increase in the number of gap junctions and their electrical transmission strength provides stronger coupling between the cells, resulting in synchronization and coordination of the contractile events. These results show clearly that the propagation of the electrical activity over the entire myometrium due to the increase in gap junction areas at term is related to successful progress of labor and delivery of the fetus.

There are two fundamental issues to be considered in this study: 1) the monitoring and 2) the interpretation of the myometrial signals recorded from the maternal abdomen. In order to have in-depth knowledge of the low level behavior, continuous monitoring is required. Therefore, a monitoring environment was developed to utilize the noninvasive detailed physiological information that is simultaneously recorded from 151 different sensors using the Squid Array for Reproductive Assessment (SARA) instrument [7]. SARA detects magnetomyographic signals that can help us to better investigate the dynamical properties of the uterus during the contraction. We implemented several approaches to study the data and understand the low level activities of uterus. There is only limited knowledge about uterine physiology, especially related to coordinated activity, so we start with a data-centered approach. Therefore, the environment is designed and implemented with respect to the following aims:
– Determining the initial points of uterine contractions and the activity spread.
– Modeling of spatio-temporal contractility patterns and myometrial activity.
– Determining the characteristics of the uterine contractions to observe and analyze the changes in the connection pattern.
– Identifying the varying properties of false and true labor.
– Classifying uterine contraction signals

2 The Architecture of Myometrial Activity Monitoring Model

The MyAM architecture, which is used to monitor the myometrial activities, is composed of three layers: *signal level, sensor level,* and *cell level.* It is clear that the sensor level, which is defined by the resolution of the recording system, is not capable of resolving single cells. We just record mass actions generated by a high number of synchronously active smooth muscle cells. This is compatible with our desire to find the macroscopic signatures of uterine contractions.

The primary function of the *signal level* is to provide an interface for conducting a reliable activity analysis via threshold algorithms on each sensor's signal, as shown in Fig. 1. The recording is performed while the mother is leaning over the 151-channel array. The recording last for 6 minutes and the sampling rate is 312.5 Hz. The data are downsampled to 25Hz offline and filtered between .25 to 1 Hz. The data are scanned at the initial stage of execution to identify the maximum of the data set. This value is important not only to define the origin of the intense activities but also to provide a reference value to determine the initial threshold[1].

Each data signal obtained from the sensors is used to define the scaled value of the curve. The highest amplitude value, v_{max}, of the contraction plays an important role in the scaled value determination and is computed as, $s = h/v_{max}$. Here s denotes the scaled value of the contraction; h denotes the magnetic strength; and v_{max} represents the maximum value.

The *sensor level,* as shown in Fig. 2, shows how the activity propagates among clusters of sensors. A set of steps that are enforced in the regional algorithm has been promoted to identify this behavior in a critical area. In the first step, the definition of a threshold for all sensors is required. It was necessary to take into account that every sensor is affected by noise. At this level, we are using a threshold value in order to differentiate active cells and passive cells. A sensor that has a value greater than the threshold is temporarily assumed to be active.

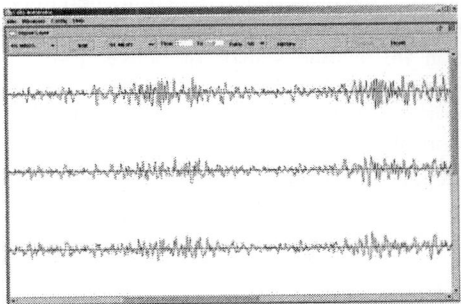

Fig. 1. Display of magnetic activity of three different sensors.

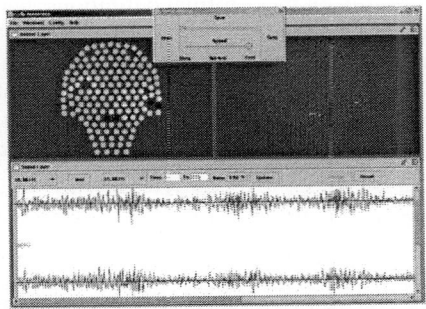

Fig. 2. Sensor and Cellular Level Activity Recording

The *Cellular level* is built on the basis of the sensor level. According to the data collected from the sensors, we developed a cellular interaction algorithm based on cellular automata [8] to discover more activity details at the lower level.

In each time tick, the active cell's position is represented by a red point in the cellular level, with yellow points representing the history of active cells in the past time tick. A red filled circle represents the critical active sensor in the sensor level, and a yellow circle is part of the region in the current time tick. A blue circle represents the sequence history of the active sensor.

In the sensor level, we have already discovered the regions in every time tick and found the critical sensor for every region. Assume that the area that the critical sensor locates is the most active area in every region. In order to find the critical active cell point from this area, we employ the cellular interaction algorithm to locate the exact position. First, we find the critical sensor from a region and its neighbors. For every time tick, we suppose S_i is the critical sensor of the ith region. X_i, Y_i are the x, y

---

[1] The threshold used here is the uniform threshold applied on the complete set of signals.

coordinates, and value_i is the signal value of the S_i. X_{ij}, Y_{ij} are the x, y coordinates, and value_{ij} is the signal value of the jth neighbor of S_i. In the algorithm, we set $X_{i0}=X_i$, $Y_{i0}=Y_i$, $\text{value}_{i0}= \text{value}_i$.

The exact position of the critical cell is determined through the contribution of all neighboring sensors in terms of values and coordinates. Since the coordinates of the critical sensor in a current region are identified with the sensor level algorithm, we suppose that the critical cell must be located somewhere nearby. In order to locate the critical cell, the sensors that are in the neighborhood of the critical sensor are analyzed to verify this assumption with a big/small value perspective, i.e., the position of critical cell should be near the neighboring sensor with a big value and far from a neighboring sensor with a small value. The formal context of this issue can be represented as:

$$V_{i\_min} = \min(v_{i\_n})$$
$$V_{i\_n} = V_{i\_neighbors} - V_{i\_min}$$
$$C_{sum} = \sum_{j=0}^{neighbor\_count} v_{ij}$$

$$C_{sum(x,y)} = \sum_{j=0}^{neighbor\_count} \{(X_{ij})(v_{ij})\}, \{(Y_{ij})(v_{ij})\}$$

$$X_i \mid Y_i = \{C_{sum(x,y)} / C_{sum}\}$$

Based on these formal definitions, we can find the critical active cell, its neighbors, and the associated propagation of every time tick, which can show more details of the signals' migration using cellular interaction inside one sensor or between several sensors. Therefore, in the targeted topology, pixels are used to represent the cellular environment in which the local interaction is controlled in discrete time. Similar to sensors, for each active cell, a neighborhood of radius r is defined. The state of an active cell, c_i^{t+1} of the cell I at time $t+1$ depends only on the states (the recording of each cell with respect to the threshold value) of cells in the neighborhood at time t.

3 Properties of Myometrial Signal Interpretation

The myometrial signal interpretation can be analyzed with respect to the following properties: *Contraction Life Cycle*, *Region Identification*, and *Contraction Detection*. In this process of marking a contraction it is necessary to scan each sensor's data signal for the identification of isolated segments and active "Valleys." Since it is possible to encounter some isolated segments that have a value greater then the threshold but are not necessarily part of the contraction activity, we remove the isolated active segments (segment's value greater than threshold) from the active segments list for the current time tick. Furthermore, we also find the signal data which is located in the Valley of the active data and add them into the active data list. More specifically, the contraction life cycle is composed of two fundamental elements: identification of windows and segments. Window identification requires that the segment's value of each sensor from starting time tick be scanned. For each value at the current time tick, t, we verify five *a priori* and *a posteriori* segment values. If there are more than five values greater than the threshold, this window is recorded to be active, otherwise inactive. On the other hand, in the segment identification all sequences of active segments with the length less than 25 are identified as inactive. (With a window size of 50, 25 windows represent a period of 50 seconds.)

In order to define localized activities, we have developed a region identification algorithm. A region represents a collection of sensors. All the sensors in this collection must contiguous and active at a given time tick. For each region, we define a sensor with maximum value inside as the center of the region. For every time tick, we scan all sensors to find several valid regions and store them into a collection of regions called the region set. Note that a valid region is a region whose sensor count is greater than 4. In every time tick, we store a region set as a history record. The pseudo code of this algorithm is:

```
for tick from 0 to Time_Tick_Count
    for i from 0 to Sensor_Count
        if(InactiveSensor.contains(i)) continue;
        if (Sensors[i].Value[tick] < threshold)
            InactiveSensor.add(i);
        else
            Current_Region = new Region();
            call FindRegion(i);
        end if
            if Current_Region.sensor_count>4)
            Region_Set.add(Current_Region);
                Current_Region.findCenter();
            end if
    end loop
    History_Record.add(Region_Set);
end loop
function FindRegion(int sn)
    if(InactiveSensor.contains(sn)) return;
    Current_Region.add(sn);
    InactiveSensor.add(sn);
    for i from 0 to 6
        FindRegion(Sensors[sn].neighbor[i]);
    end loop
end function
```

The contraction detection algorithm is developed to identify the relationship between regions to define contractions. For every time tick t_i, we have one or more regions. For each region r_i, we find a sensor s_i in the region representing r_i's center. In the next time tick, t_{i+1}, we have another region r_{i+1} with a center s_{i+1}. If $s_i \in r_{i+1}$, then r_{i+1} is a continuation of r_i, therefore, we add r_{i+1} to r_i's active segment. If r_{i+1} is not a continuation of r_i, we terminate the active segment which r_i belongs to, and create a new active segment for r_{i+1}. Furthermore, when an active segment is terminated, we check its life cycle length. If it is greater than four, we add it into the active segment set. Otherwise, we discard it. The corresponding pseudo algorithm of this definition is given below.

```
for tick from 0 to Time_Tick_Count
    Region_Set=History_record.elementAt(tick);
    for i from 0 to Region_Set.count
        Region=Region_Set.elementAt(i);
        for j from 0 to Contraction_Set.count
            contraction=Contraction_Set.count.elementAt(j);
            Boolean isContain=
                Region.CheckContains(contraction.lastCenter);
            if(isContain)
                contraction.add(Region);
            end if
```

```
      end loop
      if (!isContain)
            Contraction_Set.add(new Contraction(Region));
      end if
   end loop
end loop
```

3.1 Determining the Contraction Threshold

In analyzing the activities recorded non-invasively via 151 sensors, we have identified three fundamental properties to focus on: 1) the contraction threshold, 2) the life cycle of the contraction and 3) pre- and post- conditions of the contraction (pre- and post-gestation stages). Since 3) is one of the focuses of our future study, we will address the first two of these in this section.

The purpose of the threshold is to give a scalar standard to evaluate whether a signal from a certain sensor at a specific time belongs to a contraction. Therefore, we have developed a set of algorithms: The Variable Threshold Algorithm (VTA) and the Adaptive Threshold Algorithm (ATA).

3.1.1 Variable Threshold Algorithm

The VTA is based on a statistical approach, with the requirement of a minimum Signal Noise Ratio (SNR) between the contraction signal and the background noise. This minimum SNR can be set using statistical criteria. The key ideas of the algorithm can be summarized as follows:

Definition: The basic indexes of VTA are denoted i, j, and k, representing the sequence number of sensors (i: 0, Sensor_Count), data (j: 0, Data_Count), and windows (k: 0, Window_Count) respectively.

a) For each sensor, we get 100 continuous data points from the raw signal. Their values are less than a preset threshold.
b) Find the sample standard deviation of these 100 values, and take it as an estimate of the background noise, i.e, if $(Data\_Value_{i,j} < Present\_Threshold)$ then $Back\_Noise = STD(Data\_Value_{i,j})$.
c) Calculate the product between a SNR (a preset value) and the STD value, and take the result as the final threshold of this sensor,i.e, $Threshold\_II_i = Preset\_SNR * Back\_Noise_i$.
d) Repeat steps (a) to (c) for all sensors, and calculate the threshold value for each sensor.
e) There are two adaptive parameters: the preset threshold, and the SNR.

3.1.2 Adaptive Threshold Algorithm

ATA bases the final threshold on the active sensors rather than the background noise (also known as *take–it-or-leave-it*.) It assumes that a real contraction will lead to a set of continual and intensive signal values for some sensors, while short-term big fluctuations will not be considered as a part of contraction. The key ideas of this algorithm are summarized as follows:

a) Find the maximum absolute value of signals among all sensors (151 sensors), and take this value as the seed of the first threshold. In other words, Threshold_I = Percentage_I * Value$_{max}$
b) For each sensor, segment the signal into windows with a preset size, i.e, Windows_Count$_i$ = {Data_Count / Windows_Size}. Windows_Value$_k$=Max(Data_Count$_{i,k*window\_size}$-Data_Count$_{i,(k+1)*window\_size}$)
c) For each window, set its property as positive or negative, based on the first threshold.
d) Find the window with maximum value in each sensor. We judge whether the value is valid according to the following rule: Among 10 surrounding windows, if more than 6 windows are positive, this maximum window is valid, or it is invalid. Then, we should check the validity of the second maximum window.
e) Calculate the STD value and the average value of maximum window values from all sensors. Set the summation of these two values as the seed of the second threshold, i.e., SUM = STD(SensorMaxWindows_Value$_i$)
 + AVE(Sensor_MaxWindow_value$_i$) and
Threshold_II = Percentage_II * SUM
f) Both the first threshold and second threshold are adjustable parameters.

4 Result and Analysis

The approaches we have developed for our monitoring environment helped us to identify not only the location of the activity but also the length, the path, and the intensity, as shown in Fig. 3. One challenge was to identify the beginning and the end of a contraction. Through the use of a correlational approach we were able to isolate the activities that are above the threshold but have nothing to do with the contraction. In Fig.3, the red line (upper line) represents the region count, e.g. number of active regions, with respect to the threshold, and the blue line indicates the sensor count. A close analysis of the obtained results reveals that there are negative correlations between sensor and regional count. For example, anytime there is a strong burst, we observed a significant *decrease* in the region count and a significance *increase* in sensor count. This can be interpreted as the necessary synchronization defining a contraction, which may also lead to the production of a mechanical force. At the same time the crossover between these two properties also yield the life cycle (time, length) of the intensive activity.

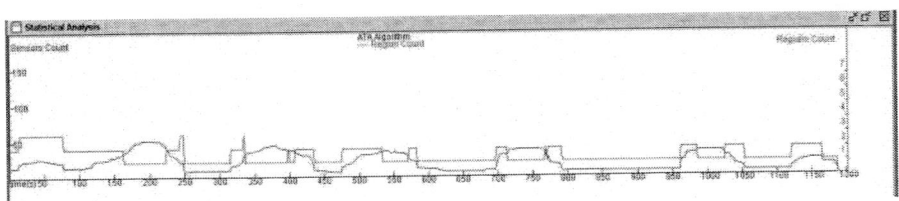

Fig. 3. Sensor and Regional Count for contraction length, and intensity.

5   Conclusions and Future Research

The project is divided into two basic research sections: a data collection and analysis section and a model adaptation and enhancement section. The focus of the first section is to collect data to enhance the capabilities of the MyAM model developed. For this purpose, we use the SARA instrument to obtain noninvasive detailed physiological information simultaneously from 151 different areas of the uterus. These recordings will help us to better formulate the low level details of the cellular interaction during the contraction through the analysis and understanding of the spatial temporal relationships.

Our preliminary findings provide some understanding in terms of where the contraction starts, its duration, its path, and its intensity. However, in this an ongoing research soon we will be focusing on the nature, characteristics, and the governing functional dependency at not only the sensor level but also at the cellular level.

References

1. Bayrak, C., Kayi, A., Lowery, C., Eswaran, H., Wilson, J. D., & Preissl, H. (2002). Modeling of myometrial activities to understand the global behavior of uterine contraction. Proceedings of ANNIE 2002, Vol. 12, November 10–13, St. Louis, Missouri.
2. Devedeux, D., Marque, C., Mansour, S. et al. (1993). Uterine electromyography – acritical review. Am. J of Ob/Gyn *169*: 1635–1653
3. Garfield, R.E., Chwalisz, K., Shi, L. et al. (1998). Instrumentation for the diagnosis of term and preterm labour – Review. J. Perinat Med *26*: 413–436
4. Bardou, A. L., P. M. Auger, P. J. Birkui, and J. L. Chasse, (1996), Modeling Cardiac Electrophysiological Mechanism: From Action Potential Genesis to its Propagation in Myocardium, *Critical Reviews in Biomedical Engineering*, 24(2/3): 141–221.
5. Garfield, R. E., Blennerhasset, M. G., & Miller, S. M. (1988). Control of myometrial contractility: Role and regulation of gap junctions. In Clarke, J. R. (Ed.). *Oxford review of reproductive biology* (pp. 436-90). Oxford: Oxford University Press.
7. Eswaran, H., Preissl, H., Wilson, J.D., Robinson, S.E , Murphy, P. & Lowery, C.L. (2002). First magnetomyographic recordings of uterine activity with spatial-temporal information using a 151 channel sensor array *Am. J of Ob/Gyn 187*: 145–151
8. Chopard, B., and Droz, M. (1998). *Cellular automata modeling of physical systems*, Cambridge, [England]; New York : Cambridge University Press.

Speed Enhancement with Soft Computing Hardware

Taher Daud, Ricardo Zebulum, Tuan Duong, Ian Ferguson, Curtis Padgett, Adrian Stoica, and Anil Thakoor

Jet Propulsion Laboratory, California Institute of Technology, Pasadena, CA, USA

Abstract. During the past few years JPL has been actively involved in soft computing research encompassing theory, architecture, and electronic hardware. There are a host of soft computing applications that require orders of magnitude enhancement in speed compared to present day simulations on digital machines. For real-time computing this is made possible by selecting suitable algorithms, designing compatible architectures and implementing them in parallel processing hardware. A compact low-power hardware design for in-situ applications uses a 3D-packaged artificial neural network (ANN) multi-chip module performing object classification and recognition with 10^{12} multiply-sum operations per second (ops). Additionally, development on evolvable hardware (EHW) implemented on reconfigurable electronic hardware has shown exciting high-speed evolution of various digital and analog circuits. We review our work to demonstrate real-time processing.

1 Introduction

The Jet Propulsion Laboratory (JPL) is conducting research in information processing using soft-computing algorithms and architectures. Our research focuses on orders of magnitude speed advantage and achieving specialized processing needs. A highly parallel neural network design was combined with a multi-chip module technique (with 64 ICs) in a 3D configuration (sugar cube size) for high-speed (10^{12} multiply-sum operations per second, ops) data processing [1].

Using soft-computing paradigms, an effective, power-miser architecture was evolved in providing solutions for sensor and data fusion in high-speed hardware. Such an application requiring low power (<10W) and real-time processing of multi-sensor data is that of object discrimination performed onboard a fast frame seeker.

In addition, the present focus for JPL's new research activity is on evolvable hardware (EHW). The theoretical, algorithmic, modeling, and analytical work has been on-going. Further, a series of test chips termed "Field-Programmable Transistor Array (FPTA)" have been designed, fabricated, and tested successfully in digital and analog circuit-evolution experiments [2]. Integration has progressed using FPTAs combined with digital signal processor (DSP) for its control that provide high-speed evolution of circuits with potential on-board fault tolerance and function morphing.

A description of these activities along with the motivation of high speed brought on by required applications is described. Selected results of the hardware implementation are presented. EHW work is described not only for the speed advantage but also its enabling promise for future long-life space missions.

2 Object Classfication/ Recognition

Present deployable object classification, recognition, and tracking applications are either bulky, power hungry, or not capable of providing reliable results in real time. This prevents the realization of a flexible, robust processor for such applications.

2.1 Test-Bed

Our, 3D packaging approach of IC chips processes large-size images (IR, UV, visible) by sequentially inputting consecutive 64x64 pixel chunks and performing high speed convolutions with 64 prestored 64x64 image templates [1]. The data processing architecture providing an image processing system in a small package performing 10^{12} ops of multiply-sum was designed and executed as a testbed [3]. It incorporates a frame grabber, a highly parallel 3D data convolver engine (performing 64x64 pixel operations with 64x64 templates in <250 ns) (Figure 1), an artificial neural network, and an output processing protocol. It can be coupled to a variety of sensors covering spectral range of ultraviolet (UV) through infrared (IR).

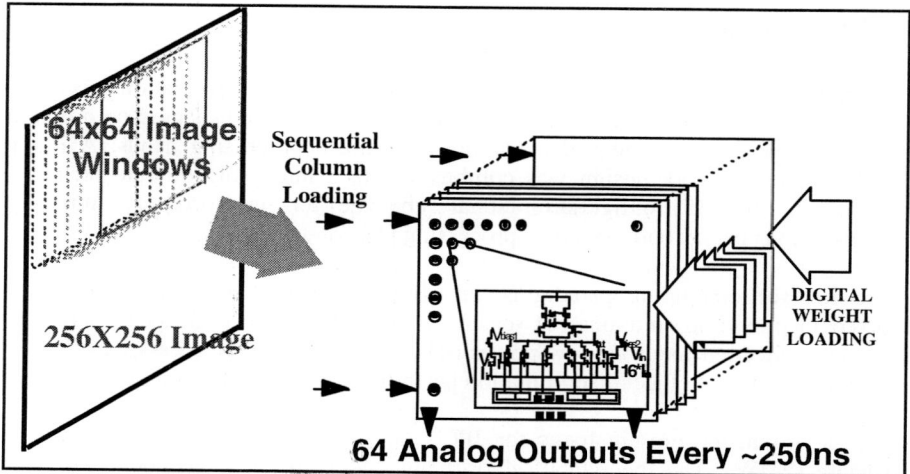

Fig. 1. The 3D MCM network consists of 64 ICs each with a 64x64 synapse array based on 8-bit multiplying D/A technology with an image input circuitry to interface with a larger size image frame. It is realized in a 10-gm, 3-cm³ package, with power consumption of ~5 W. A speed of ~10^{12} multiply-add operations/s is obtained.

2.2 Neural Networks

The ICs use a synapse design based on Multiplying Digital-to-Analog Converter (MDAC) technology using a hybrid approach [1]. Each circuit is digitally programmable, has an 8-bit resolution digital weight storage, and is a compact analog multiplier with voltage-input/current-output configuration.

2.3 Functional Description of Analog Processing

The 64 analog voltage inputs first get converted to currents by a set of V-I converters at the beginning of each row of the 64 x 64 synaptic array. These signals are then current mirrored into all 64 synapses along the row so that all the synapses in a given row receive identical input signals.

At each synapse, a byte, which controls switches to scale current copies of the input, is stored in respective local static memories (SRAM) constituting as weights. Synapses on the same column have their outputs, Iout, summed by attaching them all to the same wire. These 64 summed signals, one for each column of the array, are then sent directly out every 250 nanoseconds as shown in Figure 1. In the 3D scheme, respective column outputs of all the 64 chips are added together through edge-wise metallization, so that a 64x64-pixel incoming image multiplies with 64, 64x64 templates on 64 chips to provide 64 analog inner-product current outputs. The process is repeated by sequentially inputting the adjoining 64x64 image windows, "row-by-row" and "column-by-column". Thus a 256x256-image convolution is completed in about 16 milliseconds (equivalent speed of $\sim 10^{12}$ operations/s).

2.4 Digital Weight Programming

Before the processing can begin, the synapse weights as 64x64 templates are obtained separately. An approach based on eigenvectors was developed to evaluate the hardware. Since each data point (image) is a 4096-element vector, finding a set of 4096 orthonormal eigenvectors is possible (64 of these can then reside on 3DANN at a time). Selecting the most significant 64 eigenvectors constructed from principal component analysis of target imagery reduces dimensionality of image sets, without losing much of the information relevant for classification. The register loads from the bottom up so that the first data loaded corresponds to the first row. More details can be found in [1,3] and in their citations. Incorporating a multi-synapse circuit as an analog multiplier makes the network extremely powerful image-processing engine capable of carrying out in parallel 64 convolutions of the form:

$$c_i(x,y) = f(x,y)\, g_i(x,y); \quad i = 1, 2, ..., 64; \tag{2.1}$$

where $\mathbf{f}$ is the input image, $\mathbf{g}_i$ is the ith filter mask, and $\mathbf{c}_i$ is the ith output.

2.5 Processing Results

To estimate the speed advantage, an image-processing example was used. As a comparison, the convolution operations on a 256x256 image would only take 16 milliseconds using our 3D MCM. However, the same processing would take as much as 2.5 hours using SPARC-10, and a few minutes with digital signal processor such as SHARC. Thus, the hardware provides orders of magnitude speed advantage.

Information about the object (its class, identity, or pose) is processed iteratively in a coarse-to-fine manner using subsequent image frames. For instance, after detecting an object in a frame, a rough estimate of image pose/scale is made, a result that can then be used to limit the variation that needs to be considered during object classification (i.e., plane, helicopter, and missile). Results (Figure 2) using the technique described here have achieved nearly 97% detection rates, 94% classification rates for determining the angle of the principal dimension of an object with respect to the image (±30°), and object classification rates approaching 95%. Results on object/non-object image classification rates achieved with a helicopter/missile/plane data set were also very encouraging [3]. Also see Ref [4-6] for other application examples.

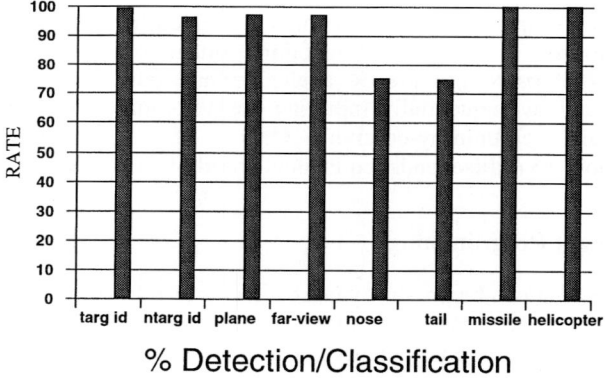

% Detection/Classification

Fig. 2. High detection/classification rates are achieved on selected data sets that include all possible orientations and scales of targets.

3 Evolvable Hardware (EHW)

An evolvable hardware system consists of two main components: the reconfigurable hardware (RH) and the reconfiguration mechanism (RM). In previously reported research, the evolutionary processor (EP) that acts as an RM was implemented on a variety of platforms including supercomputer, single PC, DSP, FPGA, and ASIC. The RH was approached as simulated model of unconstrained topology, real FPGA, FPAA model or actual chips, FPTA model or actual chip. For a survey on these different applications the reader is referred to [7,8].

Most simulation approaches have demonstrated that circuit evolution times can vary from a few seconds to hours and days. Further, real-world uses will require compact, low-power, autonomous, and stand-alone EHW, especially for a variety of NASA and DoD applications. An effort in transitioning from PC-simulated or PC-controlled evolutions to embedded and ultimately to integrated system-on-a-chip evolvable systems is required, because in general, a circuit evolution using simulation models such as SPICE take many seconds to minutes, just to go through one iteration versus a circuit in hardware that takes only a fraction of a second.

3.1 A Stand-Alone Board-Level Evolvable System (SABLES)

A board-level solution provides autonomous, fast (1,000 circuit evaluations per second), on-chip circuit reconfiguration. Its main components are a JPL-designed Field Programmable Transistor Array (FPTA) chip as a transistor-level reconfigurable hardware, and a Texas Instruments DSP implementing the evolutionary algorithm as the controller for reconfiguration. An overview of the components of SABLE is provided below, including the FPTA2 chip and the DSP system. The evolution of a half-wave rectifier circuit is presented to illustrate how the system functions.

3.2 SABLES Components

As mentioned, SABLES integrates an FPTA and a DSP implementing the Evolutionary Platform (EP). The system is stand-alone and is connected to a PC only for the purpose of receiving specifications and communicating back the results of evolution for analysis. The FPTA is an implementation of an evolution-oriented reconfigurable architecture (EORA) [7]. The lack of evolution-oriented devices, in particular for analog, has been an important stumbling block for researchers attempting evolution in intrinsic mode (with evaluation directly in hardware). Extrinsic evolution (using simulated models) is slow and scales badly when performed accurately e.g. in SPICE), and less accurate models may lead to solutions that behave differently in hardware than in software simulations. The FPTA has transistor level reconfigurability and supports any arrangement of programming bits without danger of damage to the chip (as is the case with some commercial devices).

Three generations of FPTA chips have been built and used in evolutionary experiments. The latest chip, FPTA-2, consists of an 8x8 array of reconfigurable cells. Each cell has a transistor array as well as a set of programmable resources, including programmable resistors and static capacitors. Figure 3 provides a block diagram of the chip architecture on the left and a schematic of the reconfigurable transistor array cell on the right. The reconfigurable circuitry consists of 14 transistors connected through 44 switches and is able to implement different building blocks for analog processing, such as two- and three-stage operational amplifiers, logarithmic photo detectors, or Gaussian computational circuits. It includes three capacitors, Cm1, Cm2 and Cc, of 100fF, 100fF and 5pF value respectively. The evolutionary algorithm was implemented in a DSP that directly controlled the FPTA, together forming a board-level evolvable system with fast internal communication ensured by a 32-bit bus operating at 7.5MHz. Details of the EP were presented in [9]. SABLES is compact enough to fit in a box 20x20x8 cm^3 in size.

3.3 An Evolution on SABLES

The following experiments illustrate evolution on SABLES. The objective of the first experiment is to synthesize a half-wave rectifier circuit. The testing of candidate circuits is made for an excitation input of 2kHz sine wave of amplitude 2V. A computed rectified waveform of this signal is considered as the target. The fitness function rewards those individuals exhibiting behavior closer to target (using a simple sum of differences between the response of a circuit and target) and penalizes those farther from it. After evaluation of 100 individuals, they are sorted according to fitness and a 9% portion (elite percentage) is set aside, the remaining individuals undergoing first crossover (70% rate), either among themselves or with an individual from elite, and then mutation (4% rate). In this experiment only two cells of the FPTA was allocated.

In the second experiment, evolution builds a circuit able to extract two sine waves (independent source signals) from linear combinations of these sources: the evolving circuit is excited with two different linear combinations of the source signals, and the two circuit outputs should respectively restore each source signal. In this signal separation experiment, the GA parameters were: 70% mutation rate; 20% crossover rate; replacement factor of 20%; population of 400; and 100 to 200 generations. Each execution took about 5 minutes in the SABLES system. More than 20 different GA executions were performed. The fitness was the sum of the absolute difference between the FFT of the output signals and the target values over a spectrum between 1kHz and 50kHz. Figure 4 displays snapshots of evolution in progress in the rectifier experiment, illustrating the response of the best individual in the population over a set of generations. Figure 4 a) shows the best individual of the initial population, while Figures 4. b), c), & d) show the best after 5, 50 and 82 generations, and the solution, with a fitness value below a required minimum is shown on the right in Fig. 4.

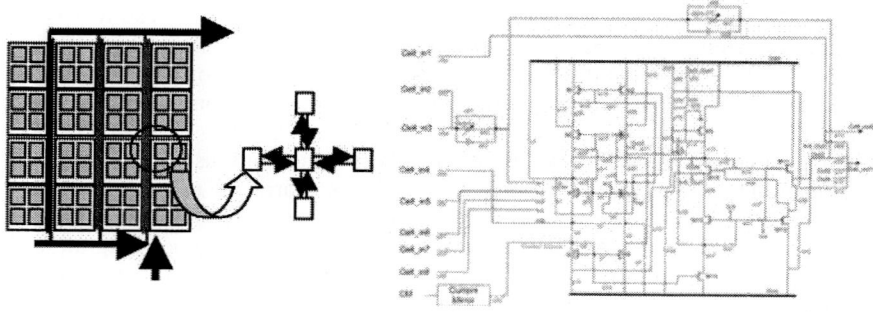

Fig. 3. FPTA 2 architecture (left) and schematic of cell transistor array (right). The cell contains additional capacitors and programmable resistors (not shown).

In the second experiment, evolution was designed to build a circuit able to extract two sine waves (independent source signals) from linear combinations of these sources: the evolving circuit is excited with two different linear combinations of the source signals, and the two circuit outputs respectively separate these source signals. Thus, in the signal separation experiment, we selected two sine waves of frequencies $f_1 = 10kHz$ and $f_2 = 20kHz$ as source signals. More than 20 different GA executions were performed. The fitness was the sum of the absolute difference between the FFT of the output signals and the target values over a spectrum between 1kHz and 50kHz.

The set of experiments was performed using 10 cells of the FPTA-2. Figure 5 depicts the inputs and outputs of the best circuit achieved in this experiment. For further details the reader can refer to [10].

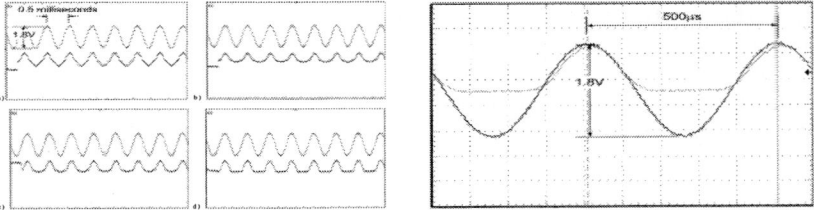

Fig. 4. Evolution of a halfwave rectifier showing the response of the best individual of generation a) 1, b) 5, c) 50 and finally the solution at generation d) 82. The final solution is illustrated on the right.

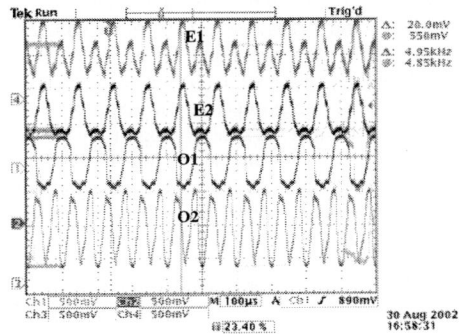

Fig. 5. Result of a signal separation experiment. At the top inputs E1, E2, & at the bottom, outputs O1 (10kHz), O2 (20kHz) are shown.

3.4 Results

SABLES achieves about 1-2 orders of magnitude reduction in memory and nearly 4 and 2 orders of magnitude speed enhancement compared to systems that evolve using respectively single and 16 CPU processor simulations [9], and about 1 order of magnitude reduction in volume and 1 order of magnitude improvement in speed (through improved communication) compared to a PC-controlled system using the same FPTA chip. In the signal separation experiment, each trial takes about 5 to 10 minutes. This means a 1 to 2 orders of magnitude speed enhancement compared to systems evolving in simulations.

4 Conclusions

Soft computing architectures have been realized in hardware. Examples of neural network and evolution based hardware have been described with their demonstrated results. They have consistently shown not only compact and low power attributes but also orders of magnitude speed enhancements including enabling nature for certain applications pertaining to on-board deployable systems.

Acknowledgements. The research described in this paper was performed at the Center for Advanced Avionics, Jet Propulsion Laboratory, California Institute of Technology and was sponsored by the National Aeronautics and Space Administration, the Missile Defense Agency, and the Defense Advanced Research Projects Agency.

References

[1] Duong, TA, Daud T, Thakoor AP (1995) United States Patent #5479579, Cascaded VLSI neural network architecture for on-line learning.
[2] Stoica A, Keymeulen D, Tawel R, Lazaro C, Li W-T (1999) Evolutionary experiments with a fine-grained reconfigurable architecture for analog and digital CMOS circuits. In Stoica A, Keymeulen D, Lohn J (eds) Proc. First NASA/DOD Workshop on Evolvable Hardware, IEEE Computer Society Press, pp. 77–84.
[3] Udomkesmalee S, Thakoor A, Padgett C, Daud T, Fang W-C, Suddarth SC (1997) VIGILANTE: An advanced sensing/processing testbed for ATR applications. In Sadjadi FA (ed) Proc. SPIE Conf. Automatic Target Recognition VII vol. 3069, pp. 82–93.
[4] Howard A, Padgett C (1999) Real time intelligent target detection and analysis with machine vision In Computational Intelligence: Methods and Applications (CIMA).
[5] Howard A, Padgett C, Brown K (1999) Intelligent target detection in hyperspectral imagery In Proceedings of the Thirteenth International Conference on Applied Geologic Remote Sensing.
[6] Howard A, Padgett C (2000) A generalized approach to real-time pattern recognition in sensed data. In Pattern Recognition.
[7] Stoica A, Zebulum R, Keymeulen D, Tawel R, Daud T, Thakoor A (2001), Reconfigurable VLSI Architectures for evolvable hardware: from experimental field programmable transistor arrays to evolution-oriented chips. In IEEE Transactions on VLSI Systems, Special Issue on Reconfigurable and Adaptive VLSI Systems, vol 9, pp. 227–232.
[8] Stoica A, Lohn J, Keymeulen D (eds) Proceedings of the First NASA/DOD Workshop on Evolvable Hardware. IEEE Computer Society Press.
[9] Ferguson MI, Stoica A, Zebulum R, Keymeulen D, Duong V (2002) An evolvable hardware platform based on DSP and FPTA. In AAAI/Proceedings of the Genetic and Evolutionary Computation Conference – Late Breaking Papers, New York, NY, pp 145–152.
[10] Zebulum RS, Stoica A, Keymeulen D, Ferguson MI, Duong V, Guo X, Vorperian V (2003), Automatic evolution of tunable filters using SABLES. In Tyrrell AM, Haddow PC, Torresen J (eds) 5th International Conference Evolvable Systems: From Biology to Hardware, Springer, pp 286–295.

Neural Networks Applied to Electromagnetic Compatibility (EMC) Simulations

Hüseyin Göksu and Donald C. Wunsch II

Applied Computational Intelligence Lab,
Department of Electrical and Computer Engineering,
University of Missouri-Rolla,
1870 Miner Circle,
G11 Emerson Electric Co. Hall,
Rolla, Missouri, 65409, USA
{hgbmf, dwunsch}@ece.umr.edu
http://www.ece.umr.edu/acil

Abstract. Data extrapolation in FDTD simulations using feedforward multi-layer Perceptron (MLP) showed promising results in a previous study. This work studies two different aspects of the problem: First is the learning aspect, including the effect of prior training with the same class of random signals, which is an attempt to find a general solution to the weight initialization problem in adaptive systems. The second aspect covers the steps to make the extrapolator fully adaptive, through optimization of the time step sensitivity and the input layer width of a sliding window extrapolator. Average mutual information is used as a performance measure in most of the work.

1 Introduction

Finite Difference Time Domain (FDTD) simulations, which are widely used for simulating EMC characteristics of systems, are computationally very expensive. In order to boost the efficiency of the algorithm by stopping the simulation after a sufficient number of time steps and having an MLP extrapolate the rest of the signal, recent work has shown successful prediction results compared to some linear eigenanalysis predictors [2]. One of the problems reported was the weight initialization, which kept the percentage of successful predictions low. This work attempts to look into this problem, which is common in all training algorithms requiring weight initialization. Another improvement to the aforementioned work is making the code adaptive for different time step sensitivities, and choosing an appropriate input layer width. This problem is overcome by using information theoretic measures. Overall results of this work are directly adaptable to analysis of other impulse response time series. Extension to other classes of signals needs further examination.

Organization of the paper is as follows: Section 2 reviews time domain EMC simulations and improvements to them; Section 3 examines the weight initialization and other training issues of the extrapolators; Section 4 applies information theoretic measures to adaptation of the NN to various signals and Section 5 is Conclusions.

2 Electromagnetic Compatibility Simulations

FDTD is a common method where impulse response of an electromagnetic system is simulated in time domain [5]. Output of the simulation is transformed to frequency domain, because measuring instruments work in this domain, and the behavior of the systems depends highly on frequency due to the resonant structures in systems.

As an example, shielding properties of enclosures can be simulated by their impulse response. Apparently, a perfect impulse is equivalent to flat white noise and shielding of an enclosure depends on the degree of attenuation it performs for different frequencies. The method is to induce an impulse from inside the enclosure and measure the attenuated signal outside.

If the geometry of the system to be tested is fully known, propagation of the impulse through the system can be simulated by FDTD through discretized Maxwell equations by computing the electric and magnetic fields, one following another, through two consecutive grids. As the system under test gets bigger, the simulation becomes computationally unaffordable. Namely, the shielding property of an enclosure might need to be simulated for as long as several weeks.

We know that FDTD simulations are not efficient but they are one of the best simulation tools at hand. The waste of resources in an FDTD simulation can be understood by considering the fact that two very different geometries having the same volume but very different complexity levels would require the same computational complexity as long as they have resonant structures. FDTD does not use the inherent symmetries in the systems, so the waste of resources is obvious.

Reducing the computational cost of such simulations would make more simulations possible, hence result in more creative and better designs. If we consider that most time domain simulations work in the same principle, any attempt for such an improvement may help improve the whole group.

An improvement model to FDTD is capturing the patterns inherent in the output time domain signal, using an extrapolator, from its partial results. The best such extrapolator reported so far are two NN models. The first work is the comparison of an FIR network with a linear ARMA extrapolator [3]. Second is the comparison between a feedforward MLP extrapolator with that of a linear matrix pencil extrapolator [2]. Like their high performance in system identification [4], NN methods performed better.

3 Learning and Parameter Initialization Issues

In supervised learning, the output of a dynamic modeler is compared with the desired output, and the network variables are optimized using the resulting cost function. The NN most likely has multiple optima, which may represent completely different systems, all corresponding to the same training sets. In almost every practical case, there is a great chance that the global minimum, which looks like the most efficient solution, is not necessarily the most effective solution, because it may restrict flexibility. An example for this case may be the overtraining of a NN which restricts generalization even if the state corresponds to the global optimum. As it is hard to embed all the desired features like 'generalization' as numerical variables and put them into the global optimization scheme, we need another way to deal with this issue.

Neural networks may not be the most efficient modeling systems. However, they are effective, because they can exploit prior information. Prior learning of a neural network corresponds to weight initialization. Typically, if one assumes existence of regions, which include local optima corresponding to solutions reachable with derivative-based training, then one of such solutions can be used as an initial weight assignment for any of the others.

Most inverse problems using global optimization have similar characteristics with the learning paradigm mentioned above, and advancements in this area may affect the outcome of all.

The signals used in prior training are of the same kind, as that of the signal for testing the NN extrapolator, namely in the form of exponentially decaying sinusoidals:

$$S(t) = \sum_i \sin(w_i t - \theta_i) e^{-t/\tau_i} \tag{1}$$

The generating variables, which are the decay constants and sinusoidal frequencies, were varied randomly in their 100% neighborhood by starting from the predicted signal, shown in Figure 1. Figure 2 shows a sample from the varied signals. The successful predictors for each of the signals were used as an initial training condition for the varied versions. The results were compared with that of random initializations in terms of successful predictions and training epochs of the Levenberg Marquardt backpropagation algorithm (Table 1). Average mutual information between the signals seems to be a significant indicator to judge whether the extrapolator of two signals can be used for initialization for the other. Results show significant improvement over random initializations.

Table 1. Comparison between predictions

Weight Initialization	Average mutual information between the actual signal and the signal used for prior training		Rate of successful predictions		Number of training epochs for convergence	
	Mean	Std. dev.	Mean	Std. dev.	Mean	Std. dev.
With prior training	5.9	1.8	88%	8%	90	32
Random	0.001	0.01	6%	2%	350	180

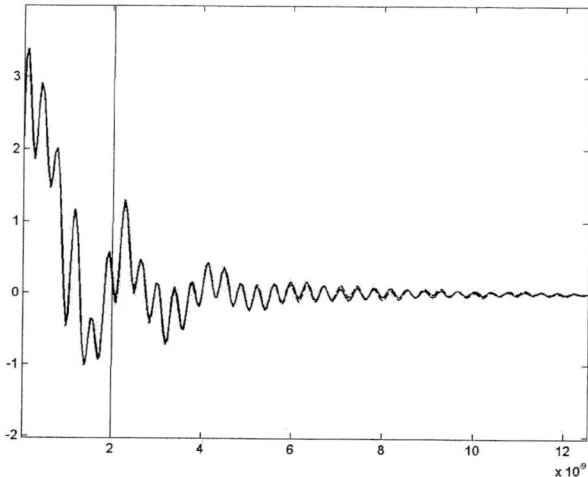

Fig. 1. Extrapolated signal sample; solid line represents the actual signal and dashed line represents the predicted signal, vertical line shows the point where prediction starts

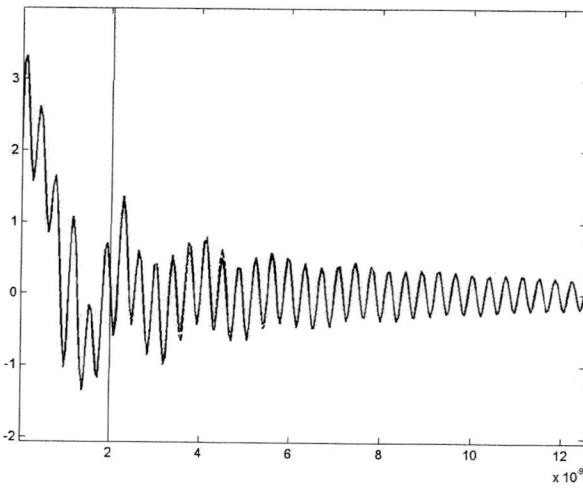

Fig. 2. Varied version of the extrapolated signal in Fig. 1; solid line represents the actual signal and dashed line represents the predicted signal, vertical line shows the point where prediction starts

4 Code Adaptivity Issues

Adaptability of the code for different time step sensitivities and avoiding oversampling are the two main problems. A previous study [1] proposed using mutual information for adapting the sampling rate and false nearest neighborhood method for the proper window size. Here, we have made an extension and used average mutual information for optimizing the window size as well. The steps are:

1. Finding a suitable input size, where we are sure that the signal is not over-sampled: For this purpose we took the first minimum of the average mutual information between sliding windows versus window size. For our signal this corresponded to 6 neurons (Figure 3).
2. Finding the optimal network topology: This was done by the method of pruning. Our network has one hidden layer of 3 neurons. We have used a feedforward architecture, not because it is better than recurrent ones, but because it is more convenient for especially training analysis made in the previous section.
3. Training the NN with a learning algorithm: We used Levenberg Marquardt version of backpropagation.
4. For a new signal, resampling the signal looking at the first minimum of the average mutual information between sliding windows versus sampling rate (Figure 4).

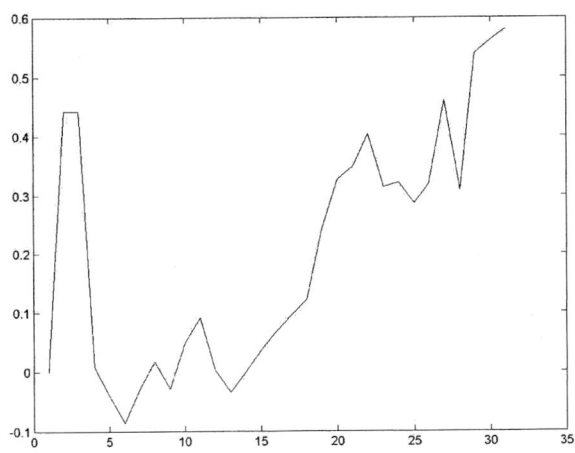

Fig. 3. Average mutual information between sliding windows versus window size

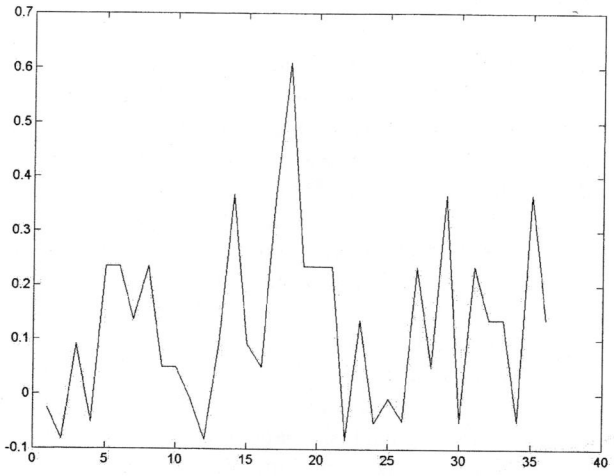

Fig. 4. Average mutual information between sliding windows versus sampling rate

5 Summary

The solution proposed at the beginning of this work for weight initialization in NN training for FDTD-type signal extrapolators seems to be promising. This weight initialization scheme, which uses the topology of successful extrapolators of different signals of the same class in weight initialization of the other, improves the extrapolation success rate and the training rate. Extension of this method to other classes of signals or systems may require further research. Average mutual information between the signals looks like a good measure to judge whether extrapolator of a signal can be used for weight initialization for the other.

Average mutual information is a good judge for deciding on sampling rate of specified time domain signals and on window size of the specified time domain sliding window NN extrapolators. Extension to different signals may require additional work.

Acknowledgements. We gratefully acknowledge the financial support received from National Science Foundation and M. K. Finley Endowment for this research.

References

1. Ababarnel, H. D. I., Brown, R., Sidorowich, J. L., Tsimring, L. S.: The analysis of observed chaotic data in physical systems. Rev. of Modern Physics. Vol. 65 (1993) 1331–1392

2. Göksu, H., Selli, G., Wunsch, D. C. II.: FDTD data extrapolation using multilayer perceptron (MLP). IEEE Symp. EMC 2003-Boston. (2003) Accepted.
3. Wu, C., Navarro, A., Litva, J.: Combination of finite impulse response neural network technique with FDTD method for simulation of electromagnetic problems. Electron. Lett., Vol. 32. (1996) 1112–1113
4. Narendra, K., Parthasarathy, K.: Identification and control of dynamical systems using neural networks. Trans. Neural Networks, Vol. 78 (1990) 4–27
5. Taflove, A., Umashankar, K. R.: Review of FDTD numerical modeling of electromagnetic wave scattering and radar cross section. Proc. IEEE, Vol. 77 (1989) 682–699

Sliding Mode Algorithm for Online Learning in Analog Multilayer Feedforward Neural Networks

Nikola G. Shakev[1], Andon V. Topalov[1,2], and Okyay Kaynak[2]

[1] Technical University Sofia, branch Plovdiv, Control Systems Department,
25, Canko Dustabanov str., 4000 Plovdiv, Bulgaria
nikolashakev@yahoo.com, topalov@mbox.digsys.bg
[2] Bogazici University, Electrical and Electronic Engineering Department, Bebek,
80815, Istanbul, Turkey
{topalov,kaynak}@boun.edu.tr

Abstract. A new dynamical sliding mode control algorithm is proposed for robust adaptive learning in analog multilayer feedforward networks with a scalar output. These type neural structures are widely used for modeling, identification and control of nonlinear dynamical systems. The zero level set of the learning error variable is considered as a sliding surface in the space of network learning parameters. The convergence of the algorithm is established and conditions are given. Its effectiveness is shown when applied to on-line learning of non-monotonic function using a two-layered feedforward neural network.

1 Introduction

In the theory of control engineering, one way of designing a robust and stable control system is to use the Variable Structure Systems (VSS) approach, which enables the designer to come up with a rigorous stability analysis. The studies demonstrating the high performance of the variable structure control in handling the uncertainties and imprecision have motivated the use of sliding mode control (SMC) scheme in training of artificial neural networks (ANN). The results presented in [1] have shown that the convergence properties of the gradient-based training strategies can be improved by utilizing the SMC scheme. The method presented can be considered as an indirect use of VSS theory. Some studies on the direct use of SMC strategy are also reported in the literature [2-5]. In [2] the zero level set of the learning error variable in Adaline neural networks is regarded as a sliding surface in the space of learning parameters. A sliding mode trajectory can then be induced, in finite time, on such a desired sliding manifold. Yu et al. [3] extend further the results of [2] by introducing adaptive uncertainty bound dynamics of the signals.

Learning algorithm for training multilayer artificial neural networks, based on direct use of SMC strategy, was recently proposed by G. G. Parma et al. [4-5]. In addition to its applicability for updating the weights of multilayer network structures it also differs from the algorithms in [2-3] due to the definition of separate sliding surfaces for the different network layers.

In the present paper the sliding mode strategy for adaptive learning in Adaline networks proposed in [2] is further extended to more general classes of multilayer neuron arrangements. The main difference of the proposed algorithm from the one presented in [4] is that only one sliding surface is defined.

The main body of the paper contains four sections. Section II presents the SMC approach to weight adaptation in perceptron-based multilayer ANN with a scalar output. Simulation results are shown in Section III. Finally, section IV summarizes the findings of this investigation.

2 A Sliding Mode Control Approach for Learning in Multilayer Feedforward Networks with a Scalar Output

2.1 Definitions and Basic Assumptions

Consider the two-layered feedforward neural network shown on Fig. 1. We will use the following definitions:

$X(t) = \left[x_1(t), \ldots, x_p(t) \right]^T$ – vector of the time-varying input signals augmented by the bias term.

$Y_H(t) = \left[y_{H1}(t), \ldots, y_{Hn}(t) \right]^T$ – vector of the output signals of the neurons in the hidden layer.

$y(t)$ – scalar signal representing the time-varying output of the network.

$W1(t)_{(n \times p)}$ – matrix of the time-varying connections' weights between the neurons in the input and the hidden layer, where each matrix's element $w1_{i,j}(t)$ means the weight of the connection of the neuron i from its input j.

$W2(t)_{(1 \times n)} = \left[w2_1(t), \ldots, w2_n(t) \right]$ – vector of the time-varying connections' weights between the neurons in the hidden layer and the output node. Both $W1(t)_{(n \times p)}$ and $W2(t)_{(1 \times n)}$ are considered augmented by including the bias weight components for the neurons in the hidden layer and the output neuron respectively.

$N1(t)$ – vector representing the time-varying output signals of the neurons in hidden layer before applying the activation functions (the neurons net input signals).

$f(\cdot)$ – nonlinear, differentiable, monotonously increasing activation function of the neurons in the hidden layer of the network (e. g. log-sigmoid or tan-sigmoid function). The neuron in the output layer of the neural network is considered with a linear activation function.

An assumption is made that the input vector $X(t) = \left[x_1(t), \ldots, x_p(t) \right]^T$ and it's time derivative $\dot{X}(t) = \left[\dot{x}_1(t), \ldots, \dot{x}_p(t) \right]^T$ are bounded, i.e.

$$\|X(t)\| = \sqrt{x_1^2(t) + \ldots + x_p^2(t)} \leq B_X \quad \forall t$$
$$\|\dot{X}(t)\| = \sqrt{\dot{x}_1^2(t) + \ldots + \dot{x}_p^2(t)} \leq B_{\dot{X}} \quad \forall t \tag{1}$$

where B_X and $B_{\dot{X}}$ are known positive constants.

It will be assumed that, due to the physical constraints, the magnitude of all vectors row $W1_i(t)$ constituting the matrix $W1(t)$ and the elements of the vector $W2(t)$ are also bounded at each instant of time t by means of

$$\|W1_i(t)\| = \sqrt{w1_{i,1}^2(t) + w1_{i,2}^2(t) + \ldots + w1_{i,p}^2(t)} \leq B_{W1} \quad \forall t$$
$$|w2_i(t)| \leq B_{W2} \quad \forall t \tag{2}$$

for some known constants B_{W1} and B_{W2}, where $i = 1, 2, \ldots, n$

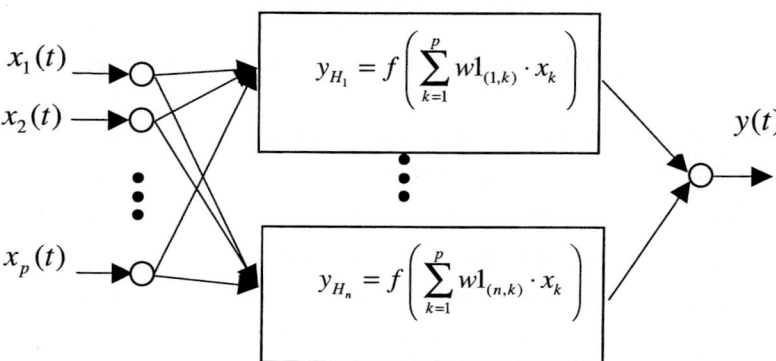

Fig. 1. Multilayer feedforward neural network with a scalar output.

The scalar signal $y_d(t)$ represents the time-varying desired output of the neural network. It will be assumed that $y_d(t)$ and $\dot{y}_d(t)$ are also bounded signals, i.e.,

$$|y_d(t)| \leq B_{y_d}, \quad |\dot{y}_d(t)| \leq B_{\dot{y}_d} \quad \forall t \tag{3}$$

where B_{y_d} and $B_{\dot{y}_d}$ are positive constants.

The output signal $y(t)$ is a scalar quantity defined as:

$$y(t) = \sum_{i=1}^{n} w2_i f\left[\sum_{j=1}^{p} w1_{i,j} \cdot x_j\right] \tag{4}$$

We define the learning error $e(t)$ as the scalar quantity obtained from

$$e(t) = y(t) - y_d(t) \tag{5}$$

2.2 Problem Formulation and Main Results

Using the SMC approach, we define the zero value of the learning error coordinate $e(t)$ as a time-varying sliding surface, i.e.,

$$S(e(t)) = e(t) = y(t) - y_d(t) = 0 \tag{6}$$

which is the condition that guarantees that the neural network output $y(t)$ coincides with the desired output signal $y_d(t)$ for all time $t > t_h$ where t_h is the hitting time of $e = 0$.

Definition 2.1. A sliding motion will have place on a sliding manifold $S(e(t)) = e(t) = 0$, after time t_h, if the condition $S(t)\dot{S}(t) = e(t)\dot{e}(t) < 0$ is true for all t in some nontrivial semi open subinterval of time of the form $[t, t_h) \subset (-\infty, t_h)$. The learning algorithm for the neural network weights $W1(t)$ and $W2(t)$ should be derived in such a way that the sliding mode condition of definition 2.1 will be enforced.

Let us denote as "$sign(e(t))$" the signum function, defined as follows

$$sign(e) = \begin{cases} 1 & \text{for } e(t) > 0 \\ 0 & \text{for } e(t) = 0 \\ -1 & \text{for } e(t) < 0 \end{cases} \tag{7}$$

To enable $S = 0$ is reached, we have the following theorem:

Theorem 2.2: If the learning algorithm for the weights $W1(t)$ and $W2(t)$ is chosen respectively as

$$\dot{w}1_{i,j} = -\left(\frac{w2_i x_j}{X^T X}\right) \alpha \, sign(e), \quad \dot{w}2_i = -\left(\frac{y_{Hi}}{Y_H^T Y_H}\right) \alpha \, sign(e) \tag{8}$$

with α being sufficiently large positive constant satisfying

$$\alpha > nB_A B_{W1} B_{\dot{X}} B_{W2} + B_{\dot{Y}_d} \tag{9}$$

then, for any arbitrary initial condition $e(0)$, the learning error $e(t)$ will converge to zero during a finite time t_h which may be estimated as

$$t_h \leq \frac{|e(0)|}{\alpha - nB_A B_{W2} B_{W1} B_{\dot{X}} - B_{\dot{Y}_d}} \tag{10}$$

and a sliding motion will be maintained on $e = 0$ for all $t > t_h$.

Proof: We choose the Lyapunov function candidate as follows:

$$V(e(t)) = \frac{1}{2} e^2(t) \tag{11}$$

Then differentiating $V(e(t))$ yields

$$\dot{V}(e(t)) = e\dot{e} = e(\dot{y} - \dot{y}_d) = e\left\{\left[\sum_{i=1}^{n} w2_i f\left(\sum_{j=1}^{p} w1_{i,j} x_j\right)\right]' - \dot{y}_d\right\} =$$

$$= e\left[\sum_{i=1}^{n} \dot{w}2_i f\left(\sum_{j=1}^{p} w1_{i,j} x_j\right) + \right.$$

$$\left. + \sum_{i=1}^{n} w2_i f'\left(\sum_{j=1}^{p} w1_{i,j} x_j\right) \sum_{j=1}^{p} \left(\dot{w}1_{i,j} x_j + w1_{i,j} \dot{x}_j\right) - \dot{y}_d\right] =$$

$$= e\left[\sum_{i=1}^{n} \dot{w}2_i y_{Hi} + \sum_{i=1}^{n} w2_i A_i \sum_{j=1}^{p} \left(\dot{w}1_{i,j} x_j + w1_{i,j} \dot{x}_j\right) - \dot{y}_d\right] =$$

$$= e\left[-\sum_{i=1}^{n} \frac{y_{Hi}}{Y_H^T Y_H} \alpha \, sign(e) y_{Hi} + \right.$$

$$\left. + \sum_{i=1}^{n} A_i \sum_{j=1}^{p} \left(-\left(\frac{w2_i x_j}{X^T X}\right) \alpha \, sign(e) x_j w2_i + w1_{i,j} \dot{x}_j w2_i\right) - \dot{y}_d\right] =$$

$$= e\left(-\alpha \, sign(e) - \sum_{i=1}^{n} A_i \alpha w2_i^2 \, sign(e) + \sum_{i=1}^{n} A_i w2_i \sum_{j=1}^{p} w1_{i,j} \dot{x}_j - \dot{y}_d\right) =$$

$$= -\alpha|e| - \alpha|e|\sum_{i=1}^{n} A_i w2_i^2 + e\sum_{i=1}^{n} A_i w2_i \sum_{j=1}^{p} w1_{i,j} \dot{x}_j - e\dot{y}_d =$$

$$= -\left(\alpha + \alpha \sum_{i=1}^{n} A_i w2_i^2\right)|e| + \left(\sum_{i=1}^{n} A_i w2_i \sum_{j=1}^{p} w1_{i,j} \dot{x}_j - \dot{y}_d\right) e \leq \tag{12}$$

$$\leq -\alpha |e| + e\left(\sum_{i=1}^{n} A_i w2_i \sum_{j=1}^{p} w1_{i,j} \dot{x}_j - \dot{y}_d\right) \leq$$

$$\leq -\alpha |e| + \left(nB_A B_{W2} B_{W1} B_{\dot{X}} + B_{\dot{Y}_d}\right)|e| =$$

$$= |e|\left(-\alpha + nB_A B_{W2} B_{W1} B_{\dot{X}} + B_{\dot{Y}_d}\right) < 0 \quad \forall e \neq 0$$

where $A_i(t)$, $0 < A_i(t) = f'\left(\sum_{j=1}^{p} w1_{i,j} x_j\right) \leq B_A \quad \forall i, j$ is the derivative of the neurons' activation function $f(.)$ and B_A corresponds to its maximum value.

The inequality (12) means that the controlled trajectories of the learning error $e(t)$ converge to zero in a stable manner.

It is possible now to be shown that such a convergence takes place in finite time. The differential equation that is satisfied by the controlled error trajectories $e(t)$ is as follows

$$\dot{e}(t) = -\alpha sign(e) - \left(\sum_{i=1}^{n} A_i w2_i^2\right)\alpha sign(e) + \sum_{i=1}^{n} A_i w2_i \sum_{j=1}^{p} w1_{i,j} \dot{x}_j - \dot{y}_d =$$

$$= -\left(1 + \sum_{i=1}^{n} A_i w2_i^2\right)\alpha \, sign(e) + \sum_{i=1}^{n} A_i w2_i \sum_{j=1}^{p} w1_{i,j} \dot{x}_j - \dot{y}_d \qquad (13)$$

For any $t \leq t_h$, the solution, $e(t)$, of this equation, with initial condition $e(0)$ at $t = 0$, satisfies

$$e(t) - e(0) = \int_0^t \dot{e}(\sigma) d\sigma =$$

$$= \int_0^t \left[-\alpha sign(e(\sigma))\left(1 + \sum_{i=1}^{n} A_i(\sigma) w2_i^2(\sigma)\right) + \right.$$

$$\left. + \sum_{i=1}^{n} A_i(\sigma) w2_i(\sigma) \sum_{j=1}^{p} w1_{i,j}(\sigma) \dot{x}_j(\sigma) - \dot{y}_d(\sigma)\right] d\sigma \qquad (14)$$

at time $t = t_a$ the solution takes zero value and, therefore,

$$-e(0) = \int_0^{t_h} \left[-\alpha \, sign(e(0))\left(1 + \sum_{i=1}^{n} A_i(t) w2_i^2(t)\right) + \right.$$

$$\left. + \sum_{i=1}^{n} A_i(t) w2_i(t) \sum_{j=1}^{p} w1_{i,j}(t) \dot{x}_j(t) - \dot{y}_d(t)\right] dt =$$

$$= -\alpha \, sign(e(0))\left[t_h + \int_0^{t_h} \left(\sum_{i=1}^{n} A_i(t) w2_i^2(t)\right) dt\right] + \qquad (15)$$

$$+\int_0^{t_h}\left(\sum_{i=1}^n A_i(t)w2_i(t)\sum_{j=1}^p w1_{i,j}(t)\dot{x}_j(t)-\dot{y}_d(t)\right)dt$$

By multiplying both sides of the equation by $-sign(e(0))$ the estimate of t_h in (10) can be found using the inequality (16).

$$|e(0)|=\alpha t_h+\alpha\int_0^{t_h}\left(\sum_{i=1}^n A_i(t)w2_i^2(t)\right)dt-$$

$$-sign(e(0))\int_0^{t_h}\left(\sum_{i=1}^n A_i(t)w2_i(t)\sum_{j=1}^p w1_{i,j}(t)\dot{x}_j(t)-\dot{y}_d(t)\right)dt\geq$$

$$\geq\alpha\left(t_h+\int_0^{t_h}\left(\sum_{i=1}^n A_i(t)w2_i^2(t)\right)dt\right)-\left(nB_AB_{W2}B_{W1}B_{\dot{X}}+B_{\dot{Y}_d}\right)t_h\geq$$

$$\geq\left[\alpha-\left(nB_AB_{W2}B_{W1}B_{\dot{X}}+B_{\dot{Y}_d}\right)\right]t_h$$

(16)

Obviously, for all times $t<t_h$, taking into account the chosen sliding mode controller gain α in (9), it follows from (13) that

$$e(t)\dot{e}(t)=-\alpha|e(t)|\left(1+\sum_{i=1}^n A_i(t)w2_i^2(t)\right)+$$

$$+\left(\sum_{i=1}^n A_i(t)w2_i(t)\sum_{j=1}^p w1_{i,j}(t)\dot{x}_j(t)-\dot{y}_d(t)\right)e(t)\leq$$

$$\leq\left(-\alpha+nB_AB_{W2}B_{W1}B_{\dot{X}}+B_{\dot{Y}_d}\right)|e(t)|<0$$

(17)

and a sliding motion exists on $e(t)=0$ for $t>t_h$.

3 Application to Online Learning of Nonlinear Functions

In this section, the effectiveness of the proposed algorithm is evaluated when compared to the standard backpropagation approach for neural network weights adaptation in one-line learning of the function $f(t)=e^{-1/3}\sin(3t)$. The latter is commonly used as benchmark since it is non-monotonic. Simulations where carried on using fixed learning rate parameters, so that the comparison is not masked by supporting improvement algorithms. The learning rates that yield the best results were chosen. In addition to this both compared algorithms where started from the same initial conditions, so that a good balance was preserved in simulations. The network topology used had five nodes in the hidden layer and a single output. A hyperbolic tangent was used as an activation function for the nodes in the hidden layer and a linear activation function for the output node.

Simulation results are presented in Figure 2. As can be seen, with both learning strategies the ANN has an adaptive behavior by adjusting itself to track the function presented. The proposed SMC-based algorithm has demonstrated to be much more efficient. The implementation of the sliding mode concept has really introduced a speed-up in network learning and after a small period of time the network error is very small.

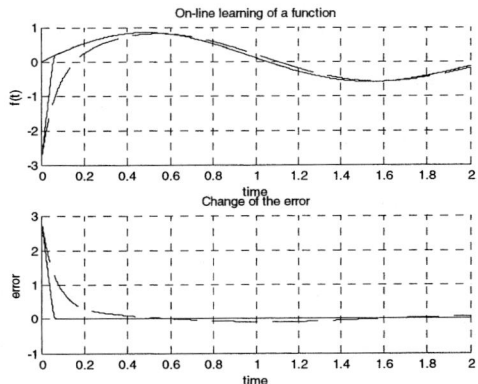

Fig. 2. Online learning of a function. The function is plotted with dash-dotted line, the output of the ANN with SMC learning algorithm is plotted with solid line and the output of the ANN using backpropagation algorithm – with dashed line.

4 Conclusion

In this paper a new learning algorithm has been proposed, for analog multilayer feedforward neural networks with scalar output, which robustly drives the learning error to zero in finite time. The weights adaptation scheme is based on sliding mode control concept and it represents a simple, yet robust, mechanism for guaranteeing finite time reachability of zero learning error condition. The convergence of the algorithm has been analyzed and simulation results have been presented to show its effectiveness. In contrast with off-line learning algorithms, the algorithm proposed can be used to train the network as it interacts with the external environment

References

1. Efe M. O., Kaynak O.: Stabilizing and Robustifying the Learning Mechanisms of Artificial Neural Networks in Control Engineering Applications. Int. Journal of Intelligent Systems, 15 (5) (2000) 365–388
2. Sira-Ramirez H., Colina-Morles E.: A Sliding Mode Strategy for Adaptive Learning in Adalines. IEEE Trans. on Circuits and Systems – I: Fundamental Theory and Applications. 42 (12) (1995) 1001–1012

3. Yu X., Zhihong M., Rahman S. M. M.: Adaptive Sliding Mode Approach for Learning in a Feedforward Neural Network. Neural Computing & Applications. 7 (1998) 289–294
4. Parma G. G., Menezes B. R., Braga A. P.: Sliding Mode Algorithm for Training Multilayer Artificial Neural Networks. Electronics Letters. 34 (1) (1998) 97–98.
5. G. G. Parma G. G., Menezes B. R., Braga A. P.: Neural Networks Learning with Sliding Mode Control: the Sliding Mode Backpropagation Algorithm. Int. Journal of Neural Systems. 9 (3) (1999) 187–194

Exploring Protein Functional Relationships Using Genomic Information and Data Mining Techniques

Jack Y. Yang, Mary Qu Yang, and Okan K. Ersoy

School of Electrical and Computer Engineering,
Purdue University, West Lafayette, IN 47907-1285 USA

Abstract. An approach that uses both supervised and unsupervised learning methods for exploring protein functional relationships is reported; we refer to this as Maximum Contrast (MC) tree. The tree is constructed by performing a hierarchical decomposition of the feature space; this step is performed regardless of complex nature of protein functions, i.e. it performs this decomposition even without knowledge of the protein functional class labels. In order to test our algorithm, we have constructed a library of Protein Phylogenetic Profiles for the proteins in the yeast Saccharomyces Cerevisiae with 60 species. Results showed our algorithm compares favorably to other classification algorithms such as the decision tree algorithms C4.5, C5, and to support vector machines.

1 Introduction

Determination of protein functions using traditional laboratory methods remains a slow, laborious process. New methods concerning determination of multiple functional relations among a large group of proteins simultaneously are based either on protein phylogenetic profiles (PPP) or DNA Microarray data.

In its simplest form, a protein phylogenetic profile (PPP) is a string of bits; given n species for which a complete genome is available, and given a target protein, this string has the form $b_1 b_2 \ldots b_n$, where a 1 in the ith bit position indicates that a homologue of the target protein is present in species i, while a 0 indicates that it is not. The idea is that functionally related proteins will tend to evolve together, and thus will have similar PPPs, while proteins that are not functionally related will tend to evolve independently, and thus are likely to have disparate PPPs.

Recently, several authors have begun to apply supervised learning techniques to genomic data; Brown et. al. applied a variety of classifiers, (including decision trees and support vector machines) to the problem of predicting the protein functional class from DNA microarray data. Vert (2002) proposed a new support vector machine kernel (which he terms a tree kernel), and showed that it outperforms the "heterogeneous" SVM kernels on heterogeneous protein phylogenetic profile and DNA microarray data that Pavlidis, Weston, Cai, and Grundy (2002) used (because the data set was heterogeneous, they used a support vector machine with an explicitly heterogeneous kernel to classify this data). Ersoy et al (Ersoy et al 2000) developed rule extraction by decision trees and neural networks in the Human Genome Projects.

In this paper, we investigate an approach that uses both supervised and unsupervised learning methods; we refer to this as *Maximum Contrast (MC) tree*. The tree is constructed by performing a hierarchical decomposition of the feature space; this step is entirely unsupervised, i.e. it performs this decomposition without knowledge of the PPP protein functional class labels. To use the tree as a classifier, given a test instance, we find the K PPP vectors in the training set that are nearest to the test instance, and assign to the test instance the majority class label of this set of K PPP vectors. Here "nearest" refers to the nearest neighbors of the test instance with respect to the tree structure, rather than to the K "true" nearest neighbors in the feature space.

2 Methodology and Algorithms

Based on the scenario of nearest neighbor classifier, the Maximum Contrast Tree (MCT) is constructed so that at each stage the two training instances with maximum contrast (that is, the two training instances with maximum separation according to some distance measure) are used as seeds from which a partition of the feature space into two sets is grown (this is called splitting a node).

The construction of the tree begins with a root node that contains all the training data. The root node is added to a list, called the UNPROCESSED list; this list consists of all the nodes that have yet to be split. The main loop of the tree construction algorithm consists of selecting the next node on the UNPROCESSED list (call it N). If N contains more than one training instance, we then split N into two new nodes, NL and NR, which are then added to the UNPROCESSED list. The next node on the UNPROCESSED list is then selected and processed as above. This process continues until the UNPROCESSED list is empty.

The details of the splitting procedure are as follows. Let N denote the node to be split, and let T be the set of training instances in node N. First we find the two instances $\vec{X}_L, \vec{X}_R$ in T that have maximum separation according to some distance measure $d(\cdot, \cdot)$, i.e.

$$d(\vec{X}_L \vec{X}_R) = \max_{i,j} d(\vec{X}_i, \vec{X}_j)$$

Let A_N^L L be a set of training instances that initially contains only the element $\vec{X}_L$, and A_N^R be a set of training instances that initially contains only the element $\vec{X}_R$. Let $d(\vec{X}, A_N^L)$ be the minimum distance of instance $\vec{X}$ to any instance in A_N^L, and let $d(\vec{X}, A_N^R)$ be the minimum distance of instance $\vec{X}$ to any instance in A_N^R.

The following pseudocode defines how the split of node N is performed: Repeat until $A_N^L \bigcup A_N^R = T$:

Let $\vec{X}_1$ be the instance in the set $T - (A_N^L \bigcup A_N^R)$ that minimizes the distance to any instance in A_N^L, i.e.

$$\vec{X}_1 = \arg \min_{\vec{X} \in T-(a_N^L \bigcup A_N^R)} d(\vec{X}, A_N^L),$$

and let $\vec{X}_2$ be the instance in the set $T - (A_N^L \cup A_N^R)$ that minimizes the distance to any instance in A_N^R, i.e.

$$\vec{X}_2 = \arg \min_{\vec{X} \in T-(a_N^L \cup A_N^R)} d(\vec{X}, A_N^R)$$

If $d(\vec{X}_1, A_N^L) < d(\vec{X}_2, A_N^R)$ then add $\vec{X}_1$ to A_N^L else add $\vec{X}_2$ to A_N^R.

Create two new nodes N_L and N_R, which are, respectively, the left and the child of node N. Initialize node N_L so that it contains all the training instances in the set A_N^L, and similarly initialize node N_R so that it contains all the training instances in the set A_N^R. This completes the description of how a node N is split.

The MCT classifier is essentially a K-NN-type classifier, but rather than choosing the nearest neighbors using a distance measure, the nearest neighbors are defined by a tree structure. As such, it performs a hierarchical decomposition similar to that used in the branch and bound implementation of the K-NN algorithm. Further details are discussed in Section 3.2.

3 Experimental Results

3.1 Data Generation

Currently there is a protein library of protein phylogenetic profiles built by Pavlidis et al (Pavlidis et al 2002) and Vert (Vert, J. 2002) based on 24 species and roughly around 1/3 genes from Yeast genome. Our library is constructed over 60 species on a complete yeast genome with hundred types of proteins and it is an improvement over that existing libraries.

For each of the 6357 ORFs (Open Reading Frames, representing a possible gene) in the yeast *Saccharomyces cerevisiae* genome[1], we constructed a phylogenetic profile over 60 complete genomes[2], which includes 12 archaeabacterial genomes, 45 eubacterial genomes and 3 eukaryotic genomes. The ith element of the phylogenetic profile for a given ORF A is obtained by using the BLASTp program (Altschul, S.F et al, 1997) to search the ith genome for the presence of ORF A. The score reported by BLASTp (means blast algorithm on proteins) is given by:

$$\max_{ORF\ B\ \text{in ith genome}} Evalue(A, B) \quad \text{where Evalue(A,B) is a matching score}$$

that lies between 0 and infinity. The Evalue is obtained from another quantity called the p-value via the transformation

Evalue(A,B) = $-\ln(1 - \text{Pvalue}(A,B))$

The Pvalue is a matching score (probability) that lies between 0 and 1; Pvalue(A,B) = 1 if internal amino-acid sequences of ORFs A and B are identical. The phylogenetic profiles were then normalized by subtracting off the mean of each attribute and dividing by the standard deviation of each attribute.

---
[1] downloaded from ftp://genome-ftp.stanford.edu.
[2] downloaded from the National Center for Biotechnology (NCBI) site ftp://ftp.ncbi.nih,gov/genomes/

Protein function descriptions and class labels were assigned according to the MIPS Comprehensive Yeast Genome Database (CYGD) using the Pedant (Protein Extraction, Description and Analysis Tools) program. Of the 6357 ORFs in the *Saccharomyces cerevisiae* genome, 3887 are functionally known and 2470 are functionally unknown or questionable; only 1084 carry a unique label. Functionally unknown ORFs are assigned label "98" and questionable ORFs are assigned label "99". Functionally known ORFs may carry more than one label, due to the multifunctional nature of proteins. Furthermore, the labeling scheme is hierarchical. For example, Table 1 shows the labels for two Open Reading Frames (ORFs).

The resulting dataset consisted of 6357 labeled instances; each instance includes a 60 element phylogenetic profile vector, along with a set of labels. The overall process results in the dataset to be fed into the MC tree structure.

3.2 Results

We compared the MCT-based classifier to the decision tree algorithms C4.5 and C5, and to support vector machines on our phylogenetic profile dataset. To make the learning task more well-defined, we treated the multi-class problem of learning into mapping a given phylogenetic profile to its functional class label by a series of twoclass problems, one for each functional class. For a given functional class label, say 67.28, we give all proteins that include that functional classification the class label 1, and all other proteins the class label 2. By training a classifier to distinguish class 1 instances from class 2 instances, we effectively construct a detector for each protein functional class.

Table 1. S.cerevisiae Multi-Functional ORFs YBR243C and YMR319C

S.cerevisiae ORF name	functional categories	Description
YBR243C	01.04.01	phosphate utilization
	01.05.01	C-compound and carbohydrate utilization
	03.03.01	Mitotic cell cycle and cell cycle control
	06.07	Protein modification
	40.07	Endoplasmic reticulum
YMR319C	13.01.01.01	homeostasis of metal ions (Na, K, Ca etc.)
	67.04.01.01	heavy metal ion transporters (Cu, Fe, etc.)
	08.19	Cellular import
	40.02	Plasma membrane

The MCT-based classifier was tested in two different modes, which we refer to as one-level-up and two-level-up. In one-level-up mode, given a test instance, we first search the leaves of the tree to find the leaf node that contains the closest training instance. We then look at the set of training instances in the parent of that leaf node, find the K instances that are nearest to the test instance from this set, and use the majority class label of these K training instances as the classification for the test instance. If the parent node does not contain K training instances, then we look to the parent of that parent node, and apply the voting strategy just described. Two-level-up mode is similar, but skips the step of

Table 2. Results of the algorithms.

Average classification accuracy *of protein* 02.13 *respiration*.				Our Tree	
Label: 2.13	C45	C5	SVM	1 Level	2Level
AVERAGE	0.556992	0.567444	0.580289	*0.653173*	*0.552118*
STD	0.067531	0.074686	0.068411	0.060416	0.059277
Average classification accuracy *of protein* 01.20.01 *metabolism of primary metabolic sugars derivatives*				Our tree	
Label: 1.20.01	C45	C5	SVM	1 Level	2Level
AVERAGE	0.647228	0.651643	0.685763	*0.711537*	*0.717163*
STD	0.093500	0.092932	0.089360	0.100229	0.105281
Average classification accuracy of *protein* 13.01 *ionic homeostasis*				Our tree	
Label: 131	C45	C5	SVM	1 Level	2Level
AVERAGE	0.693767	0.689213	0.706512	*0.735415*	*0.737424*
STD	0.081842	0.079796	0.053468	0.066802	0.065093
Average classification accuracy of *protein* 01.05.07 *C-compound, carbohydrate transport*				Our tree	
Label: 157	C45	C5	SVM	1 Level	2Level
AVERAGE	0.720587	0.722808	0.772268	*0.773178*	*0.776172*
STD	0.084490	0.082181	0.065284	0.062435	0.065022
Average classification accuracy of *protein* 13.11 *cellular sensing and response transport*				Our tree	
Label: 13.11	C45	C5	SVM	1 Level	2Level
AVERAGE	0.537677	0.553849	0.576719	*0.611462*	*0.617491*
STD	0.074537	0.082375	0.064964	.073410	00.070193
Average classification accuracy of *protein* 05.01 *ribosome biogenesis*				Our tree	
Label: 5.1	C45	C5	SVM	1 Level	2Level
AVERAGE	*0.700833*	*0.695237*	0.657565	0.682350	0.685155
STD	0.033982	0.032216	0.035005	0.036841	0.038382
Average classification accuracy of *protein* 06.01 *protein folding and stabilization*				Our tree	

looking at the parent of the leaf node, and looks directly at the parent of the parent of the leaf node to find the K nearest training instances. In out experiments we used K = 3.

Each learning algorithm was tested on each of roughly 100 protein functional classes using 3-fold cross-validation, and the tests were repeated many times with different subsamplings of the data to reduce the variability of the results. Results for a few of the

Table 2 continued

Label: 6.1	C45	C5	SVM	1 Level	2Level
AVERAGE	0.561222	0.568070	**0.585753**	0.578137	0.576069
STD	0.049356	0.046013	0.034965	0.040868	0.043029
Average classification accuracy of *protein 08.13 vacuolar transpor*				Our tree	
Label: 813	C45	C5	SVM	1 Level	2Level
AVERAGE	0.544490	0.555609	0.560525	*0.560824*	*0.561862*
STD	0.075523	0.072518	0.061885	0.075320	0.074384
Average classification accuracy of *protein 01.06.13 lipid and fatty-acid transport*				Our tree	
Label: 1.6.13	C45	C5	SVM	1 Level	2Level
AVERAGE	0.533150	0.535718	0.536973	*0.586261*	*0.589970*
STD	0.126575	0.122040	0.078373	0.125472	0.125213
Average classification accuracy of *protein 08.19 cellular import*				Our tree	
Label: 8.19	C45	C5	SVM	1 Level	2Level
AVERAGE	0.630333	0.629118	0.654826	*0.668303*	*0.669005*
STD	0.055713	0.053053	0.034129	0.048694	0.045544
Average classification accuracy of *protein 67.28 drug transporters*				Our tree	
Label: 67.28	C45	C5	SVM	1 Level	2Level
AVERAGE	0.780112	0.782809	0.729279	*0.826751*	*0.829124*
STD	0.084681	0.086370	0.101071	0.069167	0.066971
Average classification accuracy of *protein 67.04.07 anion transporters*				Our tree	
Label: 67.4.7	C45	C5	SVM	1 Level	2Level
AVERAGE	0.591504	0.588087	0.598894	*0.629478*	*0.637114*

protein functional classes are reported in the table below: the best-performing classifier is shown in boldface type.

On the basis of these results (see Table 2) we conclude that the MCT-based 3-nearest-neighbor classifier outperforms both decision trees and SVMs.

From the results for the various classes, it is evident that decision trees do not perform well on this data. A possible explanation is that decision trees only split on one feature at a time, that is, on one bit position in the phylogenetic profile. However, the fact that two phlylogenetic profiles either agree or disagree in one bit position says almost nothing about the overall similarity of one phlylogenetic profile to another. By contrast, the tree-based K-nearest neighbor classifier takes into account the overall similarity of one phylogenetic profile to another. This may explain why the tree based K-nearest neighbor methods appear to outperform decision trees on this data.

4 Conclusions and Discussion

High dimensional feature space in relation to the number of available training instances as well as the fact that instances can belong to more than one class (a consequence of the multi-functional nature of proteins) make the classification a challenging problem for traditional supervised learning methods. The MCT structure introduced here performs a hierarchical decomposition of the feature space into more localized feature spaces, for which the density of training instances in relation to the size of the localized feature space may be higher. The advantage of this approach over conventional unsupervised methods such as SOMs is that with SOMs the number of SOM neurons must be specified in advance, whereas with the hierarchical approach, the number of tree nodes can adaptively increase, thus matching to the complexity of the problem. As there is only a unique winning process for each node at each level in the hierarchical MCT scheme than would be the case with a flat clustering model, the solution achieved at each stage on MCT is unique, resulting in a more robust algorithm. Furthermore, the hierarchical structure improves the scaling properties of the algorithm by making it more computationally efficient.

Based on our experiments, our algorithm appears to perform considerably better than decision tree algorithms C4.5 and C5, and Support Vector Machines, and may provide a viable alternative to supervised or unsupervised methods alone.

In addition, the algorithm is capable of handling protein functional classes with a small number of proteins (rare events), and also handles the case that instance belong to more than one class (due to complex nature of protein-protein interactions. The ability of the MCT to handle such cases means that a larger dataset can be used, which may provide deeper insight into protein functional relationships at the genome level, and thus may lead to a better understanding of evolution at a molecular and genetic level.

References

1. Altschul, S.F., Madden, T.L., Schäffer, A.A., Zhang, J., Zhang, Z., Miller, W.& Lipman, D.J. (1997) "Gapped BLAST and PSI-BLAST: a new generation of protein database search programs." *Nucleic Acids Res.* 25:3389–3402.
2. Brown. M. P. S., Grundy, W. N., Lin, D., Cristianini, N., Sugnet, C. W., Furey, T. S., Ares M. J., and Haussler, D. (2000), *Knowledge-based analysis of microarray gene expression data by using support vector machines*, PNAS 97, p. 262–267.
3. Cover, T. M. and Hart, P. E. (1967) "Nearest Neighbor Pattern Classification" *IEEE Trans. IT* Vol. 13. No.1 P21–27, 1967.

4. Ersoy, O K., Choe W, Bina M (2000) "Neural network schemes for detecting rare events in human genomic DNA" Bioinformatics, Vol. 16 no 12 Pages 1062-1072.
5. Ersoy, O.K., Deng, S.W. (1995). *"Parallel, Self-Organizing Neural Networks with Continuous Inputs and Outputs"*, IEEE Transactions on Neural Networks Volume 6 Number 4, pp. 1037–1044.
6. Ersoy, O. K. et al (1998) in *Algorithm and Architectures* (Leondes, C. T. editor) Pages 364–401, Academic Press 1998 (ISBN: 012443861X).
7. Marcotte, E. M., Pellegrini, M., Thompson, M. J., Yeates, T. O., and Eisenberg, D. (1999), A combined algorithm for genome-wide prediction of protein function, *Nature* 402, p.83–86.
8. Pavlidis, Paul, Jason Weston, Jinsong Cai and William Noble Grundy. "Learning Gene Functional Classification from Multiple Data Types". *J. of Computational Biology*, Vol 9. pp. 401–444.
9. Pellegrini, M., Marcotte, E. M., Thompson, M. J., Eisenberg, D., and Yeates, T. O. (1999), Assigning protein functions by comparative genome analysis: Protein phylogenetic profiles, *PNAS 96*, p. 4285–4288.
10. Yang, Jack, Yang, Mary and Ersoy,O.K. (2002) "Gene finding and protein functional determination by protein phylogenetic profile and computational intelligence," *Intelligent Engineering Systems through Neural Networks*, Vol 12. Page 733–740 ASME Press (ISBN: 0791801918)
11. Vert J.(2002) "A tree kernel to analyze phylogenetic profiles", *Bioinformatics*, Vol 18 Suppl 1. pp. S276–S284.

Predicting Bad Credit Risk: An Evolutionary Approach

Susan E. Bedingfield and Kate A. Smith

School of Business Systems Monash University Clayton, Victoria 3168 Australia
{sue.bedingfield, kate.smith}@infotech.monash.edu.au

Abstract. This paper considers classification of binary valued data with unequal misclassification costs. This is a pertinent consideration in many applications of data mining, specifically in the area of credit scoring. An evolutionary algorithm is introduced and employed to generate rule systems for classification. In addition to the misclassification costs various other properties of the classification systems generated by the evolutionary algorithm, such as accuracy and coverage, are considered and discussed.

1 Introduction

Credit scoring is an applicaton where the misclassification costs are in general unequal. More specifically, the cost of misclassifying a 'bad risk' as a 'good risk' is significantly greater than the reverse. However, often the information available which we can use to classify potential 'bad risk" customers is frequently unreliable and there are usually less instances available. Significant work has been done on developing techniques for handling such situations. For example, the technique of misclassification cost sensitive boosting has been developed to aid in the accurate classification of data where differences in misclassification costs are a significant issue [1].

The evolutionary rule generation system described in this paper has been reported upon in [2,3,4]. It has been used to generate classification systems for both binary and multi-class data. The results reported in [2] were based upon the widely reported upon German credit data and showed that the system was capable of generating accurate rules for classifying 'good' applicants, but displayed a reluctance to generate accurate rules for classifying 'bad' applicants.

The purpose of this paper is to determine which is the best way of utilising the evolutionary system to accurately and comprehensively classify bad credit risks.

Previously our results have been based on using the system to generate rule systems that contain rules for classifying all values of the decision attribute [2,3,4].

In an information system where the decision attribute is binary valued, instead of using the system to generate rules predicting both values of the decision attribute, the option of only predicting one value of the decision attribute and classifying data points into the 'other' class if they do not satisfy any of the rules becomes available. This paper focuses on using our system to look at the alternative approaches, (i.e.

predict both 'goods' and 'bads', just to predict 'goods', and just to predict 'bads'), to determine which approach gives the most accurate and comprehensive rules for predicting 'bad' applicants.

2 Evolutionary Rule Generation

In this section we define the structure within which the evolutionary rule generation system operates. We then discuss the structure of the rule systems, as well as the evolutionary operators used to evolve the rules within the rule systems.

2.1 Information System Definitions

The definition of an information system originates with Pawlak [5] and provides a structure for the evolutionary algorithm to act upon.

<u>Definition 1:</u> An *information system* is a 4-tuple $S = <O,A,V,f>$, where O is a finite set of objects, A is a finite set of attributes, V_a is the set of attribute values that $a \in A$ can take,

$V = \bigcup_{a \in A} V_a$ and $f : O \times A \rightarrow V$ such that $f(x,a) \in V_a$. (f is called an information function).

We use a more specific information system called a decision table. This enables us to distinguish between two different types of attributes, condition attributes and decision attributes.

<u>Definition 2:</u> An information system $<O, A \cup \{d\}, V, f >$, where d is a function from O to a finite set V_d is called an *extension* of A by d. In this context, the attributes in A are called the *condition attributes* and d is called the *decision attribute*. For example, d might indicate whether a person was a good or bad credit risk.

2.2 Rule Structure

Each individual rule is made up of a set of atoms. An atom is a structure of the form (α, β, γ) where α represents an attribute, β is a comparison operator ($\leq$, $\geq$, $=$) and γ a is number within the range of values assumed by the attribute α.
A rule has a structure of the form *(atom1, atom2, ...,atomN)* where $N \leq M$ and $M \geq 2$ is a parameter defining the upper bound on the number of atoms allowed to make a rule. For each rule, $atom_1, atom_2, ...,atom_{N-1}$ have a condition attribute as the attribute, and $atom_N$ has a decision attribute as its attribute component.
A rule system, $\Re$, comprises a finite set of rules $\{rule_1, rule_2,...,rule_k\}$ where $1 \leq k \leq K$, K being a parameter defining the number of allowable rules in a rule set. The genetic

algorithm population consists of *P* rule systems each containing *k* individual rules. If $p \in \Re$, then we define O_p to be the subset of *O* whose members satisfy the condition attribute values associated with p.

It is assumed that the data is contained in an information system extension $S = <O, A \cup \{d\}, V, f>$.

2.3 Genetic Operators

The genetic operators used in this paper are an elitist selection criteria, and crossover and mutation operators. Crossover between individual rule systems is accomplished randomly based on a fixed crossover probability P_c. The first *C* rules from each rule system are selected and swapped. Mutation occurs to the rules within the individual rule bases and takes various forms – random changes to the components of each atom, swapping one or more atoms between two rules, adding a new atom to a specific rule, deleting a rule, adding a new rule. The probabilities of each type of mutation are parameterised (with given probabilities P_{m1}-P_{m5}). The selection criteria used is elitist - the best *P* rule systems of the current generation are selected to form the next generation. The initialisation procedure used in this paper is random initialisation; for a given population of size *P* we generate a predefined number of rules for each of the *P* rule systems as follows. An atom is produced by using a random number generator to generate the contents of each component. For example, if there are *n* attributes in the information system, each attribute is allocated an integer between 1 and *n*. For the attribute component of each atom, a random integer between 1 and *n* is generated to determine the specific attribute represented by the atom. There are three comparison operators =, >, < which are possible candidates for the second component of each atom and the comparison operator for each specific atom is generated in the same manner. The last component, the value component, is generated in a similar way. In this manner the atoms are generated for each of *K* rules in each of *P* rule systems. The number of atoms belonging to each rule is initially fixed, but allowed to vary as atoms are added and deleted from a given rule. Likewise, the number of rules in a rule system is initially fixed, but allowed to vary as rules are added and deleted during mutation.

3 Fitness Functions

In this section we present the components that comprise the fitness function, as well as two alternative ways of combining these fitness components into fitness functions.

3.1 Fitness Function Components

There are several measures of fitness of the individual rules in each rule base that we are interested in recording and improving over time. We first consider accuracy measures – both row and column accuracy – of the resulting confusion matrix. The particular information system we are experimenting with has a binary valued decision attribute (equivalent to 'good' or 'bad' risk). This leads to two row accuracy measures C_1 and C_2, and two column accuracy measures C_3 and C_4. C_1 and C_2 effectively measure the coverage by the rule system of the 'good' and 'bad' objects respectively. Whereas C_3 and C_4 measure the accuracy of the 'good' and 'bad' predictions. These four expressions should optimally be equal to 1.

C_1 and C_2 are defined as $\dfrac{Card\left(O_i \cap \bigcup_{d(\rho)=i} O_\rho\right)}{Card(O_i)}$ and C_3, C_4 as $\dfrac{Card\left(O_i \cap \bigcup_{d(\rho)=i} O_\rho\right)}{Card\left(\bigcup_{d(\rho)=i} O_\rho\right)}$

where $i = 0,1$

Analogous to the accuracy measures C1 and C2 are two measures of inaccuracy C5 and C6. The two inaccuracy measures should optimally be equal to 0. (In practice this may be difficult to achieve if the information stem itself contains inconsistencies. This may in turn lead to the generation of inconsistent rules).

3.2 Combining Fitness Function Components

The total fitness function for the genetic algorithm can be represented as the weighted function of the six components C_1-C_6, and attempts to generate rules over time with maximal coverage, maximal accuracy. All fitness components have optimal values of 1, except C_5 and C_6 which should be 0. The general form for the overall fitness function can take various forms. For the fitness function used in this paper we use a linear combination

$F = \lambda F^1 + (1-\lambda) F^2$ where $0 < \lambda < 1$ and F^1 and F^2 are defined as:

$$F^1 = \left(\dfrac{\sum_{i=1}^{4} C_i}{1 + \sum_{i=5}^{6} C_i}\right), \quad F^2 = \left(\sum_{i=1}^{4} C_i + \sum_{i=5}^{6} \dfrac{1}{1+C_i}\right) \qquad (1)$$

The value that λ takes has an impact on the behaviour of the evolutionary algorithm. It has been previously reported [3] that for a value of $\lambda = 1$, the algoritm tends to generate highly accurate rules, but the coverage (i.e. the number of data points satisfying the conditions of one or more of the rules) tends to be low. Conversely, for a value of $\lambda = 0$, the coverage of the rule systems generated is higher, but the accuracy lower.

4 Experiments

The evolutionary algorithm was used to generate the following three types of rule systems:
In the first case the algorithm was given the freedom to generate rule systems containing both 'good' and 'bad' rules (i.e. rules predicting both 'good' and 'bad' credit risk).
In the second case, the algorithm was allowed to generate only 'good' rules (i.e. rules predicting 'good' only).
In the last case, the algorithm was allowed to generate only 'bad' rules. (i.e. rules predicting 'bad' only).
In all cases the experiments were performed for values of $\lambda = 0$ and $\lambda = 1$. A five fold cross validation was performed in all cases for each value of λ. For type 1 rule systems, if a data point in the test set satisfied none of the rule conditions for any of the rules in the rule system, no prediction was given. In the second type of rule system, if no prediction was available from the rule system, a prediction of bad was given. For the third type of rule system, if no prediction was available from the rule system, a prediction of good was given.

4.1 Data and Test Sets

The data used in these experiments is the same German credit classification data available from the UCI Machine learning repository. The data contains 1000 examples of credit applicants, 700 of which are known to be good credit risks, and 300 of which are known to be bad credit risks. The attributes for each example include a combination of continuous and categorical variables such as age, marital status, bank account status, credit history, and the loan amount. There are a total of 20 attributes available with which to model the relationships between attributes and consequence, in this case good or bad credit risk. Since 70% of the credit applicants in the data set are classified as good, the default level of accuracy is 70%, obtained by simply classifying all applicants as good. Similarly, if we decide to classify all applicants as bad, the default level of accuracy is 30%.
Each of the test and training sets for the five fold cross validation contained 900 and 100 data points respectively. These were generated randomly from the data set ensuring that the ratio of 'goods' and 'bads' remained the same as the original data set and ensuring that all test sets were mutually exclusive.

4.2 Parameter Values

For the experiments reported upon in this paper, the fixed parameter values listed in table 1 were used.

Table 1.

Parameter name	Value	Explanation
PopSize	20	The number of rule sets in each population
MaxAtoms	6	The maximum initial number of atoms in each rule
RulesPerSet	40	The initial number of rules in each rule set
ChgComponent	0.5	Probabilty of changing a component of an atom
SwapAtom	0.2	Probabilty of swapping atoms between rules
DelRule	0.5	Probabilty of deleting rule from a rule set
AddRule	1	The probability of adding a new rule to a rule set – in this case a new rule is always added. Any empty rules are deleted.
AddAtom	0.2	Probability of adding an atom to a rule
CrossOver	0.2	Probabilty of crossing two rulesets

5 Results

The results were obtained by averaging the results from each of the test sets used for the five fold cross validation. Tables below give results for the first rule system in the population.

Generating 'Good' and 'Bad' Rules

We can see from tables 2 and 3 that the ability of the rule systems to make a classification varies considerably depending on the value of λ. However, in both cases it is evident that the rule systems generated were unable to classify 'bad' credit risks. The reason for this is that whilst the evolutionary algorithm was able to generate accurate rules predicting 'bad', these rules only applied to a small percentage of data points in the training sets, and none of the data points in the test sets. i.e. these rules were not generalisable. For $\lambda=0$, we can see that the rule system was able to classify on average 53.4% of the test sets. For $\lambda=1$, the percentage that could be classified is much less, 26.6%. The accuracy of prediction, however, was higher with a value of $\lambda=0$ (84%) than $\lambda=1$ (91%), so that the misclassification of 'bads' was much lower with $\lambda=1$.

Generating 'Good' Rules

In this case any data point in the test set that is not given a prediction by the rule system, is automtically given a 'bad' prediction, which means that all data points in the test set are classified. It is eveident, (tables 4 and 5), that a value of $\lambda=0$ gives the opportunity for the evolutionary system to classify more of the data points (67%) than a value of $\lambda=1$ (36.2%). However a consequence of this is that, by default, a higher percentage of the 'bad' applicants are correctly classified when $\lambda=1$ (89%) as opposed to $\lambda=0$ (56%). The misclassification rate for 'bads' with $\lambda=1$ in this case is similar to the case where both 'goods' and 'bads' are classified.

Table 2: λ= 0

	actual	
classified	good	bad
good	45	8.4
bad	0	0

Table 3: λ= 1

	actual	
classified	good	bad
good	24.2	2.4
bad	0	0

Table 4: λ= 0

	actual	
classified	good	bad
good	53.8	13.2
bad	16.2	16.8

Table 5: λ= 1

	actual	
classified	good	bad
good	32.8	3.4
bad	37.2	26.6

Table 6: λ= 0

	actual	
classified	good	bad
good	51.8	16.2
bad	18.2	13.8

Table 7: λ= 1

	actual	
classified	good	bad
good	70	29.5
bad	0	0.5

Generating 'Bad' Rules

In terms of the aim of this paper, the results for this experiment are less encouraging than the previous two experiments (see tables 6 and 7). The reason for this is that the evolutionary system was able to evolve accurate rules predicting 'bad' credit risks, however these only applied to a small percentage of the training sets and did not readily generalise to the test sets.

6 Conclusion and Further Research

With the aim of accurately predicting bads, the results indicate that for this data set there is no advantage in using the system to predict both values of the decision attribute. It appears that the effort that the algorithm expends in generating 'bad' rules as well as 'good' rules would be better utilised generating only 'good' rules and making the assumption that any unclassified data point should be classified 'bad'. When the evolutionary algorithm is used in this way, the results also indicate that with a value of $\lambda=1$, whilst not providing high coverage for actual 'goods', does provide the best coverage for 'bad' predictions. This is in accordance with previous results [3]. As a secondary aim, with a value of $\lambda=1$, generating exclusively 'good' rules rather than both 'goods' and 'bads' provides better coverage for the actual 'goods'.

A further area of experimentation is to give weights to the fitness function components (equation (1)) and vary those weights and also the parameter values (table 1). If we are only attempting to classify one value of a binary decision attribute then some of the fitness components (and hence the weights) become redundant. If we are attempting to produce rule systems that predict 'goods' only, we could increase the penalty for misclassifying 'bads' relative to the reward for correctly classifying 'goods'. Also, whilst the results for only classifying 'bads' look discouraging, it may be worth experimenting to see if the reluctance to classify 'bad' can be improved by using the weights to increase the reward for successful 'bad' classifications and reduce the penalty for classifying actual 'goods' as 'bad'.

References

1. W. Fan S.J. Stolfo J. Zhang P.K. Chan AdaCost: misclassification cost-sensitive boosting Proc. 16th Int. Conf. on Machine learning pp 97–105, 1999.
2. Bedingfield, S. E. and Smith, K. A., "Evolutionary Rule Generation in an Information System", in Dagli, C. H. et al. (eds.), Intelligent Engineering Systems Through Artificial Neural Networks, ASME Press, NY, volume 9, pp. 485–492, 1999.
3. Bedingfield, S. and Smith, K. A., "A Comparison of Fitness Functions for Evolutionary Rule Generation", in M. Mohammadian (ed.), Advances in Intelligent Systems: Theory and Applications, IOS Press, 2000.
4. Bedingfield, S. E. and Smith, K. A., "Evolutionary Rule Generation classification and its Application to multi-class data", International Conference in Computational Science 2003, in press.
5. Pawlak, Z., "Information Systems, Theoretical Foundations", Information Systems, vol. 6, no. 3, pp. 205–218, 1981.

Indirect Differentiation of Function for a Network of Biologically Plausible Neurons

Amber D. Fischer and Cihan H. Dagli

Smart Engineering Systems Laboratory, Department of Engineering Management
University of Missouri-Rolla, Rolla, MO 65401, USA

Abstract. This paper introduces a new method to model differentiation of biologically plausible neurons, introducing the capability for indirectly defining the characteristics for a network of spiking neurons. Due to its biological plausibility and greater potential for computational power, a spiking neuron model is employed as the basic functional unit in our system. The method for designing the architecture (network design, communication structure, and neuron functionality) for networks of spiking neurons has been purely a manual process. In this paper, we propose a new design for the differentiation of a network of spiking neurons, such that these networks can be indirectly specified, thus enabling a method for the automatic creation of a network for a predetermined function. In this manner, the difficulties associated with the manual creation of these networks are overcome, and opportunity is provided for the utilization of these networks more readily for applications. Thus, this paper provides a new method for indirectly constructing these powerful networks, such as could be easily linked to an evolutionary system or other optimization algorithm.

Keywords: Artificial Neural Networks, Spiking Neural Networks, Integrate-and-Fire Neuron Models, Computational Intelligence, Neuro-Modeling, Evolutionary Algorithms, Evolutionary Neural Networks

1 Introduction and Motivation

Networks of spiking neurons have potential for advanced functional capabilities in comparison to the functionality of classical neural networks. Classical neural networks contain a minimum of neurons with distinctly weighted connections. These networks are easy to implement for functional specification due to a multitude of training algorithms developed to tune the weights of predefined architectures. Additionally, evolutionary systems efficiently search out efficient architectures for optimal functionality for a predetermined problem. The vast area of application and effectiveness of these networks has been well documented in literature. Literature has also produced a large content on the limitation of these networks, such as scalability issues, functional limitations, and the difficulty in designing suitable networks for specific problems. These limitations are partly due to the simplistic functionality of the individual neuron function, the significance of weight values within the network in correlation with the difficulty in assigning this value correctly, and the over-dependence of network function on individual weight values and specific network architecture. These networks do not allow for much variation in architecture without hindering functionality. Networks of spiking neurons, on the other hand, based on a more biologically plausible neural unit, have demonstrated advanced functional capabilities overcoming many of the limitation of classical neural networks.

Experimental evidence accumulated over the last few years suggests that many biological neural systems use the timing of spikes to encode information [Maass 1997]. Additionally, there are indications that the average frequency of spike trains and their temporal correlations carry important information within neural systems [Henkel 2000]. Networks incorporating mathematical models of spiking neurons or integrate-and-fire neurons as the computational unit, in contrast to classical neuron models, attempt to simulate the synchronous and oscillatory behavior recently observed in the human brain.

In many applications, networks of spiking neurons have been found to be computationally more powerful than classical neural networks [Maass 1997, Ruf and Schmitt 1998]. Based on the correlation theory[1], networks of spiking neurons allow advanced capabilities for image and data analysis[2], in contrast to classical applications of neural networks which face combinatorial complexity of the conjunctive feature maps, known as the binding problem [Milanese 1994]. The advanced capabilities for data and image processing encompass such areas as object segmentation [Labbi, Milanese, Bosch 1999], pattern segmentation and figure/ground segregation [Campbell and Wang 1995], temporal segmentation, edge detection and data clustering [Horn and Opher 1999, Choe, Miikkulainen, Cormack 2000, Opher, Horn and Quenet 1999], coherence detection [Hopfield and Brody 2000, 2001], segregation of distinct auditory patterns [Von der Malsburg and Schneider, 1986], and stereovision [Henkel, 2000]. In addition to data and image processing, networks of integrate-and-fire neurons have demonstrated potential for application in other research areas, such as nonlinear optimization [Malaka and Buck (2000)] and robot control [Michel and Biondi (1999), Ijspeert (2000), Billard and Ijspeert (2001), Berthouze (2000).

In comparison with classical neural networks, networks of spiking neurons rely not on a minimally sized network with distinctly defined weights, but rather they depend on large quantities of functionally organized 'groups' of neurons interconnected by a simple communication structure (having simply a -1 or + 1defined weight). In other words, classical neural networks rely on the specific weight values and function of each individual neuron, whereas spiking neurons depend on the trend or organized assembly of large quantity of simply connected neurons. The following list highlights positive features associated with these neural networks compared to classical neural networks:

---

[1] The correlation theory of brain function, proposed by Von der Malsburg (1981), solves the feature integration or binding problem in sensory processing, suggesting that the activities of neurons that correspond to the same feature are synchronized while representations of different features are temporally decorrelated.

[2] Image and data analysis are an important requirement for many artificial intelligence systems used in various fields from navigation to medicine [Horn and Opher, 1999].

Classical neural networks are necessarily specific, requiring a direct encoding for functional specification (and/or requiring a training function to tune the network). Networks of spiking neurons, on the other hand, can get by with an indirect encoding of the architecture without a learning rule due to the high level of abstraction necessary for their functional specification. The method for designing the architecture (network design, communication structure, and neuron functionality) for networks of spiking neurons is generally a manual process, as suggested so far from literature. However, due to distinguished properties of spiking neurons that we have so far outlined in comparison to classical neural networks, these networks are more catered to design by indirect and autonomous methods, such as evolutionary systems.

The individual function and connection weights between neurons are not the most significant factor in defining network functionality. The spiking network design leaves much room available for variation and non-specific inexact definition (error) for the specifics of each individual neuron.

The functional capability of the network depends on the architectural organization, a higher abstraction than the detail necessary for classical neural networks.

An autonomous agent based design of these networks designed directly from brain theory and similar to the organization of ant colonies and other complex systems whose complex functionality stems from the organization and interactions between multitudes of simple systems, in this case the individual neurons, generating emergent behavior. Due to the higher abstraction for focus of functionality, these networks are more significantly catered to indirect and autonomous design, such as by means of evolution.

In this paper, we present a new method for the differentiation of a network of spiking networks. This indirect method for design suggests opportunity for coupling with an evolutionary system for effective functionality in utilization in a predetermined application. In the next section of this paper, Section 2, we outline the details for the neuron model, which is the basic functioning unit of the network. The capabilities for the individual neuron to express temporal dynamics provide opportunity for emergent behavior from the network. Thus, this model must allow for much variation dependent on simple definition. Then, in the next section, Section 3, we provide details as to the new design method for indirectly differentiating a network of neurons, based on the neuron model provided in Section 2. In conclusion, we defend this new method as an obvious solution for the autonomous design of a network of spiking neurons.

2 Introduction to the Neuron Model

There are multiple approaches to simplifying the biological properties of a neuron in a computer model [Hoppensteat 1997]. Because communication between neurons via short electrical pulses (action potentials or spikes) dictates network functionality, neural representations employing temporal information, such as spike timing, synchrony in spikes or population activities, and spiking events locked to background oscillators [Choe 2001] are the most biologically plausible for simulating network functionality. Hodgkin and Huxley (1952) developed the first quantitative representation of a neuron's membrane current, upon which most subsequent models have been based [Rinzel and Ermentrout 1999]. Spiking neurons, leaky integrators, spike accumulation neurons, leaky integrate-and-fire neurons, leaky synapse with dynamic threshold models, and the spike response model (SRM) all refer to models that simulate the occurrence of voltage spikes, dependent on the input activity overcoming the threshold of the neuron.

In this section, a new biologically plausible computational model analogous to the integrate-and-fire model of the neuron (see Gabbini and Kock (1999) for a review) is presented. Simulations of the activity of this neuron model in response to incoming signals demonstrate that this simple model captures the temporal dynamics of a biological neuron. Based on the temporal dynamics of the neuron, the integrate-and-fire neuron model is represented by a single variable corresponding to the state of a neuron's membrane potential. This section presents a computer model for the function of a single neuron and analogous to the integrate-and-fire neuron model.

At each time step, a single input signal combined from the summation of zero to multiple input sources is presented to the neuron function. In response, dynamic variables of the neuron function, a simplification of the electrochemical reaction that occurs inside the body of a neuron, may change, potentially stimulating an action potential. In conjunction with the action potential is the generation of an output signal, an all or nothing response. In this section, details of the model are expounded, and simulations are performed to observe the behavior of the neuron model in response to regular input signals and network interactions.

2.1 Electrical Properties of the Neuron's Lipid Bylayer Membrane

To model the neuron, the electrical properties of the lipid bylayer membrane of the neuron are modeled as an electrical circuit[3]; the equations for which were adapted from [Levitan and Kaczmarek, 1997]. Under normal conditions (not considering the dramatics of the action potential), the neuron voltage, V, exhibits a voltage response related to an incoming signal, S, and the neuron's membrane time constant, M. In this model of the neuron, the resting potential of the neuron's voltage is zero, and the neuron's voltage is constrained between V_{max} and V_{min}, constant values above and below zero. At each time step, the voltage responds to both excitatory (+) and inhibitory (-) incoming signals. In addition to the current incoming signal having an affect on the neuron's voltage, the voltage also reduces exponentially with time, towards the resting potential of the neuron. The normal behavior of the neuron's voltage, measured at each time step, t, where t ∈ [0, 1, 2, etc], can be represented by the following function:

$$V_t = S_t - \frac{(S_t - V_{(t-1)})}{e^{1/M}}. \tag{1}$$

---

[3] There are, of course, many different models for the biological properties of a neuron, simplifying different aspects of the chemical and/or electrical properties of the biological neuron [Hoppensteat 1997].

The voltage response plot in Figure 1 demonstrates the affect of an incoming signal on the normal behavior of the neuron's voltage. In this figure, the top plot is the voltage of the neuron in response to the bottom plot representing the value for the neuron's incoming signal.

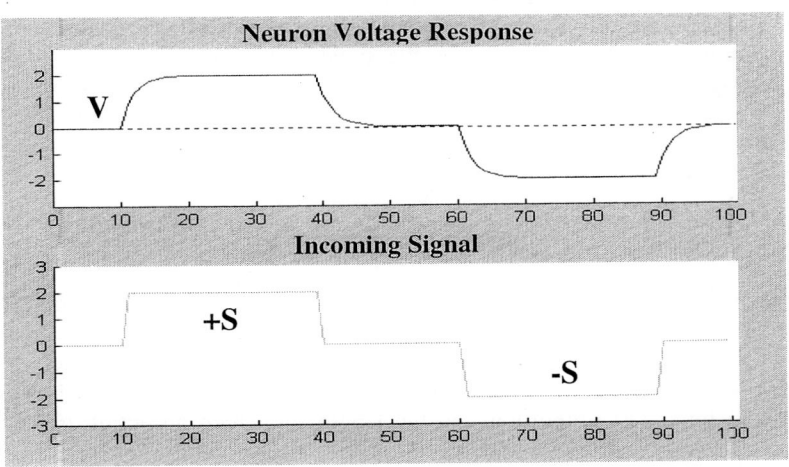

Fig. 1. Example of a Neuron's Voltage Response

2.2 The Action Potential

Normal conditions imply a neuron's voltage does not exceed the threshold level of the neuron. The threshold level of the neuron, represented as T, is the normal voltage value above which under normal conditions an action potential is initiated. An action potential is triggered at each time step that the neuron's voltage, V, is greater than the actual threshold level, T_t, of the neuron. An action potential results in the firing of a constant output signal down the neuron's axon, thus enabling communication with other neurons. This response is referred to as a spike.

2.3 Voltage Response to an Action Potential

In addition to the presence of an output signal, the behavior of the neuron voltage in response to incoming signals is not the same when an action potential is triggered. First, directly in response to triggering an action potential, the neuron's voltage increases towards V_{max}, no matter the weight of the incoming signal. Also, the actual threshold level of the neuron, T_t, increases to infinity, beginning a period called the refractory period, R. The refractory period begins with an absolute refractory period followed by a relative refractory period, $R = R_a + R_r$. During the absolute refractory period, R_a, while T_t remains at infinity, incoming signals have no affect on the neuron's voltage. Then, T_t begins to slowly fall back towards its original value, T_0, during what is called the relative refractory period, R_r. During the relative refractory period, incoming signals can initiate an action potential, but the threshold level is higher than usual making it harder to generate.

In some instances, an action potential is initiated spontaneously, based on the innate properties of the neuron. If the neuron's initial threshold value, T_0, is less than zero, the neuron will instantly spike. This spontaneous activity occurs without initiation from incoming signals, but generates the same voltage response as is induced by incoming signals. The spontaneous activity causes a patterned spike response, as the neuron's threshold after an action potential will always decay below the resting potential of the neuron. Inhibitory inputs, however, can reduce the voltage level of the neuron impeding spike activity.

2.4 Neuron Fatigue

Another property of the neuron influencing its voltage measure and resulting from the triggering of an action potential is the experience of some degree of fatigue. Under fatigue, incoming signals have less than one-half their original influence on the neuron's voltage. Fatigue, **F**, is an internal property of the neuron, however the duration of fatigue is proportional to the length for which an action potential was present. Normal conditions will not return to the neuron until after a brief period of rest in which no action potentials are triggered.

2.5 Neuron Communication

Within a network, neurons communicate via an oversimplified axodendritic synaptic connection. Each established connection allows the unidirectional transfer of an output signal to the input signal of another (or the same) neuron. When an action potential is triggered, the resulting signal is passed down each of a neuron's connections, reaching all target neurons by the beginning of the next time step. Associated with each unidirectional neuron-neuron connection is a weight, or signal value. Each of a neuron's connections has a unique weight value that is either excitatory (+1) or inhibitory (-1).

Although a neuron can have multiple input and output connections, the neuron function reacts at each time step to a single input triggering a single output. Neurons with multiple input connections sum the total input weights of all active signals at each time step. The resulting value becomes the neuron's single input signal. An output from the neuron function activates the transfer of a signal down each of the neuron's connections to the target neurons.

Networks also communicate with the external environment. A neuron can directly receive signals from sensors and output signals to actuators. Similar to connections from other neurons, the input signals from the environment are summed at each time step before being presented to the neuron function. Output connections to the environment can either be a direct affect of the firing pattern of the neuron, or some other translation from the signal value. Both input and output environmental communications need to be predetermined prior to the simulation of the network.

2.6 Simulations of Networks of Neurons

To demonstrate the variability in temporal dynamics this neuron model provides, networks of these neurons have been constructed and the communication between neurons over many time steps recorded. First, the communication between random networks of neurons is simulated. To create this network, 16 neurons are functionally differentiated based on the random assignment of the static neuron variables defined above. The communication infrastructure is arbitrarily created by selecting a random positive integer for each neuron, representing the total connection number per neuron. Then, for each neuron connection, a random target neuron (including possibly itself) is chosen, and arbitrarily assigned a (+/-) weight. To trigger a pattern of firing for the network, Neuron 1 is passed a constant input from an external source. All neuron activity from the network in response to this single input was recorded for 200 time steps. In this random network of neurons observable patterns of activity was noticed. A second simulation of a network of neurons contains a fully connected network of 8 neurons with two distinct neuron types. In this network, neurons 1 through 4 make up a group of similar neurons, and neurons 5 through 8 form the other distinct type of neuron. Both neuron 1 and neuron 5 in this example lie inside the input area, therefore both receive the external input signal (a constant input of 5). In this network, the internal connections and connection weights are the same for all the neurons, therefore, other than the external input received by neuron 1 and neuron 5, all input signals to the neurons are equivalent since the network is fully connected. The two distinct neuron groups behave similarly within their groups, but a dramatic difference in firing patterns is observable between neuron types.

3 Overview of Neuron Differentiation

In this section, we introduce a new model for neuron differentiation. In this new model a neuron functionally differentiates by the indirect specification of its five static neuron variables, which were previously defined in Section 2. Similar to biological differentiation, each cell individually interprets from the environment and its own internal genes those variables that define its function. A direct assignment for each cell's variables from the genome (a direct encoding) we know is not plausible, as this would either limit the neuron type and number (restricting scalability) or necessitate an excessively large genome (decreasing evolvability). Furthermore, the differentiation of each cell into different neuron types is a process determined not singly by the genetic code, but also from environmental cues. Therefore, a cell's genes must encode a function from which each neuron's functional variables can be defined based on environmental cues. In this manner, many neurons can utilize the same function for the derivation of neuron variable specification, reducing the necessary size of the genetic code without limiting neuron types or number.

3.1 The Differentiation Function

In this model, each neuron functionally differentiates based on its own unique location. A neuron's genetic material supplies some differentiation function, G, which takes the Cartesian coordinates representing a neuron's location as inputs and returns the neuron function variables:

$\{M, T_0, R, R_r, F\} = G(x, y)$.

Each neuron utilizes the same differentiation function. In this manner, the genome only needs to supply the genetic material for a single differentiation function. This method of indirect encoding dramatically reduces the quantity of information necessary for specification of neuron functionality in a network.

A feed-forward multilayer perceptron represents the differentiation function, G. The set of functions that can be computed by these networks is dense in the space of continuous functions [Girosi and Poggio 1990]. The networks are therefore appropriate as differentiation functions, as they can map two real input spaces to multiple real output spaces.

3.2 Simulation of Differentiated Networks of Neurons

In this section, three simulations are presented to show the variation of neuron function resulting from the differentiation of a network of evenly spaced neurons. For the 3 simulations, each consecutive simulation utilizes a larger size differentiation neural network, thus increasing the resulting complexity for neuron variable differentiation. To demonstrate the variation over the area encompassing a single network for each of the six neuron function variables (the membrane time constant, the initial threshold level, the decay factor, the total refractory period, the relative refractory period, and the absolute refractory period), surface and contour plots for each static variable value were taken for the 3 simulations. All variables but the absolute refractory period is directly output from the neural network, a classification mapped from the two-dimensional Cartesian coordinate location. The absolute refractory period is directly calculated from the total and relative refractory values. These plots demonstrated the capacity of the differentiation neural networks for complex classification of multiple variables given a two-dimensional input space.

Additionally, as part of these three simulations, 17 evenly spaced fully-connected neurons are differentiated for simulation of communication within the network. To represent graphically the location and functionality of each neuron, the contour plots were overlaid with neuron numbers, indicating the location of each of 17 neurons within the network. In this simulation, neurons one, two, three, and four are induced with an input signal to initiate the spike response pattern of the network. The first simulation utilizes a fully connected feed-forward neural network with two neurons in each of two hidden layers. Figure 2 gives the surface plot for each of the six neuron function variables. In this simulation, the neural network encompasses a total of only four hidden neurons; therefore, the resulting classification of neuron function variables is quite simple. Just below this figure, Figure 3 shows the resulting firing pattern resulting from the single network over 250 time steps. The resulting fully connected network displays very little activity. Only the four neurons presented with external signals result in the firing of action potentials.

Simulation 2 involves differentiation of the neuron functions from a more complex classification neural network. In this simulation, a fully connected feed-forward neural network was utilized which had 10 neurons in both hidden layers. The surface graphs demonstrate that the variation of the neuron function variables is more diverse than in the first simulation. In this simulation, more neurons other than the four induced from external signals respond with action potentials. Additionally, the spike response of this network demonstrates the occurrence of a synchronous firing pattern from several neurons. In the final simulation for neuron differentiation, simulation 3, the differentiation neural network's size was increased dramatically to include 30 neurons in 2 hidden layers. The large, arbitrarily initialized network's classification of neuron variables is quite complex, which contains six surface plots for the classification of these variables. The network of 17 fully connected neurons, differentiated by the classification of variables, was simulated for 250 time steps. In this case, due to the complexity of neuron variable definition, the neurons do not exhibit a noticeable pattern of synchrony in their resulting spike responses.

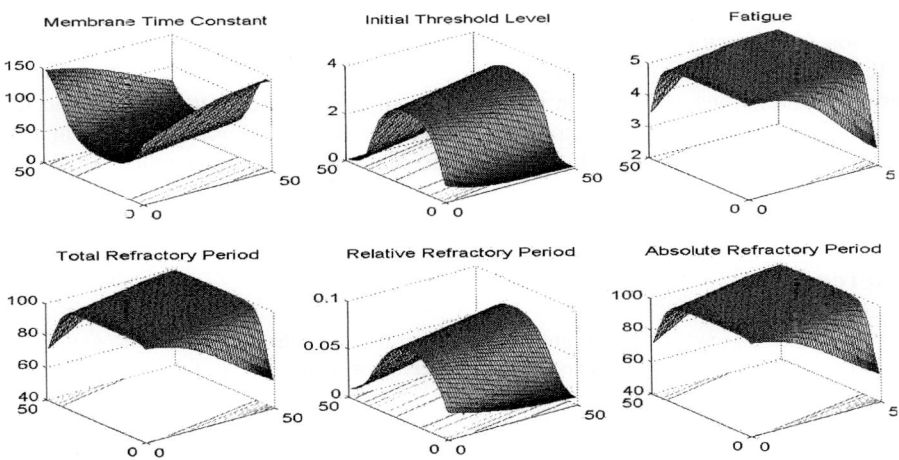

Fig. 2. Neuron Variable Surface Plots for Simulation 1

4 Conclusion

In this paper, a method for modeling neuron differentiation has been presented, paralleling biological observation of this phase of development. In this process, environmental cues from the neighborhood of each cell, in combination with genetic information, control the differentiation process. The genetic information is indirectly encoded in the form of a differentiation function, multilayer feed-forward neural network. This classical neural network is utilized by each neuron in the spiking network to translate environmental variables for the classification of neuron function

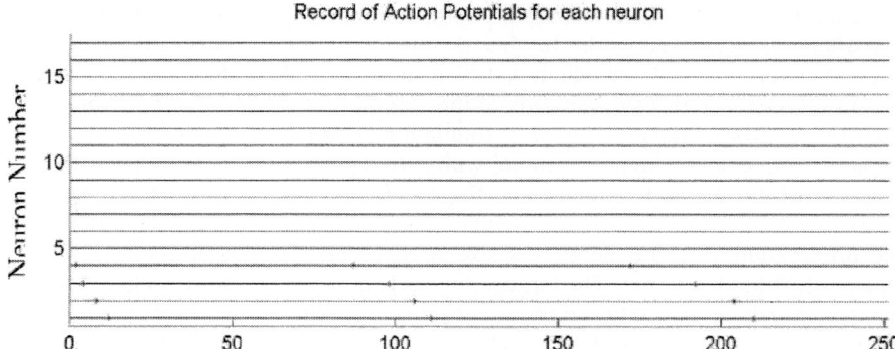

Fig. 3. Resulting Action Potentials from Simulation 1

variables. The neuron function variables, which define the differentiation of each neuron, include: Membrane Time Constant → M, Original Threshold Level → T_0, Duration of Refractory Period → R, Percentage of Refractory Period that is Relative → R_r, Fatigue Property of Neuron → F.

Network simulations, provided in this paper in support of the neuron model and the differentiation method, demonstrate the capability for the simple neuron function model introduced in Section 2 to exhibit a variation of temporal dynamics single and in concert grouped as a network

References

1. Billard, A., Ijspeert, A. J., "Biologically inspired neural controllers for motor control in a quadruped robot", Robotics Laboratory, University of Southern California, SAL 230, Los Angeles 90089, U.S.A 2001.
2. Berthouze, L., "An episodic memory model using spiking neurons", *Proceeding of the IEEE International Conference on Systems, Man, and Cybernetics*, Nashville, TN, pp. 86–91, 2000.
3. Champbell, S. , and Wang, D., Synchronization and Desynchronization in a Network of Locally Coupled Wilson-Cowan Oscillators, IEEE Trans. on Neural Networks 7(3), 1996, 541–552.
4. Choe, Yoonsuck. *Perceptual Grouping in a Self-Organizing Map of Spiking Neurons*. PhD thesis, Department of Computer Sciences, The University of Texas at Austin, Austin, TX, 2001.
5. Choe, Yoonsuck; Miikkulainen, Risto; and Cormack, Lawrence K., "Effects of presynaptic and postsynaptic resource redistribution in Hebbian weight adaptation", *Neurocomputing*, vol. 32–33, pp. 77–82, 2000.
6. Gabbini, F. and Kock, C., "Principles of Spike Train Analysis", in Kock, C and Segev, I. Editors, *Methods in Neural Modeling*, MIT Press, pps 313–360, 1999.
7. Girosi, F., Poggio, T, "Networks and the best approximation property", *Biological Cybernetics,* vol. 63, pp 169–176, 1990.
8. Henkel, Rolf, "Synchronization, Coherence-Detection and Three-Dimensional Vision", 2000.

9. Hodgkin, A. L. and Huxley, A. F. (1952) "A Quantitative Description of Membrane Current and its Application to Conduction and Excitation in Nerve" Journal of Physiology 117: 500–544
10. Hopfield, J. J., and Brody, C., "What is a moment? "Cortical" sensory integration over a brief interval, *"Proc Natl Acad Sci.* USA, vol. 97(25, pgs 13919–24 , 2000.
11. Hopfield, J. J., and Brody, C., " What is a moment? Transient synchrony as a collective mechanism for spatiotemporal integration, " *Proc Natl Acad Sci.* USA, vol. 98(3), pg 1282–7, 2001.
12. Hoppensteadt, Frank C., An Introduction to the Mathematics of Neurons, Second Edition: Modeling in the Frequency Domain, Cambridge University Press, 1997.
13. Horn, D. and Opher, I., 1999. *Collective Excitation Phenomena and their Applications*. In: Pulsed Neural Networks, Eds: W. Maass and C. B. Bishop, MIT Press, 297–316.
14. Ijspeert, A.J, "A leaky-integrator neural network for controlling the locomotion of a simulated salamander", *IEEE*, 2000.
15. Labbi A., and Milanese, R. and Bosch, H., "Asymptotic synchronization in networks of locally connected oscillators", Int. J. of Bifurcation and Chaos, World Scientific, vol. 9, no. 12, pgs. 2279–2284, 1999.
16. Levitan, Irwin B. and Kaczmarek, Leonard K., *The Neuron: Cell and Molecular Biology*, Oxford University Press, 1997.
17. Maass, W. (1997b). Networks of spiking neurons: The third generation of neural network models. Neural Networks, 10(9):1659–1671.
18. Malaka, R. and Buck, S., "Solving nonlinear optimization problems using networks of spiking neurons", *International Joint Conference on Neural Networks,* 2000.
19. Michel, Olivier and Biondi, Joelle, "From the chromosome to the neural network", In Pearson et al. pgs 80–83, 1999
20. Milanese, Ruggero, "Feature Binding through Synchronized Neuronal Oscillations: {A} Preliminary Study", Report Number TR-94-044, Berkeley, California, 1994.
21. Opher, I., Horn, D., and Quenet, B. *Clustering with Spiking Neurons*. In Proceedings of the International Conference on Artificial Neural Networks, ICANN'99, Edinburgh, Scotland September 1999, pp. 485–490.
22. Rinzel, J. and Ermentrout, B., "Analysis of neural excitability and oscillations", in Kock, C and Segev, I. Editors, *Methods in Neural Modeling*, MIT Press, pp. 251–291, 1999.
23. Ruf, B. and Schmitt, M. (1998). *Self-organization of spiking neurons using action potential timing*. IEEE Transactions on Neural Networks, 9(3):575–578.
24. Von der Malsburg, C. and Schneider, W., "*A neural cocktail-party processor*," Biol. Cybern., vol. 54, pp. 29–40, 1986.

Application of Vision Models to Traffic Sign Recognition

X.W. Gao[1], L. Podladchikova[2], and D. Shaposhnikov[2]

[1] School of Computing Science, Middlesex University, Bounds Green,
London N11 2NQ, UK.
x.gao@mdx.ac.uk
http://www.cs.mdx.ac.uk/staffpages/xiaohong

[2] Laboratory of Neuroinformatics of Sensory and Motor Systems, A.B. Kogan Research Institute for Neurocybernetics, Rostov State University, Rostov-on-Don, Russia.
nisms@krinc.ru

Abstract. A system for traffic sign recognition has been developed. Both colour and shape information from signs are utilised for extraction of features. Colour appearance model CIECAM97 has been applied to extract colour information and to segment and classify traffic signs. Whilst shape features are extracted using FOSTS model, the extension of Behaviour Model of Visions (BMV). Recognition rate is very high. For British traffic signs (n=98) obtained under various viewing conditions, the recognition rate is up to 0.95.

1 Introduction

For car drivers, correctly identifying traffic signs at right time and right place plays a crucial part in insuring themselves and their passengers' safe journey. Sometimes, due to changing weather conditions or viewing angles, traffic signs are not easily to be seen until it is too late. Development of automatic systems for recognition of traffic signs is therefore an important approach to improve driving safety [1-3]. For traffic sign recognition, feature representations should be robust and invariant of possible transformations of shapes and change of colours as happened in the real driving situation.

Due to adaptation to the environment, human can correctly identify traffic signs invariant of lighting conditions and viewing angles. Therefore invariant features can be extracted using vision models. One model is CIECAM97 for measuring colour appearance invariant of lighting conditions and is applied in this study to extract colour features. The other vision model, Foveal System for Traffic Signs (FOSTS), is developed based on BMV model (Behaviour Model of Visions) imitating some mechanisms of the real visual system for perceiving shapes[4, 5].

CIECAM97 is a standard colour appearance model recommended by CIE (International Colour Commission on Illumination) in 1997 for measuring colour appearance under various viewing conditions [6, 7]. For human perception, the most common terms used for colour or colour appearance are lightness, chroma, and hue. These measures are given in the model. The input parameters are viewing conditions including lighting source, reference white, and the background.

The BMV model [5] is initially developed on the base of biologically plausible algorithms of space-variant representation [8] of images and specific viewing trajectory formation. It has demonstrated the ability to recognise complex grey-level images invariantly with respect to shift, plain rotation, and in a certain extent to scale. One of the BMV model applications is the development of foveal visual systems for traffic sign recognition that are considered as the most prospective in solution of computational problems in real world image processing. Like other foveal systems it imitates the changes of visual acuity from the fovea to the retinal periphery and attention mechanisms during detailed process of choosing image fragments.

In this paper, new algorithms and models have been represented for sign colour and shape classification, context feature description and recognition.

2 Segmentation of Sign Images Based on CIECAM97

Segmentation is to obtain sub-images containing possible signs from the rest of scene. To recognise a traffic sign, a picture taken from the real road scene during driving condition should be segmented first as there might be more than one sign in an image to be recognised. A typical such image has size about 1680 x1680 pixels while a typical standard sign in the database is 400 x 400 pixels.

Because the image has different colour distribution combination depending on the weather conditions when the photos are taken, colour appearance model CIECAM97 is applied to perform this task. First, the colour ranges have to be found. The colours used in the traffic signs are commonly red, blue, black, and white. Images taken from real world are processed to find the range of colour vectors under different viewing conditions. In this study, the hue range for red and blue signs are 393-423, and 280-290 respectively. While the chroma range for both colour signs is between 57 –95.

3 Sign Feature Description Using FOSTS Model

The shape features of traffic signs in this study are extracted by the extension of the BMV model, called FOSTS model (Foveal System for Traffic Signs).

3.1 Classification of Traffic Signs According to External Forms

For all signs, both from standard databases and from real world images, preliminary classification is conducted according to the colour, their external shape (circle, rectangle, or triangle) by means of histograms of oriented elements detected at resolution level 3 (RL 3).

3.2 Shape Feature Vectors

Each sign in the FOSTS model is represented by specific description of sign inner content. The basic structure and operations in the FOSTS consist of: (i) an image in each sensor fixation point is described by oriented segments extracted in vicinity of each of 49 sensor nodes; (ii) the sensor nodes are located at the intersections of sixteen radiating lines and three concentric circles, each with a different radius; (iii) orientation of segments in the vicinity of each sensor node is determined by means of calculation of the difference between two oriented of Gaussian with spatially shifted centres having the step of 22.5°; (iv) space-variant representation of image features is emulated by Gaussian convolution with different kernels increasing with the distance from the sensor centre. Fig. 1 illustrates the procedure of extraction of shape feature vectors.

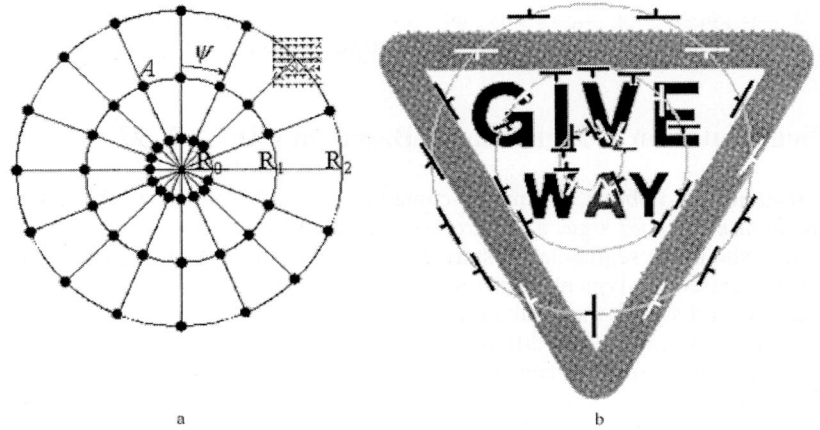

Fig. 1. (a) Schematically representation of sign shape vectors using FOSTS model, context area for a node is indicated by square (b) example of detected edges

4 Traffic Sign Recognition

4.1 Determination of Sign Centre

As it is shown during preliminary tests of the FOSTS for sign processing, sensor positioning near the sign centre increases sign recognition rate. Evidently, such location of the sensor provides the most specific sign description by detailed representation of its internal informative part. It is determined from the centre of mass for colour elements with LCH composition characters from external sign contour. This calculation provides the geometric centre for a sign with necessary accuracy (±3 pixels), the extraction of a "pure" real world sign (without background), and receiving a normalised sign with size of 40x40 pixels.

4.2 Sign Recognition

The recognition is performed in two stages. The basic procedure for both stages is comparison of the 49-dimensional vector describing a current image with template vectors stored in the database that has been classified into several colour/shape subgroups (both standard and obtained from real road conditions). Colour classification is performed according to the parameters of sign LCH composition into external colour sign contour that is determined during colour segmentation.

5 Results

5.1 Evaluation of Shape Transformation Invariance

To imitate possible sign transformations in real road conditions and obtain the quantitative estimations of recognition invariance range, several additional sign databases are created. Graduated artificial transformations (noise, scale, and perspective distortions) of traffic sign have been performed. Then, the distorted images are presented for recognition. Noise have been simulated by adding graduated Gauss noise (5%, 10%, 20%, and 50%) to the images from the standard database.

Table 1 gives the averaged results of recognition of noised and scaled traffic sign images. Recognition rate for images with perspective transformations is equal to 1 (=100% recognition) for red and blue circular signs, and 0.98 for red triangular signs. The obtained results indicate that recognition rate is relatively high for signs with artificial transformations that represent possible sign distortions in the real road conditions (up to 50% for noise level, 50 meters for distance to signs, and 5° for perspective disturbances). It is also shown that recognition rate for red triangular signs sharply decreases at the increase of distortion levels.

Table 1. Recognition rate for artificially noised and scaled traffic sign images

Sign subgroups	Transformation						
	Level of noise				Distance to signs		
	5%	10%	20%	50 %	20 m	30 m	50 m
Blue circular signs (n=14)	1	1	1	0.93	1	1	1
Red circular signs (n=24)	1	1	1	0.87	1	1	0.91
Red triangular signs (n=49)	1	1	0.98	0.40	0.91	0.96	0.70

5.2 Recognition of Real World Sign Images

93 out of 98 potential traffic sign images are correctly identified, which gives 0.95 success recognition rate. Similar results have been obtained for different viewing and environmental conditions (0.96 and 0.94 for sunny and cloudy weather respectively). Recognition time (without low-level processing procedures) varied from 0.2 up to 0.7 seconds per image on a standard Pentium III PC. The non-identified signs (n=5) are either of low resolution (taken from very far distance, more than 60 meters) or have a complex disturbing background. Examples of recognised road signs are shown in Fig. 2 (b). Fig. 2 (3c) demonstrates that a traffic sign with two kinds of distortions (shielding about 35% and perspective disturbance about 10°) is not recognized.

Fig. 2. The examples of recognized (a, b) and non-recognized (c) real world traffic signs. In: (1) the template images from standard database; (2) real world signs after colour segmentation; (3) the same signs as in (2) after colour contour determination and size normalization

6 Conclusion

Overall, the described approach based on vision models provides an accurate recognition of traffic signs located at a moderate distance (up to 60 meters) under various environmental conditions. The use of the CIECAM97 colour vision model allows the segmentation of the majority of traffic signs from the rest of the scenes. The algorithms of the FOSTS model provide essential increase of the recognition rate as compared to the former model versions (0.95 versus 0.80 and 0.87). It is interestingly noticed, that recognition rate obtained by the FOSTS are similar to that for the human observer in the same real world road conditions (0.96).

References

1. Gavrila D. M., Franke U., Gorzig S., Wohler C: Real-time Vision for Intelligent Vehicles. IEEE Instrumentation and Measurement Magazine, Vol. 4 (2001) 22–27
2. Lalonde M., Li Y: Road Sign Recognition – Survey of the State of Art, technique report for Sub-Project 2.4, CRIM-IIT-95/09-35,
   http://nannetta.ce.unipr.it/argo/theysay/rs2/#publications
3. Miura J., Kanda T., Shirai Y: An Active Vision System for Real-Time Traffic Sign Recognition. In Proc. 2000 IEEE Int. Conf. on Intelligent Transportation Systems (2000) 52–57

4. Podladchikova L.N., Gusakova V.I., Shaposhnikov D.G., Faure A., Golovan A.V., Shevtsova N.A: MARR: Active vision model, Proceedings SPIE'97, Vol. 3208 (1997) 418–425
5. Rybak I.A., Gusakova V.I., Golovan A.V., Podladchikova L.N., Shevtsova N.A.: A Model of Attention-guided Visual Perception and Recognition, Vision Research, Vol. 38 (1998) 2387–2400
6. Luo M.R., Hunt R.W.G: The structure of the CIE 1997 colour appearance model (CIECAM97s), Color Res. Appl., Vol. 23 (1998) 138–146
7. CIE: The CIE 1997 Interim Colour Appearance Model (Simple Version), CIECAM97s, CIE TC1-34, April (1998)
8. Schwartz E.L., Greve D.N., Bonmassar G: Space-variant Active Vision: Definition, Overview and Examples. // Neural Networks, Vol..8 (1995), n.7/8 1297–1308

Emotion Recognition

An Intelligent Scheme for Facial Expression Recognition

Amaryllis Raouzaiou[1], Spiros Ioannou[1], Kostas Karpouzis[1], Nicolas Tsapatsoulis[1], Stefanos Kollias[1], and Roddy Cowie[2]

[1] Department of Electrical and Computer Engineering
National Technical University of Athens, Heroon Polytechniou 9, 157 73 Zographou, Greece
Phone: +30-10-7722491, Fax: +30-10-7722492
{araouz,sivann,kkarpou,ntsap}@image.ntua.gr,
stefanos@cs.ntua.gr
[2] Department of Psychology
Queen's University of Belfast
Northern Ireland, United Kingdom
r.cowie@qub.ac.uk

Abstract. This paper addresses the problem of emotion recognition in faces through an intelligent neuro-fuzzy system, which is capable of analysing facial features extracted following the MPEG-4 standard, associating these features to symbolic fuzzy predicates, and reasoning on the latter, so as to classify facial images according to the underlying emotional states. Results are presented which illustrate the capability of the developed system to analyse and recognise facial expressions in human computer interaction applications.

1 Introduction

There has recently been high interest in affective computing, especially in interfaces which can analyse their users' emotional state and generate synthetic agents that possess convincing expression characteristics. Automatic emotion recognition in faces is a hard problem, requiring a number of pre-processing steps which attempt to detect or track the face, to locate characteristic facial regions such as eyes, mouth and nose on it, to extract and follow the movement of facial features, e.g., characteristic points in these regions, or model facial gestures using anatomic information about the face.

Most of the above techniques are based on a well-known system for describing "all visually distinguishable facial movements", called the Facial Action Coding System (FACS) [4], [6]. FACS is an anatomically oriented coding system, based on the definition of "action units" that cause facial movements. The FACS model has inspired the derivation of facial animation and definition parameters in the framework of the ISO MPEG-4 standard [7]. In particular, the Facial Definition Parameter (FDP) set and the Facial Animation Parameter (FAP) set were designed in the MPEG-4 framework to allow the definition of a facial shape and texture, as well as the animation of faces reproducing expressions, emotions and speech pronunciation. By monitoring facial gestures corresponding to FDP feature points (FP) and/or FAP movements over time, it is possible to derive cues about user's expressions/emotions [1], [3].

Research on facial expression analysis and synthesis has tended to concentrate on primary or archetypal emotions, i.e., sadness, anger, joy, fear, disgust and surprise. Very few studies which explore non-archetypal emotions have appeared in the computer science literature [2], [8]. However, psychological researchers working in different traditions [9] have investigated a broader variety of emotions. An extensive survey on emotion analysis can be found in [10]. According to these studies, emotions can be modelled as points in a space with a relatively small number of dimensions. Two dimensions, *activation* and *evaluation,* are sufficient for a first approximation. *Evaluation* summarises how positive or negative the user feels; *activation* indicates how energetically he or she is disposed to act.

In this work we present a methodology for analysing both primary and intermediate expressions, taking into account the above-mentioned results and particularly the *activation* parameter. This is performed through a neuro-fuzzy system which first translates FP movements into FAPs and reasons on the latter to recognize the underlying emotion in facial video sequences.

2 Modelling Facial Expressions Using FAPs

Two basic issues should be addressed when modelling archetypal expression: (i) estimation of FAPs that are involved in their formation, (ii) definition of the FAP intensities. Table 1 illustrates the description of "joy" and "sadness", using MPEG-4 FAPs. Descriptions for all archetypal expressions can be found in [1].

Table 1. FAP vocabulary for description of "joy" and "sadness"

Joy	open_jaw (F_3), lower_t_midlip (F_4), raise_b_midlip (F_5), stretch_l_cornerlip (F_6), stretch_r_cornerlip (F_7), raise_l_cornerlip (F_{12}), raise_r_cornerlip (F_{13}), close_t_l_eyelid (F_{19}), close_t_r_eyelid (F_{20}), close_b_l_eyelid (F_{21}), close_b_r_eyelid (F_{22}), raise_l_m_eyebrow (F_{33}), raise_r_m_eyebrow (F_{34}), lift_l_cheek (F_{41}), lift_r_cheek (F_{42}), stretch_l_cornerlip_o (F_{53}), stretch_r_cornerlip_o (F_{54})
Sadness	close_t_l_eyelid (F_{19}), close_t_r_eyelid (F_{20}), close_b_l_eyelid (F_{21}), close_b_r_eyelid (F_{22}), raise_l_i_eyebrow (F_{31}), raise_r_i_eyebrow (F_{32}), raise_l_m_eyebrow (F_{33}), raise_r_m_eyebrow (F_{34}), raise_l_o_eyebrow (F_{35}), raise_r_o_eyebrow (F_{36})

Although FAPs are practical and very useful for animation purposes, they are inadequate for analysing facial expressions from video scenes or still images. In order to measure FAPs in real images and video sequences, it is necessary to define a way of describing them through the movement of points that lie in the facial area and that can be automatically detected. Such a description could gain advantage from the extended research on automatic facial point detection [11].

Quantitative modelling of FAPs can be implemented using the features labelled as f_i ($i=1...15$) in the third column of Table 2 [12]. The feature set employs FDP feature points that lie in the facial area. It consists of distances (noted as $s(x,y)$, where x and y correspond to FDP feature points ranked in terms of their belonging to specific facial areas [14]), some of which are constant during expressions and are used as reference points. It should be noted that not all FAPs can be modelled by distances between facial protuberant points (e.g. *raise_b_lip_lm_o*, *lower_t_lip_lm_o*). In such cases, the corresponding FAPs are retained in the vocabulary and their ranges of variation are experimentally defined based on facial animations. Moreover, some features serve for the estimation of the range of variation of more than one FAP (e.g. features f_{12}-f_{15}).

Table 2. Quantitative FAP modelling: (1) $s(x,y)$ is the Euclidean distance between FPs x and y, (2) $D_{i\text{-NEUTRAL}}$ refers to distance D_i with the face in neutral position

FAP name	Main Feature for description	Utilized Main Feature
squeeze_l_eyebrow (F_{37})	$D_1=s(4.6,3.8)$	$f_1= D_{1\text{-NEUTRAL}} - D_1$
squeeze_r_eyebrow (F_{38})	$D_2=s(4.5,3.11)$	$f_2= D_{2\text{-NEUTRAL}} - D_2$
lower_t_midlip (F_4)	$D_3=s(9.3,8.1)$	$f_3= D_3 - D_{3\text{-NEUTRAL}}$
raise_b_midlip (F_5)	$D_4=s(9.3,8.2)$	$f_4= D_{4\text{-NEUTRAL}} - D_4$
raise_l_i_eyebrow (F_{31})	$D_5=s(4.2,3.8)$	$f_5= D_5 - D_{5\text{-NEUTRAL}}$
raise_r_i_eyebrow (F_{32})	$D_6=s(4.1,3.11)$	$f_6= D_6 - D_{6\text{-NEUTRAL}}$
raise_l_o_eyebrow (F_{35})	$D_7=s(4.6,3.12)$	$f_7= D_7 - D_{7\text{-NEUTRAL}}$
raise_r_o_eyebrow (F_{36})	$D_8=s(4.5,3.7)$	$f_8= D_8 - D_{8\text{-NEUTRAL}}$
raise_l_m_eyebrow (F_{33})	$D_9=s(4.4,3.12)$	$f_9= D_9 - D_{9\text{-NEUTRAL}}$
raise_r_m_eyebrow (F_{34})	$D_{10}=s(4.3,3.7)$	$f_{10}= D_{10} - D_{10\text{-NEUTRAL}}$
open_jaw (F_3)	$D_{11}=s(8.1,8.2)$	$f_{11}= D_{11} - D_{11\text{-NEUTRAL}}$
close_t_l_eyelid (F_{19}) –close_b_l_eyelid (F_{21})	$D_{12}=s(3.2,3.4)$	$f_{12}= D_{12} - D_{12\text{-NEUTRAL}}$
close_t_r_eyelid (F_{20}) –close_b_r_eyelid (F_{22})	$D_{13}=s(3.1,3.3)$	$f_{13}= D_{13} - D_{13\text{-NEUTRAL}}$
stretch_l_cornerlip (F_6) (stretch_l_cornerlip_o)(F_{53}) – stretch_r_cornerlip (F_7) (stretch_r_cornerlip_o) (F_{54})	$D_{14}=s(8.4,8.3)$	$f_{14}= D_{14} - D_{14\text{-NEUTRAL}}$
squeeze_l_eyebrow (F_{37}) AND squeeze_r_eyebrow (F_{38})	$D_{15}=s(4.6,4.5)$	$f_{15}= D_{15\text{-NEUTRAL}} - D_{15}$

3 The Facial Expression Recognition System

In general, six general categories are used, each one characterized by an archetypal emotion. Within each category, intermediate expressions are described by different emotional and optical intensities, as well as minor variations in expression details.

A hybrid intelligent emotion recognition system is presented next, consisting of a connectionist (subsymbolic) association part and a symbolic processing part as shown in Figure 1. In this modular architecture the *Connectionist Association Module* (CAM) provides the system with the ability to ground the symbolic predicates (associating them with the input features), while the *Adaptive Resource Allocating Neuro Fuzzy Inference System* (ARANFIS) [15] implements the semantic reasoning process.

The system takes as input a feature vector f that corresponds to the features f_i shown in the third column of Table 2. The particular values of f are associated to the symbolic predicates – i.e., FAP values shown in the first column of the same table- through the CAM subsystem. The CAM's outputs form the input vector G to the fuzzy inference subsystem, with the elements of G expressing the observed value of a corresponding FAP. The CAM consists of a neural network that dynamically forms the above association, providing the emotion analysis system with the capability to adapt to peculiarities of the specific user. In the training phase, the CAM learns to analyse the feature space and provide estimates of the FAP intensities (e.g. low, high, medium). This step requires: (a) Using an appropriate set of training inputs f, (b) Collecting a representative set T_I of pairs (f, s) to be used for network training, and (c) Estimating a parameter set $\mathbf{W_I}$, which maps the input space F to the symbolic predicate space S.

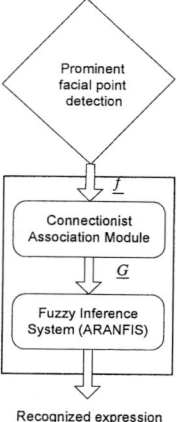

Fig. 1. The emotion analysis system

ARANFIS evaluates the symbolic predicates provided by the CAM subsystem and performs the conceptual reasoning process that finally results to the degree at which the output situations – expressions- are recognised. ARANFIS [15] is a variation of the SuPFuNIS system [5] that enables structured learning. ARANFIS embeds fuzzy rules of the form "If s_1 is LOW and s_2 is HIGH then y is [expression - e.g. anger], where LOW, and HIGH are fuzzy sets defined, respectively, on input universes of discourse (UODs) and the output is a fuzzified expression.

Input nodes represent the domain variables-predicates and output nodes represent the target variables or classes. Each hidden node represents a rule, and input-hidden node connections represent fuzzy rules antecedents. Each hidden-output node connection represents a fuzzy-rule consequent. Fuzzy sets corresponding to linguistic labels of fuzzy *if-then* rules (such as LOW and HIGH) are defined on input and output UODs and are represented by symmetric Gaussian membership functions specified by a center and spread. Fuzzy weights w_{ij} from input nodes i to rule nodes j are thus modeled by the center w_{ij}^c and spread w_{ij}^s of a Gaussian fuzzy set and denoted by $w_{ij}=(w_{ij}^c, w_{ij}^s)$. In a similar fashion, consequent fuzzy weights from rule nodes j to output nodes k are denoted by $v_{jk} = (v_{ij}^c, v_{ij}^s)$. The spread of the i-th fuzzified input element is denoted as s_i^s while s_i^c is obtained as the crisp value of the i-th input element. Knowledge in the form of *if-then* rules can be either derived through clustering of input data or be embedded directly as a-priori knowledge.

It should be noted that in the previously described emotion analysis system, no hypothesis has been made about the type of recognizable emotions, that can be either archetypal or non-archetypal ones.

4 Application Study

Let us examine the situation where a PC camera captures its user's image. In the preprocessing stage, skin color segmentation is performed and the face is extracted. A snake is then used to smooth the face mask computed at the segmentation subsystem output. Then, the facial points are extracted, and point distances are calculated. Assuming that the above procedure is first performed for the user's neutral image, storing the corresponding facial points, the differences between them and the FPs of the current facial image of the user are estimated.

An emotion analysis system is created in [13]. In the system interface shown in Figure 2, one can observe an example of the calculated FP distances, the rules activated by the neurofuzzy system and the recognised emotion ('surprise').

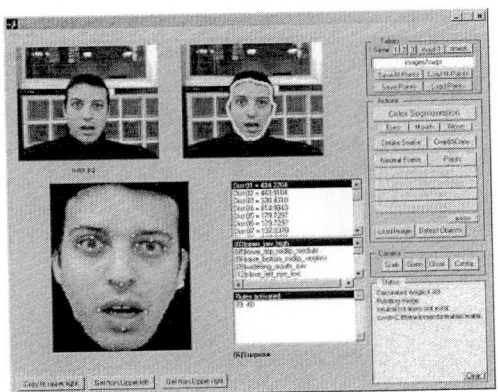

Fig. 2. System Interface

To train the CAM system, we used the PHYSTA database in [2] as training set and the EKMAN database [4], [10] as evaluation test. The coordinates of the points have been marked by hand for 300 images in the training set and 110 images in the test set.

Table 3. Training the CAM module

FAP name	Primary distance	Other distances	States (VL-VeryLow, L-Low, M-Medium, H-High)
Squeeze_l_eyebrow (F_{37})	d_2	$d_6, d_8, d_{10}, d_{17}, d_{19}, d_{15}$	L, M, H
Squeeze_r_eyebrow (F_{38})	d_1	$d_5, d_7, d_9, d_{16}, d_{18}, d_{15}$	L, M, H
Lower_t_midlip (F_4)	d_3	d_{11}, d_{20}, d_{21}	L, M
Raise_b_midlip (F_5)	d_4	d_{11}, d_{20}, d_{21}	VL, L, H
Raise_l_I_eyebrow (F_{31})	d_6	$d_2, d_8, d_{10}, d_{17}, d_{19}, d_{15}$	L, M, H
Raise_r_I_eyebrow (F_{32})	d_5	$d_1, d_7, d_9, d_{16}, d_{18}, d_{15}$	L, M, H
Raise_l_o_eyebrow (F_{35})	d_8	$d_2, d_6, d_{10}, d_{17}, d_{19}, d_{15}$	L, M, H
Raise_r_o_eyebrow (F_{36})	d_7	$d_1, d_5, d_9, d_{16}, d_{18}, d_{15}$	L, M, H
Raise_l_m_eyebrow (F_{33})	d_{10}	$d_2, d_6, d_8, d_{17}, d_{19}, d_{15}$	L, M, H
Raise_r_m_eyebrow (F_{34})	d_9	$d_1, d_5, d_7, d_{16}, d_{18}, d_{15}$	L, M, H
Open_jaw (F_3)	d_{11}	d_4	L, M, H
close_left_eye (F_{19}, F_{21})	d_{13}	-	L, H
close_right_eye (F_{20}, F_{22})	d_{12}	-	L, H
Wrinkles_between_eyebrows (F_{37}, F_{38})	d_{15}	$d_1, d_2, d_5, d_6, d_7, d_8, d_9, d_{16}, d_{17}, d_{18}, d_{19}$	L, M, H
Raise_l_cornerlip_o (F_{53})	d_{23}	$d_3, d_4, d_{11}, d_{20}, d_{21}, d_{22}$	L, M, H
Raise_r_cornerlip_o (F_{54})	d_{22}	$d_3, d_4, d_{11}, d_{20}, d_{21}, d_{23}$	L, M, H
widening_mouth (F_6, F_7)	d_{11}	d_3, d_4, d_{14}	L, M, H

The CAM consisted of 17 neural networks, each of which associated less than 10 FP input distances (from the list of 23 distances defined as in Table 1 and mentioned in Table 3) to the states (high, medium, low, very low) of a corresponding FAP, and was trained using a variant of backpropagation learning algorithm [16]. Moreover, 41 rules were appropriately defined, half of them taken from the associated literature and half of them derived through training [14], and inserted in the ARAFNIS subsystem.

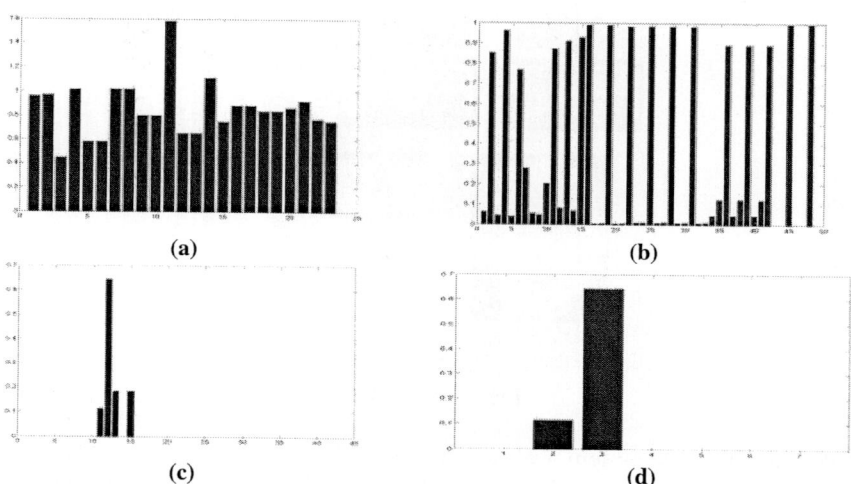

Fig. 3. (a) Example of a feature vector feeding the CAM, (b) An instance of CAM's output, (c) Activation of each of the 41 rules, (d) The final system output

Let us provide an example of the performance of the overall system. Input is *image001* of the Ekman database, showing a happy expression. Figure 3a shows the feature vector provided at the input of the CAM subsystem; Figure 3b shows the output of the CAM, which is translated as: *open_jaw*-> Medium, *lower_t_midlip*-> Low, *raise_b_midlip*->VeryLow, ..., *raise_r_cornerlip_o*->High. Figure 3c presents the activation level of each of the 41 rules inserted in ARANFIS, while Figure 3d the final system output, in terms of the archetypal emotional states.

Table 4. Results in images of different expressions

	Anger	Joy	Disgust	Surprise	Neutral
Anger	0.611	0.01	0.068	0	0
Joy	0.006	0.757	0.009	0	0.024
Disgust	0.061	0.007	0.635	0	0
Surprise	0	0.004	0	0.605	0.001
Neutral	0	0.123	0	0	0.83

Table 5. Activated rules

Expressions	Rule more often activated (% of examined photos)
Anger	[*open_jaw_low, lower_top_midlip_medium, raise_bottom_midlip_high, raise_left_inner_eyebrow_low, raise_right_inner_eyebrow_low, raise_left_medium_eyebrow_low, raise_right_medium_eyebrow_low, squeeze_left_eyebrow_high, squeeze_right_eyebrow_high, wrinkles_between_eyebrows_high, raise_left_outer_cornerlip_medium, raise_right_outer_cornerlip_medium*] (47%)
Joy	[*open_jaw_high, lower_top_midlip_low, raise_bottom_midlip_verylow, widening_mouth_high, close_left_eye_high, close_right_eye_high*] (39%)
Disgust	[*open_jaw_low, lower_top_midlip_low, raise_bottom_midlip_high, widening_mouth_low, close_left_eye_high, close_right_eye_high, raise_left_inner_eyebrow_medium, raise_right_inner_eyebrow_medium, raise_left_medium_eyebrow_medium, raise_right_medium_eyebrow_medium, wrinkles_between_eyebrows_medium*] {33%)
Surprise	[*open_jaw_high, raise_bottom_midlip_verylow, widening_mouth_low, close_left_eye_low, close_right_eye_low, raise_left_inner_eyebrow_high, raise_right_inner_eyebrow_high, raise_left_medium_eyebrow_high, raise_right_medium_eyebrow_high, raise_left_outer_eyebrow_high, raise_right_outer_eyebrow_high, squeeze_left_eyebrow_low, squeeze_right_eyebrow_low, wrinkles_between_eyebrows_low*] (71%)
Neutral	[*open_jaw_low, lower_top_midlip_medium, raise_left_inner_eyebrow_medium, raise_right_inner_eyebrow_medium, raise_left_medium_eyebrow_medium, raise_right_medium_eyebrow_medium, raise_left_outer_eyebrow_medium, raise_right_outer_eyebrow_medium, squeeze_left_eyebrow_medium, squeeze_right_eyebrow_medium, wrinkles_between_eyebrows_medium, raise_left_outer_cornerlip_medium, raise_right_outer_cornerlip_medium*] (70%)

Table 4 illustrates the confusion matrix of the mean degree of beliefs (*not the classification rates*), for each of the archetypal emotions *anger, joy, disgust, surprise* and the *neutral* condition, computed over the EKMAN dataset, which verifies the good system performance, while Table 5 shows the more often activated rule for each of the above expressions.

5 Conclusions

Facial expression recognition has been investigated in this paper, based on neuro-fuzzy analysis of facial features extracted from a user's image following the MPEG-4 standard. A hybrid intelligent system has been described that performs extraction of fuzzy predicates and inference, providing an estimate of the user's emotional state. Work is currently been done, extending and validating the above developments in the framework of the IST ERMIS project [13].

References

1. N. Tsapatsoulis, A. Raouzaiou, S. Kollias, R. Cowie and E. Douglas-Cowie, "Emotion Recognition and Synthesis based on MPEG-4 FAPs," in *MPEG-4 Facial Animation*, Igor Pandzic, R. Forchheimer (eds), John Wiley & Sons, UK, 2002.
2. EC TMR Project "PHYSTA: Principled Hybrid Systems: Theory and Applications," http://www.image.ece.ntua.gr/physta.
3. R. Cowie, E. Douglas-Cowie, N. Tsapatsoulis, G. Votsis, S. Kollias, W. Fellenz and J. Taylor, "Emotion Recognition in Human-Computer Interaction", *IEEE Signal Processing Magazine*, 18 (1), p. 32–80, January 2001.
4. P. Ekman and W. Friesen, *The Facial Action Coding System*, Consulting Psychologists Press, San Francisco, CA, 1978 (http://www.paulekman.com)
5. S. Paul and S. Kumar, "Subsethood-Product Fuzzy Neural Inference System (SuPFuNIS)," *IEEE Trans. on Neural Networks,* vol. 13, no 3, pp. 578–599, May 2002.
6. ISO/IEC JTC1/SC29/WG11 N3205, "Multi-users technology (Requirements and Applications)", December 1999, Maui
7. A.M. Tekalp, J. Ostermann, "Face and 2-D mesh animation in MPEG-4", *Signal Processing: Image Communication,* Vol. 15, No. 4-5 (Tutorial Issue on the MPEG-4 Standard), pp. 387–421, January 2000.
8. EC TMR Project PHYSTA Report, "Development of Feature Representation from Facial Signals and Speech," January 1999.
9. P. Ekman, "Facial expression and Emotion," *Am. Psychologist*, vol. 48 pp.384-392, 1993
10. P. Ekman and W.V. Friesen, "Pictures of Facial Affect", Palo Alto, CA: Consulting Psychologists Press, 1978.
11. P. Chellapa, C. Wilson and S. Sirohey, "Human and Machine Recognition of Faces: A Survey," *Proceedings of IEEE*, vol.83, no. 5, pp. 705–740, 1995.
12. K.Karpouzis, N. Tsapatsoulis and S. Kollias, "Moving to Continuous Facial Expression Space using the MPEG-4 Facial Definition Parameter (FDP) Set," *in Proc. of the Electronic Imaging 2000 Conference of SPIE,* San Jose, CA, USA, January 2000.
13. IST Project: Emotionally Rich Man-Machine Interaction Systems (ERMIS), 2001-2003
14. A. Raouzaiou, N. Tsapatsoulis, K. Karpouzis and S. Kollias, "Parameterized facial expression synthesis based on MPEG-4", EURASIP Journal on Applied Signal Processing,Vol. 2002, No. 10, pp. 1021–1038, Hindawi Publishing Corporation, October 2002.
15. M Pertselakis, N. Tsapatsoulis, S. Kollias and A. Stafylopatis, "An Adaptive Resource Allocating Neural Fuzzy Inference System," submitted for possible presentation to the "IEEE Intelligent Systems Application to Power Systems" (ISAP'03), Lemnos, Greece, 2003.
16. S. Haykin, "Neural Networks: a Comprehensive Foundation", Macmillan College Publishing Company, Inc., New York, 1994

Signal Enhancement for Continuous Speech Recognition

Theologos Athanaselis, Stavroula-Evita Fotinea, Stelios Bakamidis,
Ioannis Dologlou, and Georgios Giannopoulos

Institute for Language and Speech processing (ILSP)
6, Artemidos str. & Epidavrou, Paradissos Amaroussiou 151 25, Greece
Tel: +302106875300, Fax: +302106854270
{tathana,evita,bakam,ydol,ggia}@ilsp.gr

Abstract. This paper presents a comparison between two parametric methods for Signal Enhancement in order to address the problem of robust Automatic Speech Recognition (ASR). An SVD–based technique (ISE) and a non-linear spectral subtraction method (NSS), have been evaluated by means of the Continuous Speech Recognition system that is used in the ERMIS project. The input signal is corrupted with coloured noise with variable signal-to-noise ratio. It was found that fine-tuning of the various parameters of the enhancement techniques is crucial for efficient optimisation of their performance. Both methods provide significant improvement of the speech recogniser performance in the presence of coloured noise, with the NSS method being slightly better.

1 Introduction

The performance of commonly used speech recognisers is affected by adverse environmental conditions. Suppression of additive noise before the feature extraction stage is one important component in the development of any Speech Recogniser [6]. Considerable effort has been made to alleviate this problem using signal enhancement techniques to remove the noise prior to the recognition process. This is however a delicate procedure since denoising usually alters the spectral characteristics of speech that does not fit any more the already designed acoustic models of the recogniser. This is the reason why speech enhancement, despite the perceptual improvement that may provide, can sometimes deteriorate the performance of the recogniser [4].

Our study deals with the comparison of the Non Linear Spectral Subtraction (NSS) method with the SVD-based noise removal scheme in order to enhance impaired speech prior to feed it to the speech recognition system. The SVD-based technique of a signal is based on the eigen-analysis of its covariance matrix [3]. The signal can be seen as a vector of dimension N and it is projected onto the singular vectors of an $p \times N$ Hankel matrix, where p is the model order under consideration. This operation is equivalent to adaptive filtering the signal with a filter whose frequency response is influenced by the spectral content of the signal.

The paper is organized as follows. A short description of a non-linear spectral subtraction method is presented in section 2.1 while the general SVD approach along with an algorithmic extension, based on the combination of the SVD and an iterative process is presented in sections 2.2 and 2.2.1. Experimentation and results, can be found in section 3, under various additive noise conditions for the large vocabulary continuous recognition system developed by ILSP in the framework of the ERMIS (Emotionally Rich Man-machine Intelligent System) project, IST-2000-29319. Finally, concluding remarks are presented in section 4.

2 Noise Reduction Algorithms

2.1 Speech Enhancement Based on Non-linear Spectral Subtraction (NSS)

In additive noise, the degraded speech can be described by $y[k] = x[k] + n[k]$, where $x[k]$ and $n[k]$ represent the noise-free speech and corrupting noise sequences respectively. Assuming the speech and noise processes are uncorrelated, the relationship can be described in the short time power spectral domain by, $|Y_i(\omega_k)|^2 = |X_i(\omega_k)|^2 + |N_i(\omega_k)|^2$. Note that the index, i, is used to represent the i-th windowed frame of speech.

Non-linear spectral subtraction (NSS) takes into account the frequency-dependent signal to noise ratio (SNR) of coloured noise. Here, the algorithm reduces subtraction for spectral components of high SNR and increases subtraction for spectral components of low SNR. In addition, the noise model includes both an averaged noise spectrum. NSS enhancement can be expressed in terms of a filtering operation, $|\hat{X}_i(\omega_k)| = H_i(\omega_k)|Y_i(\omega_k)|$, where $H_i(\omega_k)$ depends on a smoothed estimate of the noise-corrupted speech magnitude spectrum $|\ddot{Y}_i(\omega_k)|$, and non-linear subtraction term, $\Phi_i(\omega_k)$, $H_i(\omega_k) = \dfrac{|\ddot{Y}_i(\omega_k)| - |\Phi_i(\omega_k)|}{|\ddot{Y}_i(\omega_k)|}$.

The subtraction term, $\Phi_i(\omega_k)$, is given by $\Phi_i(\omega_k) = \dfrac{\max_{i-40 \leq \tau \leq i}|\hat{N}_T(\omega_k)|}{1 + \gamma \rho_t(\omega_\kappa)}$ with $\rho_t(\omega_\kappa) = \dfrac{|\ddot{Y}_i(\omega_k)|}{|\hat{N}_i(\omega_k)|}$, where γ is a constant dependent on the range of $\rho_t(\omega_\kappa)$.

For practical purposes, the dynamic range of between 1 to 3 times the smoothed noise magnitude estimate (i.e., $|\ddot{N}_i(\omega_k)| \leq \Phi_i(\omega_k) \leq 3|\ddot{N}_i(\omega_k)|$) and a noise-floor is established during subtraction [5].

2.2 Outline of the Truncated SVD Procedure

Consider the clean speech signal $x[k]$ and the noise signal $n[k]$ (both unknown). If we assume the noise to be additive, we can write $y[k] = x[k] + n[k]$, where $y[k]$ corresponds to the recorded noisy signal. From the vector $\mathbf{y} = [y[0], y[1], \cdots, y[N-1]]^T$ we can construct the Hankel matrix $\mathbf{Y} \in \Re^{L \times M}$,

$$\mathbf{Y} = \begin{bmatrix} y[0] & y[1] & \cdots & y[M-1] \\ y[1] & y[2] & \cdots & y[M] \\ \vdots & \vdots & & \vdots \\ y[L-1] & y[L] & \cdots & y[N-1] \end{bmatrix}$$

with $L \geq M$ and $L = N + 1 - M$. Assuming that the clean signal $x[k]$ consists of a sum of p complex exponentials, then the Hankel matrix containing the clean signal is rank-deficient and has rank $p \leq M$. If $n[k]$ consists of broadband noise, the matrix $\mathbf{Y}$ will in general not be rank-deficient and will have rank M.

From the SVD of $\mathbf{Y}$ it is possible to construct a least-squares estimate of the Hankel matrix containing the clean signal. When we set the $M - p$ smallest singular values, corresponding to the noise, to zero and we only retain the p largest singular values, corresponding to the signal, we are able to construct the matrix $\mathbf{Y}_p$,

$$\mathbf{Y}_p = [U_1 \; U_2] \begin{bmatrix} \Sigma_1 & 0 \\ 0 & 0 \end{bmatrix} \begin{bmatrix} V_1^T \\ V_2^T \end{bmatrix} = U_1 \Sigma_1 V_1^T$$

which is the best rank-p approximation of the original matrix $\mathbf{Y}$.

In general, the matrix $\mathbf{Y}_p$ does not have a Hankel structure. A simple procedure for restoring the Hankel structure is to average along the anti-diagonals of the matrix and to construct a Hankel matrix $\hat{\mathbf{X}}$, $\hat{X} = \begin{bmatrix} \hat{x}[0] & \hat{x}[1] & \cdots & \hat{x}[M-1] \\ \hat{x}[1] & \hat{x}[2] & \cdots & \hat{x}[M] \\ \vdots & \vdots & & \vdots \\ \hat{x}[L-1] & \hat{x}[L] & \cdots & \hat{x}[N-1] \end{bmatrix}$,

$$\hat{x}[k] = \frac{1}{\beta - \alpha + 1} \sum_{i=\alpha}^{\beta} Y_p(k-i+2, i), \; \alpha = \max(1, k-L+2), \beta = \min(M, k+1).$$

Because of the averaging, the matrix $\hat{\mathbf{X}}$ in general does not have rank p any more. Still, because $\hat{\mathbf{X}}$ is closer to $\mathbf{Y}_p$ than the original matrix $\mathbf{Y}$, the signal $\hat{\mathbf{x}} = [\hat{x}[0], \hat{x}[1], \ldots, \hat{x}[N-1]]^T$ will be more compatible with the p-th order model than the signal $\mathbf{y}$. It has been shown that for speech applications this simple procedure is indeed able to reduce additive noise [2,3].

2.2.1 Iterative Signal Enhancement Algorithm (ISE)

The relatively new algorithm that is known in the literature as ISE is based on the combination of the SVD of the input signal and an iterative process that each time extracts from the signal its most energetic spectral properties. The signal is processed frame by frame and for a given frame an M-th order SVD is computed.

The algorithm begins with the calculation of the rank-1 signal decomposition $s[k]$ from the corrupted signal $y[k]$. This calculation is realised by truncating the Hankel matrix to rank one and averaging the anti-diagonals. Then the residual signal $r[k]$ is computed by subtracting the signal decomposition $s[k]$ from the input signal $y[k]$. The procedure is repeated using the residual signal as input for the next iteration. The algorithm terminates when the energy of the residual signal is equal to the energy of the noise. The enhanced signal $\hat{x}[k]$ is obtained by accumulating the signal decompositions $s[k]$ over all iterations [3,4].

3 Experimentation and Results

3.1 Description of the ASR Task

The proposed large vocabulary continuous speech recognition system being developed by ILSP, is based on Hidden Markov Models. It is a speaker independent system. The speech waveform is converted by a parameter extraction module into a sequence of acoustic vectors. Each of these vectors is a compact representation of the short-time speech spectrum covering a period of typically 10 msecs (e.g. 32 components every 10 milliseconds). In order to extract these vectors the Mel-frequency Cepstral Coefficients computation is being used. Acoustic modelling is achieved by using models which represent individual phones by hidden Markov model (HMM), with state-tying used to link states which are acoustically indistinguishable. The acoustic model is based on small units such as phonemes or phonemes in a left and right context ("triphones"). For Greek, 32 phoneme units are used to describe the pronunciation of all words. The corresponding figure for English is 45. The vocabulary size is currently 60000 words for Greek; while further expansion is foreseen in the near future. The language models are computed using very large amounts of text data (corpus). The corpus is filtered to remove obsolete words. The statistical language model consists of bigrams and trigrams. The search engine finds an optimal solution among all possible sentences using the Viterbi algorithm. The output of the speech recognition engine is ASCII text, representing what the speaker has uttered.

3.2 Experimental Scheme

The experimentation involves a continuous speech recognition task for Greek dictation with a small vocabulary. The recordings have been made using the Praat software package (doing phonetics by computer) version 3.8.63 [1]. The sampling frequency was 16 KHz and the data format was Mono. The sound files contained utterances of the following numbers: 1, 2, 3, 4, 7, 28, 40, 60, 67, 88, 99, 100. Our test-set consists of the above numbers uttered by four speakers (two male (MS1,MS2) and two female (FS1,FS2)). The speakers are natives Greeks, with no speaking or hearing disability whatsoever. They read the test numbers in ascending order, in a natural and relaxed manner. In order to evaluate the speech recognition system performance we used coloured noise, because it is more representative to the environmental noise than the white one. The sound files were degraded by adding artificially coloured noise with variable signal-to-noise ratio. We have used different levels of noise, changing each time the SNR, starting from 1db up to 45 db (step 1db). In order to create coloured noise we have used white noise filtered through a bandpass FIR filter. For experimental purposes we used different order of FIR filters and a different bandpass zone. Multiple combinations of these two parameters (FIR order and bandpass zone) were investigated. A 50th and 200th order FIR digital filters were designed with different bandpass zones. We considered two different zones, one between 500-1500Hz and another between 3000-5000Hz.

The performance of the speech recognition system is improved when the input signal is enhanced using either the non-linear spectral subtraction technique with iterative overestimation or the SVD-based method. For the ISE approach as well as for the NSS, fine-tuning of the enhancement parameters individually for each noise conditions turned out to be crucial in order to achieve best performance. It was found that the ISE method is more sensitive in determining an optimal set of the parameters. Multiple combinations of the parameters for the ISE algorithm were investigated. The analysis frame size is set to 1000 samples. For the model order the values 4, 10, 20, and 40 were considered and combined with the number of iterations which varied between 1 and 20.

3.3 Results

The Tables below, where we have presented the results, can be classified into two groups. The first group, consists of Tables 1, 2, 3 and 4, summarises results per speaker showing the recognition rate (%) achieved for input signals with different SNR values, using coloured noise derived by means of FIR filtering (50th order with a bandpass zone of 500-1500Hz). The second group, comprising Tables 5, 6, 7 and 8, summarises results per speaker showing the recognition rate (%) achieved for input signals with different SNR values, using coloured noise derived by means of FIR filtering (200th order with a bandpass zone of 3000-5000Hz). The column labelled "No Enh." in all tables, shows the recognition rate (%) when no enhancement has taken place. The column "NSS" depicts recognition rate (%) using the non-linear spectral subtraction method and "ISE" shows recognition rate (%) using the SVD-based noise reduction technique.

Each Table refers to SNR values for which the recognition performance of the non-enhanced input signals changes. Both NSS and ISE were tested for these SNR values. For example, Table 3 shows that with no speech enhancement we manage to reach the 100% recognition rate using input signals with SNR 15dB, while when the NSS method is used the 100% recognition rate is reached at SNR 11dB and for ISE the 100% recognition rate is reached at SNR 12 dB.

Table 1. Recognition rate (%) for speaker MS1, FIR order 50, bandpass zone 500-1500Hz.

Condition	Recognition rate (%)		
dB	No Enh.	NSS	ISE
SNR 4	83.33	75	83.33
SNR 9	91.66	91.66	91.66
SNR 11	91.66	100	91.66
SNR 12	91.66	100	100
SNR 15	100	100	100

Table 2. Recognition rate (%) for speaker MS2, FIR order 50, bandpass zone 500-1500Hz.

Condition	Recognition rate (%)		
dB	No Enh.	NSS	ISE
SNR 4	0	50	41.66
SNR 7	75	83.33	75
SNR 9	83.33	91.66	83.33
SNR 14	91.66	100	91.66
SNR 15	91.66	100	100
SNR 17	100	100	100

Table 3. Recognition rate (%) for speaker FS1, FIR order 50, bandpass zone 500-1500Hz.

Condition	Recognition rate (%)		
dB	No Enh.	NSS	ISE
SNR 4	33	75	41.66
SNR 8	91.66	91.66	91.66
SNR 11	91.66	100	91.66
SNR 12	91.66	100	100
SNR 15	100	100	100

Table 4. Recognition rate (%) for speaker FS2, FIR order 50, bandpass zone 500-1500Hz.

Condition	Recognition rate (%)		
dB	No Enh.	NSS	ISE
SNR 5	33	75	41.66
SNR 8	75	83.33	75
SNR 11	91.66	100	83.33
SNR 12	91.66	100	100
SNR 15	100	100	100

Table 5. Recognition rate (%) for speaker MS1, FIR order 200, bandpass zone 3000-5000Hz.

Condition	Recognition rate (%)		
dB	No Enh.	NSS	ISE
SNR 5	0	91.66	66.66
SNR 7	50	91.66	75
SNR 8	58.33	91.66	75
SNR 10	58.33	100	83.33
SNR 11	75	100	100
SNR 12	100	100	100

Table 6. Recognition rate (%) for speaker MS2, FIR order 200, bandpass zone 3000-5000Hz.

Condition	Recognition rate (%)		
dB	No Enh.	NSS	ISE
SNR 7	0	0	91.66
SNR 8	41.66	100	91.66
SNR 10	83.33	100	91.66
SNR 12	100	100	100

Table 7. Recognition rate (%) for speaker FS1, FIR order 200, bandpass zone 3000-5000Hz.

Condition	Recognition rate (%)		
dB	No Enh.	NSS	ISE
SNR 5	0	41.66	33
SNR 7	0	83.33	33
SNR 10	41.66	100	41.66
SNR 12	75	100	75
SNR 13	83.33	100	100
SNR 15	91.66	100	100
SNR 16	100	100	100

Table 8. Recognition rate (%) for speaker FS2, FIR order 200, bandpass zone 3000-5000Hz.

Condition	Recognition rate (%)		
dB	No Enh.	NSS	ISE
SNR 4	0	41.66	16.66
SNR 8	33	91.66	33
SNR 10	83.33	100	91.66
SNR 11	91.66	100	100
SNR 12	100	100	100

Fig. 1 shows that by further reducing the SNR of the input signal the optimal performance can be obtained if enhancement techniques (NSS/ISE) are used. All these results concern degraded signals using coloured noise derived by means of FIR filtering (order 50 and bandpass zone 500-1500Hz). Note that for speakers MS1, FS1, FS2, the 100% recognition rate is reached at SNR value of the input signal reduced by 26.6%, when the latter is enhanced via the NSS method. The corresponding figure for ISE is 20%. For speaker MS2 the above figures drop to 17.6% for the NSS method and 11.76% for ISE, respectively. The better performance of NSS over ISE may be due to its robustness with respect to parameters fine-tuning.

Regarding the investigation of several combinations of parameters of the ISE algorithm reported above, it can be said that the ISE algorithm seems to be speaker dependent and its performance depends on the noise level (dB).

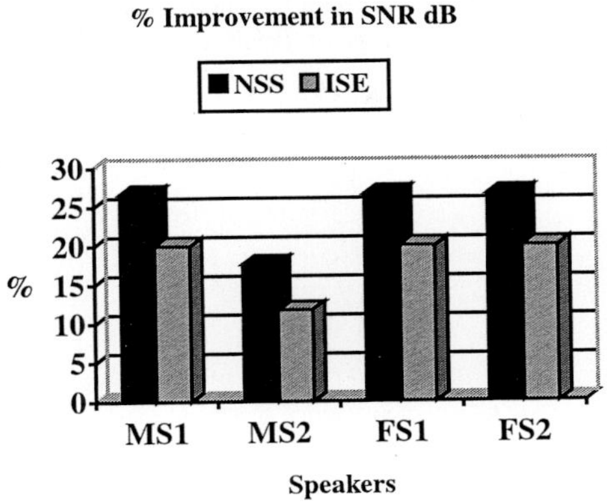

Fig. 1. The % improvement in SNR dB for different speakers.

4 Conclusions

In this paper two speech enhancement algorithms were compared for improving the performance of our speech recognition system. Our findings show that for the specific speech recognition system, the NSS method performs better compared to the ISE methodology especially at low SNR conditions. The NSS method has robust performance with respect to parameter tuning. On the other hand it is possible to improve the Word Error Rate (WER) by using the ISE algorithm, when the standard deviation of the coloured noise is known a priori. Further evaluation of the proposed technique is under way.

Acknowledgements. This work has been partially supported by the European Commission under the ERMIS Project Grant (IST-2000-29319).

References

1. Boersma, P.: Accurate short-term analysis of the fundamental frequency and the harmonics-to-noise ratio of a sampled sound. Proceedings of the Institute of Phonetic Sciences 17 (1993) 97–110
2. Dendrincs, M., Bakamidis, S., Carayannis, G.: Speech enhancement from noise: A regenerative approach. Speech Communication, Vol. 10, no.2, February (1991) 45–57
3. Doclo, S., Dologlou, I., Moonen, M.: A novel iterative signal enhancement algorithm for noise reduction in speech, Proceedings of ICSLP-98, Sydney, Australia, (1998) 1435–1439

4. Kyriakou, C., Bakamidis, S., Dologlou, I,, Carayannis, G.: Robust Continuous Speech Recognition in the Presence of Coloured Noise., Proceedings of 4th European Conference on Noise Control EURONOISE2001, Vol. 2, Patra, January 14-17 (2001) 702–705
5. Pellom, B. L., Hansen, J.H.L.: Voice Analysis in Adverse Conditions: The Centennial Olympic Park Bombing 911 Call, Proceedings of IEEE Midwest Symposium on Circuits & Systems, August (1997) 125–128
6. Uhl, C., and Leib, M.: Experiments with an Extended Adaptive SVD Enhancement Scheme for Speech Enhancement, Proceedings of IEEE ICASSP, Vol. 1, Salt Lake City, Utah, USA, May (2001) 281–284

Emotion in Speech: Towards an Integration of Linguistic, Paralinguistic, and Psychological Analysis

Stavroula-Evita Fotinea[1], Stelios Bakamidis[1], Theologos Athanaselis[1],
Ioannis Dologlou[1], George Carayannis[1], Roddy Cowie[2], E. Douglas-Cowie[2],
N. Fragopanagos[3], and John G. Taylor[3]

[1] Institute for Language and Speech processing (ILSP)
Tel:0030-210-6875300, evita@ilsp.gr
[2] Department of Psychology, Queen's University, Belfast, UK
Tel:0044-(0)28-90-274354, r.cowie@qub.ac.uk
[3] Department of Mathematics, King's College, London, UK
Tel:0044-207-848-2214, john.g.taylor@kcl.ac.uk

Abstract. If speech analysis is to detect a speaker's emotional state, it needs to derive information from both linguistic information, i.e., the qualitative targets that the speaker has attained (or approximated), conforming to the rules of language; and paralinguistic information, i.e., allowed variations in the way that qualitative linguistic targets are realised. It also needs an appropriate representation of emotional states. The ERMIS project addresses the integration problem that those requirements pose. It mainly comprises a paralinguistic analysis and a robust speech recognition module. Descriptions of emotionality are derived from these modules following psychological and linguistic research that indicates the information likely to be available. We argue that progress in registering emotional states depends on establishing an overall framework of at least this level of complexity.

1 Introduction

Speech recognition is a technically sophisticated field, with numerous commercial systems already available for transforming speech to text. However, these systems ignore a large part of the information that humans extract from speech signals – that is, information about the emotional state of the speaker. There are various specific applications for the detection of emotional and emotion-related states [1]; but probably the most important reason for addressing the issue is completely generic. In this paper we describe progress towards a system capable of recovering the emotional content of speech signals. Our general case is that understanding the emotional dimension of speech communication is a thoroughly interdisciplinary problem. Learning algorithms in general, and neural networks in particular, have an indispensable part to play. However, they need to be applied within a framework that makes use of other computational techniques, and of knowledge derived from several traditions within linguistics and psychology. In humans, there are at least two separate systems involved in the processing of information about emotion from speech. One derives information from the words that are spoken; the other derives information from the way they are spoken, particularly from the patterns of rise and fall in pitch and intensity known as prosody and the changes in fine structure known as voice quality. There are indications that these distinctions may be associated with different cortical processing streams [2]. Following this bipartite division of emotion processing in the human, our work distinguishes two basic components for the emotional speech analysis system. The first consists of a linguistic analysis system, which derives information from a word string, extracted as text from the signal. A postprocessor stage then provides an interpretation of the emotion associated with the speaker. The other component is composed of a paralinguistic analysis system. This uses different components of the raw acoustic signal to infer underlying emotion states of the speaker. The structure of the emotion recognition process depends critically on the definition of emotion-related states. There is a large body of psychological research in that area, but it is not well known in the IT communities that have expertise in the basic extraction processes. We highlight a well-established parameterisation of emotional states (into activation and valence levels) that is 'soft' in its state delineation. Using that representation makes it possible to avoid some of the problems of binary state representation (with too much dependence on a linguistic definition of emotional states). Ideas that are less well established, but much more useful than uninformed intuitions, are relevant to the extraction of information from specifically verbal sources. In the next section we describe the system that we have developed for prosodic analysis. Various emotionally important components, such as the F0 and intensity plots, are extracted, and then used to give a separate indication of the speaker's emotional state of the speaker. Section 3 describes the linguistic analyser, with subsections devoted to the explicit text recognition process and to the post-processing emotional state look-up. We conclude the paper with a discussion of the issues facing research in the immediate future.

2 Paralinguistic Analysis of Speech

The paralinguistic module extracts information about emotion that resides in the way words are spoken. The first target in this module is the extraction of phonetic structures, such as pitch and intensity contours, spectral profiles, and feature boundaries. From these are derived measures such as average pitch and energy, and parameters of timing. These are measured across sections of an utterance marked by natural endpoints. The module derives from a system called ASSESS (standing for Automatic Statistical Summary and Extraction of Speech Segments), which we have shown captures information relevant to speakers' emotional states [3]. Hence, we call the new system ASSESS MU (for modular unit).

2.1 Overall Organization

For several reasons, it is desirable to apply paralinguistic processing to units of speech which correspond roughly to sentences or phrases – lasting of the order of a second or more, and bounded by substantial breaks in speech. Some of the features that are most often associated with emotion, are only defined relative to that kind of unit. An example is declination, i.e. a pattern in which pitch shows an overall tendency to fall from the beginning of a phrase to the end. Hence a good deal of processing must be held back until such a break occurs. The linguistic analyser needs to work continuously, and so it will provide the signal that a break has occurred; and at that point, ASSESS MU will be triggered and will analyse the file, operating in three main stages, described below.

2.2 Stage 1

Stage 1 will take the plot of voltage against time specified by a pause-defined file, and output descriptions of three basic types – overall signal energy, signal spectrum, and vocal cord openings. Voltage is sampled at 22.5Khz. Overall energy and spectral properties will be described in terms of 'slices', that is, portions of the signal which span 512 points in the voltage plot. The overall energy measures will describe RMS of voltage measurements within a slice, and the basic spectral description of each slice will describe signal intensity within each of 18 bands, which are generally 1/3 octave but wider (for practical reasons) at the top and the bottom of the range. From that will be derived descriptions of the energy in four broad bands associated with measures used in [5] to capture qualities of voice such as breathiness, tension, etc; plus one lower boundary. which other work (including our own) has shown is emotion-sensitive. The bands are: #1 0-500Hz, #2 0-2kHz, #3 2-5kHz, #4 5-8kHz

Vocal cord openings form the basis on which the pitch contour (F0) will be estimated. They will be identified using an algorithm which picks up rapid upswings in the voltage/time curve. In the context of emotion detection, that approach is more appropriate than standard cepstral techniques, because it has the potential to detect local irregularities which underlie emotionally significant qualities of vocalization, such as creak. Detecting vocal cord openings reliably is a non-trivial problem. There are standard algorithms which give rough solutions, but we believe that neural net techniques may give more precise identification.

2.3 Stage 2

The core of Stage 2 will be the description of two contours, one representing the rise and fall of intensity and the other describing the rise and fall of pitch (or strictly speaking F0). Two main operations are applied to the intensity contour. It is smoothed to filter events that last much less than a syllable. A more complex problem is suggesting a reference constant for the dB scale. A histogram-based technique is currently used to give reasonable estimates of intensity given a calibration sample of normal speech. A more sophisticated approach is to use evidence indicative of vocal effort (the energy in our third spectral band is reported to correlate with perceived vocal effort). Finding appropriate functions is another task where neural net techniques are probably appropriate. Constructing a pitch contour is complex because (a) samples usually contain time periods where there is no pitch contour – most obviously pauses; and (b) stage 1 outputs may lack direct information about pitch during time periods where there is a pitch contour, or contain misleading information about pitch during time periods when there is none. Our response to these problems is based on a flexible 'string' that is (so to speak) stretched across the sample from the first slice that contains good pitch information to the last. Each point is the string is pulled towards data points on one hand, and towards its neighbours on the other. An iterative process finds a balance between the two, giving a robust estimate of the pitch contour. After contour extraction, the speech signal is divided into significant units before quantitative descriptions are formed. The main units to be considered are 'tunes', roughly phrase-like units; and pauses, i.e. silences which form the outer boundary of a tune (these must last for more than 150ms). Shorter intervals when no speech is detected are called silences.

2.4 Stage 3

Stage 3 takes the general descriptions provided by stage 2 and recovers parameters that are expected to correlate with emotional states. In general, the relevant parameters come from straightforward statistical summary of data derived in stage 2. That strategy yields both parameters that are generally regarded as basic (for instance, mean, range, and standard deviation of intensity or pitch range) and others that are at a higher level, for instance parameters related to durations of chunks, tunes and silences. A few key descriptors involve more specific operations. These involve specific properties of tunes, which we have considered under the heading 'tune shape', and some spectral properties. In the spectral domain, various measures which have been correlated with perceptual qualities will also be generated from the basic stage 2 outputs, notably; Energy in 0-500Hz region relative to total energy (see [4]). Measures from [5] based on peak energy in selected spectral bands.

Band 2 – Band 3 (correlates with perceived coarseness of voice)
Band 3 – Band 4 (correlates with perceived stability of voice)
Band 2 – Band 4 (correlates with perceived use of head register vs chest register)

The approach described up to this point defines a wide range of parameters that could in principle be passed to the emotion recognition subsystem. We have reported elsewhere on the relationships between these parameters and speakers' emotional states, using a range of learning algorithms to identify the parameters which have most predictive value.

3 Linguistic Analysis of Speech

The Linguistic Analyser processes the speech signal and provides the linguistic parameters used for the deduction of the user's emotion based on the speech signal. It consists of a Signal Enhancement/Adaptation module to provide the enhanced speech signal from the original speech input, and a robust Speech Recognition module that outputs a text string representing what the speaker has uttered. This text serves as input to the Text Postprocessing module that converts text to emotion.

3.1 Recognising Speech

To guarantee the best possible quality of speech recognition for emotionally coloured speech, the Linguistic Analyser should use uncompressed speech signals before any enhancement or recognition algorithm is being applied. The modules that need to be combined in order to recognise speech are in short presented below.

3.1.1 The Signal Enhancement/Adaptation Module

Signal Enhancement: The uncompressed speech signal is fed to the Signal Enhancement/Adaptation module and it is processed in order to enhance the signal and remove noise prior to recognition. Two methods are currently implemented. The first, is the well known non-linear spectral subtraction [6] and the second comprises a noise reduction technique presented in [7], based on the Singular Value Decomposition (SVD) approach. Validation tests are being conducted to evaluate the speech enhancement algorithms with respect to the word error rate and initial comparative results are reported in [8].

Speaker adaptation: An important source of variability in speech is due to the difference between speakers, e.g., male/female, adult/child. The performance may be improved considerably if normalisation of the input speech against speaker variability is performed. The selected strategy involves feature extraction for the current speaker be adapted to the acoustic models, instead of models being adapted to the input.

3.1.2 The Speech Recognition Module

This module allows the processing of the speech signal and the feature extraction, by converting each speech frame into a set of cepstral coefficients. Then, acoustic phoneme models provide estimates of the probability of the features, given a sequence of words. Language modelling provides a mechanism for estimating the probability of some word in an utterance given its preceding words. The output of this process is a text, representing what the speaker has uttered. The developed Speech Recognition module has been inspired by the work proposed in [9].

Parameter extraction: The prime function of the parameter extraction module is to divide the input speech into blocks; then for each block to derive a smoothed spectral estimate. (The spacing between blocks is typically 10 msecs and blocks are normally overlapped to give a longer analysis window, typically 25 msecs). In almost all cases of such processing, it is quite usual to apply a tapered window function (e.g. Hamming) to each block. Mel-Frequency Cepstral Coefficients (MFCCs) are used to model the spectral characteristictis of each block.

Acoustic modelling: The purpose of the acoustic models is to provide a method of calculating the likelihood of any vector sequence Y given a word w. In principle, the required probability distribution could be found by finding many examples of each w and collecting the statistics of the corresponding vector sequences. However, this is impractical for LVR systems and instead, word sequences are decomposed into basic sounds called phones. Each individual phone is represented by a hidden Markov model (HMM). Contextual effects cause large variations in the way that different sounds are produced. Hence, to achieve good phonetic discrimination, different HMMs have to be trained for each different context, instead for one HMM per phone. Our approach involves using triphones where every phone has a distinct HMM model for every unique pair of left and right neighbours. Moreover, state-tying techniques with continuous density HMMs are used.

Language modelling: An effective way of estimating the probability of a word given its preceding words, is to use N-grams which simultaneously encode syntax, semantics and pragmatics and they concentrate on local dependencies, which makes them very effective for languages where word order is important and the strongest contextual effects tend to come from near neighbours. We have also chosen N-grams, because the N-gram probability distributions can be computed directly from text data, yielding hence no requirement to have explicit linguistic rules (e.g. formal grammars).

Search engine: The basic recognition problem is to find the most probable sequence of words given the observed acoustic signal (based on the Bayes' rule for decomposition). In our system, we use the breadth-first approach and specifically, beam search and Viterbi decoding (it exploits Bellman's optimality principle). The dynamic performance in this search engine accomplishes a system capable of exploiting complex language models and HMM phone models depending on both the previous and succeeding acoustic context, such as coarticulation. Moreover, it can do this in a single pass, in contrast to most other Viterbi-systems that use multiple passes.

3.2 Emotion-Related Information from Text

Converting speech to text is the outcome of the Speech Recognition procedure described above. The extraction, however, of the speaker's emotional state requires conversion from text to emotion. This module of the Linguistic Analyser, being the last, in terms of sequential execution, is called the Text Post-Processing Module.

The simplest way to proceed is to assume that Text Post-Processing comprises text retrieval techniques, such as Word Spotting, in order to provide a classification of the user's emotion based on the linguistic characteristics of the user's utterance. The possible use of Emotional Lexicons is being investigated. Such lexicons exist in English, and the appropriate adaptation for the Greek language seems necessary, should we foresee emotion recognition for Greek as well. The basic process we start with here is to use a look-up table to describe the speaker's emotional state from interpreted words. We base this on the original one of Whissel, extended more recently to 8700 word, with a 90% matching rate for most documents [10]. This uses the two dimensions of activation and evaluation. The first of these is the degree of arousal associated with various emotion-relevant words, such as having a low value of 2.2 for 'bashful' and a high of over 6 for 'surprised'. The second emotion dimension is the degree of pleasantness, with low value of 1.1 for the word 'guilty', and a high value of 6.4 associated with 'delighted'. We use the two-dimensional look-up table to produce a two-dimensional activation-evaluation coding for each word in a text. This transformation produces a dynamic trajectory followed in the two-dimensional emotion space, as a string of words is successively processed. This trajectory is to be related to the associated 'feel-trace' trajectory arising by using the ASSESS system to analyse the prosodic components of the speech input string. An important question to be answered is to how these two trajectories are to be fused to produce a suitable coding of the emotional content of the speech trace. This is discussed in section 4.

4 Fusion of the Two Streams

A plethora of issues arise from the effort to fuse the emotional features extracted from the linguistic analysis and those extracted from the paralinguistic (prosody). These issues pertain to both technical intricacies and the generic complexity of the fusion task. On the technical level, there must be an effective method of synchronizing and combining the two streams of data that represent the emotional state as detected by the two types of analysis. To this end, we need to specify what the unit of analysis is and which characteristic(s) of the speech stream should trigger the different modules. On a more generic level, there is a question of harmonization of the two emotion inference procedures by means of balancing the authority of the linguistic vs. paralinguistic analysis with respect to which is apposite for deducing the emotional state at each instance. This is particularly important in cases where the two methods report incompatible emotional states. For instance, we know that the same phrase spoken with a different tone (different prosodic features) can have quite a different emotional effect. Thus, prosody can often be more informative than the actual words spoken as when one uses sarcasm or when the semantic content of the phrase spoken is neutral but the tone is highly emotional (e.g. in frustration).

The aptness of the two individual analyses is important before a merge occurs, as both linguistic and paralinguistic analysis are susceptible to emotion detection errors. In the case of the text post-processing, we have to improve our approach by removing incorrect emotion assignments by the presence of further context indicating that the speaker is not themselves experiencing the emotion state spotted. Thus, in the example 'He said to me that he was very angry' it is clear that the speaker is not angry. Thus items of reported speech containing emotion words should be treated as a separate category. They may contain implications of an emotion state that needs to be taken notice of. But that needs to be treated differently from that of recognising and responding appropriately to the emotion state of the speaker. Thus any presence of reported speech words: 'that p', 'X felt', or equivalents must be treated separately. In the case of emotion detection by prosody, it has been reported that different emotional states correspond to the same or similar prosodic patterns. Thus, special care should be given for classifying emotion based on these patterns with the utilisation of cross-referencing between the two feature streams to resolve ambiguity.

One solution to this problem of fusion is by means of a neural network, trained on a suitable training set of speech streams with known emotional state tagging. Such a set of data is being developed as part of ERMIS, with the associated emotional activation-evaluation trajectories being part of the developing FEELTRACE database. An initial version of this was already used in an earlier project (PHYSTA), using a variety of techniques; our present approach is more principled as well as involving a larger and better-defined FEELTRACE data-base. We will also take seriously the suggestion of the accompanying paper, to take lesions from the human brain. More specifically we propose to build a feedback system, essentially mimicking the ventral route (amygdala and prefrontal cortices) to emotion recognition in the human brain. This will allow attention to be directed to subsets of the overall speech features being analysed; in that way we will obtain speed-up as well as improved accuracy.

5 Conclusions

We have presented a description of the ongoing work in the ERMIS project to marry prosodic and linguistic analyses of speech so as to create an emotional recognition system. The problems of so doing are not trivial, as has been noted elsewhere in some detail [11, 12]. However we consider that we have built an expertise on both the fundamentals of emotional recognition and word recognition. Addition of feedback may help give the edge needed to obviate the difficulties noted in [11, 12].

Acknowledgements. This work has been partially supported by the European Commission under the ERMIS Project Grant (IST-2000-29319).

References

1. Cowie, R., Douglas-Cowie, E., Tsapatsoulis, N., Votsis, G., Kollias, S., Fellenz, W., Taylor, J.: Emotion Recognition in Human-Computer Interaction. IEEE Signal Processing Magazine 18 (1), (2001) 32–80
2. Taylor, J.G. et al: The Emotional Recognition Architecture in the Human Brain. Submitted to ICONIP/ICANN 2003, Istanbul, Turkey (2003)
3. McGilloway, S., Cowie, R. Douglas-Cowie, E., Gielen, S., Westerdijk and Stroeve, S.: Automatic recognition of emotion from speech: a rough benchmark. Proceedings of ISCA Workshop on Speech and Emotion: A Conceptual framework for research, Belfast: Textflow, (2000) 207–212
4. Klasmeyer, G.: An automatic description tool for time-contours and long-term average voice features in large emotional speech databases. Proceedings of ISCA Workshop on Speech and emotion: A conceptual framework for research. Belfast:Textflow, (2000) 66–71
5. Hammarberg, B., Fritzell, B., Gauffin, J., Sundberg, J., Wedin, l.: Perceptual and acoustic correlates of voice qualities. Acta Otolaryng 90, (1980) 441–451
6. Pellom, B. L., Hansen, J.H.L.: Voice Analysis in Adverse Conditions: The Centennial Olympic Park Bombing 911 Call, Proceedings of IEEE Midwest Symposium on Circuits & Systems, August (1997) 125–128
7. Doclo, S., Dologlou, I., Moonen, M.: A novel iterative signal enhancement algorithm for noise reduction in speech, Proceedings of ICSLP, Sydney, Australia, (1998) 1435–1439
8. Athanaselis, T., Fotinea, S-E., Bakamidis, S., Dologlou, I., Giannopoulos, G.: Signal Enhancement for Continuous Speech Recognition. Submitted to ICONIP/ICANN 2003, Instabul, Turkey (2003)
9. Young, S.J.: Large Vocabulary Continuous Speech Recognition IEEE Signal Processing Magazine 13(5) (1996) 45–57
10. Whissel, C.M.: The dictionary of affect in language. In R Plutchik, H Kellerman, eds, Emotion: Theory, Research and Experience: vol 4. The Measurement of Emotions New York: Academic Press (1989)
11. Russell, J.A. et al: Facial & Vocal Expressions of Emotion. Ann Rev Psychol 54 (2003) 329–349
12. McNeely, H.E. & Parlow, S.E.: Complimentarity of Linguistic and Prosodic Processes in the Intact Brain. Brain & Language 79 (2001) 473–481

An Emotional Recognition Architecture Based on Human Brain Structure

John G. Taylor[1], N. Fragopanagos[1], Roddy Cowie[2], E. Douglas-Cowie[2], Stavroula-Evita Fotinea[3], and Stefanos Kollias[4]

[1] Department of Mathematics, King's College, London, UK
Tel: +44-207-848-2214, john.g.taylor@kcl.ac.uk
[2] Department of Psychology, Queen's University, Belfast, UK
Tel: +44-289-027-4354, r.cowie@qub.ac.uk
[3] Institute for Language and Speech Processing (ILSP), Athens, Greece
Tel: +30-210-687-5300, evita@ilsp.gr
[4] IMVC, NTUA, Athens, Greece
Tel: +30-210-772-2488, stefanos@cs.ntua.gr

Abstract. Emotional experience has two distinct components in human beings: 'automatic' and 'attended'. The former of these is based more heavily on the ventral and limbic areas of the brain; the attention part is concerned with cognitive aspects of experience, and involves more dorsal components. A rapidly increasing body of knowledge on these two separate components of human experience is being developed through brain imaging, single cell recording and deficit analyses under emotional as compared to neutral inputs. We start by summarizing this data. We then incorporate the data into a recently developed engineering control model of attention and motor responses. The crucial extension of this model involves a ventral/limbic brain network building representations of salience and valence. A simulation of a simple paradigm is used to demonstrate the considerable dissociation possible between the cognitive and emotional components. The system is further extended by inclusion of the attention-based CODAM model of consciousness. This allows us to relate 'emotions' to 'feelings' and delineate expected architectures for the construction of artificial emotional recognition systems.

1 Introduction

There is growing acceptance that IT needs to incorporate various kinds of process associated with emotion [1][2]. At the interface level, systems that try to interact with people in a quasi-natural way probably need the ability to detect the emotion-related signals that the people are transmitting, and to respond with signals that carry communicatively appropriate emotional colouring. At the level of user models, systems need to represent emotion-related processes and balances within the user in ways that allow prediction of his/her likely actions. Most fundamentally, emotion seems to rest on representations that select and prioritise in a highly efficient way, and representations of that kind may be as useful to artificial agents as they are to humans.

The complexity of the domain means that there are many tasks to be addressed in designing an emotion-sensitive system. This paper addresses one which to our knowledge has not been addressed before, which is choosing whether to devote attention to the channels that carry information about agent's emotional state. The issue invites multiple perspectives. On one hand, it is practically important for systems being designed to process emotional signals, including our ERMIS project [3]. On the other, it is a topic where a substantial amount is known about the relevant brain structures in humans. We use that information to guide the design of an artificial emotion processor.

An increasing body of knowledge is being amassed about the brain structures involved in emotional experience in humans [4][5][6]. This is a crucial aspect of emotional recognition: emotionally salient inputs give rise to emotionally experienced 'simulations' in the brain, which then lead to a recognition process. At the same time there appears to be a battle between emotion and cognition, as is common to everyone: emotions cloud the intellect, and in a heightened cognitive state there is reduced emotional experience. This mutual inhibition has been studied by a number of teams, with results indicating a mutual inhibition between dorsal prefrontal 'cognitive' sites, involved in working memory goal-holding tasks, and more ventral lateral [5] or orbital prefrontal sites [6] for emotionally demanding inputs. Cingulate cortex was also observed to be involved in both the more cognitive or more emotional tasks [5], possibly acting as a monitor associated with response control [7]. Insula and somato-sensory cortex have also been observed in response to inputs causing disgust [5], again consistent with an internal simulation of the associated emotion. Finally, single neurons in human ventral prefrontal cortex have been shown especially responsive to fearful faces [8].

At the same time there are a number of important sub-cortical sites which have been studied over the previous decades and are now accepted as being involved in the generation of emotional salience [9]: the amygdala, the basal ganglia and the hypothalamus. These sites have been investigated as part of the system of reward [9], as well as being strongly anatomically linked to the ventral emotional system in the cortex. Thus these cannot be ignored; here we will only consider the amygdala, which is seen to be strongly active in a number of brain imaging studies [4][5].

Our task is first to summarize the known results from brain imaging, single cell and deficit studies on this complex interplay between emotion and cognition. This we do in the next section. If we only concentrated on emotion then we would not be able to rise to the conscious experience itself, which we propose has a cognitive element. We then turn, in section 2, to develop the joint cognitive-emotional circuit consistent with the experimental results of section 1 as well as those described elsewhere [10]. A simplified version of this is used in section 3 to simulate the results of [5], involving strong dissociation between the emotional and cognitive components. We extend our circuit to include consciousness by inserting a suitable observer following the CODAM model [11][12]. The paper concludes with a discussion on implications of our results for artificial emotional recognition systems.

2   The Emotional Brain

Present brain imaging and deficit results support the existence of two interacting but distinct circuits in the brain: a dorsal one for cognitive processing, and a ventral one for emotional content and recognition. The former of these has been extensively discussed in recent experimental reviews [13]. Parietal and dorsal prefrontal sites are involved in a network of areas creating control signals to achieve attention focusing on a specific input, or in a manner to solve a particular task. An engineering control model has been developed from these data [10][11][12][14], in which an inverse model controller in parietal cortex is created, by prefrontal goal signals, to focus attention signals which modulate activity in posterior cortical sensory (or motor) areas.

As noted in the introduction, there is a further more ventral prefrontal circuit, with good connections to various limbic and sub-cortical sites, which is involved in emotion processing. There are two components observed active: one is the canonical medial one involving anterior cingulate, medial orbito-frontal cortex, the rostral insula and the amygdala. The other is more lateral [5], consisting of infero-temporal and ventro-lateral cortex, the amygdala and anterior cingulate. One explanation (of several) of these two separate circuits [15] is that the first, medial, circuit is concerned with internally generated emotional states, the second, lateral, circuit with externally triggered emotional states. This fits with the known coding of important objects in infero-temporal, since it is these, especially faces, which function as triggers of emotions.

Brain imaging and deficit results in depressives have supported the division of processing into two separate ventral (for emotional) and dorsal (for cognitive) aspects of experience. Thus Mayberg has suggested [16] that in depression there is a failure to regulate the balance between these two components, especially through the common areas in the two associated networks. She has singled out the anterior cingulate as a specific site for such deregulation, and for which there is now support from brain imaging in patients with severe depression.

3   The Neural Architecture

We summarize the above results in a (suitably simplified) overall brain architecture.

The inverse model controller (IMC) generates a suitable attention modulation signal, as shown in the figure 1, being fed back to primary and associative sensory or motor cortical sites, as well as to amygdala [5]. This signal is guided by a signal from the goals module, in dorso-lateral prefrontal cortex. The goal module is in inhibitory competition with the ventral prefrontal activity caused by the input. This activity arises from coding of the emotion salience of the input, supported both by its more primitive emotional representation coded in the amygdala, as well as the further sensory coding in the insula (for the medial emotional circuit).

There is some discrepancy in the literature over the necessity for attention in the emotional circuitry. Figure 1 is based mainly on the results of [5], which show that amygdala is activated by 'unattended' pictures of disgusting stimuli (functioning as distracters in the paradigm). The results of [17] show that amygdala is only activated by attention to fearful faces, but is not so when they are unattended (again acting as distracters). However in the latter case these distracters are not at the spatial focus of attention, while in the former all stimuli are at the centre of the screen. The two results are thus reconciled if we assume that spatial attention is necessary for emotional stimuli to be processed by the brain. That is why attention modulation from the spatial IMC is shown sending signals to the amygdala, thereby being consistent with the results of both [5] and [17].

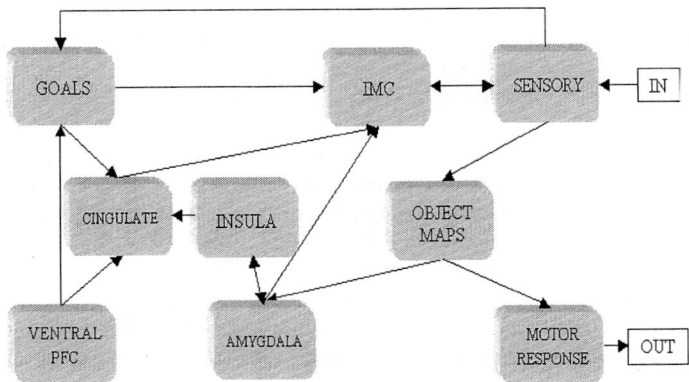

Fig. 1. Overall Brain Architecture for Emotion experience based on the attention control model of [10][11][12][14]. The extension to include sites supporting emotional experience is discussed in the text.

4 Simulating the Emotional/Cognitive Divide

We now present a simulation of the reaction times results of [5], that we present in table 1.

Table 1. Reaction Times for the Paradigm of [5].

Type of Input	Description of Input	Frequency of Input	RT (ms)
Standards	Squares of various sizes & colors	84%	536
Targets	Circles of various sizes & colors	~8%	691
Emotional	Unpleasant pictures	4%	728
Neutral	Neutral pictures	4%	680

The paradigm had various types of inputs presented to a subject lying in the bore of the magnet in an fMRI machine. The task was to press a button with the right index finger for any target, and with the right middle finger for any other input.

The basic problem presented by these results is the longer RT to the emotional stimuli than to the targets or neutral stimuli; we assume that the standards are being processed automatically (as encouraged by their preponderance, so making it easy for a subject always to press the index finger unless they notice a non-target). The explanation of emotional slowing is, we propose, caused by inhibition of the goal signal, for attention to speed analysis of the input, being inhibited by the emotional salience of the input activating the ventral prefrontal salience circuit. This is achieved by the architecture of fig 2, with the unpleasant stimuli activating the AMYGD-ORB module, which then inhibits the goal modules.

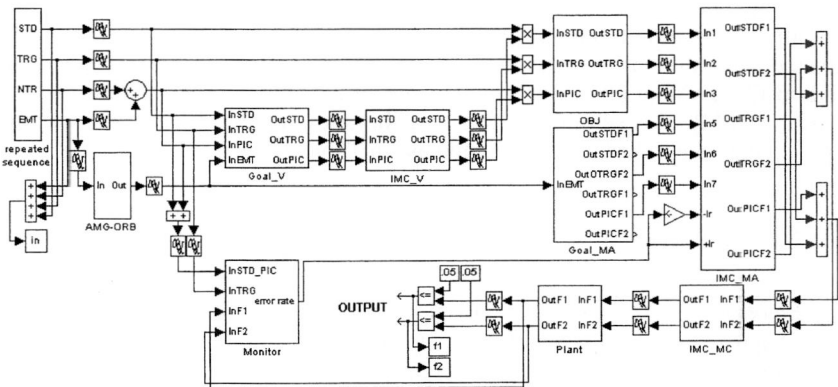

Fig. 2. Simulink architecture used for the simulation of [5].

The resulting inhibition then produces a slowing of response, by about 50 ms, to the unpleasant stimuli.

5 Extending to Consciousness

So far attention has not necessarily contained any conscious component. This is consistent with what is known about attention being captured by degraded inputs (as shown by later priming) but without awareness of the inputs. There must therefore be more to consciousness than arises purely by attention. It was suggested in [11][12] that the extra component was an observer model of the sensory cortices. This can be used for rapid guidance of the inverse model controller, as is known to occur in motor response [18][19]. The COrollary Discharge of Attention Movement model was then developed from this, in which the extra observer component was split into two parts: a buffer for the efference copy of the IMC signal, and another buffer, in competition with the first, in which the attentionally amplified input finally attains contentful consciousness. The prior efference copy signal carries with it the important components of ownership of the about-to-arrive amplified activity denoting the input. This prior signal was proposed to be the signal of the pre-reflective self of Western phenomenology.

The CODAM model thus divides consciousness into two parts: a contentful one (composed of qualia, representing the external world), and a contentless one (the pre-reflective self). In CODAM the problem of relating the intrinsic component of self with that which is only relational (or intentional) is solved by the temporal flow of the signals: first the efference copy, second (by about 150-200ms) the content.

Where does emotion come in this division of awareness? It is now well accepted that emotion can be unconscious, as in the case of blindsight subjects [20] or for subliminally experienced emotional stimuli [21]. In both cases excitation of the amygdala was observed, with attention not able to bring to awareness either the stimulus or the emotion associated with it. Thus we conclude that the ventral emotion circuit can function out of awareness. Emotional awareness (feeling), and hence its reportable recognition, could only arise if the relevant sensory buffer(s) were activated after the earlier activation of the efference copy let it through (as in the standard CODAM model). Such buffers are in the somatosensory and insula cortex for disgust [22]. We summarize this and the sites for the other basic emotions of surprise, fear, anger, sadness, and happiness in Table 2.

Table 2. Proposed Sites for the Creation of Consciousness of the Basic Emotions.

Emotion	Conjectured Siting of Main Buffer
Disgust	Secondary somatosensory cortex; Insula cortex [5]
Fear	Superior temporal sulcus [16]
Anger	Right orbitofrontal cortex [24]
Sadness	Right inferior and middle temporal gyri [24]
Happiness	Superior temporal sulcus [16]

6 Artificial Emotional Recognition Architectures

What lessons can we draw from the above about software architectures that could recognise emotions in either speech (from prosody) or facial features? We suggest that one of the important aspects of such processing is the need for speed. Much computation has to be done in general in speech or facial analysis to extract the needed emotional clues. We suggest that attention is used to help reduce this load by concentrating on the essential features leading to extraction of the emotional impact of the input. That is the essence of the control brought about the IMC feedback. However there is also further important feedback to much of cortex from the amygdala. This feedback is 'learnt on the job', so to speak, by use of dopamine-based reward signals being received in association with the input. These signals arise from primary sites in the brain stem and basal ganglia, as well as from the nucleus accumbens and amygdala themselves [9] (as well as there being an important but unknown component which is genetically determined). Thus the simplified version of figure 1 is that of figure 2. This has both an attentional IMC and an amygdala, thereby extending it beyond the present feed-forward emotion recognition proposed for ERMIS to have suitable feedback.

We therefore use the following main features to lead to the architecture of figure 3:

- Emotional experience has 2 components: 'automatic' and 'attended'
- Automatic emotion activates Paralimbic regions (amygdala, hypothalamus)
- Attended emotion activates Heteromodal regions (parietal, prefrontal, cingulate)
- Emotion classification is different from feeling (attention)
- Emotion is identified with valence (coded in paralimbic)
- Salience is identified with the attention-grabbing aspect of emotion
- Attention feedback then occurs to posterior processing sites, plus others leading to emotional experience.

The architecture can be thought of as an extension of a natural feedforward architecture that we have described elsewhere [23]. The key change is that there is a valence map (AMYG) to direct fed-back attention modulation to the three original input processing modules (which are separately for faces, linguistics and prosody). The amygdala is activated by emotionally important components of these inputs. What the emotional valence of inputs is composed of has to be learnt by suitable Hebbian learning, with a reinforcement basis. That will be developed in detail elsewhere.

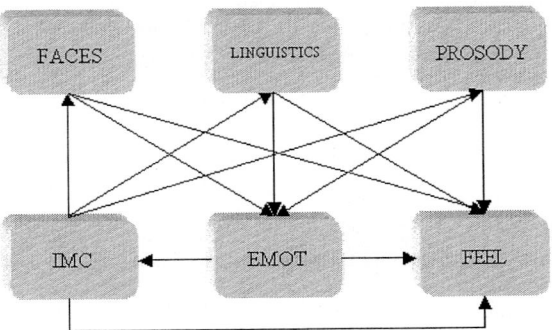

Fig. 3. A Simplified Emotional Recognition Architecture.

7 Conclusion

It is often said, quite rightly, that emotion pervades human cognition. The converse is perhaps not as widely understood as it might be: descriptions of emotion must address its interfaces with cognition in general. We have addressed the issue in a limited way, considering interfaces between emotion, attention and consciousness. If nothing else, our model stands as a useful reminder that a great many other interfaces need to be addressed before we can claim to understand emotion in any depth – with action, motivation, planning, the self-concept, semantic representation, memory, and communication [23], to name but a few.

Acknowledgements. This word has been partially supported by the European Commission under the ERMIS Project Grant (IST–2000-29319).

References

1. Picard, R.W., Vyzas, E., Healey, J. (2001). IEEE transactions on pattern analysis and machine intelligence, 23 (10), 1175–1191.
2. Douglas-Cowie, E., Cowie R., Campbell N. (2003). Speech communication, 40 (1–2), 1–3.
3. http://www.image.ntua.gr/ermis/
4. Adolphs R. (2002). Current opinion in neurobiology, 12 (2), 169–177.
5. Yamasaki, H., LaBar, K. S., McCarthy, G. (2002). Proceedings of the National Academy of Sciences USA, 99 (17), 11447–11451.
6. Perlstein, W. M., Elbert, T., Stenger, V. A. (2002). Proceedings of the National Academy of Sciences USA, 99 (3), 1736–1741.
7. Pailing, P. E., Segalowitz, S. J., Dywan, J., Davies, P. L. (2002). Psychophysiology, 39 (2), 198–206.
8. Kawasaki, H., Kaufman, O., Damasio, H., Damasio, A. R., Granner, M., Bakken, H., Hori, T., Howard, M. A. 3rd, Adolphs, R. (2001). Nature Neuroscience, 4 (1), 15–16.
9. Cardinal, R. N., Parkinson, J. A., Hall, J., Everitt, B. J. (2002). Neuroscience & Biobehavioral Reviews, 26 (3), 321–352.
10. Fragopanagos, N., Taylor, J. G. (2003). In preparation.
11. Taylor, J. G. (2002). Journal of Consciousness Studies, 9 (4), 3–22.
12. Taylor, J. G. (2002). Trends in Cognitive Sciences, 6 (5), 206–210.
13. Pessoa, L., Kastner, S., Ungerleider, L. G. (2002). Cognitive Brain Research, 15 (1), 31–45.
14. Taylor, J. G., Rogers, M. (2002). Neural Networks, 15 (3), 309–326.
15. Chen, Y.-C. (1995). Experimental Brain Research, 10, 93–107.
16. Mayberg H. (1997). Journal of neuropsychiatry, 9 (3), 471–481.
17. Pessoa, L., McKenna, M., Gutierrez, E., Ungerleider, L. G. (2002). Proceedings of the National Academy of Sciences USA, 99 (17), 11458–11463.
18. Sabes, P. N. (2000). Current opinion in neurobiology, 10 (6), 740-746.
19. Desmurget, M., Grafton, S. (2000). Trends in cognitive sciences, 4 (11), 405–440.
20. Morris, J. S., DeGelder, B., Weiskrantz, L., Dolan, R. J. (2001). Brain, 124 (6), 1241–1252.
21. Vuilleumier, P., Armony, J. L., Clarke, K., Husain, M., Driver, J., Dolan, R. J. (2002). Neuropsychologia, 40 (12), 2156–2166.
22. Winston, J. S., Strange, B. A., O'Doherty, J., Dolan, R. J. (2002). Nature Neuroscience, 5, 277–283.
23. Cowie, R., Cornelius, R. R. (2003). Speech Communication, 40 (1-2), 5–32.
24. Blair, R. J. R., Morris, J. S., Frith, C. D., Perrett, D. I., Dolan, R. J. (1999). Brain, 122 (5), 883–893.

Neural Networks for Bio-informatics Applications

Neural Network Ensemble with Negatively Correlated Features for Cancer Classification

Hong-Hee Won and Sung-Bae Cho

Dept. of Computer Science, Yonsei University, 134 Shinchon-dong, Sudaemoon-ku,
Seoul 120-749, Korea
cool@candy.yonsei.ac.kr, sbcho@cs.yonsei.ac.kr

Abstract. The development of microarray technology has supplied a large volume of data to many fields. In particular, it has been applied to prediction and diagnosis of cancer, so that it expectedly helps us to exactly predict and diagnose cancer. It is essential to efficiently analyze DNA microarray data because the amount of DNA microarray data is usually very large. Since accurate classification of cancer is very important issue for treatment of cancer, it is desirable to make a decision by combining the results of various expert classifiers rather than by depending on the result of only one classifier. In spite of many advantages of ensemble classifiers, ensemble with mutually error-correlated classifiers has a limit in the performance. In this paper, we propose the ensemble of neural network classifiers learned from negatively correlated features to classify cancer precisely, and systematically evaluate the performance of the proposed method using three benchmark datasets. Experimental results show that the neural network ensemble with negatively correlated features produces the best recognition rate on the three benchmark datasets.

1 Introduction

DNA microarray technology has advanced so much that we can simultaneously measure the expression levels of thousands of genes under particular experimental environments and conditions [1]. DNA microarray technology makes it possible to understand life on the molecular level. The development of DNA microarray technology enables to generate large-scale gene expression data. It has led to many statistical and analytical challenges from the problems in biology because it has been produced large amount of genes. We can analyze the gene information very rapidly and precisely by managing them at one time using several statistical methods and machine learning.

Cancer classification in clinical practice relied on clinical and histopathological information can be often incomplete or misleading. DNA microarray technology has been applied to the field of accurate prediction and diagnosis of cancer and expected that it would help them. Molecular level diagnostics with gene expression profiles can offer the methodology of precise, objective, and systematic cancer classification. Especially accurate classification of cancer is very important issue for treatment of cancer. Since the gene expression data usually consist of huge number of genes, several researchers have been studying many problems of cancer classification using data mining methods, machine learning algorithms and statistical methods to efficiently analyze these data [2, 3]. However, most researchers partly have evaluated only the performance of the feature selection method and classifier.

In this paper, we attempt to use the negative correlation of the features. We define two ideal feature vectors for a standard of good feature, and utilize the features selected by scoring the similarity with each ideal feature vector. Two ideal feature vectors are the one high in class A and low in class B, and the other one low in class A and high in class B. Since the vectors have negative correlation, the sets of genes similar to each ideal vector are also negatively correlated. The negatively correlated features represent two different aspects of classification boundary for gene expression data. We can search in a much wider solution space by combining these features. In this paper, we propose the ensemble classifier trained with negatively correlated features. We test the proposed method in three benchmark cancer datasets, and systematically analyze the usefulness of the negative correlation.

2 DNA Microarray

DNA arrays consist of a large number of DNA molecules spotted in a systemic order on a solid substrate. Depending on the size of each DNA spot on the array, DNA arrays can be categorized as microarrays when the diameter of DNA spot is less than 250 microns, and macroarrays when the diameter is bigger than 300 microns. The arrays with the small solid substrate are also referred to as DNA chips. It is so powerful that we can investigate the gene information in short time, because at least hundreds of genes can be put on the DNA microarray to be analyzed.

There are two representative DNA microarray technologies: cDNA microarray technology and oligonucleotide microarray technology. cDNA microarrays are composed of thousands of individual DNA sequences printed in a high density array on a glass microscope slide using a robotic arrayer. High-density oligonucleotide microarrays are made using spatially patterned, light-directed combinatorial chemical synthesis, and contain up to hundreds of thousands of different oligonucleotides on a small glass surface. For mRNA samples, the two samples are reverse-transcribed into cDNA, labeled using different fluorescent dyes mixed (red-fluorescent dye Cy5 and green-fluorescent dye Cy3). After the hybridization of these samples with the arrayed DNA probes, the slides are imaged using scanner that makes fluorescence measurements for each dye. The log ratio between the two intensities of each dye is used as the gene expression data.

$$gene\_expression = \log_2 \frac{Int(Cy5)}{Int(Cy3)} \qquad (1)$$

where Int(Cy5) and Int(Cy3) are the intensities of red and green colors. Since at least hundreds of genes are put on the DNA microarray, we can investigate the genome-wide information in short time.

3 Neural Network Ensemble with Informative Features

We propose the ensemble classifier with mutually exclusive features and negatively correlated features. The framework of the proposed ensemble classifier with mutually exclusive features and negatively correlated features is shown in Figure 1. The basic idea of ensemble classifier scheme is to develop several pairs of trained neural networks with feature sets selected on correlation analysis, and to classify a given input pattern by utilizing combination methods. Then it naturally raises the question of obtaining a consensus on the results of each individual network.

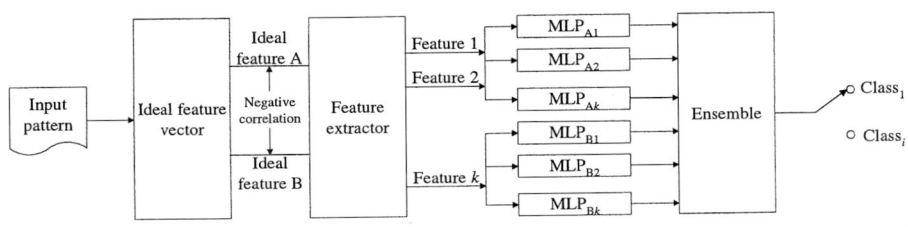

Fig. 1. Overview of the ensemble classifier with negatively correlated features

3.1 Neural Network Ensemble with Mutually Exclusive Features

Among thousands of genes whose expression levels are measured, not all are needed for classification. Microarray data consist of large number of genes in small samples. For efficient classification, we need to find out the informative features from input observation. This process is referred to as gene selection [4].

Suppose that we have a $M \times N$ training set where M is the number of samples (input vector) and N is the number of features (dimensionality of input vector). The ith feature of samples, g_i, can be expressed:

$$g_i = (e_1, e_2, e_3, \cdots, e_M) \qquad (2)$$

where e is the data and $i=1 \sim N$. We want to know the locations of informative k features out of M. Suppose g_{ideal} is an ideal vector representing class c_j. If it is possible to know representative vector g_{ideal} for class c_j, we can simply measure the correlation and similarity of g_i to classes, which tells the feature-goodness. Modeling g_{ideal}, we should use prior knowledge and intuitional experience about classes.

$$g_{ideal} = (e_1', e_2', e_3', \cdots, e_M') \qquad (3)$$

Measuring the similarity of g_i and g_{ideal} using similarity measures, Pearson's correlation coefficient (*PC*), Spearman coefficient (*SC*), Euclidean distance (*ED*), and cosine coefficient (*CC*) [4], the most similar 25 genes are used for classification. Also, the most informative 25 genes can be selected using information-theoretic feature selection methods, information gain (*IG*), mutual information (*MI*), and signal to noise ratio [5]. Using feature selection, we get a set of informative features from the data. In order to choose mutually exclusive features, we have plotted the distribution of g_i from two feature selection methods. If the two features are mutually exclusive, the distribution will be in the (-) direction, otherwise (+) direction. The mutually exclusive feature is to encourage set of classifiers to learn different aspects of data.

We have used multi-layer perceptron (MLP), self-organizing map (SOM), structure adaptive SOM (SASOM), support vector machine (SVM), decision tree (DT) and k-nearest neighbor (KNN) as classifiers [5]. For combining classifiers, a neural network and majority voting are used. A neural network combines the outputs of single classifiers in our system. Outputs of single classifiers can be thought of as CSVs (classification status values), which contain information on answer patterns of classifiers. Neural network has $m+n$ (dimensionality of CSV) input nodes and j output nodes.

3.2 Neural Network Ensemble with Negatively Correlated Features

To select negatively correlated features, we define two ideal feature vectors as the one high in class A and low in class B (1,1,...,1,0,0,...,0), and the other one low in class A and high in class B (0,0,...,0,1,1,...,1) as shown in Figure 2 and select the sets of informative genes with high similarity to each ideal gene vector. Since Pearson's correlation coefficient of two ideal gene vectors is −1, two vectors are perfectly negative-correlated. The sets of gene vectors are also highly negative-correlated. Correlation analysis and distance measure methods are used in order to measure the similarity of gene vector g_i and ideal gene vectors A and B. Similarity measures used for negative correlation are Pearson correlation coefficient, Spearman correlation coefficient, Euclidean distance, and cosine coefficient [5]. The informative features selected by negative correlation represent two different aspects of training data. We can search in a much wider solution space by combining these features.

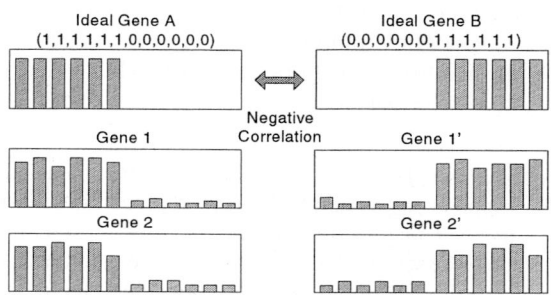

Fig. 2. Informative genes selected using negative correlation

We have chosen multi-layer perceptron for classification and the Bayesian approach for final decision of the neural network classifier because the Bayesian approach can solve the problem of tie-break in ensemble by using a priori knowledge of each combined classifier. The Bayesian approach combines classifiers with different weights by using the previous knowledge of each classifier. Where k classifiers are combined, c_i, $i=1,...,m$, is the class of a sample, $c(classifier_j)$ is the class of the *j*th classifier, and w_i is a priori possibility of the class c_i, Bayesian combination is defined as follows:

$$c_{ensemble} = \arg\max_{1 \le i \le m} \left\{ w_i \prod_{j=1}^{k} P(c_i \mid c(classifier_j)) \right\} \qquad (4)$$

4 Experiments

4.1 Datasets

Three representative datasets, leukemia cancer dataset, colon cancer dataset and lymphoma cancer dataset, are used in this paper among several microarray datasets. Leukemia dataset consists of 72 samples: 25 samples of acute myeloid leukemia (AML) and 47 samples of acute lymphoblastic leukemia (ALL). 38 out of 72 samples were used as training data and the remaining were used as test data. Each sample contains 7129 gene expression levels. Colon dataset consists of 62 samples of colon epithelial cells taken from colon-cancer patients. Each sample contains 2000 gene expression levels. 31 out of 62 samples were used as training data and the remaining were used as test data. Lymphoma dataset consists of 24 samples of GC B-like and 23 samples of activated B-like. 22 out of 47 samples were used as training data and the remaining were used as test data.

4.2 Results Analysis of Ensemble with Mutually Exclusive Features

The results of recognition rate on the test data with single feature and classifier are as shown in Table 1. The MLP seems to have the best recognition rate among the classifiers on the average. 97.1% of accuracy is the best throughout all the classifiers and features. The performance of classifiers seems to be somewhat dependent on the feature it uses. SVM, for example, has 97.1% of accuracy with Pearson's correlation, but 58.8% with information gain and mutual information.

Table 1. Recognition rates by feature and classifier (%)

	MLP	SOM	SVM	DT	KNN
PC	97.1	74.1	97.1	97.1	88.2
SC	70.6	67.4	70.6	61.8	73.5
ED	97.1	70.6	91.2	82.4	82.4
CC	79.4	70.6	70.6	73.5	76.5
IG	72.9	63.8	58.8	47.1	70.6
MI	62.1	68.8	58.8	55.9	58.8
SN	94.1	97.1	94.1	91.2	94.1

Figure 3 illustrates the dependency between two feature selection methods. In case (a), dots are distributed in negative direction. Therefore, the feature sets chosen by Pearson's correlation and Euclidean distance must be very mutually exclusive, and the classifiers with these feature selection methods are trained in independent feature spaces each other. In case (b), dots are distributed in a triangular form. We cannot explicitly see the direction of the correlation. In case (c), genes selected by one method with high score also appear in the list of top-ranking genes by the other method. Since two sets of classifiers are trained in mutually dependent feature spaces, it is hard to expect the performance improvement when the classifiers are combined.

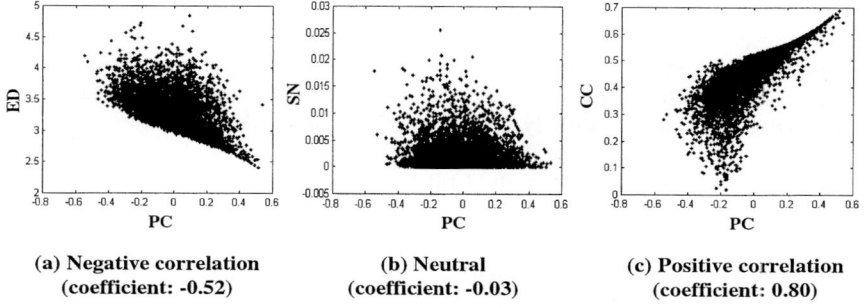

(a) Negative correlation (coefficient: -0.52)
(b) Neutral (coefficient: -0.03)
(c) Positive correlation (coefficient: 0.80)

Fig. 3. Correlations of feature selection methods in Leukemia

Table 2 is the result of the ensemble classifiers. Case (a), (b) and (c) are investigated and we also have combined all the features, for the comparison with others. Case (a) produces the best recognition rates, 97.1% in both neural network and voting method, which is also the best that we could get in the experiments with single feature/classifier. Case (b) also produces relatively high rates. Case (c) and 'all feature,' however, turn to be bad, which implies that combining independent features is efficient, producing much higher performance than when all features are considered.

Table 2. Results of ensemble classifiers in Leukemia (%)

	Neural network	Majority voting
Case (a)	97.1	97.1
Case (b)	97.1	94.1
Case (c)	91.2	85.3
All features	64.7	41.2

4.3 Results Analysis of Ensemble with Negatively Correlated Features

Table 3 shows the recognition rate of the basis classifiers in each dataset. In Leukemia dataset, MLP I with Pearson's correlation coefficient and MLP I with information gain produce the best recognition rate, 97.1%, among the feature-classifier combinations. In Colon dataset, MLP I with cosine coefficient produces the best recognition rate, 83.9%. In Lymphoma dataset, MLP II with Spearman's correlation coefficient produces the best recognition rate, 88.0%. While MLP I outperforms MLP II in Leukemia dataset and Colon dataset, MLP II outperforms MLP I in Lymphoma dataset.

Table 3. Recognition rate with features and classifiers (%)

	Leukemia		Colon		Lymphoma	
	MLP I	MLP II	MLP I	MLP II	MLP I	MLP II
PC	97.1	79.4	74.2	77.4	64.0	72.0
SC	82.4	79.4	58.1	64.5	60.0	88.0
ED	91.2	61.8	67.8	77.4	56.0	72.0
CC	94.1	76.5	83.9	77.4	68.0	76.0
Mean	91.2	74.3	71.0	74.2	62.0	77.0

Figure 4 shows the average and the best recognition rates of the ensemble classifiers for Lymphoma dataset. In case of the negatively correlated feature set (MLP I + MLP II), 8 diverse feature sets have been produced with 2 ideal feature vectors (Ideal Gene A and Ideal Gene B) and 4 similarity measures. The classifiers learned with 8 diverse feature sets have been combined using Bayesian approach. The average recognition rate means the average of all possible $_8C_k$ (k=2, 3 and 4) combinations of ensemble classifiers.

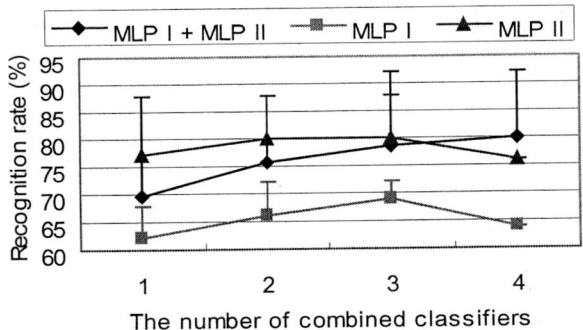

Fig. 4. Recognition rate of the ensemble in Lymphoma

The performance of the ensemble classifier is superior to the basis in all benchmark datasets. The best recognition rate of ensemble classifier is 97.1% in Leukemia dataset, 87.1% in Colon dataset, and 92.0% in Lymphoma dataset. Compared with the best recognition rates of base classifiers, 97.1%, 83.9%, and 92.0% on the datasets respectively in Table 3, the performance of ensemble is better.

Compared with the results of MLP I and MLP II, the negatively correlated features set (MLP I + MLP II) does not outperform in the average recognition rate, but outperforms in the best recognition rate. While the best recognition of the ensemble of MLP I and MLP II is decreasing as the number of combined classifiers is increasing, the best recognition of the ensemble of the negatively correlated coefficient feature set is increasing.

5 Concluding Remarks

In order to predict the cancer class of patients, we have illustrated a classification framework that combines sets of classifiers using the correlation information. The results clearly show that the suggested framework works and we may improve the classification performance by combining mutually exclusive sets of classifiers learned from two independent features and by combining independent sets of classifiers learned from negatively correlated features, even when we use simple combination method of voting and Bayesian approach.

The experimental results also imply some correlations between features, which might guide the researchers to choose or devise the best ensemble classifier for their problems in bioinformatics. Based on the results, we have developed the optimal feature-classifier combination to produce the best performance on the classification.

Moreover, the neural network classifier with negative correlation outperforms the ensemble classifiers without negative correlation. We have confirmed that mutually exclusiveness and the negative correlation enable the ensemble classifier to work better by providing appropriate information for the classification to classifiers

Acknowledgements. This work was supported by Biometrics Engineering Research Center and a grant of Korea Health 21 R&D Project, Ministry of Health & Welfare, Republic of Korea.

References

[1] Harrington, C. A., Rosenow, C., and Retief, J., "Monitoring gene expression using DNA microarrays," *Curr. Opin. Microbiol.*, vol. 3, pp. 285–291, 2000.
[2] Ben-Dor, A., Bruhn, L., Friedman, N., Nachman, I., Schummer, M. and Yakhini, N., "Tissue classification with gene expression profiles," *Journal of Computational Biology*, vol. 7, pp. 559–584, 2000.
[3] Dudoit, S., Fridlyand, J. and Speed, T. P., "Comparison of discrimination methods for the classification of tumors using gene expression data," *Technical Report 576*, Department of Statistics, University of California, Berkeley, 2000.
[4] Li, L., Weinberg, C. R., Darden, T. A. and Pedersen, L. G., "Gene selection for sample classification based on gene expression data: Study of sensitivity to choice of parameters of the GA/KNN method," *Bioinformatics*, vol. 17, no. 12, pp. 1131–1142, 2001.
[5] Cho, S.-B. and Ryu, J., "Classifying gene expression data of cancer using classifier ensemble with mutually exclusive features," *Proc. of the IEEE*, vol. 90, no. 11, pp. 1744–1753, 2002.

Feature Analysis and Classification of Protein Secondary Structure Data

S.Y.M. Shi and P.N. Suganthan

School of Electrical and Electronic Engineering
Nanyang Technological University, Republic of Singapore 639798
epnsugan@ntu.edu.sg

Abstract. In this paper, we investigate feature analysis for the prediction of the secondary structure of protein sequences using support vector machines (SVMs) and k-nearest neighbor algorithm (kNN). We apply feature selection and scaling techniques to obtain a number of distinct feature subsets with different features and each scaled differently. The feature selection and the scaling are performed using the mutual information (MI). We formulate the feature selection and scaling as combinatorial optimization problem and obtain solutions using a Hopfield-style algorithm. Our experimental results show that the feature subset selection improves the performance for both SVM and kNN while the feature scaling is consistently beneficial for kNN.

1 Introduction

More and more protein sequence data becomes available due to numerous genome projects. There is a need to determine the structure of these protein sequences [4,15]. As it is costly and time consuming to experimentally determine the structures it is important to develop accurate automatic structure prediction algorithms to determine the structure of the new sequences. In this paper, we incorporate concepts such as feature selection and feature scaling to design a protein secondary structure classification system. SVM has been demonstrated to perform well in solving a large number of classification problems. Although SVM is a strong classifier, its performance may be significantly affected if the feature set is not properly chosen. We also show that the kNN's performance can be improved by feature selection and scaling [18].

Feature selection plays an important role in pattern classification and data mining. The feature selection may reduce the cost of processing provide a better performance due to finite sample size effects [8,10] and elimination of redundancy. More generic feature extraction methods may create new features using transformations of the original features [8,10]. This paper considers feature selection and scaling.

Feature selection has been the focus of interest for quite some time and much work has been done [1,10,13]. There are three main approaches to feature subset selection [1]: embedded approach [16] wrapper approach [9] and filtering approach [11,12]. In the embedded approach the feature selection and classifier design processes are combined into one step. The wrapper approach uses two processes one searches for feature subset the other evaluates the selected feature subset using the same learning algorithm that will be used for learning on the problem domain represented with the selected features. This two-step process is repeated and directed by the performance feedback until an optimal feature subset is obtained. It is used only in the supervised learning. In the filtering approach, a feature subset is selected independently of the learning method that will use the selected features. Feature selection by filtering may be performed in supervised or unsupervised manner.

MI [11] or correlation [12] can be used to perform feature subset selection by filter approach. The correlation measure is able to determine linear relationships between features while the MI is capable of estimating arbitrary interactions between features. Hence although the MI is computationally more demanding it is expected to perform better than correlation measures.

Feature subset selection is a subset of feature scaling approaches. Feature weights can be introduced to scale features based on their relative significance within the feature subset [6]. Caruana and Freitag [2] developed the Relief algorithm, which assigned weight to each feature and used the nearest neighbor algorithm to update the weights. The Relief algorithm does not attempt to determine useful subsets of the weakly relevant features. In real domains many features may be correlated some may be weakly relevant and will not be removed by Relief.

To our best of knowledge all filter type feature selection algorithms are sequential in nature. We formulate the filter type feature selection as a combinational optimization problem. Since Hopfield and Tank [7] have quantitatively demonstrated the computational power and speed of collective analog networks of neurons in solving optimization problems rapidly we map the feature selection problem onto a single layered Hopfield neural networks and use heuristic methods to adjust the network parameters. Our experimental results show that the combinatorial optimization approach is capable of yielding better feature subset in comparison to sequential feature selection algorithms.

2 Mutual Information

The objective is to select the features with relevant information for classification decision making. In order to estimate the relevance the Shannon's information theory can be used which relates information of random variables with entropy and mutual information. Entropy of a discrete random variable X is defined as follows:

$$H(X) = -\sum_{x \in X} p(x) \log_2 p(x). \tag{1}$$

The information found in two random discrete variables is the mutual information and can be computed as follows:

$$I(X,Y) = \sum_{x \in X} \sum_{y \in Y} p(x,y) \log \frac{p(x,y)}{p(x)p(y)}. \tag{2}$$

The major problems associated with the application of the MI are the need for sufficient number of samples to estimate the probabilities and the need to quantise the continuous input features. In our experiments, the features are scaled between 0 and 1 and quantised into 10 bins to estimate various probabilities. The greedy sequential feature selection algorithm [11] starts with one best feature based on $I(C;f_k)$ where C is the class label and f_k is the kth feature that maximizes $I(C;f_*)$. Then it searches for the feature f_i to be included in the feature subset such that $I(C;f_s,f_i)$ is maximized where f_s is the existing feature subset. Instead of performing a sequential search we propose the maximize the following criterion using a combinatorial optimization method:

$$E_{obj} = \sum_{i \in S} \left(I(C;f_i) - \beta \sum_{j \in S, j \neq i} \frac{I(C;f_j)I(f_i;f_j)}{2H(f_j)} \right).$$ (3)

where S is the subset containing the selected features and β is a scale factor to balance the importance of selecting features relevant to the classification problem and eliminating features with high level correlation.

3 Hopfield Neural Networks

Hopfield neural network (HNN) is a single-layered feedback network (as shown in Figure 1) whose dynamics are governed by a system of nonlinear ordinary differential equations and by an energy function [7]. A basic artificial neuron has many inputs and weighted connections. If u_i $i=12...n$ is defined as the network input I_i an externally supplied input bias current to neuron T_{ij} the weight connection from neuron i to neuron j then the equation of motion describing the time evolution of the circuit designed by Hopfield and Tank [7] is

$$du_i/dt = -u_i/\tau + \sum_j T_{ij} \cdot V_j + I_i.$$ (4)

$\tau = RC$ and $V_j = g(u_j)$. The energy function of the Hopfield model is defined as:

$$E = -\frac{1}{2}\sum_i \sum_j T_{ij}V_iV_j + \sum_i V_i I_i.$$ (5)

For further details on these equations please refer to [7,19]. The term energy function comes from a physical analogy to magnetic systems. A central property of the HNN is that given a starting point for the neurons the energy of equation (5) will never increase as the states of the neurons change provided T is a symmetric matrix with zero diagonal elements. Thus, one of the most important uses of a HNN is in solving optimization problem in where the cost function of the optimization problem is made identical to the energy function of equation (5) by properly defining the connection weights output of neurons and biases.

4 Heuristic Hopfield Neural Networks Based Feature Selection

We use a single layered HNN to solve the feature selection problem by mapping various MIs into the cost function and the reduced feature subset size into a constraint function. After minimization of the energy function, feature subset with high degree of information for classification and low level of redundancy will be selected.

4.1 Energy Function for Feature Selection

The objective function to maximize when a subset with N features is selected from M features, is given by equation (3). To enable N neurons in the HNN to compute a solution to the problem the network must be described by an energy function in which the lowest energy state corresponds to the best subset. There are two requirements: a) the energy function must favor strongly stable states with N neurons 'on' and $(M-N)$ neurons 'off' and b) the objective, E_{obj} is maximized. An appropriate form for this function can be found by considering the high gain limit when outputs are 0 or 1. The space over which the energy function is minimized is the 2^M corners of the M-dimensional hypercube defined by $V = 0$ or 1. The minima of the energy function:

$$E = \frac{K}{2}\left(\beta\sum_{i,j}\frac{I(C;f_j)I(f_i;f_j)}{H(f_j)}V_iV_j - \sum_i I(C;f_i)V_i\right) + \frac{1}{2}(\sum_i V_i - N)^2 . \tag{6}$$

The first term is minimized if and only if the features with least similarity are selected. The second sum is zero if and only if there are N entries of "1" in the entire vector. The third term encourages the selection of features relevant to the classification problem. The quadratic terms in the energy function define a connection matrix and the linear terms define input bias currents [7,17,19]. By partial differentiation, we obtain the following equations:

$$\frac{\partial E}{\partial V_i} = K\beta\sum_{j\neq i}\frac{I(C,f_j)I(f_i;f_j)}{H(f_j)}V_j + \sum_j V_j - N - \frac{K}{2}I(C,f_i). \tag{7}$$

$$\frac{du_i}{dt} = -\frac{\partial E}{\partial V_i}. \tag{8}$$

K is the coefficient ratio between cost and constraint. Comparing with the standard HNN energy function the connection matrix and the input currents are

$$T_{ij} = -(K\beta\frac{I(C;f_j)I(f_i;f_j)}{H(f_j)} + 1)(1-\delta(i,j)). \tag{9}$$

$$I_i = N + \frac{K}{2}I(C;f_i). \tag{10}$$

4.2 Adapting the Constraint Parameter

The HNN is very sensitive to the adjustment of parameters. Improper parameter values often make the network to converge to invalid solutions [19]. Even if converged to valid solutions the obtained solutions are often far from the optimal [17]. We adjust the ratio between cost and constraint weight values K using the number of increasing output values. This adjustment procedure heuristically updates K. The constraint parameter update procedure is given below:

{Count the number of $\frac{\partial u_i}{\partial t}$ which are above 0 (N_Above_0)

If $N\_Above\_0 > N$
$$K = K \cdot K\_Scale$$
Else if $N\_Above\_0 < N$
$$K = K / K\_Scale$$
End if
} % where K_Scale is the Scaling factor of K.

4.3 The Feature Selection Algorithm

The pseudocode of the feature selection algorithm is given below (using the variables defined below in Table 1)

Table 1. Feature Selection Algorithm

Initialize the following: the Start Temperature T_ini End Temperature T_end the Temperature Scaling Coefficient T_Scale K the K Scaling Coefficient K_Scale.

While $T >$ End Temperature {
    For i =1 to Max_No_Iterations {
    Calculate the $\frac{\partial u_i(t)}{\partial t}$

$$u_i(t+1) = u_i(t) + \frac{\partial u_i}{\partial t} \cdot \Delta t \quad V_i(t+1) = \frac{1}{1+e^{-u_i(t+1)/T}}$$

% Heuristically Adjusting K
Count the number of $\frac{\partial u_i}{\partial t}$ above 0 (N_Above_0)
    If $N\_Above\_0 > N$
$$K = K \cdot K\_Scale$$
    Else if $N\_Above\_0 < N$
$$K = K / K\_Scale$$
    End if }
$T = T \cdot T\_Scale$ }

Table 2. Variable and Constant Definitions and some initial values for HHNN

Coefficient	Comments	Value
T	Temperature	
T_ini	Initial temperature value	0.5
T_end	Final temperature value	0.05
T_Scale	Adjusting Coefficient of T	0.98
K	Ratio of Constraint and Cost	
K_Scale	Adjusting Coefficient of K	1.02
u	Input of each neuron	
V	Output of each neuron	
Δt	Time interval	0.05
N	Number of features to be selected	
M	Total number of features	

4.4 Initialization of the Network and Parameters

Since we have no prior knowledge about the features, the initial values of the neural input voltages u without bias in favor of any particular feature subset. According to [7] we set $\sum_i V_i = N$. From V we deduce $u_0(i)$ ($i=12..M$). To break the symmetry that appears in magnetic phase transitions it is therefore necessary to add some noise. $u_i = u_0 + \delta \cdot u_o \quad \delta = 5\%$.

K reflects the relative significance of constraint with respect to cost function function. From experiments, we found that the initial value affects the convergence and quality of the solution. A sensible choice might seem to use only the cost to calculate the input u with all V set to 1, i.e. $K(0) = \max(u_i) \; i=1 \; to \; M;$.

There are many ways to set the initial temperature. Based on our experiments it is appropriate to set the initial temperature to 0.5 and the final temperature to 0.05 for all datasets instead of introducing additional expressions and computations.

5 Experiment Results

We use the SVM [3] and the *k*NN to perform the classification. The SVM has been shown as a promising pattern classification technique. The SVM maps the input features into a high dimensional feature space so that the classes are linearly separable. Further, the decision boundary is constructed in order to maximize the margin between the two classes. However, SVM's performance depends on the feature set used. We employ the OSU SVM Matlab toolbox to carry out our simulations.

We carried out experiments with the data sets used in [4]. There are 313 training samples and 385 testing samples. We perform classification into four secondary structures: alpha beta alpha/beta and alpha+beta. The dataset has 125 elements representing various properties of the proteins. Once a feature subset is chosen, each feature is scaled using the following scaling factor:

$$W_i = I(C; f_i) - \alpha \sum_{j \in S} \frac{I(C; f_j) I(f_i; f_j)}{H(f_j)}. \tag{11}$$

The experimental results are shown in Table 3. From the results we can observe that the performance of the SVM peaks when the feature set size is around 85-115. kNN's performance is significantly inferior to the SVM. However, the kNN appears to perform well with a smaller feature subset. Further feature scaling improves the performance of the kNN. Our preliminary experiments showed that the feature scaling did not have consistent beneficial effect on the SVM.

Table 3. Experimental Results show recognition accuracy against feature subset size.

Subset size	SVM	kNN	
		W/out Scaling	With Scaling
125	0.7688	0.6831	0.7143
115	0.7792	0.6935	0.7273
105	0.7532	0.6883	0.7169
95	0.7818	0.7221	0.7169
85	0.7714	0.7091	0.7558
75	0.7688	0.7241	0.7532
65	0.7506	0.7195	0.7662
55	0.7688	0.7299	0.7532
45	0.7481	0.7429	0.7532
35	0.7532	0.7377	0.7506
25	0.7558	0.7429	0.7506
15	0.7351	0.7403	0.7221
5	0.6779	0.7377	0.7143

Further, our results also highlight the difficulty in employing the filter approach when the objective is to improve the classification performance. We can observe that the kNN gives the best classification when the feature subset has 25-85 features while SVM performs well with 85-115 features. This suggests that we should combine the ideas of wrapper with feature filter method to improve the performance but with much less computational cost in comparison to the pure wrapper approach.

6 Conclusion

In this paper, we formulate the feature selection as a combinatorial optimization problem and map it onto a single layered HNN. The traditional HNN is sensitive to the adjustment of parameters. We developed a heuristic algorithm to adjust the weighting between the cost function and the constraint function. Our experiments showed that the feature selection and scaling improves the performance of the kNN in the prediction of the protein secondary structure. The SVM is sensitive to the selected feature set. Further experimentations are needed to evaluate the significance of feature scaling for the SVM.

References

1. Blum, A. L., Langley, P.: Selection of relevant features and examples in machine learning. Artificial Intelligence J. (1997) No. 1–2 245–271.
2. Caruana, R. Freitag, D.: Greedy Attribute Selection. Proc. 11th Int. Conf. on Machine Learning (1994) 26–28.
3. Chung, C-C., Lin C-J.: LIBSVM: A library for support vector machines. (2002) http://www.csie.ntu.edu.tw/~cjlin/ http://eewww.eng.ohio-state.edu/~maj/osu_svm/.
4. Ding, C. H. Q., Dubchak, I.: Multi-class protein fold recognition using support vector machines and neural networks. Bioinformatics (2001) 349–358 http://www.nersc.gov/~cding/protein.
5. Dash, M., Liu, H.: Feature Selection for Classification. Intelligent Data Analysis (1997) Vol. 1 131–156.
6. Duch, W., Grudzinski, K.: Search and global minimization in similarity-based methods. Int. Joint Conf. on Neural Networks. (1999) paper no. 742 Washington.
7. Hopfield, J. J., Tank, D. W.: 'Neural' Computation of Decisions in Optimization Problems. Bio. Cybernetics (1985) Vol. 52 141–152.
8. Jain, A. K., Zongker, D.: Feature selection: evaluation application and small sample performance. IEEE T. on Pattern Analysis and Machine Intelligence (1997) Vol. 19 153–158.
9. Kohavi, R., John, G. H.: Wrappers for feature subset selection. Artificial Intelligence J. (1997) No. 1-2 273–324.
10. Kudo, M., Sklansky, J.: Comparison of algorithms that selects features for pattern classifiers. Pattern Recognition (2000) Vol. 33 25–41.
11. Kwak, N., Choi, C.: Input feature selection for classification problems. IEEE Trans. on Neural Networks (2002) Vol. 13 143–159.
12. Mitra, P., Murthy, C. A., Pal, S. K.: Unsupervised feature selection using feature similarity. IEEE Trans. on Pattern Analysis and Machine Intelligence (2002) Vol. 24 1–12.
13. Pal, N. R.: Soft computing for feature analysis. Fuzzy Sets and Systems (1999) Vol. 103 201–221.
14. Rost, B.: Review: Protein secondary structure prediction continues to rise. J of Structural Biology (2001) Vol. 134 204–218.
15. Setiono R., Liu, H.: Neural network feature selector. IEEE Trans on neural networks (1997) 654–662.
16. Wang, R., Tang Z., Cao, Q.: A learning method in Hopfield neural network for combinatorial optimization problem. Neurocomputing (2002) Vol. 48 1021–1024.
17. Wettschereck, D., Aha, D. W., Mohri, T.: A review and empirical evaluation of feature weighting methods for a class of lazy learning algorithms. Artificial Intelligence Review (1997) Vol. 11 273–314.
18. Wilson, G. V., Pawley, G. S.: On the stability of the traveling salesman problem algorithm of Hopfield and Tank. Biol. Cybernet. (1988) Vol. 58 63–70.

Recognition of Structure Classification of Protein Folding by NN and SVM Hierarchical Learning Architecture

I-Fang Chung[1], Chuen-Der Huang[1,2], Ya-Hsin Shen[1], and Chin-Teng Lin[1]

[1]Department of Electrical and Control Engineering, Chiao-Tung University,
HsinChu, Taiwan, Republic of China
[2]Department of Electrical Engineering, HsiuPing Institute of Technology,
Taichung, Taiwan, Republic of China
ctlin@fnn.cn.nctu.edu.tw

Abstract. Classifying the structure of protein is a very important task in biological data. By means of the classification, the relationships and characteristics among known proteins can be exploited to predict the structure of new proteins. The study of the protein structures is based on the sequences and their similarity. It is a difficult task. Recently, due to the ability of machine learning techniques, many researchers have applied them to probe into this protein classification problem. We also apply here machine learning methods for multi-class protein fold recognition problem by proposing a novel hierarchical learning architecture. This novel hierarchical learning architecture can be formed by NN (neural networks) or SVM (support vector machine) as basic building blocks. Our results show that both of them can perform well. We use this new architecture to attack the multi-class protein fold recognition problem as proposed by Dubchak and Ding in 2001. With the same set of features our method can not only obtain better prediction accuracy and lower computation time, but also can avoid the use of the stochastic voting process in the original approach.

1 Introduction

Large-scale sequencing projects produce a massive number of putative protein sequences. However, the growing of the number of known three-dimensional protein structures is much slower. This situation makes the need to extract structural information from both the sequence database and, moreover, the structure database itself more imperative. Since the three-dimensional coordinate structures provide insight into protein's function, mechanism and evolution, there exist several classification databases such as SCOP, CATH, DDBASE, Entrez, and 3Dee, which imbue the structures with context and analysis. Different classification databases of proteins focus on their own characteristics. For example, comprehensive protein classification, such as SCOP, provides a detailed description of the structural and evolutionary relationships of the proteins of known structure [1].

Classification databases of proteins which imbue the structures with context and analysis are important for understanding the function of proteins, and also essential for the discovery of new medication and therapies. In the past, such databases were made by factitious or semi-automatic procedure such as SCOP or CATH. But recently, protein classification or protein fold prediction are solved by computer-aided methods. For example, a computational method was developed for the assignment of a protein sequence to a folding class in the SCOP [5]. This method used primary global protein sequence in terms of three descriptors as physical, chemical, and structural properties of the constituent amino acids. There have been several attempts to predict protein folds [4-6]. Researchers have also worked on distinguishing the members of the 83 folds in the 3D_ALI classification [4] and predicting protein folds in the context of the 128 folds of the SCOP classification [5].

Some authors used the one-versus-others approach, which is based on a decision tree algorithm. Methods of this kind usually spend many classifiers and involves a lot of computation [3]. For example, the number of classifiers required in the one-against-one method is $C^K_2 = K$, for K classes. Besides, these methods may cause the problem called 'False Positive,' resulting in poor classification accuracy [2]. To eliminate the 'False Positive' problem, a voting scheme was developed and included into the decisive process. The one-versus-others method was also modified to the unique one-versus-others and all-versus-all methods [6].

Machine learning tools such as neural network (NN) and support vector machine (SVM) could be very useful for such problems of bioinformatics. The SVM method, which has the advantage of fast convergence, was combined with the decision tree algorithm for multi-class protein folds recognition in order to get higher prediction accuracy [8]. Furthermore, in the paper proposed by Dubchak and Ding, both NN and SVM were combined with the decision tree algorithm separately [6].

In this paper, we consider the problem as proposed by Dubchak and Ding [6] and construct a novel hierarchical learning structure to cope with the multi-class protein fold recognition problem. The proposed structure can house a set of NNs or SVMs as basic building blocks, with each being a multi-class classifier inherently. This is in contrast to the original approach in [6], where a series of two-class classifiers and a voting scheme were used to solve the same problem. The experiments on the same datasets and protein characteristics show that the proposed approach can achieve higher prediction accuracy with smaller number of classifiers and lower computation overhead. Also, due to the removal of the voting mechanism, the numerical output value of the classifiers in the proposed hierarchical structure can indicate the reliability or confidence of the prediction. Since each protein is predicted with different reliability, such a reliability score is necessary for practical prediction systems.

2 Hierarchical Learning Structure

As discussed in [6], we find that the fold characteristics of the proteins can be separated into four typical classes named as all α, all β, α and β (α/β), α plus β ($\alpha+\beta$), respectively. Each class contains several different numbers of folds, with a total of 27 folds. The task of this work is to classify each of the proteins into one of the 27 folds. According to the classification characteristics of the protein data, a new hierarchical learning structure including two-stage of classifiers as shown in Figure 1 is proposed. In the first stage, a multi-class classifier for recognizing the four protein classes (all α, all β, α/β, $\alpha+\beta$) is used. In the second stage, we perform detailed classification on each class. There are four independent multi-class classifiers used in this stage for protein fold recognition.

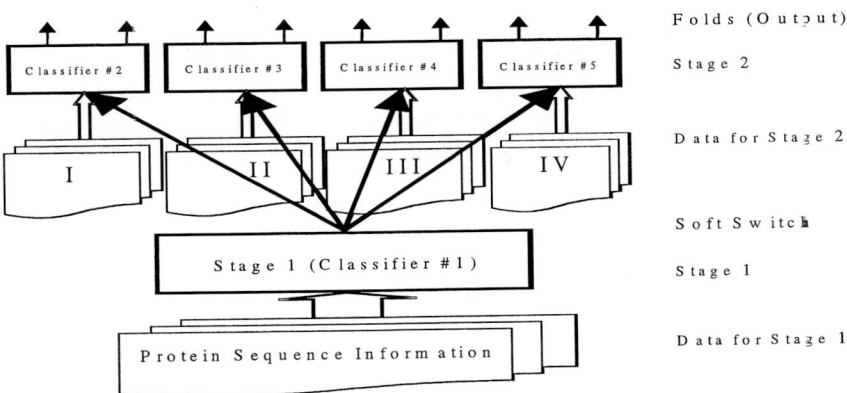

Fig. 1. Illustration of the proposed hierarchical learning structure for protein folds recognition.

In Figure 1, we also illustrate how the hierarchical structure can be used in actual experimental data. In the first stage, a multi-class classifier (Classifier #1) is used to distinguish proteins into four classes, denoted as I, II, III, and IV ($\alpha, \beta, \alpha/\beta$, and $\alpha+\beta$, correspondingly). Here we adopt proper protein sequence information as the inputs to this classifier. The protein sequence information is obtained from six kinds of protein features including composition of amino acids, predicted protein secondary structure, hydrophobicity, Van Der Waals volume, polarity, and polarizability. The second stage consists of four independent multi-class classifiers (Classifier #2--- Classifier #5), each for the fold recognition of different class of protein data classified by the Stage-1 classifier. In other words, Classifier #2 is to classify the protein data, which are classified as Class I by Classifier #1, into one of 6 fold types and so on. So, totally 27 folds are recognized by the Stage-2 classifiers.

In the proposed hierarchical learning structure, different kinds of classifiers can be the candidates of the composing building blocks. In our experiments, we use three kinds of NNs (MLP, RBFN and GRNN) and SVM, as the basic building blocks in our hierarchical model. We shall introduce these classifiers and the experimental results in the following sections. No matter what kind of classifiers we choose, the overall recognition results are better than those of the one-versus-others method with NN, and are even better than those of the existing modified one-versus-others method. Moreover, the higher recognition accuracy is obtained by using fewer classifiers with smaller size. The extra decision mechanism such as voting scheme is also avoided.

3 Machine Learning Algorithms for Multi-class Classification

For performance comparisons among different classifiers, such as that proposed in [6], we adopt two common machine-learning algorithms, SVM and NN, as the basic building blocks in the proposed hierarchical learning structure. For the NN-based classifiers, three common NN models are used individually in our experiments for extensive testing. We shall introduce these classifiers in the followings.

3.1 Support Vector Machine

Support Vector Machine (SVM) basically is a typical two-class classifier developed by Vapnik and his colleagues at Bell Laboratories [13], with algorithms improved by others [9]. It is a kind of algorithm, which constructs a hyperplane in a high-dimensional features space as the decision surface between positive and negative patterns. It can be used for pattern classification and nonlinear regression easily [13]. With further improvements by other researchers recently, the SVM has the ability to do multi-class classification directly too [10].

3.2 Neural Networks

Neural networks (NNs) has been developed for many years and been used well in various applications. Here we use three NN models (MLP, RBFN and GRNN), respectively, as the multi-class classifiers in our hierarchical learning structure.

(1) Multi-Layer-Perceptron (MLP) is a classic and widely used NN model. Such a network can solve nonlinear regression, and construct global approximation to the nonlinear input-output mapping.

(2) Radial Basis Function Network (RBFN) is a three-layer network. The hidden layer nodes use a basis function, such as a Gaussian function, as the activation function. Unlike the MLP network, the output nodes are linear [12].

(3) General Regression Neural Network (GRNN) is another type of NN coming from Probabilistic Neural Network (PNN), which is based on the probabilistic model, especially the Bayesian classifiers.

4 Datasets and Features

In our experiments, we use the same training set and test set of protein data as those used in [6]. They are introduced briefly in the followings. We shall also explain the feature vectors of the protein data used in our experiments.

4.1 Training Dataset

This training data set was built for the prediction of 128 protein folds based on the PDB select sets [7]. The data set was selected by their characteristics so that all proteins in the data set have less than 35% of the sequence identity for the aligned subsequences longer than 80 residues. Following the prior published paper, the training data was divided to 27 folds and represent all major structural classes.

Table 1. The numbers of proteins in the training and testing datasets in our experiments.

Item / Group	N_{train} (Number of Training Patterns)	N_{test} (Number of Testing Patterns)
all α	55	61
all β	109	117
α and β (α / β)	115	145
α plus β ($\alpha + \beta$)	34	62
Sum	313	385

Table 2. The Protein-fold prediction accuracy of various single-stage classification approaches, where the input PSIs fed into the classifier are C+S+H+P+V+Z.

Classifier / Prediction Accuracy	MLP	GRNN	RBFN	SVM
ϱ (C+S+H+P+V+Z)(%)	48.8	44.2	49.4	51.4

4.2 Testing Dataset

An independent dataset was also taken for testing the effect of prediction. The test dataset was based on PDB-40D set developed by the authors of the SCOP database [11]. A total of 385 proteins, same as those used by Dubchak and Ding, were selected for testing in our study. Table 1 shows the numbers of proteins in the training and test datasets for different protein classes used in our experiments.

4.3 Feature Vector Extraction

The features extraction of the analyzed data is a very important task, different extracted features may cause different classification results, better or worse. These features were obtained from the web site (http://www.nersc.gov/~cding/protein), which is available on line. The six kinds of protein sequence information (PSI), including the composition of amino acids (C), the predicted secondary structure (S), hydrophobicity (H), normalized Van Der Waals volume (V), polarity (P), and polarizability (Z), are extracted from the database. Besides the dimension of the composition of amino acids being twenty, the rest PSIs have the same dimension, twenty-one in size [6]. We feed these feature data to our classifiers from single PSI to multiple PSIs progressively. In the following result reports of our experiments, the symbol '+' denotes information combination. It means that we feed multiple PSIs into the classifiers at once. The summed dimensions of the PSIs determines the number of input nodes of the NN classifiers or the input variables of the SVM. In our experiments, we use different combinations of PSIs as input features to each classifier. Hence, the two extreme cases are (1) the use of the composition of amino acids only, and (2) the use of all six PSIs. In the first case, the feature dimension is 20, and in the second case, the feature dimension is up to 125 (20+21+21+21+21).

5 Experiments and Results

The used RBFN and GRNN have only one hidden layer. The used SVM is the multi-class SVM proposed in [10]. In each case, the whole hierarchical learning structure is trained completely. The nodes and training epochs of NNs are chosen carefully during the experiments to avoid the over-fitting problem.

In bioinformatics, there are some accuracy measurement methods [15]. Based on these, the accuracy measurement of the proposed approach is defined as follows. If the number of testing proteins belonging to the F_i^{th} fold is n_i, but the tested classifier only recognizes c_i proteins as the F_i^{th} fold, then the accuracy rate of this tested classifier is set as c_i/n_i for the F_i^{th} fold. In addition to the calculation of individual accuracy rate, the total accuracy rate is calculated as follows:

$$N = n_1 + n_2 + n_3 + \ldots + n_i \quad \text{(in this study, i=27, N=385)} \tag{1}$$

$$C = c_1 + c_2 + c_3 + \ldots + c_i \quad \text{(in this study, i=27)} \tag{2}$$

$$Q = C/N, \tag{3}$$

where N is the total number of test proteins, C is the total number of correctly classified proteins, and Q is the classification (prediction) accuracy.

In our experiments, we used six different combinations of features as the inputs to the classifier. These combination are C, CS, CSH, CSHP, CSHPV, and CSHPVZ, where each character represents a kind of PSI defined in last section. For performance comparisons, we also use each of MLP, RBFN, GRNN, and SVM to classify the proteins into 27 folds directly without using the proposed hierarchical structure. Table 2 lists the prediction rates of various single-stage approaches, where the full set of PSIs are used as input features. It is observed that the average prediction accuracy Q is only about 50%. The prediction accuracies of the proposed hierarchical learning structure with various NN or SVM classifiers with respect to different combinations of PSIs are listed in Table 3. It is observed that the hierarchical structure can increase the prediction accuracy Q by about 7%. Also, more PSIs result in higher Q values.

The results obtained by the proposed hierarchical learning structure are also better than those by the one-versus-others (OvO), unique one-versus-others (uOvO), and all-versus-all (AvA) methods proposed in [6]. These methods require a series of SVMs or NNs, and a voting mechanism. We compare the results in Table 4. Table 4 shows that the overall recognition results of the proposed approach are usually better than those of the compared counterparts. Especially, the proposed hierarchical learning structure with the RBFN classifiers achieves the best prediction accuracy, 56.4%, which is higher than the best result (53.9%) achieved by the all-versus-all method with the two-class SVM classifiers (AvA(SVM)) proposed in [6]. The higher recognition accuracy of the proposed approach is obtained by using fewer classifiers with smaller size. Also, the extra decision mechanism such as the voting scheme is avoided.

Table 4 also shows that the proposed hierarchical learning structure with the RBFN sub-classifiers achieves the highest prediction accuracy (56.4%). This structure consists of five RBFN classifiers as shown in Figure 1, with a total of 366 hidden nodes. The RBFN can find the proper number of hidden nodes by itself during the training process. In our hierarchical structure, the largest RBFN is Classifier #1 in Stage 1, which contains 145 hidden nodes. The smallest RBFN is Classifier # 5 in Stage 2, which contains only 13 hidden nodes. For comparisons, the total number of

Table 3. Protein-fold prediction accuracy of the proposed hierarchical learning structure with various NN or SVM sub-classifiers. The corresponding prediction accuracies of various single-stage classification approaches are also shown for comparisons.

Classifier and PSIs	Prediction Accuracy	Single-stage classifier (%)	Proposed Hierarchical Learning Structure (%)
RBFN	C	48.6	44.9
	C+S	50.7	53.8
	C+S+H	52.0	53.3
	C+S+H+P	50.7	54.3
	C+S+H+P+V	49.1	55.3
	C+S+H+P+V+Z	49.4	56.4
GRNN (C+S+H+P+V+Z)		44.2	45.2
SVM (C+S+H+P+V+Z)		51.4	53.8

Table 4. Protein-fold prediction accuracy comparisons of the proposed hierarchical learning structure and the existing approaches.

Method \ Features	C	C+S	C+S+H	C+S+H+P	C+S+H+P+V	C+S+H+P+V+Z
OvO(NN)*	20.5	36.8	40.6	41.1	41.2	41.8
OvO(SVM)*	43.5	43.2	45.2	43.2	44.8	44.9
uOvO(SVM)*	49.4	48.6	51.1	49.4	50.9	49.6
AvA(SVM)*	44.9	52.1	56.0	56.5	55.5	53.9
RBFN**	40.3	48.6	50.1	52.0	49.1	49.4
Hierarchical Structure (MLP)	32.7	48.6	47.5	43.2	43.6	44.7
Hierarchical Structure (RBFN)	44.9	53.8	53.3	54.3	55.3	56.4
Hierarchical Structure (GRNN)	--	--	--	--	--	45.2
Hierarchical Structure (SVM)	--	--	--	--	--	53.8

Note: * Data from the paper (Dubchak and Ding, 2001).
** Using RBFN directly to classify the proteins into 27 folds (i.e., single-stage approach).

hidden nodes used in the single-stage RBFN is 125, which achieves 49.4% prediction accuracy, and cannot be better even with more hidden nodes. Also, in the all-versus-all method with the two-class SVM classifiers (AvA(SVM)) proposed in [6], which achieves 53.9% prediction accuracy, a total of 351 two-way SVM classifiers were used. In another experiment, we also calculate the training time required by the single-stage RBFN, and the training time required by each RBFN in the hierarchical learning structure, where the training was performed in a personal computer with Intel Pentium IV CPU under 1 GHz clocks. Here the training time required by the single-stage RBFN is 95.58 seconds and the training time required by the hierarchical learning structure is 152.02 seconds, where Stage-1 RBFN uses 126.92 seconds and Stage-2 RBFNs totally use 25.1 seconds. The results indicate that although Stage-1 RBFN in the hierarchical structure consumed longer training time, the training of each Stage-2 RBFN converged very quickly.

Last but not the least, as compared to the popular OvO, and the modified unique uOvO and AvA methods proposed in [6], the proposed hierarchical learning structure with embedded multi-class classifiers has another important advantage. Due to the removal of the voting mechanism required by the OvO, uOvO, and AvA methods, the numerical output value of the classifiers in the proposed hierarchical structure can indicate the reliability or confidence of the prediction. Since each protein is predicted with different reliability, such a reliability score is necessary for practical prediction systems.

6 Conclusions

We proposed a new hierarchical learning structure to solve the multi-class protein fold recognition problem. The proposed structure can integrate a set of baseline classifiers (called "basic building blocks" in this paper) in an efficient way to attack highly complex classification/prediction problems. In our experiments, we used three neural network models and the SVM, as the basic building blocks. The extensive experimental results based on the SCOP database demonstrated the superiority of the proposed scheme over the traditional single-stage classification methods. The prediction accuracy of the new scheme is also higher than that of the popular one-versus-others, and the modified unique one-versus-others and all-versus-all methods. In addition, due to the use of the multi-class classifiers as the basic building blocks, the proposed hierarchical structure does not need a large number of two-class classifiers and a voting scheme. As a result, the computation time for a prediction can be reduced and each prediction can be associated with a reliability or confidence of the prediction.

References

[1] A. G. Murzin, S. E. Brenner, T. Hubbard, and C. Chothia, "SCOP: A structural classification of proteins database for the investigation of sequence and structures," *Journal of Molecular Biology*, Vol. 247, pp. 536–540, 1995.

[2] P. Baldi and S. Brunak, *Bioinformatics: the Machine Learning Approach*, MIT Press, 1998.

[3] K. C. Chou and C. T. Zhang, "Prediction of protein structural classes," *Critical Reviews in Biochemistry and Molecular Biology,* Vol. 30, No. 4, pp. 275–349, 1995.

[4] I. Dubchak, I. Muchnik, S. R. Holbrook, and S. H. Kim, "Prediction of protein folding class using global description of amino acid sequence," *Proc. Natl. Acad. Sci.*, USA, Vol. 92, pp. 8700–8704, 1995.

[5] I. Dubchak, I. Muchnik, C. Mayor, I. Dralyuk, and S. H. Kim "Recognition of a protein fold in the context of the SCOP classification," *Proteins*, Vol. 35, pp. 401–407, 1999.

[6] I. Dubchak and C. H. Q. Ding, "Multi-class protein fold recognition using support vector machines and neural networks," *Bioinformatics,* Vol. 17, No. 4, pp. 349–358, 2001.

[7] U. Hobohm and C. Sander, "Enlarged representative set of protein structures," *Protein Science,* Vol. 3, No. 3, pp. 522–524, 1994.

[8] T. Jaakkola, M. Diekhans, and D. Haussler, "Using the fisher kernel method to detect remote protein homologies," *Proceedings of the Seventh International Conference on Intelligent Systems for Molecular Biology*, pp. 149–158, 1999.

[9] T. Joachims, "Making large-scale SVM learning practical," in *Advances in kernel methods – Support vector learning,* B. Scholkopf, C. J. C. Burges, and A. J. Smola (editors), Cambridge, MA, MIT Press, 1998.
[10] C. J. Lin and C. W. Hsu, "A comparison of methods for multi-class support vector machines," *IEEE Transactions on Neural Networks,* Vol. 13, pp. 415–425, 2002.
[11] L. Lo Conte, B. Ailey, T. J. Hubbard, S. E. Brenner, A. G. Murzin, and C. Chothia, "SCOP: a structural classification of proteins database," *Nuclear Acid Research,* Vol. 28, No. 1, pp. 257–259, 2000.
[12] J. Moody and C. J. Darken, "Fast learning in networks of locally tuned processing units," *Neural Computation,* Vol. 1, No. 2, pp. 281–294, 1989.
[13] V. N. Vapnik, *The nature of statistical learning theory,* Springer, N.Y., 1995.
[14] C. H. Wu, Neural networks and genome informatics, Elsevier, U.K., 2000.

Machine Learning for Multi-class Protein Fold Classification Based on Neural Networks with Feature Gating

Chuen-Der Huang[2,3], I-Fang Chung[2], Nikhil Ranjan Pal[1], and Chin-Teng Lin[2]

[1]Electronics and Communication Sciences Unit, Indian Statistical Institute, Calcutta, INDIA
[2]Department of Electrical and Control Engineering, National Chiao-Tung University, Hsinchu, Taiwan, R.O.C.
[3]Department of Electrical Engineering, HsiuPing Institute of Technology, Taichung, Taiwan, R.O.C.
`ctlin@fnn.cn.nctu.edu.tw`

Abstract. The success of a classification system depends heavily on two things: the tools being used and the features considered. For the bioinformatics applications the role of appropriate features has not been paid adequate importance. In this investigation we use two novel ideas. First, we use neural networks where each input node is associated with a gate. At the beginning of the training all gates are almost closed, i.e., no feature is allowed to enter the network. During the training, depending on the requirements, gates are either opened or closed. At the end of the training, gates corresponding to good features are completely opened while gates corresponding to bad features are closed more tightly. And of course, some gates may be partially open. So the network can not only select features in an online manner when the learning goes on, it also does some feature extraction. The second novel idea is to use a hierarchical machine learning architecture. Where at the first level the network classifies the data into four major folds : all alpha, all beta, alpha + beta and alpha / beta. And in the next level we have another set of networks, which further classifies the data into twenty seven folds. This approach helps us to achieve the following. The gating network is found to reduce the number of features drastically. It is interesting to observe that for the first level using just 50 features selected by the gating network we can get a comparable test accuracy as that using 125 features using neural classifiers. The process also helps us to get a better insight into the folding process. For example, tracking the evolution of different gates we can find which characteristics (features) of the data are more important for the folding process. And, of course, it reduces the computation time. The use of the hierarchical architecture helps us to get a better performance also.

1 Introduction

For the past decades, neural networks (NNs) have been well used as an intelligent machine learning method in many fields such as pattern recognition, speech and bioinformatics. There have been several attempts to use neural networks for prediction of protein folds. Dubchak *et al.* [2] point out that when we want a broad structural classification of protein, say into four classes, all alpha, all beta, (alpha+beta) and (alpha/beta) it is easy to get more than 70% prediction accuracy using simpler feature vector for representing a protein sequence [3-5]. However, the problem becomes more and more difficult as we demand more refined classification into more classes. Dubchak *et al.* [1] used a multi-layer perceptron network for predicting protein folds using global description of the chain of amino acids representing proteins. Authors used different properties of the amino acids as features. For example, they used the relative hydrophobicity of amino acids. They also used information about the predicted secondary structure and predicted solvent accessibility. They divided the amino acids into three groups based on hydrophobicity, three groups based on secondary structure and four groups based on solvent accessibility. Now a protein sequence is then described based on three global descriptors : Composition (C), Transition (T) and Distribution (D). These descriptors essentially describe the frequencies with which the properties change along the sequence and their distribution on the chain. In [1] authors used various combination of these features and trained networks to find a good set of features. In [2] Dubchak *et al.* proposed a neural network based scheme for protein fold prediction into 27 classes. This method like the one in [1] also uses global descriptors of the primary sequence. These descriptors are also computed from the physical, chemical and structural properties of the constituent amino acids. In [2] authors used proteins from the PDB where two proteins have no more than 35% sequence identity. Here in addition to the three amino acids attributes described earlier, authors used three more attributes : normalized Van Der Walls volume, polarity and polarizability. The same set of descriptors are used for all attributes resulting in a parameter vector in 21 dimension for each attribute. They also used the percent composition of amino acids as feature vectors. Let there be M folds in the data set. For each fold, authors divided the data set into two groups, one containing points from the fold and the other containing the rest. So there are M such partitions. For each fold a NN is trained. And this procedure is repeated 7 times for each fold, each time only one set of features computed from a particular attribute is used. Then a voting mechanism is used to decide on the fold of a given protein. All these investigations clearly suggest that the choice of the right features is very important for a better prediction of protein folds.

The bioinformatics researchers, although acknowledged the importance of feature analysis, no systematic effort to find the best set of features have been done – mostly authors have used enumeration techniques. Feature analysis is more important for bioinformatics applications for two reasons, the class structure is highly complex and the data are usually in very large dimension. Most of the feature analysis techniques available in the pattern recognition literature is off-line in nature. It is known that all features that characterize a data point may not have the same impact with regard to its classification, i.e., some features may be redundant and also some may have derogatory influence on the classification task. Thus, selection of a proper subset of features from the available set of features is important for design of efficient classifiers. There are methods for selecting good features on the basis of feature ranking etc. [7-10].

The goodness of a feature depends on the problem being solved and also on the tools being used to solve the problem [7]. Therefore, feature selection simultaneously with designing classifiers can select the most appropriate features for the task and can result in a good classifier. In [6] Pal and Chintalpudi developed an integrated feature selection and classification scheme based on the multilayer perceptron architecture. We would like to use the same concept here to reduce the dimensionality of the data.

In addition to this, we use a novel hierarchical architecture [1] for achieving better classification performance.

2 Online Feature Selection through Gating

In a standard multilayer perceptron network, the effect of some features (inputs) can be eliminated by not allowing them into the network, i.e., by equipping each input node (hence each feature) with a gate and closing the gate. For good features the associated gates can be completely opened. On the other hand, if a feature is partially important, then the corresponding gate should be partially opened. Pal and Chintalapudi suggested a mechanism for realizing such a gate so that "partially useful" features be identified and attenuated according to their relative usefulness. In order to model the gates we consider an attenuation function for each feature such that for a good feature the function produces a value of 1 or nearly 1; while for a bad feature, it should be nearly 0. For a partially effective feature it should have a value that is intermediate to these extremes. To model the gate we multiply the input feature value by its gate function value and the modulated feature value is passed into the network. The gate functions attenuate the features before they propagate through the net, so we may call these gate functions attenuation functions. A simple way of identifying useful gate functions is to use sigmoidal functions with a *tunable* parameter, which can be learnt using training data. To complete the description of the method we define the following in connection with a multi-layer perceptron network.

Let $F_i : R \to [0,1]$ be the gate or attenuation function associated with the ith input feature, F_i has an argument w_i, $F'_i(w_i)$ be the value of derivative of the attenuation function at w_i; μ be the learning rate of the attenuation parameter; v be the learning rate of the connection weights, x_i be the ith input of an input vector; x' be the attenuated value of x, i.e., $x' = x F(w)$; w^0_{ij} be the weight connecting the jth node of the *first hidden* layer to the ith node of the input layer; and δ^1_j be the error term for the j-th node of the first hidden layer..

It can be easily shown that except for w^0_{ij}, the update rules for all weights remain the same as that for an ordinary MLP. Assuming that the first hidden layer has q nodes. the update rules for w^0_{ij} and w_i are :

$$w^0_{ji,new} = w^0_{ji,old} - v x_i \delta^1_j F(w_i) \tag{1}$$

$$w_{i,new} = w_{i,old} - \mu x_i (\sum_{j=1}^{q} w^0_{ji} \delta^1_j) F'(w_i) \tag{2}$$

Although for the gate function, several choices are possible, we use here the sigmoidal function $F(w) = 1.0/(1 + e^{-w})$. The p gate parameters are so initialized that when the training starts F(w) is practically zero for all gates, i.e., no feature is allowed to enter the network. As the back-propagation learning proceeds, gates for the features that can reduce the error faster are opened. Note that, the learning of the gate function continues along with other weights of the network. At the end of the training important features can be picked up based on the values of the attenuation function.

3 Learning Machines

In our experiment, we use a novel hierarchical learning structure which has been proposed by us [11]. The concept of the hierarchical structure is neither the same as the cascade network nor as the divide-and-conquer network. The constituents of the hierarchical structure are all independent networks. A hierarchical architecture is suitable for data sets that can be grouped into a smaller number of classes, where each class can further be divided into a set other classes. The multi-classification of protein structure has this characteristic.

Before training of the hierarchical classifier, data should be passed through the feature selection network to find out the important features. Figure 1 shows integrated view of the whole system. It has two major components; the gating network and the hierarchical classifier. First, the original data are used to train the gating network. At the end of the training we look at the gate function values for each feature. If the gate function value is greater than a threshold *th*, then we consider that feature important. In this way, from the initial set of p features, we get a reduced set of q important features.

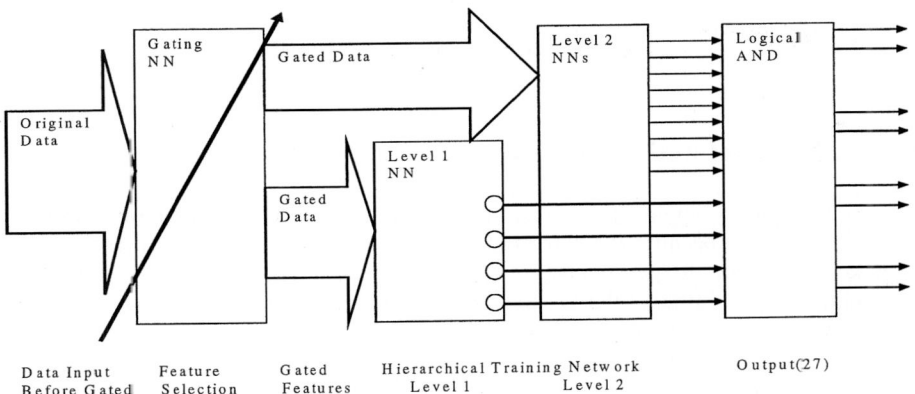

Fig. 1. Block Diagram of Learning System

Now this q-dimensional data set is used to train the hierarchical learning machine represented by Level 1 and Level 2 in Fig. 1. This hierarchical machine is blown up in Fig. 2. Let the training data be $X_{Tr}=X_1 \cup X_2 \cup X_3 \cup X_4$, where X_i is the training data corresponding to group i. First we train the Level1 NN (see figure 1). using X. The Level 1 NN divides the data into four groups. Note that the division of X made by the Level 1 NN may not exactly correspond to $X_{Tr} =X_1 \cup X_2 \cup X_3 \cup X_4$. The Level2 networks are independently trained. The i-*th* Level 2 NN is trained with X_i. Once the training of the second level networks is over, the system is ready to be tested. A test data point is first passed through the gating network, which reduces its dimension to q. This q dimensional data point is now fed the Level 1 NN which will classify the point to one of the four groups; say, it is classified to group 3. Then the training data point is fed to the 3rd network in the second level. It should be noted here that, for such an architecture, if the Level 1 NN makes any mistake, then Level 2 network cannot recover the same. The proposed architecture is quite general in nature and hence for both Level 1 and Level 2, we can use any classification network; in fact, we can use any non-neural classifier too. Although, features are selected using a feature-selection multilayer perceptron type network, we use the selected features for classification using both MLP and RBF networks.

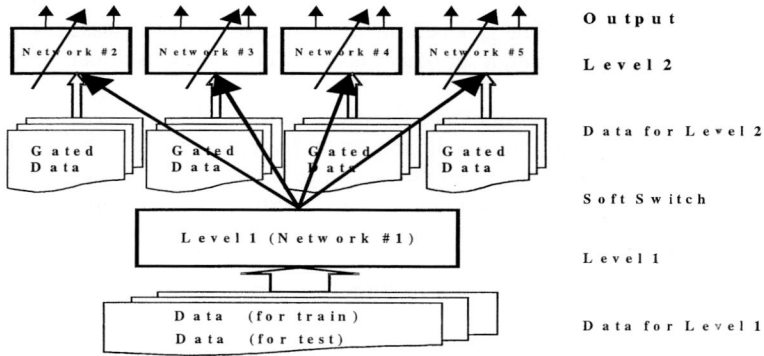

Fig. 2. Hierarchical Learning Structure.

4 The Data Set and the Features

For bioinformatics applications, feature extraction is a very important task that deserve discussion because the extracted features may have a strong influence on the accuracy. In our experiments, we use composition, secondary structure, hydrophobicity, volume, polarity and polarizability. as the characteristics of the protein. Table 1 summarizes the characteristics of descriptors that will be used by the gating network. For composition item, since there are twenty amino acids, the first set of feature contain twenty entries. But for the remaining characteristics, we obtain twenty-one features for each. So the total number of features that we use here is 125 (20+21+21+21+21). Consequently, the number of input nodes of the neural networks can be up to 125, as shown in Table 1.

The number of training proteins used in our experiment is 313. It can be divided into 4 groups with 27 folds within it. The number of proteins used in the test set is 385. This set has also representatives from all 27 folds. Table 2 depicts the distribution of training and test proteins in different groups.

5 Results

We have made several runs of the gating networks and results reported correspond to some typical output. We emphasize the fact that depending on the initialization, two different sets of features may be picked up by the gating net as important in two different runs. This is absolutely fine, as if there are two correlated features, a and b,

Table 1. Features used in the experiments.

	Descriptors			Features
Composition (C)	20 kinds of amino acids			20
Predicted Secondary Structure (S)	Alpha	Beta	Loop	21
Hydrophobicity (H)	Positive	Neutral	Negative	21
Volume (V)	Large	Middle	Small	21
Polarity (P)	Positive	Neutral	Negative	21
Polarizability (Z)	Strong	Middle	Weak	21
Total	125			

Table 2. Numbers of Pattern in the Training and Test Sets.

Fold Types	Number of Training Pattern	Numbers of Test Pattern
All Alpha	55	61
All Beta	109	117
Alpha/Beta	115	145
Alpha + Beta	34	62
Total	313	385

the net may pick up feature a in run 1 and feature b in run 2. Moreover, depending on the choice of the threshold, the number of selected features may be different. Table 3 shows 15 of the most important features of a typical run of the gating network after 1000, 1500, and 4000 iterations. It is interesting to note that after 1000 iterations, eight of the top most 15 important features come from the group, predicted secondary structure. Of these eight one of the features, No. 27, disappears from the list of important features with iterations. Probably, the gate corresponding to some other correlated feature opened faster. After 4000 iterations, of the important 15 features, nine come from the predicted secondary structure. This clearly tells that the local secondary structure, as expected, has a strong impact on the final folds. In this list of 15 important features, we have representation from polarity, polarizability, volume and hydrophobicity. In this investigation, we initialized the gating function with a value of 0.000124.

Table 4 depicts the classification performance at level 1 (into four groups) by the MLP network with different sets of features. Table 4 reveals the fact that use of more features are not necessarily good. It also says that the distribution predicted secondary structure and composition constitute a good set of features. This is also consistent with the results obtained from the gating network.

Table 5 presents classification performance of the system with different feature sets when RBF nets are used as the basic classifier unit. The level 1 performance shows that with 67 features (50% reduction), the decrease in performance is only 1.26% while with 65% features the test accuracy is reduced by only 0.76 %. This clearly

Table 3. Values of the gate functions for most important 15 features after different iterations.

Feature number	Gate function values-after 1000 iterations	Feature number	Gate function values-after 1500 iterations	Feature number	Gate function values-after 4000 iterations
30	0.002657	82	0.002903	103	1.0
81	0.002677	98	0.002995	22	1.0
41	0.002774	79	0.00305	26	1.0
40	0.002952	83	0.003197	28	1.0
77	0.002964	92	0.003634	29	1.0
103	0.00297	40	0.003697	30	1.0
82	0.003042	81	0.004338	31	1.0
92	0.003211	41	0.004585	33	1.0
98	0.003256	103	0.007582	35	1.0
27	0.0035	22	1	38	1.0
31	0.004106	26	1	41	1.0
22	0.008275	29	1	59	1.0
26	1.0	30	1	75	1.0
29	1.0	31	1	81	1.0
35	1.0	35	1	83	1.0

Table 4. Performance of ordinary MLP on different subsets of features.

	C	CS	CSH	CSHP	CSHPV	CSHPVZ
Correct classifications	243 (63.1%)	308 (80.0%)	305 (79.2%)	301 (78.2%)	302 (78.4%)	309 (80.3%)

Table 5. Performance of the hierarchical system using different feature sets selected by the gating net.

		Number of Features used							
		125		80		67		50	
		No.	%	No.	%	No.	%	No.	%
Level 1		314	81.56	311	80.8	309	80.3	305	79.2
Level 2	Group 1	41	67.2	45	73.8	31	50.8	29	47.5
	Group 2	61	52.1	66	56.4	60	51.3	56	47.9
	Group 3	85	58.6	79	54.5	77	53.1	74	51.0
	Group 4	30	48.4	54	87.1	34	54.8	30	48.4
Overall		217	56.36	204	53.0	202	52.5	189	49.1

suggests that the gating network can do an excellent job of selecting important features. Let us now consider the overall classification performance (with 27 folds). For this case we get 53% test accuracy with 67% features which is just 3% less than what we can achieve taking into account all 125 features.

Comparing our results with that of Dubchak and Ding [12] we find that their All v.s. All method with support vector machines can result in a test accuracy of 53.9% while with the RBF networks using only 67% features we can get 53% test accuracy.

6 Conclusion

In this paper, we integrated two novel ideas: an online feature selection technique and a hierarchical learning machine to deal with the multi-class protein fold recognition problem. The results showed that the proposed structure is quite effective in both reducing the dimensionality of the data and enhancing the classification performance. Such online feature selection capability can give a better insight into the folding process. So far the bioinformatics researchers did not have any tool for such online feature selection and consequently, they used to consider different intuitive combination of features. Since consideration of all possible subset is computationally not feasible, it is often impossible to find the best set of features. The proposed system opens up the possibility of computing many more features from the amino acid sequence and then allowing the system to pickup the desirable ones. Its application domain is extended to all other areas of bioinformatics also.

References

[1] I. Dubchak, I. Muchnik, S. R. Holbrook and S-H Kim, "Prediction of protein folding class using global description of amino acid sequence", *Proc. Natl. Acad. (Biophysics)* USA, Vol. 92, pp. 8700–8704, Sep., 1995.

[2] I. Dubchak, I. Muchnik, C. Mayor, I. Dralyuk, and S. H. Kim, "Recognition of a Protein Fold in the context of the SCOP Classification", *PROTEINS: Structure, Function and Genetics*, Vol. 35, pp. 401–407, 1999.

[3] P. Y. In Chou and G. D.Fashman, editor, "Prediction of protein structure and principles of protein conformation", *Plenum Press*, New York:, pp. 549–586, 1989.

[4] H. Nakashima, K. Nishikawa, and T. Ooi ,"The folding type of a protein is relevant to the amino acid composition", *J. Biochem*, Vol. 99, pp.152–162, 1986.

[5] I. Dubchak, S. R. Holbrook, and S. H. Kim, "Prediction of protein folding class from amino acid composition", *PROTEINS: Structure, Function and Genetics*, Vol. 16, pp. 79–91,1993.

[6] N. R. Pal and K. Chintalapudi, "Connectionist system for feature selection," *Neural, Parallel and Scientific Computation*, Vol. 5, No. 3, pp. 359–381, 1997.

[7] R. De, N. R. Pal, and S. K. Pal, "Feature analysis: neural network and fuzzy set theoretic approaches", *Pattern Recognition*, Vol. 30, No. 10, pp. 1579–1590, 1997.

[8] K. Fukunaga and W. Koontz, "Applications of the karhunen-Loeve expansion to feature selection and ordering", *IEEE Trans. Comp.*, Vol. C-19, 1970.

[9] K. L. Priddy, S. K. Rogers, D. W. Ruck, G. L. Tarr, and M. Kabrisby, "Bayesian Selection of Important Features for Feed-forward Neural Network", *NeuroComputing*, Vol. 5, pp. 91–103, 1993.

[10] A. Verikas and M. Bacauskiene, "Feature Selection with Neural Networks," *Pattern Recognition Letter*, Vol. 23, pp. 1323–1335, 2002.

[11] I F. Chung, C. D. Huang, Y. H. Shen, and C. T. Lin, "Recognition of Structure Classification of Protein Folding by NN and SVM Hierarchical Learning Architecture", Int. Conf. Neural Infor. Processing, ICONIP'03, Turkey, 2003.

[12] I. Dubchak and C. H. Q. Ding, "Multi-class protein fold recognition using support vector machines and neural networks," *Bioinformatics*, Vol. 17, No. 4, pp. 349–358, 2001.

Some New Features for Protein Fold Prediction

Nikhil Ranjan Pal and Debrup Chakraborty

Electronics and Communication Sciences Unit
Indian Statistical Institute, Calcutta 700108, India
{nikhil,debrup_r}@isical.ac.in

Abstract. In this paper we propose several sets of new features for protein fold prediction. The first feature set consisting of 47 features uses only the sequence information. We also define four different sets of features based on hydrophobicity of amino acids. Each such set has 400 features which are motivated by folding energy modeling. To define these features we have considered pair-wise amino acids (AA) interaction potential. The effectiveness of the proposed feature sets is tested using multilayer perceptron and radial basis function networks to solve the 4 class (level 1) and 27 class (level 2) prediction problems as defined in the context of SCOP classification. Our investigation shows that such features have good discriminating powers in predicting protein folds.

1 Introduction

One of the most important and challenging problems of bioinformatics is prediction of protein folds from the amino acid sequences. Researchers have been using machine learning techniques for solving many problems of bioinformatics including the prediction of protein folds[1-4]. Also, there have been several attempts to predict local secondary structures of proteins[2]. Success of any such method depends on the features used to characterize a residue sequence representing a protein. Among other tools, neural networks are the most successful ones for prediction of protein structures. Dubchak et al. [1] point out that when we want a broad structural classification of protein, say into four classes, all alpha, all beta, (alpha+beta) and (alpha/beta) it is easy to get more than 70% prediction accuracy using simpler feature vector for representing a protein sequence. However, the problem becomes more and more difficult as we demand more refined classification into more classes.

So far one of the most successful set of features used for protein folds consists of global description of the chain of amino-acids representing proteins. In this feature set different properties of the amino acids are used as features. For example, they used the relative hydrophobicity of amino acids. They also used information about the predicted secondary structure and predicted solvent accessibility. Here we do not like to use the predicted secondary structure because it has, inherent in it, some incorrect information. In other words, about 30% of the predicted secondary structure is incorrect. Thus it would not be meaningful to use, the predicted secondary structure as a feature. It would be better if we can use properties of the residue sequence to directly predict the folds. And that is the objective of this paper.

Here we propose five sets of new features and evaluate their performance using neural networks. We compute some features which characterize the spatial distribution of different amino acids on the sequence. For example, for a particular residue, we compute the average separation between two successive occurrences of the same residue. We also compute some entropy based features. In this way, just based on the symbols, not using any of their physico-chemical properties, we computed 47 features and this set alone is found to produce a test prediction accuracy of about 74%. We also computed four sets of features each having 400 members based on hydrophobicity of the amino acids. Here, we have considered amino acid pairs separated by just one position and taken an exponential function of the hydrophobocity of the pair to compute the feature. This is motivated by the fact that in case of structure prediction by ab-initio method hydrophobicity has been successfully used [5]. Moreover, for such approaches researchers have considered pairs, which are in "contact" but separated by at least one residue to avoid complete collapse. Out of these four sets of features two works quite well both for both level 1 and level 2 classification tasks. In fact for classification into 27 folds, both these feature sets outperform the classification accuracy reported in the literature using the popular 125 features based on the various physico-chemical properties and predicted secondary structure of the amino acid sequences.

2   Features for Protein Fold Prediction: Old and New

2.1   Some Existing Features

One of the most successful set of features for protein fold prediction contains 125 features which are extensively used in the context of SCOP classification [6]. These features are computed using the following characteristics of proteins: composition, predicted secondary structure, hydrophobicity, volume, polarity and polarizability. The amino acids (AAs) are divided into three groups based on hydrophobicity, volume, polarity, polarizability and predicted secondary structure, as shown in Table 1 [1,4]. Now a protein, that is an amino acid sequence, is described using three global descriptors [1,4] : Composition (C), Transition (T) and Distribution (D). These descriptors essentially describe the frequencies with which the properties change along the sequence and their distribution on the chain. Let us illustrate it using hydrophobicity as an example. As stated earlier, based on the hydrophobicity values, AAs are divided into three groups, polar (P), neutral (N) and hydrophobic (H). Then C, the composition descriptor consists of three values giving the percentage of the three types of AAs in the protein. Transition feature is also characterized by three transition probabilities: transition probability of P to N and N to P; transition probability of P to H and H to P and that from N to H and H to N. The computation of the feature values representing distribution is a little complex. Here for each of the three groups of AAs, five percentages are computed. These five values are: the percentage of the sequence where the first member of that group is located, and the fractions where the first 25%, 50%, 75% and 100% residues of that group are contained. In this way, based on just hydrophobicity we get 3+3+15= 21 feature values. So using five properties of AAs one gets $5 \times 21 = 105$ features and an additional 20 features representing the percentage compositions of amino acids in the protein. Thus in total one gets 125 features. Authors in [4] used various combination of these features. The data sets with these features are available at http://www.nersc.gov/~cding/protein. The 125 features and various subsets of them have been extensively used by researchers for prediction of protein folds.

Table 1. Grouping of Amino Acids based on attributes (an extended version of Table 1 in [1])

Property	Group 1	Group2	Group 3
Hydrophobicity	Polar	Neutral	Hydrophobic
	R,K,E,D,Q,N	G,A,S,T,P,H,Y	C,V,L,I,M,F,W
Volume	0 - 2.78	2.95 - 4.0	4.43 - 8.08
Polarity	4.9 - 6.2	8.0 - 9.2	10.4 - 13.0
Polarizability	0.00 - 0.108	0.128 - 0.186	0.219 - 0.409
Predicted Secondary Structure	Helix	Strand	Coil

2.2 Some New Features

Since, the native fold of a protein depends only on the residue sequence, we should be able to do a good job using just the sequence information. Keeping this in mind we shall talk about five types of features. The first set of features does not explicitly use any attribute of the AAs but is based on distribution of the residues on the chain. Let us denote the 20 residues by $x_i, i = 1, 2, ..., 20$ and their frequencies by $f_i, i = 1, 2, ..., 20$. Let N be the length of a residue sequence representing a protein $S = s_1 \ s_2 \ s_3 ... s_N$. Define $P = \{p_i = f_i/N : i = 1, 2, ..., n\}$, where p_i is the probability of residue x_i on S.

Our first set of 20 features is $F_i = p_i, i = 1, 2, ..., 20$. These 20 features have been used by other researchers also. Next we compute five features that try to characterize the shape of the histogram. These features are summarized in Table 2. The *first order energy* (F_{21}, Table 2) attains the minimum value for a uniform distribution, while the *first order entropy* (F_{22}, Table 2) attains the maximum value for a uniform distribution. The features $F_{23} - F_{25}$ characterize the shape of the histogram. The *second order energy* (F_{26}) and the *second order entropy* (F_{27}) measure the uniformity of distribution of pairs of residues. The remaining 20 features compute the average separation between two successive appearance of the same residue on the AA chain. Note that, the denominator of the *average separation of the residues* makes it independent of the length of the sequence and the frequency with which the residue type occurs. These 47 features, $F_1 - F_{47}$, constitute our first set of features.

We also compute other sets of features based on the hydrophobicity attribute of the AAs. It is believed that hydrophobicity characteristic of residues is a very important determinant of native structure of a protein. Consequently, hydrophobicity has been used by researchers for threading [5]. Motivated by this fact, we have generated features characterizing interaction between pairs of residues in contact. We consider two residues are in contact if they are separated by exactly one residue on the AA chain. So we compute the interaction potential between two residues (a, b) as

$$P_1(a,b) = \frac{1}{R} \sum_{x_i=a, x_j=b, j=i+2} e^{\frac{(h(x_i)+h(x_j))}{M}}, a, b = 1, 2, ..., 20.$$

Here $h(a)$ is the hydrophobicity of residue a and M is a constant, the role of M is to scale the value of hydrophobicity so that numerical overflow is avoided. We choose M as 24 because the maximum absolute value of hydrophobicity is 12. The same M will be used for scaling the test data, X_{Ts}. R is a normalizing constant defined as :

$$R = max_{S \in X_{Tr}} \left\{ \max_{a,b} \sum_{x_i=a, x_j=b, j=i+2} e^{\frac{(h(x_i)+h(x_j))}{M}} \right\}.$$

Note that, the normalizing constant R is computed taking into account the entire training set. In this way we shall get a feature vector of dimension 400 for each protein sequence. Researchers using energy modeling for threading or ab-initio folding do not consider adjacent residues to avoid complete collapse of the sequence. Keeping this in mind, the feature set P_1 does not consider adjacent residues. However, since we are not using energy modeling, but shall do feature based pattern recognition, we also conducted experiments considering another set of features P_2 which is computed exactly in the same manner as P_1, but taking into account only adjacent pairs of residues.

In P_1 and P_2 we defined the interaction potential for a pair of residues (a, b) in protein S as the sum of interaction potential of every occurrence of the (a, b). However, the potential energy of an ensemble is usually computed as the sum of pair-wise interaction. Keeping this in view, we propose another two sets of features P_3 and P_4 as defined in Table 2. P_3 considers pairs of residues separated by one residue while P_4 considers all adjacent pairs. Note that, P_3 and P_4 are normalized using a different constant Q. We choose

$$Q = max_{S \in X_{Tr}} \left\{ \max_{a,b} \sum_{x_i=a, x_j=b, j=i+1} (h(x_i) + h(x_j)) \right\},$$

X_{Tr} is the training data set. In other words, we find the maximum possible exponent over the entire training data.

Table 2. The new features

Histogram	$F_i = p_i, i = 1, 2, ..., 20$
First order energy	$F_{21} = \sum_{i=1}^{20} p_i^2$
First order entropy	$F_{22} = \sum_{i=1}^{20} -p_i \log p_i$
Histogram difference	$F_{23} = \sum_{i=1}^{19} |p_i - p_{i+1}|$
Weighted histogram difference-1	$F_{24} = \sum_{i=1}^{19} |p_i - p_{i+1}| p_{i+1}$
Weighted histogram difference-2	$F_{25} = \sum_{i=1}^{19} |p_i - p_{i+1}| p_i$
Second order energy	$F_{26} = \sum_{i=1}^{20} \sum_{j=1}^{20} p_{ij}^2$
Second order entropy	$F_{27} = -\sum_{i=1}^{20} \sum_{j=1}^{20} p_{ij} \log p_{ij}$
Average separation of residues	$F_{i+27} = \dfrac{1}{Nf_i} \sum_{s_j = x_i, s_k = s_i, s_l \neq x_i, \forall j < l < k} (j-k), \quad \text{if } f_i \neq 0$ $= 0, \quad \text{otherwise}, \quad i = 1, ...20$
Pairwise interaction Potential -type1	$P_1(a,b) = \dfrac{1}{R} \sum_{x_i = a, x_j = b, j = i+2} e^{\frac{(h(x_i) + h(x_j))}{M}}, \quad a, b = 1, ..., 20$
Pairwise interaction Potential -type2	$P_2(a,b) = \dfrac{1}{R} \sum_{x_i = a, x_j = b, j = i+1} e^{\frac{(h(x_i) + h(x_j))}{M}}, \quad a, b = 1, ..., 20$
Pairwise interaction Potential -type3	$P_3(a,b) = e^{\frac{1}{Q} \sum_{x_i = a, x_j = b, j = i+2} (h(x_i) + h(x_j))}, \quad a, b = 1, ..., 20$
Pairwise interaction Potential -type4	$P_4(a,b) = e^{\frac{1}{Q} \sum_{x_i = a, x_j = b, j = i+1} (h(x_i) + h(x_j))}, \quad a, b = 1, ..., 20$

3 Results

In our experiments we use a set of 698 proteins divided into 313 training and 385 test instances as used by Dubchak et al. [4]. The training data set do not have proteins with more than 35% of sequence identity for aligned subsequences [4]. Similarly, the test data contains SCOP sequences having less than 40% identity with each other. Also it does not contain any sequence with more than 35% identity with the training data. There are two levels of classifications of this data set. First, a coarse classification into four levels as shown in Table 3 are available. Each of these four classes are then further classified. All-alpha is classified into 6 folds, all-beta is classified to 9 classes, alpha/beta and alpha+beta are respectively grouped to 9 and 3 classes resulting in total 27 folds. In this investigation we shall consider classification at both levels using neural networks as the machine learning tools. We shall use both the multilayer perceptron and radial basis function network as the classifiers.

Table 3. Number of patterns in training and test sets

Fold Types	Number of Training Pattern (X_{Tr})	Number of Test Pattern (X_{Ts})
All Alpha	55	61
All Beta	109	117
Alpha/Beta	115	145
Alpha+Beta	34	62
Total	313	385

Table 4 presents the performance of the proposed features on the training and test data sets when MLP is used as the classifier. In order to compare the performance of the proposed features we also trained networks with the 125 features of Dubchak et al. [1,4]. We call this feature set D_{125}. D_{125} uses 21 features based on predicted secondary structures. We excluded these 21 features and generated a feature set named D_{104}. As we mentioned earlier that use of features which are guaranteed to have about 30% incorrect information is not desirable. This is the reason for considering D_{104}. We also experimented with this feature set. Table 4 shows that the feature set $F_1 - F_{47}$ have considerable discriminatory power, giving a classification accuracy of nearly 74%. Of these five new feature sets, the feature set P_3 seems to be the best.

The prediction accuracy obtained by the RBF networks is depicted in Table 5. We see that using RBF also P_3 performs the best among all the features we calculated. But, still while classifying into 4 folds D_{125} seems to be the best.

Next we consider the problem of detailed classification into 27 folds. For this we use here only RBF networks. Table 6 depicts effectiveness of different feature sets in conjunction with RBF networks (as implemented in MATLAB neural network toolbox). Table 7 reports the results using D_{125} by MLP, General Regression Neural Network (GRNN) and support vector machines (SVM). Table

Table 4. Performance of MLP on different feature sets for first level classification

Feature sets	Network Size	Training error	Test error
$F_1 - F_{47}$ (47 features)	47:50:20:10:4	3.83%	26.75%
P_1 (400 features)	400:80:40:10:4	8.62%	31.60%
P_2 (400 features)	400:80:40:10:4	12.46%	31.90%
P_3 (400 features)	400:80:40:10:4	1.91%	26.49%
P_4 (400 features)	400:80:40:10:4	0.00%	29.35%
D_{125} (125 features)	125:80:40:10:4	0.00%	19.48%
D_{104} (104 features)	125:80:40:10:4	3.83%	22.80%

7 have been adapted from [7]. Comparing Tables 6 and 7 it is clear that in the 2nd level of classification, i.e., classification into 27 folds, P_3 outperforms D_{125} for all four classifiers tried. The performance of P_4 is marginally less than that obtained by using SVM on D_{125} but is better than D_{125} for all other classifiers tried. The performance of P_1 and P_2 is also quite good.

Table 5. Performance of RBF on different feature sets for first level classification

Feature sets	Network Size	Training error	Test error
$F_1 - F_{47}$ (47 features)	40	19.80%	29.35%
P_1 (400 features)	150	3.19%	23.89%
P_2 (400 features)	150	2.55%	25.71%
P_3 (400 features)	150	1.91%	22.33%
P_4 (400 features)	150	2.23%	25.71%
D_{125} (125 features)	100	1.27%	18.18%
D_{104} (104 features)	80	8.31%	27.01%

Table 6. Performance of RBF on different feature sets for classification into 27 folds

Feature sets	Network Size	Training error	Test error
$F_1 - F_{47}$ (47 features)	40	39.3%	57.50%
P_1 (400 features)	150	4.79%	50.64%
P_2 (400 features)	150	6.38%	51.42%
P_3 (400 features)	150	6.70%	45.97%
P_4 (400 features)	150	5.43%	48.83%
D_{125} (125 features)	100	10.86%	49.87%
D_{104} (104 features)	80	14.37%	51.68%

4 Conclusions

We have proposed five sets of features that are defined only using characteristics of the residues and the distribution of residues on the AA sequence representing

Table 7. The Protein-fold prediction error using D_{125} for level 2 classification[7]

Method	MLP	GRNN	RBFN	SVM
Classification accuracy	51.2%	55.8%	50.6%	48.6%

a protein. As the learning machine, we used multilayer perceptron network and radial basis function network. We used the SCOP database and considered classification to four folds and twenty seven folds. Our experimental results revealed that the proposed features have reasonably good discrimination power. Of the five sets of features P3 and P4 are more effective than the other three types of features. Our investigation also revealed that while computing interaction potential type features use of adjacent pairs and pairs separated by exactly one residue produces more or less the same performance. Our next step would be to combine these feature sets and use some connectionist online feature selection scheme to select the best set of features[8,9].

References

1. I. Dubchak, I. Muchnik, C. Mayor, I. Dralyuk and S-H Kim, "Recognition of a Protein Fold in the context of the SCOP Classification. PROTEINS: Structure, Function and Genetics, vol. 35, pp. 401–407, 1999.
2. P. Baldi and S. Brunak, Bioinformatics: the Machine Learning Approach, MIT Press, 1998.
3. I. Dubchak, I. Muchnik, S. R. Holbrook, and S. H. Kim, "Prediction of protein folding class using global description of amino acid sequence", Proc. Natl. Acad. Sci., USA, Vol. 92, pp. 8700–8704, 1995.
4. I. Dubchak and C. H. Q. Ding, "Multi-class protein fold recognition using support vector machines and neural networks," Bioinformatics, Vol. 17, No. 4, pp. 349–358, 2001.
5. Antônio F. Pereira de Araújo, "Folding protein models with simple hydrophobic energy function: the fundamenta importanve of monomer inside/outside segregation", Proc. Natl. Acad. Sci., USA, vol 96, no 22, pp. 12482–12487.
6. A. G. Murzin, S. E. Brenner, T. Hubbard, and C. Chothia, "SCOP: A structural classification of proteins database for the investigation of sequence and structures. Journal of Molecular Biology, vol. 247, pp. 536–540, 1995.
7. I-Fang Chung, Chuen-Der Huang, Ya-Hsin Shen and Chin-Teng Lin, "Recognition of Structure Classification of Protein Folding by NN and SVM Hierarchical Learning Architecture, Proceedings of ICONIP 2003.
8. N.R. Pal and K.K. Chintalapudi, "A connectionist system for feature selection", Neural, Parallel & Scientific Computations, vol 5. No. 3, 359–381, 1997.
9. D. Chakraborty and Nikhil R. Pal, "Integrated feature analysis and fuzzy rule-based system identification in a neuro-fuzzy paradigm", IEEE Trans. on Systems Man Cybernetics B, vol 31, no 3, pp. 391–400, 2001.

Author Index

Acciani, Giuseppe 367
Agakov, Felix V. 107
Albayrak, Songül 695
Alonso-Betanzos, Amparo 84
Alpaydın, Ethem 69
Apolloni, B. 875
Arndt, Dirk 307
Artières, Thierry 891
Athanaselis, Theologos 1117, 1125
Aussem, Alex 523
Avedillo, Maria J. 737

Bacauskiene, Marija 35
Bakamidis, Stelios 1117, 1125
Ban, Sang-Woo 678
Bang, Sung-Yang 291
Bao, W.Y. 1026
Barber, David 92, 107
Barutçuoğlu, Zafer 76
Bax, Ingo 425
Bayrak, C. 1041
Becerikli, Yasar 710
Bedingfield, Susan E. 1081
Beiu, Valeriu 737, 745
Bekel, Holger 425
Bengio, Samy 443
Bezerianos, Anastasios 262
Bidel, Sylvain 891
Blekas, Konstantinos 702
Boekhorst, Rene te 496
Brega, A. 875
Buchtala, Oliver 43
Byorick, Jeffrey 181

Cambio, Roberta 721
Cangelosi, Angelo 763
Carayannis, George 1125
Carvalho, André C.P.L.F. de 234
Casile, Antonino 854
Castillo, Enrique 84
Cengiz, Yavuz 630
Chakraborty, Debrup 1176
Chan, Lai-Wan 132
Chen, Hsin 638
Chen, Peng 1018, 1026
Chen, Y.H. 686

Chen, Z. 1041
Cheung, Yiu-ming 165
Cho, Sung-Bae 1143
Choi, Seungjin 68
Chokshi, Kaustubh 504
Chung, I-Fang 1159, 1168
Corchado, Emilio 280
Cowie, Roddy 1109, 1125, 1133
Cutzu, Florin 375

Dagli, Cihan H. 1089
Daoudi, Khalid 452
Das, Jyotirmay 581
Daud, Taher 1049
Demir, Yakup 225
Detyniecki, Marcin 883
Deviren, Murat 452
Dockner, Engelbert J. 589
Doğan, Hatice 554
Dologlou, Ioannis 1117, 1125
Dong, Qi 515
Dorffner, Georg 589
Douglas-Cowie, E. 1125, 1133
Dragomir, Andrei 262
Duin, Robert P.W. 140, 333
Duong, Tuan 1049

Eggert, Julian 385
Erdogmus, Deniz 84
Ersoy, Okan K. 1011, 1073
Eswaran, H. 1041

Fend, Miriam 805
Ferguson, Ian 1049
Fernández-Redondo, Mercedes 670
Fischer, Amber D. 1089
Fontenla-Romero, Oscar 84
Fornarelli, Girolamo 367
Fotiadis, Dimitrios I. 702
Fotinea, Stavroula-Evita 1117, 1125, 1133
Fragopanagos, N. 1125, 1133
Frossyniotis, Dimitrios 925
Fu, Hsin-Chia 686
Fujisawa, Shoichiro 471
Fukushima, Kunihiko 393
Fyfe, Colin 280

Author Index

Gallinari, Patrick 891
Gao, X.W. 1100
Garfield, Sheila 646
Gelenbe, Erol 901
Gersten, Wendy 307
Gerstner, Wulfram 92, 839, 846
Giannopoulos, Georgios 1117
Giese, Martin 854
Göksu, Hüseyin 1057
González-Manteiga, Wenceslao 209
Grąbczewski, Krzysztof 359
Greco, Alberto 763
Gündüz, Şule 1003
Güneş, Filiz 630
Gueorguieva, Natacha 1033
Güzeliş, Cüneyt 225, 554
Gurney, Kevin N. 797
Gustafsson, Lennart 830

Hafner, Verena Vanessa 805
Hamano, Toshihiko 821
Harrington, Edward 538
Heidemann, Gunther 425
Henderson, James 19
Hendry, David C. 721
Hernández-Espinosa, Carlos 670
Herzel, Hanspeter 245
Heskes, Tom 562
Higgins, Charles M. 433
Hirose, Akira 821, 943, 959
Hoffmann, Heiko 463
Hofmann, Alexander 43, 316
Huang, Chuen-Der 1159, 1168
Huang, Kaizhu 115
Humphries, Mark D. 797

Ikeda, Kazushi 201
Inoue, Hirotaka 11
Ioannou, Spiros 1109
Ishii, Shin 123, 271
Ito, Yoshifusa 253

Jain, Brijnesh J. 299
Jankowski, Norbert 359
Jimbo, Takashi 729
Jolivet, Renaud 846
Juszczak, Piotr 140

Kamimura, Ryotaro 99
Kamps, Marc de 771

Karakahya, Hakan 1011
Karpouzis, Kostas 1109
Kasderidis, Stathis 867, 909
Katsumata, Naoto 27
Kawaguchi, Masashi 729
Kawamura, Ryo 27
Kaynak, Okyay 1064
King, Irwin 115
Kinjo, Mitsunaga 951
Knoblauch, Andreas 325
König, Peter 805
Körding, Konrad Paul 805
Körner, Edgar 385
Kollias, Stefanos 933, 1109, 1133
Konar, Ahmet Ferit 710
Kondo, Kazuyuki 729
Kouropteva, Olga 333
Kropas-Hughes, Claudia V. 1018
Kuroe, Yasuaki 985
Kurozumi, Ryota 471
Kursin, Andrei 779

Lajbcygier, Paul 615
Le, Quan 443
Lecoeuche, Stéphane 350
Lee, Minho 530, 678
Lehtimäki, Pasi 622
Lemoine, Laurent 891
Lendasse, Amaury 573
Lewis, Timothy J. 846
Likas, Aristidis 702
Likharev, Konstantin 753
Lin, Chin-Teng 1159, 1168
Liou, Cheng-Yuan 52
Liturri, Luciano 367
Long, Zhi-ying 515
Lorena, Ana Carolina 234
Lowery, C. 1041
Ludermir, Teresa B. 654
Lungarella, Max 496, 805
Lurette, Christophe 350
Lyu, Michael R. 115

MacLeod, Christopher 488
Maeda, Michiharu 546
Majumdar, Kausik 581
Malchiodi, Dario 875, 909
Malmqvist, Kerstin 35
Martin, Trevor P. 917
Martín de Diego, Isaac 217

Matías, José M.   209
Matsuda, Yoshitatsu   401
Matsuyama, Yasuo   27
Mavroudi, Seferina   262
Maxwell, Grant   488
Mayor, Julien   839
Miazhynskaia, Tatiana   589
Micheli, Alessio   173
Minami, Motoi   943
Miravet, Carlos   417
Möller, Ralf   463
Moguerza, Javier M.   217
Mori, Takehiro   985
Morikawa, Koji   786
Morita, Satoru   409
Müller, Klaus-R.   342
Muñoz, Alberto   217
Murray, Alan F.   638
Muthuraman, Sethuraman   488

Nakajima, Koji   951
Narihisa, Hiroyuki   11
Nemoto, Iku   977
Neumann, Peter   307
Nitta, Tohru   993
Norton, J.   1041
Nürnberger, Andreas   883
Nunes da Silva, Ivan   189
Núñez, Arturo   901

Oba, Shigeyuki   271
Özsu, M. Tamer   1003
Ohigashi, Yu   786
Oka, Natsuki   786
Okun, Oleg   333
Omori, Takashi   157, 786
Oohira, Takayuki   157
Ortiz-Gómez, Mamen   670
Oysal, Yusuf   710
Ozalevli, Erhan   433

Paccanaro, Alberto   149
Padgett, Curtis   1049
Pal, Nikhil Ranjan   1168, 1176
Pal, Srimanta   581
Palmas, G.   875
Pao, H.T.   686
Papadimitriou, Stergios   262
Papliński, Andrew P.   830
Park, Sang-Jae   678

Pei, Liu-qing   515
Peng, Dan-ling   515
Peng, Zou   607
Pertselakis, Minas   925
Pfeifer, Rolf   496, 805
Pfister, Jean-Pascal   92
Piat, Frédéric   891
Pietikäinen, Matti   333
Podladchikova, L.   1100
Polikar, Robi   181
Preissl, H.   1041
Prescott, Tony J.   797
Principe, J.C.   84
Prudêncio, Ricardo B.C.   654

Quintana, Jose M.   737

Raivio, Kimmo   622
Raouzaiou, Amaryllis   1109
Reen, N.S.   1026
Ridder, Dick de   333
Riedmiller, Martin   479
Riga, Thomas   763
Rincon, D.   1026
Rodríguez, Francisco B.   417

Saltan, Mehmet   662
Sato, Masa-aki   123, 271
Sato, Shigeo   951
Schmitz, Carsten   316
Schoknecht, Ralf   479
Serpen, Gürsel   3
Shakev, Nikola G.   1064
Shaposhnikov, D.   1100
Shen, Ya-Hsin   1159
Shi, S.Y.M.   1151
Shin, Jang-Kyoo   678
Sick, Bernhard   43, 307, 316
Simula, Olli   622
Singh, Reen Nripjeet   1018
Smith, Kate A.   1081
Sohn, Jun-Il   530
Sona, Diego   173
Sou, Un-Cheong   52
Sperduti, Alessandro   173
Srinivasan, Cidambi   253
Stafylopatis, Andreas   925
Stamou, Giorgos   933
Steil, Jochen J.   60
Stoica, Adrian   1049

Suárez, Alberto 597
Suganthan, P.N. 1151
Suksmono, Andriyan Bayu 959
Sung, JaeMo 291

Tang, Tong Boon 638
Tansel, Ibrahim N. 1018, 1026
Tax, David M.J. 342
Taylor, John G. 909, 1125, 1133
Terzi, Serdal 662
Thakoor, Anil 1049
Topalov, Andon V. 1064
Tsapatsoulis, Nicolas 867, 909, 1109
Tseng, C.L. 686
Türel, Özgür 753
Tzouvaras, Vassilis 933

Uçar, Ayşegül 225
Umeno, Masayoshi 729

Valova, Iren 1033
Vaucher, Gilles 967
Velde, Frank van der 771
Verikas, Antanas 35
Verleysen, Michel 573
Vidal, Carmen 597
Voort van der Kleij, Gwendid T. van der 771

Wallace, Manolis 867
Weber, Cornelius 504, 813
Weiss, Olaf 245

Wen, Dou 607
Weng, Sebastian 60
Wermter, Stefan 504, 646, 813
Wersing, Heiko 385
Wertz, Vincent 573
Wilson, J.D. 1041
Won, Hong-Hee 1143
Wunsch, Donald C. II 1057
Wysotzki, Fritz 299

Xue, Gui 515

Yamaguchi, Kazunori 401
Yamamoto, Toru 471
Yamauchi, Koichiro 157
Yan, Jia 607
Yang, Jack Y. 1073
Yang, Mary Qu 1073
Yang, S.Y. 1026
Yao, Li 515
Yazgan, Bingül 1011
Yildirim, Tulay 662
Yoshida, Mitsuo 985
Yoshimoto, Junichiro 123

Zanaboni, A.M. 875
Zebulum, Ricardo 1049
Zhang, Kun 132
Zhao, Xiao-jie 515
Zhong, Liu 607
Ziehe, Andreas 245
Zoeter, Onno 562

Lecture Notes in Computer Science

For information about Vols. 1–2609

please contact your bookseller or Springer-Verlag

Vol. 2610: C. Ryan, T. Soule, M. Keijzer, E. Tsang, R. Poli, E. Costa (Eds.), Genetic Programming. Proceedings, 2003. XII, 486 pages. 2003.

Vol. 2611: S. Cagnoni, J.J. Romero Cardalda, D.W. Corne, J. Gottlieb, A. Guillot, E. Hart, C.G. Johnson, E. Marchiori, J.-A. Meyer, M. Middendorf, G.R. Raidl (Eds.), Applications of Evolutionary Computing. Proceedings, 2003. XXI, 708 pages. 2003.

Vol. 2612: M. Joye (Ed.), Topics in Cryptology – CT-RSA 2003. Proceedings, 2003. XI, 417 pages. 2003.

Vol. 2613: F.A.P. Petitcolas, H.J. Kim (Eds.), Digital Watermarking. Proceedings, 2002. XI, 265 pages. 2003.

Vol. 2614: R. Laddaga, P. Robertson, H. Shrobe (Eds.), Self-Adaptive Software: Applications. Proceedings, 2001. VIII, 291 pages. 2003.

Vol. 2615: N. Carbonell, C. Stephanidis (Eds.), Universal Access. Proceedings, 2002. XIV, 534 pages. 2003.

Vol. 2616: T. Asano, R. Klette, C. Ronse (Eds.), Geometry, Morphology, and Computational Imaging. Proceedings, 2002. X, 437 pages. 2003.

Vol. 2617: H.A. Reijers (Eds.), Design and Control of Workflow Processes. Proceedings, 2002. XV, 624 pages. 2003.

Vol. 2618: P. Degano (Ed.), Programming Languages and Systems. Proceedings, 2003. XV, 415 pages. 2003.

Vol. 2619: H. Garavel, J. Hatcliff (Eds.), Tools and Algorithms for the Construction and Analysis of Systems. Proceedings, 2003. XVI, 604 pages. 2003.

Vol. 2620: A.D. Gordon (Ed.), Foundations of Software Science and Computation Structures. Proceedings, 2003. XII, 441 pages. 2003.

Vol. 2621: M. Pezzè (Ed.), Fundamental Approaches to Software Engineering. Proceedings, 2003. XIV, 403 pages. 2003.

Vol. 2622: G. Hedin (Ed.), Compiler Construction. Proceedings, 2003. XII, 335 pages. 2003.

Vol. 2623: O. Maler, A. Pnueli (Eds.), Hybrid Systems: Computation and Control. Proceedings, 2003. XII, 558 pages. 2003.

Vol. 2624: H.G. Dietz (Ed.), Languages and Compilers for Parallel Computing. Proceedings, 2001. XI, 444 pages. 2003.

Vol. 2625: U. Meyer, P. Sanders, J. Sibeyn (Eds.), Algorithms for Memory Hierarchies. Proceedings, 2003. XVIII, 428 pages. 2003.

Vol. 2626: J.L. Crowley, J.H. Piater, M. Vincze, L. Paletta (Eds.), Computer Vision Systems. Proceedings, 2003. XIII, 546 pages. 2003.

Vol. 2627: B. O'Sullivan (Ed.), Recent Advances in Constraints. Proceedings, 2002. X, 201 pages. 2003. (Subseries LNAI).

Vol. 2627: B. O'Sullivan (Ed.), Recent Advances in Constraints. Proceedings, 2002. X, 201 pages. 2003. (Subseries LNAI).

Vol. 2628: T. Fahringer, B. Scholz, Advanced Symbolic Analysis for Compilers. XII, 129 pages. 2003.

Vol. 2631: R. Falcone, S. Barber, L. Korba, M. Singh (Eds.), Trust, Reputation, and Security: Theories and Practice. Proceedings, 2002. X, 235 pages. 2003. (Subseries LNAI).

Vol. 2632: C.M. Fonseca, P.J. Fleming, E. Zitzler, K. Deb, L. Thiele (Eds.), Evolutionary Multi-Criterion Optimization. Proceedings, 2003. XV, 812 pages. 2003.

Vol. 2633: F. Sebastiani (Ed.), Advances in Information Retrieval. Proceedings, 2003. XIII, 546 pages. 2003.

Vol. 2634: F. Zhao, L. Guibas (Eds.), Information Processing in Sensor Networks. Proceedings, 2003. XII, 692 pages. 2003.

Vol. 2636: E. Alonso, D, Kudenko, D. Kazakov (Eds.), Adaptive Agents and Multi-Agent Systems. XIV, 323 pages. 2003. (Subseries LNAI).

Vol. 2637: K.-Y. Whang, J. Jeon, K. Shim, J. Srivastava (Eds.), Advances in Knowledge Discovery and Data Mining. Proceedings, 2003. XVIII, 610 pages. 2003. (Subseries LNAI).

Vol. 2638: J. Jeuring, S. Peyton Jones (Eds.), Advanced Functional Programming. Proceedings, 2002. VII, 213 pages. 2003.

Vol. 2639: G. Wang, Q. Liu, Y. Yao, A. Skowron (Eds.), Rough Sets, Fuzzy Sets, Data Mining, and Granular Computing. Proceedings, 2003. XVII, 741 pages. 2003. (Subseries LNAI).

Vol. 2641: P.J. Nürnberg (Ed.), Metainformatics. Proceedings, 2002. VIII, 187 pages. 2003.

Vol. 2642: X. Zhou, Y. Zhang, M.E. Orlowska (Eds.), Web Technologies and Applications. Proceedings, 2003. XIII, 608 pages. 2003.

Vol. 2643: M. Fossorier, T. Høholdt, A. Poli (Eds.), Applied Algebra, Algebraic Algorithms and Error-Correcting Codes. Proceedings, 2003. X, 256 pages. 2003.

Vol. 2644: D. Hogrefe, A. Wiles (Eds.), Testing of Communicating Systems. Proceedings, 2003. XII, 311 pages. 2003.

Vol. 2645: M.A. Wimmer (Ed.), Knowledge Management in Electronic Government. Proceedings, 2003. XI, 320 pages. 2003. (Subseries LNAI).

Vol. 2646: H. Geuvers, F. Wiedijk (Eds.), Types for Proofs and Programs. Proceedings, 2002. VIII, 331 pages. 2003.

Vol. 2647: K.Jansen, M. Margraf, M. Mastrolli, J.D.P. Rolim (Eds.), Experimental and Efficient Algorithms. Proceedings, 2003. VIII, 267 pages. 2003.

Vol. 2648: T. Ball, S.K. Rajamani (Eds.), Model Checking Software. Proceedings, 2003. VIII, 241 pages. 2003.

Vol. 2649: B. Westfechtel, A. van der Hoek (Eds.), Software Configuration Management. Proceedings, 2003. VIII, 241 pages. 2003.

Vol. 2651: D. Bert, J.P. Bowen, S. King, M, Waldén (Eds.), ZB 2003: Formal Specification and Development in Z and B. Proceedings, 2003. XIII, 547 pages. 2003.

Vol. 2652: F.J. Perales, A.J.C. Campilho, N. Pérez de la Blanca, A. Sanfeliu (Eds.), Pattern Recognition and Image Analysis. Proceedings, 2003. XIX, 1142 pages. 2003.

Vol. 2653: R. Petreschi, Giuseppe Persiano, R. Silvestri (Eds.), Algorithms and Complexity. Proceedings, 2003. XI, 289 pages. 2003.

Vol. 2655: J.-P. Rosen, A. Strohmeier (Eds.), Reliable Software Technologies – Ada-Europe 2003. Proceedings, 2003. XIII, 489 pages. 2003.

Vol. 2656: E. Biham (Ed.), Advances in Cryptology – EUROCRPYT 2003. Proceedings, 2003. XIV, 429 pages. 2003.

Vol. 2657: P.M.A. Sloot, D. Abramson, A.V. Bogdanov, J.J. Dongarra, A.Y. Zomaya, Y.E. Gorbachev (Eds.), Computational Science – ICCS 2003. Proceedings, Part I. 2003. LV, 1095 pages. 2003.

Vol. 2658: P.M.A. Sloot, D. Abramson, A.V. Bogdanov, J.J. Dongarra, A.Y. Zomaya, Y.E. Gorbachev (Eds.), Computational Science – ICCS 2003. Proceedings, Part II. 2003. LV, 1129 pages. 2003.

Vol. 2659: P.M.A. Sloot, D. Abramson, A.V. Bogdanov, J.J. Dongarra, A.Y. Zomaya, Y.E. Gorbachev (Eds.), Computational Science – ICCS 2003. Proceedings, Part III. 2003. LV, 1165 pages. 2003.

Vol. 2660: P.M.A. Sloot, D. Abramson, A.V. Bogdanov, J.J. Dongarra, A.Y. Zomaya, Y.E. Gorbachev (Eds.), Computational Science – ICCS 2003. Proceedings, Part IV. 2003. LVI, 1161 pages. 2003.

Vol. 2663: E. Menasalvas, J. Segovia, P.S. Szczepaniak (Eds.), Advances in Web Intelligence. Proceedings, 2003. XII, 350 pages. 2003. (Subseries LNAI).

Vol. 2665: H. Chen, R. Miranda, D.D. Zeng, C. Demchak, J. Schroeder, T. Madhusudan (Eds.), Intelligence and Security Informatics. Proceedings, 2003. XIV, 392 pages. 2003.

Vol. 2667: V. Kumar, M.L. Gavrilova, C.J.K. Tan, P. L'Ecuyer (Eds.), Computational Science and Its Applications – ICCSA 2003. Proceedings, Part I. 2003. XXXIV, 1060 pages. 2003.

Vol. 2668: V. Kumar, M.L. Gavrilova, C.J.K. Tan, P. L'Ecuyer (Eds.), Computational Science and Its Applications – ICCSA 2003. Proceedings, Part II. 2003. XXXIV, 942 pages. 2003.

Vol. 2669: V. Kumar, M.L. Gavrilova, C.J.K. Tan, P. L'Ecuyer (Eds.), Computational Science and Its Applications – ICCSA 2003. Proceedings, Part III. 2003. XXXIV, 948 pages. 2003.

Vol. 2670: R. Peña, T. Arts (Eds.), Implementation of Functional Languages. Proceedings, 2002. X, 249 pages. 2003.

Vol. 2671: Y. Xiang, B. Chaib-draa (Eds.), Advances in Artificial Intelligence. Proceedings, 2003. XIV, 642 pages. 2003. (Subseries LNAI).

Vol. 2672: M. Endler, D. Schmidt (Eds.), Middleware 2003. Proceedings, 2003. XIII, 513 pages. 2003.

Vol. 2673: N. Ayache, H. Delingette (Eds.), Surgery Simulation and Soft Tissue Modeling. Proceedings, 2003. XII, 386 pages. 2003.

Vol. 2674: I.E. Magnin, J. Montagnat, P. Clarysse, J. Nenonen, T. Katila (Eds.), Functional Imaging and Modeling of the Heart. Proceedings, 2003. XI, 308 pages. 2003.

Vol. 2675: M. Marchesi, G. Succi (Eds.), Extreme Programming and Agile Processes in Software Engineering. Proceedings, 2003. XV, 464 pages. 2003.

Vol. 2676: R. Baeza-Yates, E. Chávez, M. Crochemore (Eds.), Combinatorial Pattern Matching. Proceedings, 2003. XI, 403 pages. 2003.

Vol. 2678: W. van der Aalst, A. ter Hofstede, M. Weske (Eds.), Business Process Management. Proceedings, 2003. XI, 391 pages. 2003.

Vol. 2679: W. van der Aalst, E. Best (Eds.), Applications and Theory of Petri Nets 2003. Proceedings, 2003. XI, 508 pages. 2003.

Vol. 2680: P. Blackburn, C. Ghidini, R.M. Turner, F. Giunchiglia (Eds.), Modeling and Using Context. Proceedings, 2003. XII, 525 pages. 2003. (Subseries LNAI).

Vol. 2681: J. Eder, M. Missikoff (Eds.), Advanced Information Systems Engineering. Proceedings, 2003. XV, 740 pages. 2003.

Vol. 2686: J. Mira, J.R. Álvarez (Eds.), Computational Methods in Neural Modeling. Proceedings, Part I. 2003. XXVII, 764 pages. 2003.

Vol. 2687: J. Mira, J.R. Álvarez (Eds.), Artificial Neural Nets Problem Solving Methods. Proceedings, Part II. 2003. XXVII, 820 pages. 2003.

Vol. 2688: J. Kittler, M.S. Nixon (Eds.), Audio- and Video-Based Biometric Person Authentication. Proceedings, 2003. XVII, 978 pages. 2003.

Vol. 2689: K.D. Ashley, D.G. Bridge (Eds.), Case-Based Reasoning Research and Development. Proceedings, 2003. XV, 734 pages. 2003. (Subseries LNAI).

Vol. 2692: P. Nixon, S. Terzis (Eds.), Trust Management. Proceedings, 2003. X, 349 pages. 2003.

Vol. 2694: R. Cousot (Ed.), Static Analysis. Proceedings, 2003. XIV, 505 pages. 2003.

Vol. 2695: L.D. Griffin, M. Lillholm (Eds.), Scale Space Methods in Computer Vision. Proceedings, 2003. XII, 816 pages. 2003.

Vol. 2701: M. Hofmann (Ed.), Typed Lambda Calculi and Applications. Proceedings, 2003. VIII, 317 pages. 2003.

Vol. 2702: P. Brusilovsky, A. Corbett, F. de Rosis (Eds.), User Modeling 2003. Proceedings, 2003. XIV, 436 pages. 2003. (Subseries LNAI).

Vol. 2704: S.-T. Huang, T. Herman (Eds.), Self-Stabilizing Systems. Proceedings, 2003. X, 215 pages. 2003.

Vol. 2706: R. Nieuwenhuis (Ed.), Rewriting Techniques and Applications. Proceedings, 2003. XI, 515 pages. 2003.

Vol. 2707: K. Jeffay, I. Stoica, K. Wehrle (Eds.), Quality of Service – IWQoS 2003. Proceedings, 2003. XI, 517 pages. 2003.

Vol. 2709: T. Windeatt, F. Roli (Eds.), Multiple Classifier Systems. Proceedings, 2003. X, 406 pages. 2003.

Vol. 2714: O. Kaynak, E. Alpaydin, E. Oja, L. Xu (Eds.), Artificial Neural Networks and Neural Information Processing – ICANN/ICONIP 2003. Proceedings, 2003. XXII, 1188 pages. 2003.

Vol. 2716: M.J. Voss (Ed.), OpenMP Shared Memory Parallel Programming. Proceedings, 2003. VIII, 271 pages. 2003.